Design of Machine Elements II
(DME II)

Design of Machine Elements II
(DME II)

K Raghavendra M Tech
Assistant Professor
Department of Mechanical Engineering
Ballari Institute of Technology and Management (BITM)
Bellary, Karnataka

CBS Publishers & Distributors Pvt Ltd

New Delhi • Bengaluru • Chennai • Kochi • Kolkata • Mumbai
Bhopal • Bhubaneswar • Hyderabad • Jharkhand • Nagpur • Patna • Pune • Uttarakhand • Dhaka (Bangladesh)

Disclaimer

Science and technology are constantly changing fields. New research and experience broaden the scope of information and knowledge. The author has tried their best in giving information available to him while preparing the material for this book. Although, all efforts have been made to ensure optimum accuracy of the material, yet it is quite possible some errors might have been left uncorrected. The publisher, the printer and the author will not be held responsible for any inadvertent errors, omissions or inaccuracies.

Design of Machine Elements II (DME II)

ISBN: 978-81-239-2633-9

Copyright © Author and Publisher

First Edition: 2015

Reprint: 2019, 2020

All rights reserved. No part of this book may be reproduced or transmitted in any form or by any means, electronic or mechanical, including photocopying, recording, or any information storage and retrieval system without permission, in writing, from the author and the publisher.

Published by Satish Kumar Jain and Produced by Varun Jain for

CBS Publishers & Distributors Pvt Ltd
4819/XI Prahlad Street, 24 Ansari Road, Daryaganj, New Delhi 110 002, India.
Ph: 23289259, 23266861, 23266867   Fax: 011-23243014   Website: www.cbspd.com
e-mail: delhi@cbspd.com; cbspubs@airtelmail.in.

Corporate Office: 204 FIE, Industrial Area, Patparganj, Delhi 110 092
Ph: 4934 4934   Fax: 4934 4935   e-mail: publishing@cbspd.com; publicity@cbspd.com

Branches

- **Bengaluru:** Seema House 2975, 17th Cross, K.R. Road, Banasankari 2nd Stage, Bengaluru 560 070, Karnataka
  Ph: +91-80-26771678/79   Fax: +91-80-26771680   e-mail: bangalore@cbspd.com
- **Chennai:** 7, Subbaraya Street, Shenoy Nagar, Chennai 600 030, Tamil Nadu
  Ph: +91-44-26680620, 26681266   Fax: +91-44-42032115   e-mail: chennai@cbspd.com
- **Kochi:** 42/1325, 1326, Power House Road, Opp. KSEB Power House Ernakulam 682 018, Kochi, Kerala
  Ph: +91-484-4059061-65   Fax: +91-484-4059065   e-mail: kochi@cbspd.com
- **Kolkata:** 6/B, Ground Floor, Rameswar Shaw Road, Kolkata-700 014, West Bengal
  Ph: +91-33-22891126, 22891127, 22891128   e-mail: kolkata@cbspd.com
- **Mumbai:** 83-C, Dr E Moses Road, Worli, Mumbai-400018, Maharashtra
  Ph: +91-22-24902340/41   Fax: +91-22-24902342   e-mail: mumbai@cbspd.com

Representatives

• Bhopal	0-8319310552	• Bhubaneswar	0-9911037372	• Hyderabad	0-9885175004	• Jharkhand	0-9811541605
• Nagpur	0-9421945513	• Patna	0-9334159340	• Pune	0-9623451994	• Uttarakhand	0-9716462459
• Dhaka (Bangladesh)	01912-003485						

Printed at Swastik Packagings, Patparganj Industrial Area, Delhi, India

*In loving memory
of
my father
Late Sri K Sivaramulu*

Preface

It gives me a great satisfaction in presenting this book titled **Design of Machine Elements II (DME II)**, written according to the syllabus prescribed by VTU, Belagavi, for VI semester students of Mechanical Engineering and Industrial Production Engineering.

The manuscript is based on the lectures delivered by the author with reference to the third and fourth editions of *Design Data Hand Book for Mechanical Engineers* by Prof K Mahadevan and Prof K Balaveera Reddy. [Addendum given at the end of the text lists tables, figures and equations for further reference]. The concepts are presented in simple and lucid language to explain the subject within the scope of the topics given in the syllabus.

I owe my gratitude to my mother Smt B Susheela, whose blessings inspired me in bringing out this book. I am thankful to my wife Smt V Radhika and son Chi K Naga Ganesh for their continuous support and encouragement in preparing this book.

I would like to express my sincere thanks to Dr Kori Nagaraj, Prof and HOD, Department of Mechanical Engineering, RYMEC, Bellari; Dr Yadavalli Basavaraj, Prof and HOD, Department of Mechanical Engineering, BITM, Bellari, for their support and cooperation while preparing the manuscript.

Last but not the least, I would like to thank the entire team of CBS Publishers & Distributors, New Delhi, for making all possible efforts in the publication of this book.

K Raghavendra

Contents

Preface *vii*

Part A

1. Curved Beams, Cylinders and Cylinder Heads 3–118

Curved Beams
- 1.1 Introduction 3
- 1.2 Difference between a Straight Beam and a Curved Beam 3
- 1.3 Stress in Curved Beams (Winkler–Bach Equation) 4
- 1.4 Steps to Solve Curved Beam Problems 8
- 1.5 Stresses in Closed Rings 29
- 1.6 Chain Links 37
- 1.7 Condition for Bending Stress at Extreme Fibers to be Numerically Equal 50

Cylinders and Cylinder Heads
- 1.8 Thin Cylinders 57
- 1.9 Thin Cylindrical Shells Subjected to Internal Pressure 57
    - 1.9.1 Circumferential/Tangential/Hoop Stress 58
    - 1.9.2 Longitudinal Stress 59
    - 1.9.3 Maximum Shear Stress 60
- 1.10 Thick Cylinders 60
- 1.11 Difference between Thick and Thin Cylinders 60
- 1.12 Lame's Equation 61
- 1.13 Wall Thickness 66
    - 1.13.1 For Brittle Materials 66
    - 1.13.2 For Ductile Materials 67
- 1.14 Birnie's Equation 68
- 1.15 Clavarino's Equation 68
- 1.16 Barlow's Equation 68
- 1.17 Changes in Cylinder Diameter 68
- 1.18 Autofrettage/Self-hooping 69
- 1.19 Compound -or- Composite Cylinders 76
- 1.20 Total Allowance -or- Interference 79

1.21 Forces and Torque in Interference Fits 80
1.22 Stresses due to Force and Shrink Fits 81
1.23 Radial Stresses 91
1.24 Cylinder Heads (End Closures) 99
    1.24.1 Flat Heads 99
        1.24.1.1 Circular Flats with Uniformly Distributed Load 100
        1.24.1.2 Circular Flat Plates Loaded Centrally 100
        1.24.1.3 Rectangular Plates 100
        1.24.1.4 Elliptical Plates 100
    1.24.2 Spherical Dished Covers 101
    1.24.3 Shells Subjected to Internal Pressure 101
1.25 Thickness of Stayed and Braced Plates 101
1.26 Unstayed Flat Heads 101
VTU QUESTION PAPERS 105

2. Belt, Rope and Chain Drives   119–219

2.1 Introduction 119
2.2 Selection of Belt Drive 119
2.3 Materials Used for Belts 119
2.4 Flat Belt Drives 120
2.5 Length of Open Belt Drive 120
2.6 Length of Cross Belt Drive 122
2.7 Centre Distance 124
2.8 Velocity Ratio of Belt Drive 124
2.9 Ratio of Driving Tensions in Flat Belts 125
2.10 Centrifugal Tension 127
2.11 Ratio of Driving Tensions in Flat Belts Considering Centrifugal Tension 129
2.12 Power Transmitted by Flat Belts 131
2.13 Condition for Maximum Power Transmission 132
2.14 Initial Tension in the Belt 133
2.15 Effect of Initial Tension on Flat Belts 133
2.16 Forces in Flat Belt 135
2.17 Idler-or-Jockey Pulley 135
2.18 Relation between Diameter of Pulley and Thickness 135
2.19 Design Procedure for Flat Belts 145
2.20 V-Belts 154
2.21 Advantages and Disadvantages of V-belt Over Flat Belt 155
2.22 Types of V-belts 155
2.23 Dimensions of a Standard V-grooved Pulley 155
2.24 Power Transmission 156
2.25 Number of Belts (n') 156
2.26 Centre Distance 157
2.27 Pitch Length of the Belt 157

2.28 Ratio of Driving Tensions in V-Belt 157
2.29 Design Procedure for V-Belts 168
2.30 Wire Ropes 183
2.31 Choice of a Wire Rope 184
2.32 Stresses in Hoisting Ropes 184
2.33 Drum and Sheave Diameters 185
2.34 Causes of Wire Rope Failure 186
2.35 Applications of Wire Ropes 186
2.36 Chain Drives 196
2.37 Classification of Chain Drives 196
2.38 Velocity Ratio of Chain Drives 197
2.39 Minimum Number of Teeth on Sprocket 197
2.40 Centre Distance 197
2.41 Chain Length 198
2.42 Power Transmitted 198
2.43 Minimum Number of Strands in a Chain 198
2.44 Actual Factor of Safety 199
2.45 Definitions 199
2.46 Design Procedure for Chain Drives 200
VTU QUESTION PAPERS 214

3. Springs   220–323

3.1 Introduction 220
3.2 Classification 220
3.3 Terms in Compression Springs 221
3.4 Spring Materials 222
3.5 End Connections for Helical Compression Springs 224
3.6 Surge in Springs 224
3.7 Stresses in Helical Springs–Circular Wire 225
3.8 Deflection in Helical Springs–Circular Wire 227
3.9 Energy Stored in Helical Coil Springs–Circular Wire 228
3.10 Design Procedure for Helical Springs 229
3.11 Spring Scale 247
3.12 Stresses and Deflection in Helical Springs–Non-circular Wire 271
3.13 Springs Subjected to Fatigue/Fluctuating Loads 276
3.14 Helical Torsion Springs 283
3.15 Disc-or-Belleville Springs 290
3.16 Leaf Springs 294
3.17 Laminated Springs 297
3.18 Semi-elliptical Laminated Springs 298
3.19 Equalized Stresses in Springs–Nipping 301
VTU QUESTION PAPERS 315

4. Spur and Helical Gears   324–415

  4.1 Introduction to Gears 324
  4.2 Classification of Gears 324
  4.3 Advantages of Gear Drive 324
  4.4 Disadvantages of Gear Drive 324
  4.5 General Profiles of Gear Tooth 324
  4.6 System -or- Pressure Angles of Gear Tooth 325
  4.7 Terms used in Gears 325
  4.8 Gear Materials 326
  4.9 Design Considerations for Gear Drive 326
  4.10 Methods of Gear Drive 326

Spur Gears
  4.11 Introduction 327
  4.12 Beam Strength of a Gear Tooth–Lewis Equation 327
        4.12.1 Assumptions in Lewis Bending Equation 329
  4.13 Velocity Factor 330
  4.14 Allowable Stress 330
  4.15 Design Methodology for Spur Gears 330
  4.16 Strength Factor 331
  4.17 Tangential Load 331
  4.18 Forces Acting on Spur Gear 331
  4.19 Dynamic Tooth Load 332
  4.20 Dynamic Load Factor 333
  4.21 Static Tooth Load -or- Beam Strength -or- Endurance Strength (F_{en}) 333
  4.22 Wear Tooth Load (F_w) 333
  4.23 Velocity Ratio 334
  4.24 Design Procedure for Spur Gear Problems 334
  4.25 Design Alterations for a Spur Gear 335
  4.26 Problems Based on Unknown Diameter 335
  4.27 Problems Based on Known Diameter 354

Helical Gears
  4.28 Introduction 364
  4.29 Advantages and Disadvantages of Helical Gear 364
  4.30 Comparison between Spur and Helical Gears 364
  4.31 Terms Used in Helical Gears 364
  4.32 Proportions of Helical Gear 365
  4.33 Face Width (*b*) 366
  4.34 Virtual or Formative Number of Teeth (z_e) 366
  4.35 Force Analysis of Helical Gears 367
  4.36 Strength of Helical Gear 369
  4.37 Design Methodology for Helical Gears 369

4.38 Dynamic Tooth Load 370
4.39 Dynamic Strength 371
4.40 Wear Tooth Load (F_w) 371
4.41 Herringbone Gears 371
4.42 Design Procedure for Helical Gear Problems 372
4.43 Problems Based on Known Diameter 373
4.44 Problems Based on Unknown Diameter 387
4.45 Problems on Herringbone Gears 403
VTU QUESTION PAPERS 407

Part B

5. Bevel and Worm Gears 419–501

Bevel Gears
  5.1 Introduction 419
  5.2 Classification 419
  5.3 Types of Tooth on Bevel Gear 420
  5.4 Applications 420
  5.5 Advantages and Disadvantages 421
  5.6 Terminology 421
  5.7 Pitch Angle of Bevel Gears 422
  5.8 Forces Acting on Bevel Gear 423
  5.9 Other Relations 424
  5.10 Strength of Bevel Gear 424
  5.11 Dynamic Load 426
  5.12 Static Tooth Load -or- Beam Strength -or- Endurance Strength (F_{en}) 427
  5.13 Wear Tooth Load (F_w) 427
  5.14 Formative Number of Teeth (z_e) 427
  5.15 Power Transmitted 427
  5.16 Design Methodology for Bevel Gears 428
  5.17 Design Procedure for Bevel Gear Problems 429
  5.18 Problems Based on Known Diameter 433
  5.19 Problems Based on Unknown Diameter 453

Worm Gears
  5.20 Introduction 468
  5.21 Characteristics of Worm Gears 468
  5.22 Advantages and Disadvantages 469
  5.23 Applications 469
  5.24 Designation of Worm Gears 469
  5.25 Worm Gear Design Parameters 469
  5.26 Terms in Worm Gear 469
  5.27 Strength of Worm Gear (F_t) 472

- 5.28 Dynamic Strength (F_s) 472
- 5.29 Wear Tooth Load (F_w) 473
- 5.30 Efficiency of Worm Gears 473
- 5.31 Thermal Capacity of Worm Gear 474
- 5.32 Power Rating 474
- 5.33 Basic Problems 475
- 5.34 Design Procedure for Worm Gear 481
- 5.35 Center Distance is Known 482
- 5.36 Center Distance is Unknown 488
- VTU QUESTION PAPERS 495

6. Clutches and Brakes   502–605

Design of Clutches
- 6.1 Introduction 502
- 6.2 Classification of Clutches 502
    - 6.2.1 Positive Clutches 503
    - 6.2.2 Friction Clutches 503
- 6.3 Single Plate/Disc Clutch 503
- 6.4 Multiplate Clutch 504
- 6.5 Difference between Single Plate and Multiplate Clutches 504
- 6.6 Cone Clutch 504
- 6.7 Torque Analysis of Plate/Disc Clutch 505
- 6.8 Basic Problems on Plate Clutch 510
- 6.9 Design Problems on Plate Clutch 517
- 6.10 Torque Analysis of Cone Clutch 526
- 6.11 Basic Problems on Cone Clutch 531
- 6.12 Design of Cone Clutch 537

Design of Brakes
- 6.13 Introduction to Brakes 542
- 6.14 Classification of Brakes 542
    - 6.14.1 Mechanical Brakes 543
- 6.15 Brake Shoe 543
- 6.16 Brake Lining 543
- 6.17 Energy Equations 544
- 6.18 Heating of Brakes 545
- 6.19 Other Relations (To Remember) 546
- 6.20 Block/ Shoe Brakes 551
- 6.21 Double Block or Shoe Brake 562
- 6.22 Band Brakes 567
    - 6.22.1 Simple Band Brake 567
    - 6.22.2 Differential Band Brake 581
- VTU QUESTION PAPERS 591

7. Lubrication and Bearings 606–687

7.1 Introduction to Lubrication 606
7.2 Purpose of Lubricants 607
7.3 Selection of Proper Lubricant 607
7.4 Lubrication Regimes 607
    7.4.1 Hydrodynamic or Full Fluid Film Lubrication 607
    7.4.2 Boundary Lubrication -or- Thin Film Lubrication 608
    7.4.3 Mixed Film Lubrication 608
    7.4.4 Elastohydrodynamic Lubrication (EHD -or- EHL) 609
7.5 Properties of Lubricants 609
7.6 Bearings 612
    7.6.1 Classification of Bearings 612
    7.6.2 Formation of Continuous Oil Film in a Journal Bearing 614
7.7 Bearing Materials 615
    7.7.1 Properties of Bearing Materials 615
7.8 Selection of Journal -or- Antifriction Bearings 616
7.9 Petroff's Equation 616
7.10 Bearing Characteristic Number -or- Bearing Modules for Journal Bearing 619
7.11 Sommerfeld Number 620
7.12 Operating Pressure 620
7.13 Terms and Definitions 621
7.14 Heat Generated in Bearings 622
7.15 Heat Dissipated by Bearings 622
7.16 Design Procedure for Journal Bearings 659
    7.16.1 When Diameter is Unknown 659
    7.16.2 When Diameter is known 668
7.17 Thrust Bearing 675
    7.17.1 Pivot Bearing 675
    7.17.2 Collar Bearing 676
7.18 Allowable Pressures 677
VTU QUESTION PAPERS 680

8. IC Engine Parts 688–776

8.1 Piston—An Introduction 688
    8.1.1 Functions of Piston 688
8.2 Parts of a Piston 688
8.3 Materials for Piston 689
8.4 Basic Design Considerations 690
8.5 Design of Piston 690
    8.5.1 Thickness of Piston Head 690
    8.5.2 Piston Rings 692

8.5.3 Piston Barrel (Thickness) 693
8.5.4 Piston Barrel 694
8.5.5 Piston Pin 694
8.6 Connecting Rod 706
8.7 Forces Acting on Connecting Rod 707
    8.7.1 Force on the Piston due to Gas Pressure and Inertia of the Reciprocating Parts 707
    8.7.2 Force due to Inertia of the Connecting Rod 708
8.8 Design of Connecting Rod 711
    8.8.1 Dimension of Cross-section of Connecting Rod 711
    8.8.2 Dimension of the Crank Pin at the Big End and the Piston Pin at the Small End 713
    8.8.3 Size of the Bolts for Big End Cap 714
    8.8.4 Thickness of the Big End Cap 715
    8.8.5 Whipping Stress -or- Bending Force due to Inertia 715
8.9 Design of Crankshaft 724
    8.9.1 Classification 724
    8.9.2 Materials 725
8.10 Design of Centre Crankshaft 726
    8.10.1 Case 1: Centre Crankshaft at Top Dead Center Position 726
    8.10.2 Case 2: Centre Crankshaft at an Angle of Maximum Torque 731
8.11 Design of Side Crankshaft 756
    8.11.1 Case 1: Centre Crankshaft at Top Dead Centre Position 756
    8.11.2 Case 2: Centre Crankshaft at an Angle of Maximum Torque 761
VTU QUESTION PAPERS 776

Addendum for DHB Third and Fourth Editions   *777*

Index   *793*

Part - A

1. Curved Beams, Cylinders and Cylinder Heads

2. Belt, Rope and Chain Drives

3. Springs

4. Spur and Helical Gears

1

Curved Beams, Cylinders and Cylinder Heads

CURVED BEAMS

1.1 INTRODUCTION

A beam is a structural member whose length is large (longer than the width and the thickness) compared to its cross-sectional area which is loaded and supported in the direction transverse to its axis.

Curved beams in the form of C-clamps, press frames, chain links and brackets are used as machine elements. As the name indicates the beam is initially curved before the bending moment is applied. When such members are subjected to bending moment, the stress distribution is not linear since the stress increases more rapidly on the inner side.

1.2 DIFFERENCE BETWEEN A STRAIGHT BEAM AND A CURVED BEAM

Straight Beam (Fig. 1.1):
- A beam is a structural member subjected to a system of external forces acting at right angles to its axis.
- In a straight beam, there are infinite number of layers of equal length and parallel to each other.
- The neutral axis coincides with the centroidal axis.
- The stress distribution is linear.

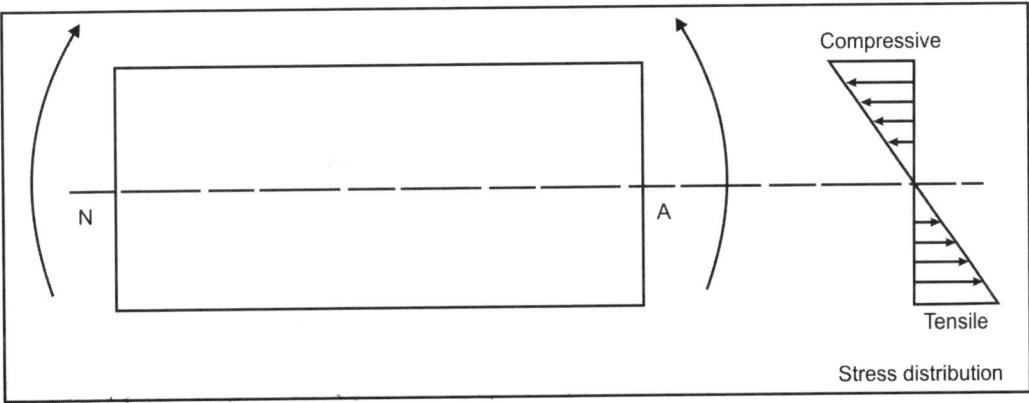

Fig. 1.1: A straight beam

- The expression for straight beam is

$$\sigma_b = \frac{M}{I} y,$$

Where,
- σ_b = is the bending stress
- M = applied bending moment
- I = moment of inertia
- y = distance of layer from neutral axis

Curved Beam (Fig. 1.2):
- Here the beam is initially curved before the bending moment is applied.
- The neutral axis does not coincide with the centroidal axis but is shifted towards the center of curvature of the beam.
- Stress distribution is not linear but is hyperbolic since neutral axis is initially curved.
- Fibres on one side of the neutral axis are in tension while on the other side the layers are in compression.

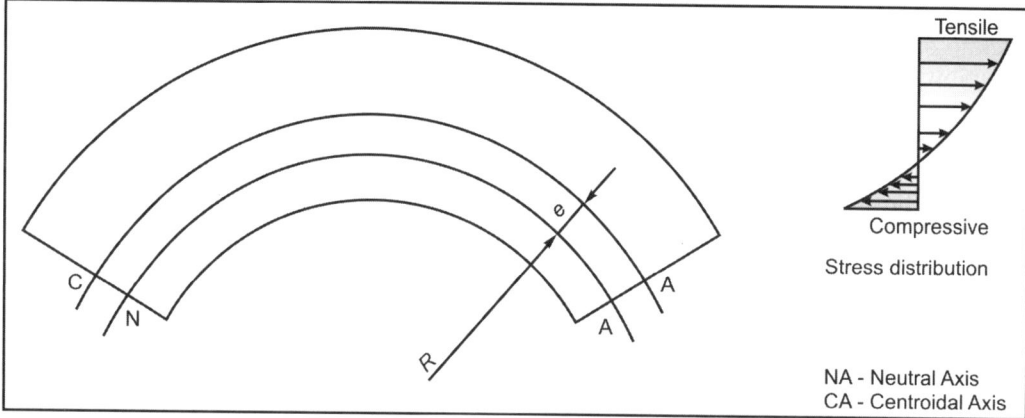

Fig. 1.2: Curved beam

- The expression for bending stress is

$$\sigma_b = \frac{Mc_i}{AeR_i} \text{ or } \sigma_b = \frac{Mc_0}{AeR_0},$$

Where,
- σ_b = bending stress
- M = applied bending moment
- c_i = distance from centroidal axis to the inner fiber
- c_0 = distance from centroidal axis to the outer fiber
- e = distance from centroidal axis to neutral axis
- y = distance of layer from neutral axis
- R_i = radius of curvature of inner fiber
- R_0 = radius of curvature of outer fiber

1.3 STRESSES IN CURVED BEAMS (WINKLER-BACH EQUATION)

Assumptions:
- The material of the beam is perfectly homogeneous and isotropic.
- The material of the beam obeys Hooke's law.

- Young's modulus is same in tension and compression.
- Each layer of the beam is free to expand -or- contract independent of the layer above -or- below it.
- The transverse sections of the beam which are plane before bending remain plane even after bending.
- Stresses induced are within the elastic limit.

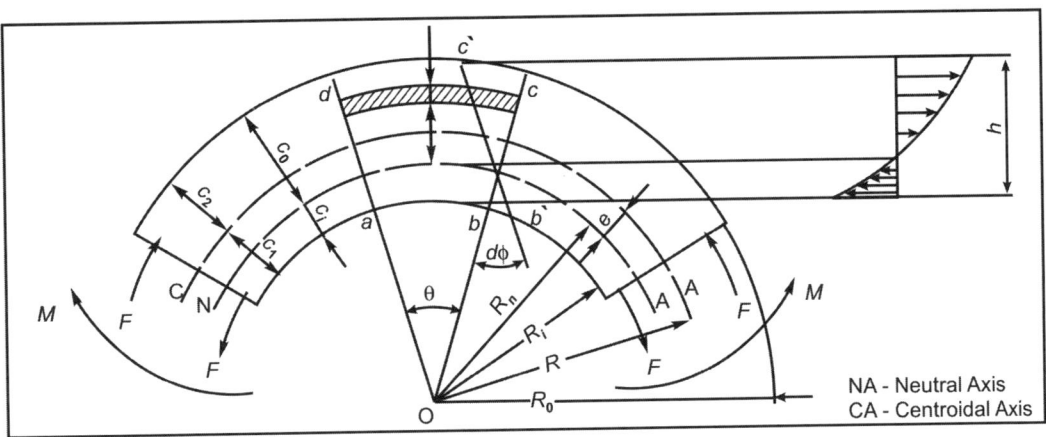

Fig. 1.3: Stress analysis in curved beam (Fig. 10.2/pg 137 DHB)

Let,
F = applied load
M = applied bending moment
A = cross-sectional area
e = distance from centroidal axis to neutral axis
R = radius of curvature of centroidal axis
R_n = radius of curvature of neutral axis
R_i = radius of curvature of inside fiber
R_o = radius of curvature of outside fiber
c_i = distance from neutral axis to inner fiber $(c_1 - e)$
c_o = distance from neutral axis to outer fiber $(c_1 + e)$ or $(h - c_i)$
c_1 = distance from centroidal axis to inner fiber
c_2 = distance from centroidal axis to outer fiber
h = depth of cross-section $(c_1 + c_2)$ or $(c_i + c_o)$
y = distance from neutral axis to fiber under consideration

Consider a segment *abcd* subtending an angle θ at the center of curvature. When the beam is subjected to a bending moment as shown in **Fig. 1.3**, the side *bc* undergoes rotation through an angle $d\phi$ about neutral axis and takes a new position $c'b'$. Due to rotation, the outer fibers are stretched while the inner fibers are compressed.

Consider a strip of thickness dy at a distance y from neutral axis and having an area dA.

The original length of strip = $(R_n + y)\, d\theta$ ... (Eq. 1.1)

And the elongation experienced by the strip = $y\, d\phi$ ... (Eq. 1.2)

Therefore the strain experienced by the strip, $\varepsilon = \dfrac{y\, d\phi}{(R_n + y)\, d\theta}$ ... (Eq. 1.3)

According to Hooke's law, $\phi = \varepsilon E$

$$\sigma = E \frac{y\, d\phi}{(R_n + y) d\theta} = E\left[\frac{d\phi}{d\theta}\right] \frac{y}{(R_n + y)} \qquad \ldots \text{(Eq. 1.4)}$$

Now force responsible for strain in the strip, $dF = \sigma dA$

$$F = \left[E\frac{d\phi}{d\theta}\right] \frac{y\, dA}{(R_n + y)} \qquad \ldots \text{(Eq. 1.5)}$$

For the beam to be in equilibrium, $\Sigma F = 0$

i.e.
$$\int dF = 0$$

$$\int \sigma dA = 0$$

$$\int \left[E\frac{d\phi}{d\theta}\right] \frac{y\, dA}{(R_n + y)} = 0$$

$$E\left[\frac{d\phi}{d\theta}\right] \int \frac{y\, dA}{(R_n + y)} = 0$$

Since $\quad E\left[\dfrac{d\phi}{d\theta}\right] \neq 0$

$$\int \frac{y\, dA}{(R_n + y)} = 0 \qquad \ldots \text{(Eq. 1.6)}$$

Taking moments about neutral axis (NA) for the strip,

$$dM = dFy$$

$$= \left[E\frac{d\phi}{d\theta}\right] \frac{y^2\, dA}{(R_n + y)} \qquad \ldots \text{(Eq. 1.7)}$$

Thus the total bending moment is $M = \int dM = \int \left[E\dfrac{d\phi}{d\theta}\right] \dfrac{y^2\, dA}{(R_n + y)}$

$$= \left[E\frac{d\phi}{d\theta}\right] \int \left[\frac{y^2\, dA}{(R_n + y)}\right]$$

$$= \left[E\frac{d\phi}{d\theta}\right] \int \left[y - \left(\frac{yR_n}{R_n + y}\right)\right] dA$$

$$= \left[E\frac{d\phi}{d\theta}\right] \left\{\int y\, dA - R_n \int \frac{y}{R_n + y} dA\right\}$$

$$M = \left[E\frac{d\phi}{d\theta}\right] \left\{\int y\, dA - 0\right\} \qquad \ldots \text{using (Eq. 1.6)}$$

but $\int y\, dA$ is the moment of inertia, which may be replaced with Ae, i.e. the product of total area and distance e from centroidal axis to neutral axis.

Therefore,
$$M = \left[E\frac{d\phi}{d\theta}\right]Ae$$

$$\left[E\frac{d\phi}{d\theta}\right] = \frac{M}{Ae} \qquad \text{...(Eq. 1.8)}$$

Substituting Eq. (1.8) in Eq. (1.4)
$$\sigma = \frac{M}{Ae}\left(\frac{y}{R_n + y}\right) \qquad \text{...(Eq. 1.9) } \mathbf{10.1/Pg\ 132,\ DHB}$$

Equation (1.9) gives the stress induced in any fibre at a distance y from the neutral axis.

y is negative, when measured towards center of curvature ($-c_i$)
y is positive, when measured away from center of curvature (c_0)
at inner fiber, $y = -c_i$

Eq. (1.9) yields
$$\sigma_i = \frac{M}{Ae}\left(\frac{-c_i}{R_n - c_i}\right)$$

$$\therefore \quad \sigma_i = \frac{-Mc_i}{AeR_i} \qquad (R_n - c_i = R_i) \qquad \text{...(Eq. 1.10)}$$

at outer fiber, $y = +c_0$

Eq. (1.9) yields
$$\sigma_0 = \frac{M}{Ae}\left(\frac{c_0}{R_n + c_0}\right)$$

$$\sigma_0 = \frac{Mc_0}{AeR_0} \qquad (R_n + c_0 = R_0) \qquad \text{...(Eq. 1.11)}$$

Based on the applied bending moment, outer fibers are subjected to compression (negative) and inner fibers are subjected to tension (positive).

Eq. (1.9) yields
$$\sigma_i = \frac{Mc_i}{AeR_i} \qquad \text{...(Eq. 1.12) } \mathbf{10.2b/Pg\ 132,\ DHB}$$

Eq. (1.11) yields
$$\sigma_0 = \frac{-Mc_0}{AeR_0} \qquad \text{...(Eq. 1.13) } \mathbf{10.2a/Pg\ 132,\ DHB}$$

Note:
- The bending stress in a curved beam is zero at a point other than at centroidal axis.
- If the section is symmetrical such as circular, rectangular, I-beam with equal flanges, then maximum bending moment will always occur at the inside fiber.
- If the section has an axial load in addition to bending, then it should be added to the bending stress to obtain the resultant stress on the section.
- On the other hand, if the line of action of force does not pass through the centre of gravity (C_g) of the section, it is referred to as eccentric load. To analyze such problems, we replace the eccentric load by an equal and parallel force through C_g of the cross-section together with a couple (C) in opposite direction as shown in **Fig. 1.4.**

Direct stress (tensile/compressive), $\sigma = \dfrac{F}{A}$

This couple $C = Fx$ produces bending stress in the cross-section and hence is a bending moment with respect to centroidal axis.

8 Design of Machine Elements II (DME II)

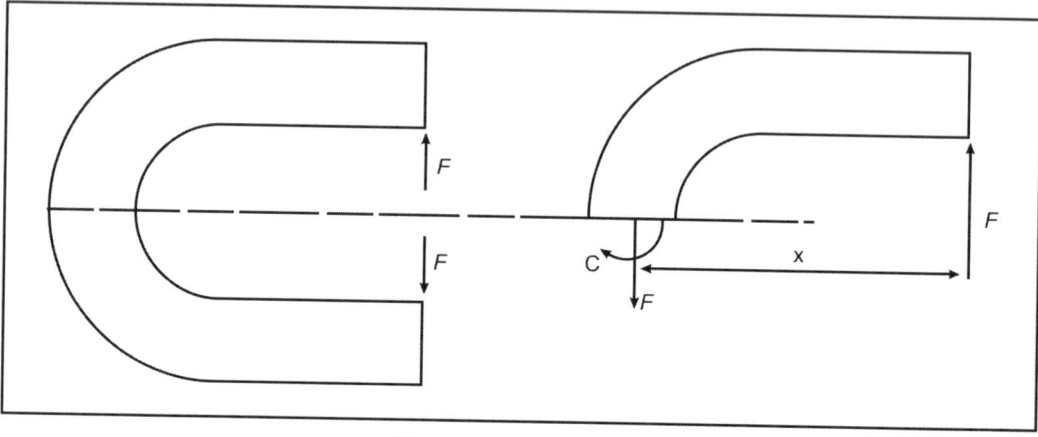

Fig. 1.4: Eccentric load

1.4 STEPS TO SOLVE CURVED BEAM PROBLEMS

1. Locate the position of C_g of cross-section with respect to the innermost fiber.

$$\bar{x} = \frac{\Sigma ax}{\Sigma a} \quad \text{or} \quad \bar{y} = \frac{\Sigma ay}{\Sigma a}$$

2. Replace the eccentric load by an equal and parallel force through C_g of the cross-section together with a couple in opposite direction.
3. Evaluate the direct stresses (σ) produced.
4. Evaluate the extreme fiber ending stress due to couple.
5. Evaluate the resultant stresses in the extreme fibers as

   Resultant stress in the inner most fiber, $(\sigma_i)_r = \sigma + \sigma_i$
   Resultant stress in the outer most fiber, $(\sigma_0)_r = \sigma + \sigma_0$

Problems of Type I–To Find Stress

1. Determine the maximum stress induced in a punch press as shown in Fig. 1.5.

Solution: $F = 120$ kN, $\sigma_i, \sigma_0 = ?$

a. To find $\bar{x}$:

$a_1 = 30 \times 10 = 300$ mm², $\quad a_2 = 8 \times 20 = 160$ mm², $\quad a_3 = 16 \times 4 = 64$ mm²,
$x_1 = 10/2 = 5$ mm, $\quad\quad x_2 = (20/2) + 10 = 20$ mm, $\quad x_3 = (4/2) + 30 = 32$ mm,
$A = \Sigma a = a_1 + a_2 + a_3 = 524$ mm²

$$\bar{x} = \frac{\Sigma ax}{\Sigma a} = \frac{(300 \times 5) + (160 \times 20) + (64 \times 32)}{(300 + 160 + 64)} = 12.87 \text{ mm}$$

b. Replace the given eccentric force by an equal and parallel force through C_g along with a couple as shown in **Fig. 1.5(a)**.

c. Direct stress $\sigma = \dfrac{F}{A} = \dfrac{120 \times 10^3}{524} = 229$ N/mm²

d. To find the bending stresses (σ_i, σ_0)

- Moment, $M = Fx$

$$= 120 \times 10^3 (900 + 200 + 12.87)$$
$$M = 133.5 \times 10^6 \text{ N-mm}$$

Curved Beams, Cylinders and Cylinder Heads

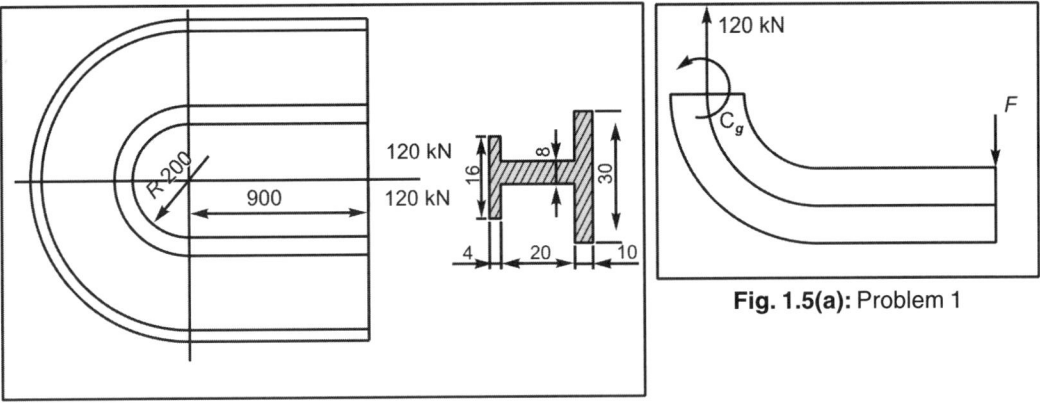

Fig. 1.5(a): Problem 1

Fig. 1.5: Problem 1

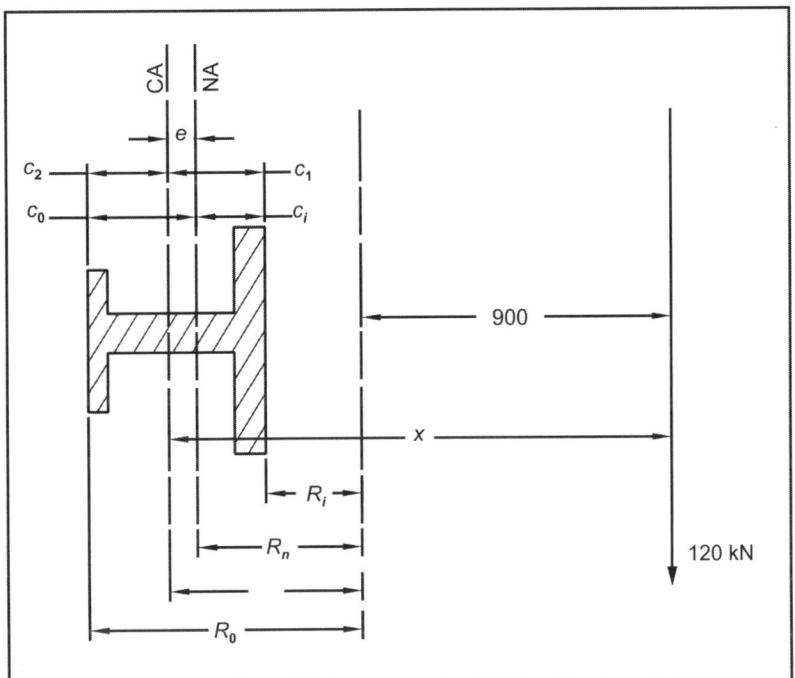

Fig. 1.5(b): Problem 1

- **Fig. 10-Tb 10.1/Pg 136, DHB**–for an I-section (Fig. 1.5(b)),
$e = R - R_n$

$$e = R - \frac{A}{B\ln^*\left(\frac{R+d-c_1}{R-c_1}\right) + b_2 \ln\left(\frac{R+c_2-d_1}{R-d-c_1}\right) = b_1 \ln\left(\frac{R+c_2}{R-c_2-d_1}\right)}$$

Here, $B = 30$ mm, $b_1 = 16$ mm, $d = 10$ mm, $d_1 = 4$ mm, $d_2 = 8$ mm,
$H = 10 + 20 + 4 = 34$ mm,

Also $R_i = 200$ mm, $R_0 = R_i + H = 200 + 34 = 234$ mm, $c_1 = \bar{x} = 12.87$ mm,

$R = c_1 + R_i = 12.87 + 200 = 212.87$ mm, $c_2 = H - c_1 = 34 - 12.87 = 21.13$ mm

---
* while doing problems, ln (natural log) is used in place of $\log_e$.

$$= 212.87 - \frac{524}{30\ln\left(\frac{212.87+10-12.87}{212.87-12.87}\right)+8\ln\left(\frac{212.87+21.13-4}{212.87+10-12.87}\right)+16\ln\left(\frac{212.87+21.13}{212.87+21.13-4}\right)}$$

$e = 0.496$ mm

Now $c_i = c_1 - e = 12.87 - 0.496 = 12.37$ mm, $c_0 = c_2 + e = 21.13 + 0.496 = 21.63$ mm

- Bending stress at inner fiber,

$$\sigma_i = \frac{Mc_i}{AeR_i} = \frac{(133.5\times 10^6)\times 12.37}{524\times 0.496\times 200} = 31.77 \text{ kN/mm}^2 \quad \ldots \text{10.2b/Pg 132, DHB}$$

- Bending stress at outer fiber,

$$\sigma_0 = \frac{-Mc_0}{AeR_0} = \frac{-(133.5\times 10^6)\times 21.63}{524\times 0.496\times 234} = -47.48 \text{ kN/mm}^2 \quad \ldots \text{10.2a/Pg 132, DHB}$$

e. Resultant stresses
  - Resultant stress in the inner most fiber,
  $$(\sigma_i)_r = \sigma + \sigma_i = 229 + 31.17 \times 10^3 = 31.40 \text{ kN/mm}^2$$
  - Resultant stress in the outer most fiber,
  $$(\sigma_0)_r = \sigma + \sigma_0 = 229 - 47.48 \times 10^3 = -47.25 \text{ kN/mm}^2$$

2. A section of a C-clamp is shown in Fig. 1.6. Determine the stresses.

Solution: $\sigma_i = 52.4$ kN/mm^2 $\sigma_0 = -57.7$ kN/mm^2 $(\sigma_i)_r = 54.6$ kN/mm^2
$(\sigma_0)_r = 55.5$ kN/mm^2

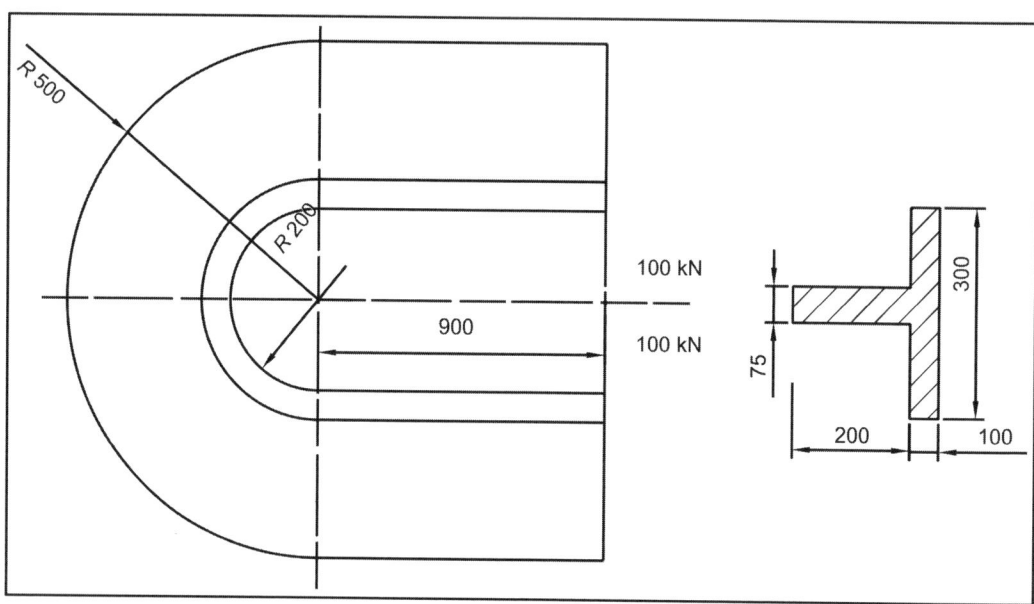

Fig. 1.6: Problem 2

3. A crane hook has a trapezoidal cross-section as:
Inside width = 87.5 mm,
Outside width = 25 mm,
Depth = 112.5 mm

The line of action of load passes through the center of curvature. The radius of curvature of inner side = 62.5 mm. Calculate the maximum stresses developed under a load of 90 kN. Also draw the stress distribution (Fig. 1.7).

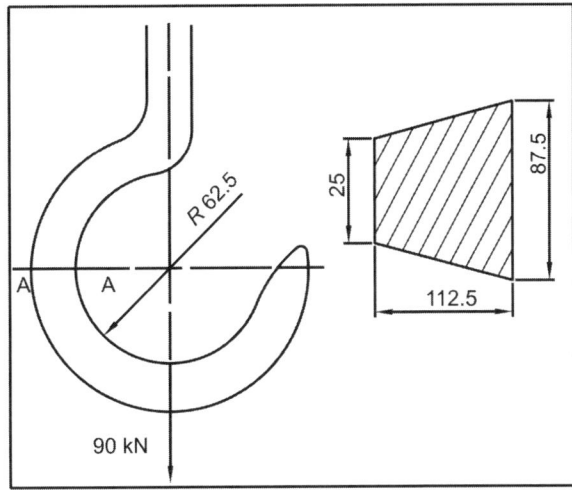

Fig. 1.7: Problem 3

Solution: $F = 90$ kN, $\sigma_i, \sigma_0 = ?$

a. To find $\bar{x}$:
   - From **Fig. f -Tb 1.3/Pg 9, DHB**

   $b = 25$ mm, $b_1 = 87.5$ mm, $h = 112.5$ mm, therefore, $b_0 = b_1 - b = 87.5 - 25 = 62.5$ mm

   $$c = \frac{(3b + 2b_0)h}{3(2b + b_0)}$$

   $$c = \frac{(3 \times 25 + 2 \times 62.5) \times 112.5}{3(2 \times 25 + 62.5)} = 66.67 \text{ mm}$$

   $\bar{x} = h - c = 112.5 - 66.67 = 45.83$ mm

b. Replace the given eccentric force by an equal and parallel force through C_g along with a couple (similar to **Fig. 1.5(a)**).

c. Direct stress, $\sigma = \dfrac{F}{A} = \dfrac{90 \times 10^3}{6328.13} = 14.22$ N/mm^2

   $$\therefore \quad A = \frac{h}{2}(b_1 + b) = \frac{112.5 \times (87.5 + 25)}{2} = 6328.13 \text{ mm}^2$$

d. To find the bending stresses (σ_i, σ_0)
   - Moment, $M = Fx = F(R_i + \bar{x})$

   $= 90 \times 10^3 \times (62.5 + 45.83)$

   $M = 9.75 \times 10^6$ N-mm

   - **Fig. 7-Tb 10.1/Pg 135, DHB**–for a trapezoidal section,

$e = R - R_n$

$$e = R - \frac{A}{\left[\left(\frac{b_1(R+c_2)-b(R-c_1)}{h}\right)\ln\left(\frac{R+c_2}{R-c_1}\right)\right]-(b_1-b)}$$

Here, $b_1 = 87.5$ mm, $b = 25$ mm, $h = 112.5$ mm, $R_i = 62.5$ mm, $c_1 = \bar{x} = 45.83$ mm,
$R = R_i + c_1 = 62.5 + 45.83 = 108.33$ mm, $R_o = R_i + h = 62.5 + 112.5 = 175$ mm,
$c_2 = h - c_1 = 112.5 - 45.83 = 66.67$ mm

$$= 108.33 - \frac{6328.13}{\left[\left(\frac{87.5(108.33+66.67)-25(108.33-45.83)}{112.5}\right)\ln\left(\frac{108.33+66.67}{108.33-45.83}\right)\right]-(87.5-25)}$$

$e = 8.43$ mm

Now, $c_0 = c_2 + e = 66.67 + 8.43 = 75.1$ mm, $c_i = c_1 - e = 45.83 - 8.43 = 37.4$ mm
- Bending stress at inner fiber,

$$\sigma_i = \frac{Mc_i}{AeR_i} = \frac{(9.75 \times 10^6) \times 37.4}{6328.13 \times 8.43 \times 62.5} = 109.37 \text{ kN/mm}^2 \quad \ldots \textbf{10.2b/Pg 132, DHB}$$

- Bending stress at outer fiber,

$$\sigma_0 = \frac{-Mc_0}{AeR_0} = \frac{-(9.75 \times 10^6) \times 75.1}{6328.13 \times 8.43 \times 175} = 78.43 \text{ kN/mm}^2 \quad \ldots \textbf{10.2a/Pg 132, DHB}$$

e. Resultant stresses
- Resultant stress in the inner most fiber,
$$\sigma_i)_r = \sigma + \sigma_i = 14.22 + 109.37 = 123.6 \text{ N/mm}^2$$
- Resultant stress in the outer most fiber,
$$\sigma_0)_r = \sigma + \sigma_0 = 14.22 - 78.43 = -64.21 \text{ N/mm}^2$$

Thus the inner most fiber is subjected to a maximum bending stress of 123.6 N/mm².
The resultant stresses are plotted as shown in **Fig. 1.7(b)**.

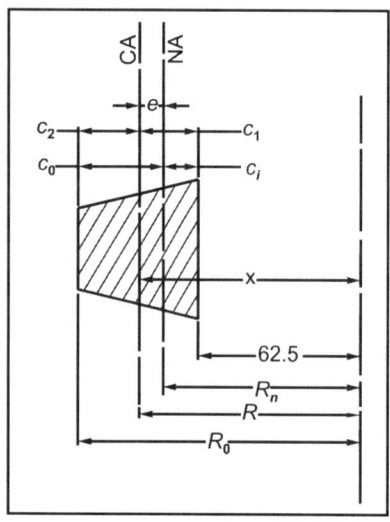

Fig. 1.7(a): Problem 3

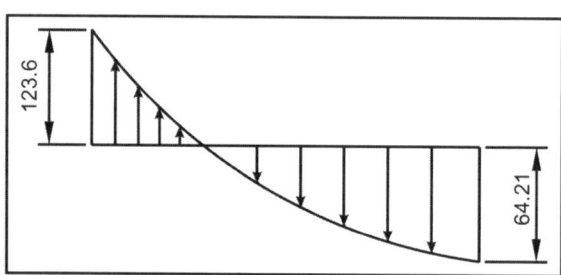

Fig. 1.7(b): Problem 3

4. If the cross-section in problem 3 is a rectangle as shown, with the load being 20 kN, find the resultant stresses. The radius of curvature on inner side is 50 mm and that on the outer side is 150 mm (Fig. 1.8).

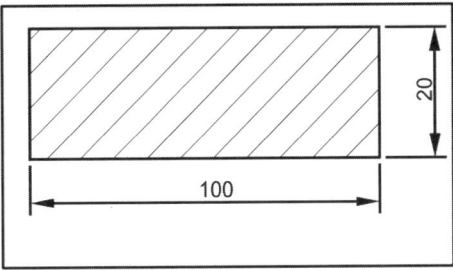

Fig. 1.8: Problem 4

Solution:

$\sigma = 10 \text{ kN/mm}^2$
$\sigma_1 = 92 \text{ kN/mm}^2$
$\sigma_0 = -44 \text{ kN/mm}^2$
$\sigma_i)_r = 102 \text{ kN/mm}^2$
$\sigma_0)_r = -32 \text{ kN/mm}^2$

5. Compute the combined stresses at the inner and outer fibres in the critical section of a crane hook which is required to lift loads up to 25 kN. The hook has trapezoidal cross-section with parallel sides 60 mm and 30 mm, the distance between them being 90 mm. The inner radius of the hook is 100 mm. The load line is nearer to the inner surface of the hook by 25 mm than the center of curvature at the critical section (Fig. 1.9). What will be the stresses at the inner and outer fibre, if the beam is treated as straight beam for the given load?

[VTU – Dec 06/Jan. 07 – 12 Marks]

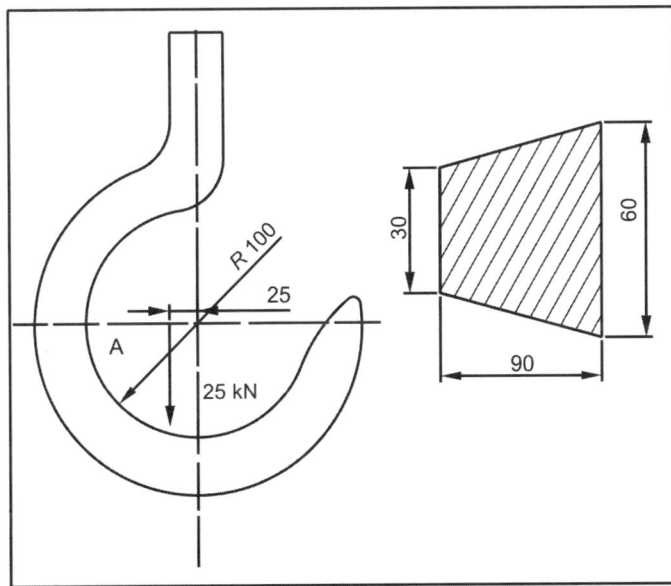

Fig. 1.9: Problem 5

14 Design of Machine Elements II (DME II)

Solution: $F = 25$ kN, $\sigma_i, \sigma_0 = ?$

Case 1: *Curved beam:*

a. To find $\bar{x}$:
- From **Fig. f -Tb 1.3/Pg 9, DHB**

  $b = 30$ mm, $b_1 = 60$ mm, $h = 90$ mm, therefore, $b_0 = b_1 - b = 60 - 30 = 30$ mm

  $$c = \frac{(3b + 2b_0)h}{3(2b + b_0)}$$

  $$c = \frac{(3 \times 30 + 2 \times 30)90}{3(2 \times 30 + 30)} = 50 \text{ mm}$$

  $$\bar{x} = h - c = 90 - 50 = 40 \text{ mm}$$

b. Replace the given eccentric force by an equal and parallel force through C_g along with a couple (similar to **Fig. 1.5(a)**).

c. Direct stress, $\sigma = \dfrac{F}{A} = \dfrac{25 \times 10^3}{4050} = 6.17$ N/mm^2

$\therefore$
$$A = \frac{h}{2}(b_1 + b) = \frac{90 \times (60 + 30)}{2} = 4050 \text{ mm}^2$$

d. To find the bending stresses (σ_i, σ_0)
- $M = Fx = F(R_i + \bar{x})$
  $= 25 \times 10^3 \times (75 + 40)$
  $M = 2.88 \times 10^6$ N-mm

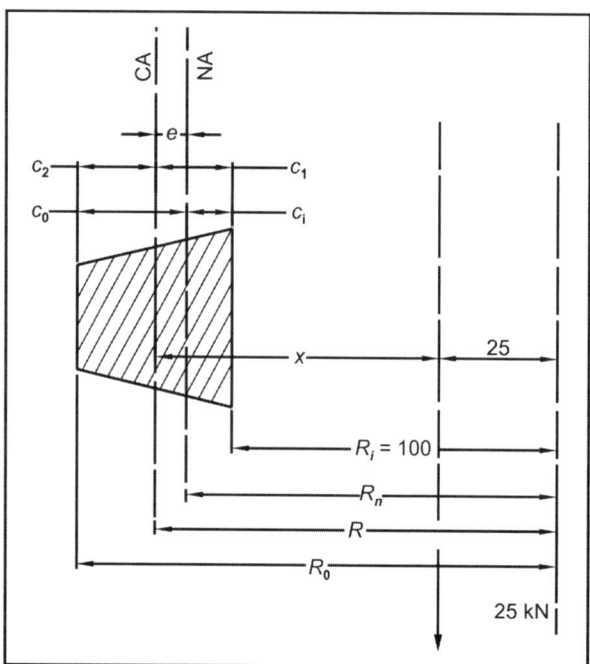

Fig. 1.9(a): Problem 5

- **Fig. 7-Tb 10.1/Pg 135, DHB** – for a trapezoidal section,

$e = R - R_n$

$$e = R - \frac{A}{\left[\left(\frac{b_1(R+c_2)-b(R+c_2)}{h}\right)\right]\ln\left(\frac{R+c_2}{R+c_1}\right)-(b_1+b)}$$

Here, $b_1 = 60$ mm, $b = 30$, $h = 90$
$R_i = 100$ mm, $c_1 = \bar{x} = 40$ mm, $\quad R = R_i + c_1 = 100 + 40 = 140$ mm
$R_0 = R_i + h = 100 + 90 = 190$ mm $\quad c_2 = h - c_1 = 90 - 40 = 50$

$$= 140 - \frac{4050}{\left(\frac{60(140+50)-30(140-40)}{90}\right)\ln\left(\frac{140+50}{140+40}\right)-(60+30)}$$

$e = 4.58$ mm

Now, $c_0 = c_2 + e = 50 + 4.58 = 54.58$ mm, $c_i = c_1 - e = 40 - 4.58 = 35.42$ mm

- Bending stress at inner fiber,

$$\sigma_i = \frac{Mc_i}{AeR_i} = \frac{(2.88 \times 10^6) \times 35.42}{4050 \times 4.58 \times 100} = 55 \text{ N/mm}^2 \quad \ldots \text{10.2b/ Pg 132, DHB}$$

- Bending stress at outer fiber,

$$\sigma_0 = \frac{-Mc_0}{AeR_0} = \frac{-(2.88 \times 10^6) \times 54.58}{4050 \times 4.58 \times 190} = 44.6 \text{ N/mm}^2 \quad \ldots \text{10.2a/ Pg 132, DHB}$$

e. Resultant stresses
 - Resultant stress in the inner most fiber, $(\sigma_i)_r = \sigma + \sigma_i = 6.17 + 55 = 61.17$ N/mm^2
 - Resultant stress in the outer most fiber, $(\sigma_0)_r = \sigma + \sigma_0 = 6.17 - 44.6 = -38.43$ mm^2

Case 2: *Straight beam:*
 - From **Fig. f-Tb 1.3/Pg 9, DHB,**
  $b = 30$ mm, $b_1 = 60$ mm, $h = 90$ mm, therefore, $b_0 = b_1 - b = 60 - 30 = 30$ mm

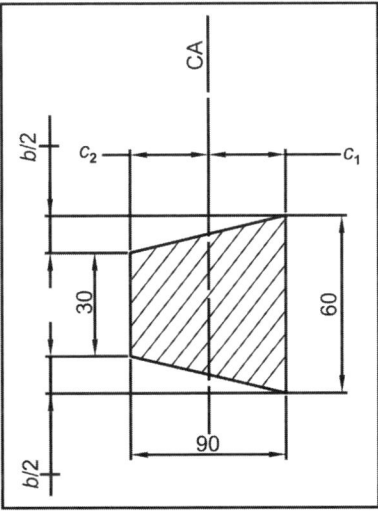

Fig. 1.9(b): Problem 5

We know that,

$$\frac{M}{I} = \frac{\sigma}{c} = \frac{E}{R}$$

But $I = \dfrac{(6b^2 + 6bb_0 + b_0^2)}{36(2b + b_0)}$ ... **Pg 9/ DHB**

$$= \frac{(6 \times 30^2 + 6 \times 30 \times 30 + 30^2) 90^3}{36(2 \times 30 + 30)}$$

$I = 2632500 \text{ mm}^4$

Also, $c = \dfrac{(3b + 2b_0)h}{2(2b + b_0)}$ ... **Pg 9/ DHB**

$$= \frac{(3 \times 30 + 2 \times 30) 90}{3(2 \times 30 + 30)}$$

$c = 50 \text{ mm}$

Comparing **Fig. f-Tb 1.3/Pg 9, DHB** with **Fig. 7-Tb 10.1/Pg 135, DHB**,

$c = c_2 = 50 \text{ mm}$
$c_1 = h - c_2 = 90 - 50 = 40 \text{ mm}$

- Bending stress at inner fiber, $\sigma_i = \dfrac{Mc_i}{I} = \dfrac{(2.88 \times 10^6) \times 40}{2632500} = 43.76 \text{ N/mm}^2$

- Bending stress at outer fiber, $\sigma_0 = \dfrac{Mc_0}{I} = \dfrac{-(2.88 \times 10^6) \times 50}{2632500} = -54.7 \text{ N/mm}^2$

6. The horizontal cross-section of a crane hook is an isosceles triangle of 120 mm deep, the inner width being 90 mm. The hook carries a load of 50 kN. Inner radius of curvature is 100 mm. The line of action of load passes through the center line of curvature. Determine the stress at the extreme fibres (Fig. 1.10).

[VTU – June/July 09 – 12 Marks]

Solution: $F = 50 \text{ kN}$, $R_i = 100 \text{ mm}$, $\sigma_i, \sigma_0 = ?$

a. To find $\bar{x}$:

- We know that, $\bar{x} = \dfrac{h}{3} = \dfrac{120}{3} = 40 \text{ mm}$

b. Replace the given eccentric force by an equal and parallel force through C_g along with a couple.

c. Direct stress. $\sigma = \dfrac{F}{A} = \dfrac{50 \times 10^3}{5400} = 9.26 \text{ N/mm}^2$

$\therefore \quad A = \dfrac{90 \times 120}{2} = 5400 \text{ mm}^2$

d. To find the bending stresses (σ_i, σ_0)

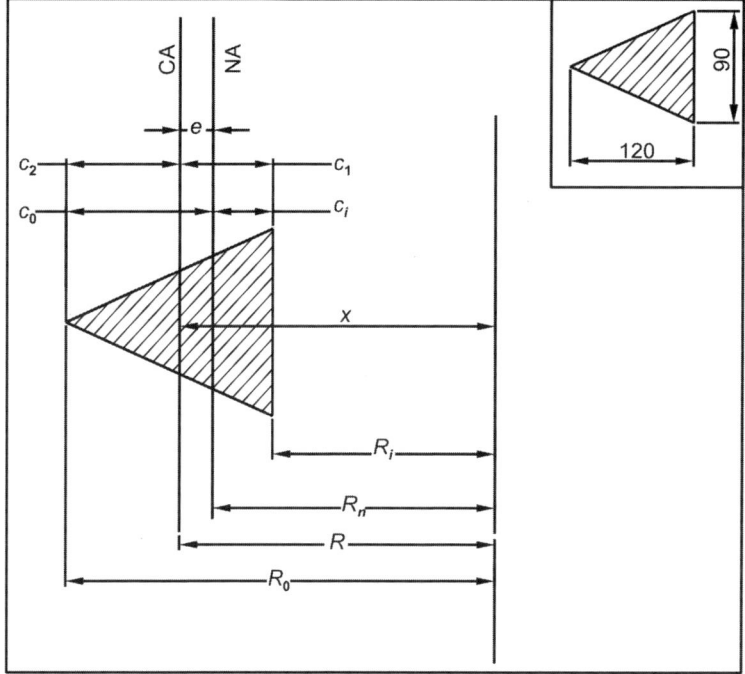

Fig. 1.10: Problem 6

- Moment, $M = Fx = F(R_i + \bar{x})$
$$= 50 \times 10^3 \times (100 + 40)$$
$$M = 7 \times 10^6 \text{ N-mm}$$

- **Fig. 6- Tb 10.1/Pg 135, DHB** – for a triangular section,

$e = R - R_n$

$$e = R - \frac{h^2/2}{\left[(R+c_2)\ln\left(\frac{R+c_2}{R-c_1}\right)\right] - h}$$

$b = 90$ mm, $h = 120$ mm, $c_1 = \bar{x} = 40$ mm, $c_2 = h - 120 - 40 = 80$ mm
$R = R_i + c_1 = 100 + 40 = 140$ mm, $R_0 = R_i + h = 100 + 120 = 220$ mm,

$$= 400 - \frac{(120^2/2)}{\left[(140+80)\ln\left(\frac{140+80}{140-40}\right)\right] - 120}$$

$e = 5.32$ mm

Now, $c_0 = c_2 + e = 80 + 5.32 = 85.32$ mm, $c_i = c_1 - e = 40 - 5.32 = 34.68$ mm

- Bending stress at inner fiber,

$$\sigma_i = \frac{Mc_i}{AeR_i} = \frac{(7 \times 10^6) \times 34.68}{5400 \times 5.32 \times 100} = 84.5 \text{ N/mm}^2 \quad \ldots \textbf{10.2b/Pg 132, DHB}$$

- Bending stress at outer fiber,

$$\sigma_0 = \frac{-Mc_0}{AeR_0} = \frac{-(7 \times 10^6) \times 85.32}{5400 \times 5.32 \times 220} = 94.50 \text{ N/mm}^2 \ldots \textbf{10.2a/Pg 132, DHB}$$

e. Resultant stresses

- Resultant stress in the inner most fiber, $(\sigma_i)_r = \sigma + \sigma_i = 9.26 + 84.5 = 93.76 \text{ N/mm}^2$
- Resultant stress in the outer most fiber, $(\sigma_0)_r = \sigma + \sigma_0 = 9.26 - 94.50 = -85.24 \text{ N/mm}^2$
- Maximum shear stress, $\tau_{max} = \dfrac{\sigma_{max}}{2} = \dfrac{93.76}{2} = 46.88 \text{ N/mm}^2$

7. Calculate the stresses at the points A and B for a circular beam as shown in Fig. 1.11. The circular beam is subjected to a compressive load of 6 kN.

[VTU – July 07 – 10 Marks]

Solution: $F = 6000 \text{ N}$ (compressive), $R_i = 40 \text{ mm}$, $d = 35 \text{ mm}$, $\sigma + \sigma_0 = ?$

a. To find $\bar{x}$:

- We know that, $\bar{x} = \dfrac{d}{2} = \dfrac{35}{2} = 17.5 \text{ mm}$

b. Replace the given eccentric force by an equal and parallel force through C_g along with a couple.

c. Direct stress, $\sigma = \dfrac{F}{A} = \dfrac{-6 \times 10^3}{962.11} = -6.24 \text{ N/mm}^2$ (compressive)

$$\because \quad A = \dfrac{\pi d^2}{4} = \dfrac{\pi \times 35^2}{4} = 962.11 \text{ mm}^2$$

d. To find the bending stresses $(\sigma + \sigma_0)$

- Moment, $M = Fx = F(R_i + \bar{x})$
  $= 6000 \times (40 + 17.5)$
  $M = 345 \times 10^3 \text{ N-mm}$

- **Fig. 2-Tb 10.1/Pg 134 DHB** – for an circular section,
  $e = R - R_n$

  $e = R - \dfrac{c^2/2}{R - \sqrt{R^2 - c^2}}$

  $R_i = 40 \text{ mm}, \ c_1 = c_2 = 17.5 \text{ mm} = \bar{x}$

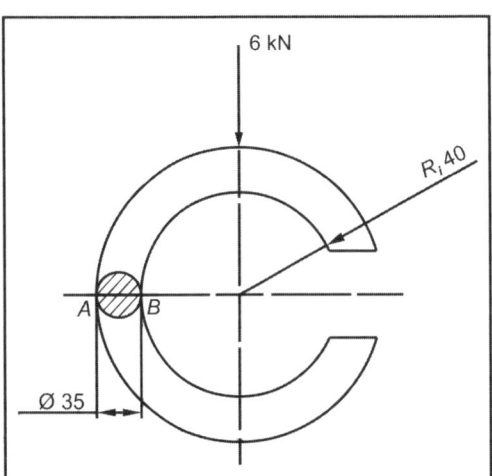

Fig. 1.11: Problem 7

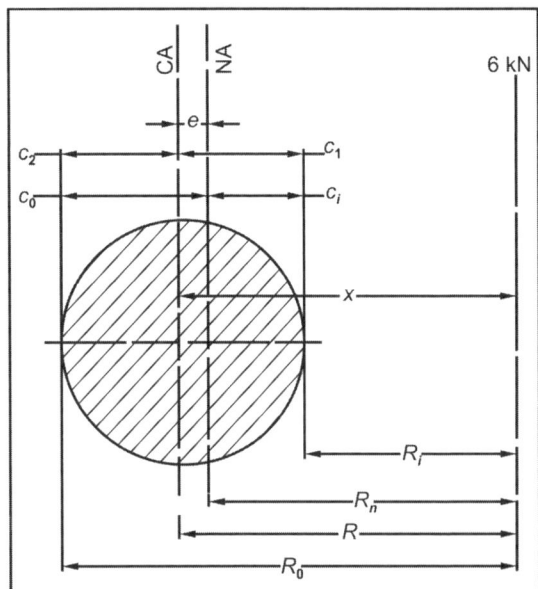

Fig. 1.11(a): Problem 7

$R = R_i + c_1 = 40 + 17.5 = 57.5$ mm, $R_0 = R_i + d = 40 + 35 = 75$ mm

$$= 57.5 - \frac{17.5^2/2}{57.5 - \sqrt{57.5^2 - 17.5^2}}$$

$e = 1.36$ mm

Now, $c_i = c_1 + e = 17.5 - 1.36 = 16.14$ mm, $c_0 = c_2 + e = 17.5 + 1.36 = 18.86$ mm

- Bending stress at inner fiber,

$$\sigma_i = \frac{Mc_i}{AeR_i} = \frac{(345 \times 10^3) \times 16.14}{962.11 \times 1.36 \times 40} = 106.4 \text{ N/mm}^2 \quad \ldots \textbf{10.2b/Pg 132, DHB}$$

- Bending stress at outer fiber,

$$\sigma_0 = \frac{-Mc_0}{AeR_0} = \frac{-(345 \times 10^3) \times 18.86}{962.11 \times 1.36 \times 40} = 66.3 \text{ N/mm}^2 \quad \ldots \textbf{10.2a/Pg 132, DHB}$$

e. Resultant stresses
  - Resultant stress in the inner most fiber, $\sigma_i)_r = \sigma + \sigma_i = -6.24 + 106.4 = 100.16$ N/mm²
  - Resultant stress in the outer most fiber, $\sigma_0)_r = \sigma + \sigma_0 = -6.24 - 66.3 = -72.54$ N/mm²

8. **An open S-link made from a rod of 25 mm is as shown in Fig. 1.12. Calculate the stresses at sections A – A and B – B.**

Solution: $F = 900$ N, $d = 25$ mm, $\sigma_i + \sigma_0 = ?$

Case 1: *Section A – A:*

a. To find $\bar{x}$:
  - We know that, $\bar{x} = \dfrac{d}{2} = \dfrac{25}{2} = 12.5$ mm

b. Replace the given eccentric force by an equal and parallel force through C_g along with a couple.

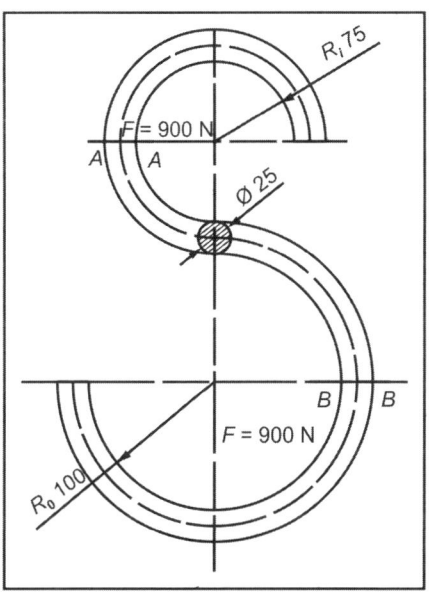

Fig. 1.12: Problem 8

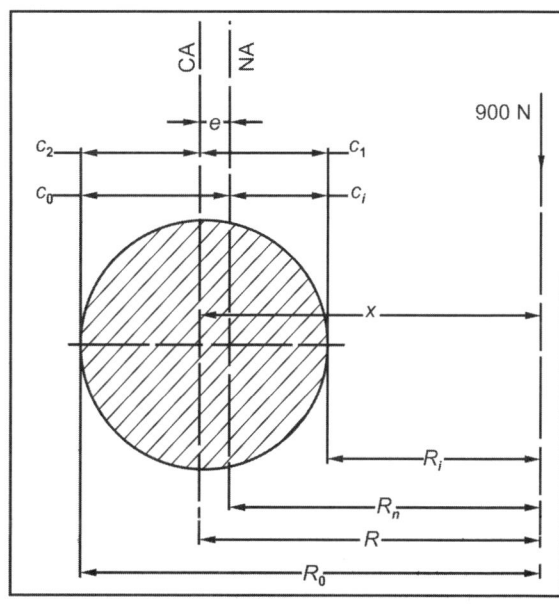

Fig. 1.12(a): Problem 8

c. Direct stress, $\sigma = F/A = \dfrac{900}{\pi \times 25^2/4} = 1.83 \text{ N/mm}^2$

d. To find the bending stresses $(\sigma_i + \sigma_0)$
- Moment, $M = Fx = F(R_i + \bar{x})$
  $= 900 \times (75 + 12.5)$
  $M = 78750$ N-mm
- **Fig. 2-Tb 10.1/Pg 134, DHB** – for a circular section, $e = R - R_n$

  $e = R - \dfrac{c^2/2}{R - \sqrt{R^2 - c^2}}$

  $R_i = 75$ mm, $c_1 = c_2 = 12.5$ mm $= \bar{x}$,
  $R = R_i + c_1 = 75 + 12.5 = 87.5$ mm,
  $R_0 = R_i + d = 75 + 25 = 100$ mm,

  $= 87.5 - \dfrac{12.5^2/2}{87.5 - \sqrt{87.5^2 - 12.5^2}}$

  $e = 0.45$ mm

  Now, $c_i = c_1 - e = 12.5 - 0.45 = 12.05$ mm, $\quad c_0 = c_2 - e = 12.5 + 0.45 = 12.95$ mm

- Bending stress at inner fiber,

  $\sigma_i = \dfrac{Mc_i}{AeR_i} = \dfrac{(78750) \times 12.05}{490.87 \times 0.45 \times 75} = 57.28 \text{ N/mm}^2$ ... **10.2b/Pg 132, DHB**

- Bending stress at outer fiber,

  $\sigma_0 = \dfrac{-Mc_0}{AeR_0} = \dfrac{-(78750) \times 12.95}{490.87 \times 0.45 \times 100} = -46.16 \text{ N/mm}^2$ ...**10.2a/Pg 132, DHB**

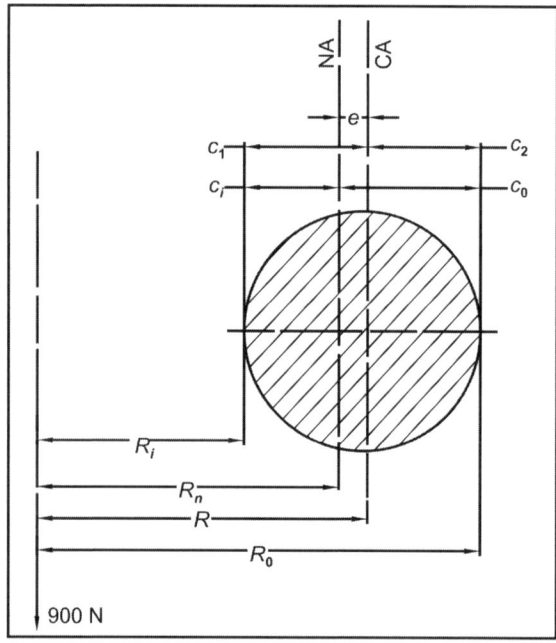

Fig. 1.12(b): Problem 8

e. Resultant stresses
- Resultant stress in the inner most fiber, $(\sigma_i)_r = \sigma + \sigma_i = 1.83 + 57.28 = 59.11 \text{ N/mm}^2$
- Resultant stress in the outer most fiber, $(\sigma_0)_r = \sigma + \sigma_0 = 1.83 - 46.16 = -44.33 \text{ N/mm}^2$
- Maximum shear stress, $\tau_{max} = \dfrac{\sigma_{max}}{2} = \dfrac{59.11}{2} = 29.56 \text{ N/mm}^2$

Case 2: *Section B – B:*

a. $\bar{x} = 25$ mm

b. $\sigma = 1.83 \text{ N/mm}^2$

c. To find the bending stresses $(\sigma_i + \sigma_0)$
- $M = Fx = F(R_i + \bar{x})$
  $= 900 \times (100 + 12.5)$
- $\therefore M = 101250$ N-mm
- **Fig. 2- Tb 10.1/Pg 134, DHB**–for a circular section,
  $e = R - R_n$

$$e = R - \dfrac{c^2/2}{R - \sqrt{R^2 - c^2}}$$

$R_i = 100$ mm, $c_1 = c_2 = 12.5$ mm $= \bar{x}$,
$R = R_i + c_1 = 100 + 12.5 = 112.5$ mm,
$R_0 = R_i + d = 100 + 25 = 125$ mm,

$$= 112.5 - \dfrac{12.5^2/2}{112.5 - \sqrt{112.5^2 - 12.5^2}}$$

$e = 0.348$ mm

Now, $c_i = c_1 - e = 12.5 - 0.348 = 12.152$ mm, $c_0 = c_2 + e = 12.5 + 0.348 = 12.848$ mm

- Bending stress at inner fiber,

$$\sigma_i = \dfrac{Mc_i}{AeR_i} = \dfrac{(101250) \times 12.152}{490.87 \times 0.348 \times 100} = 72.03 \text{ N/mm}^2 \quad \ldots \text{10.2b/Pg 132, DHB}$$

- Bending stress at outer fiber,

$$\sigma_0 = \dfrac{-Mc_0}{AeR_0} = \dfrac{-(101250) \times 12.848}{490.87 \times 0.348 \times 125} = -60.92 \text{ N/mm}^2 \quad \ldots \text{10.2a/Pg 132, DHB}$$

d. Resultant stresses
- Resultant stress in the inner most fiber, $(\sigma_i)_r = \sigma + \sigma_i = 1.83 + 72.03 = 73.86 \text{ N/mm}^2$
- Resultant stress in the outer most fiber, $(\sigma_0)_r = \sigma + \sigma_0 = 1.83 - 60.92 = -59.09 \text{ N/mm}^2$
- Maximum shear stress, $\tau_{max} = \dfrac{\sigma_{max}}{2} = \dfrac{73.86}{2} = 36.93 \text{ N/mm}^2$.

9. A curved beam is as shown in Fig. 1.13. Determine the maximum stresses.

Solution: $F_1 = 50$ kN, $F_2 = 20$ kN, $R_i = 100$ mm, $b = 50$ mm, $h = 100$ mm, $\sigma_i + \sigma_0 = ?$

Case 1: $F_1 = 50 \, kN$:

a. To find $\bar{x}$:
- We know that, $\bar{x} = \dfrac{h}{2} = \dfrac{100}{2} = 50$ mm

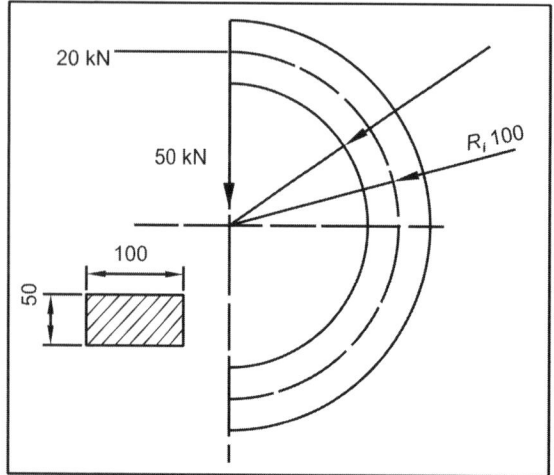

Fig. 1.13: Problem 9

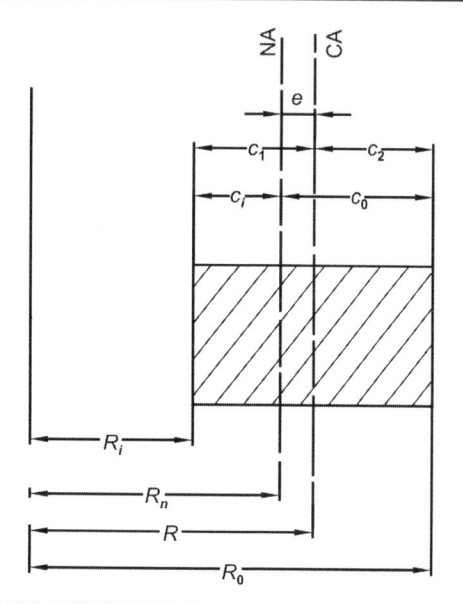

Fig. 1.13(b): Problem 9

b. Replace the given eccentric force by an equal and parallel force through C_g along with a couple.

c. Direct stress. $\sigma = \dfrac{F}{A} = \dfrac{50 \times 10^3}{100 \times 50} = 10 \text{ N/mm}^2$

d. To find the bending stresses (σ_i, σ_0)
- Moment, $M = Fx = F(R_i + \bar{x})$

$$= 50000 \times (100 + 50)$$
$$M = 7.5 \times 10^6 \text{ N-mm}$$

- **Fig. 1-Tb 10.1/Pg 134, DHB**–for a rectangular section,

$e = R - R_n$

$$e = R - \dfrac{h}{\ln\left(\dfrac{R+c}{R-c}\right)}$$

$R_i = 100$ mm, $c_1 = c_2 = 50 = \bar{x}$, $R = R_i + c_1 + 100 + 50 = 150$ mm,
$R_0 = R_i + d = 100 + 100 = 200$ mm

$$= 150 - \dfrac{100}{\ln\left(\dfrac{150+50}{150-50}\right)}$$

$e = 5.73$ mm

Now, $c_i = c_1 - e = 50 - 5.73 = 44.27$ mm, $c_0 = c_2 - e = 50 + 5.73 = 55.73$ mm

- Bending stress at inner fiber,

$$\sigma_i = \dfrac{Mc_i}{AeR_i} = \dfrac{(7.5 \times 10^6) \times 44.27}{(100 \times 50) \times 5.73 \times 100} = 115.89 \text{ N/mm}^2 \qquad \text{... 10.2b/Pg 132, DHB}$$

- Bending stress at outer fiber,

$$\sigma_0 = \dfrac{-Mc_0}{AeR_0} = \dfrac{-(7.5 \times 10^6) \times 55.73}{(100 \times 50) \times 5.73 \times 200} = -72.94 \text{ N/mm}^2 \qquad \text{... 10.2a/Pg 132, DHB}$$

e. Resultant stresses
   - Resultant stress in the inner most fiber, $\sigma_i)_r = \sigma + \sigma_i = 10 + 115.89 = 125.89 \text{ N/mm}^2$
   - Resultant stress in the outer most fiber, $\sigma_0)_r = \sigma + \sigma_0 = 10 - 72.94 = -62.94 \text{ N/mm}^2$

Case 2: $F_2 = 20$ kN

a. $\bar{x} = 50$ mm

b. Shear stress, $\tau = \dfrac{F_2}{A} = \dfrac{20 \times 10^3}{100 \times 50} = 4 \text{ N/mm}^2$

c. To find the bending stresses (σ_i, σ_0)
   - Moment,
   $$M = Fx = F(R_i + \bar{x})$$
   $$= 20000 \times (100 + 50)$$
   $$M = 3 \times 10^6 \text{ N-mm}$$

   - **Fig. 1-Tb 10.1/Pg 134, DHB,** for a rectangular section,
   $$e = R - R_n$$

   $$e = R - \dfrac{h}{\ln\left(\dfrac{R+c}{R-c}\right)}$$

   $R_i = 100$ mm, $c_1 = c_2 = 50 = \bar{x}$, $R = R_i + c_1 = 100 + 50 = 150$ mm,
   $R_0 = R_i + d = 100 + 100 = 200$ mm

   $$= 150 - \dfrac{100}{\ln\left(\dfrac{150+50}{150-50}\right)}$$

   $e = 5.73$ mm

   - Bending stress at inner fiber,
   $$\sigma_i = \dfrac{Mc_i}{AeR_i} = \dfrac{(3 \times 10^6) \times 44.27}{(100 \times 50) \times 5.73 \times 100} = 46.36 \text{ N/mm}^2 \qquad \ldots \text{10.2b/Pg 132, DHB}$$

   - Bending stress at outer fiber,
   $$\sigma_0 = \dfrac{-Mc_0}{AeR_0} = \dfrac{-(3 \times 10^6) \times 55.73}{(100 \times 50) \times 5.73 \times 200} = 29.18 \text{ N/mm}^2 \qquad \ldots \text{10.2a/Pg 132, DHB}$$

d. Resultant stresses
   - Resultant stress in the inner most fiber,

   $$\sigma_i)_r = \dfrac{\sigma_i}{2} + \sqrt{\left(\dfrac{\sigma_i}{2}\right)^2 + \tau^2} \qquad \ldots \text{1.11a/Pg 2, DHB}$$

   $$= \dfrac{46.36}{2} + \sqrt{\left(\dfrac{46.36}{2}\right)^2 + 4^2}$$

   $\sigma_i)_r = 46.7 \text{ N/mm}^2$

- Resultant stress in the outer most fiber,

$$\sigma_i)_0 = \frac{\sigma_0}{2} + \sqrt{\left(\frac{\sigma_0}{2}\right)^2 + \tau^2} \qquad \ldots \text{1.11a/Pg 2, DHB}$$

$$= \frac{-29.18}{2} + \sqrt{\left(\frac{-29.18}{2}\right)^2 + 4^2}$$

$$\sigma_i)_0 = 0.54 \text{ N/mm}^2$$

10. A trough 25 mm thick and 200 mm long is as shown in Fig. 1.14. Determine the magnitude and location of maximum tension, maximum compression and maximum shear stresses.

Solution: Comparing **Fig. 1-Tb 1.3/Pg 8, DHB**, with **Fig. 1-Tb 10.1/Pg 134, DHB**, $b = 200$ mm, $h = 25$ mm.

a. To find $\bar{x}$:

We know that, $\bar{x} = \dfrac{h}{2} = \dfrac{25}{2} = 12.5$ mm

b. To find the bending stresses (σ_i, σ_0)

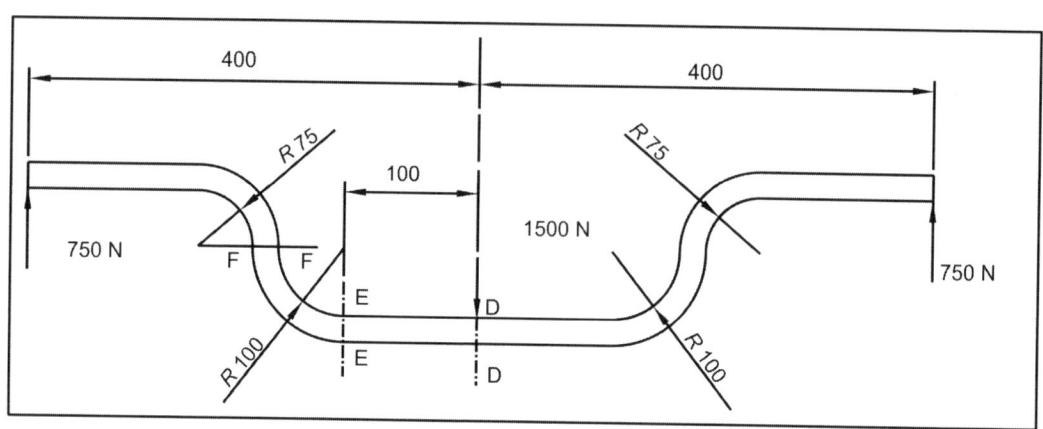

Fig. 1.14: Problem 10

Section D – D

Here the beam is straight, hence, $\sigma = \dfrac{Mc}{I}$

Moment, $M = Fx = 750 \times 400 = 3 \times 10^5$ N-mm

$c = h/2 = 25/2 = 12.5$ mm

$$I = \frac{bh^3}{12} = \frac{200 \times 25^3}{12} = 260.42 \times 10^3 \text{ mm}^4$$

$$\sigma = \frac{(20 \times 10^5) \times 12.5}{260.42 \times 10^3} = 14.4 \text{ N/mm}^2$$

Here the transverse shear stress is zero at the inner and outer fiber, as it is a straight beam.

Section E – E:
- Moment, $M = Fx = 750 \times (400 - 100)$
$$M = 225 \times 10^3 \text{ N-mm}$$

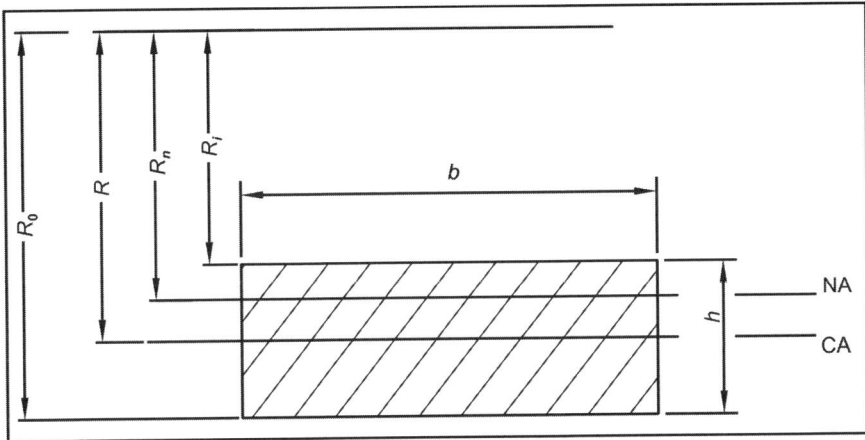

Fig. 1.14(a): Problem 10

- Referring to **Fig. 1.14(a)**,
$R_i = 100$ mm, $c_1 = c_2 = 12.5 = \bar{x}$,
$R = R_i + c_1 = 100 + 12.5 = 112.5$ mm,
$R_0 = R_i + h = 100 + 25 = 125$ mm
- **Fig. 1-Tb 10.1/Pg 134, DHB**, for a rectangular section,
$e = R - R_n$

$$e = R - \frac{h}{\ln\left(\dfrac{R+c}{R-c}\right)}$$

$$= 112.5 - \frac{25}{\ln\left(\dfrac{11.25 + 12.5}{112.5 - 12.5}\right)}$$

$e = 0.46$ mm

Now, $c_i = c_1 - e = 12.5 - 0.46 = 12.04$ mm,
$c_0 = c_2 + e = 12.5 + 0.46 = 12.96$ mm

- Bending stress at inner fiber,
$$\sigma_i = \frac{Mc_i}{AeR_i} = \frac{(225 \times 10^3) \times 12.04}{(25 \times 200) \times 0.46 \times 100} = 11.67 \text{ N/mm}^2 \text{ (compression)}$$
... **10.2b/Pg 132, DHB**

- Bending stress at outer fiber,
$$\sigma_0 = \frac{Mc_0}{AeR_0} = \frac{(225 \times 10^3) \times 12.96}{(25 \times 200) \times 0.46 \times 125} = 10.14 \text{ N/mm}^2 \text{ (tension)}$$
(don't use sign) ... **10.2a/Pg 132, DHB**

Section F – F:

- Moment, $M = Fx = 750 \times [400 - (100 + 100 + 12.5)]$
  $M = 140.63 \times 10^3$ N-mm

- Referring to **Fig. 1.14(b)**,
  $R_i = 75$ mm, $c_1 = c_2 = 12.5 = \bar{x}$, $R + R_i + c_1 = 75 + (25/2) = 87.5$ mm,
  $R_0 = R_i + h = 75 + 25 = 100$ mm

- **Fig. 1-Tb 10.1/Pg 134, DHB**–for a rectangular section,
  $e = R - R_n$

$$e = R - \frac{h}{\ln\left(\dfrac{R+c}{R-c}\right)} = 87.5 - \frac{25}{\ln\left(\dfrac{87.5+12.5}{87.5-12.5}\right)}$$

$e = 0.6$ mm

Now, $c_i = c_1 - e = 12.5 - 0.6 = 11.90$ mm,
$c_0 = c_2 + e = 12.5 + 0.6 = 13.10$ mm

- Bending stress at inner fiber,

$$\sigma_i = \frac{Mc_i}{AeR_i} = \frac{(140.63 \times 10^3) \times 11.90}{(25 \times 200) \times 0.6 \times 75} \quad \ldots 10.2b/Pg\ 132,\ DHB$$

$\sigma_i = 7.46$ N/mm^2 (tension)

- Bending stress at outer fiber,

$$\sigma_0 = \frac{Mc_0}{AeR_0} = \frac{(140.63 \times 10^3) \times 13.10}{(25 \times 200) \times 0.6 \times 100} = 6.14\ \text{N/mm}^2\ \text{(compression)}$$

$\ldots 10.2a/Pg\ 132,\ DHB$

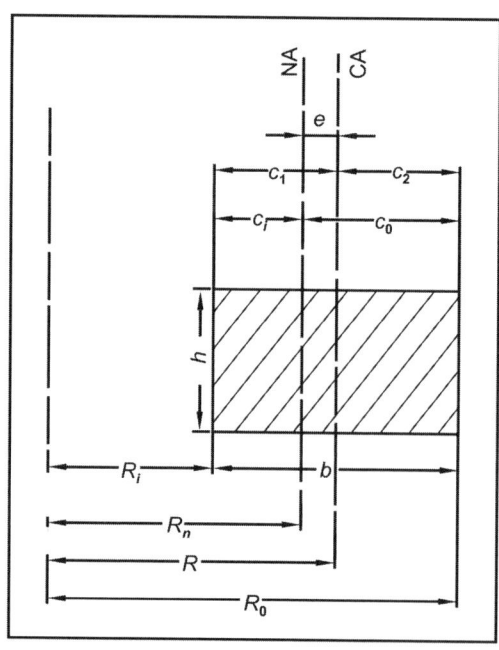

Fig. 1.14(b): Problem 10

c. Maximum stresses
- Maximum tensile stress occurs at $D-D$, $\sigma_{max} = 14.4 \text{ N/mm}^2$
- Maximum compressive stress occurs at $E-E$, $\sigma_{max} = 11.67 \text{ N/mm}^2$
- Maximum shear stress, $\tau_{max} = \dfrac{\sigma_{max}}{2} = \dfrac{14.4}{2} = 7.2 \text{ N/mm}^2$

11. An offset bar has forces applied as shown in Fig. 1.15. The bar is 25 × 50 mm. The offset of two applied forces is a pure couple that causes the same bending moment at every section of the beam. Determine the magnitude and location of maximum tension, maximum compression and maximum shear stresses.

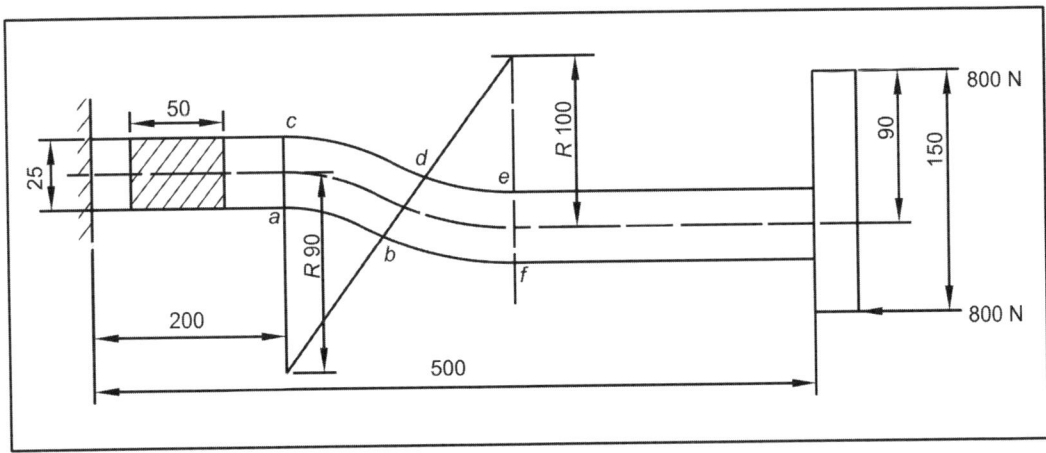

Fig. 1.15: Problem 11

Solution: Comparing **Fig. 1 -Tb 1.3/Pg 8, DHB**, with **Fig. 1-Tb 10.1/Pg 134 DHB**, $b = 50$ mm, $h = 25$ mm

a. To find $\bar{x}$:

We know that, $\bar{x} = \dfrac{h}{2} = \dfrac{25}{2} = 12.5$ mm

b. To find the bending stresses (σ_i, σ_0)

Section a - c:
- Moment, $M = Fx = 800 \times 150$

$$M = 1.20 \times 10^5 \text{ N-mm}$$

Referring to **Fig. 1.15(a)**,

$$R_i = 90 - 12.5 = 77.5 \text{ mm}, c_1 = c_2 = 12.5 = \bar{x},$$

$$R = 90 \text{ mm}$$

$$R_0 = R + \bar{x} = 90 + 12.5 = 102.5 \text{ mm}$$

- **Fig. 1-Tb 10.1/Pg 134, DHB**–for a rectangular section,

$$e = R - R_n$$

$$e = R - \dfrac{h}{\ln\left(\dfrac{R+c}{R-c}\right)}$$

$$= 90 - \frac{25}{\ln\left(\frac{90+12.5}{90-12.5}\right)}$$

$e = 0.58$ mm

Now, $c_i = c_1 - e = 12.5 - 0.58 = 11.92$ mm, $\quad c_0 = c_2 + e = 12.5 + 0.58 = 13.08$ mm

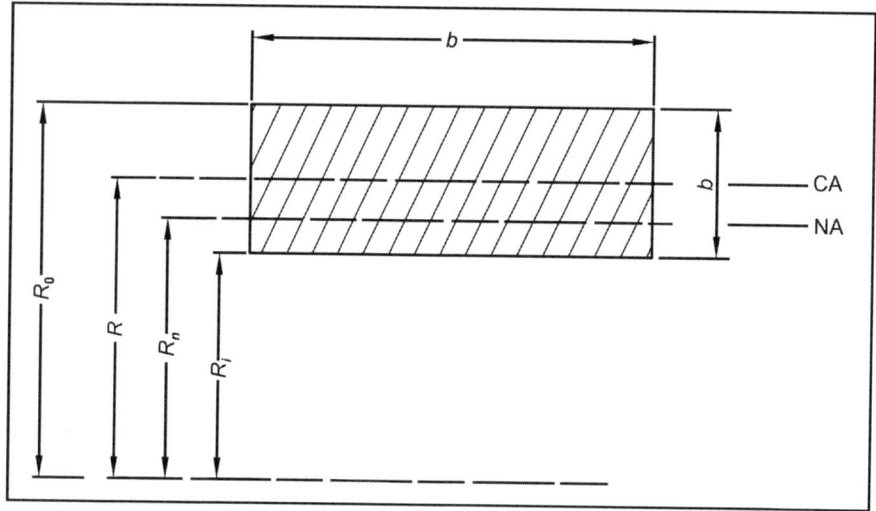

Fig. 1.15(a): Problem 11

- Bending stress at inner fiber,

$$\sigma_i = \frac{Mc_i}{AeR_i} = \frac{(1.2 \times 10^5) \times 11.92}{(25 \times 50) \times 0.58 \times 77.5} = 25.45 \text{ N/mm}^2 \text{ (compression)}$$

... **10.2b/Pg 132, DHB**

- Bending stress at outer fiber,

$$\sigma_0 = \frac{Mc_0}{AeR_0} = \frac{(1.2 \times 10^5) \times 13.08}{(25 \times 50) \times 0.58 \times 102.5} = 21.12 \text{ N/mm}^2 \text{ (tension)}$$

... **10.2a/Pg 132, DHB**

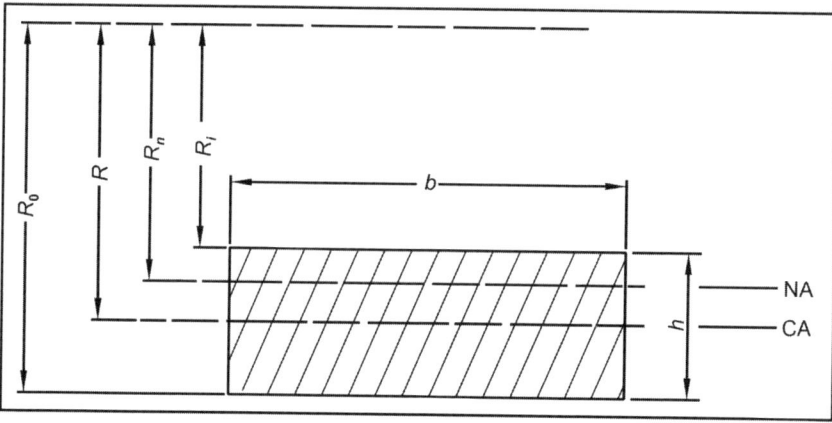

Fig. 1.15(b): Problem 11

Section e – f:
- Referring to **Fig. 1.15(b)**,
$$R_i = 100 - 12.5 = 87.5 \text{ mm},$$
$$c_1 = c_2 = 12.5 = \bar{x}, R = 100 \text{ mm}$$
$$R_0 = R + \bar{x} = 100 + 12.5 = 112.5 \text{ mm}$$

- **Fig. 1-Tb 10.1/Pg 134, DHB** –for a rectangular section,

$$e = R - R_n$$

$$e = R - \frac{h}{\ln\left(\frac{R+c}{R-c}\right)} = 100 - \frac{25}{\ln\left(\frac{100+12.5}{100-12.5}\right)}$$

$$e = 0.52 \text{ mm}$$

Now, $c_i = e_1 - e = 12.5 - 0.52 = 11.98$ mm, $\quad c_0 = c_2 + e = 12.5 + 0.52 = 13.02$ mm

- Bending stress at inner fiber,

$$\sigma_i = \frac{Mc_i}{AeR_i} = \frac{(1.2 \times 10^5) \times 11.92}{(25 \times 50) \times 0.52 \times 87.5} = 25.14 \text{ N/mm}^2 \text{ (tension)}$$

... **10.2b/ Pg 132, DHB**

- Bending stress at outer fiber,

$$\sigma_0 = \frac{Mc_0}{AeR_0} = \frac{(1.2 \times 10^5) \times 13.02}{(25 \times 50) \times 0.58 \times 112.5} = 21.37 \text{ N/mm}^2 \text{ (compression)}$$

... **10.2a/ Pg 132, DHB**

c. Maximum stresses
  - Maximum tensile stress occurs at $a - c$, $\sigma_{max} = 25.14$ N/mm^2
  - Maximum compressive stress occurs at $e - f$, $\sigma_{max} = 25.45$ N/mm^2
  - Maximum shear stress, $\tau_{max} = \dfrac{\sigma_{max}}{2} = \dfrac{25.14}{2} = 12.57$ N/mm^2

1.5 STRESSES IN CLOSED RINGS

Consider a closed ring as shown in **Fig. 1.16(a)**, subjected to a tensile load F. Due to symmetry we consider only one quadrant as shown in **Fig. 1.16(b)**. The applied load tends to stretch the vertical dimension and reduce the horizontal dimension.

- The bending moment at any cross-section of the ring is,

$$M = FR\left[\frac{1}{\pi} - \frac{\sin\theta}{2}\right] = \frac{FR}{2}\left[\frac{2}{\pi} - \sin\theta\right] \qquad \text{.... (Eq. 1.13a)}$$

R = mean radius of the ring
θ = angle with respect to load line (vertical)
F = load

- At section B – B, $\theta = 0°$ (with respect to vertical)
  Eq. (1.13a) yields, $M_B = 0.318 \; FR$ ... **10.5/Pg 133, DHB**
- At section A – A, $\theta = 90°$ (with respect to vertical)
  Eq. (1.13a) yields, $M_A = -0.182 \; FR$ ... **10.6/Pg 133, DHB**

- And the stress at D – D, $\sigma_d = \dfrac{F \sin\theta}{2A}$

30 Design of Machine Elements II (DME II)

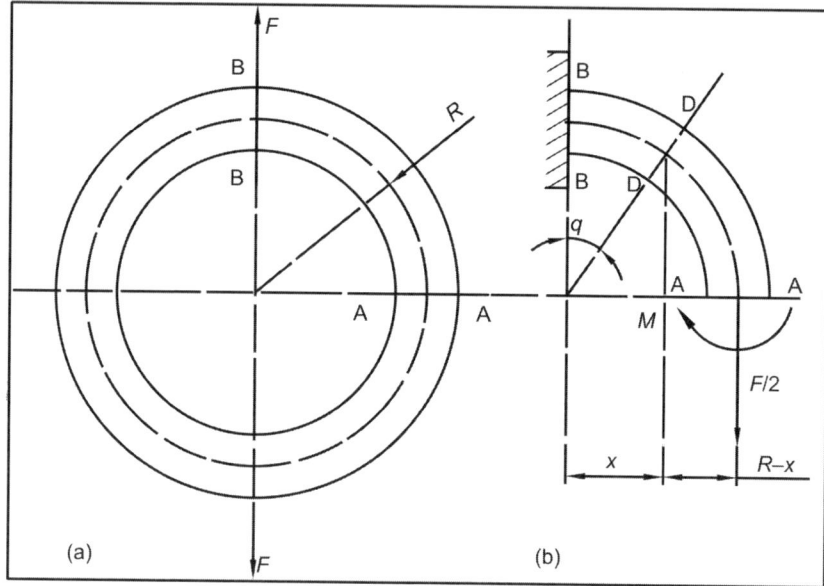

Fig. 1.16: Closed ring in tension (Fig. 10.4/pg 137, DHB)

The stress at any point in the cross-section is $\sigma = \sigma_d + \sigma_b$ ... 10.8/Pg 133, DHB

Where, $\quad \sigma_b = \dfrac{Mc_i}{AeR_i}$ or $\dfrac{Mc_0}{AeR_0}$ ... 10.2a, 10.2b/Pg 132, DHB

At load line ($\theta = 0°$), with respect to vertical):
The inner fibers are subjected to compression while the outer fibers are subjected to tension (in σ_b), hence

Resultant stress in the inner fiber, $\sigma_i)_r = \sigma_d + \dfrac{-Mc_i}{AeR_i}$

Resultant stress in the outer fiber, $\sigma_0)_r = \sigma_d + \dfrac{-Mc_0}{AeR_0}$

Away from load line ($\theta = 90°$, with respect to vertical):
The inner fibers are subjected to compression while the outer fibers are subjected to tension (in σ_b), hence

Resultant stress in the inner fiber, $\sigma_i)_r = \sigma_d + \dfrac{-Mc_i}{AeR_i}$

Resultant stress in the outer fiber, $\sigma_0)_r = \sigma_d + \dfrac{-Mc_0}{AeR_0}$

12. Determine the stresses induced in a closed ring as shown in Fig. 1.17.
Solution: $F = 25$ kN, $d = 40$ mm, $R_i = 40$ mm
  a. To find $\bar{x}$:

  We know that, $\bar{x} = \dfrac{d}{2} = \dfrac{40}{2} = 20$ mm

  $A = \dfrac{\pi d^2}{4} = \dfrac{\pi \times 40^2}{4} = 1256.64$ mm^2

Curved Beams, Cylinders and Cylinder Heads **31**

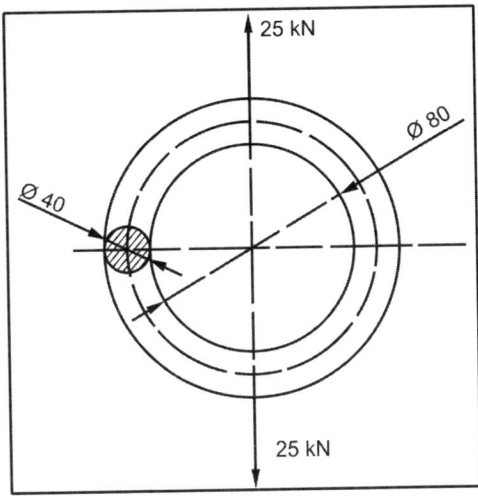

Fig. 1.17: Problem 12

b. To find maximum stresses:
(i) *At load line ($\theta = 0°$, with respect to vertical) – Section B – B:*
- Referring to **Fig. 1.17(a)**,
 $R_i = 40$ mm
 $c_1 = c_2 = 20 = \bar{x}$,
 $R = 40 + 20 = 60$ mm
 $R_0 = R + \bar{x} = 60 + 20 = 80$ mm

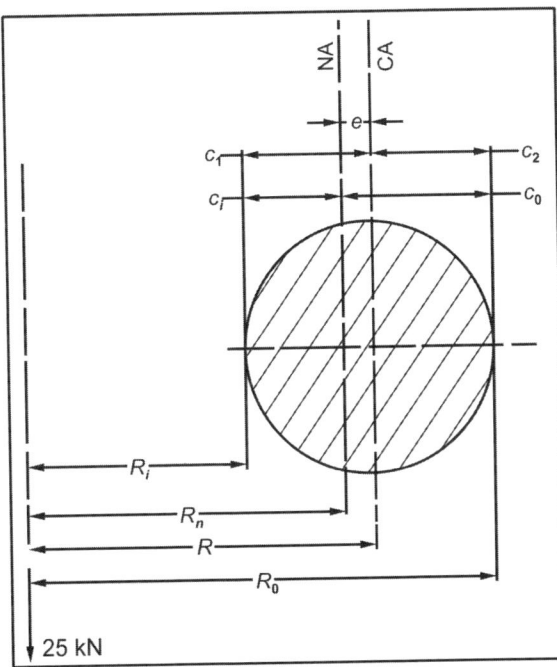

Fig. 1.17(a): Problem 12

- Moment, $M = 0.318\, FR$ ...10.5/Pg 133, DHB
  $= 0.318 \times 25000 \times 60$
  $M = 477 \times 10^3$ N-mm

- Fig. 2-Tb 10.1/Pg 134, DHB–for a circular section,
  $e = R - R_n$

  $e = R - \dfrac{c^2/2}{R - \sqrt{R^2 - c^2}}$

  $= 60 - \dfrac{20^2/2}{60 - \sqrt{60^2 - 20^2}}$

  $e = 1.72$ mm

  Now, $c_i = c_1 - e = 20 - 1.72 = 18.28$ mm, $\quad c_0 = c_2 + e = 20 + 1.72 = 21.72$ mm

- Resultant stress in the inner fiber, $\sigma_i)_r = \sigma_d + \dfrac{-Mc_i}{AeR_i}$

  $= \dfrac{F\sin\theta}{2A} + \dfrac{-Mc_i}{AeR_i}$

  $= \dfrac{25000 \times \sin(\theta)}{2 \times 1256.64} + \dfrac{-(477 \times 10^3 \times 18.28)}{1256.64 \times 1.72 \times 40}$

  $= 0 - 100.85$ ...10.8/Pg 133, DHB

  $\sigma_i)_r = -100.85$ N/mm²

- Resultant stress in the outer fiber, $\sigma_0)_r = \sigma_d + \dfrac{-Mc_0}{AeR_0} = \dfrac{F\sin\theta}{2A} + \dfrac{Mc_0}{AeR_0}$

  ...10.8/Pg 133, DHB

  $= \dfrac{25000 \times \sin(\theta)}{2 \times 1256.64} + \dfrac{(477 \times 10^3 \times 21.72)}{1256.64 \times 1.72 \times 80}$

  $= 0 + 60$

  $\sigma_0)_r = 60$ N/mm²

(ii) *Away from load line ($\theta = 90°$, with respect to vertical) – Section A – A:*

- Moment, $M = -0.182\, FR$ ...10.6/Pg 133, DHB
  $= -0.182 \times 15000 \times 60$
  $M = -273 \times 10^3$ N-mm

- Resultant stress in the inner fiber, $\sigma_i)_r = \sigma_d + \dfrac{-Mc_i}{AeR_i} = \dfrac{F\sin\theta}{2A} + \dfrac{-Mc_i}{AeR_i}$

  ...10.8/Pg 133, DHB

  $= \dfrac{25000 \times \sin(90)}{2 \times 1256.64} + \dfrac{-(-273 \times 10^3 \times 18.28)}{1256.64 \times 1.72 \times 40}$

  $= 9.95 + 57.68$

  $\sigma_i)_r = 67.67$ N/mm²

- Resultant stress in the outer fiber, $\sigma_0)_r = \sigma_d + \dfrac{-Mc_0}{AeR_0} = \dfrac{F\sin\theta}{2A} + \dfrac{Mc_0}{AeR_0}$

... **10.8/Pg 133, DHB**

$$= \dfrac{25000 \times \sin(90)}{2 \times 1256.64} + \dfrac{(-273 \times 10^3 \times 21.72)}{1256.64 \times 1.72 \times 80}$$

$$= 9.95 - 34.29$$

$$\sigma_0)_r = -24.34 \text{ N/mm}^2$$

13. A closed ring is made up of 50 mm diameter steel bar having allowable tensile stress of 200 MPa. The inner diameter of the ring is 100 mm. For a load of 30 kN, find the maximum stress in the bar and specify the location. If the ring is cut as shown in part B of Fig. 1.18, check whether it is safe to support the applied load.

[VTU-Dec 08/Jan 09 – 10 Marks]

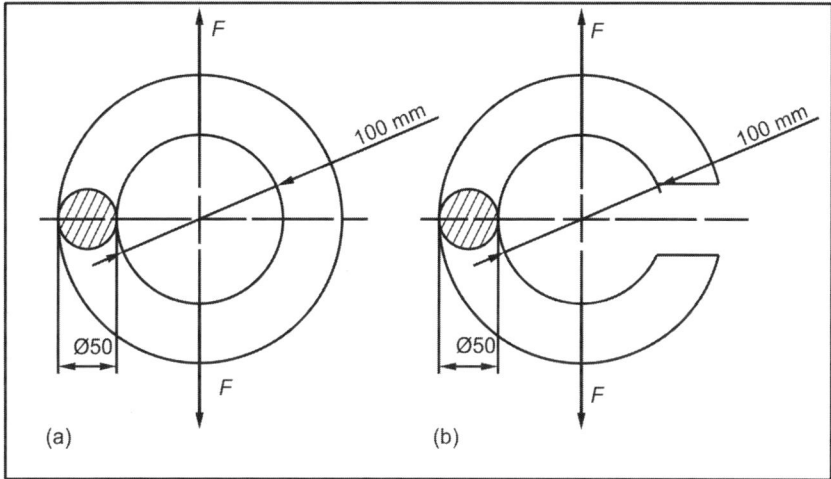

Fig. 1.18: Problem 13

Solution: $F = 30$ kN, $d = 50$ mm, $R_i = 50$ mm

a. To find $\bar{x}$:

We know that, $\bar{x} = \dfrac{d}{2} = \dfrac{50}{2} = 25$ mm

$$A = \dfrac{\pi d^2}{4} = \dfrac{\pi \times 50^2}{4} = 1963.5 \text{ mm}^2$$

b. To find maximum stresses:

(i) At load line ($\theta = 0°$, with respect to vertical) – Section B – B:

- Referring to **Fig. 1.18(a)**,
    $R_i = 50$ mm, $\qquad c_1 = c_2 = 25 = \bar{x}$,
    $R = 50\ 50 + 25 = 75$ mm
    $R_0 = R + \bar{x} = 75 + 25 = 100$ mm
- Moment, $M = 0.318\ FR$ ... **10.5/Pg 133, DHB**
    $= 0.318 \times 30000 \times 75$
    $M = 715.5 \times 10^3$ N-mm

Fig. 1.18(a): Problem 13

- **Fig. 2-Tb 10.1/Pg 134, DHB** – for a circular section,
$$e = R - R_n$$

$$e = R - \frac{c^2/2}{R - \sqrt{R^2 - c^2}}$$

$$= 75 - \frac{25^2/2}{75 - \sqrt{75^2 - 25^2}}$$

$e = 2.14$ mm

Now, $c_i = c_1 - e = 25 - 2.14 = 22.86$ mm, $\quad c_0 = c_2 + e = 25 + 2.14 = 27.14$ mm

- Resultant stress in the inner fiber, $\sigma_i)_r = \sigma_d + \frac{-Mc_i}{AeR_i} = \frac{F\sin\theta}{2A} + \frac{-Mc_i}{AeR_i}$

... **10.8/Pg 133, DHB**

$$= \frac{30000 \times \sin(0)}{2 \times 1963.5} + \frac{-(715.5 \times 10^3 \times 22.86)}{1963.5 \times 2.14 \times 50}$$

$$= 0 - 77.85$$

$\sigma_i)_r = 77.85 \text{ N/mm}^2$

- Resultant stress in the outer fiber, $\sigma_0)_r = \sigma_d + \frac{Mc_0}{AeR_0} = \frac{F\sin\theta}{2A} + \frac{Mc_0}{AeR_0}$

... **10.8/Pg 133, DHB**

$$= \frac{30000 \times \sin(0)}{2 \times 1963.5} + \frac{(715.5 \times 10^3 \times 27.14)}{1963.5 \times 2.14 \times 100}$$

$$= 0 + 46.21$$

$\sigma_0)_r = 46.21 \text{ N/mm}^2$

(ii) Away from load line ($\theta = 90°$, with respect to vertical) – Section A – A:

- Moment, $M = -0.182\, FR$ ... **10.6/Pg 133, DHB**
  $= -0.182 \times 30000 \times 75$
  $M = -409.5 \times 10^3$ N-mm

- Resultant stress in the inner fiber, $\sigma_i)_r = \sigma_d + \dfrac{-Mc_i}{AeR_i} = \dfrac{F\sin\theta}{2A} + \dfrac{-Mc_i}{AeR_i}$

       ... **10.8/Pg 133, DHB**

  $= \dfrac{30000 \times \sin(90)}{2 \times 1963.5} + \dfrac{-(-409.5 \times 10^3 \times 22.86)}{1963.5 \times 2.14 \times 50}$

  $= 7.63 + 44.50$

  $\sigma_i)_r = 52.13$ N/mm²

- Resultant stress in the outer fiber, $\sigma_0)_r = \sigma_d + \dfrac{Mc_0}{AeR_0} = \dfrac{F\sin\theta}{2A} + \dfrac{Mc_0}{AeR_0}$

       ... **10.8/Pg 133, DHB**

  $= \dfrac{30000 \times \sin(90)}{2 \times 1963.5} + \dfrac{-(-409.5 \times 10^3 \times 27.14)}{1963.5 \times 2.14 \times 100}$

  $= 7.63 - 26.44$

  $\sigma_0)_r = 18.81$ N/mm²

Thus the maximum stress is 77.85 N/mm², which is less than the allowable tensile stress of 200 N/mm². Hence the design of ring is safe.

14. Determine the maximum stress induced in a ring cross-section of 50 mm diameter rod subjected to a compressive load of 20 kN. The mean diameter of the ring is 100 mm (Fig. 1.19).   *[VTU-Dec 09/Jan 10 – 10 Marks]*

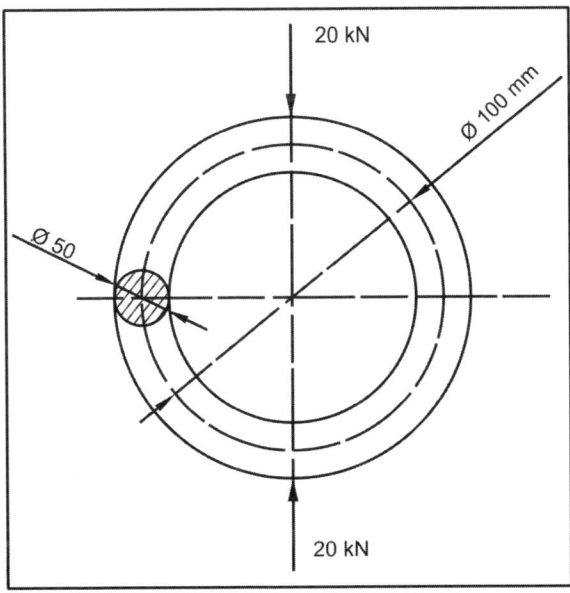

Fig. 1.19: Problem 14

Solution: $F = -20$ kN, $d = 50$ mm, $R_i = 50$ mm

a. To find $\bar{x}$:

We know that, $\bar{x} = \dfrac{d}{2} = \dfrac{50}{2} = 25$ mm

$$A = \dfrac{\pi d^2}{4} = \dfrac{\pi \times 50^2}{4} = 1963.5 \text{ mm}^2$$

b. To find maximum stresses:

(i) At load line ($\theta = 0°$, with respect to vertical) – Section B – B:

- Referring to **Fig. 1.19(a)**,
  $R_i = 50 - 25 = 25$ mm,
  $c_1 = c_2 = 25 = \bar{x}$,
  $R = 50$ mm
  $R_0 = R + \bar{x} = 50 + 25 = 75$ mm

- Moment, $M = -0.318\, FR$

  ... **10.5/ Pg 133, DHB**

  $= -0.318 \times 20000 \times 50$

  $M = -318 \times 10^3$ N-mm

- **Fig. 2-Tb 10.1/Pg 134, DHB** – for an circular section,

  $e = R - R_n$

  $e = R - \dfrac{c^2/2}{R - \sqrt{R^2 - c^2}}$

  $= 50 - \dfrac{52^2/2}{50 - \sqrt{50^2 - 25^2}}$

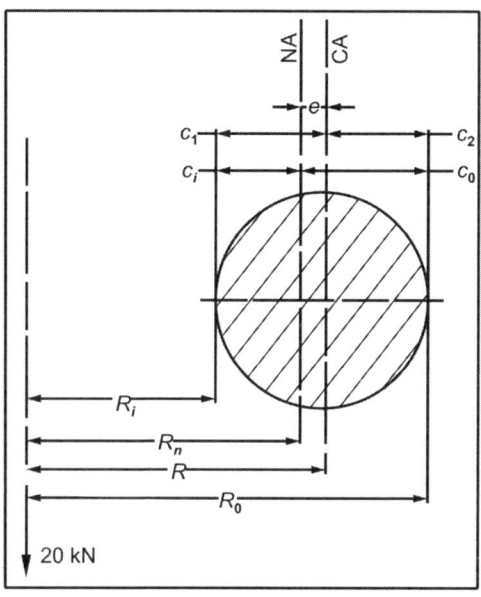

Fig. 1.19(a): Problem 14

$e = 3.35$ mm

Now, $c_i = c_1 - e = 25 - 3.35 = 21.65$ mm, $c_0 = c_2 + e = 25 + 3.35 = 28.35$ mm

- Resultant stress in the inner fiber, $\sigma_i)_r = \sigma_d + \dfrac{-Mc_i}{AeR_i}$

$$= \dfrac{F\sin\theta}{2A} + \dfrac{-Mc_i}{AeR_i} \qquad \text{... 10.8/Pg 133, DHB}$$

$$= \dfrac{-20000 \times \sin(0)}{2 \times 1963.5} + \dfrac{-(-318 \times 10^3 \times 21.65)}{1963.5 \times 3.35 \times 25}$$

$$= 0 + 41.87$$

$$\sigma_i)_r = 41.87 \text{ N/mm}^2$$

- Resultant stress in the outer fiber, $\sigma_0)_r = \sigma_d + \dfrac{Mc_0}{AeR_0} = \dfrac{F\sin\theta}{2A} + \dfrac{Mc_0}{AeR_0}$

... **10.8/Pg 133, DHB**

$$= \dfrac{-20000 \times \sin(0)}{2 \times 1963.5} + \dfrac{(-318 \times 10^3 \times 28.35)}{1963.5 \times 3.35 \times 25}$$

$$= 0 - 18.27$$
$$\sigma_0)_r = -18.94 \text{ N/mm}^2$$

(ii) Away from load line ($\theta = 90°$, with respect to vertical) – Section A – A:

- Moment, $M = 0.182 \, FR$ ... **10.6/Pg 133, DHB**
$$= 0.182 \times 20000 \times 50$$
$$M = 182 \times 10^3 \text{ N-mm}$$

- Resultant stress in the inner fiber, $\sigma_i)_r = \sigma_d + \dfrac{-Mc_i}{AeR_i} = \dfrac{F\sin\theta}{2A} + \dfrac{-Mc_i}{AeR_i}$
... **10.8/Pg 133, DHB**

$$= \dfrac{-20000 \times \sin(90)}{2 \times 1963.5} + \dfrac{-(-182 \times 10^3 \times 21.65)}{1963.5 \times 3.35 \times 25}$$
$$= -5.09 - 23.97$$
$$\sigma_i)_r = 29.05 \text{ N/mm}^2$$

- Resultant stress in the outer fiber, $\sigma_0)_r = \sigma_d + \dfrac{Mc_0}{AeR_0} = \dfrac{F\sin\theta}{2A} + \dfrac{Mc_0}{AeR_0}$
... **10.8/Pg 133, DHB**

$$= \dfrac{-20000 \times \sin(90)}{2 \times 1963.5} + \dfrac{(182 \times 10^3 \times 28.35)}{1963.5 \times 3.354 \times 75}$$
$$= -5.09 + 10.46$$
$$\sigma_0)_r = 5.37 \text{ N/mm}^2$$

1.6 CHAIN LINKS

Consider a chain link as shown in **Fig. 1.20** subjected to a tensile load F. Due to symmetry we consider only one quadrant as shown in **Fig. 1.16(b)**. The analysis is similar to closed rings.

These are used in heavy hoisting equipment and are subjected to bending moment.

- The bending moment at section **AA**, i.e. 90° away from the point of application of the load and in all the straight parts of the link is:

$$M_A = \dfrac{FR}{2}\left[\dfrac{2R - \pi R}{\pi R + l}\right] \quad \text{... 10.3a/Pg 132, DHB}$$

- The bending moment at section **BB**, i.e. at the point of application of load is:

$$M_B = \dfrac{FR}{2}\left[\dfrac{2R + l}{\pi R + l}\right] \quad \text{...10.3b/Pg 132, DHB}$$

R = mean radius of the ring
l = length of straight portion of link
F = load

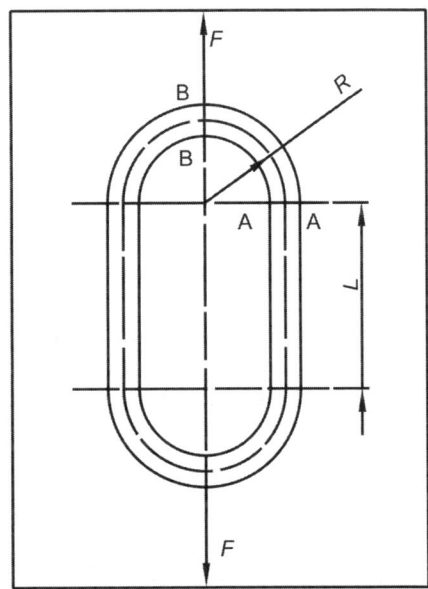

Fig. 1.20: Chain link (Fig. 10.3/pg 137, DHB)

15. A chain link made of 40 mm diameter rod is semicircular at each end, the mean diameter of which is 80 mm. The straight sides of the link are also 80 mm. If the link carries a load of 90 kN, estimate the tensile and compressive stresses in the link along the section of load line (Fig. 1.21). *[VTU-July/Aug. 03 – 10 Marks]*

Solution: $F = 90$ kN, $d = 40$ mm, Mean diameter = 80 mm, mean radius $R = 40$ mm, $l = 80$ mm

a. To find $\bar{x}$:

We know that, $\bar{x} = \dfrac{d}{2} = \dfrac{40}{2} = 20$ mm

$A = \dfrac{\pi d^2}{4} = \dfrac{\pi \times 40^2}{4} = 1256.64$ mm^2

b. To find maximum stresses:

(i) At load line ($\theta = 0°$, with respect to vertical)– Section B – B:

- Referring to **Fig. 1.19(a)**,
  $R_i = R - d/2 = R - d/2 = 40 - 20 = 20$ mm,
  $c_1 = c_2 = 25 = \bar{x}$, $R = 40$ mm
  $R_0 = R + \bar{x} = 40 + 20 = 60$ mm

- Moment, $M = \dfrac{FR}{2}\left[\dfrac{2R+l}{\pi R + l}\right]$

  ... **10.3b/Pg 132, DHB**

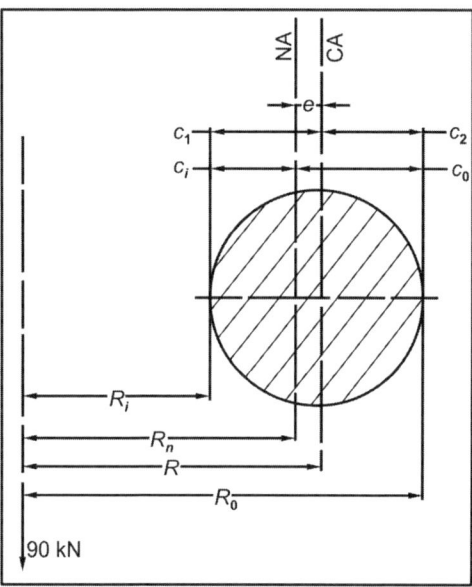

Fig. 1.21: Problem 15

$= \dfrac{90000 \times 40}{2}\left[\dfrac{(2\times 40)+80}{40\pi + 80}\right]$

$M = 14 \times 10^6$ N-mm

- **Figure 2-Tb 10.1/Pg 134, DHB** – for an circular section,

$e = R - R_n$

$e = R - \dfrac{c^2/2}{R - \sqrt{R^2 - c^2}}$

$= 40 - \dfrac{20^2/2}{40 - \sqrt{40^2 - 20^2}}$

$e = 2.68$ mm

Now, $c_i = c_1 - e = 20 - 2.68 = 17.32$ mm, $\qquad c_0 = c_2 - e = 20 + 2.68 = 22.68$ mm

- Stress in the inner fiber,

$$\sigma_i)_r = \sigma_d + \dfrac{-Mc_i}{AeR_i} = \dfrac{F\sin\theta}{2A} + \dfrac{-Mc_i}{AeR_i} \qquad \text{... 10.8/Pg 133, DHB}$$

$= \dfrac{90000 \times \sin(0)}{2 \times 1256.64} + \dfrac{-(1.4 \times 10^6 \times 22.68)}{1256.64 \times 2.68 \times 60}$

$= 0 - 360$

$\sigma_i)_r = -360$ N/mm^2

- Stress in the outer fiber, $\sigma_0)_r = \sigma_d + \dfrac{Mc_0}{AeR_0} = \dfrac{F\sin\theta}{2A} + \dfrac{Mc_0}{AeR_0}$ ... **10.8/Pg 133, DHB**

$$= \dfrac{90000 \times \sin(0)}{2 \times 1256.64} + \dfrac{-(1.4 \times 10^6 \times 22.68)}{1256.64 \times 2.68 \times 60}$$

$$= 0 + 157.14$$

$$\sigma_0)_r = 157.14 \text{ N/mm}^2$$

(ii) Away from load line ($\theta = 90°$, with respect to vertical) – Section A – A:

- Moment, $M = \dfrac{FR}{2}\left[\dfrac{2R-l}{\pi R+l}\right]$ ... **10.3a/Pg 132, DHB**

$$= \dfrac{90000 \times 40}{2}\left[\dfrac{(2 \times 40) + 40\pi}{40\pi + 80}\right]$$

$$M = 400 \times 10^3 \text{ N-mm}$$

- Stress in the inner fiber, $\sigma_i)_r = \sigma_d + \dfrac{-Mc_i}{AeR_i} = \dfrac{F\sin\theta}{2A} + \dfrac{-Mc_i}{AeR_i}$ ... **10.8/Pg 133, DHB**

$$= \dfrac{90000 \times \sin(90)}{2 \times 1256.64} + \dfrac{-(-400 \times 10^3 \times 17.32)}{1256.64 \times 2.68 \times 20}$$

$$= 35.80 + 102.86$$

$$\sigma_i)_r = 138.6 \text{ N/mm}^2$$

- Stress in the outer fiber, $\sigma_0)_r = \sigma_d + \dfrac{Mc_0}{AeR_0} = \dfrac{F\sin\theta}{2A} + \dfrac{Mc_0}{AeR_0}$ ... **10.8/Pg 133, DHB**

$$= \dfrac{90000 \times \sin(90)}{2 \times 1256.64} + \dfrac{(-400 \times 10^3 \times 22.68)}{1256.64 \times 2.68 \times 60}$$

$$= 35.80 - 44.90$$

$$\sigma_0)_r = -9.1 \text{ N/mm}^2$$

Problems of Type II – To Find Loads

16. A section of a C-clamp is as shown in Fig. 1.22. Determine the force required, if permissible stress is limited to 90 MPa.

Solution: $\sigma = 90$ MPa, $F = ?$

a. To find $\bar{x}$:

$a_1 = 20 \times 5 = 100$ mm^2

$a_2 = 25 \times 5 = 125$ mm^2

$x_1 = 5/2 = 2.5$ mm

$x_2 = 5 + (25/2) = 17.5$ mm

$A = \Sigma a = a_1 + a_2 = 100 + 125 = 225$ mm^2

$$\bar{x} = \dfrac{\Sigma ax}{\Sigma a} = \dfrac{(200 \times 2.5) + (125 \times 17.5)}{225} = 10.83 \text{ mm}$$

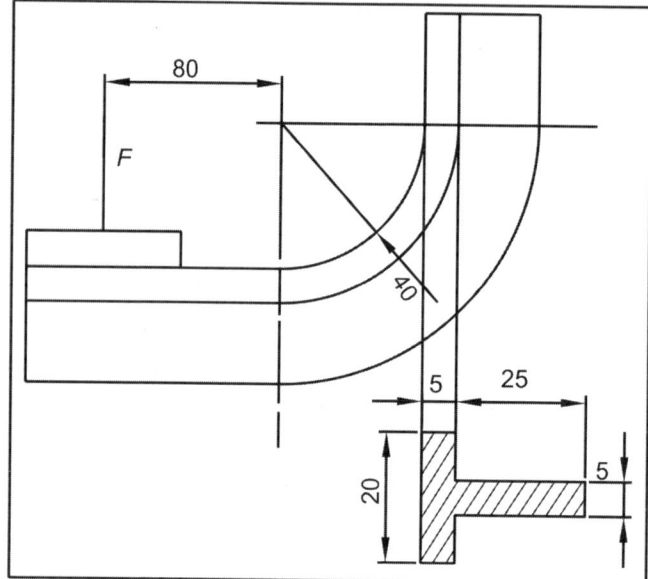

Fig. 1.22: Problem 16

b. Direct stress $\sigma = \dfrac{F}{A} = \dfrac{F}{225} = 4.45 \times 10^{-3} F \text{ N/mm}^2$

c. To find the bending stresses (σ_i, σ_0)
- Moment, $M = Fx$
$$= F \times (80 + 40 + 10.83)$$
$$M = 130.83 F \text{ N-mm}$$

- **Fig. 8-Tb 10.1/Pg 136, DHB,** for an T-section,
$e = R - R_n$

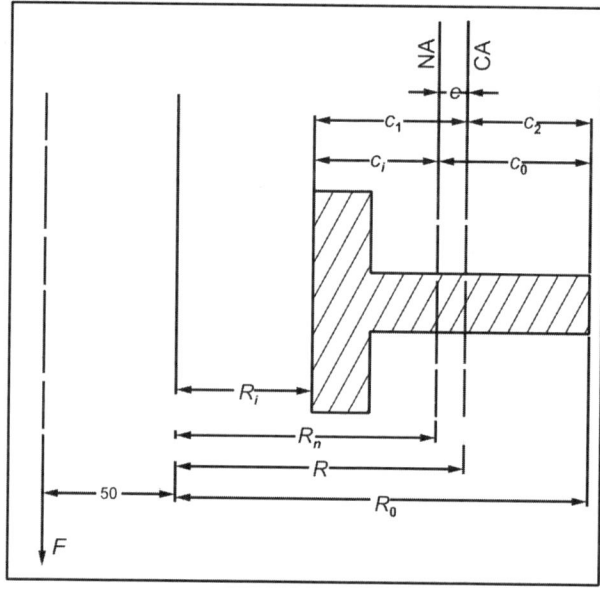

Fig. 1.22 (a): Problem 16

$$e = R - \frac{A}{B\ln\left(\frac{R+d-c_1}{R-c_1}\right) + a\ln\left(\frac{R+C_2}{R+d-c_1}\right)}$$

Here, $B = 20$ mm, $d = 5$ mm, $a = 5$ mm, $H = 5 + 25 = 30$ mm
Also $R_i = 40$ mm, $R_0 = R_i + h = 40 + 30 = 70$ mm, $c_1 = \bar{x} = 10.83$ mm,
$R = c_1 + R_i = 10.83 + 40 = 50.83$ mm, $c_2 = h - c_1 = 230 - 10.83 = 19.17$ mm

$$= 50.83 - \frac{225}{20\ln\left(\frac{50.83+5-10.83}{50.83-10.83}\right) + 5\ln\left(\frac{50.83+19.17}{50.83+5-10.83}\right)}$$

$e = 1.543$ mm

Now, $c_i = c_1 - e = 10.83 - 1.543 = 9.29$ mm, $c_0 = c_2 + e = 19.17 + 1.543 = 20.713$ mm

- Bending stress at inner fiber, $\sigma_i = \frac{Mc_i}{AeR_i} = \frac{(130.83F) \times 9.29}{225 \times 1.543 \times 40} = 0.0875 F$ N/mm^2

... **10.2b/Pg 132, DHB**

- Bending stress at outer fiber, $\sigma_0 = \frac{-Mc_i}{AeR_0} = \frac{-(130.83F) \times 20.713}{225 \times 1.543 \times 70} = 0.112 F$ N/mm^2

... **10.2a/Pg 132, DHB**

d. Resultant stresses
   - Resultant stress in the inner most fiber,
     $\sigma_i)_r \sigma + \sigma_i = 4.45 \times 10^{-3} F + 0.0875 F = 0.0920 F$ N/mm^2
   - Resultant stress in the outer most fiber,
     $\sigma_0)_r \sigma + \sigma_0 = 4.45 \times 10^{-3} F - 0.112 F = -0.107 F$ N/mm^2

e. Since maximum stress occurs in the inner fiber, $\sigma_i)_r = 0.0920 F$ N/mm^2

$$90 = 0.0920 F$$
$$F = \frac{90}{0.0920} = 978.80 \text{ N/mm}^2$$

17. The cross-section of a steel crane hook is a trapezium with an inner side of 50 mm and outer side of 25 mm. The depth of section is 64 mm. The center of curvature of the section is at a distance of 64 mm from the inner edge of the section and the line of action of the load is 50 mm from the same edge. Determine the maximum load the hook can carry if the allowable stress is limited to 60 MPa (Fig. 1.23).

[*VTU-Dec 11, June/July 2009, Jan/Feb 05 – 16 Marks*]

Solution: $\sigma = 60$ MPa, $F = ?$

a. To find $\bar{x}$:
   - From **Fig. f -Tb 1.3/Pg 9, DHB**
   $b = 25$ mm, $b_1 = 50$ mm, $h = 64$ mm, therefore, $b_0 = b_1 - b = 50 - 25 = 25$ mm
   $$c = \frac{(3b + 2b_0)h}{3(2b + b_0)}$$
   $$= \frac{(3 \times 25 + 2 \times 25)64}{3(2 \times 25 + 25)} = 35.56 \text{ mm}^2$$
   $\bar{x} = h - c = 64 - 35.56 = 28.44$ mm

b. Direct stress

$$\sigma = \frac{F}{A} = \frac{F}{2400}$$

$$= 4.167 \times 10^{-4} F \, N/mm^2$$

$$A = \frac{h}{2}(b_1 + b)$$

$$A = \frac{h}{2}(b_1 + b) = \frac{64 \times (50 + 25)}{2}$$

$$= 2400 \, mm^2$$

c. To find the bending stresses (σ_i, σ_0)

- Moment, $M = Fx$

$$= F \times (50 + 28.44)$$

$$M = 78.44 \, N\text{-}mm$$

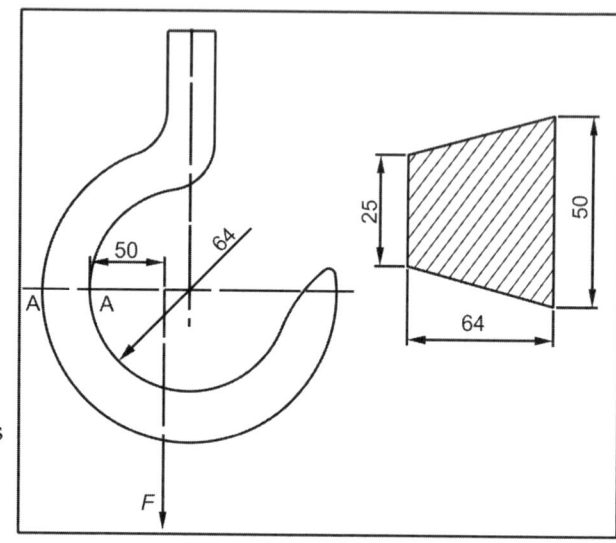

Fig. 1.23: Problem 17

- **Fig. 7-Tb 10.1/Pg 135, DHB** – for a trapezoidal section, $e = R - R_n$

$$e = R - \frac{A}{\left[\left(\frac{b_1(R+c_2) - b(R-c_1)}{h}\right) \ln\left(\frac{R+c_2}{R+c_1}\right)\right] - (b_1 - b)}$$

Here, $b_1 = 50$ mm, $b = 25$ mm, $h = 64$ mm, $R_i = 64$ mm, $c_1 = \bar{x} = 28.44$ mm, $R = R_i + c_1 = 64 + 28.44 = 92.44$ mm, $R_0 = R_i + h = 64 + 64 = 128$ mm, $c_2 = h - c_1 = 64 - 28.44 = 35.56$ mm

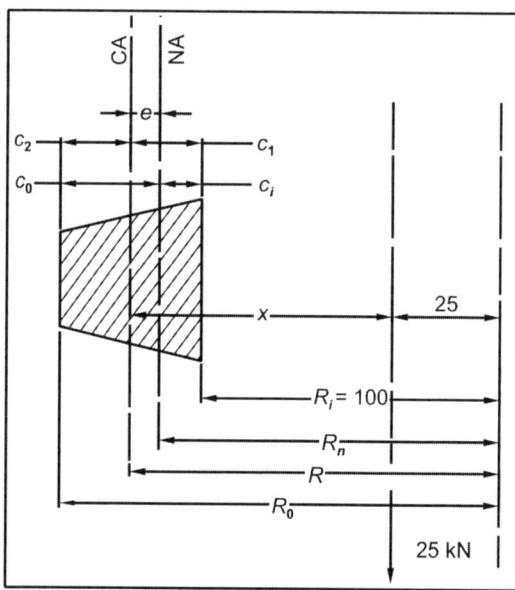

Fig. 1.23(a): Problem 17

$$= 92.44 - \cfrac{2400}{\left[\left(\cfrac{50(92.44+35.56)-25(92.44-28.44)}{64}\right)\ln\left(\cfrac{92.44+35.56}{92.44-28.44}\right)\right]-(50-25)}$$

$e = 3.51$ mm

Now, $c_i = c_1 - e = 28.44 - 3.51 = 24.93$ mm.
$c_0 = c_2 + e = 35.56 + 3.51 = 39.07$ mm,

- Bending stress at inner fiber,

$$\sigma_i = \frac{Mc_i}{AeR_i} = \frac{(78.44F)\times 24.93}{2400\times 3.51 \times 64} = (3.63\times 10^{-3})F \text{ N/mm}^2 \quad \ldots \textbf{10.2b/Pg 132, DHB}$$

- Bending stress at outer fiber,

$$\sigma_0 = \frac{Mc_0}{AeR_0} = \frac{-(78.44F)\times 39.07}{2400\times 3.51 \times 128} = -(2.84\times 10^{-3})F \text{ N/mm}^2 \quad \ldots \textbf{10.2a/Pg 132, DHB}$$

d. Resultant stresses
- Resultant stress in the inner most fiber, $(\sigma_i)_r = \sigma + \sigma = (4.167\times 10^{-4})F + (3.63\times 10^{-3})F = 4.05\times 10^{-3} F$ N/mm^2
- Resultant stress in the outer most fiber, $(\sigma_0)_r = \sigma + \sigma_0 = (4.167\times 10^{-4})F - (2.84\times 10^{-3})F = -2.43\times 10^{-3}$ N/mm^2

e. Since maximum stress occurs in the inner fiber, $(\sigma_i)_r = (4.05\times 10^{-3})F$ N/mm^2

$$60 = (4.05\times 10^{-3})F$$

$$F = \frac{60}{4.05\times 10^{-3}} = 14.83 \text{ kN}$$

18. **Determine a safe value for load P for a machine element loaded as shown in Fig. 1.24, limiting the maximum normal stress induced on the cross-section X–X to 120 MPa.** *[VTU-Jan/Feb 2006–10 Marks]*

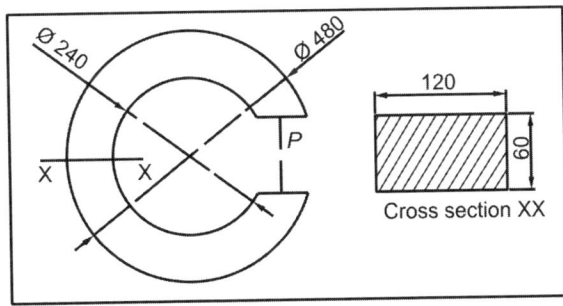

Fig. 1.24: Problem 18

Solution: $\sigma = 120$ MPa, $b = 60$ mm, $h = 120$ mm, $F = ?$

a. To find $\bar{x}$:

We know that, $\bar{x} = \dfrac{h}{2} = \dfrac{120}{2} = 60$ mm

b. Direct stress $\sigma = \dfrac{F}{A} = \dfrac{F}{120\times 60} = (1.39\times 10^{-4})F$ N/mm

c. To find the bending stresses (σ_i, σ_0)
- Moment, $M = Fx$
$$= F \times (120 + 60 + 180)$$
$$M = 362F \text{ N-mm}$$
- **Fig. 1-Tb 10.1/Pg 134, DHB** – for a rectangular section,

$$e = R - R_n$$

$$e = R - \frac{h}{\ln\left(\frac{R+c}{R-c}\right)}$$

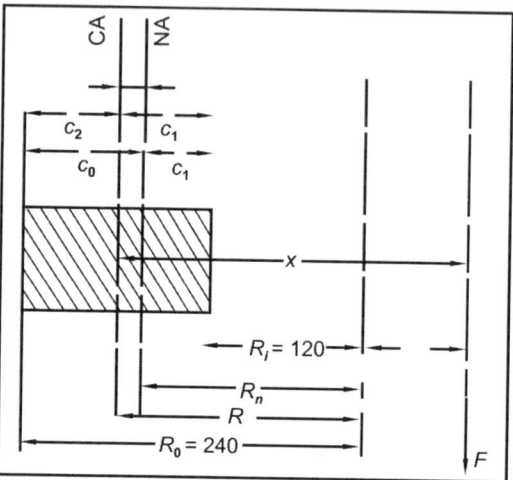

Fig. 1.24(a): Section XX Problem 18

$R_i = 120$ mm, $c_1 = c_2 = 60$ mm $= \bar{x}$,
$R = R_i + c_1 = 120 + 60 = 180$ mm,
$R_0 = R_i + h = 120 + 120 = 240$ mm,

$$= 180 - \frac{120}{\ln\left(\frac{180+60}{180-60}\right)}$$

$e = 6.88$ mm

Now, $c_i = c_1 - e = 60 - 6.88 = 53.12$ mm, $c_0 = c_2 + e = 60 + 6.88 = 66.88$ mm

- Bending stress at inner fiber,

$$\sigma_i = \frac{Mc_i}{AeR_i} = \frac{(360F) \times 53.12}{(120 \times 60) \times 688 \times 120} = (3.22 \times 10^{-3})F \text{ N/mm}^2 \quad \ldots \textbf{10.2b/Pg 132, DHB}$$

- Bending stress at outer fiber,

$$\sigma_0 = \frac{-Mc_0}{AeR_0} = \frac{(360F) \times 66.88}{(120 \times 60) \times 688 \times 240} = -(2.03 \times 10^{-3})F \text{ N/mm}^2 \quad \ldots \textbf{10.2a/Pg 132, DHB}$$

d. Resultant stresses
- Resultant stress in the inner most fiber,
$$\sigma_i)_r = \sigma + \sigma_i = (1.39 \times 10^{-4})F + (3.22 \times 10^{-3}) = (3.36 \times 10^{-3}) \text{ N/mm}^2$$
- Resultant stress in the outer most fiber,
$$\sigma_0)_r = \sigma + \sigma_0 = (1.39 \times 10^{-4})F - (2.03 \times 10^{-3}) = -(1.89 \times 10^{-3}) \text{ N/mm}^2$$

e. Since maximum stress occurs in the inner fiber, $\sigma_i)_r = (3.36 \times 10^{-3})$ N/mm^2

$$120 = (3.36 \times 10^{-3})$$

$$F = \frac{120}{3.36 \times 10^{-3}} = 35.72 \text{ kN}$$

19. An offset bar is loaded as shown in Fig. 1.25. Neglecting the weight of the bar, determine the maximum offset 'L' if allowable stress in tension is limited to 60 MPa

Solution: $\sigma = 60$ MPa, $d = 75$ mm, $F = 8000$ N, $L = ?$

a. To find $\bar{x}$:

We know that, $\bar{x} = \frac{d}{2} = \frac{75}{2} = 37.5$ mm

$$A = \frac{\pi d^2}{4} = \frac{\pi \times 75^2}{4} = 4417.86 \text{ mm}^2$$

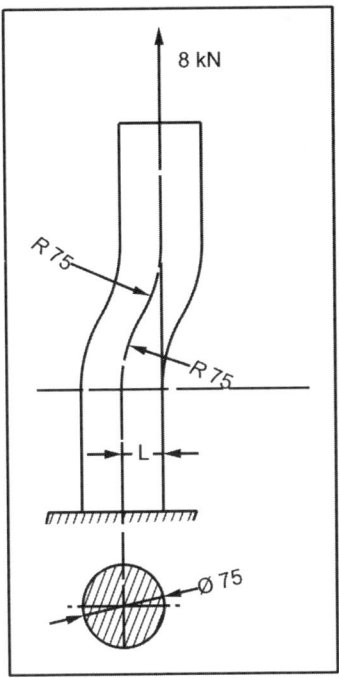

Fig. 1.25: Problem 6

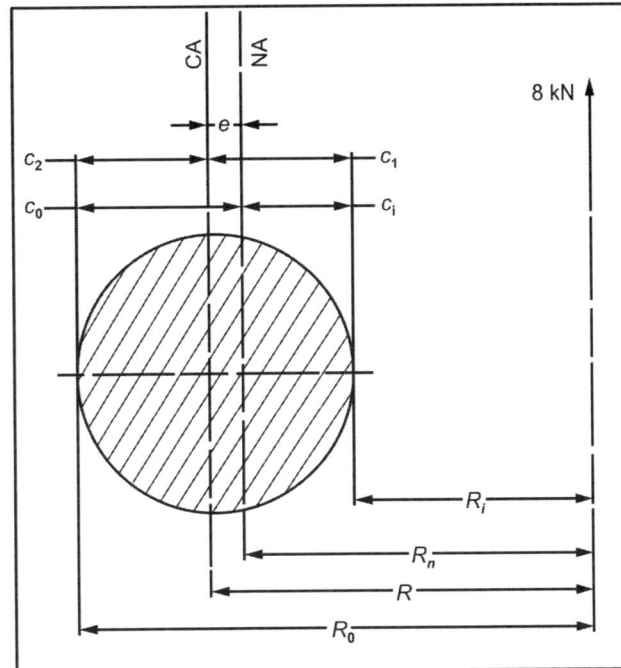

Fig. 1.25(a): Problem 6

b. Direct stress $\sigma = \dfrac{F}{A} = \dfrac{8000}{4417.8} = 1.81 \text{ N/mm}^2$

c. To find the bending stresses (σ_i, σ_0)

- Moment, $M = Fx = FL = 8000L$ N-mm
- **Fig. 2-Tb 10.1/Pg 134, DHB** – for a circular section, $e = R - R_n$

$$e = R - \dfrac{c^2/2}{R - \sqrt{R^2 - c^2}}$$

$R_i = 37.5$ mm, $c_1 = c_2 = 37.5$ mm $= \bar{x}$
$R = R_i + c_1 = 37.5 + 37.5 = 75$ mm (data)
$R_0 = R_i + d = 37.5 + 75 = 112.5$ mm

$$= 75 - \dfrac{37.5^2/2}{75 - \sqrt{75^2 - 37.5^2}}$$

$e = 5.02$ mm

Now, $c_i = c_1 - e = 37.5 - 5.02 = 32.48$ mm, $c_0 = c_2 + e = 37.5 + 5.02 = 42.52$ mm

- Bending stress at inner fiber,

$$\sigma_i = \dfrac{Mc_i}{AeR_i} = \dfrac{(8000L) \times 32.48}{4417.856 \times 5.02 \times 37.5} = (0.3124)L \text{ N/mm}^2 \quad \ldots \textbf{10.2b/Pg 132, DHB}$$

- Bending stress at outer fiber,

$$\sigma_0 = \dfrac{-Mc_0}{AeR_0} = \dfrac{-(8000L) \times 42.52}{4417.856 \times 5.02 \times 112.5} = (0.1363)L \text{ N/mm}^2 \quad \ldots \textbf{10.2a/Pg 132, DHB}$$

d. Resultant stresses
- Resultant stress in the inner most fiber, $\sigma_i)_r = \sigma + \sigma_i = 1.81 + (0.3124) L$
- Resultant stress in the outer most fiber, $\sigma_0)_r = \sigma + \sigma_0 = 1.81 - (0.1363) L$

e. Since maximum stress occurs in the inner fiber,
$$\sigma_i)_r = 1.81 + (0.3124) L \text{ N/mm}^2$$
$$60 = 1.81 + (0.3124) L$$
$$60 - 1.81 = (0.3124) L$$
$$\therefore L = 186.27 \text{ mm}$$

20. A cast iron frame of a small punch is as shown in Fig. 1.26. Determine: (a) The force that will produce a maximum tensile stress of 60 MPa at section A – A. (b) The corresponding compressive stress in the section.

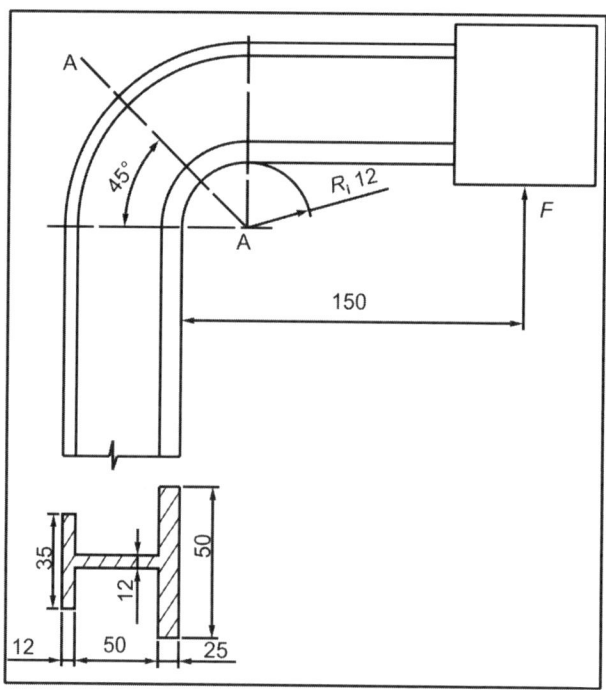

Fig. 1.26: Problem 20

Solution: $R_i = 12$ mm, $\sigma_t = 60$ MPa, $F = ?$, $\sigma_c = ?$

a. To find $\bar{x}$:

$a_1 = 50 \times 25 = 1250$ $a_2 = 12 \times 50 = 600 \text{ mm}^2$ $a_3 = 35 \times 12 = 420 \text{ mm}^2$
$x_1 = 25/2 = 12.5 \text{ mm}$ $x_2 = (50/2) + 25 = 50 \text{ mm}$ $x_3 = (12/2) + 75 = 81 \text{ mm}$

$A = \Sigma a = a_1 + a_2 + a_3 = 2270 \text{ mm}^2$

$$\bar{x} = \frac{\Sigma ax}{\Sigma a} = \frac{(1250 \times 12.5) + (600 \times 50) + (420 \times 81)}{(1250 + 600 + 420)} = 35.1 \text{ mm}$$

b. Direct stress $\sigma = \dfrac{F \cos \theta}{A} = \dfrac{F \times \cos 45}{2270} = (3.12 \times 10^{-4}) F \text{ N/mm}^2$

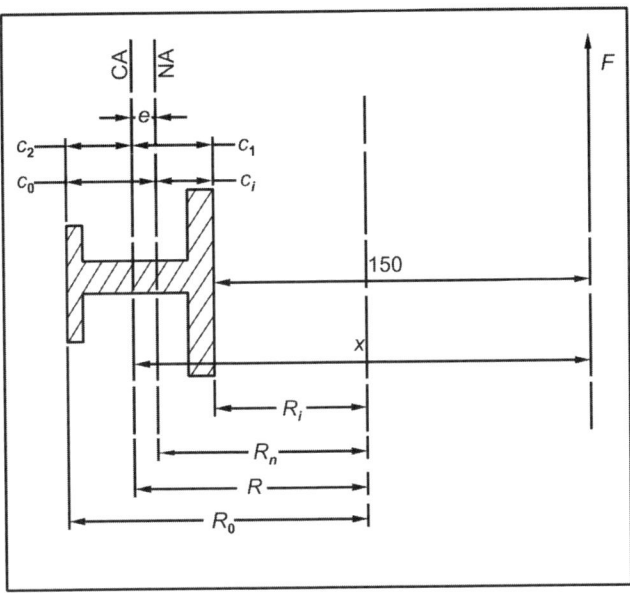

Fig. 1.26(a): Problem 20

c. To find the bending stresses (σ_i)
   - Moment, $M = F.x = F(150 + \bar{x}) = F(150 + 32) = 182\,F$ N-mm
   - **Fig. 10-Tb 10.1/Pg 136, DHB** – for an I- section,

   $e = R - R_n$

   $$e = R - \frac{A}{B\ln\left(\frac{R+d-c_1}{R-c_1}\right) + b_2\ln\left(\frac{R+c_2-d_1}{R-d-c_1}\right) + b_1\ln\left(\frac{R+c_2}{R-c_2-d_1}\right)}$$

   Here, $B = 50$ mm, $b_1 = 35$ mm, $d = 25$ mm, $d_1 = 12$ mm, $b_2 = 12$ mm,
   $H = 25 + 50 + 12 = 87$ mm,
   Also $R_i = 12$ mm, $R_0 = R_i + H = 12 + 87 = 99$ mm, $c_1 = \bar{x} = 35.1$ mm,
   $R = c_1 + R_i = 35.1 + 12 = 47.1$ mm, $c_2 = H - c_1 = 87 - 35.1 = 51.9$ mm

   $$= 47.1 - \frac{2270}{50\ln\left(\frac{47.1+25-35.1}{47.1-35.1}\right) + 12\ln\left(\frac{47.1+51.9-12}{47.1-25-35.1}\right) + 35\ln\left(\frac{47.1+51.9}{47.1+51.9-12}\right)}$$

   $e = 15.15$ mm
   Now, $c_i = c_1 - e = 35.1 - 15.15 = 19.95$ mm, $c_0 = c_2 + e = 51.9 + 15.15 = 67.05$ mm

   - Bending stress at inner fiber,

   $$\sigma_i = \frac{Mc_i}{AeR_i} = \frac{(182F) \times 19.95}{2270 \times 15.15 \times 12.5} = (8.44 \times 10^{-3})F \text{ N/mm}^2 \quad \ldots \text{10.2b/Pg 132, DHB}$$

   - Bending stress at outer fiber,

   $$\sigma_0 = \frac{Mc_0}{AeR_0} = \frac{-(182F) \times 67.05}{2270 \times 15.15 \times 99} = (-3.58 \times 10^{-3})F \text{ N/mm}^2 \quad \ldots \text{10.2a/Pg 132, DHB}$$

d. Tensile stress at inner fiber:
- Resultant stress in the inner most fiber, $\sigma_i)_r = \sigma + \sigma_i$
$$= (3.12 \times 10^{-4})F + (8.44 \times 10^{-3})F$$
$$60 = (8.752 \times 10^{-3})F$$
$$F = 6855.57 \text{ N}$$

e. To find σ_0:
- Resultant stress in the outer most fiber, $\sigma_0)_r = \sigma + \sigma_0 = (3.12 \times 10^{-4})F - (3.58 \times 10^{-3})F$
$$= (-3.268 \times 10^{-3})F$$
$$= (-3.268 \times 10^{-3}) \times 6855.57$$
$$= -22.40 \text{ N/mm}^2$$
$$\sigma_0)_r = -22.40 \text{ N/mm}^2$$

21. Taking a permissible stress in the material as 100 MPa, estimate the thickness 't' for the cross-section shown in Fig. 1.27. *[VTU-July/August 2002]*

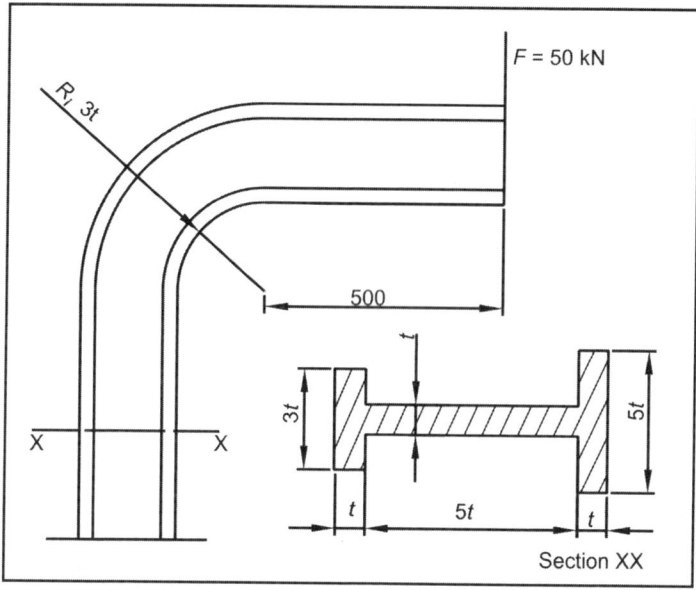

Fig. 1.27: Problem 21

Solution: $R_i = 3t$ mm, $\sigma_i)_r = 100$ MPa, $t = ?$, $F = 50 \times 10^3$ N

a. To find $\bar{x}$:
Here, $a_1 + 5t \times t = 5t^2$, $a_2 = 5t \times t = 5t^2$, $a_3 = 3t \times t = 3t^2$
$x_1 = t/2 = 0.5t$, $x_2 = (5t/2) + t = 3.5t$, $x_3 = (t/2) + 5t + t = 6.5t$
$A = \Sigma a = a_1 + a_2 + a_3 + = 13\, t^2$

$$\bar{x} = \frac{\Sigma ax}{\Sigma a} = \frac{(5t^2 \times 0.5t) + (5t^2 \times 3.5t) + (3t^2 \times 6.5t)}{(5t^2 + 5t^2 + 3t^2)} = 3.04t \text{ mm}$$

b. Direct stress $\sigma = \dfrac{F}{A} = \dfrac{50 \times 10^3}{13t^2} = \dfrac{3846.15}{t^2}$ N/mm^2

c. To find the bending stresses:
- Moment, $M = Fx$

$$= 50 \times 10^3(500 + 3t + 3.04t)$$
$$M = 25 - 10^6 + (302 \times 10^3)t \text{ N-mm}$$

- Fig. 10-Tb 10.1/Pg 136, DHB – for an I- section,
$e = R - R_n$

$$e = R - \cfrac{A}{B\ln\left(\cfrac{R+d-c_1}{R-c_1}\right) + b_2 \ln\left(\cfrac{R+c_2-d_1}{R+d-c_1}\right) + b_1 \ln\left(\cfrac{R+c_2}{R+c_2-d_1}\right)}$$

Here, $B = 5t$, $b_1 = 3t$, $d = t = d_1$, $b_2 = t = t$, $H = t + 5t + t = 7t$
Also $R_i = 3t$, $R_0 = R_i + H = 3t + 7t = 10t$, $c_1 = x = 3.04t$
$R = c_1 + R_i = 3.04t + 3t = 6.04t$, $c_2 = H - c_1 = 7t - 3.04t = 3.96t$

$$= 6.04t - \cfrac{13t^2}{5t\ln\left(\cfrac{6.04t + t - 3.04t}{6.04t - 3.04t}\right) + t\ln\left(\cfrac{6.04t + 3.96t - t}{6.04t + t - 3.04t}\right) + 3t\ln\left(\cfrac{6.04t + 3.96t}{6.04t + 3.96t - t}\right)}$$

$e = 0.973t$ mm

Now, $c_i = c_1 - e = 3.04t - 0.973t = 2.067t$, $c_0 = c_2 + e = 3.96t + 0.973t = 4.933t$

- Bending stress at inner fiber,

$$\sigma_i = \frac{Mc_i}{AeR_i} = \frac{(25 \times 10^6 + 302 \times 10^3 t) \times 2.067t}{13t^2 \times 0.973t \times 3t} \quad \ldots 10.2b/\text{Pg } 132, \text{ DHB}$$

$$= \frac{(51.68 \times 10^6 + 624.23 \times 10^3 t)}{37.95t^3} \text{ N/mm}^2$$

d. To find t:

- We know that the resultant stress in the inner most fiber, $\sigma_i)_r = \sigma + \sigma_i$

$$100 = \frac{3846.15}{t^2} + \frac{(51.68 \times 10^6 + 624.43 \times 10^3 t)}{37.95t^3} \text{ N/mm}^2$$
$$3849.3t^3 = (146 \times 10^3) + 51.68 \times 10^6 + (624.23 \times 10^3)t$$
$$3849.3t^3 - (770.2 \times 10^3) - 51.68 \times 10^6 = 0$$
$$t = 26.5 \text{ mm}$$

22. Determine the dimensions of the curved bar as shown in Fig. 1.28. Assume σ_{yt} = 400 N/mm² and FOS = 3.5.   *[VTU-June/July 2011 – 12 Marks]*

Solution: $\sigma_{yt} = 400$ N/mm² and $FOS = 3.5$, $F = 1000$ N, $R = 4D$, $D = ?$

Here, $\sigma = \cfrac{\sigma_{yt}}{FOS} = \cfrac{400}{3.5} = 114.29$ N/mm²

a. To find $\bar{x}$:

We know that, $\bar{x} = \cfrac{D}{2} = 0.5D$ mm

$$\bar{x} = \frac{\pi d^2}{4} = 0.7854 D^2 \text{ mm}^2$$

b. Direct stress $\sigma = \cfrac{F}{A} = \cfrac{1000}{0.7754 D^2} = \cfrac{1273.24}{D^2}$ N/mm²

c. To find the bending stresses (σ_i, σ_0)
- Moment, $M = Fx = FR = 1000 \times 4D = 4000D$ N-mm
- **Fig. 2-Tb 10.1/Pg 134, DHB** – for a circular section,

$e = R - R_n$

$e = R - \dfrac{c^2/2}{R - \sqrt{R^2 - c^2}}$

$R = 4D, R_i = R - \left(\dfrac{D}{2}\right) = 4D - 0.5D = 3.5D$

$R_0 = R_i + D = 3.5D + D = 4.5, \qquad c_1 = c_2 = 0.5D = \bar{x}$

$= 4D - \dfrac{(0.5D)^2/2}{4D - \sqrt{(4D)^2 - (0.5D)^2}}$

$e = 0.0157D$ mm
$c_i = c_1 - e = 0.5D - 0.0157D = 0.4843D$,
$c_0 = c_2 + e = 0.5D + 0.0157D = 0.5157D$

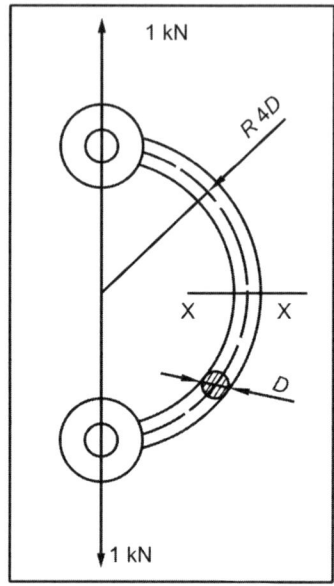

Fig. 1.28: Problem 22

- Bending stress at inner fiber,

$\sigma_i = \dfrac{Mc_i}{AeR_i} = \dfrac{(4000D) \times 0.4843D}{0.7854D^2 \times 0.0157D \times 3.5D} = \dfrac{44.88 \times 10^3}{D^2}$

... **10.2b/Pg 132, DHB**

- Bending stress at outer fiber,

$\sigma_0 = \dfrac{-Mc_0}{AeR_0} = \dfrac{-(4000D) \times 0.5157D}{0.7854D^2 \times 0.0157D \times 4.5D} = \dfrac{-37.18 \times 10^3}{D^2}$

... **10.2a/Pg 132, DHB**

d. Resultant stresses
- Resultant stress in the inner most fiber,

$$\sigma_i)_r = \sigma + \sigma_i = \dfrac{1273.24}{D^2} + \dfrac{44.88 \times 10^3}{D^2} \text{ N/mm}^2$$

e. To find D:
Since maximum stress occurs in the inner fiber,

$$\sigma_i)_r = \dfrac{1273.24}{D^2} + \dfrac{44.88 \times 10^3}{D^2}$$

$$114.29 = \dfrac{1273.24}{D^2} + \dfrac{44.88 \times 10^3}{D^2}$$

$$D = 20.11 \text{ mm}$$

1.7 CONDITION FOR BENDING STRESS AT EXTREME FIBERS TO BE NUMERICALLY EQUAL

For a curved beam subjected to bending, the extreme fiber stresses are

Bending stress at inner fiber, $\sigma_i = \dfrac{Mc_i}{AeR_i}$

Bending stress at outer fiber, $\sigma_0 = \dfrac{Mc_0}{AeR_0}$

For extreme fibers to be numerically equal, we have $\sigma_r = \sigma_0$

$$\frac{Mc_i}{AeR_i} = \frac{Mc_0}{AeR_0}$$

$$\frac{c_i}{R_i} = \frac{c_0}{R_0} \qquad \ldots \text{(Eq. 1.14)}$$

But $c_i = c_1 - e = R_n - R_i$
$c_0 = c_2 + e = R_0 - R_n$

Eq. (1.14) yields
$$\frac{R_n - R_i}{R_i} = \frac{R_0 - R_n}{R_0}$$

$$\frac{R_n}{R_i} - 1 = 1 - \frac{R_n}{R_0}$$

$$\frac{(R_0 - R_i)R_n}{R_i R_0} = 2$$

$$R_n = \frac{2R_i R_0}{(R_0 + R_i)} \qquad \ldots \text{(Eq. 1.15)}$$

23. Determine the width of larger side of a T-section shown in Fig. 1.29 for extreme fiber stresses in bending to be numerically equal.

Solution: $R_i = 60$ mm,

$R_0 = 120$ mm,

$B = ?$

Since extreme bending stresses are numerically equal, we have

$$R_n = \frac{2R_i R_0}{(R_0 + R_i)}$$

$$= \frac{2 \times 60 \times 120}{(60 + 120)}$$

$R_n = 80$ mm

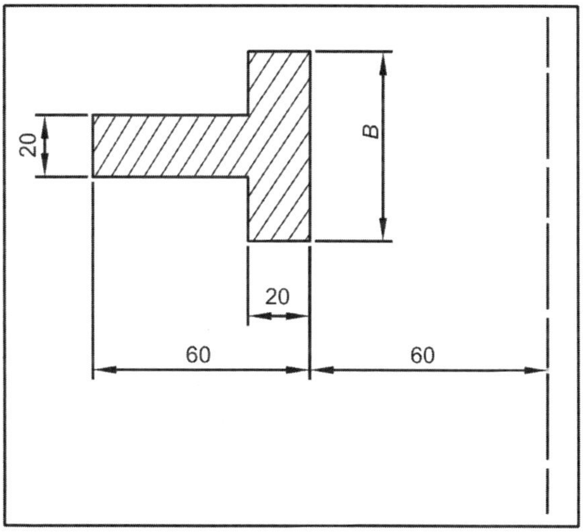

- Fig. 8-Tb 10.1/Pg 136, DHB – for a T-section, $e = R - R_n$
  Since $e = 0$, $R = R_n$

Fig. 1.29: Problem 23

$$R_n = \frac{A}{B\ln\left(\dfrac{R + d - c_1}{R - c_1}\right) + a\ln\left(\dfrac{R + c_2}{R + d - c_1}\right)}$$

Here, $d = 20$ mm, $H = 60$ mm, $a = 20$ mm
Also $R_i = 60$ mm $= R - c_1$, $R_0 = 120$ mm $= R + c_2$
Therefore, $R + d - c_1 = R_i + d = 60 + 20 = 80$ mm

$$80 = \frac{20B + (40 \times 20)}{B\ln\left(\dfrac{80}{60}\right) + 20\ln\left(\dfrac{120}{80}\right)}$$

$$80(0.287\ B + 8.109) = 20\ B + 800$$
$$22.96\ B + 648.72 = 20\ B + 800$$
$$2.96\ B = 151.28$$
$$B = 51.11 \text{ mm}$$

24. Determine the value of steam thickness 't' in the T-cross-section of a curved beam shown in Fig. 1.30 such that the normal stresses due to bending at the extreme inner and outer fibers are numerically equal.

[VTU-June/July 09–15 Marks; Jan/Feb 05–10 Marks]

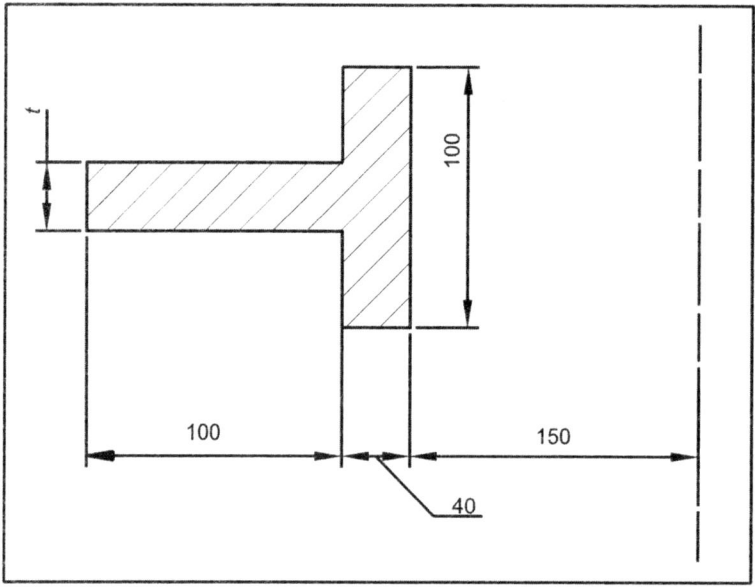

Fig. 1.30: Problem 24

Solution: $R_i = 150$ mm, $R_0 = 290$ mm, $B = 100$ mm, $t = ?$
Since extreme bending stresses are numerically equal, we have

$$R_n = \frac{2R_i R_0}{(R_0 + R_i)}$$

$$= \frac{2 \times 150 \times 290}{(290 + 150)}$$

$$R_n = 197.73 \text{ mm}$$

- **Fig. 8-Tb 10.1/Pg 136, DHB** – for a T- section, $e = R - R_n$
  Since $e = 0$, $R = R_n$

$$R_n = \frac{A}{B \ln\left(\dfrac{R + d - c_1}{R - c_1}\right) + a \ln\left(\dfrac{R + c_2}{R + d - c_1}\right)}$$

Here, $d = 40$ mm, $H = 140$ mm,
Also $R_i = 150$ mm $= R - c_1$, $R_0 = 290$ mm $= R + c_2$
Therefore, $R + d - c_1 = R_i + d = 150 + 40 = 190$ mm; ($a = t$)

$$197.73 = \frac{(100 \times 40) + 100t}{100 \ln\left(\frac{190}{150}\right) + t \ln\left(\frac{290}{190}\right)}$$

$$197.73 \,(23.638 + 0.423t) = 4000 + 100t$$
$$4673.94 + 83.61t = 4000 + 100t$$
$$673.94 = 16.389$$
$$t = 41.12 \text{ mm}$$

25. Determine the dimensions of a unsymmetrical I-beam having circular center line and subjected to pure bending in the plane of unsymmetry, such that the extreme fiber stresses due to bending are numerically equal. The dimensions are: $R_i = 75$ mm, $R_i + d = 100$ mm, $R_0 = 175$ mm, $b_2 = 25$ mm, $b_1 + B = 125$ mm, web length = 50 mm (Fig. 1.31).

Solution: From Fig. 10-Tb 10.1/Pg 136, DHB
$R_i = 75$ mm, $R_i + d = 100$ mm, $R_0 = 175$ mm,
$b_2 = 25$ mm, $b_1 + B = 125$ mm, web length = 50 mm.

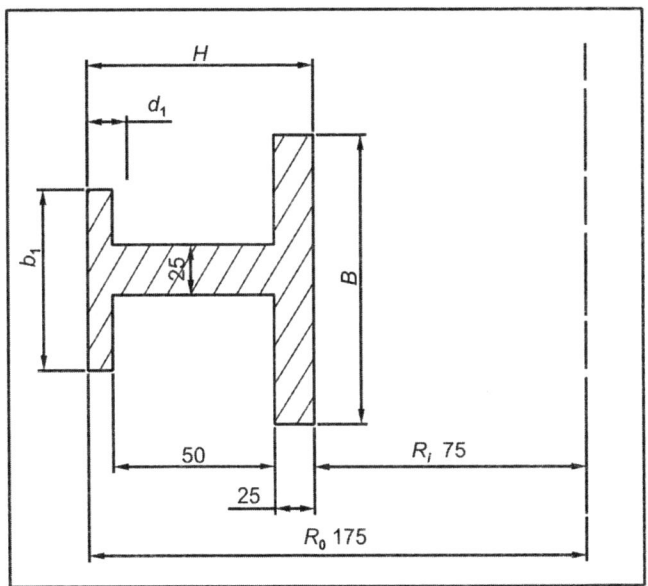

Fig. 1.31: Problem 25

Since extreme bending stresses are numerically equal, we have

$$R_n = \frac{2R_i R_0}{(R_0 + R_i)} = \frac{2 \times 75 \times 1750}{(275 + 75)}$$

$$R_n = 105 \text{ mm}$$

- Fig. 10-Tb 10.1/Pg 136, DHB – for an I-section,
$$e = R - R_n$$
Since $e = 0$, $R = R_n$

$$\therefore R_n = \cfrac{A}{B\ln\left(\cfrac{R+d-c_1}{R-c_1}\right) + b_2\ln\left(\cfrac{R+c_2-d_1}{R+d-c_1}\right) + b_1\ln\left(\cfrac{R+c_2}{R+c_2-d_1}\right)}$$

Here, $b_i = b_1, d = 25$ mm, $b_2 = 25$ mm, $H = 175 - 75 = 100$ mm, $d_1 = H - 75 = 100 - 75 = 25$ mm

Also $R_i = 75$ mm $= R - c_1$, $R_0 = R_i + H = 75 + 100 = 175$ mm

$R + d - c_1 = R + d = 75 + 25 = 100$ mm

$R + c_2 - d = R_0 - d = 175 - 25 = 150$ mm

$A = (b_1 d_1 + b_2 \times 50 + B.d) = (25b_1 + 25 \times 50 + 25)$

$= 25(b_1 + B) + 1250 = (25 \times 125) + 1250$

$A = 4375$ mm^2

$$105 = \cfrac{4375}{B\ln\left(\cfrac{100}{75}\right) + 25\ln\left(\cfrac{150}{100}\right) + b_1\ln\left(\cfrac{175}{150}\right)}$$

$105\,(0.287B + 10.14 + 0.154b_1) = 4375$

$0.287B + 10.14 + 0.154b_1 = \cfrac{4375}{105}$

$0.287B + 0.154b_1 = 41.67 - 10.14$

$0.287\,(125 - b_1) + 0.154 b_1 = 31.526$ [since $b_1 + B = 125$ mm hence, $B = 125 - b_1$]

$-0.133 b_1 + 35.875 = 31.526 - 35.875$

$-0.133 b_1 = -4.349$

$b_1 = 32.70$ mm and $B = 125 - 32.70 = 92.30$ mm

26. **The section of a crane hook is a trapezium having the following dimensions. Width on inner side = b_1, width on outer side = 40 mm, depth of cross-section = 80 mm. The center of curvature is at a distance of 150 mm from inner edge. Determine the value of b_1, if extreme fiber stresses are numerically equal (Fig. 1.32).**

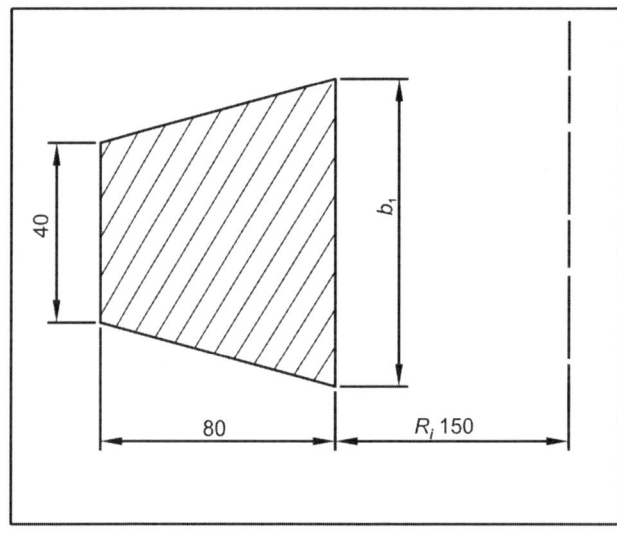

Fig. 1.32: Problem 26

Solution: From Fig. 7-Tb 10.1/Pg 135, DHB

$b = 40$ mm, $h = 80$ mm,
$R_i = 150$ mm, $b_1 = ?$
$R_0 = R_i + h = 150 + 80 = 230$ mm

Since extreme bending stresses are numerically equal, we have

$$R_n = \frac{2R_i R_0}{(R_0 + R_i)}$$

$$= \frac{2 \times 150 \times 230}{(230 + 150)}$$

$$R_n = 181.6 \text{ mm}$$

- **Fig. 7-Tb 10.1/Pg 136 DHB**–for a trapezoidal section,
$e = R - R_n$
Since $e = 0$, $R = R_n$

$$R = \frac{A}{\left[\left(\frac{b_1(R+c_2) - b(R-c_1)}{h}\right)\ln\left(\frac{R+c_2}{R-c_1}\right)\right] - (b_1 - b)}$$

Also, $R_i = 150$ mm $= R - c_1$, $R_0 = 230$ mm $= R + c_2$

$$A = \frac{h}{2}(b_1 + b) = \frac{80 \times (b_1 + 40)}{2} = 40(b_1 + b)$$

$$181.6 = \frac{40(b_1 + 40)}{\left(\frac{23b_1 - (40 \times 150)}{80}\right)\ln\left(\frac{230}{150}\right) - (b_1 - 40)}$$

$$= \frac{40b_1 + 1600}{[1.23b_1 - 32.06] - b_1 - 40}$$

$$= \frac{40b_1 + 1600}{0.23b_1 + 7.9440}$$

$41.77b_1 + 1442 = 40 b_1 + 1600$
$1.77 b_1 = 158$
$b_1 = 89.26$ mm
$b_1 \approx 90$ mm

27. Determine the value of 't' in the cross-section of a curved machine member shown in Fig. 1.33, so that the normal stresses due to bending at extreme fibers are numerically equal. Also determine the normal stresses so induced at extreme fibers due to bending moment of 10 kN-m.   *[VTU-Dec 2010 – 12 Marks]*

Solution: From Fig. 7-Tb 10.1/Pg 136 DHB

$b = t = ?$, $h = 100$ mm,
$R_i = 150$ mm, $b_1 = 80$ mm
$R_0 = R_i + h = 150 + 100 = 250$ mm

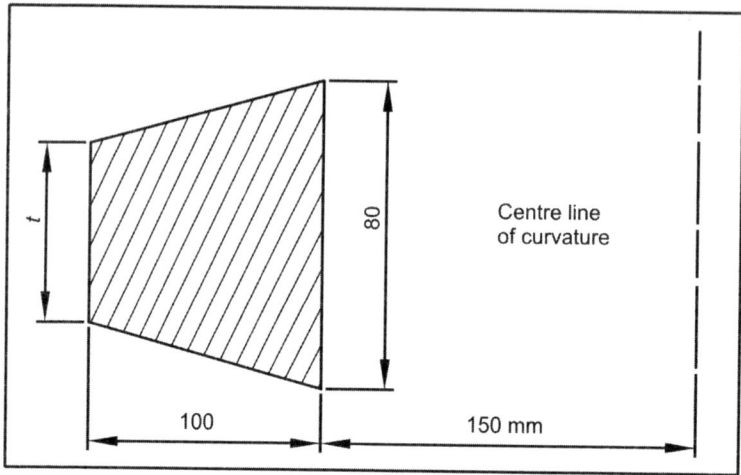

Fig. 1.33: Problem 27

Since extreme bending stresses are numerically equal, we have

$$R_n = \frac{2R_i R_0}{(R_0 + R_i)}$$

$$= \frac{2 \times 150 \times 250}{(250 + 150)}$$

$$R_n = 187.5 \text{ mm}$$

- **Fig. 7-Tb 10.1/Pg 135, DHB**–for a trapezoidal section,
  $e = R - R_n$
  Since $e = 0$, $R = R_n$

$$R = \frac{A}{\left[\left(\frac{b_1(R+c_2)-b(R-c_1)}{h}\right)\ln\left(\frac{R+c_2}{R-c_1}\right)\right]-(b_1-b)}$$

Also, $R_i = 150$ mm $= R - c_1$, $R_0 = 250$ mm $= R + c_2$

$$A = \frac{h}{2}(b_1 + b) = \frac{100 \times (80+t)}{2} = 50(80+t)$$

$$187.5 = \frac{50(80+t)}{\left[\left(\frac{(80 \times 250)-150t}{100}\right)\ln\left(\frac{250}{150}\right)\right]-(80-t)}$$

$$= \frac{4000 + 50t}{[102.17 - 0.766t] - 80 + t}$$

$$= \frac{4000 + 50t}{22.17 + 0.234t}$$

$$4156.88 + 43.88t = 4000 + 50t$$

$$153.88 = 6.12t$$

$$t = 25.14 \text{ mm} = b$$

Curved Beams, Cylinders and Cylinder Heads

CYLINDERS AND CYLINDER HEADS

1.8 THIN CYLINDERS

Cylindrical and spherical shells are most commonly used in engineering works such as steam air compressors, boilers, tanks, reservoirs, engine cylinders, gas cylinders, roof domes, airplane wings, submarine hulls, etc. The walls of the shell are subjected to pressures from fluids, gases–or–dry materials. When gas is used, pressure is constant in all parts of the vessel. In case of liquids, the pressure is lowest at the top and increases with depth. On the other hand if the vessels are empty, they are subjected to atmospheric pressure both internally and externally and hence the resultant effect of atmospheric pressure is zero (nil).

The shells are classified into two types based on the ratio of wall thickness to that of the diameter of the shell as:

- **Thin shells:** Here the normal stresses (tensile/compressive) are assumed to be uniformly distributed through the thickness of the wall. The operating pressure is around 30 MPa and more.

$$\frac{d}{10} < t > \frac{d}{15}, \qquad \frac{t}{d} \leq 0.07 \qquad \ldots \text{7.1/Pg 75, DHB}$$

t-thickness of shell

Examples: Boilers, tanks, steam pipes, water pipes, etc.

- **Thick shells:** Here the normal stresses (tensile/compressive) vary along the thickness of the wall. The analysis of thick shells is more complex than that of thin shells. The operating pressure is more than 250 MPa.

$$t > \frac{d}{15}$$

1.9 THIN CYLINDRICAL SHELLS SUBJECTED TO INTERNAL PRESSURE

When a cylinder is subjected to internal pressure, the following types of stresses are developed:
1. **Hoop/circumferential stress:** These act in a tangential direction to the circumference of the shell.
2. **Longitudinal stress:** These act parallel to the longitudinal axis of the shell.
3. **Radial stress:** These act radially and are too small and hence can be neglected.

A problem in which combined stresses are present is that of a cylindrical shell under internal pressure. Consider a thin cylinder subjected to an internal pressure 'p', which may be due to a fluid –or– gas enclosed within the cylinder as shown in **Fig. 1.34**. The

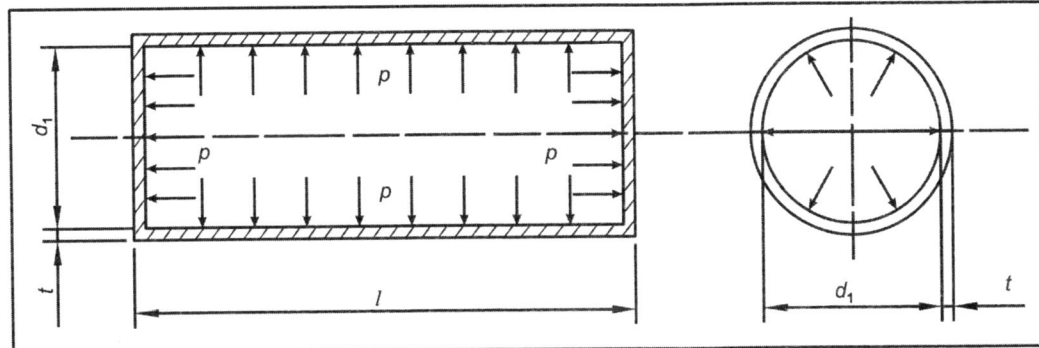

Fig. 1.34: Long thin cylindrical shell with closed ends under internal pressure

internal pressure acting on the long sides of the cylinder gives rise to a circumferential stress in the wall of the cylinder (σ_t) and if the ends of the cylinder are closed, the pressure acting on these ends is transmitted to the walls of the cylinder, thus producing a longitudinal stress (σ_l) in the walls.

1.9.1 Circumferential/Tangential/Hoop Stress

Consider the cross-section of a cylinder as shown in **Fig. 1.35** subjected to internal pressure.

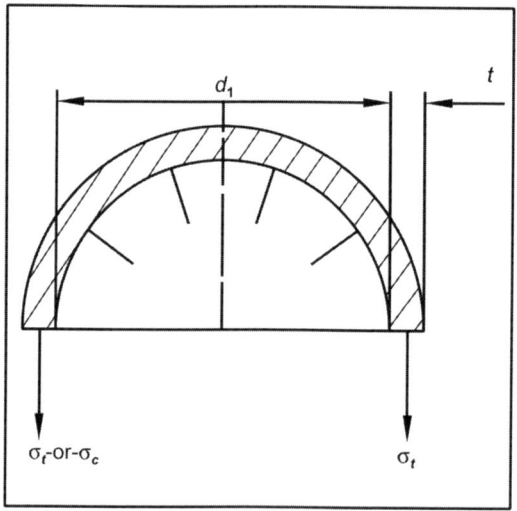

Fig. 1.35: Circumferential stress

Let,
- d_i = inside diameter of the cylinder
- t = thickness of the cylinder
- p = internal/working pressure in the cylinder
- σ_t = the circumferential/hoop stress
- l = length of the cylinder

The bursting force is equal to ($p d_i l$). Due to this bursting force, the cylinder has a tendency to get split into two parts along the horizontal diameter. The resistance to this action is offered by the development of hoop stress (σ_t) as shown in **Fig. 1.35**.

For equilibrium,

$$\text{Bursting force} = \text{resisting strength}$$

i.e.
$$\text{pressure} \times \text{area} = \text{resisting strength}$$

$$p(d_i l) = \sigma_t (2tl)$$

$$\sigma_t = \frac{pd_i}{2t} \qquad \ldots 7.2a/\text{Pg } 75, \text{DHB}$$

- When there is a seam/joint in the cylinder, the tangential stress,

$$\sigma_t = \frac{pd_i}{2t\eta} \qquad \ldots 7.2b/\text{Pg } 75, \text{DHB}$$

η is the efficiency of the riveted joint.

- While designing engine and press cylinders, a value from 6–12 mm is added to permit for reboring,

$$t = \frac{pd_i}{2\sigma_t} + 8 \text{ mm} \qquad \ldots \text{7.6/Pg 76, DHB}$$

$\sigma_t = 8.825$ MPa for ordinary grade cast iron.
For, ductile materials, $\sigma_t = 0.8\,\sigma_y$ $\sigma_y =$ yield stress
        brittle materials, $\sigma_t = 0.125\,\sigma_u$ $\sigma_u =$ ultimate stress

1.9.2 Longitudinal Stress

Consider the cross-section of a cylinder as shown in **Fig. 1.36** subjected to internal pressure. Since the ends of the cylinder are closed at its ends, the bursting force is equal to $\left\{p \times \left(\frac{\pi}{4}d_i^2\right)\right\}$. Due to this bursting force, the cylinder has a tendency to be split into two smaller cylinders, longitudinally.

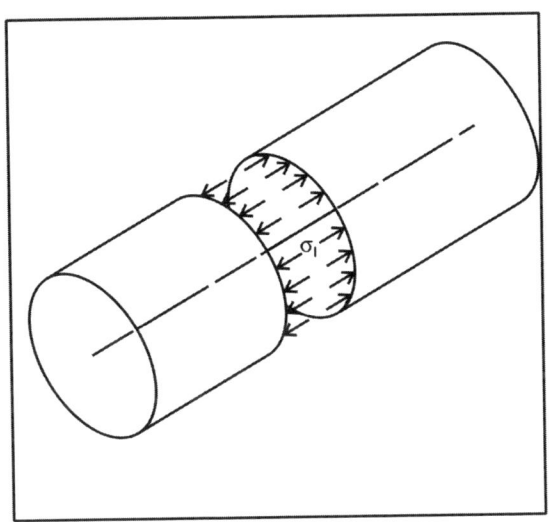

Fig. 1.36: Longitudinal stress

For equilibrium,
            Bursting force = resisting strength
i.e.   pressure × area = resisting strength

$$p\left(\frac{\pi}{4}d_i^2\right) = \sigma_l(\pi d_i t)$$

$$\sigma_l = \frac{pd_i}{4t} \qquad \ldots \text{7.3/Pg 75, DHB}$$

If η is the efficiency of the riveted joint then,

$$\sigma_l = \frac{pd_i}{4t\eta}$$

Thus the longitudinal stress is half that of circumferential stress or circumferential stress is twice that of longitudinal stress.

Note: The above formulae [Eqs (7.2) and (7.3)] are based on the following assumptions:
- The stress induced in the cylinder wall is uniform throughout its thickness, since $t \ll d$.
- The effect of curvature of the cylinder wall is neglected.

1.9.3 Maximum Shear Stress

The stresses acting on an element of the wall of the cylinder consist of a circumferential stress (σ_t), a longitudinal stress (σ_l), and a radial stress σ_r on the internal face of the element. If p is neglected, the state of stress in the wall of the cylinder approximates then to a simple two-dimensional system with principal stresses (σ_t) and (σ_l).

Therefore, the maximum shear stress,

$$\tau_{max} = \frac{\sigma_t - \sigma_l}{2}$$

$$= \frac{1}{2}\left(\frac{pd_i}{2t} - \frac{pd_i}{4t}\right)$$

$$\tau_{max} = \frac{pd_i}{8t}$$

1.10 THICK CYLINDERS

The thin cylinders are basically used for low internal pressure. Due to this the pressure was considered negligible compared to the circumferential and longitudinal stresses. On the other hand thick cylinders are subjected to high internal pressures and hence the radial stresses cannot be neglected. Further the circumferential stress varies across the thickness of the shell, i.e. maximum at inner surface and minimum at outer surface. Radial stress varies from the inner surface where it is equal to the magnitude of the fluid pressure to the outer surface where usually it is equal to zero if exposed to atmosphere.

The following equations are mostly used in the design of thick cylinders:
1. Lame's equation
2. Birnie's equation
3. Clavarino's equation
4. Barlow's equation

The use of above equations depends upon the type of material used and the end connections.

1.11 DIFFERENCE BETWEEN THICK AND THIN CYLINDERS

Sl. No	Thin cylinder	Thick cylinder
1	Here the normal stresses (tensile/compressive) are assumed to be uniformly distributed through the thickness of the wall	Here the normal stresses (tensile/compressive) vary along the thickness of the wall
2	Thickness: $\frac{d}{10} < t > \frac{d}{15}$	Thickness: $t > \frac{d}{15}$
3	The operating pressure is around 30 MPa and more	The operating pressure is more than 250 MPa

Conti...

Sl. No	Thin cylinder	Thick cylinder
4	Radial stress varies from zero at the outside surface to a value equal to the internal pressure at the inside surface	Radial stress varies from the inner surface where it is equal to the magnitude of the fluid pressure to the outer surface where usually it is equal to zero if exposed to atmosphere, the circumferential stress also varies with thickness
5	Analysis is simple	Complex
6	The thin cylinder is likely fail in two ways: a. Split up into two troughs b. Split up into two cylinders	
7	**Examples:** Boilers, tanks, steam pipes, water pipes, etc.	

1.12 LAME'S EQUATION

Assumptions

- The material of the shell is homogeneous and isotropic.
- Plane sections of the cylinder, perpendicular to the longitudinal axis remain plane under the pressure.
- The longitudinal strain is assumed to be constant.

Figure 1.37 shows a thick cylinder subjected to internal pressure p_i and external pressure p_0. These pressures are compressive and act radially. Consider an elementary ring of radius 'r' and thickness 'dr' as shown.

Let,

r_0 = be the outer radius of the cylinder.

r_i = be the inner radius of the cylinder.

l = the length of the cylinder.

σ_r = be the internal radial stress of the ring.

$(\sigma_r + d\sigma_r)$ = be the external radial stress of the ring.

σ_t = the hoop/circumferential stress induced in the elementary ring.

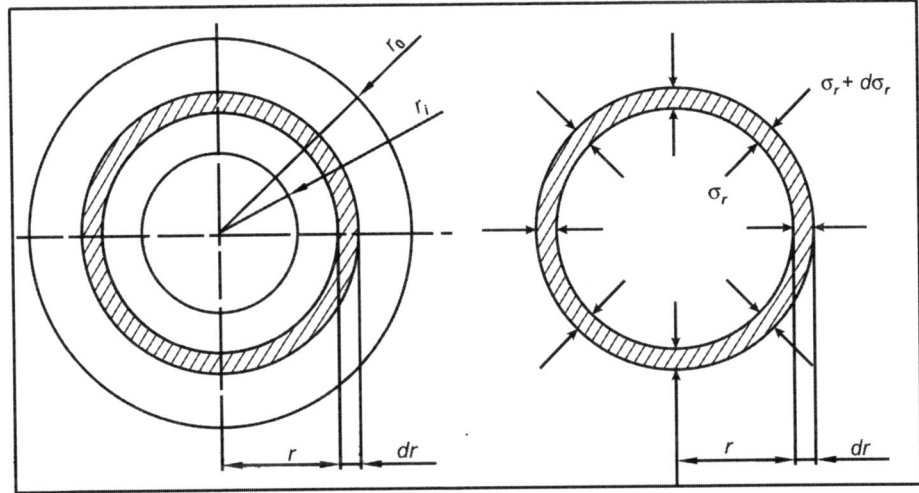

Fig. 1.37: Thick cylinder subjected to internal pressure

The bursting force = $\sigma_r (2rl) - [(\sigma_r + d\sigma_r) 2l (r + dr)]$ ... (Eq. 1.16)
and resisting force = $\sigma_t (2l) dr$ ... (Eq. 1.17)
equating Eqs (1.16) and (1.17), we have
$$\sigma_t (2l) dr = \sigma_r (2rl) - [(\sigma_r + d\sigma_r) 2l (r + dr)]$$
Dividing throughout by $2l$
$$\sigma_t dr = \sigma_r r - [(\sigma_r + d\sigma_r)(r + dr)]$$
$$= \sigma_r r - (\sigma_r r + \sigma_r dr + r d\sigma_r + d\sigma_r dr)$$
$$\sigma_t dr = -\sigma_r dr - r d\sigma_r - d\sigma_r dr$$
Neglecting $d\sigma_r dr$
$$\sigma_t dr = -\sigma_r dr - r d\sigma_r$$
Therefore,
$$\sigma_t = -\sigma_r - r\left(\frac{d\sigma_r}{dr}\right) \qquad \text{... (Eq. 1.18)}$$

Now at any point in the section of the elemental ring, the following three principal stresses exist:

a. Radial stress (σ_r)
b. Tangential stress (σ_t)
c. Longitudinal stress (σ_l)

Since longitudinal strain is constant and independent of radius, we have
$$\varepsilon_l = \frac{\sigma_l}{E} - \mu\sigma_t + \mu\sigma_r = \text{Constant} \qquad \text{...(Eq. 1.19)}$$

In the above equation, μ, E and σ_l constants
$$-\sigma_t + \sigma_r = \text{constant} = 2a$$
$$\therefore \quad \sigma_t = 2a + \sigma_r \qquad \text{... (Eq. 1.20)}$$

Substituting Eq. (1.20) in Eq. (1.18)
$$2a + \sigma_r = -\sigma_r - r\left(\frac{d\sigma_r}{dr}\right)$$
$$2a + 2\sigma_r = -r\left(\frac{d\sigma_r}{dr}\right)$$
$$-2\left(\frac{dr}{r}\right) = \left(\frac{d\sigma_r}{a + \sigma_r}\right) \qquad \text{... (Eq. 1.21)}$$

Integrating the above equation, we have
$$\log_e (a + \sigma_r) = 2 \log_e r + \log_e b \qquad \text{where, } \log_e b \text{ is integration constant}$$
$$= \log_e r^2 + \log_e b \qquad [n \log_e x = \log_e x^n]$$

$$\log_e (a + \sigma_r) = \left(\frac{b}{r^2}\right)$$

Therefore, $(a + \sigma_r) = \left(\dfrac{b}{r^2}\right)$

Thus,
$$\sigma_r = \left(\frac{b}{r^2}\right) - a \qquad \text{... (Eq. 1.21a)}$$

Since σ_r is compressive, we have $\sigma_r = a - \left(\dfrac{b}{r^2}\right)$ ... (Eq. 1.22)

Substituting Eq. (1.21a) in Eq. (1.20) yields, $\sigma_t = 2a + \left(\dfrac{b}{r^2}\right) - a$

$$\sigma_t = a + \left(\dfrac{b}{r^2}\right) \qquad \text{... (Eq. 1.23)}$$

These constants 'a' and 'b' are evaluated by applying the boundary conditions and are known as **"Lame's constants"**.

Boundary conditions:

Case 1: *Internal pressure* $= p_i$, *external pressure* $= p_0$

@ $r = r_0$, $\quad \sigma_0 = -p_0 \quad$ (negative because, σ_r is compressive)
@ $r = r_i$, $\quad \sigma_i = -p_i$

Eq. (1.22) yields, $\quad -p_0 = a - \left(\dfrac{b}{r_0^2}\right)$ ... (Eq. 1.24)

$$-p_i = a - \left(\dfrac{b}{r_i^2}\right) \qquad \text{... (Eq. 1.25)}$$

Eqs (1.24) and (1.25) gives,

$$-p_0 + p_i = -\left(\dfrac{b}{r_0^2}\right) + \left(\dfrac{b}{r_i^2}\right)$$

$$p_i - p_0 = +\left(\dfrac{b}{r_i^2}\right) - \left(\dfrac{b}{r_0^2}\right) = \dfrac{b(r_0^2 - r_i^2)}{(r_0^2\, r_i^2)}$$

$$b = \dfrac{(p_i - p_0)(r_0^2\, r_i^2)}{(r_0^2 - r_i^2)} \qquad \text{... (Eq. 1.26)}$$

Substituting Eq. (1.26) in Eq. (1.24) yields

$$a = \left(\dfrac{b}{r_0^2}\right) - p_0$$

$$= \dfrac{(p_i - p_0)(r_0^2\, r_i^2)}{r_0^2(r_0^2 - r_i^2)} - p_0$$

$$= \dfrac{(p_i - p_0)r_i^2 - p_0(r_0^2 - r_i^2)}{(r_0^2 - r_i^2)} = \dfrac{p_i r_i^2 - p_0 r_i^2 - p_0 r_0^2 + p_0 r_i^2}{(r_0^2 - r_i^2)}$$

$$\therefore \quad a = \dfrac{p_i r_i^2 - p_0 r_0^2}{(r_0^2 - r_i^2)} \qquad \text{... (Eq. 1.27)}$$

In terms of diameter,

Eq. (1.26) yields ...
$$b = \dfrac{(p_i - p_0)\left(\dfrac{d_0}{2}\right)^2 \left(\dfrac{d_i}{2}\right)^2}{\left(\dfrac{d_0}{2}\right)^2 - \left(\dfrac{d_i}{2}\right)^2} = \dfrac{(p_i - p_0) d_0^2\, d_i^2 / 16}{(d_0^2 - d_i^2)/4}$$

∴ $$b = \frac{(p_i - p_0)d_0^2 d_i^2}{4(d_0^2 - d_i^2)}$$ ... (Eq. 1.28) **7.15b/Pg 79, DHB**

Eq. (1.27) yields ... $$a = \frac{p_i\left(\frac{d_i}{2}\right)^2 - p_0\left(\frac{d_0}{2}\right)^2}{\left(\frac{d_0}{2}\right)^2 - \left(\frac{d_i}{2}\right)^2} = \frac{(p_i d_i^2 - p_0 d_0^2)/4}{(d_0^2 - d_i^2)/4}$$

∴ $$a = \frac{(p_i d_i^2 - p_0 d_0^2)}{(d_0^2 - d_i^2)}$$ ... (Eq. 1.29) **7.15a/Pg 79, DHB**

Substituting Eq. (1.28) and Eq. (1.29) in Eq. (1.22) and Eq. (1.23)

Eq. (1.22) yields ... $$\sigma_r = \frac{(p_i d_i^2 - p_0 d_0^2)}{d_0^2 - d_i^2} - \frac{(p_i - p_0)d_0^2 d_i^2}{4r^2(d_0^2 - d_i^2)}$$

... (Eq. 1.30) **7.15/Pg 79, DHB**

Eq. (1.23) yields ... $$\sigma_t = \frac{(p_i d_i^2 - p_0 d_0^2)}{d_0^2 - d_i^2} + \frac{(p_i - p_0)d_0^2 d_i^2}{4r^2(d_0^2 - d_i^2)}$$

... (Eq. 1.31) **7.14/Pg 78, DHB**

Equations (1.30) and (1.31) give the value of σ_r, and σ_t at any radius.

Case 2: *Internal pressure = p_i, external pressure = zero*

@ $r = r_0$, $\sigma_r = 0$
@ $r = r_i$, $\sigma_r = -p_i$

Eq. (1.22) yields ... $$0 = a - \left(\frac{b}{r_0^2}\right)$$

$$a = \left(\frac{b}{r_0^2}\right)$$ ... (Eq. 1.32)

$$-p_i = a - \left(\frac{b}{r_i^2}\right)$$ ... (Eq. 1.33)

Substituting Eq. (1.32) in Eq. (1.33)

$$-p_i = \left(\frac{b}{r_0^2}\right) - \left(\frac{b}{r_i^2}\right)$$

$$= \frac{p_i(r_i^2 - r_0^2)}{r_0^2 r_i^2} = \frac{-b(r_0^2 - r_i^2)}{r_0^2 r_i^2}$$

$$b = \frac{p_i(r_0^2 r_i^2)}{(r_0^2 - r_i^2)}$$ ... (Eq. 1.34)

Substituting Eq. (1.34) in Eq. (1.32)

$$a = \frac{p_i \left(r_0^2 \, r_i^2 \right)}{r_0^2 \left(r_0^2 - r_i^2 \right)}$$

$$\therefore \quad a = \frac{p_i \, r_i^2}{\left(r_0^2 - r_i^2 \right)} \quad \ldots \text{(Eq. 1.35)}$$

Substituting Eq. (1.34) and Eq. (1.35) in Eq. (1.22) and Eq. (1.23)

Eq. (1.22) yields ...

$$\sigma_r = \frac{p_i \, r_i^2}{\left(r_0^2 - r_i^2 \right)} - \frac{p_i \left(r_i^2 \, r_0^2 \right)}{r^2 \left(r_0^2 - r_i^2 \right)}$$

$$= \frac{p_i \, r_i^2}{\left(r_0^2 - r_i^2 \right)} \left(1 - \frac{r_0^2}{r^2} \right)$$

$$= \frac{p_i \, d_i^2}{\left(d_0^2 - d_i^2 \right)} \left(1 - \frac{d_0^2}{4 r^2} \right) = \frac{p_i \, d_i^2}{\left(d_0^2 - d_i^2 \right)} \left(\frac{4 r^2 - d_0^2}{4 r^2} \right)$$

$$\therefore \quad \sigma_r = \frac{p_i \, d_i^2}{4 r^2} \left(\frac{4 r^2 - d_0^2}{d_0^2 - d_i^2} \right) \quad \ldots \text{(Eq. 1.36)} \; \textbf{7.17/Pg 79, DHB}$$

On similar lines, Eq. (1.23) yields

$$\sigma_t = \frac{p_i \, d_i^2}{4 r^2} \left(\frac{4 r^2 + d_0^2}{d_0^2 - d_i^2} \right) \quad \ldots \text{(Eq. 1.37)} \; \textbf{7.16/Pg 79, DHB}$$

Equations (1.36) and (1.37) give the value of σ_r, and σ_t at any radius.

The stress distribution and variation of the hoop and radial pressure are shown in **Figs 1.38** and **1.39** respectively.

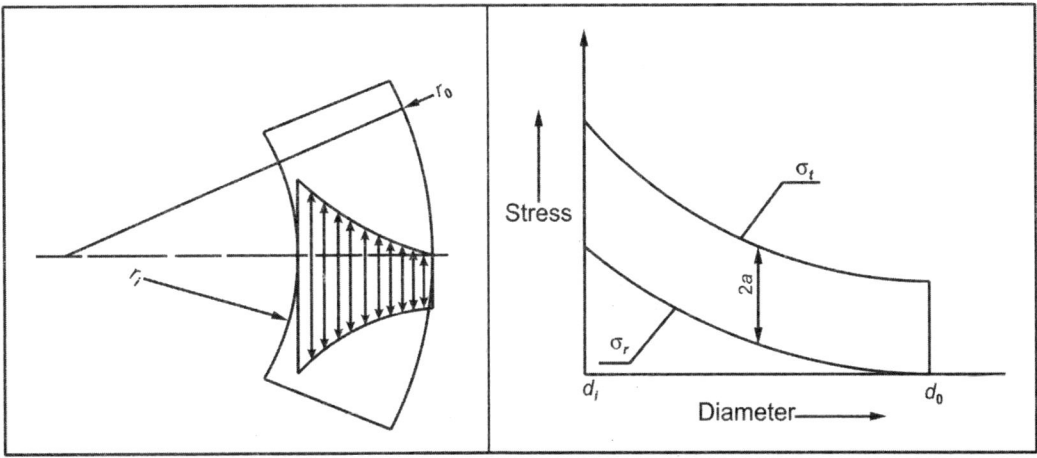

Fig. 1.38: Hoop and radial pressure distribution   **Fig. 1.39:** Hoop and radial pressure variation

Maximum stress: The maximum stress occurs at $r = d_i/2$

- Thus from Eq. (1.36), the maximum radial stress at $r = d_i/2$ is

$$\sigma_r)_{max} = \frac{p_i d_i^2}{4\left(\frac{d_i}{2}\right)^2}\left[\frac{4\left(\frac{d_i}{2}\right)^2 - d_0^2}{d_0^2 - d_i^2}\right] = \frac{p_i(d_i^2 - d_0^2)}{d_0^2 - d_i^2} = \frac{-p_i(d_i^2 - d_0^2)}{d_0^2 - d_i^2}$$

$$\sigma_r)_{max} = -p_i \qquad \ldots \text{(Eq. 1.38) } \mathbf{7.19/Pg\ 79,\ DHB}$$

- And from Eq. (1.37), the maximum tangential stress at $r = d_i/2$ is

$$\sigma_t)_{max} = \frac{p_i d_i^2}{4\left(\frac{d_i}{2}\right)^2}\left[\frac{4\left(\frac{d_i}{2}\right)^2 + d_0^2}{d_0^2 - d_i^2}\right] = \frac{p_i(d_i^2 + d_0^2)}{d_0^2 - d_i^2}$$

$$\sigma_t)_{max} = \frac{p_i(d_0^2 + d_i^2)}{d_0^2 - d_i^2} \qquad \ldots \text{(Eq. 1.39) } \mathbf{7.18/Pg\ 79,\ DHB}$$

- The maximum shear stress at inner surface is

$$\tau_{max} = \frac{\sigma_t)_{max} - \sigma_r)_{max}}{2} = \frac{\left[\frac{p_i(d_0^2 + d_i^2)}{d_0^2 - d_i^2}\right] - (-p_i)}{2}$$

$$\tau_{max} = \frac{p_i d_0^2}{d_0^2 - d_i^2} \qquad \ldots \text{(Eq. 1.40) } \mathbf{7.20/Pg\ 79,\ DHB}$$

- The equivalent maximum tension in the cylinder wall, according to maximum shear stress theory is

$$\sigma_t)_{max} = 2\tau_{max} = \frac{2 p_i d_0^2}{d_0^2 - d_i^2} \qquad \ldots \text{(Eq. 1.41) } \mathbf{7.21/\ Pg\ 79,\ DHB}$$

1.13 WALL THICKNESS
1.13.1 For Brittle Materials

In designing a cylinder of brittle material such as cast iron, hard steel and cast aluminium with open -or- closed ends and in accordance with maximum normal stress theory, the tangential stress

$$\sigma_t = \sigma_t)_{max} = \frac{p_i(d_0^2 + d_i^2)}{d_0^2 - d_i^2} \qquad \ldots \text{from (Eq. 1.39)}$$

Now $\qquad d_0 = d_i + 2t; \ t = \dfrac{d_0 - d_i}{2}$

$$\sigma_t = \frac{p_i\left[(d_i+2t)^2 + d_i^2\right]}{\left[(d_i+2t)^2 - d_i^2\right]}$$

$$\sigma_t\left[(d_i+2t)^2 - d_i^2\right] = p_i\left[(d_i+2t)^2 + d_i^2\right]$$

$$(d_i+2t)^2(\sigma_t - p_i) = d_i^2(p_i + \sigma_t)$$

$$\frac{(d_i+2t)^2}{d_i^2} = \frac{(\sigma_t + p_i)}{(\sigma_t - p_i)}$$

$$\frac{d_i+2t}{d_i} = \sqrt{\frac{(\sigma_t + p_i)}{(\sigma_t - p_i)}}$$

$$1 + \frac{2t}{d_i} = \sqrt{\frac{(\sigma_t + p_i)}{(\sigma_t - p_i)}}$$

$$t = \frac{d_i}{2}\left[\sqrt{\frac{(\sigma_t + p_i)}{(\sigma_t - p_i)}} - 1\right] \qquad \ldots\text{(Eq. 1.42) } \mathbf{7.22/Pg\ 79,\ DHB}$$

1.13.2 For Ductile Materials

This is based on maximum shear stress theory.
We know that

$$\sigma_t = \sigma_t)_{max} = \frac{2p_i d_0^2}{d_0^2 - d_i^2} \qquad \ldots\textit{from (Eq. 1.41)}$$

$$d_0 = d_i + 2t$$

$$\sigma_t = \frac{2p_i(d_i+2t)^2}{\left[(d_i+2t)^2 - d_i^2\right]}$$

$$\sigma_t\left[(d_i+2t)^2 - d_i^2\right] = 2p_i(d_i+2t)^2$$

$$(d_i+2t)^2(\sigma_t - 2p_i) = \sigma_t d_i^2$$

$$\frac{(d_i+2t)^2}{d_i^2} = \frac{\sigma_t}{(\sigma_t - 2p_i)}$$

$$\frac{d_i+2t}{d_i} = \sqrt{\frac{\sigma_t}{(\sigma_t - 2p_i)}}$$

$$1 + \frac{2t}{d_i} = \sqrt{\frac{\sigma_t}{(\sigma_t - 2p_i)}}$$

$$\therefore \quad t = \frac{d_i}{2}\left[\sqrt{\frac{\sigma_t}{(\sigma_t - 2p_i)}} - 1\right] \qquad \ldots\text{(Eq. 1.43) } \mathbf{7.23/Pg\ 79,\ DHB}$$

1.14 BIRNIE'S EQUATION

In case of open end cylinders such as gun barrels, rams, pumps cylinder, etc. made of ductile materials such as low carbon steels, brass, bronze and aluminium alloys, the allowable stress cannot be determined by maximum stress theory. In such cases, maximum strain theory is used. The wall thickness is calculated as:

$$t = \frac{d_i}{2} = \left[\sqrt{\frac{\sigma_t' + (1-\mu)p_i}{\sigma_t' - (1+\mu)p_i}} - 1\right] \quad \ldots \text{(Eq. 1.44) 7.29/Pg 80, DHB}$$

Where, $\sigma_t' = 0.125\, \sigma_u$

For open end cylinder,

- Tangential stress at radius 'r', $\sigma_t' = (1-\mu)a + (1+\mu)\dfrac{b}{r^2}$ ... 7.27/Pg 80, DHB

- Radial stress at radius 'r', $\sigma_t' = (1-\mu)a - (1+\mu)\dfrac{b}{r^2}$ ... 7.28/Pg 80, DHB

  Values of are obtained from **7.15a and 7.15b/Pg 79, DHB**

1.15 CLAVARINO'S EQUATION

This is based on maximum strain theory of failure and is applicable to ductile materials with closed end cylinders.

$$t = \frac{d_i}{2} \times \left[\sqrt{\frac{\sigma_t' + (1-2\mu)p_i}{\sigma_t' - (1+\mu)p_i}} - 1\right], \quad \ldots \text{7.26/Pg 80, DHB}$$

Where, $\sigma_t' = 0.125\, \sigma_u$

- Tangential stress at radius 'r' $\sigma_t' = (1-2\mu)a + (1+\mu)\dfrac{b}{r^2}$ ... 7.24/Pg 79, DHB

- Radial stress at radius 'r' $\sigma_r' = (1-2\mu)a - (1+\mu)\dfrac{b}{r^2}$ ... 7.25/Pg 80, DHB

$\sigma_u = \sigma_u$, for brittle materials and
$\sigma_u = \sigma_y$, for ductile materials

1.16 BARLOW'S EQUATION

This equation is generally used for high pressure oil and gas pipes.

$$\sigma_t = \frac{p_i d_0}{2t} \quad \ldots \text{7.30/Pg 80, DHB}$$

Values of σ_t ... **Table 7.2/Pg 84, DHB**

1.17 CHANGES IN CYLINDER DIAMETER

- For cylinders subjected to internal pressure, increase in internal diameter:

$$\Delta d_i = \frac{p_i d_i}{E}\left[\frac{d_0^2 + d_i^2}{d_0^2 + d_i^2} + \mu\right] \quad \ldots \text{7.31/Pg 80, DHB}$$

- For cylinders subjected to internal pressure, increase in internal diameter:

$$\Delta d_0 = \frac{p_0 d_0}{E}\left[\frac{d_0^2 + d_i^2}{d_0^2 - d_i^2} - \mu\right] \qquad \text{...7.32/Pg 80, DHB}$$

1.18 AUTOFRETTAGE/SELF-HOOPING

Thick-walled cylinders are widely used as critical components in pneumatic and hydraulic systems and as storage and processing vessels, such as high-pressure pump cylinders, battleship and tank cannon barrels, and fuel injection systems for diesel engines. These components require a strict analysis for optimum design to ensure reliable and safe operational performance. In the design of thick-walled cylinders, there are two main objectives to be achieved:

- Increasing its strength-weight ratio, and
- Extending its fatigue life.

Autofrettage is a process of pre-stressing (generating residual stresses) in the wall of a thick-walled cylinder prior to use. When a component is pressurized by an autofrettage pressure, which is much higher than the working pressure and is dependent on the material used, hardness, and the geometry of the component, the inner boring will be formed plastically and the deeper areas of the component wall will be formed elastically.

After relieving the autofrettage pressure from the component, the elastically formed areas try to return to their original state while the plastically formed areas prevent this process. Therefore internal stresses (compressive residual circumferential stress) are created in a huge part of the wall thickness which tries to work against the stresses that arise from normal working pressure. These residual stresses serve to reduce the tensile stresses developed as a result of subsequent application of an operating pressure, thus increasing the load bearing capacity and the endurance strength.

Under working pressure the stresses inside the component do not move between zero and a maximum value any more, but start in the pressure area below zero and end at a much lower maximum value.

Following are the three methods of pre-stressing the cylinder:
1. Using compound cylinder.
2. Using theory of plasticity.
3. Wounding the cylinder with a tension wire.

1. **Using Compound Cylinder/Shrunk Cylinder:** Here, the outer cylinder is shrunk fit over the inner cylinder by heating and cooling. On cooling, the contact pressure is developed at the junction of the two cylinders, which induces compressive tangential stress in the material of the inner cylinder and tensile tangential stress in the material of the outer cylinder. When the cylinder is loaded, the compressive stresses are first relieved and then tensile stresses are induced. Thus, a compound cylinder is effective in resisting higher internal pressure than a single cylinder with the same overall dimensions.

    Example: Design of gun tubes.

2. **Using Theory of Plasticity/Overloading the Cylinder:** In the theory of plasticity, a temporary high internal pressure is applied till the plastic stage is reached near the inside of the cylinder wall, while the outer portion is still in the elastic range. When

the internal pressure is released, the outer portion contracts exerting pressure on the inner portion which has deformed permanently. This results in a residual compressive stress, thereby making the cylinder more effective to withstand a higher internal pressure.

3. **Wounding the Cylinder with a Tension Wire:** Here a wire under tension is wound around the cylinder thereby resulting in residual compressive stresses.

28. Calculate the thickness of metal necessary for a cylindrical shell of internal diameter 150 mm to withstand 25 MPa. The maximum permissible tensile stress is 120 MPa. Assume that the material is brittle

Solution: $d_i = 150$ mm, $p_i = 25$ MPa, $\sigma_t = 120$ MPa, $t = ?$

For brittle material,

$$t = \frac{d_i}{2}\left[\sqrt{\frac{(\sigma_t + p_i)}{(\sigma_t - p_i)}} - 1\right] \quad \ldots \text{7.22/Pg 79, DHB}$$

$$= \frac{150}{2}\left[\sqrt{\frac{120+25}{120-25}} - 1\right]$$

$$= 17.66 \text{ mm}$$

$$\therefore \quad t \approx 18 \text{ mm}$$

29. A thick walled closed end cylinder has internal and external diameters as 200 mm and 800 mm. The cylinder is subjected to an internal fluid pressure of 150 MPa. If $E = 72$ GPa and $\mu = 0.33$, determine the principal stresses and the maximum shear stress. Also find the increase in internal diameter due to fluid pressure.

Solution: $d_i = 200$ mm, $d_0 = 800$ mm, $p_i = 150$ MPa, $E = 72$ GPa $= 72 \times 10^3$ N/mm² and $\mu = 0.33$.

a. Principal stresses: $\sigma_t)_{max}$, $\sigma_t)_{min}$
b. Shear stress: τ_{max}
c. Increase in internal diameter: Δd_i

a. To find principal stresses: $\sigma_t)_{max}$, $\sigma_t)_{min}$

We know that at any radius 'r' $\sigma_t = \dfrac{p_i d_i^2}{4r^2}\left(\dfrac{4r^2 + d_0^2}{d_0^2 - d_i^2}\right)$ ... Eq. (i) **7.16/Pg 79, DHB**

At $r = r_i$, $\sigma_t = \sigma_t)_{max}$,

Eq. (i) Yields ...
$$\sigma_t)_{max} = \frac{p_i\left(d_0^2 + d_1^2\right)}{d_0^2 - d_1^2} \quad \ldots \text{7.18/Pg 79, DHB}$$

$$= \frac{150 \times (800^2 + 200^2)}{(800^2 - 200^2)}$$

$$\sigma_t)_{max} = 170 \text{ N/mm}^2$$

At $r = r_0$, $\sigma_t = \sigma_t)_{min}$,

Eq. (i) Yields ...
$$\sigma_t)_{min} = \frac{p_i d_i^2}{4r_0^2}\left(\frac{4r_0^2 + d_0^2}{d_0^2 - d_i^2}\right) = \frac{150 \times 200^2}{4 \times 400^2}\left(\frac{4 \times 400^2 \times 800^2}{800^2 - 200^2}\right)$$

$$\sigma_t)_{min} = 20 \text{ N/mm}^2$$

Curved Beams, Cylinders and Cylinder Heads

b. To find shear stress: τ_{max}

We know that, $\tau_{max} = \dfrac{\sigma_t)_{max} - \sigma_r)_{max}}{2} = \dfrac{170 - 20}{2} = 75 \text{ N/mm}^2$

c. To find increase in internal diameter: Δd_i

We know that increase in internal diameter:

$$\Delta d_i = \dfrac{p_i d_i}{E}\left[\dfrac{d_0^2 + d_i^2}{d_0^2 - d_i^2} + \mu\right] \qquad \ldots 7.31/\text{Pg } 80, \text{DHB}$$

$$= \dfrac{150 \times 200}{72 \times 10^3}\left[\left(\dfrac{800^2 + 200^2}{800^2 - 200^2}\right) + 0.33\right]$$

$$\Delta d_i = 0.6097 \text{ mm}$$

30. A steel cylinder of 1 m inside diameter is to be designed for an internal pressure of 8 MPa. Calculate the thickness if maximum shear stress is not to exceed 35 MPa.

Solution: $d_i = 1 \text{ m} = 1000 \text{ mm}$, $p_i = 8 \text{ MPa}$, $t_{max} = 35 \text{ MPa}$, $t = ?$

We know that, $\tau_{max} = \dfrac{p_i d_0^2}{d_0^2 - d_i^2} \qquad \ldots 7.20/\text{Pg } 79, \text{DHB}$

$$35 = \dfrac{8 \times d_0^2}{d_0^2 - 1000^2}$$

$$35\left(d_0^2 + 1000^2\right) = 8 d_0^2$$

$$27 d_0^2 = 35 \times 10^6$$

$$d_0 = 1138.55$$

$$d_0 = 1140 \text{ mm}$$

But $t = \dfrac{d_0 - d_i}{2} = \dfrac{1140 - 1000}{2}$

$$t = 70 \text{ mm}$$

31. A thick cylinder of internal diameter 200 mm and 300 mm external diameter is subjected to an internal pressure of 60 MPa and an external pressure of 30 MPa. Calculate the maximum shear stress in the cylinder at inner radius.

Solution: $d_i = 200 \text{ mm}$, $d_0 = 300 \text{ mm}$, $p_i = 60 \text{ MPa}$, $p_0 = 30 \text{ MPa}$, $\tau_{max})r_i = ?$

We know that, $\tau_{max}) = \dfrac{\sigma_t - \sigma_r}{2}$

Therefore at inner radius, $r = r_i$, hence $\tau_{max})_{r_i} = \dfrac{\sigma_{t_i} - \sigma_{r_i}}{2} \qquad \ldots \text{Eq. (i)}$

But $\sigma_t = a + \left(\dfrac{b}{r^2}\right) \qquad \ldots \text{Eq. (ii) } 7.14/\text{Pg } 78, \text{DHB}$

$$a = \dfrac{\left(p_i d_i^2 - p_0 d_0^2\right)}{d_0^2 - d_i^2} \qquad \ldots 7.15a/\text{Pg } 79, \text{DHB}$$

$$= \left(\frac{60 \times 200^2 - 30 \times 300^2}{300^2 - 200^2}\right)$$

$$a = -6$$

$$b = \frac{(p_i - p_0)d_0^2 d_i^2}{4(d_0^2 - d_i^2)} \quad \ldots 7.15b/Pg\ 79,\ DHB$$

$$= \frac{(60-30) \times 300^2 \times 200^2}{4(300^2 - 200^2)}$$

$$b = 540 \times 10^3$$

Eq. (ii) yields
$$\sigma_t = -6 + \left(\frac{540 \times 10^3}{100^2}\right) \quad r = r_i = 100\ mm$$

$$\sigma_t = 48\ MPa$$

Also
$$\sigma_t = a - \left(\frac{b}{r^2}\right) = -6 - \left(\frac{540 \times 10^3}{100^2}\right)$$

$$\sigma_r = -60\ MPa$$

Eq. (i) yields ... $\tau_{max})_{r_i} = \dfrac{48-(-60)}{2} = 54\ MPa$

32. An external pressure of 12 MPa is applied to a thick cylinder of internal diameter 160 mm and external diameter 320 mm. if the maximum hoop stress is limited to 36 MPa, calculate the maximum internal pressure that can be applied?

Solution: $p_0 = 12\ MPa,\ d_i = 160\ mm,\ d_0 = 320\ mm,\ \sigma_t = 36\ MPa,\ p_i = ?$

We know that
$$\sigma_t = \frac{(p_i d_i^2 - p_0 d_0^2)}{d_0^2 - d_i^2} + \frac{(p_i - p_0)d_0^2 d_i^2}{4r^2(d_0^2 - d_i^2)} \quad \ldots 7.14/Pg\ 78,\ DHB$$

Here $r = r_i = 80\ mm$

$$36 = \frac{1}{320^2 - 160^2}\left[(p_i \times 160^2) - (12 \times 320^2) + \frac{(p_i - 12)160^2 \times 320^2}{4 \times 80^2}\right]$$

$$= \frac{1}{76800}\left(25600 p_i - 1.229 \times 10^6 + (102.4 \times 10^3)p_i - 1.229 \times 10^6\right)$$

$$2.765 \times 10^6 = 128 \times 10^3 p_i - 2.458 \times 10^6$$

$$p_i = 40.73\ MPa$$

33. A cast iron cylinder of internal diameter 200 mm and thickness 50 mm is subjected to a pressure of 5 N/mm². Calculate the tangential and radial stresses at the inner, middle and outer surface (Fig. 1.40). [VTU-Dec. 09/Jan. 10–10 Marks]

Solution: $d_i = 200\ mm,\ t = 50\ mm,\ p = 5\ N/mm^2$

a. Tangential stress σ_t at inner, mean and outer radius = ?
b. Radial stress σ_r at inner, mean and outer radius = ?

a. To find σ_t at inner, mean and outer radius:

Now $d_0 = d_i + 2t = 200 + 2 \times 50 = 300$ mm;

$$d_m = \frac{d_0 + d_i}{2} = \frac{300 + 200}{2} = 250 \text{ mm}$$

$r_i = 100$ mm, $r_m = 125$ mm, $r_0 = 150$ mm

We know that at any radius r,

$$\sigma_t = \frac{p_i d_i^2}{4r^2}\left(\frac{4r^2 + d_0^2}{d_0^2 - d_i^2}\right) \qquad \ldots \text{Eq. } (i)\ \mathbf{7.16/Pg\ 79, DHB}$$

At $r = r_i$, Eq. (i) yields ... $\sigma_t)_{r_i} = \dfrac{p_i(d_0^2 + d_i^2)}{d_0^2 - d_i^2}$ \hspace{1em} ....**7.18/Pg 79, DHB**

$$= \frac{5 \times (300^2 + 200^2)}{(300^2 - 200^2)}$$

$$\therefore \sigma_t)_{r_i} = 13 \text{ N/mm}^2$$

At $r = r_m$, Eq. (i) yields ...

$$\sigma_t)_{r_m} = \frac{p_i d_i^2}{4r_m^2}\left(\frac{4r_m^2 + d_0^2}{d_0^2 - d_i^2}\right) = \frac{5 \times 200^2 (4 \times 125^2 + 300^2)}{4 \times 125^2 (300^2 - 200^2)}$$

$$\sigma_t)_{r_m} = 9.76 \text{ N/mm}^2$$

At $r = r_0$, Eq. (i) yields ... $\sigma_t)_{r_0} = \dfrac{p_i d_i^2}{4r_0^2}\left(\dfrac{4r_0^2 + d_0^2}{d_0^2 - d_i^2}\right) = \dfrac{5 \times 200^2}{4 \times 150^2}\left(\dfrac{(4 \times 150^2 + 300^2)}{(300^2 - 200^2)}\right)$

$$\sigma_t)_{r_0} = 8 \text{ N/mm}^2$$

b. To find σ_r at inner, mean and outer radius:

We know that at any radius 'r',

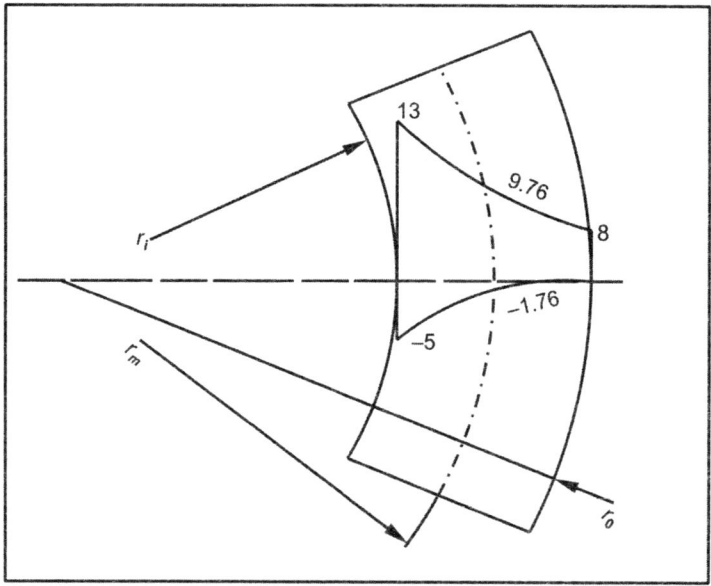

Fig. 1.40: Problem 33 (Hoop and radial pressure distribution)

$$\sigma_r = \frac{p_i d_i^2}{4r^2}\left(\frac{4r^2 - d_0^2}{d_0^2 - d_i^2}\right) \qquad \text{... Eq. (ii) 7.17/Pg 79, DHB}$$

At $r = r_i$, Eq. (i) yields ... $\sigma_r)_{r_i} = -p_i = -5\,\text{N/mm}^2$ ... 7.19/Pg 79, DHB

At $r = r_m$, Eq. (ii) yields ... $\sigma_t)_{r_m} = \dfrac{p_i d_i^2}{4r_m^2}\left(\dfrac{4r_m^2 - d_0^2}{d_0^2 - d_i^2}\right)$

$$= \frac{5 \times 200^2\,(4 \times 125^2 - 300^2)}{4 \times 125^2\,(300^2 - 200^2)}$$

$\sigma_t)_{r_m} = -1.76\,\text{N/mm}^2$

At $r = r_0$, Eq. (ii) yields ... $\sigma_r)_{r_0} = \dfrac{p_i d_i^2}{4r_0^2}\left(\dfrac{4r_0^2 - d_0^2}{d_0^2 - d_i^2}\right)$

$$= \frac{5 \times 200^2}{4 \times 150^2}\left(\frac{4 \times 150^2 - 300^2}{300^2 - 200^2}\right)$$

$\sigma_t)_{r_0} = 0\,\text{N/mm}^2$

34. A steel tank used for shipping gas has an inside diameter of 400 mm and the gas pressure is 20 MPa. If permissible stress is limited to 60 MPa, determine the thickness of the tank. Take μ = 0.3

Solution: $d_i = 400$ mm, $p_i = 20$ MPa, $\sigma_t = 60$ MPa, $t = ?$, $\mu = 0.3$

Since, the material used is ductile, and the ends are closed (to transport gas), the thickness is found using Clavarino's equation as

$$t = \frac{d_i}{2}\left[\sqrt{\frac{\sigma_t' + (1 - 2\mu)p_i}{\sigma_t' - (1+\mu)p_i}} - 1\right] \qquad \text{... 7.26/Pg 80, DHB}$$

$$= \frac{400}{2}\left[\sqrt{\frac{60 + (1 - 2 \times 0.3)20}{60 - (1 + 0.3)20}} - 1\right]$$

Here $\sigma_t = \sigma_t' = 60$ MPa

$t = 82.8$ mm ≈ 85 mm

35. The cylinder of a portable hydraulic riveter is 250 mm. The gauge pressure of the fluid is 15 MPa. Determine the thickness of the cylinder wall assuming that the permissible tensile stress is not to exceed 120 MPa and μ = 0.25.

Solution: $d_i = 250$ mm, $p_i = 15$ MPa, $t = ?$, $\sigma_t = 120$ MPa, $\mu = 0.25$

For a hydraulic riveter, the ends are open and the pressure is high. Hence, the thickness is found Birnie's equation as

$$t = \frac{d_i}{2}\left[\sqrt{\frac{\sigma_t' + (1-\mu)p_i}{\sigma_t' - (1+\mu)p_i}} - 1\right] \qquad \text{... 7.29/Pg 80, DHB}$$

$$= \frac{250}{2}\left[\sqrt{\frac{120 + (1 - 0.25)15}{120 - (1 + 0.25)15}} - 1\right]$$

$t = 17.32$ mm ≈ 18 mm

36. **The piston rod of a hydraulic cylinder exerts an operating force of 12 kN. The friction due to piston packing and stuffing box is equivalent to 10% of operating force. The pressure inside the cylinder is 10 MPa. The cylinder is made up of cast iron having σ_{ut} = 200 MPa and FOS = 5. Determine the thickness of the cylinder.**

Solution: Force, F = 12000 N, Friction effect = 10% of (F) = 1.1F = 13200 N, p_i = 10 MPa, t = ?, σ_{ut} = 200 MPa, FOS = 5

To find t: We know that, $\text{FOS} = \dfrac{\sigma_{ut}}{\sigma_t}$

$$\sigma_t = \dfrac{200}{5} = 40 \text{ MPa}$$

For brittle materials (cast iron)

$$t = \dfrac{d_i}{2}\left[\sqrt{\dfrac{\sigma_t + p_i}{\sigma_t - p_i}} - 1\right] \qquad \text{... Eq. (i) 7.22/Pg 80, DHB}$$

Now, pressure = force/area

$$p = \dfrac{F}{A}$$

$$A = \dfrac{F}{p} = \dfrac{13200}{10} = 1320 \text{ mm}^2$$

But

$$A = \dfrac{\pi d_i^2}{4} = 1320 \text{ mm}^2$$

Hence

$$d_i = 40.9 \text{ mm} \approx 42 \text{ mm}$$

Eq. (i) yields ...

$$t = \dfrac{42}{2}\left[\sqrt{\dfrac{40 + 10}{40 - 10}} - 1\right]$$

$$t = 6.1 \text{ mm} \approx 6 \text{ mm}.$$

37. **In an air operated press, the piston rod of a operating cylinder must exert a force of 4000 N. The air pressure in the cylinder is 0.7 MPa. Calculate the bore of the cylinder, assuming that the overall friction due to stuffing box and piston is equivalent to 8% of maximum force exerted by the piston rod. Determine the thickness of the cylinder assuming that it is a seamless tube with an allowable stress of 21 MPa.** *[VTU-June 2012–06 Marks]*

Solution: Force, F = 4000 N, Friction effect = 8% of (F) = 1.08F = 4320 N, p_i = 0.7 MPa, σ_u = 21 MPa, d_i = ?, t = ?,

a. To find d_i: We know that, pressure = force/area

$$p = \dfrac{F}{A}$$

$$A = \dfrac{F}{p_i} = \dfrac{4320}{0.7} = 6171.43 \text{ mm}^2$$

But

$$A = \dfrac{\pi d_i^2}{4} = 1320 \text{ mm}^2$$

Hence

$$d_i = 8864 \text{ mm} \approx 90 \text{ mm}$$

b. To find t: Assuming the material as brittle, we have

$$t = \frac{d_i}{2}\left[\sqrt{\frac{\sigma_t + p_i}{\sigma_t - p_i}} - 1\right] \quad \ldots 7.22/\text{Pg 80, DHB}$$

$$= \frac{90}{2}\left[\sqrt{\frac{21+0.7}{21-0.7}} - 1\right]$$

$$t = 1.526 \text{ mm} \approx 2 \text{ mm}$$

1.19 COMPOUND—OR COMPOSITE CYLINDERS

A compound cylinder is made by shrinking –or- press fitting –or- interference fitting an outer cylinder over an inner cylinder, a shown in **Figs 1.41** and **1.42**. Due to shrinking there exists a contact pressure (p_c) at the junction of two cylinders, which induces compressive tangential stress in the material of the inner cylinder and tensile tangential stress in the material of the outer cylinder.

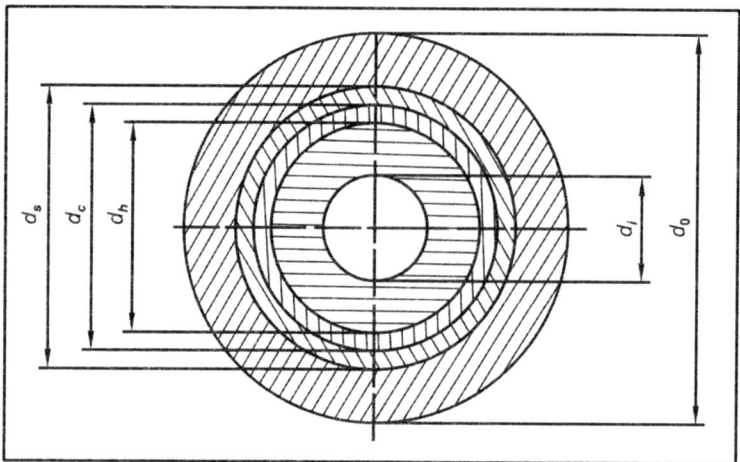

Fig. 1.41: Compound cylinder (Pg 81-DHB)

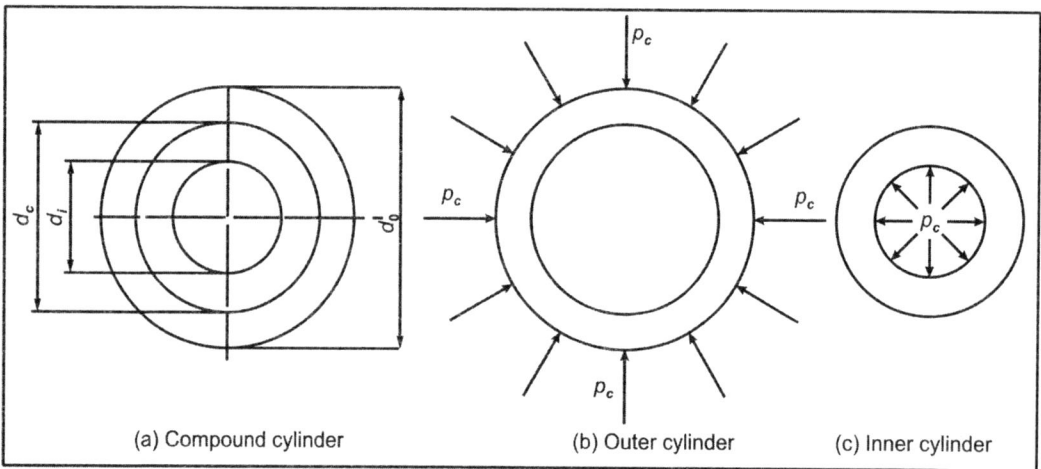

Fig. 1.42: Stresses in compound cylinder

Let,
- d_i = inside diameter of inner cylinder
- d_0 = outside diameter of outer cylinder
- d_c = common diameter after shrinking -or- contact diameter
- d_s = outside diameter of inner cylinder -or- diameter of shaft
- d_h = inside diameter of outer cylinder -or- diameter of hub
- p_c = pressure at contact surface
- σ_t = hoop/circumferential/tangential stress
- μ = Poisson's ratio

The stresses due to contact pressure (p_c) may be determined by Birnie's equation as follows:

We know that, for an open cylinder,

Tangential stress at radius r, $\sigma'_t = (1-\mu)a + (1+\mu)\dfrac{b}{r^2}$ ...**7.27/Pg 80, DHB**

Substituting 'a' and 'b' from **7.15a and 7.15b/Pg 80, DHB**

We get, $\quad \sigma_t = \sigma'_t = (1-\mu)\dfrac{p_i d_i^2 - p_0 d_0^2}{d_0^2 - d_i^2} + (1+\mu)\dfrac{(p_i - p_0)d_0^2 d_i^2}{4r^2(d_0^2 - d_i^2)}$ ... (Eq. 1.44a)

Considering only the internal pressure, (a) yields

$$\sigma_t = (1-\mu)\dfrac{p_i d_i^2}{d_0^2 - d_i^2} + (1+\mu)\dfrac{p_i d_0^2 d_i^2}{4r^2(d_0^2 - d_i^2)} \quad \text{...(Eq. 1.44b) 7.33/Pg 80, DHB}$$

Considering only the external pressure, Eq. (1.44a) yields

$$\sigma_t = (1-\mu)\dfrac{(-p_0 d_0^2)}{d_0^2 - d_i^2} + (1+\mu)\dfrac{(-p_0)d_0^2 d_i^2}{4r^2(d_0^2 - d_i^2)}$$

$$\sigma_t = -(1-\mu)\dfrac{p_0 d_0^2}{d_0^2 - d_i^2} - (1+\mu)\dfrac{+p_0 d_0^2 d_i^2}{4r^2(d_0^2 - d_i^2)} \quad \text{... (Eq. 1.45)}$$

Case 1: *Tangential stress at outer surface of outer cylinder:*

Substituting $p_i = p_c$, $d_i = d_c$, and $r = \dfrac{d_0}{2}$ in Eq. (1.29) yields

$$\sigma_{t-0} = (1-\mu)\dfrac{p_c d_c^2}{d_0^2 - d_c^2} + (1+\mu)\dfrac{p_c d_0^2 d_c^2}{4\left(\dfrac{d_0}{2}\right)(d_0^2 - d_c^2)}$$

$$= \dfrac{p_c d_c^2}{d_0^2 - d_c^2}\left[(1-\mu) + (1+\mu)\right]$$

$$\sigma_{t-0} = \dfrac{2p_c d_c^2}{d_0^2 - d_c^2} \quad \text{... (Eq. 1.46) 7.38/Pg 81, DHB}$$

Case 2: *Tangential stress at inner surface of outer cylinder:*

Substituting $p_i = p_c$, $d_i = d_c$, and $r = \dfrac{d_c}{2}$ in Eq. (1.44b) yields

$$\sigma_{t-c} = (1-\mu)\frac{p_c d_c^2}{d_0^2 - d_c^2} + (1+\mu)\frac{p_c d_0^2 d_c^2}{4\left(\dfrac{d_c}{2}\right)(d_0^2 - d_c^2)}$$

$$= \frac{p_c d_c^2}{d_0^2 - d_c^2}\left[(1-\mu) + (1+\mu)\left(\frac{d_0}{d_c}\right)^2\right]$$

$$= \frac{p_c d_c^2}{d_0^2 - d_c^2}\left[\frac{d_c^2(1-\mu) + d_0^2(1+\mu)}{d_c^2}\right]$$

$$= \frac{p_c}{d_0^2 - d_c^2}\left[d_c^2 - \mu d_c^2 + d_0^2 + \mu d_0^2\right]$$

$$= \frac{p_c}{d_0^2 - d_c^2}\left[(d_0^2 + d_c^2) + \mu(d_0^2 - d_c^2)\right]$$

$$\sigma_{t-c} = p_c\left(\frac{d_0^2 + d_c^2}{d_0^2 - d_c^2} + \mu\right) = \sigma_{t-c})_0 \quad \ldots \text{(Eq. 1.47) } \mathbf{7.47/Pg\ 81,\ DHB}$$

Case 3: Tangential stress at inner surface of inner cylinder (σ_{t-i}):

Substituting $p_0 = p_c$, $d_0 = d_c$, and $r = \dfrac{d_i}{2}$ in Eq. (1.45) yields

$$\sigma_{t-i} = -(1-\mu)\frac{p_c d_c^2}{d_c^2 - d_i^2} - (1+\mu)\frac{p_c d_c^2 d_i^2}{4\left(\dfrac{d_i}{2}\right)^2(d_c^2 - d_i^2)}$$

$$= \frac{p_c d_c^2}{d_c^2 - d_i^2}\left[-(1-\mu) - (1+\mu)\right]$$

$$\boldsymbol{\sigma_{t-i} = \frac{-2 p_c d_c^2}{d_c^2 - d_i^2}} \quad \ldots \text{(Eq. 1.48) } \mathbf{7.35/Pg\ 81,\ DHB}$$

Case 4: Tangential stress at outer surface of inner cylinder (σ_{t-c}):

Substituting $p_0 = p_c$, $d_0 = d_c$, and $r = \dfrac{d_c}{2}$ in Eq. (1.45) yields

$$\sigma_{t-c} = -(1-\mu)\frac{p_c d_c^2}{d_c^2 - d_i^2} - (1+\mu)\frac{p_c d_c^2 d_i^2}{4\left(\dfrac{d_c}{2}\right)(d_c^2 - d_i^2)}$$

$$= \frac{p_c d_c^2}{d_c^2 - d_i^2}\left[(1-\mu) + (1+\mu)\left(\frac{d_i}{d_c}\right)^2\right]$$

$$= \frac{p_c d_c^2}{d_c^2 - d_i^2}\left[\frac{d_c^2(1-\mu) + d_i^2(1+\mu)}{d_c^2}\right]$$

$$= \frac{p_c}{d_c^2 - d_i^2}\left[d_c^2 - \mu d_c^2 + d_i^2 + \mu d_i^2\right]$$

$$= \frac{p_c}{d_c^2 - d_i^2}\left[(d_c^2 + d_i^2) - \mu(d_c^2 - d_i^2)\right]$$

$$\sigma_{t-c} = -p_c\left(\frac{d_c^2 + d_i^2}{d_c^2 - d_i^2} - \mu\right) = \sigma_{t-c})_i \quad \ldots\text{(Eq. 1.49)} \text{ 7.36/Pg 81, DHB}$$

Note

- All the above equations cannot be solved until p_c is known.
- Equations **7.35 to 7.38/DHB** are in accordance with Birnie's equation, based on maximum strain theory.
- In the absence of μ from equations **7.35 to 7.38/DHB**, these reduce to Lame's equation based on maximum shear theory.
- Values of μ are obtained from **Tb 1.1/Pg 7**.

1.20 TOTAL ALLOWANCE -OR- INTERFERENCE

Equations **7.35 to 7.38/DHB** cannot be solved until p_c is known. In obtaining a shrink fit, the outside diameter of inner cylinder (shaft) is made larger than the inside diameter of the outside cylinder (sleeve/jacket/hub). This difference in diameters is known as *interference*.

The contact pressure is caused by the interference between the outer and inner cylinder due to which the radius of outside cylinder increases while that of inner cylinder decreases.

i.e. Decrease in diameter of inner cylinder, $\Delta d_i = \dfrac{-p_c d_c}{E}\left[\dfrac{d_c^2 + d_i^2}{d_c^2 - d_i^2} - \mu\right]$ ...(Eq. 1.50)

Increase in diameter of outer cylinder, $\Delta d_0 = \dfrac{p_c d_c}{E}\left[\dfrac{d_0^2 + d_c^2}{d_0^2 - d_c^2} + \mu\right]$ ...(Eq. 1.51)

Thus the total interference is $\quad B = \Delta d_i - \Delta d_0$ ...(Eq. 1.52)

Referring to **Fig. 1.43 -or- Pg 81/DHB**, the radial interference -or- shrinkage allowance according to Eq. (1.51) is

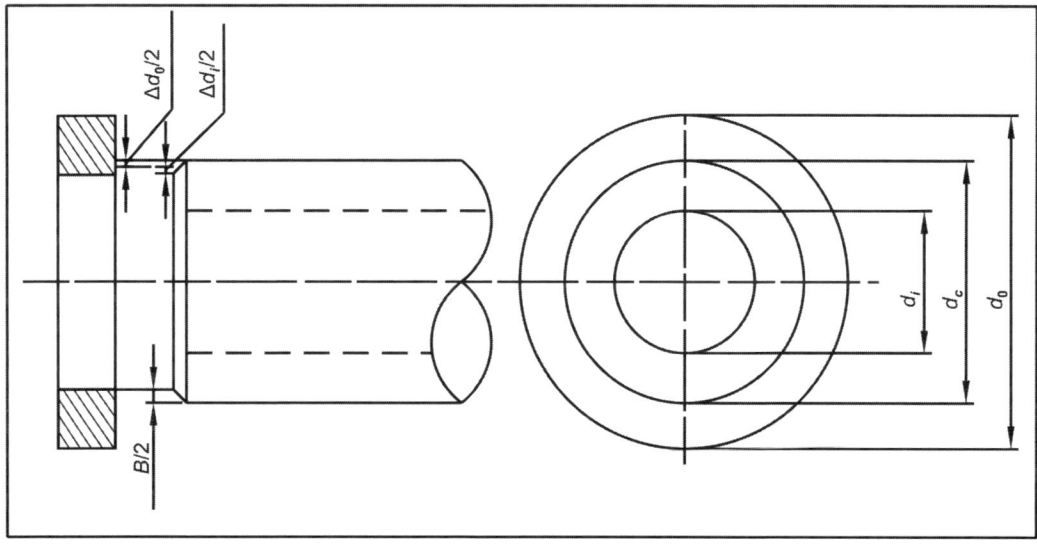

Fig. 1.43: Shrink and press fits

$$B = \frac{p_c d_s}{E_s}\left[\frac{d_s^2 + d_i^2}{d_s^2 - d_i^2} - \mu_s\right] + \frac{p_c d_h}{E_h}\left[\frac{d_0^2 + d_h^2}{d_0^2 - d_h^2} - \mu_h\right]$$

$$B \approx p_c d_s\left[\frac{d_c^2 + d_i^2}{E_s(d_s^2 - d_i^2)} + \frac{d_0^2 + d_c^2}{E_h(d_0^2 - d_c^2)} - \frac{\mu_s}{E_s} + \frac{\mu_h}{E_h}\right] \quad \ldots\text{(Eq. 1.53)} \ \mathbf{7.39/Pg\ 81,\ DHB}$$

Where,

$d_0 = (d_c + \Delta d_i)$ diameter of the shaft -or- outer diameter of inner cylinder
$d_h = (d_c + \Delta d_0)$ diameter of the hub -or- inner diameter of outer cylinder
d_c = contact -or- common diameter
d_i = inner diameter of inner cylinder
d_0 = outer diameter of outer cylinder
p_c = contact pressure
B = radial interference -or- total shrinkage allowance
μ_h = Poisson's ratio for inner cylinder/hub material
μ_s = Poisson's ratio for outer cylinder/shaft material
E_h = Young's modulus for inner cylinder/hub material
E_s = Young's modulus for outer cylinder/shaft material

If both cylinders are made of same material, then $E_s = E_h = E$ and $\mu_s = \mu_h = \mu$

Eq. (1.53) yields ... $$B = \frac{2 d_c^3 (d_0^2 - d_i^2) p_c}{E(d_0^2 - d_c^2)(d_c^2 - d_i^2)} \quad \text{-or-}$$

$$p_c = \frac{BE(d_0^2 - d_c^2)(d_c^2 - d_i^2)}{2 d_c^3 (d_0^2 - d_i^2)} \quad \ldots\text{(Eq. 1.54)} \ \mathbf{7.40/Pg\ 82,\ DHB}$$

Thus for a given value of interference (B), p_c is evaluated from Eq. (1.54).

1.21 FORCES AND TORQUES IN INTERFERENCE FITS

The maximum axial force (F_a) required to assemble a force fit varies directly as the thickness of outer member, length of the outer member, the coefficient of friction and the difference in diameters of shaft and hub.

i.e. $$F_a = \pi d L f p_c \quad \ldots\text{(Eq. 1.55)} \ \mathbf{7.55/Pg\ 82,\ DHB}$$

and the torque transmitted, $$T = F_a\left(\frac{d}{2}\right)$$

$$= \pi d L f p_c F_a\left(\frac{d}{2}\right)$$

$$T = \frac{\pi d^2 L f p_c}{2} \quad \ldots\text{(Eq. 1.56)} \ \mathbf{7.42/Pg\ 82,\ DHB}$$

Where,
L = length of outer member –or– hub
d = external diameter of inner member –or– nominal diameter of shaft
f = coefficient of friction (0.04 – 0.25)
  average value of $f = 0.08$ ...**Pg 75/DHB**

1.22 STRESSES DUE TO FORCES AND SHRINK FITS

For obtaining a shrink fit, the common procedure is to heat the outer member (hub) so as to expand it beyond the interference and then slip it over the inner component (shaft). Cooling will then contract the outer component. This change in temperature produces thermal strain even in the absence of stress.

If, t_1 = original temperature of the parts

t_2 = final temperature to which the parts must be heated for shrinking

Then, change in temperature, $= \Delta t = t_2 - t_1 = \dfrac{B}{\alpha d_c}$

$$t_2 \geq \left(\dfrac{B}{\alpha d_c} + t_1\right) \qquad \ldots \text{(Eq. 1.57) 7.44/Pg 82, DHB}$$

Where, α coefficient of expansion

The shrinkage stress in the band, $\sigma_t = E\delta = \dfrac{EB}{d_c}$ ....7.43/Pg 82, DHB

38. A 200 diameter steel shaft is to have a press fit with a 400 mm diameter × 300 mm long hub made of cast iron. The maximum tangential stress is limited to 40 MPa. If young's modulus for steel and cast iron are 2×10^5 MPa and 110 GPa, with $\mu = 0.25$ for both materials and $f = 0.12$, determine

a. The maximum diametral interference.
b. The torque transmitted by the fit.

Solution: Outer diameter (C.I) $d_0 = 400$ mm (hub), contact diameter (steel) $d_c = 200$ mm (shaft), $L = 300$ mm, $\sigma_t)_{max} = 40$ MPa, $E_s = 2 \times 10^5$ N/mm², $E_h = 110 \times 10^3$ N/mm², $\mu_s = \mu_h = 0.25, f = 0.12$.

a. $B = ?$
b. $T = ?$

a. To find B:

We know that,

$$B = p_c d_c \left[\dfrac{d_c^2 + d_i^2}{E_s(d_c^2 - d_i^2)} + \dfrac{d_0^2 + d_c^2}{E_h(d_0^2 - d_c^2)} - \dfrac{\mu_s}{E_s} + \dfrac{\mu_h}{E_h}\right] \qquad \ldots \text{Eq. (i) 7.39/Pg 81, DHB}$$

Here $d_i = 0$. The maximum tangential stress occurs at the inside surface of outer cylinder, i.e.

$$\sigma_{t-c} = p_c\left(\dfrac{d_0^2 + d_c^2}{d_0^2 - d_c^2} + \mu\right) \qquad \ldots 7.37\text{/Pg 81, DHB}$$

$$40 = p_c\left(\dfrac{400^2 + 200^2}{400^2 - 200^2} + 0.25\right)$$

$$p_c = 20.86 \text{ N/mm}^2$$

Eq. (i) yields ...

$$B = 20.86 \times 200 \left[\dfrac{200^2}{2 \times 10^5 (200^2)} + \dfrac{400^2 + 200^2}{110 \times 10^3 (400^2 - 200^2)} - \dfrac{0.25}{2 \times 10^5} + \dfrac{0.25}{110 \times 10^3}\right]$$

$$B = 0.08834 \text{ mm}$$

b. To find torque (T):

We know that, $T = F_a\left(\dfrac{d}{2}\right) = \dfrac{\pi d^2 L f p_c}{2}$ ... 7.42/Pg 82, DHB

$$= \dfrac{\pi \times 200^2 \times 300 \times 0.12 \times 20.86}{2} \text{ here } d = d_c$$

$T = 47.18 \times 10^6$ N-mm $= 47.18$ kN-m

39. A steel shaft of inner diameter 300 mm and outer diameter 600 mm is to be press fit in a C.I hub having an outer diameter of 1500 mm and an axial length of 1.2 m. Determine:

a. The radial interference
b. The torque capacity of the joint.

Take $E = 210$ GPa and 90 GPa for steel and C.I, $\mu_s = 0.3$, $\mu_h = 0.25$, $f = 0.15$. The maximum tangential stress is not to exceed 35 MPa.

Solution: Inner diameter, $d_i = 300$ mm, contact diameter, $d_c = 600$ mm, outer diameter, $d_0 = 1500$ mm, $L = 1200$ mm, $E_s = 2.1 \times 10^5$ N/mm², $E_h = 90 \times 10^3$ N/mm², $\mu_s = 0.3$, $\mu_h = 0.25$, $f = 0.15$

a. Radial clearance $(B/2) = ?$
b. $T = ?$

a. To find radial clearance (B/2):

We know that,

$$B = p_c d_c \left[\dfrac{d_c^2 + d_i^2}{E_s(d_c^2 - d_i^2)} + \dfrac{d_0^2 + d_c^2}{E_h(d_0^2 - d_c^2)} - \dfrac{\mu_s}{E_s} + \dfrac{\mu_h}{E_h} \right] \quad \text{... Eq. (i) 7.39/Pg 81, DHB}$$

Here $d_i = 0$. The maximum tangential stress occurs at the inside surface of outer cylinder, i.e.

$$\sigma_{t-c} = p_c \left(\dfrac{d_0^2 + d_c^2}{d_0^2 - d_c^2} + \mu \right) \quad \text{... 7.37/Pg 81, DHB}$$

Here, $\mu = \mu_h = 0.25$

$$35 = p_c \left(\dfrac{1500^2 + 600^2}{1500^2 - 600^2} + 0.25 \right)$$

$p_c = 21.45$ N/mm²

Eq. (i) yields ...

$$B = 21.45 \times 600 \left[\dfrac{600^2 + 300^2}{2.1 \times 10^5 (600^2 - 300^2)} + \dfrac{1500^2 + 600^2}{90 \times 10^3 (1500^2 - 600^2)} - \dfrac{0.3}{2.1 \times 10^5} + \dfrac{0.25}{90 \times 10^3} \right]$$

$B = 0.3170$ mm

Hence, the radial clearance $= B/2 = 0.3170/2 = 0.1585$ mm.

b. To find torque (T)

We know that, $T = F_a\left(\dfrac{d}{2}\right) = \dfrac{\pi d^2 L f p_c}{2}$ ... 7.42/Pg 82, DHB

$$= \frac{\pi \times 600^2 \times 1200 \times 0.15 \times 21.45}{2} \quad \text{here } d = d_c$$

$T = 2.183 \times 10^9$ N-mm $= 2183$ kN-m

40. It is desired to assemble two steel cylinders having nominal diameters of 40 × 80 mm and 80 × 120 mm, with the tangential stress at inner surface of outer member limited to 80 MPa. Determine the tangential stress at the inner, outer and surfaces of both the members. Also find the interference required. The material used is steel with young's modulus of 20 GPa, and μ = 0.3

Solution: $d_i = 40$ mm, $d_c = 80$ mm, $d_0 = 120$ mm, $\sigma_{t-c} = 80$ N/mm², $E = 20 \times 10^3$ N/mm², μ = 0.3

a. $\sigma_{t-i} = ?$ b. $(\sigma_{t-c})_i = ?$ c. $(\sigma_{t-c})_0 = ?$ d. $\sigma_{t-0} = ?$ e. $B = ?$

We know that, the tangential stress at the inside surface of outer cylinder is

$$\sigma_{t-c} = p_c\left(\frac{d_0^2 + d_c^2}{d_0^2 - d_c^2} + \mu\right) = (\sigma_{t-c})_0 \quad \ldots 7.37/\text{Pg 81, DHB}$$

$$80 = p_c\left(\frac{120^2 + 80^2}{120^2 - 80^2} + 0.3\right)$$

$p_c = 27.59$ N/mm²

a. *Tangential stress at inner surface of inner cylinder* (σ_{t-i}):

$$\sigma_{t-i} = \frac{-2p_c d_c^2}{d_c^2 - d_i^2} \quad \ldots 7.35/\text{Pg 81, DHB}$$

$$= \frac{-2 \times 27.59 \times 80^2}{80^2 - 40^2}$$

$\sigma_{t-i} = -73.56$ N/mm²

b. *Tangential stress at outer surface of inner cylinder* (σ_{t-c}):

$$\sigma_{t-c} = -p_c\left(\frac{d_c^2 + d_i^2}{d_c^2 - d_i^2} - \mu\right) = (\sigma_{t-c})_i \quad \ldots 7.36/\text{Pg 81, DHB}$$

$$= -27.59\left(\frac{80^2 + 40^2}{80^2 - 40^2} - 0.3\right)$$

$\sigma_{t-c} = -37.71$ N/mm²

c. *Tangential stress at the inside surface of outer cylinder* (σ_{t-c}):

$\sigma_{t-c} = (\sigma_{t-c})_0 = 80$ N/mm² ... (data)

d. *Tangential stress at outer surface of outer cylinder* (σ_{t-0}):

$$\sigma_{t-0} = \frac{2p_c d_c^2}{d_0^2 - d_c^2} \quad \ldots 7.38/\text{Pg 81, DHB}$$

$$= \frac{2 \times 27.59 \times 80^2}{120^2 - 80^2}$$

$\sigma_{t-0} = 44.14$ N/mm²

e. Interference (B):

Since both cylinders are made of same material,

$$p_c = \frac{BE(d_0^2 - d_c^2)(d_c^2 - d_i^2)}{2d_c^3(d_0^2 - d_i^2)} \quad \ldots 7.40/\text{Pg 82, DHB}$$

$$27.59 = \frac{B \times (2 \times 10^5) \times (120^2 - 80^2) \times (80^2 - 40^2)}{2 \times 80^3 (120^2 - 40^2)}$$

$$B = 0.0471 \text{ mm}$$

41. A compound tube is made by shrinking a tube of 100 mm internal diameter and 20 mm wall thickness on to another tube of 100 mm external diameter and 20 mm wall thickness. The shrinkage allowance based on radius is 0.01 mm. if both the tubes have the same modulus as 210 GPa, calculate the radial pressure at the junction.

Solution: Tube 1: $d_i = 100$ mm, $t = 20$ mm; Tube 2: $d_0 = 100$ mm, $t = 20$ mm;

Hence $d_c = 100$ mm, $d_i = d_c - 2t = 100 - (2 \times 20) = 60$ mm,

$d_0 = d_c + 2t = 100 + (2 \times 20) = 140$ mm

$E = 210$ MPa, $(B/2) = 0.01$ mm, thus $B = 0.02$ mm, $p_c = ?$

Since both cylinders are made of same material,

$$p_c = \frac{BE(d_0^2 - d_c^2)(d_c^2 - d_i^2)}{2d_c^3(d_0^2 - d_i^2)} \quad \ldots 7.40/\text{Pg 82, DHB}$$

$$p_c = \frac{0.02 \times (210 \times 10^3) \times (140^2 - 100^2) \times (100^2 - 60^2)}{2 \times 100^3 \times (140^2 - 60^2)}$$

$$p_c = 8.064 \text{ mm}$$

42. Two steel rings of radial thickness 25 mm, common radius 50 mm and length 40 mm are shrunk together to form a compound ring. It is found that the axial force required to separate the rings is 120 kN. Determine the shrinkage allowance if 200 GPa and 0.15

Solution: $t = 25$ mm, $r_c = 50$ mm, $L = 40$ mm, $F_a = 120$ kN, $B = ?$, $E = 2 \times 10^5$ MPa, $f = 0.15$

Since both cylinders are made of same material,

$$p_c = \frac{BE(d_0^2 - d_c^2)(d_c^2 - d_i^2)}{2d_c^3(d_0^2 - d_i^2)} \quad \ldots \text{Eq. }(i)\ 7.40/\text{Pg 82, DHB}$$

Here $d_c = 2r_c = 100$ mm, $d_0 = d_c + 2t = 100 + (2 \times 25) = 150$ mm

$d_i = d_c - 2t = 100 - (2 \times 25) = 50$ mm

Also, $F_a = \pi d L f p_c$ $\quad \ldots 7.41/\text{Pg 82, DHB}$

$120 \times 10^3 = \pi \times 100 \times 40 \times 0.15) p_c,$ here $d = d_c$

$p_c = 63.66$ MPa

Eq. (i) yields $63.66 = \dfrac{B \times (2 \times 10^5) \times (150^2 - 100^2) \times (100^2 - 50^2)}{2 \times 100^3 \times (150^2 - 50^2)}$

$B = 0.1358$ mm

43. A steel sleeve 180 mm outside diameter is to be shrunk on to a solid steel shaft of 120 mm diameter. If shrinkage pressure is 20 MPa, find the difference between the diameters of compound cylinder. Take $E = 210$ GPa and $\mu = 0.25$.

Solution: $d_0 = 180$ mm, $d_c = 120$ mm, $p_c = 20$ MPa, $(\Delta d_0 - \Delta d_i) = ?$, $E = 2.1 \times 10^5$ MPa, $\mu = 0.25$

To find $(\Delta d_0 - \Delta d_i)$:

We know that, decrease in diameter of inner cylinder,

$$\Delta d_i = \dfrac{-p_c d_c}{E}\left[\dfrac{d_c^2 + d_i^2}{d_c^2 - d_i^2} - \mu\right]$$

$$= \dfrac{-20 \times 120}{120 \times 10^3}\left(\dfrac{120^2 + 0}{120^2 - 0} - 0.25\right)$$

$\Delta d_i = -8.57 \times 10^{-3}$ mm

Also, increase in diameter of outer cylinder,

$$\Delta d_0 = \dfrac{p_c d_c}{E}\left[\dfrac{d_0^2 + d_c^2}{d_0^2 - d_c^2} + \mu\right]$$

$$= \dfrac{20 \times 120}{210 \times 10^3}\left(\dfrac{180^2 + 120^2}{180^2 - 120^2} - 0.25\right)$$

$\Delta d_0 = 0.0326$ mm

Therefore, $(\Delta d_0 - \Delta d_i) = 0.0326 - (-8.57 \times 10^{-3}) = 0.04115$ mm

44. A steel shaft of 80 mm diameter is pressed into a steel hub of 120 mm outside diameter and 250 mm long such that an applied torque of 8 kN–m relative slip is just avoided. Find the interference fit assuming a common diameter of 80 mm and the maximum circumferential stress in the hub. Take $f = 0.2$ and $E = 210$ GPa, Poison's ratio = 0.3.

Solution: $d_c = 80$ mm, $d_0 = 120$ mm, $L = 250$ mm, $T = 8$ kN–m $= 8 \times 10^6$ N–mm, $f = 0.2$, $E = 210 \times 10^3$ MPa, $\mu = 0.3$,
   a. $B = ?$,   b. $\sigma_{t-c})_0 = ?$

a. To find B:

Since both cylinders are made of same material,

$$p_c = \dfrac{BE(d_0^2 - d_c^2)(d_c^2 - d_i^2)}{2d_c^3(d_0^2 - d_i^2)} \quad \ldots \text{Eq. (i) 7.40/Pg 82, DHB}$$

But, $\quad T = \dfrac{\pi d^2 L f p_c}{2} \quad \ldots$ 7.42/Pg 82, DHB

$2 \times (8 \times 10^6) = \pi \times 80^2 \times 250 \times 0.2 \times p_c$,   here $d = d_c$

$p_c = 15.92$ mm

86 Design of Machine Elements II (DME II)

Eq. (*i*) yields ... $15.92 = \dfrac{B \times (210 \times 10^3) \times (120^2 - 80^2) \times (80^2 - 0^2)}{2 \times 80^3 \times (120^2 - 0^2)}$

$$B = 0.0218 \text{ mm}$$

b. To find $\sigma_{t-c})_0$:

We know that, the tangential stress at the inside surface of outer cylinder is

$$\sigma_{t-c} = p_c \left(\dfrac{d_0^2 + d_c^2}{d_0^2 - d_c^2} + \mu \right) = \sigma_{t-c})_0 \qquad \text{...7.37/Pg 81, DHB}$$

$$= 15.92 \times \left(\dfrac{120^2 + 80^2}{120^2 - 80^2} + 0.3 \right)$$

$$\sigma_{t-c} = 46.17 \text{ N/mm}^2 \qquad = \sigma_{t-c})_0$$

45. A steel cylindrical plug of 100 mm diameter is forced into a sleeve of 180 mm external diameter and 150 mm long. If the greatest circumferential stress in the sleeve *i* 5–75 MPa, Find the torque required to turn the sleeve, assuming $f = 0.2$, and Poisson's ratio as 0.3.

Solution: $d_c = 100$ mm, $d_0 = 180$ mm, $L = 150$ mm, $\sigma_t)_{max} = 75$ MPa, $T = ?, f = 0.2, \mu = 0.3$,

We know that, $\qquad T = \dfrac{\pi d^2 L f p_c}{2} \qquad$ ... Eq. (*i*) 7.42/Pg 82, DHB

But the maximum tangential stress occurs at the inside surface of outer cylinder, i.e.

$$\sigma_{t-c} = p_c \left(\dfrac{d_0^2 + d_c^2}{d_0^2 - d_c^2} + \mu \right) = \sigma_{t-c})_0 \qquad \text{...7.37/Pg 81, DHB}$$

$$75 = p_c \left(\dfrac{180^2 + 100^2}{180^2 - 100^2} + 0.3 \right)$$

$$p_c = 34.2 \text{ N/mm}^2$$

Eq. (*i*) yields ... $\qquad T = \dfrac{\pi \times 100^2 \times 150 \times 0.2 \times 34.2}{2}, \quad$ here $d = d_c$

$$T = 16.12 \times 10^6 \text{ N} - \text{mm} = 16.12 \text{ kN} - \text{mm}$$

46. A steel plug of 75 mm diameter is forced into a steel ring of 125 mm external diameter and 50 mm width. From a reading taken by fixing in a circumferential direction, an electrical resistance strain gauge on the external surface of the ring, the strain was found to be 1.49×10^{-4}. Assuming $f = 0.2$, find the force required to push the plug out of the ring. Also find the greatest hoop stress in the ring. Take $E = 210$ GPa, Poisson's ratio = 0.3.

Solution: $d_c = 75$ mm, $d_0 = 125$ mm, $L = 50$ mm, strain on outer surface, $\varepsilon_0 = 1.49 \times 10^{-4}$, $f = 0.2, E = 210$ MPa,
$F_a = ?, \sigma_t)_{max} = ?, \mu = 0.3$

a. To find F_a:

We know that, $\qquad F_a = \pi d L f p_c \qquad$ ... Eq. (*i*) 7.41/Pg 82, DHB

But, $\qquad E = \dfrac{\sigma}{\varepsilon} = \dfrac{\sigma_t - 0}{\varepsilon_0}$

$$210 \times 10^3 = \frac{\sigma_{t-0}}{1.49 \times 10^{-4}}$$

$$\sigma_{t-0} = 31.29 \text{ MPa}$$

Also,
$$\sigma_{t-0} = \frac{2 p_c d_c^2}{d_0^2 - d_c^2} \qquad \text{...7.38/Pg 81, DHB}$$

$$31.29 = \frac{2 \times p_c \times 75^2}{125^2 - 75^2}$$

$$p_c = 27.81 \text{ N/mm}^2$$

Eq. (i) yields ... $F_a = \pi \times 75 \times 50 \times 0.2 \times 27.81$ \qquad here $d = d_c$

$$F_a = 65.53 \text{ kN}$$

b. To find $\sigma_t)_{\max}$:

We know that the maximum tangential stress occurs at the inside surface of outer cylinder, i.e.

$$\sigma_{t-c} = p_c \left(\frac{d_0^2 + d_c^2}{d_0^2 - d_c^2} + \mu \right) \qquad \text{...7.37/Pg 81, DHB}$$

$$= 27.81 \times \left(\frac{125^2 + 75^2}{125^2 - 75^2} + 0.3 \right)$$

$$\sigma_{t-c} = 67.44 \text{ N/mm}^2$$

47. A shrink fit assembly, formed by shrinking one cylinder over another, is subjected to an external pressure of 60 N/mm². Before the fluid is admitted, the internal and external diameters of the assembly are 120 mm and 200 mm respectively and the diameter at the junction is 160 mm. If after shrinking on, the contact pressure at the junction is 8 N/mm², determine using Lame's equation, the stresses at the inner, mating and outer surfaces of the assembly after the fluid has been admitted. *[VTU-Dec-10–12 Marks]*

Solution: $p_i = 60$ N/mm², $d_i = 120$ mm; $p_c = 8$ N/mm², $d_0 = 200$ mm, $d_c = 160$ mm

Case 1: a. $\sigma_{t-i} = ?$ \quad b. $\sigma_{t-c})_i = ?$ \quad c. $\sigma_{t-c})_0 = ?$ \quad d. $\sigma_{t-0} = ?$, based on p_c
Case 2: a. $\sigma_{t-i} = ?$ \quad b. $\sigma_{t-c})_i = ?$ \quad c. $\sigma_{t-c})_0 = ?$ \quad d. $\sigma_{t-0} = ?$, based on p_i

Case 1: *Based on p_c*

Substituting $\mu = 0$, in Lame's equation

a. Tangential stress at inner surface of inner cylinder (σ_{t-i}):

$$\sigma_{t-i} = \frac{-2 p_c d_c^2}{d_c^2 - d_i^2} \qquad \text{...7.35/Pg 81, DHB}$$

$$= \frac{-2 \times 8 \times 160^2}{160^2 - 120^2}$$

$$\sigma_{t-i} = -36.57 \text{ N/mm}^2$$

b. Tangential stress at outer surface of inner cylinder (σ_{t-i}):

$$\sigma_{t-c} = -p_c \left(\frac{d_c^2 + d_i^2}{d_c^2 - d_i^2} - \mu \right) = \sigma_{t-c})_i \qquad \text{...7.36/Pg 81, DHB}$$

$$= -8 \times \left(\frac{160^2 + 120^2}{160^2 - 120^2} - 0 \right)$$

$$\sigma_{t-c} = -28.57 \text{ N/mm}^2$$

c. *Tangential stress at the inside surface of outer cylinder* (σ_{t-c}):

$$\sigma_{t-c} = p_c \left(\frac{d_0^2 + d_c^2}{d_0^2 - d_c^2} + \mu \right) = \sigma_{t-c})_0 \qquad \text{...7.37/Pg 81, DHB}$$

$$= 8 \times \left(\frac{200^2 + 160^2}{200^2 - 160^2} + 0 \right)$$

$$\sigma_{t-c} = 36.44 \text{ N/mm}^2 \qquad = \sigma_{t-0})$$

d. *Tangential stress at outer surface of outer cylinder* (σ_{t-0}):

$$\sigma_{t-0} = \frac{2 p_c d_c^2}{d_0^2 - d_c^2} \qquad \text{...7.38/Pg 81, DHB}$$

$$= \frac{2 \times 8 \times 160^2}{200^2 - 160^2}$$

$$\sigma_{t-0} = 28.44 \text{ N/mm}^2$$

Case 2: Based on p_i

We know that at any radius the tangential stress is

$$\sigma_t = \frac{p_i d_i^2}{4r^2} \left(\frac{4r^2 + d_0^2}{d_0^2 - d_i^2} \right) \qquad \text{... Eq. (}i\text{) 7.16/Pg 79, DHB}$$

a. *Tangential stress at inner surface of inner cylinder* (σ_{t-i}):

Here $r = r_i$

Eq. (*i*) yields ... $\qquad \sigma_{t-i} = p_i \left(\frac{d_i^2 + d_0^2}{d_0^2 - d_i^2} \right)$

$$= 60 \times \left(\frac{120^2 + 200^2}{200^2 - 120^2} \right)$$

$$\sigma_{t-i} = 127.5 \text{ N/mm}^2$$

b. and c. *Tangential stress at outer surface of inner cylinder -or- at the inside surface of outer cylinder* (σ_{t-c}):

Eq. (*i*) yields ... $\qquad \sigma_{t-c})_i = \sigma_{t-c})_0 = \frac{p_i d_i^2}{d_c^2} \left(\frac{d_0^2 + d_c^2}{d_0^2 - d_i^2} \right)$

$$= \frac{60 \times 120^2}{160^2} \times \left(\frac{200^2 + 160^2}{200^2 - 120^2} \right)$$

$$\sigma_{t-c})_i = \sigma_{t-c})_0 = 86.48 \text{ N/mm}^2$$

d. *Tangential stress at outer surface of outer cylinder* (σ_{t-0}):

Eq. (*i*) yields ... $\qquad \sigma_{t-0} = \frac{2 p_i d_i^2}{d_0^2 - d_i^2}$

$$= \frac{2 \times 60 \times 120^2}{200^2 - 120^2}$$

$$\sigma_{t-0} = 67.5 \text{ N/mm}^2$$

Thus the resultant stresses are

$\sigma_{t-i} = -36.57 + 127.5 = 90.93 \text{ N/mm}^2$
$(\sigma_{t-c})_i = -28.57 + 86.48 = 57.91 \text{ N/mm}^2$
$(\sigma_{t-c})_0 = 36.44 + 86.48 = 122.92 \text{ N/mm}^2$
$\sigma_{t-0} = 28.44 + 67.5 = 95.94 \text{ N/mm}^2$.

48. A compound cylinder is formed by shrinking a tube of 250 mm internal diameter and 25 mm wall thickness onto another tube of 250 mm external diameter and 25 mm wall thickness both tubes being made of same material. The stress at the junction owing to shrinkage is 10 MPa. The compound tube is then subjected to an internal pressure of 80 MPa (Fig. 1.44).

a. Determine the stresses developed in compound and represent them graphically.
b. Calculate the necessary difference in diameter of two members.
c. Calculate the minimum temperature to which the outer tube should be heated before it can be slipped on.

Take $E = 200$ GPa, $\mu = 0.3$ and $\alpha = 11 \times 10^{-6}/°C$

Solution: $d_i = 250$ mm, $t = 25$ mm; $d_0 = 250$ mm, $p_c = 10$ N/mm^2, $p_i = 80$ N/mm^2, $E = 2 \times 10^5$ N/mm^2, $\mu = 0.3$ and $\alpha = 11 \times 10^{-6}/°C$

a. Resultant stresses = ?   b. $\Delta d_0 - \Delta d_i = ?$ c. $t_1 = ?$

a. To find resultant stresses:

Hence, $d_c = 250$ mm, $d_0 = d_0 + 2t = 300$ mm, $d_i = d_c - 2t = 200$ mm

Case 1: *Based on p_c:* Substituting $\mu = 0$, in Lame's equation

i. *Tangential stress at inner surface of inner cylinder (σ_{t-i}):*

$$\sigma_{t-i} = \frac{-2p_c d_c^2}{d_c^2 - d_i^2} \qquad \ldots 7.35/\text{Pg 81, DHB}$$

$$= \frac{-2 \times 10 \times 250^2}{250^2 - 200^2}$$

$$\sigma_{t-i} = -55.56 \text{ N/mm}^2$$

ii. *Tangential stress at outer surface of inner cylinder (σ_{t-c}):*

$$\sigma_{t-c} = -p_c\left(\frac{d_c^2 + d_i^2}{d_c^2 - d_i^2} - \mu\right) = (\sigma_{t-c})_i \qquad \ldots 7.36/\text{Pg 81, DHB}$$

$$= -10 \times \left(\frac{250^2 + 200^2}{250^2 - 200^2} - 0\right)$$

$$\sigma_{t-c} = -45.55 \text{ N/mm}^2 \qquad = (\sigma_{t-c})_i$$

iii. *Tangential stress at the inside surface of outer cylinder σ_{t-c}:*

$$\sigma_{t-c} = p_c\left(\frac{d_0^2 + d_c^2}{d_0^2 - d_c^2} + \mu\right) = (\sigma_{t-c})_0 \qquad \ldots 7.37/\text{Pg 81, DHB}$$

$$= 10 \times \left(\frac{300^2 + 250^2}{300^2 - 250^2} + 0 \right)$$

$$\sigma_{t-c} = 55.45 \text{ N/mm}^2 \qquad = \sigma_{t-c})_0$$

iv. Tangential stress at outer surface of outer cylinder (σ_{t-0}):

$$\sigma_{t-0} = \frac{2 p_c d_c^2}{d_0^2 - d_c^2} \qquad \ldots 7.38/\text{Pg 81, DHB}$$

$$= \frac{2 \times 10 \times 250^2}{300^2 - 250^2}$$

$$\sigma_{t-0} = 45.45 \text{ N/mm}^2$$

Case 2: Based on p_i:

We know that at any radius the tangential stress is

$$\sigma_t = \frac{p_i d_i^2}{4r^2} \left(\frac{4r^2 + d_0^2}{d_0^2 - d_i^2} \right) \qquad \ldots \text{Eq. (}i\text{) 7.16/Pg 79, DHB}$$

i. Tangential stress at inner surface of inner cylinder (σ_{t-i}): Here $r = r_i$

Eq. (i) yields ...

$$\sigma_{t-i} = p_i \left(\frac{d_i^2 + d_0^2}{d_0^2 - d_i^2} \right)$$

$$= 80 \times \left(\frac{200^2 + 300^2}{300^2 - 200^2} \right)$$

$$\sigma_{t-i} = 208 \text{ N/mm}^2$$

ii. and iii. Tangential stress at outer surface of inner cylinder -or- at the inside surface of outer cylinder (σ_{t-i}):

Eq. (i) yields ...

$$\sigma_{t-c})_i = \sigma_{t-c})_0 = \frac{p_i d_i^2}{d_c^2} \left(\frac{d_0^2 + d_c^2}{d_0^2 - d_i^2} \right)$$

$$= \frac{80 \times 200^2}{250^2} \times \left(\frac{300^2 + 250^2}{300^2 - 200^2} \right)$$

$$\sigma_{t-c})_i = \sigma_{t-c})_0 = 156.16 \text{ N/mm}^2$$

iv. Tangential stress at outer surface of outer cylinder (σ_{t-0}):

Eq. (i) yields ...

$$\sigma_{t-0} = \frac{2 p_i d_i^2}{d_0^2 - d_i^2}$$

$$= \frac{2 \times 80 \times 200^2}{300^2 - 200^2}$$

$$\sigma_{t-0} = 128 \text{ N/mm}^2$$

Thus the resultant stresses are

$\sigma_{t-i} = -55.56 + 208 = 152.44 \text{ N/mm}^2$

$\sigma_{t-c})_i = -45.55 + 156.16 = 110.61 \text{ N/mm}^2$

$\sigma_{t-c})_0 = 55.45 + 156.16 = 211.61 \text{ N/mm}^2$

$\sigma_{t-0} = 45.45 + 128 = 173.45 \text{ N/mm}^2$.

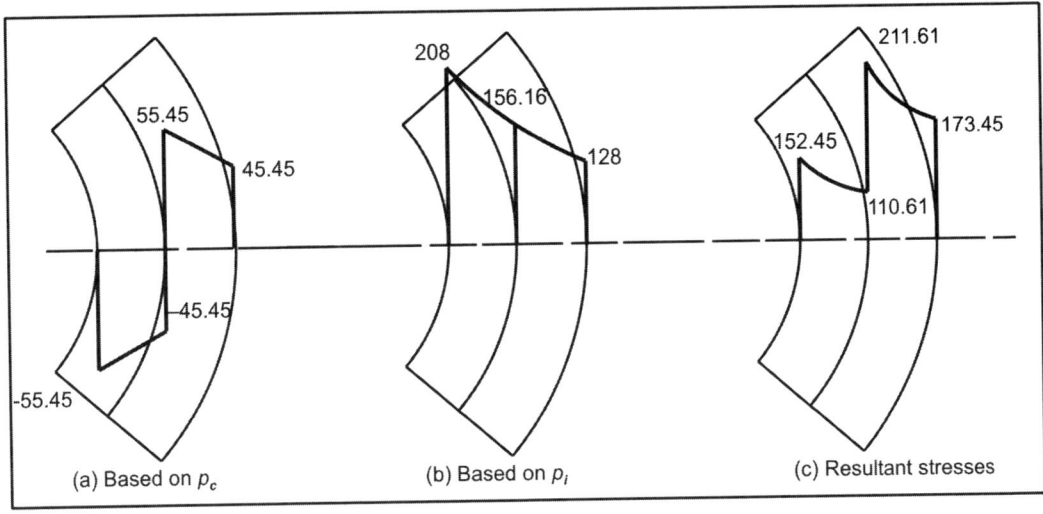

Fig. 1.44: Graphs for problem 48

b. To find difference in diameter:

We know that, Decrease in diameter of inner cylinder,

$$\Delta d_i = \frac{-p_c d_c}{E}\left[\frac{d_c^2 + d_i^2}{d_c^2 - d_i^2} - \mu\right]$$

$$= \frac{-10 \times 250^2}{2 \times 10^5}\left(\frac{250^2 + 200^2}{250^2 - 200^2} - 0.3\right)$$

$$\Delta d_i = -0.05319 \text{ mm}$$

Also, increase in diameter of outer cylinder,

$$\Delta d_0 = \frac{p_c d_c}{E}\left[\frac{d_0^2 + d_c^2}{d_c^2 - d_c^2} + \mu\right]$$

$$= \frac{10 \times 250^2}{2 \times 10^5}\left(\frac{300^2 + 250^2}{300^2 - 250^2} + 0.3\right)$$

$$\Delta d_0 = 0.07306 \text{ mm}$$

Therefore, $(\Delta d_0 - \Delta d_i) = 0.07306 - (-0.05319) = 0.1263$ mm

c. To find minimum temperature:

We know that, $t_2 = \left(\dfrac{B}{\alpha d_c} + t_1\right)$ ...7.44/Pg 82, DHB

here, $t_1 = 0$, $B = \Delta d_0 - \Delta d_i = 0.1263$ mm

$$t_2 = \left(\frac{0.1263}{(11 \times 10^{-6} \times 250)} + 0\right)$$

$$t_2 = 46°C$$

1.23 RADIAL STRESSES

We know that, Radial stress at radius 'r', $\sigma'_r = (1-\mu)a - (1+\mu)\dfrac{b}{r^2}$ ...7.28/Pg 80, DHB

Substituting values of 'a' and 'b' from **7.15a and 7.15b/Pg 80, DHB**

$$\sigma_r = \sigma'_r = (1-\mu)\frac{(p_i d_i^2 - p_0 d_0^2)}{d_0^2 - d_i^2} - (1+\mu)\frac{(p_i - p_0)d_0^2 d_i^2}{4r^2(d_0^2 - d_i^2)} \quad \text{... (Eq. 1.57a)}$$

Considering only the internal pressure, Eq. (1.57a) yields

$$\sigma_r = (1-\mu)\frac{p_i d_i^2}{d_0^2 - d_i^2} - (1+\mu)\frac{p_i d_0^2 d_i^2}{4r^2(d_0^2 - d_i^2)} \quad \text{...(Eq. 1.58) 7.34/Pg 81, DHB}$$

Considering only the external pressure, Eq. (1.57a) yields

$$\sigma_r = -(1-\mu)\frac{p_0 d_0^2}{d_0^2 - d_i^2} - (1+\mu)\frac{(-p_0)d_0^2 d_i^2}{4r^2(d_0^2 - d_i^2)}$$

$$\sigma_r = -(1-\mu)\frac{p_0 d_0^2}{d_0^2 - d_i^2} + (1+\mu)\frac{p_0 d_0^2 d_i^2}{4r^2(d_0^2 - d_i^2)} \quad \text{... (Eq. 1.59)}$$

Substituting the boundary conditions and simplifying yields

a. Radial stress at inner surface of inner cylinder (σ_{r-i}):
$$\sigma_{r-i} = 0$$

b. Radial stress at outer surface of inner cylinder (σ_{r-c}):
$$\sigma_{r-c} = -p_c \quad = \sigma_{r-c})_i$$

c. Radial stress at the inside surface of outer cylinder (σ_{r-c}):
$$\sigma_{r-c} = -p_c \quad = \sigma_{r-c})_o$$

d. Radial stress at outer surface of outer cylinder (σ_{r-0}):
$$\sigma_{r-0} = 0$$

... (Eq. 1.60)

Note: Equation (1.60) has to be remembered

49. Design a shrink fit joint to join two cylinders of diameter 150 × 200 mm and 200 × 250 mm. Maximum tangential stress in the components due to shrink fitting is to be limited to 40 MPa. Also determine the axial force necessary to disengage the joint if the length of the joint is 200 mm and the maximum power that can be transmitted at the rated speed of 1000 rpm. The cylinder material has a modulus of elasticity of 210 GPa and Poisson's ratio 0.3.

[VTU-June/July 2009-15 Marks]

Solution: Dimensions are 150 × 200 mm and 200 × 250 mm; thus $d_i = 150$ mm, $d_c = 200$ mm, $d_0 = 250$ mm, $\sigma_t)_{max} = 40$ MPa, $\mu = 0.3$, $L = 200$ mm, $N = 1000$ rpm, $E = 2.1 \times 10^5$ N/mm², $\mu = 0.3$

a. Design the joint   b. $F_a = ?$ c. $P = ?$

a. Design the joint

Case 1: *To find tangential stresses:*

We know that, the tangential stress at the inside surface of outer cylinder is

$$\sigma_{t-c} = p_c\left(\frac{d_0^2 + d_c^2}{d_0^2 - d_c^2} + \mu\right) = \sigma_{t-c})_0 \quad \text{... 7.37/Pg 81, DHB}$$

$$40 = p_c \times \left(\frac{250^2 + 200^2}{250^2 - 200^2} + 0.3\right)$$

$$p_c = 8.24 \text{ N/mm}^2$$

i. Tangential stress at inner surface of inner cylinder (σ_{t-i}):

$$\sigma_{t-i} = \frac{-2p_c d_c^2}{d_c^2 - d_i^2} \quad \text{...7.35/Pg 81, DHB}$$

$$= \frac{-2 \times 8.24 \times 200^2}{200^2 - 150^2}$$

$$\sigma_{t-c} = -37.67 \text{ N/mm}^2$$

ii. Tangential stress at outer surface of inner cylinder (σ_{t-c}):

$$\sigma_{t-c} = p_c \left(\frac{d_c^2 + d_i^2}{d_c^2 - d_i^2} - \mu \right) = (\sigma_{t-c})_i \quad \text{...7.36/Pg 81, DHB}$$

$$= -8.24 \left(\frac{200^2 + 150^2}{200^2 - 150^2} - 0.3 \right)$$

$$\sigma_{t-c} = -27 \text{ N/mm}^2$$

iii. Tangential stress at the inside surface of outer cylinder (σ_{t-c}):

$$\sigma_{t-c} = (\sigma_{t-c})_0 = 40 \text{ N/mm}^2 \quad \text{...(data)}$$

iv. Tangential stress at outer surface of outer cylinder σ_{t-0}:

$$\sigma_{t-0} = \frac{2p_c d_c^2}{d_0^2 - d_c^2} \quad \text{...7.38/Pg 81, DHB}$$

$$= \frac{2 \times 8.24 \times 200^2}{250^2 - 200^2}$$

$$\sigma_{t-0} = 29.29 \text{ N/mm}^2$$

Case 2: *To find radial stresses:*
  i. Radial stress at inner surface of inner cylinder σ_{r-i}: $\quad \sigma_{r-i} = 0$
  ii. Radial stress at outer surface of inner cylinder σ_{r-c}: $\quad \sigma_{r-c} = -p_c = -8.24 \text{ N/mm}^2 = (\sigma_{t-c})_i$
  iii. Radial stress at the inside surface of outer cylinder σ_{r-c}: $\quad \sigma_{r-c} = -p_c = -8.24 \text{ N/mm}^2 = (\sigma_{t-c})_0$
  iv. Radial stress at outer surface of outer cylinder σ_{r-0}: $\quad \sigma_{r-0} = 0$

Case 3: *To find B:*
Since both cylinders are made of same material,

$$p_c = \frac{BE(d_0^2 - d_c^2)(d_c^2 - d_i^2)}{2d_c^2(d_0^2 - d_i^2)} \quad \text{...7.40/Pg 82, DHB}$$

$$8.24 = \frac{B \times (2.1 \times 10^5) \times (250^2 - 200^2) \times (200^2 - 150^2)}{2 \times 200^3 \times (250^2 - 150^2)}$$

$$B = 0.067 \text{ mm}$$

b. To find F_a:
We know that,
Since f is not given

$$F_a = \pi d L f p_c \quad \text{...7.41/Pg 82, DHB}$$
$$f_{avg} = 0.08, \quad d = d_c \quad \text{...Pg 75/DHB}$$
$$F_a = \pi \times 200 \times 200 \times 0.08 \times 8.24$$
$$F_a = 82.84 \text{ kN}$$

c. To find power (P):

We know that the general equation for power is

$$P = \frac{2\pi NT}{60} \qquad \ldots \text{Eq. }(i)$$

$$\text{but } T = F_a\left(\frac{d}{2}\right) \qquad \ldots 7.42/\text{Pg 82, DHB}$$

$$= (82.84 \times 10^3)\frac{200}{2}, \quad \text{here } d = d_c$$

$$T = 8.284 \times 10^6 \text{ N-mm}$$

$$T = 8.284 \times 10^3 \text{ N-m}$$

Eq. (i) yields …

$$P = \frac{2\pi \times 1000 \times (8.284 \times 10^3)}{60}$$

$$P = 867.47 \text{ kW.}$$

50. A high pressure cylinder consists of an inner cylinder of ID and OD 200 mm and 300 mm respectively. It is jacketed by an outer cylinder of OD 400 mm. the difference between the OD and the ID of inner cylinder and inner dia. of the jacket before assembly is 0.25 mm. E = 2.07 × 10⁵ MPa. Calculate the shrinkage pressure and stress induced in cylinders due to shrinkage pressure. In service, the cylinder is further subjected to an internal pressure of 200 MPa. Plot the resultant stress distribution (Fig. 1.45). **[VTU–May/June10–16 Marks]**

Solution: $d_i = 200$ mm, $d_c = 300$ mm, $d_0 = 400$ mm, $B = 0.25$ mm, $E = 2.07 \times 10^5$ N/mm²,
a. $p_c = ?$ b. $\sigma_t = ?$, at p_c c. $\sigma_t = ?$, at $p_i = 200$ N/mm²

a. To find p_c:

Since both cylinders are made of same material,

$$p_c = \frac{BE(d_0^2 - d_c^2)(d_c^2 - d_i^2)}{2d_c^3(d_0^2 - d_i^2)} \qquad \ldots 7.40/\text{Pg 82, DHB}$$

$$p_c = \frac{0.25 \times (2.07 \times 10^5) \times (400^2 - 300^2) \times (300^2 - 200^2)}{2 \times 300^3 \times (400^2 - 200^2)}$$

$$p_c = 28 \text{ N/mm}^2$$

b. To find $\sigma_t = ?$, based on p_c:

Substituting $\mu = 0$, in Lame's equation

i. Tangential stress at inner surface of inner cylinder (σ_{t-i}):

$$\sigma_{t-i} = \frac{-2p_c d_c^2}{d_c^2 - d_i^2} \qquad \ldots 7.35/\text{Pg 81, DHB}$$

$$= \frac{-2 \times 28 \times 300^2}{300^2 - 200^2}$$

$$\sigma_{t-i} = -100.8 \text{ N/mm}^2$$

ii. Tangential stress at outer surface of inner cylinder (σ_{t-c}):

$$\sigma_{t-c} = -p_c\left(\frac{d_0^2 + d_c^2}{d_0^2 - d_c^2} - \mu\right) = \sigma_{t-c})_i \qquad \ldots 7.36/ \text{Pg 81, DHB}$$

$$= -28 \times \left(\frac{300^2 + 200^2}{300^2 - 200^2} - 0\right)$$

$$\sigma_{t-c} = -72.8 \text{ N/mm}^2 \quad = (\sigma_{t-c})_i$$

iii. Tangential stress at the inside surface of outer cylinder (σ_{t-0}):

$$\sigma_{t-c} = p_c\left(\frac{d_0^2 + d_c^2}{d_0^2 - d_c^2} + \mu\right) = \sigma_{t-c})_0 \qquad \ldots 7.37/\text{Pg 81, DHB}$$

$$= 28 \times \left(\frac{400^2 + 300^2}{400^2 - 300^2} + 0\right)$$

$$\sigma_{t-c} = 100 \text{ N/mm}^2 \quad = (\sigma_{t-c})_0$$

iv. Tangential stress at outer surface of outer cylinder (σ_{t-0}):

$$\sigma_{t-0} = \frac{2p_c d_c^2}{d_0^2 - d_c^2} \qquad \ldots 7.38/\text{Pg 81, DHB}$$

$$= \frac{+2 \times 28 \times 300^2}{400^2 - 300^2}$$

$$\sigma_{t-0} = 72 \text{ N/mm}^2$$

c. To find σ_t = ?, based on p_i = 200 N/ mm²

We know that the tangential stress at any radius is

$$\sigma_t = \frac{p_i d_i^2}{4r^2}\left(\frac{4r^2 + d_0^2}{d_0^2 - d_i^2}\right) \qquad \ldots \text{Eq. } (i) \text{ 7.16/Pg 79, DHB}$$

i. Tangential stress at inner surface of inner cylinder (σ_{t-i}):
Here $r = r_i$

Eq. (i) yields ... $\quad p_{t-i} = p_i\left(\dfrac{d_i^2 + d_0^2}{d_0^2 - d_i^2}\right)$

$$= 200 \times \left(\frac{200^2 + 400^2}{400^2 - 200^2}\right)$$

$$\sigma_{t-i} = 333.34 \text{ N/mm}^2$$

ii. and iii. Tangential stress at outer surface of inner cylinder (σ_{t-c}) -or- at the inside surface of outer cylinder (σ_{t-c}):

Eq. (i) yields ... $\quad \sigma_{t-c})_i = \sigma_{t-c})_0 = \dfrac{p_i d_i^2}{d_c^2}\left(\dfrac{d_0^2 + d_c^2}{d_0^2 - d_i^2}\right)$

$$= \frac{200 \times 200^2}{300^2} \times \left(\frac{400^2 + 300^2}{400^2 - 200^2}\right)$$

$$\sigma_{t-c})_i = \sigma_{t-c})_0 = 185.18 \text{ N/mm}^2$$

iv. Tangential stress at outer surface of outer cylinder (σ_{t-0}):

Eq. (i) yields ...

$$\sigma_{t-0} = \frac{2p_i d_i^2}{d_0^2 - d_c^2}$$

$$= \frac{2 \times 200 \times 200^2}{400^2 - 200^2}$$

$\sigma_{t-0} = 133.34 \text{ N/mm}^2$

Thus the resultant stresses are

$\sigma_{t-i} = -100.8 + 333.34 = 232.54 \text{ N/mm}^2$

$(\sigma_{t-c})_i = -72.8 + 133.34 = 112.38 \text{ N/mm}^2$

$(\sigma_{t-c})_0 = -100 + 185.18 = 285.18 \text{ N/mm}^2$

$\sigma_{t-0} = 100 + 133.34 = 205.34 \text{ N/mm}^2$

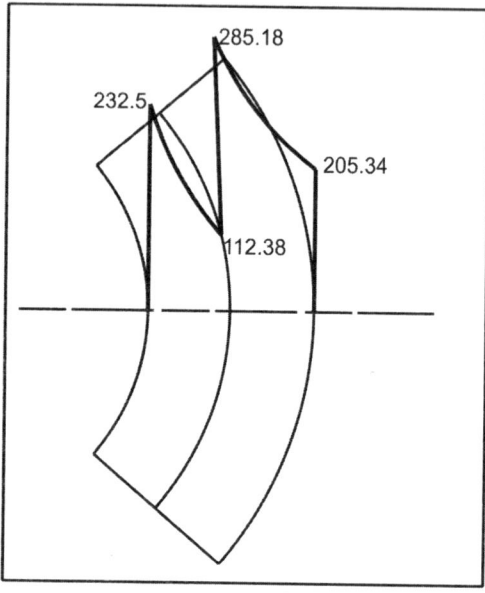

Fig. 1.45: Resultant stresses for problem 50

51. A tube with 50 mm and 75 mm inner and outer diameters respectively is reinforced by shrinking a jacket of outer diameter 100 mm. The compound tube has to withstand an internal pressure of 35 MPa. Calculate the shrinkage allowance such that the maximum tangential stress in each tube has same magnitude. Also calculate the shrinkage pressure and show the distribution of tangential stresses. Assume $E = 207 \text{ kN/mm}^2$.

[VTU–June/July 11–20 Marks]

Solution: $d_i = 50$ mm, $d_c = 75$ mm, $d_0 = 100$ mm, $p_i = 35 \text{ N/mm}^2$, $E = 207 \times 10^3 \text{ N/mm}^2$
 a. $B = ?$, if $(\sigma_{t-max})_{hub} = (\sigma_{t-max})_{shaft}$ b. $p_c = ?$

a. To find B:

Here B depends upon which in turn is dependent on the resultant stresses (as per data)

Case 1: *Based on p_i:*

We know that the tangential stress at any radius is

$$\sigma_t = \frac{p_i d_i^2}{4r^2} \left(\frac{4r^2 + d_0^2}{d_0^2 - d_1^2} \right) \quad \text{... (Eq. 1.1) 7.16/Pg 79, DHB}$$

i. Tangential stress at inner surface of inner cylinder (σ_{t-i}): Here $r = r_i$

Eq. (i) yields ...

$$\sigma_{t-i} = p_i \left(\frac{d_0^2 + d_i^2}{d_0^2 - d_i^2} \right)$$

$$= 35 \times \left(\frac{100^2 + 50^2}{100^2 - 50^2} \right)$$

$\sigma_{t-i} = 58.34 \text{ N/mm}^2$

ii. and iii. Tangential stress at outer surface of inner cylinder (σ_{t-c}) -or- at the inside surface of outer cylinder (σ_{t-c}):

Eq. (i) yields ...
$$\sigma_{t-c})_i = \sigma_{t-c})_o = \frac{p_i d_i^2}{d_c^2}\left(\frac{d_o^2 + d_c^2}{d_o^2 - d_i^2}\right)$$

$$= \frac{35 \times 50^2}{75^2} \times \left(\frac{100^2 + 75^2}{100^2 - 50^2}\right)$$

$$\sigma_{t-c})_i = \sigma_{t-c})_o = 32.41 \text{ N/mm}^2$$

iv. Tangential stress at outer surface of outer cylinder (σ_{t-c}):

Eq. (i) yields ...
$$\sigma_{t-o} = \frac{2p_i d_i^2}{d_o^2 - d_i^2}$$

$$= \frac{2 \times 35 \times 50^2}{100^2 - 50^2}$$

$$\sigma_{t-o} = 23.34 \text{ N/mm}^2$$

Case 2: Based on p_c: Substituting $\mu = 0$, in Lame's equation

i. Tangential stress at inner surface of inner cylinder (σ_{t-i}):

$$\sigma_{t-i} = \frac{-2p_c d_c^2}{d_c^2 - d_i^2} \quad \text{...7.35/Pg 81, DHB}$$

$$= \frac{-2p_c \times 75^2}{75^2 - 50^2}$$

$$\sigma_{t-c} = -3.6\, p_c \text{ N/mm}^2$$

ii. Tangential stress at outer surface of inner cylinder (σ_{t-c}):

$$\sigma_{t-c} = +p_c\left(\frac{d_c^2 + d_i^2}{d_c^2 - d_i^2} - \mu\right) = \sigma_{t-c})_i \quad \text{...7.36/Pg 81, DHB}$$

$$= -10 \times \left(\frac{75^2 + 50^2}{75^2 - 50^2} - 0\right)$$

$$\sigma_{t-c} = -2.6\, p_c \text{ N/mm}^2 \quad = \sigma_{t-c})_i$$

iii. Tangential stress at the inside surface of outer cylinder (σ_{t-c}):

$$\sigma_{t-c} = -p_c\left(\frac{d_o^2 + d_c^2}{d_o^2 - d_c^2} + \mu\right) = \sigma_{t-c})_o \quad \text{...7.37/Pg 81, DHB}$$

$$= p_c\left(\frac{100^2 + 75^2}{100^2 - 75^2} + 0\right)$$

$$\sigma_{t-c} = 3.57\, p_c \text{ N/mm}^2 = \sigma_{t-c})_i$$

iv. Tangential stress at outer surface of outer cylinder (σ_{t-o}):

$$\sigma_{t-o} = \frac{2p_c d_c^2}{d_o^2 - d_c^2} \quad \text{...7.38/Pg 81, DHB}$$

$$= \frac{2 \times p_c \times 75^2}{100^2 - 75^2}$$

$$\sigma_{t-o} = 2.57\, p_c \text{ N/mm}^2$$

Thus the resultant stresses are

$\sigma_{t-i} = 58.34 - 3.6\, p_c$

$\sigma_{t-c)i} = 32.41 - 2.6\, p_c$

$\sigma_{t-c)o} = 32.41 + 3.57\, p_c$

$\sigma_{t-c} = 23.34 + 2.57\, p_c$

Given, $\sigma_{t-max})_{hub} = \sigma_{t-max})_{shaft}$

$\sigma_{t-i} = \sigma_{t-c)o}$

$58.34 - 3.6\, p_c = 32.41 + 3.57\, p_c$

$p_c = 3.616\ \text{N/mm}^2$

Since both cylinders are made of same material,

$$p_c = \frac{BE(d_0^2 - d_c^2)(d_c^2 - d_i^2)}{2 d_c^3 (d_0^2 - d_i^2)} \qquad \text{...7.40/Pg 82, DHB}$$

$$3.616 = \frac{B \times (207 \times 10^3) \times (100^2 - 75^2) \times (75^2 - 50^2)}{2 \times 75^3 \times (100^2 - 50^2)}$$

$B = 8.086 \times 10^{-3}$ mm

52. A steel hub 440 mm outside diameter, 250 mm inside diameter and 300 mm length has an interference fit with a shaft of 250 mm diameter. The torque to be transmitted is 30×10^4 N-m. The permissible stress for the material of the shaft and hub is 120 MPa. The coefficient of friction is 0.18. Determine:

a. The contact pressure
b. Interference required
c. The tangential stress at the inner and outer surfaces of the hub
d. Force required to assemble
e. Radial stress at the inner and outer diameter of the hub. *[VTU–June 12–14 Marks]*

Solution: $d_c = 250$ mm, $d_0 = 440$ mm, $L = 300$ mm, $T = 30 \times 10^4$ N-m $= 3 \times 10^8$ N-mm, $\sigma = 120$ MPa, $f = 0.18$

a. $p_c = ?$ b. $B = ?$ c. $\sigma_{t-c}, \sigma_{t-0}$, for hub d. $F_a = ?$
e. σ_r at inner and outer radii for hub

a. To find p_c:

We know that, $F_a = \pi dLF p_c$ ...7.41/Pg 82, DHB

$2.4 \times 10^6 = \pi \times 250 \times 300 \times 0.18 \times p_c$, here $d = d_c$

$p_c = 56.58$ N/mm^2

b. To find B:

Since both cylinders are made of same material,

$$p_c = \frac{BE(d_0^2 - d_c^2)(d_c^2 - d_i^2)}{2 d_c^3 (d_0^2 - d_i^2)} \qquad \text{...7.40/Pg 82, DHB}$$

$$56.58 = \frac{B \times (2.1 \times 10^5) \times (440^2 - 250^2) \times (250^2 - 0)}{2 \times 250^3 \times (440^2 - 0)}$$

assume $E = 2.1 \times 10^5$ MPa

$B = 0.199$ mm

Note: For this problem, first find (F_a), is case (d)

c. To find tangential stress at the inner and outer surfaces of the hub:

i. Tangential stress at the inside surface of outer cylinder (σ_{t-c}):

$$\sigma_{t-c} = p_c \left(\frac{d_0^2 + d_c^2}{d_0^2 - d_c^2} + \mu \right) = \sigma_{t-c})_0 \qquad \ldots 7.37/\text{Pg 81, DHB}$$

$$= 56.58 \times \left(\frac{440^2 + 250^2}{440^2 - 250^2} + 0 \right)$$

$$\sigma_{t-c} = 110.57 \text{ N/mm}^2 \quad = \sigma_{t-c})_0 < 120 \text{ MPa}$$

ii. Tangential stress at outer surface of outer cylinder (σ_{t-0}):

$$p_{t-0} = \frac{2 p_c d_c^2}{d_0^2 - d_c^2} \qquad \ldots 7.38/\text{Pg 81, DHB}$$

$$= \frac{2 \times 56.58 \times 250^2}{440^2 - 250^2}$$

$$\sigma_{t-0} = 53.97 \text{ N/mm}^2 \qquad < 120 \text{ MPa}$$

d. To find F_a:

We know that $\quad T = F_a \left(\dfrac{d}{2} \right) \qquad \ldots 7.42/\text{Pg 82, DHB}$

$$3 \times 10^8 = F_a \left(\frac{250}{2} \right), \quad \text{here } d = d_c$$

$$F_a = 2.4 \times 10^6 \text{ N}$$

e. Radial stress at the inner and outer diameter of the hub:

i. Radial stress at outer surface of inner cylinder (σ_{r-c}): $\sigma_{r-c} = -p_c = -56.58 \text{ N/mm}^2 = \sigma_{t-c})_i$
ii. Radial stress at outer surface of outer cylinder (σ_{r-0}): $\sigma_{r-0} = 0$.

1.24 CYLINDER HEADS (END CLOSURES)

The heads of cylinders, pistons, boilers as well as the sides of a tank (rectangular -or- square) may have flat -or- slightly dished plates. These plates may be cast integral with the cylinder walls -or- fixed to them by means of bolts, welds -or- rivets.

The end closures may be formed in the following shapes:
1. Flat end
2. Conical end
3. Domed end
   a. Hemi-spherical   b. Semi-ellipsoidal   c. Dished and flanged

1.24.1 Flat Heads

The design of flat heads depends upon two factors
   a. Type of connection with supporting member
      i. Simply supported at edges -or- center
      ii. Rigidly fixed
   b. Nature of loading
      i. Concentrated load
      ii. Uniformly distributed load

1.24.1.1 Circular Flats with Uniformly Distributed Load

The thickness of the plate of diameter 'D' supported at the circumference and subjected to uniformly distributed pressure over the total area is calculated as:

$$t_1 = c_1 D \sqrt{p/f} \quad \quad \text{...8.10/Pg 88, DHB}$$

f = allowable design stress
c_1 = coefficient, which depends upon the material and the method of holding the edges
...Tb 8.5/Pg 97, DHB

D = diameter of the plate

And the maximum deflection is $y = \dfrac{c_2 D^4 p}{E t^3}$ ...8.11/Pg 88, DHB

values of c_1, c_2 ...Tb 8.5/Pg 97, DHB

The maximum stress in circular plate is

- For edge supported: $\sigma_{max} = \sigma_t = \dfrac{-3F(3m+1)}{8\pi m t^2}$ ...Tb 8.7-(1)/Pg 98, DHB

- For edge fixed: $\sigma_{max} = \sigma_t = \dfrac{3F}{4\pi t^2}$ ...Tb 8.7-(2)/Pg 98, DHB

F = Total load = $\pi r_0^2 p$
$1/m$ = Poisson's ratio

1.24.1.2 Circular Flat Plates Loaded Centrally

The thickness of a flat cast iron plate supported freely at the circumference with diameter 'D' and subjected to a load, distributed uniformly over an area ($\pi D_0^2 / 4$) is given as:

- For freely supported plate:

$$t = 1.2 \sqrt{\left(1 - \dfrac{0.67 D_0}{D}\right) \dfrac{F}{f}} \quad \quad \text{...8.12/Pg 88, DHB}$$

- For rigidly fixed plate: $t = 0.65 \sqrt{\dfrac{F}{f} \log_e (D/D_0)}$ ...8.14/Pg 88, DHB

1.24.1.3 Rectangular Plates

According to Grashof and Bach, the thickness of the plate is calculated as:

- For uniform load, $t = abc_3 \sqrt{\dfrac{p}{f(a^2 + b^2)}}$ ...8.15/Pg 89, DHB

- For concentrated load: $t = c_4 \sqrt{\dfrac{abF}{f(a^2 + b^2)}}$ ...8.16/Pg 89, DHB

a = length of the plate (mm)
b = breadth of the plate (mm)
c_3, c_4 = coefficient ...Tb 8.5/Pg 97, DHB

1.24.1.4 Elliptical Plates

The thickness of uniformly loaded elliptical plate is calculated as:

$$t = abc_5\sqrt{\frac{p}{f(a^2+b^2)}}$$ ...8.17/Pg 89, DHB

a = minor axis (mm)
b = major axis (mm)
c_5 = coefficient ...Tb 8.5/Pg 97, DHB

1.24.2 Spherical Dished Covers

The thickness of spherically dished ends secured to the shell to a flange connection by means of bolts is calculated as:

$$t = \frac{3pD_i}{2fJ}$$ ...8.8/Pg 87, DHB

J = joint factor ...Tb 8.2/Pg 93, DHB
D_i = inside diameter of shell

The above equation is valid if, $R \leq 1.3 D_i$

and $\dfrac{100t}{R} \leq 10$

R = radius of the crown

1.24.3 Shells Subjected to Internal Pressure

a. Standard cylindrical head: The minimum thickness of the shell shall be

$$t = \frac{pD_i}{2fJ-p} = \frac{pD_0}{2fJ+p}$$ ...8.1/Pg 86, DHB

if corrosion allowance (C) is considered,

$$t = \frac{pD_i}{2fJ-p} + C$$

b. Standard spherical shells:

$$t = \frac{pD_i}{2fJ-p} = \frac{pD_0}{2fJ+p}$$ ...8.2/Pg 86, DHB

if corrosion allowance (C) is considered,

$$t = \frac{pD_i}{4fJ-p} + C$$

1.25 THICKNESS OF STAYED AND BRACED PLATES

The thickness of stayed and braced plates shall be calculated as:

$$t = C_1 D_1 \sqrt{p/f}$$ ...8.9/Pg 88, DHB

D_1 = diameter of largest circle, inscribed between supporting points of plate. [Fig. 8.2/Pg 101, DHB]
C_1 = factor depending upon mode of support
[Fig. 8.3 (A-F)/Pg 102, DHB]

1.26 UNSTAYED FLAT HEADS

a. Circular flat heads: The thickness of flat unstayed circular heads and covers shall be calculated as:

$$t = CD\sqrt{p/f}$$ ...8.6/Pg 87, DHB

The above equation is used when the head -or- cover is attached by bolts causing an edge movement.

b. Non-circular flat heads:

$$t = CZa\sqrt{p/f}$$ ... 8.7/Pg 87, DHB

values of C and D ... Tb 8.1/Pg 90, DHB

Z = factor depending on the ratio of $\dfrac{\text{Short span}}{\text{long span}} = \dfrac{a}{b}$ [Fig. 8.1/Pg 101, DHB]

Note: Also refer Table 8.7 for more formulae, DHB.

53. The steam chest of a stem engine is covered by a flat rectangular plate of size 250 × 500 mm. The plate is made of cast iron and subjected to a steam pressure of 1.5 MPa. If the plate is uniformly loaded and freely supported at the edges, determine the thickness of the plate for an allowable stress of 40 MPa.

Solution: Rectangular plate: 250 × 500 mm; $a = 500$ mm, $b = 250$ mm, $p = 1.5$ MPa, $t = ?$, $f = 40$ MPa

For a rectangular plate, uniformly loaded, the thickness is calculated as:

$$t = abc_3\sqrt{\dfrac{p}{f(a^2+b^2)}}$$ ... 8.15/Pg 89, DHB

$c_3 = 0.75$, for CI ... Tb 8.5/Pg 97, DHB

$$t = (500 \times 250 \times 0.75) \times \sqrt{\dfrac{1.5}{40(500^2+250^2)}}$$

$t = 32.48$ mm.

Also for a rectangular plate with all edges supported,

$$\sigma_b = \dfrac{0.75 b^2 p}{t^2\left[1+1.61\left(\dfrac{b^3}{a^6}\right)\right]}$$ ... Tb 8.7-(12)/Pg 100, DHB

$$40 = \dfrac{0.75 \times 250^2 \times 1.5}{t^2\left[1+1.61\left(\dfrac{250^3}{500^3}\right)\right]}$$

$t = 38.25$ mm.

Adopt higher value for design, we have $t = 38.25$ mm ≈ 40 mm.

54. Repeat the above problem, if the plate is uniformly loaded and fixed at the edges.

Solution: For a rectangular plate, uniformly loaded, the thickness is calculated as:

$$t = abc_3\sqrt{\dfrac{p}{f(a^2+b^2)}}$$ ... 8.15/Pg 89, DHB

$c_3 = 0.62$, for CI ... Tb 8.5/Pg 97, DHB

$$t = (500 \times 250 \times 0.62) \times \sqrt{\dfrac{1.5}{40(500^2+250^2)}}$$

$t = 26.85$ mm.

Also for a rectangular plate with all edges supported,

$$\sigma_b = \frac{0.5b^2 p}{t^2\left[1+0.623\left(\dfrac{b^6}{a^6}\right)\right]} \quad \ldots \text{Tble 8.7-(13)/ Pg100, DHB}$$

$$40 = \frac{0.5 \times 250^2 \times 1.5}{t^2\left[1+0.623\left(\dfrac{250^6}{500^6}\right)\right]}$$

$t = 34.06$ mm.

Selecting higher value for design, we have $t = 34.06$ mm ≈ 35 mm.

55. Determine the thickness of a CI pipe 400 m inside diameter subjected to an internal pressure of 0.6 MPa. The allowable stress for the pipe material is 14 MPa and the joint factor is 0.85. Take corrosion allowance as 1.5 mm.

Solution: $d_i = 400$ mm, $p = 0.6$ MPa, $f = 14$ MPa, $J = 0.85$, $C = 1.5$ mm

We know that the minimum thickness is

$$t = \frac{pD_i}{2fJ - p} \quad \ldots \text{8.1/Pg 86, DHB}$$

$$t = \frac{0.6 \times 400}{2 \times 14 \times 0.85 - 0.6}$$

$t = 10.35$ mm ≈ 10.5 mm

56. A cast steel cylinder of 300 mm internal diameter is to contain liquid at a pressure of 12.5 N/mm². It is closed at both ends by unstayed flat cover plates rigidly bolted to the shell flange. Determine the thickness of the cover plates if the allowable working stress for the cover material is 75 N/mm².

[VTU–June/July 2009–05 Marks]

Solution: Material: Cast steel—brittle; unstayed flat plate, $d_i = 300$ mm, $p = 12.5$ N/mm², $f = 75$ N/mm², $t = ?$

For an unstayed flat circular plate, $t = CD\sqrt{p/f}$ ... 8.6/Pg 87, DHB

Here $D = d_i$, $p = p_i$

$C = 0.42$ (bolted)   ... Tb 8.1/Pg 91, DHB

$t = 0.42 \times 300\sqrt{12.5/75}$

$t = 51.4$ mm

Also, $\sigma_t = \dfrac{3F}{4\pi t^2}$ ... Eq. (i) Tb 8.7-(2)/Pg 98, DHB

$F = \pi r_0^2 p$ ... Tb 8.7-(2)/Pg 98, DHB

$= \pi \times 150^2 \times 12.5$ ... ($r_0 = r_i = d_i/2$)

$F = 883.57 \times 10^3$ N

Eq. (i) yields ... $75 = \dfrac{3 \times 883.57 \times 10^3}{4\pi t^2}$

$t = 53$ mm.

Adopt higher value for design, we have $t = 53$ mm ≈ 55 mm.

57. A cast steel cylinder of 350 mm inside diameter is to contain liquid at a pressure of 13.5 N/mm². It is closed at both ends by flat cover plates which are made of alloy steel and are attached by bolts.

i. Determine the wall thickness of the cylinder, if the maximum hoop stress in the cylinder is limited to 55 MPa.
ii. Calculate the minimum thickness necessary of the cover plates if the working stress is not to exceed 65 MPa.   *[VTU-Dec 10–8 Marks]*

Solution: Material: Cast steel—brittle; $p_i = 13.5$ N/mm², $d_i = 350$ mm
i. $t = ?$, $\sigma_t = 55$ MPa   ii. $t = ?$, $f = 65$ MPa

i. *To find t, when* $\sigma_t = 55$ MPa

We know that for a brittle material,

$$t = \frac{d_i}{2}\left[\sqrt{\frac{\sigma_t + p_i}{\sigma_t - p_i}} - 1\right]$$ ...7.22/Pg 80, DHB

$$= \frac{350}{2}\left[\sqrt{\frac{55 + 13.5}{55 - 13.5}} - 1\right]$$

$t = 49.83$ mm ≈ 50 mm

ii. *To find t, when* $f = 65$ MPa

For an unstayed flat circular plate,

$$t = CD\sqrt{(p/f)}$$ ...8.6/Pg 87, DHB

$D = d_i$, $p = p_i$
$C = 0.42$ (bolted)   ...Tb 8.1/Pg 91, DHB

$t = 0.42 \times 350\sqrt{13.5/65}$
$t = 67$ mm

58. A circular plate made of steel and of diameter 200 mm with thickness 10 mm is subjected to a load inducing a pressure of 4 MPa. Taking $E = 201$ kN/mm², Poisson's ratio = 0.3, determine:

i. The maximum stress, its location and maximum deflection when the edges of the plate are supported.
ii. The maximum stress, its location and maximum deflection when the edge of the plate is fixed.   *[VTU-Dec 11–10 Marks]*

Solution: $d_i = 200$ mm, $t = 10$ mm, $p = 4$ MPa, $E = 201 \times 10^3$ N/mm², $\mu = 0.3 = 1/m$, hence $m = 3.34$

σ_{max} and its location y_{max};
  i. Edges are supported
  ii. Edges are fixed

i. *Edges are supported:*

The maximum stress in a circular plate when the edge is supported is

$$\sigma_{max} = \sigma_t = \frac{-3F(m+1)}{8\pi m t^2}$$ ...Tb 8.7-(1)/Pg 98, DHB

$$F = \pi r_0^2 p$$ ...Tb 8.7-(1)/Pg 98, DHB

$$= \pi \times 100^2 \times 4 \qquad \ldots (r_0 = r_i = d_i/2)$$
$$F = 125.66 \times 10^3 \text{ N}$$
$$\sigma_{max} = \frac{-3 \times 125.66 \times 10^3 (3.34 + 1)}{8\pi \times 3.34 \times 10^2}$$
$$\sigma_{max} = -195 \text{ MPa (compressive)}$$

Deflection, $y_{max} = \dfrac{3F(m-1)(5m+1)r_0^2}{16\pi E m^2 t^3}$ ...Tb8.7-(1)/Pg 98, DHB

$$= \frac{3 \times 125.66 \times 10^3 (3.34-1)(5 \times 3.34 + 1)100^2}{16\pi \times 201 \times 10^3 \times 3.34^2 \times 10^3}$$
$$y_{max} = 1.385 \text{ mm}$$

ii. Edges are fixed: The maximum stress in a circular plate when the edge is supported is

$$\sigma_{max} = \sigma_t = \frac{3F}{4\pi t^2} \qquad \ldots \text{Tb 8.7-(2)/Pg 98, DHB}$$
$$= \frac{3 \times 125.66 \times 10^3}{4\pi \times 10^2}$$
$$\sigma_{max} = 300 \text{ MPa}$$

Deflection, $y_{max} = \dfrac{3F(m^2-1)r_0^2}{16\pi E m^2 t^3}$ ... Tb 8.7-(2)/Pg 98, DHB

$$= \frac{3 \times 125.66 \times 10^3 (3.34^2 - 1) \times 100^2}{16\pi \times 201 \times 10^3 \times 3.34^2 \times 10^3}$$
$$y_{max} = 0.339 \text{ mm}.$$

VTU QUESTION PAPERS

Feb. 2002 (ME6T2)

1. a. Discuss the stress distribution pattern in curved beams when compared to straight beams with sketches. **(4 Marks)**
   b. A machine member has a *T* shaped cross-section and is loaded as shown in **Fig. 1.46**. If the allowable compressive stress is 50 MPa, determine the largest force '*P*' which may be applied to the member safely. **(16 Marks)**

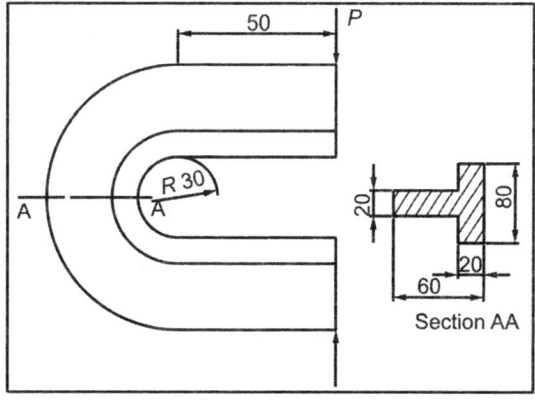

Fig. 1.46

July/August 2002 (ME6T2)

2. Taking a permissible stress in the material as 100 MPa, estimate the thickness "t" for the cross-section shown in **Fig. 1.47**. Determine the maximum stress induced in the material of the member shown considering curved beam effect. By how much the factor of safety is reduced if the ultimate strength of the material is 440 MPa.

(20 Marks)

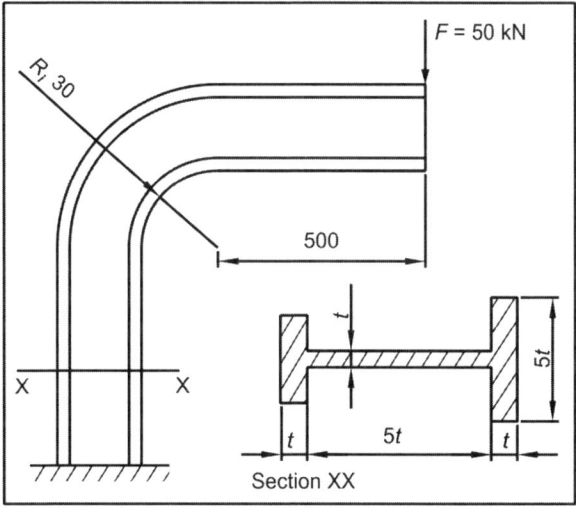

Fig. 1.47

Jan./Feb. 2003 (ME6T2)

3. a. List the main differences between straight and curved beams. **(05 Marks)**
   b. A crane hook has a section which, for purpose of analysis, is considered as trapezoidal. The dimensions are shown in **Fig. 1.48**. Determine the maximum stresses and the location. **(15 Marks)**

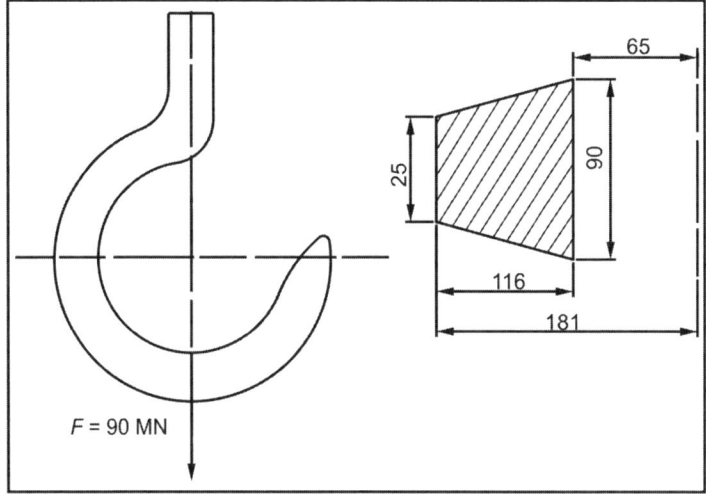

Fig. 1.48

July/August 2003 (ME6T2)

4. a. Using usual notations, prove the moment of resistance M of a curved beam of initial radius R_1 when bent to radius R_2 by uniform bending moment is

$$M = EAh^2 \left(\frac{1}{R_2} - \frac{1}{R_1} \right)$$ (10 Marks)

b. A chain link made of 40 mm diameter rod is semicircular at each end, the mean diameter of which is 80 mm. The straight sides of the link are also 80 mm. If the link carries a load of 90 kN, estimate the tensile and compressive stresses in the link along the section of load line. (10 Marks)

July/August 2004 (ME6T2)

5. a. Discuss the stress distribution pattern in curved and straight beams with appropriate sketches. (04 Marks)

b. Determine the safe load 'F' that the frame of a punch press shown in **Fig. 1.49** can carry considering the cross-section along section A – A for an allowable tensile stress of 100 MPa. What is the stress at the outer fiber for the above load? What will be the stress at the inner fiber, if the beam is a straight beam for the above load? (16 Marks)

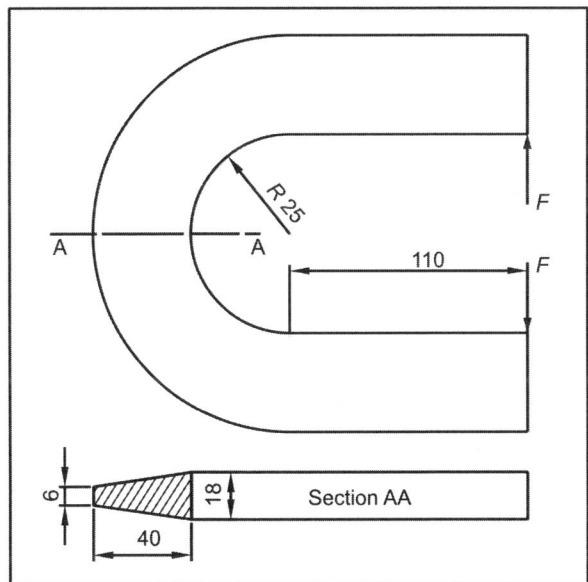

Fig. 1.49

Jan./Feb. 2005 (ME6T2)

6. a. Give the differences between a straight beam and a curved beam. (04 Marks)

b. The cross-section of steel crane hook is a trapezium with an inner side of 50 mm and outer side of 25 mm. The depth of the section is 64 mm. The center of curvature of the section is at a distance of 64 mm from the inner edge of the section and the line of action of load is 50 mm from the same edge. Determine the maximum load the hook can carry if the allowable strength is limited to 60 MPa. (16 Marks)

Jan./Feb. 2005 (AU53)

7. Determine the value of t in the cross-section of a curved beam as shown in **Fig. 1.50**, such that the normal stresses due to bending at the extreme fibers are numerically equal. **(10 Marks)**

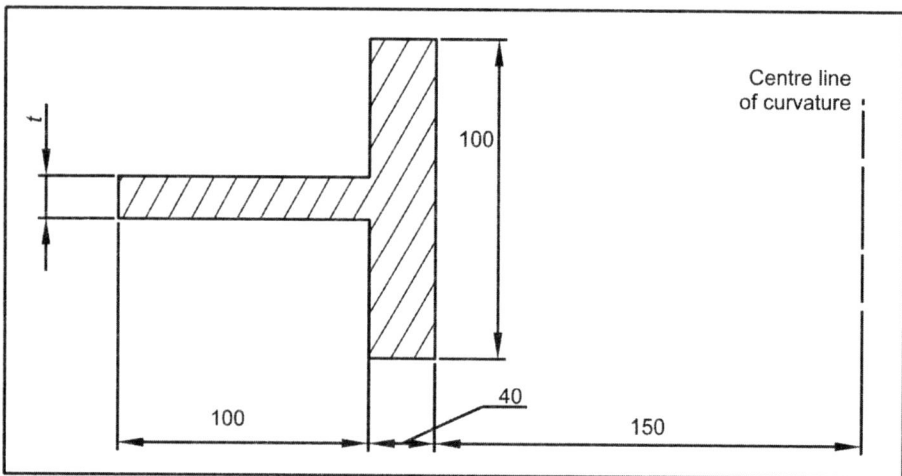

Fig. 1.50

July/August 2005 (AU53)

8. The section of a crane hook is a trapezium, whose inner and outer sides are 80 mm and 40 mm respectively and has a depth of 100 mm. The center of curvature of the section is at a distance of 120 mm from the inner side of the section and the load line is 110 mm from the same point. Find the maximum load the hook can carry if the maximum stress is not to exceed 70 MPa. **(10 Marks)**

Jan./Feb. 2006 (AU53)

9. Determine a safe value for load P for a machine element loaded as shown in **Fig. 1.51**, limiting the maximum normal stress induced on the cross-section XX to 120 MPa. **(10 Marks)**

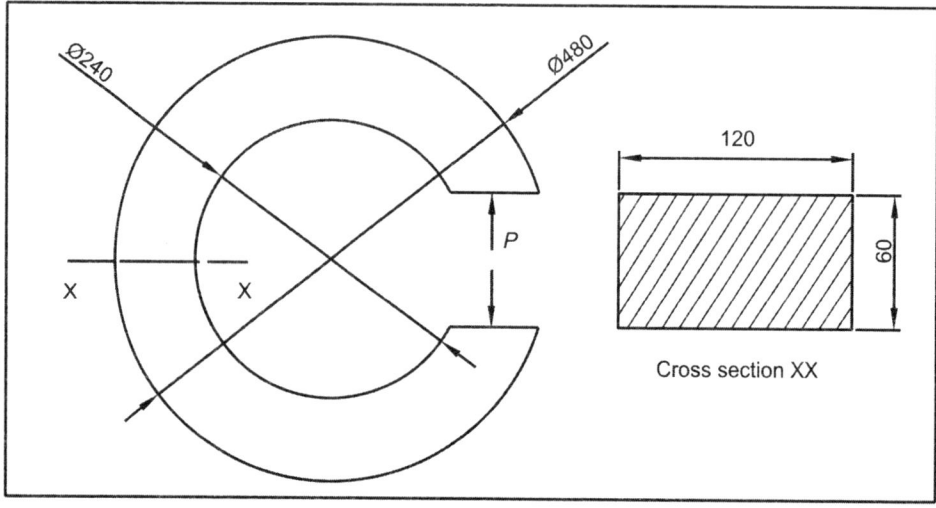

Fig. 1.51

July 2006 (AU53)

10. a. Explain why curved beams have to be analyzed for stresses specially when we already have straight beam equations for determining the stresses? **(04 Marks)**
    b. The beam shown in **Fig. 1.52** is subjected to a load of 50 kN. Determine the stresses at the inner and outer fibers. Plot the stress distribution. **(16 Marks)**

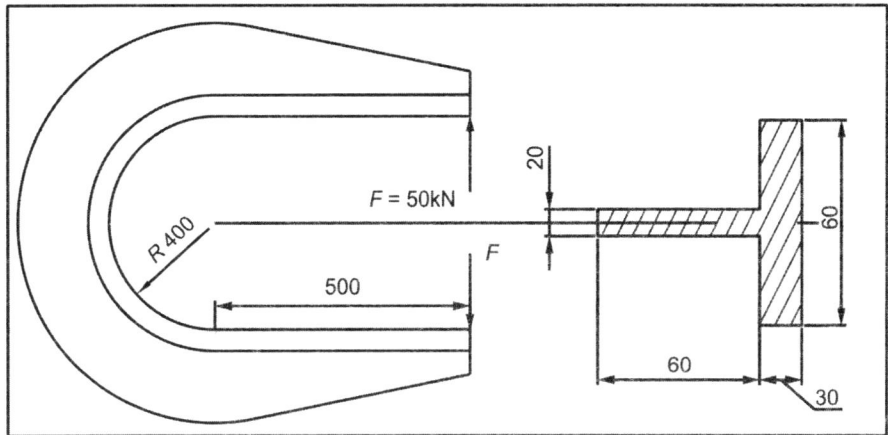

Fig. 1.52

Dec. 06/Jan. 07 (AU53)

11. Compute the combined stresses at the inner and outer fibres in the critical section of a crane hook which is required to lift loads up to 25 kN. The hook has trapezoidal cross-section with parallel sides 60 mm and 30 mm, the distance between them being 90 mm. The inner radius of the hook is 100 mm. The load line is nearer to the inner surface of the hook by 25 mm than the center of curvature at the critical section. What will be the stresses at the inner and outer fibre, if the beam is treated as straight beam for the given load? **(12 Marks)**

July 2007 (AU53)

12. Calculate the stresses at the points A and B for a circular beam as shown in **Fig. 1.53**. The circular beam is subjected to a compressive load of 6 kN. **(10 Marks)**

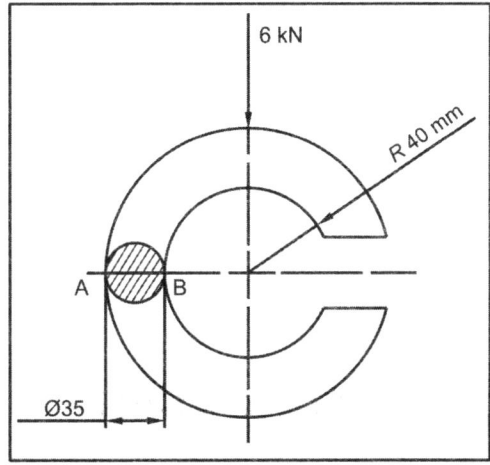

Fig. 1.53

Dec. 07/Jan. 08 ((AU53)

13. The section of a crane hook is trapezoidal, whose inner and outer sides are 90 mm and 25 mm respectively and has a depth of 116 mm. The center of curvature of the section is at a distance of 65 mm from the inner side of the section and the load line passes through the center of curvature. Find the maximum load the hook can carry, if the maximum stress is not to exceed 70 MPa. **(12 Marks)**

Dec. 07/Jan. 08 (ME6T2)

14. a. Derive an expression for normal stresses due to bending, across the cross-section of a curved beam. **(08 Marks)**
    b. Compute the stresses in critical section of a crane hook which is required to lift loads up to 50 kN. The hook has trapezoidal cross-section with parallel sides 100 mm and 60 mm. The distance between them is 120 mm. Inner radius of the hook is 150 mm. **(12 Marks)**

June/July 08 (AU53)

15. a. Differentiate between a straight beam and a curved beam with stress distribution in each of the beam. **(04 Marks)**
    b. **Figure 1.54** shows a 100 kN crane hook with a trapezoidal section. Determine stress in the outer, inner, and also at the neutral fiber and draw the stress distribution across the section AB. **(16 Marks)**

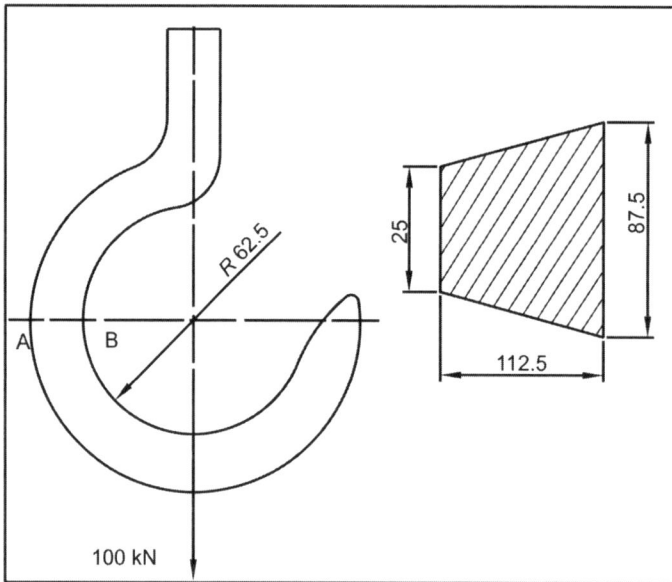

Fig. 1.54

Dec. 08/Jan. 09 (ME6T2)

16. a. Derive an expression for normal stress due to bending, across the section of a curved beam. **(08 Marks)**
    b. Compute the stresses in critical section of a crane hook which is required to lift loads up to 50 kN. The hook has trapezoidal cross-section with parallel sides 100 mm and 60 mm. The distance between them is 120 mm, inner radius of the hook is 150 mm. **(12 Marks)**

June-July 2009 (ME6T2)

17. a. Give the differences between a straight beam and a curved beam. **(04 Marks)**

    b. The cross-section of a steel crane hook is a trapezium with an inner side of 50 mm and outer side of 25 mm. The depth of section is 64 mm. The center of curvature of the section is at a distance of 64 mm from the inner edge of the section and the line of action of the load is 50 mm from the same edge. Determine the maximum load the hook can carry if the allowable stress is limited to 60 MPa. **(16 Marks)**

Dec. 08/Jan. 09 (AU53)

18. A closed ring is made up of 50 mm diameter steel bar having allowable tensile stress of 200 MPa. The inner diameter of the ring is 100 mm. For a load of 30 kN, find the maximum stress in the bar and specify the location. If the ring is cut as shown in **part B** of **Fig. 1.55**, check whether it is safe to support the applied load. **(10 Marks)**

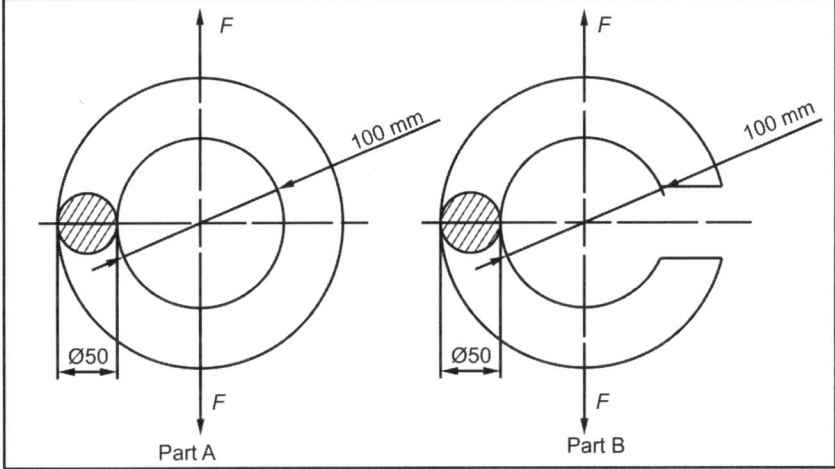

Fig. 1.55

June-July 2009 (AU53)

19. The horizontal cross-section of a crane hook is an isosceles triangle of 120 mm deep, the inner width being 90 mm. The hook carries a load of 50 kN. Inner radius of curvature is 100 mm. The line of action of load passes through the center line of curvature. Determine the stress at the extreme fibres. **(12 Marks)**

June-July 2009 (06ME61)

20. a. What are the assumptions made in finding stress distribution for a curved flexural member? Also state two major differences between a straight beam and a curved beam. **(05 Marks)**

    b. Determine the value of thickness in the T-cross-section of a curved beam shown in **Fig. 1.56** such that the normal stresses due to bending at the extreme inner and outer fibers are numerically equal. **(15 Marks)**

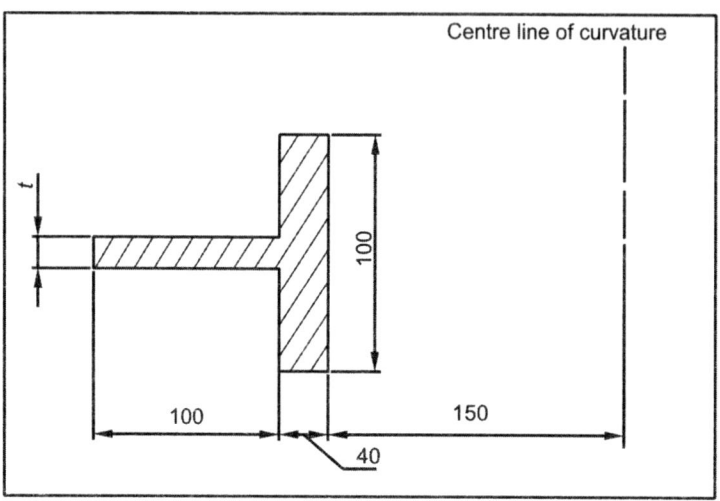

Fig. 1.56

21. a. A cast steel cylinder of 300 mm internal diameter is to contain liquid at a pressure of 12.5 N/mm². It is closed at both ends by unstayed flat cover plates rigidly bolted to the shell flange. Determine the thickness of the cover plates if the allowable working stress for the cover material is 75 N/mm². **(05 Marks)**

b. Design a shrink fit joint to join two cylinders of diameter 150 × 200 mm and 200 × 250 mm. The maximum tangential stress in the components due to shrink fitting is to be limited to 40 MPa. Also determine the axial force necessary to disengage the joint if the length of the joint is 200 mm and the maximum power that can be transmitted at the rated speed of 1000 rpm. The cylinder material has a modulus of elasticity of 210 GPa and Poison's ratio is 0.3. **(15 Marks)**

Dec. 09/Jan. 10 (06ME61)

22. a. Determine the maximum stress induced in a ring cross-section of 50 mm diameter rod subjected to a compressive load of 20 kN. The mean diameter of the ring is 100 mm. **(10 Marks)**

b. A cast iron cylinder of internal diameter 200 mm and thickness 50 mm is subjected to a pressure of 5 N/mm². Calculate the tangential and radial stresses at the inner, middle and outer surface. **(10 Marks)**

May/June 2010 (AU53)

23. The frame of a punch press is shown in **Fig. 1.57**. Find the stresses at the inner and outer fibers at section X – X of the frame, if W = 5000 N. **(10 Marks)**

Dec. 2010 (AU53)

24. A central horizontal section of a crane hook is a symmetrical trapezium of 100 mm deep, the inner width being 60 mm and the outer width being 40 mm. The crane hook carries a load of 25 kN. The inner radius of the hook is 75 mm. The load line is nearer to the inner surface of the hook by 25 mm than the center of curvature at the critical section. Determine the extreme fiber stresses. **(10 Marks)**

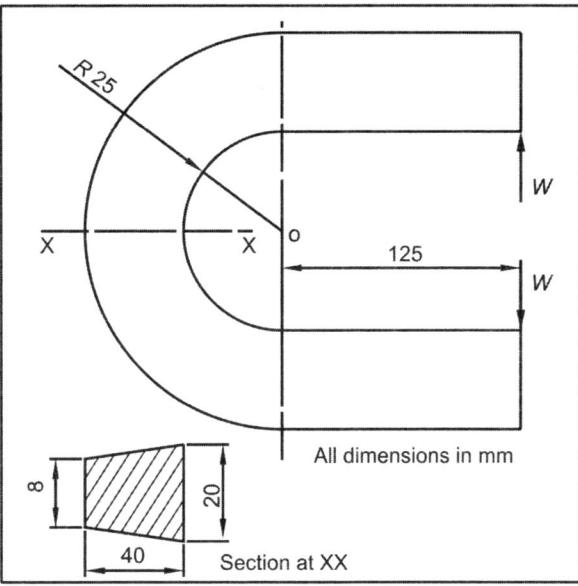

Fig. 1.57

May/June 2010 (06ME61)

25. a. Derive expression for extreme fiber stresses in a curved beam subjected to pure bending. **(08 Marks)**

    b. Determine the combined stresses at the inner and outer fibers at the critical section of a crane hook which is required to lift loads up to 50 kN. The hook has trapezoidal cross-section with inner and outer sides of 90 mm and 40 mm respectively. Depth is 120 mm. The center of curvature of the section is at a distance of 100 mm from the inner side of the section and the load line passes through the center of curvature. Also, determine the factor of safety according to max shear stress theory if $\tau_{allow} = 80$ MPa. **(12 Marks)**

26. a. With reference to pressure vessels, what is autofrettage? Explain. **(04 Marks)**

    b. A high pressure cylinder consists of an inner cylinder of ID and OD 200 mm and 300 mm respectively. It is jacketed by an outer cylinder of OD 400 mm. The difference between the OD and the ID of inner cylinder and inner diameter of the jacket before assembly is 0.25 mm. $E = 2.07 \times 10^5$ MPa. Calculate the shrinkage pressure and stress induced in cylinders due to shrinkage pressure. In service, the cylinder is further subjected to an internal pressure of 200 MPa. Plot the resultant stress distribution. **(16 Marks)**

Dec. 2010 (06ME61)

27. a. Derive an expression for normal stresses due to bending at the extreme fibers on the cross-section of a curved machine member. **(08 Marks)**

    b. Determine the value of 't' in the cross-section of a curved machine member shown in **Fig. 1.58**, so that the normal stresses due to bending at extreme fibers are numerically equal. Also determine the normal stresses so induced at extreme fibers due to bending moment of 10 kN-m. **(12 Marks)**

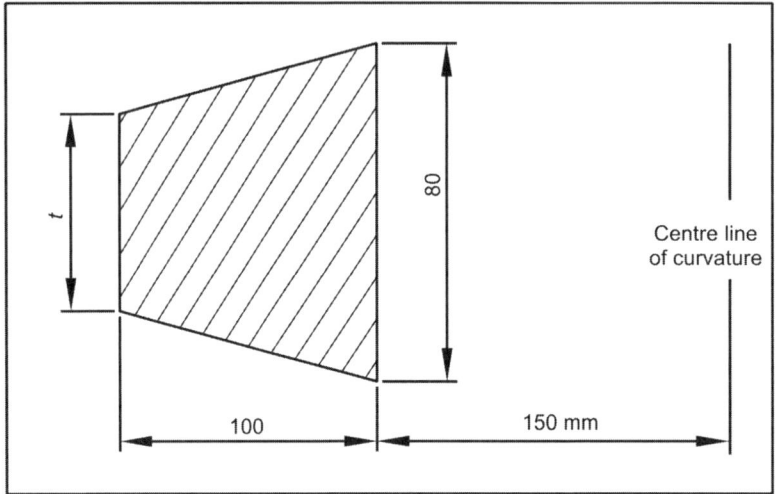

Fig. 1.58

28. a. A cast steel cylinder of 350 mm inside diameter is to contain liquid at a pressure of 13.5 N/mm². It is closed at both ends by flat cover plates which are made of alloy steel and are attached by bolts.
   i. Determine the wall thickness of the cylinder, if the maximum hoop stress in the cylinder is limited to 55 MPa.
   ii. Calculate the minimum thickness necessary of the cover plates if the working stress is not to exceed 65 MPa. **(08 Marks)**
   b. A shrink fit assembly, formed by shrinking one cylinder over another, is subjected to an external pressure of 60 MPa. Before the fluid is admitted, the internal and external diameters of the assembly are 120 mm and 200 mm respectively and the diameter at the junction is 160 mm. If after shrinking on, the contact pressure at the junction is 8 MPa, determine using Lame's equation, the stresses at the inner, mating and outer surfaces of the assembly after the fluid has been admitted. **(12 Marks)**

June/July 2011 (06ME61)

29. a. Determine the dimensions of the curved bar as shown in **Fig. 1.59**. Assume $\sigma_{yt} = 400$ N/mm² and FOS = 3.5. **(12 Marks)**
   b. Briefly discuss about any four types of springs, with suitable sketches. **(08 Marks)**

30. A tube with 50 mm and 75 mm inner and outer diameters respectively is reinforced by shrinking a jacket of outer diameter 100 mm. The compound tube has to withstand an internal pressure of 35 MPa. Calculate the shrinkage allowance such that the maximum tangential stress in each tube has same magnitude. Also calculate the shrinkage pressure and show the distribution of tangential stresses. Assume $E = 207$ kN/mm². **(20 Marks)**

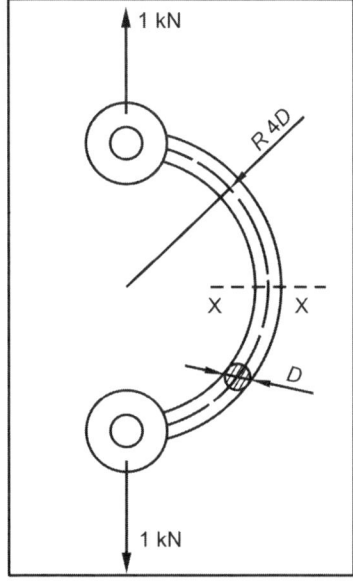

Fig. 1.59

Dec. 2011 (06ME61)

31. a. Give the differences between a straight beam and a curved beam. **(04 Marks)**
  b. The cross-section of a steel crane hook is a trapezium with an inner side of 50 mm and outer side of 25 mm, the depth of the section is 64 mm. The center of curvature of the section is at a distance of 64 mm from the inner edge of the section and the line of action of the load is 50 mm from the same edge. Determine the maximum load the hook can carry if the allowable strength is limited to 60 MPa. **(16 Marks)**

32. a. Derive Lame's equation for thick cylinder. **(10 Marks)**
  b. A circular plate made of steel and of diameter 200 mm with thickness 10 mm is subjected to a load inducing a pressure of 4 MPa. Taking $E = 201 kN/mm^2$, Poisson's ratio = 0.3, determine:
  i. The maximum stress, its location and maximum deflection when the edges of the plate are supported.
  ii. The maximum stress, its location and maximum deflection when the edge of the plate is fixed. **(10 Marks)**

June 2012 (06ME61)

33. a. Compare the stresses due to bending moment applied in a straight beam and a curved beam. **(05 Marks)**
  b. The parallel sides of a trapezoidal cross-section of a crane hook of capacity 50 kN are 100 mm and 60 mm. The depth of the section being 120 mm. The radius of curvature of inner fiber is 150 mm as shown in **Fig. 1.60.** Determine the stresses at the extreme members of the cross-section of the crane hook. **(15 Marks)**

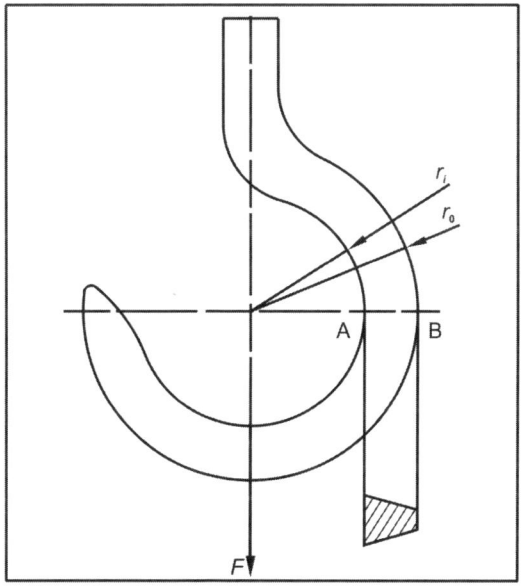

Fig. 1.60

34. a. In an air operated press, the piston rod of the operating cylinder must exert a force of 4000 N. the air pressure in the cylinder is 0.7 MPa. Calculate the bore of the cylinder, assuming that overall friction due to stuffing box and piston packaging is equivalent to 8% of the maximum force exerted by the piston rod.

Determine the thickness of the cylinder assuming it as seamless tubing with an allowable stress of 21MPa. **(06 Marks)**

b. A steel hub 440 mm outside diameter, 250 mm inside diameter and 300 mm length has an interference fit with a shaft of 250 mm diameter. The torque to be transmitted is 30×10^4 N-m. The permissible stress for the material of the shaft and hub is 120 MPa. The coefficient of friction is 0.18. Determine:
  i. The contact pressure
  ii. Interference required
  iii. The tangential stress at the inner and outer surfaces of the hub
  iv. Force required to assemble
  v. Radial stress at the inner and outer diameter of the hub. **(14 Marks)**

December 2012 (06ME12)

35. a. Differentiate between a straight beam and a curved beam. **(04 Marks)**
   b. Compute the combined stresses at the inner and outer fibres in a critical cross-section of a crane hook which is required to lift loads upto 25 kN. The hook has trapezoidal cross-section with parallel sides 60 mm and 30 mm, the distance between them being 90 mm. The inner radius of the hook is 100 mm. The load line is nearer to the inner surface of the hook by 25 mm than the center of curvature at the critical section. What will be the stresses at the inner and outer fiber, if the beam is treated as straight beam for the given load? **(16 Marks)**

36. a. A cast iron cylindrical pipe of outside diameter 300 mm and inside diameter 200 mm is subjected to an internal fluid pressure of 20 N/mm² and external fluid pressure of 5 N/mm². Determine the tangential and radial stresses at the inner, middle and outer surface. **(10 Marks)**
   b. A cylinder is provided with a head of flat circular steel plate of 500 mm diameter and is supported around the edge. It is subjected to a uniform pressure of 5 N/m². The allowable working stress for the material is 70 N/mm² and Poisson's ratio is 0.3. Determine:
   i. Thickness of the thick cylinder wall and
   ii. Thickness of circular flat cylinder head. **(10 Marks)**

June/July 2013 (AU53)

37. A link of S – shape made of steel bar is shown in **Fig. 1.61**. It is made of steel 45C8 with 380 MPa and factor of safety is 4.5. Calculate the dimensions of the link. **(10 Marks)**

June/July 2013 (06ME61)

38. a. Clearly state five assumptions used in determining the stress distribution in a curved flexural member. **(05 Marks)**

   b. **Figure 1.62** shows a frame of a punching machine and its various dimensions.

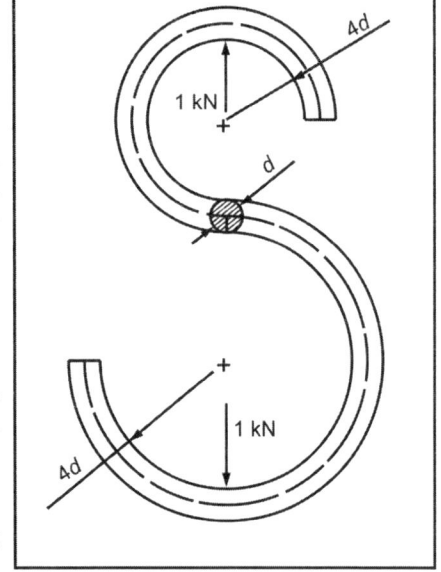

Fig. 1.61

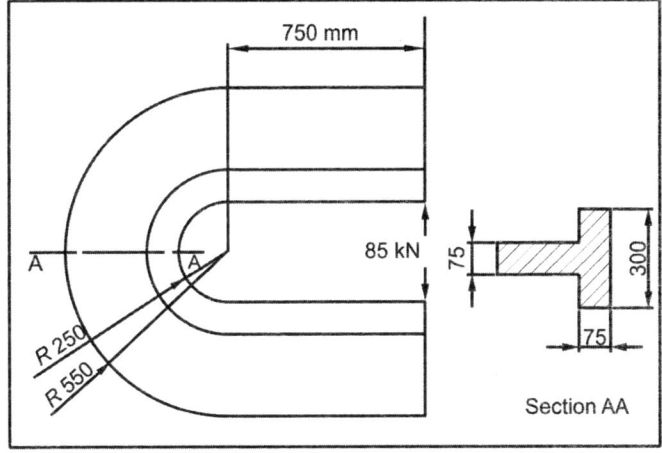

Fig. 1.62

Determine the combined stress at the inner and outer fibers. Also find the maximum shear stress and its location. Take the force as 85 kN. **(15 Marks)**

39. a. A domestic gas cylinder made of CI has an allowable tensile stress of 45 MPa. If the internal pressure is 1.5 MPa, find the wall thickness of the cylinder. Take cylinder diameter as 300 mm. **(05 Marks)**
    b. A CI cylinder of ID 300 mm and wall thickness 40 mm carries a fluid under pressure of 6 MPa. Find the tangential and radial stresses across the wall of the cylinder at every 10 mm. Also plot the stress distribution. **(15 Marks)**

June/July 2013 (10ME62)

40. a. The cross-section of a steel crane hook is a trapezium with an inner side of 50 mm and outer side of 25 mm, the depth of the section is 64 mm. The center of curvature of the section is at a distance of 64 mm from the inner edge of the section and the line of action of the load is 50 mm from the same edge. Determine the maximum load the hook can carry if the allowable strength is limited to 60 MPa. **(10 Marks)**
    b. A cast iron cylindrical pipe of outside diameter 300 mm and inside diameter 200 mm is subjected to an internal fluid pressure of 20 N/mm² and external fluid pressure of 5 N/mm². Determine the tangential and radial stresses at the inner, middle and outer surface. Sketch the tangential and radial distribution across its thickness. **(15 Marks)**

Dec. 2013/Jan. 2014 (10ME62)

41. a. A curved link mechanism made from a round steel bar is shown in **Fig. 1.63**. The material for the link is plain carbon steel 30C8 with an allowable yield strength of 400 MPa. Determine the factor of safety. **(10 Marks)**
    b. A high pressure cylinder consists of a steel tube with inner and outer diameters of 20 mm and 40 mm respectively. It is jacketed by an outer steel tube with an outer diameter of 60 mm. The tubes are assembled by shrinking process in such a way that the maximum principal stress induced in any tube is limited to 100 MPa. Calculate the shrinkage pressure and the original dimensions of the tubes. Take the Young's modulus as 207 GPa. **(10 Marks)**

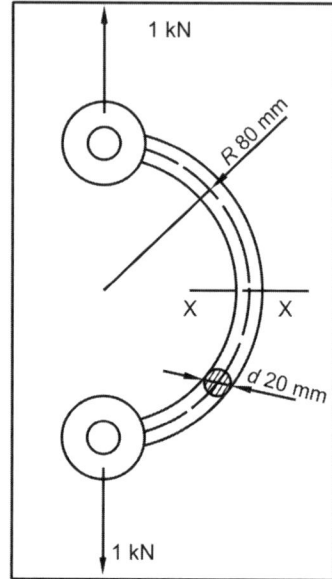

Fig. 1.63

Dec. 2013/Jan. 2014 (AU53)

42. A curved machine member is loaded as shown in **Fig. 1.64**. Determine the maximum tensile stress induced and locate that point. **(10 Marks)**

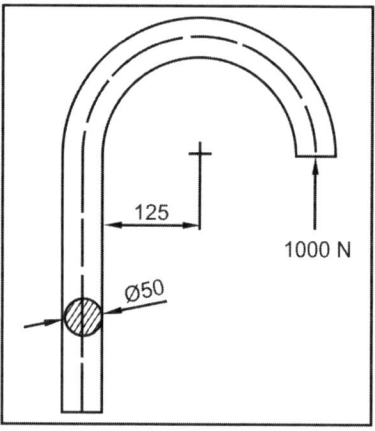

Fig. 1.64

2

Belt, Rope and Chain Drives

2.1 INTRODUCTION

Power transmission from one shaft to another may be accomplished in many ways; some of them include belt drives, chain drives, gear drives, timing belts, etc. These elements are referred to as flexible elements -or- power transmission elements and employ friction for transmission of power.

Power transmission elements may be of flexible type -or-non-flexible type. Flexible elements are those wherein the center distance between the members (driving and driven) can be changed and if the center distance is fixed then we refer them as non-flexible members/elements.

Examples of flexible members include–belt drives (flat and V-type), chain drives and rope drives (wire and rope), while gears drives, couplings and clutches refer to non-flexible elements.

Flexible members are usually employed when the distance between the centers is too large. Since these elements are elastic, they play an important part in absorbing shock loads and in damping out the effects of vibration.

2.2 SELECTION OF A BELT DRIVE

The selection of a belt drive depends on various factors such as:
- Space available.
- Service conditions.
- Power to be transmitted.
- Speed of the driving and driven shafts.
- Speed reduction ratio.
- Centre distance between the shafts.

2.3 MATERIALS USED FOR BELTS

The material used for belts and ropes must be strong, flexible, and durable. It must have a high coefficient of friction. The belts, according to the material used, are classified as follows:
1. Leather belts
   a. Oak tanned
   b. Chrome tanned
2. Cotton –or- fabric belts
3. Rubber belts
4. Balata belts
5. Camel's hair belts.

2.4 FLAT BELT DRIVES

A flat belt drive is one wherein the width of the belt is larger than the thickness. These are used where a large amount of power has to be transmitted between pulleys. The flat belt is the simplest type, often made from leather -or- rubber-coated fabric. This is typically limited to low torque applications since the driving force is restricted -or- limited by the pure friction between the belt and the sheave.

A flat belt is said to be open type if the pulleys rotate in the same direction and cross type if the pulleys rotate in opposite direction.

2.5 LENGTH OF OPEN BELT DRIVE

Consider an open belt drive as shown in **Fig. 2.1**. Let

R = radius of the larger pulley (driver)
r = radius of smaller pulley (driven)
C = center distance between pulleys
L = total length of the belt
ϕ = angle of wrap
θ_S = angle of contact of smaller pulley
θ_L = angle of contact of larger pulley.

From **Fig. 2.1**, the total length of the belt is,

$L = arc\ (ABC) + CD + arc\ (DEF) + FA$
$= 2[arc\ (AB) + CD + arc\ (DE)]$

[since $arc\ (AB) = arc\ (BC)$, $arc\ (DE) = arc\ (EF)$ and $CD = AF$]

$$L = 2\left[\left(\frac{\pi}{2}+\phi\right)R + CD + \left(\frac{\pi}{2}-\phi\right)r\right] \qquad \ldots \text{(Eq. 2.1)}$$

From $\Delta\ C_1C_2G$, $\sin\phi = \dfrac{GC_1}{C_1G_2} = \dfrac{CC_1 - CG}{C_1C_2} = \dfrac{R-r}{C}$

$$\phi = \sin^{-1}\left(\frac{R-r}{C}\right) \qquad \ldots \text{(Eq. 2.1a)}$$

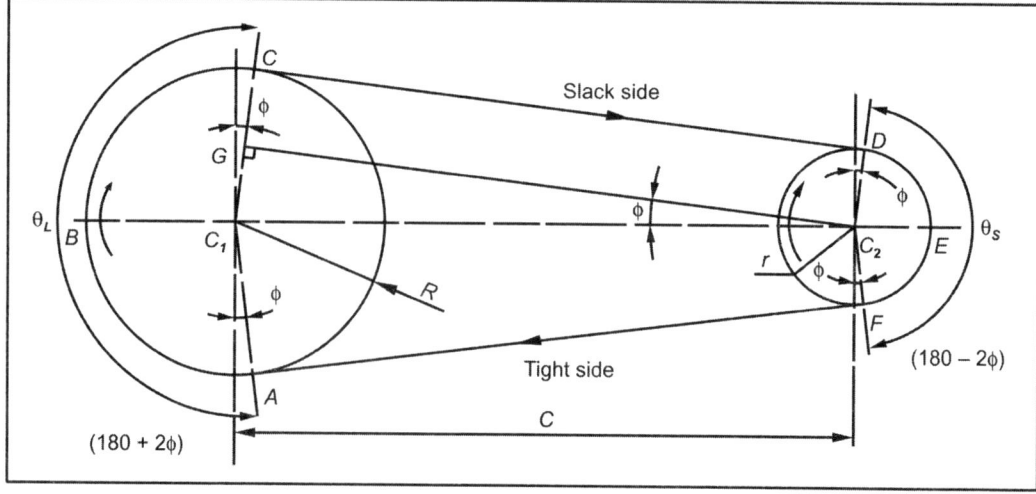

Fig. 2.1: Open belt drive

Since ϕ is very small, therefore $\sin \phi \approx \phi$, thus $\phi = \left(\dfrac{R-r}{C}\right)$

Also length CD = length GC_2

Therefore, $\cos \phi = \dfrac{GC_2}{C_1 G_2} = \dfrac{GC_2}{C}$ ... (Eq. 2.2)

$CD = GC_2 = C(\cos \phi)$ ... (Eq. 2.3)

But $\cos \phi = \sqrt{1 - \sin^2 \phi} = \left(1 - \sin^2 \phi\right)^{1/2}$

Eq. (2.3) yields ... $CD = C\{1 - \sin^2\phi\}^{1/2}$

Expanding Eq. (2.3) (using Binomial theorem) we have,

$$CD = C\left\{1 - \dfrac{\sin^2 \phi}{2} + \ldots\right\}$$

Substituting CD in Eq. (2.1) yields

$$L = 2\left[\left(\dfrac{\pi}{2} + \phi\right)R + C\left\{1 - \dfrac{\sin^2 \phi}{2} + \ldots\right\} + \left(\dfrac{\pi}{2} - \phi\right)r\right]$$

Neglecting higher order terms, we have

$$L = 2\left[\dfrac{\pi R}{2} + \phi R + C - \dfrac{C(\sin^2 \phi)}{2} + \dfrac{\pi r}{2} - \phi r\right]$$

$$= 2\left[\dfrac{\pi(R+r)}{2} + \phi(R-r) + C - \dfrac{C(\sin^2 \phi)}{2}\right]$$

$$= \pi(R+r) + 2\phi(R-r) + 2C - C(\sin^2\phi)$$

$$= \pi(R+r) + 2(R-r)\left(\dfrac{R-r}{C}\right) + 2C - C\left(\dfrac{R-r}{C}\right)^2 \quad \ldots \text{using (Eq. 2.1a)}$$

$$= \pi(R+r) + 2\dfrac{(R-r)^2}{C} + 2C - \dfrac{(R-r)^2}{C}$$

$$L = \pi(R+r) + \dfrac{(R-r)^2}{C} + 2C \quad \ldots \text{(Eq. 2.4)}$$

In terms of diameter,

$$L = \dfrac{\pi(D+d)}{2} + \dfrac{(D-d)^2}{2C} + 2C \quad \ldots \text{(Eq. 2.4a) } \textbf{14.3/Pg 238, DHB}$$

Note:
- *Angle of contact of larger pulley,*

$$\boldsymbol{\theta_L = \pi + 2\sin^{-1}\left(\dfrac{D-d}{2C}\right)} \quad \ldots \text{(degrees) } \textbf{14.1b/Pg 238, DHB}$$

$$\boldsymbol{\theta_L \approx \pi + \left(\dfrac{D-d}{C}\right)} \quad \ldots \text{(radians) } \textbf{14.1b/Pg 238, DHB}$$

- *Angle of contact of smaller pulley,*

$$\boldsymbol{\theta_S = \pi - 2\sin^{-1}\left(\dfrac{D-d}{2C}\right)} \quad \ldots \text{(degrees) } \textbf{14.1a/Pg 238, DHB}$$

$$\theta_s \approx \pi - \left(\frac{D-d}{C}\right) \quad \ldots \text{(radians)} \ \textbf{14.1a/Pg 238, DHB}$$

2.6 LENGTH OF CROSS BELT DRIVE

Consider a cross belt drive as shown in **Fig. 2.2**. Let
- R = radius of the larger pulley (driver)
- r = radius of smaller pulley (driven)
- C = center distance between pulleys
- L = total length of the belt
- ϕ = angle of wrap
- θ_s = angle of contact of smaller pulley
- θ_L = angle of contact of larger pulley.

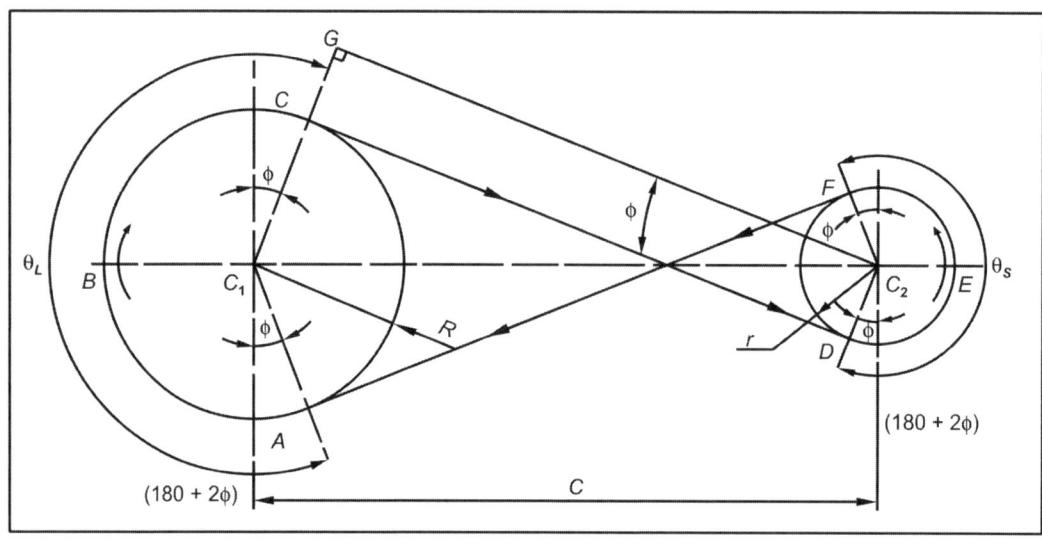

Fig. 2.2: Cross belt drive

From **Fig. 2.2**, the total length of the belt is,
$$L = arc\ (ABC) + CD + arc\ (DEF) + FA$$
$$= 2[arc\ (AB) + CD + arc\ (DE)]$$
[since $arc\ (AB) = arc\ (BC)$, $arc\ (DE) = arc\ (EF)$ and $CD = AF$]

$$L = 2\left[\left(\frac{\pi}{2}+\phi\right)R + CD + \left(\frac{\pi}{2}+\phi\right)r\right] \quad \ldots \text{(Eq. 2.5)}$$

From $\Delta\ C_1C_2G$, $\quad \sin\phi = \dfrac{GC_1}{C_1C_2} = \dfrac{CC_1 + CG_1}{C_1C_2} = \dfrac{R+r}{C}$

$$\phi = \sin^{-1}\left(\frac{R+r}{C}\right) \quad \ldots \text{(Eq. 2.5a)}$$

Since ϕ is very small, therefore $\sin\phi \approx \phi$, thus $\phi = \left(\dfrac{R+r}{C}\right)$

Also length $\quad CD = $ length GC_2 $\quad \ldots \text{(Eq. 2.6)}$

Therefore,
$$\cos\phi = \frac{GC_2}{C_1C_2} = \frac{GC_2}{C}$$
$$CD = GC_2 = C(\cos\phi) \qquad \text{...(Eq. 2.7)}$$

But
$$\cos\phi = \sqrt{1-\sin^2\phi} = (1-\sin^2\phi)^{1/2}$$

Eq. (2.7) yields ... $CD = C\{(1-\sin^2\phi)^{1/2}\}$

Expanding Eq. (2.7) (using Binomial theorem) we have,
$$CD = C\left\{1 - \frac{\sin^2\phi}{2} + ...\right\}$$

Substituting CD in Eq. (2.5) yields
$$L = 2\left[\left(\frac{\pi}{2}+\phi\right)R + C\left\{1 - \frac{\sin^2\phi}{2} + ...\right\} + \left(\frac{\pi}{2}+\phi\right)r\right]$$

Neglecting higher order terms, we have
$$L = 2\left[\frac{\pi R}{2} + \phi R + C - \frac{C(\sin^2\phi)}{2} + \frac{\pi R}{2} + \phi r\right]$$
$$= 2\left[\frac{\pi(R+r)}{2} + \phi(R+r) + C - \frac{C(\sin^2\phi)}{2}\right]$$
$$= \pi(R+r) + 2\phi(R+r) + 2C - C(\sin^2\pi)$$
$$= \pi(R+r) + 2(R+r)\left(\frac{R+r}{C}\right) + 2C - C\left(\frac{R+r}{C}\right)^2$$
$$\text{...using (Eq. 2.5a)}$$
$$= \pi(R+r) + 2\frac{(R+r)^2}{C} + 2C - \frac{(R+r)^2}{C}$$
$$L = \pi(R+r) + \frac{(R+r)^2}{C} + 2C \qquad \text{...(Eq. 2.8)}$$

In terms of diameter,
$$L = \frac{\pi(D+d)}{2} + \frac{(D+d)^2}{4C} + 2C \qquad \text{....(Eq. 2.8a)}$$

or
$$L = \left[\frac{\pi}{2} + \frac{(D+d)}{2C}\right](D+d) + \sqrt{2C^2 - (D+d)^2}$$
$$\text{...(Eq. 2.8b) } \mathbf{14.4/Pg\ 238,\ DHB}$$

Note:
- Angle of contact for larger as well as smaller pulleys for cross belt drive is

$$\theta_s = \theta_L = \pi + 2\sin^{-1}\left(\frac{(D+d)}{2C}\right) \quad \text{...(degrees) } \mathbf{14.2/Pg\ 238,\ DHB}$$

$$\theta_s = \theta_L \approx \pi + \left(\frac{(D+d)}{C}\right) \quad \text{...(radians) } \mathbf{14.2/Pg\ 238,\ DHB}$$

- In order to provide initial tension in belt, the actual length of the belt is made slightly less than the calculated length. The decrease in length depends upon the initial tension to be given in the belt and the belt material. *The reduction in length for a leather belt varies from 0.25 to 1.0% of calculated length.*

2.7 CENTER DISTANCE

The life of a belt is a function of center distance between the driver and driven pulleys. If the belt is shorter, it will be subjected to additional bending stresses thereby leading to failure.

- For smaller width pulleys, center distance: $C > (2 \times \text{diameter of larger pulley})$
- For larger width pulleys, center distance: $C > (4 \times \text{diameter of larger pulley})$, for cross drive
  $C < (20 \times \text{width of pulley})$

In case of flat belt drives, the center distance may be 15 meters but the best center distance ranges from 6 m to 7.5 m. The center distance may also be found by the following relations:

$$C = (0.07 \text{ to } 0.01)v$$
-or-
$$C \geq (1.5 - 2)(D + d) \qquad \ldots \textbf{14.5/Pg 238, DHB}$$

v = belt speed (m/s),
D = diameter of larger pulley,
d = diameter of smaller pulley.

2.8 VELOCITY RATIO OF BELT DRIVE

Consider a belt drive as shown in **Fig. 2.1**
Let
D = diameter of larger pulley
d = diameter of smaller pulley
N_L = speed of larger pulley (rpm)
N_S = speed of smaller pulley (rpm)

The velocity of the larger pulley per minute, $v_L = \dfrac{\pi D N_L}{60}$

The velocity of the smaller pulley per minute, $v_S = \dfrac{\pi d N_S}{60}$

Assuming that there is no slip between the belt and the pulleys,
$$v_L = v_S$$
$$\frac{\pi D N_L}{60} = \frac{\pi D N_S}{60}$$
$$N_L D = N_S d$$

The *velocity ratio* is defined as the ratio of speed of driver pulley to that of driven pulley. Assuming that the smaller pulley is the driver pulley and the larger as driven pulley, we have

$$\text{Velocity ratio} = \frac{N_S}{N_L} = \frac{D}{d} \qquad \ldots \text{(Eq. 2.9)}$$

If the thickness of the belt is considered, then

$$\text{Velocity ratio} = \frac{N_S}{N_L} = \frac{D+t}{d+t} \qquad \ldots \text{(Eq. 2.10)}$$

If slip is taken into account, then

$$\text{Velocity ratio} = \frac{N_S}{N_L} = \frac{(D+t)\times(1-\epsilon)}{d+t} \quad \ldots \text{(Eq. 2.11)}$$

ϵ = slip factor (0.01 – 0.03)

Slip: Slip is defined as the relative motion between the pulley and the belt, i.e. the difference between the linear speeds of pulley and the belt. Slip can be avoided by increasing the coefficient of friction or by increasing the angle of contact between pulley and belt.

2.9 RATIO OF DRIVING TENSIONS IN FLAT BELTS

Consider a driven pulley rotating in clockwise direction as shown in **Fig. 2.3**.

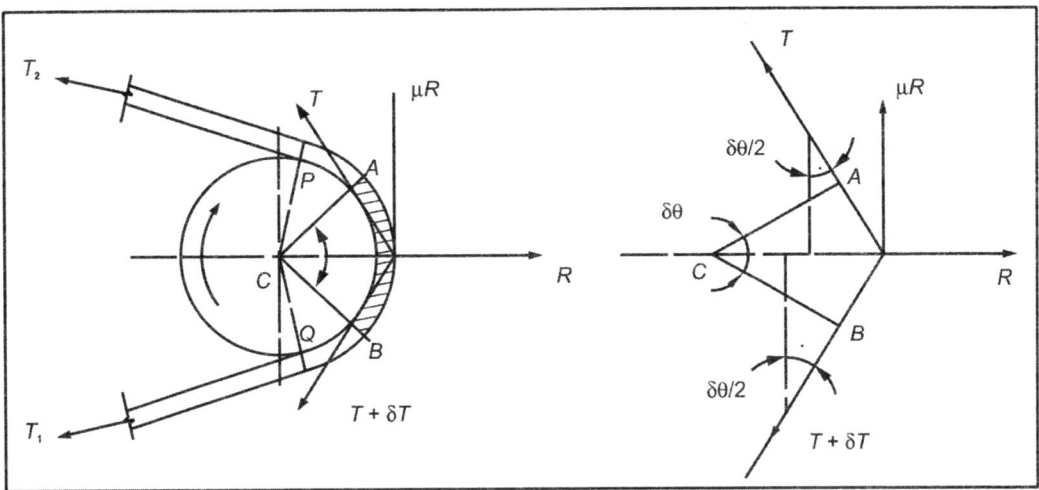

Fig. 2.3: Ratio of driving tensions in flat belts

Let
 T_1 = tension on tight side of the belt
 T_2 = tension on slack side of the belt
 θ = angle of contact -or- lap angle
 μ = coefficient of friction between the pulley and the belt.

Consider a small element AB subtending an angle $\delta\theta$ at the center of the pulley. This element is in equilibrium under the following forces.
- Tension T in the belt at A
- Tension $(T + \delta T)$ in the belt at B
- Normal reaction R
- Frictional force μR

The components of force are shown in **Fig. 2.4**

Resolving the forces horizontally, we have

$$R = x + x'$$
$$= T \sin(\delta\theta/2) + (T + \delta T)\sin(\delta\theta/2)$$
$$R = 2T \sin(\delta\theta/2) + \delta T \sin(\delta\theta/2)$$

Since $\delta\theta$ is very small, letting $\sin(\delta\theta/2) \approx \delta\theta/2$

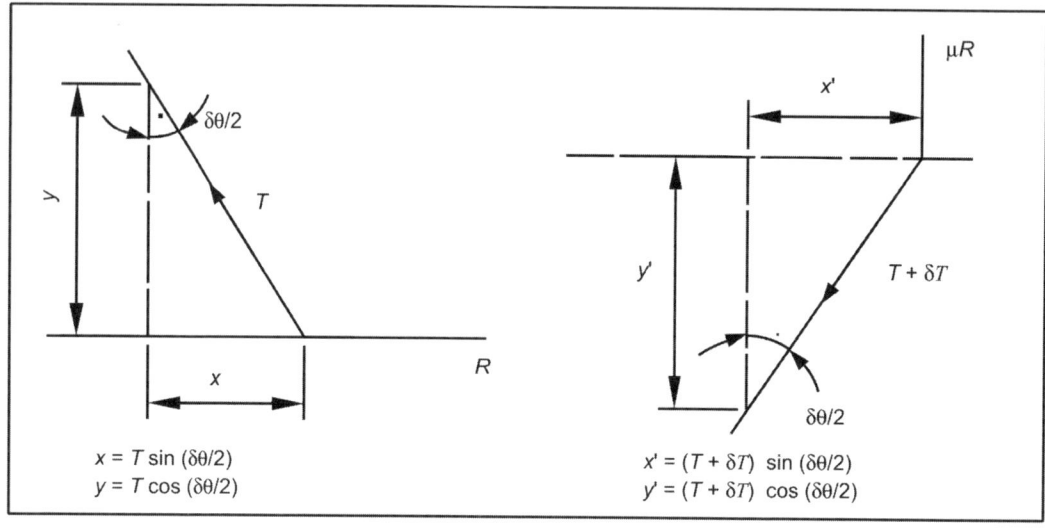

Fig. 2.4: Components of force

$$R = 2T(\delta\theta/2) + \delta T \sin(\delta\theta/2)$$

Neglecting $\delta T(\delta\theta/2)$, we have

$$R = 2T(\delta\theta/2)$$
$$R = T\,\delta\theta \quad \ldots \text{(Eq. 2.12)}$$

Resolving the forces vertically, we have

$$\mu R + y = y'$$
$$\mu R = (T + \delta T)\cos(\delta\theta/2) - T\cos(\delta\theta/2)$$
$$\mu R = \delta T \cos(\delta\theta/2)$$

Since $\cos(\delta\theta/2) \approx 1$, we have

$$\mu R = \delta T \quad \ldots \text{(Eq. 2.13)}$$

Substituting Eq. (2.12) in Eq. (2.13) yields

$$\mu(T\,\delta\theta) = \delta T$$
$$\mu\,\delta\theta = \delta T/T \quad \ldots \text{(Eq. 2.13a)}$$

Integrating between the limits T_1 and T_2

$$\int_0^\theta \mu\,d\theta = \int_{T_2}^{T_1} \frac{\delta T}{T}$$

$$\mu\theta = \ln T \Big|_{T_2}^{T_1} = \ln(T_1 - T_2)$$

$$\mu\theta = \ln\left(\frac{T_1}{T_2}\right)$$

$$\frac{T_1}{T_2} = e^{\mu\theta} \quad \ldots \text{(Eq. 2.14) } \mathbf{14.6a/Pg\ 238,\ DHB}$$

In terms of stress,

$$\frac{\sigma_1}{\sigma_2} = e^{\mu\theta} \quad \ldots \text{(Eq. 2.15) } \mathbf{14.6b/Pg\ 238,\ DHB}$$

σ_1 = unit tension on tight side of the belt (N/mm²)
σ_2 = unit tension on slack side of the belt (N/mm²)

μ = coefficient of friction and depends upon material of the belt, material of the pulley, slip of the belt and speed of the belt

According to CG Barth, $\mu = 0.54 - \dfrac{0.712}{2.542 + V}$ ... **14.6d/Pg 238, DHB**

Note:
- *The design is based on pulley having smaller value of "$\mu\theta$"*
- *If μ is unknown, then select the value of μ based on velocity of belt from* **Table 14.4/Pg 253, DHB**
- *In general the term diameters (D and d) refer to pitch diameter of pulleys.*
- *Table 14.1/Pg 251, DHB gives the data for leather belt.*
- *Table 14.2/Pg 252, DHB gives values of $e^{\mu\theta}$, for various values of $\mu\theta$.*
- *Table 14.3/Pg 253, DHB gives coefficients of friction for various Belt and Pulley materials.*
- *Table 14.4/Pg 253, DHB gives values of μ based on velocity of leather belt on iron pulleys.*
- *Table 14.5/Pg 254, DHB gives allowable tension in N per mm width of belt.*
- *Table 14.6/Pg 254, DHB gives the relative strength (efficiency) of belt based on the type of joint.*
- *Table 14.10a/Pg 258, DHB gives the nominal belt widths of friction surface rubber transmission belting (mm).*
- *Table 14.10b/Pg 258, DHB gives the thickness of friction surface rubber transmission belting.*
- *Table 14.10e/Pg 259, DHB gives the minimum pulley diameters for given belt speeds and belt plies (mm).*
- *Table 14.7/Pg 255, DHB gives the rating in kW/mm of width = Oak-tanned leather belts.*
- *Table 14.11b/Pg 260, DHB gives the nominal diameters of cast iron and mild steel pulleys.*

2.10 CENTRIFUGAL TENSION

Whenever a particle of mass m is rotated in a circular path of radius r at a uniform angular velocity ω, there exist a centripetal acceleration of $\omega^2 r$ and the force causing this is called the centripetal force $= \dfrac{m}{g}\omega^2 r$.

This centripetal force is applied by the radial inward component of tension T_c acting at either ends of the elementary piece of belt as shown in **Fig. 2.5**. The centrifugal force

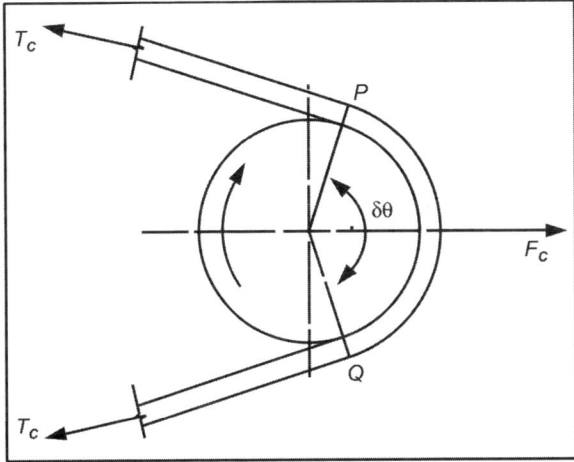

Fig. 2.5: Centrifugal tension

F_c acting radially outwards is balanced by the components of T_c acting radially inwards. This tension T_c is called the *centrifugal tension* and may be found by the forces acting on elemental piece when no power is being transmitted.

Consider an elemental length of belt subtending an angle as shown in **Fig. 2.5**. Let

w' = weight of the belt per meter length (N/m)
v = linear velocity of the belt
b = width of the belt
t = thickness of the belt
r = radius of pulley

From **Fig. 2.5**, length of the belt $PQ = r\,\delta\theta$
Weight of elemental length = $w'(r\,\delta\theta)$

Therefore, centrifugal force, $F_c = \dfrac{w'(r\,\delta\theta)}{g}\omega^2 r$

But
$$\omega = \dfrac{v}{r} \qquad \ldots \text{(Eq. 2.16)}$$

$$F_c = \dfrac{w'(r\,\delta\theta)}{g}\left(\dfrac{v}{r}\right)^2 r$$

$$F_c = \dfrac{w'v^2}{g}\delta\theta \qquad \ldots \text{(Eq. 2.17)}$$

The element of the belt is in equilibrium under the two forces T_c acting tangentially at extremities and the force F_c.

Resolving the forces horizontally

$$F_c = T_c \sin(\delta\theta/2) + T_c \sin(\delta\theta/2)$$
$$\therefore\ F_c = 2T_c \sin(\delta\theta/2)$$

Since $\delta\theta$ is very small, letting $\sin(\delta\theta/2) \approx \delta\theta/2$

$$F_c = 2T_c (\delta\theta/2)$$
$$F_c = 2T_c\,\delta\theta$$

i.e. $\dfrac{w'v^2}{g}\delta\theta = T_c\,\delta\theta$ \qquad ...using (Eq. 2.17)

$$T_c = \dfrac{w'v^2}{g}\,N \qquad \ldots \text{(Eq. 2.18)}\ \mathbf{14.7a/Pg\ 239,\ DHB}$$

w' – N/m [(w'/l), $l = 1$ meter]

Also weight density $\quad w = \dfrac{w'}{\text{volume}} = \dfrac{w'}{(bt)l} = \dfrac{w'}{(bt)} \qquad (l = 1\ \text{meter})$

Eq. (2.18) yields ... $\quad T_c = \dfrac{v^2}{g}(w = \text{volume})$

$$= \dfrac{w(bt)v^2}{g} \qquad (\text{Here } b \text{ and } t \text{ are in mm})$$

$$T_c = \dfrac{wbtv^2}{10^6\,g}\,N \qquad \ldots \text{(Eq. 2.19)}\ \mathbf{14.7a/Pg\ 239,\ DHB}$$

Here b and t are in meters, W–N/m^3, $\omega = \rho g$

We know that stress in the belt is $\sigma = \dfrac{T}{a} = \dfrac{T}{bt}$

Hence centrifugal stress, $\sigma = \dfrac{T}{a} = \dfrac{wbtv^2}{10^6 g}\left(\dfrac{1}{a}\right)$

$$\sigma_c = \dfrac{wbtv^2}{10^6 g}\left(\dfrac{1}{bt}\right)$$

$$\sigma_c = \dfrac{wv^2}{10^6 g} \qquad \ldots \text{(Eq. 2.20)} \ \ \textbf{14.7b/Pg 239, DHB}$$

From Eqs (2.18) and (2.19) it is observed that T_c is independent of T_1 and T_2, but depends upon velocity of the belt. The effect of centrifugal tension is to reduce the driving power of belt.

Note:
- *Centrifugal tension is considered if $v > 10$ m/s*
- *Maximum tension on tight side of the belt, $T = T_{max} = T_1 + T_c$* ... (Eq. 2.20a)
- *Maximum tension on slack side of the belt, $T = T_{max} = T_2 + T_c$* ... (Eq. 2.20b)

2.11 RATIO OF DRIVING TENSIONS IN FLAT BELTS CONSIDERING CENTRIFUGAL TENSION

Consider a pulley rotating in clockwise direction as shown in **Fig. 2.6**.

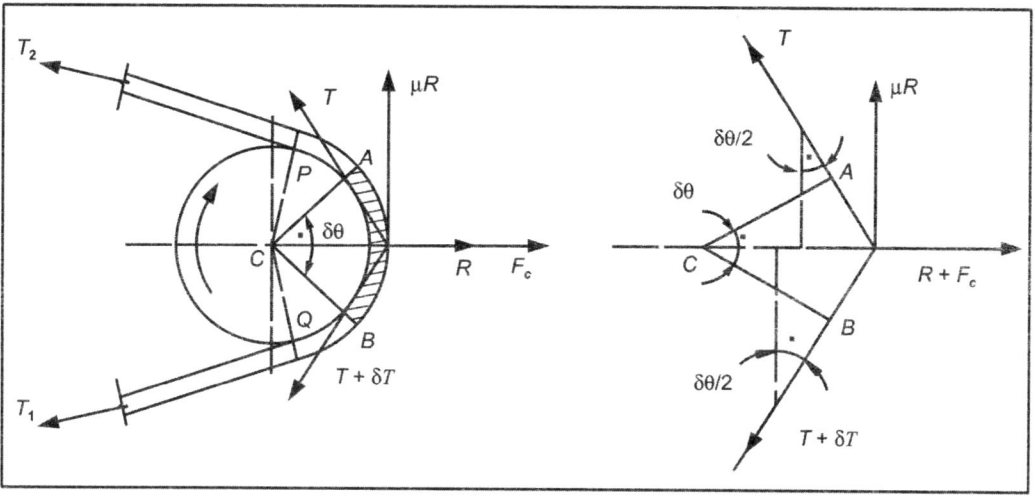

Fig. 2.6: Ratio of driving tensions in flat belts considering centrifugal tension

Let
  T_1 = tension on tight side of the belt
  T_2 = tension on slack side of the belt
  θ = angle of contact -or- lap angle
  μ = coefficient of friction between the pulley and the belt.

Consider a small element AB subtending an angle $\delta\theta$ at the center of the pulley. This element is in equilibrium under the following forces.
- Tension T in the belt at A
- Tension $(T + \delta T)$ in the belt at B

- Normal reaction R and centrifugal force F_c
- Frictional force μR.

The components of force are shown in **Fig. 2.7.**

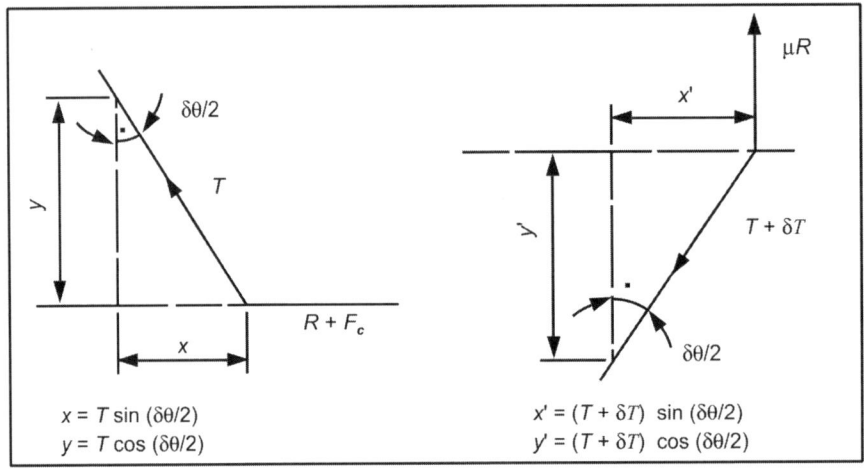

$x = T \sin(\delta\theta/2)$
$y = T \cos(\delta\theta/2)$

$x' = (T + \delta T) \sin(\delta\theta/2)$
$y' = (T + \delta T) \cos(\delta\theta/2)$

Fig. 2.7: Components of force considering centrifugal tension

Resolving the forces horizontally, we have
$$R + F_c = x + x'$$
$$= T \sin(\delta\theta/2) + (T + \delta T) \sin(\delta\theta/2)$$
$$R + F_c = 2T \sin(\delta\theta/2) + \delta T \sin(\delta\theta/2)$$

Since $\delta\theta$ is very small, letting $\sin(\delta\theta/2) \approx \delta\theta/2$
$$R + F_c = 2T (\delta\theta/2) + \delta T (\delta\theta/2)$$

Neglecting $\delta T (\delta\theta/2)$, we have
$$R + F_c = 2T (\delta\theta/2)$$
$$R + F_c = T \delta\theta \qquad \ldots \text{(Eq. 2.21)}$$

But
$$F_c = \frac{w'v^2}{g} \delta\theta = T_c \delta\theta \qquad \ldots \text{using (Eq. 2.17)}$$

$$R = T \delta\theta = T_c \delta\theta$$
$$R = (T - T_c) \delta\theta \qquad \ldots \text{(Eq. 2.22)}$$

Resolving the forces vertically, we have
$$\mu R + y = y'$$
$$\mu R = (T + \delta T) \cos(\delta\theta/2) - T \cos(\delta\theta/2)$$
$$\mu R = \delta T \cos(\delta\theta/2)$$

Since $\cos(\delta\theta/2) \approx 1$, we have
$$\mu R = \delta T \qquad \ldots \text{(Eq. 2.23)}$$

Substituting Eq. (2.22) in Eq. (2.23) yields
$$\mu(T - T_c) \delta\theta = \delta T$$
$$\mu \delta\theta = \delta T/(T - T_c) \qquad \ldots \text{(Eq. 2.23a)}$$

Integrating between the limits T_1 and T_2

ρ = density
σ = stress

$$\int_0^\theta \mu d\theta = \int_{T_2}^{T_1} \frac{\delta T}{T - T_c}$$

$$\mu\theta = \ln(T - T_c)\Big|_{T_2}^{T_1} = \left[\ln(T_1 - T_c) - \ln(T_2 - T_c)\right]$$

$$\mu\theta = \ln\left(\frac{T_1 - T_c}{T_2 - T_c}\right)$$

$$\frac{T_1 - T_c}{T_2 - T_c} = e^{\mu\theta} \qquad \ldots \text{(Eq. 2.24) } \mathbf{14.6c/Pg\ 238,\ DHB}$$

In terms of stress,

$$\frac{\sigma_1 - \sigma_c}{\sigma_2 - \sigma_c} = e^{\mu\theta} \qquad \ldots \text{(Eq. 2.25) } \mathbf{14.6d/Pg\ 238,\ DHB}$$

2.12 POWER TRANSMITTED BY FLAT BELTS

Let,
T_1 = tension on tight side of the belt
T_2 = tension on slack side of the belt
v = velocity of the belt

then effective pull -or- effective tension in the belt,

$$F_t = (T_1 - T_2) \qquad \ldots \text{(Eq. 2.26) } \mathbf{14.8/Pg\ 239,\ DHB}$$

and work done per second, = Power, $P = F_t v = (T_1 - T_2)v$

i.e. work done,

$$P = \frac{(T_1 - T_2)}{1000}(\text{kW}) \qquad \ldots \text{(Eq. 2.27)}$$

-or-

$$P = \frac{btv}{1000}\left[\rho_d - \frac{wv^2}{16^6 g}\right]\left(\frac{e^{\mu\theta} - 1}{e^{\mu\theta}}\right) \quad (\text{kW})$$

$$\ldots \text{(Eq. 2.28) } \mathbf{14.9a/Pg\ 239,\ DHB}$$

Where,
σ_d = design stress in leather belt (20.6 MPa)
b = width of the belt (mm)
t = thickness of the belt (mm)
w = density of the belt material (N/m³)

Note: $\dfrac{wv^2}{g} = \dfrac{(N/m^3)(m^2/s^2)}{m/s^2} = \dfrac{N}{m^2} = \dfrac{1}{10^6} N/mm^2$

Also power transmitted per mm² of belt is obtained using the following relations:
- At high velocity,

$$P = \frac{(\sigma_d - \sigma_c)v}{1000} = \left(\frac{e^{\mu\theta} - 1}{e^{\mu\theta}}\right) \text{ kW/mm}^2 \quad \ldots \text{(Eq. 2.29) } \mathbf{14.10a/Pg\ 239,\ DHB}$$

- At low velocity,

$$P = \frac{\sigma_d v}{1000}\left(\frac{e^{\mu\theta} - 1}{e^{\mu\theta}}\right) \text{ kW/mm}^2 \quad \ldots \text{(Eq. 2.30) } \mathbf{14.10c/Pg\ 239,\ DHB}$$

2.13 CONDITION FOR MAXIMUM POWER TRANSMISSION

The effect of centrifugal tension is to decrease the driving power of the belt. T_c increases with increase in velocity which in turn increases the power transmitted; but the value of T_1 and consequently the value of $(T_1 - T_2)$ diminishes. Hence power transmitted increases with increase in speed up to a certain value of velocity and then decreases. Thus there exists a certain velocity at which the power transmitted by the belt is maximum.

Let,

T_{max} = maximum permissible tension in a given belt.
T_1 = tension on tight side of the belt
T_2 = tension on slack side of the belt
T_c = centrifugal tension
v = velocity of the belt

We know that the power transmitted b the belt,

$$P = \frac{(T_1 - T_2)v}{1000} \quad \text{...using 14.9a/Pg 239, DHB}$$

But

$$\frac{T_1}{T_2} = e^{\mu\theta} \quad \text{...using 14.6a/Pg 238, DHB}$$

$$\frac{T_1}{e^{\mu\theta}} = T_2$$

$$p = \left(T_1 - \frac{T_1}{e^{\mu\theta}}\right)\frac{v}{1000}$$

$$p = \frac{T_1 v}{1000}\left(\frac{e^{\mu\theta} - 1}{e^{\mu\theta}}\right)$$

Let, $\quad k = \frac{1}{1000}\left(\dfrac{e^{\mu\theta} - 1}{e^{\mu\theta}}\right)$

Therefore, $\quad P = T_1 k v \quad$ ...(Eq. 2.31)

But the maximum tension in the belt is

$$T_{max} = T_1 + T_c \quad \text{...(Eq. 2.32)}$$

Substituting Eq. (2.32) in Eq. (2.31) yields

$$P = (T_{max} - T_c)kv$$

$$P = \left(T_{max} - \frac{w'v^2}{g}\right)kv$$

...(Eq. 2.33) using **14.7a/Pg 239, DHB**

For maximum power, differentiating the above Eq. (2.33) with respect to v and equating to zero

i.e.

$$\frac{dP}{dv} = 0$$

$$\frac{d}{dv}\left\{\left(T_{max} - \frac{w'v^2}{g}\right)kv\right\} = 0$$

$$\frac{d}{dv}\left(T_{max}v - \frac{w'v^3}{g}\right) = 0$$

$$\left(T_{max} - \frac{3w'v^2}{g}\right) = 0$$

$$T_{max} = \frac{3w'v^2}{g} = 3T_c \qquad \ldots \text{(Eq. 2.34)}$$

or
$$v = \sqrt{\frac{T_{max}\, g}{3w'}} \qquad \ldots \text{(Eq. 2.34a)}$$

Thus the power transmitted is maximum, when 1/3rd of maximum tension is absorbed as centrifugal tension $T_c = \dfrac{T_{max}}{3}$

Equation (2.32) yields …
$$T_1 = 2T_c = \frac{2T_{max}}{3} \qquad \ldots \text{(Eq. 2.35)}$$

or
$$T_c = \frac{T_1}{2} \text{ or } T_c = \frac{T_{max}}{3} \qquad \ldots \text{(Eq. 2.35a)}$$

2.14 INITIAL TENSION IN THE BELT

In order to transmit the required amount of power, the belt is given an initial tension (T_0) by reducing the length of the belt through a small percentage than that of calculated value. When the power is being transmitted between pulleys, the tight side of the belt stretches until the pull is increased from T_0 to T_1 and slack side shortens until the pull reduces from T_0 to T_2.

i.e. tension on tight side of the belt = $(T_1 - T_0)$
tension on slack side of the belt = $(T_0 - T_2)$

Since the belt remains unchanged, the mean tension should also remain unchanged,
i.e. tension on tight side of the belt = tension on slack side of the belt
-or- increase of stretch on tight side = decrease of stretch on slack side

$$(T_1 - T_0) = (T_0 - T_2)$$

$$\frac{T_1 + T_2}{2} = 2T_0 \qquad \ldots \text{(Eq. 2.36)}$$

If is considered, we have,
$$T_0 = \frac{T_1 + T_2 + 2T_c}{2} \qquad \ldots \text{(Eq. 2.37)}$$

Eq. (2.36) is based on the assumption that the belt material is perfectly elastic. In actual practice the belt is not perfectly elastic, therefore $(T_1 + T_2) > 2T_0$.

According to Barth, Eq. (2.36) is written as
$$\sqrt{T_1} + \sqrt{T_2} = 2\sqrt{T_0} \qquad \ldots \text{(Eq. 2.38)} \ \textbf{14.12/Pg 240, DHB}$$

2.15 EFFECT OF INITIAL TENSION ON FLAT BELTS

We know that the initial tension considering centrifugal tension is
$$T_0 = \frac{T_1 + T_2 + 2T_c}{2} \qquad \ldots using \text{ (Eq. 2.37)}$$

i.e.
$$(T_1 + T_2) = 2(T_0 + T_c) \qquad \ldots \text{(Eq. 2.39)}$$

But
$$\frac{T_1}{T_2} = e^{\mu\theta} = k \text{ (Say)} \qquad \ldots \text{using } \textbf{14.6a/Pg 238, DHB}$$

Eq. (1.39) yields ...

$$\left(T_1 + \frac{T_1}{k}\right) = 2(T_0 - T_c)$$

$$T_1\left(\frac{k+1}{k}\right) = 2(T_0 - T_c)$$

$$T_1 = \frac{2k(T_0 - T_c)}{k+1} \quad \text{... (Eq. 2.40)}$$

On similar lines,
$$T_2 = \frac{2(T_0 - T_c)}{k+1} \quad \text{... (Eq. 2.41)}$$

Therefore,
$$T_1 - T_2 = \frac{2k(T_0 - T_c)}{k+1} - \frac{2(T_0 - T_c)}{k+1}$$

$$T_1 - T_2 = \frac{2(T_0 - T_c)}{k+1}(k-1) \quad \text{... (Eq. 2.42)}$$

We know that the power transmitted in the belt,

$$P = \frac{(T_1 - T_2)v}{1000} \quad \text{... using \textbf{14.9a/Pg 239, DHB}}$$

Substituting Eq. (2.42) yields
$$P = \frac{v}{1000}\left[\frac{2(T_0 - T_c)}{(k+1)}(k-1)\right]$$

$$= \left[\frac{2v(T_0 - T_c)(k-1)}{1000(k+1)}\right]$$

$$P = \left[\frac{2(k-1)}{1000(k+1)}\right]\left(T_0 - \frac{w'v^2}{g}\right)v \quad \text{... (Eq. 2.43)}$$

For maximum power, differentiating the above Eq. (2.43) with respect to v and equating to zero

i.e.
$$\frac{dP}{dv} = 0$$

$$\frac{d}{dv}\left\{\left[\frac{2(k-1)}{1000(k+1)}\right]\left(T_0 - \frac{w'v^2}{g}\right)v\right\} = 0$$

$$\frac{d}{dv}\left(T_0 v - \frac{w'v^3}{g}\right) = 0$$

$$\left(T_0 - \frac{3w'v^2}{g}\right) = 0$$

$$T_0 = \frac{3w'v^2}{g} = 3T_c \quad \text{... (Eq. 2.44)}$$

or
$$v = \sqrt{\frac{T_0 g}{3w'}} \quad \text{... (Eq. 2.44a)}$$

Thus the power transmitted is maximum, when initial tension is 3 times the centrifugal tension $T_0 = 3T_c$.

From Eq. (2.40), limiting friction condition occurs when T_1 is maximum, i.e. $v = 0$

Eq. (2.40) yields ... $$T_1 = \left(\frac{2k}{k+1}\right)T_c \qquad \text{...(Eq. 2.45)}$$

2.16 FORCES IN FLAT BELT

The relation between stress (σ) and elongation (e) is given by the relation
$$\sigma = C_1^2 e^2 \qquad \text{... 14.11/Pg 240, DHB}$$

C_1 – a constant = 70, for leather belts.

2.17 IDLER -OR- JOCKEY PULLEY

Due to constant usage, the belt is stretched in length thereby reducing the initial tension and the power capacity of the drive. In such cases, the initial tension in the belt is restored by increasing the center distance or by using a idler pulley on the slack side of the belt as shown in **Fig. 2.8**.

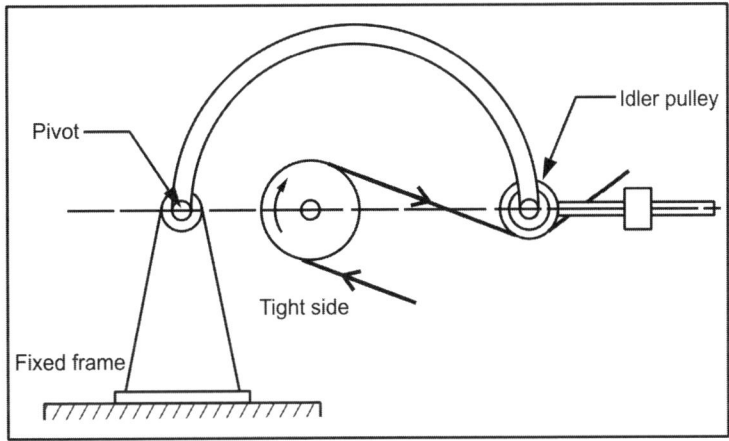

Fig. 2.8: Idler or Jockey pulley

The idler pulley is free to turn about pivots in a fixed frame, supported on an arm. The pressure of this pulley on the belt is maintained by means of a hanging weight or spring weight.

2.18 RELATION BETWEEN DIAMETER OF PULLEY AND THICKNESS

The thickness of the belt is determined using the following relations:

- For leather belts, $\quad t \leq \dfrac{D_{min}}{50}$
- For rubber belts, $\quad t \leq \dfrac{D_{min}}{30}$
- For woven cotton, $\quad t \leq \dfrac{D_{min}}{25}$

Where, D_{min} refers to smaller diameter.

Note:

$v = \dfrac{\pi X N}{60}$, here X refers to the driver pulley, i.e. d or D

1. Two pulleys 200 mm in diameter and the other 150 mm in diameter are connected by means of a cross belt drive, 2 meters apart. Find the length of the belt required and the lap angle between each pulley and the belt.

   If the larger pulley rotates at 300 rpm, find the power transmitted assuming that the maximum tension in the belt as 1 kN and coefficient of friction between the belt and pulley as 0.3.

Solution: Larger pulley diameter, D = 300 mm, smaller pulley diameter, d = 150 mm, 2 m = 2000 mm, N = 300 rpm, T_{max} = 1 kN = 1000 N, μ = 0.3,
    a. L = ?,   b. θ_s, θ_L = ?   c. P = ?

a. To find length of belt:

We know that for a cross belt drive,

$$L = \left[\frac{\pi}{2} + \frac{D+d}{2C}\right](D+d) + \sqrt{2C^2 - (D+d)^2} \quad \ldots 14.4/\text{Pg } 238, \text{DHB}$$

$$= \left[\frac{\pi}{2} + \frac{(300+150)}{2 \times 2000}\right](300+150) + \sqrt{4 \times 2000^2 - (300+150)^2}$$

$$= 4732.1 \text{ mm}$$

$$L = 4.73 \text{ m}$$

b. Angle of contact:

For a cross belt drive, angle of contact for both the pulleys is same

$$\theta_S = \theta_L \approx \pi + \frac{(D+d)}{C} \quad \ldots 14.2/\text{Pg } 238, \text{DHB}$$

$$\theta_S = \theta_L \approx \pi + \frac{(300+150)}{2000}$$

$$\theta_S = \theta_L = 3.37 \text{ rad (radians)}$$

c. To find power:

We know that power transmitted, $P = \dfrac{(T_1 - T_2)v}{1000}$ (kW)   ...Eq. (i) 14.9a/Pg 239, DHB

But velocity of belt $v = \dfrac{\pi DN}{60}$ (here the diameter of the driver is to be used)

$$v = \frac{\pi \times 0.3 \times 300}{60} = 4.712 \text{ m/s}$$

Since $v < 10$ m/s, the effect of centrifugal tension (T_c) is neglected
But Maximum tension, $T_{max} = T_1 + T_c$

$$T_{max} = 1000 \text{ N} = T_1 \quad \text{(neglecting } T_c\text{)}$$

Also, $\dfrac{T_1}{T_2} = e^{\mu\theta}$ ...14.6a/Pg 238, DHB

$$\frac{T_1}{e^{\mu\theta}} = T_2$$

$$T_2 = \frac{100}{e^{\mu\theta(0.3 \times 3.37)}} = 363.85 \text{ N}$$

Eq. (i) ...
$$P = \frac{(1000 - 363.85) \times 4.712}{1000}$$
$$P = 3 \text{ kW}$$

2. **A leather belt 9 × 250 mm is to drive a CI pulley 800 mm in diameter at 400 rpm. If active arc on smaller pulley is 150° and the stress in the tight side is 1.5 MPa, find the power transmitted. Take the density of leather as 1000 kg/m³ and μ = 0.25.**

Solution: Thickness, $t = 9$ mm, width, $b = 250$ mm, $D = 800$ mm, $N = 400$ rpm, $\theta_S = 150° = 2.617$ rad, $\sigma_1 = 1.5$ MPa $= \sigma_d$, $\rho = 1000$ kg/m³, $\mu = 0.25$, $P = ?$

To find power:

We know that, velocity of belt $v = \dfrac{\pi D N}{60}$

Since the thickness of the belt is known, we have
$$v = \frac{\pi(D+t)N}{60} = \frac{\pi \times (0.8 + 0.009) \times 400}{60} = 16.94 \text{ m/s}$$

Since $v > 10$ m/s, the effect of centrifugal tension (T_c) has to be considered

Therefore, $\dfrac{ptv}{1000}\left[\sigma_d - \dfrac{wv^2}{10^6 g}\right]\left[\dfrac{e^{\mu\theta}-1}{e^{\mu\theta}}\right]$ ... **14.9a/Pg 239, DHB**

$w = \rho g = 1000 \times 9.81 = 9810$ N/m³ or $\rho = \dfrac{w}{g}$

$$P = \frac{250 \times 9 \times 16.94}{1000}\left[1.5 - \frac{9810 \times 16.94^2}{10^2 \times 9.81}\right]\left(\frac{e^{0.25 \times 2.617}-1}{e^{0.25 \times 2.617}}\right)$$
$$P = 22.21 \text{ kW}$$

3. **A flat belt is required to transmit 25 kW from a pulley 1 m effective diameter at 400 rpm. The angle of contact is spread over 11/24 of the circumference. If thickness of the belt is 8 mm, μ = 0.25, ρ = 1000 kg/m³ and working stress = 3 MPa, determine the width of the belt required.**

Solution: $P = 25$ kW, effective diameter, $D_e = 1000$ mm, $N = 400$ rpm, $\theta = \dfrac{11}{24} \times 360 = 165° = 2.88$ rad, $t = 8$ mm, $\mu = 0.25$, $\rho = 1000$ kg/m³, $\sigma_d = 3$ MPa, $b = ?$

To find width of belt:

We know that, velocity of belt $v = \dfrac{\pi D_e N}{60} = \dfrac{\pi(1+0.008) \times 400}{60} = 21.11$ m/s

Since $v > 10$ m/s, the effect of centrifugal tension (T_c) has to be considered

Therefore, $P = \dfrac{btv}{1000}\left[\sigma_d - \dfrac{wv^2}{10^6 g}\right]\left(\dfrac{e^{\mu\theta}-1}{e^{\mu\theta}}\right)$ ... **14.9a/Pg 239, DHB**

$$25 = \frac{b \times 8 \times 21.11}{1000}\left[3 - \frac{1000 \times 21.11^2}{10^6}\right]\left(\frac{e^{0.25 \times 2.88}-1}{e^{0.25 \times 2.88}}\right)$$
Where, $\rho = \dfrac{w}{g}$

$P = 113$

Therefore, standard width $b \approx 112$ mm ... **Tb 14.10a/Pg 258, DHB**

138 Design of Machine Elements II (DME II)

4. **An electric motor is to drive an exhaust fan by means of a flat leather belt. The following data is known:**

	Motor pulley	Fan pulley
Diameter	400 mm	1200 mm
Contact angle	2.5 rad	3.75 rad
Coefficient of friction	0.3	0.25
Speed	900 rpm	
Power transmitted	25 kW	

The thickness of the belt is 6 mm and the maximum permissible stress is 2.1 MPa. Take density as 1000 kg/m³. Find the width of the belt.

Solution:

	Motor (Driver)	Fan (Driven)
Diameter	$D = 400$ mm	$d = 1200$ mm
Contact angle	$\theta_L = 2.5$ rad	$\theta_S = 3.75$ rad
Coefficient of friction	$\mu_L = 0.3$	$\mu_S = 0.25$
Speed	900 rpm	
Power transmitted	25 kW	
$t = 6$ mm, $\rho = 1000$ kg/m³, $\sigma_d = 2.1$ MPa, $b = ?$		

To find power:

We know that, velocity of belt $v = \dfrac{\pi(D+t)N_L}{60} = \dfrac{\pi \times (0.4 + 0.006) \times 900}{60} = 19.13$ m/s

Since $v > 10$ m/s, the effect of centrifugal tension (T_c) has to be considered.

Since μ is different for both pulleys, design is based on pulley having smaller value of "$\mu\theta$" or "$e^{\mu\theta}$"

For motor pulley, $\mu_L \theta_L = 0.3 \times 2.5 = 0.75$
For fan pulley, $\mu_S \theta_S = 0.25 \times 3.75 = 0.938$
Here design is based on larger pulley, having $\mu\theta = 0.75$

We know that, $\quad P = \dfrac{btv}{1000}\left[\sigma_d - \dfrac{wv^2}{10^6 g}\right]\left(\dfrac{e^{\mu\theta} - 1}{e^{\mu\theta}}\right)$ ...14.9a/Pg 239, DHB

$25 = \dfrac{b \times 6 \times 19.13}{1000}\left[2.1 - \dfrac{1000 \times 19.13^2}{10^6}\right]\left(\dfrac{e^{0.75} - 1}{e^{0.75}}\right) \quad \because \rho = \dfrac{w}{g}$

$b = 238.06$ mm

Therefore, standard width $b \approx 250$ mm ... Tb 14.10a/Pg 258, DHB

5. **A belt 125 mm wide and 10 mm thick is transmitting power at 900 rpm. The net driving tension is 2 times the tension on slack side. If same permissible stress on the belt is 1.5 MPa, calculate the maximum power that can be transmitted at this speed. Take density of belt material as 1000 kg/m³. Also find the power that can be transmitted by this belt and the speed at which this can be transmitted.**

Solution: $b = 125$ mm, $t = 10$ mm, $v = 900$ rpm $= 15$ m/s, $(T_1 - T_2) = 2T_2$, $\sigma_d = 1.5$ MPa,
$\rho = 1000$ kg/m³ 　　a. Power $P = ?$ 　b. $P_{max} = ?$, $v_{max} = ?$

a. To find power P:

Given, $(T_1 - T_2) = 2T_2$

Since $v > 10$ m/s, the effect of centrifugal tension (T_c) has to be considered

i.e. $(T_1 - T_c) - (T_2 - T_c) = 2(T_2 - T_c)$

$$(T_1 - T_c) = 3(T_2 - T_c)$$

$$\frac{(T_1 - T_c)}{(T_2 - T_c)} = 3 \text{ or}$$

$$\frac{(\sigma_1 - \sigma_c)}{(\sigma_2 - \sigma_c)} = 3 \qquad \ldots \text{Eq. (i)}$$

Comparing Eq. (i) with **14.6d/Pg 238, DHB**, we have $e^{\mu\theta} = 3$

We know that, $\quad P = \dfrac{btv}{1000}\left[\sigma_d - \dfrac{wv^2}{10^6 g}\right]\left(\dfrac{e^{\mu\theta}-1}{e^{\mu\theta}}\right) \qquad \ldots$ **14.9a/Pg 239, DHB**

$$= \frac{125 \times 10 \times 15}{1000}\left[1.5 - \frac{1000 \times 19.13^2}{10^6}\right]\left(\frac{3-1}{3}\right) \quad \because \rho = \frac{w}{g}$$

$$P = 15.94 \text{ kW}$$

b. To find absolute maximum power, P_{max} = ? and its speed, v_{max}

For maximum power, $T_1 = 3T_c$

or $\quad T_c = T_1/3$

or $\quad \sigma_c = \dfrac{\sigma_1}{3} = 1.5/3$

$\quad \sigma_c = 0.5$ MPa

But $\quad \sigma_c = \dfrac{wv^2}{10^6 g} \qquad \ldots$ **14.7b/Pg 239, DHB**

$$0.5 = \frac{1000 \times v^2}{10^6}$$

$$v = 22.36 \text{ m/s}$$

Now maximum power transmitted per mm² of belt is

$$P_{max} = \frac{(\sigma_1 - \sigma_c)v}{1000}\left(\frac{e^{\mu\theta}-1}{e^{\mu\theta}}\right) \qquad \ldots \textbf{14.10a/Pg 239, DHB}$$

$$= \frac{(1.5 - 0.5) \times 22.36}{1000}\left(\frac{3-1}{3}\right)$$

$P_{max} = 0.0149$ kW/mm²

$= 0.0149 \times$ area

$= 0.0149 \times (125 \times 10)$

$P_{max} = 18.63$ kW

6. A compressor is driven by 900 rpm motor by means of 250 mm × 10 mm flat belt. The motor pulley is 0.3 m in diameter and the compressor pulley is 1.5 m diameter. The distance between the centers of the pulleys is 2 m. A jockey pulley is used to make the angle of wrap on the smaller pulley 220° and the larger pulley 270°. The coefficient of friction between the belt and the smaller pulley is 0.3 and between the belt and the larger pulley is 0.5. The maximum allowable

belt stress is 2 MN/m² and the specific weight of the belt material is 9.515 kN/m³. Determine the power that can be transmitted by the belt drive.

[VTU-Dec. 09/Jan.10–10 Marks]

Solution: $N_S = 900$ rpm, $b = 250$ mm, $t = 10$ mm, driver (motor) $d = 0.3$ m $= 300$ mm, driven (compressor), $D = 1.5$ m $= 1500$ mm, $C = 2$ m $= 2000$ mm, $\theta_S = 220° = 3.84$ rad, $\theta_S = 270° = 4.71$ rad, $\mu_S = 0.3$, $\mu_L = 0.25$, $\sigma_d = 2$ MN/m² $= 2$ N/mm², $w = 9.515$ kN/m³, Power, $P = ?$

To find power:

We know that, velocity of belt $v = \dfrac{\pi(d+t)N_S}{60} = \dfrac{\pi \times (0.3 + 0.01) \times 900}{60} = 14.61$ m/s

Since $v > 10$ m/s, the effect of centrifugal tension (T_c) has to be considered

Since μ is different for both pulleys, design is based on pulley having smaller value of "$\mu\theta$" or "$e^{\mu\theta}$"

For motor pulley, $\mu_L \theta_L = 0.25 \times 4.71 = 1.178$
For fan pulley, $\mu_S \theta_S = 0.3 \times 3.84 = 1.152$

Here design is based on compressor pulley, having $\mu\theta = 1.152$

We know that, $P = \dfrac{btv}{1000}\left[\sigma_d - \dfrac{wv^2}{10^6 g}\right]\left(\dfrac{e^{\mu\theta} - 1}{e^{\mu\theta}}\right)$ ... 14.9a/Pg 239, DHB

$$= \dfrac{250 \times 10 \times 14.61}{1000}\left[2 - \dfrac{9.515 \times 10^3 \times 14.61^2}{10^6 \times 9.81}\right]\left(\dfrac{e^{1.152} - 1}{e^{1.152}}\right)$$

$P = 44.80$ kW

7. A leather belt 125 mm wide and 6 mm thick transmits power from a pulley 750 mm diameter which runs at 500 rpm. The angle of lap is 150° and the coefficient of fiction between the belt and the pulley is 0.3. If the belt density is 1000 kg/m³ and the stress in the belt is not to exceed 2.75 N/mm², find the power that can be transmitted by the belt.

Also find the initial tension in the belt. [VTU-Dec 10–08 Marks]

Solution: $b = 125$ mm, $t = 6$ mm, $D = 750$ mm, $N = 500$ rpm, $\theta = 150° = 2.62$ rad, $\mu_S = 0.3$, $\rho = 1000$ kg/m³, $\rho_d = 2.75$ N/mm², $P = ?$

a. To find power:

We know that, velocity of belt

$$v = \dfrac{\pi(D+t)N}{60} = \dfrac{\pi \times (0.75 + 0.06) \times 500}{60} = 19.79 \text{ m/s}$$

Since $v > 10$ m/s, the effect of centrifugal tension (T_c) has to be considered

We know that, $P = \dfrac{btv}{1000}\left[\sigma_d - \dfrac{wv^2}{10^6 g}\right]\left(\dfrac{e^{\mu\theta} - 1}{e^{\mu\theta}}\right)$

$$= \dfrac{125 \times 6 \times 19.97}{1000}\left[2.75 - \dfrac{1000 \times 19.79^2}{10^6}\right]\left(\dfrac{e^{(0.3 \times 2.62)} - 1}{e^{(0.3 \times 2.62)}}\right) \quad \because \rho = \dfrac{w}{g}$$

... 14.9a/Pg 239, DHB

$P = 19.05$ kW

b. To find initial tension:

We know that, initial tension, $\sqrt{T_1} + \sqrt{T_2} = 2\sqrt{T_0}$ ... Eq. (i) **14.12/Pg 240, DHB**

But, $P = (T_1 - T_2)v$

$$(T_1 - T_2) = \frac{19.05 \times 10^3}{19.97} = 962.61 \text{ N} \quad \text{... Eq. (ii)}$$

Also, $\dfrac{(T_1 - T_c)}{(T_2 - T_c)} = e^{\mu\theta}$ ... Eq. (iii) **14.6c/Pg 238, DHB**

and, $T_c = \dfrac{wbtv^2}{10^6 g}$ ... **14.7a/Pg 239, DHB**

$$= \frac{(1000 \times 9.81) \times 125 \times 6 \times 19.79^2}{10^6 \times 9.81}$$

$T_c = 293.73$ N

Eq. (iii) yields ...
$(T_1 - T_c) = e^{\mu\theta}(T_2 - T_c)$
$= e^{(0.3 \times 2.62)}(T_2 - T_c)$
$(T_1 - T_c) = 2.195\,(T_2 - T_c)$

i.e. $(T_1 - 2.195\,T_2) = -1.195 \times 293.73$
$(T_1 - 2.195\,T_2) = -350.89$ ... Eq. (iv)

Solving Eqs (ii) and (iv) gives,

$T_1 = 2061.77 \approx 2062$ N and
$T_2 = 1100$ N

Eq. (i) yields ... $\sqrt{2062} + \sqrt{1100} = 2\sqrt{T_0}$
$T_0 = 1543.53$ N

8. **A flat belt drive is required to transmit 20 kW of power at 1440 rpm. The driver and the driven shafts are approximately 3 m apart. The dimensions of the pulley mounted on driver and driven shafts are 300 and 450 respectively. The weight density of selected belt material is 9.7 × 10³ N/m³, allowable design stress $\sigma_d = 2$ N/mm² and coefficient of friction = 0.3. Determine:**
   i. **Width of the belt, if thickness = 6 mm**
   ii. **Length of the belt**
   iii. **Initial tension in the belt**
   iv. **Centrifugal tension in the belt.** *[VTU-Dec 08/Jan 09–10Marks]*

Solution: $P = 20$ kW, $N = 1440$ rpm, $C = 3000$ mm, driver pulley, $d = 300$ mm, driven pulley, $D = 450$ mm, $w = 9.7 \times 10^3$ N/m³, $\sigma_d = 2$ N/mm², $\mu = 0.3$, $t = 6$ mm

a. Width of belt, b b. $L = ?$ c. $T_0 = ?$ d. $T_c = ?$

a. To find b:

We know that, velocity of belt $v = \dfrac{\pi(d+t)N}{60} = \dfrac{\pi \times (0.3 + 0.006) \times 1440}{60} = 23.07$ m/s

Since $v > 10$ m/s, the effect of centrifugal tension (T_c) has to be considered

We know that, $P = \dfrac{btv}{1000}\left[\sigma_d - \dfrac{wv^2}{10^6 g}\right]\left(\dfrac{e^{\mu\theta} - 1}{e^{\mu\theta}}\right)$ ... Eq. (i) **14.9a/Pg 239, DHB**

But
$$\theta_S = \pi - \frac{(D-d)}{C} \quad \text{... 14.1a/Pg 238, DHB}$$
$$= \pi - \frac{(0.45 - 0.3)}{3}$$
$$\theta_S = 3.092 \text{ rad}$$

Eq. (i) yields ...
$$20 = \frac{b \times 6 \times 23.07}{1000}\left[2 - \frac{9.7 \times 10^3 \times (23.07)^2}{10^6 \times 9.81}\right]\left(\frac{e^{(0.3 \times 3.09)} - 1}{e^{(0.3 \times 3.09)}}\right)$$
$$b = 162.25 \text{ mm}$$

Therefore, standard width $b \approx 180$ mm ... Tb 14.10a/Pg 258, DHB

b. To find L:

The type of belt is based on the value of θ, i.e. $\theta = \frac{3.09 \times 180}{\pi} = 177.04° < 180°$, hence open belt.

We know that for an open belt drive,
$$L = \frac{\pi(D+d)}{2} + \frac{(D-d)^2}{4C} + 2C \quad \text{... 14.3/Pg 238, DHB}$$
$$= \frac{\pi(450 + 300)}{2} + \frac{(450 - 300)^2}{4 \times 3000} + (2 \times 3000)$$
$$L = 7180 \text{ mm} = 7.18 \text{ m}$$

c. To find T_c:

We know that,
$$T_c = \frac{wbtv^2}{10^6 g} \quad \text{... 14.7a/Pg 239, DHB}$$
$$= \frac{9.7 \times 10^3 \times 180 \times 6 \times 23.07^2}{10^6 \times 9.81}$$
$$T_c = 568.36 \text{ N}$$

d. To find initial tension:

We know that, initial tension,
$$\sqrt{T_1} + \sqrt{T_2} = 2\sqrt{T_0} \quad \text{... Eq. (ii) 14.12 Pg 240, DHB}$$

But,
$$P = (T_1 - T_2)v$$
$$(T_1 - T_2) = \frac{20 \times 10^3}{23.07} = 866.93 \text{ N} \quad \text{... Eq. (iii)}$$

Also,
$$\frac{(T_1 - T_c)}{(T_2 - T_c)} = e^{\mu\theta}$$
$$(T_1 - T_c) = e^{\mu\theta}(T_2 - T_c)$$
$$= e^{(0.3 \times 3.09)}(T_2 - T_c)$$
$$(T_1 - T_c) = 2.527(T_2 - T_c)$$

i.e.
$$(T_1 - 2.527 T_2) = -1.527 \times 568.36$$
$$(T_1 - 2.527 T_2) = -867.89 \quad \text{... Eq. (iv)}$$

Solving Eqs (*iii*) and (*iv*) gives,
$$T_1 = 2003.5 \text{ and}$$
$$T_2 = 1136 \text{ N}$$
Eq. (*ii*) yields ... $\sqrt{2003.5} + \sqrt{1136} = 2\sqrt{T_0}$
$$T_0 = 1539 \text{ N}$$

9. **The layout of leather belt drive transmitting a power of 15 kW is as shown in Fig. 2.9. The center distance between the pulleys is twice the diameter of the big pulley. The belt should operate at a velocity of 20 m/sec and the stress in the belt should not exceed 2.25 MPa. The density of the leather belt is 0.95 gm/cc and the coefficient of friction is 0.35. The thickness of the belt is 5 mm. Calculate:**
   i. diameter of the pulleys
   ii. the length and width of the belt
   iii. belt tensions
   [VTU-June 2012–15 Marks]

Solution: $P = 15$ kW, $C = 2D$, $v = 20$ m/s, $\sigma_d = 2.25$ MPa, $\rho = 0.95$ gm/cc $= 950$ kg/m^3, 0.35, $t = 5$ mm, $N_S = 1440$ rpm, $N_L = 480$ rpm

a. Diameters: $D, d = ?$ b. Length $L = ?$ c. $b = ?$ d. Tensions $T_1, T_2 = ?$

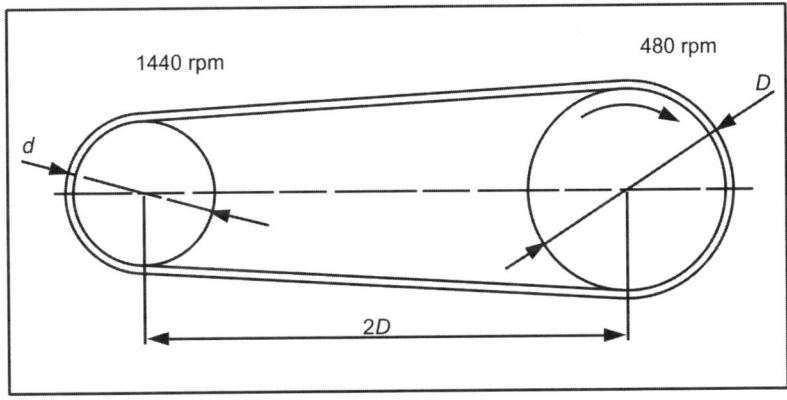

Fig. 2.9: Problem 9

a. To find diameters, D, d:

We know that, $v = \dfrac{\pi d N}{60}$

$$20 = \dfrac{\pi \times d \times 1440}{60}$$

$$d = 265.26 \text{ mm}$$

Therefore, standard diameter, $d \approx 280$ mm   ... Tb 14.11b/Pg 260, DHB

Also, velocity ratio, $= \dfrac{N_S}{N_L} = \dfrac{D}{d}$

i.e. $\dfrac{1440}{480} = \dfrac{D}{280}$

$$D = 840 \text{ mm}$$

Note: The value 840 mm is not standardized as it leads to change in velocity ratio

b. To find length L:

Given $C = 2D = 2 \times 840 = 1680$ mm
But for an open belt drive,

$$L = \frac{\pi(D+d)}{2} + \frac{(D-d)^2}{4C} + 2C \qquad \text{... 14.3/Pg 238, DHB}$$

$$= \frac{\pi(840+280)}{2} + \frac{(840-280)^2}{4 \times 1680} + 2 \times 1680$$

$$L = 5166 \text{ mm} = 5.166 \text{ m}$$

c. To find width b:

Based on standardized diameters, actual velocity of the belt is belt

$$v = \frac{\pi(d+t)N_s}{60} = \frac{\pi \times (0.28 + 0.006) \times 1440}{60} = 21.56 \text{ m/s}$$

Since $v > 10$ m/s, the effect of centrifugal tension (T_c) has to be considered
We know that,

$$P = \frac{btv}{1000}\left[\sigma_d - \frac{wv^2}{10^6 g}\right]\left(\frac{e^{\mu\theta}-1}{e^{\mu\theta}}\right) \qquad \text{... 14.9a/Pg 239, DHB}$$

But $\quad \theta_s = \pi - \frac{(D-d)}{C} \qquad \text{... 14.1a/Pg 238, DHB}$

$$= \pi - \frac{(840-280)}{1680}$$

$$\theta_s = 2.81 \text{ rad}$$

$$15 = \frac{b \times 5 \times 21.56}{1000}\left[2.25 - \frac{950 \times 21.56^2}{10^6}\right]\left(\frac{e^{(0.35 \times 2.81)}-1}{e^{(0.35 \times 2.81)}}\right)$$

$$b = 123 \text{ mm}$$

Therefore, standard width $b \approx 125$ mm $\qquad \text{... Tb14.10a/Pg 258, DHB}$

d. To find tensions T_1, T_2:

We know that, $\quad P = \frac{(T_1 - T_2)v}{1000} \qquad \text{... 14.9a/Pg 239, DHB}$

$$(T_1 - T_2) = \frac{15 \times 10^3}{21.56} = 695.73 \text{ N} \qquad \text{... Eq. }(i)$$

Also, $\quad \dfrac{(T_1 - T_c)}{(T_2 - T_c)} = e^{\mu\theta} \qquad \text{... }(ii) \text{ 14.6c/Pg 238, DHB}$

But, $\quad T_c = \dfrac{wbtv^2}{10^6 g} \qquad \text{... 14.7a/Pg 239, DHB}$

$$= \frac{(950 \times 9.81) \times 125 \times 5 \times 21.56^2}{10^6 \times 9.81}$$

$$T_c = 276 \text{ N}$$

Eq. (*ii*) yields ... $(T_1 - T_c) = e^{\mu\theta}(T_2 - T_c)$
$$= e^{(0.35 \times 2.81)}(T_2 - T_c)$$
$$(T_1 - T_c) = 2.673(T_2 - T_c)$$

i.e. $(T_1 - 2.673\ T_2) = -1673\ T_c$
$$= -1.673 \times 276$$
$$(T_1 - 2.673\ T_2) = -461.75 \qquad \text{... Eq. (}iii\text{)}$$

Solving Eqs (*i*) and (*iii*) gives,
$$T_1 = 1387.56 \text{ N and}$$
$$T_2 = 691.86 \text{ N}$$

2.19 DESIGN PROCEDURE FOR FLAT BELTS

1. Make a preliminary decision regarding:
   a. The material used for belt
      (generally oak tanned/mineral tanned leather, with $\sigma_d = 2$ MPa),
   b. The material used for pulley   (generally CI, because of damping property),
   c. The type of joint required,   (generally cemented with $\eta_j = 100\%$), or
      ... **Table 14.6/Pg 254, DHB**
   d. The service conditions (C_s)   [= 1.2, in general]
      Service factor,
      $C_S = C_1 C_2 C_3 C_4 C_5$ ... **Table 14.9/Pg 257, DHB**
   e. Calculate the design power, $P_d = P(\text{kW}) = P \times C_S$ ... **(in kW)**

2. Find the diameter of the motor pulley (driver) using the relation:
$$d = 630 \times \sqrt[3]{\frac{P_d(\text{kW})}{\omega_{max}}} \qquad \text{... 14.13a/Pg 240, DHB}$$

Where, $\omega_{max} = 2\pi n_{max} = \dfrac{2\pi N_{max}}{60}$ (rad/s)
$$n = \text{speed (rps)},$$
$$N = \text{speed (rpm)}$$

- $d = D_{min}$, only in step-down device.
- $D_{min} = D$, for a step-up device. Here instead of selecting the diameter of the pulley, the belt velocity v may be specified and then d is determined.

3. Calculate the diameter of the driven pulley by considering the slip in belt (1 to 3%) and neglecting belt thickness as:
$$D = (1 - \epsilon) \times d \times i \qquad \text{... 14.13b/Pg 240, DHB}$$
$$i = \text{velocity ratio}$$
$$\epsilon = \text{Slip or creep in the belt (1 - 3\%)}$$

4. Standardize the pulley diameters in steps 2 and 3, using **Table 14.11b/Pg 260, DHB**.

5. Calculate the belt speed as:
$$v = \frac{\pi D_1 N_1 (1 - \epsilon)}{60}$$
$$D_1 = \text{diameter of driver},$$
$$N_1 = \text{rpm of driver}.$$

6. Determine the center distance as $C \geq 2(D+d)$ ... **14.5/Pg 238, DHB**
7. Determine the coefficient of friction between the pulley and the belt using Barth's formula as

$$\mu = 0.54 - \frac{0.712}{2.542 + v}$$

   ... (for leather) **14.6/Pg 238, DHB** or from **Table 14.4/Pg 253, DHB**
   - On the other hand, if the belt is made of different material other than leather, select from **Table 14.3/Pg 253, DHB**
     ◆ If $v > 10$ m/s, consider the centrifugal tension (T_c)
8. Determine the length of the belt (open/cross). ...**14.3 or 14.4/Pg 238, DHB**
9. Determine the angle of contact (open/cross). ... **14.1 or 14.2/Pg 238, DHB**
10. Calculate the width (b) of the belt by selecting suitable belt thickness from **Table 14.1/Pg 251** in the power equation as

$$P_d = P(\text{kW}) = \frac{btv}{1000}\left[\sigma_d - \frac{wv^2}{10^6 g}\right]\left(\frac{e^{\mu\theta} - 1}{e^{\mu\theta}}\right) \times \eta_j \quad ... \text{14.9a/Pg 239, DHB}$$

η_j efficiency of the joint ... **Table 14.6/Pg 254, DHB**
- The relation between the diameter of the pulley and thickness is given (thumb rule) as,

$$\frac{D_{\min}}{t} < 50$$

$D_{\min}$ = refers to smaller diameter

11. Calculate the values of T_1, T_2 and T_0 using the relations:

$$P_d = P(\text{kW}) = \frac{(T_1 - T_2)v}{1000}, \quad \frac{(T_1 - T_c)}{(T_1 - T_c)} = e^{\mu\theta}, \quad \sqrt{T_1} + \sqrt{T_2} = 2\sqrt{T_0}$$

10. A horizontal drive is required to drive a compressor by means of an electric motor. Select a suitable flat belt drive from the following details:

Power = 6 kW, slip = 2.5%, speed of motor pulley = 1400 rpm, service factor = 1.2, working stress = 2 MPa, joint efficiency = 90%, speed of compressor = 500 rpm.

Solution: $P = 6$ kW, slip, $\epsilon = 2.5\% = 0.025$, speed of motor pulley (driver) $N_S = 1400$ rpm, service factor, $C_S = 1.2$, $\sigma_d = 2$ MPa, $\eta_j = 90\%$, speed of compressor (driven) $N_L = 500$ rpm

1. *Preliminary decision:*
   a. Given, $\sigma_d = 2$ MPa.
   b. Assume that the pulley is made of cast iron (damping property).
   c. Given $\eta_j = 90\%$.
   d. Given, service factor as $C_s = 1.2$.
   e. The design power is $C_d = P(\text{kW}) = P \times C_s = 6 \times 1.2 = 7.2$ kW.

2. *Diameter of driving pulley (motor):*

$$d = 630 \times \sqrt[3]{\frac{P_d(\text{kW})}{\omega_{\max}}} \quad ... \text{14.13a/Pg 240, DHB}$$

Where, $\omega_{\max} = 2\pi n_{\max} = \dfrac{2\pi \times N_{\max}}{60} = \dfrac{2\pi \times 1400}{60} = 146.61$ rad/s

$$d = 630 \times \sqrt[3]{\frac{7.2}{146.61}}$$

$$d = 230.71 \text{ mm}$$

Therefore, standard size, $d = 250$ mm. ... **Tb 14.11b/Pg 260, DHB**

3. Diameter of driven pulley:

$$D = (1 - \epsilon) \times d \times i \qquad \text{...14.13b/Pg 240, DHB}$$

Slip, $\epsilon = 2.5\% = 0.025$

Velocity ratio, $i = \dfrac{N_{\text{driver}}}{N_{\text{driven}}} = \dfrac{1400}{500} = 2.8$

$$D = (1 - 0.025) \times 250 \times 2.8$$
$$D = 682.5 \text{ mm}$$

Therefore, standard size, $d = 710$ mm. ... **Tb 14.11b/Pg 260, DHB**

4. Standard sizes:

Driver pulley (motor) $d = 250$ mm, Driven pulley, $D = 710$ mm

5. Belt speed:

$$v = \frac{\pi d N (1 - \epsilon)}{60}$$

$$= \frac{\pi \times 0.25 \times 1400 \times (1 - 0.025)}{60}$$

$$v = 17.87 \text{ m/s}$$

6. Center distance:

$$C \geq 2(D + d) \qquad \text{...14.5/Pg 238, DHB}$$
$$C = 2 \times (710 + 250)$$
$$C = 1920 \text{ mm} = 19.2 \text{ m}$$

7. Coefficient of friction:

According to Barth
$$\mu = 0.54 - \frac{0.712}{2.542 + v} \quad \text{... (for leather) } \textbf{14.6d/Pg 238, DHB}$$

$$= 0.54 - \frac{0.712}{2.542 + 17.87}$$

$$\mu = 0.505$$

8. Length of the belt:

Assuming open belt we have,

$$L = \frac{\pi(D + d)}{2} + \frac{(D - d)^2}{4C} + 2C \qquad \text{...14.3/Pg 238, DHB}$$

$$= \frac{\pi(710 + 250)}{2} + \frac{(710 - 250)^2}{4 \times 1920} + (2 \times 1920)$$

$$L = 5375.52 \text{ mm} \approx 5.4 \text{ m}$$

9. Angle of contact:

For smaller pulley,

$$\theta_S = \pi - \frac{(D-d)}{C} \quad \ldots \text{14.1a/Pg 238, DHB}$$

$$= \pi - \frac{(710-250)}{1920}$$

$$\theta_S = 2.9 \text{ rad}$$

For larger pulley,

$$\theta_L = \pi + \frac{(D-d)}{C} \quad \ldots \text{14.1b/Pg 238, DHB}$$

$$= \pi + \frac{(710-250)}{1920}$$

$$\theta_L = 3.38 \text{ rad}$$

10. To find width b:

$$P_d = P(kW) = \frac{btv}{1000}\left[\sigma_d - \frac{wv^2}{10^6 g}\right]\left(\frac{e^{\mu\theta}-1}{e^{\mu\theta}}\right) \times \eta_j \quad \ldots \text{14.9a/Pg 239, DHB}$$

- Here, $\eta_j = 90\%$ (data)
- Assuming density of leather belt as $\rho = 1000 \text{ kg/m}^3$, $w = 9810 \text{ N/m}^3$

For motor pulley, $\mu_S \theta_S = 0.505 \times 2.9 = 1.465$
For winch pulley, $\mu_L \theta_L = 0.505 \times 3.38 = 1.707$
Here design is based on motor pulley having $\mu\theta = 1.465$

$$7.2 = \frac{bt \times 17.87}{1000}\left[2 - \frac{9810 \times 17.87^2}{9.81 \times 10^6}\right]\left(\frac{e^{1.465}-1}{e^{1.465}}\right) \times 0.9$$

$$bt = 346.42 \text{ mm}^2 \quad \ldots \text{Eq. (i)}$$

- The relation between the diameter of the pulley and thickness is given (thumb rule) as,

$$\frac{d}{t} < 50$$

i.e. $\quad t \geq 0.02d$

$$t = 0.02 \times 250$$

$$t = 5 \text{ mm (say 6 mm)}$$

Eq. (i) yields ... $b = \frac{346.42}{6} = 57.74$ mm

Now $b = 57.74$ lies in the range of (24 to 102 mm) with an increment of 6 mm.
Thus the standard width, $b = 60$ mm (for light loads). ...Tb 14.1/Pg 251, DHB

11. To find tensions:

We know that, $\quad P_d = P(kW) = \frac{(T_1 - T_2)v}{1000} \quad \ldots \text{14.9a/Pg 239, DHB}$

$$(T_1 - T_2) = \frac{7.2 \times 10^3}{17.87} = 403 \text{ N} \quad \ldots \text{Eq. (ii)}$$

Also, $\quad \frac{(T_1 - T_c)}{(T_2 - T_c)} = e^{\mu\theta} \quad \ldots \text{Eq. (iii) 14.6c/Pg 238, DHB}$

But, $\quad T_c = \frac{wbtv^2}{10^6 g} \quad \ldots \text{14.7a/Pg 239, DHB}$

$$= \frac{(9810) \times 60 \times 6 \times 17.87^2}{10^6 \times 9.81}$$

$$T_c = 114.96 \text{ N}$$

Eq. (*iii*) yields ... $(T_1 - T_c) = e^{\mu\theta}(T_2 - T_c)$
$$= e^{(1.465)}(T_2 - T_c)$$
$$(T_1 - T_c) = 4.327(T_2 - T_c)$$
i.e. $(T_1 - 4.327\,T_2) = -3.327\,T_c$
$$= -3.327 \times 114.96$$
$$(T_1 - 4.327\,T_2) = -382.87 \qquad \ldots \text{Eq. }(iv)$$

Solving Eqs (*ii*) and (*iv*) gives,
$$T_1 = 639.21 \text{ N and}$$
$$T_2 = 236.21 \text{ N}$$

We know that, initial tension,
$$\sqrt{T_1} + \sqrt{T_2} = 2\sqrt{T_0} \qquad \ldots \textbf{14.12/Pg 240, DHB}$$
$$\sqrt{639.21} + \sqrt{236.21} = 2\sqrt{T_0}$$
$$T_0 = 413.14 \text{ N}$$

11. **Design a flat belt to drive a winch from an electric motor of 12 kW having a speed ratio of 3. The speed of the motor shaft is 900 rpm. Assume a service factor of 1.5.**

Solution: $P = 12$ kW, $i = 3$, motor speed (driver) $N = 900$ rpm, $C_S = 1.5$

1. *Preliminary decision:*
   a. Assume that the belt is made of oak tanned leather, with $\sigma_d = 2$ MPa.
   b. Assume that the pulley is made of cast iron (damping property).
   c. Assume that the belt is made endless at the factory by means of cemented joint having a joint efficiency (η_j) of 100%, using **Tb 14.6/Pg 254, DHB.**
   d. Given, service factor $C_S = 1.5$
   e. The design power is $P_d = P(\text{kW}) = P \times C_S = 12 \times 1.5 = 18$ kW.

2. *Diameter of driving pulley (motor):*
$$d = 630 \times \sqrt[3]{\frac{P_d(\text{kW})}{\omega_{max}}} \qquad \ldots \textbf{14.13a/Pg 240, DHB}$$

Where, $\omega_{max} = 2\pi n_{max} = \dfrac{2\pi \times N_{max}}{60} = \dfrac{2\pi \times 900}{60} = 94.25$ rad/s

$$d = 362.81 \text{ mm}$$
Therefore, standard size, $d = 400$ mm. ... **Tb 14.11b/Pg 260, DHB**

3. *Diameter of driven pulley:*
$$D = (1 - \epsilon) \times d \times i \qquad \ldots \textbf{14.13b/Pg 240, DHB}$$
Assuming slip $\epsilon = 2\% = 0.02$
$$D = (1 - 0.02) \times 400 \times 3$$
$$D = 1176 \text{ mm}$$
Therefore, standard size, $D = 1250$ mm. ... **Tb 4.11b/Pg 260, DHB**

4. *Standard sizes:*
Driver pulley (motor) $d = 400$ mm,   driven pulley $D = 1250$ mm

5. Belt speed:

$$v = \frac{\pi d N (1-\epsilon)}{60}$$

$$= \frac{\pi \times 0.4 \times 900 \times (1-0.02)}{60}$$

$$v = 18.48 \text{ m/s}$$

6. Center distance:

$$C \geq 2(D+d) \quad \ldots \text{14.5/Pg 238, DHB}$$

$$C = 2 \times (1250 + 400)$$

$$C = 3300 \text{ mm} = 3.30 \text{ m}$$

7. Coefficient of friction:

According to Barth

$$\mu = 0.54 - \frac{0.712}{2.542 + v} \quad \ldots \text{(for leather) } \textbf{14.6d/Pg 238, DHB}$$

$$= 0.54 - \frac{0.712}{2.542 + 18.48}$$

$$\mu = 0.506$$

8. Length of the belt:

Assuming open belt we have,

$$L = \frac{\pi(D+d)}{2} + \frac{(D-d)^2}{4C} + 2C \quad \ldots \text{14.3/Pg 238, DHB}$$

$$= \frac{\pi(1250 + 400)}{2} + \frac{(1250 - 400)^2}{4 \times 3300} + (2 \times 3300)$$

$$L = 9246.5 \text{ mm} \approx 9.25 \text{ m}$$

9. Angle of contact:

For smaller pulley,

$$\theta_S = \pi - \frac{(D-d)}{C} \quad \ldots \text{14.1a/Pg 238, DHB}$$

$$= \pi - \frac{(1250 - 400)}{3300}$$

$$\theta_S = 2.88 \text{ rad}$$

For larger pulley,

$$\theta_L = \pi + \frac{(D-d)}{C} \quad \ldots \text{14.1b/Pg 238, DHB}$$

$$= \pi + \frac{(1250 - 400)}{3300}$$

$$\theta_L = 3.40 \text{ rad}$$

10. To find width b:

$$P_d = P(\text{kW}) = \frac{btv}{1000} \left[\sigma_d - \frac{wv^2}{10^6 g} \right] \left(\frac{e^{\mu\theta} - 1}{e^{\mu\theta}} \right) \times \eta_j \quad \ldots \text{14.9a/Pg 239, DHB}$$

- Here, $\eta_j = 100\%$ (step 1c) ... **Tb 14.6/Pg 254, DHB**
- Assuming density of leather belt as $\rho = 1000 \text{ kg/m}^3$, $w = 9810 \text{ N/m}^3$
  For motor pulley, $\mu_S \theta_S = 0.506 \times 2.88 = 1.46$
  For winch pulley, $\mu_L \theta_L = 0.506 \times 3.44 = 1.71$
  Here design is based on motor pulley, having $\mu\theta = 1.46$

$$18 = \frac{bt \times 18.48}{1000} \left[2 - \frac{9810 \times 18.48^2}{9.81 \times 10^6} \right] \left(\frac{e^{1.46} - 1}{e^{1.46}} \right) \times 1$$

$$bt = 765 \text{ mm} \quad \text{Eq. } (i)$$

- The relation between the diameter of the pulley and thickness is given (thumb rule) as,

$$\frac{d}{t} < 50$$

i.e.
$$t \geq 0.02d$$
$$t = 0.02 \times 400$$
$$t = 8 \text{ mm}$$

Eq. (i) yields ...
$$b = \frac{765}{8} = 95.63 \text{ mm}$$

Now $b = 95.63$ lies in the range of (24 to 102 mm) with an increment of 6 mm. Thus the standard width, 96 mm (for light loads). ... **Tb 14.1/Pg 251, DHB**

11. *To find tensions:*

We know that,
$$P_d = P(\text{kW}) = \frac{(T_1 - T_2)v}{1000} \qquad \ldots \textbf{14.9a/Pg 239, DHB}$$

$$(T_1 - T_2) = \frac{18 \times 10^3}{18.48} = 974.42 \text{ N} \qquad \ldots \text{Eq. (ii)}$$

Also,
$$\frac{(T_1 - T_c)}{(T_2 - T_c)} = e^{\mu\theta} \qquad \ldots \text{Eq. (iii) } \textbf{14.6c/Pg 238, DHB}$$

But,
$$T_c = \frac{wbtv^2}{10^6 g} \qquad \ldots \textbf{14.7a/Pg 239, DHB}$$

$$= \frac{(9810) \times 96 \times 8 \times 18.48^2}{10^6 \times 9.81}$$

$$T_c = 262.27 \text{ N}$$

Eq. (iii) yields ...
$$(T_1 - T_c) = e^{\mu\theta}(T_2 - T_c)$$
$$= e^{(1.46)}(T_2 - T_c)$$
$$(T_1 - T_c) = 4.304(T_2 - T_c)$$

i.e.
$$(T_1 - 4.304 T_2) = -3.304 T_c$$
$$= -3.304 \times 262.27$$
$$(T_1 - 4.304 T_2) = -866.54 \qquad \ldots \text{Eq. (iv)}$$

Solving Eqs (ii) and (iv) gives,
$$T_1 = 1531.67 \text{ N and}$$
$$T_2 = 557.20 \text{ N}$$

We know that, initial tension,
$$\sqrt{T_1} + \sqrt{T_2} = 2\sqrt{T_0} \qquad \ldots \textbf{14.12/Pg 240, DHB}$$

$$\sqrt{1531.67} + \sqrt{557.20} = 2\sqrt{T_0}$$

$$T_0 = 984.12 \text{ N}.$$

12. A 50 kW, 1200 rpm squirrel cage motor is used to drive a punch press. The motor pulley is of 350 mm diameter and that the driven pulley is 1050 mm in diameter. The center distance is 2.5 m. Design a flat belt drive, assuming a service factor of 1.2.

Solution: $P = 50$ kW, driver (motor) pulley, $d = 350$ mm, $N_{motor} = 1200$ rpm, driven (press) pulley, $D = 1050$ mm, $C = 2.5$ m.

1. *Preliminary decision:*
   a. Assume that the belt is made of oak tanned leather, with $\sigma_d = 2$ MPa.
   b. Assume that the pulley is made of cast iron (damping property).
   c. Assume that the belt is made endless at the factory by means of cemented joint having a joint efficiency (η_j) of 100%, using **Tb14.6/Pg 254, DHB**.
   d. Service factor, $C_S = 1.2$ ... (data)
   e. The design power is $P_d = P(kW) = P \times C_S = 50 \times 1.2 = 60$ kW.

2. *Diameter of driving pulley (motor):* $d = 350$ mm ... (data)

3. *Diameter of driven pulley:* $D = 1050$ mm ... (data)

4. *Standard sizes:*
   Driver pulley (motor), $d = 350$ mm,
   Driven (press) pulley, $D = 1050$ mm

5. *Belt speed:*
$$v = \frac{\pi d N(1-\epsilon)}{60}$$
$$= \frac{\pi \times 0.35 \times 1200 \times (1-0.02)}{60} \quad \text{(assuming a slip of 2\%)}$$
$$v = 21.55 \text{ m/s}$$

6. *Center distance:* $C = 2500$ mm, $\quad [> 1.5(D+d)] \quad$ ... **14.5/Pg 238, DHB**

7. *Coefficient of friction:*

   According to Barth $\quad \mu = 0.54 - \dfrac{0.712}{2.542 + v} \quad$ ... (for leather) **14.6d/Pg 238, DHB**

$$= 0.54 - \frac{0.712}{2.542 + 21.55}$$
$$\mu = 0.51$$

8. *Length of the belt:*

   Assuming open belt we have,
$$L = \frac{\pi(D+d)}{2} + \frac{(D-d)^2}{4C} + 2C \quad \text{... \textbf{14.3/Pg 238, DHB}}$$
$$= \frac{\pi(1050+350)}{2} + \frac{(1050-350)^2}{4 \times 2500} + (2 \times 2500)$$
$$L = 7248.11 \text{ mm} \approx 7.25 \text{ m}$$

9. Angle of contact:

For smaller pulley,

$$\theta_S = \pi - \frac{(D-d)}{C} \quad \text{...14.1a/Pg 238, DHB}$$

$$= \pi - \frac{(1050-350)}{2500}$$

$$\theta_S = 2.86 \text{ rad}$$

For larger pulley,

$$\theta_L = \pi + \frac{(D-d)}{C} \quad \text{...14.1b/Pg 238, DHB}$$

$$= \pi + \frac{(1050-350)}{2500}$$

$$\theta_L = 3.42 \text{ rad}$$

10. To find width b:

$$P_d = P(\text{kW}) = \frac{btv}{1000}\left[\sigma_d - \frac{wv^2}{10^6 g}\right]\left(\frac{e^{\mu\theta}-1}{e^{\mu\theta}}\right) \times \eta_j \quad \text{...14.9a/Pg 239, DHB}$$

- Here, η_j = Efficiency of the joint =100% (step 1c) ... Tb 14.6/Pg 254, DHB
- Assuming density of leather belt as $\rho = 1000$ kg/m³, $w = 9810$ N/m³
  For motor pulley, $\mu_S\theta_S = 0.51 \times 2.86 = 1.46$
  For winch pulley, $\mu_L\theta_L = 0.51 \times 3.42 = 1.74$
  Here design is based on motor pulley, having $\mu\theta = 1.46$

$$60 = \frac{bt \times 21.55}{1000}\left[2 - \frac{9810 \times 21.55^2}{9.81 \times 10^6}\right]\left(\frac{e^{1.46}-1}{e^{1.46}}\right) \times 1$$

$$bt = 2361.59 \text{ mm}^2 \quad \text{...Eq. (i)}$$

- The relation between the diameter of the pulley and thickness is given (thumb rule) as,

$$\frac{d}{t} < 50$$

i.e. $t \geq 0.02d$

$t = 0.02 \times 250$

$t = 7$ mm (Say 8 mm)

Eq. (i) yields ... $b = \frac{2361.56}{8} = 295.20$

Now $b = 295.20$ lies in the range of (200 to 800 mm) with an increment of 25 mm. Thus the standard width, $b = 300$ mm (for light loads).   ... Tb 14.1/Pg 251, DHB

11. To find tensions:

We know that, $P_d = P(\text{kW}) = \frac{(T_1 - T_2)v}{1000} \quad \text{...14.9a/Pg 239, DHB}$

$$(T_1 - T_2) = \frac{60 \times 10^3}{21.55} = 2784.22 \text{ N} \quad \text{...Eq. (ii)}$$

Also, $\frac{(T_1 - T_c)}{(T_2 - T_c)} = e^{\mu\theta} \quad \text{...Eq. (iii) 14.6c/Pg 238, DHB}$

But, $T_c = \frac{wbtv^2}{10^6 g} \quad \text{...14.7a/Pg 239, DHB}$

$$= \frac{(9810) \times 300 \times 8 \times 21.55^2}{10^6 \times 9.81}$$

$$T_c = 1114.57 \text{ N}$$

Eq. (*iii*) yields ... $(T_1 - T_c) = e^{\mu\theta} (T_2 - T_c)$

$$= e^{(1.46)} (T_2 - T_c)$$

$$(T_1 - T_c) = 4.306 (T_2 - T_c)$$

i.e. $(T_1 - 4.3067 \, T_2) = -3.306 \, T_c$

$$= -3.306 \times 1114.77$$

$(T_1 - 4.306 \, T_2) = -3687.77$ ... Eq. (*iv*)

Solving Eqs (*ii*) and (*iv*) gives,

$$T_1 = 4740.96 \text{ N and}$$

$$T_2 = 1956.74 \text{ N}$$

We know that, initial tension,

$$\sqrt{T_1} + \sqrt{T_2} = 2\sqrt{T_0} \qquad \text{... 14.12/Pg 240, DHB}$$

$$\sqrt{4740.96} + \sqrt{1956.74} = 2\sqrt{T_0}$$

$$T_0 = 3197.32 \text{ N.}$$

2.20 V-BELTS

A V-belt is widely used in automotive and industrial machines, such as compressors, pumps, fans, machine tools, etc. These are used to transmit large amount of power when the distance between the two pulleys is small. The profile of the belts and pulleys are such that the belt comes in contact with the sides of pulley grooves and not at the base of the grooves. The V shape causes the belt to wedge tightly into the pulley, increasing friction and allowing higher operating torque.

V-belts are made of fabric and cords moulded with rubber and covered with fabric in the form of a trapezium as shown in **Fig. 2.10**, and are made endless by cementing.

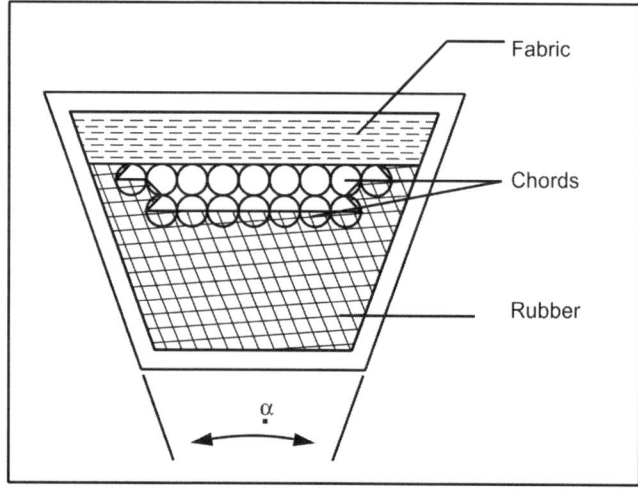

Fig. 2.10: Cross-section of a V-belt

The chords are located near the center of gravity of the belt and transmit the force from driving to driven pulley. Since the chords are nearer to the neutral axis of the belt, the bending stress of the belt is almost negligible. These are particularly suitable for short drives with velocity ratio up to 10:1. The included angle of V-belt is 40° and that of the grooved pulley is 34° to 38°. The groove angle of a sheave is 40° made somewhat smaller than the belt-section angle. This causes the belt to wedge itself into the groove, thus increasing friction. The exact value of this angle depends on the belt section, the sheave diameter, and the angle of contact.

2.21 ADVANTAGES AND DISADVANTAGES OF V-BELT OVER FLAT BELT

Advantages of V-belts
- These are particularly suitable for short drives thereby resulting in compact construction.
- The belts are made endless resulting in smooth and quite operation.
- Higher velocity ratio up to 7 or 8 can be achieved, maximum being 10.
- The drive is positive, because the slip between the belt and the pulley groove is negligible due to wedge action.
- The power transmitted by V-belts is more than flat belts for the same coefficient of friction, arc of contact and allowable tension in the belts.
- The V-belt may be operated in any position.

Disadvantages of V-belt drives
- The V-belt drive cannot be used with large centre distances.
- The efficiency of V-belt is less than flat belt.
- The design of V-grooved pulleys is complicated than pulleys of flat belt drive.

2.22 TYPES OF V-BELTS

According to Indian standards IS: 2494 – 1974, V-belts are classified into five standard sections viz. A, B, C, D, E. These are widely used as general purpose belts. The selection of a particular cross-section depends upon two factors, viz. the power to be transmitted and the speed of the smaller pulley or sheave. V-belts are designated by the symbol of cross-section and the nominal pitch length.

For example **B 4013** represents a belt of cross-section 'B' having a nominal inside length of 4013 mm.

- *Table 14.12/Pg 261, DHB gives the dimensions of the belt(s) along with their power range.*
- *Table 14.13/Pg 262, DHB gives the data regarding nominal inside length, nominal pitch length and permissible length variations for various classification of the belts.*

2.23 DIMENSIONS OF A STANDARD V GROOVED PULLEY

Figure 2.11 shows the dimensions of a standard V grooved pulley, where
  l_p = pitch width (mm)
  b = minimum height of groove above the pitch line (mm)
  h = minimum depth of groove below the pitch line (mm)
  e = center to center distance of grooves (mm)
  f_p = edge of pulley to the first groove center (mm)
- *Table 14.23/Pg 274, DHB gives the minimum pitch diameters in relation to groove angles.*

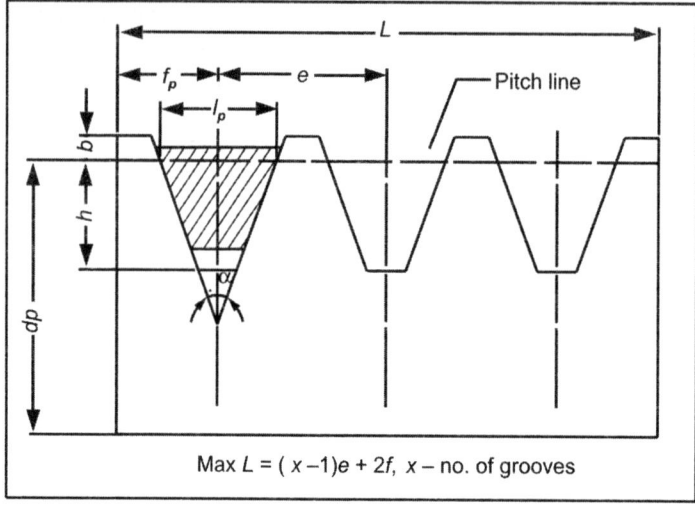

Fig. 2.11: Dimensions of standard V-grooved pulleys **(Fig. 14.24/Pg 274, DHB)**

- *Table 14.24/Pg 274, DHB gives the dimensions for standard V- grooved pulleys.*
- *Table 14.25/Pg 275, DHB gives the standard pulley pitch diameters for various types of belts.*

2.24 POWER TRANSMISSION

The maximum power in kilowatts (kW) which the V-belts of various types or sections can transmit shall be calculated using Equations **14.27a to 14.27e/Pg 243, DHB**.

Example: For belt A, the maximum power that the belt can transmit is

$$kW = \left[\left(0.61v^{-0.09}\right) - \frac{26.68}{d_e} - \left(1.04 \times 10^{-4}\right)v^2\right] \times 0.7355v \qquad \text{... 14.27a/Pg 243, DHB}$$

Where,
kW maximum power in kilowatts at 180° arc of contact for a belt of average length
v = belt speed (m/s).
d_S = equivalent pitch diameter = $d \times K_d$ (mm)
d = diameter of the smaller pulley (mm).
K_d = small diameter factor from **Table 14.19/Pg 269, DHB**

2.25 NUMBER OF BELTS (n')

The number of belts is calculated as $n' = \dfrac{PK_s}{K_L K_a (\text{kW})}$ ... **14.28/Pg 244, DHB**

Where,
P = power in kW
K_s = correction factor according to service ... **Table 14.20/Pg 269, DHB**
K_L = correction factor for belt length ... **Table 14.21/Pg 271, DHB**
K_a = correction factor for arc of contact ... **Table 14.22/Pg 273, DHB**
kW = ratings of V-belt ... **(Equations 14.27 a – e)** and
...**Tables 14.14 to 14.18/Pg 264–268, DHB**

In the absence of tables from manufacturers', the power rating is determined as

$$P(\text{kW}) = \frac{n'av}{1000}\left[\sigma_d - \frac{wv^2}{10^6 g}\right]\left(\frac{e^{\mu_1\theta}-1}{e^{\mu_1\theta}}\right) \qquad \ldots 14.31a/\text{Pg 244, DHB}$$

Where,
 a = area of the belt ($b.t$), mm^2,
 σ_d = working stress = 2.26 MPa
 w = weight density of the belt material = 10.89×10^3 N/m^3
 n' = number of belts

The number of belts should not exceed 8 to 12; if so the next larger belt section should be used. This is because as the number of belts increases, the load distribution is difficult to maintain due to variations in actual length of the belts and in the dimensions of the individual pulley grooves.

2.26 CENTER DISTANCE

The exact center distance o V-belts is calculated as

$$C = A + \sqrt[2]{(A^2 - B)} \qquad \ldots 14.29/\text{Pg 244, DHB}$$

Where,
$$A = \frac{L}{4} - \frac{\pi(D-d)}{8}$$

$$B = \left[\frac{D-d}{8}\right]^2$$

 d = pitch diameter of smaller pulley
 D = pitch diameter of larger pulley.

2.27 PITCH LENGTH OF THE BELT

According to IS, pitch length is defined as the circumferential length of the belt at pitch width of the belt (i.e. the width at neutral axis). The value of pitch width remains constant for each type of belt irrespective of groove angle.

The pitch length of the belt is calculated as

$$L = 2C + 1.57(D+d) + \frac{(D-d)^2}{4C} \qquad \ldots 14.30/\text{Pg 244, DHB}$$

Or ... **14.3/Pg 238, DHB**

The nominal inside lengths and nominal pitch lengths are given in
 ... **Table 14.13/Pg 262, DHB**

2.28 RATIO OF DRIVING TENSIONS IN V-BELT

Figure 2.12 shows a V-belt in a grooved pulley
Let,
 α = groove angle of the pulley
 R = Normal reaction between the belt and side of pulley groove
 R_1 = total reaction in the plane of the groove
 μ = coefficient of friction between the belt and the pulley surface
Resolving the forces vertically,
$$R_1 = R\sin(\alpha/2) + R\sin(\alpha/2)$$

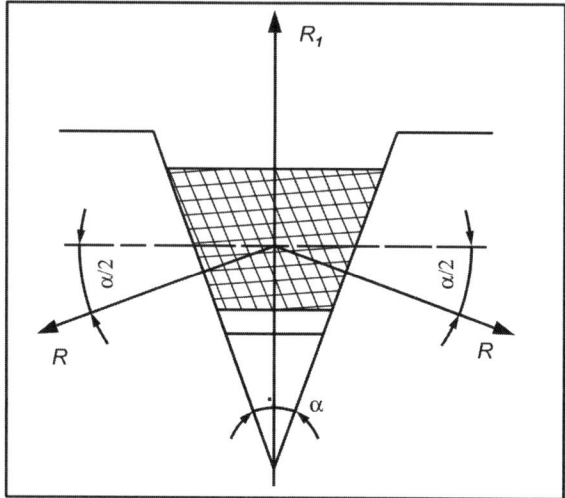

Fig. 2.12: Components in V-belts

$$R_1 = 2R \sin(\alpha/2) \quad \ldots \text{(Eq. 2.46)}$$

The total frictional force $= \mu R + \mu R = 2\mu R \quad \ldots \text{(Eq. 2.47)}$

Consider a driven pulley rotating in clockwise direction as shown in **Fig. 2.13**.

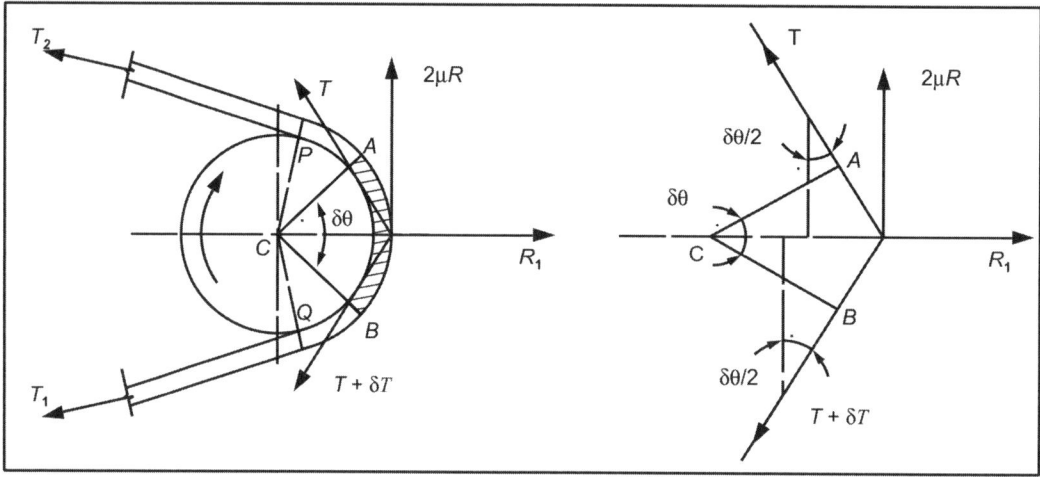

Fig. 2.13: Ratio of driving tensions in V-belts

Let,

T_1 = tension on tight side of the belt

T_2 = tension on slack side of the belt

θ = angle of contact –or- lap angle

μ = coefficient of friction between the pulley and the belt.

Consider a small element AB subtending an angle $\delta\theta$ at the center of the pulley. This element is in equilibrium under the following forces.

- Tension T in the belt at A
- Tension $(T + \delta T)$ in the belt at B

- Normal reaction $R_1 = 2R \sin(\alpha/2)$
- Frictional force $2\mu R$

The components of force are shown in **Fig. 2.14**

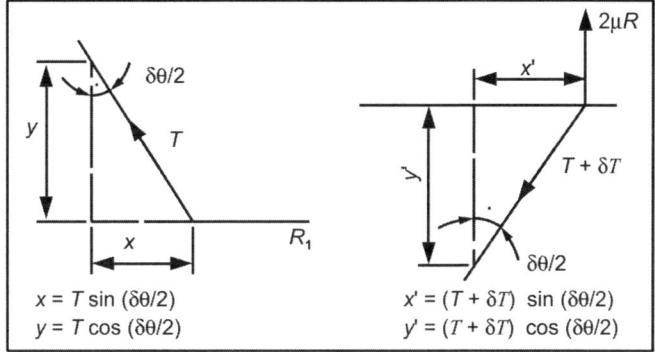

Fig. 2.14: Components of force in V-belts

Resolving the forces horizontally, we have
$$R_1 = x + x'$$
$$= T \sin(\delta\theta/2) + (T + \delta T) \sin(\delta\theta/2)$$
$$R_1 = 2T \sin(\delta\theta/2) + \delta T \sin (T + \delta T)$$

Since $\delta\theta$ is very small, letting $\sin(\delta\theta/2) \approx \delta\theta/2$
$$R_1 = 2T (\delta\theta/2) + \delta T (\delta\theta/2)$$

Neglecting $\delta T (\delta\theta/2)$, we have
$$R_1 = 2T (\delta\theta/2)$$
$$2R \sin(\alpha/2) = T\, \delta\theta$$
$$R = \frac{T\,\delta\theta}{2\sin(\alpha/2)} \qquad \ldots \text{(Eq. 2.48)}$$

Resolving the forces vertically, we have
$$2\mu R + y = y'$$
$$2\mu R = (T + \delta T)\cos(\delta\theta/2) - T\cos(\delta\theta/2)$$
$$2\mu R = \delta T \cos(\delta\theta/2)$$

Since $\cos(\delta\theta/2) \approx 1$, we have
$$2\mu R = \delta T \qquad \ldots \text{(Eq. 2.49)}$$

Substituting Eq. (2.48) in Eq. (2.49) yields
$$2\mu \cdot \left[\frac{T \cdot \delta\theta}{2\sin(\alpha/2)}\right] = \delta T$$

$$\frac{\mu\,\delta\theta}{\sin(\alpha/2)} = \delta T/T \qquad \ldots \text{(Eq. 2.49a)}$$

Integrating between the limits T_1 and T_2
$$\int_0^\theta \frac{\mu\,\delta\theta}{\sin(\alpha/2)} = \int_{T_2}^{T_1} \frac{\delta T}{T}$$

$$\frac{\mu\delta\theta}{\sin(\alpha/2)} = \ln T \bigg|_{T_2}^{T_1} = \ln(T_1 - T_2)$$

$$\frac{\mu\cdot\theta}{\sin(\alpha/2)} = \ln\left(\frac{T_1}{T_2}\right)$$

$$\frac{T_1}{T_2} = e^{\frac{\mu\theta}{\sin(\alpha/2)}}$$

$$\frac{T_1}{T_2} = e^{\mu_1\theta} \qquad \ldots \text{(Eq. 2.50)}$$

If centrifugal tension is considered, then,

$$\frac{T_1 - T_c}{T_2 - T_c} = e^{\mu_1\theta} \qquad \ldots \text{(Eq. 2.51) } \mathbf{14.26/Pg\ 242, DHB}$$

In terms of stress,

$$\frac{\sigma_1 - \sigma_c}{\sigma_2 - \sigma_c} = e^{\mu_1\theta} \qquad \ldots \text{(Eq. 2.52)}$$

Where,

$\mu_1 = \dfrac{\mu}{\sin(\alpha/2)}$ is the apparent coefficient of friction.

13. A V-belt drive is designed to connect two shafts 1000 mm apart. The diameter of driving pulley is 400 mm and transmits 60 kW at 900 rpm. The follower pulley rotates at 300 rpm. The angle of groove is 40° and the coefficient of friction between the belt and the pulley rim is 0.25. The area of belt section is 270 mm² and the permissible stress is 2 MPa. Density of belt is 1000 kg/m³. Calculate the number of belts required and the length of the belt. Also find the initial tension in the belt.

Solution: $C = 1000$ mm, $P = 60$ kW, (driver speed) $N_L = 900$ rpm, $d = 400$ mm, (driven speed) $N_S = 300$ rpm, $\alpha = 40°$, $\mu = 0.25$, $a = 270$ mm², $\sigma_d = 2$ MPa, $\rho = 1000$ kg/m³, $n' = ?$, $T_0 = ?$

a. To find n':

We know that, $\quad P = \dfrac{n'av}{1000}\left[\sigma_d - \dfrac{wv^2}{10^6 g}\right]\left(\dfrac{e^{\mu_1\theta} - 1}{e^{\mu_1\theta}}\right) \qquad \ldots$ Eq. (i) **14.31a/Pg 244, DHB**

Since μ is same for both the pulleys, design is based on smaller pulley.

Now velocity ratio, $i = \dfrac{900}{300} = \dfrac{D}{400}$

$$D = 1200 \text{ mm}$$

Velocity, $\quad v = \dfrac{\pi d N_L}{60} = \dfrac{\pi \times 0.4 \times 900}{60} = 18.85$ m/s

Angle of contact of smaller pulley, $\theta_S = \pi - \dfrac{(D-d)}{C}$ ... **14.1a/Pg 238, DHB**

$$= \pi - \dfrac{(1200 - 400)}{1000}$$

$$D = 2.342 \text{ rad}$$

Also, apparent coefficient of friction,

$$\mu_1 = \dfrac{\mu}{\sin(\alpha/2)} \qquad \ldots \mathbf{14.26/Pg\ 242, DHB}$$

$$= \frac{0.25}{\sin(40/2)}$$
$$\mu_1 = 0.731$$

Eq. (i) yields ... $60 = \frac{n' \times 270 \times 18.85}{1000}\left[2 - \frac{1000 \times 18.85^2}{10^6}\right]\left(\frac{e^{0.731 \times 2.342} - 1}{e^{0.731 \times 2.342}}\right)$ $\left(\rho = \frac{w}{g}\right)$

$$n' = 8.75 \simeq 9 \text{ belts}$$

b. To find T_0:

We know that, $\quad P = \dfrac{(T_1 - T_2)v}{1000}$

$$(T_1 - T_2) = \frac{60 \times 10^3}{18.85} = 3183.02 \text{ N} \qquad \ldots \text{Eq. (ii)}$$

Also, $\quad \dfrac{(T_1 - T_c)}{(T_2 - T_c)} = e^{\mu_1 \theta} \qquad \ldots$ Eq. (iii) **14.26/Pg 242, DHB**

But, $\quad T_c = \dfrac{wbtv^2}{10^6 g} \qquad \ldots$ **14.7a/Pg 239, DHB**

$$= \frac{(9810) \times 270 \times 18.85^2}{10^6 \times 9.81}$$

$$T_c = 95.94 \text{ N}$$

Eq. (iii) yields ...

$$(T_1 - T_c) = e^{\mu_1 \theta}(T_2 - T_c)$$
$$= e^{(0.731 \times 2.342)}(T_2 - T_c)$$
$$(T_1 - T_c) = 5.54(T_2 - T_c)$$

i.e. $\quad (T_1 - 5.54 T_2) = -5.54 T_c$
$$= -4.54 \times 95.94$$
$$(T_1 - 5.54 T_2) = -435.58 \qquad \ldots \text{Eq. (iv)}$$

Solving Eqs (ii) and (iv) gives,
$$T_1 = 3980 \text{ N and}$$
$$T_2 = 797 \text{ N}$$

We know that, initial tension,
$$\sqrt{T_1} + \sqrt{T_2} = 2\sqrt{T_0} \qquad \ldots \textbf{14.12/Pg 240, DHB}$$
$$\sqrt{3980} + \sqrt{797} = 2\sqrt{T_0}$$
$$T_0 = 2084.76 \text{ N}.$$

14. Two shafts 1 meter apart are connected by V-belt to transmit 90 kW at 1200 rpm of a driver pulley of 300 mm effective diameter. The driven pulley rotates at 400 rpm. The angle of groove is 40° and the coefficient of friction between the belt and the pulley rim is 0.25. The area of belt section is 400 mm² and the permissible stress is 2.1 MPa. Density of belt is 1100 kg/m³. Calculate the number of belts required and the length of the belt. *[VTU- June/July 2009–15 Marks]*

Solution: $C = 1$ m, $P = 90$ kW, (driver speed) $N_L = 1200$ rpm, $d = 300$ mm, (driven speed) $N_S = 400$ rpm, $\alpha = 40°$, $\mu = 0.25$, $a = 400$ mm², $\sigma_d = 2.1$ MPa, $\rho = 1100$ kg/m³, $n' = ?$, $L = ?$

a. To find n':

We know that, $P = \dfrac{n'av}{1000}\left[\sigma_d - \dfrac{wv^2}{10^6 g}\right]\left(\dfrac{e^{\mu_1\theta}-1}{e^{\mu_1\theta}}\right)$ ... Eq. (i) **14.31a/Pg 244, DHB**

Since μ is same for both the pulleys, design is based on smaller pulley.

Now velocity ratio, $i = \dfrac{1200}{400} = \dfrac{D}{400}$

$D = 1200$ mm

Velocity, $v = \dfrac{\pi d N_L}{60} = \dfrac{\pi \times 0.4 \times 1200}{60} = 25.13$ m/s

Angle of contact of smaller pulley,

$\theta_S = \pi - \dfrac{(D-d)}{C}$ ... **14.1a/Pg 238, DHB**

$= \pi - \dfrac{(1200-400)}{1000}$

$\theta_S = 2.342$ rad

Also, apparent coefficient of friction,

$\mu_1 = \dfrac{\mu}{\sin(\alpha/2)}$ ... **14.26/ Pg 242, DHB**

$= \dfrac{0.25}{\sin(40/2)}$

$\mu_1 = 0.731$

Eq. (i) yields ...

$90 = \dfrac{n' \times 400 \times 25.13}{1000}\left[2.1 - \dfrac{1100 \times 25.13^2}{10^6}\right]\left(\dfrac{e^{0.731\times 2.342}-1}{e^{0.731\times 2.342}}\right)\quad \left(\because \rho = \dfrac{w}{g}\right)$

$n' = 7.77 \approx 8$ belts

b. To find length of belt:

Assuming that the belt is of open type, we have,

$L = \dfrac{\pi(D+d)}{2} + \dfrac{(D-d)^2}{4C} + 2C$ ... **14.3/Pg 238, DHB**

$= \dfrac{\pi(1200+400)}{2} + \dfrac{(1200-400)^2}{4\times 1000} + 2\times 1000$ or ... **14.30/Pg 244, DHB**

$= 4673.27$ mm

$L = 4.67$ m

15. A compressor requiring 90 kW is to run at 250 rpm. The drive is by V-belt from an electric motor running at 750 rpm. The diameter of the pulley on the compressor shaft is 1 m, while the center distance between the pulleys is limited to 1.75 m. The belt speed should not exceed 1600 m/min. Determine the number

Belt, Rope and Chain Drives **163**

of V-belts required to transmit the power if each belt has a cross-sectional area of 375 mm² and density of 1 mg/m³ and has an allowable stress of 2.5 N/mm². The groove angle of the pulley is 35° and the coefficient of friction between the belt and the pulley is 0.25. *[VTU-Dec 09/Jan 10–10 Marks]*

Solution: $P = 90$ kW, driven (compressor) speed $N_L = 250$ rpm, driver (motor) speed $N_S = 750$ rpm, Driven diameter, $D = 1$ m $= 1000$ mm, $C = 1.75$ m $= 1750$ mm, $v = 1600$ m/min $= 26.67$ m/s, $n' = ?$, $a = 375$ mm², $\rho = 1$ mg/m³ $= 1000$ kg/m³, $\sigma_d = 2.5$ MPa, $\alpha = 35°$, $\mu = 0.25$.

We know that, $P = \dfrac{n'av}{1000}\left[\sigma_d - \dfrac{wv^2}{10^6 g}\right]\left(\dfrac{e^{\mu_1\theta}-1}{e^{\mu_1\theta}}\right)$ ... Eq. (i) **14.31a/Pg 244, DHB**

Since μ is same for both the pulleys, design is based on smaller pulley.

Now velocity ratio, $i = \dfrac{750}{250} = \dfrac{1000}{d}$

$d = 333.33$ mm ≈ 330 mm

Angle of contact of smaller pulley,

$$\theta_S = \pi - \dfrac{(D-d)}{C} \qquad \text{...14.1a/Pg 238, DHB}$$

$$= \pi - \dfrac{(1000-330)}{1750}$$

$$\theta_S = 2.76 \text{ rad}$$

Also, apparent coefficient of friction,

$$\mu_1 = \dfrac{\mu}{\sin(\alpha/2)} \qquad \text{...14.26/Pg 242, DHB}$$

$$= \dfrac{0.25}{\sin(35/2)}$$

$$\mu_1 = 0.8314$$

Eq. (i) yields ...

$$90 = \dfrac{n' \times 375 \times 26.67}{1000}\left[2.5 - \dfrac{9810 \times 26.67^2}{10^6 \times 9.81}\right]\left(\dfrac{e^{0.834 \times 2.76}-1}{e^{0.8314 \times 2.76}}\right)$$

$n' = 5.59 \approx 6$ belts

16. A belt drive consists of two V-belts in parallel, on grooved pulleys of same size. The angle of the groove is 30°. The cross-sectional area of each belt is 740 mm² and μ = 0.13. The density of the belt material is 1200 kg/m³ and the maximum safe stress is 7000 kN/m². Calculate the power that can be transmitted between pulleys of 300 mm diameter rotating at 1200 rpm. Also, find the shaft speed in rpm at which the power transmitted would be maximum?
[VTU- May/June 2010–12 Marks]

Solution: $n' = 2, \alpha = 30°, a = 740$ mm², $\mu = 0.13, \rho = 1200$ kg/m³, $\sigma_d = 7000$ kN/m² $= 7$ N/mm², $P = ?, D = d = 300$ mm (data), $N_L = N_S = 1200$ rpm, $N_{max} = ?$

a. To find P:

We know that, $P = \dfrac{n'av}{1000}\left[\sigma_d - \dfrac{wv^2}{10^6 g}\right]\left(\dfrac{e^{\mu_1\theta}-1}{e^{\mu_1\theta}}\right)$ ...Eq. (i) **4.31a/Pg 244, DHB**

Since μ is same for both the pulleys, design is based on smaller pulley.

Velocity, $v = \dfrac{\pi d N}{60} = \dfrac{\pi \times 0.3 \times 1200}{60} = 18.85$ m/s

Angle of contact of smaller pulley,

$$\theta_s = \pi - \dfrac{(D-d)}{C} = \pi - 0 \qquad \text{... 14.1a/Pg 238, DHB}$$

$\therefore \theta_s = 3.142$ rad $\qquad (D = d = 300$ mm$)$

Also, apparent coefficient of friction,

$$\mu_1 = \dfrac{\mu}{\sin(\alpha/2)} \qquad \text{... 14.26/Pg 242, DHB}$$

$$= \dfrac{0.13}{\sin(30/2)}$$

$\mu_1 = 0.502$

Eq. (i) yields ... $P = \dfrac{2 \times 740 \times 18.85}{1000}\left[7 - \dfrac{1200 \times 18.85^2}{10^6}\right]\left(\dfrac{e^{0.502 \times 3.142} - 1}{e^{0.502 \times 3.142}}\right) \qquad \left(\because \rho = \dfrac{w}{g}\right)$

$P = 145.51$ kW

b. To find N_{max}:

We know that for maximum power transmission,

$$T_c = \dfrac{T}{3}$$

$$= \dfrac{\sigma_d a}{3} = \dfrac{7 \times 740}{3}$$

$T_c = 1726.67$ N

But, $T_c = \dfrac{wbtv'^2}{10^6 g} = \dfrac{wav'^2}{10^6 g} \qquad \text{... 14.7a/Pg 239, DHB}$

$1726.67 = \dfrac{1200 \times 740 \times v'^2}{10^6}$

$v' = 44.1$ m/s

Now maximum velocity,

$$v' = \dfrac{\pi d N_{max}}{60} = \dfrac{\pi \times 0.3 \times N_{max}}{60}$$

$N_{max} = 2807.23$ rpm

17. The following data is given for a V-belt connecting 20 kW motor pulley to a compressor;

	Motor pulley	Compressor pulley
Pitch diameter (mm)	300	900
Speed (rpm)	1440	480
Coefficient of friction	0.2	0.2

The center distance between the pulleys is 1 m. CS of belt is trapezoidal with parallel sides being 12 mm and 22 mm respectively and the depth is 14 mm. The density of the composite belt is 0.97 gm/cc and the allowable tension per belt is 850 N. determine the number of belts required for this application.

[VTU-May/June 2010–12 Marks]

Solution:

Driver (motor): $d = 300$ mm, $N_S = 440$ rpm, $\mu_S = 0.2 = \mu_L$, $P = 20$ kW

Driven (compressor): $D = 900$ mm, $N_S = 480$ rpm, $C = 1$m $= 1000$ mm, $\rho = 0.97$ gm/cc $= 970$ kg/m³, $T_1 = 850$ N,

Belt details: $b_1 = 22$mm, $b = 12$ mm, $h = 14$ mm, $n' = ?$

We know that, $P = \dfrac{n'av}{1000}\left[\sigma_d - \dfrac{wv^2}{10^6 g}\right]\left(\dfrac{e^{\mu_1\theta}-1}{e^{\mu_1\theta}}\right)$ ... Eq. (i) **14.31a/Pg 244, DHB**

Since µ is same for both the pulleys, design is based on smaller pulley.
Angle of contact of smaller pulley,

$$\theta_S = \pi - \dfrac{(D-d)}{C} \quad \text{... 14.1a/ Pg 238, DHB}$$

$$= \pi - \dfrac{(900-300)}{1000}$$

$$\theta_S = 2.542 \text{ rad}$$

Also, apparent coefficient of friction,

$$\mu_1 = \dfrac{\mu}{\sin(\alpha/2)} \quad \text{... 14.26/Pg 242, DHB}$$

$$= \dfrac{0.2}{\sin(40/2)} \quad \text{(assume } \alpha = 40°\text{)}$$

$$\mu_1 = 05847$$

Area of the belt, $a = \dfrac{h}{2}(b_1 + b) = \dfrac{14 \times (22+12)}{2} = 238$ mm²

Velocity of the belt, $v = \dfrac{\pi dN}{60} = \dfrac{\pi \times 0.3 \times 1440}{60} = 22.62$ m/s

Design stress, $\sigma_d = \dfrac{T_1}{a} = \dfrac{850}{238} = 3.57$ N/mm²

Eq. (i) yields ... $20 = \dfrac{n' \times 238 \times 22.62}{1000}\left[3.57 - \dfrac{970 \times 22.62^2}{10^6}\right]\left(\dfrac{e^{0.5847\times 2.542}-1}{e^{0.5847\times 2.542}}\right)$

$n' = 1.561 \simeq 2$ belts

18. A V-belt drive is required to transmit 19 kW at 1500 rpm from a 250 mm pitch diameter sheave to a 900 mm diameter flat pulley. The center distance between the shafts is 1 m. The groove angle is 40° and the coefficient of friction between the belt and the sheave is 0.2 and that between the belt and flat pulley is 0.2. The cross-section of the belt is 40 mm wide at the top, 20 mm wide at bottom and 25 mm deep. Each belt weighs 9810 kN/m and the allowable tension in the belt is 1000 N Determine the number of belts.

Solution: $P = 19$ kW, $N_S = 1500$ rpm, sheave diameter $d = 250$ mm, flat pulley diameter, $D_f = 900$ mm, $C = 1$m, $\alpha = 40°$, $\mu_S = 0.2 = \mu_L$, $w = 9810$ kN/m³, $T_1 = 1000$ N **(Fig. 2.15)**.

Belt details: $b_1 = 40$ mm, $b = 20$ mm, $h = 25$ mm, $n' = ?$

We know that, $\quad P = \dfrac{n'av}{1000}\left[\sigma_d - \dfrac{wv^2}{10^6 g}\right]\left(\dfrac{e^{\mu_1 \theta} - 1}{e^{\mu_1 \theta}}\right)$ ... Eq. (*i*) **14.31a/Pg 244, DHB**

Area of the belt, $\quad a = \dfrac{h}{2}(b_1 + b) = \dfrac{25 \times (40 + 20)}{2} = 750$ mm²

Velocity of the belt, $v = \dfrac{\pi dN}{60} = \dfrac{\pi \times 0.25 \times 1500}{60} = 19.63$ m/s

Design stress, $\quad \sigma_d = \dfrac{T_1}{a} = \dfrac{1000}{750} = 1.33$ N/mm²

In general the thickness of the flat belt is negligible compared to the diameter of the pulley, but is not the case in V-belts. Hence the pitch diameter of the V-belt on the flat pulley is calculated by assuming that the pitch diameter is measured at the centroid of the belt section.

i.e. The pitch diameter of larger pulley is $D = D_f + 2\bar{x}$ ... Eq. (*ii*)

From **Fig. f-Tb 1.3/Pg 9, DHB**, $b = 20$ mm, $b_1 = 40$ mm, $h = 25$ mm, therefore, $b_0 = b_1 - b = 40 - 20 = 20$ mm

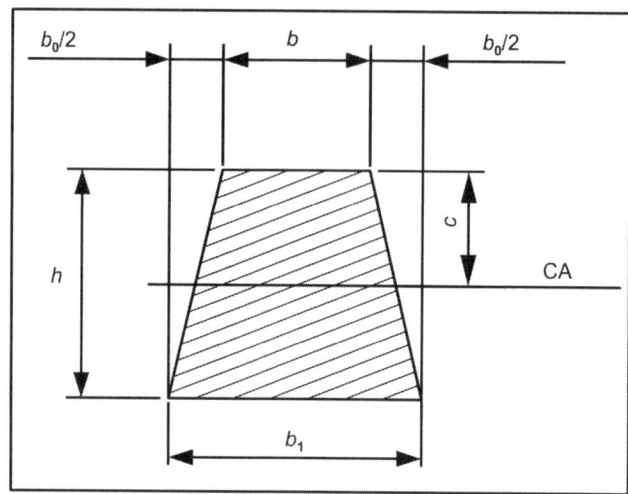

Fig. 2.15: Trapezoidal section (Problem 18)

$$C = \bar{x} = \dfrac{(3b + 2b_0)h}{3(2b + b_0)}$$

$$\bar{x} = \dfrac{(3 \times 20 + 2 \times 20)25}{3(3 \times 20 + 20)}$$

$\bar{x} = 13.9$ mm

Eq. (*ii*) yields ... $\quad D = 900 + 2 \times 13.9 = 927.8$ mm

Thus the pitch diameters are, $d = 250$ **mm and** $D = 930$ **mm**

Angle of contact

V-belt:

Angle of contact of smaller pulley, $\theta_s = \pi - \dfrac{(D - d)}{C}$ ... **14.1a/Pg 238, DHB**

$$= \pi - \frac{(930-250)}{1000}$$

$$\theta_S = 2.462 \text{ rad}$$

Therefore, $$e^{\mu_s \theta} = \frac{\mu_s \theta_S}{\sin(\alpha/2)}$$

$$= \frac{0.2 \times 2.464}{\sin(40/2)} \quad \ldots \text{Eq. }(iii)$$

$$e^{\mu_s \theta} = 4.22$$

Flat belt:
Angle of contact of larger pulley,

$$\theta_L = \pi + \frac{(D-d)}{C} \quad \ldots \text{14.1a/Pg 238, DHB}$$

$$= \pi + \frac{(930-250)}{1000}$$

$$\theta_S = 3.822 \text{ rad}$$

Therefore, $$e^{\mu_L \theta} = e^{(0.2 \times 3.822)}$$

$$e^{\mu_L \theta} = 2.147 \quad \ldots \text{Eq. }(iv)$$

Comparing Eqs (*iii*) and (*iv*), select the least value for design, i.e. $e^{\mu_L \theta} = \mathbf{2.147}$

Eq. (*i*) yields … $$19 = \frac{n' \times 750 \times 19.63}{1000} \left[1.33 - \frac{9810 \times 19.63^2}{10^6 \times 9.81}\right]\left(\frac{2.147-1}{2.147}\right)$$

$$n' = 2.56 \approx \mathbf{3 \text{ belts}}$$

19. **Determine the percentage increase in power capacity made possible in changing over from a flat belt to a V-belt. The diameter of the flat pulley is same as the pitch diameter of grooved pulley. The pulley rotates at the same speed as that of the grooved pulley. The coefficient of friction is 0.3, same for flat and v-belts. The groove angle is 60° and the angle of wrap is 150° in each case. The belts are made of same material and have the same cross-section.**

Solution:

Parameters	Flat belt	V-belt
Diameter	$d = D$	$d = D$
Speed (rpm)	$N_S = N_L$	$N_S = N_L$
Coefficient of friction, μ	$\mu_S = \mu_L = 0.3$	$\mu_S = \mu_L = 0.3$
Groove angle, α	–	60°
Angle of wrap, θ	150°	–
Area, a	a	a

Percentage increase in power = ?
We know that, percentage increase in power

$$= \frac{P_v - P_{\text{flat}}}{P_{\text{flat}}} = \frac{P_v}{P_{\text{flat}}} - 1 \quad \ldots \text{Eq. }(i)$$

Now,
$$\frac{P_v}{P_{flat}} = \frac{\left(\frac{e^{\mu_1\theta}-1}{e^{\mu_1\theta}}\right)}{\left(\frac{e^{\mu\theta}-1}{e^{\mu\theta}}\right)} \quad \ldots \text{Eq. (ii)}$$

(All other parameters are same and get cancelled)

$$\left(\frac{e^{\mu\theta}-1}{e^{\mu\theta}}\right) = \frac{e^{(0.3\times 150\pi/180)}-1}{e^{(0.3\times 150\pi/180)}} = 0.5441$$

$$\left(\frac{e^{\mu_1\theta}-1}{e^{\mu_1\theta}}\right) = \frac{e^{[0.3\times 150\pi/(180\times \sin(30))]}-1}{e^{[0.3\times 150\pi/(180\times \sin(30))]}} = 0.7921$$

Eq. (ii) yields ...
$$\frac{P_v}{P_{flat}} = \frac{0.7921}{0.5441} = 1.456$$

Eq. (i) yields ... Percentage increase in power = $1.456 - 1 = 0.456 = 45.6\%$.

2.29 DESIGN PROCEDURE FOR V-BELTS

1. Make a preliminary decision regarding:
   a. The material used for pulley (generally CI),
   b. The service conditions (K_s) K_s service factor   ... **Table 14.20/ Pg 269, DHB** based on combination of driving and driven pulleys/ members.
   c. Calculate the design power, $P_d = P$ (kW) $= P \times K_S$ ... (in kW)
2. *Belt Selection:* Based on design power (P_d), select the type of belt from **Table 14.12/ Pg 261, DHB** and note down the nominal top width, nominal thickness of the belt and maximum velocity.
3. Find the pitch diameter of the motor pulley (driver) using the relation:

$$d = 630 \times \sqrt[3]{\frac{P_d(kW)}{w_{max}}} \quad \ldots \text{14.13a/Pg 240, DHB}$$

Where, $w_{max} = 2\pi n_{max} = \dfrac{2\pi N_{max}}{60}$ (rad/s)

n = speed (rps), N = speed (rpm)
- $d = D_{min}$, only in step-down device.
- $D_{min} = D$, for a step-up device. Here instead of selecting the diameter of the pulley, the belt velocity v may be specified and then d is determined.

Note: If the belt type does not tally with that selected in step 2, then the next lower belt type has to be chosen,   ...(*Refer Problem 22*)

4. Calculate the pitch diameter of the driven pulley as:
$$D = (1-\epsilon) \times d \times i = d \times i \quad \text{(neglecting '}\epsilon\text{')} \ldots \text{14.13b/Pg 240, DHB}$$
i = velocity ratio
5. Standardize the pitch diameters of pulley in steps 3 and 4, using:
  ... **Table 14.25/Pg 275, DHB** (Preference – 1, in DHB)
- Find the revised velocity ratio, i', using standardized values.

6. Calculate the belt speed as:

$$v = \frac{\pi D_1 N_1}{60}$$ ... *[Should be $\leq v_{max}$ in 14.27 (a – e)]* i.e. in step 2

D_1 = diameter of driver (D or d), N – rpm of driver.

7. Determine the approximate center distance as:
$$C_{appr} \geq 1.5 (D + d)$$ ... **14.5/Pg 238, DHB**

8. Determine the pitch length of the belt using: ... **14.30/Pg 244, DHB**
   - Note down the standard values of pitch length and nominal length based on the type of belt in step 2, from ... **Table 14.13/Pg 262, DHB**

9. Calculate the exact center distance using: ... **14.29/Pg 244, DHB**

10. Calculate the angle of contact of driver pulley (larger/smaller):
    $[\theta > 120°]$ ... **14.1/Pg 238, DHB**

11. Calculate the number of belts as:

$$n' = \frac{PK_S}{(kW)K_L K_a} = \frac{P_d}{(kW)K_L K_a} \quad [\theta > 120°]... \textbf{14.28/Pg 244, DHB}$$

K_S = service factor ... (step 1) ... **Table 14.20/Pg 269, DHB**
K_L = correction factor for length ... **Table 14.21/ Pg 271, DHB**
K_a = correction factor for arc of contact ... **Table 14.22/ Pg 273, DHB**
(kW) To be calculated from (14.27a – 14.27e)/ **Pg 243, DHB** - based on the type of belt selected, as in step 2.

- In equations **(14.27a–14.27e)/Pg 243, DHB**
  Equivalent pitch diameter, $d = K_d d$
  K_d = smaller diameter factor, based on ...**Table 14.19/Pg 269, DHB**
  d = pitch diameter of smaller pulley,
  v = velocity of driver pulley as calculated in step 6.

12. Specify the belt by the cross-section selected in step 2 and the nominal inside length as in step 8.

Note:
- If the calculated value of is greater than the maximum value in *14.27(a – e)*, then select the maximum value, i.e. as given in ... **(14.27a – 14.27e)/Pg 243, DHB**
- The calculated value of (kW) in step 11, should be approximately equal to the power ratings as given in **Tables (14.14 – 14.18)/ Pg (264 – 268)** for respective belt selected in step (2), based on belt speed (maximum velocity).
- All the calculations are made assuming that $\alpha = 40°$. If the groove angle is varied then refer **Table 14.23/Pg 274, DHB** for the minimum pitch diameters for the corresponding type of belt.

20. **Select a suitable V-belt to transmit 15 kW to a compressor. The motor speed is 1200 rpm and compressor pulley runs at 400 rpm (Fig. 2.16).**

Solution: $P = 15$ kW, motor speed (driver) $N_S = 1200$ rpm, $N_L = 400$ rpm, velocity ratio,

$$i = \frac{N_L}{N_S} = \frac{1200}{400} = 3$$

1. **Preliminary decision:**
   a. Assume that the pulley is made of cast iron (damping property).
   b. Based on given power and combination of driving and driven members, the service factor for driven member (compressor) is taken as $K_S = 1.2$ [(column 5), assuming light service and operating continuously].

   ... **Tb 14.20/ Pg 269, DHB**

   c. The design power is $P_d = P$ (kW) $= P \times K_S = 15 \times 1.2 = 18$ kW.

2. **Belt selection:**

   Referring to **Table 14.12/ Pg 261, DHB**, $P_d = 18$ kW lies in the range of 10 to 70 kW. Hence select Type 'C' belt having

   Nominal top width = 22 mm,   Nominal thickness = 14 mm,
   Maximum velocity, $v_{max} = 25$ m/s.

3. **Pitch diameter of the motor pulley (driver):**

   $$d = 630 \times \sqrt[3]{\frac{P_d(\text{kW})}{w_{max}}} \quad \ldots \text{14.13a/Pg 240, DHB}$$

   Where, $\quad w_{max} = 2\pi n_{max} = \dfrac{2\pi \times 1200}{60} = 125.66$ (rad/s)

   $$d = 630 \times \sqrt[3]{\frac{18}{125.66}}$$

   $$d = 329.66 \text{ mm}$$

   Therefore, standard pitch diameter for 'C' size belt is $d = 400$ mm.

   ... **Tb 14.25/ Pg 275, DHB** *(Preference – 1, in DHB)*

4. **Pitch diameter of the driven pulley:**

   $D = d \times i$ (Neglecting '$\in$')   ... **14.13b/Pg 240, DHB**

   $D = 400 \times 3 = 1200$ mm

   Therefore, standard size, $D = 1250$ mm.   ... **Tb 14.25/Pg 275, DHB**

5. **Standard sizes:**

   Driver pulley (motor) $d = 400$ mm   driven pulley, $D = 250$ mm

   - Revised velocity ratio, $\quad i' = \dfrac{D}{d} = \dfrac{1250}{400} = 3.125$

6. **Belt speed:**

   $$v = \frac{\pi d N}{60} = \frac{\pi \times 0.4 \times 1200}{60} = 25.13 \text{ m/s} \approx v_{max} \text{ in step (2)}$$

7. **Approximate center distance:**

   $C_{appr} \geq 1.5$ (D + d)   ... **14.5/Pg 238, DHB**

   $C_{appr} = 1.5 \times (1250 + 400)$

   $C_{appr} = 2475$ mm

8. **Pitch length of the belt:**

   $$L = 2C + 1.57(D+d) + \frac{(D-d)^2}{4C} \quad \ldots \text{14.30/Pg 244, DHB}$$

   $$= 2 \times 2475 + 1.57(1250 + 400) + \frac{(1250 - 400)^2}{4 \times 2475}$$

   $$L = 7613.5 \text{ mm}$$

For C-belt (step 2), the nearest standard nominal pitch length is $L = 7625$ mm
and nominal inside length = 7569 mm ... **Tb 14.13/Pg 262, DHB**

9. *Exact center distance:*

$$C = A + \sqrt[2]{(A^2 - B)} \quad \text{... Eq. }(i) \text{ } \textbf{14.29/Pg 244, DHB}$$

Where,
$$A = \frac{L}{4} - \frac{\pi(D+d)}{8} = \frac{7625}{4} - \frac{\pi(1250+400)}{8} = 1258.3 \text{ mm}$$

$$B = \left[\frac{D-d}{8}\right]^2 = \left[\frac{1250-400}{8}\right]^2 = 11289 \text{ mm}$$

Eq. (i) Yields ...
$$C = 1258.3 + \sqrt[2]{(1258.3^2 - 11289)}$$
$$C = 2512.08 \text{ mm}$$

10. *Angle of contact of driver pulley:*

Angle of contact of smaller pulley,

$$\theta_S = \pi - 2\sin^{-1}\frac{(D-d)}{2C} \quad \text{... } \textbf{14.1a/Pg 238, DHB}$$

$$= \pi - 2\sin^{-1}\left(\frac{1250-400}{2 \times 2512.08}\right)$$

$$\theta_S = 160.52° \quad (\theta > 120°)$$

11. *Number of belts:*

$$n' = \frac{PK_S}{(kW)K_L K_a} = \frac{P_d}{(kW)K_L K_a} \quad \text{... Eq. }(ii) \text{ } \textbf{14.28/Pg 244, DHB}$$

For a 'C' belt,

$$(kW) = \left[(2.01v^{-0.09}) - \frac{194.8}{d_e} - (3.18 \times 10^{-4})v^2\right] \times 0.7355v$$

... Eq. (iii) **14.27c/Pg 243, DHB**

- Equivalent pitch diameter, $d_e = K_d d$
  For $i' = 3.125$, smaller diameter factor $K_d = 1.14$, ... **Tb 14.19/Pg 269, DHB**
  $d_e = 1.14 \times 400 = 456$ mm
  But the maximum value of d_e is 300 mm for a C-belt, ... **14.27c/Pg 243, DHB**
  Hence adopt $d_e = 300$ mm

Eq. (iii) yields ...

$$(kW) = \left[(2.01 \times 25.13^{-0.09}) - \frac{194.8}{300} - (3.18 \times 10^{-4}) \times 25.13^2\right] \times (0.7355 \times 25.13)$$

(kW) = 12 kW [*same as in* **Table 14.16/ Pg 266, DHB**, *for v = 25 m/s and d_e = 300 mm*]

For a 'C' belt having a nominal inside length of 7569 mm,

Correction factor for length, $K_L = 1.16$ ... **Tb 14.21/Pg 271, DHB**

For $\theta_S = 160°$, assuming V – V transmission,

Correction factor for arc of contact, $K_a = 0.95$ ... **Tb 14.22/ Pg 273, DHB**

Eq. (ii) yields ...
$$n' = \frac{18}{12 \times 1.16 \times .095}$$

$$n' = 1.36 \approx 2 \text{ belts}$$

12. *Belt specification:*
    C 7569

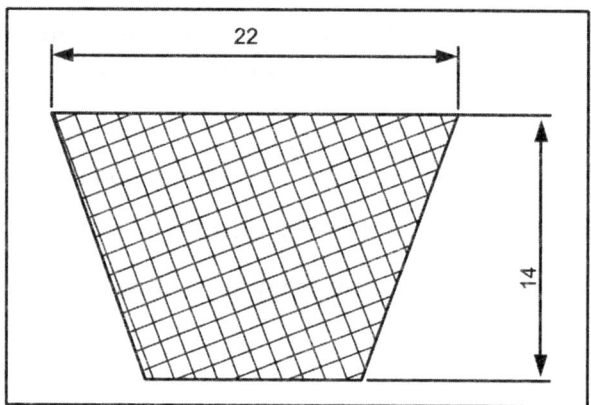

Fig. 2.16: Cross-section of a V-belt

21. **Select type of V-belt and number of belts required for 10 kW, 750 rpm induction motor to drive an exhaust fan in a steel plant at 250 rpm. The center distance between shafts is 1.2 m. Pitch diameter of the motor pulley is 200 mm.**

    [VTU – Dec.08/Jan.09 – 10 Marks]

Solution: $P = 10$ kW, motor speed (driver) $N_S = 750$ rpm, $N_L = 250$ rpm, $C_{appr} = 1.2$ m, motor pulley, $d = 200$ mm.

Therefore, velocity ratio $\quad i = \dfrac{750}{250} = 3$

1. *Preliminary decision:*
   a. Assume that the pulley is made of cast iron (damping property).
   b. Based on given power and combination of driving and driven members, the service factor for driven member (exhaust fan) is taken as $K_s = 1.4$ [(column 8), assuming medium service (>7.5 kW) and operating continuously]

   ... **Tb 14.20/Pg 269, DHB**
   c. The design power is $P_d = P$ (kW) $= P \times K_s = 10 \times 1.4 = 14$ kW.

2. *Belt selection:*

   Referring to **Table 14.12/Pg 261, DHB**, $P_d = 14$ kW lies in the range of 1.5 to 15 kW. Hence select Type 'B' belt having
   Nominal top width = 17 mm, Nominal thickness = 11 mm,
   Maximum velocity, $v_{max} = 25$ m/s.

3. *Pitch diameter of the motor pulley (driver):*
   $d = 200$ mm (data)
   Therefore, standard pitch diameter for 'B' size belt is $d = 200$ mm

   ... **Tb 14.25/Pg 275, DHB** *(Preference – 1, in DHB)*

4. *Pitch diameter of the driven pulley:*
   $D = d \times i$ (Neglecting 'ϵ') ... **14.13b/Pg 240, DHB**
   $D = 200 \times 3 = 600$ mm

   Therefore, standard size, $D = 630$ mm. ... **Tb 14.25/Pg 275, DHB**

5. Standard sizes:
Driver pulley (motor) $d = 200$ mm driven pulley, $D = 630$ mm

- Revised velocity ratio, $i' = \dfrac{D}{d} = \dfrac{630}{200} = 315$

6. Belt speed:
$$v = \frac{\pi d N}{60} = \frac{\pi \times 0.2 \times 750}{60} = 7.85 \text{ m/s} < v_{max} \text{ in step (2)}$$

7. Approximate center distance:
$$C_{appr} = 1200 \text{ mm} \quad \text{(data)}$$

8. Pitch length of the belt:
$$L = 2C + 1.57(D+d) + \frac{(D-d)^2}{4C} \quad \ldots 14.30/\text{Pg 244, DHB}$$

$$= 2 \times 1200 + 1.57(630+200) + \frac{(630-200)^2}{4 \times 1200}$$

$$L = 3741.62 \text{ mm}$$

For B- belt (step 2), the nearest standard nominal pitch length is
L = 4056 mm
and nominal inside length = 4013 mm $\ldots$ Tb 14.13/Pg 262, DHB

9. Exact center distance:
$$C = A + \sqrt[2]{(A^2 - B)} \quad \ldots \text{Eq. (i) } 14.29/\text{Pg 244, DHB}$$

Where,
$$A = \frac{L}{4} - \frac{\pi(D+d)}{8} = \frac{4056}{4} - \frac{\pi(630+200)}{8} = 688.06 \text{ mm}$$

$$B = \left[\frac{D-d}{8}\right]^2 = \left[\frac{630-200}{8}\right]^2 = 2889.06 \text{ mm}$$

Eq. (i) yields $\ldots$
$$C = 688.06 + \sqrt[2]{(688.06^2 - 2889.06)}$$
$$C = 1374 \text{ mm}$$

10. Angle of contact of driver pulley:
Angle of contact of smaller pulley,
$$\theta_s = \pi - 2\sin^{-1}\left(\frac{D-d}{2C}\right) \quad \ldots 14.1a/\text{Pg 238, DHB}$$

$$= \pi - 2\sin^{-1}\left(\frac{630-200}{2 \times 1374}\right)$$

$$\theta_s = 162° \quad (\theta > 120°)$$

11. Number of belts:
$$n' = \frac{P K_s}{(\text{kW}) K_L K_a} = \frac{P_d}{(\text{kW}) K_L K_a} \quad \ldots \text{Eq. (ii) } 14.28/\text{Pg 244, DHB}$$

For a 'B' belt,
$$(\text{kW}) = \left[(1.08 v^{-0.09}) - \frac{96.68}{d_e} - (1.78 \times 10^{-4})v^2\right] \times 0.7355 v$$
$$\ldots \text{Eq. (iii) } 14.27b/\text{Pg 243, DHB}$$

- Equivalent pitch diameter, $d_e = K_d d$
  For $i' = 3.15$, smaller diameter factor $K_d = 1.14$, ... **Tb 14.19/Pg 269, DHB**
  $d_e = 1.14 \times 200 = 228$ mm
  But the maximum value of d_e is 175 mm for a B-belt, ... **14.27b/Pg 243, DHB**
  Hence adopt $d_e = \mathbf{175}$ **mm**

Eq. (*iii*) yields ...

$$(\text{kW}) = \left[(1.08 \times 7.58^{-0.09}) - \frac{96.68}{175} - (1.78 \times 10^{-4}) \times 7.85^2 \right] \times (0.7355 \times 7.85)$$

$(\text{kW}) = 2.82$ kW

[≈ *the power in* **Table 14.15/Pg 265, DHB**, *for* $v = 7.85 \approx 8$ m/s *and mm*]

For a 'B' belt having a nominal inside length of 4013 mm,
Correction factor for length, $K_L = 1.13$ ... **Tb 14.21/Pg 271, DHB**
For $\theta_s = 162°$, assuming V – V transmission, from **Table 14.22/Pg 273, DHB**

θ	V – V
163	0.96
160	0.95

For 1 deg, $K_a = \dfrac{0.96 - 0.95}{163 - 160} = 3.33 \times 10^{-3}$

Therefore, for $162°$, $K_a = 0.95 + [(162 - 160) \times (3.33 \times 10^{-3})] = 0.956$

Eq. (*ii*) yields ... $n' = \dfrac{14}{2.82 \times 1.13 \times 0.956}$

$n' = 4.59 \approx 5$ belts

12. *Belt specification:*

    B 4013   (*Figure similar to* **Fig. 2.16**)

22. Select the type and number of V-belts required to drive a crusher, which works 8 hours a day. The power transmitted is 65 kW. The motor shaft runs at 900 rpm and carries a pulley of 250 mm diameter, the crusher shaft rotates at 300 rpm and the center distance is 700 mm. Determine the pitch length of the belt.

[VTU-July 06–15 Marks]

Solution: Service = 8 h/day, $P = 65$ kW, motor speed (driver) $N_s = 900$ rpm, $d = 250$ mm, $N_L = 300$ rpm, $C_{appr} = 700$ mm, velocity ratio

$$i = \frac{900}{300} = 3$$

1. *Preliminary decision:*
   a. Assume that the pulley is made of cast iron (damping property).
   b. Based on given power and combination of driving and driven members, the service factor for driven member (crusher) is taken as $K_s = 1.5$ [(column 6), assuming extra heavy duty service, operating up to 10 h (data: 8 h/day]
   ... **Tb 14.20/Pg 269, DHB**
   c. The design power is
      $P_d = P(\text{kW}) = P \times K_s = 65 \times 1.5 = 97.5$ kW.

2. *Belt selection:*

Referring to **Table 14.12/Pg 261, DHB,** $P_d = 97.5$ kW lies in the range of 35 to 150 kW. Hence select type 'D' belt having

Nominal top width = 32 mm, Nominal thickness = 19 mm,
Maximum velocity, v_{max} = 30 m/s.

3. *Pitch diameter of the motor pulley (driver):* 250 mm   (data)

   Since the belt type (D) does not have any preference based on the given pitch diameter (250 mm), the next lower belt type has to be chosen (i.e. Belt 'C'). From Table 14.12/Pg 261, DHB, for Type 'C' belt we have

   Nominal top width = 22 mm,
   Nominal thickness = 14 mm,
   Maximum velocity, v_{max} = 25 m/s.

   Therefore, standard pitch diameter for 'C' size belt is 250 mm
   $\qquad$ ... **Tb 14.25/Pg 275, DHB** *(Preference – 1, in DHB)*

4. *Pitch diameter of the driven pulley:*

   $D = d \times i$ $\qquad$ (Neglecting 'ϵ') $\qquad$ ... **14.13b/Pg 240, DHB**

   $D = 250 \times 3 = 750$ mm

   Therefore, standard size, $D = 800$ mm. $\qquad$ ... **Tb 14.25/Pg 275, DHB**
   $\qquad\qquad\qquad\qquad\qquad$ *(Preference – 1, in DHB)*

5. *Standard sizes:*

   Driver pulley (motor) $d = 250$ mm $\qquad$ driven pulley, $D = 800$ mm

   - Revised velocity ratio, $i' = \dfrac{D}{d} = \dfrac{800}{250} = 3.2$

6. *Belt speed:*

   $$v = \frac{\pi d N}{60} = \frac{\pi \times 0.25 \times 900}{60}$$

   $v = 11.78$ m/s $< v_{max}$ in step (3)

7. *Approximate center distance:*

   $$C_{appr} = 700 \text{ mm} \qquad \text{(data)}$$

8. *Pitch length of the belt:*

   $$L = 2C + 1.57(D+d) + \frac{(D-d)^2}{4C} \qquad \text{... 14.30/Pg 244, DHB}$$

   $$= 2 \times 700 + 1.57(800+250) + \frac{(800-250)^2}{4 \times 700}$$

   $L = 3156.54$ mm

   For C- belt (step 2), the nearest standard nominal pitch length is
   $$L = 3205 \text{ mm}$$
   and nominal inside length = 3150 mm $\qquad$ ... **Tb 14.13/Pg 262, DHB**

9. *Exact center distance:*

   $$C = A + \sqrt{(A^2 - B)} \qquad \text{... Eq. (i) 14.29/Pg 244, DHB}$$

   Where, $A = \dfrac{L}{4} - \dfrac{\pi(D+d)}{8} = \dfrac{3205}{4} - \dfrac{\pi(800+250)}{8} = 389$ mm, $B = \left(\dfrac{D-d}{8}\right)^2 = \left(\dfrac{800-250}{8}\right)^2$

   Eq. (i) yields ... $\quad C = 389 + \sqrt{(389^2 - 4726.56)}$, $B = 4726.56$ mm

   $C = 772$ mm

10. Angle of contact of driver pulley:

Angle of contact of smaller pulley,

$$\theta_s = \pi - 2\sin^{-1}\left(\frac{D-d}{2C}\right) \quad \ldots \text{14.1a/Pg 238, DHB}$$

$$= \pi - 2\sin^{-1}\left(\frac{800-250}{2\times 772}\right)$$

$$\theta_s = 138.26° \quad (\theta > 120°)$$

11. Number of belts:

$$n' = \frac{PK_s}{K_L K_a (\text{kW})} = \frac{P_d}{K_L K_a (\text{kW})} \quad \ldots \text{Eq. }(ii)\text{ 14.28/Pg 244, DHB}$$

For a 'C' belt,

$$(\text{kW}) = \left[(2.01v^{-0.09}) - \frac{194.8}{d_e} - (3.18\times 10^{-4})v^2\right] \times 0.7355v$$

$$\ldots \text{Eq. }(iii)\text{ 14.27c/Pg 243, DHB}$$

- Equivalent pitch diameter, $d_e = K_d d$
  For $i' = 3.2$, smaller diameter factor $K_d = 1.14$, ... Tb 14.19/Pg 269, DHB
  $$d_e = 1.14 \times 250 = 285 \text{ mm}$$
  But the maximum value of d_e is 300 mm for a C-belt, ... 14.27b/Pg 243, DHB
  Hence adopt $d_e = 285$ mm

Method 1

$$d_e = 285 \text{ mm}$$

Eq. (iii) yields ...

$$(\text{kW}) = \left[(2.01\times 11.78^{-0.09}) - \frac{194.8}{285} - (3.18\times 10^{-4})11.78^2\right] \times (0.7355 \times 11.78)$$

$$(\text{kW}) = 7.64 \text{ kW}$$

[≈ the power in **Table 14.15/Pg 265, DHB**, for $v = 11.85$ m/s and $d_e = 280$–300 mm]

For a 'C' belt having a nominal inside length of 4013 mm,
Correction factor for length, $K_L = 0.97$ ... Tb 14.21/Pg 271, DHB
For $\theta_s = 138.26°$, assuming V – V transmission, from **Table 14.22/ Pg 273, DHB**

θ	V – V
139	0.89
136	0.88

For 1 deg,
$$K_a = \frac{0.89 - 0.88}{139 - 136} = 3.33 \times 10^{-3}$$

Therefore, for 138.26°, $K_a = 0.88 + [(138.26 - 136) \times (3.18 \times 10^{-4})] = 0.8875$

Eq. (ii) yields ...
$$n' = \frac{97.5}{7.64 \times 0.97 \times 0.8875}$$

$$n' = 14.82 \approx 15 \text{ belts}$$

Method 2

$$d_e = 285 \text{ mm from } \textbf{Method 1}$$

From **Table 14.16/Pg 266, DHB** for 'C' belts, the equivalent pitch diameters are (mm): 180, 200, 220, 240, 260, 280, 300.

Rounding off to the nearest value, we have $d_e = 280$ mm.
Eq. (*iii*) yields ...

$$(kW) = \left[(2.01 \times 11.78^{-0.09}) - \frac{194.8}{280} - (3.18 \times 10^{-4})11.78^2\right] \times (0.7355 \times 11.78)$$

$(kW) = 7.54$ kW

[≈ *the power in* **Table 14.15/ Pg 265, DHB**, *for* $v = 11.85$ *m/s and* $d_e = 280$ *mm*]

Eq. (*ii*) yields ...

$$n' = \frac{97.5}{7.64 \times 0.97 \times 0.8875}$$

$n' = 15.02 \approx 15$ belts

12. *Belt specification:*
    C 3150   (*Figure similar to* **Fig. 2.16**)

23. **Select a V-belt drive to connect a 15 kW, 2880 rpm motor to a centrifugal pump, running at approximately 2400 rpm, for a service of 18 h per day. The center distance should be approximately 400 mm. Assume the pitch diameter of driving pulley as 125 mm.** *[VTU-June/July 2011–08 Marks]*

Solution: Service = 18 h/ day, P = 15 kW, motor speed (driver) Ns = 2880 rpm, d = 125 mm, N_L = 2400 rpm, C_{appr} = 400 mm,

$$i = \frac{2880}{2400} = 1.2$$

1. *Preliminary decision:*
   a. Assume that the pulley is made of cast iron (damping property).
   b. Based on given power and combination of driving and driven members, the service factor for driven member (pump) is taken as K_s = 1.2 [(column 5), operating continuously (data: 18 h/day]   ...**Tb 14.20/Pg 269, DHB**
   c. The design power is
        $P_d = P(kW) = P \times K_s = 15 \times 1.2 = 18$ kW.

2. *Belt selection:*

   Referring to **Table 14.12/ Pg 261, DHB**, P_d = 18 kW lies in the range of 10 to 70 kW. Hence select Type 'C' belt having

   Nominal top width = 22 mm,
   Nominal thickness = 14 mm,
   Maximum velocity, v_{max} = 25 m/s.

3. *Pitch diameter of the motor pulley (driver):* d = 125 mm   (data)

   Since the belt type (C) does not have any preference based on the given pitch diameter (125 mm), the next lower belt type has to be chosen (i.e. Belt 'B'), i.e. from Table 14.12/Pg 261, DHB, for Type 'B' belt we have.

   Nominal top width = 17 mm,
   Nominal thickness = 11 mm,
   Maximum velocity, v_{max} = 25 m/s.

   Therefore, standard pitch diameter for '**B**' size belt is d = 125 mm
   ... **Tb 14.25/Pg 275, DHB** (*Preference – 2, in DHB*)

4. **Pitch diameter of the driven pulley:**

   $D = d \times i$ (Neglecting '$\in$')   ... **14.13b/Pg 240, DHB**

   $D = 125 \times 1.2 = 150$ mm

   Therefore, standard size, $D = 150$ mm.

   ... **Tb 14.25/Pg 275, DHB** *(Preference – 2, in DHB)*

5. **Standard sizes:**

   Driver pulley (motor) $d = 125$ mm   driven pulley, $D = 150$ mm

   - Revised velocity ratio, $i' = \dfrac{D}{d} = \dfrac{150}{125} = 1.2$

6. **Belt speed:**

   $$v = \frac{\pi d N}{60} = \frac{\pi \times 0.125 \times 2880}{60} = 18.85 \text{ m/s} < v_{max} \text{ in step (3)}$$

7. **Approximate center distance:** $C_{appr} = 400$ mm   (data)

8. **Pitch length of the belt:**

   $$L = 2C + 1.57(D + d) + \frac{(D-d)^2}{4C} \quad \text{... } \textbf{14.30/Pg 244, DHB}$$

   $$= 2 \times 400 + 1.57(150 + 125) + \frac{(150-125)^2}{4 \times 400}$$

   $L = 1232.14$ mm

   For B-belt (step 2), the nearest standard nominal pitch length is

   $$L = 1262 \text{ mm}$$

   and nominal inside length = 1219 mm   ... **Tb 14.13/Pg 262, DHB**

9. **Exact center distance:**

   $$C = A + \sqrt[2]{(A^2 - B)} \quad \text{... Eq. (i) } \textbf{14.29/ Pg 244, DHB}$$

   Where, $A = \dfrac{L}{4} - \dfrac{\pi(D+d)}{8} = \dfrac{1262}{4} - \dfrac{\pi(150+125)}{8} = 207.51$ mm

   $$B = \left(\frac{D-d}{8}\right)^2 = \left(\frac{150-125}{8}\right)^2, \quad B = 9.77$$

   Eq. (i) yields ... $C = 207.51 + \sqrt[2]{(207.51^2 - 9.77)}$, $C = 415$ mm

10. **Angle of contact of driver pulley:**

    Angle of contact of smaller pulley,

    $$\theta_s = \pi - 2\sin^{-1}\left(\frac{D-d}{2C}\right) \quad \text{... } \textbf{14.1a/Pg 238, DHB}$$

    $$= \pi - 2\sin^{-1}\left(\frac{150-125}{2 \times 415}\right)$$

    $\theta_s = 176.55°$ ($\theta > 120°$)

11. **Number of belts:**

    $$n' = \frac{PK_s}{K_L K_a (\text{kW})} = \frac{P_d}{K_L K_a (\text{kW})}$$

    ... Eq. (ii) **14.28/Pg 244, DHB**

For a '**B**' belt,

$$(kW) = \left[\left(1.08v^{-0.09}\right) - \frac{96.68}{d_e} - \left(1.78 \times 10^{-4}\right)v^2\right] \times 0.7355v$$

Eq. (*iii*) **14.27c/Pg 243, DHB**

- Equivalent pitch diameter, $d_e = K_d d$
  For $i' = 1.2$, smaller diameter factor $K_d = 1.07$ ... **Tb 14.19/Pg 269, DHB**
  $d_e = 1.07 \times 125 = 133.75$ mm
  But the maximum value of d_e is 175 mm for a B-belt, ... **14.27b/Pg 243, DHB**
  Hence adopt $d_e = 133.75$ mm

From **Table 14.16/Pg 266, DHB** for 'B' belts, the equivalent pitch diameters are (mm): 130, 140, 150, 160, 170, 180.
Rounding off d_e to the nearest value, we have $d_e = 140$ mm.
Eq. (*iii*) yields...

$$(kW) = \left[\left(1.08 \times 18.85^{-0.09}\right) - \frac{69.68}{140} - \left(1.78 \times 10^{-4}\right) \times 18.85^2\right] \times (0.7355 \times 18.85)$$

kW = 3.72 kW
[≈ *the power in* **Table 14.15/Pg 265, DHB**, *for v = 18.85 m/s and = 140 mm*]
For a 'B' belt having a nominal inside length of 1219 mm,
Correction factor for length, $K_L = 0.88$ ... **Tb 14.21/Pg 271, DHB**
For $\theta_s = 176.55° \approx 177°$ assuming V – V transmission,
Correction factor for arc of contact, $K_a = 0.99$ ... **Tb 14.22/Pg 273, DHB**

Eq. (*ii*) yields ... $n' = \dfrac{18}{3.72 \times 0.88 \times 0.99}$

$n' = 5.55 \approx 6$ belts

12. *Belt specification:* B 1219 (*Figure similar to* **Fig. 2.16**)

24. **Two shafts whose center distances are 1100 mm apart are connected by means of a V-belt. The driving pulley is 355 mm in diameter and runs at 1100 rpm, with 90 kW. The driven pulley runs at 1000 rpm. Determine the number of V-belts required using 'D' type belts.**

Solution: $C_{appr} = 1100$ mm, $d = 355$ mm, $P = 90$ kW, $n' = ?$, $N_s = 1100$ rpm, $N_L = 1000$ rpm.
Use belt 'D'

Therefore, velocity ratio, $i = \dfrac{1100}{1000} = 1.1$

1. *Preliminary decision:*
   a. Assume that the pulley is made of cast iron (damping property).
   b. Based on given power and combination of driving and driven members, the service factor for driven member is taken as $K_s = 1.3$ [(column 5), operating continuously] ... **Tb 14.20/Pg 269, DHB**
   c. The design power is $P_d = P(kW) = P \times K_s = 90 \times 1.3 = 117$ kW.

2. *Belt selection:* Given type 'D' belt
   Referring to **Table 14.12/Pg 261, DHB, for t**ype 'D' belt, we have
   Nominal top width = 32 mm,   Nominal thickness = 19 mm,
   Maximum velocity, $v_{max} = 30$ m/s.

3. **Pitch diameter of the motor pulley (driver):** $d = 355$ mm   (data)
   ... Tb 14.25/Pg 275, DHB *(Preference – 1, in DHB)*

4. **Pitch diameter of the driven pulley:**
   $D = d \times i$ (Neglecting '$\in$')   ...14.13b/Pg 240, DHB
   $D = 355 \times 1.1 = 390.5$ mm
   Therefore, standard size, $D = 400$ mm.
   ... Tb 14.25/Pg 275, DHB *(Preference – 1, in DHB)*

5. **Standard sizes:**
   Driver pulley (motor) $d = 355$ mm,   driven pulley $D = 400$ mm
   Revised velocity ratio, $i' = \dfrac{D}{d} = \dfrac{400}{355} = 1.13$

6. **Belt speed:**
   $$v = \frac{\pi dN}{60} = \frac{\pi \times 0.335 \times 1100}{60} = 20.45 \text{ m/s} < v_{max} \text{ in step (3)}$$

7. **Approximate center distance:** $C_{appr} = 1100$ mm   (data)

8. **Pitch length of the belt:**
   $$L = 2C + 1.57(D+d) + \frac{(D-d)^2}{4C} \quad \text{...14.30/Pg 244, DHB}$$
   $$= 2 \times 1100 + 1.57(400 + 355) + \frac{(400-355)^2}{4 \times 1100}$$
   $L = 3385.81$ mm
   For D-belt (step 2), the nearest standard nominal pitch length is
   $L = 3736$ mm
   and nominal inside length = 3658 mm   ... Tb 14.13/ Pg 262, DHB

9. **Exact center distance:**
   $$C = A + \sqrt[2]{(A^2 - B)} \quad \text{... Eq. }(i)\text{ 14.29/Pg 244, DHB}$$
   Where, $A = \dfrac{L}{4} - \dfrac{\pi(D+d)}{8} = \dfrac{3736}{4} - \dfrac{\pi(400+355)}{8} = 31.64$ mm
   $B = \left[\dfrac{D-d}{8}\right]^2 = \left[\dfrac{400-355}{8}\right]^2 = 31.64$ mm
   Eq. (i) yields ... $C = 637.5 + \sqrt[2]{(637.5^2 - 31.64)}$
   $C = 1275$ mm

10. **Angle of contact of driver pulley:**
    Angle of contact of smaller pulley,
    $$\theta_s = \pi - 2\sin^{-1}\left(\frac{D-d}{2C}\right) \quad \text{...14.1a/Pg 238, DHB}$$
    $$= \pi - 2\sin^{-1}\left(\frac{400-355}{2 \times 1275}\right)$$
    $\theta_s = 178°$ ($\theta > 120°$)

11. Number of belts:

$$n' = \frac{PK_s}{(kW)K_L K_a} = \frac{P_d}{(kW)K_L K_a} \quad \ldots \text{Eq. } (ii) \text{ } 14.28/\text{Pg } 244, \text{DHB}$$

For a 'D' belt,

$$(kW) = \left[(4.29v^{-0.09}) - \frac{690}{d_e} - (6.48 \times 10^{-4})v^2\right] \times 0.7355v$$

... Eq. (iii) 14.27d/Pg 243, DHB

- Equivalent pitch diameter, $d_e = K_d d$
  For $i' = 1.13$, smaller diameter factor $K_d = 1.05$ ... Tb 14.19/Pg 269, DHB
  $d_e = 1.05 \times 355 = 372.75$ mm
  But the maximum value of d_e is 425 mm for a D-belt, ... 14.27b/Pg 243, DHB

From **Table 14.16/Pg 267, DHB** for 'D' belts, the equivalent pitch diameters are (mm): 300, 320, 340, 360, 380, 400, 420, 430.

Rounding off d_e to the nearest value, we have $d_e = $ **380 mm**.

Eq. (iii) yields ...

$$(kW) = \left[(4.29 \times 20.45^{-0.09}) - \frac{690}{380} - (6.48 \times 10^{-4}) \times 20.45^2\right] \times (0.7355 \times 20.45)$$

(kW) = 17.79 kW [≈ *the power in* **Table 14.17/ Pg 267, DHB**, *for* $v \approx 21$ *m/s and* $d_e = 380$ *mm*]

For a 'D' belt having a nominal inside length of 3658 mm,
Correction factor for length, $K_L = 0.90$ ... Tb 14.21/Pg 271, DHB
For $\theta_s = 178°$, assuming V – V transmission, from **Table 14.22/Pg 273, DHB**
Correction factor for arc of contact, $K_a \approx 0.993$ ... Tb 14.22/Pg 273, DHB

Eq. (ii) yields ... $\quad n' = \dfrac{117}{17.79 \times 0.90 \times 0.993}$

$n' = 7.35 \simeq $ **8 belts**

12. Belt specification: D 4013 *(Figure similar to* **Fig. 2.16**)

25. The drive from a motor to a machine consists of three V-belts of Type- 'B'. The motor pulley has a pitch diameter of 160 mm, while that of the machine pulley is 500 mm. If centre distance is 1.3 m, determine the specifications of V-belt.

Solution: $C_{appr} = 1300$ mm, $d = 160$ mm, $D = 500$ mm, $n' = 3$, Type – 'B',

$$i = \frac{500}{160} = 3.125$$

a. **To find P':**
  For a type- B belt,

$$(kW) = \left[(1.08v^{-0.09}) - \frac{69.68}{d_e} - (1.78 \times 10^{-4})v^2\right] \times 0.7355v$$

... Eq. (i) 14.27c/Pg 243, DHB

- Equivalent pitch diameter, $d_e = k_d d$
  For $i' = 3.125$, smaller diameter factor $K_d = 1.14$ ... Tb 14.19/Pg 269, DHB
  $d_e = 1.14 \times 160 = 182.4$ mm

But the maximum value of d_e is 175 mm for a B-belt, ... **14.27b/Pg 243, DHB**
Hence adopt d_e = 175 mm

- Referring to **Table 14.12/Pg 261, DHB,** for type 'B' belt we have
  Nominal top width = 17 mm,
  Nominal thickness = 11 mm,
  Maximum velocity, v_{max} = 25 m/s.

Eq. (i) yields ... $(kW) = \left[(1.08 \times 25^{-0.09}) - \dfrac{69.68}{175} - (1.78 \times 10^{-4}) \times 25^2\right] \times (0.7355 \times 25)$

$(kW) = 5.5$ kW   (per belt)

b. **Pitch length of the belt:**

$$L = 2C + 1.57(D+d) + \dfrac{(D-d)^2}{4C} \quad \text{... 14.30/Pg 244, DHB}$$

$$= 2 \times 1300 + 1.57(500+160) + \dfrac{(500-160)^2}{4 \times 1300}$$

For D-belt (step 2), the nearest standard nominal pitch length is
$$L = 3701 \text{ mm}$$
and nominal inside length = 3658 mm   ... **Tb 14.13/Pg 262, DHB**

c. **Exact center distance:**

$$C = A + \sqrt[4]{(A^2 - B)} \quad \text{... Eq. (ii) 14.29/Pg 244, DHB}$$

Where, $A = \dfrac{L}{4} - \dfrac{\pi(D+d)}{8} = \dfrac{3701}{4} - \dfrac{\pi(500+160)}{8} = 666.07$

$B = \left[\dfrac{D-d}{8}\right]^2 = \left[\dfrac{500-160}{8}\right]^2 = 1806.25$ mm

Eq. (ii) yields ... $C = 666.07 + \sqrt[4]{(666.07^2 - 1806.25)}$
$C = 1330.78$ mm

d. **Angle of contact of driver pulley:**
Angle of contact of smaller pulley,

$$\theta_s = \pi - 2\sin^{-1}\left(\dfrac{D-d}{2C}\right) \quad \text{... 14.1a/Pg 238, DHB}$$

$$= \pi - 2\sin^{-1}\left(\dfrac{500-160}{2 \times 1300}\right)$$

$\theta_s = 165°$ ($\theta > 120°$)

e. **Number of belts:**

$$n' = \dfrac{P K_s}{K_L K_a (\text{kW})} = \dfrac{P_d}{K_L K_a (\text{kW})} \quad \text{... Eq. (ii) 14.28/Pg 244, DHB}$$

For a 'D' belt having a nominal inside length of 3658 mm,
Correction factor for length, $K_L = 1.11$ ... **Tb 14.21/Pg 271, DHB**

For $\theta_s = 165°$ assuming V – V transmission, from **Table 14.22/Pg 273, DHB**

θ	V – V
166	0.97
163	0.96

For 1 deg, $\quad n' = \dfrac{P K_s}{K_L K_a (\text{kW})} = \dfrac{P_d}{K_L K_a (\text{kW})}$

Therefore, for 165°, $\quad 0.96 + [(165 - 163) \times (3.33 \times 10^{-3})] = 0.9667$

Eq. (ii) yields ... $\quad 3 = \dfrac{P_d}{5.5 \times 0.667 \times 1.11}$

$\qquad P_d = 17.70$ kW

Hence for 1 belt, $\quad P_d = 5.9$ kW

But design power $P_d = P(\text{kW}) = P K_s$

$\quad$ Assuming $\quad K_s = 1.2$

$\qquad 17.70 = P \times 12$

$\qquad P = 14.75$ kW

[in the range of 1.5–15 kW ... **Tb 14.12/ Pg 261, DHB**, *for Type 'B' belt*]

2.30 WIRE ROPES

Wire ropes are used where a large amount of power has to be transmitted (up to 150 m). These are widely used in elevators, cranes, suspension bridges, mine hoists, conveyors, etc. The wire ropes are made from cold drawing in order to increase its strength and durability. The various materials used for wire ropes are wrought iron, cast steel, plow steel, and alloy steel.

A wire rope is made up of strands and a strand is made up of one –or- more layers of wires as shown in **Fig. 2. 17.** The number of strands in a rope denotes the number of groups of wires that are laid over the central core.

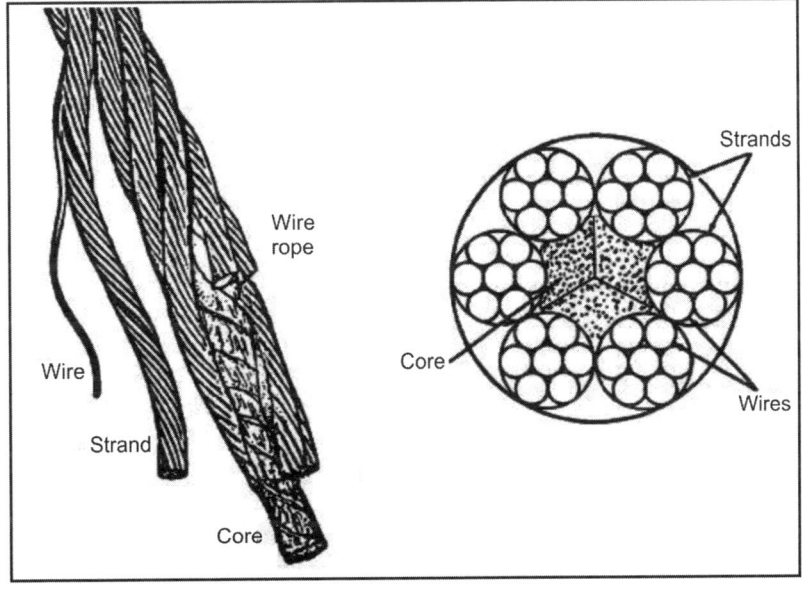

Fig. 2.17: Details of wire rope

184 Design of Machine Elements II (DME II)

For example: a 6 × 19 construction (designation) means that the rope has 6 strands and each strand is composed of 19 (12/6/1) wires. The central part of the wire rope is called the core and may be of fiber, wire, plastic, paper or asbestos. The fiber core is very flexible and very suitable for all conditions. The wire core is used where the wire rope is subjected to severe heat or crushing conditions.

2.31 CHOICE OF A WIRE ROPE

Following points have to be considered while selecting a wire rope:
- Strength.
- Flexibility.
- Fatigue strength.
- Corrosion resistance.
- Abrasion resistance.
- Resistance to crushing.

2.32 STRESSES IN HOISTING ROPES

1. Direct stress due to load hoisted and the weight of the rope.
2. Stresses due to bending of the rope over the sheave.
3. Starting stresses.
4. Stresses due to change of rope speed including stops.

All these stresses are explained in terms of loads as follows:

Design procedure

♦ Factor of safety, $FS = n\left\{\dfrac{F_u}{F_{max}}\right\}$

where, n = no. of ropes
- The value of FS is selected from ... **Table 14.33/Pg 285, DHB**
- If the diameter of the rope is specified, then take the value of F_u, from the tables

or
- Calculate F_u as, $F_u = \sigma_u A$

$\sigma_u = 1800$ MPa

A = net area of the rope, from

... **Table 14.34/Pg 285, DHB** *(Based on construction)*

♦ F_{max} is calculated as follows:

1. *Dead weight (F):* The dead weight of the rope includes the weight to be lifted and the weight of the skip.
2. *The weight of the rope is calculated as:*
   F_r = weight of the rope = $n(w'\,l)$ (N)
   D' = w' Weight/meter (N/m),
   l = l Length of rope (m)
3. **Bending load** (F_b):

$$F_b = n\left\{KA\left(\dfrac{d_w}{D}\right)\right\}$$ ... **14.44/Pg 246, DHB**

K = Constant of proportionality = 82.8 GPa $\quad$ A = Net area of wire in rope (mm^2)
d_w = diameter of the wire (mm) $\quad$ D = Diameter of the sheave (mm)

...**Table 14.34/Pg 285, DHB** *(Based on construction)*

4. *Loads due to acceleration:*

$$F_a = (F + F_r)\left(\frac{a}{g}\right)$$

a = acceleration = v/t (m/s²)
t = time (sec)
v = velocity (m/s)
F = Load to be lifted (N)

5. *Starting load (F_s):*

- $$F_s = (F + F_r)\left\{1 + \sqrt{1 + \left(\frac{2ahK}{\sigma_d g l}\right)}\right\}$$ (with slack condition)

h = slackness in the rope

$$\sigma_d = \frac{(F + F_r)}{A}$$

- If $h = 0$, then $F_s = 2(F + F_r)$ (without slack condition)

6. The maximum load can be determined as follows:
   a. Effective load on rope = $F + F_r + F_b$ ... Eq. (i)
   b. Load on the rope during starting = $F_s + F_b$ ... Eq. (ii)
   c. Load on the rope during acceleration = $F + F_r + F_b + F_a$ ... Eq. (iii)

The *largest value* of the above three equations gives F_{max}

Note:
- **Tb 14.27 & 27a/Pg 277 and 279, DHB** – *Specification of steel wire ropes for general engineering purposes.*
- **Tb 14.28/Pg 280, DHB** – *Specification for steel wire for lifts and hoists (suspension ropes).*
- **Tb 14.29/Pg 281, DHB** – *Specifications of small wire ropes.*
- **Tb 14.30/Pg 282, DHB** – *Specifications of round wire ropes for shipping purposes.*
- **Tb 14.31/Pg 283, DHB** – *Specifications of flat hoisting wire ropes used in mines.*
- **Tb 14.32/Pg 284, DHB** – *Ratio of drum and sheave diameter to rope diameter.*
- **Tb 14.33/Pg 285, DHB** – *Factor of safety for wire ropes.*
- **Tb 14.34/Pg 285, DHB** – *Approximate wire rope and sheave data.*

2.33 DRUM AND SHEAVE DIAMETERS

When the rope passes around the periphery of the sheave or drum, the length of the wires on the outer portion increases (tension) while that on the inner portion decreases (compression). The bending of the rope over the drum and straightening as it leaves the drum results in fluctuating stresses, thereby leading to failure due to fatigue or wear. In order to reduce the effects of bending, the diameter of the drum should be large. The minimum value of drum diameters are given in **Tb 14.32/ Pg 284, DHB.**

The ratios specified in the **Table 14.32** are valid for rope speeds up to 50 m/min. For speeds above 50 m/min, the drum or sheave diameter should be increased approximately by 8% for every additional 50 m/min of rope speed. This is because above 50 m/min, fatigue action will affect the life of the rope.

2.34 CAUSES OF WIRE ROPE FAILURE

- Using incorrect size, construction or grade.
- Dragging over obstacles.
- Improper lubrication.
- Operating over sheaves and drums of inadequate size.
- Overriding or cross winding on drums.
- Operating over sheaves and drums with improperly fitted grooves or broken flanges.
- Jumping off sheaves.
- Exposure to acid fumes
- Being subjected to severe or continuing overload.

2.35 APPLICATIONS OF WIRE ROPES

Standard designation	Type	Application
6 × 7	Standard coarse laid rope	Mines, tramways, power transmission
6 × 19	Standard hoisting rope	(Hoisting rope)-Mines, quarries, cranes, dredges, elevators, tramways, well drilling.
6 × 37	Extra flexible hoisting rope	(Hoisting rope)-Steel mill ladles, cranes, and high speed elevators.
8 × 19	Extra flexible hoisting rope	(Hoisting rope)

26. A 25 mm, 6 × 37 steel wire rope is used in a mine of 80 m deep. The velocity of cage is 2 m/s and the time required to accelerate the cage to the desired velocity is 10 sec. The diameter of sheave is 1.25 m. Determine the safe load, neglecting the impact on the load.   *[VTU – Dec. 2010/12 Marks, June/July 08–10 Marks]*

Solution: Diameter of the rope, $d = 25$ mm, type of construction: 6×37, $l = 80$ mm, $v = 2$ m/s, $t = 10$ sec, sheave diameter, $D = 1.25$ m, safe load, $F = ?$, $a = v/t = 2/10 = 0.2$ m/s².

From **Table 14.34/Pg 285, DHB**, for 6×37 construction,

Weight/m, $w' = 0.0343 d^2 = 0.0343 \times 25^2 = 21.4375$ N/mm²
Wire diameter, $d_w = 0.045 d = 0.045 \times 25 = 1.125$ mm
Area of wire, $A = 0.38 d^2 = 0.38 \times 25^2 = 237.5$ mm²

To find safe load (F):

We know that, Factor of safety, $F_s = \dfrac{F_u}{F_{max}}$ ... Eq. (i)

For $l = 80$ mm, $FS = 8$ ... **Tb 14.33/Pg 285, DHB**

To find F_{max}:
1. Dead weight $= F$
2. Weight of the rope, $F_r = w' l = 21.4375 \times 80 = 1715$ N
3. Bending load, $F_b = KA\left(\dfrac{d_w}{D}\right)$ ... **14.44/Pg 246, DHB**

$$= 82.8 \times 10^3 \times 237.5 \times \left(\dfrac{1.125}{12.50}\right) \quad K = 82.8 \times 10^3 \text{ N/mm}^2$$

$F_b = 17698.5$ N

4. Load due to acceleration, $F_a = (F + F_r)\left(\dfrac{a}{g}\right)$

$$F_s = (F + 1715)\left(\dfrac{0.2}{9.81}\right)$$

$$F_b = 0.0204(F + 1715)$$

5. Total load:
$$F_{max} = F + F_r + F_b + F_a$$
$$= F + 1715 + 17698.5 + 0.0204\,(F + 1715)$$
$$F_{max} = 1.0204F + 19448.48$$

For 6×37 construction @ $d = 25$ mm, assuming $\sigma_u = 1716 - 1863$ MPa, we have $F_u = 349.12$ kN ... **Tb 14.27/Pg 277, DHB**

Eq. (i) yields ...
$$8 = \dfrac{349.12 \times 10^3}{1.0204F + 19448.48}$$

$$F = 23707.8 \text{ N}$$

27. **A 8×19 steel wire rope is to hoist 50 kN of load from a depth of 1000 m. Determine the number of ropes required if the maximum speed is 2.5 m/s and acceleration is 1.25 m/s², assuming the rope to be made of 25 mm diameter. Neglect the weight of the tackle.**

Solution: Type of construction: 8×19. $F = 50$ kN, $l = 1000$ m $n' = ?$, $v = 2.3$ m/s, $a = 1.25$ m/s², $d = 25$ mm.

Table 14.34/ Pg 285, DHB, for 8×19 construction,

Weight/m, $w' = 0.0339d^2 = 0.0339 \times 25^2 = 21.1874$ N/mm²
Wire diameter, $d_w = 0.050d = 0.050 \times 25 = 1.25$ mm
Area of wire, $A = 0.38d^2 = 0.38 \times 25^2 = 237.5$ mm²
Average sheave diameter, $D = 31d = 31 \times 25 = 775$ mm

To find number of ropes (n):

We know that, Factor of safety, $FS = n\left\{\dfrac{F_u}{F_{max}}\right\}$ ... Eq. (i)

For $l = 1000$ mm, $FS = 5$ ... **Tb 14.33/Pg 285, DHB**

To find F_{max}:
1. Dead weight, $F = 50{,}000$ N
2. Weight of the rope, $F_r = (w'l)n = 21.1875 \times 1000 \times n = (21187.5)n$
3. Bending load, $F_b = nKA\left(\dfrac{d_w}{D}\right)$ ... **14.44/Pg 246, DHB**

$$= n \times 82.8 \times 10^3 \times 237.5 \times \left(\dfrac{1.25}{775}\right)$$

$K = 82.8 \times 10^3$ N/mm²

$$F_b = (31717.74)n$$

4. Load due to acceleration, $F_a = (F + F_r)\left(\dfrac{a}{g}\right)$

$$= \left[50000 + (21187.5)n\right]\left(\dfrac{1.25}{9.81}\right)$$

5. Total load:
$$\therefore F_a = 6371 + (2700)n$$
$$F_{max} = F + F_r + F_b + F_a$$
$$= 50000 + (21187.5)n + (31717.74)n + 6371 + (2700)n$$
$$F_{max} = 65371 + (55605.24)n$$

For 8×19 construction @ $d = 25$ mm, assuming $\sigma_u = 1226 - 1373$ MPa, we have
$F_u = 235.36$ kN   ... **Tb 14.28/Pg 280, DHB**

Eq. (i) yields ...
$$5 = \frac{n \times 235.362 \times 10^3}{56371 + 55605.24n}$$
$$56371 = (-8533.24)n \quad \text{(Neglecting sign)}$$
$$n = 6.6 \approx 7$$

28. An oil well has to be drilled to a depth of 900 mm using 100 drill pipe. Assume 200 N for every 15 m length of pipe. The rope sheaves are of 800 mm diameter and the acceleration is 2.5 m/s². Determine the size of 6×37 wire rope for lifting the string of pipes using a factor of safety as 3 and ultimate stress of 1800 MPa.

Solution: $l = 900$ mm, $D = 800$ mm, $a = 2.5$ m/s², $FS = 3$, $\sigma_u = 1800$ MPa, Type of construction, 6×37, load = 200 N for every 15 m, Thus for 900 m, load $F = 12000$ N

From **Table 14.34/Pg 285, DHB**, for 6×37 construction,

Weight/m, $w' = 0.0343d^2$
Wire diameter, $d_w = 0.045d$
Area of wire, $A = 0.38d^2$

To find wire diameter (d):

We know that, Factor of safety, $FS = \dfrac{F_u}{F_{max}}$ ... Eq. (i)

$$F_u = \sigma_u A = 1800 \times (0.38d^2) = 684d^2$$

To find F_{max}:
1. Dead weight, $F = 12000$ N
2. Weight of the rope, $F_r = w'l = 0.0343d^2 \times 900 = 30.87d^2$
3. Bending load, $F_b = KA\left(\dfrac{d_w}{D}\right)$ ... **14.44/Pg 246, DHB**

$$= 82.8 \times 10^3 \times 0.38d^2 \times \left(\frac{0.045d}{800}\right) \quad K = 82.8 \times 10^3 \text{ N/mm}^2$$
$$F_b = 1.769d^3$$

4. Load due to acceleration,
$$F_a = (F + F_r)\left(\frac{a}{g}\right)$$
$$= (12000 \times 30.87d^2)\left(\frac{2.5}{9.81}\right)$$
$$F_a = 3058.1 + 7.867d^2$$

5. Starting load, $F_s = 2(F + F_r)$
$$= 2 \times (12000 + 30.87d^2)$$
$$F_s = (24 \times 10^3) + 61.74d^2$$

6. a. Effective load on rope = $F + F_r + F_b$
$$= 12000 + 30.87d^2 + 1.769d^3 \quad \ldots \text{Eq. } (ii)$$
b. Load on the rope during starting = $F_s + F_b$
$$= 24 \times 10^3 + 61.74d^2 + 1.769d^3 \quad \ldots \text{Eq. } (iii)$$
c. Load on the rope during acceleration
$$= F + F_r + F_b + F_a$$
$$= 12000 + 30.87d^2 + 1.769d^3 + (3058.1 + 7.867d^2)$$
$$= 15.06 \times 10^3 + 38.74d^2 + 1.769d^3 \quad \ldots \text{Eq. } (iv)$$

Thus the largest value of equations Eqs (ii), (iii), and (iv) gives
$$F_{max} = 24 \times 10^3 + 61.74d^2 + 1.769d^3$$

Eq. (i) yields ... $3 = \dfrac{684d^2}{24 \times 10^3 + 61.74d^2 + 1.769d^3}$

$d = 13$ mm

For 6×19 construction, the standard wire diameter is $d = 14$ mm.
$$\ldots \text{Tb } 14.27/\text{Pg } 277, \text{DHB}$$

29. **Determine the size of a 6 × 19 steel wire rope to be used with a lifting machine of capacity 75 kN and a lifting height of 120 m. Assume a rope speed of 6 m/s and an acceleration of 3 m/s², when starting:**
   a. With no slack condition
   b. With a slack of 1.2 m.

Solution: Type of construction: 6×19. $F = 75$ kN, $l = 120$ m, $v = 6$ m/s, $a = 3$ m/s², $d = ?$,
(i) $h = 0$, (ii) $h = 1.2$ m

Table 14.34/ Pg 285, DHB, for 6×19 construction,

Weight/m, $w' = 0.0363d^2$
Wire diameter, $d_w = 0.063d$
Area of wire, $A = 0.38d^2 = 0.38 \times 25^2 = 237.5$ mm²
Average sheave diameter, $D = 45d$

To find wire diameter (d):

We know that, Factor of safety,
$$FS = \dfrac{F_u}{F_{max}} \quad \ldots \text{Eq. } (i)$$

For $l = 120$ m, $FS = 8$ ... Tb 14.33/Pg 285, DHB
Assuming $\sigma_u = 1800$ MPa, we have
$$F_u = \sigma_u A = 1800 \times (0.38d^2) = 684d^2$$

To find F_{max}:
1. Dead weight, $F = 75000$ N
2. Weight of the rope, $F_r = w'l = 0.0363d^2 \times 120 = 4.356d^2$
3. Bending load, $F_b = KA\left(\dfrac{d_w}{D}\right)$ ... 14.44/Pg 246, DHB

$$= 82.8 \times 10^3 \times 0.38 d^2 \times \left(\frac{0.063 d}{45 d} \right)$$

$$F_b = 44.05 d^2$$

4. Load due to acceleration, $F_a = (F + F_r)\left(\dfrac{a}{g}\right)$

$$= \left[75000 + 4.356 d^2\right]\left(\frac{3}{9.81}\right)$$

$$F_a = 22.94 \times 10^3 + 1.3321 d^2$$

5. Starting load,
   a. Without slack,
   $$F_s = 2(F + F_r)$$
   $$= 2 \times (75000 + 4.356 d^2)$$
   $$F_s = 150 \times 10^3 + 8.712 d^2$$

   b. With slack,
   $$F_s = (F + F_r)\left\{1 + \sqrt{1 + \left(\frac{2ahk}{\sigma_d g l}\right)}\right\}$$

   but $\sigma_d = \dfrac{(F + F_r)}{A} = \dfrac{75000 + 4.356 d^2}{0.38 d^2} = \dfrac{197.4 \times 10^3}{d^2} + 11.46$

   $$= (75000 + 4.356 d^2)\left\{1 + \sqrt{1 + \left[\frac{2 \times 3 \times 1.2 \times 82.8 \times 10^3}{\left(\dfrac{197.4 \times 10^3}{d^2} + 11.46\right) \times 9.81 \times 120}\right]}\right\}$$

   $$F_s = (75000 + 4.356 d^2)\left\{1 + \sqrt{1 + \left[\frac{506.42 d^2}{197.43 \times 10^3 + 11.46 d^2}\right]}\right\}$$

6. a. Effective load on rope $= F + F_r + F_b$
   $$= (75000 + 4.356 d^2) + 44.05 d^2$$
   $$= 75 \times 10^3 + 48.406 d^2 \qquad \ldots \text{Eq. }(ii)$$

   b. Load on the rope during starting $= F_s + F_b$
   i. $h = 0$:
   $$= (150 \times 10^3 + 8.712 d^2) + 44.05 d^2$$
   $$= 150 \times 10^3 + 52.762 d^2 \qquad \ldots \text{Eq. }(iii)$$

   ii. $h = 1.2 m$:
   $$= (75000 + 4.356 d^2)\left\{1 + \sqrt{1 + \left[\frac{506.42 d^2}{197.43 \times 10^3 + 11.46 d^2}\right]}\right\} + 44.05 d^2$$

   $$\ldots \text{Eq. }(iiia)$$

   c. Load on the rope during acceleration $= F + F_r + F_b + F_a$
   $$= (75000 + 4.356 d^2) + 44.05 d^2 + (22.94 \times 10^3 + 1.3321 d^2)$$
   $$= 97.94 \times 10^3 + 49.74 d^2 \qquad \ldots \text{Eq. }(iv)$$

Case 1: when h = 0:
$$F_{max} = 150 \times 10^3 + 52.762d^2$$

Eq. (i) yields ...$8 = \dfrac{684d^2}{150 \times 10^3 + 52.762d^2}$

$$d = 67.68 \text{ mm} \simeq 68 \text{ mm}$$

Case 2: when h = 1.2 m:
$$F_{max} = (75000 + 4.356d^2)\left\{1 + \sqrt{1 + \left[\dfrac{506.42d^2}{197.43 \times 10^3 + 11.46d^2}\right]}\right\} + 44.05d^2$$

Assuming d = 70 mm for h = 1.2 m, we have

$$= (75000 + 4.356 \times 70^2)\left\{1 + \sqrt{1 + \left[\dfrac{506.42 \times 70^2}{197.43 \times 10^3 + 11.46 \times 70^2}\right]}\right\} + 44.05 \times 70^2$$

$$F_{max} = 628.6 \times 10^3 \text{ N}$$

Eq. (i) yields ...$FS = \dfrac{684 \times 70^2}{628.6 \times 10^3}$

$$FS = 5.33 < 8$$

Hence the assumed value of d is safe, i.e. $d = 70$ mm for $h = 1.2$ m.

30. **Select a suitable size of a wire rope to lift a cage of a vertical mine hoist 500 m deep. The cage weights 15 kN and has to lift a load of 25 kN of ore at 10 m/s, which is to be attained in 10 sec. The sheave diameter may be assumed as 80 times the diameter of rope.**

Solution: $l = 500$ m, weight of cage, $F_{cage} = 1.5$ kN, ore to be lifted, $F_{ore} = 25$ kN, $v = 10$ m/s, acceleration time, $t = 10$ sec, sheave diameter, $D = 80d$

For mining operation, the type of wire used is 6 × 19 –or– 8 × 19
Select wire as 6 × 19: From **Table 14.34/Pg 285, DHB**, for 6 × 19 construction.

Weight/m, $w' = w' = 0.0363d^2$
Wire diameter, $d_w = 0.063d$
Area of wire, $A = 0.38d^2$
Sheave diameter, $D = 80d$ (data)

To find wire diameter (d):

We know that, Factor of safety, $FS = \dfrac{F_u}{F_{max}}$ ... Eq. (i)

For 500 m, $FS = 7$ ... Tb 14.33/ Pg 285, DHB

Assuming $\sigma_u = 1800$ MPa, we have
$$F_u = \sigma_u A = 1800 \times (0.38d^2) = 684d^2$$

To find F_{max}

1. Dead weight, $F = F_{cage} + F_{ore}$
   $= 15000 + 25000$
   $= 40000$ N $= 40$ kN

2. Weight of the rope, $F_r = w'l = 0.0363d^2 \times 500 = 18.15d^2$

3. Bending load, $F_b = KA\left(\dfrac{d_w}{D}\right)$ ... 14.44/ Pg 246, DHB

$$= 82.8 \times 10^3 \times (0.38d^2) \times \left(\dfrac{0.063d}{80d}\right) \quad K = 82.8 \times 10^3 \text{ N/mm}^2$$

$$F_b = 24.78d^2$$

4. Load due to acceleration, $F_a = (F + F_r)\left(\dfrac{a}{g}\right)$

$$= (40000 + 18.15d^2)\left(\dfrac{1}{9.81}\right) \quad (\because v = at)$$

$$F_a = 4077.5 + 1.85d^2$$

5. Starting load, $F_s = 2(F + F_r)$

$$= 2 \times (40000 + 18.15d^2)$$

$$F_s = 80 \times 10^3 + 36.3d^2$$

6. a. Effective load on rope $= F + F_r + F_b$

$$= (40000 + 18.15d^2) + 24.78d^2$$

$$= 40 \times 10^3 + 42.93d^2 \qquad \ldots \text{Eq. } (ii)$$

   b. Load on the rope during starting $= F_s + F_b$

$$= (80 \times 10^3 + 36.3d^2) + 24.78d^2$$

$$= 80 \times 10^3 + 61.08d^2 \qquad \ldots \text{Eq. } (iii)$$

   c. Load on the rope during acceleration $= F + F_r + F_b + F_a$

$$= (40000 + 18.15d^2) + 24.78d^2 + (4077.5 + 1.85d^2)$$

$$= 44.07 \times 10^3 + 44.78d^2 \qquad \ldots \text{Eq. } (iv)$$

Thus the largest value of Eqs (ii), (iii), and (iv) gives F_{max}

i.e. $F_{max} = 80 \times 10^3 + 61.08d^2$

Eq. (i) yields ...$7 = \dfrac{684d^2}{80 \times 10^3 + 61.08d^2}$

$$d = 46.73 \text{ mm}$$

For 6 × 19 construction, the standard wire diameter is d = **48 mm**.
... Tb 14.27/ Pg 277, DHB

31. Select a wire rope for a vertical mine hoist to lift 7 MN of ore in 8 h shift from a depth of 900 m. Assume a two compartment shaft with the hoisting skips in balance. The maximum velocity is 720 m/min with acceleration and retardation periods of 15 seconds each; and 10 seconds as rest period for discharging and loading the skips. The hoisting skip weighs approximately 0.6 the load capacity.

Solution: Ore to be lifted, F_{ore} = 7 MN, for 8 h, l = 900 mm, v = 720 m/min = 12 m/s, acceleration time, t_1 = 15 sec, retardation time, t_1 = 15 sec, rest period, t_2 = 10 sec. $F_{hoist} = 0.6\, F_{ore}$

For mining operation, the type of wire used is 6 × 19 –or– 8 × 19
... Tb 14.28/ Pg 280, DHB

Select wire as 6 × 19. From **Table 14.34/ Pg 285, DHB**, for 6 × 19 construction,

Weight/m, $w' = 0.0363d^2$

Wire diameter, $d_w = 0.063d$
Area of wire, $A = 0.38d^2$
Average sheave diameter, $D = 45d$

◆ *Time required for one trip*:

- Distance travelled during acceleration, $s_1 = \dfrac{at_1^2}{2}$

  $= \dfrac{0.8 \times 15^2}{2}$ [acceleration, $a = v/t_1 = 12/15 = 0.8 \text{ m/s}$]

  $s_1 = 90$ m

- Distance travelled during retardation, $s_2 = \dfrac{at_2^2}{2}$

  $= \dfrac{0.8 \times 15^2}{2}$ [deceleration, $a = v/t_2 = 15 = 0.8 \text{ m/s}$]

- Thus the net distance, $s = l - (s_1 + s_2)$

  $= 900 - (90 + 90)$

  $s = 720$ m.

- Time required to travel net distance, $t = \dfrac{s}{v} = \dfrac{720}{12} = 60$ s

- Thus the time taken for one complete trip = time for (acceleration + retardation + loading and unloading + net time)

  $= (15 + 15 + 10 + 60)$

  $= 100$ s

◆ Number of trips in 8 h shift $= \dfrac{8 \times 3600}{100} = 288$ trips

◆ Ore lifted per trip, $F_{ore} = \dfrac{7 \times 10^6}{288} = 24305.5$ N

◆ Weight of hoist, $F_{hoist} = 0.6 F_{ore} = 0.6 \times 24305.5 = 14583.34$ N

To find wire diameter (d):

We know that, Factor of safety, $FS = \dfrac{F_u}{F_{max}}$ ...Eq. (i)

For $l = 900$ m, $FS = 6$ ...Tb 14.33/ Pg 285, DHB

Assuming $= \sigma_u = 1800$ MPa, we have

$F_u = \sigma_u A = 1800 \times (0.38 d^2) = 684 d^2$

To find F_{max}

1. Dead weight, $F = F_{hoist} + F_{ore}$

   $= 14583.34 + 24305.5$

   $F = 38888.8$ N ≈ 38.88 kN

2. Weight of the rope, $F_r = w'l = 0.0363 d^2 \times 900 = 32.67 d^2$

3. Bending load, $F_b = KA\left(\dfrac{d_w}{D}\right)$ ...14.44/ Pg 246, DHB

$$= 82.8 \times 10^3 \times (0.38d^2) \times \left(\frac{0.063d}{45d}\right) \quad K = 82.8 \times 10^3 \, \text{N/mm}^2$$

$$F_b = 44.05d^2$$

4. Load due to acceleration, $F_a = (F + F_r)\left(\dfrac{a}{g}\right)$

$$= (38.88 \times 10^3 + 32.67d^2)\left(\frac{0.8}{9.81}\right)$$

$$F_a = 3170.64 + 2.664d^2$$

5. Starting load, $\quad F_s = 2(F + F_r)$

$$= 2 \times (38888.8 + 32.67d^2)$$

$$F_s = 77.76 \times 10^3 + 65.34d^2$$

6. a. Effective load on rope $= F + F_r + F_b$

$$= (38888.8 + 32.67d^2) + 44.05d^2$$

$$= 38.88 \times 10^3 + 76.72d^2 \qquad \text{...Eq. (ii)}$$

b. Load on the rope during starting $= F_s + F_b$

$$= (77.76 \times 10^3 + 65.34d^2) + 44.05d^2$$

$$= 77.76 \times 10^3 + 109.39d^2 \qquad \text{...Eq. (iii)}$$

c. Load on the rope during acceleration $= F + F_r + F_b + F_a$

$$= (38888.8 + 32.67d^2) + 44.05d^2 + (3170.64 + 2.664d^2)$$

$$= 42.05 \times 10^3 + 79.38d^2 \qquad \text{...Eq. (iv)}$$

Thus the largest value of Eqs (ii), (iii), and (iv) gives F_{max}

i.e. $F_{max} = 77.76 \times 10^3 + 109.35d^2$

Eq. (i) yields ... $6 = \dfrac{684d^2}{77.76 \times 10^3 + 109.39d^2}$

$$d = 53.26 \text{ mm}$$

For 6×19 construction, the standard wire diameter is **$d = 54$ mm.**

...Tb 14.27/ Pg 277, DHB

32. **Select a wire rope of an elevator in the building using the following details:**
    Weight of elevator = 30 kN,
    Weight of passengers = 12 kN,
    Total lift = 250 m,
    Rope velocity = 5 m/s to be reached in a distance of 10 meters.
    Factor of safety = 7.

Solution: Weight of elevator, $F_1 = 30$ kN, Weight of passengers, $F_2 = 12$ kN, $l = 250$ m, $v = 5$ m/s, distance, $s = 10$ m, $a = \dfrac{v^2}{2s} = \dfrac{5^2}{2 \times 10} = 1.25$ mm, $FS = 7$

For elevators/ hoist operation, the type of wire used is 6×19 –or– 8×19

...Tb 14.28/ Pg 280, DHB

Select wire as 6×19. From **Table 14.34/ Pg 285, DHB**, for 6×19 construction,
    Weight/m, $\quad w' = 0.0363d^2$
    Wire diameter, $d_w = 0.063d$
    Area of wire, $\quad A = 0.063d$
Average sheave diameter, $D = 45d$

To find wire diameter (d):

We know that, Factor of safety, $FS = \dfrac{F_u}{F_{max}}$ ...Eq. (*i*)

$FS = 7$ (data)

Assuming $\sigma_u = 1800$ MPa, we have
$$F_u = \sigma_u A = 1800 \times (0.38 d^2) = 684\, d^2$$

To find F_{max}

1. Dead weight, $F = \dfrac{F_1 + F_2}{n}$ (here $n = 4$, i.e. an elevator has 4 ropes)

   $= \dfrac{30 + 12}{4}$

   $= 10500$ N $= 10.5$ kN.

2. Weight of the rope, $F_r = w'l = 0.0363\, d^2 \times 250 = 9.075\, d^2$

3. Bending load, $F_b = KA\left(\dfrac{d_w}{D}\right)$ ...14.44/ Pg 246, DHB

   $= 82.8 \times 10^3 \times (0.38 d^2) \times \left(\dfrac{0.063 d}{45 d}\right)$ $K = 82.8 \times$ N/mm^2

   $F_b = 44.05\, d^2$

4. Load due to acceleration, $F_a = (F + F_r)\left(\dfrac{a}{g}\right)$

   $= (30000 + 12000 + 9.075 d^2)\left(\dfrac{1.25}{9.81}\right)$

   $F_a = 5351.68 + 1.156\, d^2$

5. Starting load, $F_s = 2(F + F_r)$

   $= 2 \times (10500 + 9.075\, d^2)$

   $F_s = 21000 + 18.15\, d^2$

6. a. Effective load on rope $= F + Fr + F_b$

   $= (10500 + 9.075\, d^2) + 44.05\, d^2$

   $= 10.5 \times 10^3 + 53.12\, d^2$ ...Eq. (*ii*)

   b. Load on the rope during starting $= F_s + F_b$

   $= (21000 + 18.15\, d^2) + 44.05\, d^2$

   $= 21 \times 10^3 + 62.2\, d^2$ ...Eq. (*iii*)

   c. Load on the rope during acceleration

   $= F + F_r + F_b + F_a$

   $= (10500 + 9.075\, d^2) + 44.05\, d^2 + (5351.68 + 1.156\, d^2)$

   $= 15851.68 + 54.28\, d^2$ ...Eq. (*iv*)

Thus the largest value of Eqs (*ii*), (*iii*), and (*iv*) gives F_{max}

i.e. $F_{max} = 77.76 \times 10^3 + 109.35\, d^2$

Eq. (*i*) yields ... $7 = \dfrac{684 d^2}{21 \times 10^3 + 62.2 d^2}$

$d = 24.32$ mm

For 6 × 19 construction, the standard wire diameter is **$d = 25$ mm.**

...Tb 14.27/ Pg 277, DHB

2.36 CHAIN DRIVES

Chain drives are used to transmit rotational motion and torque from one shaft to another. They provide the flexibility of a belt drive with the positive engagement feature of a gear drive. It consists of an endless chain wrapped around two sprockets – or- sprocket wheels. The chains are made up of number of rigid links which are hinged together by pin joints. The power is transmitted between parallel shafts only.

These find applications in agricultural machinery, bicycles, motor cycles, conveying machinery, rolling mills, etc. These can be used with chain speeds up to 25 m/s and speed ratios of up to 8.

Advantages:
- It transmits more power than belt drives.
- It permits high speed ratio of 8 to 10.
- Suitable for long as well as short center distances; these are particularly suitable for medium center distances.
- They perform better than gears under shock loads.
- They occupy less space.
- Transmission efficiency is high.
- It gives fewer loads on the shafts since chains do not require initial tension.
- Since there is no slip, hence perfect velocity ratio is obtained.
- It can be operated under adverse temperature and atmospheric conditions.
- Long service life because metal chain ordinarily doesn't deteriorate with age and is unaffected by atmospheric conditions.

Disadvantages:
- Requires lubrication since there is metal to metal contact.
- Noise is usually higher than with belts –or- gears.
- Chain drives can elongate due to wearing of link and sprocket teeth contact surfaces.
- Manufacturing cost is high.
- It needs accurate mounting and careful maintenance.

2.37 CLASSIFICATION OF CHAINS

Chains are classified into the following three groups:
1. Driving –or- Power transmitting chains.
   a. Block chain.   b. Roller chain.   c. Silent chain.
2. Crane –or- Hoisting and hauling chains:
   a. Chains with oval links   b. Square link chains.
3. Pulling –or- conveyor –or- tractive chains:
   a. Detachable/ Hook joint type.   b. Closed joint type.
   - Power transmitting chains are used to transmit power from one shaft to another and operate at a maximum speed of 900 m/min. These are also known as *driving chains*
   - Hoisting and hauling chains are used for suspending and hoisting (lifting) loads and operate at a maximum speed of 150 m/min. These are commonly known as *crane chains*.
   Applications: Cranes, hoists, conveyors, dredges, etc.
   - Conveyor chains are used for moving loads in elevators, conveyors, material handling equipment etc. and operate at a maximum speed of 120 m/min. These are also known as *tractive chains*.
   Applications: Conveyors, mines, mills, etc.

2.38 VELOCITY RATIO OF CHAIN DRIVES

Let z_1 = Number of teeth on smaller sprocket
z_2 = Number of teeth on larger sprocket
N_1 = speed of smaller sprocket (rpm)
N_2 = speed of larger sprocket (rpm)

Velocity –or– transmission ratio, $i = \dfrac{N_1}{N_2} = \dfrac{z_2}{z_1}$

The value of i varies from 1 to 7 ...**Table 14.37a/ Pg 286, DHB**

In general, the average speed of the chain is given as $v = \dfrac{\pi DN}{60} = \dfrac{pzN}{60}$ N – rpm

-or- $v = \dfrac{pzn}{1000}$ ...**14.49/ Pg 247, DHB**

Where,
p = pitch of the chain
n = speed of sprocket in rps

The empirical formula to determine pitch is $p \leq 10\left(\dfrac{60.67}{n_1}\right)^{2/3}$ ...**14.50/ Pg 247, DHB**

Where, n_1 = speed of smaller sprocket in rps

2.39 MINIMUM NUMBER OF TEETH ON SPROCKET

The minimum number of teeth on smaller sprocket based on transmission ratio is obtained from **Table 14.37a/ Pg 286, DHB**. When space is a problem, the minimum value of $z_1 = 7$ and $z_2 = i.z_1$. It is observed that the velocity ratio of a chain drive does not remain constant during operation thereby causing variation in angular speed of the sprocket.

The minimum number of teeth on the smaller sprocket should always be odd (17, 19, -or- 21).
i.e.
$z_1 = 17$, for smooth operation at moderate speeds
$z_2 = 19$, for durability and noise considerations,
$z_3 = 21$, for high speeds

With odd number of teeth on smaller sprocket and an even number of pitches in the chain, the frequency of contact between a particular tooth and a particular roller is minimum and thus the wear is distributed uniformly.

2.40 CENTRE DISTANCE

In order to have an arc of contact greater than ($\geq$) 120° on the smaller sprocket, the minimum center distance is given as

$$C_{min} = K_1 C_1$$ ...**14.56/ Pg 248, DHB**

Where, $C_1 = \dfrac{d_{01} + d_{02}}{2}$

d_{01} = tip diameter of smaller sprocket
d_{01} = tip diameter of larger sprocket
K_1 = a constant ...**Table 14.37b/ Pg 286, DHB**

The optimum center distance between the sprockets in terms of pitches is
$C = p.C_p$ ...**14.55/ Pg 248, DHB**
Where, C_p = 30 to 50
i.e. $C = (30 \text{ to } 50)p$.

2.41 CHAIN LENGTH

- The chain length in pitches is given as

$$L_p = 2C_p \cos \alpha + \frac{1}{2}(z_1 + z_2) + \alpha\left(\frac{z_2 - z_1}{180}\right) \quad \text{(exact)} \quad \text{...14.57a/ Pg 248, DHB}$$

$$L_p = 2C_p + 0.5(z_1 + z_2) + \frac{0.026(z_2 - z_1)^2}{C_p} \quad \text{(approx.)} \quad \text{...14.57b/ Pg 248, DHB}$$

Where, C_p – center distance in pitches
z_2, z_1 – number of teeth on larger and smaller sprockets respectively.
α – angle between tangent to the sprocket pitch circle and the center line

$$\alpha = \sin^{-1}\left(\frac{D_2 - D_1}{2C}\right)$$

D_2, D_1 – pitch diameters of larger and smaller sprockets

Pitch diameter of sprocket, $D = \dfrac{p}{\sin(180/z)}$ ...14.59/ Pg 248, DHB

i.e., $D_1 = \dfrac{p}{\sin(180/z_1)}$ and $D_2 = \dfrac{p}{\sin(180/z_2)}$

- The chain length $L = p\, L_p$ ...14.58/ Pg 248, DHB

2.42 POWER TRANSMITTED

The tangential force –or- the allowable tension in the chain is given as

$$F = \frac{1000P}{v} \quad \text{...14.51a/ Pg 247, DHB}$$

Thus the power can be calculated as $P = \dfrac{Fv}{1000}$ ... (kW)

2.43 MINIMUM NUMBER OF STRANDS IN A CHAIN

The minimum number of strands in a chain for is

$$j = \frac{F}{F_w} \quad \text{...14.54/ Pg 248, DHB}$$

Where, F – Tangential force
F_w – Allowable working load per strand

$$F_w = \frac{F_u}{(FS)K_s} \quad \text{...14.52/ Pg 247, DHB}$$

F_u – ultimate strength of the chain (N/strand)
K_s – service factor depending upon nature of load, efficiency of lubrication and position of chain
...Table 14.36/ Pg 286, DHB
(FS) – factor of safety ...Table 14.38/ Pg 287, DHB

- According to AGMA, the formula for allowable working load per strand (neglecting centrifugal force) is

$$F_w = \frac{98.07 A}{v + 3.05} \qquad \text{...14.53a/ Pg 248, DHB}$$

A – projected bearing area of the pun bushing joint (mm²)
v – chain speed (m/s).

2.44 ACTUAL FACTOR OF SAFETY

The actual factor of safety is calculated as

$$FS = \frac{F_u}{F + F_c + F_s} \qquad \text{...14.60/ Pg 249, DHB}$$

Where, F_u – Breaking load of the chain (N) F – tangential force (N)

F_c – Centrifugal force = $\dfrac{w'v^2}{g}$ (N)

w' – weight per meter length of chain (N) v – chain velocity (m/s)
F_s – tension due to sagging of chain (N)
   = $K_2 w' C_1$
K_2 – coefficient for sag   **...Table 14.39/ Pg 287A, DHB**
C_1 – center distance (m)

2.45 DEFINITIONS

- **Pitch:** The linear distance between the axes of adjacent rollers is known as pitch of the chain.
- **Pitch circle diameter (PCD):** The PCD of the sprocket is the diameter of imaginary circle that passes through the centers of link pins when the chain is wrapped round the sprocket.
- **Breaking load:** Refers to the maximum load at which the chain undergoes failure.

Note:
- **Fig. 14.14/ Pg 298, DHB** *gives the details of precision roller chains.*
- **Fig. 14.16/ Pg 298, DHB** *gives the details of precision Bush chains.*
- **Fig. 14.19/ Pg 298, DHB** *gives the details of leaf chains.*
- **Table 14.11b/ Pg 260, DHB** *gives the nominal diameters of pulleys.*
- **Table 14.40a/ Pg 287b, DHB** *gives details of base chains.*
- **Table 14.40b/ Pg 288, DHB** *gives details of roller chains.*
- **Table 14.41/ Pg 289, DHB** *gives details of bush chains.*
- **Table 14.42/ Pg 290, DHB** *gives the details of pitch circle diameter.*
- **Table 14.43/ Pg 293, DHB** *gives the details of leaf chains.*
- **Table 14.44/ Pg 295, DHB** *gives the dimensions of leaf chain sheaves.*
- In **Tables 14.40a, 14.40b –or– 14.41/ Pg 287b – 289, DHB** *the suffix at the end of each chain number represents the series.*
    Example: 208A –or– 208B
        208 – indicates chain number
         A – American Standard ANSI series
         B – British standard series

2.46 DESIGN PROCEDURE FOR CHAIN DRIVES

1. Find the velocity ratio as $i = \dfrac{N_1}{N_2} = \dfrac{z_2}{z_1}$

2. To find z:
   Based on the velocity ratio, select the number of teeth on the smaller sprocket (z_1) using **Tb 14.37a/ Pg 286, DHB,** and obtain $z_2 = i.z_1$ (z_1 should always be odd)

3. Calculate the pitch as:

   $$p \leq 10\left(\dfrac{60.67}{n_1}\right)^{2/3} \qquad \text{...14.50/ Pg 247, DHB}$$

   Where n_1 – speed of smaller sprocket in rps
   - Standardize the pitch to the nearest value, referring to **Tables 14.40a, 14.40b –** or– **14.41/ Pg 287b – 289, DHB** and note down the corresponding values of:
     Chain number: ....
     Measuring load, (w'):   .... (N)
     Breaking –or–ultimate load, F_u: .... (kN)

4. Calculate the PCD of sprockets as:

   $$D = \dfrac{p}{\sin\left(180/z\right)} \quad \text{(...value of } p \text{ from step 3)} \qquad \text{...14.59/ Pg 248, DHB}$$

5. Find the velocity of chain as:

   $$v = \dfrac{pz_1n_1}{1000} \qquad \text{...14.49/ Pg 247, DHB}$$

   Where, n_1 – speed of smaller sprocket in rps,
   z_1 – number of teeth on smaller sprocket

6. Calculate the tangential force as:

   $$F = \dfrac{1000P}{v} \qquad \text{...14.51a/ Pg 247, DHB}$$

7. Calculate the allowable working load per strand as:

   $$F_w = \dfrac{F_u}{(FS)K_s} \qquad \text{...14.52/ Pg 247, DHB}$$

   Where, F_u – .... (from step 3)
   K_s – Service factor   ...Table 14.36/ Pg 286, DHB
   (FS) – Factor of safety   ...Table 14.38/ Pg 287, DHB

8. Calculate the number of strands as

   $$j = \dfrac{F}{F_w} \qquad \text{...14.54/ Pg 248, DHB}$$

9. Calculate the actual factor of safety as: $(FS)_a = j\left[\dfrac{F_u}{F + F_c + F_s}\right]$ ...14.60/ Pg 249, DHB

Where, $F_c = F_c = \dfrac{w'v^2}{g}$, is the centrifugal force

w' .... (step 3)

$F_s = K_2 w' C_1$, is the tension due to sagging of chain

K_2 – coefficient for sag ...Table 14.39/ Pg 287A, DHB

C_1 – center distance

$\quad = C$ ... (if given in data)

$\quad = p\, C_p = (30\ \text{to}\ 50)p$ ... (for best result)

$\quad = D_1 + D_2$ ...(if center distance is as short as possible)

$\quad = \left(\dfrac{d_{01} + d_{02}}{2}\right) K_1$ ...(if sprocket tip diameters are known)

Value of K_1 ...Table 14.37b/ Pg 287A, DHB

- If $(FS)_a > FS$ (tables), then the selected chain is safe.
- If $(FS)_a < FS$ (tables), then the selected chain is not safe and design needs to be modified. The options are:
  (i) Increase the number of strands
  (ii) Change the chain

10. Calculate the chain length in pitches as:

$$L_p = 2C_p \cos\alpha + \dfrac{1}{2}(z_1 + z_2) + \alpha\left(\dfrac{z_2 - z_1}{180}\right) \quad \text{...14.57a/ Pg 248, DHB}$$

Where, $C_p = C/p$ ...14.55/ Pg 248, DHB

$$\alpha = \sin^{-1}\left(\dfrac{D_2 - D_1}{2C}\right) \quad \text{...14.57b/ Pg 248, DHB}$$

Round off L_p to the nearest *even* number.

11. Find the chain length as:

$$L = p.L_p \quad \text{...14.58/ Pg 248, DHB}$$

12. From the obtained value of L_p, determine the exact center distance (C_e) by replacing (C_p) with $\left(\dfrac{C_e}{p}\right)$ in step 10 as:

i.e. $L_p = 2\left(\dfrac{C_e}{p}\right)\cos\alpha + \dfrac{1}{2}(z_1 + z_2) + \alpha\left(\dfrac{z_2 - z_1}{180}\right).$

33. A 800 rpm, 25 kW squirrel cage induction motor is to drive a reciprocating pump at 200 rpm. The pump is to run at full load for 24 hours a day. Select a suitable roller chain drive, if the center distance is as short as possible.

Solution: Driver speed (smaller sprocket), $N_1 = 800$ rpm, $P = 25$ kW, driven speed (larger sprocket), $N_2 = 200$ rpm. Service condition = 24 h a day.

1. *Velocity ratio:*

   We know that, $i = \dfrac{N_1}{N_2} = \dfrac{800}{200} = 4$

2. *Number of teeth:*

   Referring to **Table 14.37a/ Pg 286, DHB**, $i = 4$ lies in the range of (3 – 4).
   Hence the number of teeth on smaller sprocket, $z_1 = 23$
   and $4 \times 23 = 92.$

3. *Pitch:*

We know that, $\quad p \leq 10\left(\dfrac{60.67}{n_1}\right)^{2/3}$ ...14.50/ Pg 247, DHB

$$\leq 10\left(\dfrac{60.67}{800/60}\right)^{2/3}$$

$p \leq 27.46$ mm

- From **Table 14.40b/ Pg 288,** for a roller chain, the nearest standard pitch is $p = 25.40$ mm, for chains 208A and 208B. Hence adopt:
  Chain number: 208B   Measuring load: 127.50 N   Breaking –or–ultimate load, $F_u = 17.85$ kN

4. *PCD of sprockets:*

We know that, pitch diameter of sprocket, $D = \dfrac{p}{\sin(180/z)}$ ...14.59/ Pg 248, DHB

i.e. For smaller sprocket, $D_1 = \dfrac{p}{\sin(180/z_1)} = \dfrac{25.4}{\sin(180/23)} = 186.54$ mm

and for larger sprocket, $D_2 = \dfrac{p}{\sin(180/z_2)} = \dfrac{25.4}{\sin(180/92)} = 744$ mm.

5. *Velocity of chain:*

$v = \dfrac{p z_1 n_1}{1000} = \dfrac{25.4 \times 23 \times (800/60)}{1000} = 7.79$ m/s ...14.49/ Pg 247, DHB

6. *Tangential force:*

$F = \dfrac{1000 P}{v} = \dfrac{1000 \times 25}{7.79} = 3209.52$ N ...14.51a/ Pg 247, DHB

7. *Allowable working load per strand:*

$$F_w = \dfrac{F_u}{(FS) K_s}$$ ...14.52/ Pg 247, DHB

Where, $F_u = 17.85$ kN   (from step 3)
Service factor, $K_s = 2.2$, for continuous operation   ...Tb 14.36/ Pg 286, DHB
Factor of safety, (FS) 11.7   [for $p = 25$ & $N_1 = 800$ rpm]   ...Tb 14.38/ Pg 287, DHB

$$= \dfrac{17.85 \times 10^3}{11.7 \times 2}$$

$= 635.68$ N
$F_w = 635.68$ N

8. *Number of strands:*

$j = \dfrac{F}{F_w} = \dfrac{3209.52}{635.68} = 4.21 \approx 5$ strands ...14.54/ Pg 248, DHB

9. *Actual factor of safety:*

$$(FS) = j\left[\frac{F_u}{F + F_c + F_s}\right] \qquad \text{...14.60/ Pg 249, DHB}$$

- $F_c = \dfrac{w'v^2}{g} = \dfrac{127.5 \times 7.79^2}{9.81} = 788.7 \text{ N} \qquad [w' = 127.50 \text{ N} \ldots\ldots \text{ (step 3)}]$
- $F_s = K_2 w' C_1$

For shortest center distance, $C_1 = D_1 + D_2$
$$= 186.5 + 744$$
$$= 930.54 \text{ mm} = 0.930 \text{ m}$$

coefficient for sag, $K_2 = 6$, for horizontal drive
...Tb 14.39/ Pg 287A, DHB

$$F_s = 6 \times 127.5 \times 0.9305$$
$$F_s = 711.84 \text{ N}$$

Therefore, $\qquad (FS) = 5\left[\dfrac{17.85 \times 10^3}{3209.52 + 788.7 + 711.84}\right]$

$(FS)_a = 18.95$

Since $(FS)_a > FS$ (tables), the selected chain is safe.

10. *Chain lengths:*

$$L_p = 2C_p \cos\alpha + \frac{1}{2}(z_1 + z_2) + \alpha\left(\frac{z_2 - z_1}{180}\right) \qquad \text{...Eq. (i) ...14.57a/ Pg 248, DHB}$$

Where, $C_p = \dfrac{C}{p} = \dfrac{600}{19.05} \; 36.6 = 3 \qquad \text{...14.55/ Pg 248, DHB}$

$$\alpha = \sin^{-1}\left(\frac{D_2 - D_1}{2C}\right) = \sin^{-1}\left(\frac{744 - 186.54}{2 \times 600}\right) = 17.43°$$
...14.57b/ Pg 248, DHB

Eq. (i) yields ... $L_p = 2C_p \cos\alpha + \dfrac{1}{2}(z_1 + z_2) + \alpha\left(\dfrac{z_2 - z_1}{180}\right)$

$$= 2 \times 31.5 \times \cos(25.74) + \frac{1}{2}(23 + 92) + 17.43\left(\frac{92 - 23}{180}\right)$$

$L_p = 134$ pitches $\qquad \qquad \text{... Eq. (ii)}$

11. *Chain length:*

$$L = p.L_p \qquad \text{...14.58/ Pg 248, DHB}$$
$$= 25.4 \times 134$$
$$L = 3403.6 \text{ mm}$$

12. *Exact center distance:*

Substituting (ii) in (i), we have

$$134 = 2 \times \left(\frac{C_e}{19.05}\right) \times \cos(25.74) + \frac{1}{2}(23 + 92) + 17.43\left(\frac{92 - 23}{180}\right)$$

$C_e = 930$ mm.

34. A 15 kW, 1100 rpm motor drives a line shaft at 200 rpm. The shaft center distance is approximately 600 mm. The motor shaft has a diameter of 50 mm. The starting torque on motor is 2 times the running torque. The load is applied with moderate shocks. Select a suitable roller chain drive.

Solution: 15 kW, driver speed (smaller sprocket), $N_1 = 1100$ rpm, driven speed (larger sprocket), $N_2 = 200$ rpm, $C_1 = 600$ mm $= 0.6$ m, shaft diameter, $d_1 = 50$ mm, service condition: Moderate shocks.

1. *Velocity ratio:*

    We know that, $$i = \frac{N_1}{N_2} = \frac{1100}{200}$$
    $$i = 5.5$$

2. *Number of teeth:*

    Referring to **Table 14.37a/ Pg 286, DHB**, $i = 5.5$ lies in the range of $(5 - 7)$. Hence the number of teeth on smaller sprocket,
    $$z_1 = 19$$
    and $$z_2 = i.z_1 = 5.5 \times 19 = 104.5 \approx 105$$

3. *Pitch:*

    We know that, $$p \leq 10\left(\frac{60.67}{n_1}\right)^{2/3} \qquad \text{...14.50/ Pg 247, DHB}$$

    $$\leq 10\left(\frac{60.67}{1100/60}\right)^{2/3}$$

    $$p = 22.21 \text{ mm}$$

- From **Table 14.40a/ Pg 287B**, the nearest standard pitch is 19.05 mm. Hence Adopt

    Chain number: 208B

    Measuring load, $w' = 29$ kg $= 284.50$ N (simplex type)
    Breaking –or–ultimate load, $F_u = 2950$ kg $= 28939.5$ N (simplex type)

4. *PCD of sprockets:*

    We know that, pitch diameter of sprocket, $D = \dfrac{p}{\sin(180/z)}$ ...14.59/ Pg 248, DHB

    i.e. For smaller sprocket, $D_1 = \dfrac{p}{\sin(180/z_1)} = \dfrac{19.05}{\sin(180/19)} = 115.74$ mm

    and for larger sprocket, $D_2 = \dfrac{p}{\sin(180/z_2)} = \dfrac{19.05}{\sin(180/105)} = 636.8$ mm

5. *Velocity of chain:*

    $$v = \frac{pz_1 n_1}{1000} = \frac{19.05 \times 19 \times (1100/60)}{1000} = 6.636 \text{ m/s} \qquad \text{...14.49/ Pg 247, DHB}$$

6. *Tangential force:*

    $$F = \frac{2(M_t)_{max}}{d} \qquad \text{...Eq. (i)}$$

But $(M_t)_{max} = 2M_t$ ...Eq. (ii)

Also $P = \dfrac{2\pi N M_t}{60}$

$$15 \times 10^3 = \dfrac{2\pi \times 1100 \times M_t}{60}$$

$M_t = 130.22$ N-m

Eq. (ii) yields ... $(M_t)_{max} = 2 \times 130.22 = 260.44$ N-m

$(M_t)_{max} = 260.44 \times 10^3$ N-mm

Eq. (i) yields ... $F = \dfrac{2(M_t)_{max}}{d} = \dfrac{2 \times 260.44 \times 10^3}{50}$

$F = 10417.6$ N

7. *Allowable working load per strand:*

$$F_w = \dfrac{F_u}{(FS)K_s} \qquad \text{...14.52/ Pg 247, DHB}$$

$F_u = 28939.5$ N (from step 3)

Service factor, $K_s = 1.9$, assuming 10 h per day and moderate shocks.

...Tb 14.36/ Pg 286, DHB

Factor of safety, (FS)

For $N_1 = 1100$ rpm, from **Tb 14.38/ Pg 287, DHB**

N	FS
1200	14
1000	12.9

For $N = 1$ rpm, $FS = \dfrac{14 - 12.9}{1200 - 1000} = 5.5 \times 10^{-3}$

Therefore, for $N = 1100$ rpm, $FS = 12.9 + [(1100 - 1000) \times (5.5 \times 10^{-3})] = 13.45$

Factor of safety, $(FS) = 13.45$

$$\therefore F_w = \dfrac{28939.5}{13.45 \times 1.9}$$

$F_w = 1132.44$ N.

8. *Number of strands:*

$$j = \dfrac{F}{F_w} = \dfrac{10417.6}{1132.44} = 9.19 \approx 10 \text{ strands} \qquad \text{...14.54/ Pg 248, DHB}$$

9. *Actual factor of safety:*

$$(FS)_a = j\left[\dfrac{F_u}{F + F_c + F_s}\right] \qquad \text{...14.60/ Pg 249, DHB}$$

- $F_c = \dfrac{w'v^2}{g} = \dfrac{284.5 \times 6.636^2}{9.81} = 1278.64$ N $[w' = 127.50$ N ...(step 3)]

- $FS = K_2 w' C_1$

Here, $C_1 = 600$ mm $= 0.6$ m (data)
Coefficient for sag, $K_2 = 6$, for horizontal drive ...Tb 14.39/ Pg 287A, DHB
$$F_s = 6 \times 284.5 \times 0.6$$
$$F_s = 1024.2 \text{ N}$$

Therefore, $$(FS)_a = 10\left[\frac{28939.5}{10417.6 + 1278.64 + 1024.2}\right]$$
$$(FS)_a = 22.75$$

Since $(FS)_a > FS$ (tables), the selected chain is safe.

10. *Chain lengths:*

$$L_p = 2C_p \cos\alpha + \frac{1}{2}(z_1 + z_2) + \alpha\left(\frac{z_2 - z_1}{180}\right) \qquad \text{...Eq. }(iii)\ 14.57a/\text{ Pg 248, DHB}$$

Where, $$C_p = \frac{C}{p} = \frac{600}{19.05} = 31.5 \qquad \text{...14.55/ Pg 248, DHB}$$

$$\alpha = \sin^{-1}\left(\frac{D_2 - D_1}{2C}\right) = \sin^{-1}\left(\frac{636.8 - 115.74}{2 \times 600}\right) = 25.74°$$
...14.57b/ Pg 248, DHB

Eq. (*iii*) yields ... $$L_p = 2C_p \cos\alpha + \frac{1}{2}(z_1 + z_2) + \alpha\left(\frac{z_2 - z_1}{180}\right)$$

$$= 2 \times 31.5 \times \cos(25.74) + \frac{1}{2}(19 + 105) + 25.74\left(\frac{105 - 19}{180}\right)$$
$$L_p = 131.05 \text{ pitches} \approx 132 \text{ pitches} \qquad \text{...Eq. }(iv)$$

11. *Chain length:*
$$L_p = p.L_p \qquad \text{...14.58/ Pg 248, DHB}$$
$$= 19.05 \times 132$$
$$L = 2514.6 \text{ mm}$$

12. *Exact center distance:*
Substituting (*iv*) in (*iii*), we have

$$132 = 2 \times \left(\frac{C_e}{19.05}\right) \times \cos(25.74) + \frac{1}{2}(19 + 105) + 25.74\left(\frac{105 - 19}{180}\right)$$

Where, $$C_p = \frac{C_e}{p} = \frac{C_e}{19.05}$$

$$C_e = 610.15 \text{ mm.}$$

35. **A roller chain is to transmit 60 kW from a 17 tooth sprocket running at 400 rpm to a 34 tooth sprocket. The load characteristics are moderate shock with abnormal service conditions. The equipment is to run 10 hours per day. Design a roller chain assuming a center distance of 30 pitches.**

Solution: $P = 60$ kW, number of teeth on smaller sprocket $z_1 = 17$, number of teeth on larger sprocket $z_2 = 34$, service condition: abnormal service with moderate shocks working for 10 hours per day, center distance, $C_1 = 30p$, $N_1 = 400$ rpm.

1. *Velocity ratio:*

We know that, $$i = \frac{N_1}{N_2} = \frac{z_2}{z_1}$$

$$i = \frac{34}{17} = 2.$$

2. *Number of teeth:*

    Number of teeth on smaller sprocket, $z_1 = 17$
    Number of teeth on larger sprocket, $z_1 = 34$ (data)

3. *Pitch:*

    We know that, $\quad p \le 10\left(\dfrac{60.67}{400/60}\right)^{2/3}$ ...**14.50/ Pg 247, DHB**

    $$\le 10\left(\dfrac{60.67}{400/60}\right)^{2/3}$$

    $p \le 43.59$ mm.

    - From **Table 14.40b/ Pg 288**, the nearest standard pitch is 38.10 mm. Hence adopt Chain number: 212A   Measuring load $w' = 284.39$ N   Breaking –or–ultimate load $F_u = 31.19$ kN

4. *PCD of sprockets:*

    We know that, Pitch diameter of sprocket, $D = \dfrac{p}{\sin(180/z)}$ ...**14.59/ Pg 248, DHB**

    i.e. For smaller sprocket, $D_1 = \dfrac{p}{\sin(180/z_1)} = \dfrac{38.10}{\sin(180/17)} = 207.35$ mm

    and for larger sprocket, $D_2 = \dfrac{p}{\sin(180/z_2)} = \dfrac{38.10}{\sin(180/34)} = 413$ mm.

5. *Velocity of chain:*

    $v = \dfrac{p z_1 n_1}{1000} = \dfrac{38.10 \times 17 \times (400/60)}{1000} = 4.32$ m/s   ...**14.49/ Pg 247, DHB**

6. *Tangential force:*

    $$F = \dfrac{1000P}{v} = \dfrac{1000 \times 60}{4.32} = 13889 \text{ N} \quad \text{...14.51a/ Pg 247, DHB}$$

7. *Allowable working load per strand:*

    $$F_w = \dfrac{F_u}{(FS)K_s} \quad \text{...14.52/ Pg 247, DHB}$$

    Where, $F_u = 31.19$ kN   (from step 3)
    Service factor, $K_s = 1.9$, for moderate shocks up to 10 h/ day
    ...**Tb 14.36/ Pg 286, DHB**
    Factor of safety, $(FS) = 10.2$ [for $p = 35$ & $N_1 = 400$ rpm]
    ...**Tb 14.38/ Pg 287, DHB**

$$= \frac{31.19 \times 10^3}{10.2 \times 1.9}$$

$$F_w = 1609.39 \text{ N}.$$

8. *Number of strands:*

$$j = \frac{F}{F_w} = \frac{13889}{1609.39} = 8.63 \approx 9 \text{ strands} \qquad \text{...14.54/ Pg 248, DHB}$$

9. *Actual factor of safety:*

$$(FS)_a = j\left[\frac{F_u}{F + F_c + F_s}\right] \qquad \text{...14.60/ Pg 249, DHB}$$

- $F_c = \dfrac{w'v^2}{g} = \dfrac{284.39 \times 4.32^2}{9.81} = 541 \text{ N} \quad [w' = 127.50\text{N} \ldots\ldots (\text{step 3})]$

- $FS = K_2 w' C_1$

For shortest center distance, $C_1 = 30p$
$$= 30 \times 38.10$$
$$= 1143 \text{ mm} = 1.143 \text{ m}$$

coefficient for sag, $K_2 = 6$, for horizontal drive ...Tb 14.39/ Pg 287A, DHB

$$F_s = 6 \times 284.39 \times 1.143$$
$$F_s = 1950.35 \text{ N}$$

Therefore, $(FS)_a = 9\left[\dfrac{31.19 \times 10^3}{13889 + 541 + 1950.35}\right]$

$$(FS)_a = 17.14$$

Since $(FS)_a > FS$ (tables), the selected chain is safe.

10. *Chain length:*

$$L_p = 2C_p \cos\alpha + \frac{1}{2}(z_1 + z_2) + \alpha\left(\frac{z_2 - z_1}{180}\right) \qquad \text{...Eq. }(i)\text{ ...14.57a/ Pg 248, DHB}$$

Where, $C_p = \dfrac{C}{p} = \dfrac{1143}{38.10} = 30$ \qquad ...14.55/ Pg 248, DHB

$$\alpha = \sin^{-1}\left(\frac{D_2 - D_1}{2C}\right) = \sin^{-1}\left(\frac{413 - 207.35}{2 \times 1143}\right) = 5.16° \qquad \text{...14.57b/ Pg 248, DHB}$$

Eq. (i) yields ... $L_p = 2C_p \cos\alpha + \dfrac{1}{2}(z_1 + z_2) + \alpha\left(\dfrac{z_2 - z_1}{180}\right)$

$$= 2 \times 30 \times \cos(5.16) + \frac{1}{2}(17 + 34) + 5.16\left(\frac{34 - 17}{180}\right)$$

$$L_p = 85.31 \text{ pitches} \approx 86 \text{ pitches} \qquad \text{...Eq. }(ii)$$

11. *Chain length:*

$L = p.L_p = 38.10 \times 86 = 3276.6 \text{ mm}$ \qquad ...14.58/ Pg 248, DHB

12. *Exact center distance:*
Substituting (ii) in (i), we have

$$86 = 2 \times \left(\frac{C_e}{38.10}\right) \times \cos(5.16) + \frac{1}{2}(17 + 34) + 5.16\left(\frac{34-17}{180}\right)$$

$$\text{Where, } C_p = \frac{C_e}{p} = \frac{C_e}{25.4}$$

$$C_e = 1148 \text{ mm.}$$

36. Select a roller chain for a bucket elevator to be driven by a gear motor. The gear motor has 6 kW and runs at 120 rpm. The speed of bucket elevator is 60 rpm. The center distance is 1100 mm. The elevator operates 10 hours per day with mild shock.

Solution: $P = 6$ kW, $N_1 = 120$ rpm, $N_2 = 60$ rpm, $C_1 = 1100$ mm, service condition: mild shock working for 10 hours per day.

1. *Velocity ratio:*

   We know that, $\quad i = \dfrac{N_1}{N_2} = \dfrac{120}{60} = 2$

2. *Number of teeth:*
   Referring to **Table 14.37a/ Pg 286, DHB**, $i = 2$ lies in the range of $(1 - 2)$.
   Hence the number of teeth on smaller sprocket,
   $$z_1 = 27$$
   and $\quad z_2 = i.z_1 = 27 \times 2 = 54$

3. *Pitch:*

   We know that, $\quad p \leq 10\left(\dfrac{60.67}{n_1}\right)^{2/3}$ ...**14.50/ Pg 247, DHB**

   $$\leq 10\left(\dfrac{60.67}{120/60}\right)^{2/3}$$

   $p \leq 97.26$ mm.

   - From **Table 14.40b/ Pg 288,** the nearest standard pitch is $p = 88.90$ mm. Hence
     Adopt
     Chain number: 228B   Measuring load $w' = 1510.22$ N   Breaking –or–ultimate load $F_u = 129.06$ kN

4. *PCD of sprockets:*

   We know that, pitch diameter of sprocket, $D = \dfrac{p}{\sin(180/z)}$ ...**14.59/ Pg 248, DHB**

   i.e. For smaller sprocket, $\quad D_1 = \dfrac{p}{\sin(180/z_1)} = \dfrac{88.90}{\sin(180/27)} = 766$ mm

   and for larger sprocket, $\quad D_2 = \dfrac{p}{\sin(180/z_2)} = \dfrac{88.90}{\sin(180/54)} = 1529$ mm

5. *Velocity of chain:*

$$v = \frac{pz_1n_1}{1000} = \frac{88.90 \times 27 \times \left(\frac{120}{60}\right)}{1000} = 4.80 \text{ m/s} \qquad \text{...14.49/ Pg 247, DHB}$$

6. *Tangential force:*

$$F = \frac{1000P}{v} = \frac{1000 \times 6}{480} = 1250 \text{ N} \qquad \text{...14.51a/ Pg 247, DHB}$$

7. *Allowable working load per strand:*

$$F_w = \frac{F_u}{(FS)K_s} \qquad \text{...14.52/ Pg 247, DHB}$$

Where, F_u = 129.06 kN   (from step 3)
Service factor, K_s = 1.9, for moderate shocks up to 10 h/ day
...Tb 14.36/ Pg 286, DHB

Factor of safety, (FS)
For N_1 = 120 rpm, from **Tb 14.38/ Pg 287, DHB**

N	FS
200	8.55
50	7.0

For $\qquad N = 1$ rpm, $FS = \dfrac{8.55 - 7}{200 - 50} = 10.33 \times 10^{-3}$

Therefore, for $\qquad N = 120$ rpm, $FS = 7 + [(120 - 50) \times (10.33 \times 10^{-3})] = 7.72$
Factor of safety, $\qquad (FS) = 7.72$

$$F_w = \frac{129.06 \times 10^3}{7.72 \times 1.9}$$

$$F_w = 8798.7 \text{ N}$$

8. *Number of strands:*

$$j = \frac{F}{F_w} = \frac{1250}{8798.7} = 0.142 \simeq 1 \text{ strand} \qquad \text{...14.54/ Pg 248, DHB}$$

9. *Actual factor of safety*

$$(FS)_a = j\left[\frac{F_u}{F + F_c + F_s}\right] \qquad \text{...14.60/ Pg 249, DHB}$$

- $F_c = \dfrac{w'v^2}{g} = \dfrac{1510.22 \times 4.80^2}{9.81} = 3547 \text{ N} \qquad [w' = 1510.22 \text{ N ...(step 3)}]$

- $FS = K_2 w' C_1$
C_1 = 1100 mm = 1.1 m   (data)
coefficient for sag, K_2 = 6, for horizontal drive   ...Tb 14.39/ Pg 287A, DHB
$FS = 6 \times 1510.22 \times 1.1$
$FS = 9967.45$ N

Therefore, $\qquad (FS)_a = 1\left[\dfrac{129.06 \times 10^3}{1250 + 3547 + 9967.45}\right]$

$(FS)_a = 8.78$

Since $(FS)_a > FS$ (tables), the selected chain is safe.

10. *Chain lengths:*

$$L_p = 2C_p \cos \alpha + \frac{1}{2}(z_1 + z_2) + \alpha\left(\frac{z_2 - z_1}{180}\right) \qquad \text{...Eq. (}i\text{) ...14.57a/ Pg 248, DHB}$$

Where, $C_p = \dfrac{C}{p} = \dfrac{1100}{88.90} = 12.37$ ...14.55/ Pg 248, DHB

$$\alpha = \sin^{-1}\left(\frac{D_2 - D_1}{2C}\right) = \sin^{-1}\left(\frac{1529 - 766}{2 \times 1100}\right) 20.29° \text{ ...14.57b/ Pg 248, DHB}$$

Eq. (*i*) yields ... $L_p = 2C_p \cos \alpha + \dfrac{1}{2}(z_1 + z_2) + \alpha\left(\dfrac{z_2 - z_1}{180}\right)$

$$= 2 \times 12.37 \times \cos(20.29) + \frac{1}{2}(27 + 54) + 20.29\left(\frac{54 - 27}{180}\right)$$

$L_p = 66.75$ pitches ≈ 66 pitches ...Eq. (*ii*)

11. *Chain length:*

$$L = p.L_p \qquad \text{...14.58/ Pg 248, DHB}$$
$$= 88.90 \times 66$$
$$L = 5867.4 \text{ mm.}$$

12. *Exact center distance:*

Substituting (*ii*) in (*i*), we have

$$66 = 2 \times \left(\frac{C_e}{88.90}\right) \times \cos(20.29) + \frac{1}{2}(27 + 54) + 20.29\left(\frac{54 - 27}{180}\right)$$

Where, $C_p = \dfrac{C_e}{p} = \dfrac{C_e}{88.90}$

$C_e = 1064.23$ mm.

37. Select a suitable roller chain drive to transmit 10 kW from a 1200 rpm motor to a compressor at 400 rpm. The center distance is adjustable to 800 mm. The service is 24 hours per day. Assume a factor of safety as 14.

Solution: $P = 10$ kW, $N_1 = 1200$ rpm, $N_2 = 400$ rpm, $C_1 = 800$ mm, Service condition: 24 h (continuous), $FS = 14$

1. *Velocity ratio:*

We know that $\qquad i = \dfrac{N_1}{N_2} = \dfrac{1200}{400} = 3$

2. *Number of teeth:*

Referring to **Table 14.37a/ Pg 286, DHB**, $i = 3$ lies in the range of (3 – 4). Hence the number of teeth on smaller sprocket,

$z_1 = 25$

and $\qquad z_1 = i.z_1 = 3 \times 25 = 75$

3. *Pitch:*

We know that, $\qquad p \leq 10\left(\dfrac{60.67}{n_1}\right)^{2/3}$ ...14.50/ Pg 247, DHB

$$\leq 10\left(\frac{60.67}{1200/60}\right)^{2/3}$$

$p \leq 20.95$ mm.

- From **Table 14.40a/ Pg 287B,** the nearest standard pitch is 19.05 mm. Hence Adopt
  Chain number: 208B

  Measuring load, $w' = 29$ kg $= 284.50$ N (simplex type)
  Breaking –or–ultimate load, $F_u = 2950$ kg $= 28939.5$ N (simplex type)

4. *PCD of sprockets:*

We know that, pitch diameter of sprocket, $D = \dfrac{p}{\sin\left(180/z\right)}$ ...14.59/ Pg 248, DHB

i.e. For smaller sprocket, $D_1 = \dfrac{p}{\sin\left(180/z_1\right)} = \dfrac{19.05}{\sin\left(180/25\right)} = 152$ mm

and for larger sprocket, $D_2 = \dfrac{p}{\sin\left(180/z_2\right)} = \dfrac{19.05}{\sin\left(180/75\right)} = 455$ mm

5. *Velocity of chain:*

$$v = \frac{pz_1n_1}{1000} = \frac{19.05 \times 25 \times (1200/60)}{1000} = 9.525 \text{ m/s} \qquad \text{...14.49/ Pg 247, DHB}$$

6. *Tangential force:*

$$F = \frac{1000P}{v} = \frac{1000 \times 10}{9.525} = 1049.87 \text{ N} \qquad \text{...14.51a/ Pg 247, DHB}$$

7. *Allowable working load per strand:*

$$F_w = \frac{F_u}{(FS)K_s}, \qquad \text{...14.52/ Pg 247, DHB}$$

Where, $F_u = 28939.5$ N (from step 3)
Service factor, $K_s = 2.4$, continuous service ...Tb 14.36/ Pg 286, DHB
Factor of safety, $(FS) = 14$ (data)

$$= \frac{28939.5}{14 \times 2.4}$$

$F_w = 861.3$ N

8. *Number of strands:*

$$j = \frac{F}{F_w} = \frac{1049.87}{861.3} = 1.218 \approx 2 \text{ strands} \qquad \text{...14.54/ Pg 248, DHB}$$

9. *Actual factor of safety:*

$$(FS)_a = j\left[\frac{F_u}{F + F_c + F_s}\right] \qquad \text{...14.60/ Pg 249, DHB}$$

- $$F_c = \frac{w'v^2}{g} = \frac{284.5 \times 9.525^2}{9.81} = 2631.04 \text{ N} \quad [w' = 127.50\text{N} \ldots(\text{step 3})]$$

- $FS = K_2 w' C_1$

  Here, $C_1 = 800 \text{ mm} = 0.8 \text{ m}$ (data)

  Coefficient for sag, $K_2 = 6$, for horizontal drive ...Tb 14.39/ Pg 287A, DHB

  $FS = 6 \times 284.5 \times 0.8$
  $FS = 1365.6 \text{ N}$

Therefore, $(FS)_a = 2\left[\dfrac{28939.5}{1049.87 + 2631.04 + 1365.5}\right]$

$(FS)_a = 11.47$

Since $(FS)_a < FS$ (tables), **the selected chain is not safe** and design needs to be modified. The options are:

(i) Increase the number of strands
(ii) Change the chain

Increase the number of strands to 3 yields, $FS = 3 \times 11.7 = 34.40$

10. *Chain lengths:*

$$L_p = 2C_p \cos\alpha + \frac{1}{2}(z_1 + z_2) + \alpha\left(\frac{z_2 - z_1}{180}\right) \quad \ldots\text{Eq. } (i) \ldots 14.57a/ \text{ Pg 248, DHB}$$

Where, $C_p = \dfrac{C}{p} = \dfrac{800}{19.05} = 42$ ...14.55/ Pg 248, DHB

$$\alpha = \sin^{-1}\left(\frac{D_2 - D_1}{2C}\right) = \sin^{-1}\left(\frac{455 - 152}{2 \times 800}\right) = 10.92°$$

...14.57b/ Pg 248, DHB

Eq. (i) yields, $L_p = 2C_p \cos\alpha + \dfrac{1}{2}(z_1 + z_2) + \alpha\left(\dfrac{z_2 - z_1}{180}\right)$

$= 2 \times 42 \times \cos\cos(10.92) + \dfrac{1}{2}(25 + 75) + 10.92\left(\dfrac{75 - 25}{180}\right)$

$L_p = 135.51 \text{ pitches} \approx 136 \text{ pitches}$ ...Eq. (ii)

11. *Chain length:*

$L = p.L_p$ ...14.58/ Pg 248, DHB
$= 19.05 \times 136$
$L = 2590.8 \text{ mm}$

12. *Exact center distance:*

Substituting Eq. (ii) in Eq. (i), we have

$$136 = 2 \times \left(\frac{C_e}{19.05}\right) \times \cos(10.92) + \frac{1}{2}(25 + 75) + 10.92\left(\frac{75 - 25}{180}\right)$$

Where, $C_p = \dfrac{C_e}{p} = \dfrac{C_e}{19.05}$

$C_e = 804.83 \text{ mm}.$

VTU QUESTION PAPERS

Feb. 2002 (ME6T2)

1. a. Select a V belt drive to transmit a power of 6 kW from a shaft rotating at 1500 rpm to a parallel shaft to be run at 375 rpm. The distance between the shaft centers is 500 mm. The pitch diameter of the smaller grooved pulley can be taken to be 150 mm. The factor of application is to be taken as 1.2. **(10 Marks)**

   b. Select a wire rope to lift a load of 10 kN by 200 m. the desired velocity of 20 m/min is to be achieved while travelling through a distance of 10 m.
   (10 Marks)

July/ August 2005 (AU 53)

2. a. Select a standard V belt to transmit a power of 30 kW from an AC induction motor rotating at 1500 rpm to a centrifugal pump rotating at 750 rpm. The drive operates continuously for 8 hours per day. Calculate the number of belts.
   (10 Marks)

   b. Select a 6 × 19 steel rope to lift 15 kN of debris from a tunnel 200 m deep. The bucket weighs 8 kN. The velocity of the rope is 100 m/min to be attained in 20 seconds. What will be the maximum load on the rope when there is a slack of 10 m in the rope. **(10 Marks)**

Jan./ Feb 2006 (AU 53)

3. a. Select a V belt drive to transmit a load of 6 kW from a shaft rotating at 1000 rpm to a parallel shaft to be rotated at 350 rpm. The space limits the center distance between shafts to 500 mm. The pitch diameter of the smaller pulley could be assumed to be 150 mm. **(10 Marks)**

   b. Select a suitable wire rope of a standard strand to raise a load of 10 kN through 400 m. The load has to achieve a desired linear speed of 20 m/min while traversing through a distance of 15 m from the start. **(10 Marks)**

July 2006 (AU 53)

4. a. Show that in flat belts drives the ratio of belt tensions is given by $\dfrac{T_1}{T_2} = e^{\mu\theta}$ where T_1 and T_2 are the belt tensions, μ – coefficient of friction and θ – is the angle of wrap. **(05 Marks)**

   b. Select the type and number of V- belts required to drive a crusher, which works 8 hours a day. The power transmitted is 65 kW. The motor shaft runs at 900 rpm and carries a pulley of 250 mm diameter, the crusher shaft rotates at 300 rpm and the center distance is 700 mm. Determine the pitch length of the belt required.
   (15 Marks)

Dec. 06/ Jan. 07 (AU 53)

5. a. Select a V-belt drive to transmit 10 kW of power from a pulley of 200 mm diameter mounted on an electric motor running at 720 rpm to another pulley mounted on compressor running at 200 rpm. The approximate center distance between the two pulleys is 600 mm. The correction factor for service is 1.3. Find the number of belts and the correct enter distance. **(10 Marks)**

Belt, Rope and Chain Drives **215**

b. Select a suitable wire rope of standard strand to lift a load of 10 kN through a height of 600 mm from a mine. The weight of the bucket is 2.5 KN. The load should attain a maximum speed of 50 m/min in 2 seconds. **(14 Marks)**

July 2007 (AU 53)

6. a. Derive the equation $\dfrac{T_1}{T_2} = e^{\mu\theta}$, where T_1 – tension in the belt on the tight side, T_2 – tension in the belt on the slack side, coefficient of friction and θ is the angle of contact in radians. **(08 Marks)**
   b. A compressor requiring 85 kW is to run at 250 rpm. The drive is by V-belts from an electric motor running at 800 rpm. The diameter of the pulley on the compressor shaft must not be greater than 1 meter while the center distance between the pulleys is limited to 1.8 m. The belt speed should not exceed 1500 m/min. Determine the number of V-belts required to transmit the power if each has a cross-sectional area of 360 mm², density 1000 kg/m³ and an allowable tensile stress of 2.5 N/mm². The groove angle of the pulley is 35°. The coefficient of fiction between the belt and the pulley is 0.25. **(12 Marks)**

Dec. 07/ Jan. 08 (AU 53)

7. a. Derive an expression for the ratio of tension in V-belt drive. **(06 Marks)**
   b. Two shafts one meter apart are connected by a V-belt drive to transmit 90 kW at 1200 rpm of a driver pulley of 300 mm effective diameter. The driver pulley rotates at 400 rpm. The angle of the groove is 40° and coefficient of friction between the belt and the pulley rim is 0.25. Area of the belt section is 400 mm² and the permissible stress is 2.1 MPa. Density of the belt material = 1100 kg/m³. Calculate the number of belts required and length of the belt. **(14 Marks)**

June/ July 08 (AU 53)

8. A 25 mm diameter 6 × 37 steel rope is used in a mine of 80 meters deep. The velocity of the cage is 2 m/sec and the time required to accelerate the cage to the desired velocity is 10 seconds. The diameter of the drum is 1.25 m. Determine the safe load that the hoist can handle by assuming a factor of safety as 8. **(10 Marks)**

Dec. 08/ Jan. 09 (AU 53)

9. a. A flat belt drive is required to transmit 20 kW of power at 1440 rpm. The driver and the driven shafts are approximately 3 m apart. The dimensions of the pulley mounted on driver and driven shafts are 300 and 450 respectively. The weight density of selected belt material is 9.7×10^6 N/m³, allowable design stress 2 N/mm² and coefficient of friction = 0.3. Determine:
   i. Width of the belt if thickness = 6 mm, ii. Length of the belt
   iii. Initial tension in the belt iv. Centrifugal tension in the belt.
   (10 Marks)
   b. Select type of V-belt and number of belts required for 10 kW, 750 rpm induction motor to drive an exhaust fan in a steel plant at 250 rpm. The maximum center distance is 1.2 m. Pitch diameter of the motor pulley is 200 mm. **(10 Marks)**

June – July 2009 (AU 53)

10. a. Derive an expression for centrifugal tension in belt drive. **(08 Marks)**
    b. A belt drive consists of two V-belts in parallel, on ground pulleys of same size. The angle of groove is 30°. The cross-sectional area of each belt is 750 mm² and $\mu = 0.12$. The density of belt material is 1.2 gm/cc and the safe stress in the material is 7 MPa. Calculate the power that can be transmitted between the pulleys of 300mm diameter rotating at 1500 rpm. Find the shaft speed at which the power transmitted would be maximum? **(14 Marks)**

Dec. 09/ Jan. 10 (06ME61)

11. a. A compressor is driven by 900 rpm motor by means of 250 mm × 10 mm flat belt. The motor pulley is 0.3 m in diameter and the compressor pulley is 1.5 m diameter. The distance between the centers of the pulleys is 2 m. A jockey pulley is used to make the angle of wrap on the smaller pulley 220° and the larger pulley 270°. The coefficient of friction between the belt and the smaller pulley is 0.3 and between the belt and the larger pulley is 0.22. The maximum allowable belt stress is 2 MN/m² and the specific weight of the belt material is 9.515 KN/m³. Determine the power that can be transmitted by the belt drive. **(10 Marks)**
    b. A compressor requiring 90 kW is to run at 250 rpm. The drive is by V-belt from an electric motor running at 750 rpm. The diameter of the pulley on the compressor shaft is 1m, while the center distance between the pulleys is limited to 1.75 m. The belt speed should not exceed 1600 m/min. Determine the number of V-belts required to transmit the power if each belt has a cross-sectional area of 375 mm² and density of 1 mg/m³ and has an allowable stress of 2.5 N/mm². The groove angle of the pulley is 35° and the coefficient of friction between the belt and the pulley is 0.25. **(10 Marks)**

May/ June 2010 (AU 53)

12. A belt drive consists of two V-belts in parallel, on grooved pulleys of same size. The angle of the groove is 300. The cross-sectional area of each belt is 740 mm² and $\mu = 0.13$. The density of the belt material is 1200 kg/m³ and the maximum safe stress is 7000 kN/m². Calculate the power that can be transmitted between pulleys of 300 mm diameter rotating at 1200 rpm. Also, find the shaft speed in rpm at which the power transmitted would be maximum? **(12 Marks)**

May/ June 2010 (06ME61)

13. a. Derive an expression for power rating of a V-belt drive. **(08 Marks)**
    b. The following data is given for a V-belt connecting 20 kW motor pulley to a compressor;

	Motor pulley	Compressor pulley
Pitch dia (mm)	300	900
Speed (rpm)	1440	480
Coefficient of friction	0.2	0.2

    The center distance between the pulleys is 1m. CS of belt is trapezoidal with parallel sides being 12 mm and 22 mm respectively and the depth is 14 mm. The density of the composite belt is 0.97 gm/cc and the allowable tension per belt is 850 N. Determine the number of belts required for this application. **(12 Marks)**

December 2010 (AU 53)

14. a. Write the procedure to design a V-belt. **(06 Marks)**
    b. Design a V- belt for transmitting 74 kW with the following specifications:
    Speed of driver pulley = 1440 rpm   Speed of driven pulley = 400 rpm
    Diameter of the driver = 300 mm   Center distance = 2500 mm
    Service condition = 16 h/ day
    Drive is required for an AC motor driving unit for heavy duty services. Specify the number of belts and the type of the section. **(14 Marks)**

December 2010 (06ME61)

15. a. A 25 mm, 6 × 37 steel wire rope is used in a mine of 80 m deep. The velocity of the cage is 2 m/sec, and the time required to accelerate the cage to the desired velocity is 10 sec. The diameter of the drum is 1.25 m. Determine the safe load that the hoist can handle by assuming a factor of safety as 8. Neglect the impact load on the rope. **(12 Marks)**
    b. A leather belt 125 mm wide and 6 mm thick transmits power from a pulley 750 mm diameter which runs at 500 rpm. The angle of lap is 150° and the coefficient of fiction between the belt and the pulley is 0.3. If the belt density is 1000 kg/m³ and the stress in the belt is not to exceed 2.75 N/mm², find the power that can be transmitted by the belt. **(08 Marks)**

June/ July 2011 (06ME61)

16. a. Select a wire rope for a vertical mine hoist to lift a load of 55 kN from a depth of 300 meters. A rope speed of 500 m/min is to be attained in 10 sec. **(12 Marks)**
    b. Select a V-belt drive to connect a 15 kW, 2880 rpm motor to a centrifugal pump, running at approximately 2400 rpm, for a service of 18 h per day. The center distance should be approximately 400 mm. Assume the pitch diameter of driving pulley as 125 mm. **(08 Marks)**

December 2011 (06ME61)

17. a. Select a V-belt drive to transmit a power of 6 kW from a shaft rotating at 1500 rpm to a parallel shaft to be run at 375 rpm. The distance between the shaft centers is 500 mm. The pitch diameter of the smaller grooved pulley car may be taken as 150 mm and the factor of application is to be taken as 1.2. **(10 Marks)**
    b. Select a standard V belt to transmit 30 kW from an AC induction motor rotating at 1500 rpm to a centrifugal pump rotating at 750 rpm. The drive operates continuously for 8 h/day. Calculate the number of belts. **(12 Marks)**

June 2012 (06ME61)

18. a. Explain the advantages and applications of chain drive. **(05 Marks)**
    b. The layout of leather belt drive transmitting a power of 15 kW is as shown in **Fig. 2.18**. The center distance between the pulleys is twice the diameter of the big pulley. The belt should operate at a velocity of 20 m/s and the stress in the belt should not exceed 2.25 MPa. The density of the leather belt is 0.95 gm/cc and the coefficient of friction is 0.35. The thickness of the belt is 5 mm. Calculate:

i. Diameter of the pulleys ii. The length and width of the belt
iii. Belt tensions (15 Marks)

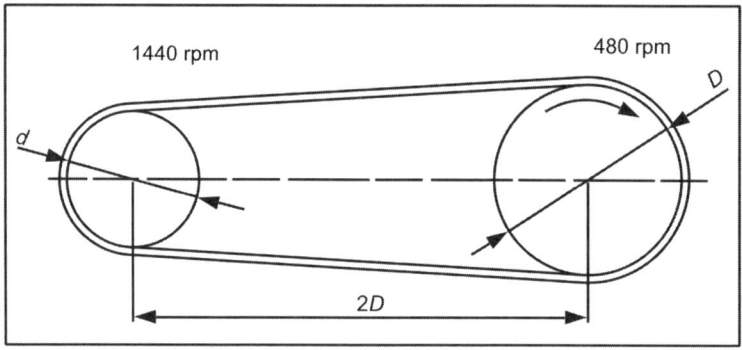

Fig. 2.18

December 2012 (06ME12)

19. a. A nylon core flat belt 200 mm wide weighing 20 N/m, connects a 300 diameter pulley to a 900 mm diameter driven pulley at a shaft spacing of 6 m, transmits 55.2 kW at a belt speed of 25 m/s.
    i. calculate the belt length and the angles of wrap
    ii. compute the belt tensions based on coefficient of friction 0.38. (10 Marks)
    b. A compressor is driven by a motor of 2.5 kW running at 1200 rpm to a 400 rpm compressor. Select a suitable V- belt. (10 Marks)

June/ July 2013 (AU53)

20. a. A flat belt is required to transmit 30 kW from a pulley of 1.5 m effective diameter running at 300 rpm. The angle of contact is spread over 11/24 of circumference. The coefficient of friction between the belt and the pulley surface is 0.3. Determine, taking centrifugal tension into account, width of the belt required. It is given that the belt thickness is 9.5 mm. Density of its material is 1100 kg/m^3 and the permissible working stress is 2.5 MPa.
    (10 Marks)
    b. A V-belt is required for 15 kW, 1440 rpm electric motor which drives a centrifugal pump running at 360 rpm for a service of 24 h per day. From space considerations, the center distance should be approximately 1 m. Determine:
    i. Belt specifications ii. Number of belts
    iii. correct center distance iv. Pulley diameters
    (10 Marks)

June/ July 2013 (06ME61)

21. a. State three advantages and two disadvantages of V-belt drive over flat belt drive. (05 Marks)
    b. A V-belt is used between two shafts 3 m apart. The driving pulley has 850 mm effective diameter and is supplied with 75 kW at 960 rpm. The driven pulley runs at 480 rpm. Given that the area of belt section = 400 mm^2, weight of the belt = 10×10^{-6} N/mm^3, safe working tensile stress = 2.1 N/mm^2, 0.27 and groove angle of pulley = 40°, determine the number of belts required. Also, calculate the initial tension in each belt. (15 Marks)

June/ July 2013 (10ME62)

22. a. Select a V-belt drive to transmit 40 kW power from a pulley of 200 mm diameter mounted on an electric motor running at 750 rpm to another pulley mounted on compressor running at 200 rpm. The service is heavy duty varying from 10 h to 14 h per day and distance between centers of pulley is 600 mm. **(10 Marks)**
    b. A roller chain is to transmit 66.24 kW from a 17 tooth sprocket to a 34 tooth sprocket at a pinion speed of 300 rpm. The loads are moderate shock. The equipment is to run 18 h/day. Specify the length and size of the chain required for a center distance of about 25 pitches. **(10 Marks)**

Dec. 2013/ Jan.2014 (10ME62)

23. a. Write a note on construction of flat and 'V' belt. **(05 Marks)**
    b. It is required to design a V-belt to connect a 7.5 kW, 1440 r/min induction motor to a fan, running at approximately 480 r/min for a service of 24 h/day. Space is available for a center distance of about 1 m. Determine the pitch length of the belt and the number of belts required. **(15 Marks)**

Dec. 2013/ Jan. 2014 (AU53)

24. a. Select a V belt and number of belts required for a belt drive to transmit 10 kW power from an induction motor through a pulley of 150 mm diameter rotating at 750 r/min to another pulley. The driven pulley is to run at 30 r/min. The center distance between the pulleys is approximately 300 mm. Service is heavy duty and the drive has to operate for 10 to 14 hours per day. **(12 Marks)**
    b. A hoist in a mine, lifts ore to a maximum height of 600 m. The weight of the carriage is 270 kN and 180 kN of ore is to be lifted per trip. The maximum rope speed is 600 m/min. The time taken for acceleration is 6 s. The diameter of the drum is 1800 mm. Determine the size of the 6 × 19 steel ropes. The equivalent modulus of elasticity of the rope may be taken as 82.8 GPa. Expected factor of safety is 5. **(08 Marks)**

3
Springs

3.1 INTRODUCTION
Spring is an elastic member designed and constructed to give a relatively large deformation under a given load. –or– Spring is defined as a resilient member whose primary function is to deflect/distort under the load. These are used to exert force –or– torque, as well as store energy. The force can be a linear push or pull, or it can be radial. The torque can be used to cause rotation. They operate with high values for working stresses and with loads that are continuously varying.

Functions/Applications:
- To absorb shocks and vibrations. Ex: Automobiles, railway buffer springs, etc.
- To store energy. Ex: Watches, toys, cameras, etc.
- To measure forces. Ex: Spring balances, engine indicators, etc.
- To apply forces and control the motion. Ex: Brakes, clutches, cams and followers, etc.

3.2 CLASSIFICATION
1. Helical springs
   a. Closed coil helical springs   b. Open coil helical springs
   c. Helical springs:
      i. Tension helical springs   ii. Compression helical springs
                                           (Helical: Round, Spiral, and Rectangle)
2. Laminated/ Leaf springs
   a. Full elliptic   b. Semi elliptic   c. Cantilever
3. Torsion springs
4. Circular springs
5. Disc –or– Belleville springs
6. Flat springs
7. Conical –or– Volute springs.
8. Special purpose springs: Rubber springs, air –or– liquid springs, ring springs, etc.
   - *Helical compression/extension springs:* These are made of wire coiled into a helical form, the load being applied along the axis of the helix. The major stress is torsional shear stress due to twisting and the deflection is linear.
   - *Helical torsion spring:* These are similar in from to helical compression springs, the torque being applied about the axis of the helix. The major stresses are tensile and compressive due to bending while the deflection is circular.

A helical spring is said to be of *closed type* if the spring wire is coiled such that the plane containing each coil is at right angles to the axis of helix. i.e. helix angle < 10°.

A helical spring is said to be of *open type* if the spring is coiled such that there is a large gap between the adjacent coils. i.e. helix angle > 10°.

- *Spiral springs:* It consists of a flat strip wound in the form of a spiral and loaded in torsion. The major stresses are tensile and compressive due to bending while the deflection is angular.
- *Leaf springs:* These are composed of flat bars of varying lengths clamped together so as to obtain greater resilience. These may be full elliptic, semi-elliptic –or– cantilever. The deflection is linear.
- *Belleville springs:* These are composed of coned discs which are stacked up to give a variety of spring load deflection characteristics. The major stresses are tensile and compressive, while the deflection is linear.

3.3 TERMS IN COMPRESSION SPRINGS

- *Solid length:* It refers to the length of the compression spring when all the coils are in contact with each other under the action of the load **(Fig. 3.1)**.

   Solid length = id i – no. of active coils d – diameter of wire
- *Compressed length:* It refers to the axial length of the spring which is subjected to maximum compressive force.
- *Active coil:* It refers to coils which are free to deflect under the load.
- *Inactive coil:* It refers to the springs in contact with the seat and does not contribute to spring action (deflection).

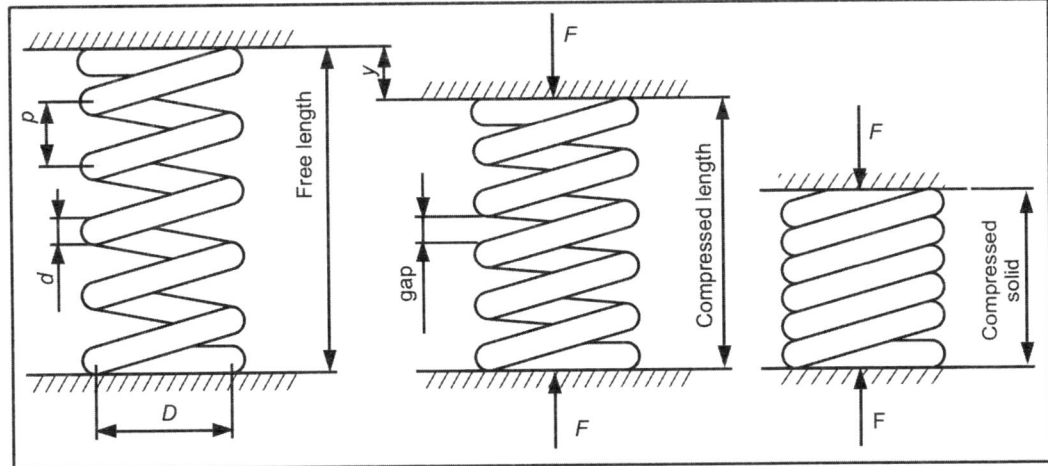

Fig. 3.1: Nomenclature of compression spring

- *Free length:* It refers to the overall length of spring when no load is acting on it.
  - If the ends are bent before grinding, $l_0 = (i+2)d + y + a$

    ...11.20a/ Pg 142, DHB
  - If the ends are either bent –or– ground $l_0 = (i+1)d + y + a$

    ...11.20b/ Pg 142, DHB
  - If the ends are neither ground nor bent, $l_0 = id + y + a$

    ...11.20c/ Pg 142, DHB

    a – clearance/ clash allowance (mm) y - deflection (mm)

Table 11.7/ Pg 152, DHB *gives different types of coil ends for a spring.*
- *Deflection (y):* It is the axial displacement of the spring under a given load.
- *Spring rate (F_0):* It is defined as the load required per unit deflection. It is also called rate of spring –or- stiffness –or- spring gradient –or- spring constant –or- spring scale

Spring rate, $\quad F_0 = \dfrac{F}{y} = \dfrac{Gd^4}{8iD^3} \quad$ ...**11.7a/ Pg 139, DHB**

G – Modulus of rigidity (MPa), D – Mean diameter of coil (mm)
- *Spring Index (C):* It is defined as the ratio of mean diameter of coil to the wire diameter

$$C = \dfrac{D}{d} \quad \text{(for circular wire)} \quad \text{...11.2c/ Pg 139, DHB}$$

d – Diameter of the wire, D – mean diameter of the coil

The value of C:
    For industrial purposes   : 4 to 12
    For valves   : 8 to 10
    For clutch springs   : 5

The minimum value of C is 3, which is used in extreme cases. As the value of 'C' reduces, the stresses increases rapidly.
- *Pitch:* It is defined as the axial distance between adjacent coils in uncompressed state. This is generally calculated using end conditions from **Tb 11.7/ Pg 152, DHB**
- *Total number of coils:* It refers to the sum of the number of active and inactive coils in a spring body.
- *Natural frequency:* It is defined as the lowest inherent rate of free vibration of a spring vibrating between its own ends.

- When one end of the spring is at rest, $\quad f = \dfrac{1}{2\pi}\sqrt{\dfrac{2gF_0}{W}}$

$$f = 22.3\sqrt{\dfrac{F_0}{W}} \quad \text{...}\textbf{11.24a/ Pg 143, DHB}$$

- When both ends of the spring are fixed, $\quad f = 44.6\sqrt{\dfrac{F_0}{W}} \quad$ ...**11.24b/ Pg 144, DHB**

Where, F_0 = Stiffness (N/ mm)

$$\text{Weight of spring } W = m/g = (Al)\rho/g = \dfrac{\pi^2 d^2 D i \gamma}{4g}$$

3.4 SPRING MATERIALS

The material of the spring should have high fatigue strength, high ductility, high resilience and creep resistant. It largely depends upon the service for which they are used, i.e. severe service, average service –or- light service.
- *Severe service:* refers to rapid continuous loading (above 1 million cycles).
  Ex: Engine valve springs.
- *Average service:* refers to moderate rate of loading (up to 1 million cycles) with intermittent operation.
  Ex: Automobile suspension springs, engine governor springs.

- *Light service:* It refers to static loads –or- up to 1 million cycles.
  Ex: Safety valve springs, spring couplings.

  - **Table 11.6/ Pg151, DHB** *gives design stresses for springs based on the type of service*

Springs are manufactured either by hot working –or- cold working processes depending upon the size of wire, spring index and desirable properties. Winding of the springs causes residual stresses owing to bending and hence the springs are heat treated to relieve the stresses. Non-ferrous materials like brass, phosphor bronze, beryllium copper, monel metal, brass, etc., are used in special cases to increase fatigue resistance and corrosion resistance.

BIS has recommended 4 basic varieties of steels for various applications:
1. Patented and cold drawn steel – unalloyed
2. Oil hardened and tempered spring steel and valve spring wires – unalloyed
3. Oil hardened and tempered steel wires – alloyed
4. Stainless spring steel wire for normal corrosion resistance

1. *Patented and cold drawn steel – unalloyed* ...**Tb 11.14/ Pg 155C, DHB**

   It is also known as high- carbon hard- drawn spring steel. Patenting refers to heating the steel above the critical temperature and cooling it rapidly thereby producing a structure which is uniform and tough.
   - Most widely used spring material, made of high carbon steel containing 0.85 – 0.95 % carbon.
   - Has high strength and can withstand high stresses under fatigue loading.
   - We have 4 grades of this material:

     Grade 1: used for springs subjected to static loads.

     Grade 2: used for springs subjected to moderate static load cycles.

     Grade 3: used for springs subjected to moderate dynamic load.

     Grade 4: used for springs subjected to severe operating conditions.
   - The modulus of rigidity of these springs is 81370 MPa.

2. *Oil hardened and tempered spring steel and valve spring wires – unalloyed*
   ...**Tb 11.12/ Pg 155B, DHB**
   - These are made of steel wires containing 0.55 – 0.75% carbon.
   - The wires are cold drawn followed by hardening and tempering.
   - Has excellent surface finish.
   - Used for springs subjected to static and fatigue loads.
   - We have 2 grades of this material:

     Grade SW: This is suitable for springs subjected to moderate fatigue loads.

     Grade VW: This refers to valve spring grade and is recommended for springs subjected to high magnitude of fluctuating stresses.
   - The modulus of rigidity of these springs is 81370 MPa.

3. *Oil hardened and tempered steel wires – alloyed*
   - Used for applications involving higher stresses and springs subjected to impact –or- shock loads.
   - We have two varieties of alloy steel wires: chromium – vanadium steel and chromium – steel.

4. *Stainless steel:* ...**Tb 11.13/ Pg 155B, DHB**

   This is Ni-Cr steel mainly used for resistance to corrosion and creep at high temperatures.

Note:
- **Table 11.2/ Pg 149, DHB** *gives applications of the above mentioned wires as per their grades and sizes.*
- **Table 11.3a/ Pg 150, DHB** *gives standard dimensions of the wire.*
- **Table 11.6/ Pg 151, DHB** *gives design stresses for springs based on the type of service.*
- **Table 11.8/ Pg 153, DHB** *gives physical properties of various spring materials.*
- **Table 11.12/ Pg 155B, DHB** *gives physical properties of oil hardened and tempered spring steel wire and valve spring wire – unalloyed.*
- **Table 11.13/ Pg 155B, DHB** *gives physical properties of stainless steel wire for normal corrosion resistance.*
- **Table 11.14/ Pg 155C, DHB** *gives physical properties of patented and cold drawn steel wire – unalloyed.*
- **Table 1.18/ Pg 428, DHB** *gives properties of typical carbon and alloy steels.*

3.5 END CONNECTIONS FOR HELICAL COMPRESSION SPRINGS

The spring ends may be plain, plain-ground, square , -or- square end as given in **Table 11.7/ Pg 152, DHB.**
- *Plain ends:* Here the end coils of a helical spring have a constant pitch and with their ends not squared.
- *Plain ends – ground:* It is similar as plain ends, except that wire ends are ground square with the axis.
- *Square –or- closed ends:* Here the spring ends are coiled with pitch angle reduced so that they are square with the spring axis and touch the adjacent coils.
- *Square and ground ends:* It is similar to closed ends, except that the first and last coils are ground to provide a flat bearing surface.

The end coils produce an eccentric application of the load, increasing the stress on one side of the spring. Under certain conditions, especially where the number of coils is small, this effect must be taken into account. The nearest approach to an axial load is secured by squared and ground ends, where the turns are squared and then ground perpendicular to the helix axis.

Note: In all springs there is eccentricity of loading introduced by the end connections. This eccentricity can be avoided in compression springs having squared and ground ends, with large spring indices and having 6 –or- more active coils.

3.6 SURGE IN SPRINGS

When a spring is compressed suddenly, a compression wave is formed which travels along the spring and is reproduced at the far end. This wave of vibration, when it approaches resonance is termed surging. This results in very large deflections of the coils and very high stresses, thereby leading to failure of the spring. To prevent this condition the spring should not be cycled at a frequency close to its natural frequency. Typically the natural frequency of the spring should be greater than 15 times that of any applied forcing frequency.

The natural frequency of a helical compression spring depends upon its end conditions. It is observed that in case of a spring guided at both ends and periodically compressed by the stroke h, the natural frequency is

$$f = \frac{d}{2\pi i D^2} \sqrt{\frac{Gg}{2\gamma}} \qquad \text{...11.24c/ Pg 144, DHB}$$

Where, d = diameter of the wire (mm),
D = mean diameter of the spring (mm),
i = number of active turns,
G = modulus of rigidity (N/mm²),
g = acceleration due to gravity (mm/s²), and
γ = density of the material of the spring (N/mm³)

For commercial springs made of steel wire having 81370 MPa, the natural frequency is

$$f = 3.59 \times 10^5 \left(\frac{d}{iD^2} \right)$$

$$= 13.56 \left(\frac{\tau_r}{hK} \right) \qquad \text{...11.24d/ Pg 144, DHB}$$

Where, $\tau_r = 2\tau_a$ – stress range corresponding to stroke (amplitude of stress)
...Fig. 11.3H and 11.3I/ Pg 157B, DHB
h – stroke (lift), i.e. difference between two deflections –or–
two load lengths
K – stress concentration factor

The surge of a spring decreases the ability of the spring to control the motion of the machine part involved. In addition, the spring material under compression wave is subjected to higher stresses thereby leading to early failure. Thus it is obvious that the springs used in high-speed machinery must have natural frequencies of vibration considerably excess than the natural frequency of the motion they control.

The surge in springs may be eliminated by using the following methods:
1. Designing the springs such that the natural frequency of the spring is 15 to 20 times that of any applied forcing frequency.
2. Using friction dampers on the central coils.

3.7 STRESSES IN HELICAL COIL SPRINGS—CIRCULAR WIRE

Figure 3.2(a) shows a helical compression spring subjected to axial load.

Let d = diameter of the wire
D = mean diameter of the coil
D_i = inside diameter of the coil
(= D – d)
D_0 = outside diameter of the coil
(= D + d)
i = number of active coils
p = pitch of the spring
G = modulus of rigidity
F = axial load acting on the spring
y = axial deflection
τ = shear stress induced in the wire.

Now consider a portion of the spring as shown in **Fig. 3.2(b)**, the effect of removed portion being replaced by net internal reactions. The load (F) tends to rotate the wire due to the twisting moment set up in the wire. Thus the spring will be in equilibrium under the action of two forces (F) and the twisting moment (T).

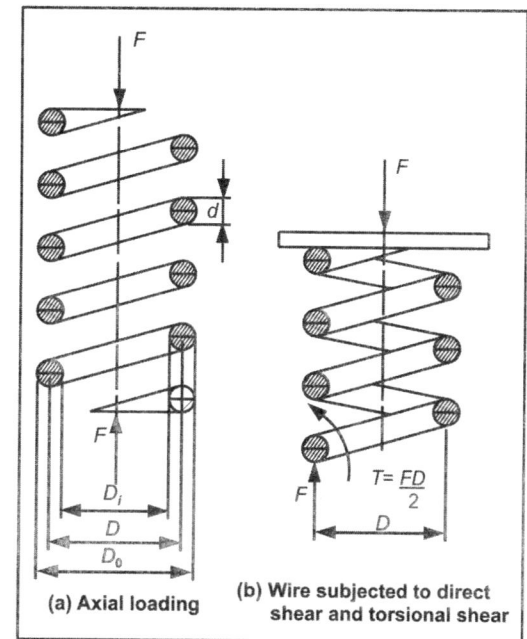

(a) Axial loading

(b) Wire subjected to direct shear and torsional shear

Fig. 3.2: Helical springs–circular wire

The torsional shear stress setup in the material of the wire and the maximum value of shear stress induced in the material may be obtained as

$$T = F\left(\frac{D}{2}\right) = \left(\frac{\pi}{16}\right)d^3\tau \qquad \text{...(Eq. 3.1)}$$

Therefore the torsional shear stress is, $\tau = \dfrac{8FD}{\pi d^3}$ ...(Eq. 3.2)

Fig 3.3(a) shows the torsional shear stress diagram.

In addition to this there is a direct shear stress acting on the wire, $\tau = \dfrac{4F}{\pi d^2}$ ...(Eq. 3.3)

Fig 3.3(b) shows the direct shear stress diagram.

Thus, the maximum shear stress = torsional shear stress + direct shear stress

$$\tau_{xy} = \frac{8FD}{\pi d^3} + \frac{4F}{\pi d^2}$$

$$= \frac{8FD}{\pi d^3}\left(1 + \frac{d}{2D}\right)$$

But $C = \dfrac{D}{d}$

Therefore, $\tau_{xy} = \dfrac{8FD}{\pi d^3}\left(1 + \dfrac{1}{2C}\right)$

$$\tau_{xy} = \frac{8FD}{\pi d^3}K_s \qquad \text{...(Eq. 3.4)}$$

Where, $K_s = 1 + \dfrac{1}{2C}$ known as shear stress factor.

Figure 3.3(c) shows the combined diagram of torsional shear stress and direct shear stress.

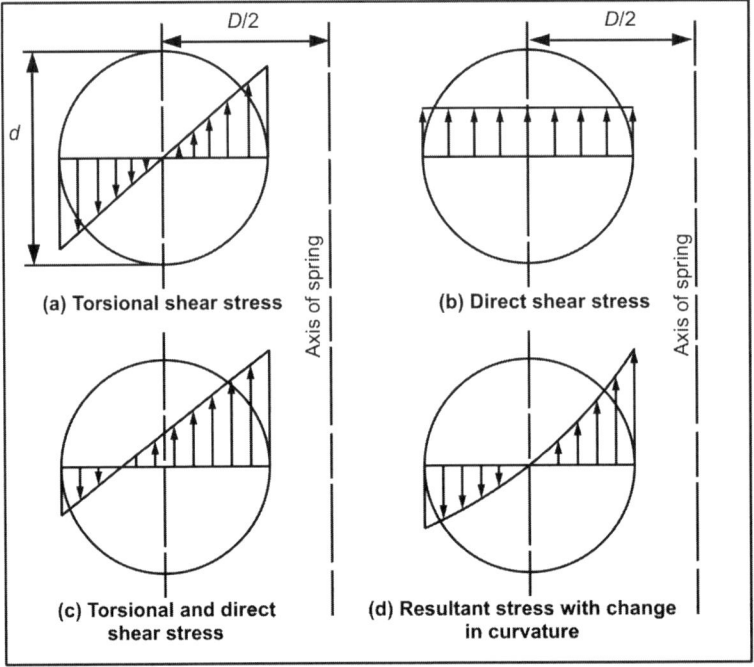

(a) Torsional shear stress
(b) Direct shear stress
(c) Torsional and direct shear stress
(d) Resultant stress with change in curvature

Fig. 3.3: Stress distribution across helical spring of circular wire

Equation (3.4) is applicable to both static and dynamic loads for springs of smaller spring index (C) and is based on the wire being straight. On the other hand, for a curved wire, the curvature of the wire increases the stresses on the inside and decreases slightly on the outer side. The curvature stress is very important in fatigue because the loads are lower and hence localized yielding does not occur. For static loads these stresses are generally neglected.

To account for the curvature effects of direct shear and change in coil curvature as shown in **Fig 3.3(d)**, a stress factor defined by A H Wahl is introduced, as

$$K = \frac{4C-1}{4C-4} + \frac{0.615}{C} \qquad \text{...(Eq. 3.5)} \quad \textbf{11.2b/ Pg 139, DHB}$$

The first term accounts for the effects of curvature and is basically a stress concentration factor. The second term gives a correction factor for direct shear only.

Another factor was introduced by Bergstroessar as

$$K = \frac{4C+2}{4C-3} \qquad \text{...(Eq. 3.6)} \quad \textbf{11.2a/ Pg 139, DHB}$$

Equations (3.5) and (3.6) differ by less than 1% and hence (3.5) is normally preferred. Therefore the maximum shear,

$$\tau_{xy} = \frac{8FD}{\pi d^3} K \qquad \text{...(Eq. 3.7)} \quad \textbf{11.1a/ Pg 139, DHB}$$

The values of K for a given spring index (C) may be obtained from the graph as shown in ...**Fig. 11.1/ Pg 156, DHB**

A very close approximation to K is

$$K = \frac{2}{C^{0.25}} = 2\left(\frac{d}{D}\right)^{0.25} \qquad \text{...(Eq. 3.8)} \quad \textbf{11.2d/ Pg 139, DHB}$$

3.8 DEFLECTION IN HELICAL COIL SPRINGS—CIRCULAR WIRE

As a compression spring is compressed under an axial load, the wire is twisted. Therefore the stress developed in the wire is torsional shear stress, and it can be derived from the torsional equation as follows.

We know that the torsional equation is, $\dfrac{T}{J} = \dfrac{G\theta}{L} = \dfrac{\tau}{R}$

Consider $\theta = \dfrac{TL}{GJ}$

$$= \frac{F \times (D/2) \times (\pi D i)}{G(\pi d^4/32)} \qquad (L = \pi D i)$$

$$\theta = \frac{16FD^2 i}{Gd^4} \qquad \text{...(Eq. 3.9)} \quad \textbf{11.4/ Pg 139, DHB}$$

If θ is the angular deflection of the wire, then axial deflection,

$$y = \theta (D/2)$$

$$= \frac{16FD^2 i}{Gd^4}\left(\frac{D}{2}\right)$$

$$y = \frac{8FD^3 i}{Gd^4} = \frac{8FC^3 i}{Gd} \qquad \text{...(Eq. 3.10) \textbf{11.5a/ Pg 139, DHB}}$$

We know that spring rate –or- stiffness $= \dfrac{\text{Force}}{\text{Unit deflection}}$

$$F_0 = \frac{F}{y} = \frac{Gd^4}{8iD^3} \qquad \text{...(Eq. 3.11) \textbf{11.7a/ Pg 139, DHB}}$$

3.9 ENERGY STORED IN HELICAL COIL SPRINGS—CIRCULAR WIRE

Springs are used to store energy which is equal to the work done on it by some external load.

Let, F = load applied on the spring
y = deflection of the spring due to load.

Assuming that the load is applied gradually the energy stored in the spring is

$$U = \frac{1}{2} Fy \qquad \text{...(Eq. 3.12) \textbf{11.8/ Pg 139, DHB}}$$

$$\text{But } \tau_{xy} = \frac{8FD}{\pi d^3} K \qquad \text{...using (3.7) \textbf{11.1a/ Pg 139, DHB}}$$

$$\text{Therefore, } F = \frac{\pi d^3 \tau}{8DK} \qquad \text{...(Eq. 3.13)}$$

Also deflection $\quad y = \dfrac{8FD^3 i}{Gd^4} \qquad \text{...using (3.10) \textbf{11.5a/ Pg 139, DHB}}$

Substituting Eq. (3.13) in Eq. (3.10), we have

$$y = \frac{8D^3 i}{Gd^4} \times \frac{\pi d^3 \tau}{8DK}$$

$$y = \frac{\pi \tau D^2 i}{GdK} \qquad \text{...(Eq. 3.14) \textbf{11.5b/ Pg 139, DHB}}$$

Substituting Eqs (3.13) and (3.14) in (3.12), we have

$$U = \frac{1}{2} \times \frac{\pi d^3 \tau}{8DK} \times \frac{\pi \tau D^2 i}{GdK}$$

$$= \frac{\pi^2 d^2 \tau^2 D i}{16 G K^2}$$

$$= \frac{\tau^2}{4GK^2} \times \left[\frac{\pi d^2}{4} \times (\pi D i) \right]$$

$$U = \frac{\tau^2 V}{4GK^2} \qquad \text{...(Eq. 3.15) ...\textbf{11.8/ Pg 139, DHB}}$$

Where, V – volume of the spring = area × length

$$= \left[\frac{\pi d^2}{4} \times (\pi D i) \right] \qquad \text{...(Eq. 3.16) \textbf{11.9/ Pg 140, DHB}}$$

In terms of deflection, $$U = \frac{y^2 d^4 G}{16 i D^3}$$ ...(Eq. 3.17) ...**11.8/ Pg 139, DHB**

Note:
1. When a load falls on the spring through a height 'h', then the energy absorbed by the spring is

$$U = F_1(h+y) = \frac{1}{2}F_e y$$

Where, F_e – equivalent static load, i.e. the gradually applied load which produces te same effect as that of falling load, F_1.

2. *For good design, value of C between 8 and 10 is preferred* ...**11.13b/ Pg 140, DHB**

3.10 DESIGN PROCEDURE FOR HELICAL SPRINGS

1. Find the diameter of the wire using $\tau = \dfrac{8FDK}{\pi d^3}$ ...**11.1a/ Pg 139, DHB**

   Where, $K = \dfrac{4C-1}{4C-4} + \dfrac{0.615}{C}$ ...**11.2b/ Pg 139, DHB**

2. Standardize the wire diameter using **Table 11.3a/ Pg 150, DHB.**
   Also calculate the mean diameter, inner diameter and outer diameter of the coil

3. Calculate the number of coils as: $i = \dfrac{yGd}{8FC^3}$ ...**11.6/ Pg 139, DHB**

   The actual number of coils is calculated by assuming square and ground ends, round-off 't' as $i_T = i + 2$ ...**Table 11.7/ Pg 152, DHB**

4. The free length of the spring is calculated as:
   $l_0 = (i+1)d + y + a$ ...or square and ground ends **11.20b/ Pg 142, DHB**
   Here a is the clearance between coils assumed as 1 mm per coil.
   $a = (i-1) \times 1$ mm per coil

5. The pitch of the spring is calculated as
   $l_0 = ip + 2d$ ...for square and ground ends **Table 11.7/ Pg 152, DHB**

6. Calculate the stiffness of the spring as
   $$F_0 = \frac{F}{y}$$ ...**11.7a/ Pg 139, DHB**

Note:
- In general the ends of the spring are assumed to be squared and ground as indicated in steps 3 to 5. If the end condition is different, then the corresponding relations should be used as given in ...**Table 11.7/ Pg 152, DHB**
- If C is assumed, check for shear stress. If the design fails, adopt higher value of d.
- While designing the problems, curvature effect (Wahl's factor) has to be considered.

1. **A helical spring is made from a 8 mm diameter wire and has a outer diameter of 100 mm. if the permissible shear stress is 420 MPa and modulus of rigidity is 84 GPa. Find the axial load the spring can carry and the deflection per active turn: (a) neglecting curvature effect (b) considering curvature effect.**

Solution: $d = 8$ mm, $D_0 = 100$ mm, $\tau = 420$ MPa $= 420$ N/mm², $G = 84$ GPa $= 84 \times 10^3$ N/mm².

Therefore, mean diameter, $D = D_0 - d = 100 - 8 = 92$ mm, and $C = D/d = 92/8 = 11.5$ mm.

Case 1: Neglecting curvature effect:
a. To find F:

We know that, $\tau = \dfrac{8FDK}{\pi d^3}$ ...11.1a/ Pg 139, DHB

When the curvature effect is neglected $K = K_s = 1 + \dfrac{1}{2C}$

$$K_s = 1 + \dfrac{1}{2 \times 11.5} = 1.0435$$

Therefore, $420 = \dfrac{8F \times 92 \times 1.0435}{\pi \times 8^3}$

$$F = 879.6 \text{ N}$$

b. Deflection per coil:

We know that deflection, $y = \dfrac{8FC^3 i}{Gd}$ ...11.5a/ Pg 139, DHB

$$\dfrac{y}{i} = \dfrac{8 \times 879.6 \times 11.5^3}{84 \times 10^3 \times 8} = 15.93 \text{ mm}$$

Case 2: Considering curvature effect:
a. To find F:

We know that, $\tau = \dfrac{8FDK}{\pi d^3}$ ...11.1a/ Pg 139, DHB

Here, $K = \dfrac{4C-1}{4C-4} + \dfrac{0.615}{C} = \dfrac{4 \times 11.5 - 1}{4 \times 11.5 - 4} + \dfrac{0.615}{11.5}$ ...11.2b/ Pg 139, DHB

$$K = 1.125$$

Therefore, $420 = \dfrac{8F \times 92 \times 1.125}{\pi \times 8^3}$

$$F = 816 \text{ N}$$

b. Deflection per coil:

We know that deflection, $y = \dfrac{8FC^3 i}{Gd}$ ...11.5a/ Pg 139, DHB

$$\dfrac{y}{i} = \dfrac{8 \times 816 \times 11.5^3}{84 \times 10^3 \times 8} = 14.77 \text{ mm.}$$

2. **Design a closed coil helical spring subjected to a load of 800 N deflects by 40 mm. The diameter of each coil is 10 times that of wire and the maximum shear stress is not to exceed 350 MPa. Take 84 GPa.**

Solution: $F = 800$ N, $y = 40$ mm, $D = 10d$, i.e. $C = 10$, $\tau = 350$ MPa, $G = 84$ GPa $= 84 \times 10^3$ N/mm². *Design:* (d, D, i, l_0, p, F_0)

1. To find diameter of wire:

We know that, $\tau = \dfrac{8FDK}{\pi d^3}$ ...11.1a/ Pg 139, DHB

Here,
$$K = \frac{4C-1}{4C-4} + \frac{0.615}{C} \qquad \text{...11.2b/ Pg 139, DHB}$$

$$= \frac{4 \times 10 - 1}{4 \times 10 - 4} + \frac{0.615}{10}$$

$$K = 1.145.$$

Therefore,
$$350 = \frac{8 \times 800 \times 10d \times 1.145}{\pi \times d^3}$$

$$d = 8.16 \text{ mm.}$$

2. Diameters:
Standard wire diameter is $d = 8.5$ mm ...Tb 11.3a/ Pg 150, DHB
Mean diameter of coil, $D = 10d = 10 \times 8.5 = 85$ mm
Inner diameter of coil, $D_i = D - d = 85 - 8.5 = 76.5$ mm
Outer diameter of coil, $D_0 = D + d = 85 + 8.5 = 93.5$ mm

3. Number of coils:

We know that,
$$i = \frac{yGd}{8FC^3} \qquad \text{...11.6/ Pg 139, DHB}$$

$$= \frac{40 \times 84 \times 10^3 \times 8.5}{8 \times 800 \times 10^3}$$

$$i = 4.463 \approx 5 \text{ turns}$$

Assuming square and ground ends, the actual number of coils,
$$i_T = i + 2 \qquad \text{...Tb 11.7/ Pg 152, DHB}$$
$$= 5 + 2$$
$$i_T = 7$$

4. Free length:
For square and ground ends, $l_0 = (i+1)d + y + a$ ...11.20b/ Pg 142, DHB
Here, $a = (i-1) \times 1$ mm per coil
$a = (5-1) \times 1$
$= 4$ mm
Therefore, $l_0 = (5+1) \times 8.5 + 40 + 4$
$l_0 = 95$ mm

5. Pitch of the spring:
For square and ground ends, $l_0 = ip + 2d$ ...Tb 11.7/ Pg 152, DHB
$95 = 5p + 2 \times 8.5$
$p = 15.6$ mm ≈ 16 mm.

6. Spring stiffness:

We know that,
$$F_0 = \frac{F}{y} = \frac{800}{40} = 20 \text{ N/mm.} \qquad \text{...11.7a/ Pg 139, DHB}$$

3. **Design a helical compression spring for a maximum load of 1000 N and for a deflection of 25 mm. the maximum permissible shear stress for the spring wire is 420 N/mm², modulus of rigidity is 0.84 × 10⁵ N/mm² and value of spring index is 6.** *[VTU – Dec. 07/ Jan. 08–10 Marks; May/ June 2010 – 15 Marks]*

Solution: $F = 1000$ N, $y = 25$ mm, $C = 6 = \frac{D}{d}$, $\tau = 420$ N/mm², $G = 0.84 \times 10^5$ N/mm².

1. To find diameter of wire:

We know that, $\tau = \dfrac{8FDK}{\pi d^3}$ ...11.1a/ Pg 139, DHB

Therefore, $\tau = \dfrac{8FCK}{\pi d^2}$ ($C = D/d$)

Here, $K = \dfrac{4C-1}{4C-4} + \dfrac{0.615}{C}$ ...11.2b/ Pg 139, DHB

$ = \dfrac{4 \times 6 - 1}{4 \times 6 - 4} + \dfrac{0.615}{6}$

$K = 1.253$

Therefore, $420 = \dfrac{8 \times 1000 \times 6 \times 1.253}{\pi \times d^2}$

$d = 6.75$ mm.

2. Diameters:

Standard wire diameter is $d = 7$ mm ...Tb 11.3a/ Pg 150, DHB
Mean diameter of coil, $D = 10d = 6 \times 7 = 42$ mm
Inner diameter of coil, $D_i = D - d = 42 - 7 = 35$ mm
Outer diameter of coil, $D_0 = D + d = 42 + 7 = 49$ mm

3. Number of coils:

We know that, $i = \dfrac{yGd}{8FC^3}$ ...11.6/ Pg 139, DHB

$ = \dfrac{25 \times 0.84 \times 10^5 \times 7}{8 \times 1000 \times 6^3}$

$i = 8.51 \approx 9$ turns

Assuming square and ground ends, the actual number of coils,

$i_T = i + 2$ ...Tb 11.7/ Pg 152, DHB
$ = 9 + 2$
$i_T = 11$

4. Free length:

For square and ground ends, $l_0 = (i+1)d + y + a$ ...11.20b/ Pg 142, DHB
Here, $a = (i-1) \times 1$ mm per coil
$a = (9-1) \times 1$
$a = 8$ mm

Therefore, $l_0 = (9+1) \times 7 + 25 + 8$
$l_0 = 103$ mm.

5. Pitch of the spring:

For square and ground ends, $l_0 = ip + 2d$ ...Tb 11.7/ Pg 152, DHB

$103 = 9p + 2 \times 7$

$p = 9.88$ mm ≈ 10 mm.

6. Spring stiffness:

We know that, $F_0 = \dfrac{F}{y} = \dfrac{1000}{25} = 40$ N/mm ...11.7a/ Pg 139, DHB

4. A helical coil spring made from 6.3 mm diameter steel wire has an outside diameter of 57.3 mm with squared and ground ends and has 12 coils. The length of the spring is such that when it is compressed solid the torsional stress is 827 MPa. Determine the:

i. spring rate   ii. free length   iii. critical frequency.

The density of the material is 7800 kg/m³ and modulus of rigidity 0.8×10^5 MPa.

[VTU – July / Aug 2002–15 Marks]

Solution: $d = 6.3$ mm, $D_0 = 57.3$ mm, $i = 12$-square and ground ends, $\tau = 827$ MPa, $\gamma = 7800$ kg/m³, $G = 0.8 \times 10^5$ MPa,

a. Spring rate, $F_0 = ?$ b. Free length, $l_0 = ?$ c. Frequency, $f = ?$

a. To find F_0:

We know that, $\quad F_0 = \dfrac{F}{y} \quad$ ...Eq. (i) **11.7a/ Pg 139, DHB**

Given,   Outer diameter of coil, $D_0 = D + d = 57.3$ mm
            Mean diameter of coil, $D = D_0 - d = 57.3 - 6.3 = 51$ mm
            Inner diameter of coil, $D_i = D - d = 51 - 6.73 = 44.7$ mm

Therefore spring index, $C = \dfrac{D}{d} = \dfrac{51}{6.3} = 8.1$

- But $\tau = \dfrac{8FDK}{\pi d^3} = \dfrac{8FCK}{\pi d^2} \quad$ ...**11.1a/ Pg 139, DHB**

here, $K = \dfrac{4C-1}{4C-4} + \dfrac{0.615}{C} \quad$ ...**11.2b/ Pg 139, DHB**

$= \dfrac{4 \times 8.1 - 1}{4 \times 8.1 - 4} + \dfrac{0.615}{8.1}$

$K = 1.182$

Therefore, $\quad 827 = \dfrac{8F \times 8.1 \times 1.182}{\pi \times 6.3^2}$

$F = 1346.31$ N

Also deflection, $\quad y = \dfrac{8FC^3 i}{Gd} \quad$ ...**11.5a/ Pg 139, DHB**

$= \dfrac{8 \times 1346.31 \times 8.1^3 \times 12}{0.8 \times 10^5 \times 6.3}$

$y = 136.28$ mm

Eq. (i) yields ... $F_0 = \dfrac{1346.31}{136.28}$

$F_0 = 9.88$ N/mm.

b. To find l_0:

For square and ground ends, $\quad l_0 = (i+1)d + y + a \quad$ ...**11.20b/ Pg 142, DHB**

Here, $a = (i-1) \times 1$ mm per coil

$$a = (12 - 1) \times 1$$
$$a = 11 \text{ mm.}$$
Therefore, $l_0 = (12 + 1) \times 6.3 + 136.28 + 1.1$
$$l_0 = 229.18 \text{ mm.}$$

c. To find f:

We know that,
$$f = \frac{d}{2\pi i D^2} \sqrt{\frac{Gg}{2\gamma}} \quad \text{...11.24c/ Pg 144, DHB}$$

$$= \frac{6.3}{2\pi \times 12 \times 51^2} \sqrt{\frac{0.8 \times 10^5 \times 9810}{2 \times 7800 \times 10^{-9}}}$$

$$f = 227.85 \text{ cps.}$$

5. **Design a closed coil helical spring to have a mean diameter of 125 mm and a spring rate of 75 N/mm. The total axial force is 9 kN and the allowable shear stress is 400 MPa. Take G = 84 GPa.**

Solution: $D = 125$ mm, $F_0 = 75$ N/mm, $F = 9000$ N, $\tau = 400$ MPa, $G = 84$ GPa = 84×10^3 MPa. Design: (d, D, i, l_0, p, F_0).

1. To find diameter of wire:

We know that,
$$\tau = \frac{8FDK}{\pi d^3} \quad \text{...11.1a/ Pg 139, DHB}$$

Therefore,
$$400 = \frac{8 \times 9000 \times 125 \times K}{\pi \times d^3}$$

$$K = (1.39 \times 10^{-4}) \, d^3 \quad \text{...Eq. (}i\text{)}$$

Also
$$K = 2\left(\frac{d}{D}\right)^{0.25} \quad \text{...11.2d/ Pg 139, DHB}$$

$$= 2\left(\frac{d}{125}\right)^{0.25}$$

$$K = (0.5981) \, d^{0.25} \quad \text{...Eq. (}ii\text{)}$$

From Eqs (i) and (ii), we have
$$(1.39 \times 10^{-4}) \, d^3 = (0.5981) \, d^{0.25}$$
$$d = 21 \text{ mm.}$$

2. Diameters:

Wire diameter is $= 21$ mm.
Mean diameter of coil, $D = 125$ mm (data)
Inner diameter of coil, $D_i = D - d = 125 - 21 = 104$ mm
Outer diameter of coil, $D_0 = D + d = 125 + 21 = 146$ mm

3. Number of coils:

We know that,
$$F_0 = \frac{F}{y} = \frac{Gd^4}{8iD^3} \quad \text{...11.7a/ Pg 139, DHB}$$

$$75 = \frac{84 \times 10^3 \times 21^4}{8 \times i \times 125^3}$$

$$i = 13.94 \approx 14 \text{ turns}$$

Assuming square and ground ends, the actual number of coils,
$$i_T = i + 2 \quad \text{...Tb 11.7/ Pg 152, DHB}$$
$$= 14 + 2$$
$$i_T = 16$$

4. Free length:

For square and ground ends, $l_0 = (i + 1)d + y + a$ ...11.20b/ Pg 142, DHB

Here, $a = (i - 1) \times 1 \, mm \, per \, coil$
$$a = (14 - 1) \times 1$$
$$a = 13 \, mm$$

But $F_0 = \dfrac{F}{y}$

$$75 = \dfrac{9000}{y}$$
$$y = 120 \, mm$$

Therefore, $l_0 = (14 + 1) \times 21 + 120 + 13$
$$l_0 = 448 \, mm.$$

5. Pitch of the spring:

For square and ground ends, $l_0 = ip + 2d$ ...Tb 11.7/ Pg 152, DHB
$$448 = 14p + 2 \times 12$$
$$p = 29 \, mm$$

6. Spring stiffness: $F_0 = 75 \, N/mm$ (data)

6. An automobile helical coil spring is to have a mean diameter of 80 mm and stiffness of 200 N/mm. The total axial force is 8000 N and allowable shear stress of spring material is 320 N/mm^2 and 8×10^4 N/mm^2. Calculate:

i. Diameter of the wire
ii. Number of effective coils
iii. Free length of spring and
iv. Maximum energy which can be stored in the spring

[VTU – Dec 08/ Jan 09 – 8 Marks]

Solution: $D = 80 \, mm$, $F_0 = 200 \, N/mm$, $F = 8000 \, N$, $\tau = 320 \, N/mm^2$, $G = 8 \times 10^4 \, N/mm^2$.
Find: D, i, l_0, U.

1. To find diameter of wire:

We know that, $\tau = \dfrac{8FDK}{\pi d^3}$ ...11.1a/ Pg 139, DHB

Therefore, $320 = \dfrac{8 \times 8000 \times 80 \times K}{\pi \times d^3}$

$K = (1.96 \times 10^{-4}) d^3$ ...Eq. (i)

Also $K = 2\left(\dfrac{d}{D}\right)^{0.25}$ ...11.2d/ Pg 139, DHB

$= 2\left(\dfrac{d}{80}\right)^{0.25}$

$K = (0.6687) d^{0.25}$ ...Eq. (ii)

Equating Eqs (i) and (ii), we have
$$(1.96 \times 10^{-4}) d^3 = (0.6687) d^{0.25}$$
$$d = 19.26 \, mm \approx 20 \, mm$$

Hence the diameters are:
Wire diameter is $d = 20$ mm.
The mean diameter of coil, $D = 80$ mm (data)
Inner diameter of coil, $D_i = D - d = 80 - 20 = 60$ mm
Outer diameter of coil, $D_0 = D + d = 80 + 20 = 100$ mm

2. Number of effective coils:

We know that,
$$F_0 = \frac{F}{y} = \frac{Gd^4}{8iD^3} \qquad \text{...11.7a/ Pg 139, DHB}$$

$$200 = \frac{8 \times 10^4 \times 20^4}{8 \times i \times 80^3}$$

$$i = 15.63 \approx 16 \text{ turns}$$

Assuming square and ground ends, the actual number of coils,
$$i_T = i + 2 \qquad \text{...Tb 11.7/ Pg 152, DHB}$$
$$= 16 + 2$$
$$i_T = 18$$

3. Free length:

For square and ground ends, $l_0 = (i + 1)d + y + a$ ...11.20b/ Pg 142, DHB

Here, $a = (i - 1) \times$ mm per coil
$$a = (16 - 1) \times 1$$
$$a = 15 \text{ mm}$$

But $F_0 = \dfrac{F}{y}$

$$200 = \frac{8000}{y}$$

$$y = 40 \text{ mm}$$

Therefore, $l_0 = (16 + 1) \times 20 + 40 + 15$
$$l_0 = 395 \text{ mm.}$$

4. Energy stored:

We know that,
$$U = \frac{1}{2}Fy \qquad \text{...11.8/ Pg 139, DHB}$$
$$= \frac{1}{2} \times 8000 \times 40$$
$$U = 160 \times 10^3 \text{ N-mm.}$$

7. A railway wagon weighing 3 tons is moving with a velocity of 3 m/s. It is brought to rest by two buffer springs of 200 diameter. The maximum deflection allowed is 160 mm. The allowable shear stress in spring material is 600 MPa. Take 84 GPa. Design the spring.

Solution: $m = 3$ tons $= 3000$ kg, $v = 3$ m/s, $n = 2$, $D = 200$ mm, $y = 160$ mm, $\tau = 600$ N/mm², $G = 84 \times 10^3$ N/mm². Design: $(d, D, i, l_0, p\, F_0)$

1. To find diameter of wire:

Kinetic energy of the wagon, $\text{K.E} = \dfrac{mv^2}{2} = \dfrac{3000 \times 3^2}{2} = 13500$ N-m

$$\text{K.E} = 13.5 \times 10^6 \text{ N-mm} \qquad \text{...Eq. (i)}$$

Also energy absorbed by the spring $= U \times n$

$$= \left(\frac{Fy}{2}\right)n$$

$$= \left(\frac{F \times 160}{2}\right) \times 2$$

$$= 160\, F \qquad \text{...Eq. }(ii)$$

Since the energy lost by the wagon = energy absorbed by the springs, equating Eqs (i) and (ii), we have

$$13.5 \times 10^6 = 160\, F$$

$$F = 84375\text{ N}$$

Method -1(Neglecting K)

We know that, $\qquad T = F\left(\dfrac{D}{2}\right) = \left(\dfrac{\pi}{16}\right)d^3 \tau$

Therefore, $\qquad \tau = \dfrac{8FD}{\pi d^3}$

$$600 = \dfrac{8 \times 84375 \times 200}{\pi d^3}$$

$$d = 41.53 \text{ mm} \approx 42 \text{ mm}.$$

Method -2 (Considering K) ...(Preferred)

We know that, $\qquad \tau = \dfrac{8FDK}{\pi d^3} \qquad$ ...11.1a/ Pg 139, DHB

Therefore, $\qquad 600 = \dfrac{8 \times 84375 \times 200 \times K}{\pi \times d^3}$

$$K = (1.39 \times 10^{-5})\, d^3 \qquad \text{...Eq. }(iii)$$

Also $\qquad K = 2\left(\dfrac{d}{D}\right)^{0.25} \qquad$ ...11.2d/ Pg 139, DHB

$$= 2\left(\dfrac{d}{200}\right)^{0.25}$$

$$K = (0.5318)\, d^{0.25} \qquad \text{...Eq. }(iv)$$

Equating Eq. (iii) and Eq. (iv), we have

$$(1.39 \times 10^{-5})\, d^3 = (0.5318)\, d^{0.25}$$

$$d = 46.4 \text{ mm} \approx 48 \text{ mm}.$$

2. Diameters:

Wire diameter is $\qquad d = 48$ mm.
The mean diameter of coil, $D = 200$ mm (data)
Inner diameter of coil, $\quad D_i = D - d = 200 - 48 = 152$ mm
Outer diameter of coil, $\quad D_0 = D + d = 200 + 48 = 248$ mm
$$C = D/d = 200/48 = 4.17$$

3. Number of coils:

We know that, $\qquad i = \dfrac{yGd}{8FC^3} \qquad$ ...11.6/ Pg 139, DHB

$$= \frac{160 \times 84 \times 10^3 \times 48}{8 \times 84375 \times 4.17^3}$$

$$i = 13.18 \approx 14 \text{ turns}$$

Assuming square and ground ends, the actual number of coils,

$$i_T = i + 2 \qquad \text{...Tb 11.7/ Pg 152, DHB}$$
$$= 14 + 2$$
$$i_T = 16$$

4. Free length:

For square and ground ends, $l_0 = (i + 1)d + y + a$ ...11.20b/ Pg 142, DHB

Here, $a = (i - 1) \times 1$ mm per coil
$$a = (14 - 1) \times 1$$
$$a = 13 \text{ mm}$$

Therefore, $l_0 = (14 + 1) \times 48 + 160 + 13$

$$l_0 = 893 \text{ mm}$$

5. Pitch of the spring:

For square and ground ends, $l_0 = ip + 2d$ ...Tb 11.7/ Pg 152, DHB

$$893 = 14p + 2 \times 48$$
$$p = 57 \text{ mm}.$$

6. Spring stiffness:

We know that, $F_0 = \dfrac{F}{y} = \dfrac{84375}{160} = 527.34 \text{ N/mm}$ ...11.7a/ Pg 139, DHB

Note: Method -1 is preferred if the curvature effects are neglected.

8. **A railway wagon weighing 40 kN and moving with a speed of 10 km/hr has to be stopped by four buffer springs in which the maximum compression allowed is 200 mm. Find the number of active turns in each spring of mean diameter 150 mm. The diameter of spring wire is 25 mm. Take 82.7×10^3 MPa.**

[VTU – June/ July 08 – 08 Marks; Dec. 09 / Jan. 10 – 10 Marks; (similar) VTU – Dec. 06 / Jan. 07 – 08 Marks]

Solution: $W = 40$ kN, $v = 10$ kms/ hr $= 2.78$ m/s, $n = 4$, $y = 200$ mm, $D = 150$ mm, $d = 25$ mm, $G = 82.7 \times 10^3$ N/mm², $i = ?$

1. To find number of active turns:

We know that, $i = \dfrac{yGd}{8FC^3}$ ...Eq. (i) ...11.6/ Pg 139, DHB

$$C = \frac{D}{d} = \frac{150}{25} = 6$$

Also, Kinetic energy of the wagon, K.E $= \dfrac{mv^2}{2} = \dfrac{\left(W/g\right)v^2}{2} = \dfrac{40000 \times 2.78^2}{2 \times 9.81}$

$$= 15756.16 \text{ N-m}$$

$$\text{K.E} = 15.76 \times 10^6 \text{ N-mm} \qquad \text{...Eq. (ii)}$$

and energy absorbed by the spring = $U \times n$

$$= \left(\frac{Fy}{2}\right)n$$

$$= \left(\frac{F \times 200}{2}\right) \times 4$$

i.e. energy absorbed by the spring = $400 F$ ...Eq. (iii)

Since the energy lost by the wagon = energy absorbed by the springs, equating Eqs (ii) and (iii), we have

$$15.76 \times 10^6 = 400 F$$
$$F = 39400 \text{ N}$$

Eq. (i) yields ... $i = \dfrac{200 \times 82.7 \times 10^3 \times 25}{8 \times 39400 \times 6^3} = 6.08$

$i = 6.08 \approx 7$

Assuming square and ground ends, the actual number of coils,

$i_T = i + 2$ ...Tb 11.7/ Pg 152, DHB
$= 7 + 2$
$i_T = 9$.

9. **A carriage weighing 25000 N is moving on a track with a linear velocity of 3.6 km/hour. It is brought to rest by two helical compression springs in the form of a bumper by undergoing a compression of 180 mm. The springs may be assumed to have a spring index of 6 and permissible shear strength of 450 MPa. Design the spring and determine the diameter of the wire, mean coil diameter and the length of the spring. Assume modulus of rigidity of the spring material as 81.4 GPa.** *[VTU – June 12 – 14 Marks]*

Solution: $W = 25000$ N, $v = 3.6$ km/h $= 1$ m/s, $n = 2$, $y = 180$ mm, $C = 6$, $\tau = 450$ N/mm², $G = 81.4 \times 10^3$ N/mm², Design: (d, D, i, l_0, p, F_0).

1. To find diameter of wire:

We know that, $\tau = \dfrac{8FDK}{\pi d^3} = \dfrac{8FCK}{\pi d^2}$ ...Eq. (i) 11.1a/ Pg 139, DHB

Here, $K = \dfrac{4C - 1}{4C - 4} + \dfrac{0.615}{C}$ ...11.2b/ Pg 139, DHB

$= \dfrac{4 \times 6 - 1}{4 \times 6 - 4} + \dfrac{0.615}{6}$

$K = 1.2525$

Also, kinetic energy of the wagon, K.E $= \dfrac{mv^2}{2} = \dfrac{(W/g)v^2}{2} = \dfrac{25000 \times 1^2}{2 \times 9.81}$

$= 1274.21$ N-m

K.E $= 1.27 \times 10^6$ N-mm ...Eq. (ii)

and energy absorbed by the spring = $U \times n$

$$= \left(\frac{Fy}{2}\right)n$$

$$= \left(\frac{F \times 180}{2}\right) \times 2$$

i.e.   energy absorbed by the spring = 180 F ...Eq. (iii)

Since the energy lost by the wagon = energy absorbed by the springs, equating Eq. (ii) and Eq. (iii), we have

$$1.27 \times 10^6 = 180 F \qquad \text{...Eq. (iv)}$$
$$F = 7079 \text{ N}$$

Eq. (i) yields... $450 = \dfrac{8 \times 7079 \times 6 \times 1.2525}{\pi d^2}$

$$\therefore d = 17.35 \text{ mm} \approx 18 \text{ mm}$$

2. Diameters:

Wire diameter is $\quad d \approx 18$ mm.
The mean diameter of coil, $D = Cd = 6 \times 18 = 108$ mm
Inner diameter of coil, $\quad D_i = D - d = 108 - 18 = 90$ mm
Outer diameter of coil, $\quad D_0 = D + d = 108 + 18 = 126$ mm

3. Number of coils:

We know that, $\quad i = \dfrac{yGd}{8FC^3}$ ...11.6/ Pg 139, DHB

$$= \frac{180 \times 81.4 \times 10^3 \times 18}{8 \times 7079 \times 6^3}$$

$$i = 21.56 \approx 22 \text{ turns}$$

Assuming square and ground ends, the actual number of coils,

$$i_T = i + 2 \qquad \text{...Tb 11.7/ Pg 152, DHB}$$
$$= 22 + 2$$
$$i_T = 24$$

4. Free length:

For square and ground ends, $l_0 = (i + 1)d + y + a$ ...11.20b/ Pg 142, DHB
Here, $a = (i - 1) \times 1$ mm per coil
$a = (22 - 1) \times 1$
$a = 21$ mm
Therefore, $l_0 = (22 + 1) \times 18 + 180 + 21$
$l_0 = 615$ mm

5. Pitch of the spring:

For square and ground ends, $l_0 = ip + 2d$ ...Tb 11.7/ Pg 152, DHB
$615 = 22p + 2 \times 18$
$p = 26.32$ mm

6. Spring stiffness:

We know that, $\quad F_0 = \dfrac{F}{y} = \dfrac{7079}{180} = 39.33$ N/mm ...11.7a/ Pg 139, DHB

10. A load of 2 kN is dropped axially on a closed soil helical spring from a height of 250 mm. The spring has 20 effective turns and it is made of 25 mm diameter wire. The spring index is 8. Find the maximum shear stress induced in the spring and the amount of compression produced. Take $G = 82.7$ GPa.

[VTU – Dec. 2010–10 Marks]

Solution: $W = 2000$ N, $h = 250$ mm, $i = 20$, $d = 25$ mm, $C = 8$, $\tau = ?$, $y = ?$, $G = 82.7 \times 10^3$ MPa

1. To find shear stress:

We know that, $\tau = \dfrac{8FDK}{\pi d^3} = \dfrac{8FCK}{\pi d^2}$ ...Eq. (i) **11.1a/ Pg 139, DHB**

Here, $K = \dfrac{4C-1}{4C-4} + \dfrac{0.615}{C}$ ...**11.2b/ Pg 139, DHB**

$= \dfrac{4 \times 8 - 1}{4 \times 8 - 4} + \dfrac{0.615}{8}$

$K = 1.184$

Also Energy lost by falling weight $= W(h+y)$

$= 2000(250+y)$

$= 500000 + 2000y$ ...Eq. (ii)

and energy absorbed/ gained by the spring $= U \times n$

$= \left(\dfrac{Fy}{2}\right)n$ ...Eq. (iii)

Since the energy lost by the falling weight = energy absorbed by the springs, equating Eqs (ii) and (iii), we have

$500000 + 2000 y = \left(\dfrac{Fy}{2}\right)n$ $(n = 1)$

$1000000 + 4000 y = F.y$ ...Eq. (iv)

Also deflection, $y = \dfrac{8FC^3 i}{Gd}$ ...**11.5a/ Pg 139, DHB**

$= \dfrac{8F \times 8^3 \times 20}{82.7 \times 10^3 \times 25}$

$y = 0.03962 F$ ...Eq. (v)

Substituting Eq. (v) in Eq. (iv), we have

$1000000 + 4000 (0.03962 F) = F(0.03962 F)$

$1000000 + 158.5 F = 0.03962 F^2$

$\therefore$ $0.03962 F^2 - 158.5 F - 1000000 = 0$

Solving the above quadratic equation, we have $F = 7407.72$ N, -3407.22 N

Thus $F = 7407.72$ N

Eq. (i) yields... $\tau = \dfrac{8 \times 7407.72 \times 8 \times 1.184}{\pi \times 25^2} = 285.86$ MPa

2. To find deflection:

Eq. (v) yields... $y = 0.03962 \times 7407.22$

$y = 293.5$ mm.

11. A weight of 1200 N located at a position of 900 mm above the center of the spring is dropped on it. Calculate the deflection of the spring if spring scale is 80 N. Also calculate the maximum shear stress if spring has 18 coils. Take as 84 GPa, wire diameter = 25 mm and Mean diameter = 300 mm.

Solution: $W = 1200$ N, $h = 900$ mm, $F_0 = 80$ N, $i = 18$, wire diameter, $d = 25$ mm, mean diameter, $D = 300$ mm, $C = D/d = 12$, $y = ?$, $\tau = ?$, $G = 84 \times 10^3$ MPa

1. To find deflection:

We know that,

Energy lost by falling weight $= W(h + y)$
$$= 1200(900 + y)$$
$$= 1.08 \times 10^6 + 1200y \quad \text{...Eq. (i)}$$

and energy absorbed/gained by the spring $= U \times n$
$$= \left(\frac{Fy}{2}\right)n \quad \text{...Eq. (ii)}$$

Since the energy lost by the falling weight = energy absorbed by the springs, equating Eqs (i) and (ii), we have

$$1.08 \times 10^6 + 1200y = \left(\frac{Fy}{2}\right)n \quad (n = 1)$$

$$2.16 \times 10^6 + 2400y = F.y \quad \text{...Eq. (iii)}$$

Also spring scale, $\quad F_0 = \dfrac{F}{y}$

$$F = 80y \quad \text{...Eq. (iv)}$$

Substituting (iv) in (iii), we have
$$2.16 \times 10^6 + 2400y = 80y^2$$
$$80y^2 - 2400y - 2.16 \times 10^6 = 0$$

Solving the above quadratic equation we have $y = 180$ mm, -150 mm

Thus $\quad y = 180$ mm

2. To find shear stress:

We know that, $\quad \tau = \dfrac{8FDK}{\pi d^3} = \dfrac{8FCK}{\pi d^2}$

[*This formula can't be used since it does not involve number of active turns (i)*]

Now, deflection in term of shear stress is $y = \dfrac{\pi i \tau D^2}{KGd}$ ...**11.5b/ Pg 139, DHB**

Here, $K = \dfrac{4C - 1}{4C - 4} + \dfrac{0.615}{C}$ ...**11.2b/ Pg 139, DHB**

$$= \dfrac{4 \times 12 - 1}{4 \times 12 - 4} + \dfrac{0.615}{12}$$

$K = 1.119$

Therefore, $\quad 180 = \dfrac{\pi \times 18 \times \tau \times 300^2}{1.119 \times 84000 \times 25}$

$\tau = 84.13$ MPa.

12. A weight of 800 N in to be dropped on the center of a platen from a height of 300 mm. The platen is supported on four identically placed helical springs. Assuming that the deflection allowed for each spring is 60 mm, spring rate of 5 and maximum allowable shear stress equal to 400 MPa, determine the diameter of the wire and design the springs completely and also tabulate the specifications for manufacturing. Take $G = 80$ GPa for the spring material.

[VTU – Dec.08 / Jan. 09 – 15 Marks]

Solution: $W = 800$ N, $h = 300$ mm, $n = 4$, $y = 60$ mm, $F_0 = 5$, $\tau = 400$ MPa, $G = 80 \times 10^3$ MPa. Design (d, D, i, l_0, p, F_0).

1. To find diameter of wire:

We know that, $\quad \tau = \dfrac{8FDK}{\pi d^3} = \dfrac{8FCK}{\pi d^2} \quad$ ...Eq. (i) **11.1a/ Pg 139, DHB**

Energy lost by falling weight $= W(h + y)$
$$= 800(300 + 60)$$
$$= 288 \times 10^3 \text{ N-mm} \quad\quad \text{...Eq. (ii)}$$

and energy absorbed/ gained by the spring $\cup . n$

$$= \left(\dfrac{Fy}{2}\right) n \quad\quad \text{...Eq. (iii)}$$

Since the energy lost by the falling weight = energy absorbed by the springs, equating Eqs (ii) and (iii), we have

$$288 \times 10^3 = \left(\dfrac{Fy}{2}\right) n$$

$$288 \times 10^3 = \left(\dfrac{F \times 60}{2}\right) 4$$

$$F = 2400 \text{ N}$$

Also, $\quad K = \dfrac{4C-1}{4C-4} + \dfrac{0.615}{C} \quad$ ...**11.2b/ Pg 139, DHB**

$$= \dfrac{4 \times 6 - 1}{4 \times 6 - 4} + \dfrac{0.615}{6} \quad (\text{Assume } C = 6)$$

$$K = 1.2525$$

Eq. (i) yields... $400 = \dfrac{8 \times 2400 \times 6 \times 1.2525}{\pi \times d^2}$

$$d = 10.72 \text{ mm}$$

2. Diameters:

Standard wire diameter is $d = 11$ mm. $\quad$ ...**Tb 11.3a/ Pg 150, DHB**
Mean diameter of coil, $D = 10d = 6 \times 11 = 66$ mm
Inner diameter of coil, $D_i = D - d = 66 - 11 = 55$ mm
Outer diameter of coil, $D_0 = D + d = 66 + 11 = 77$ mm

- Since C was assumed, **Check for :**

Now, $\quad\quad C = D/d = 66/11 = 6$

And $\quad\quad K = \dfrac{4C-1}{4C-4} + \dfrac{0.615}{C}$

$$= \dfrac{4 \times 6 - 1}{4 \times 6 - 4} + \dfrac{0.615}{6}$$

$$K = 1.2525$$

Eq. (i) yields, ... $\tau = \dfrac{8 \times 2400 \times 6 \times 1.2525}{\pi \times 11^2}$

[Values of C & K from step 2(diameters)]

$$\tau = 379.57 \text{ MPa} < 400 \text{ MPa}.$$

Hence safe.

3. Number of coils:

We know that, $\quad i = \dfrac{yGd^4}{8FD^3} \quad$ ...11.6/ Pg 139, DHB

$$= \dfrac{60 \times 80 \times 10^3 \times 11^4}{8 \times 2400 \times 66^3}$$

(*Since C was assumed, don't use C in the formula*)
$i = 12.73 \approx 13$ turns

Assuming square and ground ends, the actual number of coils,
$$i_T = i + 2 \quad \text{...Tb 11.7/ Pg 152, DHB}$$
$$= 13 + 2$$
$$i_T = 15$$

4. Free length:

For square and ground ends, $\quad l_0 = (i + 1)d + y + a \quad$ ...11.20b/ Pg 142, DHB

Here, $a = (i - 1) \times 1$ *mm per coil*

$a = 12$ mm

Therefore, $l_0 = (13 + 1) \times 11 + 60 + 12$

$l_0 = 226$ mm.

5. Pitch of the spring:

For square and ground ends, $l_0 = ip + 2d \quad$ ...Tb 11.7/ Pg 152, DHB

$226 = 13p + 2 \times 11$

$p = 15.7$ mm ≈ 16 mm.

6. Specifications for manufacturing:

Material	:	Cold drawn steel wire - unalloyed
Wire diameter, d	:	11 mm
Mean coil diameter, D	:	66 mm
Free length l_0	:	226 mm
Total number of active turns, i	:	13
Type of ends	:	square and ground
Pitch, p	:	16 mm
Spring rate, F_0	:	5 N/mm

13. At the bottom of an elevator shaft, a group of 12 identical springs are set in parallel to absorb the shock in case of failure. The elevator weighs 40 kN. Assuming the elevator has a free fall of 1200 mm from rest and that the springs are compressed by 400 mm, determine:
   a. Load on each spring
   b. Wire diameter, mean diameter and
   c. Number of active turns. Assume $C = 6$, $G = 80$ GPa, $\tau = 450$ MPa.

Solution: $n = 12$, $W = 40000$ N, $h = 1200$ mm, $y = 400$ mm, $C = 6$, $G = 80 \times 10^3$ MPa, $\tau = 450$ MPa. a) $F = ?$ b) $d, D = ?$ c) $i = ?$

a. To find F:

We know that, Energy lost by falling weight $= W(h + y)$

$\qquad = 40000 (1200 + 400)$

$\qquad = 64 \times 10^6$ N-mm $\qquad$ ...Eq. (*i*)

and energy absorbed/gained by the spring = $U \times n$

$$= \left(\frac{Fy}{2}\right) n \qquad \text{...Eq. (ii)}$$

Since the energy lost by the falling weight = energy absorbed by the springs, equating Eqs (i) and (ii), we have

$$64 \times 10^6 = \left(\frac{Fy}{2}\right) n$$

$$64 \times 10^6 = \left(\frac{F \times 400}{2}\right) 12$$

$$F = 26.67 \text{ kN}$$

b. To find diameters:

We know that, $\tau = \dfrac{8FDK}{\pi d^3} = \dfrac{8FCK}{\pi d^2}$ ...Eq. (iii) **11.1a/ Pg 139, DHB**

Also, $K = \dfrac{4C-1}{4C-4} + \dfrac{0.615}{C}$ ...**11.2b/ Pg 139, DHB**

$$= \dfrac{4 \times 6 - 1}{4 \times 6 - 4} + \dfrac{0.615}{6}$$

$$K = 1.2525$$

Eq. (iii) yields... $450 = \dfrac{8 \times 26.67 \times 10^3 \times 6 \times 1.2525}{\pi \times d^2}$

$$d = 33.67 \text{ mm}$$
$$d \approx 34 \text{ mm}$$

Mean diameter of coil, $D = C.d = 6 \times 34$
$$= 204 \text{ mm}$$

c. Number of coils:

We know that, $i = \dfrac{yGd}{8FC^3}$ ...**11.6/ Pg 139, DHB**

$$= \dfrac{400 \times 80 \times 10^3 \times 34}{8 \times 26.67 \times 10^3 \times 6^3}$$

$$i = 23.61 \approx 24 \text{ turns.}$$

14. At the bottom of an elevator shaft, a group of 16 identical springs are set in parallel to absorb the shock in case of failure. Assuming a free fall of 1 meter, springs of wire diameter 10 mm, mean coil diameter 100 mm, number of active coils 20, determine the load on each spring and maximum shear stress induced in the spring. The weight of the elevator with the passengers may be taken as 10,000 N. *[VTU – Dec. 2010–14 Marks]*

Solution: $W = 10000$ N, $n = 16$, $h = 1000$ mm, $d = 10$ mm, $D = 100$ mm, therefore $C = D/d = 10$, $i = 20$, $F = ?$, $\tau = ?$

1. To find F:

We know that, Energy lost by falling weight = $W(h+y)$
$$= 10000(1000 + y)$$
$$= 10 \times 10^6 + 10000\, y \qquad \text{...Eq. (i)}$$

and energy absorbed/gained by the spring = $U \times n$
$$= \left(\frac{Fy}{2}\right)n = \left(\frac{Fy}{2}\right)16$$
$$= 8\,Fy \qquad \text{...Eq. (ii)}$$

Since the energy lost by the falling weight = energy absorbed by the springs, equating Eqs (i) and (ii), we have
$$10 \times 10^6 + 10000\,y = 8\,Fy \qquad (n = 1)$$
$$1.25 \times 10^6 + 1250\,y = Fy \qquad \text{...Eq. (iii)}$$

Also deflection, $\quad y = \dfrac{8FC^3 i}{Gd} \qquad$ ...11.5a/ Pg 139, DHB

$$= \frac{8F \times 10^3 \times 20}{80 \times 10^3 \times 10} \qquad \text{(Assume } G = 80\text{ GPa)}$$
$$y = 0.2\,F \qquad \text{...Eq. (iv)}$$

Substituting (iv) in (iii), we have
$$1.25 \times 10^6 + 1250\,(0.2\,F) = F\,(0.2\,F)$$
$$1.25 \times 10^6 + 250\,F = 0.2\,F^2$$
$$0.2\,F^2 - 250\,F - 1.25 \times 10^6 = 0$$

Solving the above quadratic equation we have $F = 3202$ N, -1952 N

Thus $\qquad F = 3202$ N

Eq. (iv) yields... $y = 0.2 \times 3202 = 640.4$ mm

2. To find shear stress:

We know that, $\quad \tau = \dfrac{8FDK}{\pi d^3} = \dfrac{8FCK}{\pi d^2} \qquad$ ...Eq. (v) **11.1a/ Pg 139, DHB**

Also, $\quad K = \dfrac{4C-1}{4C-4} + \dfrac{0.615}{C} \qquad$ ...**11.2b/ Pg 139, DHB**

$$= \frac{4 \times 10 - 1}{4 \times 10 - 4} + \frac{0.615}{10}$$
$$K = 1.145$$

Eq. (v) yields... $\tau = \dfrac{8 \times 3202 \times 10 \times 1.145}{\pi \times 10^2}$

$$\tau = 933.48 \text{ MPa.}$$

15. At the bottom of a mine shaft a group of 20 identical springs are set in parallel to absorb shock by failing of cage in case of failure. The load cage weighs 15 kN while the counter weigh weighs 6 kN. If the load cage falls through a height of 10 m from rest, find the maximum shear stress induced in each spring. Take wire diameter = 25 mm, $C = 8$, $i = 12$, $G = 84$ GPa.

Solution: $n = 20$, weight of cage, $W_1 = 15$ kN, counter weight, $W_2 = 6$ kN, $h = 10$ m, $d = 25$ mm, $C = 8$, $i = 12$, $G = 84 \times 10^3$ MPa, $\tau = ?$

1. To find diameter of wire:

We know that, $\tau = \dfrac{8FDK}{\pi d^3} = \dfrac{8FCK}{\pi d^2}$ ...Eq. (i) **11.1a/ Pg 139, DHB**

Here, $K = \dfrac{4C-1}{4C-4} + \dfrac{0.615}{C}$ ...**11.2b/ Pg 139, DHB**

$= \dfrac{4 \times 8 - 1}{4 \times 8 - 4} + \dfrac{0.615}{8}$

$K = 1.184$

Also Energy lost by falling weight $= W(h + y)$

$= 9000(10000 + y)$

$[W = W_1 - W_2 = 15 - 6 = 9 \text{ kN}]$

$= 9 \times 10^6 + 9000\, y$ ...Eq. (ii)

And energy absorbed/ gained by the spring $= U \times n$

$= \left(\dfrac{Fy}{2}\right) n = \left(\dfrac{Fy}{2}\right) 20$

$= 10\, Fy$ ...Eq. (iii)

Since the energy lost by the falling weight = energy absorbed by the springs, equating Eqs (ii) and (iii), we have

$9 \times 10^6 + 9000\, y = 10\, Fy$ $(n = 1)$

$9 \times 10^6 + 900\, y = Fy$ ...Eq. (iv)

Also deflection, $y = \dfrac{8FC^3 i}{Gd}$ ...**11.5a/ Pg 139, DHB**

$= \dfrac{8F \times 8^3 \times 12}{84 \times 10^3 \times 25}$

$y = 0.0234\, F$ ...Eq. (v)

Substituting (v) in (iv), we have

$9 \times 10^6 + 900\,(0.0234\, F) = F(0.0234\, F)$

$9 \times 10^6 + 21.07\, F = 0.0234\, F^2$

$0.0234\, F^2 - 21.07\, F - 9 \times 10^6 = 0$

Solving the above quadratic equation, we have $F = 20.06$ kN, -19.17 kN

Thus $F = 20.06$ kN

Eq. (v) yields... $y = 0.0234 \times 20.06 \times 10^3$

$y = 469.40$ mm

and Eq. (i) yields... $\tau = \dfrac{8 \times 20.06 \times 10^3 \times 8 \times 1.184}{\pi \times 25^2}$

$\tau = 774.16$ MPa.

3.11 SPRING SCALE

It is defined as the load required per unit deflection. It is also called as *'rate of spring'* – or- *'stiffness'* –or- *'spring gradient'* –or- *'spring constant'* –or-*' spring scale'*.

Spring rate, $$F_0 = \frac{F}{y} = \frac{Gd^4}{8iD^3}$$ ...11.7a/ Pg 139, DHB

From **Fig. 3.4 (Fig. 11.2a/ Pg 156, DHB)**, we have

$$F_0 = \frac{F}{y} = \frac{F_b - F_a}{y'}$$ ...11.7b/ Pg 139, DHB

Combining the above equations we have,

$$F_0 = \frac{F}{y} = \frac{F_2 - F_1}{y_2 - y_1} = \frac{Gd^4}{8iD^3}$$

$F_2 = F_b$ – Maximum load
$F_1 = F_a$ – Minimum load
y_2 – Maximum deflection
y_1 – Minimum –or- initial deflection
y' – Deflection for the load range = $(y_2 - y_1)$

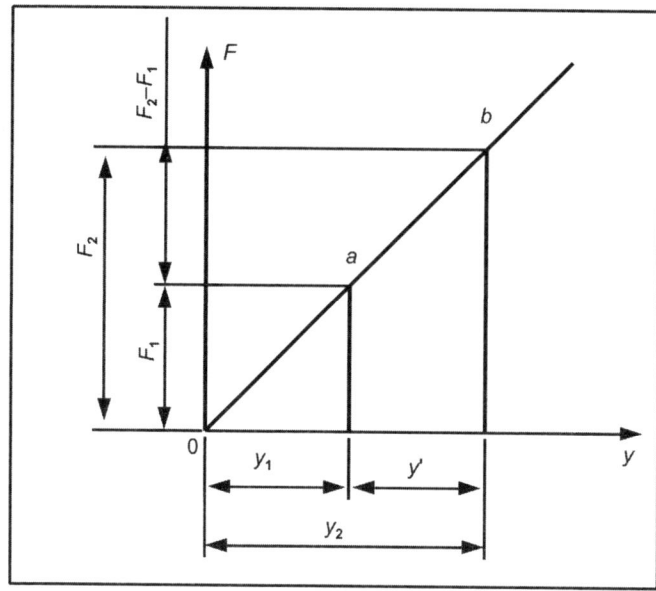

Fig. 3.4: Spring scale (Relation between loads and deflection in a helical spring, (Fig. 11.2a/Pg 156, DHB)

16. A helical spring whose mean diameter is 8 times the wire diameter is to absorb 600 N-m of energy. The initial compression of the spring is 70 mm and compresses additional of 90 mm while absorbing the shock. The maximum allowable stress is 420 MPa and 84 GPa. Design the spring.

Solution: $D = 8d$, $U = 600$ N-m $= 6 \times 10^5$ N-mm, $y_1 = 70$ mm, $y' = 90$ mm, $\tau = 420$ MPa, $G = 84 \times 10^3$ MPa. *Design:* (d, D, i, l_0, p, F_0).

Design is Based on Maximum Load

1. **To find diameter of wire:**

We know that, $$\tau = \frac{8FDK}{\pi d^3} = \frac{8F_{max}CK}{\pi d^2}$$ ...Eq. (*i*) 11.1a/ Pg 139, DHB

But $$K = \frac{4C-1}{4C-4} + \frac{0.615}{C} \quad \text{...11.2b/ Pg 139, DHB}$$
$$= \frac{4\times 8-1}{4\times 8-4} + \frac{0.615}{8}$$
$$= 1.184$$

Also $$F_0 = \frac{F_1}{y_1} = \frac{F_2}{y_1}$$
Therefore, $F_1 = F_0 y_1 = 70 F_0$ ...Eq. (ii)
$F_2 = F_0 y_2 = 160 F_0$ ...Eq. (iii)
Where, $y_2 = y_1 + y' = 70 + 90 = 160$ mm $= y_{max}$

$$F_{mean} = \frac{F_1 + F_2}{2}$$
$$= \frac{70 F_0 + 160 F_0}{2}$$
$$F_{mean} = 115 \times F_0 \quad \text{...Eq. (iv)}$$

Strain energy, $U = Fy = F_{mean} \cdot y'$
$6 \times 10^5 = F_{mean} \times 90$
$F_{mean} = 6666.67$ N ...Eq. (v)

Equating Eqs (iv) and (v), we have
$6666.67 = (115 \times F_0)$
$F_0 = 57.97 \approx 58$ N/mm
Eq. (iii) yields... $F_2 = 160 \times 58 = 9280$ N
Eq. (ii) yields... $F_1 = 70 \times 58 = 4060$ N
Eq. (i) yields... $420 = \dfrac{8 \times 9280 \times 8 \times 1.184}{\pi \times d^2}$ ($F_{max} = 9280$ N)
$d = 23.08$ mm.

2. Diameters:

Wire diameter is $d \approx 23$ mm.
Mean diameter of coil, $D = Cd = 8 \times 23 = 184$ mm
Inner diameter of coil, $D_i = D - d = 184 - 23 = 161$ mm
Outer diameter of coil, $D_0 = D + d = 184 + 23 = 207$ mm

3. Number of coils:

We know that, spring rate, $F_0 = \dfrac{Gd^4}{8iD^3}$ ...11.7a/ Pg 139, DHB

$$58 = \frac{84 \times 10^3 \times 23^4}{8 \times i \times 184^3}$$

$i = 8.13 \approx 9$ turns

Assuming square and ground ends, the actual number of coils,
$i_T = i + 2$ ...Tb 11.7/ Pg 152, DHB
$= 9 + 2$
$i_T = 11$

4. Free length:

For square and ground ends, $l_0 = (i + 1)d + y_{max} + a$ ...11.20b/ Pg 142, DHB

Here, $a = (i-1) \times 1$ mm per coil
$a = (9-1) \times 1$
$a = 8$ mm
Therefore, $l_0 = (9+1) \times 23 + 160 + 8$ $(y_2 = 160$ mm $= y_{max})$
$l_0 = 398$ mm.

5. Pitch of the spring:
For square and ground ends, $l_0 = ip + 2d$ ...Tb 11.7/ Pg 152, DHB
$398 = 9p + 2 \times 23$
$p = 39.11$ mm ≈ 39 mm

6. Spring stiffness:
$F_0 = 57.97 \simeq 58$ N/ mm.

17. A helical compression spring of circular cross-section is initially compressed by 25 mm. On further compression by 40 mm, the spring stores energy of 72 N-m. The spring stiffness is to be 40 N/mm. Design the spring completely.

[VTU – Dec.07 / Jan. 08 – 10 Marks]

Solution: $U = 72$ N-m $= 72 \times 10^3$ N-mm, $y_1 = 25$ mm, $y' = 40$ mm, $F_0 = 40$ N/mm.
Design: (d, D, i, l_0, p, F_0).
Material properties: Assume 420 MPa, 84×10^3 MPa

1. To find diameter of wire:

We know that, $\tau = \dfrac{8FDK}{\pi d^3} = \dfrac{8F_{max}CK}{\pi d^2}$ ...Eq. (i) 11.1a/ Pg 139, DHB

But $K = \dfrac{4C-1}{4C-4} + \dfrac{0.615}{C}$ ...11.2b/ Pg 139, DHB

$= \dfrac{4 \times 6 - 1}{4 \times 6 - 4} + \dfrac{0.615}{6}$ (Assume $C = 6$)

$K = 1.2525$

Also $F_0 = \dfrac{F_1}{y_1} = \dfrac{F_2}{y_2}$

Therefore, $F_1 = F_0 y_1 = 40 \times 25 = 1000$ N
$F_2 = F_0 y_2 = 40 \times 65 = 2600$ N
Where, $y_2 = y_1 + y' = 25 + 40 = 65$ mm $= y_{max}$

Eq. (i) yields... $420 = \dfrac{8 \times 2600 \times 6 \times 1.2525}{\pi \times d^2}$ $(F_{max} = 2600$ N$)$

$d = 10.88$ mm.

2. Diameters:
Standard wire diameter is $d = 11$ mm   ...Tb 11.3a/ Pg 150, DHB
Mean diameter of coil, $D = 6 \times 11 = 66$ mm
Inner diameter of coil, $D_i = D - d = 66 - 11 = 55$ mm
Outer diameter of coil, $D_0 = D + d = 66 + 11 = 77$ mm

- Since C was assumed, **Check for :**
Now, $C = D/d = 66/11 = 6$

And $\quad K = \dfrac{4C-1}{4C-4} + \dfrac{0.615}{C}$

$\quad\quad\quad\quad = \dfrac{4\times 6 - 1}{4\times 6 - 4} + \dfrac{0.615}{6}$

$\quad K = 1.2525$

Eq. (i) yields... $\tau = \dfrac{8\times 2600\times 6\times 1.2525}{\pi \times 11^2}$ *[Values of C & K from step 2(diameters)]*

$\quad\quad \tau = 411.20$ MPa < 420 MPa

Hence safe.

3. Number of coils:

We know that, spring rate, $F_0 = \dfrac{Gd^4}{8iD^3}$ ...**11.7a/ Pg 139, DHB**

$\quad\quad\quad 40 = \dfrac{84\times 10^3 \times 11^4}{8\times i \times 66^3}$

(Since C was assumed, don't use C in the formula)

$\quad\quad i = 13.36 \approx 14$ turns

Assuming square and ground ends, the actual number of coils,

$\quad\quad i_T = i + 2$ ...**Tb 11.7/ Pg 152, DHB**

$\quad\quad\quad = 14 + 2$

$\quad\quad i_T = 16$

4. Free length:

For square and ground ends, $l_0 = (i + 1)d + y_{max} + a$ ...**11.20b/ Pg 142, DHB**

Here, $a = (i - 1) \times 1$ mm per coil

$\quad\quad a = (14 - 1) \times 1$

$\quad\quad a = 13$ mm

Therefore, $l_0 = (14 + 1) \times 11 + 65 + 13$

$\quad\quad l_0 = 243$ mm

5. Pitch of the spring:

For square and ground ends, $l_0 = ip + 2d$ ...**Tb 11.7/ Pg 152, DHB**

$\quad\quad 243 = 14p + 2 \times 11$

$\quad\quad p = 15.78 \approx 16$ mm

6. Spring stiffness:

$\quad\quad F_0 = 40$ N/mm (data)

18. Design a valve spring for a petrol engine under the following conditions:
Spring load (valve is open) = 40 N, spring load (valve is closed) = 25 N
Spring length (valve is open) = 40 mm, spring length (valve is closed) = 50 mm
Maximum inside diameter of spring = 25 mm, shear stress = 40 MPa, modulus of rigidity = 84 GPa.

[(Similar) VTU – July/ Aug. 2005 – 16 Marks]

Solution: Maximum load, $F_{max} = F_2 = 40$ N, minimum load, $F_{min} = F_1 = 25$ N, minimum length, $l_1 = 40$ mm, maximum length, $l_2 = 50$ mm, $D_i = 25$ mm, $\tau = 40$ MPa, $G = 84$ GPa = 80×10^3 MPa.

1. To find diameter of wire:

We know that, $\quad \tau = \dfrac{8FDK}{\pi d^3} = \dfrac{8F_{max}CK}{\pi d^2}$ ...Eq. (*i*) **11.1a/ Pg 139, DHB**

But $\quad K = \dfrac{4C-1}{4C-4} + \dfrac{0.615}{C}$ ...**11.2b/ Pg 139, DHB**

$\qquad = \dfrac{4 \times 6 - 1}{4 \times 6 - 4} + \dfrac{0.615}{6} \qquad$ (Assume $C = 6$)

$K = 1.2525$

Eq. (*i*) yields... $40 = \dfrac{8 \times 40 \times 6 \times 1.2525}{\pi \times d^2} \qquad (F_{max} = 40$ N$)$

$d = 4.37$ mm

2. Diameters:

Standard wire diameter is $d = 4.5$ mm   ...**Tb 11.3a/ Pg 150, DHB**
Mean diameter of coil, $D = D_i + d = 25 + 4.5 = 29.5$ mm
Inner diameter of coil, $D_i = 25$ mm (data)
Outer diameter of coil, $D_0 = D + d = 29.5 + 4.5 = 34$ mm

- Since C was assumed, check for τ:

Now, $\qquad\qquad C = D/d = 29.5/4.5 = 6.56$

And $\qquad\qquad K = \dfrac{4C-1}{4C-4} + \dfrac{0.615}{C}$

$\qquad\qquad\quad = \dfrac{4 \times 6.56 - 1}{4 \times 6.56 - 4} + \dfrac{0.615}{6.56}$

$\qquad\qquad\quad = 1.228$

Eq. (*i*) yields... $\tau = \dfrac{8 \times 40 \times 6.56 \times 1.228}{\pi \times 4.5^2}$ [Values of C & K from step 2(diameters)]

$\tau = 40.52$ MPa > 40 MPa.

Here the design fails. Hence adopt the next higher value of d.

Hence adopt $d = 4.75$ mm. Therefore $D = 25 + 4.75 = 29.75$, $D_i = 25$ mm, $D_0 = 34.5$ mm, $C = 6.26$, $K = 1.241$

Eq. (*i*) yields... $\tau = \dfrac{8 \times 40 \times 6.26 \times 1.241}{\pi \times 4.75^2}$

$\tau = 35.09$ MPa < 40 MPa.

3. Number of coils:

We know that, $\qquad i = \dfrac{yGd^4}{8FD^3}$ ...**11.6/ Pg 139, DHB**

Here $y = y' = l_2 - l_1 = 50 - 40 = 10$ mm
$F = F_2 - F_1 = 40 - 25 = 15$ N

$$= \frac{10 \times 84 \times 10^3 \times 4.75^4}{8 \times 15 \times 29.75^3}$$

(Since C was assumed, don't use C in the formula)

$i = 135.33 \approx 136$ turns

Assuming square and ground ends, the actual number of coils,

$i_T = i + 2$ ...Tb 11.7/ Pg 152, DHB
$= 136 + 2$
$i_T = 138$

4. Free length:

For square and ground ends, $l_0 = (i + 1)d + y_{max} + a$ ...11.20b/ Pg 142, DHB

But, $\dfrac{F_{max}}{y_{max}} = \dfrac{F_2 - F_1}{y'}$

$y_{max} = \dfrac{F_{max} \cdot y'}{F_2 - F_1} = \dfrac{40 \times 10}{15} = 26.67$ mm

Also, $a = (136 - 1) \times 1$ mm per coil
$a = (136 - 1) \times 1$
$a = 135$ mm

Therefore, $l_0 = (136 + 1) \times 4.75 + 26.67 + 135$
$l_0 = 812.42$ mm

5. Pitch of the spring:

For square and ground ends, $l_0 = ip + 2d$ ...Tb 11.7/ Pg 152, DHB
$812.42 = 136p + 2 \times 4.75$
$p = 5.9$ mm ≈ 6 mm

6. Stiffness:

We know that, $F_0 = \dfrac{F_2 - F_1}{y'} = \dfrac{40 - 25}{10} = 1.5$ N/mm ...11.7b/ Pg 139, DHB

19. The following data refers to the valve of a petrol engine:
Length of the spring when the valve is open = 40 mm
Length of the spring when the valve is closed = 48 mm
Spring load when the valve is open = 220 N
Spring load when the valve is closed = 350 N
Spring index, C = 6.8, τ = 150 MPa, G = 84 GPa.
The ends are square and ground and the gap between the adjacent coils is 0.1 times the wire diameter, when the spring is free. Determine the following:
   a. Wire diameter   b. Mean coil diameter
   c. Number of active coils   d. Free length of the spring
   e. Pitch of coils.   *[VTU – July/ Aug. 2004 – 16 Marks]*

Solution: Maximum load, $F_{max} = F_2 = 350$ N, minimum load, $F_{min} = F_1 = 220$ N, minimum length, $l_1 = 40$ mm, maximum length, $l_2 = 48$ mm, $C = 6.8$, $\tau = 150$ MPa, $G = 84$ GPa $= 80 \times 10^3$ MPa, clearance, $a = (0.1d) \times i$, Design, (d, D, i, l_0, p, F_0).

1. To find diameter of wire:

We know that, $\tau = \dfrac{8FDK}{\pi d^3} = \dfrac{8F_{max}CK}{\pi d^2}$ ...Eq. (*i*) 11.1a/ Pg 139, DHB

But $K = \dfrac{4C-1}{4C-4} + \dfrac{0.615}{C}$ ...11.2b/ Pg 139, DHB

$= \dfrac{4 \times 6.8 - 1}{4 \times 6.8 - 4} + \dfrac{0.615}{6.8}$

$K = 1.219$

Eq. (i) yields... $150 = \dfrac{8 \times 350 \times 6.8 \times 1.219}{\pi \times d^2}$ ($F_{max} = 350$ N)

$d = 7.01$ mm

2. Diameters:

Standard wire diameter is $d = 7$ mm ...Tb 11.3a/ Pg 150, DHB
Mean diameter of coil, $D = Cd = 6.8 \times 7 = 47.6$ mm
Inner diameter of coil, $D_i = D - d = 47.6 - 7 = 40.6$ mm
Outer diameter of coil, $D_0 = D + d = 47.6 + 7 = 54.6$ mm

3. Number of coils:

We know that, $i = \dfrac{yGd^4}{8FD^3}$ ...11.6/ Pg 139, DHB

Here $y = y' = l_2 - l_1 = 48 - 40 = 8$ mm
$F = F_2 - F_1 = 350 - 220 = 130$ N

$i = \dfrac{8 \times 84 \times 10^3 \times 7^4}{8 \times 130 \times 47.6^3}$

$i = 14.38 \approx 15$ turns

Assuming square and ground ends, the actual number of coils,
$i_T = i + 2$ ...Tb 11.7/ Pg 152, DHB
$= 15 + 2$
$i_T = 17$

4. Free length:

For square and ground ends, $l_0 = (i + 1)d + y_{max} + a$ ...11.20b/ Pg 142, DHB

But, $\dfrac{F_{max}}{y_{max}} = \dfrac{F_2 - F_1}{y'}$

$y_{max} = \dfrac{F_{max} \cdot y'}{F_2 - F_1} = \dfrac{350 \times 8}{130} = 21.54$ mm

Also, $a = (0.1d) \times i$
$a = (0.1 \times 7) \times 15$
$a = 10.5$ mm.

Therefore, $l_0 = (15 + 1) \times 7 + 21.54 + 10.5$
$l_0 = 144.04$ mm.

5. Pitch of the spring:

For square and ground ends, $l_0 = ip + 2d$ ...Tb 11.7/ Pg 152, DHB
$144.04 = 15p + 2 \times 7$
$p = 8.67$ mm

6. Stiffness:

We know that, $F_0 = \dfrac{F_2 - F_1}{y'} = \dfrac{350 - 220}{8} = 16.25 \text{ N/mm}$ ...**11.7b/ Pg 139, DHB**

20. The spring used in an automobile engine has to exert 500 N when the valve is closed and 600 N when the valve is open. The displacement of the valve is 5 mm. The engine crankshaft rotates at 8000 rpm. Design the spring if permissible stress in the material of the spring is 300 MPa. The ratio of mean coil diameter to the wire diameter is 6. The specific weight and the modulus of rigidity of the spring material are 7.35×10^{-5} N/mm³, and 8×10^4 MPa, respectively. The ends of the spring are square and ground. Inspect the suitability of the spring for this engine. At what speed of the engine does the spring resonate?

[VTU – July 2006 – 14 Marks]

Solution: Minimum load, $F_{min} = F_1 = 500$ N, Maximum load, $F_{max} = F_2 = 600$ N, displacement, $y' = 5$ mm, $N = 8000$ rpm, $C = 6$, $\tau = 300$ MPa, $\gamma = 7.35 \times 10^{-5}$ N/mm³, $G = 8 \times 10^4$ MPa, Square and ground ends. *Design:* (d, D, i, l_0, p, F_0), Resonating speed = ?

1. To find diameter of wire:

We know that, $\tau = \dfrac{8FDK}{\pi d^3} = \dfrac{8F_{max}CK}{\pi d^2}$ ...Eq. (*i*) **11.1a/ Pg 139, DHB**

But $K = \dfrac{4C-1}{4C-4} + \dfrac{0.615}{C}$ ...**11.2b/ Pg 139, DHB**

$= \dfrac{4 \times 6 - 1}{4 \times 6 - 4} + \dfrac{0.615}{6}$

$K = 1.2525$

Eq. (*i*) yields... $300 = \dfrac{8 \times 600 \times 6 \times 1.2525}{\pi \times d^2}$ ($F_{max} = 600$ N)

$d = 6.18$ mm

2. Diameters:

Standard wire diameter is $d = 6.30$ mm ...**Tb 11.3a/ Pg 150, DHB**
Mean diameter of coil, $D = Cd = 6 \times 6.30 = 37.8$ mm
Inner diameter of coil, $D_i = D - d = 37.8 - 6.3 = 31.5$ mm
Outer diameter of coil, $D_0 = D + d = 37.8 + 6.3 = 44.1$ mm

3. Number of coils:

We know that, $\dfrac{F_2 - F_1}{y_2 - y_1} = \dfrac{Gd^4}{8iD^3}$ using ...**11.7 a and b/ Pg 139, DHB**

$\dfrac{600 - 500}{5} = \dfrac{8 \times 10^4 \times 6.3^4}{8 \times i \times 37.8^3}$

$i = 14.58 \approx 15$ turns

-Or-

$i = \dfrac{yGd}{8FC^3}$ ...**11.6/ Pg 139, DHB**

Here $y = y' = y_2 - y_1 = 5$ mm
$F = F_2 - F_1 = 600 - 500 = 100$ N

$$= \frac{5 \times 8 \times 10^4 \times 6.3}{8 \times 100 \times 6^3}$$

$$= 14.58 \approx 15 \text{ turns}$$

Given: square and ground ends, the actual number of coils,

$$i_T = i + 2 \quad \text{...Tb 11.7/ Pg 152, DHB}$$
$$= 15 + 2$$
$$i_T = 17$$

4. Free length:

For square and ground ends, $l_0 = (i + 1) d + y_{max} + a$ ...11.20b/ Pg 142, DHB

But, $\dfrac{F_{max}}{y_{max}} = \dfrac{F_2 - F_1}{y'}$

$$y_{max} = \frac{F_{max} \cdot y'}{F_2 - F_1} = \frac{600 \times 5}{600 - 500} = 30 \text{ mm}$$

Here, $a = (15 - 1) \times 1$ mm per coil
$a = (15 - 1) \times 1$
$a = 14$ mm.

Therefore, $l_0 = (15 + 1) \times 6.3 + 30 + 14 = 144.8$ mm

5. Pitch of the spring:

For square and ground ends, $l_0 = ip + 2d$
$$144.8 = 15p + 2 \times 6.3 \quad \text{...Tb 11.7/ Pg 152, DHB}$$
$$p = 8.81 \text{ mm} \approx 9 \text{ mm}$$

6. Stiffness:

We know that, $F_0 = \dfrac{F_2 - F_1}{y'} = \dfrac{600 - 500}{5} = 20 \text{ N/mm}$ ...11.7b/ Pg 139, DHB

7. Resonating speed (N'):

We know that critical speed, $N_c = f \times N$ ...Eq. (ii)

But, $f = \dfrac{d}{2\pi i D^2} \sqrt{\dfrac{Gg}{2\gamma}}$ ...11.24c/ Pg 144, DHB

$$= \frac{6.3}{2\pi \times 15 \times 37.8^2} \sqrt{\frac{8 \times 10^4 \times 9810}{2 \times 7.35 \times 10^{-5}}}$$

$$f = 108 \text{ cps}$$

Eq. (ii) yields... $N_c = 108 \times 60 = 6480$ rpm

Assuming that the automobile is a four stroke engine, we have

$$N_c = \frac{N'}{2}$$
$$= 2 \times 6480$$
$$= 12960 \text{ rpm.}$$

Springs

21. Design a helical compression spring for a service load ranging from 2250 N to 2750 N. The axial deflection of the spring for the load range is 6 mm. assume a spring index of 5, permissible shear stress of 420 MPa and modulus of rigidity of 84 kN/mm². *[VTU – June / July 2011 – 12 Marks]*

Solution: Minimum load, $F_{min} = F_1 = 2250$ N, Maximum load, $F_{max} = F_2 = 2750$ N, displacement, $y' = 6$ mm, $C = 5$, $\tau = 420$ MPa, $G = 84 \times 10^3$ N/mm². Design: (d, D, i, l_0, p, F_0).

1. To find diameter of wire:

We know that, $\quad \tau = \dfrac{8FDK}{\pi d^3} = \dfrac{8F_{max}CK}{\pi d^2}$ ...Eq. (i) **11.1a/ Pg 139, DHB**

$$\text{But } K = \dfrac{4C-1}{4C-4} + \dfrac{0.615}{C} \qquad \text{...11.2b/ Pg 139, DHB}$$

$$= \dfrac{4\times5-1}{4\times5-4} + \dfrac{0.615}{5}$$

$$K = 1.3105$$

Eq. (i) yields... $420 = \dfrac{8 \times 2750 \times 5 \times 1.3105}{\pi \times d^2} \qquad (F_{max} = 2750 \text{ N})$

$$d = 10.45 \text{ mm.}$$

2. Diameters:

Standard wire diameter is $d = 10.5$ mm ...**Tb 11.3a/ Pg 150, DHB**
Mean diameter of coil, $D = Cd = 5 \times 10.5 = 52.5$ mm
Inner diameter of coil, $D_i = D - d = 52.5 - 10.5 = 42$ mm
Outer diameter of coil, $D_0 = D + d = 52.5 + 10.5 = 63$ mm

3. Number of coils:

We know that, $\quad \dfrac{F_2 - F_1}{y_2 - y_1} = \dfrac{Gd^4}{8iD^3} \qquad$ using... **11.7 a & b/ Pg 139, DHB**

$$\dfrac{2750-2250}{6} = \dfrac{84 \times 10^3 \times 10.5^4}{8 \times i \times 52.5^3}$$

$$i = 10.58 \approx 11 \text{ turns}$$

Assuming square and ground ends, the actual number of coils,
$$i_T = i + 2 \qquad \text{...Tb 11.7/ Pg 152, DHB}$$
$$= 11 + 2$$
$$i_T = 13$$

4. Free length:

For square and ground ends, $\quad l_0 = (i+1)d + y_{max} + a \qquad$ ...**11.20b/ Pg 142, DHB**

But, $\quad \dfrac{F_{max}}{y_{max}} = \dfrac{F_2 - F_1}{y'}$

$$y_{max} = \dfrac{F_{max} \cdot y'}{F_2 - F_1} = \dfrac{2750 \times 6}{2750 - 2250} = 33 \text{ mm}$$

Here, $a = (i-1) \times 1$ mm per coil
$a = (11-1) \times 1$
$a = 10$ mm
Therefore, $l_0 = (11+1) \times 10.5 + 33 + 10$
$l_0 = 169$

5. Pitch of the spring:

For square and ground ends, $l_0 = ip + 2d$ ...Tb 11.7/ Pg 152, DHB
$169 = 11p + 2 \times 10.5$
$p = 13.45$ mm ≈ 14 mm

6. Stiffness:

We know that, $F_0 = \dfrac{F_2 - F_1}{y'} = \dfrac{2750 - 2250}{6} = 83.34$ N/mm ...**11.7b/ Pg 139, DHB**

22. Design a valve spring for an automobile engine, when the valve is closed, the spring produces a force of 45 N and when it opens, produces a force of 55 N. The spring must fit over the valve bush which has an outside diameter of 20 mm and must go inside a space of 35 mm. The lift of the valve is 6 mm. The spring index is 12. The allowable stress may be taken as 330 MPa and modulus of rigidity, = 80 GPa. *[VTU – June/ July 2009 – 15 Marks]*

Solution: Minimum load, $F_{min} = F_1 = 45$ N, Maximum load, $F_{max} = F_2 = 55$ N, bush diameter = 20 mm, maximum space = 35 mm, displacement, $y' = 6$ mm, $C = 12$, $\tau = 330$ MPa, $G = 80 \times 10^3$ N/mm^2, *Design:* (d, D, i, l_0, p, F_0).

1. To find diameter of wire:

We know that, $\tau = \dfrac{8FDK}{\pi d^3} = \dfrac{8F_{max}CK}{\pi d^2}$ ...Eq. (i) **11.1a/ Pg 139, DHB**

But $K = \dfrac{4C-1}{4C-4} + \dfrac{0.615}{C}$ ...**11.2b/ Pg 139, DHB**

$= \dfrac{4 \times 12 - 1}{4 \times 12 - 4} + \dfrac{0.615}{12}$

$K = 1.119$

Eq. (i) yields... $330 = \dfrac{8 \times 55 \times 12 \times 1.119}{\pi \times d^2}$ $(F_{max} = 55$ N$)$

$d = 2.39$ mm

2. Diameters:

Standard wire diameter is $d = 2.40$ mm ...Tb 11.3a/ Pg 150, DHB
Mean diameter of coil, $D = Cd = 12 \times 2.40 = 28.8$ mm
Inner diameter of coil, $D_i = D - d = 28.8 - 2.40 = 26.4$ mm
Outer diameter of coil, $D_0 = D + d = 28.8 + 2.4 = 31.2$ mm

Check: As per given data bush diameter = 20 mm, maximum space = 35 mm.

Therefore, $D_i = 26.4$ mm > 20 mm ...Thus safe
$D_0 = 31.2$ mm < 35 mm ...Thus safe

3. Number of coils:

We know that, $\dfrac{F_2 - F_1}{y_2 - y_1} = \dfrac{Gd^4}{8iD^3}$ *using* ...**11.7 a and b/ Pg 139, DHB**

$$\frac{55-45}{6} = \frac{80 \times 10^3 \times 2.4^4}{8 \times i \times 28.8^3}$$
$$i = 8.33 \approx 9 \text{ turns}$$

Assuming square and ground ends, the actual number of coils,
$$i_T = i + 2 \qquad \text{...Tb 11.7/ Pg 152, DHB}$$
$$= 9 + 2$$
$$i_T = 11$$

4. Free length:

For square and ground ends, $l_0 = (i+1)d + y_{max} + a$ ...11.20b/ Pg 142, DHB

But, $\dfrac{F_{max}}{y_{max}} = \dfrac{F_2 - F_1}{y'}$

$$= \frac{F_{max} \cdot y'}{F_2 - F_1} = \frac{55 \times 6}{55 - 45} = 33 \text{ mm}$$

Here, $a = (i-1) \times 1$ mm per coil
$$a = (9-1) \times 1$$
$$a = 8 \text{ mm}$$

Therefore, $l_0 = (9+1) \times 2.4 + 33 + 8$
$$l_0 = 65 \text{ mm}.$$

5. Pitch of the spring:

For square and ground ends, $l_0 = ip + 2d$ ...Tb 11.7/ Pg 152, DHB
$$65 = 9p + 2 \times 2.4$$
$$p = 6.68 \text{ mm} \approx 7 \text{ mm}$$

6. Stiffness:

We know that, $F_0 = \dfrac{F_2 - F_1}{y'} = \dfrac{55 - 45}{6} = 1.67$ N.mm ...11.7b/ Pg 139, DHB

23. Design a helical spring for a spring loaded safety valve (Ram's bottom safety valve) for the following conditions:

Diameter of valve seat = 60 mm, operating pressure = 0.7 N/mm²,
Maximum pressure when the valve blows off freely = 0.75 N/mm²,
Maximum lift of the valve when the pressure rises from 0.7 to 0.75 N/mm² = 3.5 mm,
Maximum allowable stress = 550 N/mm², modulus of rigidity = 84 kN/mm², spring index = 6. *[VTU – July 2007 – 15 Marks]*

Solution: Diameter of valve, $d_v = 65$ mm, operating pressure, $p_1 = 0.7$ MPa, maximum pressure, $p_2 = 0.75$ MPa, $y' = 3.5$ mm, $\tau = 550$ MPa, $G = 84 \times 10^3$ N/mm², $C = 6$.
Design: (d, D, i, l_0, p, F_0).

1. To find diameter of wire:

We know that, $\tau = \dfrac{8FDK}{\pi d^3} = \dfrac{8F_{max}CK}{\pi d^2}$ ...Eq. (i) 11.1a/ Pg 139, DHB

But $K = \dfrac{4C-1}{4C-4} + \dfrac{0.615}{C}$ ...11.2b/ Pg 139, DHB

$$K = \frac{4 \times 6 - 1}{4 \times 6 - 4} + \frac{0.615}{6}$$

$$K = 1.2525$$

Also $p = \frac{F}{A_v}$

Therefore, $F_1 = p_1 A_v = \frac{\pi}{4} \times 65^2 \times 0.7 = 2322.82$ N

$$F_2 = p_2 A_v = \frac{\pi}{4} \times 65^2 \times 0.75 = 2488.73 \text{ N}$$

Eq. (i) yields... $550 = \dfrac{8 \times 2488.73 \times 6 \times 1.2525}{\pi \times d^2}$

$d = 9.31$ mm

2. Diameters:

Standard wire diameter is $d = 9.50$ mm ...Tb 11.3a/ Pg 150, DHB
Mean diameter of coil, $D = Cd = 6 \times 9.50 = 57$ mm
Inner diameter of coil, $D_i = D - d = 57 - 9.5 = 47.50$ mm
Outer diameter of coil, $D_0 = D + d = 57 + 9.5 = 66.50$ mm

3. Number of coils:

We know that, $\quad \dfrac{F_2 - F_1}{y_2 - y_1} = \dfrac{Gd^4}{8iD^3} \qquad$ using ...**11.7 a and b/ Pg 139, DHB**

$$\frac{2488.73 - 2322.82}{3.5} = \frac{84 \times 10^3 \times 9.5^4}{8 \times i \times 57^3}$$

$i = 9.74 \approx 10$ turns

- For a tension spring, the ends are bent to form loops at both ends.
  Therefore, $i_T = i + 1$
  $= 10 + 1$
  $i_T = 11$

4. Free length:

For ends bent before grinding, $\quad l_0 = (i + 2)d + y_{max} + a \qquad$ ...11.20a/ Pg 142, DHB

But, $\dfrac{F_{max}}{y_{max}} = \dfrac{F_2 - F_1}{y'}$

$$y_{max} = \frac{F_{max} \cdot y'}{F_2 - F_1} = \frac{2488.73 \times 3.5}{2488.73 - 2322.82} = 52.50 \text{ mm}$$

Here, $a = (i - 1) \times 1$ mm per coil
$a = (10 - 1) \times 1$
$a = 9$ mm

Therefore, $l_0 = (10 + 2) \times 9.5 + 52.50 + 9$
$l_0 = 175.5$ mm

5. Pitch of the spring:

For square and ground ends, $l_0 = ip + 2d$ ...Tb 11.7/ Pg 152, DHB

$$175.5 = 10p + 2 \times 9.5$$
$$p = 15.65 \text{ mm}$$

6. Stiffness:

We know that, $F_0 = \dfrac{F_2 - F_1}{y'} = \dfrac{2488.73 - 2322.82}{3.5} = 47.40 \text{ N/mm}$ ...**11.7b/ Pg 139, DHB**

TYPICAL PROBLEMS–MATERIAL PROPERTIES UNKNOWN

24. A helical valve spring is to be designed for an operating load between 100 N to 150 N. The valve lift is 7.5 mm in this load range. Assuming C = 10, design the spring.

Solution: $F_1 = F_{min} = 100$ N, $F_2 = F_{max} = 150$ N, $y' = 6$ mm, $C = 10$. Design: (d, D, i, l_0, p, F_0).

1. To find diameter of wire:

We know that, $\quad \tau = \dfrac{8FDK}{\pi d^3} = \dfrac{8F_{max}CK}{\pi d^2}$ ...Eq. (i) **11.1a/ Pg 139, DHB**

$$\text{But } K = \dfrac{4C - 1}{4C - 4} + \dfrac{0.615}{C} \qquad \text{...11.2b/ Pg 139, DHB}$$

$$= \dfrac{4 \times 10 - 1}{4 \times 10 - 4} + \dfrac{0.615}{10}$$

$$K = 1.145$$

Since the material properties are unknown, assume suitable material from tables.

Trial- 1:

Material	Oil hardened and tempered steel	
Grade	VW	
Wire diameter	2.5 to 2.8 mm	**Tb 11.12/ Pg 155B, DHB**
Tensile strength, σ	1470 to 1570 MPa	
Rigidity modulus, G	81370 MPa	

Here shear stress, $\quad \tau = 0.5, \sigma = 0.5 \times \left(\dfrac{1470 + 1570}{2}\right) = 760$ MPa

Eq. (i) yields... $760 = \dfrac{8 \times 150 \times 10 \times 1.145}{\pi \times d^2} \qquad (F_{max} = 150 \text{ N})$

$$d = 2.4 \text{ mm}$$

Since the obtained value of 'd' does not fall in the range, trial 1 fails.
Trial- 1 fails but gives the range of 'd' to start the problem.

Trial- 2:

Material	Oil hardened and tempered steel	
Grade	VW	
Wire diameter	2.0 to 2.4 mm	**Tb 11.12/ Pg 155B, DHB**
Tensile strength, σ	1520 to 1620 MPa	
Rigidity modulus, G	81370 MPa	

Here shear stress, $\tau = 0.5\sigma = 0.5 \times \left(\dfrac{1520+1620}{2}\right) = 785$ MPa

Eq. (i) yields... $785 = \dfrac{8 \times 150 \times 10 \times 1.145}{\pi \times d^2}$

$d = 2.36$ mm

Thus, $2.0 < 2.36 < 2.4$ mm

2. Diameters:

Standard wire diameter is $d = 8.5$ mm ...Tb 11.3a/ Pg 150, DHB
Mean diameter of coil, $D = Cd = 10 \times 2.4 = 24$ mm
Inner diameter of coil, $D_i = D - d = 24 - 2.4 = 21.60$ mm
Outer diameter of coil, $D_0 = D + d = 24 + 2.4 = 26.40$ mm

3. Number of coils:

We know that, $\dfrac{F_2 - F_1}{y_2 - y_1} = \dfrac{Gd^4}{8iD^3}$ using ...11.7 a and b/ Pg 139, DHB

$\dfrac{150 - 100}{7.5} = \dfrac{81370 \times 2.4^4}{8 \times i \times 24^3}$

$\tau = 3.66 \approx 4$ turns

Assuming square and ground ends, the actual number of coils,

$i_T = i + 2$ ...Tb 11.7/ Pg 152, DHB
$= 4 + 2$
$i_T = 6$

4. Free length:

For square and ground ends, $l_0 = (i + 1)d + y_{max} + a$ ...11.20b/ Pg 142, DHB

But, $\dfrac{F_{max}}{y_{max}} = \dfrac{F_2 - F_1}{y'}$

$y_{max} = \dfrac{F_{max} \cdot y'}{F_2 - F_1} = \dfrac{150 \times 7.5}{150 - 100} = 22.5$ mm

Here, $a = (i - 1) \times 1$ mm per coil
$a = (4 - 1) \times 1$
$a = 3$ mm..

Therefore, $l_0 = (4 + 1) \times 2.4 + 22.5 + 3$
$l_0 = 37.5$ mm.

5. Pitch of the spring:

For square and ground ends, $l_0 = ip + 2d$ ...Tb 11.7/ Pg 152, DHB
$37.5 = 4p + 2 \times 2.4$
$p = 8.18$ mm ≈ 9 mm.

6. Stiffness:

We know that, $F_0 = \dfrac{F_2 - F_1}{y'} = \dfrac{150 - 100}{7.5} = 6.67$ N/mm   ...11.7b/ Pg 139, DHB

7. Specifications for manufacturing:

Material	:	Oil hardened and tempered steel
Grade	:	Valve spring wire (VW)
Wire diameter, d	:	2.4 mm
Mean coil diameter, D	:	24 mm
Free length, l_a	:	37.5 mm
Total number of active turns, i	:	4
Type of ends	:	square and ground
Pitch, p	:	9 mm
Spring rate, F_0	:	6.67 N/mm

25. Design a helical compression spring to sustain an axial load that fluctuates between 1.5 kN and 2 kN with an associated deflection of 15 mm during the fluctuation of the load.

[VTU – Dec. 2011 – 10 Marks; Dec.07 / Jan. 08 – 10 Marks; Jan/ Feb 2005 – 10 Marks]

Solution: $F_1 = F_{min} = 1500$ N, $F_2 = F_{max} = 2000$ N, $y' = 15$ mm. Design: (d, D, i, l_0, F_0).

1. To find diameter of wire:

We know that,
$$\tau = \frac{8FDK}{\pi d^3} = \frac{8F_{max}CK}{\pi d^2} \quad \text{...Eq. (i) 11.1a/ Pg 139, DHB}$$

$$\text{But } K = \frac{4C-1}{4C-4} + \frac{0.615}{C} \quad \text{...11.2b/ Pg 139, DHB}$$

$$= \frac{4 \times 8 - 1}{4 \times 8 - 4} + \frac{0.615}{8} \quad \text{(Assume } C = 8\text{)}$$

$$K = 1.184$$

Since the material properties are unknown, assume suitable material from tables.

Trial- 1:

Material	Oil hardened and tempered steel	
Grade	VW	
Wire diameter	6.5 to 7.5 mm	**Tb 11.12/ Pg 155B, DHB**
Tensile strength, σ	1300 to 1400 MPa	
Rigidity modulus, G	81370 MPa	

Here shear stress, $\tau = 0.5, \sigma = 0.5 \times \left(\frac{1300 + 1400}{2}\right) = 675$ MPa

Eq. (i) yields... $675 = \dfrac{8 \times 2000 \times 8 \times 1.184}{\pi \times d^2}$ ($F_{max} = 2000$ N)

$d = 8.45$ mm

Since the obtained value of 'd' does not fall in the range, trial 1 fails.
Trial- 1 fails but gives the range of 'd' to start the problem.

Trial-2:

Material	Oil hardened and tempered steel	
Grade	VW	
Wire diameter	8.0 to 9.5 mm	**Tb 11.12/ Pg 155B, DHB**
Tensile strength, σ	1290 to 1400 MPa	
Rigidity modulus, G	81370 MPa	

Here shear stress, $\tau = 0.5, \sigma = 0.5 \times \left(\dfrac{1290 + 1400}{2}\right) = 672.5$ MPa

Eq. (i) yields... $672.5 = \dfrac{8 \times 2000 \times 8 \times 1.184}{\pi \times d^2}$

$d = 8.46$ mm

Thus, $8.0 < 8.46 < 9.5$

2. Diameters:

Standard wire diameter is $d = 8.5$ mm ...Tb 11.3a/ Pg 150, DHB
Mean diameter of coil, $D = Cd = 8 \times 8.5 = 68$ mm
Inner diameter of coil, $D_i = D - d = 68 - 8.5 = 59.5$ mm
Outer diameter of coil, $D_0 = D + d = 68 + 8.5 = 76.50$ mm

- Since C was assumed, Check for τ:

Now, $C = D/d = 68/8.5 = 8$

And $K = \dfrac{4C - 1}{4C - 4} + \dfrac{0.615}{C}$

$= \dfrac{4 \times 8 - 1}{4 \times 8 - 4} + \dfrac{0.615}{8}$

$K = 1.184$

Eq. (i) yields... $\tau = \dfrac{8 \times 2000 \times 8 \times 1.184}{\pi \times 8.5^2}$ *[Values of C and K from step 2 (diameters)]*

$\tau = 667.59 < 672.50$ MPa.

Hence safe.

3. Number of coils:

We know that, $\dfrac{F_2 - F_1}{y_2 - y_1} = \dfrac{Gd^4}{8iD^3}$ using ...11.7 a and b/ Pg 139, DHB

$\dfrac{2000 - 1500}{15} = \dfrac{81370 \times 8.5^4}{8 \times i \times 68^3}$

$i = 5.06 \approx 5$ turns

Assuming square and ground ends, the actual number of coils,
$i_T = i + 2$ ...Tb 11.7/ Pg 152, DHB
$= 5 + 2$
$i_T = 7$

4. Free length:

For square and ground ends, $l_0 = (i + 1)d + y_{max} + a$ ...11.20b/ Pg 142, DHB

But, $K = \dfrac{F_{max}}{y_{max}} = \dfrac{F_2 - F_1}{y'}$

$= \dfrac{F_{max} \cdot y'}{F_2 - F_1} = \dfrac{2000 \times 15}{2000 - 1500} = 60$ mm

Here, $a = (i - 1) \times 1$ mm per coil
$a = (5 - 1) \times 1$
$a = 4$ mm

Therefore, $l_0 = (5+1) \times 85 + 60 + 4$

$l_0 = 115$ mm

5. Pitch of the spring:

For square and ground ends, $l_0 = ip + 2d$ ...Tb 11.7/ Pg 152, DHB

$$115 = 5p + 2 \times 8.5$$
$$p = 19.6 \text{ mm} \approx 20 \text{ mm}$$

6. Stiffness:

We know that, $F_0 = \dfrac{F_2 - F_1}{y'} = \dfrac{2000 - 1500}{15} = 33.34$ N/mm ...11.7b/ Pg 139, DHB

7. Specifications for manufacturing:

Material	:	Oil hardened and tempered steel
Grade	:	Spring wire (SW)
Wire diameter, d	:	8.5 mm
Mean coil diameter, D	:	68 mm
Free length, l_0	:	115 mm
Total number of active turns, i	:	5
Type of ends	:	square and ground
Pitch, p	:	20 mm
Spring rate, F_0	:	33.34 N/mm

26. The valve spring of a petrol engine is 40 mm long when the valve is open and 48 mm when the valve is closed. The spring loads are 200 N when the valve is closed and 400 N when the valve is open. The inside diameter of the spring should not be less than 25 mm. Design the spring.

[VTU – June/ July 2009 – 20 Marks]

Solution: Maximum load, $F_2 = F_{max} = 400$ N, minimum load, $F_1 = F_{min} = 200$ N, minimum length, $l_1 = 40$ mm, $l_2 = 48$ mm, $D_i \geq 25$ mm. *Design:* (d, D, i, l_0, p, F_0).

1. To find diameter of wire:

We know that, $\tau = \dfrac{8FDK}{\pi d^3} = \dfrac{8F_{max}CK}{\pi d^2}$ ...Eq. (i) 11.1a/ Pg 139, DHB

But $K = \dfrac{4C-1}{4C-4} + \dfrac{0.615}{C}$ ...11.2b/ Pg 139, DHB

$= \dfrac{4 \times 8 - 1}{4 \times 8 - 4} + \dfrac{0.615}{8}$ (Assume $C = 8$)

$K = 1.184$

Since the material properties are unknown, assume suitable material from tables.

Trial- 1:

Material	Oil hardened and tempered steel	
Grade	VW	
Wire diameter	3.6 to 4.0 mm	Tb 11.12/ Pg 155B, DHB
Tensile strength, σ	1400 to 1500 MPa	
Rigidity modulus, G	81370 MPa	

Here shear stress, $\tau = 0.5$, $\sigma = 0.5 \times \left(\dfrac{1400 + 1500}{2}\right) = 725$ MPa

Eq. (i) yields... $725 = \dfrac{8 \times 400 \times 8 \times 1.184}{\pi \times d^2}$ $(F_{max} = 400$ N$)$

$d = 3.65$ mm

Thus, $3.6 < 3.65 < 4.0$

2. Diameters:

Standard wire diameter is $d = 3.80$ mm ...**Tb 11.3a/ Pg 150, DHB**
Mean diameter of coil, $D = Cd = 8 \times 3.8 = 30.40$ mm
Inner diameter of coil, $D_i = D - d = 30.4 - 3.8 = 26.60$ mm ≥ 25 mm
Outer diameter of coil, $D_0 = D + d = 30.4 + 3.8 = 34.20$ mm

- Since C was assumed, check for τ:

Now, $C = D/d = 30.4/3.8 = 8$

And $K = \dfrac{4C - 1}{4C - 4} + \dfrac{0.615}{C}$

$= \dfrac{4 \times 8 - 1}{4 \times 8 - 4} + \dfrac{0.615}{8}$

$K = 1.184$

Eq. (i) yields... $\tau = \dfrac{8 \times 400 \times 8 \times 1.184}{\pi \times 3.8^2}$ *[Values of C and K from step 2(diameters)]*

$\tau = 668.15 < 725$ MPa.

Hence safe.

3. Number of coils:

We know that, $\dfrac{F_2 - F_1}{y_2 - y_1} = \dfrac{Gd^4}{8iD^3}$ using ...**11.7 a and b/ Pg 139, DHB**

$\dfrac{400 - 200}{8} = \dfrac{81370 \times 3.8^4}{8 \times i \times 30.4^3}$ $(y' = l_2 - l_1 = 48 - 40 = 8$ mm$)$

$i = 3.02 \approx 3$ turns

Assuming square and ground ends, the actual number of coils,

$i_T = i + 2$ ...**Tb 11.7/ Pg 152, DHB**
$= 3 + 2$
$i_T = 5$

4. Free length:

For square and ground ends, $l_0 = (i + 1)d + y_{max} + a$ ...**11.20b/ Pg 142, DHB**

But, $\dfrac{F_{max}}{y_{max}} = \dfrac{F_2 - F_1}{y'}$

$y_{max} = \dfrac{F_{max} \cdot y'}{F_2 - F_1} = \dfrac{400 \times 8}{400 - 200} = 16$ mm

Here, $a = (i-1) \times 1$ mm per coil
$a = (3-1) \times 1$
$a = 2$ mm

Therefore, $l_0 = (3+1) \times 3.8 + 16 + 2$
$l_0 = 33.2$ mm

5. Pitch of the spring:

For square and ground ends, $l_0 = ip + 2d$ ...Tb 11.7/ Pg 152, DHB
$33.2 = 3p + 2 \times 3.8$
$p = 8.53$ mm ≈ 9 mm

6. Stiffness:

We know that, $F_0 = \dfrac{F_2 - F_1}{y'} = \dfrac{400 - 200}{18} = 25$ N/mm ...11.7b/ Pg 139, DHB

7. Specifications for manufacturing:

Material	:	Oil hardened and tempered steel
Grade	:	Valve spring wire (VW)
Wire diameter, d	:	3.8 mm
Mean coil diameter, D	:	30.4 mm
Free length l_0	:	33.2 mm
Total number of active turns, i	:	3
Type of ends	:	square and ground
Pitch, P	:	9 mm
Spring rate, F_0	:	25 N/mm

27. Design a helical compression spring to support a load of 3 kN. The frequency of the system is 1.5 Hz. Take C = 6.

Solution: $F = 3000$ N, $C = 6$, $f = 1.5$ Hz. *Design:* (d, D, i, l_0, p, F_0).

1. To find diameter of wire:

We know that, $\tau = \dfrac{8FDK}{\pi d^3}$ ...Eq. (i) 11.1a/ Pg 139, DHB

But $K = \dfrac{4C-1}{4C-4} + \dfrac{0.615}{C}$ ...11.2b/ Pg 139, DHB

$= \dfrac{4 \times 6 - 1}{4 \times 6 - 4} + \dfrac{0.615}{6}$

$K = 1.2525$

Since the material properties are unknown, assume suitable material from tables.

Trial- 1:

Material	Patented and cold drawn steel wire-Unalloyed	
Grade	2	Tb 11.12/ Pg 155B, DHB
Wire diameter	10	
Tensile strength, σ	1130 MPa	
Rigidity modulus, G	88370 MPa	

Here shear stress, $\tau = 0.5 \sigma = 0.5 \times 1130 = 565$ MPa

Eq. (i) yields... $565 = \dfrac{8 \times 3000 \times 6 \times 1.2525}{\pi \times d^2}$

$$d = 10.08 \text{ mm} \approx 10 \text{ mm}$$

2. Diameters:

Standard wire diameter is $d = 10$ mm ...Tb 11.3a/ Pg 150, DHB
Mean diameter of coil, $D = Cd = 6 \times 10 = 60$ mm
Inner diameter of coil, $D_i = D - d = 60 - 10 = 50$ mm
Outer diameter of coil, $D_0 = D + d = 60 + 10 = 70$ mm

3. Number of coils:

We know that, $\quad F_0 = \dfrac{Gd^4}{8iD^3}$ ...Eq. (ii) 11.7a/ Pg 139, DHB

Also, $\quad f = 22.3\sqrt{\dfrac{F_0}{W}}$ ...11.24a/ Pg 143, DHB

$$1.5 = 22.3\sqrt{\dfrac{F_0}{3000}}$$

$$F_0 = 13.58 \text{ N/mm}$$

Eq. (ii) yields... $13.58 = \dfrac{88370 \times 10^4}{8 \times i \times 60^3}$

$$i = 37.68 \approx 38 \text{ turns}$$

Assuming square and ground ends, the actual number of coils,
$\quad i_T = i + 2$ ...Tb 11.7/ Pg 152, DHB
$\quad\quad = 38 + 2$
$\quad i_T = 40$

4. Free length:

For square and ground ends, $l_0 = (i + 1)d + y + a$ ...11.20b/ Pg 142, DHB
Here, $a = (i - 1) \times 1$ mm per coil
$\quad a = (38 - 1) \times 1$
$\quad a = 37$ mm
And $y = F/F_0 = 3000/13.58 = 221$ mm
Therefore, $l_0 = (38 + 1) \times 10 + 221 + 37$
$\quad l_0 = 648$ mm

5. Pitch of the spring:

For square and ground ends, $\quad l_0 = ip + 2d$ ...Tb 11.7/ Pg 152, DHB
$\quad\quad 648 = 38p + 2 \times 10$
$\quad\quad p = 16.52$ mm

6. Stiffness:

We know that, $\quad F_0 = 13.58$ N/ mm $\quad$ [from step (2)]

7. Specifications for manufacturing:

Material : Patented and cold drawn steel wire - unalloyed
Grade : 2
Wire diameter, d : 10 mm

Mean coil diameter, D	: 60 mm
Free length, l_0	: 648 mm
Total number of active turns, i	: 38
Type of ends	: square and ground
Pitch, p	: 16.52 mm
Spring rate, F_0	: 13.58 N/mm

28. A bullet of 2 N is fired from a gun. The bullet travels a distance of 12 meters. The compression of the spring when the gun is loaded is 150 mm and the diameter of the barrel is 25 mm. Design the spring.

Solution: Weight of bullet, $W = 2$ N, distance $s = 12\ m = 12000$ mm, $y = 150$ mm, $D = 25$ mm. Design: (d, D, i, l_0, p, F_0).

1. To find diameter of wire:

We know that,
$$\tau = \frac{8FDK}{\pi d^3} \quad \text{...Eq. (i) 11.1a/ Pg 139, DHB}$$

But
$$K = \frac{4C-1}{4C-4} + \frac{0.615}{C} \quad \text{...11.2b/ Pg 139, DHB}$$

$$= \frac{4\times 6 -1}{4\times 6 - 4} + \frac{0.615}{6} \quad \text{(Assume } C = 6\text{)}$$

$$K = 1.2525$$

Work done by bullet $= W.s = 2 \times 12000 = 24000$ N – mm

Energy stored by spring $= \left(\dfrac{Fy}{2}\right) n \quad \text{...Eq. (ii)}$

$$= \left(\frac{F\times 150}{2}\right) \times 1 \quad (n = 1)$$

$$= 75\ F \quad \text{...Eq. (iii)}$$

Since the work done = energy stored by the springs, equating Eqs (ii) and (iii), we have
$$24000 = 75\ F$$
$$\therefore F = 320\ \text{N}$$

Since the material properties are unknown, assume suitable material from tables.

Trial- 1:

Material	Patented and cold drawn steel wire-Unalloyed	
Grade	2	Tb 11.14/ Pg 155C, DHB
Wire diameter	2.5	
Tensile strength, σ	1640 MPa	
Rigidity modulus, G	88370 MPa	

Here shear stress, $\tau = 0.5\ \sigma = 0.5 \times 1640 = 820$ MPa

Eq. (i) yields... $820 = \dfrac{8 \times 320 \times 6 \times 1.2525}{\pi \times d^2}$

$$d = 2.73\ \text{mm} < 2.5\ \text{mm}$$

Trial- 1 fails.

Trial- 2:

Material	Patented and cold drawn steel wire-Unalloyed	
Grade	2	Tb 11.14/ Pg 155C, DHB
Wire diameter	2.8	
Tensile strength, σ	1600 MPa	
Rigidity modulus, G	88370 MPa	

Here shear stress, $\tau = 0.5, \sigma = 0.5 \times 1600 = 800$ MPa

Eq. (i) yields... $800 = \dfrac{8 \times 320 \times 6 \times 1.2525}{\pi \times d^2}$

$d = 2.77$ mm ≈ 2.8 mm

2. Diameters:

Standard wire diameter is $d = 2.8$ ...Tb 11.3a/ Pg 150, DHB
Mean diameter of coil, $D = Cd = 6 \times 2.8 = 16.8$ mm
Inner diameter of coil, $D_i = D - d = 16.8 - 2.8 = 14$ mm
Outer diameter of coil, $D_0 = D + d = 16.8 + 2.8 = 19.6$ mm

- Since C was assumed, Check for τ :

Now, $C = D/d = 16.8/2.8 = 6$

And $K = \dfrac{4C-1}{4C-4} + \dfrac{0.615}{C}$

$= \dfrac{4 \times 6 - 1}{4 \times 6 - 4} + \dfrac{0.615}{6}$

$K = 1.2525$

Eq. (i) yields... $\tau = \dfrac{8 \times 320 \times 6 \times 1.2525}{\pi \times 2.8^2}$ [Values of C and K from step 2(diameters)]

$\tau = 781.1$ MPa < 800 MPa.

Hence safe.

3. Number of coils:

We know that, $i = \dfrac{yGd^4}{8FD^3}$ ...11.6/ Pg 139, DHB

$= \dfrac{150 \times 88370 \times (2.8)^4}{8 \times 320 \times 16.8^3}$

$i = 67.1 \approx 67$ turns

Assuming square and ground ends, the actual number of coils,

$i_T = i + 2$ ...Tb 11.7/ Pg 152, DHB
$= 67 + 2$
$i_T = 69$

4. Free length:

For square and ground ends, $l_0 = (i + 1)d + y + a$ ...11.20b/ Pg 142, DHB

Here, $a = (i - 1) \times 1$ mm per coil
$a = (67 - 1) \times 1$
$a = 66$ mm
And $y = 150$ mm (data)
Therefore, $l_0 = (67 + 1) \times 2.8 + 150 + 66$
$l_0 = 406.4$ mm

5. Pitch of the spring:
For square and ground ends, $l_0 = ip + 2d$ ...Tb 11.7/ Pg 152, DHB
$406.4 = 67p + 2 \times 2.8$
$p = 5.98$ mm ≈ 6 mm

6. Stiffness:
We know that, $\quad F_0 = F/y = 320/150 = 2.13$ N/mm ...11.7a/ Pg 139, DHB

7. Specifications for manufacturing:

Material	:	Patented and cold drawn steel wire- Un alloyed
Grade	:	2
Wire diameter, d	:	2.8 mm
Mean coil diameter, D	:	16.8 mm
Free length l_0	:	406.4 mm
Total number of active turns, i	:	67
Type of ends	:	square and ground
Pitch, p	:	6 mm
Spring rate, F_0	:	2.13 N/mm

3.12 STRESSES AND DEFLECTION IN HELICAL SPRINGS—NON-CIRCULAR WIRE

Non- circular helical springs are used to provide greater resilience in a given space and to provide predetermined altering of spring stiffness **(Fig. 3.5)**. These are used in cases where a large amount of energy has to be stored within a given space. These are not recommended until the space limitations make it necessary.

The non-circular helical springs are generally rectangular –or- square in cross-section.

Springs made of rectangular wire with the long side of the wire cross-section perpendicular to the axis of the coils can store more energy in a smaller space than an equivalent, round-wire spring.

Disadvantages:
- The shape of the spring changes to trapezoidal cross-section while forming the helix, thereby reducing the energy absorbing capacity.
- The stress distribution is not favorable as that of circular wires.

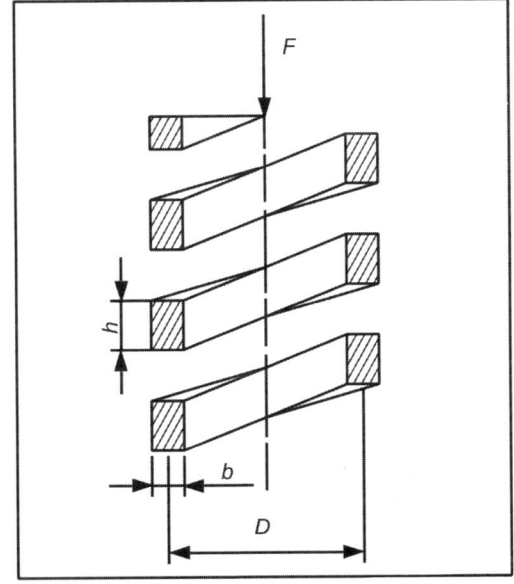

Fig. 3.5: Non circular helical springs [Fig. 11.2(b)/Pg 156, DHB]

Design formulae:

Let b – side of cross-section perpendicular to the axis of the spring
  h – side of cross-section parallel to the axis of spring
  D – mean diameter of the coil
  C – spring index
  $1/m$ = Poisson's ratio

Rectangular section springs:

- Shear stress

$$\tau' = \frac{KFD(1.5h + 0.96b)}{b^2 h^2} = \frac{KFD(1.5 + 0.9m)}{m^2 h^3} \quad \ldots 11.14/\text{ Pg 140, DHB}$$

Where, $K = \frac{4C-1}{4C-4} + \frac{0.615}{C}$

$C = \frac{D}{b}$ and

$m = \frac{b}{h} \leq 1$

- Deflection, $y = \frac{2.83 i F D^3 (b^2 + h^2)}{b^3 h^3 G} = \frac{2.83 i F D^3 (1 + m^2)}{m^3 h^4 G}$ ...11.14a/ Pg 141, DHB

- Spring rate, $F_0 = \frac{m^3 h^4 G}{2.83 i D^3 (1 + m^2)}$ ...11.14b/ Pg 141, DHB

Square section springs:

- Shear stress, $\tau' = \frac{2.4 KFD}{h^3}$ ...11.16/ Pg 141, DHB

- Deflection, $y = \frac{5.66 i F D^3}{h^4 G}$ ...11.17/ Pg 141, DHB

Note: Design of noncircular springs is same as that of circular springs except that wire diameter 'd' has to be replaced with 'h'.

29. A loaded narrow car of mass 1600 kg moving with a velocity of 1.2 m/s is brought to rest by a bumper consisting of two helical steel springs of square section. The mean coil diameter of the spring is 6 times the side of square. In bringing the car to rest, the springs are compressed by 200 mm, τ = 400 MPa and G = 84 GPa.

Determine: i. mean load on each spring   ii. side of the square section wire.
      iii. mean coil diameter   iv. active number of coils.

[VTU – Feb 2002 – 14 Marks]

Solution: m = 1600 kg, v = 1.2 m/s, n = 2, D = $6b$ (square c/s), y = 200 mm, τ = 400 N/mm², G = 84 × 10³ N/mm². Find: F, b, D, i.

i. To find load on each spring:

Kinetic energy of the wagon, $\quad K.E = \dfrac{mv^2}{2} = \dfrac{1600 \times 1.2^2}{2} = 1152$ N-m

$$K.E = 1.152 \times 10^6 \text{ N-mm} \quad \ldots \text{Eq. }(i)$$

Also energy absorbed by the spring $= U \cdot n$

$$= \left(\dfrac{Fy}{2}\right)n = \left(\dfrac{F \times 200}{2}\right) \times 2$$

$$= 200\,F \quad \ldots \text{Eq. }(ii)$$

Since the energy lost by the wagon = energy absorbed by the springs, equating Eqs (i) and (ii), we have

$$1.152 \times 10^6 = 200\,F$$
$$F = 5760 \text{ N}$$

ii. To find side of wire:

We know that, $\quad \tau' = \dfrac{2.4 KFD}{h^3} \quad \ldots$Eq. (iii) **11.16/ Pg 141, DHB**

$$K = \dfrac{4C-1}{4C-4} + \dfrac{0.615}{C}$$

$$= \dfrac{4 \times 6 - 1}{4 \times 6 - 4} + \dfrac{0.615}{6}$$

$$K = 1.2525$$

Eq. (iii) yields... $400 = \dfrac{2.4 \times 1.2525 \times 5760 \times 6b}{b^3} \quad (b = h, \text{ for square section})$

$$b = 16.12 \text{ mm} \approx 16.5 \text{ mm}$$

iii. Cross-section and diameters:

Side of square wire, $\quad h = b = 16.5$ mm
Mean diameter of coil, $\quad D = Cb = 6 \times 16.5 = 99$ mm
Inner diameter of coil, $\quad D_i = D - b = 99 - 16.5 = 82.5$ mm
Outer diameter of coil, $\quad D_0 = D + b = 99 + 16.5 = 115.5$ mm

iv. Number of coils:

We know that deflection, $\quad y = \dfrac{5.66\,iFD^3}{h^4 G} \quad \ldots$**11.17/ Pg 141, DHB**

$$200 = \dfrac{5.66 \times i \times 5760 \times 99^3}{16.5^4 \times 84 \times 10^3}$$

$$i = 39.36 \approx 40 \text{ turns}$$

Assuming square and ground ends, the actual number of coils,

$$i_T = i + 2 \quad \ldots \text{Tb 11.7/ Pg 152, DHB}$$
$$= 40 + 2$$
$$i_T = 42$$

274 Design of Machine Elements II (DME II)

30. A helical spring made of square steel wire is to absorb 360 N-m of energy while being compressed 150 mm. The coils have a mean diameter of seven times the side of square and the maximum induced shear stress is not to exceed 420 MPa. Take 84 GPa. Design the spring.

Solution: Energy, $U = 360$ N-m $= 360 \times 10^3$ N-mm, $y = 150$ mm, $D = 7b$, $\tau = 400$ N/mm², $G = 84 \times 10^3$ N/mm². *Design:* $(b = h, D, i, l_0, p, F_0)$.

1. To find side of wire:

We know that,
$$\tau' = \frac{2.4KFD}{h^3} \qquad \text{...Eq. (i) 11.16/ Pg 141, DHB}$$

$$K = \frac{4C-1}{4C-4} + \frac{0.615}{C}$$

$$= \frac{4 \times 7 - 1}{4 \times 7 - 4} + \frac{0.615}{7}$$

$$K = 1.213$$

Also energy absorbed by the spring $= U \cdot n$

$$= \left(\frac{Fy}{2}\right)n$$

$$360 \times 10^3 = \left(\frac{F \times 150}{2}\right) \times 1$$

$$F = 4800 \text{ N}$$

Eq. (i) yields... $400 = \dfrac{2.4 \times 1.213 \times 4800 \times 7b}{b^3}$ ($b = h$, for square section)

$$b = 15.63 \text{ mm} \approx 16 \text{ mm}$$

2. Cross-section and diameters:

Side of square wire, $h = b = 16$ mm
Mean diameter of coil, $D = Cb = 7 \times 16 = 112$ mm
Inner diameter of coil, $D_i = D - b = 112 - 16 = 96$ mm
Outer diameter of coil, $D_0 = D + b = 112 + 16 = 128$ mm

3. Number of coils:

We know that, Deflection, $y = \dfrac{5.66iFD^3}{h^4G}$ ...11.17/ Pg 141, DHB

$$150 = \frac{5.66 \times i \times 4800 \times 112^3}{16^4 \times 84 \times 10^3}$$

$$i = 21.63 \approx 22 \text{ turns}$$

Assuming square and ground ends, the actual number of coils,
$$i_T = i + 2 \qquad \text{...Tb 11.7/ Pg 152, DHB}$$
$$= 22 + 2$$
$$i_T = 24$$

4. Free length:

For square and ground ends, $l_0 = (i+1)h + y + a$ ...11.20b/ Pg 142, DHB
Here, $a = (i-1) \times 1$ mm per coil
$$a = 21 \text{ mm}$$

And $y = 150$ mm (data)

Therefore, $l_0 = (22 + 1) \times 16 + 150 + 21$

$l_0 = 539$ mm

5. Pitch of the spring:

For square and ground ends, $l_0 = ip + 2h$ ...Tb 11.7/ Pg 152, DHB

$539 = 22p + 2 \times 16$

$p = 23.04$ mm ≈ 23 mm

6. Stiffness:

We know that, $F_0 = F/y = 4800/150 = 32$ N/mm ...11.7a/ Pg 139, DHB

31. Design a rectangular section helical spring to mount to a buffer to sustain a load of 30 kN. The initial compression in the spring upon mounting is 50 mm and further deflection upon load is limited to 100 mm. The spring is made of Z-Nickel. The longer side of the section is made twice the shorter side and the spring is formed with longer side parallel to the axis. The clearance between each coil is to be 5 mm and the spring index is to be 10. Take G = 76 GPa and factor of safety 2. *[VTU – July / August 2003– 14 Marks]*

Solution: Load, $F = 30$ kN, $y_1 = 50$ mm, $y' = 100$ mm, $y_2 = y_1 + y' = 150$ mm, Material: Z- Nickel, $h = 2b$, $a = 5$ mm for each coil, $C = D/b = 10$, $G = 76 \times 10^3$ N/mm², FOS = 2. *Design*: $(b, h, D, i, l_0, p, F_0)$.

Material properties:

From **Table 11.8/ Pg 155, DHB**, for Z- Nickel,

Ultimate tensile in torsion, $\tau_u = 830$ MPa

Elastic limit in torsion, $\tau_y = 414$ MPa

Therefore, $\tau = \tau_y/FOS = 414/2 = 207$ MPa

1. To find side of wire:

We know that, $\tau' = \dfrac{KFD(1.5h + 0.96b)}{b^2 h^2}$ ...Eq. (i) **11.14/ Pg 140, DHB**

$K = \dfrac{4C - 1}{4C - 4} + \dfrac{0.615}{C}$

$= \dfrac{4 \times 10 - 1}{4 \times 10 - 4} + \dfrac{0.615}{10}$

$K = 1.145$

Eq. (i) yields... $207 = \dfrac{1.145 \times 30000 \times 10b(1.5 \times 2b + 0.96b)}{b^2 (2b)^2}$

$= \dfrac{340065 b^2}{b^4}$

$b = 40.53$ mm ≈ 41 mm

2. Cross-section and diameters:

Shorter side, $b = 41$ mm

Longer side, $h = 2b = 82$ mm

Mean diameter of coil, $D = Cb = 10 \times 41 = 410$ mm

Inner diameter of coil, $D_i = D - b = 410 - 41 = 369$ mm
Outer diameter of coil, $D_0 = D + b = 410 + 41 = 451$ mm

3. Number of coils:

We know that, Deflection, $y = \dfrac{2.83 iFD^3 (b^2 + h^2)}{b^3 h^3 G}$ ...11.14a/ Pg 141, DHB

$$150 = \dfrac{2.83 \times i \times 30000 \times 410^3 \times (41^2 + 82^2)}{41^3 \times 82^3 \times 76 \times 10^3}$$

$i = 8.81 \approx 9$ turns

Assuming square and ground ends, the actual number of coils,

$i_T = i + 2$ ...Tb 11.7/ Pg 152, DHB
$= 9 + 2$
$i_T = 11$

4. Free length:

For square and ground ends, $l_0 = (i + 1)h + y + a$ ...11.20b/ Pg 142, DHB

Here, $a = (i - 1) \times 5$ mm per coil
$a = (9 - 1) \times 5$
$a = 40$ mm

And $y = 150$ mm (data)

Therefore, $l_0 = (9 + 1) \times 82 + 150 + 40$
$l_0 = 1010$ mm

5. Pitch of the spring:

For square and ground ends, $l_0 = ip + 2h$ ...Tb 11.7/ Pg 152, DHB
$1010 = 9p + 2 \times 82$
$p = 94$ mm

6. Stiffness:

We know that, $F_0 = F/y = 30000/150 = 200$ N/mm

3.13 SPRINGS SUBJECTED TO FATIGUE/ FLUCTUATING LOADS

In many applications, compression springs are subjected to variable –or- fatigue loads. For example the valve spring of an IC engine is subjected to several millions of stress reversal during its life cycle. On the other hand, springs in linkages and mechanisms are subjected to comparatively less number of stress cycles **(Fig. 3.6)**. Other examples include the suspension systems in case of automobiles, railway carriages, etc.

Springs which carry at least 10 million stress reversal cycles before fatigue failure are called infinite life springs. Springs subjected to fluctuating loads are designed on the basis of two criteria; design for infinite life and design for finite life.

Consider a spring subjected to external fluctuating force, that changes it's magnitude from F_{max} to F_{min} as shown in **Fig 3.6(b)**. The mean force and the alternating forces are calculated as follows:

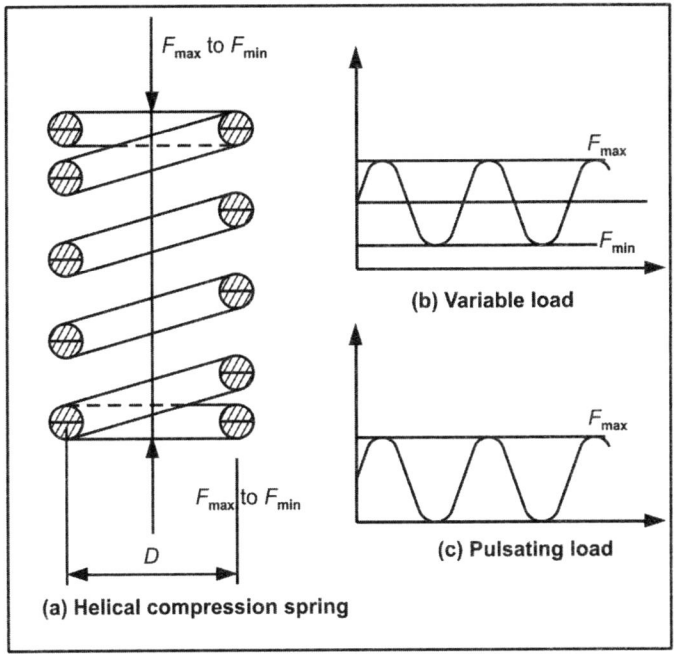

Fig. 3.6: Helical springs subjected to fluctuating load

Mean –or- average load, $\quad F_m = \dfrac{F_{max} + F_{min}}{2} \quad$ ...11.18f/ Pg 142, DHB

Alternating –or- variable load, $\quad F_a = \dfrac{F_{max} - F_{min}}{2} \quad$ ...11.18g/ Pg 142, DHB

F_m is calculated from $\tau_m = \dfrac{8 F_m D K_s}{\pi d^3} \quad$ ...11.1a/ Pg 139, DHB

Shear stress concentration factor, $K_s = 1 + \dfrac{1}{2C}$

F_a is calculated from $\tau_a = \dfrac{8 F_a D K}{\pi d^3} \quad$ ...11.1a/ Pg 139, DHB

Wahl's stress factor, $K = \dfrac{4C-1}{4C-4} + \dfrac{0.615}{C} \quad$ ...11.2b/ Pg 139, DHB

As springs are often used under continuously fluctuating loading conditions it is necessary to consider fatigue loading and stress concentration factors. Helical springs are never used under conditions of load reversals. They are either normally in tension or normally in compression. In addition springs are often pre-stressed as part of the forming process or/and preloaded, thus preventing the stress from being zero.

Figure 3.7 shows the fatigue diagram for the spring with mean stress plotted on abscissa and the variable stress on the ordinate. The value of stress at A indicates the pulsating load condition while the value of stress at B indicates the static load condition. The line joining A and B is called the *'failure line'* –or –the *'original Soderberg failure line'*. To account for the factor of safety a line CD is drawn parallel to line AB from D on the x-axis which corresponds to $\tau_y/\text{FOS} = \tau_y/n$, where n – factor of safety (FOS). The line CD is called the *'design line'* –or- the *'Modified Soderberg line'*. According to Soderberg hypothesis any point lying on the line CD –or- within the triangle CRD (ΔCRD) is considered safe.

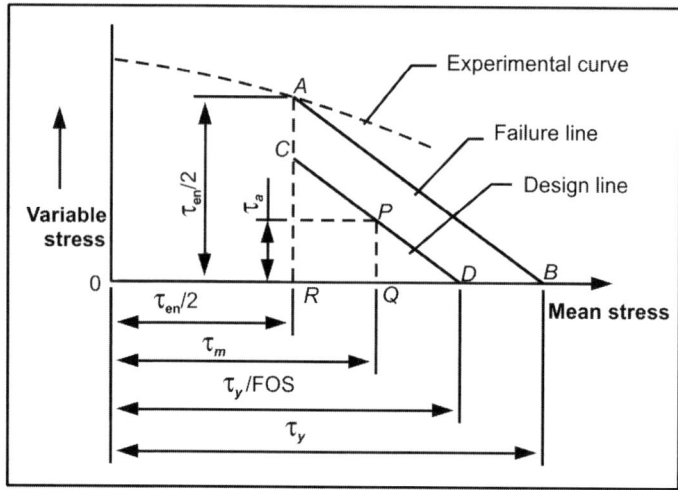

Fig. 3.7: Modified Soderberg criteria for springs

The modified design equation for springs subjected to fatigue loads is given as

$$\frac{1}{n} = \frac{\tau_m - \tau_a}{\tau_y} + \frac{2\tau_a}{\tau_{en}} \qquad \text{...(Eq. 3.18)}$$

the above equation can also be written as

$$n = \frac{\tau_y}{(\tau_m - \tau_a) + \left(\dfrac{2\tau_a \tau_y}{\tau_{en}}\right)} \qquad \text{...(Eq. 3.19)}$$

The value of τ_{en} is:

$$\tau_{en} = (0.5 - 0.6)\sigma_{en} \qquad \text{...2.19a/ Pg 17, DHB}$$
$$\sigma_{en} = 0.5\,\sigma_u \qquad \text{...(Eq. 3.20) 2.17a/ Pg 17, DHB}$$

Note: *The factor of safety in springs is less than –or- equal to 1.5.*

32. A coiled spring made of cold drawn steel wire has a mean coil diameter of 36 mm formed by 6 mm wire. it is subjected to a continuous alternating load between 500 N and 300 N. Assume ultimate shear strength as 1130 MPa, shear stress at yield point as 0.42 ultimate shear strength, and elastic strength as 0.21 ultimate shear strength. Determine the factor of safety under which the spring is operating from stand point of endurance.

Solution: Mean diameter, $D = 36$ mm, wire diameter, $d = 6$ mm, $C = 36/6 = 6$, $F_{max} = 500$ N, $F_{min} = 300$ N, $\tau_u = 1130$ MPa, $\tau_y = 0.42\,\tau_u = 474.6$ MPa, elastic –or- endurance strength $\tau_{en} = 0.21\,\tau_u = 237.6$ MPa

To find n:

We know that, $$n = \frac{\tau_y}{(\tau_m - \tau_a) + \left(\dfrac{2\tau_a \tau_y}{\tau_{en}}\right)} \qquad \text{...Eq. (i)}$$

- Shear stress concentration factor, $K_s = 1 + \dfrac{1}{2C} = 1 + \dfrac{1}{2 \times 6} = 1.083$

- Wahl's stress factor, $K = \dfrac{4C-1}{4C-4} + \dfrac{0.615}{C}$ ...**11.2b/ Pg 139, DHB**

$$= \dfrac{4 \times 6 - 1}{4 \times 6 - 4} + \dfrac{0.615}{6}$$

$$K = 1.2525$$

- Mean –or– average load, $F_m = \dfrac{F_{max} + F_{min}}{2}$ ...**11.18f/ Pg 142, DHB**

$$= \dfrac{500 + 300}{2}$$

$$F_m = 400 \text{ N}$$

- Alternating –or– variable load, $F_a = \dfrac{F_{max} - F_{min}}{2}$ ...**11.18g/ Pg 142, DHB**

$$= \dfrac{500 - 300}{2}$$

$$F_a = 100 \text{ N}$$

- Mean –or– average stress, $\tau_m = \dfrac{8F_m D K_s}{\pi d^3}$ ...**11.1a/ Pg 139, DHB**

$$= \dfrac{8 \times 400 \times 36 \times 1.083}{\pi \times 6^3}$$

$$\tau_m = 184 \text{ MPa}$$

- Alternating –or– variable stress, $\tau_a = \dfrac{8F_a D K}{\pi d^3}$ ...**11.1a/ Pg 139, DHB**

$$= \dfrac{8 \times 100 \times 36 \times 1.2525}{\pi \times 6^3}$$

$$\tau_a = 53.16 \text{ MPa}$$

Eq. (*i*) yields... $n = \dfrac{474.6}{(184 - 53.16) + \left(\dfrac{2 \times 53.16 \times 474.6}{237.3}\right)}$

$$n = 1.38$$

33. **A helical compression spring of 5.7 mm diameter carries a fluctuating load. The spring index is 6 and FOS = 1.5. if the mean load on the spring is 533 N, find the permissible values of maximum and minimum loads. Assume $\tau_u = 1620$ MPa, $\tau_y = 0.4\ \tau_u$, $\tau_{en} = 0.23\ \tau_u$.**

Solution: $d = 5.7$ mm, $C = 6$, (FOS) $n = 1.5$, $F_m = 533$ N, $\tau_u = 1620$ MPa, $\tau_y = 0.4\ \tau_u = 648$ MPa, $\tau_{en} = 0.23\ \tau_u = 372.6$ MPa, $F_{max} = ?$, $F_{min} = ?$

To find loads:

We know that, $$n = \frac{\tau_y}{(\tau_m - \tau_a) + \left(\frac{2\tau_a \tau_y}{\tau_{en}}\right)}$$ ...Eq. (i)

- Shear stress concentrationz factor, $K_s = 1 + \frac{1}{2C} = 1 + \frac{1}{2 \times 6} = 1.083$

- Wahl's stress factor, $K = \frac{4C-1}{4C-4} + \frac{0.615}{C}$ ...11.2b/ Pg 139, DHB

$$= \frac{4 \times 6 - 1}{4 \times 6 - 4} + \frac{0.615}{6}$$

$K = 1.2525$

- Mean –or- average stress, $\tau_m = \frac{8F_m D K_s}{\pi d^3} = \frac{8F_m C K}{\pi d^2}$ ...11.1a/ Pg 139, DHB

$$= \frac{8 \times 533 \times 6 \times 1.083}{\pi \times 5.7^2}$$

$\tau_m = 271.54$ MPa

Eq. (i) yields... $1.5 = \frac{648}{(271.54 - \tau_a) + \left(\frac{2\tau_a \times 648}{372.63}\right)}$

$432 = (271.54 - \tau_a) + 3.48\tau_a$

$\tau_a = 64.7$ MPa

But, alternating –or- variable stress, $\tau_a = \frac{8F_a D K}{\pi d^3} = \frac{8F_a C K}{\pi d^2}$ ...11.1a/ Pg 139, DHB

$$64.7 = \frac{8 \times F_a \times 6 \times 1.2525}{\pi \times 5.7^2}$$

$F_a = 109.85$ N

Now, mean load, $F_m = \frac{F_{max} + F_{min}}{2} = 533$ N ...11.18f/ Pg 142, DHB

$F_{max} + F_{min} = 1066$ N ...Eq. (ii)

Alternating load, $F_a = \frac{F_{max} - F_{min}}{2} = 109.85$ N ...11.18g/ Pg 142, DHB

$F_{max} - F_{max} = 217.7$ N ...Eq. (iii)

Solving Eqs (ii) and (iii) yields... $F_{max} = 642.85$ N and $F_{min} = 423.15$ N

34. A compression spring is used in service where the load is fluctuating and the maximum load on the spring is three times the amplitude. The dimensions of the spring are: coil diameter = 50 mm, wire diameter = 10 mm, factor of safety = 1.25, yield point of the spring material is 600 MPa and endurance limit = 300 MPa. Determine the maximum load permitted by Soderberg criterion for failure.

Solution: $F_{max} = 3F$, $F_{min} = F$, $d = 10$ mm, $D = 50$ mm, $C = D/d = 5$, $n = 1.25$ $\tau_y = 600$ MPa, $\tau_{en} = 300$ MPa, $F_{max} = ?$

To find loads:

We know that, $\qquad n = \dfrac{\tau_y}{(\tau_m - \tau_a) + \left(\dfrac{2\tau_a \tau_y}{\tau_{en}}\right)}$ ...Eq. (i)

- Shear stress concentration factor, $\quad K_s = 1 + \dfrac{1}{2C} = 1 + \dfrac{1}{2 \times 5} = 1.1$

- Wahl's stress factor, $\qquad K = \dfrac{4C-1}{4C-4} + \dfrac{0.615}{C}$ ...**11.2b/ Pg 139, DHB**

$$= \dfrac{4 \times 5 - 1}{4 \times 5 - 4} + \dfrac{0.615}{5}$$

$$K = 1.3105$$

- Mean load, $\qquad F_m = \dfrac{F_{max} + F_{min}}{2}$ ...**11.18f/ Pg 142, DHB**

$$= \dfrac{3F + F}{2}$$

$$F_m = 2F$$

- Alternating load, $\qquad F_a = \dfrac{F_{max} - F_{min}}{2}$ ...**11.18g/ Pg 142, DHB**

$$= \dfrac{3F - F}{2}$$

$$F_a = F$$

- Mean –or- average stress, $\qquad \tau_m = \dfrac{8 F_m D K_s}{\pi d^3}$ ...**11.1a/ Pg 139, DHB**

$$= \dfrac{8 \times 2F \times 50 \times 1.1}{\pi \times 10^3}$$

$$\tau_m = 0.280\,F$$

- Alternating –or- variable stress, $\tau_a = \dfrac{8 F_a D K}{\pi d^3}$ ...**11.1a/ Pg 139, DHB**

$$= \dfrac{8 \times F \times 50 \times 1.3105}{\pi \times 10^3}$$

$$\tau_a = 0.167\,F$$

Eq. (i) yields... $1.25 = \dfrac{600}{(0.280F - 0.167F) + \left(\dfrac{2 \times 0.167F \times 600}{300}\right)}$

$$F = 615\,\text{N}$$

Therefore, $F_{max} = 3F = 3 \times 615 = 1845\,\text{N}$
$F_{min} = F = 615\,\text{N}$

35. A helical compression spring made of oil-tempered carbon steel is subjected to a load, which varies from 400 N to 1000 N. The spring index is 6 and factor of safety is 1.25. If the yield strength in shear is 770 MPa, endurance strength in shear is 350 MPa, deflection at maximum load is 30 mm and $G = 80$ GPa, design the spring.

Solution: $F_{max} = 1000$ N, $F_{min} = 400$ N, $C = 6$, $n = 1.25$, $\tau_y = 770$ MPa, $\tau_{en} = 350$ MPa, $y = 30$ mm, $G = 80$ GPa $= 80 \times 10^3$ MPa. *Design:* $(b, h, D, i, l_0, p, F_0)$.

1. To find side of wire:

We know that, $n = \dfrac{\tau_y}{(\tau_m - \tau_a) + \left(\dfrac{2\tau_a \tau_y}{\tau_{en}}\right)}$ ...Eq. (i)

- Shear stress concentration factor, $K_s = 1 + \dfrac{1}{2C} = 1 + \dfrac{1}{2 \times 6} = 1.083$

- Wahl's stress factor, $K = \dfrac{4C - 1}{4C - 4} + \dfrac{0.615}{C}$ ...11.2b/ Pg 139, DHB

$$= \dfrac{4 \times 6 - 1}{4 \times 6 - 4} + \dfrac{0.615}{6}$$

$K = 1.2525$

- Mean –or- average load, $F_m = \dfrac{F_{max} + F_{min}}{2}$ ...11.18f/ Pg 142, DHB

$$= \dfrac{1000 + 400}{2}$$

$$= 700 \text{ N}$$

- Alternating –or- variable load, $F_a = \dfrac{F_{max} - F_{min}}{2}$ ...11.18g/ Pg 142, DHB

$$= \dfrac{1000 - 400}{2}$$

$F_a = 300$ N

- Mean –or- average stress, $\tau_m = \dfrac{8 F_m D K_s}{\pi d^3} = \dfrac{8 F_m C K_s}{\pi d^2}$ ...11.1a/ Pg 139, DHB

$$= \dfrac{8 \times 700 \times 6 \times 1.083}{\pi \times d^2}$$

$\tau_m = 11583.5/d^2$

- Alternating –or- variable stress, $\tau_a = \dfrac{8 F_a D K}{\pi d^3} = \dfrac{8 F_a C K}{\pi d^2}$ ...11.1a/ Pg 139, DHB

$$= \dfrac{8 \times 300 \times 6 \times 1.2525}{\pi \times d^2}$$

$\tau_a = 5741/d^2$

Eq. (i) yields... $1.25 = \dfrac{770}{\left(\dfrac{11583.5}{d^2} - \dfrac{5741}{d^2}\right) + \left[\dfrac{2 \times 770 \times \left(\dfrac{5741}{d^2}\right)}{350}\right]}$

$$d = 7.11 \text{ mm}$$

2. Diameters:

Standard wire diameter is $d = 7.5$ ...Tb 11.3a/ Pg 150, DHB
Mean diameter of coil, $D = 6d = 6 \times 7.5 = 45$ mm
Inner diameter of coil, $D_i = D - d = 45 - 7.5 = 37.5$ mm
Outer diameter of coil, $D_0 = D + d = 45 + 7.5 = 52.5$ mm

3. Number of coils:

We know that, $\quad i = \dfrac{yGd}{8FC^3}$ ...11.6/ Pg 139, DHB

$$= \dfrac{30 \times 80 \times 10^3 \times 7.5}{8 \times 1000 \times 6^3} \quad (F = F_{max})$$

$i = 10.42 \approx 11$ turns

Assuming square and ground ends, the actual number of coils,
$$i_T = i + 2 \quad \text{...Tb 11.7/ Pg 152, DHB}$$
$$= 11 + 2$$
$$i_T = 13$$

4. Free length:

For square and ground ends, $l_0 = (i + 1)d + y + a$ ...11.20b/ Pg 142, DHB
Here, $a = (i - 1) \times 1$ mm per coil
$a = (11 - 1) \times 1$
$a = 10$ mm
Therefore, $l_0 = (11 + 1) \times 7.5 + 30 + 10$
$l_0 = 130$ mm

5. Pitch of the spring:

For square and ground ends, $l_0 = ip + 2d$ ...Tb 11.7/ Pg 152, DHB
$130 = 11p + 2 \times 8.5$
$p = 10.27$ mm ≈ 12 mm

6. Spring stiffness:

We know that, $\quad F_0 = \dfrac{F}{y} = \dfrac{F_{max}}{y_{max}} = \dfrac{1000}{30} = 33.34$ N/mm ...11.7a/ Pg 139, DHB

3.14 HELICAL TORSION SPRINGS

These are similar to helical compression springs in form and are loaded by a torque (twisting moment) about the axis of the helix. The primary stresses in helical torsion spring are the bending (flexural) stress. These are used for transmitting smaller torques in door hinges, clock pins, window shades, automobile starters, etc. **Figure 3.8** shows one form of helical torsion spring.

Their cross-section may be circular –or- rectangular.

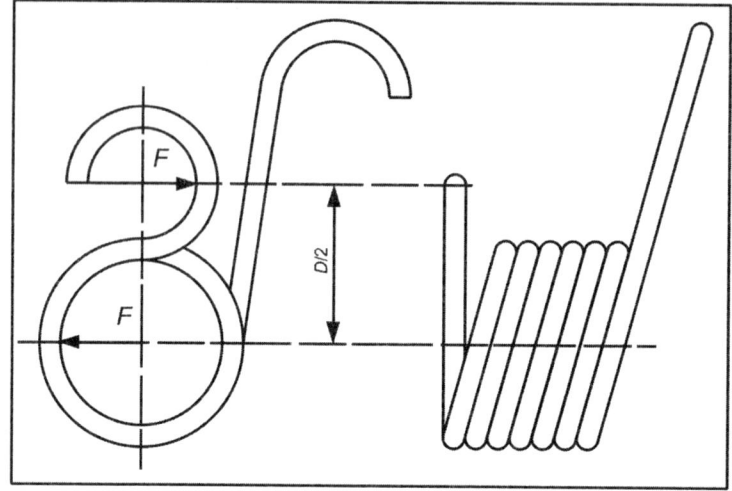

Fig. 3.8: Helical torsion spring

Circular wire:

Bending stress, $\sigma = \dfrac{8T(4K_1 D + d)}{\pi D d^3}$ ...**11.29a/ Pg 144A, DHB**

Where, T – torsional moment of the spring
D – mean diameter of the coil
d – wire diameter

K_1 – Stress factor $= \dfrac{4C - 1}{4C - 4}$ -or- $\dfrac{4C^2 - C - 1}{4C(C - 1)}$ ...**11.29b/ Pg 144A, DHB**

-or- **Fig. 11.1/ Pg 156, DHB**

Rectangular wire:

Bending stress, $\sigma = \dfrac{6K_2 T}{b^2 h} + \dfrac{2T}{DBh}$ ...**11.30/ Pg 144A, DHB**

Where, $C = D/b$
b – width of spring
h – thickness of spring
K_1 – stress factor, **Fig. 11.1/ Pg 156, DHB**

In general, deflection $y = \dfrac{TLD}{2EI}$ ...**11.28/ Pg 144A, DHB**

Where, L – length of the coil part of the spring $= \pi Di$,
I – moment of inertia of the wire

$= \dfrac{\pi d^4}{64}$ ... circular cross-section

$= \dfrac{bh^3}{12}$ ... rectangular cross-section

Angular deflection, $\theta = \dfrac{y}{R}$ ... radians

36. A helical torsion spring of mean diameter 80 mm is made of a round wire of 8 mm. If a torque of 9 N-m is applied on this spring, find the bending stress induced and the angular defection. Take E = 210 GPa and number of effective turns as 8.

Solution: $D = 80$ mm, $d = 8$ mm, $C = D/d = 80/8 = 10$, $T = 9$ N–m $= 9000$ N–mm, $E = 210$ GPa $= 210 \times 10^3$ MPa, $i = 8$, $\sigma = ?$, $\theta = ?$

a. To find σ:

We know that, $\sigma = \dfrac{8T(4K_1 D + d)}{\pi D d^3}$ ...Eq. (i) ...**11.29a/ Pg 144A, DHB**

But $K_1 = \dfrac{4C^2 - C - 1}{4C(C-1)}$ ...**11.29b/ Pg 144A, DHB**

$= \dfrac{4 \times 10^2 - 10 - 1}{4 \times 10 \times (10-1)}$

$K_1 = 1.081$

Eq. (i) yields... $\sigma = \dfrac{8 \times 9000 \times (4 \times 1.081 \times 80 + 8)}{\pi \times 80 \times 8^3}$

$\sigma = 198$ MPa

b. To find θ:

We know that, $\theta = \dfrac{y}{R}$ ...Eq. (ii)

But deflection, $y = \dfrac{TLD}{2EI}$ ...**11.28/ Pg 144A, DHB**

$= \dfrac{9000 \times (\pi \times 80 \times 8) \times 80}{2 \times 210 \times 10^3 \times \left(\dfrac{\pi \times 8^4}{64}\right)}$

$y = 17.14$ mm

Eq. (ii) yields... $\theta = \dfrac{17.14}{(80/2)}$

$\theta = 0.43$ rad $= 24.56°$.

37. The free end of a torsional spring deflects through 90 degrees when subjected to a torque of 6 N-m. If the spring index is 6 find the effective number of turns. Assume E = 200 GPa, and bending stress as 450 MPa.

Solution: $\theta = 90° = 1.57$ rad, $T = 6$ N-m, $= 6000$ N-mm, $C = 6$, $d = ?$, $i = ?$, $E = 200$ GPa $= 2 \times 10^5$ MPa, $\sigma = 450$ MPa.

a. To find i:

We know that, $\theta = \dfrac{y}{R}$

Therefore, $y = R\theta$
$= (D/2) \times 1.57$
$y = 0.785\, D$ ...Eq. (i)

but $\sigma = \dfrac{8T(4K_1 D + d)}{\pi D d^3}$ ...Eq. (ii) **11.29a/ Pg 144A, DHB**

$K_1 = \dfrac{4C^2 - C - 1}{4C(C-1)}$ ...**11.29b/ Pg 144A, DHB**

$= \dfrac{4 \times 6^2 - 6 - 1}{4 \times 6 \times (6-1)}$

$K_1 = 1.142$

Eq. (ii) yields... $450 = \dfrac{8 \times 6000 \times (4 \times 1.1421 \times 6d + d)}{\pi \times 6d \times d^3}$ ($D = 6d$)

$d^3 = 160.71$
$d = 5.44$ mm

Therefore, standard size, $d = 5.6$ mm, ...**Tb 11.3a. Pg 150, DHB**
$D = 33.6$ mm

Eq. (i) yields... $y = 0.785 \times 33.6 = 26.4$ mm

Also, $y = \dfrac{TLD}{2EI}$ ...**11.28/ Pg 144A, DHB**

$26.4 = \dfrac{6000 \times (\pi \times 33.6 \times i) \times 33.6}{2 \times 200 \times 10^3 \times \left(\dfrac{\pi \times 5.6^4}{64}\right)}$ ($L = \pi D_i / 1 = \pi d^4/64$)

$i = 23.95 \approx 24$ coils.

38. A pivoted roller follower is held in contact with a cam by a torsion spring. The moment exerted by the spring varies from 3 N-m to 5 N-m as the follower oscillates through 30°. Design a suitable spring using a factor of safety of 1.5, based on Soderberg line. Take C = 6, ultimate tensile strength of steel = 1400 MPa, yield strength as 1200 MPa, E = 210 GPa.

Solution: $T_{max} = 5000$ N-mm, $T_{min} = 3000$ N-mm, $\theta = 30° = 0.524$ rad, $C = 6$, $n = 1.5$, $\sigma_u = 1400$ MPa, $\sigma_y = 1200$ MPa, $E = 210$ GPa $= 210 \times 10^3$ MPa. *Design:* (d, D, i, y, L) $\sigma_{en} = \sigma_u/2 = 700$ MPa.

1. To find side of wire:

We know that, $n = \dfrac{\sigma_y}{(\sigma_m - \sigma_a) + \left(\dfrac{2\sigma_a \sigma_y}{\sigma_{en}}\right)}$ ...Eq. (i)

- Wahl's stress factor, $K_1 = \dfrac{4C^2 - C - 1}{4C(C-1)}$ ...11.29b/ Pg 144A, DHB

$$= \dfrac{4 \times 6^2 - 6 - 1}{4 \times 6 \times (6-1)}$$

$$K_1 = 1.142$$

- Mean torque, $T_m = \dfrac{T_{max} + T_{min}}{2}$ (in terms of torque) ...11.18f/ Pg 142, DHB

$$= \dfrac{5000 + 3000}{2}$$

$$T_m = 4000 \text{ N}$$

- Alternating torque, $T_a = \dfrac{T_{max} - T_{min}}{2}$ ...11.18g/ Pg 142, DHB

$$= \dfrac{5000 - 3000}{2}$$

$$T_a = 1000 \text{ N}$$

- Mean stress, $\sigma_m = \dfrac{8T_m(4K_1 D + d)}{\pi D d^3}$ ...11.29a/ Pg 144A, DHB

$$= \dfrac{8 \times 4000 \times (4 \times 1.142 \times 6d + d)}{\pi \times 6d \times d^3}$$

$$\sigma_m = 48213.3 \, d^3$$

- Alternate stress, $\sigma_a = \dfrac{8T_a(4K_1 D + d)}{\pi D d^3}$ ...11.29a/ Pg 144A, DHB

$$= \dfrac{8 \times 1000 \times (4 \times 1.142 \times 6d + d)}{\pi \times 6d \times d^3}$$

$$\sigma_a = 12053.3 \, d^3$$

Eq. (i) yields... $1.5 = \dfrac{1200}{(48213.3 - 12053.3)d^3 + \dfrac{2 \times 12053.3 d^3 \times 1200}{700}}$

$$d = 4.59 \text{ mm}$$

a. Diameters:
Standard wire diameter is $d = 4.75$ mm
Mean diameter of coil, $D = Cd = 6 \times 4.75 = 28.5$ mm

b. To find y:

We know that, $\theta = \dfrac{y}{R}$ ...Tb 11.3a/ Pg 150, DHB

Therefore, $y = R\theta$

$$= (28.5/2) \times 0.524$$
$$y = 7.461 \text{ mm}$$

c. To find i:

We know that, $\quad y = y_{max} = \dfrac{T_{max} L D}{2EI}$ ...11.28/ Pg 144A, DHB

$$7.461 = \dfrac{5000 \times (\pi \times 28.5 \times i) \times 28.5}{2 \times 210 \times 10^3 \times \left(\dfrac{\pi \times 4.75^4}{64}\right)} \quad (L = \pi D i, \text{ and } I = \pi d^4/64)$$

$$i = 6.1 \approx 6$$

d. Length of the coil:

We know that, $\quad L = \pi D i = \pi \times 28.5 \times 6 = 537.2 \text{ mm}$.

39. Design a helical torsion spring for a window shade made from patented and cold drawn steel wire of grade 4. The yield strength of the material is 60% of the ultimate tensile strength and the FOS = 2. Due to space considerations, the mean diameter is kept as 18 mm. The maximum bending moment acting on the spring is 250 N-mm. The stiffness of the spring should be 3 N-mm/rad.

Solution: $\sigma_y = 0.6\ \sigma_u$, $n = 2$, $D = 18$ mm, $T = 250$ N–mm, $F_0 = 3$ N–mm/rad.

Material: Patented and cold drawn steel wire – Grade 4.

Trial- 1:

Material	Patented and cold drawn steel wire-Unalloyed	
Grade	4	Tb 11.14/ Pg 155C, DHB
Wire diameter	1.5	
Tensile strength, σ	2260 MPa	
Rigidity modulus, G	210790 MPa	

We know that, $\quad \sigma_t = \dfrac{\sigma_{yt}}{n} = \dfrac{0.6 \sigma_u}{n}$

$$= \dfrac{0.6 \times 2260}{2}$$

$$\sigma_t = 678 \text{ MPa}$$

But $\quad \sigma = \dfrac{8T(4K_1 D + d)}{\pi D d^3}$ ...Eq. (*i*) 11.29a/ Pg 144A, DHB

$$K_1 = \dfrac{4C^2 - C - 1}{4C(C-1)} \quad \text{...11.29b/ Pg 144A, DHB}$$

$$= \dfrac{4 \times 12^2 - 12 - 1}{4 \times 12 \times (12-1)} \quad (C = D/d = 18/1.5 = 12)$$

$$K_1 = 1.066$$

Eq. (i) yields... $\sigma = \dfrac{8 \times 250 \times (4 \times 1.066 \times 18 + 1.5)}{\pi \times 18 \times 1.5^3}$

$\sigma = 820.25$ MPa > 678 MPa.

Hence the selected diameter is not safe.

Trial- 2:

Material	Patented and cold drawn steel wire-Unalloyed	
Grade	4	
Wire diameter	1.7	Tb 11.14/ Pg 155C, DHB
Tensile strength, σ	2220 MPa	
Rigidity modulus, G	210790 MPa	

We know that, $\quad \sigma_t = \dfrac{\sigma_{yt}}{n} = \dfrac{0.6\sigma_u}{n}$

$= \dfrac{0.6 \times 2220}{2}$

$\sigma_t = 666$ MPa

But $\sigma = \dfrac{8T(4K_1 D + d)}{\pi D d^3}$ ...Eq. (ii) **11.29a/ Pg 144A, DHB**

$K_1 = \dfrac{4C^2 - C - 1}{4C(C - 1)}$ ...**11.29b/ Pg 144A, DHB**

$= \dfrac{4 \times 10.6^2 - 10.6 - 1}{4 \times 10.6 \times (10.6 - 1)} \quad (C = D/d = 18/1.7 = 10.6)$

$K_1 = 1.076$

Eq. (ii) yields... $\sigma = \dfrac{8 \times 250 \times (4 \times 1.076 \times 18 + 1.7)}{\pi \times 18 \times 1.7^3}$

$\sigma = 569.7$ MPa < 666 MPa.

Hence the selected diameter is safe.

Thus the standard diameter is $d = 1.7$ mm

a. To find i:

The stiffness of a torsional spring is $\quad F_0 = \dfrac{T}{\theta}$ ...Eq. (iii)

But, $\theta = \dfrac{y}{R}$ ...Eq. (iv)

Also, $y = \dfrac{TLD}{2EI}$ ...Eq. (v) **11.28/ Pg 144A, DHB**

Substituting Eq. (iv) in Eq. (iii) yields,

$\theta = \dfrac{64Di}{Ed^4} T$

Eq.(iii) yields... $F_0 = \dfrac{T}{\theta} = \dfrac{Ed^4}{64Di}$ ...Eq. (iv)

$$3 = \dfrac{210790 \times 1.7^4}{64 \times 18 \times i}$$

$i = 509.42 \approx 510$ coils

b. To find y:

We know that, $y = \dfrac{TLD}{2EI}$ ...11.28/ Pg 144A, DHB

$$= \dfrac{250 \times (\pi \times 18 \times 510) \times 18}{2 \times 210790 \times \left(\dfrac{\pi \times 1.7^4}{64}\right)} \quad (L = \pi Di, \text{ and } I = \pi d^4/64)$$

$y = 750.86$ mm

c. Length of the coil:

We know that, $L = \pi Di$
$= \pi \times 18 \times 510$
$L = 28839.82$ mm

3.15 DISC -OR- BELLEVILLE SPRINGS

These are also called as *coned disc springs –or- Belleville washers* and are used to support large loads with small deflection. Their cross-section is coned with a thickness of 't' and an inside height of cone as 'h' as shown in **Fig. 3.9(a)**. When load is applied, the disk tends to flatten and the elastic deformation constitutes the spring action. These may be stacked in series –or- parallel –or- a combination of both as shown in **Fig 3.9 (b) and (c).**

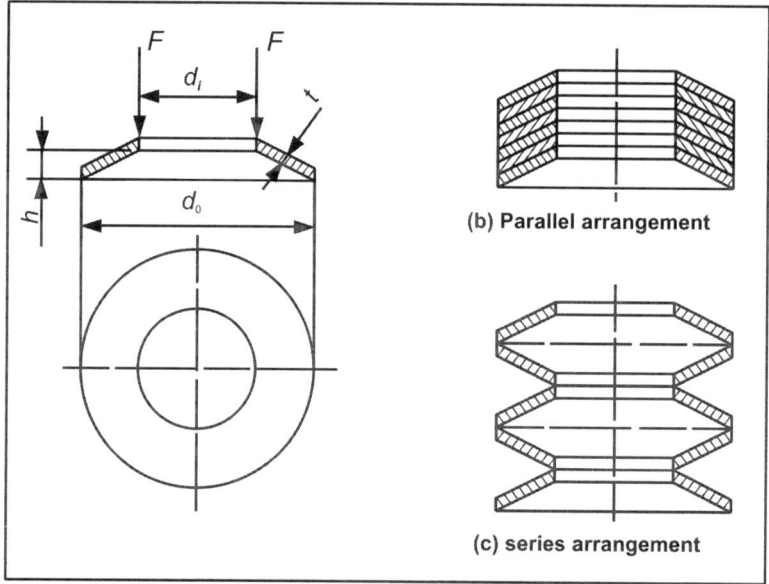

Fig. 3.9: (a) Disc -or- belleville spring (b) parallel arrangement (c) series arrangement
(Fig. 11.7a/Pg 15C, DHB)

Applications:

Bolted connections, clutch plate supports, gun recoil mechanism, etc.

Let, F = Load on the spring, $\qquad$ t = Thickness of the disc,
h = Free height of the truncated cone, d_0 = Outside diameter of the disc,
d_i = Inside diameter of the disc, $\qquad$ E = Young's modulus,
μ = Poisson's ratio, $\qquad$ σ_0 = Maximum stress at outer edge,
σ_i = Maximum stress at inner edge, $\qquad$ y = Deflection of the disc.

When the load is applied uniformly around the edge, the relation between the applied load and the axial deflection is [**Fig. 11.7/ Pg 157C, DHB**]

$$F = \frac{4Ey}{(1-\mu^2)Md_0^2}\left[(h-y)(h-0.5y)t + t^3\right] \qquad \text{...11.44/ Pg 146, DHB}$$

The maximum stress at the inner edge is

$$\sigma_i = \frac{4Ey}{(1-\mu^2)Md_0^2}\left[C_1\left(h-\frac{y}{2}\right) + C_2 t\right] \qquad \text{...11.45a/ Pg 146, DHB}$$

The stress at the outer edge is

$$\sigma_0 = \frac{4Ey}{(1-\mu^2)Md_0^2}\left[C_1\left(h-\frac{y}{2}\right) - C_2 t\right] \qquad \text{...11.45b/ Pg 146, DHB}$$

M, C_1, C_2 – Constants which depend upon (d_0/d_i) ...**Fig. 11.7/ Pg 157C, DHB**
-or- The values of M, C_1, C_2 can also be obtained using equations
$\qquad\qquad\qquad\qquad\qquad\qquad\qquad\qquad\qquad\qquad$ ...**11.45c to 11.45e/ Pg 146, DHB**

40. A disc spring is made of 3 mm sheet steel with an outside diameter of 130 mm and an inside diameter of 50 mm. The spring is dished 5 mm. The maximum stress is 600 MPa. Determine:

a. the safe axial load carried by the spring
b. deflection at this load.
c. stress produces at the inner edge. Take μ = 0.3 and E = 200 GPa.

Solution: t = 3 mm, d_0 = 130 mm, d_i = 50 mm, h = 5 mm, maximum stress, σ_i = 600 MPa. μ = 0.3, E = 2 × 10^5 MPa. a. F = ?, b. y = ? c. σ_0 = ?

a. To find F:

We know that, $F = \dfrac{4Ey}{(1-\mu^2)Md_0^2}\left[(h-y)(h-0.5y)t + t^3\right]$ ...Eq. (*i*) **11.44/ Pg 146, DHB**

Also maximum stress at inner edge,

$$\sigma_i = \frac{4Ey}{(1-\mu^2)Md_0^2}\left[C_1\left(h-\frac{y}{2}\right) + C_2 t\right] \qquad \text{...Eq. (}ii\text{) 11.45a/ Pg 146, DHB}$$

Here M, C_1, C_2 – constants which depend upon d_0/d_i
Therefore, $\qquad d_0/d_i = 130/50 = 2.6$,
$\qquad\qquad\qquad M = 0.75, C_1 = 1.35, C_2 = 1.58$ ...**Fig. 11.7/ Pg 157C, DHB**

Eq. (ii) yields... $600 = \dfrac{4 \times 2 \times 10^5 \times y}{(1-0.3^2) \times 0.75 \times 130^2}[1.35(5-0.5y)+1.58 \times 3]$

$= 69.36y\,(11.49 - 0.675y)$

$8.65 = 11.49y - 0.675y^2$

$0.675y^2 - 11.49y + 8.65 = 0$

Solving the above quadratic equation we have $y = 16.23$ mm, 0.79 mm.
Taking minimum value, we have $y = 0.79$ mm.

Eq. (i) yields... $F = \dfrac{4 \times 2 \times 10^5 \times 0.79}{(1-0.3^2) \times 0.75 \times 130^2}\big[(5-0.79)(5-0.5 \times 0.79)3 + 3^3\big]$

$F = 4666.26$ N

b. To find y: $y = 0.79$ mm.

c. To find σ_0:

We know that, $\sigma_0 = \dfrac{4Ey}{(1-\mu^2)Md_0^2}\left[C_1\left(h-\dfrac{y}{2}\right)-C_2 t\right]$ ...11.45b/ Pg 146, DHB

$= \dfrac{4 \times 2 \times 10^5 \times 0.79}{(1-0.3^2) \times 0.75 \times 130^2}\big[1.35(5 - 0.5 \times 0.79) - 1.58 \times 3\big]$

$\sigma_0 = 80.92$ MPa.

41. A steel Belleville spring is compressed flat by exerting a load of 1 kN. For maximum compression, the induced stress is 1200 MPa. Calculate the thickness and outside diameter of the spring if the ratio of height to thickness is 1.6 and the ratio of outside diameter to inside diameter is 5.

Solution: $F = 1000$ N, maximum stress, $\sigma_i = 1200$ MPa, $d_0/d_i = 5$, $h/t = 1.6$. $t = ?$, $d_0 = ?$
Material properties: For steel, $E = 2 \times 10^5$ MPa, $\mu = 0.3$

a. To find t:

As per given data for maximum compression, i.e. the spring is compressed flat, we have $y = h$

We know that, $F = \dfrac{4Ey}{(1-\mu^2)Md_0^2}\big[(h-y)(h-0.5y)t + t^3\big]$ ...Eq. (i)

...11.44/ Pg 146, DHB

For $d_0/d_i = 5$, we have
$M = 0.78$, $C_1 = 1.75$ $C_2 = 2.35$ ...Fig. 11.7/ Pg 157C, DHB

Substituting $y = h$ and $h = 1.6t$

Eq. (i) yields... $1000 = \dfrac{4 \times 2 \times 10^5 \times 1.6t}{(1-0.3^2) \times 0.78 \times d_0^2}[0 + t^3]$

$= (1803.32 \times 3.755)\left(\dfrac{t^4}{d_0^2}\right)$

$$d_0^2 = 1803.32\, t^4 \qquad \text{...Eq. (ii)}$$

Also, $\sigma_i = \dfrac{4Ey}{(1-\mu^2)Md_0^2}\left[C_1\left(h-\dfrac{y}{2}\right)+C_2 t\right]$ ...**11.45a/ Pg 146, DHB**

$$1200 = \dfrac{4\times 2\times 10^5 \times 1.6t}{(1-0.3^2)\times 0.78 \times d_0^2}\left[1.75(1.6t - 0.5\times 1.6t)+2.35t\right]$$

$$= (1803.32\times 10^3)\times 3.755\left(\dfrac{t^2}{d_0^2}\right)$$

$$d_0^2 = 5635.38\, t^2 \qquad \text{...Eq. (iii)}$$

Equating Eqs (ii) and (iii)

$$1803.32\, t^4 = 5635.38\, t^2$$
$$t = 1.76\text{ mm} \approx 2\text{ mm}$$

b. To find d_0:
substituting t in Eq. (ii) –or– Eq. (iii) yields,
$$d_0^2 = 5635.38 \times 2^2$$
$$d_0 = 150.14 \text{ mm} \simeq 150 \text{ mm}.$$

42. A Belleville spring made of steel is subjected to a load of 2.5 kN. For deflection of the spring is equal to half the height, the stress induced is 560 MPa. Calculate the size parameters of the spring, if the ratio of height to thickness is 2 and the ratio of outside diameter to inside diameter is 1.5.

Solution: $F = 2500$ N, $y = h/2$, maximum stress, $\sigma_i = 560$ MPa, $h/t = 2$, $d_0/d_i = 1.5$
   a. $t = ?$,   b. $h = ?$,   c. $y = ?$,   d. $d_0 = ?$,   e. $d_i = ?$

Material properties: For steel, $E = 2\times 10^5$ MPa, $\mu = 0.3$

a. To find t:

We know that, $F = \dfrac{4Ey}{(1-\mu^2)Md_0^2}\left[(h-y)(h-0.5y)t + t^3\right]$ ...Eq. (i) **11.44/ Pg 146, DHB**

For $d_0/d_i = 1.5$, we have
$$M = 0.53,\quad C_1 = 1.08,\quad C_2 = 1.18 \qquad \text{...Fig. 11.7/ Pg 157C, DHB}$$
Given, $y = h/2$ and $h/t = 2$, i.e. $h = 2t$ and

Simplifying the given relations we have
$$y = 2t/2$$
$$y = t \qquad \text{...Eq. (ii)}$$

Eq. (i) yields... $2500 = \dfrac{4\times 2\times 10^5 \times t}{(1-0.3^2)\times 0.53 \times d_0^2}\left[(2t-t)(2t-0.5t)t + t^3\right]$

$$= 4.15 \times 10^6\left(\dfrac{t^4}{d_0^2}\right)$$

$$d_0^2 = 1658.7\, t^4 \qquad \text{...Eq. (iii)}$$

Also, $\sigma_i = \dfrac{4Ey}{(1-\mu^2)Md_0^2}\left[C_1\left(h-\dfrac{y}{2}\right)+C_2 t\right]$ ...11.45b/ Pg 146, DHB

$$560 = \dfrac{4\times 2\times 10^5 \times t}{(1-0.3^2)\times 0.53 \times d_0^2}\left[1.08(2t-0.5\times t)+1.18t\right]$$

$$= 4.64\times 10^6 \left(\dfrac{t^2}{d_0^2}\right)$$

$$d_0^2 = 8293.6\ t^2 \qquad \text{...Eq. (iv)}$$

Equating Eqs (ii) and (iii)

$$1658.7\ t^4 = 8293.6\ t^2$$

$$t = 2.23\text{ mm} \approx 3\text{ mm}$$

Eq. (ii) yields... $y = t = 3$ mm

Eq. (iv) yields... $d_0^2 = 8293.6 \times 3^2$

$$d_0 = 273.20\text{ mm} \approx 274\text{ mm}$$

Given, $h/t = 2$, therefore $h = 2t = 6$ mm

$$d_0/d_i = 1.5$$

i.e. $274/1.5 = d_i$

$$d_i = 182.67\text{ mm} \approx 184\text{ mm}$$

b. To find σ_0:

We know that, $\sigma_0 = \dfrac{4Ey}{(1-\mu^2)Md_0^2}\left[C_1\left(h-\dfrac{y}{2}\right)-C_2 t\right]$ ...11.45b/ Pg 146, DHB

$$= \dfrac{4\times 2\times 10^5 \times 3}{(1-0.3^2)\times 0.53 \times 274^2}\left[1.08(6-0.5\times 3)-1.18\times 3\right]$$

$$\sigma_0 = 87.50\text{ MPa}.$$

3.16 LEAF SPRINGS

The term *leaf spring* –or- *flat spring* applies to a wide variety of shapes made out of flat strip. An advantage of leaf spring over helical spring is that the ends of the spring may be guided along a definite path as it deflects. Thus the spring may act as a structural member in addition to energy absorbing device. Thus the leaf springs may carry lateral loads, brake torque, driving torque etc., in addition to shocks.

Leaf springs can be designed to have progressive spring rates. This "non-linear spring constant" is useful for vehicles which must operate with widely varying loads, such as trucks.

The leaf spring may be arranged as a cantilever –or- a simply supported member.

Case 1: Cantilever arrangement:

Consider a rectangular flat strip of uniform width as shown in **Fig. 3.10 (a)**.

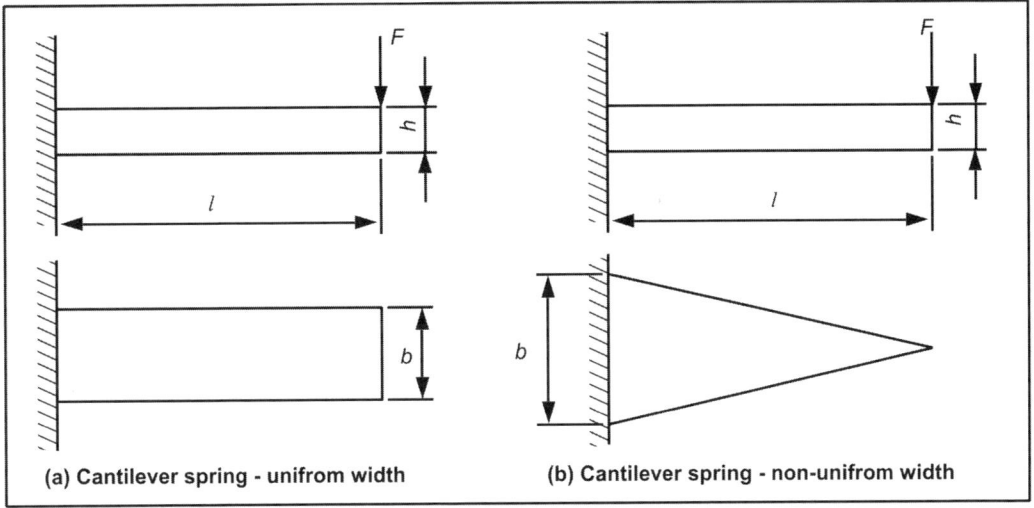

Fig. 3.10: Beams with rectangular section
(Fig. 11.6 a and b/ Pg 157C, DHB)

Let, F = applied load
b = width of flat spring.
h = depth/ thickness of spring.
l = length of the plate

We know that the bending stress is

$$\sigma = \frac{M}{Z}$$

$$= \frac{Wl}{I/y} = \frac{Fl}{\dfrac{bh^3}{12} \Big/ \dfrac{h}{2}} \qquad (W - \text{load in general terms})$$

$$\sigma = \frac{6Fl}{bh^2} = \frac{C_1 Fl}{bh^2} \qquad (C_1 = 6) \quad \text{...(Eq. 3.21)}\ \textbf{11.31/ Pg 144A, DHB}$$

And the deflection of the cantilver with a concnetrated load at free end is

$$y = \frac{Wl^3}{3EI} \qquad \text{...Tb 1.4 - Fig. 1/ Pg 10, DHB}$$

$$= \frac{Fl^3}{3E\left(\dfrac{bh^3}{12}\right)}$$

$$y = \frac{4Fl^3}{Ebh^3} = \frac{C_2 Fl^3}{Ebh^3} \qquad (C_2 = 4) \quad \text{...(Eq. 3.22)}\ \textbf{11.32/ Pg 144A, DHB}$$

The thickness of the spring plate is obtained by equating Eq. (3.21) and Eq. (3.22) in terms of 'b'

$$\frac{C_1 Fl}{\sigma h^2} = \frac{C_2 Fl^3}{Eyh^3}$$

$$h = \frac{C_2 \sigma l^2}{C_1 Ey} \qquad \text{...(Eq. 3.23) 11.33/ Pg 144A, DHB}$$

The width of the plate is found from (Eq. 3.21) as

$$h = \frac{C_1 Fl}{\sigma h^2} \qquad \text{...(Eq. 3.24) 11.34/ Pg 144A, DHB}$$

Here C_1 and C_2 are constants obtained from **Table 11.1/ Pg 149, DHB** for various types of beams, as shown in **Fig 11.6/ Pg 157C, DHB**.

Case 2: Simply supported arrangement:

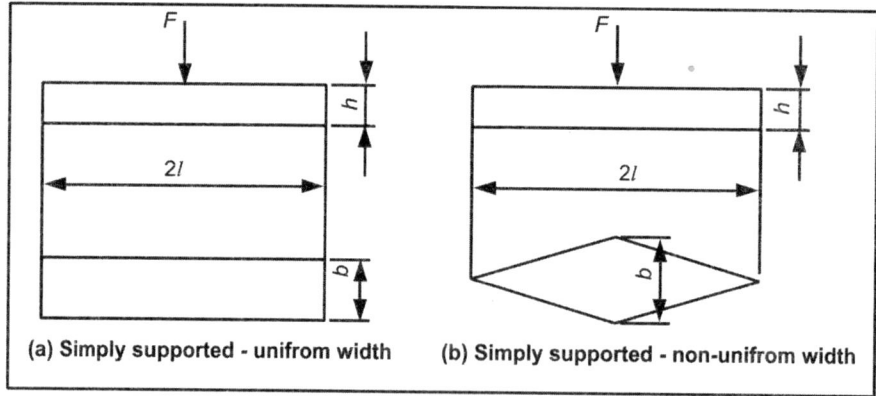

Fig. 3.11: Beam with rectangular section
(Fig. 11.6 d and e/Pg 157C, DHB)

On similar lines, for **Fig. 3.11 (a)**, we have

$$\text{Bending stress, } \sigma = \frac{Wl}{I/y} = \frac{(F/2)l}{\dfrac{bh^3}{2} / \dfrac{h}{2}} \qquad (W - \text{load in general terms})$$

Here, using **Fig. 3.11(a)**

$$\sigma = \frac{3Fl}{bh^2} \qquad (C_1 = 3) \qquad \text{...(Eq. 3.25)}$$

...Tb 11.1/ Pg 149, DHB and Fig 11.6 d/ Pg 157C, DHB

$$\text{Deflection, } y = \frac{Wl^3}{48EI} \qquad \text{...Tb 1.4 - Fig. 4/ Pg 10, DHB}$$

$$= \frac{\left(\dfrac{F}{2}\right)l^3}{48E\left(\dfrac{bh^3}{12}\right)}$$

$$y = \frac{2Fl^3}{Ebh^3} \qquad (C_2 = 2) \qquad \text{...(Eq. 3.26)}$$

...Tb 11.1/ Pg 149, DHB & Fig 11.6 d/ Pg 157C, DHB

It is observed that in beams of uniform width, the stresses act heavily at one specific point rather than equally along the length of the plate. Thus, uniform strength is achieved either by keeping the thickness –or– the width as constant. The general procedure adopted is to keep the thickness constant and vary the width as shown in **Figs 3.10 (b) and 3.11 (b).**

3.17 LAMINATED SPRING

Beams of uniform strength permit a considerable saving in material and at the same time provide greater deflection. Thus their resilience and capacity for absorbing shocks is greater. In designing a spring of uniform strength, the width of the spring is increased which becomes too large in case of a single leaf spring. In order to decrease the width, a diamond shaped plate in case of simply supported beams and a triangular shape plate for cantilever can be used which is cut into several strips as shown in **Fig 3.12.** The central strip, marked 1 is the master leaf which is placed at the top. Then two pieces, marked 2 are put together, side by side to form another leaf and placed below the top leaf. In the similar manner other pairs of strips, marked 3 and 4 respectively are placed in the decreasing order of strip length to form a laminated spring. The width of each leaf is $b' = b/i$, where i is the number of leaves.

These are commonly used in automobiles, railway cars, etc. The maximum bending stress and deflection values for these springs are same as that of the original plate, except that width b is replaced with Nb.

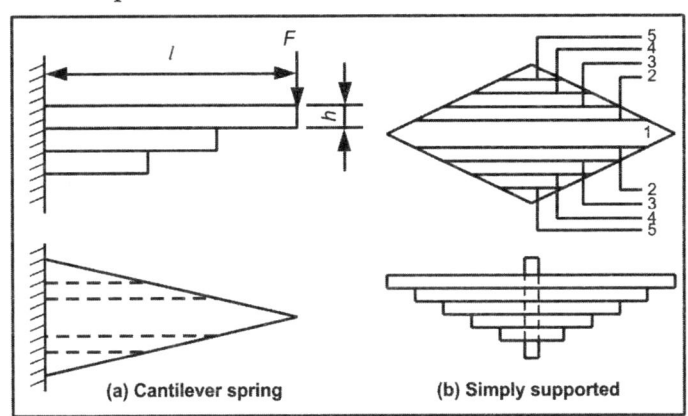

Fig. 3.12: Laminated springs

For cantilever spring:

$$\text{Bending stress, } \sigma = \frac{6Fl}{ib'h^2} \qquad (C_1 = 6) \qquad \text{...11.36/ Pg 144A, DHB}$$

and

$$\text{Deflection, } y = \frac{6Fl^3}{Eib'h^3} \qquad (C_2 = 6) \qquad \text{...11.37/ Pg 145, DHB}$$

...Tb 11.1/ Pg 149, DHB and Fig 11.6 b/ Pg 157C, DHB

For simply supported spring:

$$\text{Bending stress, } \sigma = \frac{3Fl}{ib'h^2} \qquad (C_1 = 3) \qquad \text{...11.36/ Pg 144A, DHB}$$

and

$$\text{deflection, } y = \frac{3Fl^3}{Eib'h^3} \qquad (C_2 = 3) \qquad \text{...11.37/ Pg 145, DHB}$$

...Tb 11.1/ Pg 149, DHB and Fig 11.6 e/ Pg 157C, DHB

3.18 SEMI-ELLIPTICAL LAMINATED SPRING

Construction:

The most common type of leaf spring is the semi-elliptic leaf spring as shown in **Fig. 3.13**, used in suspensions of automobiles and railway wagons. A multi-leaf spring consists of a series of flat plates, usually of semi-elliptical shape known as leaves of the spring and have graduated lengths. The top most leaf has the maximum length and the length gradually decreases from top leaf to the the bottom leaf. The longest leaf is called the *master leaf –or- main leaf* and has its ends bent in the form of a of an eye. The shorter leaves are known as *graduated leaves*. The leaves are held together by two U-bolts and a center clip. Rebound clips are provided to keep the leaves in alignment and prevent lateral shifting of the leaves during operation. In adddition to the master leaf, one –or- two extra full length leaves are stacked between the master leaf and the graduated leaves to suuport the transverse shear force.

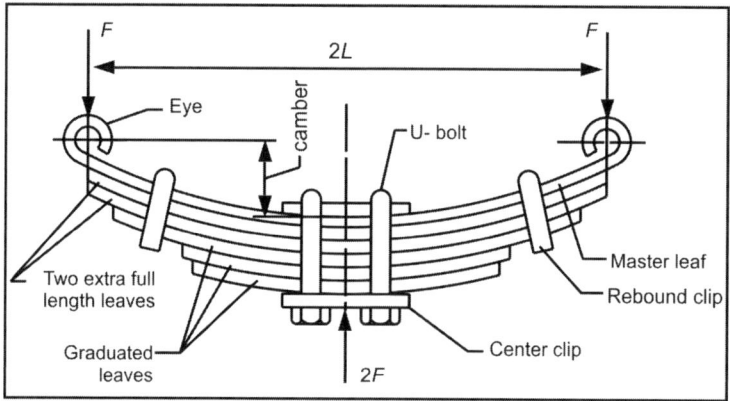

Fig. 3.13: Laminated springs (semi-elliptical)

Analysis:

Let, i_f = be the number of Main/ Full length leaves

i_g = be the number of graduated length leaves

i = be the total number of leaves $(i_f + i_g)$

$2l$ = length of cantilever

l = distance from center of eye to edge of spring band –or- half length of spring

F_f = be the load shared by full leaves

F_g = be the load shared by graduated leaves

F = be the total load on spring $(F_f + F_g)$

σ_f = be the stress in full length leaves

σ_g = be the stress in graduated leaves

b' = be the width of laminated spring $(b' = b/i)$

b = width of flat spring, i = no. of springs/ leaves.

h = be the thickness of spring.

For analysis, half portion of the spring is considered as cantilever. The graduated leaves along with master leaf are treated as a triangular plate of thickness h and maximum width at the support as $i_g b'$, as shown in **Fig. 3.14 (a).**

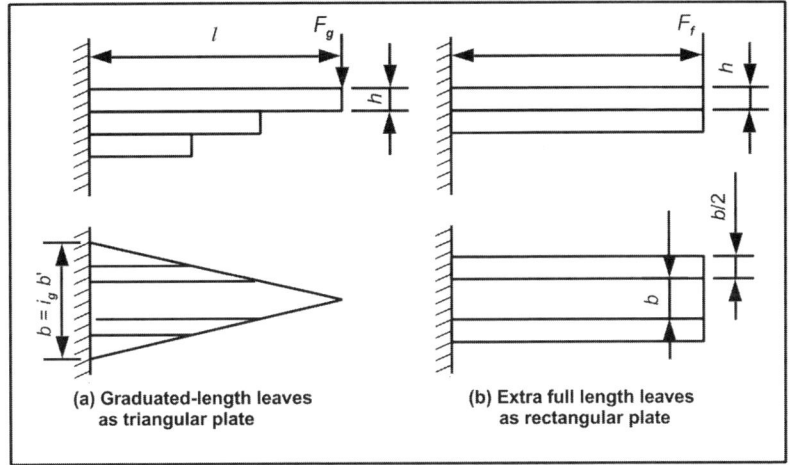

Fig. 3.14: Analysis of laminated springs

We know that, for a leaf spring $\sigma = \dfrac{C_1 Fl}{bh^2}$ *[as in equation (3.21)]* ...**11.31/ Pg 144A, DHB**

For a laminated spring, $\quad b = ib'$, $\hspace{4cm}$ ...**11.35/ Pg 144A, DHB**

$$\text{Therefore,} \quad \sigma = \dfrac{C_1 Fl}{ib'h^2} \qquad \text{...(Eq. 3.27)}$$

$$F = \dfrac{\sigma ib'h^2}{C_1 l} \qquad \text{...(Eq. 3.28)} \; \textbf{11.36/ Pg 144A, DHB}$$

Here $(C_1 = 6)$ $\hspace{3cm}$ ...**Tb 11.1/ Pg 149, DHB** and **Fig 11.6 b/ Pg 157C, DHB**

Thus for graduated leaves, Eq. (3.27) yields...

$$\sigma_g = \dfrac{6 F_g l}{i_g b' h^2} \qquad \text{...(Eq. 3.29)}$$

Also, for a leaf spring deflection $y = \dfrac{C_2 Fl^3}{Ebh^3}$ *[as in equation (3.22)]* ...**11.32/ Pg 144A, DHB**

Substituting $b = ib'$ for a laminated spring, we have

$$y = \dfrac{C_2 Fl^3}{Eib'h^3} \qquad \text{...(Eq. 3.30)} \; \textbf{11.37/ Pg 145, DHB}$$

Here $(C_2 = 6)$ $\hspace{3cm}$ ...**Tb 11.1/ Pg 149, DHB** and **Fig 11.6 b/ Pg 157C, DHB**

Thus for graduated leaves, Eq. (3.30) yields...

$$y_g = \dfrac{6 F_g l^3}{E i_g b' h^3} \qquad \text{...(Eq. 3.31)}$$

Similarly the extra full length leaves can be treated as a rectangular plate of thickness h and uniform width $i_f b'$, as shown in **Fig. 3.14 (b)**.

$$\sigma_f = \dfrac{6 F_f l}{i_f b' h^2} \qquad \text{...(Eq. 3.32)} \quad \textit{[as in equation (3.21)]}$$

$$y_f = \frac{4F_f l^3}{E i_f b'h^3} \quad \text{...(Eq. 3.33) [as in equation (3.22)]}$$

Since the graduated leaves and full length leaves are clamped together, their deflection is same.

$$y_f = y_g$$

$$\frac{4F_f l^3}{E i_f b'h^3} = \frac{6F_g l^3}{E i_g b'h^3}$$

$$\frac{2F_f}{i_f} = \frac{3F_g}{i_g}$$

$$\frac{F_g}{F_f} = \frac{2i_g}{3i_f} \quad \text{...(Eq. 3.34)}$$

But $F = F_f + F_g$ ...(Eq. 3.35) **11.39c/ Pg 145, DHB**

$$= F_f \left[1 + \frac{F_g}{F_f} \right]$$

$$= F_f \left[1 + \frac{2i_g}{3i_f} \right] \quad \text{...using (Eq. 3.34)}$$

$$= F_f \left[\frac{3i_f + 2i_g}{3i_f} \right]$$

$$F_f = \left[\frac{3i_f}{3i_f + 2i_g} \right] F$$

...(Eq. 3.36) **11.39b/ Pg 145, DHB**

Substituting Eq. (3.36) in Eq. (3.35) yields

$$F_g = \left[\frac{2i_g}{3i_f + 2i_g} \right] F$$

...(Eq. 3.37) **11.39a/ Pg 145, DHB**

Substituting Eq. (3.37) in Eq. (3.29) yields

$$\sigma_g = \frac{6l}{i_g b'h^2} \left[\frac{2i_g}{3i_f + 2i_g} \right] F$$

$$\sigma_g = \frac{12Fl}{b'h^2 (3i_f + 2i_g)} \quad \text{...(Eq. 3.38) \textbf{11.40b/ Pg 145, DHB}}$$

Similarly substituting Eq. (3.36) in Eq. (3.32) yields

$$\sigma_f = \frac{6l}{i_g b'h^2} \left[\frac{3i_f}{3i_f + 2i_g} \right] F$$

$$\sigma_f = \frac{18Fl}{b'h^2\left(3i_f + 2i_g\right)} \quad \text{...(Eq. 3.39)} \quad \textbf{11.40a/ Pg 145, DHB}$$

Dividing Eq. (3.39) with Eq. (3.38) yields,

$$\frac{\sigma_f}{\sigma_g} = \frac{\left[\dfrac{18Fl}{b'h^2\left(3i_f + 2i_g\right)}\right]}{\left[\dfrac{12Fl}{b'h^2\left(3i_f + 2i_g\right)}\right]}$$

$$\frac{\sigma_f}{\sigma_g} = \frac{18}{12}$$

$$\sigma_f = \frac{3}{2}\sigma_g \quad \text{...(Eq. 3.40)} \quad \textbf{11.38/ Pg 145, DHB}$$

From Eq. (3.40) it is seen that the stress developed in full length leaves is 50% greater than that developed in graduated leaves.

Substituting Eq. (3.36) in Eq. (3.33) yields

$$y_f = \frac{4l^3}{Ei_f b'h^3}\left[\frac{3i_f}{3i_f + 2i_g}\right]F$$

$$y_f = \frac{12Fl^3}{Eb'h^3\left(3i_f + 2i_g\right)} \quad \text{...(Eq. 3.41)}$$

Similarly substituting Eq. (3.37) in Eq. (3.31) yields

$$y_g = \frac{6l^3}{Ei_f b'h^3}\left[\frac{2i_g}{3i_f + 2i_g}\right]F$$

$$y_g = \frac{12Fl^3}{Eb'h^3\left(3i_f + 2i_g\right)} \quad \text{...(Eq. 3.42)}$$

From Eqs (3.41) and (3.42), it is seen that the deflection in graduated and full length leaves are the same.

i.e. $y_f = y_g = y = \dfrac{12Fl^3}{Eb'h^3\left(3i_f + 2i_g\right)}$ ...(Eq. 3.43) ...**11.40C/ Pg 145, DHB**

3.19 EQUALIZED STRESSES IN SPRINGS—NIPPING

In the previous section that the stress developed in full length leaves is 50% greater than that developed in graduated leaves. In order to stress all the leaves to the same extent, the full length leaves are given greater radii of curvature than that of graduated leaves, before the leaves are assembled with the center clip to form a spring as shown in **Fig. 3.15**. This leaves a gap between the leaves known as 'Nip'.

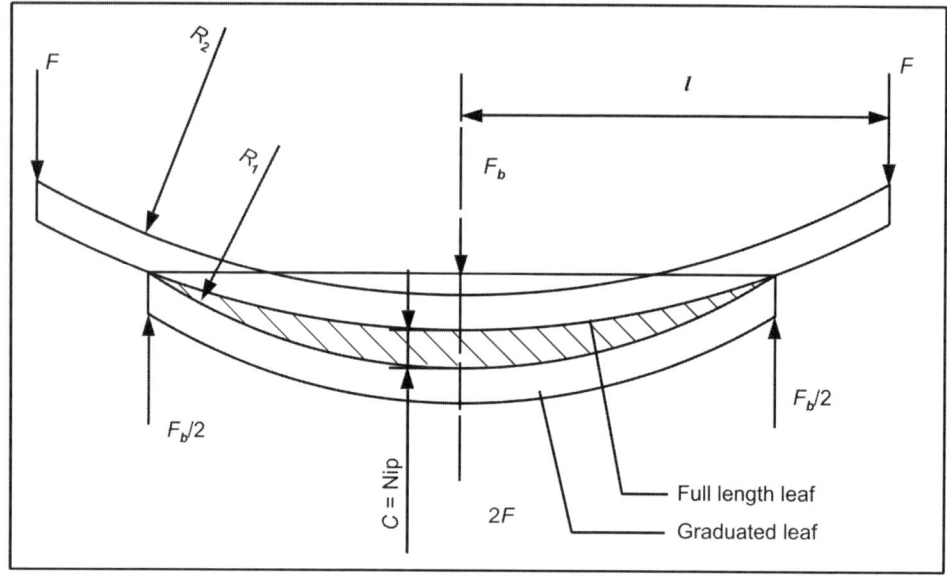

Fig. 3.15 Nipping of leaf spring

When the central bolt is tightened, the upper leaf will bend back and have an initial stress in a direction opposite to that of the normal load, while the lower leaf will have an initial stress in the same direction as that of the normal load. Thus on loading, the upper leaf will have lower value of resultant stress than that of lower leaf. The initial gap between the leaves may be adjusted so that under maximum load condition the stress in all the leaves is equal. This is desirable in automobile springs in which full length leaves are designed for lower stress because the full length leaves carry additional loads caused by the swaying of the car, twisting and in some cases due to driving the car through the rear springs.

For equal stresses between the graduated and full length leaves at maximum load, the total deflection of the graduated leaves will exceed the deflection of the full length leaves by an amount equal to the initial gap 'c'.

i.e.
$$c + y_f = y_g$$
$$c = y_a - y_f \qquad \text{...(Eq. 3.44)}$$
$$= \frac{6F_g l^3}{E i_g b' h^3} - \frac{4F_f l^3}{E i_f b' h^3} \qquad \text{[using (Eq. 3.31) and (Eq. 3.33)]}$$

$$c = \frac{l^3}{E b' h^3} \left[\frac{6F_g}{i_g} - \frac{4F_f}{i_f} \right] \qquad \text{...(Eq. 3.45)}$$

Since the stresses are equal, we have
$$\sigma_g = \sigma_f$$
$$\frac{6F_g l}{i_g b' h^2} = \frac{6F_f l}{i_f b' h^2} \qquad \text{[using (Eq. 3.29) and (Eq. 3.32)]}$$

$$\frac{F_g}{i_g} = \frac{F_f}{i_f} \qquad \text{-or-}$$

$$\frac{F_g}{F_f} = \frac{i_g}{i_f}$$

Adding '1' on both sides, we have

$$1 + \frac{F_g}{F_f} = 1 + \frac{i_g}{i_f}$$

$$\frac{F_f + F_g}{F_f} = \frac{i_f + i_g}{i_f}$$

since $F_f + F_g = F$, and $i = i_f + i_g$

$$\frac{F}{F_f} = \frac{i}{i_f}$$

Therefore, $F_f = \left(\dfrac{i_f}{i}\right)F$ and $F_g = \left(\dfrac{i_g}{i}\right)F$ ...(Eq. 3.46)

Substituting Eq. (3.46) in Eq. (3.45), we have

$$c = \frac{l^3}{Eb'h^3}\left[\frac{6}{i_g}\left(\frac{i_g}{i}\right)F - \frac{4}{i_f}\left(\frac{i_f}{i}\right)F\right]$$

$$c = \frac{2Fl^3}{Eib'h^3} \qquad \text{...(Eq. 3.47) } \mathbf{11.42a/\,Pg\,145,\,DHB}$$

Equation (3.47) gives the initial gap between the full length and graduated leaves with pre-stress.

Now the load (F_b) required on the clip bolt to close the gap is given as

$$c = y_g + y_f$$

$$\frac{2Fl^3}{Eib'h^3} = \left[\frac{6l^3}{Ei_g b'h^3} + \frac{4l^3}{Ei_f b'h^3}\right]\left(\frac{F_b}{2}\right)$$

$$\frac{4F}{i} = \left[\frac{6}{i_g} + \frac{4}{i_f}\right]F_b$$

$$\frac{4F}{i} = 2F_b\left(\frac{3i_f + 2i_g}{i_f \cdot i_g}\right)$$

$$F_b = \frac{2Fi_f \cdot i_g}{i(3i_f + 2i_g)} \qquad \text{...(Eq. 3.48) } \mathbf{11.42b/\,Pg\,146,\,DHB}$$

Equation (3.48) gives the load to close the initial gap using clip bolts.
The final stress in the spring is $\sigma = \sigma_f - \text{initial stress}$

304 Design of Machine Elements II (DME II)

$$= \frac{6F_f l}{i_f b'h^2} - \left[\frac{6l}{i_f b'h^2}\left(\frac{F_b}{2}\right)\right]$$

$$= \frac{6l}{i_f b'h^2}\left[F_f - \left(\frac{F_b}{2}\right)\right]$$

$$= \frac{6l}{i_f b'h^2}\left[\frac{3i_f F}{(3i_f + 2i_g)} - \frac{Fi_f \cdot i_g}{i(3i_f + 2i_g)}\right] \quad \text{...using (Eq. 3.48)}$$

$$= \frac{6Fi_f l}{i_f b'h^2}\left[\frac{3}{(3i_f + 2i_g)} - \frac{i_g}{i(3i_f + 2i_g)}\right]$$

$$= \frac{6Fl}{b'h^2(3i_f + 2i_g)}\left[3 - \frac{i_g}{i}\right]$$

$$= \frac{6Fl}{b'h^2(3i_f + 2i_g)}\left[\frac{3i - i_g}{i}\right]$$

$$= \frac{6Fl}{b'h^2(3i_f + 2i_g)}\left[\frac{3(i_f + i_g) - i_g}{i}\right]$$

$$= \frac{6Fl}{b'h^2(3i_f + 2i_g)}\left[\frac{3i_f + 2i_g}{i}\right]$$

$$\sigma = \frac{6Fl}{ib'h^2} \quad \text{...(Eq. 3.49)}$$

Since the stresses are equal, Eq. (3.49) can be written as

$$\sigma_g = \sigma_f = \frac{6Fl}{ib'h^2} \quad \text{...(Eq. 3.50) } \mathbf{11.42c/ Pg\ 146, DHB}$$

Equation Eq. (3.50) gives maximum stress in the spring with the full length leaves pre-stressed.

Note:
- **Table 11.1/ Pg 149, DHB** *gives values of C_1, C_2 and strain energy for various types of beams, as shown in* **Fig 11.6/ Pg 157C, DHB.**
- **Table 11.4/ Pg 150, DHB** *gives the normal sizes of flats (Laminated springs for automotive suspension).*
- **Table 11.5/ Pg 151, DHB** *gives standard sections of flats (Laminated springs for railway rolling stock).*
- ****** *The constants derived in the equations (3.47), (3.48) and (3.49), i.e.* **11.42a, 11.42b, and 11.42c, DHB** *are based on the fact that the total load acting on the spring is 2F and the support reactions are F. Comparing these equations with* **Fig. 11.6(d)/ Pg 157C, DHB,** *the force acting on the spring is F and the support reactions are each equal to F/2. Then these equations reduced to:*

$$c = \frac{Fl^3}{Eib'h^3} \qquad \text{...11.42a/ Pg 145, DHB}$$

$$F_b = \frac{Fi_f \cdot i_g}{i(3i_f + 2i_g)} \qquad \text{...11.42b/ Pg 146, DHB}$$

$$\sigma_g = \sigma_f = \frac{3Fl}{ib'h^2} \qquad \text{...11.42c/ Pg 146, DHB}$$

- Based on **, the stress in semi-elliptical spring without pre-stress are

$$\sigma_f = \frac{9Fl}{b'h^2(3i_f + 2i_f)} \qquad \text{...11.41a/ Pg 145, DHB}$$

$$\sigma_g = \frac{6Fl}{b'h^2(3i_f + 2i_g)} \qquad \text{...11.41b/ Pg 145, DHB}$$

And deflection, $y = \dfrac{6Fl^3}{Eb'h^3(3i_f + 2i_g)}$ ...11.41c/ Pg 145, DHB

43. **Determine the width and thickness of leaves for a six leaf cantilever spring, 400 mm long to carry a load of 3 kN and having a deflection of 40 mm. The allowable stress in the spring material is 320 MPa and the Young's modulus is 200 GPa.**

Solution: $b' = ?$, $h = ?$, $n = 6$, $l = 400$ mm, $F = 3000$ N, $y = 50$ mm, $\sigma = 320$ MPa, $E = 2 \times 10^5$ N/mm^2

a. **To find h:**

We know that, $\qquad F = \dfrac{\sigma i b' h^2}{C_1 l}$ ...11.36/ Pg 144A, DHB

Here $C_1 = 6$, $C_2 = 4$ ...Tb 11.1-a/ Pg 149, and Fig 11.6 a/ Pg 157C, DHB

$$3000 = \frac{320 \times 6 \times b'h^2}{6 \times 400}$$

$b'h^2 = 3750$ mm^2 ...Eq. (i)

Also deflection, $\qquad y = \dfrac{C_2 F l^3}{E i b' h^3}$ ...11.37/ Pg 145, DHB

$$40 = \frac{4 \times 3000 \times 400^3}{2 \times 10^5 \times 6 \times b'h^3}$$

$b'h^3 = 16000$ mm^4 ...Eq. (ii)

Dividing Eq. (ii) by Eq. (i), we have

$$\frac{b'h^3}{b'h^2} = \frac{16000}{3750}$$

$h = 4.27$ mm

Thus the standard thickness, $h = 5$ mm ...Tb 11.4/ Pg 150, DHB

b. To find b':

Substituting h in Eq. (i) yields ... $b' = 150$ mm

in Eq. (ii) yields ... $b' = 128$ mm

Selecting higher value for design, we have $b' = 150$ mm   ...Tb 11.4/ Pg 150, DHB

44. Design a cantilever spring to absorb 620 N-m of energy without exceeding the deflection of 150 mm and an allowable stress of 800 MPa. The length of the spring is 600 mm and Young's modulus is 210 GPa.

Solution: Energy $U = 620 \times 10^3$ N-mm, $y = 150$ mm, $\sigma = 800$ MPa, $l = 600$ mm, $E = 210 \times 10^3$ N/mm^2 *Design:* (b', h, i).

a. To find h:

We know that, Resilience –or– energy stored, $= \dfrac{1}{2} Fy$ ...11.8/ Pg 139, DHB

$$620 \times 10^3 = F \times (150/2)$$
$$F = 8266.67 \text{ N}$$

But $F = \dfrac{\sigma i b' h^2}{C_1 l}$ ...11.36/ Pg 144A, DHB

Here $C_1 = 6, C_2 = 6$ ...Tb 11.1-b/ Pg 149 & Fig 11.6 b/ Pg 157C, DHB

$$8266.67 = \dfrac{800 \times i \times b' h^2}{6 \times 600}$$

$$ib'h^2 = 37200 \text{ mm}^3 \qquad \text{...Eq. (i)}$$

Also resilience $= \dfrac{\sigma^2}{6E} \times volume$ ...Tb 11.1-b/ Pg 149, DHB

$$620 \times 10^3 = \dfrac{800^2}{6 \times 2.1 \times 10^5} \times \left(\dfrac{1}{2} \times b'h\right) il$$

$$= 0.254 \times (600 \, ib'h)$$

$$ib'h = 4068.75 \text{ mm}^2 \qquad \text{...Eq. (ii)}$$

Dividing Eq. (i) by Eq. (ii), we have

$$\dfrac{ib'h^2}{ib'h} = \dfrac{37200}{4068.75}$$

$$h = 9.14$$

Thus, the standard thickness $h = 10$ mm   ...Tb 11.4/ Pg 150, DHB

b. To find b':

Substituting in Eq. (i) yields... $ib' = 406.875$ mm

Assume a width of 60 mm, we have   ...Tb 11.4/ Pg 150, DHB

$$i = \dfrac{406.875}{60}$$

$$i = 6.78 \approx 7.$$

45. A 1 m long cantilever spring is composed of 8 graduated leaves and one extra full length leaf. The leaves are 45 mm wide. A load of 2000 N at the end of spring causes a deflection of 75 mm. Determine the thickness of the leaves and the maximum bending stress in the full length leaf assuming first that the extra full length has been pre-stressed to give the same stress in all the leaves and then determine the stress in the full extra length leaf assuming no pre-stress.

[VTU – Jan/Feb 2005 – 12 Marks; Dec/Jan 2008 – 06 Marks]

Solution: $l = 1000$ mm, $i_g = 8$, $i_f = 1$, $b' = 45$ mm, $F = 2000$ N, $y = 75$ mm.

a. $h = ?$,   b. $\sigma_f = ?$ –Pre-stressed   c. $\sigma_f = ?$ –No pre-stress.

a. Thickness:

We know that,
$$y = \frac{12 F l^3}{E b' h^3 (3 i_f + 2 i_g)}$$ ...11.40c/ Pg 145, DHB

$$75 = \frac{12 \times 2000 \times 1000^3}{2 \times 10^5 \times 45 \times h^3 (3 \times 1 + 2 \times 8)}$$

$$h = 12.32 \text{ mm}$$

Thus, the standard thickness $h = 14$ mm   ...Tb 11.4/ Pg 150, DHB

b. Stress in full length leaf – Pre-stressed:

We know that, $\sigma_g = \sigma_f = \dfrac{3 F l}{i b' h^2}$ ...11.42c/ Pg 146, DHB

$$= \frac{3 \times 2000 \times 1000}{9 \times 45 \times 14^2} \qquad (i = i_f + i_g)$$

$\sigma_f = 75.59$ MPa

c. Stress in full length leaf – No pre-stress:

We know that, $\sigma_f = \dfrac{9 F l}{b' h^2 (3 i_f + 2 i_g)}$ ...11.41a/ Pg 145, DHB

$$= \frac{9 \times 2000 \times 1000}{45 \times 14^2 [3 \times 1 + 2 \times 8]} \qquad (i = i_f + i_g)$$

$\sigma_f = 107.41$ MPa.

46. The free end of a horizontal, constant strength steel cantilever beam is directly over it and in contact with a vertical coil helical spring. The width of the beam at its fixed end is 600 mm, length is 900 mm, and has a thickness of 10 mm. The coil spring has 12 active coils of 13 mm diameter and an outside diameter of 100 mm (Fig. 3.16). Take 84 GPa:
   a. What force, if gradually applied to the end of the cantilever beam is required to cause a deflection of 50 mm?
   b. What is the bending stress in the beam at mid-span?
   c. What is the amount of energy absorbed by the coil spring? Take $E = 210$ GPa

Solution: $b' = 600$ mm, $l = 900$ mm, $h = 10$ mm, active coils (helical) $i = 12$, wire diameter, $d = 13$ mm, $D_0 = 100$ mm, $G = 84$ GPa, $i' = 1$ (Cantilever), $E = 210$ GPa, for steel.

   a. $F = ?$ on the cantilever, if $y = 50$ mm.   b. $\sigma = ?$ at mid span,   c. $U = ?$

a. To find F:

Since both springs have the same deflection,

Force required, $F = F_{coil} + F_{canti}$ ...Eq. (i)

For a coil spring, deflection, $y = \dfrac{8 \times F_{coil} D^3 i}{G d^4}$

...11.5a/ Pg 139, DHB

$D = D_0 - d = 100 - 13 = 87$ mm

$50 = \dfrac{8 \times F_{coil} \times 87^3 \times 12}{84 \times 10^3 \times 13^4}$

$F_{coil} = 1897.55$ N

For a cantilever spring, deflection,

$$y = \dfrac{C_2 \times F_{canti} \cdot l^3}{E i' b' h^3}$$ ...11.37/ Pg 145, DHB

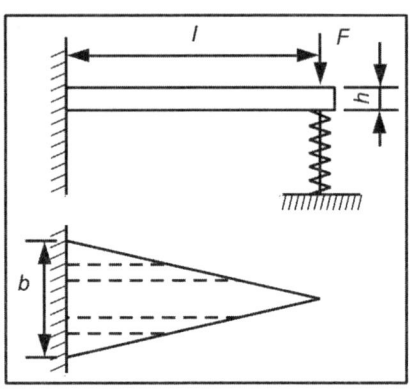

Fig. 3.16: Problem 46

Here $C_1 = 6$, $C_2 = 6$ ...Tb 11.1-b/ Pg 149 and Fig 11.6 b/ Pg 157C, DHB

$50 = \dfrac{6 \times F_{canti} \times 900^3}{2.1 \times 10^5 \times 1 \times 600 \times 10^3}$ ($i' = 1, f$ or cantilever, from Fig. 3.16)

$F_{canti} = 1440.33$ N

Eq. (i) yields... $F = 1897.55 + 1440.33$

$F = 3337.9$ N

b. Bending stress, σ at mid span:

We know that, $\dfrac{M}{I} = \dfrac{\sigma}{c} = \dfrac{E}{R}$ ...1.16/ Pg 5, DHB

$\therefore \sigma = \dfrac{Mc}{I}$

But, $c = \dfrac{h}{2} = \dfrac{10}{2} = 5$ mm, and

$I = \dfrac{bh^3}{12} = \dfrac{(600/2) \times 10^3}{12} = 25000$ mm

$M = F_{canti} x = 1440.33 \times 450 = 648148$ N-mm

(average $b = 300$ mm, x – distance from free end)

Therefore, $\sigma = \dfrac{648148 \times 5}{25000}$

$\sigma = 129.63$ MPa

c. Energy stored –or- resilience:

We know that, Resilience, $U = \dfrac{F_{coil} y}{2}$ ...11.8/ Pg 139, DHB

$= \dfrac{1897.55 \times 50}{2}$

$U = 47.44 \times 10^3$ N-mm 47.44 N-m.

47. A 100 mm OD steel coil spring having 10 active coils of 15 mm diameter wire is in contact with a 800 mm long steel cantilever spring having six graduated leaves of 150 mm wide and 8 mm thick as shown in Fig. 3.17. Find:

   a. What force if gradually applied to the top of the coil spring will cause a deflection of 25 mm in the cantilever?
   b. What will be the maximum shear stress in the coil spring? Take 2.1×10^5 MPa

Solution: $D_0 = 100$ mm, $i = 10$, $d = 15$ mm, $l = 800$ mm, $i' = 6$, $b' = 150$ mm, $h = 8$ mm, $y = 25$ mm, $E = 2.1 \times 10^5$ MPa

a. Force on the cantilever spring:

We know that, deflection $y = \dfrac{C_2 \times F_{canti} \times l^3}{E i' b' h^3}$ ...11.37/ Pg 145, DHB

Here $C_1 = 6, C_2 = 6$ ...Tb 11.1-b/ Pg 149, and Fig 11.6 b/ Pg 157C, DHB

$$25 = \dfrac{6 \times F_{canti} \times 800^3}{2.1 \times 10^5 \times 6 \times 150 \times 8^3}$$

$F_{canti} = 787.5$ N

a. Shear stress on coil spring:

We know that, $D = \dfrac{8FDK}{\pi d^3}$ ...11.1a/ Pg 139, DHB

Here, $D = D_0 - d = 100 - 15 = 85$ mm

$C = D/d = 85/15 = 5.67$

$K = \dfrac{4C-1}{4C-4} + \dfrac{0.615}{C}$

...11.2b/ Pg 139, DHB

$= \dfrac{4 \times 5.67 - 1}{4 \times 5.67 - 4} + \dfrac{0.615}{5.67}$

$K = 1.269$

Therefore, $\tau = \dfrac{8 \times 787.5 \times 85 \times 1.269}{\pi \times 15^3}$

$\tau = 64.1$ MPa.

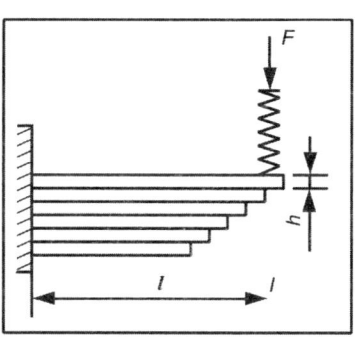

Fig. 3.17: Problem 47

48. Determine the thickness and deflection of a cantilever leaf spring for the following specifications:

   Load on the spring = 4000 N   Total number of leaves = 12
   Number of extra full length leaves = 3   Width of each leaf = 90 mm
   Length of the spring = 600 mm   Design stress = 400 MPa, $E = 2 \times 10^5$ MPa

Solution: $h = ?$, $y = ?$, $F = 4000$ N, $i_f + i_g = 12$, $i_f = 3$, $b' = 90$ mm, $l = 600$, $\sigma = 400$ MPa, $E = 2 \times 10^5$ MPa

a. To find h:

We know that, $F = \dfrac{\sigma i b' h^2}{C_1 l}$ ...11.36/ Pg 144A, DHB

Here $C_1 = 6, C_2 = 6$ ...Tb 11.1-b/ Pg 149 and Fig 11.6 b/ Pg 157C, DHB

$$400 = \frac{400 \times 12 \times 90 \times h^2}{6 \times 600}$$

$$h = 5.77 \text{ mm}$$

Thus the standard thickness, $h = 6$ mm ...Tb 11.4/ Pg 150, DHB

b. To find y:

We know that, $y = \dfrac{C_2 F l^3}{E i' b' h^3}$ ...11.37/ Pg 145, DHB

$$= \frac{6 \times 4000 \times 600^3}{2 \times 10^5 \times 12 \times 90 \times 6^3}$$

$$y = 111.11 \text{ mm} \approx 112 \text{ mm}.$$

49. Design a truck spring that has 12 number of leaves, two of which are full length leaves. The spring supports are 1meter apart and the central band is 70 mm wide. The central load is to be 6 kN with a permissible stress of 200 MPa. Determine the thickness, width and deflection of the spring leaves if the ratio of total depth to width of the spring is 3.

[VTU – June/ July 2008 – 12 Marks; (Similar) June/ July 2011 – 08 Marks]

Solution: $i = 12, i_f = 2, i_g = 12 - 2 = 10, 2l_1 = 1000$ mm, band width, $l_2 = 70$ mm, $F = 6000$ N, $\sigma = 200$ MPa, $h = ?, b = ?, y = ?, l = \dfrac{2l_1 - l_2}{2} = 3$, effective length, $l = 465$ mm, $\dfrac{ih}{b'} = 3$.

Design: (i, b', h, c, F_b)

(Note: Permissible stress indicates no pre-stress)

a. To find h:

Given $\dfrac{ih}{b'} = 3$

$$\dfrac{12h}{b'} = 3$$

$$b' = 4h \quad\quad \text{...Eq. (i)}$$

Since the leaves are initially stressed,

$$\sigma_f = \dfrac{9Fl}{b'h^2 (3i_f + 2i_g)} \quad\quad \text{...11.41a/ Pg 145, DHB}$$

$$200 = \dfrac{9 \times 6000 \times 465}{(4h) \times h^2 \times (3 \times 2 + 2 \times 10)}$$

$$h = 10.65 \text{ mm}$$

Thus the standard thickness, $h = 12$ mm ...Tb 11.4/ Pg 150, DHB

b. To find b':

Eq. (i) yields... $b' = 4 \times 12 = 48$ mm

Thus the standard width, $b' = 50$ mm ...Tb 11.4/ Pg 150, DHB

c. To find y:

We know that,
$$y = \frac{6Fl^3}{Eb'h^3(3i_f + 2i_g)} \qquad \text{...11.41c/ Pg 145, DHB}$$

$$= \frac{6 \times 6000 \times 465^3}{2 \times 10^5 \times 50 \times 12^3 \times (3 \times 2 + 2 \times 10)}$$

$$y = 8.06 \text{ mm.}$$

50. A semielliptical laminated leaf spring with two full length leaves and ten graduated leaves are to be designed to support a central load of 6 kN over two points 1000 mm apart. The central band width is 100 mm. The ratio of total depth of the spring to its width is 2.5. The design normal stress of the material of the leaves is 400 MPa and the modulus of elasticity is 208 GPa. Determine:

i. Width and thickness of the leaves;
ii. The initial gap between full length and graduated leaves;
iii. The central bolt load.

[VTU Jan./ Feb. 2006 – 10 Marks; (Similar) Dec. 2006/ Jan. 2007 – 08 Marks; (Similar)Jan./ Feb. 2005 – 10 Marks; (Similar) Dec. 2010 – 10 Marks; (Similar) Dec. 2011 – 10 Marks.]

Solution: $i_f = 2$, $i_g = 10$, $i = i_f + i_g = 12$, $F = 6000$ N, $2l_1 = 1000$ mm, band width, $l_2 = 100$ mm,

effective length, $l = \dfrac{2l_1 - l_2}{2} = 450$ mm, $\dfrac{ih}{b'} = 2.5$, $\sigma = 400$ MPa, $E = 208 \times 10^3$ MPa.

i. $h = ?, b' = ?,$ ii. $c = ?$ iii. $F_b = ?$

i. To find b', h:

Given $\dfrac{ih}{b'} = 2.5$

$$\frac{12h}{b'} = 2.5$$

$$b' = 4.8h \qquad \text{...Eq. (i)}$$

Since the leaves are not initially stressed,

$$\sigma_g = \sigma_f = \frac{3Fl}{ib'h^2} \qquad \text{...11.42c/ Pg 146, DHB}$$

$$400 = \frac{3 \times 6000 \times 450}{12 \times (4.8h) \times h^2}$$

$$h^3 = 351.53$$

$$h = 7.05 \text{ mm}$$

Thus the standard thickness, **h = 8 mm** ...Tb 11.4/ Pg 150, DHB

Substituting in Eq. (i) yields ... $b' = 4.8 \times 8 = 38.4$ mm

Thus the standard width, **b' = 40 mm** ...Tb 11.4/ Pg 150, DHB

ii. To find c:

We know that,
$$c = \frac{Fl^3}{Eib'h^3} \qquad \text{...11.42a/ Pg 145, DHB}$$

$$= \frac{6000 \times 450^3}{208 \times 10^3 \times 12 \times 40 \times 8^3}$$

$$c = 10.7 \text{ mm}$$

iii. To find F_b:

We know that, $\quad F_b = \dfrac{Fi_f \cdot i_g}{i(3i_f + 2i_g)} \quad$ ...11.42b/ Pg 146, DHB

$$= \frac{6000 \times 2 \times 10}{12 \times (3 \times 2 + 2 \times 10)}$$

$$F_b = 384.62 \text{ N.}$$

51. A laminated semi elliptical leaf spring under central load of 10 kN is to have an effective length of 1 m and not to deflect more than 75 mm. The spring has 10 leaves, 2 of which are full length and have been pre-stressed so that all leaves have same stress at full load condition. All the leaves have same width and thickness. The maximum allowable stress in the leaves is 350 N/mm². Calculate the width and thickness of the leaves.

[VTU – Dec. 08/ Jan. 2009 – 08 Marks]

Solution: $F = 10 \times 10^3$ N, $2l = 1000$ mm, $y = 75$ mm, $i = 10$, $i_f = 2$, $i_g = 8$, $\sigma = 350$ MPa, $b', h = ?$

a. To find h:

Since the leaves are initially stressed, $\quad \sigma_g = \sigma_f = \dfrac{3Fl}{ib'h^2} \quad$ ...11.42c/ Pg 146, DHB

$$350 = \frac{3 \times 10000 \times 500}{10 \times b' \times h^2}$$

$$b'h^2 = 4285.71 \text{ mm}^3 \qquad \text{...Eq. }(i)$$

Also, $\quad y = \dfrac{6Fl^3}{Eb'h^3(3i_f + 2i_g)} \quad$ ...11.41c/ Pg 145, DHB

$$75 = \frac{6 \times 10000 \times 500^3}{2 \times 10^5 \times b' \times h^3 \times (3 \times 2 + 2 \times 8)}$$

$$b'h^3 = 22727.27 \text{ mm}^4 \qquad \text{...Eq. }(ii)$$

Dividing Eq. (*ii*) by Eq. (*i*), we have

$$\frac{b'h^3}{b'h^2} = \frac{22727.27}{4285.71}$$

$$h = 5.30 \text{ mm}$$

Thus, the standard thickness **$h = 6$ mm** ...Tb 11.4/ Pg 150, DHB

b. To find b':

Substituting h in Eq. (*i*) yields ... $b' = 119.05$ mm
in Eq. (*ii*) yields ... $b' = 105.21$ mm

Selecting higher value for design we have, $b' = 119.05$ mm ...Tb 11.4/ Pg 150, DHB
Thus, the standard width **$b' = 120$ mm** ...Tb 11.4/ Pg 150, DHB

52. A multi-leaf spring with camber is fitted to the chassis of an automobile over a span of 1.2 meter to absorb shocks due to a maximum load of 20 kN. The spring material can sustain a maximum stress of 0.4 GPa. All the leaves of the spring were to receive the same stress. The spring should have at least 2 full length leaves out of 8 leaves. The leaves are assembled with bolts over a span of 150 mm width at the middle. Design the spring for a maximum deflection of 50 mm.

[VTU –Dec.09/ Jan. 10 – 10 Marks]

Solution: $2l_1 = 1200$ mm, band width, $l_2 = 150$ mm, effective length, $l = \dfrac{2l_1 - l_2}{2}$
$= 525$ mm, $F = 20 \times 10^3$ N, $\sigma = 400$ MPa, $y = 50$ mm, $i_f = 2$, $i = 8$, $i_g = 6$, Design: (i, b', h, c, F_b).

a. To find h:

Since the leaves are initially stressed, $\sigma_g = \sigma_f = \dfrac{3Fl}{ib'h^2}$ ...11.42c/ Pg 146, DHB

$$400 = \dfrac{3 \times 20000 \times 525}{8 \times b' \times h^2}$$

$$b'h^2 = 9843.75 \text{ mm}^3 \quad \text{...Eq. (i)}$$

Also, $y = \dfrac{6Fl^3}{Eb'h^3(3i_f + 2i_g)}$ ...11.41c/ Pg 145, DHB

$$50 = \dfrac{6 \times 20000 \times 525^3}{2 \times 10^5 \times b' \times h^3 \times (3 \times 2 + 2 \times 6)} \qquad \text{assume } E = 2 \times 10^5 \text{ MPa}$$

$$b'h^3 = 96468.75 \text{ mm}^4 \quad \text{...Eq. (ii)}$$

Dividing Eq. (ii) by Eq. (i), we have

$$\dfrac{b'h^3}{b'h^2} = \dfrac{96468.75}{9843.75}$$

$$h = 9.8 \text{ mm}$$

Thus, the standard thickness $h = 10$ mm ...Tb 11.4/ Pg 150, DHB

b. To find b':

Substituting in Eq. (i) yields ...$b' = 98.44$ mm
in Eq. (ii) yields ...$b' = 96.47$ mm
Selecting higher value for design we have, $b' = 98.44$ mm ...Tb 11.4/ Pg 150, DHB
Thus the standard width, $b' = 100$ mm ...Tb 11.4/ Pg 150, DHB

c. To find c:

We know that, $c = \dfrac{Fl^3}{Eib'h^3}$ ...11.42a/ Pg 145, DHB

$$= \dfrac{20000 \times 525^3}{2 \times 10^5 \times 8 \times 100 \times 10^3}$$

$$c = 18.08 \text{ mm}$$

d. To find F_b:

We know that, $$F_b = \frac{Fi_f \cdot i_g}{i(3i_f + 2i_g)}$$ ...11.42b/ Pg 146, DHB

$$= \frac{20000 \times 2 \times 6}{8 \times (3 \times 2 + 2 \times 6)}$$

$$F_b = 1666.67 \text{ N}.$$

53. A semielliptical multi leaf spring is used for the suspension of the rear axle of a truck. It consists of two extra full length leaves and 10 graduated leaves including the master leaf. The center to center distance between the spring eyes is 1.2 m. The leaves are made of steel with σ_{yt} = 1500 MPa, E = 2.07 × 10^5 MPa and FOS = 2.5. The spring is to be designed for a maximum force of 30 kN. The leaves are pre-stressed so as to equalize stresses in all leaves. Determine:

  i. C/S of the leaves;
  ii. initial nip;
  iii. initial pre-load required to close the gap.

[VTU –May/ June 2010 – 10 Marks]

Solution: $i_f = 2$, $i_g = 10$, $i = 12$, $2l_1 = 1200$ mm, effective length, $l = 600$ mm, $F = 30 \times 10^3$ N, $\sigma_{yt} = 1500$ MPa, FOS = 2.5, $E = 2.07 \times 10^5$ MPa, (b', h, c, F_b)

a. To find h:

We know that, $$FOS = \frac{\sigma_{yt}}{\sigma}$$

$$\sigma = \frac{1500}{2.5}$$

$$\sigma = 600 \text{ MPa}.$$

Since the leaves are initially stressed, $\sigma_g = \sigma_f = \dfrac{3Fl}{ib'h^2}$ ...11.42c/ Pg 146, DHB

$$600 = \frac{3 \times 30000 \times 600}{12 \times b' \times h^2}$$

$$b'h^2 = 7500 \text{ mm}^3 \quad \text{...Eq. }(i)$$

Assume a width of 60 mm, we have $h^2 = \dfrac{7500}{60}$ ...Tb 11.4/ Pg 150, DHB

$$h = 11.8 \text{ mm}$$

Thus, the standard width $h = 12$ mm ...Tb 11.4/ Pg 150, DHB

b. To find c:

We know that, $c = \dfrac{Fl^3}{Eib'h^3}$ ...11.42a/ Pg 145, DHB

$$= \frac{30000 \times 600^3}{2.07 \times 10^5 \times 12 \times 60 \times 12^3}$$

$$c = 25.16 \text{ mm}$$

c. To find F_b:

We know that, $\quad F_b = \dfrac{F i_f \cdot i_g}{i(3i_f + 2i_g)} \quad$ ...11.42b/ Pg 146, DHB

$$= \dfrac{30000 \times 2 \times 10}{12 \times (3 \times 2 + 2 \times 10)}$$

$F_b = 1923.08$ N

d. To find y:

We know that, $\quad y = \dfrac{6Fl^3}{Eb'h^3(3i_f + 2i_g)}$

$$= \dfrac{6 \times 30000 \times 600^3}{2.07 \times 10^5 \times 60 \times 12^3 \times (3 \times 2 + 2 \times 10)}$$

$y = 69.68$ mm

VTU QUESTION PAPERS

Feb. 2002 (ME6T2)

1. a. Derive an expression for the shear stress induced in a helical compression spring, with usual notations. **(6 Marks)**
   b. A loaded narrow car of mass 1600 kg and moving with a velocity of 1.2 m/s is brought to rest by a bumper consisting of two helical steel springs of square section. The mean coil diameter of the spring is 6 times the side of square. In bringing the car to rest, the springs are compressed by 200 mm, $\tau = 400$ MPa and $G = 84$ GPa.
   Determine:
      i. Mean load on each spring   ii. Side of the square section wire
      iii. Mean coil diameter   iv. Active number of coils, **(14 Marks)**

July/ August 2002 (ME6T2)

2. a. Derive an expression for the coil spring $\tau = 8FDK/\pi d^3$ **(05 Marks)**
   b. A helical coil spring made from 6.3 mm diameter steel wire has an outside diameter of 57.3 mm with squared and ground ends and has 12 coils. The length of the spring is such that when it is compressed solid the torsional stress is 827 MPa.
      i. Determine the spring rate   ii. Determine the free length
      iii. Determine the critical frequency.
   The density of the material is 7800 kg/m³ and modulus of rigidity $G = 0.8 \times 10^5$ MPa. **(15 Marks)**

Jan./ Feb. 2003 (ME6T2)

3. a. What are the requirements of spring material? What are the spring materials? **(06 Marks)**

b. In a semielliptical laminated spring the given effective length is 900 mm, the total load is 3600 N. The maximum deflection is 75 mm and maximum stress due to bending is 360 N/mm². Decide the number of leaves and their breadth and thickness. Take $E = 0.20 \times 10^6$ N/mm² for the material of the spring.
(14 Marks)

July/ August 2003 (ME6T2)

4. a. With usual notations derive the equations for deflection and bending stresses in full length leaves and graduated leaves of a laminated spring. **(06 Marks)**
   b. Design a rectangular section helical spring to mount to a buffer to sustain a load of 30 kN. The initial compression in the spring upon mounting is 50 mm and further deflection upon load is limited to 100 mm. The spring is made of Z Nickel. The longer side of the section is made twice the shorter side and the spring is formed with longer side parallel to the axis. The clearance between each coil is to be 5 mm and the spring index is to be 10. Take $G = 76$ GPa and factor of safety 2. **(14 Marks)**

July/ August 2004 (ME6T2)

5. a. With usual notations derive an equation for the deflection of helical compression spring. **(04 Marks)**
   b. The following data refers to the valve of a petrol engine:
   - Length of the spring when the valve is open = 40 mm
   - Length of the spring when the valve is closed = 48 mm
   - Spring load when the valve is open = 220 N
   - Spring load when the valve is closed = 350 N
   - Spring index $C = 6.8$, $\tau = 150$ MPa, $G = 84$ GPa.

   The ends are square and ground and the gap between the adjacent coils is 0.1 times the wire diameter, when the spring is free. Determine the following:
   a. Wire diameter   b. Mean coil diameter
   c. Number of active coils d. Free length of the spring
   e. Pitch of coils.   **(16 Marks)**

Jan./ Feb. 2005 (ME6T2)

6. a. Derive an expression for shear stress induced in a helical compression spring considering curvature effects. **(08 Marks)**
   b. A one meter long cantilever spring is composed of 8 graduated leaves and one extra full length leaf. The leaves are 45 mm wide. A load of 2000 N at the end if the spring causes a deflection of 75 mm. Determine the thickness of the leaves and the maximum bending stress in the full length leaf assuming that the extra full length leaf is pre-stressed. **(12 Marks)**

Jan./ Feb. 2005 (AU 53)

7. a. Design a helical compression spring to sustain an axial load that fluctuates between 1.5 kN and 2 kN with an associated deflection of 15 mm during the fluctuation of load. **(10 Marks)**
   b. An automotive leaf spring is to be designed to consist of 10 graduated leaves and 2 full length leaves. The spring is to support a central load of 5 kN over a span of 1100 mm with the central bandwidth of 100 mm. The ratio of total depth of spring to its width is to be 2.5. Determine the width and thickness of leaves

limiting the maximum equalized stress induced in the leaves to 350 MPa. Also determine the initial gap to be provided between the full length and graduated leaves before the assembly. **(10 Marks)**

July/ August 2005 (AU 53)

8. a. Following particulars refer to a valve spring, assume static loading. Ends are ground and flat
   Length when the valve is open = 41 mm
   Length, when the valve is closed = 49 mm
   Spring load when the valve is open = 360 N
   Spring load when the valve is closed = 220 N
   Maximum inside diameter of the spring is not to exceed 25 mm.
   Take $G = 8.3 \times 10^4$ MPa. Find the wire diameter, number of turns and pitch of the coil. The allowable shear stress is 650 MPa. **(15 Marks)**
   b. Derive the expression for the stress in graduated leaf spring of a semi-elliptical spring without pre-stress. **(05 Marks)**

Jan./ Feb. 2006 (AU 53)

9. a. Design a helical compression spring required for a spring loaded safety valve mounted on a pressure vessel. The spring is subjected to an initial compression of 50 mm at the time of assembly and will open by 10 mm when the pressure approaches 6 MPa. The diameter of the valve is 25 mm. **(10 Marks)**
   b. A semi elliptical laminated leaf spring with two full length leaves and ten graduated leaves are to be designed to support a central load of 6 kN over two points 1000 mm apart. The central band width is 100 mm. The ratio of total depth of the spring to its width is 2.5. The design normal stress of the material of the leaves is 400 MPa and the modulus of elasticity is 208 GPa. Determine:
   i. Width and thickness of the leaves
   ii. The initial gap between full length and graduated leaves.
   iii. The central bolt load **(10 Marks)**

July 2006 (AU 53)

10. a. Explain about stress concentration in helical coil springs, how is it being take care of? **(03 Marks)**
    b. What is surging in springs and how it can be overcome? **(03 Marks)**
    c. The spring used in an automobile engine has to exert 500 N when the valve is closed and 600 N when the valve is open. The displacement of the valve is 5 mm. The engine crankshaft rotates at 8000 rpm. Design the spring if permissible stress in the material of the spring is 300 MPa. The ratio of mean coil diameter to the wire diameter is 6. The specific weight and the modulus of rigidity of the spring material are 7.35×10^{-5} N/mm^3, and 8×10^4 MPa, respectively. The ends of the spring are square and ground. Inspect the suitability of the spring for this engine. At what speed of the engine does the spring resonate? **(14 Marks)**

Dec. 06/ Jan. 07 (AU 53)

11. a. What is surging in helical springs and how it can be eliminate? **(04 Marks)**
    b. A railway wagon weighing 50 kN and moving with a speed of 8 km/h has to be stopped by four buffer springs in which the maximum compression allowed is

220 mm. Find the number of active turns in each spring of mean diameter 150 mm. The diameter of the spring wire is 25 mm. Also determine the maximum shear stress in each spring. Take $E = 84$ GPa. **(08 Marks)**

c. A locomotive spring has an overall length of 1100 mm and sustains a load of 75 kN at its center. The spring has 3 full length leaves and 15 graduated leaves with a central band of 100 mm. All the leaves are stressed at 0.4 GPa, when fully loaded. The ratio of total depth of spring to its width is to be 2. Determine i) Width and thickness of the leaves ii) The initial gap between full length and graduated leaves. Take $E = 206.8$ GPa. **(08 Marks)**

July 2007 (AU 53)

12. a. Derive an equation for energy stored in a helical spring. **(05 Marks)**
    b. Design a helical spring for a spring loaded safety valve (Ram's bottom safety valve) for the following conditions:
       Diameter of valve seat = 60 mm, operating pressure = 0.7 N/mm², maximum pressure when the valve blows off freely = 0.75 N/mm², maximum lift of the valve when the pressure rises from 0.7 to 0.75 N/mm² = 3.5 mm, maximum allowable stress = 550 N/mm², modulus of rigidity = 84 kN/mm², spring index = 6. **(15 Marks)**

Dec. 07/ Jan. 08 (AU 53)

13. a. Derive an expression for the stress induced in helical coil spring. **(04 Marks)**
    b. Design a helical compression spring for a maximum load of 1000 N and for a deflection of 25 mm. The maximum permissible shear stress for the spring wire is 420 N/mm², modulus of rigidity is 0.84×10^5 N/mm² and value of spring index is 6. **(10 Marks)**
    c. A one meter long cantilever spring is composed of 8 graduated leaves and one extra full length leaf. The leaves are 45 mm wide. A load of 2000 N at the end of the spring causes a deflection of 75 mm. Determine the thickness of the leaves and maximum bending stress in the full length leaf assuming that leaves are not pre-stressed. **(06 Marks)**

Dec. 07/ Jan. 08 (ME6T2)

14. a. Design a helical compression spring of circular cross-section to sustain a load that fluctuates between 2 kN and 1.5 kN undergoing a deflection of 12 mm during the fluctuation of the load. **(10 Marks)**
    b. A helical compression spring of circular cross-section is initially compressed by 25 mm. On further compression by 40 mm, the spring stores energy of 72 N-m. The spring stiffness is to be 40 N/mm. Design the spring completely. **(10 Marks)**

June/ July 08 (AU 53)

15. a. A railway wagon weighing 40 kN and moving with a speed of 10 km/hr has to be stopped by four buffer springs in which the maximum compression allowed is 200 mm, find the number of turns in each spring of mean diameter 150 mm. the diameter of spring wire is 25 mm. Take $G = 82.7 \times 10^3$ MPa. **(08 Marks)**
    b. Design a truck spring that has 12 number of leaves two of which are full length leaves. The spring supports are 1meter apart and the central band is 70 mm wide. The central load is to be 6 kN with a permissible stress of 200 MPa.

Determine the thickness, width and deflection of the spring leaves if the ratio of total depth to width of the spring is 3. **(12 Marks)**

Dec. 08/ Jan. 09 (ME6T2)

16. a. What do you understand by surge in helical springs and how can it be eliminated? **(05 Marks)**
    b. A weight of 800 N is to be dropped on the center of a platen from a height of 300 mm. the platen is supported on four identically placed helical springs. Assuming that the deflection allowed for each spring is 60 mm, spring rate of 5 and maximum allowable shear stress equal to 400 MPa, determine the diameter of the wire and design the springs completely and also tabulate the specifications for manufacturing. Take G = 80 GPa for the spring material. **(15 Marks)**

June – July 2009 (ME6T2)

17. The valve spring of a petrol engine is 40 mm long when the valve is open and 48 mm when the valve is closed. The spring loads are 200 N when the valve is closed and 400 N when the valve is open. The inside diameter of the spring should not be less than 25 mm. Design the spring. **(20 Marks)**

Dec. 08/ Jan. 09 (AU 53)

18. a. Derive an expression for the maximum strain energy stored in the closed coil spring under axial load in terms of maximum shear stress, modulus of rigidity and volume of the spring. **(04 Marks)**
    b. An automobile helical coil spring is to have a mean diameter of 80 mm and stiffness of 200 N/mm. The total axial force is 8000 N and allowable shear stress of spring material is 320 N/mm^2 and G = 8 × 10^4 N/mm^2. Calculate:
    i. Diameter of the coil, ii. Number of effective coils,
    iii. Free length of spring and iv. Maximum energy which can be stored in the spring **(08 Marks)**
    c. A laminated semi elliptical leaf spring under central load of 10 kN is to have an effective length of 1m and not to deflect more than 75 mm. The spring has 10 leaves, 2 of which are full length and have been pre-stressed so that all leaves have same stress at full load condition. All the leaves have same width and thickness. The maximum allowable stress in the leaves is 350 N/mm^2. Calculate the width and thickness of the leaves. **(08 Marks)**

June – July 2009 (AU53)

19. a. Prove that the stress in full length leaves of leaf spring is 2 times the stress in graduated leaves. **(08 Marks)**
    b. Design a spring for a balance to measure 0 to 1000 N over a scale of length 80 mm. The spring is to be enclosed in a casing of 25 mm diameter. The approximate number of turns is 30. The modulus of rigidity is 85 kN/mm^2. Also calculate the maximum shear stress induced. **(12 Marks)**

June – July 2009 (06ME61)

20. a. Derive the expression for stress induced in helical coil spring. **(05 Marks)**
    b. Design a valve spring for an automobile engine, when the valve is closed, the spring produces a force of 45 N and when it opens, produces a force of 55 N. The spring must fit over the valve bush which has an outside diameter of 20 mm

and must go inside a space of 35 mm. The lift of the valve is 6 mm. The spring index is 12. The allowable stress may be taken as 330 MPa and modulus of rigidity, $G = 80$ GPa. **(15 Marks)**

Dec. 09/ Jan. 10 (06ME61)

21. a. A railway wagon weighing 40 kN and moving with a speed of 10 km/hour has to be stopped by four buffer springs in which the maximum compression allowed is 200 mm. Find the number of turns in each spring of mean diameter 150 mm. The diameter of the spring wire is 25 mm. Take $G = 82.7 \times 10^3$ MN/m². **(10 Marks)**

b. A multi-leaf spring with camber is fitted to the chassis of an automobile over a span of 1.2 meter to absorb shocks due to a maximum load of 20 kN. The spring material can sustain a maximum stress of 0.4 GPa. All the leaves of the spring were to receive the same stress. The spring should have at least 2 full length leaves out of 8 leaves. The leaves are assembled with bolts over a span of 150 mm width at the middle. Design the spring for a maximum deflection of 50 mm. **(10 Marks)**

May/ June 2010 (AU 53)

22. a. Derive the expression for the energy stored in helical springs of circular wire. **(05 Marks)**

b. Design a helical compression spring for a maximum load of 1000 N for a deflection of 22 mm using the value of spring index as 5. The maximum permissible shear stress for the spring wire is 420 N/mm² and modulus of rigidity is 84 kN/mm². Take Wahl's factor, $K = \dfrac{4C-1}{4C-4} + \dfrac{0.615}{C}$, C – spring index. **(15 Marks)**

December 2010 (AU 53)

23. a. Derive an expression for the shear stress induced in a helical compression spring, with usual notation. **(06 Marks)**

b. At the bottom of an elevator shaft, a group of 16 identical springs are set in parallel to absorb the shock in case of failure. Assuming a free fall of 1 mt, springs of wire diameter 10 mm, mean coil diameter 100 mm, number of active coils 20, determine the load on each spring and maximum shear stress induced in the spring. The weight of the elevator with the passengers may be taken as 10,000 N. **(14 Marks)**

May/ June 2010 (06ME61)

24. a. Derive an expression for shearing stress induced in a helical spring subjected to a compressive load. **(07 Marks)**

b. Write a note on Wahl stress factor. **(03 Marks)**

c. A semi elliptical multi leaf spring is used for the suspension of the rear axle of a truck. It consists of two extra full length leaves and 10 graduated leaves including the master leaf. The center to center distance between the spring eyes is 1.2 m. The leaves are made of steel with $\sigma_{yt} = 1500$ MPa, $E = 2.07 \times 10^5$ MPa and $FOS = 2.5$. The spring is to be designed for a maximum force of 30 kN. The leaves are pre-stressed so as to equalize stresses in all leaves.

Determine:
i. C/S of the leaves
ii. initial nip
iii. initial pre-load required to close the gap
iv. deflection of the spring. **(10 Marks)**

December 2010 (06ME61)

25. a. A semi-elliptical laminated spring has effective length of 1m. The spring has to sustain a load of 75 kN. The spring has 3 full length leaves and 16 graduated leaves. If the leaves are pre-stressed such that the stress induced in all the leaves is same and are limited to 400 MPa, when maximum load is applied. The width of the leaves is 9 times the thickness. Assume $E = 200$ GPa. Determine:
   i. The width and thickness of the leaves.
   ii. The initial space that has to be provided between full length leaves and the graduated leaves before the band is applied.
   iii. Load on the clip to close the initial gap. **(10 Marks)**
   b. A load of 2 kN is dropped axially on a closed coil helical spring from a height of 250 mm. The spring has 20 effective turns and it is made of 25 mm diameter wire. The spring index is 8. Find the maximum shear stress induced in the spring and the amount of compression produced. Take $G = 82.7$ GPa. **(10 Marks)**

June/ July 2011 (06ME61)

26. a. Design a helical compression spring for a service load ranging from 2250 N to 2750 N. The axial deflection of the spring for the load range is 6 mm. Assume a spring index of 5, permissible shear stress of 420 MPa and modulus of rigidity of 84 kN/mm². **(12 Marks)**
   b. A truck spring has 12 leaves, two of which are full length leaves. The spring supports are 1.05 m apart and the central band is 85 mm wide. The central band is 5.4 kN and the permissible stress in the spring material is 280 MPa. If the ratio of total depth to the width of the spring is 3, determine the thickness and width of the spring leaves and also the deflection of the spring. **(08 Marks)**

December 2011 (06ME61)

27. a. Design a helical compression spring to sustain a axial load that fluctuates between 1.5 kN and 2 kN with an associated deflection of 15 mm during the fluctuation of the load. **(10 Marks)**
   b. An automotive leaf spring is to be designed to consist of 10 graduated leaves and 2 full length leaves. The spring is to support a central load of 5 kN over a span of 1100 mm with the actual band width of 100 m. the width and thickness of the leaves limiting the maximum equalized stress induced in the leaves to 350 MPa. Also determine the initial gap to be provided between the full length and graduate leaves before the assembly. **(10 Marks)**

June 2012 (06ME61)

28. a. Derive an expression for the stress induced in a helical spring, with usual notations. **(06 Marks)**
   b. A carriage weighing 25000 N is moving on a track with a linear velocity of 3.6 km/hour. It is brought to rest by two helical compression springs in the form of a bumper by undergoing a compression of 180 mm. The springs may be

assumed to have a spring index of 6 and permissible shear strength of 450 MPa. Design the spring and determine the diameter of the wire, mean coil diameter and the length of the spring. Assume modulus of rigidity of the spring material as 81.4 GPa. **(14 Marks)**

December 2012 (06ME12)

29. a. Derive an expression for strain energy in a body when the lad is applied gradually. **(05 Marks)**
    b. A railway wagon weighing 40 kN and moving with a speed of 10 km/hour has to be stopped by 4 buffer springs in which the maximum compression allowed is 200 mm. Find the number of turns in each spring of mean diameter 150 mm. the diameter of the spring wire is 25 mm. Take $G = 82.7$ GPa. **(08 Marks)**
    c. A truck spring has 12 leaves of which 2 are full length leaves. The spring supports are 1.05 m apart and the central load is 85 mm wide. The central load is to be 5400 N with a permissible stress of 0.28 GPa. The ratio of total depth to width of spring is 4. Assume $E = 210$ GPa. Determine the maximum deflection in the spring. **(07 Marks)**

June/ July 2013 (AU53)

30. a. A helical compression spring of a mechanism is subjected to an initial preload of 50 N and the maximum force during the load cycle is 300 N. The wire diameter is 5 mm, while the spring index is 5. The spring is made of oil-hardened and tempered steel wire of grade SW. Determine the factor of safety from fatigue considerations. **(10 Marks)**
    b. A semi-elliptical multi-leaf spring has two extra full length leaves and ten graduated leaves including the master leaf. The center to center distance between the spring eyes is 1.2 m. The leaves are made of steel with $\sigma_{ut} = 1500$ MPa and $E = 207$ GPa. The factor of safety is 2.5. The spring is to be designed for a maximum force of 30 kN. The leaves are prestressed so as to equalize stresses in all leaves. Determine the cross-section of leaves and the deflection at the end of the spring. **(10 Marks)**

June/ July 2013 (06ME61)

31. a. A Belleville spring is made of 3 mm sheet metal with OD 125 mm and ID 50 mm. the spring is dished 5 mm. The maximum stress is to be 500 MPa. assuming Poisson's ratio = 0.3 and $E = 200$ GPa, determine:
    i. Safe load carried by the spring
    ii. Deflection for this load
    iii. Stress developed at the outer edge
    iv. Load required to flatten the spring. **(10 Marks)**
    b. Determine the complete specifications of a helical compression spring to sustain an axial load of 3 kN. The deflection is 60 mm and the spring index is 6. Shear stress is not to exceed 300 MPa. Take $G = 81$ GPa, clearance, $\alpha = 0.25y$. Assume square and round ends. **(10 Marks)**

June/ July 2013 (10ME62)

32. a. The laminated leaf spring has an overall length of 1.1 m and has a central load of 160 kN. The spring has 3 full length leaves and 15 graduated leaves with a central band of 100 mm wide. All the leaves are to be stressed to 400 N/mm², when fully loaded. The ratio of total spring depth to width is approximately 2.

Determine:
i. The width and thickness of the leaves.
ii. Initial space to be provided between full length and graduated leaves.
iii. What load is exerted on the band when the leaves are assembled?
(10 Marks)

b. Design a valve spring for an automobile engine, when the valve is closed, the spring produces a force of 45 N and when it opens produces a force of 55 N. The spring must fit over the valve bush which has an outside diameter of 20 mm and must go inside a space of 35 mm. the lift of the valve is 6 mm. the spring index is 12. The allowable stress may be taken as 0.33 GPa. Modulus of rigidity = 80 GPa. **(10 Marks)**

Dec.2013/ Jan.2014 (10ME62)

33. a. Enumerate the applications of springs. Also derive an equation for the deflection of a closed coiled helical spring. **(06 Marks)**
b. A spring is subjected to a load varying from 500 N and 1200 N. It is to be made of oil tempered cold drawn wire. Design factor based on Wahl's line is 1.25. The spring index is to be 6. The compression in the spring for the maximum load is 30 mm. Determine the wire diameter, mean coil diameter and free length of the spring. Take the yield stress in shear as 700 MPa and endurance stress in shear as 350 MPa for the material of the wire. **(14 Marks)**

Dec. 2013/ Jan. 2014 (AU53)

34. a. A helical compression spring with spring rate (stiffness) of 18 N/mm gets compressed by 30 mm when the coils touch each other. The allowable shear stress is 345 MPa. The spring index is 8; the ends are squared and ground. The modulus of rigidity of the material is 83 GPa. Calculate the following:
i. wire diameter
ii. mean coil diameter
iii. number of active coils
iv. solid length of spring.
(10 Marks)

b. A semi-elliptical leaf spring used for automobile suspension consists of 3 extra length full leaves and fifteen graduated leaves. The effective distance between the supports is 1000 mm. The maximum load on the spring is 75 kN. The modulus of elasticity of the material is 210 GPa. The breadth of each leaves is 9 times the thickness. The leaves are pre-stressed such that the maximum stress induced in the leaves is 450 MPa. Determine the following:
i. the width and thickness of the leaves.
ii. initial gap (nip) between the full length and graduated leaves.
iii. the load on the clip bolts to close the initial gap.
(10 Marks)

4

Spur and Helical Gears

4.1 INTRODUCTION TO GEARS

Gears are defined as toothed wheels, which transmit power and motion from one shaft to another by means of successive engagement of teeth. Hence, gear drives are also called positive drives. In any pair of gears, the smaller one is called pinion and the larger one is called gear, immaterial of which is driving the other.

When pinion is the driver, it results in step down drive in which the output speed decreases and the torque increases. On the other hand, when the gear is the driver, it results in step up drive in which the output speed increases and the torque decreases.

4.2 CLASSIFICATION OF GEARS

1. According to the position of axes shafts:
   a. parallel   b. intersecting   c. non-parallel and non-intersecting.
2. According to peripheral velocity of gears:
   a. Low velocity b. medium velocity   c. high velocity gears.
3. According to the type of gearing:
   a. external   b. internal   c. rack and pinion.
4. According to the position of the teeth:
   a. straight   b. inclined   c. curved.

4.3 ADVANTAGES OF GEAR DRIVE

- It transmits exact velocity ratio.
- Can be used to transmit very large amount of power.
- Can be used for small center distances between shafts.
- It has high efficiency.
- It has reliable service.
- It has a compact layout.

4.4 DISADVANTAGES OF GEAR DRIVE

- It is costlier since it requires special tools and equipment to manufacture them.
- Error in cutting teeth may cause vibration and noise during operation.
- Requires suitable lubricant for proper operation.

4.5 GENERAL PROFILES OF GEAR TOOTH

There are two profiles of gear tooth:

1. Cycloidal teeth
2. Involute teeth.
   - A Cycloidal tooth is a curve traced by a point on the circumference of a circle which rolls without slipping on a fixed straight line.
   - An involute tooth of a circle is a plane curve generated by a point on a circle tangent, which rolls on the circle without slipping –or- by a point on a taut string which is unwrapped from a reel.

4.6 SYSTEM –OR– PRESSURE ANGLES OF GEAR TOOTH

1. 14 ½° composite system — 12 ⎫
2. 14 ½° full depth involute system — 32 ⎬ minimum no. of teeth.
3. 20° full depth involute system — 18 ⎪
4. 20° stub involute system — 14 ⎭

1. **14 ½° composite system:** is used for general purpose gears. It is the strongest but has no interchangeability. The tooth profile is a cycloidal curve at the top and bottom while the middle portion is a involute curve. This system is based on a 12 tooth pinion as the smallest that will give satisfactory tooth action. The teeth are produced by hobs or milling cutters.
2. **14 ½° full depth involute system:** This system is used with gear hobs for spur and helical gears. The minimum number of teeth is 32 with pinion as the smallest for full involute action with a rack.
3. **20° full depth involute system:** This system has the same proportion as that of 14 ½° full depth involute system, except that the pressure angle has been increased to 20° to avoid interference and undercutting. An 18 tooth pinion is the smallest for full involute action with a rack.
4. **20° stub involute system:** This was developed to produce a strong tooth so as to take heavy loads free from undercutting. The tooth is made shorter than the full depth tooth. This is extensively used in automotive industry because of its ruggedness.

4.7 TERMS USED IN GEARS

- **Pitch circle:** It is an imaginary circle which by pure rolling action would give the same motion as that of an actual gear. All the calculations are based on pitch circle.
- **Pitch circle diameter (PCD) or- (d):** It refers to the diameter of pitch circle
- **Circular pitch (p):** It is the distance measured on the circumference of pitch circle from a point on one tooth to a corresponding point on the next tooth.
$$p = \pi d/z \qquad \ldots 12.1/ \text{Pg 162, DHB}$$
- **Diametrical pitch (P):** It is the ratio of number of teeth to the PCD.
$$P = z/d = \pi/p \qquad \ldots 12.2/ \text{Pg 162, DHB}$$
$$\text{-or- } Pp = \pi \qquad \ldots 12.3/ \text{Pg 162, DHB}$$
- **Module (m):** It is defined as the ratio of pitch circle diameter (PCD) to the number of teeth.
  Mathematically, $m = d/z = 1/P$ $\qquad \ldots 12.4/ \text{Pg 162, DHB}$
  d – pitch diameter, z – no. of teeth.
- **Pressure angle or angle of obliquity:** It is the angle between the line of action and a perpendicular to the center line of a pair of gears. Standard pressure angles commonly used are 14 ½°, 20°.

- **Backlash:** is the difference between tooth space and tooth thickness as measured on pitch circle.
- **Interference:** refers to the phenomena when the tip of a tooth undercuts the root of its mating gear.

4.8 GEAR MATERIALS

The material used for gears depends upon the strength and service conditions like wear, noise, etc. The gears can be manufactured from metallic or nonmetallic materials. *Metallic gears* include cast iron, steel, and bronze. *Nonmetallic gears* include wood, compressed paper, synthetic resins, etc

- CI is widely used due to its good damping properties, excellent machinability, wear characteristics, and ease of producing complicated shapes by casting.
- Steel is used for high strength gears. These are heat treated to combine toughness and tooth hardness.
- Phosphor- bronze is widely used for worm gears in order to reduce the wear of the worms.

4.9 DESIGN CONSIDERATIONS FOR GEAR DRIVE

In designing the gear drive, the following data/specifications are usually given:
- The power to be transmitted.
- The speed of driving gear.
- The speed of driven gear or the velocity ratio and
- The center distance.

The following requirements have to be met by the gear drive:
- The gear teeth should have sufficient strength so that they do not fail under static/dynamic loading during normal operating conditions.
- The gear teeth should have good wear characteristics.
- The drive should be compact.
- Lubrication of gears should be satisfactory.
- Alignment of gears and deflections of shafts must be considered since the performance is affected.
- The drive should be properly aligned.

4.10 METHODS OF GEAR DRIVE

We have two methods of designing a gear drive:
1. **Beam Strength Theory:** Here the design is based on the assumption that the gear tooth is a cantilever beam of uniform strength. "Lewis" formulated the equations for evaluating the gear parameters such as addendum, tooth depth, module, face width, etc. This theory is known as *"Beam strength theory"*.
2. **Contact Stress Theory:** The two sides of a gear are usually curved and have involutes. During power transmission, the curved surfaces are in contact. Considering the stresses due to curved surface in contact, "Hertz" has developed an equation to evaluate the gear parameters, known as *"Contact stress theory"*.

Since Lewis theory is simple and gives results on safer side, usually this theory is used for designing the gears.

SPUR GEARS

4.11 INTRODUCTION

Spur gears have teeth parallel to the axis of rotation and are used to transmit motion between parallel shafts. The spur gear is the simplest and easy to design. However due to their design spur gears create large stress on the gear teeth.

Spur gears are known as *slow speed gears*. Spur gears are noisy due to their design; and if noise is not a problem spur gears can be used at almost any speed. Spur gears are noisy because every time a gear tooth engages a tooth on the other gear, the teeth collide, and this impact makes a noise.

Applications: Washing machines, electric screw drivers, etc.

4.12 BEAM STRENGTH OF A GEAR TOOTH—LEWIS EQUATION

The teeth of a pinion are subjected to large number of load cycles than that of the gear wheel and wears out more quickly. For this reason, the material used for pinion should possess higher mechanical characteristics than the material used for gear. The beam strength of gear teeth is determined by using Lewis equation; and the load carrying capacity of toothed gear determined by this equation gives satisfactory results.

In Lewis equation each tooth is considered to be a cantilever beam as shown in **Fig. 4.1** with load acting at an outer corner of tooth or distributed across the active face of the tooth. Further it is assumed that any of the tooth pair transmits the entire load. When the contact begins, the load is assumed to be at the end of driven teeth and as the contact ceases, the load is at the beginning of the driving teeth. This may not be the case if the load is distributed among several teeth.

Figure 4.1 shows a gear tooth with face acting at the tip of tooth. The normal force (F_n) is resolved into two components viz, the tangential component (F_t) and the radial component (F_r) acting perpendicular and parallel to the centre line of the tooth. The radial component induces a compressive stress of very small magnitude and hence its effect is neglected. The tangential component induces bending stress and tends to weaken break the tooth and thus forms the basis for design considerations.

The maximum bending stress or the stress at the critical section may be obtained by drawing a parabola through A and tangential to the tooth curves at C and B respectively, as represented by dotted lines and outlines a beam of uniform strength, i.e. if the tooth are shaped like a parabola it will have the same stress at all sections. The maximum value of bending stress at BC (critical section) is obtained as follows.

We know that, $\quad \dfrac{M}{I} = \dfrac{\sigma}{c} = \dfrac{E}{R}$

Therefore, $\sigma = \dfrac{Mc}{I}$ ...(Eq. 4.1)

Where, $M = F_t h$ – the maximum bending moment at the critical section
F_t – tangential load assumed to be uniformly distributed across the face of the gear
h – height of the tooth
b – face width of the tooth
t – tooth thickness
$I = bt^3/12$ – moment of inertia about center line of the tooth

$c = t/2$ – half length of tooth thickness
σ – allowable stress

Eq. (4.1) yields ... $\sigma = \dfrac{(F_t h) \times (t/2)}{bt^3/12}$

$$\sigma = \dfrac{6F_t h}{bt^2} \qquad \text{...(Eq. 4.2)}$$

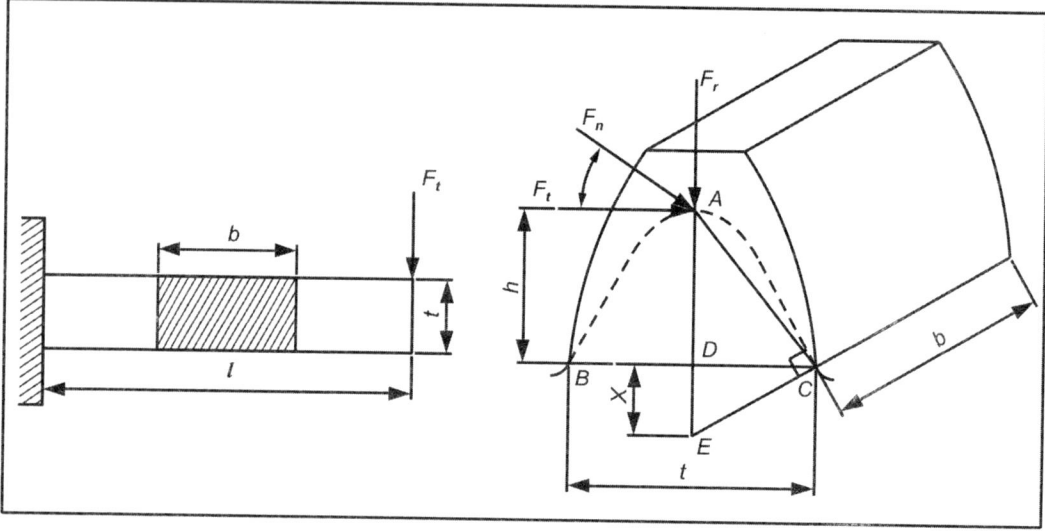

Fig. 4.1: Beam strength of a gear tooth

To find F_t:

Method I:

From similar triangles ACD and DCE, we have

$$\dfrac{x}{t/2} = \dfrac{t/2}{h}$$

$$h = \dfrac{t^2}{4x}$$

Eq. (4.2) yields ... $\sigma = \dfrac{6F_t}{bt^2} \times \dfrac{t^2}{4x} = \dfrac{3F_t}{2bx}$

$$\sigma = \dfrac{F_t}{(2x/3)b} \qquad \text{...(Eq. 4.3)}$$

Multiply and divide Eq. (4.3) with circular pitch (p), we have

$$\sigma = \dfrac{F_t \times p}{(2x/3)b \times p}$$

$$= \dfrac{F_t}{pb \times \left(\dfrac{2x}{3p}\right)}$$

$$\sigma = \dfrac{F_t}{pby}$$

or $\quad F_t = \sigma b y p$ ... *"Original LEWIS equation"*: ...(Eq. 4.4)... **12.15/ Pg 163, DHB**

Where, $y = \left(\dfrac{2x}{3p}\right)$ is the Lewis form factor

Method II:

From Eq. (4.2), we have $F_t = \dfrac{\sigma b t^2}{6h}$

Multiply and divide with circular pitch (p), we have

$$= \dfrac{\sigma b t^2}{6h} \times \left(\dfrac{p}{p}\right)$$

$$= \sigma b p \times \left(\dfrac{t^2}{6hp}\right)$$

$$= \sigma b p \times \left[\dfrac{t^2}{6h \times (\pi m)}\right] \quad \text{because } p = \pi m$$

...using **12.3 and 12.4/ Pg 162, DHB**

$$F_t = \sigma b y p \qquad \text{... (Eq. 4.5)... Same as (Eq. 4.4)}$$

Where, $y = \left[\dfrac{t^2}{6h\pi m}\right]$ is the Lewis form factor

...**12.16/ Pg 163, DHB**

Note:
- Values of y ...**Eqs 12.17a – 12.17c/ Pg 163, DHB** and **Table 12.5/ Pg 184, DHB**
- Values of module, m ...**Table 12.2/ Pg 182, DHB**
- As per American gear manufacturing association (AGMA) standards, the ratio b/m is

$$9.5 \leq b/m \leq 12.5$$
$$9.5m \leq b \leq 12.5m \qquad \text{...}\textbf{12.18/ Pg 164, DHB}$$
And $k = b/m$ ...**12.16/ Pg 163, DHB**

4.12.1 Assumptions in Lewis Bending Equation

Following are the general assumption used for deriving the Lewis bending equation:
- The tooth is assumed to be a simple cantilever beam.
- The tangential component of force is uniformly distributed across the face width. This assumption is valid for small face widths in the range of
- The effect of radial component which produces direct compressive stress is neglected.
- The maximum stress occurs when the entire load is at the tip of the tooth. This is not true because more than one pair of teeth will be in contact.
- The effect of stress concentration and manufacturing errors are neglected.

4.13 VELOCITY FACTOR (C_V)

Slight inaccuracies in tooth profile and tooth spacing, teeth being not absolutely rigid, variations in applied load and load repetitions will cause impact and fatigue stresses that become much severe as the pitch line velocity increases. To allow for these additional stresses, a velocity factor is introduced in the Lewis equation.

The values of velocity factor, (C_v)   **...Eqs 12.19a – 12.19e/ Pg 164, DHB**, for various velocities

                                 ...**Table 12.9/ Pg 188, DHB**, for peripheral speeds

4.14 ALLOWABLE STRESS (σ)

The allowable stress (σ) for a gear tooth depends upon the selected material, pitch line velocity and the loading conditions. To take care of these, we have

$$\sigma = \sigma_d C_v \quad \text{...(Eq. 4.6)}$$

Eq. (4.4) or Eq. (4.5) yields ... $F_t = pby\,(\sigma_d C_v)$

    i.e. $F_t = \sigma_d C_v\, byp$ ...(Eq. 4.6a) **12.15/ Pg 163, DHB**

Since $p = \pi m$, we have

    $F_t = \pi \sigma_d C_v\, bym$ ...(Eq. 4.6b) **12.15/ Pg 163, DHB**

Also Form factor, $Y = \pi y$ ...**12.16/ Pg 163, DHB**

    $F_t = \sigma_d C_v\, bYm$ ...(Eq. 4.6c) ...**12.15/ Pg 163, DHB**

Further $p = \pi / P$ ...**12.3/ Pg 164, DHB**

(Eq. 4.5a) yields... $F_t = \sigma_d C_v\, by \times \dfrac{\pi}{P}$

    $F_t = \sigma_d C_v\, bY/P$ ...(Eq. 4.6d)... **12.15/ Pg 163, DHB**

Where, σ_d – allowable static stress

                                 ...**Table 12.7/ Pg 186, DHB**

For steels, $\sigma_d = \sigma_u / 3$

4.15 DESIGN METHODOLOGY FOR SPUR GEARS

There are two methods of designing a spur gear problem as discussed below.

Method 1: If the pitch diameter is known:

We know that, $F_t = \sigma_d C_v\, bYm$ ...using (Eq. 4.6c) ...**12.15/ Pg 163, DHB**

But $k = b/m$ ...**12.16/ Pg 163, DHB**

i.e. $F_t = \sigma_d C_v\, (km)Ym$

      $= \sigma_d C_v\, kYm^2$ ...(Eq. 4.7)

Therefore, $m = \sqrt{\dfrac{F_t}{\sigma_d C_v k Y}}$ ...(Eq. 4.8) **12.16/ Pg 163, DHB**

Method 2: If the pitch diameter is unknown:

We know that *torque = Force × distance*

$$M_t = F_t \times (d/2)$$

$$F_t = \dfrac{2M_t}{d} \quad \text{...12.22/ Pg 165, DHB}$$

$$\sigma_d C_v\, kYm^2 = \dfrac{2M_t}{d} \quad \text{...using (Eq. 4.7)}$$

But $m = d/z$, and $d = mz$

Therefore, $\sigma_d C_v kYm^2 = \dfrac{2M_t}{mz}$

$$m^3 = \dfrac{2M_t}{\sigma_d C_v kYz}$$

$$m = \sqrt[3]{\dfrac{2M_t}{\sigma_d C_v kYz}} \qquad \text{...(Eq. 4.9) } \mathbf{12.16/\ Pg\ 163,\ DHB}$$

Where, $Y = \pi y$ and $k = b/m$

In both the cases discussed above, the smallest possible module will provide the *most economical design.*

In general,

When diameter is known,   *...design for the smallest pitch diameter.*
When diameter is unknown   *...design for the largest number of teeth.*

4.16 STRENGTH FACTOR

The amount of force transmitted to a gear tooth is a function of the product of allowable static stress (σ_d) and the Lewis form factor (y), known as strength factor.

     i.e. strength factor = $\sigma_d y$

When two gears are in mesh, the weaker gear will have the smallest value of $\sigma_d \cdot y$.

- When both pinion and gear are made of *same material,* then pinion is weaker
- When both pinion and gear are made of *different materials,* then ($\sigma_d y$) will be the deciding factor for the weaker part.

4.17 TANGENTIAL LOAD

The tangential load at pitch line may be obtained from the power equation as

     Power, $P = F_t \cdot v$ watts (W)   ...(Eq. 4.10)

     Where, $v = \dfrac{\pi d N}{60}$ m/s

$$P = \dfrac{F_t \cdot v}{1000} \text{ kW} \qquad \text{...12.14a/ Pg 163, DHB}$$

or $\qquad F_t = \dfrac{1000 P}{v} \qquad \text{...(Eq. 4.11)}$

For gears subjected to shock and operating continuously for more than 10 hours/day, Eq. (4.11) is modified by using a service factor C_s,

     i.e. $\mathbf{F_t = \dfrac{1000 P C_s}{v}} \qquad \text{...(Eq. 4.12) } \mathbf{12.20a/\ Pg\ 164,\ DHB}$

Where, C_s – service factor   ...**Table 12.8/ Pg 187, DHB**

4.18 FORCES ACTING ON SPUR GEAR

- Tangential force, $F_t = \dfrac{2M_t}{d}$ ...**12.22/ Pg 165, DHB**
- Radial force, $F_r = F_t \tan \alpha$ ...**12.23/ Pg 165, DHB**

     Where, α – pressure angle
     F_r is always directed towards the center of the gear.

332 Design of Machine Elements II (DME II)

- Normal force acting on tooth, $F_n = \dfrac{2M_t}{d_2 \cos \alpha}$ ...12.24a/ Pg 165, DHB

$$= \dfrac{M_t(i+1)}{ai \cos \alpha}$$ ...12.24b/ Pg 165, DHB

- Pitch diameter of pinion, $d_1 = \dfrac{2a}{(i+1)}$ ...12.25/ Pg 165, DHB

- Pitch diameter of gear, $d_2 = \dfrac{2ai}{(i+1)}$ ...12.25/ Pg 165, DHB

- Gear ratio $i = z_2/z_1$ ...Table 12.8a/ Pg 187, DHB

Note: **Suffix "1" refers to pinion and "2" refers to gear.**

4.19 DYNAMIC TOOTH LOAD (F_d)

The velocity factor discussed in the previous section was used to take care of the effect of dynamic loading. The dynamic loading is due to the following reasons:
- The teeth are not perfectly straight.
- The profiles are never perfect involutes.
- The load distribution is not uniform across the face.
- The tooth deflects under the load.
- The elements of the face are not perfectly parallel to the axis.

Due to the above irregularities there will be dynamic load due to shock and impact and hence the dynamic load on gear tooth will be greater than the transmitted load.

The most widely used expression for dynamic load (maximum instantaneous load) was proposed by Buckingham and is given as

$$F_d = F_t + F_i \qquad \text{...(Eq. 4.13)}$$

i.e. the actual tooth load is composed of applied or transmitted load (F_t) and an incremental load (F_i). This incremental load is caused by changes in velocity of gears resulting from machining errors, inertia forces and impact loads on the teeth,

i.e. $\quad F_d = F_t + \dfrac{K_3 v(Cb + F_t)}{K_3 v + \sqrt{Cb + F_t}}$ ...(Eq. 4.14) **12.33/ Pg 166, DHB**

Where, F_t – tangential tooth load
$K_3 = 20.67$ – Constant
v – pitch line velocity (m/s)
b – face width
C – dynamic factor depending upon machining errors
...Table 12.12/ Pg 190, DHB

- For a given pitch line velocity, the maximum allowable error 'e' can be obtained from **Table 12.14/ Pg 191, DHB**. From the obtained value of e, C can be calculated as per the given material from **Table 12.12/ Pg 190, DHB**.
- On the other hand if the Young's modulus is specified for the gears and pinion, then C is calculated as

$$C = \dfrac{e}{k_1 \left[\dfrac{1}{E_1} + \dfrac{1}{E_2} \right]}$$ ...12.33/ Pg 166, DHB

Where, k_1 = 9.345 for 14.5° full depth teeth
= 9.000 for 20° full depth teeth
= 8.700 for 20° for stub teeth
e – maximum error between gears
...**Table 12.13/ Pg 191, DHB**
and Fig. 12.3/ Pg 205, DHB
E_1 and E_2 – Young's modulus for pinion and gear

4.20 DYNAMIC LOAD FACTOR

Dynamic load factor = F_d/F_t ...(Eq. 4.15)

This is a function of accuracy, peripheral velocity and tooth surface hardness. As the degree of hardness increases, the dynamic load factor increases. It also increases with increase in the peripheral velocity.

With increase in tooth strength, the load transmitted increases and the dynamic load factor decreases.

4.21 STATIC TOOTH LOAD –OR– BEAM STRENGTH –OR– ENDURANCE STRENGTH (F_{en})

The maximum load the gears can transmit without undergoing failure (fatigue) is called the endurance strength. This is obtained by substituting the flexural endurance limit or elastic limit stress in place of permissible working stress

We know that, $F_t = \sigma_d C_v bym$ ...*using* (Eq. 4.5c) **12.15/ Pg 163, DHB**

Substituting $F_t = F_{en}$, $C_v = 1$ and $\sigma_d = \sigma_{en}$, we have

$$F_{en} = \sigma_{en} bYm$$ ...(Eq. 4.16) **12.34/ Pg 166, DHB**

The values of σ_{en} ...**Table 12.15/ Pg 192, DHB**

For steady loads, $F_{en} = 1.25\ F_d$
For pulsating loads, $F_{en} = 1.35\ F_d$
For shock loads, $F_{en} = 1.50\ F_d$ ...**12.35(a-c)/ Pg 166, DHB**

For safety against static tooth load, $F_{en} \geq F_d$ ...(Eq. 4.17)

4.22 WEAR TOOTH LOAD (F_W)

Wear is defined as the progressive removal of material from a surface due to relative motion between that surface and the contacting substance.

The amount of wear depends upon:
- Material
- Curvature of tooth surfaces
- Surface finish
- Lubrication and
- The amount of sliding action in the tooth surface

The load limit for wear is determined by the surface endurance limit of the materials, curvature of the surface and the relative surface hardness. When mating gears of different materials are used, the harder material will work-harden the softer material, thereby raising its endurance limit. For steels this is in direct proportion to the Brinell hardness. Hence the pinion should always be harder to preserve the involute profile, to allow for greater abrasive wear and decrease the possibility of seizure.

The limiting load of wear, $F_w = d_1 bQK = mz_1 bQK$ ...(Eq. 4.18) **12.36a/ Pg 167, DHB**

Where, d_1 – diameter of pinion

K – load stress factor

...Table 12.16 and 12.17/ Pg 193-194, DHB

$$= \frac{\sigma_{es}^2 \sin \alpha}{1.4} \left[\frac{1}{E_1} + \frac{1}{E_2} \right] \quad \text{...12.36b/ Pg 167, DHB}$$

Q – ratio factor

$$= \frac{2d_2}{d_2 + d_1} = \frac{2z_2}{z_2 + z_1} \quad \text{...12.36c/ Pg 167, DHB}$$

σ_{es} – surface endurance limit

For steels, $\sigma_{es} = [2.75(BHN) - 70]$ ...12.36d/ Pg 167, DHB

(BHN) = average Brinell hardness number for gear and pinion

$$= \frac{BHN_1 + BHN_2}{2}$$

For safety against wear, $F_w \geq F_d$ ...(Eq. 4.19)

4.23 VELOCITY RATIO

It is defined as the ratio of angular velocity of pinion to that of the gear.

i.e. $$VR = \frac{\omega_p}{\omega_g} = \frac{N_p}{N_g} \quad \text{...(Eq. 4.20)}$$

for spur gears, the velocity ratio is inversely proportional to the pitch diameter, we have

$$VR = \frac{N_p}{N_g} = \frac{d_g}{d_p}$$

But $m = dz$

Thus $$VR = \frac{N_p}{N_g} = \frac{d_g}{d_p} = \frac{z_g}{z_p} = i \quad \text{...(Eq. 4.21)}$$

Note: Suffix "1 –or- p" refers to pinion and "2 –or- g" refers to gear.

4.24 DESIGN PROCEDURE FOR SPUR GEAR PROBLEMS

1. Material selection:
- Select suitable material if not given from **Table 12.7/ Pg 186, DHB**.
- **Identifying weaker part (pinion/gear):**
  → If the material used for both pinion and gear is same, then the pinion is weaker.
  → If the material used for both pinion and gear are different, then the strength factor $(\sigma_d y)$ is used to determine the weaker part.
- Design is based on weaker part.

2. **To find module:**

   a. if the diameter is known, use $m = \sqrt{\dfrac{F_t}{\sigma_d C_v kY}}$ Where, $F_t = \dfrac{1000\, PC_s}{v}$

   b. if the diameter is unknown, use $m = \sqrt[3]{\dfrac{2M_t}{\sigma_d C_v kYz}}$ Where, $F_t = \dfrac{2M_t}{d}$

   Where, $Y = \pi y$ and $k = b/m$

   c. check for σ_d in both the cases

   d. If σ_d > permissible value, design fails. Hence adopt/ change the module and repeat (2c)

3. **Calculate the dynamic load (F_d).**
4. **Calculate the endurance limit (F_{en}).**

   For safe design, $F_{en} > F_d$

5. **Calculate the wear load (F_w)**
   - For safe design, $F_w > F_d$
   - If $F_w < F_d$, then equate $F_w = F_d$

     i.e. $d_1 b Q K = F_d$

   Find the value of K, and choose suitable hardness for gear and pinion using **Table 12.16/ Pg 193, DHB**

Note:
- If in the problem, diameter is known and z is unknown, calculate m assuming suitable value of z. After obtaining m, find the value of z again.

4.25 DESIGN ALTERATIONS FOR A SPUR GEAR

If the gear tooth is not strong enough (statically/dynamically), the design can be altered as follows:
- The module can be increased (this increases the tooth size).
- The face width can be increased (this increases the load carrying capacity).
- By changing the material of gears.

   If the gear tooth is over designed, the designer can change any or all of the above mentioned factors.

4.26 PROBLEMS BASED ON UNKNOWN DIAMETER

1. A pair of straight teeth spur gear is to transmit 20 kW when pinion rotates at 300 rpm. The velocity ratio is 3:1. The allowable static stress for pinion and gear materials are 120 MPa and 100 MPa respectively. The pinion has 15 teeth and its face width is 10 times the module. The tooth form factor is $y = 0.154 - \dfrac{0.912}{z}$, velocity factor, $C_v = \dfrac{3}{3+v}$, v – velocity in m/s. Determine: a. Module, b. face width, c. PCD of gears, from standpoint of strength only.

   (Similar) [VTU-June/ July - 2009 - 14 Marks]

Solution: $P = 20$ kW, speed of pinion, N_p or $N_1 = 300$ rpm, $i = 3:1$, σ_{dp} or $\sigma_{d1} = 120$ MPa, σ_{dg} or $\sigma_{d2} = 100$ MPa, number of teeth on pinion, z_p or $z_1 = 15$, face width, $b = 10\, m$, $y = 0.154 - \dfrac{0.912}{z}$, $C_v = \dfrac{3}{3+v}$ then, find

a. $m = ?$ b. $b = ?$ c. $d_p, d_g = ?$
We know that, $i = s$
$\therefore$ $z_g = iz_p = 3 \times 15 = 45$ teeth

Identifying weaker part (pinion/gear):

We know that strength factor $= \sigma_d \cdot y$

- But $\qquad y = 0.154 - \dfrac{0.912}{z}$ ... (data)

  i.e. $y_p = 0.154 - \dfrac{0.912}{z_p}$

  $y_p = 0.154 - \dfrac{0.912}{15} = 0.0932$

  $y_g = 0.154 - \dfrac{0.912}{45} = 0.1337$

$\therefore$ for pinion $\quad \sigma_{dp} \cdot y_p = 120 \times 0.0932 = 11.18$ MPa
for gear, $\quad \sigma_{dg} \cdot y_g = 100 \times 0.1337 = 13.37$ MPa

Since $\sigma_{dp} \cdot y_p$ is less, design is based on **pinion**.

Note: Suffix "1 –or- p" refers to pinion and "2 –or- g" refers to gear.

a. To find module (m):

Since the diameter is unknown, we have $m = \sqrt[3]{\dfrac{2M_t}{\sigma_d C_v k Y z}}$

...Eq. (i) **12.16/ Pg 163, DHB**

- Now $\qquad k = b/m = 10$
- Form factor, $\qquad Y = \pi y_p = 0.0932\pi$ ...**12.16/ Pg 163, DHB**

- $v = \dfrac{\pi d_p N_p}{60} = \dfrac{\pi \times (mz_p) N_p}{60} = \dfrac{\pi m \times 15 \times 300}{60}$

  $= 235.6m$ mm/s $= 0.235m$ m/s

- $C_v = \dfrac{3}{3+v} = \dfrac{3}{3+0.235m}$

- $P = \dfrac{2\pi N_p M_t}{60}$

  $20 \times 10^3 = \dfrac{2\pi \times 300 \times M_t}{60}$

  $M_t = 636.62$ N-m -or- 636.62×10^3 N-mm

Eq. (i) yields... $m^3 = \dfrac{2 \times 636.62 \times 10^3}{120 \times \left(\dfrac{3}{3+0.235m}\right) \times 10 \times 0.0932\pi \times 15}$

$= 80.53(3 + 0.235m)$

$$m^3 - 18.92m - 241.59 = 0$$
$$m = 7.23 \text{ mm}$$
Therefore, standard module, $m = 8$ mm ...Tb. 12.2/ Pg 182, DHB

b. To find face width (b):
$$\text{Given } k = b/m = 10$$
$$b = 10 \times 8 = 80 \text{ mm}$$

c. Pitch circle diameters:

We know that, $m = d/z$
PCD of pinion, $d_p = mz_p = 8 \times 15 = 120$ mm
PCD of gear, $d_g = mz_g = 8 \times 45 = 360$ mm.

2. **A pair of spur gears has to transmit 20 kW from a shaft rotating at 1000 rpm to a parallel shaft which is to rotate at 310 rpm. Number of teeth on pinion is 31 with 20° full depth involute tooth form. The material for pinion is steel SAE 1040 untreated with allowable static stress 206.81 MPa and the material for the gear is cast steel 0.20%C untreated with allowable static stress 137.34 MPa. Determine the module and face width of the gear pair. Also find the dynamic tooth load on the gears. Take the service factor as 1.5.**

[VTU- Dec. 06/ Jan. 07 – 16 Marks; (similar) Dec. 08/ Jan. 09 – 12 Marks; (similar) Dec. 11 – 16 Marks]

Solution: $P = 20$ kW, driver (pinion), $N_1 = 1000$ rpm, driver (gear), $N_2 = 310$ rpm, number of teeth on pinion, z_p or $z_1 = 31$, $\alpha = 20°$ FDI, σd_p or $\sigma_{d1} = 206.81$ MPa, σ_{dg} or $\sigma_{d2} = 137.34$ MPa, service factor, $C_s = 1.5$.

a. $m = ?$ b. $b = ?$ c. $F_d = ?$

We know that, $$i = \frac{N_1}{N_2} = \frac{d_2}{d_1} = \frac{z_2}{z_1}$$

$$i = \frac{1000}{310} = 3.23$$

$\therefore$ $z_2 = iz_1 = 3.23 \times 31 = 100$ teeth

Identifying weaker part (pinion/gear):

We know that strength factor = $\sigma_d \cdot y$

For α = FDI tooth, $y = 0.154 - \dfrac{0.912}{z}$ ...**12.17b/ Pg 163, DHB**

i.e. $y_1 = 0.154 - \dfrac{0.912}{z_1}$

$y_1 = 0.154 - \dfrac{0.912}{31} = 0.1246$

and, $y_2 = 0.154 - \dfrac{0.912}{100} = 0.1449$

$\therefore$ for pinion, $\sigma_{d1} \cdot y_1 = 206.81 \times 0.1246 = 25.77$ MPa
for gear, $\sigma_{d2} \cdot y_2 = 137.34 \times 0.1449 = 19.90$ MPa

Since $\sigma d_2 \cdot y_2$ is less, design is based on **gear**.

a. To find module (m)

Since the diameter is unknown, we have $m = \sqrt[3]{\dfrac{2M_t}{\sigma_d C_v k Y z}}$ ...Eq. (i) **12.16/ Pg 163, DHB**

- $$P = \dfrac{2\pi N_2 M_t}{60}$$

$$20 \times 10^3 = \dfrac{2\pi \times 310 \times M_t}{60}$$

$$M_t = 616.08 \text{ N-m -or- } 616.08 \times 10^3 \text{ N-mm}$$

- Assume, $k = b/m = 10$
- Assume, $C_v = 0.5$
- Form factor, $Y = \pi y_2 = 0.1449\pi$ ...**12.16/ Pg 163, DHB**

∴ Eq. (i) yields... $m^3 = \dfrac{2 \times 616.08 \times 10^3}{137.34 \times 0.5 \times 10 \times 0.1449\pi \times 100}$

Trial 1:

$$m = 3.4 \text{ mm}$$

Therefore, standard module, $m = 3.5$ mm ...**Tb. 12.2/ Pg 182, DHB**

∴ PCD of pinion, $d_1 = m z_1 = 3.5 \times 31 = 108.5$ mm
PCD of gear, $d_2 = m z_2 = 3.5 \times 100 = 350$ mm
Face width, $b = 10m = 10 \times 3.5 = 35$ mm

Since C_v was assumed, Check for σ_{d2}

We know that, $F_t = \pi \sigma_d C_v b y m$ ...Eq. (ii) **12.15/ Pg 163, DHB**

- $$v = \dfrac{\pi d_2 N_2}{60} = \dfrac{\pi \times 350 \times 310}{60} = 5681 \text{ mm/s} = 5.681 \text{ m/s}$$

- For $v < 8$ m/s, $C_v = \dfrac{3.05}{3.05 + v}$ ...**12.19a/ Pg 164, DHB**

$$= \dfrac{3.05}{3.05 + 5.681}$$

$$C_v = 0.349$$

- $$F_t = \dfrac{2M_t}{d}$$ ...**12.22/ Pg 165, DHB**

$$= \dfrac{2M_t}{d_2} \times C_s \qquad \text{(here } d \text{ – weaker member)}$$

$$= \dfrac{2 \times 616.08 \times 10^3}{350} \times (1.5) \qquad C_s = 1.5 \text{ (data)}$$

$$F_t = 5280.68 \text{ N}$$

∴ Eq. (ii) yields... $5280.68 = \pi \times \sigma_{d2} \times 0.349 \times 35 \times 0.1449 \times 3.5$

$$\sigma_{d2} = 271.34 \text{ MPa} \not< 137.374 \text{ MPa} \qquad \text{... } \textbf{\textit{not safe.}}$$

Since calculated values are ≮ permissible values, the assumed values are not satisfactory.
Hence change the module.

Trial 2:

∴ Adopt $m = 5$ mm
PCD of pinion, $d_1 = mz_1 = 5 \times 31 = 155$ mm
PCD of gear, $d_2 = mz_2 = 5 \times 100 = 500$ mm
Face width, $b = 10m = 10 \times 5 = 50$ mm

- $$v = \frac{\pi d_2 N_2}{60} = \frac{\pi \times 0.5 \times 310}{60} = 8.12 \text{ m/s}$$

- For $v > 8$ m/s, $C_v = \dfrac{4.58}{4.58 + v}$ ...12.19b/ Pg 164, DHB

$$= \frac{4.58}{4.58 + 8.12}$$

$$C_v = 0.3606$$

- $$F_t = \frac{2M_t}{d}$$ ...12.22/ Pg 165, DHB

$$= \frac{2M_t}{d_2} \times C_s$$

$$= \frac{2 \times 616.08 \times 10^3}{500} \times 1.5$$

$$F_t = 3696.48 \text{ N}$$

∴ Eq. (ii) yields... $3696.48 = \pi \times \sigma_{d2} \times 0.3606 \times 50 \times 0.1449 \times 5$

$\sigma_{d2} = 90$ MPa < 137.34 MPa ...hence safe.

Since calculated values are < permissible values, the assumed values are satisfactory.

b. To find face width (b) $b = 50$ mm

c. To find dynamic tooth load (F_d)

We know that, $$F_d = \frac{K_3 v (Cb + F_t)}{K_3 v + \sqrt{Cb + F_t}} + F_t$$ ...Eq. (iii) **12.33/ Pg 166, DHB**

here $K_3 = 20.67$

@ $v = 8$ m/s	Error, $e = 0.05$ mm	...Tb. 12.14/ Pg 191, DHB
For $\alpha = 20°$ FDI teeth and steel – steel combination		
@ $e = 0.04$ mm	$C = 457.8$ N/mm	...Tb. 12.12/ Pg 190, DHB
$e = 0.05$ mm	$C = ?$	

∴   at $v = 8.12$ m/s, $C = \dfrac{0.05 \times 457.8}{0.04} = 572.25$ N/mm

∴ Eq. (iii) yields... $F_d = 3696.48 + \dfrac{(20.67 \times 8.12) \times [(572.25 \times 50) + 3696.48]}{(20.67 \times 8.12) + \sqrt{[(572.25 \times 50) + 3696.48]}}$

$F_d = 19.30$ kN.

340 Design of Machine Elements II (DME II)

3. In a spur gear arrangement a pinion made of cast steel is rotating at 900 rpm and is driving a cast iron gear at 150 rpm. The teeth are to have standard 20° stub involute profiles and the maximum power to be transmitted is 25 kW. Determine the module and face width. Find the dynamic and wear load also. The pinion has 16 teeth with surface hardness of 250 BHN, take static stress for pinion as 103 MPa and for gear as 55 MPa. Assume $E_P = 96$ GN/m² and $E_G = 207$ GN/m².

[VTU- Dec.10 – 20 Marks; (similar) May/ June.10 - 15 Marks; (similar) Dec.07/ Jan. 08 - 20 Marks]

Solution: Pinion speed, $N_1 = 900$ rpm, gear speed, $N_2 = 150$ rpm, $\alpha = 20°$ Stub, $P = 25$ kW, $z_1 = 16$, $BHN_1 = 250$, $\sigma_{d1} = 103$ MPa, $\sigma_{d2} = 55$ MPa, $E_P = E_1 = 96$ GN/m² $= 96 \times 10^3$ MPa, $E_G = E_2 = 207$ GN/m² $= 207 \times 10^3$ MPa.

a. $m = ?$ b. $b = ?$ c. $F_d = ?$ d. $F_w = ?$

We know that, $i = \dfrac{N_1}{N_2} = \dfrac{d_2}{d_1} = \dfrac{z_2}{z_1}$

$$i = \dfrac{900}{150} = 6$$

$\therefore \quad z_2 = iz_1 = 6 \times 16 = 96$ teeth

Identifying weaker part (pinion/gear)

We know that strength factor $= \sigma_d \cdot y$

- For $\alpha = 20°$ stub tooth, $y = 0.175 - \dfrac{0.95}{z}$ ...**12.17c/ Pg 163, DHB**

i.e. $y_1 = 0.175 - \dfrac{0.95}{z_1}$

$y_1 = 0.175 - \dfrac{0.95}{16} = 0.1156$

and, $y_2 = 0.175 - \dfrac{0.95}{96} = 0.1651$

$\therefore$ for pinion $\quad \sigma_{d1} \cdot y_1 = 103 \times 0.1156 = 11.91$ MPa
for gear, $\quad \sigma_{d2} \cdot y_2 = 55 \times 0.1651 = 9.08$ MPa

Since $\sigma_{d2} \cdot y_2$ is less, design is based on **gear**.

a. To find module (m)

Since the diameter is unknown, we have

$$m = \sqrt[3]{\dfrac{2M_t}{\sigma_d C_v k Y z}} \quad \text{...Eq. (i) 12.16/ Pg 163, DHB}$$

- $P = \dfrac{2\pi N_2 M_t}{60}$

$$25 \times 10^3 = \dfrac{2\pi \times 150 \times M_t}{60}$$

$M_t = 1591.55$ N-m $= 1591.55 \times 10^3$ N-mm

- Assume, $K = b/m = 10$
- Assume, $C_v = 0.5$
- Form factor, $Y = \pi y_2 = 0.1651\pi$ ...**12.16/ Pg 163, DHB**

∴ Eq. (i) yields... $m^3 = \dfrac{2 \times 1591.55 \times 10^3}{55 \times 0.5 \times 10 \times 0.1651\pi \times 96}$

$$m = 6.15 \text{ mm}$$

Therefore, standard module, $m = 8$ mm ...Tb. 12.2/ Pg 182, DHB

∴ PCD of pinion, $d_1 = mz_1 = 8 \times 16 = 128$ mm
PCD of gear, $d_2 = mz_2 = 8 \times 96 = 768$ mm
Face width, $b = 10m = 10 \times 8 = 80$ mm

- Since C_v was assumed, check for σ_{d2} ::

We know that, $F_t = \pi \sigma_d C_v b y m$ ...Eq. (ii) 12.15/ Pg 163, DHB

- $v = \dfrac{\pi d_2 N_2}{60} = \dfrac{\pi \times 0.768 \times 150}{60} = 6$ m/s

- For $v < 8$ m/s, $C_v = \dfrac{3.05}{3.05 + v}$ ...12.19a/ Pg 164, DHB

$$= \dfrac{3.05}{3.05 + 6}$$

$$C_v = 0.337$$

- $F_t = \dfrac{2M_t}{d}$ ...12.22/ Pg 165, DHB

$$= \dfrac{2M_t}{d_2}$$

$$= \dfrac{2 \times 1591.55 \times 10^3}{768}$$

$$F_t = 4144.66 \text{ N}$$

∴ Eq. (ii) yields... $4144.66 = \pi \times \sigma_{d2} \times 0.337 \times 80 \times 0.1651 \times 8$

$\sigma_{d2} = 37$ MPa < 55 MPa ...hence safe.

Since calculated values are < permissible values, the assumed values are satisfactory.

b. To find face width (b) $b = 80$ mm

c. To find dynamic tooth load (F_d)

We know that, $F_d = F_t + \dfrac{K_3 v (Cb + F_t)}{K_3 v + \sqrt{Cb + F_t}}$ ...Eq. (iii) 12.33/ Pg 166, DHB

here $K_3 = 20.67$

@ $v = 6$ m/s, error $e = 0.0590$ mm ...Tb. 12.14/ Pg 191, DHB

Since Young's modulus is specified for the gears and pinion, we have

$$C = \dfrac{e}{k_1 \left[\dfrac{1}{E_1} + \dfrac{1}{E_2}\right]}$$ ...12.33/ Pg 166, DHB

$$C = \frac{0.059}{8.7 \times \left[\dfrac{1}{96 \times 10^3} + \dfrac{1}{207 \times 10^3}\right]}$$

$C = 444.77$ N/mm

Eq. (*iii*) yields... $F_d = 4144.66 + \dfrac{(20.67 \times 6) \times \left[(444.77 \times 80) + 4144.66\right]}{(20.67 \times 6) + \sqrt{\left[(444.77 \times 80) + 4144.66\right]}}$

$F_d = 19.38$ kN

d. To find wear load (F_w)

We know that, $\quad F_w = d_1 b Q K \quad$ ...Eq. (*iv*) **12.36a/ Pg 167, DHB**

- Diameter of pinion, $\quad d_1 = 128$ mm

- Load stress factor, $\quad K = \dfrac{\sigma_{es}^2 \sin\alpha}{1.4}\left[\dfrac{1}{E_1} + \dfrac{1}{E_2}\right] \quad$ ...**12.36b/ Pg 167, DHB**

For cast steel pinion (BHN = 250) and CI gear (say, BHN = 180),
Surface endurance limit, $\sigma_{es} = 617.8$ MPa $\qquad$ ...**Tb. 12.16/ Pg 193, DHB**

$$\therefore K = \frac{(617.8)^2 \sin(20)}{1.4}\left[\frac{1}{96 \times 10^3} + \frac{1}{207 \times 10^3}\right]$$

$K = 1.42$

- Ratio factor, $Q = \dfrac{2d_2}{d_2 + d_1} = \dfrac{2z_2}{z_2 + z_1} \quad$ ...**12.36c/ Pg 167, DHB**

$$= \frac{2 \times 96}{96 + 16}$$

$Q = 1.714$

$\therefore$ Eq. (*iv*) yields... $F_w = 128 \times 80 \times 1.714 \times 1.42$

$F_w = 24.92$ kN

For safety against wear, $F_w \geq F_d$

i.e. 24.92 kN > 19.38 kN

Since $F_w > F_d$, the material is safe against wear.

---

4. **Design a pair of spur gears to transmit 20 kW of power while operating for 8 to 10 hours per day sustaining medium shock, from a shaft rotating at 1000 rpm to a parallel shaft which is to rotate at 310 rpm. Assume the number of teeth on pinion to be 31 and 20° full depth involute tooth profile. The material of the pinion is C40 steel, untreated whose $\sigma_0 = 206.81$ N/mm² and for gear is cast steel, 0.2%C untreated whose $\sigma_0 = 137.34$ N/mm². Check the design for dynamic load if load factor $C = 522.464$ N/mm and also for wear load taking load stress factor, $K = 0.279$ N/mm². Suggest suitable hardness.**

   [VTU - June/July.09 – 15 Marks; (similar) Dec.09/ Jan.10 – 20 Marks; (similar) July. 07 – 15 Marks; (similar) June/July 09 – 20 Marks]

Solution: $P = 20$ kW, service – 8 to 10 hours per day- medium shock, driver speed (pinion), $N_1 = 1000$ rpm, driven speed (gear), $N_2 = 310$ rpm, $z_1 = 31$, $\alpha = 20°$ FDI, $\sigma_{d1} = 206.81$ N/mm², $\sigma_{d2} = 137.34$ N/mm², $C = 522.464$ N/mm, $K = 0.279$ N/mm².
Design:(m, F_d, F_{en}, F_w).

We know that, $i = \dfrac{N_1}{N_2} = \dfrac{d_2}{d_1} = \dfrac{z_2}{z_1}$

$$i = \dfrac{1000}{310} = 3.23$$

∴ $z_2 = iz_1 = 3.23 \times 31 = 100$ teeth

Identifying weaker part (pinion/gear):

We know that, strength factor = $\sigma_d \cdot y$

- For $\alpha = 20°$ FDI, $y = 0.154 - \dfrac{0.912}{z}$ ...12.17b/ Pg 163, DHB

  i.e. $y_1 = 0.154 - \dfrac{0.912}{z_1}$

  $y_1 = 0.154 - \dfrac{0.912}{31} = 0.1246$

  and, $y_2 = 0.154 - \dfrac{0.912}{100} = 0.1449$

∴ for pinion $\sigma_{d1} \cdot y_1 = 206.81 \times 0.1246 = 25.77$ MPa
for gear, $\sigma_{d2} \cdot y_2 = 137.34 \times 0.1449 = 19.90$ MPa

Since $\sigma_{d2} \cdot y_2$ is less, design is based on **gear**.

a. To find module (m)

Since the diameter is unknown, we have $m = \sqrt[3]{\dfrac{2M_t}{\sigma_d C_v kYz}}$

...Eq. (i) 12.16/ Pg 163, DHB

- $P = \dfrac{2\pi N_2 M_t}{60}$

  $20 \times 10^3 = \dfrac{2\pi \times 310 \times M_t}{60}$

  $M_t = 616.08$ N-m $= 616.08 \times 10^3$ N-mm

- Assume, $k = b/m = 10$
- Assume, $C_v = 0.5$

  Form factor, $Y = \pi y_2 = 0.1449\pi$ ...12.16/ Pg 163, DHB

Eq. (i) yields... $m^3 = \dfrac{2 \times 616.08 \times 10^3}{137.34 \times 0.5 \times 10 \times 0.1449\pi \times 100}$

$m = 3.4$ mm

Therefore, standard module, $m = 5$ mm ...Tb. 12.2/ Pg 182, DHB
(based on the solution observed in problem 2)

∴ PCD of pinion, $d_1 = mz_1 = 5 \times 31 = 155$ mm
PCD of gear, $d_2 = mz_2 = 5 \times 100 = 500$ mm
Face width, $b = 10m = 10 \times 5 = 50$ mm

- Since was assumed, check for σ_{d2}:
  We know that, $\quad F_t = \pi\sigma_d C_v bym \quad$ ...Eq. (ii) **12.15/ Pg 163, DHB**

- $$v = \frac{\pi d_2 N_2}{60} = \frac{\pi \times 0.5 \times 310}{60} = 8.12 \text{ m/s}$$

- For $v > 8$ m/s, $\quad C_v = \dfrac{4.58}{4.58 + v} \quad$ ...**12.19b/ Pg 164, DHB**

$$= \frac{4.58}{4.58 + 8.12}$$

$$C_v = 0.3606$$

- $$F_t = \frac{2M_t}{d} \quad$$ ...**12.22/ Pg 165, DHB**

$$= \frac{2M_t}{d_2} \times C_s$$

For 8 to 10 hours service per day with medium shock $C_s = 1.5$
...**Tb. 12.8/ Pg 187, DHB**

$$= \frac{2 \times 616.08 \times 10^3}{500} \times 1.5$$

$$F_t = 3696.48 \text{ N}$$

∴ Eq. (ii) yields... $3696.48 = \pi \times \sigma_{d2} \times 0.3606 \times 50 \times 0.1449 \times 5$

$\sigma_{d2} = 90$ MPa < 137.34 MPa ...hence safe.

Since calculated values are < permissible values, the assumed values are satisfactory.

b. To find face width (b) $b = 50$ mm

c. To find dynamic tooth load (F_d)

We know that, $\quad F_d = F_t + \dfrac{K_3 v(Cb + F_t)}{K_3 v + \sqrt{Cb + F_t}} \quad$ ...Eq. (iii) **12.33/ Pg 166, DHB**

here $K_3 = 20.67$
$C = 522.464$ N/mm   ...(data)

∴ Eq. (iii) yields... $F_d = 3696.48 + \dfrac{(20.67 \times 8.12) \times [(522.464 \times 50) + 3696.48]}{(20.67 \times 8.12) + \sqrt{[(522.464 \times 50) + 3696.48]}}$

$$F_d = 18.4 \text{ kN}$$

d. To find endurance strength (F_{en})

We know that, $F_{en} = \sigma_{en} bYm \quad$ ...**12.34/ Pg 166, DHB**

- Since BHN is unknown, referring to the material of the weaker part, i.e. gear: cast steel 0.2%C untreated, we have, $BHN = 180 \quad$ ...**Tb.12.7/ Pg 186, DHB**
- @ $BHN = 180$, σ_{en} value is not available in the table ...**(Tb.12.15/ Pg 192, DHB)**
  From **Table 12.15/ Pg 192, DHB,** we have

BHN	σ_{en}
150	259
200	345

For 1 BHN, $\sigma_{en} = \dfrac{345-259}{200-150} = 1.72$

∴ for BHN = 180, $\sigma_{en} = 259 + [(180-150) \times (1.72)] = 310.6$ MPa
∴ $F_{en} = 310.6 \times 50 \times (0.1449 \times \pi) \times 5$
$F_{en} = 35.35$ kN

Since $F_{en} > F_d$, the material is safe against static tooth load.

e. To find wear load (F_w)

We know that, $F_w = d_1 b Q K$ ...Eq. (iv) **12.36a/ Pg 167, DHB**
- Diameter of pinion, $d_1 = 155$mm
- Load stress factor, $K = 0.279$ N/mm² ...(data)

- Ratio factor, $Q = \dfrac{2 d_2}{d_2 + d_1} = \dfrac{2 z_2}{z_2 + z_1}$ ...**12.36c/ Pg 167, DHB**

$= \dfrac{2 \times 100}{100 + 31}$

$Q = 1.527$

∴ Eq. (iv) yields... $F_w = 155 \times 50 \times 1.527 \times 0.279$
$F_w = 3.31$ kN

For safety against wear, $F_w \geq F_d$
i.e. 3.32 kN ≥ 18.4 kN ...hence unsafe.

Since $F_w < F_d$, the pinion is subjected to rapid wear and hence has to be surface hardened to higher BHN.

i.e. $F_w \geq F_d$
$d_1 b Q K \geq 18.4$ kN
$155 \times 50 \times 1.527 \times K \geq 18.4 \times 10^3$
$K \geq 1.55$

Therefore, for steel – steel combination, having $\alpha = 20°$ and $K \geq 1.55$, we have
BHN of pinion = 350, BHN of gear = 300 ...**Tb. 12.16/ Pg 193, DHB**

5. Specify the details of a spur gear to transmit 20 kW at 1200 rpm. The teeth are of 20° full depth involute system, having 16 teeth on pinion and a speed ratio of 3:1. Assume that the starting torque is 20% more than the mean torque.

Solution: $P = 20$ kW, $N_1 = 1200$ rpm, $i = 3:1$, $z_1 = 16$, $\alpha = 20°$ FDI, $M_{t\max} = 1.2 M_t$. *Design:* m, F_d, F_{en}, F_w.

We know that, $i = \dfrac{N_1}{N_2} = \dfrac{d_2}{d_1} = \dfrac{z_2}{z_1}$

∴ $N_2 = N_1/i = 1200/3 = 400$ rpm
And $z_2 = i z_1 = 3 \times 16 = 48$ teeth

Material properties:
Since the material is not specified, let us assume that both pinion and gear are made of same material,
i.e. Steel C45, untreated having
$\sigma_{d1} = \sigma_{d2} = 233.4$ MPa and $BHN_1 = BHN_2 = 200$ ...**Tb. 12.7/ Pg 186, DHB**

Identifying weaker part (pinion/gear):
We know that strength factor = $\sigma_d \cdot y$

Since both pinion and gear are made of same material, the pinion is weaker, i.e. $\sigma_{d1} \cdot y_1 < \sigma_{d2} \cdot y_2$.

Hence design is based on **pinion**.

a. To find module (m)

Since the diameter is unknown, we have

$$m = \sqrt[3]{\frac{2M_{t)max}}{\sigma_d C_v kYz}} \qquad \text{...Eq. (i) 12.16/ Pg 163, DHB}$$

- But $M_{t)max} = 1.2\, M_t$ ...Eq. (ii)

- $P = \dfrac{2\pi N_1 M_t}{60}$

$$20 \times 10^3 = \frac{2\pi \times 1200 \times M_t}{60}$$

$$M_t = 159.15 \text{ N-m} = 159.15 \times 10^3 \text{ N-mm}$$

∴ Eq. (ii) yields... $M_{t)max} = 1.2 \times 159.15 \times 10^3$

$$M_{t)max} = 191 \times 10^3 \text{ N-mm}$$

- Assume, $k = b/m = 10$
- Assume, $C_v = 0.5$
- Form factor, $Y = \pi y_1$ ...12.16/ Pg 163, DHB

$$= \pi \left[0.154 - \frac{0.912}{z_1} \right] \qquad \text{...12.17b/ Pg 163, DHB}$$

$$= \pi \left[0.154 - \frac{0.912}{16} \right]$$

$$Y = 0.3047$$

∴ Eq. (i) yields... $m^3 = \dfrac{2 \times 191 \times 10^3}{233.4 \times 0.5 \times 10 \times 0.3047 \times 16}$

$$m = 4.06 \text{ mm}$$

Therefore, standard module, $m = 5$ mm ...Tb. 12.2/ Pg 182, DHB

∴ PCD of pinion, $d_1 = mz_1 = 5 \times 16 = 80$ mm

PCD of gear, $d_2 = id_1 = 3 \times 80 = 240$ mm

Face width, $b = 10m = 10 \times 5 = 50$ mm

- Since C_v was assumed, check for σ_{d1}:

We know that, $F_t = \pi \sigma_d C_v bym = \sigma_d C_v bYm$ ...Eq. (iii) 12.15/ Pg 163, DHB

- $v = \dfrac{\pi d_1 N_1}{60} = \dfrac{\pi \times 0.08 \times 1200}{60} = 5.03$ m/s

- For $v < 8$ m/s, $C_v = \dfrac{3.05}{3.05 + v}$ ...12.19a/ Pg 164, DHB

$$= \frac{3.05}{3.05 + 5.03}$$

$$C_v = 0.3775$$

- $$F_t = \frac{2M_{t)\max}}{d}$$ ...12.22/ Pg 165, DHB

$$= \frac{2M_{t)\max}}{d_1}$$

$$= \frac{2 \times 191 \times 10^3}{80}$$

$$F_t = 4775 \text{ N}$$

∴ Eq. (iii) yields... $4775 = \sigma_{d1} \times 0.3775 \times 50 \times 0.3047 \times 5$

$\sigma_{d1} = 166$ MPa < 233.4 MPa ...hence safe.

Since calculated values are < permissible values, the assumed values are satisfactory.

b. To find face width (b) $b = 50$ mm

c. To find dynamic tooth load (F_d)

We know that, $\quad F_d = F_t + \dfrac{K_3 v(Cb + F_t)}{K_3 v + \sqrt{Cb + F_t}}$ ...Eq. (iv) 12.33/ Pg 166, DHB

here $\quad K_3 = 20.67$

@ $v = 5$ m/s	Error, $e = 0.0640$ mm	...Tb. 12.14/ Pg 191, DHB
For $\alpha = 20°$ FDI teeth and steel – steel combination		
@ $e = 0.06$ mm	$C = 686.7$ N/mm	...Tb. 12.12/ Pg 190, DHB
$e = 0.0640$ mm	$C = ?$	

∴ at $v = 5.03$ m/s, $C = \dfrac{0.064 \times 686.7}{0.06} = 732.48$ N/mm

∴ Eq. (iv) yields... $F_d = 4775 + \dfrac{(20.67 \times 5.03) \times [(732.48 \times 50) + 4775]}{(20.67 \times 5.03) + \sqrt{(732.48 \times 50) + 4775}}$

$$F_d = 18.76 \text{ kN}$$

d. To find endurance strength (F_{en})

We know that, $\quad F_{en} = \sigma_{en} bYm$ ...12.34/ Pg 166, DHB

@ BHN = 200, $\sigma_{en} = 345$ MPa ...Tb.12.15/ Pg 192, DHB

∴ $\quad F_{en} = 345 \times 50 \times 0.3047 \times 5$

$\quad F_{en} = 26.28$ kN

Since $F_{en} > F_d$, the material is safe against static tooth load.

e. To find wear load (F_w)

We know that, $\quad F_w = d_1 bQK$ ...Eq. (v) 12.36a/ Pg 167, DHB

- Diameter of pinion, $d_1 = 80$ mm

- Ratio factor, $\quad Q = \dfrac{2d_2}{d_2 + d_1} = \dfrac{2z_2}{z_2 + z_1}$ ...12.36c/ Pg 167, DHB

$$z_2 = iz_1 = 3 \times 16 = 48$$

$$= \frac{2 \times 48}{48 + 16}$$

$$Q = 1.5$$

- For $\alpha = 20°$ and steel – steel combination of $BHN = 200$, $K = 0.539$
...Tb.12.16/ Pg 193, DHB

∴ Eq. (v) yields... $F_w = 80 \times 50 \times 1.5 \times 0.539$

$$F_w = 3.23 \text{ kN}$$

Since $F_w < F_d$, the pinion is subjected to rapid wear and hence has to be surface hardened to higher BHN.

i.e. $F_w \geq F_d$

$$d_1 b Q K \geq 18.76 \text{ kN}$$

$$80 \times 50 \times 1.5 \times K \geq 18.76 \times 10^3$$

$$K \geq 3.126$$

Therefore, for steel – steel combination, having $\alpha = 200$ and $K \geq 3.126$, we have
BHN of pinion = 450 = BHN of gear   ...Tb. 12.16/ Pg 193, DHB

6. **Design a spur gear drive required to transmit 55 kW at 800 rpm of the pinion. The speed ratio is to be 3.2:1. The teeth are to be 20° full depth involute.**

[VTU – Jan./ Feb 2003 – 16 Marks]

Solution: $P = 55$ kW, $N_1 = 800$ rpm, $i = 3.2:1$, $\alpha = 20°$ FDI, *Design:* m, F_d, F_{en}, F_w

We know that, $i = \dfrac{N_1}{N_2} = \dfrac{d_2}{d_1} = \dfrac{z_2}{z_1}$

∴ $N_2 = N_1/i = 800/3.2 = 250$ rpm

Material properties:

Since the material is not specified, let us assume that both pinion and gear are made of same material,

i.e. Cast steel 0.20% C, heat treated having

$\sigma_{d1} = \sigma_{d2} = 193.2$ MPa and $BHN_1 = BHN_2 = 250$ ...Tb. 12.7/ Pg 186, DHB

Identifying weaker part (pinion/gear):

We know that strength factor = $\sigma_d \cdot y$

Since both pinion and gear are made of same material, the pinion is weaker, i.e. $\sigma_{d1} \cdot y_1 < \sigma_{d2} \cdot y_2$

Hence design is based on **pinion**.

a. To find module (m)

Since the diameter is unknown, we have $m = \sqrt[3]{\dfrac{2M_t}{\sigma_d C_v k Y z}}$

...Eq. (i) 12.16/ Pg 163, DHB

- $$P = \frac{2\pi N_1 M_t}{60}$$

$$55 \times 10^3 = \frac{2\pi \times 800 \times M_t}{60}$$

$$M_t = 656.5 \text{ N-m} = 656.5 \times 10^3 \text{ N-mm}$$

Trial 1:

- Assume, $\quad k = b/m = 10$
- Assume, $\quad C_v = 0.5$
- Assume $\quad z_1 = 20$
- $\therefore \quad\quad\quad z_2 = iz_1 = 3.2 \times 20 = 64$ teeth
- Form factor, $\quad Y = \pi y_1$ ...12.16/ Pg 163, DHB

$$= \pi\left[0.154 - \frac{0.912}{z_1}\right] \quad \text{...12.17b/ Pg 163, DHB}$$

$$= \pi\left[0.154 - \frac{0.912}{20}\right]$$

$$Y = 0.3405$$

$\therefore$ Eq. (i) yields... $m^3 = \dfrac{2 \times 656.5 \times 10^3}{193.2 \times 0.5 \times 10 \times 0.3405 \times 20}$

$m = 5.84$ mm

Therefore, standard module, $m = 6$ mm ...Tb. 12.2/ Pg 182, DHB

$\therefore \quad$ PCD of pinion, $d_1 = mz_1 = 6 \times 20 = 120$ mm
PCD of gear, $d_2 = mz_2 = 6 \times 64 = 384$ mm
Face width, $b = 10m = 10 \times 6 = 60$ mm

- Since was assumed, check for σ_{d1}:
We know that, $\quad F_t = \pi\sigma_d C_v bym = \sigma_d C_v bYm \quad$ ...Eq. (ii) 12.15/ Pg 163, DHB

- $\quad v = \dfrac{\pi d_1 N_1}{60} = \dfrac{\pi \times 0.12 \times 800}{60} = 5.03$ m/s

- For $v < 8$ m/s, $\quad C_v = \dfrac{3.05}{3.05 + v}$ ...12.19a/ Pg 164, DHB

$$= \dfrac{3.05}{3.05 + 5.03}$$

$C_v = 0.3775$

- $\quad F_t = \dfrac{2M_t}{d}$ ...12.22/ Pg 165, DHB

$$= \dfrac{2M_t}{d_1}$$

$$= \dfrac{2 \times 656.5 \times 10^3}{120}$$

$F_t = 10941.67$ N

$\therefore \quad$ Eq. (ii) yields... $10941.67 = \sigma_{d1} \times 0.3775 \times 60 \times 0.3405 \times 6$
$\sigma_{d1} = 236.45$ MPa $\not<$ 193.2 MPa ...*not safe.*

Since calculated values are $\not<$ permissible values, the assumed values are not satisfactory.
Hence change the module.

Trial 2:

Adopt $m = 8$ mm

∴ PCD of pinion, $d_1 = mz_1 = 8 \times 20 = 160$ mm
PCD of gear, $d_2 = mz_2 = 8 \times 64 = 512$ mm
Face width, $b = 10m = 10 \times 8 = 80$ mm

- $$v = \frac{\pi d_1 N_1}{60} = \frac{\pi \times 0.16 \times 800}{60} = 6.7 \text{ m/s}$$

- For $v < 8$ m/s, $\quad C_v = \dfrac{3.05}{3.05 + v}$ ...12.19a/ Pg 164, DHB

$$= \frac{3.05}{3.05 + 6.7}$$

$$C_v = 0.3128$$

- $$F_t = \frac{2M_t}{d}$$

$$= \frac{2M_t}{d_1}$$

$$= \frac{2 \times 656.5 \times 10^3}{160}$$

$$F_t = 8206.25 \text{ N}$$

∴ Eq. (ii) yields... $8206.25 = \sigma_{d1} \times 0.3128 \times 80 \times 0.3405 \times 8$
$\sigma_{d1} = 120.38$ MPa < 193.2 MPa ...hence safe.

Since calculated values are < permissible values, the assumed values are satisfactory.

b. To find face width (b) $\quad b = 80$ mm

c. To find dynamic tooth load (F_d)

We know that, $\quad F_d = F_t + \dfrac{K_3 v(Cb + F_t)}{K_3 v + \sqrt{Cb + F_t}}$ ...Eq. (iii) **12.33/ Pg 166, DHB**

here $K_3 = 20.67$

@ $v = 6$ m/s	Error, $e = 0.0590$ mm	...Tb. 12.14/ Pg 191, DHB
For $\alpha = 20°$ FDI teeth and steel – steel combination		
@ $e = 0.06$ mm	$C = 686.7$ N/mm	...Tb. 12.12/ Pg 190, DHB
$e = 0.0590$ mm	$C = ?$	

∴ at $v = 6.7$ m/s, $C = \dfrac{0.0590 \times 686.7}{0.06} = 675.26$ N/mm

∴ Eq. (iii) yields... $F_d = 8206.25 + \dfrac{(20.67 \times 6.7) \times \left[(675.26 \times 80) + 8206.25\right]}{(20.67 \times 6.7) + \sqrt{\left[(675.26 \times 80) + 8206.25\right]}}$

$F_d = 30.43$ kN

d. To find endurance strength (F_{en})

We know that, $\quad F_{en} = \sigma_{en} bYm \quad$ ...12.34/ Pg 166, DHB
$\quad @ BHN = 250, \sigma_{en} = 429$ MPa $\quad$ ...Tb.12.15/ Pg 192, DHB
$\quad F_{en} = 93.5$ kN

Since $F_{en} > F_d$, the material is safe against static tooth load.

e. To find wear load (F_w)

We know that, $\quad F_w = d_1 bQK \quad$ ...Eq. (iv) 12.36a/ Pg 167, DHB
- Diameter of pinion, $d_1 = 80$ mm

- Ratio factor, $Q = \dfrac{2d_2}{d_2 + d_1} \quad$ ...12.36c/ Pg 167, DHB

$$= \dfrac{2 \times 512}{512 + 160}$$

$Q = 1.524$

- For $\alpha = 20°$ and steel – steel combination of $BHN = 250$, $K = 0.902$
...Tb.12.16/ Pg 193, DHB

∴ Eq. (iv) yields... $F_w = 160 \times 80 \times 1.524 \times 0.902$
$\quad F_w = 17.6$ kN

Since $F_w < F_d$, the pinion is subjected to rapid wear and hence has to be surface hardened to higher BHN.

i.e. $\quad F_w \geq F_d$
$\quad d_1 bQK \geq 30.43$ kN
$\quad 160 \times 80 \times 1.524 \times K \geq 30.43 \times 10^3$
$\quad K \geq 1.559$

Therefore for steel – steel combination, having $\alpha = 20°$ and $K \geq 1.559$, we have
$\quad BHN$ of pinion $= 350 = BHN$ of gear $\quad$ ...Tb. 12.16/ Pg 193, DHB
$\quad (K = 1.893)$ for BHN of pinion $= BHN$ of gear

7. **A 12 kW motor running at 1170 rpm drives a fan through a pair of spur gears (forged steel SAE 1030 pinion and CI gear) with a reduction ratio of 3.9:1. Design the gear and check for dynamic and wear loads.**

[VTU – June/ July 2011 – 20 Marks.]

Solution: $P = 12$ kW, $N_1 = 1170$ rpm, $i = 3.9:1$, Pinion: forged steel SAE 1030 pinion, gear: CI *Design*: m, F_d, F_{en}, F_w.

We know that, $\quad i = \dfrac{N_1}{N_2} = \dfrac{d_2}{d_1} = \dfrac{z_2}{z_1}$

∴ $\quad N_2 = 1170/3.9 = 300$ rpm

Material Properties:

Pinion: Forged steel SAE 1030: $\sigma_{d1} = 220$ MPa, $BHN_1 = 200$
Gear: Cast iron: $\quad \sigma_{d2} = 78.5$ MPa, $BHN_2 = 300$ ...Tb. 12.7/ Pg 186, DHB
- Assume $\quad \alpha = 14.5°$ involute system.
- Assume $\quad z_1 = 20$
∴ $\quad z_2 = iz_1 = 3.9 \times 20 = 78$

Identifying weaker part (pinion/gear):

We know that strength factor = $\sigma_d \cdot y$

- For $\alpha = 14.5°$ involute system, $y = 0.124 - \dfrac{0.684}{z}$ ...12.17b/ Pg 163, DHB

$$\text{i.e. } y_1 = 0.124 - \dfrac{0.684}{z_1}$$

$$y_1 = 0.124 - \dfrac{0.684}{20} = 0.0898$$

$$y_2 = 0.124 - \dfrac{0.684}{78} = 0.1152$$

∴ for pinion $\sigma_{d1} \cdot y_1 = 220 \times 0.0898 = 19.76$ MPa
for gear, $\sigma_{d2} \cdot y_2 = 78.5 \times 0.1152 = 9.05$ MPa
Since $\sigma_{d2} \cdot y_2$ is less, design is based on **gear**.

a. To find module (m)

Since the diameter is unknown, we have

$$m = \sqrt[3]{\dfrac{2M_t}{\sigma_d C_v kYz}}$$ ...Eq. (i) 12.16/ Pg 163, DHB

- $$P = \dfrac{2\pi N_2 M_t}{60}$$

$$12 \times 10^3 = \dfrac{2\pi \times 300 \times M_t}{60}$$

$$M_t = 382 \text{ N-m} = 382 \times 10^3 \text{ N-mm}$$

- Assume, $k = b/m = 10$
- Assume, $C_v = 0.5$
- Form factor, $Y = \pi y_2 = 0.1152\,\pi$ ...12.16/ Pg 163, DHB

∴ Eq. (i) yields... $m^3 = \dfrac{2 \times 382 \times 10^3}{78.5 \times 0.5 \times 10 \times 0.1152 \times \pi \times 78}$

$$m = 4.1 \text{ mm}$$

Therefore, standard module, $m = 5$ mm ...Tb. 12.2/ Pg 182, DHB

∴ PCD of pinion, $d_1 = mz_1 = 5 \times 20 = 100$ mm
PCD of gear, $d_2 = mz_2 = 5 \times 78 = 390$ mm
Face width, $b = 10m = 10 \times 5 = 50$ mm

- Since C_v was assumed, check for σ_{d2}:

We know that, $F_t = \pi \sigma_d C_v b y m$ ...Eq. (ii) 12.15/ Pg 163, DHB

- $$v = \dfrac{\pi d_2 N_2}{60} = \dfrac{\pi \times 0.39 \times 300}{60} = 6.13 \text{ m/s}$$

- For v upto 13 m/s, $C_v = \dfrac{4.58}{4.58 + v}$ ...12.19b/ Pg 164, DHB

$$= \dfrac{4.58}{4.58 + 6.13}$$

$$C_v = 0.4276$$

- $$F_t = \frac{2M_t}{d} = \frac{2M_t}{d_2} \qquad \text{...12.22/ Pg 165, DHB}$$

$$= \frac{2 \times 382 \times 10^3}{390}$$

$$F_t = 1959 \text{ N}$$

∴ Eq. (ii) yields... $1959 = \pi \times \sigma_{d2} \times 0.4276 \times 50 \times 0.1152 \times 5$

$$\sigma_{d2} = 50.63 \text{ MPa} < 78.5 \text{ MPa} \qquad \text{...hence safe.}$$

Since calculated values are < permissible values, the assumed values are satisfactory.

b. To find face width (b) $b = 50$ mm

c. To find dynamic tooth load (F_d)

We know that, $\qquad F_d = F_t + \dfrac{K_3 v(Cb + F_t)}{K_3 v + \sqrt{Cb + F_t}} \qquad$ ...Eq. (iii) **12.33/ Pg 166, DHB**

here $K_3 = 20.67$

@ $v = 6$ m/s	Error, $e = 0.0640$ mm	...Tb. **12.14/ Pg 191, DHB**
For $\alpha = 14.5°$ FDI teeth and CI – steel combination		
@ $e = 0.06$ mm	$C = 454.8$ N/mm	...Tb. **12.12/ Pg 190, DHB**
$e = 0.0590$ mm	$C = ?$	

∴   at $v = 6.13$ m/s, $C = \dfrac{0.0590 \times 454.87}{0.06} = 447.22$ N/mm

∴   Eq. (iii) yields... $F_d = 1959 + \dfrac{(20.67 \times 6.13) \times \left[(447.22 \times 50) + 1959\right]}{(20.67 \times 6.13) + \sqrt{\left[(447.22 \times 50) + 1959\right]}}$

$$F_d = 12.86 \text{ kN}$$

d. To find endurance strength (F_{en})

We know that, $\qquad F_{en} = \sigma_{en} b Y m \qquad$ ...**12.34/ Pg 166, DHB**

- @ $BHN = 300$, the value of σ_{en} is not available in **Tb. 12.15/ Pg 192, DHB**
- Referring to **Tb 12.16/ Pg 193, DHB**, the value of BHN for CI is 180 (maximum).
- For $\alpha = 14.5°$ and CI – steel combination of $BHN_1 = 200$ and $BHN_2 = 180$, we have

$$\sigma_{en} = 392.5 \text{ MPa and } K = 0.598 \qquad \text{...Tb.12.16/ Pg 193, DHB}$$

∴ $F_{en} = 392.5 \times 50 \times (\pi \times 0.1152) \times 5$

$$F_{en} = 35.51 \text{ kN}$$

Since $F_{en} > F_d$, the material is safe against static tooth load.

e. To find wear load (F_w)

We know that, $\qquad F_w = d_1 b Q K \qquad$ ...Eq. (iv) **12.36a/ Pg 167, DHB**

- Diameter of pinion, $d_1 = 100$ mm

- Ratio factor, $\qquad Q = \dfrac{2 d_2}{d_2 + d_1} \qquad$ ...**12.36c/ Pg 167, DHB**

$$= \frac{2 \times 390}{390 + 100}$$

$$Q = 1.592$$

∴ Eq. (iv) yields... $F_w = 100 \times 50 \times 1.592 \times 0.598$

$$F_w = 4.76 \text{ kN}$$

Since $F_w < F_d$, the pinion is subjected to rapid wear and hence has to be surface hardened to higher BHN.

4.27 PROBLEMS BASED ON KNOWN DIAMETER

8. Specify the details of a 14 ½° involute spur gear to transmit 20 kW at 1200 rpm of the pinion. The gear ratio is 3:1 and the center distance is 400 mm. the pinion is made of C30 heat treated steel and the gear of 0.3% C heat treated forged steel. The drive is to be safe for continuous operation.

[VTU – (Similar) July/ Aug. 2005 - 20 Marks]

Solution: $\alpha = 14.5°$ involute teeth, $P = 20$ kW, $N_1 = 1200$ rpm, $i = 3:1$, center distance = 400 mm, pinion: C 30 heat treated steel, gear: 0.3%C heat treated forged steel, service - continuous operation. *Design*: m, F_d, F_{en}, F_w.

We know that,
$$i = \frac{N_1}{N_2} = \frac{d_2}{d_1} = \frac{z_2}{z_1}$$

$$3 = \frac{1200}{N_2} = \frac{d_2}{d_1}$$

$$N_2 = 400 \text{ rpm and } d_2 = 3d_1$$

Also, center distance = $\frac{d_1 + d_2}{2}$

$$400 = \frac{d_1 + d_2}{2}$$

$$d_1 + 3d_1 = 800$$
$$d_1 = 200 \text{ mm and}$$
$$d_2 = 600 \text{ mm.}$$

Material properties:

Pinion: C30 heat treated steel: $\sigma_{d1} = 220.6$ MPa, $BHN_1 = 300$
Gear: 0.3% C heat treated forged steel: $\sigma_{d2} = 220$ MPa, $BHN_2 = 200$
...Tb. 12.7/ Pg 186, DHB

Identifying weaker part (pinion/gear):

We know that strength factor = $\sigma_d \cdot y$

- Assume $z_1 = 20$ teeth
∴ $z_2 = iz_1 = 3 \times 20 = 60$ teeth

- For $\alpha = 14.5°$ involute system, $y = 0.124 - \dfrac{0.684}{z}$ ...12.17b/ Pg 1 63, DHB

i.e. $y_1 = 0.124 - \dfrac{0.684}{z_1}$

$$y_1 = 0.124 - \frac{0.684}{20} = 0.0898$$

$$y_2 = 0.124 - \frac{0.684}{60} = 0.1126$$

∴ for pinion $\quad \sigma_{d1}.y_1 = 220.6 \times 0.0898 = 19.81$ MPa
for gear, $\quad \sigma_{d2}.y_2 = 220 \times 0.1126 = 24.77$ MPa

Since $\sigma_{d1}.y_1$ is less, design is based on **pinion**.

a. To find module (m)

Since the diameter is known, we have $m = \sqrt{\dfrac{F_t}{\sigma_d C_v k Y}}$ ...Eq. (i) **12.16/ Pg 163, DHB**

- $v = \dfrac{\pi d_1 N_1}{60} = \dfrac{\pi \times 0.2 \times 1200}{60} = 12.57$ m/s

- For v upto 13 m/s, $\quad C_v = \dfrac{4.58}{4.58 + v}$ ...**12.19b/ Pg 164, DHB**

$$= \frac{4.58}{4.58 + 12.57}$$

$$C_v = 0.2671$$

- Form factor, $\quad Y = \pi y_1 = 0.0898\pi$ ...**12.16/ Pg 163, DHB**

- $F_t = \dfrac{1000\, PC_s}{v}$ ...**12.20a/ Pg 164, DHB**

For continuous operation, assuming light shocks, service factor $C_s = 1.5$
...**Tb. 12.8/ Pg 187, DHB**

∴ $\quad F_t = \dfrac{1000 \times 20 \times 1.5}{12.57}$

$$F_t = 2.39 \text{ kN}$$

∴ Eq. (i) yields... $m = \sqrt{\dfrac{2.39 \times 10^3}{220.6 \times 0.2671 \times 10 \times 0.0898 \times \pi}}$

$$m = 3.79 \text{ mm}$$

Therefore, standard module $m = 5$ mm ...**Tb. 12.2/ Pg 182, DHB**

∴ Number of teeth on pinion, $z_1 = \dfrac{d_1}{m} = \dfrac{200}{5} = 40$ teeth

Number of teeth on gear, $z_2 = \dfrac{d_2}{m} = \dfrac{600}{5} = 120$ teeth ...Eq. (ii)

Face width, $\quad b = 10 \times 5 = 50$ mm

- Check for i:

We know that, $i = \dfrac{z_2}{z_1} = \dfrac{120}{40}$

$i = 3$ (same as given in data)

356 Design of Machine Elements II (DME II)

Note:
> → If the value of i does not match with that as given in data, then change the values of i in Eq. (ii) to obtain the same value.
> → Use the calculated values of z for further calculations.

- Check for σ_{d1}:

    We know that, $F_t = \sigma_d C_v b Y m$ ...Eq. (*iii*) **12.15/ Pg 163, DHB**

- Here $Y = \pi y_1$ ...**12.16/ Pg 163, DHB**

$$= \pi\left[0.124 - \frac{0.684}{z_1}\right] \quad \text{...12.17b/ Pg 163, DHB}$$

$$= \pi\left[0.124 - \frac{0.684}{40}\right]$$

$$Y = 0.1069\pi$$

∴ Eq. (*iii*) yields... $2.39 \times 10^3 = \sigma_{d1} \times 0.2671 \times 50 \times (0.1069 \times \pi) \times 5$

$$\sigma_{d1} = 106.58 \text{ MPa} < 220.6 \text{ MPa} \quad \text{...hence safe.}$$

Since calculated values are < permissible values, the assumed values are satisfactory.

b. To find face width (b) $b = 50$ mm

c. To find dynamic tooth load (F_d)

We know that, $F_d = F_t + \dfrac{K_3 v(Cb + F_t)}{K_3 v + \sqrt{Cb + F_t}}$ ...Eq. (*iv*) **12.33/ Pg 166, DHB**

here $K_3 = 20.67$

@ $v = 12$ m/s	Error, $e = 0.0330$ mm	...Tb. **12.14/ Pg 191, DHB**
For $\alpha = 14.5°$ FDI teeth and steel – steel combination		
@ $e = 0.03$ mm	$C = 330.9$ N/mm	...Tb. **12.12/ Pg 190, DHB**
$e = 0.0330$ mm	$C = ?$	

∴   at $v = 12.57$ m/s, $C = \dfrac{0.0330 \times 330.9}{0.03} = 364$ N/mm

∴   Eq. (*iv*) yields... $F_d = 2390 + \dfrac{(20.67 \times 12.57) \times [(364 \times 50) + 2390]}{(20.67 \times 12.57) + \sqrt{[(364 \times 50) + 2390]}}$

$$F_d = 15.65 \text{ kN}$$

d. To find endurance strength (F_{en})

We know that, $F_{en} = \sigma_{en} b Y m$ ...**12.34/ Pg 166, DHB**

    @ BHN = 300, $\sigma_{en} = 515$ MPa   ...Tb.**12.15/ Pg 192, DHB**

∴ $F_{en} = 515 \times 50 \times 0.1069\pi \times 5$

$$F_{en} = 43.24 \text{ kN}$$

Since $F_{en} > F_d$, the material is safe against static tooth load.

e. To find wear load (F_w)

We know that, $F_w = d_1 b Q K$ ...Eq. (*v*) **12.36a/ Pg 167, DHB**

- Diameter of pinion, $d_1 = 200$ mm
- Ratio factor, $Q = \dfrac{2d_2}{d_2 + d_1}$ ...12.36c/ Pg 167, DHB

$$= \dfrac{2 \times 600}{600 + 200}$$

$$Q = 1.5$$

- For $\alpha = 14.5°$ and steel – steel combination having

$BHN_1 = 300$ and $BHN_2 = 200$, $K = 0.657$ ...Tb.12.16/ Pg 193, DHB

∴ Eq. (v) yields... $F_w = 200 \times 50 \times 1.5 \times 0.657$

$F_w = 9.86$ kN

For safety against wear, $F_w \geq F_d$

i.e. $9.86 \geq 15.56$ kN ...hence unsafe.

Since $F_w < F_d$, the pinion is subjected to rapid wear and hence has to be surface hardened to higher BHN.

i.e. $F_w \geq F_d$

$d_1 b Q K \geq 15.65$ kN

$200 \times 50 \times 1.5 \times K \geq 15.65 \times 10^3$

$K \geq 1.043$

Therefore, for steel – steel combination, having $\alpha = 14.5°$ and $K \geq 1.043$, we have

$BHN_1 = 350$ and $BHN_2 = 300$ ...Tb. 12.16/ Pg 193, DHB

9. **It is required to transmit 25 kW of power from a shaft running at 1000 rpm to a parallel shaft with speed reduction 2.5:1. The center to center distance of the shaft is to be about 300 mm. The material used for pinion is steel ($\sigma_d = 200$ N/mm², BHN = 250) and for gear is cast iron ($\sigma_d = 180$ N/mm², BHN = 200). Considering class-II gear with tooth profile 20° full depth involute, design the spur gear and check for dynamic load and wear load.**

[*VTU – Dec. 08/ Jan. 2009 – 20 Marks; (similar) May/ June 2011 – 17 Marks*]

Solution: $P = 25$ kW, $N_1 = 1000$ rpm, $i = 2.5:1$, center distance = 300 mm, pinion, $\sigma_{d1} = 200$ N/mm², $BHN_1 = 250$, gear: pinion, $\sigma_{d2} = 180$ N/mm², $BHN_2 = 200$, Class – II gear, Full depth involute system. *Design*: m, F_d, F_{en}, F_w.

We know that, $\quad i = \dfrac{N_1}{N_2} = \dfrac{d_2}{d_1} = \dfrac{z_2}{z_1}$

$$2.5 = \dfrac{1000}{N_2}$$

$N_2 = 400$ rpm and $d_2 = 2.5\, d_1$

Also, center distance $= \dfrac{d_1 + d_2}{2}$

$$300 = \dfrac{d_1 + d_2}{2}$$

$d_1 + 2.5 d_1 = 600$

$d_1 = 171.43$ mm and

$d_2 = 428.57$ mm.

Round-off 'd':

Let
$$d_1 = 180 \text{ mm},$$
$$d_2 = i d_1 = 2.5 \times 180 = 450 \text{ mm}.$$

Identifying weaker part (pinion/gear):

We know that strength factor = $\sigma_d \cdot y$
- Assume $z_1 = 20$ teeth
- ∴ $z_2 = iz_1 = 2.5 \times 20 = 50$ teeth

- For $\alpha = 20°$ FDI, $\quad y = 0.154 - \dfrac{0.912}{z}$ ...12.17b/ Pg 163, DHB

$$\text{i.e. } y_1 = 0.154 - \dfrac{0.912}{z_1}$$

$$y_1 = 0.154 - \dfrac{0.912}{20} = 0.1084$$

$$y_2 = 0.154 - \dfrac{0.912}{50} = 0.1357$$

∴ for pinion $\quad \sigma_{d1} \cdot y_1 = 200 \times 0.1084 = 21.68$ MPa
for gear, $\quad \sigma_{d2} \cdot y_2 = 180 \times 0.1357 = 24.44$ MPa

Since $\sigma_{d1} \cdot y_1$ is less, design is based on **pinion**.

a. To find module (m)

Since the diameter is known, we have $m = \sqrt{\dfrac{F_t}{\sigma_d C_v k Y}}$ ...Eq. (i) 12.16/ Pg 163, DHB

- $v = \dfrac{\pi d_1 N_1}{60} = \dfrac{\pi \times 0.18 \times 1000}{60} = 9.43$ m/s

- For v upto 13 m/s, $C_v = \dfrac{4.58}{4.58 + v}$ ...12.19b/ Pg 164, DHB

$$= \dfrac{4.58}{4.58 + 9.43}$$

$$C_v = 0.3269$$

- Form factor, $Y = \pi y_1 = 0.1084\pi$ ...12.16/ Pg 163, DHB

- $F_t = \dfrac{1000 \, PC_s}{v}$ ...12.20a/ Pg 164, DHB

Assuming a service of 8 – 10 h per day with medium shocks.
service factor $C_s = 1.5$ ...Tb. 12.8/ Pg 187, DHB

∴ $F_t = \dfrac{1000 \times 25 \times 1.5}{9.43}$

$F_t = 3.98$ kN

∴ Eq. (i) yields... $m = \sqrt{\dfrac{3.98 \times 10^3}{200 \times 0.3269 \times 10 \times 0.1084\pi}}$

$m = 4.23$ mm

Therefore, standard module $m = 5$ mm ...Tb. 12.2/ Pg 182, DHB

$\therefore$ Number of teeth on pinion, $z_1 = \dfrac{d_1}{m} = \dfrac{180}{5} = 36$ teeth

Number of teeth on gear, $z_2 = \dfrac{d_2}{m} = \dfrac{450}{5} = 90$ teeth ...Eq. (ii)

Face width, $b = 10m = 10 \times 5 = 50$ mm

- Check for i:

  We know that, $i = \dfrac{z_2}{z_1} = \dfrac{90}{36}$

  $\therefore$ $i = 2.5$ same as given in data)

- Check for σ_{d1}:

  We know that, $F_t = \sigma_d C_v b Y m$ ...Eq. (iii) 12.15/ Pg 163, DHB
- Here $Y = \pi y_1$ ...12.16/ Pg 163, DHB

  $= \pi \left[0.154 - \dfrac{0.912}{z_1} \right]$ ...12.17b/ Pg 163, DHB

  $= \pi \left[0.154 - \dfrac{0.912}{36} \right]$

  $Y = 0.1287\pi$

$\therefore$ Eq. (iii) yields... $3.98 \times 10^3 = \sigma_{d1} \times 0.3269 \times 50 \times (0.1287 \times \pi) \times 5$

$\sigma_{d1} = 120.47$ MPa < 200 MPa ...hence safe.

Since calculated values are $<$ permissible values, the assumed values are satisfactory.

b. To find face width (b) $b = 50$ mm

c. To find dynamic tooth load (F_d)

We know that, $F_d = F_t + \dfrac{K_3 v (Cb + F_t)}{K_3 v + \sqrt{Cb + F_t}}$ ...Eq. (iv) 12.33/ Pg 166, DHB

here $K_1 = 20.67$
for class – II gears (data),

@ $v = 5$ m/s	Error, $e = 0.0277$ mm	...Tb. 12.14/ Pg 191, DHB
For $\alpha = 20°$ FDI teeth and steel – CI combination		
@ $e = 0.02$ mm	$C = 157.3$ N/mm	...Tb. 12.12/ Pg 190, DHB
$e = 0.0277$ mm	$C = ?$	

i.e. $C = \dfrac{0.0277 \times 157.3}{0.02} = 217.86$ N/mm

$\therefore$ Eq. (iv) yields... $F_d = 3980 + \dfrac{(20.67 \times 9.43) \times \left[(217.86 \times 50) + 3980 \right]}{(20.67 \times 9.43) + \sqrt{\left[(217.86 \times 50) + 3980 \right]}}$

$F_d = 13.13$ kN

d. To find endurance strength (F_{en})

We know that, $\quad F_{en} = \sigma_{en} b Y m \quad$ ...12.34/ Pg 166, DHB

@ $BHN_1 = 250$, $\sigma_{en} = 429$ MPa $\quad$ ...Tb.12.15/ Pg 192, DHB

$\therefore \quad F_{en} = 429 \times 50 \times 0.1287\pi \times 5$

$F_{en} = 43.36$ kN

Since $F_{en} > F_d$, the material is safe against static tooth load.

e. To find wear load (F_w)

We know that, $\quad F_w = d_1 b Q K \quad$ ...Eq. (v) 12.36a/ Pg 167, DHB

- Diameter of pinion, $d_1 = 180$ mm

- Ratio factor, $\quad Q = \dfrac{2d_2}{d_2 + d_1} \quad$ ...12.36c/ Pg 167, DHB

$$= \dfrac{2 \times 450}{450 + 180}$$

$Q = 1.428$

- For $\alpha = 20°$ and steel – CI combination having $BHN_1 = 250$ and $BHN_2 = 200$,

$K = 1.344$ (Max. $BHN_2 = 180$), [refer Problem 7]

...Tb.12.16/ Pg 193, DHB

$\therefore \quad$ Eq. (v) yields... $F_w = 180 \times 50 \times 1.428 \times 1.344$

$F_w = 17.28$ kN

Since $F_w > F_d$, the material is safe against wear.

---

10. Design a pair of spur gears to transmit a power of 25 kW from a shaft running at 1200 rpm to a parallel shaft to be run at 300 rpm maintaining a center distance of 160 mm.

[VTU – Dec. 07/ Jan. 2008 - 20 Marks; (similar) Jan./ Feb. 2005 – 20 Marks; (similar) Jan./ Feb. 2006 – 20 Marks]

Solution: $P = 25$ kW, $N_1 = 1200$ rpm, $N_2 = 300$ rpm, center distance = 160 mm

Design: m, F_d, F_{en}, F_w.

We know that, $\quad i = \dfrac{N_1}{N_2} = \dfrac{d_2}{d_1} = \dfrac{z_2}{z_1}$

$i = \dfrac{1200}{300}$

$i = 4$ and $d_2 = 4d_1$

Also, center distance $= \dfrac{d_1 + d_2}{2}$

$160 = \dfrac{d_1 + d_2}{2}$

$d_1 + 4d_1 = 320$

$d_1 = 64$ mm and

$d_2 = 256$ mm.

Material properties:

Since the material is not specified, let us assume that both pinion and gear are made of same material,

i.e. Cr-Va steel, 0.45%C, heat treated having
$\sigma_{d1} = \sigma_{d2} = 516.8$ MPa and $BHN_1 = BHN_2 = 450$ ...Tb. 12.7/ Pg 186, DHB

Identifying weaker part (pinion/gear):

We know that strength factor = $\sigma_d \cdot y$

Since both pinion and gear are made of same material, the pinion is weaker, i.e. $\sigma_{d1} \cdot y_1 < \sigma_{d2} \cdot y_2$.

Hence design is based on **pinion**.

- Assume $\alpha = 20°$ FDI system.
- Assume $z_1 = 20$ teeth
- $\therefore$ $z_2 = iz_1 = 4 \times 20 = 80$ teeth

a. To find module (m)

Since the diameter is known, we have $m = \sqrt{\dfrac{F_t}{\sigma_d C_v k Y}}$ ...Eq. (i) 12.16/ Pg 163, DHB

- $v = \dfrac{\pi d_1 N_1}{60} = \dfrac{\pi \times 0.064 \times 1200}{60} = 4.02$ m/s

- For $v < 8$ m/s, $C_v = \dfrac{3.05}{3.05 + v}$ ...12.19a/ Pg 164, DHB

$$= \dfrac{3.05}{3.05 + 4.02}$$

$C_v = 0.4314$

- Here $Y = \pi y_1$ ...12.16/ Pg 163, DHB

$$= \pi \left[0.154 - \dfrac{0.912}{z_1} \right]$$ ...12.17b/ Pg 163, DHB

$$= \pi \left[0.154 - \dfrac{0.912}{20} \right]$$

$Y = 0.1084\pi$

- $F_t = \dfrac{1000 \, P C_s}{v}$ ...12.20a/ Pg 164, DHB

Assuming a service of 8 – 10 hours per day with medium shocks.

Service factor $C_s = 1.5$ ...Tb. 12.8/ Pg 187, DHB

$\therefore$ $F_t = \dfrac{1000 \times 25 \times 1.5}{4.02}$

$F_t = 9328.36$ N

$\therefore$ Eq. (i) yields... $m = \sqrt{\dfrac{9328.36}{516.8 \times 0.4313 \times 10 \times 0.1084\pi}}$

$m = 3.51$ mm

Therefore, standard module, $m = 4$ mm   ...Tb. 12.2/ Pg 182, DHB

$\therefore$ Number of teeth on pinion, $z_1 = \dfrac{d_1}{m} = \dfrac{64}{4} = 16$ teeth

Number of teeth on gear, $z_2 = \dfrac{d_2}{m} = \dfrac{256}{4} = 64$ teeth ...Eq. (ii)

Face width, $b = 10m = 10 \times 4 = 40$ mm

- Check for i:

We know that $\quad i = \dfrac{z_2}{z_1} = \dfrac{64}{16}$

$\therefore \quad i = 4$ (same as given in data)

- Check for σ_{d1}:

We know that, $\quad F_t = \sigma_d C_v b Y m \qquad$ ...Eq. (iii) **12.15/ Pg 163, DHB**
- Here $\qquad Y = \pi y_1 \qquad\qquad\qquad\qquad\quad$ **...12.16/ Pg 163, DHB**

$\qquad\qquad = \pi \left[0.154 - \dfrac{0.912}{z_1} \right] \qquad$ **...12.17b/ Pg 163, DHB**

$\qquad\qquad = \pi \left[0.154 - \dfrac{0.912}{20} \right]$

$\qquad Y = 0.097\pi$

$\therefore$ Eq. (iii) yields... $9328.36 = \sigma_{d1} \times 0.4313 \times 40 \times (0.097 \times \pi) \times 4$

$\qquad\qquad \sigma_{d1} = 443.6$ MPa < 516.8 MPa ...hence safe.

Since calculated values are < permissible values, the assumed values are satisfactory.

b. To find face width (b) $\qquad b = 40$ mm

c. To find dynamic tooth load (F_d)

We know that, $\quad F_d = F_t + \dfrac{K_3 v (Cb + F_t)}{K_3 v + \sqrt{Cb + F_t}} \quad$ ...Eq. (iv) **12.33/ Pg 166, DHB**

here $K_3 = 20.67$

@ $v = 4$ m/s	Error, $e = 0.0710$ mm	...Tb. 12.14/ Pg 191, DHB
For $\alpha = 20°$ FDI teeth and steel – steel combination		
@ $e = 0.06$ mm	$C = 686.7$ N/mm	...Tb. 12.12/ Pg 190, DHB
$e = 0.0710$ mm	$C = ?$	

$\therefore \qquad$ at $v = 4.02$ m/s, $C = \dfrac{0.0710 \times 686.7}{0.06} = 812.59$ N/mm

$\therefore$ Eq. (iv) yields... $F_d = 9328.36 + \dfrac{(20.67 \times 4.02) \times \left[(812.59 \times 40) + 9328.36 \right]}{(20.67 \times 4.02) + \sqrt{\left[(812.59 \times 40) + 9328.36 \right]}}$

$\qquad\qquad F_d = 21.41$ kN

d. To find endurance strength (F_{en})

We know that, $\qquad F_{en} = \sigma_{en} b Y m \qquad\qquad$ **...12.34/ Pg 166, DHB**

@ $BHN_1 = 450$, $\sigma_{en} = 686.5$ MPa $\qquad$ **...Tb.12.15/ Pg 192, DHB**

$\therefore \qquad\qquad F_{en} = 686.5 \times 40 \times 0.097\pi \times 4$

$\qquad\qquad F_{en} = 33.47$ kN

Since $F_{en} > F_d$, the material is safe against static tooth load.

e. To find wear load (F_w)

We know that, $\quad F_w = d_1 b Q K \quad$ ...Eq. (v) **12.36a/ Pg 167, DHB**

- Diameter of pinion, $d_1 = 64$ mm

- Ratio factor, $Q = \dfrac{2d_2}{d_2 + d_1} \quad$ ...**12.36c/ Pg 167, DHB**

$$= \dfrac{2 \times 256}{256 + 64}$$

$$Q = 1.6$$

- For $\alpha = 20°$ and steel – steel combination having $BHN_1 = BHN_2 = 450$,

$K = 3.226 \quad$ ...**Tb.12.16/ Pg 193, DHB**

∴ Eq. (v) yields... $F_w = 64 \times 40 \times 1.6 \times 3.226$

$$F_w = 13.21 \text{ kN}$$

Since $F_w < F_d$, the pinion is subjected to rapid wear and hence has to be surface hardened to higher BHN,

i.e. $F_w \geq F_d$

$d_1 b Q K \geq 21.41$ kN

$64 \times 40 \times 1.6 \times K \geq 21.41 \times 10^3$

$K \geq 5.227$

Therefore, for steel – steel combination, having $\alpha = 20°$ and $K \geq 5.227$, we have

$$BHN_1 = BHN_2 = 600 \quad \text{...\textbf{Tb. 12.16/ Pg 193, DHB}}$$

HELICAL GEARS

4.28 INTRODUCTION

Helical gears are used to transmit motion between parallel or crossed shafts or between a shaft and a rack by meshing teeth that lie along a helix at an angle to the axis of the shaft. Due to this angle, mating of the teeth occurs such that two or more teeth of each gear are always in contact. This condition permits smoother action than that of spur gears. Unlike spur gears, helical gears generate axial thrust, which causes slight loss of power and requires thrust bearings.

In helical gears the teeth are in the form of a helix. The helixes may be right handed on one gear and left handed on the other. This provides gradual engagement and continuous contact of engaging teeth. Hence helical gears give smooth drive with high transmission efficiency.

Helical gears may be of single helical or double helical type. In case of single helical gears, there is some axial thrust between the teeth. In order to eliminate this, double helical gears (Herringbone gears) are used.

4.29 ADVANTAGES AND DISADVANTAGE OF HELICAL GEAR

- This gradual engagement and disengagement of teeth reduces the noise and dynamic load.
- Drive is smooth, shock less and without noise, vibration and impact.
- Suitable for transmitting low and medium power at high speeds.
- Gears can be surface hardened to higher *BHN*.
- Due to helical shape, the gears are subjected to axial, radial and tangential loads.
- The axial load can be eliminated by using herringbone gears.

4.30 COMPARISON BETWEEN SPUR AND HELICAL GEARS

Sl. No.	Spur gears	Helical gears
1.	Spur gears have straight teeth	Helical gears have their teeth cut in the form of a helix
2.	Used with parallel shafts	Parallel and non-parallel shafts
3.	Operate at low speeds	High speeds
4.	Load is suddenly applied	Gradually applied
5.	Operation is noisy	Smooth
6.	Dynamic stresses are high.	Low
7.	Pitch line velocity up to 8 m/s	20 – 30 m/s
8.	When the spur gears begin to engage, the contact extends across the entire tooth on a line parallel to the gear axis	Here the contact begins at one end of the entering tooth and gradually extends along a diagonal line across the tooth face as the gear rotates
9.	—	Can sustain greater tangential loads than spur gears of same size
10.	Applications: washing machines and electric screwdrivers	Turbine and automobile gears

4.31 TERMS USED IN HELICAL GEARS

- Helix angle (β): is the angle made by the helices with axis of rotation.
- Axial pitch ($p = p_c$): is same as the circular pitch and therefore is defined as the circular pitch in the plane of rotation.

- Normal pitch ($p_n = p_{cn}$): is the distance between similar faces on adjacent teeth along a helix on the pitch cylinders normal to the teeth.
  It is also defined as the circular pitch in the normal plane perpendicular to the teeth.

4.32 PROPORTIONS OF HELICAL GEAR

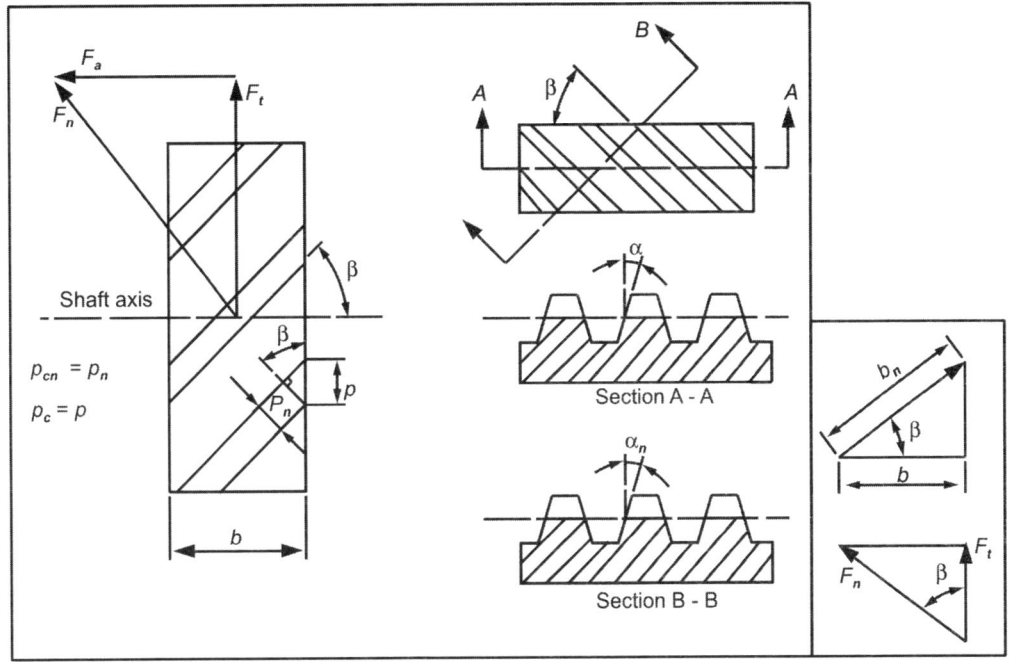

Fig. 4.2: Helical gear (Fig. 12.5/Pg 206, DHB)

Let, β – helix angle
  F_t – torque producing force
  F_a – end thrust
  F_n – normal force
  $p_c (= p)$ – circular pitch
  $p_n (= p_{cn})$ – normal circular pitch
  b – face width
  m – module
  m_n – normal module in a plane normal to tooth.

- Here we are concerned with two pitches: the normal pitch (p_n) and the real pitch (p). The relation between the normal pitch and the real pitch is given as follows:

$$p_n = p \cos \beta \quad \text{(Section B – B)}$$

$$= \frac{\pi d}{z} \times \cos \beta$$

$$p_n = \pi m \cos \beta \quad (\because p = \pi d/z, \, m = d/z)$$

...**12.43/ Pg 168, DHB**

- The helix angle (β) is the angle between a line drawn through one of the teeth and the axis of shaft on which the gear is mounted.
  Since there are no standard values of β, the following values are recommended
  For single helix, $20° < \beta < 35°$
  For herringbone gears, $\beta \leq 45°$

- The normal diametrical pitch is given as $P_n = \dfrac{P}{\cos \beta} = \dfrac{z}{d \cos \beta}$

...12.44/ Pg 168, DHB

- The normal module is $m_n = m \cos \beta = \dfrac{d}{z} \cos \beta$ ...12.45/ Pg 168, DHB

Note:
→ The values in Table 12.2/ Pg 182, DHB give the standard values of module (m), i.e. standard module for spur gears and normal module (m_n) for helical gears.
→ Values of (m_n) should be used for design in helical gears.

- The number of teeth is calculated as $z = \dfrac{d}{m_n} \cos \beta = dP_n \cos \beta$

...12.46/ Pg 168, DHB

- The pitch circle diameter is calculated as $d = mz = \dfrac{z}{P} = \dfrac{z}{P_n \cos \beta} = \dfrac{zm_n}{\cos \beta}$

...12.47/ Pg 168, DHB

- The relation between the pressure angles measured in transverse and normal planes is given as
$$\tan \alpha_n = \tan \alpha \cdot \cos \beta$$ ...12.52b/ Pg 169, DHB

- The center distance as given as $\alpha = \dfrac{(z_1 + z_2) m_n}{2 \cos \beta}$ ...12.50/ Pg 169, DHB

- The end or axial thrust is calculated as $F_a = F_t \tan \beta$ ...12.51/ Pg 169, DHB

4.33 FACE WIDTH (b)

In order that contact be maintained across the entire face width of the gear, the minimum value of face width must be

$$b = \dfrac{p}{\tan \beta}$$ ...(Eq. 4.22)

AGMA recommends a minimum face width of 15% higher than that of Eq. (4.22)

i.e. $\quad b_{min} = \dfrac{1.15 p}{\tan \beta} = \dfrac{(1.15) \pi m}{\tan \beta} = \dfrac{(1.15) \pi m_n}{\sin \beta}$ ...12.54/ Pg 169, DHB

and the range is $b = 12.5 m_n$ to $20 m_n$ ...12.58a/ Pg 169, DHB

On the other hand for double helical or Herringbone gears,

$$b_{min} \geq \dfrac{(2.3) \pi m}{\tan \beta} = \dfrac{(2.3) \pi m_n}{\sin \beta}$$ ...12.56/ Pg 169, DHB

and the range is $b = 20 m_n$ to $30 m_n$ ...12.58b/ Pg 169, DHB

4.34 VIRTUAL OR FORMATIVE NUMBER OF TEETH (z_e)

As shown in **Fig. 4.3**, the plane normal to the gear teeth intersects the pitch cylinder to form an ellipse. The gear tooth profile generated in this plane using the radius of curvature of ellipse would be a spur gear having the same properties as an actual helical gear.

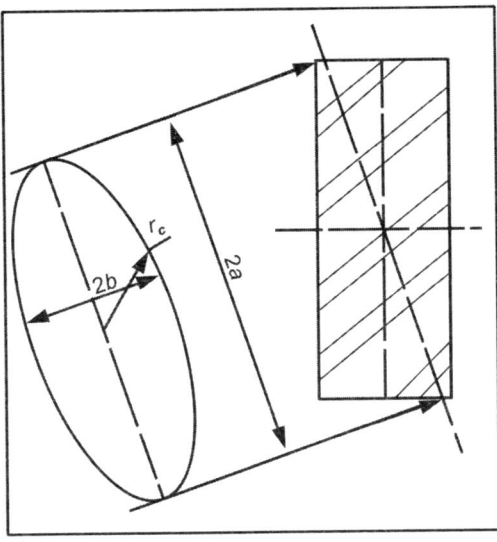

Fig. 4.3: Virtual number of teeth

The radius of curvature of an ellipse is $r_c = \dfrac{d}{\cos^2 \beta}$ ...(Eq. 4.23)

The virtual number of teeth on equivalent spur gear in normal plane is called the virtual or formative or equivalent number of teeth.

i.e. $\quad z_e = P_n \times 2r_c$

$$= \dfrac{z}{d \cos \beta} \times \dfrac{2d}{2\cos^2 \beta}$$

$$z_e = \dfrac{z}{\cos^3 \beta} \quad ...(\text{Eq. 4.24})\ \textbf{12.52a/ Pg 169, DHB}$$

Where, z = Actual number of teeth on a helical gear
β = helix angle.

Note: Design of helical gear is based on normal module and the virtual number of teeth.

4.35 FORCE ANALYSIS OF HELICAL GEARS

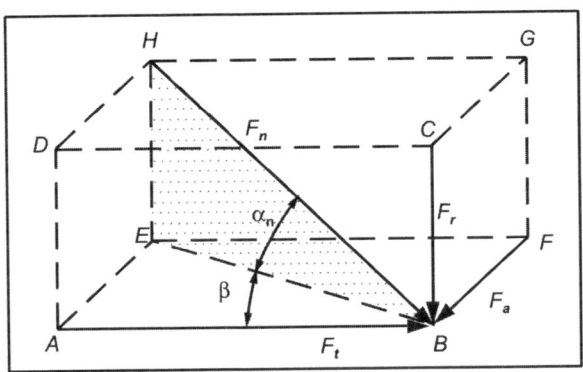

Fig. 4.4: Force analysis in helical gear

The condition for two helical gears to have a perfect mesh is that they should have the same pressure angle, same pitch and the same helix angle. The components of force are expressed in two ways:

a. The pressure angle measured in a plane perpendicular to the gear axis:

Tangential force, $\quad F_t = \dfrac{2M_t}{d}$ ...12.12/ Pg 165, DHB

Axial or thrust force or end thrust,
$$F_a = F_t \tan \beta \quad \text{...12.51/ Pg 169, DHB}$$

Radial component, $\quad F_r = F_t \tan \alpha$ ...(Eq. 4.25)

α – pressure angle $\quad \beta$ – helix angle

b. The pressure angle measured in a plane perpendicular to the tooth:

Tangential force, $\quad F_t = \dfrac{2M_t}{d} = F_n \cos \alpha_n \cos \beta$

Axial or thrust force, $\quad F_a = F_t \tan \beta = F_n \cos \alpha_n \sin \beta$

Radial component, $\quad F_r = \dfrac{F_t \tan \alpha_n}{\cos \beta} = F_n \sin \alpha_n$

...(Eq. 4.26) using **12.52b/ Pg 169, DHB**

From $\triangle BEH$

$\sin \alpha_n = F_r/F_n \Rightarrow F_r = F_n \sin \alpha_n$ ...(Eq. 4.27)
$\cos \alpha_n = BE/F_n \Rightarrow BE = F_n \cos \alpha_n$ ...(Eq. 4.28)

From $\triangle EAB$

$\sin \beta = F_a/BE = F_a/F_n \cos \alpha_n \Rightarrow F_a = F_n \cos \alpha_n \sin \beta$ ...(Eq. 4.29)
$\cos \beta = F_t/BE = F_t/F_n \cos \alpha_n \Rightarrow F_t = F_n \cos \alpha_n \cos \beta$ ...(Eq. 4.30)

Dividing Eq. (4.29) with Eq. (4.30) yields,

$$\dfrac{F_a}{F_t} = \dfrac{F_n \cos \alpha_n \sin \beta}{F_n \cos \alpha_n \cos \beta}$$

$$F_a = F_t \tan \beta \quad \text{...(Eq. 4.31) } \textbf{12.51/ Pg 169, DHB}$$

Dividing Eq. (4.26) with Eq. (4.30) yields,

$$\dfrac{F_r}{F_t} = \dfrac{F_n \sin \alpha_n}{F_n \cos \alpha_n \cos \beta} = \dfrac{\tan \alpha_n}{\cos \beta}$$

$$F_r = \dfrac{\tan \alpha_n}{\cos \beta} \cdot F_t$$

$$= F_n \cdot \cos \alpha_n \cdot \cos \beta \cdot \left(\dfrac{1}{\cos \beta}\right)\left(\dfrac{\sin \alpha_n}{\cos \alpha_n}\right)$$

$$F_r = F_n \sin \alpha_n \quad \text{...(Eq. 4.32) same as (Eq. 4.26)}$$

The component $F_t \tan \beta$ along the gear axis is called the end thrust, which is not preferred, but can be neutralized using two helical gears with teeth in opposite direction or by using a herringbone gear.

4.36 STRENGTH OF A HELICAL GEAR

We know that the Lewis equation is given as
$$F_t = \sigma_d C_v b Y m \quad \text{...Using (4.5c) ...(4.33)} \quad \textbf{12.15/ Pg 163, DHB}$$

As a rule Lewis's equation is applied in a plane normal to the teeth.

$\therefore$ Eq. (4.33) yields ... $F_{tn} = \sigma_d C_v b_n Y m_n$ ...(Eq. 4.34)

but, $m_n = m \cos \beta$
$b_n = b/\cos \beta$
$F_{tn} = F_t/\cos \beta$

$\therefore$ Eq. (4.34) yields... $\dfrac{F_t}{\cos \beta} = \sigma_d C_v b_n Y m_n \dfrac{b}{\cos \beta}$

$$F_t = \sigma_d C_v b Y m_n \quad \text{...(Eq. 4.35)}$$

Since helical gears operate at high speeds, we introduce a factor for wear and lubrication (C_w) in Eq. (4.35).

$\therefore \quad F_t = \dfrac{\sigma_d C_v b Y m_n}{C_w}$ ...(Eq. 4.36) **12.59/ Pg 169, DHB**

Where, σ_d – allowable static stress ...**Table 12.7/ Pg 186, DHB**
C_w – wear and lubrication factor ...**Table 12.21/ Pg 196, DHB**

4.37 DESIGN METHODOLOGY FOR HELICAL GEARS

There are two methods of designing a helical gear problem as discussed below.

Method 1: If the pitch diameter is known:

We know that, $F_t = \dfrac{\sigma_d C_v b Y m_n}{C_w}$ ...using (4.36) **12.59/ Pg 169, DHB**

But, $k = b/m_n$ ...**12.60/ Pg 170, DHB**

$\therefore$ Eq. (4.36) yields ... $F_t = \dfrac{\sigma_d C_v (k m_n) Y m_n}{C_w}$

$= \dfrac{\sigma_d C_v k Y m_n^2}{C_w}$

$m_n = \dfrac{F_t C_w}{\sigma_d C_v k Y}$

$\therefore \quad m_n = \sqrt{\dfrac{F_t C_w}{\sigma_d C_v k Y}}$ ...(Eq. 4.37) **12.60/ Pg 170, DHB**

Method 2: If the pitch diameter is unknown:

We know that *torque* = force × distance
$M_t = F_t \times (d/2)$

$F_t = \dfrac{2 M_t}{d}$ ...**12.22/ Pg 165, DHB**

$\dfrac{\sigma_d C_v b Y m_n}{C_w} = \dfrac{2 M_t}{d}$ ...using (4.36)

But, $k = b/m_n$

and $d = \dfrac{zm_n}{\cos\beta}$ ...12.47/ Pg 168, DHB

$$\therefore M_t = \dfrac{\sigma_d C_v (km_n) Y m_n}{2C_w}\left(\dfrac{m_n z}{\cos\beta}\right)$$

$$= \dfrac{\sigma_d C_v k Y z m_n^3}{2 C_w \cos\beta}$$

$$m_n^3 = \dfrac{2 M_t C_w \cos\beta}{\sigma_d C_v k Y z}$$

$$m_n = \sqrt[3]{\dfrac{2 M_t C_w \cos\beta}{\sigma_d C_v k Y z}} \qquad \text{..(Eq. 4.38) 12.60/ Pg 170, DHB}$$

Where, $Y = \pi y$

$k = b/m_n$

C_v = velocity factor, ...**Eqs 12.61a – 12.61e/ Pg 164, DHB**

4.38 DYNAMIC TOOTH LOAD

The dynamic load is calculated as:

$$F_d = F_t + \dfrac{K_3 v \left(Cb\cos^2\beta + F_t\right)\cos\beta}{K_3 v + \sqrt{\left(Cb\cos^2\beta + F_t\right)}} \qquad \text{...(Eq. 4.39) 12.62/ Pg 170, DHB}$$

Where, F_t = tangential tooth load

K = Constant

v = pitch line velocity (m/s)

b = face width

C = dynamic factor depending upon machining errors (as in spur gears) ...**Table 12.12/ Pg 190, DHB**

- For a given pitch line velocity, the maximum allowable error 'e' can be obtained from **Table 12.14/ Pg 191, DHB**. From the obtained value of e, C can be calculated as per the given material from **Table 12.12/ Pg 190, DHB**.
- On the other hand if the Young's modulus is specified for the gears and pinion, then C is calculated as

$$C = \dfrac{e}{k_1\left[\dfrac{1}{E_1} + \dfrac{1}{E_2}\right]} \qquad \text{...12.33/ Pg 166, DHB}$$

Where, k_1 = 9.345 for 14.5° full depth teeth

= 9.000 for 20° full depth teeth

= 8.700 for 20° stub teeth

e – maximum error between gears

...**Table 12.13/ Pg 191, DHB and Fig. 12.3/ Pg 205, DHB**

E_1 and E_2 – Young's modulus for pinion and gear respectively.

4.39 DYNAMIC STRENGTH –OR– ENDURANCE STRENGTH (F_{en} or F_s)

The dynamic load is calculated as:
$$F_s = \sigma_{en} b Y m_n,$$ ...(Eq. 4.40) **12.63/ Pg 170, DHB**

Endurance strength, σ_{en} ...**Table 12.15/ Pg 192, DHB**

For safety against dynamic load, $F_s \geq F_d$ ...(Eq. 4.41)

4.40 WEAR TOOTH LOAD (F_w)

The limiting load for wear is, $(F_w) = \dfrac{d_1 b Q K}{\cos^2 \beta}$ ...(Eq. 4.42) **12.64/ Pg 170, DHB**

Where, d_1 – diameter of pinion

$$= \dfrac{m_n z}{\cos \beta}$$ ...**12.47/ Pg 168, DHB**

K – load stress factor ...**Tb. 12.16 and 12.17/ Pg 193-194, DHB**

$$= \dfrac{\sigma_{es}^2 \sin \alpha_n}{1.4}\left[\dfrac{1}{E_1} + \dfrac{1}{E_2}\right]$$ ...**12.65/ Pg 170, DHB**

$\tan \alpha_n = \tan \alpha \, \cos \beta$ ...**12.52b/ Pg 169, DHB**

Q – ratio factor

$$= \dfrac{2 d_2}{d_2 + d_1} = \dfrac{2 z_2}{z_2 + z_1}$$ ...**12.36c/ Pg 167, DHB**

σ_{es} = surface endurance limit

For steel, $\sigma_{es} = [2.75(BHN) - 70]$ ...**12.36d/ Pg 167, DHB**

(BHN) – average Brinell hardness number for gear and pinion

$$= \dfrac{BHN_1 + BHN_2}{2}$$

For safety against wear, $F_w \geq F_d$ ...(Eq. 4.43)

4.41 HERRINGBONE GEARS

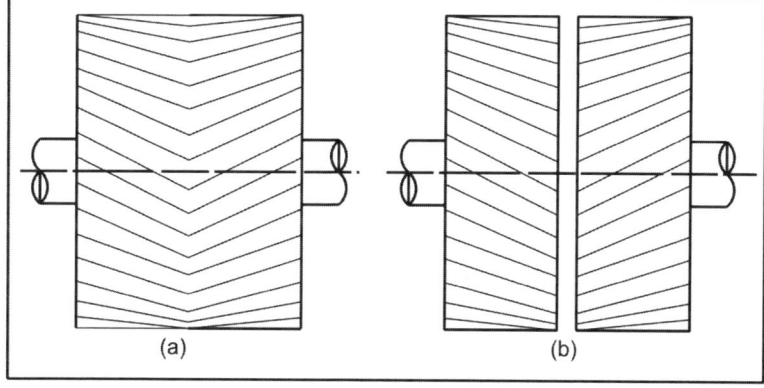

Fig. 4.5: (a) Herringbone gear (b) Double helical gear

Herringbone gears as shown in **Fig. 4.5(a)** sometimes called double helical gears, are used to transmit motion between parallel shafts. In herringbone gears, tooth engagement is progressive, and two or more teeth share the load at all times. Because they have right-hand and left-hand helixes, herringbone gears are usually not subjected to end thrust.

Double helical gears as shown in **Fig. 4.5(b)** use two tracks of mirrored, angled teeth. This arrangement cancels out the net axial thrust, since each half of the gear thrusts in the opposite direction resulting in a net axial force or thrust of zero. These tracks are often separated by a gap for different machining purposes, but can be in direct contact with one another. Double helical gears are stronger than single helical gears and have zero sideways force.

The basic difference between a herringbone gear and a double helical gear is that the double helical gear has a groove while herringbone gear has no groove.

4.42 DESIGN PROCEDURE FOR HELICAL GEARS PROBLEMS

The procedure used for helical gears is same as that of spur gears, except that
- Module (m) is replaced with normal module (m_n) and all the calculations are based on normal module.
- Lewis form factor includes virtual number of teeth (z_e)

Note:
- *The values of module given in* **Table 12.2/ Pg 182, DHB** *apply to both spur and helical gear.*
- *In case of helical gears and double helical gears, these modules represent the normal modules (m_n).*

11. A helical gear of 250 mm diameter transmits a torque of 200 N-m. The pressure angle in a plane normal to the teeth is 20°. The helix angle is 30°. Determine the gear tooth loads. *[VTU - Jan./ Feb. 2005 - 06 Marks]*

Solution: $d = 250$ mm, $M_t = 200$ N-m, $\alpha_n = 20°$ (normal to teeth), helix angle, $\beta = 45°$.

a. $F_t = ?$ b. $F_a = ?$ c. $F_r = ?$

When the pressure angle measured in a plane perpendicular to the tooth, we have

a. Tangential force, $F_t = \dfrac{2M_t}{d}$ ...12.22/ Pg 165, DHB

$$= \dfrac{2 \times 200 \times 10^3}{250}$$

$F_t = 1600$ N

b. Axial or thrust force, $F_a = F_t \tan \beta$ ...12.51/ Pg 169, DHB

$= 1600 \times \tan 45$

$F_a = 1600$ N

c. Radial component, $F_r = \dfrac{F_t \tan \alpha_n}{\cos \beta}$ (To remember)

$$= \dfrac{1600 \times \tan 20}{\cos 45}$$

$F_r = 823.57$ N.

4.43 PROBLEMS BASED ON KNOWN DIAMETER

12. A pair of helical gears are to transmit 15 kW. The teeth are 20° stub in diametral plane and have a helix angle of 45°. The pinion runs at 10000 rpm and has 80 mm pitch diameter. The gear has a pitch diameter of 320 mm. If gears are made of cast steel having allowable static strength of 100 MPa; determine module and face width from static strength considerations and check the gears for wear, given σ_{es} = 618 MPa. *[VTU - July 2007 - 15 Marks]*

Solution: P = 15 kW, α = 20°-stub teeth, helix angle, β = 45°, pinion speed, N_1 = 10000 rpm, pitch diameter of pinion, d_1 = 80 mm, pitch diameter of gear, d_2 = 320 mm, σ_{d1} = σ_{d2} = 100 MPa, σ_{es} = 618 MPa.

a. m_n = ?   b. b = ?   c. F_w = ?

$$\text{We know that, } i = \frac{N_1}{N_2} = \frac{d_2}{d_1} = \frac{z_2}{z_1}$$

$$i = \frac{d_2}{d_1} = \frac{320}{80} = 4$$

Identifying weaker part (pinion/gear):

We know that strength factor = $\sigma_d \cdot y$

Since both pinion and gear are made of same material, the pinion is weaker, i.e. $\sigma_{d1} \cdot y_1 < \sigma_{d2} \cdot y_2$.

Hence design is based on **pinion**.

- Assume z_1 = 20 teeth
  ∴ $z_2 = iz_1 = 4 \times 20 = 80$ teeth

- Virtual number of teeth, $z_e = \dfrac{z}{\cos^3 \beta}$ ...**12.52a/ Pg 169, DHB**

$$z_{e1} = \frac{z_1}{\cos^3 \beta} = \frac{20}{\cos^3 45}$$

$$z_{e1} = 56.57 \approx 57$$

a. To find module (m_n)

Since the diameter is known, we have $m_n = \sqrt{\dfrac{F_t C_w}{\sigma_d C_v k Y}}$ ...Eq. (i) **12.60/ Pg 170, DHB**

- $v = \dfrac{\pi \times 0.08 \times 10000}{60} = 41.89$ m/s

- For $v > 20$ m/s, $C_v = \dfrac{5.55}{5.55 + \sqrt{v}}$ ...**12.61d/ Pg 170, DHB**

$$= \frac{5.55}{5.55 + \sqrt{41.89}}$$

$$C_v = 0.4616$$

∴ $F_t = \dfrac{1000 \, PC_s}{v}$ ...**12.20a/ Pg 164, DHB**

Assuming 8 – 10 hours service and steady load, service factor $C_s = 1$

$$\therefore \quad F_t = \frac{1000 \times 15 \times 1}{41.89} \quad \text{...Tb. 12.8/ Pg 187, DHB}$$

$$F_t = 358 \text{ N}$$

- Form factor, Here $Y = \pi y_1$ ...12.16/ Pg 163, DHB

$$= \pi \left[0.175 - \frac{0.95}{z_{e1}} \right] \quad \text{...12.17c/ Pg 163, DHB}$$

$$= \pi \left[0.175 - \frac{0.95}{57} \right]$$

$$Y = 0.4974$$

- Assume, $k = b/m_n = 15$
- Assume, $C_w = 1.15$ ...Tb. 12.21/ Pg 196, DHB

$$\therefore \quad \text{Eq. } (i) \text{ yields... } m_n = \sqrt{\frac{358 \times 1.15}{100 \times 0.4616 \times 15 \times 0.4974}}$$

$$m_n = 1.09 \text{ mm}$$

Therefore, standard module, $m_n = 1.25$ mm ...Tb. 12.2/ Pg 182, DHB

$$\therefore \quad \text{Number of teeth on pinion, } z_1 = \frac{d_1 \cos \beta}{m_n} = \frac{80 \times \cos 45}{1.25} = 45.25 \approx 46 \text{ teeth}$$

...12.46/ Pg 168, DHB

Number of teeth on gear, $z_2 = iz_1 = 4 \times 49 = 184$ teeth

- Virtual number of teeth, $z_2 = \dfrac{z}{\cos^3 \beta}$ ...12.52a/ Pg 169, DHB

$$z_{e1} = \frac{z_1}{\cos^3 \beta} = \frac{46}{\cos^3 45}$$

$$z_{e1} = 130.10$$

and $z_{e2} = i.z_{e1} = 4 \times 130.10 = 520.4$
- Face width, $b = 15 m_n = 15 \times 1.25 = 18.75$ mm ≈ 19 mm
- **Check for b:**

$$\text{i.e. } b_{\min} = \frac{(1.15) \pi m_n}{\sin \beta} \quad \text{...12.54/ Pg 169, DHB}$$

$$= \frac{(1.15) \times \pi \times 1.25}{\sin 45}$$

$$b_{\min} = 6.38 \text{ mm}$$

Since $b > b_{\min}$, the calculated value of b is safe.
- **Check for σ_{d1}:**

We know that, $F_t = \dfrac{\sigma_d C_v b Y m_n}{C_w}$ ...Eq. (ii) 12.59/ Pg 169, DHB

- Here $Y = \pi y_1$ ...12.16/ Pg 163, DHB

$$= \pi \left[0.175 - \frac{0.95}{z_{e1}} \right] \quad \text{...12.17c/ Pg 163, DHB}$$

$$= \pi\left[0.175 - \frac{0.95}{130.10}\right]$$

$$Y = 0.5268$$

∴ Eq. (ii) yields... $358 = \dfrac{\sigma_{d1} \times 0.4616 \times 19 \times 0.5268 \times 1.25}{1.15}$

$\sigma_{d1} = 71.28$ MPa < 100 MPa   hence safe.

Since calculated values are < permissible values, the assumed values are satisfactory.

b. To find face width (b) $b = 19$ mm

c. To find dynamic tooth load (F_d)

We know that, $F_d = F_t + \dfrac{K_3 v\left(Cb\cos^2\beta + F_t\right)\cos\beta}{K_3 v + \sqrt{\left(Cb\cos^2\beta + F_t\right)}}$

...Eq. (iii) 12.62/ Pg 170, DHB

here $K_3 = 20.67$

@ $v > 26$ m/s	Error, $e = 0.0127$ mm	...Tb. 12.14/ Pg 191, DHB
For α = 20° Stub teeth and steel – steel combination		
@ $e = 0.01$ mm	$C = 118.7$ N/mm	...Tb. 12.12/ Pg 190, DHB
$e = 0.0127$ mm	$C = ?$	

∴   at $v = 41.89$ m/s. $C = \dfrac{0.0127 \times 118.7}{0.01} = 150.75$ N/mm

∴ Eq. (iii) yields... $F_d = 358 + \dfrac{(20.67 \times 41.89) \times \left[(150.75 \times 19 \times \cos^2 45) + 358\right] \times \cos 45}{(20.67 \times 41.89) + \sqrt{\left[(150.75 \times 19 \times c\cos^2 45) + 358\right]}}$

$F_d = 1564.84$ N.

d. To find dynamic tooth load (F_w)

We know that, $F_w = \dfrac{d_1 b Q K}{\cos^2\beta}$ ...Eq. (iv) 12.64/ Pg 170, DHB

- Diameter of pinion, $d_1 = 80$ mm

- Ratio factor, $Q = \dfrac{2 d_2}{d_2 + d_1}$ ...12.36c/ Pg 167, DHB

$$= \dfrac{2 \times 320}{320 + 80}$$

$Q = 1.6$

- Here BHN is not given. Since both the gears are made of steel, assuming $E = 2.1 \times 10^5$ MPa, we have

$$K = \dfrac{\sigma_{es}^2 \sin\alpha_n}{1.4}\left[\dfrac{1}{E_1} + \dfrac{1}{E_2}\right]$$

...12.65/ Pg 170, DHB

$$\tan \alpha_n = \tan \alpha \cos \beta \qquad \text{...12.52b/ Pg 169, DHB}$$
$$= \tan 20 \times \cos 45$$
$$\alpha_n = 14.43 \text{ deg}$$

$$K = \frac{618^2 \times \sin(14.43)}{1.4} \left[\frac{1}{2.1 \times 10^5} + \frac{1}{2.1 \times 10^5} \right]$$

$$K = 0.6474$$

$\therefore$ Eq. (iv) yields $F_w = \dfrac{80 \times 19 \times 1.6 \times 0.6474}{\cos^2 45}$

$$F_w = 3149 \text{ N}$$

Since $F_w > F_d$, the material is safe against wear.

13. **The following data refers to the design of a helical gear drive:**
    i. Power transmitted 34 kW at 2800 rpm of pinion
    ii. Speed ratio 4.5, number of teeth on pinion 18
    iii. Helix angel 25°, pressure angle $\alpha = 20°$ stub
    iv. Material for both pinion and gear is medium carbon steel whose allowable stress may be taken as 230 MPa.
    v. Pinion diameter is limited to 125 mm.
    Determine the axial thrust on the shaft and check the gears for dynamic and wear loads. **[VTU –Dec. 2010 – 20 Marks.]**

Solution: $P = 34$ kW, pinion speed, $N_1 = 2800$ rpm, $i = 4.5$, $z_1 = 18$ teeth, helix angle, $\beta = 25°$ $\alpha = 20°$-stub teeth, pitch diameter of pinion, $d_1 = 125$ mm, $\sigma_{d1} = \sigma_{d2} = 230$ MPa,

We know that, $\qquad i = \dfrac{N_1}{N_2} = \dfrac{d_2}{d_1} = \dfrac{z_2}{z_1}$

$$4.5 = \frac{d_2}{d_1} = \frac{d_2}{125}$$

$$d_2 = 562.5 \text{ mm}$$
and $\qquad iz_2 = 4.5 \times 18 = 81 \text{ teeth}$

Identifying weaker part (pinion/gear):
We know that strength factor $= \sigma_d \cdot y$
Since both pinion and gear are made of same material, the pinion is weaker,
i.e. $\qquad \sigma_{d1} \cdot y_1 < \sigma_{d2} \cdot y_2$
Hence design is based on **pinion**.

- Virtual number of teeth, $z_e = \dfrac{z}{\cos^3 \beta}$ \qquad ...12.52a/ Pg 170, DHB

$$z_{e1} = \frac{z_1}{\cos^3 \beta} = \frac{18}{\cos^3 25}$$

$$z_{e1} = 24.17$$

- And $z_{e2} = i \cdot z_{e1} = 24.17 \times 4.5 = 108.81$

a. To find module

Since the diameter is known, we have $m_n = \sqrt{\dfrac{F_t C_w}{\sigma_d C_v k Y}}$ \quad ...Eq. (i) **12.60/ Pg 169, DHB**

- $$v = \frac{\pi d_1 N_1}{60} = \frac{\pi \times 0.125 \times 2800}{60} = 18.33 \text{ m/s}$$

- For $10 < v < 20$ /ms, $C_v = \dfrac{15.25}{15.25 + v}$ ...12.61c/ Pg 170, DHB

$$= \frac{15.25}{15.25 + 18.33}$$

$$C_v = 0.4541$$

- $$F_t = \frac{1000 \, P C_s}{v}$$ ...12.20a/ Pg 164, DHB

Assuming moderate shocks and 8 – 10 hours service, service factor, $C_s = 1.5$
...Tb. 12.8/ Pg 187, DHB

$$\therefore \quad F_t = \frac{1000 \times 34 \times 1.5}{18.33}$$

$$F_t = 2782.32 \text{ N}$$

- Form factor,   Here $Y = \pi y_1$ ..12.16/ Pg 163, DHB

$$= \pi \left[0.175 - \frac{0.95}{z_{e1}} \right]$$ ...12.17c/ Pg 163, DHB

$$= \pi \left[0.175 - \frac{0.95}{24.17} \right]$$

$$Y = 0.4263$$

- Assume, $k = b/m_n = 15$
- Assume, $C_w = 1.15$ ...Tb. 12.21/ Pg 196, DHB

$\therefore \quad$ Eq. (i) yields... $m_n = \sqrt{\dfrac{2782.32 \times 1.15}{230 \times 0.4541 \times 15 \times 0.4263}}$

$$m_n = 2.19 \text{ mm}$$

Therefore, standard module, $m_n = 2.5$ mm   ...Tb. 12.2/ Pg 182, DHB

- Face width, $b = 15 m_n = 15 \times 2.5 = 37.5$ mm

  Check for b:

  i.e. $b_{\min} = \dfrac{(1.15) \pi m_n}{\sin \beta}$ ...12.54/ Pg 169, DHB

  $$= \frac{(1.15) \times \pi \times 2.5}{\sin 25}$$

  $$b_{\min} = 21.37 \text{ mm}$$

  Since $b > b_{\min}$, the calculated value of b is safe.

- **Check for σ_{d1}:**

  We know that, $F_t = \dfrac{\sigma_d C_v b Y m_n}{C_w}$ ...12.59/ Pg 169, DHB

  $$2782.32 = \frac{\sigma_{d1} \times 0.4541 \times 37.5 \times 0.4263 \times 2.5}{1.15}$$

$\sigma_{d1} = 176.31$ MPa < 230 MPa ...hence safe.

Since calculated values are < permissible values, the assumed values are satisfactory.

b. To find face width (b) $\quad b = 37.5$ mm

c. To find dynamic tooth load (F_d)

We know that, $F_d = F_t + \dfrac{K_3 v \left(Cb \cos^2 \beta + F_t\right) \cos \beta}{K_3 v + \sqrt{\left(Cb \cos^2 \beta + F_t\right)}}$ ...Eq. (ii) **12.62/ Pg 170, DHB**

here $K_3 = 20.67$ kN

@ $v > 15$ m/s	Error, $e = 0.0230$ mm	...Tb. **12.14/ Pg 191, DHB**
For $\alpha = 20°$ Stub teeth and steel – steel combination		
@ $e = 0.02$ mm	$C = 237.3$ N/mm	...Tb. **12.12/ Pg 190, DHB**
$e = 0.0230$ mm	$C = ?$	

$\therefore \quad$ at $v = 18.33$ m/s, $C = \dfrac{0.0230 \times 237.3}{0.02}$

$\therefore$ Eq. (ii) yields...

$F_d = 2782.32 + \dfrac{(20.67 \times 18.33) \times \left[\left(272.9 \times 37.5 \times \cos^2 25\right) + 2782.32\right] \times \cos 25}{(20.67 \times 18.33) + \sqrt{\left[\left(272.9 \times 37.5 \times \cos^2 25\right) + 2782.32\right]}}$

$F_d = 10.71$ kN

d. To find dynamic tooth load (F_w)

We know that, $\quad F_w = \dfrac{d_1 b Q K}{\cos^2 \beta}$ ...Eq. (iii) **12.64/ Pg 170, DHB**

- Diameter of pinion, $\quad d_1 = 125$ mm

- Ratio factor, $\quad Q = \dfrac{2 d_2}{d_2 + d_1}$ ...**12.36c/ Pg 167, DHB**

$\qquad = \dfrac{2 \times 562.5}{562.5 + 125}$

$Q = 1.64$

- Surface endurance limit, $\sigma_{es} = [2.75 \times (BHN) - 70]$ ...**12.36d/ Pg 167, DHB**

$(BHN) = \dfrac{BHN_1 + BHN_2}{2}$

Referring to Tb 1.18 for medium carbon steel having $\sigma_{es} = 218$ MPa, we have $BHN = 120$

$(BHN) = \dfrac{120 + 120}{2}$

= 120

$$\sigma_{es} = [2.75 \times (120) - 70]$$
$$\sigma_{es} = 260 \text{ MPa}.$$

- Here BHN is not given. Since both the gears are made of steel, assuming
$E = 2.1 \times 10^5$ MPa, we have

$$K = \frac{\sigma_{es}^2 \sin \alpha_n}{1.4}\left[\frac{1}{E_1} + \frac{1}{E_2}\right] \qquad \text{...12.65/ Pg 170, DHB}$$

$$\tan \alpha_n = \tan \alpha \cos \beta \qquad \text{...12.52b/ Pg 169, DHB}$$
$$= \tan 20 \times \cos 25$$
$$\alpha_n = 18.26°$$

$$K = \frac{260^2 \times \sin(18.26)}{1.4}\left[\frac{1}{2.1\times 10^5} + \frac{1}{2.1\times 10^5}\right]$$

$$K = 0.1441$$

∴ Eq. (iii) yields... $F_w = \dfrac{125 \times 37.5 \times 1.64 \times 0.1441}{\cos^2 25}$

$$F_w = 1348.65 \text{ N}$$

Since $F_w < F_d$, the pinion is subjected to rapid wear and hence has to be surface hardened to higher BHN.

i.e. $F_w \geq F_d$

$$\frac{d_1 bQK}{\cos^2 \beta} \geq 10.71 \times 10^3$$

$$\frac{125 \times 37.5 \times 1.64 \times K}{\cos^2 25} \geq 10.71 \times 10^3$$

$$K \geq 1.144$$

Therefore for steel – steel combination, having $\alpha = 20°$ and $K \geq 1.788$, we have

$$BHN_1 = BHN_2 = 300 \qquad \text{...Tb. 12.16/ Pg 193, DHB}$$

d: Axial or thrust force, $F_a = F_t \tan \beta$ ...12.51/ Pg 169, DHB
$$= 2782.32 \times \tan 25$$
$$F_a = 1297.42 \text{ N}.$$

14. **Design a pair of equal diameter 20° stub teeth helical gears to transmit 37.5 kW with moderate shocks at 1200 rpm. The two shafts are parallel and 0.45 m apart. Each gear is made of steel with β = 30°.**

Solution: $\alpha = 20°$-stub teeth, $P = 37.5$ kW, pinion speed, $N_1 = 1200$ rpm, service – moderate shocks, center distance = 0.45 m = 450 mm, equal diameter, helix angle, $\beta = 30°$. Design: m_n, b, F_d, F_{en}, F_w.

We know that, $\qquad i = \dfrac{N_1}{N_2} = \dfrac{d_2}{d_1} = \dfrac{z_2}{z_1}$

Since the diameters are equal (data), we have
$d_1 = d_2$, $z_1 = z_2$ and $N_1 = N_2$

∴ $i = 1$

Also, center distance = $\dfrac{d_1 + d_2}{2}$

$$450 = \dfrac{d_1 + d_2}{2}$$
$$d_1 + d_2 = 900$$
$$d_1 = d_2 = 450 \text{ mm}$$

Material properties:

Since both pinion and gear are made of same material (steel), let us assume C45 untreated steel having

$\sigma_{d1} = \sigma_{d2} = 233.4$ MPa and $BHN_1 = BHN_2 = 200$ ...Tb. 12.7/ Pg 186, DHB

Identifying weaker part (pinion/gear):

We know that strength factor = $\sigma_d \cdot y$

Since both pinion and gear are made of same material, the pinion is weaker, i.e.

$$\sigma_{d1} \cdot y_1 < \sigma_{d2} \cdot y_2$$

Hence design is based on **pinion**.

- Assume $z_1 = 20$ teeth
  $\therefore$ $z_2 = iz_1 = 1 \times 20 = 20$ teeth

- Virtual number of teeth, $z_e = \dfrac{z}{\cos^3 \beta}$ ...12.52a/ Pg 169, DHB

$$z_{e1} = \dfrac{z_1}{\cos^3 \beta} = \dfrac{20}{\cos^3 30}$$
$$z_{e1} = 30.79 \approx 31$$

a. To find module (m)

Since the diameter is known, we have $m_n = \sqrt{\dfrac{F_t C_w}{\sigma_d C_v k Y}}$ ...Eq. (i) 12.60/ Pg 170, DHB

- $v = \dfrac{\pi d_1 N_1}{60} = \dfrac{\pi \times 0.450 \times 1200}{60} = 28.27$ m/s

- For $v > 20$ m/s, $C_v = \dfrac{5.55}{5.55 + \sqrt{v}}$ ...12.61d/ Pg 170, DHB

$$= \dfrac{5.55}{5.55 + \sqrt{28.27}}$$
$$C_v = 0.5107$$

- $F_t = \dfrac{1000 \, PC_s}{v}$ ...12.20a/ Pg 164, DHB

For moderate shocks, assuming 8 – 10 hours service, service factor, $C_s = 1.5$
...Tb. 12.8/ Pg 187, DHB

$\therefore$ $F_t = \dfrac{1000 \times 37.5 \times 1.5}{28.27}$

$F_t = 1989.74$ N

- Form factor, Here $Y = \pi y_1$ ...12.16/ Pg 163, DHB

$$= \pi\left[0.175 - \frac{0.95}{z_{e1}}\right] \quad \text{...12.17c/ Pg 163, DHB}$$

$$= \pi\left[0.175 - \frac{0.95}{31}\right]$$

$$Y = 0.4535$$

- Assume, $k = b/m_n = 15$
- Assume, $C_w = 1.15$ ...Tb. 12.21/ Pg 196, DHB

∴ Eq. (i) yields... $m_n = \sqrt{\dfrac{1989.74 \times 1.15}{233.4 \times 0.5107 \times 15 \times 0.4535}}$

$$m_n = 1.68 \text{ mm}$$

Therefore standard module, $m_n = 2$ mm ...Tb. 12.2/ Pg 182, DHB

∴ Number of teeth on pinion, $z_1 = \dfrac{d_1 \cos\beta}{m_n} = \dfrac{450 \times \cos 30}{2} = 194.8 \approx 195$ teeth

...12.46/ Pg 168, DHB

Number of teeth on gear, $z_2 = z_1 = 195$ teeth

- Virtual number of teeth, $z_e = \dfrac{z}{\cos^3\beta}$ ...12.52a/ Pg 169, DHB

$$z_{e1} = \frac{z_1}{\cos^3\beta} = \frac{195}{\cos^3 30}$$

$$z_{e1} = 300$$

and $z_{e1} = z_{e2} = 300$

- Face width, $b = 15 m_n = 15 \times 2 = 30$ mm

Check for b:

i.e. $b_{\min} = \dfrac{(1.15)\pi m_n}{\sin\beta}$ ...12.54/ Pg 169, DHB

$$= \frac{(1.15) \times \pi \times 2}{\sin 30}$$

$$b_{\min} = 14.45 \text{ mm}$$

Since $b > b_{\min}$, the calculated value of b is safe

- Check for σ_{d1}:

We know that, $F_t = \dfrac{\sigma_d C_v b Y m_n}{C_w}$ ...Eq. (ii) 12.59/ Pg 169, DHB

- Here $Y = \pi y_1$ ...12.16/ Pg 163, DHB

$$= \pi\left[0.175 - \frac{0.95}{z_{e1}}\right] \quad \text{...12.17c/ Pg 163, DHB}$$

$$= \pi\left[0.175 - \frac{0.95}{300}\right]$$

$$Y = 0.5398$$

∴ Eq. (ii) yields... $1989.74 = \dfrac{\sigma_{d1} \times 0.5107 \times 30 \times 0.5398 \times 2}{1.15}$

$$\sigma_{d1} = 138.34 \text{ MPa} \le 100 \text{ MPa} \quad \text{...hence safe.}$$

Since calculated values are < permissible values, the assumed values are satisfactory.

b. To find face width (b) $b = 30$ mm

c. To find dynamic tooth load (F_d)

We know that, $F_d = F_t + \dfrac{K_3 v\left(Cb\cos^2\beta + F_t\right)\cos\beta}{K_3 v + \sqrt{\left(Cb\cos^2\beta + F_t\right)}}$ ...Eq. (iii) **12.62/ Pg 170, DHB**

here $K_3 = 20.67$

@ $v > 26$ m/s	Error, $e = 0.0127$ mm	...Tb. 12.14/ Pg 191, DHB
For $\alpha = 20°$ Stub teeth and steel – steel combination		
@ $e = 0.01$ mm	$C = 118.7$ N/mm	...Tb. 12.12/ Pg 190, DHB
$e = 0.0127$ mm	$C = ?$	

∴ at $v = 28.27$ m/s, $C = \dfrac{0.0127 \times 118.7}{0.01} = 150.75$ N/m

∴ Eq. (iii) yields...

$$F_d = 1989.74 + \frac{(20.67 \times 28.27) + \left[(150.75 \times 30 \times \cos^2 30) + 1989.74\right] + \cos 30}{(20.67 \times 28.27) + \sqrt{(150.75 \times 30 \times \cos^2 30) + 1989.74}}$$

∴ $F_d = 6130.51$ N

d. To find endurance strength (F_s or F_{en})

We know that, $F_s = \sigma_{en} b Y m_n$ ...**12.63/ Pg 170, DHB**

@ $BHN_1 = 200$, $\sigma_{en} = 345$ MPa   ...**Tb.12.15/ Pg 192, DHB**

∴ $F_s = 345 \times 30 \times 0.5398 \times 2$

$F_s = 11.17$ kN

Since $F_s > F_d$, the material is safe against static tooth load.

e. To find dynamic tooth load (F_w)

We know that, $F_w = \dfrac{d_1 b Q K}{\cos^2\beta}$ ...Eq. (iv) **12.64/ Pg 170, DHB**

- Diameter of pinion, $d_1 = 450$ mm
- Ratio factor, $Q = \dfrac{2 d_2}{d_2 + d_1}$ ...**12.36c/ Pg 167, DHB**

$$= \frac{2 \times 450}{450 + 450}$$
$$Q = 1.0$$

- For $\alpha = 20°$ and steel – steel combination having $BHN_1 = BHN_2 = 200$,
$$K = 0.539 \qquad \text{...Tb.12.16/ Pg 193, DHB}$$

∴ Eq. (iv) yields... $F_w = \dfrac{450 \times 30 \times 1 \times 0.539}{\cos^2 30}$

$$F_w = 9702 \text{ N}$$

Since $F_w > F_d$, the material is safe against wear.

15. A compressor running at 350 rpm is driven by a 120 kW motor running at 1400 rpm. The center distance is 400 mm and helix angle is 25°. The motor pinion is made of forged steel and the driven gear is cast steel design the gear using 20° FDI system.

Solution: motor/pinion speed (driver), $N_1 = 1400$ rpm, compressor speed (driven), $N_2 = 350$ rpm, $P = 120$ kW, center distance = 400 mm, $\beta = 25°$, $\alpha = 20°$ FDI.
Design: m_n, b, F_d, F_{en}, F_w.

We know that, $i = \dfrac{N_1}{N_2} = \dfrac{d_2}{d_1} = \dfrac{z_2}{z_1}$

$$i = \frac{N_1}{N_2} = \frac{1400}{350} = 4$$

Also, center distance $= \dfrac{d_1 + d_2}{2}$

$$400 = \frac{d_1 + d_2}{2}$$
$$d_1 + 4d_1 = 800$$
$$d_1 = 160 \text{ mm and}$$
$$d_2 = 640 \text{ mm}$$

Material properties

Pinion: forged steel: $\sigma_{d1} = 220$ MPa, $BHN_1 = 200$
Gear: Cast steel: $\sigma_{d2} = 193.2$ MPa, $BHN_2 = 250$ ...Tb. 12.7/ Pg 186, DHB

- Assume $z_1 = 20$
∴ $z_2 = iz_1 = 4 \times 20 = 80$

- Virtual number of teeth, $z_e = \dfrac{z}{\cos^3 \beta}$ ...12.52a/ Pg 169, DHB

$$z_{e1} = \frac{z_1}{\cos^3 \beta} = \frac{20}{\cos^3 25}$$
$$z_{e1} = 26.86 \approx 27$$

and $z_{e2} = iz_1 = 27 \times 4 = 108$

Identifying weaker part (pinion/gear)

We know that strength factor = $\sigma_d \cdot y$

- For $\alpha = 20°$ FDI tooth, $y = \left[0.154 - \dfrac{0.912}{z}\right]$ ...**12.17b/ Pg 163, DHB**

$$\text{i.e. } y = \left[0.154 - \dfrac{0.912}{z_{e1}}\right]$$

$$y_1 = \left[0.154 - \dfrac{0.912}{27}\right] = 0.1202$$

$$y_2 = \left[0.154 - \dfrac{0.912}{108}\right] = 0.1456$$

∴ for pinion, $\sigma_{d1} \cdot y_1 = 220 \times 0.1202 = 26.44$ MPa
 for gear, $\sigma_{d2} \cdot y_2 = 193.21 \times 0.1456 = 28.21$ MPa

Since $\sigma_{d1} \cdot y_1$ is less, design is based on **pinion**.

a. To find module (m_n)

Since the diameter is known, we have $m_n = \sqrt{\dfrac{F_t C_w}{\sigma_d C_v k Y}}$ ...Eq. (i) **12.60/ Pg 170, DHB**

- $v = \dfrac{\pi d_1 N_1}{60} = \dfrac{\pi \times 0.16 \times 1400}{60} = 11.72$ m/s

- For $10 < v < 20$ m/s, $C_v = \dfrac{15.25}{15.25 + v}$ ...**12.61c/ Pg 170, DHB**

$$= \dfrac{15.25}{15.25 + 11.72}$$

$$C_v = 0.5654$$

- $F_t = \dfrac{1000 \, P C_s}{v}$ ...**12.20a/ Pg 164, DHB**

Assuming moderate shocks with 8 – 10 hours service, service factor, $C_s = 1.5$
...**Tb. 12.8/ Pg 187, DHB**

∴ $F_t = \dfrac{1000 \times 120 \times 1.5}{11.72}$

$F_t = 15.36$ kN

- Form factor, Here $Y = \pi y_1$ ...**12.16/ Pg 163, DHB**
  $= \pi \times 0.1202$
  $Y = 0.3776$

- Assume, $k = b/m_n = 15$
- Assume, $C_w = 1.15$ ...**Tb. 12.21/ Pg 196, DHB**

∴ Eq. (i) yields... $m_n = \sqrt{\dfrac{15.36 \times 10^3 \times 1.15}{220 \times 0.5654 \times 15 \times 0.3776}}$

$m_n = 5$

Therefore, standard module $m = 5$ mm ...Tb. 12.2/ Pg 182, DHB

∴ Number of teeth on pinion, $z_1 = \dfrac{d_1 \cos \beta}{m_n} = \dfrac{160 \times \cos 25}{5} = 29$ teeth

...12.46/ Pg 168, DHB

Number of teeth on gear, $z_2 = iz_1 = 29 \times 4 = 116$ teeth

- Virtual number of teeth, $z_e = \dfrac{z}{\cos^3 \beta}$ ...12.52a/ Pg 169, DHB

$$z_{e1} = \dfrac{z_1}{\cos^3 \beta} = \dfrac{29}{\cos^3 25}$$

$$z_{e1} = 38.9 \approx 39$$

and $z_{e2} = iz_{e1} = 4 \times 39 = 156$

- Face width, $b = 15 m_n = 15 \times 5 = 75$ mm

  Check for b:

  i.e. $b_{min} = \dfrac{(1.15)\, \pi m_n}{\sin \beta}$ ...12.54/ Pg 169, DHB

  $= \dfrac{(1.15) \times \pi \times 5}{\sin 25}$

  $b_{min} = 42.74$ mm

Since $b > b_{min}$, the calculated value of b is safe.

- Check for σ_{d1}:

  We know that, $F_t = \dfrac{\sigma_d C_v b Y m_n}{C_w}$ ...Eq. (ii) 12.59/ Pg 169, DHB

- Here $Y = \pi y_1$ ...12.16/ Pg 163, DHB

  $= \pi \left[0.154 - \dfrac{0.912}{z_{e1}} \right]$ ...12.17b/ Pg 163, DHB

  $= \pi \left[0.154 - \dfrac{0.912}{39} \right]$

  $Y = 0.4104$

∴ Eq. (ii) yields... $15.36 \times 10^3 = \dfrac{\sigma_{d1} \times 0.5654 \times 75 \times 0.4104 \times 52}{1.15}$

$\sigma_{d1} = 203$ MPa < 220 MPa ..hence safe.

Since calculated values are < permissible values, the assumed values are satisfactory.

b. To find face width (b) $b = 75$ mm

c. To find dynamic tooth load (F_d)

We know that, $F_d = F_t + \dfrac{K_3 v \left(Cb \cos^2 \beta + F_t \right) \cos \beta}{K_3 v + \sqrt{\left(Cb \cos^2 \beta + F_t \right)}}$ ...Eq. (iii) 12.62/ Pg 170, DHB

here $K_3 = 20.67$

@ $v > 10$ m/s	Error, $e = 0.0386$ mm	...Tb. 12.14/ Pg 191, DHB
For $\alpha = 20°$ FDI and steel – steel combination		
@ $e = 0.03$ mm	$C = 343.4$ N/mm	...Tb. 12.12/ Pg 191, DHB
$e = 0.0386$ mm	$C = ?$	

$\therefore$ at $v = 11.72$ m/s. $C = \dfrac{0.0386 \times 343.4}{0.03} = 441.84$ N/mm

$\therefore$ Eq. (*iii*) yields...

$$F_d = \dfrac{(20.67 \times 11.72) \times \left[(441.84 \times 75 \times \cos^2 25) + 15.36 \times 10^3\right] \times \cos 25}{(20.67 \times 11.72) + \sqrt{\left[(441.84 \times 75 \times \cos^2 25) + 15.36 \times 10^3\right]}}$$

$F_d = 36.2 \times 10^3$ N

d. To find endurance strength (F_s)

We know that, $F_s = \sigma_{en} b Y m_n$ ...12.63/ Pg 170, DHB

@ $BHN_1 = 200$, $\sigma_{en} = 345$ MPa   ...Tb.12.15/ Pg 192, DHB

$\therefore$ $F_s = 345 \times 75 \times 0.4104 \times 5$

$F_s = 53.1 \times 10^3$ N

Since $F_s > F_d$, the material is safe against static tooth load.

e. To find dynamic tooth load (F_w)

We know that, $F_w = \dfrac{d_1 b Q K}{\cos^2 \beta}$ ...Eq. (*iv*) 12.64/ Pg 170, DHB

- Diameter of pinion $d_1 = 450$ mm

- Ratio factor, $Q = \dfrac{2 d_2}{d_2 + d_1}$ ...12.36c/ Pg 167, DHB

$= \dfrac{2 \times 640}{640 + 160}$

$Q = 1.6$

- Since given BHN combination is not available in **Tb 12.16/ Pg 193, DHB**, assuming $E = 2.1 \times 10^5$ MPa, we have

Load stress factor, $K = \dfrac{\sigma_{es}^2 \sin \alpha}{1.4} \left[\dfrac{1}{E_1} + \dfrac{1}{E_2}\right]$ ...12.36b/ Pg 167, DHB

$\tan \alpha_n = \tan \alpha \cos \beta$ ...12.52b/ Pg 169, DHB

$= \tan 20 \times \cos(25)$

$\alpha_n = 18.26$ deg

$\therefore$ $K = \dfrac{(345)^2 \times \sin(18.26)}{1.4} \left[\dfrac{1}{2.1 \times 10^5} + \dfrac{1}{2.1 \times 10^5}\right]$

$K = 0.2537$

$\therefore$ Eq. (*iv*) yields... $F_w = \dfrac{160 \times 75 \times 1.6 \times 0.2537}{\cos^2 25}$

$F_w = 5.9 \times 10^3$ N

Since $F_w < F_d$, the pinion is subjected to rapid wear and hence has to be surface hardened to higher BHN.

i.e. $F_w \geq F_d$

$$\frac{d_1 b Q K}{\cos^2 \beta} \geq 36.2 \times 10^3$$

$$\frac{160 \times 75 \times 1.6 \times K}{\cos^2 25} \geq 36.2 \times 10^3$$

$$K \geq 1.548$$

Therefore for steel – steel combination, having 20° and $K \geq 1.548$, we have

$$BHN_1 = 350 \text{ and } BHN_2 = 300 \quad \text{...Tb. 12.16/ Pg 193, DHB}$$

4.44 PROBLEMS BASED ON UNKNOWN DIAMETER

16. A helical cast steel gear with 30° helix angle has to transmit 35 kW at 1500 rpm. If the gear has 24 teeth, determine the necessary module, pitch diameter and face width for 20° full depth teeth. The static stress for cast steel may be taken as 56 MPa. The width of the face may be taken as 3 times the normal pitch. What would be the end thrust on the gear? The tooth factor for 20° full depth involute gears may be taken as $0.154 - \dfrac{0.912}{z_e}$, where z_e is the equivalent number of teeth.

[VTU – June/ July 2009 – 16 Marks; May/ June 2010 – 15 Marks]

Solution: helix angle, $\beta = 30°$, $P = 35$ kW, pinion speed, $N_1 = 1500$ rpm, $z_1 = 24$ teeth, $\alpha = 30°$- FDI teeth, $b = 3p_n$, $\sigma_{d1} = \sigma_{d2} = 56$ MPa, $y = 0.154 - \dfrac{0.912}{z_e}$

a. $m_n = ?$ b. $b = ?$ c. End thrust, $F_t = ?$

Identifying weaker part (pinion/gear)

We know that strength factor $= \sigma_d \cdot y$
Since both pinion and gear are made of same material, the pinion is weaker,
i.e. $\sigma_{d1} \cdot y_1 < \sigma_{d2} \cdot y_2$
Hence design is based on **pinion**.

- Virtual number of teeth, $z_e = \dfrac{z}{\cos^3 \beta}$ ...12.52a/ Pg 169, DHB

$$z_{e1} = \frac{z_1}{\cos^3 \beta} = \frac{24}{\cos^3 30}$$

$$z_{e1} = 37$$

a. To find module (m_n)

Since the diameter is unknown, we have

$$m_n = \sqrt[3]{\frac{2 M_t C_w \cos \beta}{\sigma_d C_v k Y z}} \quad \text{...Eq. } (i) \text{ 12.60/ Pg 170, DHB}$$

- $$P = \frac{2\pi N_1 M_t}{60}$$

$$35 \times 10^3 = \frac{2\pi \times 1500 \times M_t}{60}$$

$$M_t = 222.82 \text{ N-m} = 222.82 \times 10^3 \text{ N-mm}$$

- but, $k = b/m_n$

  $b = 3p_n$ ...(data)

  $$k = \frac{3p_n}{m_n}$$

  $$= \frac{3(\pi m \cos \beta)}{m_n}$$ ...12.43/ Pg 168, DHB

  $$= \frac{3(\pi m \cos \beta)}{m \cos \beta}$$ ...12.45/ Pg 168, DHB

  $k = 3\pi$

- Assume, $C_v = 0.5$
- Assume, $C_w = 1.15$ ...Tb. 12.21/ Pg 196, DHB
- Form factor, $Y = \pi y_1$

  $$= \pi \left[0.154 - \frac{0.912}{z_{e1}} \right]$$ ...(data)

  $$= \pi \left[0.154 - \frac{0.912}{37} \right]$$

  $Y = 0.4064$

∴ Eq. (i) yields... $m_n = \sqrt[3]{\dfrac{2 \times 222.82 \times 10^3 \times 1.15 \times \cos 30}{56 \times 0.5 \times 3\pi \times 0.4064 \times 24}}$

(here z – weaker member)

$m_n = 5.57$

Therefore, standard module $m_n = 6$ mm ...Tb. 12.2/ Pg 182, DHB

∴ PCD of pinion, $d_1 = \dfrac{m_n z_1}{\cos \beta} = \dfrac{6 \times 24}{\cos 30} = 166.27$ mm ≈ 168 mm

...12.47/ Pg 168, DHB

- Face width, $b = 3p_n = 3(\pi m_n) = 3 \times \pi \times 6 = 56.55$ mm ≈ 57 mm

b. Check for b:

i.e. $b_{min} = \dfrac{(1.15)\pi m_n}{\sin \beta}$ ...12.54/ Pg 169, DHB

$$= \frac{(1.15) \times \pi \times 6}{\sin 30}$$

$b_{min} = 43.35$ mm

Since $b > b_{min}$, the calculated value of is safe.

- Since C_v was assumed, Check for σ_{d1}:

    We know that, $\quad F_t = \dfrac{\sigma_d C_v b Y m_n}{C_w}$ ...Eq. (ii) **12.59/ Pg 169, DHB**

- $v = \dfrac{\pi d_1 N_1}{60} = \dfrac{\pi \times 0.168 \times 1500}{60} = 13.19 \text{ m/s}$

- For $10 < v < 20$ m/s. $\quad C_v = \dfrac{15.25}{15.25 + v}$ ...**12.61c/ Pg 170, DHB**

    $= \dfrac{15.25}{15.25 + 13.19}$

    $C_v = 0.5361$

- $F_t = \dfrac{2M_t}{d}$ ...**12.22/ Pg 165, DHB**

    $= \dfrac{2 \times 222.82 \times 10^3}{168}$ (here d – weaker member)

    $F_t = 2652.62$ N

∴ Eq. (ii) yields... $2652.62 = \dfrac{\sigma_{d1} \times 0.5361 \times 57 \times 0.4064 \times 6}{1.15}$

$\sigma_{d1} = 41$ MPa < 56 MPa ...hence safe.

Since calculated values are $<$ permissible values, the assumed values are satisfactory.

c. Axial or thrust force

$F_a = F_t \tan \beta$ ...**12.51/ Pg 169, DHB**

$= 2652.62 \times \tan 30$

∴ $F_a = 1531.5$ N.

17. A helical gear is required to transmit 35 kW at 1500 rpm. The helix angle is 30° and 20° FDI system is used. Both gears are made of same material having design stress of 56 MPa and BHN = 200. The starting torque is 20% greater than the mean torque. The drive is to be safe for continuous operation. The speed reduction is 3:1. Specify the details of the drive. Use 24 teeth on pinion.

Solution: $P = 35$ kW, pinion speed, $N_1 = 1500$ rpm, helix angle, $\beta = 30°$, $\alpha = 20°$- FDI teeth, $\sigma_{d1} = \sigma_{d2} = 56$ MPa, $BHN_1 = BHN_2 = 200$, $M_{t)\max} = 1.2 M_t$, $i = 3:1$, service – continuous operation, $z_1 = 24$ teeth.

Identifying weaker part (pinion/gear)

We know that strength factor = $\sigma_d \cdot y$

Since both pinion and gear are made of same material, the pinion is weaker,

i.e. $\sigma_{d1} \cdot y_1 < \sigma_{d2} \cdot y_2$

Hence design is based on **pinion**.

- Virtual number of teeth, $z_e = \dfrac{z}{\cos^3 \beta}$ ...**12.52a/ Pg 169, DHB**

    $z_{e1} = \dfrac{z_1}{\cos^3 \beta} = \dfrac{24}{\cos^3 30}$

    $z_{e1} = 37$

a. To find module (m_n)

Since the diameter is unknown, $m_n = \sqrt[3]{\dfrac{2M_{t)max}C_w \cos \beta}{\sigma_d C_v k Y z}}$

...Eq. (*i*) **12.60/ Pg 170, DHB**

- But $M_{t)max} = 1.2\, M_t$ ...Eq. (*ii*)

- $P = \dfrac{2\pi N_1 M_t}{60}$

$$35 \times 10^3 = \dfrac{2\pi \times 1500 \times M_t}{60}$$

$$M_t = 222.82 \text{ N-m} = 222.82 \times 10^3 \text{ N-mm}$$

∴ Eq. (*ii*) yields... $M_{t)max} = 1.2 \times 222.82 \times 10^3$

$$M_{t)max} = 267.38 \times 10^3 \text{ N-mm}$$

- Assume $k = b/m_n = 15$
- Assume, $C_v = 0.5$
- For continuous operation (data), $C_w = 1.15$ ...Tb. **12.21/ Pg 196, DHB**
- Form factor, $Y = \pi y_1$ ...**12.16/ Pg 163, DHB**

$$= \pi\left[0.154 - \dfrac{0.912}{z_{e1}}\right] \quad \text{...12.17b/ Pg 163, DHB}$$

$$= \pi\left[0.154 - \dfrac{0.912}{37}\right]$$

$$Y = 0.4064$$

∴ Eq. (*i*) yields... $m_n = \sqrt[3]{\dfrac{2 \times 267.38 \times 10^3 \times 1.15 \times \cos 30}{56 \times 0.5 \times 15 \times 0.4064 \times 24}}$

$$m_n = 5.06 \text{ mm}$$

Therefore, standard module, $m_n = 6$ mm ...Tb. **12.2/ Pg 182, DHB**

∴ PCD of pinion, $d_1 = \dfrac{m_n z_1}{\cos \beta} = \dfrac{6 \times 24}{\cos 30} = 166.27 \text{ mm} \approx 168 \text{ mm}$

...**12.47/ Pg 168, DHB**

We know that, $i = \dfrac{d_2}{d_1}$

$$3 = \dfrac{d_2}{168}$$

PCD of gear, $d_2 = 504$ mm

- Face width, $b = 15 m_n = 15 \times 6 = 90$ mm

Check for *b*:

i.e. $b_{min} = \dfrac{(1.15)\pi m_n}{\sin \beta}$ ...**12.54/ Pg 169, DHB**

$$= \frac{(1.15) \times \pi \times 6}{\sin 30}$$

$$b_{min} = 43.35 \text{ mm}$$

Since $b > b_{min}$, the calculated value of b is safe.

- **Check for σ_{d1}:**

  We know that, $\quad F_t = \dfrac{\sigma_d C_v b Y m_n}{C_w} \quad$ ...Eq. (iii) **12.59/ Pg 169, DHB**

  - $v = \dfrac{\pi d_1 N_1}{60} = \dfrac{\pi \times 0.168 \times 1500}{60} = 13.19 \text{ m/s}$

  - For $10 < v < 20$ m/s. $C_v = \dfrac{15.25}{15.25 + v}$ ...**12.61c/ Pg 170, DHB**

    $$= \frac{15.25}{15.25 + 13.19}$$

    $$C_v = 0.5361$$

  - $F_t = \dfrac{2 M_{t)max}}{d} \times C_s$ ...**12.22/ Pg 165, DHB**

  For continuous operation, assuming light shocks, $C_s = 1.5$
  ...**Tb. 12.8/ Pg 187, DHB**

  $$= \frac{2 \times 267.38 \times 10^3}{168} \times 1.5$$

  $$F_t = 4774.64 \text{ N}$$

  ∴ Eq. (iii) yields... $4774.64 = \dfrac{\sigma_{d1} \times 0.5361 \times 90 \times 0.4064 \times 6}{1.15}$

  $\sigma_{d1} = 46.67$ MPa < 56 MPa ...hence safe.

b. To find face width (b) $\quad b = 90$ mm

c. To find dynamic tooth load (F_d)

We know that, $\quad F_d = F_t + \dfrac{K_3 v (Cb \cos^2 \beta + F_t) \cos \beta}{K_3 v + \sqrt{(Cb \cos^2 \beta + F_t)}} \quad$ ...Eq. (iv) **12.62/ Pg 170, DHB**

here $K_3 = 20.67$

@ $v = 12$ m/s	Error, $e = 0.0330$ mm	...Tb. 12.14/ Pg 191, DHB
For $\alpha = 20°$ FDI and steel – steel combination		
@ $e = 0.03$ mm	$C = 343.4$ N/mm	...Tb. 12.12/ Pg 190, DHB
$e = 0.0330$ mm	$C = ?$	

∴ at $v = 13.19$ m/s, $C = \dfrac{0.0330 \times 343.4}{0.03} = 377.63$ N/mm

∴ Eq. (iv) yields...

$$F_d = 4774.64 + \frac{(20.67 \times 13.19) \times \left[(377.63 \times 90 \times \cos^2 30) + 4774.64\right] \times \cos 30}{(20.67 \times 13.29) + \sqrt{\left[(377.63 \times 90 \times \cos^2 30) + 4774.64\right]}}$$

$$F_d = 20.78 \times 10^3 \text{ N}$$

d. To find endurance strength (F_s)

We know that, $\quad F_s = \sigma_{en} b Y m_n \quad$ ...12.63/ Pg 170, DHB

@ $BHN_1 = 200$, $\sigma_{en} = 345$ MPa $\quad$ ...Tb.12.15/ Pg 192, DHB

∴ $\quad F_s = 345 \times 90 \times 0.4064 \times 6$

$F_s = 75.71$ kN

Since $F_s > F_d$, the material is safe against static tooth load.

e. To find dynamic tooth load (F_w)

We know that, $\quad F_w = \dfrac{d_1 b Q K}{\cos^2 \beta} \quad$ ...Eq. (v) 12.64/ Pg 170, DHB

- Diameter of pinion, $d_1 = 168$ mm

- Ratio factor, $\quad Q = \dfrac{2 d_2}{d_2 + d_1} \quad$ ...12.36c/ Pg 167, DHB

$$= \frac{2 \times 504}{504 + 168}$$

$Q = 1.5$

- For $\alpha = 20°$ and steel – steel combination having $BHN_1 = BHN_2 = 200$,

$K = 0.539 \quad$ ...Tb.12.16/ Pg 193, DHB

∴ Eq. (v) yields... $F_w = \dfrac{168 \times 90 \times 1.5 \times 0.539}{\cos^2 30}$

$F_w = 16.3$ kN

Since $F_w < F_d$, the pinion is subjected to rapid wear and hence has to be surface hardened to higher BHN.

i.e. $F_w \geq F_d$

$$\frac{d_1 b Q K}{\cos^2 \beta} \geq 20.78 \times 10^3$$

$$\frac{168 \times 90 \times 1.5 \times K}{\cos^2 30} \geq 20.78 \times 10^3$$

$K \geq 0.687$

Therefore, for steel – steel combination, having $\alpha = 20°$ and $K \geq 0.687$, we have

$BHN_1 = 250$ and $BHN_2 = 200 \quad$ ...Tb. 12.16/ Pg 193, DHB

18. Design a helical gear pair to transmit a power of 15 kW from a shaft rotating at 1000 rpm to another shaft to be run at 360 rpm. Assume involute profile with a pressure angle of 20°. The material of the pinion is forged steel SAE 1030 whose $\sigma_d = 172.375$ MPa and the material for gear is cast steel 0.2% C untreated with σ_d

= 137.4 MPa. The gears operate under a condition of medium shocks for a period of 10 hours per day. Check for dynamic load, if load factor C = 580 N/mm and also for wear load. *[VTU – Dec. 2010 – 16 Marks]*

Solution: P = 15 kW, pinion speed, N_1 = 1000 rpm, driven speed, N_2 = 360 rpm, helix angle, α = 20°-FDI teeth, σ_{d1} = 172.375, σ_{d2} = 137.4 MPa, service – medium shock, continuous operation 10 h per day, C = 580 N/mm.

We know that, $\quad i = \dfrac{N_1}{N_2} = \dfrac{d_2}{d_1} = \dfrac{z_2}{z_1}$

$$i = \dfrac{1000}{360} = 2.78$$

Identifying weaker part (pinion/gear)

We know that strength factor $\sigma_d \cdot y$

- Assume $\quad \beta = 25°$
- Assume $\quad z_1 = 20$
- $\therefore \quad z_2 = iz_1 = 2.78 \times 20 = 55.6 \approx 56$

- Virtual number of teeth, $z_e = \dfrac{z}{\cos^3 \beta}$ ...12.52a/ Pg 169, DHB

$$z_{e1} = \dfrac{z_1}{\cos^3 \beta} = \dfrac{20}{\cos^3 25}$$

$$z_{e1} = 26.86 \approx 27$$

and $\quad z_{e2} = iz_{e1} = 27 \times 2.78 = 75$

- For α = 20° FDI tooth, $\quad y = 0.154 - \dfrac{0.912}{z}$ ...12.17b/ Pg 163, DHB

i.e. $\quad y_1 = 0.154 - \dfrac{0.912}{z_{e1}} \quad$ or $\quad y_1 = 0.154 - \dfrac{0.912}{27} = 0.1202$

$\quad y_2 = 0.154 - \dfrac{0.912}{z_{e2}} \quad$ or $\quad y_2 = 0.154 - \dfrac{0.912}{75} = 0.1418$

$\therefore$ for pinion, $\quad \sigma_{d1} \cdot y_1 = 172.375 \times 0.1202 = 20.72$ MPa
for gear, $\quad \sigma_{d2} \cdot y_2 = 137.34 \times 0.1418 = 19.48$ MPa

Since $\sigma_{d2} \cdot y_2$ is less, design is based on **gear**.

a. To find module (m_n)

Since the diameter is unknown, we have $m_n = \sqrt[3]{\dfrac{2M_t C_w \cos \beta}{\sigma_d C_v k Y z}}$

...Eq. (i) 12.60/ Pg 170, DHB

- $\quad P = \dfrac{2\pi N_2 M_t}{60}$

$$15 \times 10^3 = \dfrac{2\pi \times 360 \times M_t}{60}$$

- Assume, $M_t = 397.88$ N-m $= 397.88 \times 10^3$ N-mm
- Assume, $k = b/m_n = 15$
- Assume, $C_v = 0.5$
- For continuous operation (data), $C_w = 1.15$ ...Tb. 12.21/ Pg 196, DHB
- Form factor, $Y = \pi y_2$ ...12.16/ Pg 163, DHB
  $= \pi \times 0.1418$
  $Y = 0.4455$

Eq. (i) yields... $m_n = \sqrt[3]{\dfrac{2 \times 397.88 \times 10^3 \times 1.15 \times \cos 25}{137.34 \times 0.5 \times 15 \times 0.4455 \times 56}}$

$m_n = 3.18$ mm

Therefore standard module, $m_n = 4$ mm ...Tb. 12.2/ Pg 182, DHB

$\therefore$ PCD of pinion, $d_1 = \dfrac{m_n z_1}{\cos \beta} = \dfrac{4 \times 20}{\cos 25} = 88.27$ mm ≈ 90 mm

...12.47/ Pg 168, DHB

PCD of gear, $d_2 = id_1 = 2.78 \times 90 = 250$ mm

- Face width, $b = 15 m_n = 15 \times 4 = 60$ mm

Check for b:

i.e. $b_{min} = \dfrac{(1.15)\pi m_n}{\sin \beta}$ ...12.54/ Pg 169, DHB

$= \dfrac{(1.15)\pi \times 4}{\sin(25)}$

$b_{min} = 34.2$ mm

Since $b > b_{min}$, the calculated value of b is safe.

- Check for σ_{d2}:

We know that, $F_t = \dfrac{\sigma_d C_v b Y m_n}{C_w}$ ...Eq. (ii) 12.59/ Pg 169, DHB

- $v = \dfrac{\pi d_2 N_2}{60} = \dfrac{\pi \times 0.250 \times 360}{60} = 4.71$ m/s

- For $v < 5$ m/s, $C_v = \dfrac{4.58}{4.58 + v}$ ...12.61a/ Pg 170, DHB

  $= \dfrac{4.58}{4.58 + 4.71}$

  $C_v = 0.4928$

- $F_t = \dfrac{2 M_t}{d} \times C_s$ ...12.22/ Pg 165, DHB

For medium shocks and operating 10 h per day, $C_s = 1.5$
...Tb. 12.8/ Pg 187, DHB

$= \dfrac{2 \times 397.88 \times 10^3}{250} \times 1.5$

$F_t = 4774.65$ N

∴ Eq. (ii) yields... $4774.56 = \dfrac{\sigma_{d2} \times 0.4928 \times 60 \times 0.4455 \times 4}{1.15}$

$$\sigma_{d2} = 104.21 \text{ MPa} < 137.34 \text{ MPa} \qquad \text{...hence safe.}$$

b. To find face width (b) $\quad b = 60$ mm

c. To find dynamic tooth load (F_s)

We know that, $\quad F_d = F_t + \dfrac{K_3 v \left(Cb \cos^2 \beta + F_t\right) \cos \beta}{K_3 v + \sqrt{\left(Cb \cos^2 \beta + F_t\right)}} \quad$ ...12.62/ Pg 170, DHB

here $K_3 = 20.67$
$C = 580$ N/mm $\qquad$ ...(data)

∴ $F_d = 4774.56 + \dfrac{(20.67 \times 4.71) \times \left[\left(580 \times 60 \times \cos^2 25\right) + 4774.56\right] \times \cos 25}{(20.67 \times 4.71) + \sqrt{\left[\left(580 \times 60 \times \cos^2 25\right) + 4774.56\right]}}$

$$F_d = 15.29 \times 10^3 \text{ N}$$

d. To find endurance strength (F_s)

We know that, $\quad F_s = \sigma_{en} b Y m_n \qquad$ ...12.63/ Pg 170, DHB

- For forged steel- pinion, $BHN_1 \approx 150$ and
  gear- cast steel 0.2% C untreated, $BHN_1 \approx 180 \qquad$ ...Tb. 12.7/ Pg 186, DHB
- Surface endurance limit, $\sigma_{en} = [2.75 \times (BHN) - 70] \qquad$ ...12.36d/ Pg 167, DHB

$$(BHN) = \dfrac{BHN_1 + BHN_2}{2}$$

$$= \dfrac{150 + 180}{2} = 165$$

$\sigma_{es} = [2.75 \times (165) - 70]$
$\sigma_{es} = 383.75$ MPa $= \sigma_{en}$

∴ $F_s = 383.75 \times 60 \times 0.4455 \times 4$
$F_s = 41.05$ kN

Since $F_s > F_d$, the material is safe against static tooth load.

e. To find dynamic tooth load (F_w)

We know that, $\quad F_w = \dfrac{d_1 b Q K}{\cos^2 \beta} \qquad$ ...Eq. (iii) 12.64/ Pg 170, DHB

- Diameter of pinion, $d_1 = 90$ mm

- Ratio factor, $Q = \dfrac{2 d_2}{d_2 + d_1} \qquad$ ...12.36c/ Pg 167, DHB

$$= \dfrac{2 \times 250}{250 + 90}$$

$$Q = 1.47$$

- Here BHN is not given. Since both the gears are made of steel, assuming $E = 2.1 \times 10^5$ MPa, we have

$$K = \frac{\sigma_{es}^2 \sin \alpha_n}{1.4}\left[\frac{1}{E_1} + \frac{1}{E_2}\right] \qquad \text{...12.65/ Pg 170, DHB}$$

$$\tan \alpha_n = \tan \beta \cos \beta \qquad \text{...12.52b/ Pg 169, DHB}$$

$$= \tan 20 \times \cos 25$$

$$\alpha_n = 18.26 \text{ deg}$$

$$\therefore \quad K = \frac{(383.75)^2 \sin(18.26)}{1.4}\left[\frac{1}{2.1 \times 10^5} + \frac{1}{2.1 \times 10^5}\right]$$

$$K = 0.3138$$

$\therefore$ Eq. (iii) yields... $F_w = \dfrac{90 \times 60 \times 1.47 \times 0.3138}{\cos^2 25}$

$$F_w = 3.03 \text{ N}$$

Since $F_w < F_d$, the pinion is subjected to rapid wear and hence has to be surface hardened to higher BHN.

i.e. $F_w \geq F_d$

$$\frac{d_1 b Q K}{\cos^2 \beta} \geq 15.29 \times 10^3$$

$$\frac{90 \times 60 \times 1.47 \times K}{\cos^2 25} \geq 20.78 \times 10^3$$

$$K \geq 1.582$$

Therefore, for steel – steel combination, having $\alpha = 20°$ and $K \geq 1.582$, we have

$$BHN_1 = 350 \text{ and } BHN_2 = 300 \qquad \text{...Tb. 12.16/ Pg 193, DHB}$$

19. A pair of carefully cut helical gears for a turbine has a transmission ratio of 10:1. The teeth are 20° stub involute in the normal plane. Pinion has 25 teeth and rotates at 5000 rpm. Material for pinion and gear is 0.4%C steel untreated with allowable static stress of 69.66 MPa. Helix angle = 30°. Power transmitted = 90 kW. Service factor = 1.25. Wear and lubrication factor = 1.25. Determine the module in normal plane and face width of the gears. Suggest suitable surface hardness for the gear pair. **[VTU – Dec. 06/ Jan. 2007 – 20 Marks]**

Solution: $i = 10:1$, $\alpha = 20°$- stub teeth, pinion speed, $N_1 = 5000$ rpm, $z_1 = 25$, $\sigma_{d1} = \sigma_{d2} = 69.66$ MPa, $\beta = 30°$, $P = 90$ kW, $C_s = 1.25$, $C_w = 1.25$,

a. $m_n = ?$ b. $b = ?$ c. $BHN = ?$

We know that, $t = \dfrac{N_1}{N_2} = \dfrac{d_2}{d_1} = \dfrac{z_2}{z_1}$

$$10 = \frac{5000}{N_2}$$

$$N_2 = 500 \text{ rpm}$$

And $z_2 = i z_1 = 10 \times 25 = 250$ teeth

Identifying weaker part (pinion/gear)

We know that strength factor = $\sigma_d \cdot y$

Since both pinion and gear are made of same material, the pinion is weaker,

i.e. $\sigma_{d1} \cdot y_1 < \sigma_{d2} \cdot y_2$

Hence design is based on **pinion**.

- Virtual number of teeth, $\quad z_e = \dfrac{z}{\cos^3 \beta} \qquad$ ...12.52a/ Pg 169, DHB

$$z_{e1} = \dfrac{z_1}{\cos^3 \beta} = \dfrac{25}{\cos^3 30}$$

$$z_{e1} = 39$$

a. To find module (m_n)

Since the diameter is unknown, we have

$$m_n = \sqrt[3]{\dfrac{2M_t C_w \cos \beta}{\sigma_d C_v kYz}} \qquad \text{...Eq. (i) 12.60/ Pg 170, DHB}$$

- $$P = \dfrac{2\pi N_1 M_t}{60}$$

$$90 \times 10^3 = \dfrac{2\pi \times 5000 \times M_t}{60}$$

$$M_t = 171.89 \text{ N-m} = 171.89 \times 10^3 \text{ N-mm}$$

- Assume, $\quad k = b/m_n = 15$
- Assume, $\quad C_v = 0.5$
- $\quad\quad\quad\quad C_w = 1.25 \qquad$ ...(data)
- Form factor, $\quad Y = \pi y_1 \qquad$ ...12.16/ Pg 163, DHB

$$= \pi \left[0.175 - \dfrac{0.95}{z_{e1}} \right] \qquad \text{...12.17c/ Pg 163, DHB}$$

$$= \pi \left[0.175 - \dfrac{0.95}{39} \right]$$

$$Y = 0.4733$$

$\therefore$ Eq. (i) yields... $m_n = \sqrt[3]{\dfrac{2 \times 171.89 \times 10^3 \times 1.25 \times \cos 30}{69.66 \times 0.5 \times 15 \times 0.4733 \times 25}}$

$$m_n = 3.92 \text{ mm}$$

Therefore, standard module, $m_n = 4$ mm $\qquad$ ...Tb. 12.2/ Pg 182, DHB

$\therefore$ PCD of pinion, $\quad d_1 = \dfrac{m_n z_1}{\cos \beta} = \dfrac{4 \times 25}{\cos 30} = 115.47$ mm ≈ 116 mm

...12.47/ Pg 168, DHB

PCD of gear, $\quad d_2 = i_{d1} = 116 \times 10 = 1160$ mm

- Face width, $\quad b = 15 m_n = 15 \times 4 = 60$ mm

Check for b:

i.e. $b_{min} = \dfrac{(1.15)\pi m_n}{\sin \beta}$ ...**12.54/ Pg 169, DHB**

$= \dfrac{(1.15) \times \pi \times 4}{\sin 30}$

$b_{min} = 28.9$ mm

Since $b > b_{min}$, the calculated value of b is safe.

- **Check for σ_{d1}:**

We know that, $F_t = \dfrac{\sigma_d C_v bYm_n}{C_w}$ ...Eq. (*iii*) **12.59/ Pg 169, DHB**

- $v = \dfrac{\pi d_1 N_1}{60} = \dfrac{\pi \times 0.116 \times 5000}{60} = 30.37$ m/s

- For $v > 20$ m/s, $C_v = \dfrac{5.55}{5.55 + \sqrt{v}}$ ...**12.61d/ Pg 170, DHB**

$= \dfrac{5.55}{5.55 + \sqrt{30.37}}$

$C_v = 0.5017$

- $F_t = \dfrac{2M_t}{d} \times C_s$ ...**12.22/ Pg 165, DHB**

- $C_s = 1.25$ ...(data)

$= \dfrac{2 \times 171.89 \times 10^3}{116} \times 1.25$

$F_t = 3704.53$ N

∴ Eq. (*iii*) yields... $3704.53 = \dfrac{\sigma_{d1} \times 0.5017 \times 60 \times 0.4733 \times 4}{1.25}$

$\sigma_{d1} = 81.26$ MPa > 56 MPa ...hence not safe.

Trial 2:

Let $m_n = 5$ mm

∴ PCD of pinion, $d_1 = \dfrac{m_n z_1}{\cos \beta} = \dfrac{5 \times 25}{\cos 30} = 144.33$ mm ≈ 145 mm

...**12.47/ Pg 168, DHB**

∴ PCD of gear, $d_2 = i_{d1} = 145 \times 10 = 1450$ mm

Face width, $b = 15m_n \times 5 = 75$ mm

Check for b:

i.e. $b_{min} = \dfrac{(1.15)\pi m_n}{\sin \beta}$ ...**12.54/ Pg 169, DHB**

$= \dfrac{(1.15) \times \pi \times 5}{\sin 30}$

$b_{min} = 36.12$ mm

Since $b > b_{min}$, the calculated value of b is safe

- $$v = \frac{\pi d_1 N_1}{60} = \frac{\pi \times 0.145 \times 5000}{60} = 38 \text{ m/s}$$

- For $v > 20$ m/s, $C_v = \dfrac{5.55}{5.55 + \sqrt{v}}$ ...12.61d/ Pg 170, DHB

$$= \frac{5.55}{5.55 + \sqrt{38}}$$

$$C_v = 0.4737$$

- $$F_t = \frac{2M_t}{d} \times C_s \qquad \text{...12.22/ Pg 165, DHB}$$

- $C_s = 1.25$ ...(data)

$$= \frac{2 \times 171.89 \times 10^3}{145} \times 1.25$$

$$F_t = 2963.62 \text{ N}$$

∴ Eq. (iii) yields... $2963.62 = \dfrac{\sigma_{d1} \times 0.4737 \times 75 \times 0.4733 \times 5}{1.25}$

$\sigma_{d1} = 44.06$ MPa < 56 MPa ...hence safe.

b. To find face width (b) $b = 75$ mm

c. To find dynamic tooth load (F_d)

We know that, $F_d = F_t + \dfrac{K_3 v \left(Cb \cos^2 \beta + F_t \right) \cos \beta}{K_3 v + \sqrt{\left(Cb \cos^2 \beta + F_t \right)}}$ ...12.62/ Pg 170, DHB

here $K_3 = 20.67$

@ $v > 26$ m/s	Error, $e = 0.0127$ mm	...Tb. 12.14/ Pg 191, DHB
For $\alpha = 20°$ stub teeth and steel – steel combination		
@ $e = 0.01$ mm	$C = 118.7$ N/mm	...Tb. 12.12/ Pg 190, DHB
$e = 0.0127$ mm	$C = ?$	

∴ at $v = 36$ m/s, $C = \dfrac{0.0127 \times 118.7}{0.01} = 150.75$ N/mm

∴ $F_d = 2963.62 + \dfrac{(20.67 \times 38) \times \left[(150.75 \times 75 \times \cos^2 30) + 2963.62 \right] \times \cos 30}{(20.67 \times 38) + \sqrt{\left[(150.75 \times 75 \times \cos^2 30) + 2963.62 \right]}}$

$F_d = 11.68 \times 10^3$ N

d. To find BHN

We know that, $F_w \geq F_d$

$$\frac{d_1 b Q K}{\cos^2 \beta} \geq 11.68 \times 10^3$$

$$\text{Ratio factor, } Q = \frac{2d_2}{d_2 + d_1} \qquad \text{...12.36c/ Pg 167, DHB}$$

$$= \frac{2 \times 1450}{1450 + 145}$$

$$Q = 1.82$$

$$\frac{145 \times 75 \times 1.82 \times K}{\cos^2 30} \geq 11.68 \times 10^3$$

$$K \geq 0.4428$$

Therefore for steel – steel combination, having $\alpha = 20°$ and $K \geq 0.4428$, we have
$$BHN_1 = 250 \text{ and } BHN_2 = 150 \qquad \text{...Tb. 12.16/ Pg 193, DHB}$$

20. Design a pair of helical gears to transmit a power of 20 kW from a shaft running at 1000 rpm to a parallel shaft to be run at 350 rpm.

[VTU – Dec. 07/ Jan. 2008 – 20 Marks; (similar) Jan./ Feb. 2006 – 20 Marks; (similar) Jan./ Feb. 2005 – 20 Marks.]

Solution: $P = 20$ kW, pinion speed, $N_1 = 1000$ rpm, $N_2 = 350$ rpm

We know that,
$$i = \frac{N_1}{N_2} = \frac{d_2}{d_1} = \frac{z_2}{z_1}$$

$$i = \frac{1000}{350}$$

$$i = 2.86$$

Material properties:

Since the material is not specified, let us assume that both pinion and gear are made of same material.

i.e. steel, C30 heat treated $\sigma_{d1} = \sigma_{d2} = 220.6$ MPa and $BHN_1 = BHN_2 = 300$
...Tb. 12.7/ Pg 186, DHB

Identifying weaker part (pinion/gear):

We know that strength factor
Since both pinion and gear are made of same material, the pinion is weaker,
i.e. $\sigma_{d1} \cdot y_1 < \sigma_{d2} \cdot y_2$
Hence design is based on **pinion**.

- Assume $z_1 = 21$ teeth
- $\therefore \quad z_2 = iz_1 = 2.86 \times 21 = 60$ teeth
- Assume $\beta = 25°$ and $\alpha = 20°$ FDI system

- Virtual number of teeth, $z_e = \dfrac{z}{\cos^3 \beta}$ ...12.52a/ Pg 169, DHB

$$z_{e1} = \frac{z_1}{\cos^3 \beta} = \frac{21}{\cos^3 25}$$

$$z_{e1} = 28.21 \approx 29$$

a. To find module (m_n)

Since the diameter is unknown, we have $m_n = \sqrt[3]{\dfrac{2M_t C_w \cos \beta}{\sigma_d C_v k Y z}}$

...Eq. (i) **12.60/ Pg 170, DHB**

- $$P = \dfrac{2\pi N_1 M_t}{60}$$

$$20 \times 10^3 = \dfrac{2\pi \times 1000 \times M_t}{60}$$

$$M_t = 191 \text{ N-m} = 191 \times 10^3 \text{ N-mm}$$

- Assume, $k = b/m_n = 15$
- Assume, $C_v = 0.5$
- Assume, $C_w = 1.15$ ...Tb. **12.21/ Pg 196, DHB**
- Form factor, $Y = \pi y_1$ ...**12.16/ Pg 163, DHB**

$$= \pi \left[0.154 - \dfrac{0.912}{z_{e1}} \right]$$ ...**12.17b/ Pg 163, DHB**

$$= \pi \left[0.154 - \dfrac{0.912}{29} \right]$$

$$Y = 0.3850$$

∴ Eq. (i) yields... $m_n = \sqrt[3]{\dfrac{2 \times 191 \times 10^3 \times 1.15 \times \cos 25}{220.6 \times 0.5 \times 15 \times 0.3850 \times 21}}$

$$m_n = 3.10 \text{ mm}$$

Therefore, standard module, $m_n = 4$ mm ...Tb. **12.2/ Pg 182, DHB**

∴ PCD of pinion, $d_1 = \dfrac{m_n z_1}{\cos \beta} = \dfrac{4 \times 21}{\cos 25} = 92.68$ mm ≈ 95 mm

...**12.47/ Pg 168, DHB**

PCD of gear, $d_2 = i_{d1} = 2.86 \times 95 = 271.7$ mm ≈ 272 mm

- Face width, $b = 15 m_n = 15 \times 4 = 60$ mm

Check for b:

i.e. $b_{\min} = \dfrac{(1.15)\, \pi m_n}{\sin \beta}$ ...**12.54/ Pg 169, DHB**

$$= \dfrac{(1.15) \times \pi \times 4}{\sin 25}$$

$$b_{\min} = 34.2 \text{ mm}$$

Since $b > b_{\min}$, the calculated value of b is safe.

- Check for σ_{d1}:

We know that, $F_t = \dfrac{\sigma_d C_v b Y m_n}{C_w}$ ...Eq. (iii) **12.59/ Pg 169, DHB**

- $$v = \frac{\pi d_1 N_1}{60} = \frac{\pi \times 0.95 \times 1000}{60} = 4.97 \text{ m/s}$$

- For $v < 5$ m/s, $\quad C_v = \dfrac{4.58}{4.58 + v}$ ...12.61a/ Pg 170, DHB

$$= \frac{4.58}{4.58 + 4.97}$$

$$C_v = 0.4796$$

- $$F_t = \frac{2M_t}{d}$$ ...12.22/ Pg 165, DHB

$$= \frac{2 \times 191 \times 10^3}{95}$$

$$F_t = 4021 \text{ N}$$

∴ Eq. (*iii*) yields... $4021 = \dfrac{\sigma_{d1} \times 0.4796 \times 60 \times 0.3850 \times 4}{1.15}$

$\sigma_{d1} = 104.35$ MPa < 220.6 MPa ...hence safe.

b. To find face width
$b = 60$ mm

c. To find dynamic tooth load (F_d)

We know that, $\quad F_d = F_t + \dfrac{K_3 v \left(Cb \cos^2 \beta + F_t\right) \cos \beta}{K_3 v + \sqrt{\left(Cb \cos^2 \beta + F_t\right)}}$ ...12.62/ Pg 170, DHB

here $K_3 = 20.67$

@ $v = 4$ m/s	Error, $e = 0.0710$ mm	...Tb. 12.14/ Pg 191, DHB
For $\alpha = 20°$ FDI teeth and steel – steel combination		
@ $e = 0.06$ mm	$C = 686.7$ N/mm	...Tb. 12.12/ Pg 190, DHB
$e = 0.0710$ mm	$C = ?$	

∴ at $v = 4.97$ m/s, $C = \dfrac{0.0710 \times 686.7}{0.06} = 812.6$ N/mm

∴ $F_d = 4021 + \dfrac{(20.67 \times 4.97) \times \left[(812.6 \times 60 \times \cos^2 25) + 4021\right] \times \cos 25}{(20.67 \times 4.97) + \sqrt{\left[(812.6 \times 60 \times \cos^2 25) + 4021\right]}}$

$F_d = 17.15 \times 10^5$ N

d. To find endurance strength (F_s)

We know that, $\quad F_s = \sigma_{en} b Y m_n$ ...12.63/ Pg 170, DHB

@ $BHN_1 = 300$, $\sigma_{en} = 515$ MPa ...Tb.12.15/ Pg 192, DHB

∴ $F_s = 515 \times 60 \times 0.3850 \times 4$

$F_s = 47.59$ kN

Since $F_s > F_d$, the material is safe against static tooth load.

e. To find dynamic tooth load (F_w)

We know that, $$F_w = \frac{d_1 b Q K}{\cos^2 \beta}$$ ...Eq. (iii) **12.64/ Pg 170, DHB**

- Diameter of pinion, $d_1 = 95$ mm
- Ratio factor, $$Q = \frac{2 d_2}{d_2 + d_1}$$ ...**12.36c/ Pg 167, DHB**

$$= \frac{2 \times 272}{272 + 95}$$

$$Q = 1.48$$

- For and steel – steel combination having $BHN_1 = BHN_2 = 300$,
$$K = 1.344$$ ...**Tb.12.16/ Pg 193, DHB**

∴ Eq. (iii) yields... $$F_w = \frac{95 \times 60 \times 1.48 \times 1.344}{\cos^2 25}$$

$$F_w = 13.80 \text{ N}$$

Since $F_w < F_d$, the pinion is subjected to rapid wear and hence has to be surface hardened to higher BHN.

i.e. $F_w \geq F_d$

$$\frac{d_1 b Q K}{\cos^2 \beta} \geq 17.15 \times 10^3$$

$$\frac{95 \times 60 \times 1.48 \times K}{\cos^2 25} \geq 17.15 \times 10^3$$

$$K \geq 1.669$$

Therefore for steel – steel combination, having $\alpha = 20°$ and $K \geq 1.669$, we have
$$BHN_1 = 400 \text{ and } BHN_2 = 300 \quad ...\text{Tb. 12.16/ Pg 193, DHB}$$

4.45 PROBLEMS ON HERRINGBONE GEARS

Note: The design of herringbone gear or double helical gear is same as that of helical gear, except the face width.

i.e. $$b_{min} \geq \frac{(2.3) \pi m}{\tan \beta} = \frac{(2.3) \pi m_n}{\sin \beta}$$ ...**12.56/ Pg 169, DHB**

and the range is $$b = 20 m_n \text{ to } 30 m_n$$ ...**12.58b/ Pg 169, DHB**

21. A pair of herringbone gears is used to transmit 50 kW of power. The pinion rotates at 2800 rpm. The number of teeth on the pinion and gear are 21 and 109 respectively. The tooth form is 20° FDI and the helix angle is 25°. The material for the gear is cast steel with a hardness of 150 BHN and for the pinion is steel. The wear and lubrication factor may be taken as 1.15. The normal module employed for the gears is 4 mm and the face width of the gears is 20 times the normal module. Determine the required hardness for the pinion for continuous operation of the drive. Also recommend the class of gears.

[VTU - July 2006 – 15 Marks]

Solution: $P = 50$ kW, $N_1 = 2800$ rpm, $z_1 = 21$ teeth, $z_2 = 109$ teeth, $\alpha = 20°$ FDI, $\beta = 25°$, gear: cast steel- $BHN_2 = 150$; pinion: steel, $C_w = 1.15$, $m_n = 4$ mm, $b = 20 m_n = 20 \times 4 = 80$ mm, $BHN_1 = ?$

404 Design of Machine Elements II (DME II)

We know that, $\quad i = \dfrac{N_1}{N_2} = \dfrac{d_2}{d_1} = \dfrac{z_2}{z_1}$

$$i = \dfrac{z_2}{z_1} = \dfrac{109}{21}$$

$$i = 5.2 \text{ and } N_2 = \dfrac{N_1}{i} = \dfrac{2800}{5.2} = 538.46 \approx 540 \text{ rpm}$$

Material properties:
  Pinion: steel – C30 heat treated: $\sigma_{d1} = 220.6$ MPa, $BHN_1 = 300$
  Gear: Cast steel: $\sigma_{d2} = 138.3$ MPa (@ $BHN = 180$), $BHN_2 = 150$
  ...**Tb. 12.7/ Pg 186, DHB**

- Virtual number of teeth, $\quad z_e = \dfrac{z}{\cos^3 \beta} \qquad$ ...**12.52a/ Pg 169, DHB**

$$z_{e1} = \dfrac{z_1}{\cos^3 \beta} = \dfrac{21}{\cos^3 25}$$

$$z_{e1} = 28.20 \approx 28$$
and $\quad z_{e2} = i z_{e1} = 5.2 \times 28 = 145.6 \approx 146$

We know that strength factor $= \sigma_d \cdot y$

- For $\alpha = 20°$ FDI tooth, $y = 0.154 - \dfrac{0.912}{z} \qquad$ ...**12.17b/ Pg 163, DHBs**

i.e. $y_1 = 0.154 - \dfrac{0.912}{z_{e1}}$

$$y_1 = 0.154 - \dfrac{0.912}{28} = 0.1214$$

$$y_2 = 0.154 - \dfrac{0.912}{146} = 0.1478$$

∴ for pinion $\quad \sigma_{d1} \cdot y_1 = 220.6 \times 0.1214 = 26.78$ MPa
  for gear, $\quad \sigma_{d2} \cdot y_2 = 138.3 \times 0.1478 = 28.55$ MPa

Since $\sigma_{d1} \cdot y_1$ is less, design is based on **gear**.

a. To find module (m_n)
  Given, $\quad m_n = 4$ mm

∴ PCD of pinion, $\quad d_1 = \dfrac{m_n z_1}{\cos \beta} = \dfrac{4 \times 21}{\cos 25} = 92.68$ mm ≈ 95 mm
  ...**12.47/ Pg 168, DHB**

  PCD of gear, $\quad d_2 = i d_1 = 5.2 \times 95 = 494$ mm ≈ 495 mm
- Face width, $\quad b = 15 m_n = 20 \times 4 = 80$ mm
  Check for b:

i.e. $b_{\min} = \dfrac{(2.3) \pi m_n}{\sin \beta} \qquad$ ...**12.56/ Pg 169, DHB**

$$= \frac{(2.3) \times \pi \times 4}{\sin 25}$$

$$b_{min} = 68.38 \text{ mm}$$

Since $b > b_{min}$, the given value of b is safe

- **Check for σ_{d2}:**

  We know that, $\quad F_t = \dfrac{\sigma_d C_v b Y m_n}{C_w}$ ...Eq. (*iii*) **12.59/ Pg 169, DHB**

- $$P = \frac{2\pi N_2 M_t}{60}$$

  $$50 \times 10^3 = \frac{2\pi \times 540 \times M_t}{60}$$

  $$M_t = 884.2 \text{ N-m} = 884.2 \times 10^3 \text{ N-mm}$$

- $$v = \frac{\pi d_2 N_2}{60} = \frac{\pi \times 0.495 \times 540}{60} = 14 \text{ m/s}$$

- For $10 < v < 20$ m/s, $C_v = \dfrac{15.25}{15.25 + v}$ ...**12.61c/ Pg 170, DHB**

  $$= \frac{15.25}{15.25 + 14}$$

  $$C_v = 0.5214$$

- $$F_t = \frac{2M_t}{d} \qquad \text{...12.22/ Pg 165, DHB}$$

  $$= \frac{2 \times 884.2 \times 10^3}{495}$$

  $$F_t = 3572.52 \text{ N}$$

∴ Eq. (*iii*) yields... $3572.52 = \dfrac{\sigma_{d2} \times 0.5214 \times 80 \times (0.1478 \times \pi) \times 4}{1.15}$

$$\sigma_{d2} = 53.03 \text{ MPa} < 138.3 \text{ MPa} \qquad \text{...hence safe.}$$

b. To find face width (b) $\quad b = 80$ mm

c. To find dynamic tooth load (F_d)

We know that, $\quad F_d = F_t + \dfrac{K_3 v \left(Cb \cos^2 \beta + F_t\right) \cos \beta}{K_3 v + \sqrt{\left(Cb \cos^2 \cos^2 \beta + F_t\right)}}$ ...**12.62/ Pg 170, DHB**

here $K_3 = 20.67$

@ $v = 12$ m/s	Error, $e = 0.0330$ mm	...Tb. **12.14/ Pg 191, DHB**
For $\alpha = 20°$ FDI teeth and steel – steel combination		
@ $e = 0.03$ mm	$C = 343.3$ N/mm	...Tb. **12.12/ Pg 190, DHB**
$e = 0.0330$ mm	$C = ?$	

$$\therefore \quad \text{at } v = 14 \text{ m/s}, \ C = \frac{0.0330 \times 343.34}{0.03} = 377.67 \text{ N/mm}$$

$$\therefore \quad F_d = 3572.52 + \frac{(20.67 \times 14) \times \left[\left(377.67 \times 80 \times \cos^2 25\right) + 3572.52\right] \times \cos 25}{(20.67 \times 14) + \sqrt{\left[\left(377.67 \times 80 \times \cos^2 25\right) + 3572.52\right]}}$$

$$F_d = 19.83 \times 10^3 \text{ N}$$

e. To find dynamic tooth load (F_w)

We know that, $\quad F_w = \dfrac{d_1 b Q K}{\cos^2 \beta} \quad$ ...Eq. (iii) **12.64/ Pg 170, DHB**

- Diameter of pinion, $d_1 = 95$ mm

- Ratio factor, $\quad Q = \dfrac{2 d_2}{d_2 + d_1} \quad$ ...**12.36c/ Pg 167, DHB**

$$= \frac{2 \times 495}{495 + 95}$$

$$Q = 1.677$$

- Surface endurance limit, $\sigma_{es} = [2.75 \times (BHN) - 70] \quad$ ...**12.36d/ Pg 167, DHB**

$$(BHN) = \frac{300 + 150}{2}$$

$$= 225$$

$$\sigma_{es} = [(2.75 \times 225) - 70]$$

$$\sigma_{es} = 548.75 \text{ MPa}$$

- $\quad K = \dfrac{\sigma_{es}^2 \sin \alpha_n}{1.4} \left[\dfrac{1}{E_1} + \dfrac{1}{E_2} \right] \quad$ ...**12.65/ Pg 170, DHB**

$$\tan \alpha_n = \tan \alpha \cos \beta \quad \text{...12.52b/ Pg 169, DHB}$$
$$= \tan 20 \times \cos 25$$
$$\alpha_n = 18.26 \text{ deg}$$

$$\therefore \quad K = \frac{(548.75)^2 \sin (18.26)}{1.4} \left[\frac{1}{2.1 \times 10^5} + \frac{1}{2.1 \times 10^5} \right]$$

$$K = 0.6418$$

$\therefore \quad$ Eq. (iii) yields... $F_w = \dfrac{95 \times 80 \times 1.677 \times 0.6418}{\cos^2 25}$

$$F_w = 9958.5 \text{ kN}$$

Since $F_w < F_d$, the pinion is subjected to rapid wear and hence has to be surface hardened to higher *BHN*.

i.e. $F_w \geq F_d$

$$\frac{d_1 b Q K}{\cos^2 \beta} \geq 19.83 \times 10^3$$

$$\frac{95 \times 80 \times 1.677 \times K}{\cos^2 25} \geq 19.83 \times 10^3$$

$$K \geq 1.277$$

Therefore for steel – steel combination, having $\alpha = 20°$ and $K \geq 1.277$, we have

$$BHN_1 = 350 \text{ and } BHN_2 = 250 \quad \text{...Tb. 12.16/ Pg 193, DHB}$$

VTU QUESTION PAPERS

Feb. 2002 (ME6T2)

1. A pair of carefully cut spur gears with 20° FDI profile is used to transmit 12 kW at 1200 rpm of pinion. The gear has to rotate at 300 rpm. The material used for pinion and gear is medium carbon steel whose allowable bending stress may be taken as 230 MPa. Determine the module and the face width of the spur pinion and gear. Check the pair for wear strength against dynamic load. Suggest suitable hardness. Take 24 teeth on pinion. Modulus of elasticity may be taken as 210 GPa. **(20 Marks)**

2. The following data refers to a helical gear drive
   a. Power transmitted 34 kW at 2800 r/min of pinion.
   b. Speed reduction ratio 4.5.
   c. helix angle 25°.
   d. Material for both pinion and gear is medium carbon steel whose allowable bending stress may be taken as 230 MPa.
   e. Pinion diameter is limited to 125 mm.
   Determine module and face width. Check the design for wear strength against dynamic loading. Determine also the axial thrust on the shaft. **(20 Marks)**

July/ Aug. 2002 (ME6T2)

3. A compressor receives power through a pair of spur gears. The compressor shaft runs at 350 rpm while that of motor shaft at 1450 rpm, delivering 50 kW power. The power transmission is moderate shock and operates 10 h per day. Select the number of teeth on the gear such that the drive is compact and the velocity ratio should not deviate, use material for pinion as C45 untreated and for gear cast steel C30. Determine the hardness required for the pinion teeth for continuous operation. **(20 Marks)**

Jan./ Feb 2003 (ME6T2)

4. a. Derive an expression for beam strength of a spur gear tooth with standard notations. **(04 Marks)**
   b. Design a spur gear drive required to transmit 55 kW at 800 rpm of the pinion. The speed ratio is to be 3.2:1. The teeth are to be 20° full depth involute. **(16 Marks)**

July/ Aug. 2003 (ME6T2)

5. A pair of spur gears transmitting power from a motor to a pump impeller shaft is to be designed for minimum center distance. The forged steel pinion is to transmit 4 kW at 600 rpm to a cast steel gear with a transmission ratio of 4.5:1 and 20° full depth involute teeth are to be used. Design the gears for strength and check for module, strength, dynamic and wear loads. **(20 Marks)**

July/ Aug. 2004 (ME6T2)

6. a. Following are the details of a pair of spur gears:

Details	Pinion	Gear
Rotational speed	1440 r/min	720 r/min
Allowable bending stress	200 MPa	180 MPa
Surface hardness	250 BHN	200 BHN
Modulus of elasticity	200 GPa	200 GPa
Tooth profile	20° full depth involute	
Center distance	132 mm	
Face width	32 mm.	

   The pinion has 22 teeth. Determine the power that can be transmitted based on:
   a. Bending strength b. Surface endurance strength
   Gears are manufactured to have error in action less than 0.02 mm. What should be the endurance limit in bending of the weaker one to have endurance strength of 1.25 times the dynamic load? **(16 Marks)**

   b. With sketch explain formative or virtual number of teeth applicable to helical gear; also derive an expression for virtual number of teeth in terms of helix angle and he actual number of teeth. **(04 Marks)**

7. A pair of steel helical gears is to transmit 15 kW at 5000 r/min of the pinion. Both the gears are made of the same material, hardened steel with allowable bending stress of 120 MPa. The gears have to operate at a center distance of 200 mm. Speed reduction ratio is 4:1. The teeth are 20° full depth involute profile on transverse plane (plane of rotation) (diametral plane). Helix angle is 45°. The gears are manufactured to class III accuracy (precision class). Face width can be taken as 16 times the normal module, if the wear strength has to be more than the dynamic load. Determine the following:
   i. Normal module
   ii. Transverse module
   iii. Number of teeth on pinion and gear
   iv. Face width
   v. Required surface endurance limit. **(20 Marks)**

Jan./ Feb. 2005 (ME6T2)

8. A helical gear of 250 mm diameter transmits a torque of 200 N-m. The pressure angle in a plane normal to the teeth is 20°. The helix angle is 30°. Determine the gear tooth loads. **(06 Marks)**

Jan./ Feb. 2005 (AU53)

9. Design a pair of spur gears to transmit a power of 18 kW from a shaft running at 1000 rpm to a parallel shaft to be run at 250 rpm maintaining a distance of 160 mm between the shaft centers. Suggest suitable surface hardness for the gear pair. **(20 Marks)**

10. Design a pair of helical gears to transmit a power of 20 kW from a shaft running at 1500 rpm to a parallel shaft to be run at 450 rpm. Suggest suitable surface hardness for the gear pair. **(20 Marks)**

July/ Aug. 2005 (AU53)

11. Design a pair of spur gears to transmit 27 kW for an oil pump with the gear ratio of 3:1. The rpm of the pinion is 1200. The center distance is 400 mm. The gears are to

be of forged steel and untreated with 14 ½° FDI. Check the design for dynamic and wear considerations. **(20 Marks)**

12. a. Explain formative number of teeth in helical gears. **(05 Marks)**
    b. Design a pair of helical gears to transmit 73.5 kW power with a velocity of 4.25:1. The pinion rotates at 1750 rpm. Helix angle is 15°. The teeth are 20° FDI. The gears are lubricated randomly. Check for beam strength of tooth only. Calculate the gear forces. **(15 Marks)**

Jan./ Feb. 2006 (AU53)

13. A shaft rotating at a speed of 1000 rpm is to transmit a power of 40 kW to a parallel shaft to be rotated at 350 rpm. The distance between the shaft centers is 160 mm. Design a pair of spur gears to connect these two shafts. **(20 Marks)**
14. Design a pair of helical gears to transmit a power of 30 kW from a shaft rotating at 1500 rpm to a parallel shaft to be rotated at 450 rpm. **(20 Marks)**

July 2006 (AU53)

15. a. Give reasons for the selection of involute profile for gears more commonly. While generating less number of teeth on gear wheels the problem of interference prevails in involute tooth gearing, does such a problem really exist in cycloidal tooth gearing? **(05 Marks)**
    b. A pair of spur gears is required to transmit 5 kW of power. The pinion rotates at a speed of 1620 rpm and the gear is required to run at 420 rpm. Determine the least number of teeth on the gear and the pinion such that velocity ratio does not deviate at all. The tooth form is 20° full depth involute, therefore the number of teeth selected on the pinion should not be less than the theoretical minimum. The permissible stresses in the material of the gear and the pinion are 55 MPa and 65 MPa respectively. Design the gears for beam strength only and determine all the proportions of the gearing. **(15 Marks)**
16. A pair of herringbone gears is used to transmit 50 kW of power. The pinion rotates at 2800 rpm. The number of teeth on the pinion and gear are 21 and 109, respectively. The tooth form is 20° FDI and the helix angle is 25°. The material for the gear is cast steel with a hardness of 150 BHN and for the pinion is steel. The wear and lubrication factor may be taken as 1.15. The normal module employed for the gears is 4 mm and the face width of the gears is 20 times the normal module. Determine the required hardness for the pinion for continuous operation of the drive. Also recommend the class of gears. **(15 Marks)**

Dec. 06/ Jan. 2007 (AU53)

17. a. Derive an expression for beam strength of a spur gear tooth with standard notations. **(04 Marks)**
    b. A pair of spur gears has to transmit 20 kW from a shaft rotating at 1000 rpm to a parallel shaft which is to rotate at 310 rpm. Number of teeth on pinion is 31 with 20° full depth involute tooth form. The material for pinion is steel SAE 1040 untreated with allowable static stress 206.81 MPa and the material for the gear is cast steel 0.20%C untreated with allowable static stress 137.34 MPa. Determine the module and face width of the gear pair. Also find the dynamic tooth load on the gears. Take the service factor as 1.5. **(16 Marks)**
18. A pair of carefully cut helical gears for a turbine has a transmission ratio of 10:1. The teeth are 20° stub involute in the normal plane. Pinion has 25 teeth and rotates

at 5000 rpm. Material for pinion and gear is 0.4%C steel untreated with allowable static stress of 69.66 MPa. Helix angle = 30°. Power transmitted = 90 kW. Service factor = 1.25. Wear and lubrication factor = 1.25. Determine the module in normal plane and face width of the gears. Suggest suitable surface hardness for the gear pair. **(20 Marks)**

July 2007 (AU53)

19. a. Determine an expression for beam strength of a spur gear tooth. **(05 Marks)**
    b. Design a pair of spur gears to transmit 15 kW from a shaft rotating at 1000 rpm to a parallel shaft which is to rotate at 310 rpm. Assume number of teeth on pinion as 31 and 20° full depth tooth form. The material for pinion is C-40 steel untreated and for gear, cast steel 0.20%C untreated. **(15 Marks)**
20. a. Explain formative number of teeth in helical gears. **(05 Marks)**
    b. A pair of helical gears are to transmit 15 kW. The teeth are 20° stub in diametral plane and have a helix angle of 45°. The pinion runs at 10000 rpm and has 80 mm pitch diameter. The gear has a pitch diameter of 320 mm. If gears are made of cast steel having allowable static strength of 100 MPa; determine module and face width from static strength considerations and check the gears for wear, given σ_{es} = 618 MPa. **(15 Marks)**

Dec. 07/ Jan. 2008 (AU53)

21. A cast steel pinion rotating at 900 rpm is to dive a cast iron gear at 144 rpm. The static design stresses for the pinion and gear materials are 103 MPa and 55 MPa respectively. The teeth are to have standard 20° stub involute profiles and the maximum power to be transmitted is 25 kW. Design the spur gears completely and check for dynamic and wear loads. The gear surfaces are hardened to BHN 250. Use 16 teeth on the pinion. **(20 Marks)**
22. a. Explain formative number of teeth in helical gears. **(04 Marks)**
    b. A pair of helical gears with a 23° helix angle is to transmit 2.5 kW at 10,000 rpm of the pinion. The velocity ration is 4:1. Both the gears are made of hardened steel with an allowable stress of 100 MPa for each gear. The gears are 20° stub and the pinion is to have 24 teeth. Design the gears and determine the required *BHN*. **(16 Marks)**

Dec. 07/ Jan. 2008 (ME6T2)

23. Design a pair of spur gears to transmit a power of 25 kW from a shaft running at 1200 rpm to a parallel shaft to be run at 300 rpm maintaining a center distance of 160 mm. **(20 Marks)**
24. Design a pair of helical gears to transmit a power of 20 kW from a shaft running at 1000 rpm to a parallel shaft to be run at 350 rpm. **(20 Marks)**

June/ July 2008 (AU53)

25. A machine running at 360 rpm is drive by 12 kW, 1440 rpm motor through a 14 ½ involute gear. The center distance between the drive is 250 mm. The pinion is made of heat treated cast steel with allowable stress of 191.2 MPa and 450 *BHN*. The bearing is made of untreated cast steel with allowable static stress of 137.3 MPa and *BHN* of 300. Assuming gears are working 8 hours/day and subjected to light loads determine the module, face width and number of teeth on each gear. Also check the design for wear. **(20 Marks)**

26. Design a steel helical gear pair from the following data:
    Power transmitted = 30 kW
    Speed of pinion = 1500 rpm
    Velocity ratio = 1:4
    Number of teeth on pinion = 24
    Helix angle $\beta = 30°$
    Static stress for steel $\sigma_{d1} = \sigma_{d2} = 50.7$ MPa. BHN for gear material = 350. Check the design from wear point of view also. **(20 Marks)**

Dec. 08/ Jan. 2009 (ME6T2)

27. a. Derive Lewis equation for the beam strength of a gear tooth. Also list the assumptions. **(08 Marks)**
    b. Design a pair of spur gears to transmit 20 kW of power at a pinion speed of 1000 rpm. The required velocity ratio is 3.5:1. Stub involute tooth profile of 20° is used. The static design stress for the pinion is 100 MPa and for the gear is 70 MPa. The pinion has 16 teeth. Determine the module, face width, and pitch circle diameters of the gears based on a service factor of 1.25. **(12 Marks)**
28. a. Derive the Lewis strength equation for sour gears. State the assumptions made. **(06 Marks)**
    b. Design a pair of spur gears to have the following specifications:
    Power to be transmitted = 10 kW, rpm of the pinion = 1000, rpm of the gear = 200, material of the pinion – Cr-Ni steel, material of the gear - cast steel, minimum number of teeth on pinion to avoid interference. **(14 Marks)**
29. A pair of double helical gears (herringbone gears) have the following specifications:
    Module in the normal plane – 5 mm, Number of teeth on pinion – 17, Number of teeth on gear – 51, Helix angle – 30°, Class of gears – precision cut, BHN of gears – 300, Face width of gears – 75 mm. Determine the load capacity of the gears if they work under medium shocks 8 to 10 hrs per day. **(14 Marks)**

June/ July 2009 (ME6T2)

30. A cast iron spur gear is driven by a cast steel untreated pinion transmitting a power of 4 kW at a speed of 1500 rpm. The gear rotates at a speed of 500 rpm. The drive operates for 8 to 10 hours per day with medium shock. Design stress for pinion is 190 MPa and for the gear is 100 MPa. The pinion is of 200 BHN and gear is of 180 BHN. The teeth are 20° full depth involute profile. Design the gears and check for dynamic and wear tooth load. **(20 Marks)**

Dec. 08/ Jan. 2009 (AU53)

31. It is required to transmit 25 kW of power from a shaft running at 1000 rpm to a parallel shaft with speed reduction 2.5:1. The center to center distance of the shaft is to be about 300 mm. The material used for pinion is steel ($\sigma_d = 200$ N/mm², BHN = 250) and for gear is cast iron ($\sigma_d = 180$ N/mm², BHN = 200). Considering class-II gear with tooth profile 20° full depth involute, design the spur gear and check for dynamic load and wear load. **(20 Marks)**
32. Design a single reduction parallel helical gear speed reducer having speed ratio 5:1. It is to be capable of transmitting the full load rating of 18.75 kW at 1200 rpm of pinion. Use nickel chrome steel for pinion and C45 steel for gear. Select class III precision gears. The helix angle for the gear wheels is 23°. The normal pressure

angle of the tooth is 20° and the profile is full depth involute. Check the design for dynamic and wear load. **(20 Marks)**

June/ July 2009 (AU53)

33. a. Derive an expression for Lewis equation for strength of a spur gear tooth. **(06 Marks)**
    b. A pair of spur gears, having 20° involute full depth teeth is to transmit 12 kW at 300 rpm of the pinion. The speed ratio is 3:1. The allowable static stress for gear of cast iron and pinion of steel are 60 MPa and 105 MPa respectively, use the following data: Number of teeth of pinion = 16, face width = 14 times module, velocity factor, $C_v = \dfrac{4.5}{4.5 + v}$, v being the pitch line velocity in m/s and tooth form factor, $y = 0.154 - \dfrac{0.912}{z}$, where z = number of teeth. **(14 Marks)**

34. a. Define formative number of teeth of helical gear. **(04 Marks)**
    b. A helical cast steel gear with 30° helix angle has to transmit 35 kW at 1500 rpm. If the gear has 24 teeth, determine the necessary module, pitch diameter and face width for 20° full depth teeth. The static stress for cast steel may be taken as 56 MPa. The width of the face may be taken as 3 times the normal pitch. What would be the end thrust on the gear? The tooth factor for 20° full depth involute gear may be taken as $0.154 - \dfrac{0.912}{z_e}$, where z_e is the equivalent number of teeth. **(16 Marks)**

June/ July 2009 (06ME61)

35. a. Define "Formative number of teeth" as applied to helical gears and explain its importance in the design of helical gears. **(05 Marks)**
    b. Design a pair of spur gears to transmit 20 kW of power while operating for 8 to 10 hours per day sustaining medium shock, from a shaft rotating at 1000 rpm to a parallel shaft which is to rotate at 310 rpm. Assume the number of teeth on pinion to be 31 and 20° full depth involute tooth profile. The material of the pinion is C40 steel, untreated whose $\sigma_0 = 206.81$ N/mm² and for gear is cast steel, 0.2%C untreated whose 137.34 N/mm². Check the design for dynamic load if load factor 522.464 N/mm and also for wear load taking load stress factor, 0.279 N/mm². Suggest suitable hardness. **(15 Marks)**

Dec. 09/ Jan. 2010 (06ME61)

36. Design a pair of spur gears to transmit 20 kW from a shaft rotating at 1000 rpm to a parallel shaft which is to rotate at 310 rpm. Assume number of teeth on pinion as 31 and 20° full depth tooth form. **(20 Marks)**

37. Design a pair of helical gears to transmit power of 15 kW at 3200 rpm with speed reduction 4:1 pinion is made of cast steel 0.4% C untreated. Gear made of high grade CI. Helix angle is limited to 26° and not less than 20 teeth are to be used on either gear. Check he gears for dynamic and wear considerations. **(20 Marks)**

May/ June 2010 (AU53)

38. a. Derive the Lewis equation for the beam strength of a gear tooth. **(05 Marks)**
    b. A pair of straight teeth spur gears, having 20° involute full depth teeth is to transmit 10 kW at 300 rpm of the pinion. The speed ratio is 3:1. The allowable

static stress for gear of cast iron and pinion of steel are 60 MPa and 105 MPa respectively. Assume the following:

Number of teeth on pinion = 16

Face width = 12 time module

Velocity factor $(C_v) = 4.5/(4.5 + V)$, V being the pitch line velocity in m/s and

tooth form factor $(y) = 0.154 - \dfrac{0.912}{\text{No. of teeth}}$

Determine the module, face width and pitch diameter of the gears. Check the gear for wear, given $\sigma_{es} = 600$ MPa, $E_p = 200$ kN/mm² and $E_G = 100$ kN/mm².
(15 Marks)

39. a. Explain the formative number of teeth in helical gears. **(05 Marks)**
   b. A helical cast steel gear with 30° helix angle has to transmit 40 kW at 1500 rpm. If the gear has 24 teeth, determine module, pitch diameter and face width for 20^0 full depth teeth. The static stress for cast steel may be taken as 56 MPa. The width of the face may be taken as 3 times the normal pitch. What would be the end thrust on the gear? The tooth factor for 20° full depth involute gear may be taken as $0.154 - (0.912/T_E)$, where T_E represents the equivalent number of teeth.
   (15 Marks)

Dec. 2010 (AU53)

40. In a spur gear arrangement a pinion made of cast steel is rotating at 900 rpm and is driving a cast iron gear at 150 rpm. The teeth are to have standard 20° stub involute profiles and the maximum power to be transmitted is 25 kW. Determine the module and face width. Find the dynamic and wear load also. The pinion has 16 teeth with surface hardness of 250 *BHN*, take static stress for pinion as 103 MPa and for gear as 55 MPa. Assume $E_p = 96$ GN/m² and $E_G = 207$ GN/m².
(20 Marks)

41. The following data refers to the design of a helical gear drive:
   i. Power transmitted 34 kW at 2800 rpm of pinion
   ii. Speed ratio 4.5, number of teeth on pinion 18
   iii. Helix angel 25°, pressure angle $\alpha = 20°$ stub
   iv. Material for both pinion and gear is medium carbon steel whose allowable stress may be taken as 230 MPa
   v. Pinion diameter is limited to 125 mm
   Determine the axial thrust on the shaft and check the gears for dynamic and wear loads. **(20 Marks)**

May/ June 2011 (06ME61)

42. a. List the advantages and disadvantages of helical gears. **(03 Marks)**
   b. It is required to transmit 15 kW power from a shaft running at 1200 rpm to a parallel shaft with speed reduction of 3. The center distance of shafts is to be 300 mm. The material used for pinion is steel (200 MPa) and for gear is CI (140 MPa). Service factor is 1.25 and tooth profile is 20° full depth involute. Design the spur gear and check the design for dynamic load wear. **(17 Marks)**

Dec. 2010 (06ME61)

43. a. State the advantages of gear drives when compared to chain drives. **(04 Marks)**
   b. Design a helical gear pair to transmit a power of 15 kW from a shaft rotating at 1000 rpm to another shaft to be run at 360 rpm. Assume involute profile with a

pressure angle of 20°. The material of the pinion is forged steel SAE 1030 whose σ_d = 172.375 MPa and the material for gear is cast steel 0.2% C untreated with σ_d = 137.4 MPa. The gears operate under a condition of medium shocks for a period of 10 hours per day. Check for dynamic load, if load factor 580 N/mm and also for wear load. **(16 Marks)**

June/ July 2011 (06ME61)

44. A 12 kW motor running at 1170 rpm drives a fan through a pair of spur gears (forged steel SAE 1030 pinion and CI gear) with a reduction ratio of 3.9:1. Design the gear and check for dynamic and wear loads. **(20 Marks)**

Dec. 2011 (06ME61)

45. a. Derive the Lewis equation for the beam strength of a gear tooth. Also list the assumptions. **(04 Marks)**
   b. Design a pair of spur gears to transmit 20 kW of power at a pinion speed of 1000 rpm. The required velocity ratio is 3.5:1. 20° stub involute tooth profile to be used. The static design stress for the pinion is 100 MPa and for the gear is 70 MPa. The pinion has 16 teeth. Determine the module, face width, and pitch circle diameters of the gears based on a service factor of 1.25. **(16 Marks)**

June 2012 (06ME61)

46. a. Sketch and explain the different forms of involute gear tooth. **(05 Marks)**
   b. A cast steel pinion with an allowable stress of 103 MPa rotating at 900 r/min is to drive a cast iron gear at 1440 r/min. the teeth are 20° stub involute and maximum power to be transmitted is 25 kW. The allowable stress for cast iron gear is 56 MPa. Determine the module, number of teeth on the gears and face width from the stand-point of strength, dynamic load and wear. **(15 Marks)**

December 2012 (06ME12)

47. a. Two spur gears are to be used for a rock crusher drive and are to be of minimum size. The gears are to be designed for the following requirements. Power to be transmitted is 20 kW; speed of pinion is 1200 rpm, velocity ratio is 3.5:1, tooth profile 20° stub involute. Determine module and face width for strength requirements only. **(10 Marks)**
   b. A pair of mating helical gears have 20° pressure angle in the normal plane. The normal module is 5 mm and the module in the diametral plane is 5.7735 mm. the pitch diameter of the smaller gear is 115.47 mm. if the transmission ratio is 4:1, calculate;

   i. Helix angle
   ii. Normal pitch
   iii. Transverse pitch
   iv. Number of teeth for each gear
   v. Addendum
   vi. Deddendum
   vii. Hole depth
   viii. Clearance
   ix. Tooth thickness
   x. Working depth
   xi. outside diameters
   xii. center distance
   xiii. Root circle diameters
   xiv. Base circle diameters.

   (10 Marks)

June/ July 2013 (AU53)

48. a. Derive the expression for beam strength of a gear tooth. **(05 Marks)**
   b. A pair of straight teeth spur gears, having 20° involute full depth teeth is to transmit 12 kW at 300 rpm of the pinion. The speed ratio is 3:1. The allowable

static stresses for gear of cast iron and pinion of steel are 60 MPa and 105 MPa respectively. Number of teeth on pinion = 16, face width = 16 times module. Determine the module, face width and pitch diameters of the gears. Check the gear for wear. **(15 Marks)**

49. a. Write a short note on formative number of teeth for helical gears. **(05 Marks)**
    b. A helical cast steel gear with 300 helix angle has to transmit 35 kW at 1500 rpm. If the gear has 24 teeth, determine the necessary module for 20° full depth teeth. Also calculate the end thrust in the gear and specifications of the gear. **(15 Marks)**

June/ July 2013 (06ME61)

50. Design a pair of spur gears to transmit 12 kW at 1200 rpm of the pinion. The velocity ratio required is 4:1. The pitch line velocity of the gears is limited to 12 m/s. Take allowable static stress 138 MPa for both gears and pressure angle as 20° full depth involute, also assume face width is 10 times the module and service factor as 1.5. **(20 Marks)**

June/ July 2013 (10ME62)

51. It is required to transmit 15 kW power from a shaft running at 1200 rpm to a parallel shaft with speed reduction of 3. The center distance of shafts is to be 300 mm. the material used for pinion is steel and for gear is CI. Service factor is 1.25 and tooth profile is 20° full depth involute. Design the spur gear and check the design for dynamic and wear. **(20 Marks)**

Dec.2013/ Jan.2014 (10ME62)

52. a. Write a note on design of gears based on dynamic loading and wear. **(06 Marks)**
    b. A cast steel 24 teeth spur pinion operating at 1150 r/min transmits 3 kW to a cast steel 56 teeth spur gear. The gears have the following specifications:
    Module = 3 mm   Allowable stress = 100 MPa
    Face width = 35 mm   Tooth form = 14 ½° full depth profile
    Factor of dynamic loading, C = 350 N/mm, Wear load factor, K = 0.28 MPa
    Determine the induced stress in the weaker gear. Also determine the dynamic load and wear load. Comment on the results. **(14 Marks)**

Dec. 2013/ Jan. 2014 (AU53)

53. A pair of helical gears used in a speed reduce is to be driven by an IC engine. The related power of the speed reducer is 75 kW at a pinion speed of 1200 r/min. the output speed of the reducer is 400 r/min. the loading may be assumed to be medium shock condition with 10 to 14 hours of working condition. The peripheral velocity is restricted to 10 m/s. The gear tooth profile is 20 degree full depth involute on the normal plane. Helix angle is 25 degree. Both the gears are to be of same steel with an allowable bending stress of 240 MPa. The gears are manufactured such that the error in action is limited to 0.032 mm. the modulus of elasticity of the gear material is 210 GPa. Face width is 15 times the normal module. Determine the following:
    i. Module   ii. Number of teeth on pinion and gear
    iii. Face width   iv. Surface hardness of the teeth
    (20 Marks)

Part – B

5. Bevel and Worm Gears
6. Clutches and Brakes
7. Lubrication and Bearings
8. IC Engine Parts

5

Bevel and Worm Gears

BEVEL GEARS

5.1 INTRODUCTION

Bevel gears are used to transfer power between intersecting shafts, whose axes are not parallel. The teeth of these gears are formed on a conical surface (frustums of cone) Bevel gears are most often mounted on shafts that are 90° apart, but can be designed to work at other angles as well **(Fig. 5.1)**.

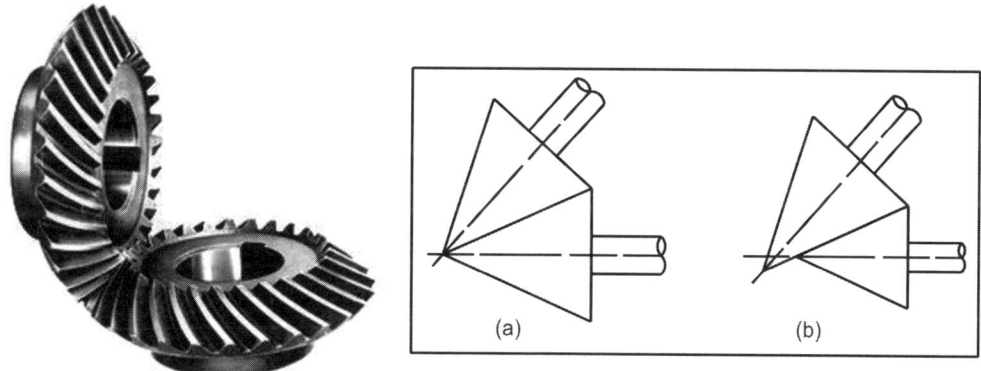

Fig. 5.1: Bevel gear   **Fig. 5.2:** Forms of bevel gear

Figure 5.2 shows two pairs of cone in contact. Since the cone elements **[Fig. 5.2(b)]** do not intersect at the point of intersection of the axis of rotation, these types of cones can't be used as pitch surfaces since it is impossible to have positive driving and sliding in the same direction at the same time. Thus in order to have a positive drive, the elements of the bevel gear pitch cones and shafts must intersect at the same point **[Fig. 5.2 (a)]**.

5.2 CLASSIFICATION

Depending upon the angle between the shafts and pitch surfaces, bevel gears are classified as:

1. **Miter Gears:** These are bevel gears with equal numbers of teeth and with axes at right angles. These are specifically designed for operating in pairs. It has a set of tooth that is identical in number, diametral pitches.

These are suitable for applications where torque ratings have been precisely calculated. For high efficiency, miter bears are put to use as right angle drives.

2. **Spiral or Angular Gears**: These gears connect two shafts when the axis intersects at an angle other than right angle as shown in **Fig. 5.1**. When compared to straight bevel gears they have a higher potential for load transmission. This is made possible by cutting the teeth in the shape of a curve. Spiral bevel gears have curved and oblique teeth that comes in contact with each other in a gradual and smooth manner from one end to the other.

    These gears are recommended for higher speeds and where the noise level is an important consideration.

3. **Crown Bevel Gear:** These gears have a pitch angle of 90°.
4. **Internal Bevel Gears:** These gears have pitch angles greater than 90°.
5. **External Bevel Gears:** These gears have pitch angles less than 90°.
6. **Zero Bevel Gear:** It is a special type of spiral bevel gear, where the spiral angle is of zero degree. It shows both the characteristics of straight and spiral bevel gears.

5.3 TYPES OF TOOTH ON BEVEL GEAR

The teeth on bevel gears can be straight, spiral or "zero".

1. **Straight Tooth Lines:** In straight bevel gears the teeth are straight and parallel to the generators of the cone. This is the simplest form of bevel gear and resembles a spur gear, which is conical rather than cylindrical.
2. **Spiral Tooth Lines:** Spiral bevel gears have their teeth formed along spiral lines. They are somewhat analogous to cylindrical type helical gears in that the teeth are angled; however with spiral gears the teeth are also curved.

    The advantage of the spiral tooth over the straight tooth is that they engage more gradually. The contact between the teeth starts at one end of the gear and then spreads across the whole tooth. This results in a less abrupt transfer of force when a new pair of teeth come in to play. With straight bevel gears, the abrupt tooth engagement causes noise, especially at high speeds, and impact stress on the teeth which makes them unable to take heavy loads at high speeds without breaking.

3. **Zero Tooth Lines:** Zero bevel gears are an intermediate type between straight and spiral bevel gears. Their teeth are curved, but not angled.

5.4 APPLICATIONS

The bevel gear finds applications in locomotives, marine applications, automobiles, printing presses, cooling towers, power plants, steel plants, railway track inspection machines, etc.

- Used in differential drives for transmitting power to two axles spinning at different speeds, such as those on a cornering automobile.
- Used as the main mechanism for a hand drill. The bevel gears change the rotation of the chuck to a horizontal rotation when the handle of the drill is turned in a vertical direction.

    The bevel gears in a hand drill have the advantage of increasing the speed of rotation of the chuck and this makes it possible to drill a range of materials.

- These gears permit minor adjustment during assembly and allow for some displacement due to deflection under operating loads without concentrating the load on the end of the tooth.

Bevel and Worm Gears **421**

- Spiral bevel gears are important components on rotorcraft drive systems, which operate at high speeds, high loads, and for a large number of load cycles.

5.5 ADVANTAGES AND DISADVANTAGES

Advantages:

- This gear makes it possible to change the operating angle.
- It can be used to change the direction of drive in a gear system by 90° (Ex: Hand drill)
- Smooth operation

Disadvantages:

- Must be precisely mounted.
- The axes must be capable of supporting significant forces.

5.6 TERMINOLOGY

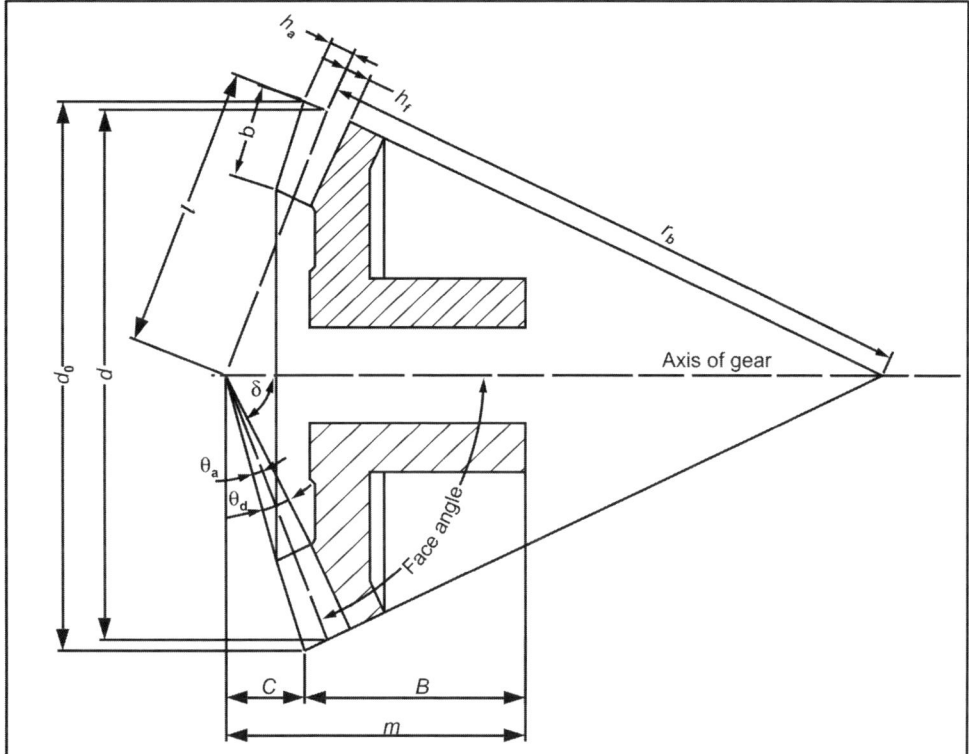

Fig. 5.3: Definitions and dimensions relating to bevel gear (Fig. 12.7/Pg 206, DHB)

1. **Pitch Cone:** refers to the pitch surface of a bevel gear in a gear pair.
2. **Cone Distance or Pitch Cone Radius (*L*):** is the length of pitch cone element.
3. **Back Cone:** is an imaginary cone, the elements of which are perpendicular to the elements of the pitch cone at the larger end of the tooth.
4. **Back Cone Radius:** length of the back cone element is called the back cone radius.
5. **Pitch Angle (δ):** is the angle made by the pitch line of the gear with gear axis.

Note: *The bevel gears may have straight or spiral teeth. Unless otherwise stated, it is assumed that bevel gears have straight teeth and the shaft axes intersect at right angles (Fig. 5.3).*

5.7 PITCH ANGLE OF BEVEL GEARS

Figure. 5.4 shows a sectional view of two bevel gears in mesh.

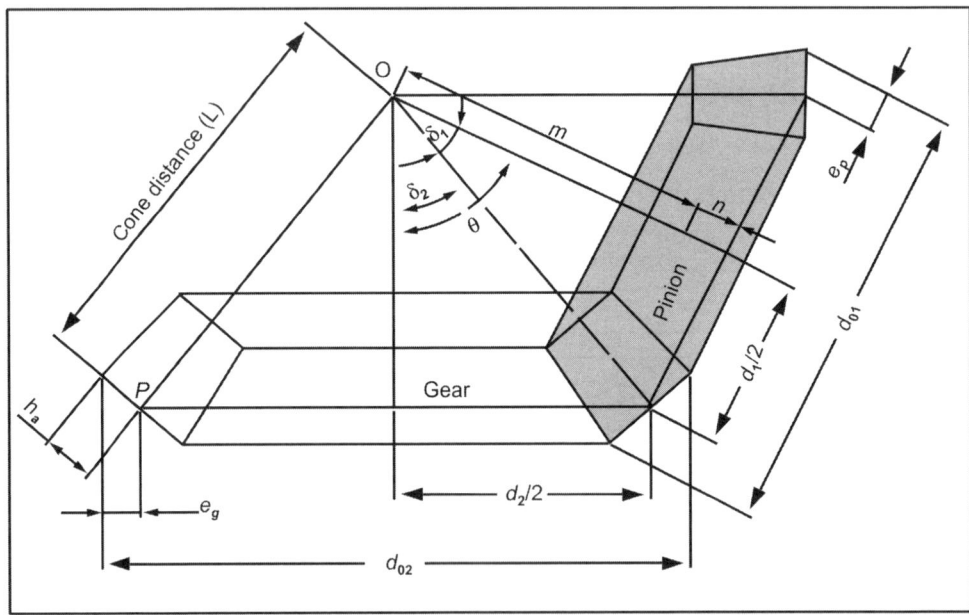

Fig. 5.4: Acute angle bevel gear (Fig. 12.8/Pg 207, DHB)

Let, δ_1 = pitch angle for pinion
δ_2 = pitch angle for gear
θ = angle between two axes of the shaft = $(\delta_1 + \delta_2)$
d_1 = pitch diameter of pinion
d_2 = pitch diameter of gear

$$i = \frac{d_2}{d_1} = \frac{z_2}{z_1} = \frac{N_1}{N_2} - \text{velocity ratio} \qquad \text{...(Eq. 5.1)}$$

From **Fig. 5.4**, $\theta = \delta_1 + \delta_2$
$\delta_2 = \theta - \delta_1$

∴ $\sin \delta_2 = \sin(\theta - \delta_1)$

$\sin \delta_2 = \sin \theta \cdot \cos \delta_1 - \cos \theta \cdot \sin \delta_1$ ...(Eq. 5.2)

Also, $\sin \delta_1 = \dfrac{\text{pitch radius}}{\text{cone distance}}$

i.e. $\sin \delta_1 = \dfrac{d_1/2}{OP} = \dfrac{d_1/2}{L} \Rightarrow L = \dfrac{d_1/2}{\sin \delta_1}$ ...(Eq. 5.3)

similarly, $L = \dfrac{d_2/2}{\sin \delta_2}$ ...(Eq. 5.4)

Equating Eq. (5.3) and Eq. (5.4), we have

$$\frac{d_1/2}{\sin\delta_1} = \frac{d_2/2}{\sin\delta_2}$$

$$\sin\delta_2 = \sin\delta_1\left(\frac{d_2}{d_1}\right) = i \times \sin\delta_1 \qquad \text{...(Eq. 5.5)}$$

Equating Eq. (5.5) and Eq. (5.2), we have

$$i \times \sin\delta_1 = \sin\theta \cdot \cos\delta_1 - \cos\theta \cdot \sin\delta_1$$

Divide throughout with $\cos\delta_1$

$$i \times \tan\delta_1 = \sin\theta - \cos\theta \cdot \tan\delta_1$$

$$\tan\delta_1 (i + \cos\theta) = \sin\theta$$

$$\therefore \quad \tan\delta_1 = \frac{\sin\theta}{(i + \cos\theta)} \qquad \text{...(Eq. 5.6) 12.67/ Pg 171, DHB}$$

On similar lines, $\tan\delta_2 = \dfrac{\sin\theta}{\left(\dfrac{1}{i}\right) + \cos\theta}$ ...(Eq. 5.7) **12.68/ Pg 171, DHB**

Note:

- If $\theta = 90°$ $\quad \tan\delta_1 = \left(\dfrac{1}{i}\right)$ ...(Eq. 5.8) **12.72a/ Pg 172, DHB**

    $\tan\delta_2 = i$ ...(Eq. 5.9) **12.72b/ Pg 172, DHB**

- If $\theta > 90°$ $\quad \tan\delta_1 = \dfrac{\sin(180-\theta)}{i - \cos(180-\theta)}$ ...(Eq. 5.10) **12.73a/ Pg 172, DHB**

    $\tan\delta_2 = \dfrac{\sin(180-\theta)}{\left(\dfrac{1}{i}\right) - \cos(180-\theta)}$ ...(Eq. 5.11) **12.73b/ Pg 172, DHB**

5.8 FORCES ACTING ON BEVEL GEAR

Consider a straight tooth bevel gear with force components as shown in **Fig. 5.5.**

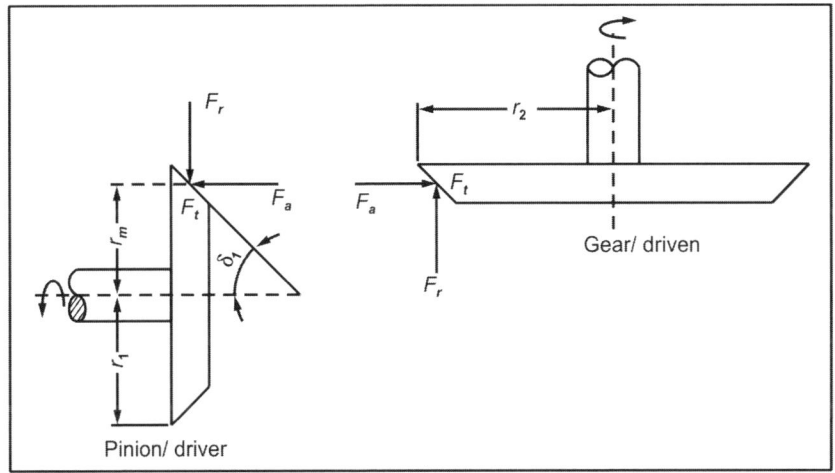

Fig. 5.5: Forces acting on bevel gear

- The tangential force is $F_t = \dfrac{2M_t}{r_m}$
- Radial load on the gear, $F_r = F_{te} \tan \alpha \cos \delta_1$ ...(Eq. 5.12) **12.93/ Pg 175, DHB**
- Axial thrust on the gear, $F_a = F_{te} \tan \alpha \sin \delta_1$ ...(Eq. 5.13) **12.94/ Pg 175, DHB**
- The effective tooth load, $F_{te} = F_n \cos \alpha = \dfrac{F_t L}{L - 0.5b}$ ...(Eq. 5.14) **12.92/ Pg 175, DHB**

5.9 OTHER RELATIONS

1. Cone distance, $L = \dfrac{1}{2}\sqrt{d_1^2 + d_2^2} = \dfrac{d_2}{2\sin \delta_2} = \dfrac{d_1}{2\sin \delta_1}$

   ...(Eq. 5.15) **12.74/ Pg 172, DHB**

2. Pitch circle diameter, $d = mz$ ...(Eq. 5.16) **12.75/ Pg 172, DHB**

3. Mean diameter, $d_m = \left[1 - \dfrac{0.5}{k_2}\right]d$ ...(Eq. 5.17) **12.76/ Pg 172, DHB**

4. Mean module, $m_m = \left[1 - \dfrac{0.5}{k_2}\right]m$ ...(Eq. 5.18) **12.77/ Pg 173, DHB**

   Where, $k_2 = \dfrac{L}{b}$

5. Proportions of bevel teeth ...**Table 12.22/ Pg 196, DHB**
6. Standard module of bevel gears ...**Table 12.23/ Pg 197, DHB**
7. Recommended series of diametral pitches ...**Table 12.24/ Pg 197, DHB**

5.10 STRENGTH OF A BEVEL GEAR

Figure 5.6 (a) shows load acting on a bevel gear tooth which varies linearly along the face of the tooth. The tooth thickness also varies along the face of the gear and converges to apex (O) of the cone. This variation in turn results in variation of circular and diametrical pitch respectively.

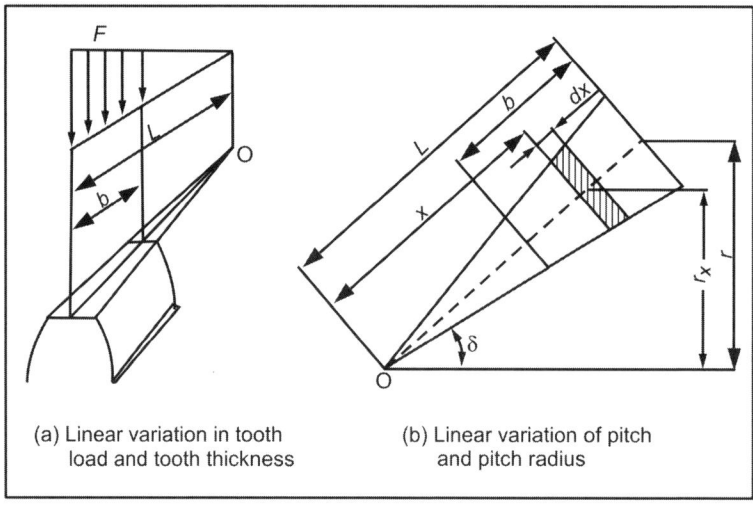

(a) Linear variation in tooth load and tooth thickness

(b) Linear variation of pitch and pitch radius

Fig. 5.6: Strength of a bevel gear

In order to take care of these variations, consider an element of thickness dx at a distance x from apex as shown in **Fig. 5.6 (b)**, along the face of the tooth.

The Lewis equation for this element is $F_x \cdot d = \sigma Y m_x \cdot dx$ ...(Eq. 5.19)

σ = allowable stress = $\sigma_d C_v$
m_x = module at a distance x from apex
$Y = \pi y$ – form factor
y = Lewis form factor based on z_e and tooth profile

Multiplying with r_x and integrating Eq. (5.19), we have

$$\int r_x (F_x \cdot d) = \int r_x (\sigma Y m_x \, dx) \qquad \text{...(Eq. 5.20)}$$

Since module varies directly as diametrical pitch $\left[m = \dfrac{1}{P} = \dfrac{d}{z} \right]$, it follows that the module varies directly with x.

i.e. $\qquad \dfrac{m}{m_x} = \dfrac{L}{x}$

$\therefore \qquad m_x = \dfrac{x \cdot m}{L}$ ...(Eq. 5.21)

From **Fig. 5.6(b)**, $\dfrac{r_x}{x} = \dfrac{r}{L}$

$\therefore \qquad r_x = \dfrac{x \cdot r}{L}$ ...(Eq. 5.22)

Substituting Eq. (5.21) and Eq. (5.22) in Eq. (5.20) yields

$$\int r_x (F_x \cdot d) = \int_{L-b}^{L} \left(\dfrac{x \cdot r}{L} \right) \left(\dfrac{x \cdot m}{L} \right) \sigma Y \, dx$$

i.e. torque, $\qquad T = \int_{L-b}^{L} \left(\dfrac{\sigma \cdot Y \cdot m \cdot r}{L^2} \right) x^2 \, dx$

$$= \left(\dfrac{\sigma \cdot Y \cdot m \cdot r}{L^2} \right) \left[\dfrac{x^3}{3} \right]_{L-b}^{L}$$

$\therefore \qquad T = \sigma \cdot Y \cdot m \cdot r \left[1 - \dfrac{b}{L} + \dfrac{b^2}{3L^2} \right] \times b$ ...(Eq. 5.23)

Since face width is limited to $1/3^{rd}$ of cone distance ($b \leq L/3$), the term $\left(\dfrac{b^2}{3L^2} \right)$ can be neglected, since it is small compared to other terms.

i.e. $\qquad T = \sigma \cdot b \cdot Y \cdot m \cdot r \left[1 - \dfrac{b}{L} \right]$

$\qquad = \sigma \cdot b \cdot Y \cdot m \cdot r \left[\dfrac{L - b}{L} \right]$ ...(Eq. 5.24)

But torque, $T = F_t \cdot (d/2) = F_t \cdot r$ ...(Eq. 5.25)

Therefore, Eq. (5.24) yields... $F_t \cdot r = \sigma b Y m r \left[\dfrac{L-b}{L} \right]$

$$F_t = \sigma b Y m \left[\dfrac{L-b}{L} \right] \qquad \text{...(Eq. 5.26)}$$

... *"is the general equation for bevel gear"*

Since allowable stresses for a gear tooth depend upon pitch line velocity, material chosen and load condition, we have

$$\sigma = \sigma_d C_v$$

∴ $\quad F_t = \sigma_d C_v b Y m \left[\dfrac{L-b}{L} \right]$ -or-

$$F_t = \dfrac{\sigma_d C_v b Y}{P} \left[\dfrac{L-b}{L} \right] \qquad \text{...(Eq. 5.27) } \textbf{12.85/ Pg 173, DHB}$$

Where, $\qquad m = \dfrac{1}{P} = \dfrac{d}{z} \qquad$ ...**12.4/ Pg 162, DHB**

P = diametral pitch at larger end
m = module at large end
σ_d = allowable static stress $\qquad$ ...**Table 12.7/ Pg 186, DHB**
C_v = velocity factor $\qquad$ ...**12.86(a & c)/ Pg 174, DHB**
b = face width of gear
$\qquad b \geq 6\,m; \quad b \leq 10\,m;$ $\qquad$ ...**12.83a/ Pg 173, DHB**
$\qquad b \leq L/3$ $\qquad$ ... **12.83b/ Pg 173, DHB**

In practice, $\quad b = 6\,m$ to $7\,m$, if $L < 30$ m,
$\qquad\qquad b = 7\,m$ to $10\,m$, if $L > 30$ m $\qquad$ ...**12.84/ Pg 173, DHB**

$Y = \pi y$ – Form factor based on formative number of teeth

Cone distance, $L = \dfrac{1}{2}\sqrt{d_1^2 + d_2^2} = \dfrac{d_2}{2\sin\delta_2} = \dfrac{d_1}{2\sin\delta_1}$ $\qquad$ ...**12.74/ Pg 172, DHB**

z_e – Formative number of teeth $= \dfrac{z}{\cos\delta}$ $\qquad$ ...**12.81/ Pg 173, DHB**

5.11 DYNAMIC LOAD

$$F_d = F_t + \dfrac{K_3 v (Cb + F_t)}{K_3 v + \sqrt{Cb + F_t}} \qquad \text{...(Eq. 5.28) } \textbf{12.88/ Pg 174, DHB}$$

Where, $\quad F_t$ = tangential tooth load
$\qquad K_3 = 20.67$ – constant
$\qquad v$ = pitch line velocity (m/s)
$\qquad b$ = face width
$\qquad C$ = dynamic factor depending upon machining errors
$\qquad\qquad$ ...**Table 12.12/ Pg 190, DHB**

5.12 STATIC TOOTH LOAD -OR- BEAM STRENGTH -OR- ENDURANCE STRENGTH (F_{en})

$$F_{en} = \sigma_{en} \, b \, Y m \left[\frac{L-b}{L} \right] \quad \text{...(Eq. 5.29) } \mathbf{12.87/\ Pg\ 174,\ DHB}$$

The values of σ_{en} ...**Table 12.15/ Pg 192, DHB**
For safety against static tooth load, $F_{en} \geq F_d$ ...(Eq. 5.30)

5.13 WEAR TOOTH LOAD (F_w)

The limiting load of wear, $F_w = \dfrac{d_1 \, b \, Q_e \, K}{\cos \delta_1}$ ...(Eq. 5.31) **12.89/ Pg 174, DHB**

Q – ratio factor

$$= \frac{2 z_{e_2}}{z_{e_2} + z_{e_1}}$$

For safety against wear, $F_w \geq F_d$ ...(Eq. 5.32)

5.14 FORMATIVE NUMBER OF TEETH (z_e)

It is defined as the number of teeth having the same pitch as the actual gear that could be cut on a gear having a pitch radius equal to the radius of the back cone.

- For a straight tooth bevel gear,

formative number of teeth, $z_e = \dfrac{z}{\cos \delta}$ ...(Eq. 5.33) **12.81/ Pg 173, DHB**

i.e. for pinion, $\quad z_{e1} = \dfrac{z_1}{\cos \delta_1}$

and for gear, $\quad z_{e2} = \dfrac{z_2}{\cos \delta_2}$

- For a spiral bevel gear,

$$z_e = \frac{z}{\cos \delta \cdot \cos^3 \beta_m} \quad \text{...(Eq. 5.34) } \mathbf{12.82/\ Pg\ 173,\ DHB}$$

β_m – angle of tooth inclination at middle of face width

$$= \left[1 + \frac{0.5}{k_2} \right] \beta$$

And $\tan \beta \geq \left(\dfrac{\pi m}{v} \right) \left[1 - \dfrac{1}{k_2} \right]$

5.15 POWER TRANSMITTED

The power transmitted is given as $P = \dfrac{F_t \, v}{1000}$ ...**12.91a/ Pg 174, DHB**

5.16 DESIGN METHODOLOGY FOR BEVEL GEARS

There are two methods of designing a bevel gear problem as discussed below.

Method 1: If the pitch diameter is known:

We know that,
$$F_t = \sigma_d C_v bYm \left[\frac{L-b}{L}\right]$$

$$\therefore m = \frac{F_t}{\sigma_d C_v bY}\left[\frac{L}{L-b}\right] \quad \text{...(Eq. 5.35)}$$

Substitute $L = \frac{1}{2}\sqrt{d_1^2 + d_2^2}$ and $b = L/m$ in Eq. (5.35)

$$F_t = \frac{1000 P}{v} \quad \text{...(Eq. 5.36)} \; \textbf{12.91a/ Pg 174, DHB}$$

Method 2: If the pitch diameter is unknown:

We know that,
$$F_t = \sigma_d C_v bYm \left[\frac{L-b}{L}\right]$$

$$\therefore m = \frac{F_t}{\sigma_d C_v bY}\left[\frac{L}{L-b}\right] \quad \text{... same as (5.35)}$$

Substitute $b = L/3$, $\therefore \frac{L}{L-b} = 3/2$ and $F_t = \frac{2M_t}{d} = \frac{2M_t}{mz}$ in Eq. (5.35)

$$\therefore m^2 = \frac{9M_t}{\sigma_d \cdot C_v \cdot Y \cdot z \cdot L} \quad \text{...(Eq. 5.36a)}$$

Substituting $L = \frac{1}{2}\sqrt{d_1^2 + d_2^2} = \frac{m}{2}\sqrt{z_1^2 + z_2^2}$, we have

$$m^3 = \frac{18 M_t}{\sigma_d \cdot C_v \cdot Y \cdot z \cdot \sqrt{z_1^2 + z_2^2}} \quad \text{-or-}$$

$$m = \sqrt[3]{\frac{18 M_t}{\sigma_d \cdot C_v \cdot Y \cdot z \cdot \sqrt{z_1^2 + z_2^2}}} \quad \text{...(Eq. 5.37)}$$

z – refers to number of teeth of weaker member.

Note:

- *When the diameter is unknown the students are advised to remember Eq. (5.37) rather than remembering the steps to get the module.*
- *Unless otherwise stated, it is assumed that then bevel gears have straight teeth and the shafts intersect at right angles.*
- *Standard module of bevel gears.*   ...Table 12.23/ Pg 197, DHB

5.17 DESIGN PROCEDURE FOR BEVEL GEAR PROBLEMS

1. **Material selection:**
   - Select suitable material if not given from **Table 12.7/ Pg 186, DHB**.
   - **Identifying weaker part (pinion/gear):**
     → If the material used for both pinion and gear is same, then the pinion is weaker.
     → If the material used for both pinion and gear are different, then the strength factor is used to determine the weaker part.
   - Design is based on weaker part.

2. **To find module:**

   a. If the diameter is known, use $m = \dfrac{F_t}{\sigma_d C_v bY}\left[\dfrac{L}{L-b}\right]$, where, $F_t = \dfrac{1000\, PC_s}{v}$

   b. If the diameter is unknown, use $m^3 = \dfrac{18 M_t}{\sigma_d \cdot C_v \cdot Y \cdot z \cdot \sqrt{z_1^2 + z_2^2}}$, where, $M_t = \dfrac{F_t d}{2}$

   c. Check for σ_d in both the cases

   d. If $\sigma_d >$ permissible value, design fails. Hence adopt/change the module and repeat (2c).

3. Calculate the dynamic load (F_d).
4. Calculate the endurance limit (F_{en}).

   For safe design, $F_{en} > F_d$

5. Calculate the wear load (F_w)
   - For safe design, $F_w > F_d$
   - If $F_w < F_d$, then equate $F_w = F_d$

   i.e. $d_1 b Q K = F_d$

   Find the value of K and choose suitable material for gear and pinion using **Table 12.16/ Pg 193, DHB**

Note:
- If in the problem, diameter is known and z is unknown, calculate m assuming suitable value of z. After obtaining m, find the value of z again.

1. Two shafts intersect at right angles and connected by a pair of bevel gears of gear ratio 2.5:1. The module for 20° full depth involute teeth at outer radius is 5 mm and the number of teeth on pinion is 30. If 10 kW of power is to be transmitted at 400 rpm of pinion and face width is 67 mm, determine:

   a. tangential force at mean radius   c. axial thrust on pinion
   d. axial thrust on gear.

Solution: $\theta = 90°$, $i = 2.5:1$, $\alpha = 20°$ FDI, $m = 5$ mm, $z_1 = z_p = 30$ teeth, $P = 10$ kW, $N_1 = N_p = 400$ rpm, $b = 67$ mm

a. Axial thrust at mean radius, $F_t = ?$
b. Axial thrust on pinion, $F_r = ?$
c. Axial thrust on gear, $F_a = ?$

To find diameters:

We know that, $d = mz$

Pitch diameter of pinion, $d_1 = mz_1 = 5 \times 30 = 150$ mm

Pitch diameter of gear, $d_2 = mz_2 = m \times (iz_1) = 5 \times (2.5 \times 30) = 375$ mm

a. To find tangential force at mean radius:

We know that, $$F_t = \frac{1000\, P}{v} \qquad \text{...12.91a/ Pg 174, DHB}$$

∴ At mean radius, $$F_{tm} = \frac{1000\, P}{v_m} \qquad \text{...Eq. (i)}$$

But $$v_m = \frac{\pi d_{m_1} N_1}{60} \qquad \text{...Eq. (ii)}$$

And $$d_m = \left(1 - \frac{0.5}{k_2}\right) d \qquad \text{...Eq. (iii) 12.76/ Pg 172, DHB}$$

$$k_2 = L/b \qquad \text{...Eq. (iv)}$$

Cone distance, $$L = \frac{1}{2}\sqrt{d_1^2 + d_2^2} \qquad \text{...12.74/ Pg 172, DHB}$$

$$= \frac{1}{2}\sqrt{150^2 + 375^2}$$

$$L = 202 \text{ mm}$$

∴ Eq. (iv) yields... $$k_2 = \frac{202}{67} = 3.01$$

∴ Eq. (iii) yields... $$d_m = \left(1 - \frac{0.5}{3.01}\right) \times 150 = 125.08 \text{ mm}$$

∴ Eq. (ii) yields... $$v_m = \frac{\pi \times 0.12508 \times 400}{60} = 2.62 \text{ m/s}$$

∴ Eq. (i) yields... $$F_{tm} = \frac{1000 \times 10}{2.62}$$

$$F_{tm} = 3816.8 \text{ N}$$

b. Axial thrust on pinion, $F_r = ?$

We know that, $F_r = F_{te} \tan \alpha \cos \delta_1$ ...12.93/ Pg 175, DHB

But $$F_{te} = \frac{F_t L}{L - 0.5 b} \qquad \text{...12.92/ Pg 175, DHB}$$

$$= \frac{3818.25 \times 202}{202 - (0.5 \times 67)}$$

$$F_{te} = 4575.63 \text{ N}$$

For $\theta = 90°$ $\tan \delta_1 = \left(\dfrac{1}{i}\right)$ ...12.72a/ Pg 172, DHB

$$= \left(\dfrac{1}{2.5}\right)$$

$$\delta_1 = 21.8°$$

$\therefore F_r = 4575.63 \times \tan(20) \cos(21.8)$
$F_r = 1546.28 \text{ N}$

c. Axial thrust on gear, $F_a = ?$

We know that, $F_a = F_{te} \tan \alpha \sin \delta_1$ ...12.94/ Pg 175, DHB
$= 4575.63 \times \tan(20) \sin(21.8)$
$F_a = 618.47 \text{ N}$

2. **A pair of bevel gears transmitting 7.5 kW at 300 rpm of the pinion. The pressure angle is 20°. The pitch diameters of the pinion and gear at their large ends are 150 mm and 200 mm respectively. The face width of the gears is 40 mm. Determine the components of the resultant gear tooth force and draw free body diagram of the forces acting on the pinion and the gear.**

VTU-Dec. 09/Jan. 2010 – 10 Marks; June/July 2013 – 10 Marks

Solution: $P = 7.5$ kW, $N_1 = N_p = 300$ rpm, $\alpha = 20°$, $d_1 = 150$ mm, $d_2 = 200$ mm, $b = 40$ mm. Components of force = ?

a. To find tangential force at mean radius:

We know that, $F_t = \dfrac{1000 P}{v}$ ...Eq. (i) 12.91a/ Pg 174, DHB

But $v = \dfrac{\pi d_1 N_1}{60}$

$v = \dfrac{\pi \times 0.150 \times 300}{60} = 2.36 \text{ m/s}$

$\therefore$ Eq. (i) yields... $F_t = \dfrac{1000 \times 7.5}{2.36}$

$F_t = 3183.10 \text{ N}$

b. Axial thrust on pinion, $F_r = ?$

We know that, $F_r = F_{te} \tan \alpha \cos \delta_1$ ...12.93/ Pg 175, DHB

But $F_{te} = \dfrac{F_t L}{L - 0.5 b}$ ...Eq. (ii) 12.92/ Pg 175, DHB

Also cone distance, $L = \dfrac{1}{2}\sqrt{d_1^2 + d_2^2}$ ...12.74/ Pg 172, DHB

$= \dfrac{1}{2}\sqrt{150^2 + 200^2}$

$L = 125 \text{ mm}$

∴ Eq. (ii) yields... $F_{te} = \dfrac{3183.10 \times 125}{125 - (0.5 \times 40)}$

$F_{te} = 3789.40$ N

For $\theta = 90°$ $\tan \delta_1 = \left(\dfrac{1}{i}\right)$ ...12.72a/ Pg 172, DHB

$= \left(\dfrac{1}{1.33}\right)$

$\delta_1 = 36.87°$

∴ $F_r = 3789.40 \times \tan(20) \cos(36.87)$
$F_r = 1103.38$ N

c. Axial thrust on gear, $F_a = ?$

We know that, $F_a = F_{te} \tan \alpha \sin \delta_1$ ...12.94/ Pg 175, DHB
$= 3789.40 \times \tan(20) \sin(36.87)$
$F_a = 827.54$ N

3. Determine the cone pitch angles and pitch diameters of the following bevel gears:

a. $\theta = 77°$ b. $\theta = 147°$.   Take $m = 5$, $z_1 = 12$ teeth, $z_2 = 42$ teeth

Solution: $m = 5$, $z_1 = 12$ teeth, $z_2 = 42$ teeth

$$i = \dfrac{z_2}{z_1} = \dfrac{42}{12} = 3.5$$

a. $\theta = 77°$ – acute angle.

We know that, for $\theta > 90°$

Pitch angle of pinion, $\tan \delta_1 = \dfrac{\sin \theta}{(i + \cos \theta)}$ ...12.67/ Pg 171, DHB

$= \dfrac{\sin 77}{(3.5 + \cos 77)}$

$\delta_1 = 14.65°$

Pitch angle of gear, $\tan \delta_2 = \dfrac{\sin \theta}{(1/i) + \cos \theta}$ ...12.68/ Pg 171, DHB

$= \dfrac{\sin 77}{\left(\dfrac{1}{3.5}\right) + \cos 77}$

$\delta_2 = 62.34°$

b. $\theta = 147°$ – obtuse angle.

We know that, for $\theta > 90°$

Pitch angle of pinion, $\tan \delta_1 = \dfrac{\sin(180 - \theta)}{i - \cos(180 - \theta)}$ ...12.73a/ Pg 172, DHB

$$= \frac{\sin(180-147)}{3.5 - \cos(180-147)}$$

$$\delta_1 = 11.56°$$

Pitch angle of gear, $\quad \tan \delta_2 = \dfrac{\sin(180-\theta)}{\left(\dfrac{1}{i}\right) - \cos(180-\theta)}$ ...12.73b/ Pg 172, DHB

$$= \frac{\sin(180-147)}{\left(\dfrac{1}{3.5}\right) - \cos(180-147)}$$

$$\delta_2 = -44.56°$$
$$\therefore \quad \delta_2 = -44.56 + 180$$
$$\delta_2 = 135.57°$$

For free body diagram, refer **Fig. 5.5**.

5.18 PROBLEMS BASED ON KNOWN DIAMETER

4. A pair of straight tooth bevel gears at right angles is to transmit 5 kW at 1200 rpm of the pinion. The diameter of the pinion is 80 mm and the velocity ratio is 3.5. The tooth form is 14 ½°. Both the pinion and gear are cast iron with allowable stress of 55 MN/m². Determine the module, face width from the standpoint of strength and also check the design from standpoint of dynamic load and wear.

VTU- June / July – 2008 – 20 Marks; (Similar) May / June 2010 – 20 Marks

Solution: $\theta = 90°$, $P = 5$ kW, pinion speed (driver), $N_p = N_1 = 1200$ rpm, diameter of pinion, $d_p = d_1 = 80$ mm, $i = 3.5$, $\alpha = 14\,½°$, $\sigma_{d1} = \sigma_{d2} = 55$ MN/m² = 55 N/mm². $m = ?$, $b = ?$, $F_w = ?$

We know that, $\quad i = \dfrac{N_1}{N_2} = \dfrac{d_2}{d_1} = \dfrac{z_2}{z_1}$

$$3.5 = \frac{d_2}{d_1} = \frac{d_2}{80}$$

$$d_2 = 280 \text{ mm}$$

Identifying weaker part (pinion/gear):

We know that strength factor = $\sigma_d \cdot y$

Since both pinion and gear are made of same material, the pinion is weaker, i.e. $\sigma_{d_1} \cdot y_1 < \sigma_{d_2} \cdot y_2$

Hence design is based on **pinion**.

- For $\theta = 90°$:

$$\tan \delta_1 = \left(\frac{1}{i}\right) \qquad \text{...12.72a/ Pg 172, DHB}$$

$$= \left(\frac{1}{3.5}\right)$$

$$\delta_1 = 15.95°$$

$$\tan \delta_2 = i \qquad \text{...12.72b/ Pg 172, DHB}$$
$$= 3.5$$
$$\delta_2 = 74.05°$$

- Assume $z_1 = 24$ teeth
- ∴ $z_2 = iz_1 = 3.5 \times 24 = 84$ teeth

- Virtual number of teeth, $z_e = \dfrac{z}{\cos \delta}$ ...12.81/ Pg 173, DHB

for pinion $\quad z_{e1} = \dfrac{z}{\cos \delta_1} = \dfrac{24}{\cos 15.95} = 24.96 \approx 25$

and for gear, $\quad z_{e2} = \dfrac{z_2}{\cos \delta_2} = \dfrac{84}{\cos 74.05} = 305.67$

a. To find module (m):

Since the diameter is known, we have $m = \dfrac{F_t}{\sigma_d\, C_v\, bY}\left[\dfrac{L}{L-b}\right]$

...Eq. (i) **12.85/ Pg 173, DHB**

- $v = \dfrac{\pi d_1 N_1}{60} = \dfrac{\pi \times 0.08 \times 1200}{60} = 5.03 \text{ m/s}$

- For generated teeth, $C_v = \dfrac{6.1}{6.1 + v}$ ...12.86b/ Pg 174, DHB

$$= \dfrac{6.1}{6.1 + 5.03}$$
$$C_v = 0.5482$$

- $F_t = \dfrac{1000 P}{v}$ ...12.91a/ Pg 174, DHB

$$= \dfrac{1000 \times 5}{5.03}$$
$$F_t = 994.04 \text{ N}$$

- Form factor, $\quad Y = \pi y_1$ ...12.16/ Pg 163, DHB

$$= \left[0.124 - \dfrac{0.684}{z_{e1}}\right] \qquad \text{...12.17a/ Pg 163, DHB}$$

$$= \pi\left[0.124 - \dfrac{0.684}{25}\right]$$

$$Y = 0.3036$$

- Cone distance, $\quad L = \dfrac{1}{2}\sqrt{d_1^2 + d_2^2}$ ...12.74/ Pg 172, DHB

$$= \dfrac{1}{2}\sqrt{80^2 + 280^2}$$

$L = 145.6$ mm

- Face width, $\quad b = \dfrac{L}{3} \quad$ ...**12.83b/ Pg 173, DHB**

$$= \dfrac{145.6}{3}$$

$$b = 48.53 \text{ mm} \approx 50 \text{ mm}$$

∴ Eq. (*i*) yields... $\quad m = \dfrac{994.04}{55 \times 0.5482 \times 50 \times 0.3036}\left[\dfrac{145.6}{145.6 - 50}\right]$

$$m = 3.31 \text{ mm}$$

Therefore, standard module, $m = 4$ mm $\quad$ ...**Tb. 12.23/ Pg 197, DHB**

∴ Number of teeth on pinion, $z_1 = \dfrac{d_1}{m} = \dfrac{80}{4} = 20$ teeth

Number of teeth on gear, $\quad z_2 = \dfrac{d_2}{m} = \dfrac{280}{4} = 70$ teeth

- Virtual number of teeth, $z_e = \dfrac{z}{\cos \delta} \quad$ ...**12.81/ Pg 173, DHB**

$$z_{e1} = \dfrac{z_1}{\cos \delta_1} = \dfrac{20}{\cos 15.95} = 20.80$$

and $\quad z_{e2} = \dfrac{z_2}{\cos \delta_2} = \dfrac{70}{\cos 74.05} = 254.73$

- Face width, $b = 50$ mm
- Check for σ_{d_1}:

We know that, $\quad \sigma_d = \dfrac{F_t}{mC_v bY}\left[\dfrac{L}{L-b}\right] \quad$ ...Eq. (*ii*) **12.85/ Pg 173, DHB**

Here, $Y = \pi y_1 \quad$ ...**12.16/ Pg 163, DHB**

$$= \pi\left[0.124 - \dfrac{0.684}{z_{e1}}\right] \quad \text{...}\textbf{12.17a/ Pg 163, DHB}$$

$$= \pi\left[0.124 - \dfrac{0.684}{20.80}\right]$$

$$Y = 0.2862$$

∴ Eq. (*ii*) yields... $\quad \sigma_{d1} = \dfrac{994.04}{4 \times 0.5482 \times 50 \times 0.2862}\left[\dfrac{145.6}{145.6 - 50}\right]$

$$\sigma_{d1} = 48.25 \text{ MPa} < 55 \text{ MPa} \quad \text{...hence safe.}$$

Since calculated values are < permissible values, the assumed values are satisfactory.

b. To find face width(b): $\quad b = 50$ mm

c. To find dynamic tooth load (F_d):

We know that,
$$F_d = F_t + \frac{K_3 v (Cb + F_t)}{K_3 v + \sqrt{Cb + F_t}} \quad \text{...Eq. (iii) 12.88/ Pg 174, DHB}$$

here $K_3 = 20.67$

@ $v = 5$ m/s	Error, $e = 0.0640$ mm	...Tb. 12.14/ Pg 191, DHB
For $\alpha = 14.5°$ system and CI – CI combination		
@ $e = 0.06$ mm	$C = 331.3$ N/mm	...Tb. 12.12/ Pg 190, DHB
$e = 0.0640$ mm	$C = ?$	

$\therefore$ at $v = 5.03$ m/s, $C = \dfrac{0.064 \times 331.3}{0.06} = 353.39$ N/mm

$\therefore$ Eq. (iii) yields...
$$F_d = 994.04 + \frac{(20.67 \times 5.03) \times [(353.39 \times 50) + 994.04]}{(20.67 \times 5.03) + \sqrt{[(353.39 \times 50) + 994.04]}}$$

$$F_d = 9060 \text{ N}$$

d. To find wear load (F_w):

We know that,
$$F_w = \frac{d_1 b Q_e K}{\cos \delta_1} \quad \text{...Eq. (iv) 12.89/ Pg 174, DHB}$$

- Diameter of pinion, $\delta_1 = 80$ mm

- Ratio factor,
$$Q_e = \frac{2 z_{e_2}}{z_{e_2} + z_{e_1}} \quad \text{...12.89/ Pg 174, DHB}$$

$$= \frac{2 \times 254.73}{254.73 + 20.80}$$

$$Q = 1.849$$

- Since BHN is unknown, referring to the material of the weaker part i.e. CI pinion whose value of $\sigma_d \leq 55$ MPa, we have BHN = 220
  ...Tb.12.7/ Pg 186, DHB
- @ BHN = 220, σ_{en} value is not available in the **Tb.12.15/ Pg 192, DHB**.
- Referring to **Tb 12.16/ Pg 193, DHB**, the value of BHN for CI is 180 (maximum).
- For $\alpha = 14.5°$ and CI – CI combination of $BHN_1 = BHN_2 = 180$, we have
$$\sigma_{en} = 617.8 \text{ MPa and } K = 1.324 \quad \text{...Tb.12.16/ Pg 193, DHB}$$

$\therefore$ Eq. (iv) yields...
$$F_w = \frac{80 \times 50 \times 1.849 \times 1.324}{\cos 15.95}$$

$$F_w = 10.18 \text{ kN}$$

For safety against wear, $F_w \geq F_d$
i.e. $\qquad$ 10.18 kN $\geq$ 9.06 kN $\qquad$ ...hence safe.

5. A pair of straight bevel gears transmits 15 kW at 1250 rpm of 120 mm diameter pinion. The speed reduction is 3.5. Use 14.5° involute tooth system. The angle between the shaft axes is 90°. The pinion is made of case hardened alloy steel

with allowable static stress of 343.34 MPa and gear is cast steel of 0.20%C heat treated with allowable static stress of 191.295 MPa. Determine module, face width, number of teeth on pinion and gear. Suggest suitable surface hardness for the gear pair. Take the service factor as 1.5 and assume the teeth are generated.   *VTU- Dec. 06/ Jan.07 – 17 Marks*

Solution: $P = 15$ kW, pinion speed, $N_1 = 1250$ rpm, diameter of pinion, $d_1 = 120$ mm, $i = 3.5$, $\alpha = 14\frac{1}{2}°$, $\theta = 90°$, $\sigma_{d1} = 343.34$ MPa, $\sigma_{d2} = 191.295$ MPa, $m = ?, b = ?, z_1, z_2 = ?$, $BHN = ?, C_s = 1.5$.

We know that,
$$i = \frac{N_1}{N_2} = \frac{d_2}{d_1} = \frac{z_2}{z_1}$$

$$3.5 = \frac{d_2}{d_1} = \frac{d_2}{120}$$

$d_2 = 420$ mm and $N_2 = N_1/i = 1250/3.5 = 357.14$ rpm

Identifying weaker part (pinion/gear):

We know that strength factor $= \sigma_d \cdot y$
- For $\theta = 90°$:

$$\tan \delta_1 = \left(\frac{1}{i}\right) \qquad \text{...12.72a/ Pg 172, DHB}$$

$$= \left(\frac{1}{3.5}\right)$$

$\delta_1 = 15.95°$

$\tan \delta_2 = i \qquad \text{...12.72b/ Pg 172, DHB}$
$\quad = 3.5$
$\delta_2 = 74.05°$

- Assume $z_1 = 24$ teeth
∴ $z_2 = iz_1 = 3.5 \times 24 = 84$ teeth

- Virtual number of teeth, $z_e = \dfrac{z}{\cos \delta} \qquad \text{...12.81/ Pg 173, DHB}$

for pinion $\quad z_{e1} = \dfrac{z_1}{\cos \delta_1} = \dfrac{24}{\cos 15.95} = 24.96 \approx 25$

and for gear, $\quad z_{e2} = \dfrac{z_2}{\cos \delta_2} = \dfrac{84}{\cos 74.05} = 305.67$

- For $\alpha = 14.5°$ involute system, $y = 0.124 - \dfrac{0.684}{z_e} \qquad \text{...12.17a/ Pg 163, DHB}$

i.e. $\quad y_1 = 0.124 - \dfrac{0.684}{z_{e1}}$

$$y_1 = 0.124 - \dfrac{0.684}{25} = 0.0966$$

$$y_2 = 0.124 - \frac{0.684}{305.67} = 0.1218$$

∴ for pinion, $\sigma_{d1} \cdot y_1 = 343.34 \times 0.0966 = 33.17$ MPa

for gear, $\sigma_{d2} \cdot y_2 = 191.295 \times 0.1218 = 23.29$ MPa

Since $\sigma_{d2} \cdot y_2$ is less, design is based on **gear**.

a. To find module (m):

Since the diameter is known, we have $m = \dfrac{F_t}{\sigma_d C_v bY}\left[\dfrac{L}{L-b}\right]$

...Eq. (i) **12.85/ Pg 173, DHB**

- $v = \dfrac{\pi d_2 N_2}{60} = \dfrac{\pi \times 0.420 \times 357.14}{60} = 7.85$ m/s

- For generated teeth, $C_v = \dfrac{6.1}{6.1+v}$ ...**12.86b/ Pg 174, DHB**

$$= \dfrac{6.1}{6.1+7.85}$$

$$C_v = 0.4372$$

- $F_t = \dfrac{1000P}{v} \times C_s$ ...**12.91a/ Pg 174, DHB**

$$= \dfrac{1000 \times 15}{7.85} \times 1.5$$

$F_t = 2866.24$ N

- Form factor, $Y = \pi y$ ...**12.16/ Pg 163, DHB**

$= \pi \times y_2$

$= \pi \times 0.1218$

$Y = 0.3826$

- Cone distance, $L = \dfrac{1}{2}\sqrt{d_1^2 + d_2^2}$ ...**12.74/ Pg 172, DHB**

$$= \dfrac{1}{2}\sqrt{120^2 + 420^2}$$

$L = 218.4$ mm

- Face width, $b = \dfrac{L}{3}$ ...**12.83b/ Pg 173, DHB**

$$= \dfrac{218.4}{3}$$

$b = 72.8$ mm ≈ 75 mm

∴ Eq. (i) yields... $m = \dfrac{2866.24}{191.295 \times 0.4372 \times 75 \times 0.3826}\left[\dfrac{218.4}{218.4 - 75}\right]$

$$m = 1.82 \text{ mm}$$
Therefore, standard module, $m = 2$ mm ...Tb. 12.23/ Pg 197, DHB

∴ Number of teeth on pinion, $z_1 = \dfrac{d_1}{m} = \dfrac{120}{2} = 60$ teeth

Number of teeth on gear, $z_2 = \dfrac{d_2}{m} = \dfrac{420}{2} = 210$ teeth

- Virtual number of teeth, $z_e = \dfrac{z}{\cos \delta}$ ...12.81/ Pg 173, DHB

$$z_{e1} = \dfrac{z_1}{\cos \delta_1} = \dfrac{60}{\cos 15.95} = 62.40$$

and $\quad z_{e2} = \dfrac{z_2}{\cos \delta_2} = \dfrac{210}{\cos 74.05} = 764.2$

- Face width, $b = 75$ mm
- Check for σ_{d2}:

We know that, $\quad \sigma_d = \dfrac{F_t}{mC_v bY}\left[\dfrac{L}{L-b}\right]$ ...Eq.(ii) 12.85/ Pg 173, DHB

- Here $\quad Y = \pi y_1$ ...12.16/ Pg 163, DHB

$$= \pi\left[0.124 - \dfrac{0.684}{z_{e2}}\right]$$ ...12.17a/ Pg 163, DHB

$$= \pi\left[0.124 - \dfrac{0.684}{764.2}\right]$$

$$Y = 0.3867$$

∴ Eq. (ii) yields... $\quad \sigma_{d2} = \dfrac{2866.24}{2 \times 0.4372 \times 75 \times 0.3867}\left[\dfrac{218.4}{218.4-75}\right]$

$\sigma_{d2} = 172.14$ MPa < 191.295 MPa ...hence safe.

Since calculated values are < permissible values, the assumed values are satisfactory.

b. To find face width (b): $\quad b = 75$ mm

c. To find dynamic tooth load (F_d):

We know that, $\quad F_d = F_t + \dfrac{K_3 v(Cb + F_t)}{K_3 v + \sqrt{Cb + F_t}}$ ...Eq. (iii) 12.88/ Pg 174, DHB

here $\quad K_3 = 20.67$

@ $v = 6$ m/s	Error, $e = 0.0590$ mm	...Tb. 12.14/ Pg 191, DHB
For $\alpha = 14.5°$ system and steel – steel combination		
@ $e = 0.04$ mm	$C = 441.3$ N/mm	...Tb. 12.12/ Pg 190, DHB
$e = 0.0590$ mm	$C = ?$	

∴ at $v = 7.85$ m/s, $C = \dfrac{0.059 \times 441.3}{0.04} = 650.92$ N/mm

∴ Eq. (*iii*) yields... $F_d = 2866.24 + \dfrac{(20.67 \times 7.85) \times [(650.92 \times 75) + 2866.24]}{(20.67 \times 7.85) + \sqrt{[(650.92 \times 75) + 2866.24]}}$

$F_d = 24.39$ kN

d. To find BHN:

We know that, $F_w = \dfrac{d_1 b Q_e K}{\cos \delta_1}$ ...Eq. (*iv*) **12.89/ Pg 174, DHB**

- Diameter of pinion, $d_1 = 120$ mm

- Ratio factor, $Q_e = \dfrac{2 z_{e_2}}{z_{e_2} + z_{e_1}}$ ...**12.89/ Pg 174, DHB**

$= \dfrac{2 \times 764.2}{764.2 + 62.40}$

$Q = 1.849$

For safety against wear, $F_w \geq F_d$

∴ Eq. (*iv*) yields... $\dfrac{120 \times 75 \times 1.849 \times K}{\cos 15.95} \geq 24.39$

$K \geq \dfrac{24.39 \times 10^3 \times \cos 15.95}{120 \times 75 \times 1.849}$

$K \geq 1.409$

Therefore, for steel – steel combination, having $\alpha = 14.5°$ and $K \geq 1.409$, we have
BHN of pinion = 400,   BHN of gear = 350   ...**Tb. 12.16/ Pg 193, DHB**

6. A pair of straight tooth bevel gears at right angles is to transmit 5 kW at 1500 rpm of the pinion at a speed ratio of 3. Diameter of pinion is 75 mm. The tooth form is 14 ½° involute. Pinion is made of steel ($\sigma_d = 160$ MPa) and gear of CI ($\sigma_d = 80$ MPa). Design the gear pair and check the design for dynamic load wear.

VTU- May/ June 2010 – 17 Marks

Solution: $\theta = 90°$, $P = 5$ kW, pinion speed, $N_1 = 1500$ rpm, $i = 3$, diameter of pinion, $d_1 = 75$ mm, $\alpha = 14.5°$.

Material properties:

Pinion: steel: $\sigma_{d1} = 160$ MPa
Gear: CI: $\sigma_{d2} = 80$ MPa

We know that, $i = \dfrac{N_1}{N_2} = \dfrac{d_2}{d_1} = \dfrac{z_2}{z_1}$

$3 = \dfrac{d_2}{d_1} = \dfrac{d_2}{75}$

∴ $d_2 = 225$ mm

And $N_2 = N_1/i = 1500/3 = 500$ rpm

Identifying weaker part (pinion/gear):

We know that strength factor $\sigma_d \cdot y$

- For $\theta = 90°$:

$$\tan \delta_1 = \left(\frac{1}{i}\right) \quad \text{...12.72a/ Pg 172, DHB}$$

$$= \left(\frac{1}{3}\right)$$

$$\delta_1 = 18.43°$$

$$\tan \delta_2 = i \quad \text{...12.72b/ Pg 172, DHB}$$

$$= 3$$

$$\delta_2 = 71.57°$$

- Assume $z_1 = 24$ teeth
- $\therefore$ $z_2 = iz_1 = 3 \times 24 = 72$ teeth

- Virtual number of teeth, $z_e = \dfrac{z}{\cos \delta}$ ...12.81/ Pg 173, DHB

for pinion, $z_{e1} = \dfrac{z_1}{\cos \delta_1} = \dfrac{24}{\cos 18.43} = 25.30$

and for gear, $z_{e2} = \dfrac{z_2}{\cos \delta_2} = \dfrac{72}{\cos 71.57} = 227.74$

- For $\alpha = 14.5°$ involute, $y = 0.124 - \dfrac{0.684}{z_e}$ ...12.17a/ Pg 163, DHB

i.e. $y_1 = 0.124 - \dfrac{0.684}{z_{e1}}$

$y_1 = 0.124 - \dfrac{0.684}{25.30} = 0.0969$

$y_2 = 0.124 - \dfrac{0.684}{227.74} = 0.1210$

$\therefore$ for pinion, $\sigma_{d1} \cdot y_1 = 160 \times 0.0969 = 15.50$ MPa

for gear, $\sigma_{d2} \cdot y_2 = 80 \times 0.1210 = 9.68$ MPa

Since $\sigma_{d2} \cdot y_2$ is less design is based on **gear**.

a. To find module (m):

Since the diameter is known, we have $m = \dfrac{F_t}{\sigma_d C_v bY} \left[\dfrac{L}{L-b}\right]$

...Eq. (i) 12.85/ Pg 173, DHB

- $v = \dfrac{\pi d_2 N_2}{60} = \dfrac{\pi \times 0.225 \times 500}{60} = 5.89$ m/s

- For generated teeth, $C_v = \dfrac{6.1}{6.1+v}$ ...12.86b/ Pg 174, DHB

$$= \dfrac{6.1}{6.1+5.89}$$
$$C_v = 0.5087$$

- $F_t = \dfrac{1000\,P}{v}$ ...12.91a/ Pg 174, DHB

$$= \dfrac{1000 \times 5}{5.89}$$
$$F_t = 848.90 \text{ N}$$

- Form factor, $Y = \pi y$ ...12.16/ Pg 163, DHB
$$= \pi \times y_2$$
$$= \pi \times 0.1210$$
$$Y = 0.3801$$

- Cone distance, $L = \dfrac{1}{2}\sqrt{d_1^2 + d_2^2}$ ...12.74/ Pg 172, DHB

$$= \dfrac{1}{2}\sqrt{75^2 + 225^2}$$
$$L = 118.58 \text{ mm}$$

- Face width, $b = \dfrac{L}{3}$ ...12.83b/ Pg 173, DHB

$$= \dfrac{118.58}{3}$$
$$b = 39.53 \text{ mm} \approx 40 \text{ mm}$$

∴ Eq. (i) yields...
$$m = \dfrac{848.90}{80 \times 0.5087 \times 40 \times 0.3801}\left[\dfrac{118.58}{118.58 - 40}\right]$$
$$m = 2.07 \text{ mm}$$

Therefore, standard module, $m = 2.5$ mm ...Tb. 12.23/ Pg 197, DHB

∴ Number of teeth on pinion, $z_1 = \dfrac{d_1}{m} = \dfrac{75}{2.5} = 30$ teeth

Number of teeth on gear, $z_2 = \dfrac{d_2}{m} = \dfrac{225}{2.5} = 90$ teeth

- Virtual number of teeth, $z_e = \dfrac{z}{\cos \delta}$ ...12.81/ Pg 173, DHB

for pinion, $z_{e1} = \dfrac{z_1}{\cos \delta_1} = \dfrac{30}{\cos 18.43} = 31.62$

and for gear, $z_{e2} = \dfrac{z_2}{\cos \delta_2} = \dfrac{90}{\cos 71.57} = 284.68$

- Face width, $b = 40$ mm
- Check for σ_{d2}:

We know that, $\sigma_d = \dfrac{F_t}{mC_v bY}\left[\dfrac{L}{L-b}\right]$ ...using Eq. (i) **12.85/ Pg 173, DHB**

- Here $Y = \pi y_2$ ...**12.16/ Pg 163, DHB**

$= \pi\left[0.124 - \dfrac{0.684}{z_{e2}}\right]$ ...**12.17a/ Pg 163, DHB**

$= \pi\left[0.124 - \dfrac{0.684}{284.68}\right]$

$Y = 0.3820$

∴ Eq. (i) yields... $\sigma_{d2} = \dfrac{848.90}{2.5 \times 0.5087 \times 40 \times 0.3820}\left[\dfrac{118.58}{118.58 - 40}\right]$

$\sigma_{d2} = 66$ MPa < 80 MPa ...hence safe.

Since calculated values are < permissible values, the assumed values are satisfactory.

b. To find face width (b): $b = 40$ mm

c. To find dynamic tooth load (F_d):

We know that, $F_d = F_t + \dfrac{K_3 v(Cb + F_t)}{K_3 v + \sqrt{Cb + F_t}}$ ...Eq. (ii) **12.88/ Pg 174, DHB**

here $K_3 = 20.67$

@ $v = 5$ m/s	Error, $e = 0.0640$ mm	...Tb. **12.14/ Pg 191, DHB**
For $\alpha = 14.5°$ system and steel – CI combination		
@ $e = 0.06$ mm	$C = 454.8$ N/mm	...Tb. **12.12/ Pg 190, DHB**
$e = 0.0640$ mm	$C = ?$	

∴ at $v = 5.89$ m/s, $C = \dfrac{0.064 \times 454.8}{0.06} = 485.12$ N/mm

∴ Eq. (ii) yields... $F_d = 848.90 + \dfrac{(20.67 \times 5.89) \times [(485.12 \times 40) + 848.90]}{(20.67 \times 5.89) + \sqrt{[(485.12 \times 40) + 848.90]}}$

$F_d = 10.19$ kN

d. To find wear load (F_w):

We know that, $F_w = \dfrac{d_1 b Q_e K}{\cos \delta_1}$ ...Eq. (iii) **12.89/ Pg 174, DHB**

- Diameter of pinion, $d_1 = 75$ mm

- Ratio factor, $Q_e = \dfrac{2 z_{e_2}}{z_{e_2} + z_{e_1}}$ ...**12.89/ Pg 174, DHB**

$= \dfrac{2 \times 284.68}{284.68 + 31.62}$

$$Q = 1.800$$

For safety against wear, $F_w \geq F_d$

∴ Eq. (iii) yields... $\dfrac{75 \times 40 \times 1.80 \times K}{\cos 18.43} \geq 10.19 \times 10^3$

$$K \geq \dfrac{10.19 \times 10^3 \times \cos 18.43}{75 \times 40 \times 1.80}$$

$$K \geq 1.7902$$

7. **A pump is driven by a 30 kW motor through a pair of right angled bevel gears. The speed of the motor is 1200 rpm. The pinion of the motor has a pitch circle diameter of 150 mm and carries 30 teeth and the gear on the pump shaft carries 40 teeth. The pinion is made of C45 steel untreated whereas the gear is made of 0.2% cast steel untreated. The teeth are generated to have 20° full depth involute. Check whether the gear pair is safe from standpoint of bending strength.**

   VTU- Dec. 11 – 16 Marks; Dec. 10 - 14 Marks; Jan. / Feb. 2005 - 14 Marks

Solution: $P = 30$ kW, $\theta = 90°$, pinion speed, $N_1 = 1200$ rpm, diameter of pinion, $d_1 = 150$ mm, number of teeth on pinion, $z_1 = 30$, number of teeth on gear, $z_2 = 40$, $\alpha = 20°$.

We know that, $\quad i = \dfrac{N_1}{N_2} = \dfrac{d_2}{d_1} = \dfrac{z_2}{z_1}$

$$i = \dfrac{z_2}{z_1} = \dfrac{40}{30}$$

∴ $\quad i = 1.33$

And $\quad d_2 = i d_1 = 1.33 \times 150 = 200$ mm

$\quad N_2 = N_1 / i = 1200 / 1.33 = 900$ rpm

Material properties

Pinion: steel – C45 untreated: $\quad \sigma_{d1} = 233.4$ MPa, $BHN_1 = 200$
Gear: 0.2% Cast steel, untreated: $\sigma_{d2} = 138.3$ MPa, $BHN_2 = 180$

...**Tb. 12.7/ Pg 186, DHB**

Identifying weaker part (pinion/gear):

We know that strength factor $= \sigma_d \cdot y$
- For $\theta = 90°$:

$$\tan \delta_1 = \left(\dfrac{1}{i}\right) \qquad \text{...12.72a/ Pg 172, DHB}$$

$$= \left(\dfrac{1}{1.33}\right)$$

$$\delta_1 = 36.86°$$

$$\tan \delta_2 = i \qquad \text{...12.72b/ Pg 172, DHB}$$

$$= 1.33$$

$$\delta_2 = 53.13°$$

- Virtual number of teeth, $z_e = \dfrac{z}{\cos \delta}$ ...12.81/ Pg 173, DHB

  for pinion, $z_{e1} = \dfrac{z_1}{\cos \delta_1} = \dfrac{30}{\cos 36.86} = 37.49$

  and for gear, $z_{e2} = \dfrac{z_2}{\cos \delta_2} = \dfrac{40}{\cos 53.13} = 66.67$

- For $\alpha = 20°$ FDI tooth, $y = 0.154 - \dfrac{0.912}{z_e}$ ...12.17b/ Pg 163, DHB

  i.e. $y_1 = 0.154 - \dfrac{0.912}{z_{e1}}$

  $y_1 = 0.154 - \dfrac{0.912}{37.49} = 0.1297$

  $y_2 = 0.154 - \dfrac{0.912}{66.67} = 0.1403$

∴ for pinion, $\sigma_{d1} \cdot y_1 = 233.4 \times 0.1297 = 30.27$ MPa
  for gear, $\sigma_{d2} \cdot y_2 = 138.3 \times 0.1403 = 19.41$ MPa

Since $\sigma_{d2} \cdot y_2$ is less, design is based on **gear**.

a. To find module (m):

Since the diameter is known, we have $m = \dfrac{F_t}{\sigma_d C_v b Y} \left[\dfrac{L}{L-b} \right]$

...Eq. (i) 12.85/ Pg 173, DHB

- $v = \dfrac{\pi d_2 N_2}{60} = \dfrac{\pi \times 0.2 \times 900}{60} = 9.43$ m/s

- For generated teeth, $C_v = \dfrac{6.1}{6.1 + v}$ ...12.86b/ Pg 174, DHB

  $= \dfrac{6.1}{6.1 + 9.43}$

  $C_v = 0.3928$

- $F_t = \dfrac{1000 P}{v}$ ...12.91a/ Pg 174, DHB

  $= \dfrac{1000 \times 30}{9.43}$

  $F_t = 3181.34$ N

- Form factor, $Y = \pi y$ ...12.16/ Pg 163, DHB

  $= \pi \times y_2$

  $= \pi \times 0.1403$

$Y = 0.4408$

- Cone distance, $\quad L = \dfrac{1}{2}\sqrt{d_1^2 + d_2^2} \qquad$ ...12.74/ Pg 172, DHB

$$= \dfrac{1}{2}\sqrt{150^2 + 200^2}$$

$L = 125$ mm

- Face width, $\quad b = \dfrac{L}{3} \qquad$ ...12.83b/ Pg 173, DHB

$$= \dfrac{125}{3}$$

$b = 41.67$ mm ≈ 40 mm

∴ Eq. (i) yields... $\quad m = \dfrac{3181.34}{138.3 \times 0.3928 \times 40 \times 0.4408}\left[\dfrac{125}{125 - 40}\right]$

$m = 4.88$ mm

Therefore, standard module, $m = 5$ mm $\qquad$ ...Tb. 12.23/ Pg 197, DHB

∴ Number of teeth on pinion, $z_1 = \dfrac{d_1}{m} = \dfrac{150}{5} = 30$ teeth

...(same as that given in data)

Number of teeth on gear, $z_2 = \dfrac{d_2}{m} = \dfrac{200}{5} = 40$ teeth

...(same as that given in data)

- Virtual number of teeth, $z_e = \dfrac{z}{\cos \delta} \qquad$ ...12.81/ Pg 173, DHB

for pinion $\quad z_{e1} = \dfrac{z_1}{\cos \delta_1} = \dfrac{30}{\cos 36.86} = 37.49$

and for gear, $\quad z_{e2} = \dfrac{z_2}{\cos \delta_2} = \dfrac{40}{\cos 53.13} = 66.67 \quad$ ...(as calculated earlier)

- Face width, $\quad b = 40$ mm
- Check for σ_{d2}:

We know that, $\quad \sigma_d = \dfrac{F_t}{mC_v bY}\left[\dfrac{L}{L-b}\right] \qquad$ ...12.85/ Pg 173, DHB

$$= \dfrac{3181.34}{5 \times 0.3928 \times 40 \times 0.4408}\left[\dfrac{125}{125 - 40}\right]$$

$\sigma_{d2} = 135.1$ MPa < 138.3 MPa $\qquad$ ...hence safe.

Since calculated values are < permissible values, the values given in data is satisfactory.

b. Check for bending strength:

According to Dobrovolsky, the allowable bending stress is given as

$$\sigma = \frac{k_2^2 M_t K_c K_d \left(\sqrt{i^2 + 1}\right)}{m i Y (k_2 - 0.5)^2 L^2 \cos \alpha} \leq \sigma_d \qquad \ldots \text{12.90/ Pg 174, DHB}$$

Where,

- $k_2 = \dfrac{L}{b} = \dfrac{125}{40} = 3.125$

- $P = \dfrac{2\pi N_2 M_t}{60}$

$$30 \times 10^3 = \frac{2\pi \times 900 \times M_t}{60}$$

$$M_t = 318.3 \text{ N-m} = 318.3 \times 10^3 \text{ N-mm}$$

-or-

$$M_t = \frac{F_t d}{2} \qquad \ldots \text{12.22/ Pg 165, DHB}$$

$$= \frac{3181.34 \times 200}{2}$$

$$M_t = 318.3 \times 10^3 \text{ N-mm}$$

- K_c – Load concentration factor- based on b/d

Now $\quad \dfrac{b}{d} = \dfrac{40}{200} = 0.2$

For $\quad b/d = 0.2$, $K_c = 1.19$, assuming cantilever. $\quad$ ...Tb. 12.10/ Pg 189, DHB

- K_d – Dynamic load factor = 1.4 $\qquad$ ...Tb. 12.11/ Pg 189, DHB

$$\therefore \quad \sigma = \frac{3.125^2 \times 318.3 \times 10^3 \times 1.19 \times 1.4 \times \left(\sqrt{1.33^2 + 1}\right)}{5 \times 1.33 \times 0.4408 \times (3.125 - 0.5)^2 \times 125^2 \times \cos 20}$$

$$\sigma = 29.06 \text{ MPa} < 138.3 \text{ MPa} \qquad \ldots \text{hence safe.}$$

8. **A pair of meter gears having pitch diameter 280 mm and face width of 36 mm run at 250 rpm. The teeth are 14½° involute and accurately cut and transmit 6 kW. Neglect friction angle, find the following:**
   i. **Outside diameter the gears**
   ii. **Resultant tooth load tangent to pitch cone**
   iii. **Resultant radial load on the bearings and**
   iv. **Resultant thrust on shafts.**

   VTU- July/ Aug. 2003 – 20 Marks

Solution: Meter gears $\Rightarrow z_1 = z_2$, $d_1 = d_2$; $N_1 = N_2$; $i = 1.$, $d_1 = d_2 = 280$ mm, $b = 36$ mm, $N_1 = N_2 = 250$ rpm, $P = 6$ kW.

a. Outside diameter of gears, d_{01}, $d_{02} = ?$
b. Resultant/ Effective tooth load, $F_{te} = ?$

c. Resultant radial load on bearings, $F_r = ?$
d. Resultant thrust on shafts, $F_a = ?$

Material properties

Since the material is not specified, let us assume that both pinion and gear are made of same material.
i.e. steel, C30 heat treated $\sigma_{d1} = \sigma_{d2} = 220.6$ MPa and $BHN_1 = BHN_2 = 300$
...Tb. 12.7/ Pg 186, DHB

Identifying weaker part (pinion/gear):

We know that strength factor $= \sigma_d \cdot y$

Since both pinion and gear are made of same material, the pinion is weaker, i.e. $\sigma_{d1} \cdot y_1 < \sigma_{d2} \cdot y_2$

Hence design is based on **pinion**.

- For $\theta = 90°$:

$$\tan \delta_1 = \left(\frac{1}{i}\right) \qquad ...12.72a/ \text{ Pg 172, DHB}$$

$$= \left(\frac{1}{1}\right)$$

$$\delta_1 = 45°$$
$$= 1 \qquad ...12.72b/ \text{ Pg 172, DHB}$$
$$\delta_2 = 45°$$

- Assume $\quad z_1 = 24$ teeth
  ∴ $\quad z_2 = iz_1 = 1 \times 24 = 24$ teeth

- Virtual number of teeth, $z_e = \dfrac{z}{\cos \delta}$ \qquad ...12.81/ Pg 173, DHB

  for pinion $\quad z_{e1} = \dfrac{z_1}{\cos \delta_1} = \dfrac{24}{\cos 45} = 34$

  and for gear, $\quad z_{e2} = 34$

To find module (m):

Since the diameter is known, we have $m = \dfrac{F_t}{\sigma_d C_v b Y}\left[\dfrac{L}{L-b}\right]$

...Eq. (i) ...12.85/ Pg 173, DHB

- $v = \dfrac{\pi d_1 N_1}{60} = \dfrac{\pi \times 0.28 \times 250}{60} = 3.67$ m/s

- For generated teeth, $C_v = \dfrac{6.1}{6.1 + v}$ \qquad ...12.86b/ Pg 174, DHB

  $= \dfrac{6.1}{6.1 + 3.67}$

  $C_v = 0.6244$

- $F_t = \dfrac{1000P}{v}$ ...12.91a/ Pg 174, DHB

  $= \dfrac{1000 \times 6}{3.67}$

  $F_t = 1634.88$ N

- Form factor, $\quad Y = \pi y_1$ ...12.16/ Pg 163, DHB

  $\quad\quad\quad\quad\quad = \pi\left[0.214 - \dfrac{0.684}{z_{e1}}\right]$ ...12.17a/ Pg 163, DHB

  $\quad\quad\quad\quad\quad = \pi\left[0.214 - \dfrac{0.684}{34}\right]$

  $\quad\quad\quad\quad\quad Y = 0.3264$

- Cone distance, $\quad L = \dfrac{1}{2}\sqrt{d_1^2 + d_2^2}$ ...12.74/ Pg 172, DHB

  $\quad\quad\quad\quad\quad = \dfrac{1}{2}\sqrt{280^2 + 280^2}$

  $\quad\quad\quad\quad\quad L = 198$ mm

- Face width, $\quad b = 36$ mm (data)

∴ Eq. (*i*) yields... $\quad m = \dfrac{1634.88}{220.6 \times 0.6244 \times 36 \times 0.3264}\left[\dfrac{198}{198-36}\right]$

$\quad\quad\quad\quad\quad\quad\quad m = 1.24$ mm

Therefore, standard module, $m = 2$ mm ...Tb. 12.23/ Pg 197, DHB

∴ Number of teeth on pinion, $z_1 = \dfrac{d_1}{m} = \dfrac{280}{2} = 140$ teeth

Number of teeth on gear, $z_2 = \dfrac{d_2}{m} = \dfrac{280}{2} = 140$ teeth

- Virtual number of teeth, $z_e = \dfrac{z}{\cos \delta}$ ...12.81/ Pg 173, DHB

  $z_{e1} = z_{e2} = \dfrac{z_1}{\cos \delta_1} = \dfrac{140}{\cos 15.9545} = 198$

- Check for σ_{d1}:

  We know that, $\quad \sigma_d = \dfrac{F_t}{mCvbY}\left[\dfrac{L}{L-b}\right]$ ...Eq. (*ii*) 12.85/ Pg 173, DHB

- Here $\quad Y = \pi y_1$ ...12.16/ Pg 163, DHB

  $\quad\quad\quad = \pi\left[0.124 - \dfrac{0.684}{z_{e2}}\right]$ ...12.17a/ Pg 163, DHB

$$= \pi\left[0.124 - \frac{0.684}{198}\right]$$

$$Y = 0.3787$$

∴ Eq.(*ii*) yields... $\quad \sigma_{d1} = \dfrac{1634.88}{2 \times 0.6244 \times 36 \times 0.3787}\left[\dfrac{198}{198-36}\right]$

$$\sigma_{d1} = 117.37 \text{ MPa} < 191.295 \text{ MPa} \qquad \text{...hence safe.}$$

Since calculated values are < permissible values, the assumed values are satisfactory.

a. Outside diameter of gears, d_{01}, d_{02}:

Since the diameters are same, therefore outside diameters of gears is

$$d_{01} = d_1 + 2h_{a1}\tan\delta_1 \qquad \text{...12.71a/ Pg 172, DHB}$$

But addendum, $\quad h_a = m = 2$ mm $\qquad$ ...Tb. 12.22/ Pg 196, DHB

∴ $\qquad d_{01} = 280 + (2 \times 2 \times \tan 45)$

$$d_{01} = d_{02} = 284 \text{ mm}$$

b. Resultant / Effective tooth load, F_{te}:

We know that, $\qquad F_{te} = \dfrac{F_t L}{L - 0.5b} \qquad$ ...12.92/ Pg 175, DHB

$$= \dfrac{1634.88 \times 198}{198 - (0.5 \times 36)}$$

$$F_{te} = 1798.37 \text{ N}$$

c. Resultant radial load on bearings, F_r:

We know that, $\qquad F_r = F_{te}\tan\alpha \cos\delta_1 \qquad$ ...12.93/ Pg 175, DHB

$$= 1798.37 \times \tan(14.5) \times \cos(45)$$

$$F_r = 328.87 \text{ N}$$

d. Axial thrust on gear, F_a:

We know that, $\qquad F_a = F_{te}\tan\alpha \sin\delta_1 \qquad$ ...12.94/ Pg 175, DHB

$$= 1798.37 \times \tan(14.5) \times \sin(45)$$

$$F_a = 328.87 \text{ N}$$

9. Two steel bevel gears connect shafts at 90°, the pinion has a surface hardness of 300 *BHN* and the gear has a surface hardness of 200 *BHN*. The tooth profile is to be 14 ½° full depth involute profile and the module is 4 mm. The number of teeth on the pinion is 30 and the gear has 48 teeth. The face width is 40 mm. Determine the wear strength of the pair. What would be the power that can be transmitted based on the above wear strength, if the pinion rotates at 1440 rpm?

VTU- July / Aug. 04 – 08 Marks; (similar) Jan./ Feb 2003 – 20 Marks

Solution: $\theta = 90°$, pinion $BHN_1 = 300$, gear $BHN_2 = 200$, $\alpha = 14.5°$, $m = 4$ mm, $z_1 = 30$ teeth, $z_2 = 48$, $b = 40$ mm, $N_1 = 1440$ rpm, $F_w = ?$, $P = ?$

We know that, $\qquad i = \dfrac{N_1}{N_2} = \dfrac{d_2}{d_1} = \dfrac{z_2}{z_1}$

$$i = \frac{z_2}{z_1} = \frac{48}{30}$$

∴ $i = 1.6$

And $N_2 = N_1/i = 1440/1.6 = 900$ rpm

a. To find F_w:

We know that,
$$F_w = \frac{d_1 b Q_e K}{\cos \delta_1} \qquad \text{...Eq. (i) } \mathbf{12.89/\ Pg\ 174,\ DHB}$$

- Diameter of pinion, $d_1 = mz_1 = 4 \times 30 = 120$ mm
- Diameter of gear, $d_2 = mz_1 = 4 \times 48 = 192$ mm
- For $\theta = 90°$:

$$\tan \delta_1 = \left(\frac{1}{i}\right) \qquad \text{...12.72a/ Pg 172, DHB}$$

$$= \left(\frac{1}{1.6}\right)$$

$$\delta_1 = 32°$$

$$\tan \delta_2 = i \qquad \text{...12.72b/ Pg 172, DHB}$$

$$= 1.6$$

$$\delta_2 = 58°$$

- Virtual number of teeth, $z_e = \dfrac{z}{\cos \delta}$ ...**12.81/ Pg 173, DHB**

for pinion
$$z_{e1} = \frac{z_1}{\cos \delta_1} = \frac{30}{\cos 32} = 35.38$$

and for gear,
$$z_{e2} = \frac{z_2}{\cos \delta_2} = \frac{48}{\cos 58} = 90.58$$

- Ratio factor,
$$Q_e = \frac{2 z_{e_2}}{z_{e_2} + z_{e_1}} \qquad \text{...12.89/ Pg 174, DHB}$$

$$= \frac{2 \times 90.58}{90.58 + 35.38}$$

$$Q = 1.4382$$

- Load stress factor,
$$K = \frac{\sigma_{es}^2 \sin \alpha}{1.4} \left[\frac{1}{E_1} + \frac{1}{E_2}\right] \qquad \text{...12.36b/ Pg 167, DHB}$$

$$\sigma_{es} = [(2.75 \times BHN) - 70] \qquad \text{...12.36d/ Pg 167, DHB}$$

$$= \left[2.75 \times \left(\frac{BHN_1 + BHN_2}{2}\right)\right] - 70$$

$$= \left[2.75 \times \left(\frac{300+200}{2}\right)\right] - 70$$

$$\sigma_{es} = 617.5 \text{ MPa}$$

Assume $E = 210$ GPa for steel

$$\therefore \quad K = \frac{(617.5)^2 \times \sin(14.50)}{1.4}\left[\frac{1}{210 \times 10^3} + \frac{1}{210 \times 10^3}\right]$$

$$K = 0.6495$$

$\therefore$ Eq. (*i*) yields...
$$F_w = \frac{120 \times 40 \times 1.4382 \times 0.6495}{\cos 32}$$

$$F_w = 5286.84 \text{ N}$$

b. To find F_t:

We know that,
$$F_d = F_t + \frac{K_3 v(Cb + F_t)}{K_3 v + \sqrt{Cb + F_t}} \quad \text{...12.88/ Pg 174, DHB}$$

For safety against wear, $F_w \geq F_d$

i.e.
$$5286.8 \geq F_t + \frac{K_3 v(Cb + F_t)}{K_3 v + \sqrt{Cb + F_t}} \quad \text{...Eq. (ii)}$$

- $v = \dfrac{\pi d_1 N_1}{60} = \dfrac{\pi \times 0.120 \times 1440}{60} = 9.05 \text{ m/s}$
- $K_3 = 20.67$

@ $v = 8$ m/s	Error, $e = 0.0500$ mm	...Tb. 12.14/ Pg 191, DHB
For $\alpha = 14.5°$ system and steel – steel combination		
@ $e = 0.04$ mm	$C = 441.3$ N/mm	...Tb. 12.12/ Pg 190, DHB
$e = 0.0500$ mm	$C = ?$	

$\therefore$ at $v = 9.05$ m/s, $C = \dfrac{0.050 \times 441.3}{0.04} = 551.63$ N/mm

$\therefore$ Eq. (*ii*) yields ... $5286.8 = F_t + \dfrac{(20.67 \times 9.05) \times [(551.63 \times 40) + F_t]}{(20.67 \times 9.05) + \sqrt{[(551.63 \times 43) + F_t]}}$

Which upon solving gives
$$F_t \approx 4835.43 \text{ N}$$

c. To find P:

We know that,
$$F_t = \frac{1000\, P}{v} \quad \text{...12.91a/ Pg 174, DHB}$$

$$4835.43 = \frac{1000\, P}{9.05}$$

$$P = 43.92 \text{ kW}$$

5.19 PROBLEMS BASED ON UNKNOWN DIAMETER

10. A pair of 20° full depth involute teeth bevel gears connect two shafts at right angles having velocity ratio 3:1. The gear is made of cast steel, 0.20% untreated and the pinion material is of steel, C30 heat treated. The pinion has 20 number of teeth and transmits 40 kW at 750 rpm. Determine: i) module, ii) face width, iii) pitch diameters. Assume width of gear face as 1/3rd of the length of pitch cone.
VTU- July 07/ 20 Marks

Solution: $\alpha = 20°$ FDI, $\theta = 90°$, $i = 3:1$, Gear material: cast steel-0.20% untreated, pinion material: steel, C30- heat treated, number of teeth on pinion, $z_p = z_1 = 20$, $P = 40$ kW, pinion speed (driver), $N_p = N_1 = 750$ rpm, $b = L/3$

a. $m = ?$, b. $b = ?$ c. $d_1, d_2 = ?$

We know that,
$$i = \frac{N_1}{N_2} = \frac{d_2}{d_1} = \frac{z_2}{z_1}$$

$$i = \frac{z_2}{z_1}$$

$$3 = \frac{z_2}{20}$$

$z_2 = z_g = 60$ teeth and $\quad N_2 = N_1/i = 750/3 = 250$ rpm

Material properties

Pinion: steel, C30- heat treated: $\quad \sigma_{d1} = 220.6$ MPa, $BHN_1 = 300$
Gear: cast steel, 0.20% untreated: $\quad \sigma_{d2} = 138.3$ MPa, $BHN_2 = 180$
...Tb. 12.7/ Pg 186, DHB

Identifying weaker part (pinion/gear):

We know that strength factor $= \sigma_d \cdot y$
- For $\theta = 90°$:

$$\tan \delta_1 = \left(\frac{1}{i}\right) \qquad \text{... 12.72a/ Pg 172, DHB}$$

$$= \left(\frac{1}{3}\right)$$

$\delta_1 = 18.43°$
$\tan \delta_2 = i \qquad \text{...12.72b/ Pg 172, DHB}$
$= 1.33$
$\delta_2 = 71.56°$

- Virtual number of teeth, $z_e = \dfrac{z}{\cos \delta} \qquad \text{...12.81/ Pg 173, DHB}$

for pinion, $\quad z_{e1} = \dfrac{z_1}{\cos \delta_1} = \dfrac{20}{\cos 18.43} = 21.08$

and for gear, $\quad z_{e2} = \dfrac{z_2}{\cos \delta_2} = \dfrac{60}{\cos 71.56} = 189.68$

- For $\alpha = 20°$ FDI tooth, $y = 0.154 - \dfrac{0.912}{z_e}$ ...12.17b/ Pg 163, DHB

  i.e. $\qquad y_1 = 0.154 - \dfrac{0.912}{z_{e1}}$

  $\qquad y_1 = 0.154 - \dfrac{0.912}{21.08} = 0.1107$

  $\qquad y_2 = 0.154 - \dfrac{0.912}{189.68} = 0.1492$

  $\therefore$ for pinion, $\qquad \sigma_{d1} \cdot y_1 = 220.6 \times 0.1107 = 24.42$ MPa
  for gear, $\qquad \sigma_{d2} \cdot y_2 = 138.3 \times 0.1492 = 20.63$ MPa

  Since $\sigma_{d2} \cdot y_2$ is less, design is based on **gear**.

a. To find module (m):

We know that, $\qquad m = \dfrac{F_t}{\sigma_d C_v bY}\left[\dfrac{L}{L-b}\right]$ ...Eq.(i) 12.85/ Pg 173, DHB

Since diameter is unknown, substituting

$$b = L/3, \quad \therefore \dfrac{L}{L-b} = 3/2$$

$$F_t = \dfrac{2M_t}{d} = \dfrac{2M_t}{mz} \quad \text{and}$$

$$L = \dfrac{1}{2}\sqrt{d_1^2 + d_2^2} = \dfrac{m}{2}\sqrt{z_1^2 + z_2^2} \quad \text{in Eq. }(i), \text{ we have}$$

$$m^3 = \dfrac{18 M_t}{\sigma_d \cdot C_v \cdot Y \cdot z \cdot \sqrt{z_1^2 + z_2^2}} \quad \text{-or-} \quad m = \sqrt[3]{\dfrac{18 M_t}{\sigma_d \cdot C_v \cdot Y \cdot z \cdot \sqrt{z_1^2 + z_2^2}}} \quad \text{...Eq. }(ii)$$

z – refers to number of teeth of weaker member.

- $P = \dfrac{2\pi N_2 M_t}{60}$

  $40 \times 10^3 = \dfrac{2\pi \times 250 \times M_t}{60}$

  $M_t = 1527.88$ N-m $= 1527.88 \times 10^3$ N-mm

- Assume, $\qquad C_v = 0.5$
- Form factor, $\qquad Y = \pi y_2$ ...12.16/ Pg 163, DHB
  $\qquad\qquad\qquad = \pi \times 0.1492$
  $\qquad\qquad Y = 0.4687$

$\therefore$ Eq. (ii) yields... $\quad m = \sqrt[3]{\dfrac{18 \times 1527.88 \times 10^3}{138.3 \times 0.5 \times 0.4687 \times 60 \times \sqrt{20^2 + 60^2}}}$

$\qquad\qquad\qquad m = 6.06$ mm

Therefore, standard module, $m = 8$ mm ...Tb. 12.23/ Pg 197, DHB

∴ PCD of pinion, $d_1 = mz_1 = 8 \times 20 = 160$ mm ...12.75/ Pg 172, DHB

PCD of gear, $d_2 = id_1 = 3 \times 150 = 480$ mm

- Cone distance, $L = \dfrac{1}{2}\sqrt{d_1^2 + d_2^2}$ ...12.74/ Pg 172, DHB

$$= \dfrac{1}{2}\sqrt{160^2 + 480^2}$$

$L = 253$ mm

- Face width, $b = \dfrac{L}{3}$ ...12.83b/ Pg 173, DHB

$$= \dfrac{2531}{3}$$

$b = 84.33$ mm ≈ 85 mm

- Check for σ_{d2}:

We know that, $\sigma_d = \dfrac{F_t}{mC_v bY}\left[\dfrac{L}{L-b}\right]$ ...Eq. (iii) 12.85/ Pg 173, DHB

- $v = \dfrac{\pi d_2 N_2}{60} = \dfrac{\pi \times 0.480 \times 250}{60} = 6.28$ m/s $(\because v_1 = v_2)$

- For generated teeth, $C_v = \dfrac{6.1}{6.1+v}$ ...12.86b/ Pg 174, DHB

$$= \dfrac{6.1}{6.1+6.28}$$

$C_v = 0.4927$

- $F_t = \dfrac{2M_t}{d_2}$ ...12.22/ Pg 165, DHB

$$= \dfrac{2 \times 1527.88 \times 10^3}{480}$$

$F_t = 6366.17$ N

∴ Eq. (iii) yields... $\sigma_{d2} = \dfrac{6366.17}{8 \times 0.4927 \times 85 \times 0.4687}\left[\dfrac{253}{253-85}\right]$

$\sigma_{d2} = 61.05$ MPa < 138.3 MPa ...hence safe.

Since calculated values are < permissible values, the assumed values are satisfactory.

b. To find face width (b): $b = 85$ mm

c. Pitch diameters:

PCD of pinion, $d_1 = 160$ mm

PCD of gear, $d_2 = 480$ mm

456 Design of Machine Elements II (DME II)

11. The vertical spindle of a drilling machine is to be driven by a pair of straight bevel gears with 20° involute teeth. The speed reduction is 4:1. The drill requires a power of 50 kW at 720 rpm. A service factor of 1.35 may be taken, and choose suitable materials for the gear and pinion. Design the gear pair.

VTU- June/ July 2009 – 15 Marks

Solution: $\alpha = 20°$ FDI, $\theta = 90°$, $i = 4:1$, $N_2 = 720$ rpm, $P = 50$ kW, $C_s = 1.35$, *Design.*

We know that,
$$i = \frac{N_1}{N_2} = \frac{d_2}{d_1} = \frac{z_2}{z_1}$$

$$i = \frac{N_1}{N_2}$$

$$4 = \frac{N_1}{720}$$

$$N_1 = 2880 \text{ rpm}$$

Material properties:

Since the material is not specified, let us assume that both pinion and gear are made of same material.

i.e. steel, C30 heat treated $\sigma_{d1} = \sigma_{d2} = 233.4$ MPa and $BHN_1 = BHN_2 = 200$

...Tb. 12.7/ Pg 186, DHB

Identifying weaker part (pinion/gear):

We know that strength factor = $\sigma_d \cdot y$

Since both pinion and gear are made of same material, the pinion is weaker, i.e. $\sigma_{d1} \cdot y_1 < \sigma_{d2} \cdot y_2$

Hence design is based on **pinion**.

- For $\theta = 90°$:

$$\tan \delta_1 = \left(\frac{1}{i}\right) \qquad \text{...12.72a/ Pg 172, DHB}$$

$$= \left(\frac{1}{4}\right)$$

$$\delta_1 = 14.04°$$

$$\tan \delta_2 = i \qquad \text{...12.72b/ Pg 172, DHB}$$

$$= 4$$

$$\delta_2 = 76°$$

- Assume $z_1 = 24$ teeth
- ∴ $z_2 = iz_1 = 4 \times 24 = 96$ teeth

- Virtual number of teeth, $z_e = \dfrac{z}{\cos \delta}$ ...12.81/ Pg 173, DHB

∴ for pinion, $z_{e1} = \dfrac{z_1}{\cos \delta_1} = \dfrac{24}{\cos 14.04} = 24.74$

for gear, $z_{e1} = \dfrac{z_1}{\cos \delta_1} = \dfrac{96}{\cos 76} = 396.82$

a. To find module (m):

We know that,
$$m = \sqrt{\frac{18 M_t}{\sigma_d \cdot C_v \cdot Y \cdot z \cdot \sqrt{z_1^2 + z_2^2}}} \quad \text{...Eq. (i)}$$

z – refers to number of teeth of weaker member.

- $P = \dfrac{2\pi N_1 M_t}{60}$

$$50 \times 10^3 = \frac{2\pi \times 2880 \times M_t}{60}$$

$M_t = 165.78$ N-m 165.78×10^3 N-mm

- Assume, $C_v = 0.5$
- Form factor, $Y = \pi_{y1}$ ...12.16/ Pg 163, DHB

$$= \pi \left[0.154 - \frac{0.912}{z_{e1}} \right]$$

$$= \pi \left[0.154 - \frac{0.912}{24.74} \right] \quad \text{...12.17b/ Pg 163, DHB}$$

$Y = 0.3680$

∴ Eq. (i) yields...
$$m = \sqrt[3]{\frac{18 \times 165.78 \times 10^3}{233.4 \times 0.5 \times 0.3680 \times 24 \times \sqrt{24^2 + 96^2}}}$$

$m = 3.08$ mm

Therefore, standard module, $m = 4$ mm   ...Tb. 12.23/ Pg 197, DHB

∴ PCD of pinion, $d_1 = m z_1 = 4 \times 24 = 96$ mm ≈ 100 mm

...12.75/ Pg 172, DHB

PCD of gear, $d_2 = i d_1 = 4 \times 100 = 400$ mm

- Cone distance, $L = \dfrac{1}{2}\sqrt{d_1^2 + d_2^2}$ ...12.74/ Pg 172, DHB

$$= \frac{1}{2}\sqrt{100^2 + 400^2}$$

$L = 206.15$ mm

- Face width, $b = \dfrac{L}{3}$ ...12.83b/ Pg 173, DHB

$$= \frac{206.15}{3}$$

$b = 68.72$ mm ≈ 70 mm

- Check for σ_{d1}:

We know that, $\sigma_d = \dfrac{F_t}{m C_v b Y}\left[\dfrac{L}{L-b}\right]$ Eq. (ii) 12.85/ Pg 173, DHB

- $v = \dfrac{\pi d_1 N_1}{60} = \dfrac{\pi \times 0.400 \times 720}{60} = 15.08$ m/s

- For generated teeth, $C_v = \dfrac{6.1}{6.1 + v}$ ...**12.86b/ Pg 174, DHB**

$$= \dfrac{6.1}{6.1 + 15.08}$$

$$C_v = 0.2880$$

- $F_t = \dfrac{2M_t}{d_1} \times C_s$ ...**12.22/ Pg 165, DHB**

$$= \dfrac{2 \times 165.78 \times 10^3}{100} \times 1.35$$

$$F_t = 4476.06 \text{ N}$$

∴ Eq. (*ii*) yields... $\sigma_{d1} = \dfrac{4476.06}{4 \times 0.2880 \times 70 \times 0.3680} \left[\dfrac{206.15}{206.15 - 70} \right]$

$$\sigma_{d1} = 228 \text{ MPa} < 233.6 \text{ MPa} \qquad \text{...hence safe.}$$

Since calculated values are < permissible values, the assumed values are satisfactory.

b. To find face width (b): $b = 70$ mm

c. To find dynamic tooth load (F_d):

We know that, $F_d = F_t + \dfrac{K_3 v (Cb + F_t)}{K_3 v + \sqrt{Cb + F_t}}$ ...Eq. (*iii*) **12.88/ Pg 174, DHB**

here $K_3 = 20.67$

@ v = 15 m/s	Error, e = 0.0230 mm	...**Tb. 12.14/ Pg 191, DHB**
For $\alpha = 20°$ system and steel – steel combination		
@ e = 0.02 mm	C = 228.9 N/mm	...**Tb. 12.12/ Pg 190, DHB**
e = 0.0230 mm	C = ?	

∴ at $v = 15.08$ m/s, $C = \dfrac{0.023 \times 228.9}{0.02} = 263.24$ N/mm

∴ Eq. (*iii*) yields... $F_d = 4476.06 + \dfrac{(20.67 \times 15.08) \times [(263.24 \times 70) + 4476.06]}{(20.67 \times 15.08) + \sqrt{[(263.24 \times 70) + 4476.06]}}$

$$F_d = 19.89 \text{ kN}$$

d. To find endurance strength (F_{en}):

We know that, $F_{en} = \sigma_{en} \, bYm \left[\dfrac{L - b}{L} \right]$ ...**12.87/ Pg 174, DHB**

- $\sigma_{es} = [(2.75 \times BHN) - 70)$ ...**12.36d/ Pg 167, DHB**

$$= \left[2.75 \times \left(\dfrac{BHN_1 + BHN_2}{2} \right) \right] - 70$$

$$= \left[2.75 \times \left(\frac{200+200}{2}\right)\right] - 70$$

$\sigma_{es} = 480$ MPa

- Load stress factor, $\quad K = \dfrac{\sigma_{es}^2 \sin \alpha}{1.4}\left[\dfrac{1}{E_1} + \dfrac{1}{E_2}\right]$ ...**12.36b/ Pg 167, DHB**

Assume $\quad E = 210$ GPa for steel

$\therefore \quad K = \dfrac{(480)^2 \times \sin(20)}{1.4}\left[\dfrac{1}{210 \times 10^3} + \dfrac{1}{210 \times 10^3}\right]$

$K = 0.5360$

-OR-

- For $\alpha = 20°$ and steel – steel combination having $BHN_1 = BHN_2 = 200$,

$K = 0.539 \quad$ and $\quad \sigma_{en} = 480.5$ MPa

...**Tb.12.16/ Pg 193, DHB**

$\therefore F_{en} = 480 \times 70 \times 0.3680 \times 4 \times \left[\dfrac{206.15 - 70}{206.15}\right]$

$F_{en} = 32.67$ kN

Since $F_{en} > F_d$, the material is safe against static tooth load.

e. To find BHN:

We know that, $\quad F_w = \dfrac{d_1 b Q_e K}{\cos \delta_1}$ ...Eq. (*iv*) **12.89/ Pg 174, DHB**

- Diameter of pinion, $\quad d_1 = 100$ mm

- Ratio factor, $\quad Q_e = \dfrac{2 z_{e_2}}{z_{e_2} + z_{e_1}}$ ...**12.89/ Pg 174, DHB**

$= \dfrac{2 \times 396.82}{396.82 + 24.94}$

$Q = 1.8817$

$\therefore$ Eq. (*iv*) yields... $\quad F_w = \dfrac{100 \times 70 \times 1.8817 \times 0.5360}{\cos 14.04}$

$F_w = 7.28$ kN

Since $F_w < F_d$, the pinion is subjected to rapid wear and hence has to be surface hardened to higher *BHN*.

i.e. $\quad F_w \geq F_d$

$\dfrac{d_1 b Q_e K}{\cos \delta_1} \geq 19.89$ kN

i.e. $\quad \dfrac{100 \times 70 \times 1.8817 \times 0.5360}{\cos 14.04} \geq 19.89 \times 10^3$

$$K \geq \frac{19.89 \times 10^3 \times \cos 15.95}{100 \times 70 \times 1.8817}$$

$$K \geq 1.465$$

Therefore, for steel – steel combination, having $\alpha = 20°$ and $K \geq 1.465$, we have
BHN of pinion = 350,   BHN of gear = 300   ...Tb. 12.16/ Pg 193, DHB

12. **A pair of straight bevel gears are to transmit 15 kW at 1500 rpm input speed. The number of teeth on pinion is 20 and the speed ratio is 5. Design the gears assuming 14 ½° full depth form.**

VTU- June/ July 2011 – 20 Marks; (similar) Jan./ Feb. 2006 – 20 Marks; (similar) Jan./ Feb. 2005 – 20 Marks; (similar) July/ Aug. 2005 – 20 Marks

Solution: $P = 15$ kW, $N_1 = 1500$ rpm, $z_1 = 20$, $i = 5$, $\alpha = 14.5°$. *Design*

We know that, $i = \dfrac{N_1}{N_2} = \dfrac{d_2}{d_1} = \dfrac{z_2}{z_1}$

$$i = \frac{z_2}{z_1}$$

$$5 = \frac{z_2}{20}$$

$z_2 = 100$ teeth

Material properties:

Since the material is not specified, let us assume that both pinion and gear are made of same material.

i.e. Forged steel 0.30%C, heat treated with $\sigma_{d1} = \sigma_{d2} = 220$ MPa and $BHN_1 = BHN_2 = 200$.   ...Tb. 12.7/ Pg 186, DHB

Identifying weaker part (pinion/gear):

We know that strength factor = $\sigma_d \cdot y$

Since both pinion and gear are made of same material, the pinion is weaker, i.e. $\sigma_{d1} \cdot y_1 < \sigma_{d2} \cdot y_2$

Hence design is based on **pinion**.

- For $\theta = 90°$:

$$\tan \delta_1 = \left(\frac{1}{i}\right) \quad \text{...12.72a/ Pg 172, DHB}$$

$$= \left(\frac{1}{5}\right)$$

$\delta_1 = 11.31°$ ...12.72b/ Pg 172, DHB

$\tan \delta_2 = i$

$= 5$

$\delta_2 = 78.69°$

- Virtual number of teeth, $z_e = \dfrac{z}{\cos \delta}$ ...12.81/ Pg 173, DHB for pinion, $\quad z_{e1} = \dfrac{z_1}{\cos \delta_1} = \dfrac{20}{\cos 11.31} = 20.40$

and for gear, $\quad z_{e1} = \dfrac{z_1}{\cos \delta_1} = \dfrac{100}{\cos 78.69} = 510$

a. To find module (m):

We know that, $\quad m = \sqrt[3]{\dfrac{18 M_t}{\sigma_d \cdot C_v \cdot Y \cdot z \cdot \sqrt{z_1^2 + z_2^2}}}$ ...Eq. (i)

z – refers to number of teeth of weaker member.

- $P = \dfrac{2\pi N_1 M_t}{60}$

$15 \times 10^3 = \dfrac{2\pi \times 1500 \times M_t}{60}$

$M_t = 95.49$ N-m $= 95.49 \times 10^3$ N-mm

- Assume, $\quad C_v = 0.5$
- Form factor, $\quad Y = \pi y_1$ ...12.16/ Pg 163, DHB

$= \pi \left[0.124 - \dfrac{0.684}{z_{e1}} \right]$ ...12.17a/ Pg 163, DHB

$= \pi \left[0.124 - \dfrac{0.684}{20.4} \right]$

$Y = 0.2842$

∴ Eq. (i) yields... $\quad m = \sqrt[3]{\dfrac{18 \times 95.49 \times 10^3}{220 \times 0.5 \times 0.2842 \times 20 \times \sqrt{20^2 + 100^2}}}$

$m = 2.99$ mm

Therefore, standard module, $m = 3$ mm ...Tb. 12.23/ Pg 197, DHB

∴ PCD of pinion, $\quad d_1 = m z_1 = 3 \times 20 = 60$ mm ...12.75/ Pg 172, DHB
PCD of gear, $\quad d_2 = i d_1 = 5 \times 60 = 300$ mm

- Cone distance, $\quad L = \dfrac{1}{2}\sqrt{d_1^2 + d_2^2}$ ...12.74/ Pg 172, DHB

$= \dfrac{1}{2}\sqrt{60^2 + 300^2}$

$L = 153$ mm

- Face width, $\quad b = \dfrac{L}{3}$ ...12.83b/ Pg 173, DHB

$= \dfrac{153}{3}$

$b = 51$ mm ≈ 50 mm

- Check for σ_{d2}: ($\sigma_{d1} = \sigma_{d2}$)

  We know that, $\quad \sigma_d = \dfrac{F_t}{mC_v bY}\left[\dfrac{L}{L-b}\right] \quad$ ...Eq. (ii) 12.85/ Pg 173, DHB

- $v = \dfrac{\pi d_1 N_1}{60} = \dfrac{\pi \times 0.06 \times 1500}{60} = 4.71$ m/s

- For generated teeth, $\quad C_v = \dfrac{6.1}{6.1 + v} \quad$ ...12.86b/ Pg 174, DHB

  $= \dfrac{6.1}{6.1 + 4.71}$

  $C_v = 0.5642$

- $F_t = \dfrac{2M_t}{d_1} \quad$ ...12.22/ Pg 165, DHB

  $= \dfrac{2 \times 95.49 \times 10^3}{60}$

  $F_t = 3183$ N

∴ Eq. (ii) yields... $\quad \sigma_{d2} = \dfrac{3183}{3 \times 0.5642 \times 50 \times 0.2842}\left[\dfrac{153}{153-50}\right]$

$\sigma_{d2} = 196.58$ MPa < 220 MPa $\quad$ ...hence safe.

Since calculated values are < permissible values, the assumed values are satisfactory.

b. To find face width (b): $\quad b = 50$ mm

c. To find dynamic tooth load (F_d):

We know that, $\quad F_d = F_t + \dfrac{K_3 v (Cb + F_t)}{K_3 v + \sqrt{Cb + F_t}} \quad$ ...Eq. (iii) 12.88/ Pg 174, DHB

here $\quad K_3 = 20.67$

@ v = 4 m/s	Error, e = 0.0710 mm	...Tb. 12.14/ Pg 191, DHB
For α = 14.5° system and steel – steel combination		
@ e = 0.06 mm	C = 662 N/mm	...Tb. 12.12/ Pg 190, DHB
e = 0.0710 mm	C = ?	

∴ at $v = 4.71$ m/s, $C = \dfrac{0.0710 \times 662}{0.06} = 783.37$ N/mm

∴ Eq. (iii) yields... $\quad F_d = 3183 + \dfrac{(20.67 \times 4.71) \times [(783.37 \times 50) + 3183]}{(20.67 \times 4.71) + \sqrt{[(783.37 \times 50) + 3183]}}$

$F_d = 16.78$ kN

d. To find endurance strength (F_{en}):

We know that, $\quad F_{en} = \sigma_{en} bYm \left[\dfrac{L-b}{L}\right] \quad$ ...12.87/ Pg 174, DHB

- For $\alpha = 14.5°$ and steel – steel combination having $BHN_1 = BHN_2 = 200$,
$$K = 0.402 \quad \text{and} \quad \sigma_{en} = 480.5 \text{ MPa}$$
...Tb.12.16/ Pg 193, DHB

$\therefore \quad F_{en} = 480.5 \times 50 \times 0.2842 \times 3 \times \left[\dfrac{153 - 50}{153}\right]$

$\therefore \quad F_{en} = 13.79$ kN

Since $F_{en} < F_d$, the material is unsafe against static tooth load.

e. To find BHN:

We know that, $\quad F_w = \dfrac{d_1 b Q_e K}{\cos \delta_1} \quad$ ...Eq. (iv) 12.89/ Pg 174, DHB

- Diameter of pinion, $\quad d_1 = 60$ mm

- Ratio factor, $\quad Q_e = \dfrac{2 z_{e_2}}{z_{e_2} + z_{e_1}} \quad$ ...12.89/ Pg 174, DHB

$$= \dfrac{2 \times 510}{510 + 20.40}$$

$$Q = 1.9231$$

$\therefore$ Eq. (iv) yields... $\quad F_w = \dfrac{60 \times 50 \times 1.9231 \times 0.402}{\cos 11.31}$

$$F_w = 2.37 \text{ kN}$$

Since $F_w < F_d$, the pinion is subjected to rapid wear and hence has to be surface hardened to higher BHN.

i.e. $\quad F_w \geq F_d$

$$\dfrac{d_1 b Q_e K}{\cos \delta_1} \geq 19.89 \text{ kN}$$

i.e. $\quad \dfrac{60 \times 50 \times 1.9231 \times K}{\cos 11.31} \geq 16.78 \times 10^3$

$$K \geq \dfrac{16.78 \times 10^3 \times \cos 11.31}{60 \times 50 \times 1.9231}$$

$$K \geq 2.852$$

Therefore, for steel – steel combination, having $\alpha = 14.5°$ and $K \geq 2.852$, we have

BHN of pinion = 500, $\quad$ BHN of gear = 500 $\quad$ ...Tb.12.16/ Pg 193, DHB

13. **Design a pair of bevel gears to connect two shafts at 60°. The power transmitted is 25 kW at 900 rpm of pinion. The reduction ratio is 5:1. The teeth are 20° full depth involute and pinion has 24 teeth. Check the design for dynamic and wear considerations.** *VTU- Dec. 2010 – 20 Marks*

Solution: $\theta = 60°$, $P = 25$ kW, $N_1 = 900$ rpm, $i = 5:1$, $a = 20°$ FDI, $z_1 = 24$, Design.

We know that, $\quad i = \dfrac{N_1}{N_2} = \dfrac{d_2}{d_1} = \dfrac{z_2}{z_1}$

$$i = \dfrac{z_2}{z_1}$$

$$5 = \frac{z_2}{z_4}$$

$$z_2 = 120 \text{ teeth}$$

Material properties:

Since the material is not specified, let us assume that both pinion and gear are made of same material.

i.e. Forged steel 0.30%C, heat treated with $\sigma_{d1} = \sigma_{d2} = 220$ MPa and $BHN_1 = BHN_2 = 200$

...**Tb. 12.7/ Pg 186, DHB**

Identifying weaker part (pinion/gear):

We know that strength factor = $\sigma_d \cdot y$

Since both pinion and gear are made of same material, the pinion is weaker, i.e. $\sigma_{d1} \cdot y_1 < \sigma_{d2} \cdot y_2$.

Hence design is based on **pinion**.

- For $\theta < 90°$:

$$\tan \delta_1 = \left(\frac{\sin \theta}{i + \cos \theta} \right) \qquad ...\textbf{12.67/ Pg 171, DHB}$$

$$= \left(\frac{\sin 60}{5 + \cos 60} \right)$$

$$\delta_1 = 8.95° \qquad ...\textbf{12.68/ Pg 171, DHB}$$

$$\tan \delta_2 = \left(\frac{\sin \theta}{\dfrac{1}{i} + \cos \theta} \right)$$

$$= \left(\frac{\sin 60}{\dfrac{1}{5} + \cos 60} \right)$$

$$\delta_2 = 51.05°$$

- Virtual number of teeth, $z_e = \dfrac{z}{\cos \delta}$ ...**12.81/ Pg 173, DHB**

for pinion $\qquad z_{e1} = \dfrac{z_1}{\cos \delta_1} = \dfrac{24}{\cos 8.95} = 24.30$

and for gear, $\qquad z_{e2} = \dfrac{z_1}{\cos \delta_1} = \dfrac{120}{\cos 51.05} = 190.88 \approx 191$

a. To find module (m):

We know that, $\qquad m = \sqrt[3]{\dfrac{18 M_t}{\sigma_d \cdot C_v \cdot Y \cdot z \cdot \sqrt{z_1^2 + z_2^2}}} \qquad$ ...Eq. (i)

z - refers to number of teeth of weaker member.

- $P = \dfrac{2\pi N_1 M_t}{60}$

  $25 \times 10^3 = \dfrac{2\pi \times 900 \times M_t}{60}$

  $M_t = 265.26$ N-m $= 265.26 \times 10^3$ N-mm

- Assume, $\quad C_v = 0.5$
- Form factor, $\quad Y = \pi y_1$ ...12.16/ Pg 163, DHB

  $= \pi \left[0.154 - \dfrac{0.912}{z_{e1}} \right]$ ...12.17b/ Pg 163, DHB

  $= \pi \left[0.154 - \dfrac{0.912}{24.30} \right]$

  $Y = 0.3658$

∴ Eq. (i) yields...

$$m = \sqrt[3]{\dfrac{18 \times 265.26 \times 10^3}{220 \times 0.5 \times 0.3658 \times 24 \times \sqrt{24^2 + 120^2}}}$$

$m = 3.43$ mm

Therefore, standard module, $m = 4$ mm ...Tb. 12.23/ Pg 197, DHB

∴ PCD of pinion, $d_1 = m z_1 = 4 \times 24 = 96$ mm ≈ 100 mm ...12.75/ Pg 172, DHB

PCD of gear, $d_2 = i d_1 = 5 \times 100 = 500$ mm

- Cone distance, $\quad L = \dfrac{1}{2} \sqrt{d_1^2 + d_2^2}$ ...12.74/ Pg 172, DHB

  $= \dfrac{1}{2} \sqrt{100^2 + 500^2}$

  $L = 255$ mm

- Face width, $\quad b = \dfrac{L}{3}$ ...12.83b/ Pg 173, DHB

  $= \dfrac{255}{3}$

  $b = 85$ mm

- Check for σ_{d1}:

  We know that, $\quad \sigma_d = \dfrac{F_t}{m C_v b Y} \left[\dfrac{L}{L - b} \right]$ Eq. (ii) 12.85/ Pg 173, DHB

- $v = \dfrac{\pi d_1 N_1}{60} = \dfrac{\pi \times 0.1 \times 900}{60} = 4.71$ m/s

- For generated teeth, $\quad C_v = \dfrac{6.1}{6.1 + v}$ ...12.86b/ Pg 174, DHB

  $= \dfrac{6.1}{6.1 + 4.71}$

  $C_v = 0.5642$

- $F_t = \dfrac{2M_t}{d_1}$ ...12.22/ Pg 165, DHB

$$= \dfrac{2 \times 265.26 \times 10^3}{100}$$

$F_t = 5305.2$ N

∴ Eq. (ii) yields... $\sigma_{d1} = \dfrac{5305.2}{4 \times 0.5642 \times 85 \times 0.3658} \times \left[\dfrac{255}{255-85}\right]$

$\sigma_{d1} = 113.4$ MPa < 220 MPa ...hence safe.

Since calculated values are < permissible values, the assumed values are satisfactory.

b. To find face width (b): $b = 85$ mm

c. To find dynamic tooth load (F_d):

We know that, $F_d = F_t + \dfrac{K_3 v (Cb + F_t)}{K_3 v + \sqrt{Cb + F_t}}$ ...Eq. (iii) 12.88/ Pg 174, DHB

here $K_3 = 20.67$

@ v = 4 m/s	Error, e = 0.0710 mm	...Tb. 12.14/ Pg 191, DHB
For α = 20° system and steel – steel combination		
@ e = 0.06 mm	C = 686.7 N/mm	...Tb. 12.12/ Pg 190, DHB
e = 0.0710 mm	C = ?	

∴ at $v = 4.71$ m/s, $C = \dfrac{0.0710 \times 686.7}{0.06} = 812.60$ N/mm

∴ Eq. (iii) yields... $F_d = 5305.2 + \dfrac{(20.67 \times 4.71) \times [(812.60 \times 85) + 5305.2]}{(20.67 \times 4.71) + \sqrt{[(812.60 \times 85) + 5305.2]}}$

$F_d = 24.87$ kN

d. To find endurance strength (F_{en}):

We know that, $F_{en} = \sigma_{en} \, bYm \left[\dfrac{L-b}{L}\right]$ ...12.87/ Pg 174, DHB

- For α = 20° and steel – steel combination having $BHN_1 = BHN_2 = 200$,
  $K = 0.539$ and 480.5 MPa ...Tb.12.16/ Pg 193, DHB

∴ $F_{en} = 480.5 \times 85 \times 0.3658 \times 4 \times \left[\dfrac{255-85}{255}\right]$

$F_{en} = 39.84$ kN

Since $F_{en} > F_d$, the material is safe against static tooth load.

e. To find BHN:

We know that, $F_w = \dfrac{d_1 b Q_e K}{\cos \delta_1}$ ...Eq. (iv) 12.89/ Pg 174, DHB

- Diameter of pinion, $d_1 = 60$ mm

- Ratio factor, $$Q_e = \frac{2z_{e_2}}{z_{e_2} + z_{e_1}} \qquad \text{...12.89/ Pg 174, DHB}$$

$$= \frac{2 \times 191}{191 + 24.30}$$

$$Q = 1.7743$$

∴ Eq. (*iv*) yields... $$F_w = \frac{100 \times 85 \times 1.7743 \times 0.539}{\cos 8.95}$$

$$F_w = 8.23 \text{ kN}$$

Since $F_w = F_d$, the pinion is subjected to rapid wear and hence has to be surface hardened to higher *BHN*.

i.e. $$F_w \geq F_d$$

$$\frac{d_1 b Q_e K}{\cos \delta_1} \geq 24.87 \text{ kN}$$

i.e. $$\frac{100 \times 85 \times 1.7743 \times K}{\cos 8.95} \geq 24.87 \times 10^3$$

$$K \geq \frac{24.87 \times 10^3 \times \cos 8.95}{100 \times 85 \times 1.7743}$$

$$K \geq 1.6289$$

Therefore, for steel – steel combination, having $\alpha = 20°$ and $K \geq 1.6289$, we have

BHN of pinion = 400,   *BHN* of gear = 300   ...**Tb. 12.16/ Pg 193, DHB**

WORM GEARS

5.20 INTRODUCTION

These are widely used for transmitting power at high velocity ratios between non-intersecting shafts that are generally but not necessarily at right angles. Velocity ratios as high as 300:1 and more can be achieved but with low efficiency. These are mostly used as speed reducers which consist of a worm and a worm gear/wheel as shown in **Fig. 5.7**. The worm (driving member) is similar to a screw and the worm wheel is essentially a helical gear with a face curved to fit the portion of worm periphery. As the worm is rotated the worm wheel is caused to rotate due to the screw like action of the worm. The size of the worm gear set is generally based on the centre distance between the worm and the worm wheel.

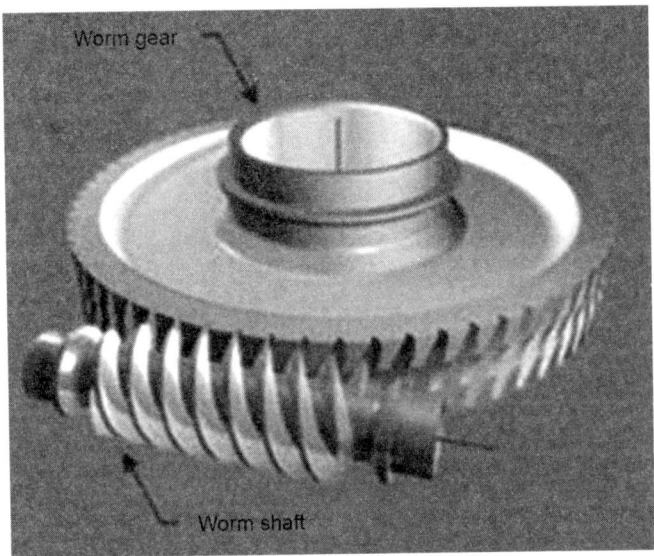

Fig. 5.7: Worm shaft and worm gear

The worm is shown with the worm above the worm wheel. The gear set can also be arranged with the worm below the worm wheel. Other alignments are used less frequently.

Worms and worm gears provide solutions to a wide range of drive problems, particularly when the following factors need to be considered:
- High ratio speed reduction
- Space limitations
- Right angle shafts
- Non-intersecting shafts

5.21 CHARACTERISTICS OF WORM GEARS

The worm gears shows the following distinct characteristics **(Fig. 5.8)**:
- Worm gears are cut helically for maximum mating.
- Perfect for accurate movement of load.
- Occurrence of pure sliding motion.
- Single step conversion of high speed inputs to low speeds and high torque outputs.
- Large speed reductions.

5.22 ADVANTAGES AND DISADVANTAGES

Advantages:
- Smooth and quiet operation.
- Small in size.
- Self locking ability.
- High speed ratios can be achieved.

Disadvantages:
- Efficiency is less.
- The drive gets heated due to conversion of friction losses into thermal energy.

5.23 APPLICATIONS

The worm gear system finds application in small-motorized instrument and toys. Most of these are battery operated and have a small motor. Though the speed produced is higher, the torque is less. The reduction in speed and increase in torque can be achieved by application of the worm gear system. They are also used in conveyor belts due to their non-reversibility. However their application in vehicles in not wide spread since their gear reduction is larger than required.

Other applications include re-circulating ball bearings, electric motors, presses. The most common uses of worm gears are for rolling mills, conveyor engineering and also for automotive parts. These worm gears are used as speed reducers. In turn, the torque is increased. In most cases, electric motors have a very high speed and a low torque level. The worm gear works the opposite and this makes it ideal to use for different applications.

5.24 DESIGNATION OF WORM GEARS

Worm gears are designated as: $z_1/z_2/q/m$

z_1 – no. of worm starts/teeth z_2 – no. of teeth on worm gear
q – diameter quotient m – module

5.25 WORM GEAR DESIGN PARAMETERS

Worm gears provide a normal single reduction range of 5:1 to 75:1. The pitch line velocity is ideally up to 30 m/s. The efficiency of a worm gear ranges from 98% for the lowest ratios to 20% for the highest ratios. Worm gears at the higher ratios are inherently self locking - the worm can drive the gear but the gear cannot drive the worm. A worm gear can provide a 50:1 speed reduction but not a 1:50 speed increase. *(In practice a worm should not be used a braking device for safety linked systems ex. hoists. Some material and operating conditions can result in a worm gear back sliding)*

The worm gear action is a sliding action and results in significant frictional losses. The ideal combination of gear materials is to opt a case hardened alloy steel worm (ground finished) with a phosphor bronze gear. Other combinations are used for gears with comparatively light loads.

5.26 TERMS IN WORM GEAR

1. **Axial or Linear Pitch (p):** It is the distance measured from any point on one thread to corresponding point on adjacent thread parallel to the axis of the worm.

   When the shafts are at right angles, the axial pitch (p) is equal to the circular pitch (p_c) of the mating gear.

2. **Lead (l):** It refers to the distance a thread advances for one completer revolution of the worm.

   i.e. lead = pitch × number of turns

   i.e.
   $$l = p_c \times z_1$$
   $$l = (\pi m) z_1 \quad \text{...(Eq. 5.38)} \ \textbf{12.98/ Pg 175, DHB}$$

   The term normal pitch is used for a worm having single start threads and for a worm having multiple start threads, the term normal lead (l_n) is normally used.

   i.e.
   $$l_n = l \cos \gamma \quad \text{...(Eq. 5.39)} \ \textbf{12.99/ Pg 175, DHB}$$

3. **Lead angle (γ):** It is defined as the angle between the tangent to the thread helix and the plane of rotation of the worm.

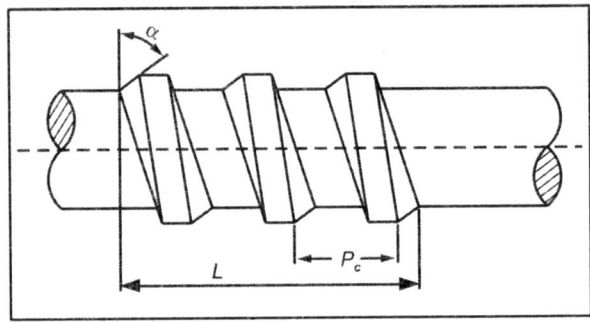 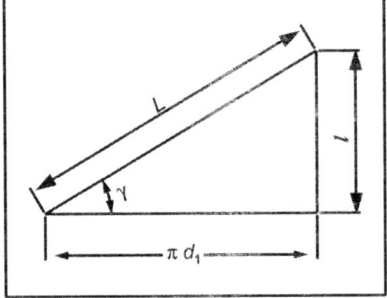

Fig. 5.8: Terms relating to worm gear   **Fig. 5.9:** Lead angle

From **Fig. 5.9**, $\tan \gamma = \dfrac{\text{lead}}{\text{circumferential pitch of the worm}}$

$$= \frac{l}{\pi d_1} \quad \text{...(Eq. 5.40)} \ \textbf{12.100/ Pg 175, DHB}$$

$$= \frac{(\pi m) z_1}{\pi d_1} \quad \text{...(Eq. 5.41)} \ \textbf{12.97a/ Pg 175, DHB}$$

$$= \frac{m z_1}{d_1}$$

Where, $d_1 = m_c z_1$ – pitch diameter of the worm ...(Eq. 5.42)
m_c – circumferential module of the worm
z_1 – number of worm starts –or– number of threads on the worm.

i.e. $\tan \gamma = \dfrac{m z_1}{m_c z_1}$

$$\tan \gamma = \frac{m}{m_c} \quad \text{...(Eq. 5.43)} \ \textbf{12.96/ Pg 175, DHB}$$

For compact design, lead angle $\tan \gamma = \sqrt[3]{\dfrac{n_2}{n_1}}$ ...(Eq. 5.44) **12.105/ Pg 176, DHB**

Where, n_1 and n_2 – speed of worm and worm gear in rev/s

Eq. (5.38) can also be written as $l = (\pi m_c \tan \gamma) z_1$ ...(Eq. 5.44a) **12.98/ Pg 175, DHB**

Eq. (5.40) can also be written as $\tan \gamma = \dfrac{l}{\pi(m_c z_1)}$

...(Eq. 5.44b) ...**12.100/ Pg 175, DHB**

Note:

The lead angle (γ) may vary from 9° to 45°. It has been shown by FA Halsey that a lead angle less than 9° results in rapid wear and the safe value of γ is 12½°.

- *Proportions of worms* ...**Table 12.25/ Pg 198, DHB**
- *Proportions of worm gears* ...**Table 12.26/ Pg 199, DHB**
- *Recommended values of pressure and lead angles are available in*
   ...**Table 12.27/ Pg 199, DHB**
- *Based on velocity ratio, number of threads in worm are available in*
   ...**Table 12.28/ Pg 199, DHB**
- *Based on normal pressure angle, values of y are available in*
   ...**Table 12.29/ Pg 199, DHB**
- *Dimensions of the worm are available in*
   ...**Table 12.30/ Pg 199, DHB**

4. **Module (m):**

   The module is calculated as $m = \dfrac{2a}{q + z_2}$ ...(Eq. 5.45) **12.101/ Pg 175, DHB**

   z_2 – number of teeth in worm gear
   q – number of modules in the pitch diameter of the worm

   $= \dfrac{d_1}{m} = 6 \text{ to } 13$

   a – centre distance

   $= \dfrac{d_1 + d_2}{2}$

   $= \left[\dfrac{z_2}{q} + 1\right]\left[\left(\dfrac{540}{\dfrac{z_2}{q}\sigma_{sur}}\right)^2 M_t K_c K_d\right]^{1/3}$ (Dobrovolsky)

   σ_{sur} = allowable surface stress ...(Eq. 5.46) **Table 12.10/ Pg 189, DHB**
   M_t = torque
   K_c = Load concentration factor ...**Table 12.10/ Pg 189, DHB**
   K_d = dynamic load factor ...**Table 12.11/ Pg 189, DHB**
   d_2 = pitch diameter of worm gear = $m z_2$ ...**Table 12.97/ Pg 175, DHB**

5. **Pitch diameters:**

   - The pitch diameter of the worm is, $d_1 = m_c z_1 = \dfrac{m z_1}{\tan \gamma}$ ...**12.97a/ Pg 175, DHB**

For speed reducers with integral worms, AGMA recommends:

- mean (pitch) worm diameter as: $d_1 = \dfrac{a^{0.875}}{1.466}$ ...**12.103/ Pg 176, DHB**

- face width as: $b = \dfrac{a^{0.875}}{2}$ ...**12.125/ Pg 180, DHB**

- The pitch diameter of the worm gear is $d_2 = mz_2$ ...**12.97b/ Pg 175, DHB**

5.27 STRENGTH OF A WORM GEAR (F_t)

The power transmitting capacity of a worm gear is decided by the strength, ability to resist wear and abrasion as well as the heat radiating capacity. In determining the tooth size and strength, it is assumed that the teeth of worm gear are always weaker than the threads of the worm. The worm is made of steel while the worm gear is made of bronze or cast iron.

In worm gearing, two or more teeth are usually in contact, but due to uncertainty of load distribution among themselves it is assumed that the load is transmitted by one tooth only.

According to Lewis equation, $F_t = \sigma_d C_v b Y m$ ...(Eq. 5.47) **12.106/ Pg 176, DHB**

Where $\quad Y = \pi y$ – form factor

y – Lewis form factor ...**Table 12.5/ Pg 184, DHB**

- If the number of teeth in worm gear + the number of threads in a length of 25 mm of worm is greater than 40, then

$$Y = 0.314 + [0.015 (\alpha - 14.5°)] \quad \text{...12.107/ Pg 176, DHB}$$

- Velocity factor, $C_v = \dfrac{3.05}{3.05 + v}$

$\quad = \dfrac{6.1}{6.1 + v}$ ...takes care of dynamic load. ...**12.108/ Pg 176, DHB**

- b – face width

For worm gears, $\quad b = 7.48\, m + 6.35$ mm for ($z_g = 1$ and 2)
$\quad\quad\quad\quad\quad\quad\quad\quad b = 6.758\, m + 5.08$ mm for ($z_g = 3$ and 4)

...**Table 12.26/ Pg 199, DHB**

- When torque is known/given, $F_t = \dfrac{2 M_{te}}{d_2}$ ...(Eq. 5.48) **12.109/ Pg 177, DHB**

Where, $\quad M_{te}$ – effective torque $= M_t K_l$
$\quad\quad\quad\quad K_l$ – Load factor ...**Table 12.34/ Pg 203, DHB**

5.28 DYNAMIC STRENGTH (F_s)

The dynamic strength is calculated as $F_s = \sigma_d b Y m = \dfrac{F_t}{C_v}$

...(Eq. 5.49) **12.110/ Pg 177, DHB**

Due to sliding action between the worm and worm gear teeth, the dynamic forces are not so severe as in regular forms of gearing because the engagement tooth in the worm set is through the worm thread sliding into contact with the worm gear teeth. Hence this need not be calculated.

5.29 WEAR TOOTH LOAD (F_w)

- The limiting load of wear, $F_w = d_2 b K$ ...(Eq. 5.50) **12.122/ Pg 179, DHB**
  d_2 – PCD of worm gear, b – face width,
  K – load stress factor ...**Table 12.31/ Pg 202, DHB**

  For safety against wear, $F_w \geq F_s$ ...(Eq. 5.51)

- Another formula which assumes the use of proper lubricant along with various other gear data is given as

$$F_w = \frac{A \cos \gamma \cdot C_v \cdot \sigma_c}{C_s} \quad \text{...(Eq. 5.52)} \textbf{ 12.123/ Pg 179, DHB}$$

$A = \dfrac{h d_1 \psi}{57.3}$ – projected tooth area of contact (mm²)

h – depth of the tooth (mm) ...**Table 12.25/ Pg 198, DHB**
d_1 – pitch diameter of the worm
ψ – one-half of face angle (deg.)

$$\tan \psi \leq \frac{\tan \alpha}{\tan \gamma} \quad \text{...12.104/ Pg 176, DHB}$$

C_s – service factor ...**Table 12.32/ Pg 202, DHB**
σ_c – allowable surface pressure (MPa) ...**Table 12.33/ Pg 203, DHB**

$$C_v = \frac{3.05}{3.05 + v}$$

5.30 EFFICIENCY OF WORM GEARS

It is defined as the ratio of work done by the worm gear to that of the worm.

- When the worm drives the worm gear, $\eta = \dfrac{\cos \theta - \mu \tan \gamma}{\cos \theta + \mu \cot \gamma}$

  ...(Eq. 5.53) **12.115/ Pg 177, DHB**

- When the worm gear drives the worm, $\eta = \dfrac{\cos \theta - \mu \cot \gamma}{\cos \theta + \mu \tan \gamma}$

  ...(Eq. 5.54) **12.116/ Pg 177, DHB**

- Barr's formula for worm gearing, $\eta = \dfrac{\tan \gamma (1 - \mu \tan \gamma)}{\mu + \tan \gamma}$ (for square threads)

  ...(Eq. 5.55) **12.117/ Pg 177, DHB**

γ = lead angle α – pressure angle
μ = coefficient of friction between the worm and the worm gear
  = 0.02 – for very carefully machined worms
  = 0.05 – for ordinary industrial worm with well lubrication
  = 015 – for low speed and indifferent lubrication

Also, $\mu = \dfrac{0.0422}{(v_r)^{0.28}}$, for $0.2 < v < 2.8$ m/s ...**12.120a/ Pg 178, DHB**

$$= 0.025 + \frac{3.281 v_r}{1000} - \text{for speeds} > 2.8 \text{ m/s} \quad \text{...12.120b/ Pg 178, DHB}$$

$$v_r = \text{rubbing velocity} = \frac{v_1}{\cos \gamma} = \frac{\pi d_1 n_1}{1000 \times \cos \gamma} \quad \text{...12.121/ Pg 179, DHB}$$

Note: The worm is said to be self-locking, if the efficiency is < 50%, i.e. it cannot be driven by applying torque to the wheel. Example: Hoists

Conditions for maximum efficiency:
- When the worm drives the worm gear/wheel, $\gamma = 45 - 0.5 \tan^{-1}(\mu/\cos\theta)$
  ...**12.118a/ Pg 178, DHB**
- When the worm gear/wheel drives the worm, $\gamma = 45 + 0.5 \tan^{-1}(\mu/\cos\theta)$
  ...**12.118b/ Pg 178, DHB**

5.31 THERMAL CAPACITY OF WORM GEARS

In order to avoid overheating of the drive and the lubricating oil, the heat generated in the worm gear due to friction must be dissipated.

The amount of heat dissipated (Watts) is given as

$$Q_d = 1000 \text{ (kW)} (1 - \eta) \quad \text{...(Eq. 5.56)} \; \textbf{12.124b/ Pg 180, DHB}$$

Eq. **12.124b/ Pg 180, DHB** is used for equations **12.115/ Pg 117, DHB**

Another equation for heat dissipation (watts) is

$$Q_d = \frac{0.407}{1000}(A_g + A_w)(t_2 - t_1)$$

...(Eq. 5.57) **12.124c/ Pg 180, DHB**

where
$A_w = L_w d_1$ – projected area of the worm (mm^2)
L_w – face length of worm   ...**Table 12.25/ Pg 198, DHB**

$$A_g = \frac{\pi d_2^2}{4} - \text{area of the worm gear (mm}^2\text{)}$$

t_2 – Gear or lubricating oil temperature °C
t_1 – room temperature °C

The amount of heat generated is given as $Q_g = \dfrac{\mu F_n v_r}{\cos \gamma}$

... (Eq. 5.58) **12.124a/ Pg 179, DHB**

F_n – Force normal to the tooth surface $= \dfrac{F_t}{\cos\gamma \cos\alpha}$

Artificial cooling is required if $Q_d < Q_g$ ...(Eq. 5.59)

5.32 POWER RATING

According AGMA, the limiting input power rating in a plain worm gear unit from standpoint of heat dissipation for worm gear speeds up to 2000 rpm is given as

$$P(\text{kW}) = \frac{0.02905 \, a^{1.7}}{(i' + 5)} \quad \text{... (Eq. 5.60)} \; \textbf{12.130a/Pg 180, DHB}$$

a = center distance

$$= \frac{d_1 + d_2}{2}$$

$$= \left[\frac{z_2}{q} + 1\right]\left[\left(\frac{540}{\frac{z_2}{q}\sigma_{sur}}\right)^2 M_t K_c K_d\right]^{1/3} \quad \text{(Dobrovolsky)}$$

...from (Eq. 5.46) 12.102/ Pg 176, DHB

σ_{sur} = allowable surface stress
M_t = torque
K_c = Load concentration factor ...Table 12.10/ Pg 189, DHB
K_d = dynamic load factor ...Table 12.11/Pg 189, DHB
d_2 = pitch diameter of worm gear = mz_2 ...12.97b/Pg 175, DHB
z_2 = number of teeth in worm gear
q = number of modules in the pitch diamter of the worm

$$= \frac{d_1}{m} = 6 \text{ to } 13 \quad \text{...12.106/ Pg 175, DHB}$$

t' – transmission ratio = $\dfrac{n_w}{n_g} = \dfrac{n_1}{n_2} = i$ n – speed in rps

5.33 BASIC PROBLEMS

14. A triple threaded worm has a pitch diameter of 80 mm and an axial pitch of 30 mm. Determine the lead angle.

Solution: $z_1 = 3$, pitch diameter of worm, $d_1 = 80$ mm, axial pitch, $p = 30$ mm, lead angle, $\gamma = ?$

We know that, $\tan \gamma = \dfrac{l}{\pi d_1} = \dfrac{z_1 p}{\pi d_1}$ ...12.100/ Pg 175, DHB

$$= \frac{3 \times 30}{\pi \times 80}$$

$$\gamma = 19.07°$$

15. A triple threaded worm has teeth of 6 mm module and pitch circle diameter of 50 mm. If the worm gear has 30 teeth of 14 ½ and coefficient of friction of the worm gearing is 0.05, find:

i. the lead angle of the worm, ii. velocity ratio, iii. center distance, iv. efficiency of the worm gearing.

VTU – June / July 2009 – 14 Marks

Solution: $z_1 = 3$, $m = 6$ mm, $d_1 = 50$ mm, $z_2 = 30$, $\alpha = 14.5°$, $\mu = 0.05$.
  i. $\gamma = ?$ ii. $i' = ?$ iii. $a = ?$ iv. $\eta = ?$

i. Lead angle (γ):

We know that, $\tan\gamma = \dfrac{l}{\pi d_1} = \dfrac{\pi m z_1}{\pi d_1} = \dfrac{m z_1}{d_1}$ ...12.97a/ Pg 175, DHB

$$= \dfrac{6 \times 3}{50}$$

$\gamma = 19.79°$

ii. Velocity ratio (i'):

We know that, $i' = \dfrac{n_1}{n_2} = \dfrac{d_2}{d_1} = \dfrac{z_2}{z_1}$ .... 12.130b/ Pg 180, DHB

$i' = \dfrac{z_2}{z_1} = \dfrac{30}{3}$ (N – rpm, n – rps)

$i' = 10$

iii. Center distance (a):

We know that centre distance $a = \dfrac{d_1 + d_2}{2} = \dfrac{d_1 + m \cdot z_2}{2}$

$$= \dfrac{50 + (6 \times 30)}{2}$$

$a = 115$ mm

iv. Efficiency of the worm gearing (η):

Barr's formula for worm gearing, $\eta = \dfrac{\tan\gamma\,(1 - \mu\tan\gamma)}{\mu + \tan\gamma}$ ...12.117/ Pg 177, DHB

$$= \dfrac{\tan 17.97\,[1 - (0.05 \times \tan 19.79)]}{0.05 + \tan 19.79}$$

$= 0.8622$

$\eta = 86.22\%$

16. A two teeth right hand worm transmits 2 kW at 1500 rpm to a 36 teeth wheel. The module of the wheel is 5 mm and the pitch diameter of the worm is 60 mm. The pressure angle is 14.5°. The coefficient of friction is found to be 0.06.
   a. Find the center distance, the lead and the lead angle
   b. Determine the forces.
   c. Determine the efficiency of the drive.

VTU – Dec. 09/ Jan. 2010 – 10 Marks; July/ Aug. 2002 – 10 Marks.

Solution: $z_1 = 2$, $P = 2$ kW, $N_1 = 1500$ rpm $\Rightarrow n_1 = 25$ rps, $z_2 = 36$, $m = 5$ mm, $d_1 = 60$ mm, $\alpha = 14.5°$, $\mu = 0.06$

i. $a = ?$, $l = ?$, $\gamma = ?$ ii. Force = ? iii. $\eta = ?$

We know that, $i' = \dfrac{n_1}{n_2} = \dfrac{d_2}{d_1} = \dfrac{z_2}{z_1}$ ...12.130b/ Pg 180, DHB

Bevel and Worm Gears

$$i' = \frac{z_2}{z_1} = \frac{36}{2} \quad (N-\text{rpm}, \ n-\text{rps})$$

$$i' = 18$$

Also
$$i' = \frac{n_1}{n_2}$$

$$18 = \frac{25}{n_2}$$

$$n_2 = 1.38 \text{ rps}$$

a. Center distance, the lead and the lead angle:

- We know that centre distance $a = \dfrac{d_1 + d_2}{2} = \dfrac{d_1 + m \cdot z_2}{2}$

$$= \frac{60 + (5 \times 36)}{2}$$

$$a = 120 \text{ mm}$$

- Lead, $\quad l = \pi m z_1 \quad$ ...12.98/ Pg 175, DHB

$$= \pi \times 5 \times 2$$

$$l = 31.42 \text{ mm}$$

- Lead angle $\quad \tan\gamma = \dfrac{l}{\pi d_1} \quad$ ...12.100/ Pg 175, DHB

$$= \frac{31.42}{\pi \times 60}$$

$$\gamma = 9.46°$$

b. Forces:

- Resulting turning force on the worm wheel, when the wheel turns the worm:

$$F_x = F_t \left[\frac{\cos\theta\cos\gamma + \mu\sin\gamma}{\cos\theta\sin\gamma - \mu\cos\gamma} \right] \quad \text{...Eq. (}i\text{) 12.112/ Pg 177, DHB}$$

- But $\quad \tan\theta = \tan\alpha\cos\gamma$

$$= \tan(14.5) \times \cos(9.46)$$

$$\theta = 14.31°$$

- Also, $\quad F_t = \dfrac{2M_{te}}{d_2} = \dfrac{2M_t K_l}{d_2} \quad$ ...Eq. (ii) 12.109/ Pg 177, DHB

  Here $\quad d_2 = mz_2 = 5 \times 36 = 180$ mm $\quad$ ...12.97b/ Pg 175, DHB

  $K_l = 1 -$ load factor (assumed)

- $P = 2\pi n_2 M_t$

  $2 \times 10^3 = 2\pi \times 1.38 \times M_t$

  $M_t = 230.65$ N-m $= 230.65 \times 10^3$ N-mm

∴ Eq. (ii) yields...
$$F_t = \frac{2 \times 230.65 \times 10^3 \times 1}{180}$$

$$F_t = 2562.78 \text{ N}$$

∴ Eq. (i) yields... $F_x = 2562.78 \times \left[\dfrac{(\cos 14.31 \times \cos 9.46) + (0.06 \times \sin 9.46)}{(\cos 14.31 \times \sin 9.46) - (0.06 \times \cos 9.46)}\right]$

$F_x = 24.73$ kN

- Separating force, $F_y = F_t \left[\dfrac{\sin \theta}{\cos \theta . \cos \gamma - \mu \cos \gamma}\right]$ ...12.113/ Pg 177, DHB

$$= \dfrac{2562.78 \times \sin 14.31}{(\cos 14.31 \times \cos 9.46) - (0.06 \times \sin 9.46)}$$

$F_y = 669.6$ N

- Resulting turning force on the worm, when the worm turns the wheel:

$$F_z = F_t \left[\dfrac{\cos \theta . \sin \gamma + \mu \cos \gamma}{\cos \theta . \cos \gamma - \mu \cos \gamma}\right] \quad \text{...12.114/ Pg 177, DHB}$$

$$= 2562.78 \times \left[\dfrac{(\cos 14.31 \times \sin 9.46) + (0.06 \times \cos 9.46)}{(\cos 14.31 \times \cos 9.46) - (0.06 \times \cos 9.46)}\right]$$

$F_z = 624.38$ N

17. A pair of worm and worm gear is designated as 3/60/10/8. The worm is transmitting 5 kW at 1500 rpm to the worm wheel. The coefficient of friction is 0.1 and normal pressure angle is 20°. Determine the components of gear tooth force acting on the worm and worm wheel.

Solution: 3/60/10/8 $\Rightarrow z_1/z_2/q/m$. $z_1 = 3$, $z_2 = 60$, $q = 10$, $m = 8$, $P = 5$ kW, $N_1 = 1500$ rpm $\Rightarrow n_1 = 25$ rps, $\alpha = 20°$, $\mu = 0.1$. Force components = ?

- We know that $i' = \dfrac{n_1}{n_2} = \dfrac{d_2}{d_1} = \dfrac{z_2}{z_1}$ ...12.130b/ Pg 180, DHB

$$i' = \dfrac{z_2}{z_1} = \dfrac{60}{3} \quad (N-\text{rpm}, \ n-\text{rps})$$

$i' = 20$ and $n_2 = 1.25$ rps

Also $q = \dfrac{d_1}{m}$ ...12.101/ Pg 175, DHB

$d_1 = mq = 8 \times 10 = 80$ mm

- $d_2 = mz_2 = 8 \times 60 = 480$ mm ...12.97b/ Pg 175, DHB

- We know that, $\tan \gamma = \dfrac{l}{\pi d_1} = \dfrac{mz_1}{d_1}$ ...12.97a/ Pg 175, DHB

$$= \dfrac{8 \times 3}{80}$$

$\gamma = 16.7°$

Forces:
- Resulting turning force on the worm wheel, when the wheel turns the worm:

$$F_x = F_t \left[\frac{\cos\theta \cos\gamma + \mu \sin\gamma}{\cos\theta \sin\gamma - \mu \cos\gamma} \right] \quad \text{...Eq. (i) 12.112/ Pg 177, DHB}$$

- But
$$\tan\theta = \tan\alpha \cos\gamma$$
$$= \tan(20) \times \cos(16.7)$$
$$\theta = 19.22°$$

- Also,
$$F_t = \frac{2M_{te}}{d_2} = \frac{2M_t K_l}{d_2} \quad \text{...Eq. (ii) 12.109/ Pg 177, DHB}$$
$$K_l = 1 - \text{load factor (assumed)}$$

- $P = 2\pi n_2 M_t$
$$5 \times 10^3 = 2\pi \times 1.25 \times M_t$$
$$M_t = 636.62 \text{ N-m} = 636.62 \times 10^3 \text{ N-mm}$$

∴ Eq. (ii) yields...
$$F_t = \frac{2 \times 636.62 \times 10^3 \times 1}{480}$$
$$F_t = 2652.58 \text{ N}$$

∴ Eq. (i) yields...
$$F_x = 2562.78 \times \left[\frac{(\cos 19.22 \times \cos 16.7) + (0.1 \times \sin 16.7)}{(\cos 19.22 \times \sin 16.7) - (0.1 \times \cos 16.7)} \right]$$
$$F_x = 14.1 \text{ kN}$$

- Separating force,
$$F_y = F_t \left[\frac{\sin\theta}{\cos\theta \cdot \cos\gamma - \mu \cos\gamma} \right] \quad \text{...12.113/ Pg 177, DHB}$$
$$= \frac{2652.58 \times \sin 19.22}{(\cos 19.22 \times \cos 16.7) - (0.1 \times \sin 16.7)}$$
$$F_y = 998.67 \text{ N}$$

- Resulting turning force on the worm, when the worm turns the wheel:
$$F_z = F_t \left[\frac{\cos\theta \cdot \sin\gamma + \mu \cos\gamma}{\cos\theta \cdot \cos\gamma - \mu \cos\gamma} \right] \quad \text{...12.114/ Pg 177, DHB}$$
$$= 2652.58 \times \left[\frac{(\cos 19.22 \times \sin 16.7) + (0.1 \times \cos 16.7)}{(\cos 19.22 \times \cos 16.7) - (0.1 \times \cos 16.7)} \right]$$
$$F_z = 1204.26 \text{ N}$$

18. One kW of power at 740 rpm is supplied to worm shaft. The number of starts for threads of worm are 6 with a pitch circle diameter of 60 mm. the worm gear has 32 teeth with 6 mm module. The normal pressure angle is 20°. Calculate the efficiency of worm gear drive and the power lost in friction.

VTU – Dec. 08/ Jan. 2009 – 06 Marks

Solution: $P = 1$ kW, $N_1 = 740$ rpm $\Rightarrow n_1 = 12.34$ rps, $z_1 = 6$, $d_1 = 60$ mm, $z_2 = 32$, $m = 6$, $\alpha = 20°$.

   i. $\eta = ?$ ii. Power lost in friction = ?

i. To find efficiency:

When the worm drives the worm gear, $\eta = \dfrac{\cos\theta - \mu \tan\gamma}{\cos\theta + \mu \cot\gamma}$

...Eq. (i) **12.115/ Pg 177, DHB**

- Also $\tan\gamma = \dfrac{1}{\pi d_1} = \dfrac{mz_1}{d_1}$ ...**12.97a/ Pg 175, DHB**

$$= \dfrac{6 \times 6}{60}$$

$$\gamma = 31°$$

- $\tan\theta = \tan\alpha \cos\gamma$

  $= \tan(20) \times \cos(31)$

  $\theta = 17.33°$

- μ – depends upon rubbing velocity v_r

$$v_r = \dfrac{\pi d_1 n_1}{1000 \times \cos\gamma}$$

...**12.121/ Pg 179, DHB**

$$v_r = \dfrac{\pi \times 60 \times 12.34}{1000 \times \cos 31}$$

$$v_r = 2.71 \text{ m/s}$$

And $v = \dfrac{\pi d_1 n_1}{1000}$

$$= \dfrac{\pi \times 60 \times 12.34}{1000}$$

$$v = 2.32 \text{ m/s}$$

$\therefore \quad \mu = \dfrac{0.0422}{(vr)^{0.28}}$, for $0.2 < v < 2.8$ m/s ...**12.120a/ Pg 178, DHB**

$$= \dfrac{0.0422}{(2.71)^{0.28}}$$

$$\mu = 0.032$$

$\therefore$ Eq. (i) yields... $\eta = \dfrac{\cos 17.33 - (0.032 \times \tan 31)}{\cos 17.33 + (0.032 \times \cot 31)} = 0.9281$

$$\eta = 92.81 \%$$

ii. Power lost in friction:

We know that, $Q_d = 1000 \text{ (kW)} (1 - h)$ ...**12.124b/ Pg 180, DHB**

$= 1000 \times 1 \times (1 - 0.9281)$

$= 72 \text{ J/s}$

$Q_d = 0.072 \text{ kW}$

5.34 DESIGN PROCEDURE FOR WORM GEAR

Material selection:
- Select suitable material if not given from **Table 12.7/ Pg 186, DHB**.
- **The material for the worm is hardened steel and that for worm wheel is phosphor bronze.**
- Design is based on Worm wheel (weaker part).

The worm gear is assumed to be weaker than the worm since it is subjected to sliding action, thereby resulting in overheating and leading to failure.

a. To find diameters:
  i. When the centre distance is known:

  - Pitch diameter of the worm $d_1 = \dfrac{a^{0.875}}{1.466}$ ...12.103/ Pg 176, DHB

  - The pitch diameter of the worm gear is $d_2 = 2a - d_1$ $\left[\because a = \dfrac{d_1 + d_2}{2}\right]$

  ii. When the centre distance is unknown:

  - Find a using $P(kW) = \dfrac{0.02905\, a^{1.7}}{(i' + 5)}$ ...12.130a/ Pg 180, DHB

  - Pitch diameter of the worm $d_1 = \dfrac{a^{0.875}}{1.466}$ ...12.103/ Pg 176, DHB

  - The pitch diameter of the worm gear is, $d_2 = 2a - d_1$ $\left[\because a = \dfrac{d_1 + d_2}{2}\right]$

b. To find module:
$$F_t = \sigma_d C_v b Y m = \sigma_d C_v b \pi y m \quad \text{...12.106/ Pg 176, DHB}$$

- $v = \pi d_2 n_2$ (since worm gear is weaker)

- $C_v = \dfrac{6.1}{6.1 + v}$ ...12.108/ Pg 176, DHB

- face width $b = \dfrac{a^{0.875}}{2}$ ...12.125/ Pg 180, DHB

- $F_t = \dfrac{2 M_{te}}{d_2} = \dfrac{2 M_t K_l}{d_2}$ ...12.109/ Pg 177, DHB

  $K_l = 1 -$ load factor ...Table 12.34/ Pg 203, DHB

- $P = 2\pi n_2 M_t$
- Value of z_1, based on i' ...Table 12.28/ Pg 199, DHB
- Value of α based on γ ...Table 12.27/ Pg 199, DHB
- Value of Lewis form factor (y) based on α ...Table 12.29/ Pg 199, DHB

c. Lead angle:
$$\tan \gamma = \dfrac{m z_1}{d_1} \quad \text{...12.97a/ Pg 175, DHB}$$

d. To find dynamic tooth load:
$$F_s = \sigma_d b Y m \qquad \text{...12.110/ Pg 177, DHB}$$

e. To find Wear tooth load:
$$F_w = d_2 b K \qquad \text{...12.122/ Pg 179, DHB}$$

K – load stress factor ...Table 12.31/ Pg 202, DHB

$F_w > F_s$, the material is safe against wear.

f. To find efficiency:
When the worm drives the worm gear, $\eta = \dfrac{\cos\theta - \mu\tan\gamma}{\cos\theta + \mu\cot\gamma}$ ...12.115/ Pg 177, DHB

- $\tan\theta = \tan\alpha \cos\gamma$
- μ – depends upon rubbing velocity v_r

$$v_r = \frac{\pi d_1 n_1}{1000 \times \cos\gamma} \qquad \text{...12.121/ Pg 179, DHB}$$

$$\mu = \frac{0.0422}{(v_r)^{0.28}}, \text{ for } 0.2 < v < 2.8 \text{ m/s} \qquad \text{...12.120a/ Pg 178, DHB}$$

$$= 0.025 + \frac{3.281\, v_r}{1000} - \text{ for speeds } > 2.8 \text{ m/s} \qquad \text{...12.120b/ Pg 178, DHB}$$

g. Heat generated:
We know that heat generated $Q_g = \dfrac{\mu F_n v_r}{\cos\gamma}$ ...12.124a/ Pg 179, DHB

$$F_n = \frac{F_t}{\cos\gamma \cos\alpha}$$

h. Heat dissipated:
We know that heat dissipated $Q_d = 1000\,(kW)(1-\eta)$ ...12.124b/ Pg 180, DHB

-OR- $Q_d = \dfrac{0.407}{1000}(A_g + A_w)(t_2 - t_1)$ ...12.124c/ Pg 180, DHB

If $Q_d > Q_g$, artificial cooling is not necessary

5.35 CENTER DISTANCE IS KNOWN

19. Design a suitable worm gearing with the following details:

Power = 3.75 kW, speed ratio = 27, pressure angle = 14.5°, center distance = 180 mm, worm speed = 1200 rpm. The material for the worm is hardened steel with design stress as 45 MPa and that for worm wheel is phosphor bronze with a design stress of 52 MPa.

Solution: $P = 3.75$ kW, $i' = 27$, $\alpha = 14.5°$, $a = 180$ mm, $N_1 = 1200$ rpm $\Rightarrow n_1 = 20$ rps, worm material – hardened steel, $\sigma_{d1} = 45$ MPa, Worm sheel – phosphor bronze, $\sigma_{d2} = 52$ MPa. *Design.*

We know that, $\qquad i' = \dfrac{n_1}{n_2} = \dfrac{d_2}{d_1} = \dfrac{z_2}{z_1}$ ...12.130b/ Pg 180, DHB

$$27 = \frac{20}{n_2}$$

$$n_2 = 0.741 \text{ rps}$$

Identifying weaker part (pinion/gear):

The worm gear is assumed to be weaker than the worm since it is subjected to sliding action, thereby resulting in overheating and leading to failures.

a. To find diameters:

- Pitch diameter of the worm $d_1 = \dfrac{a^{0.875}}{1.466}$ ...12.103/ Pg 176, DHB

$$= \frac{180^{0.0875}}{1.466}$$

$$d_1 = 64.15 \text{ mm} \approx 65 \text{ mm}$$

- The pitch diameter of the worm gear is $d_2 = 2a - d_1$ $\left[\because a = \dfrac{d_1 + d_2}{2}\right]$

$$= (2 \times 180) - 65$$

$$d_2 = 295 \text{ mm}$$

b. To find module:

We know that, $F_t = \sigma_d C_v b Y m = \sigma_d C_v b \pi y m$ ...Eq. (i) 12.106/ Pg 176, DHB

- $v = \pi d_2 n_2 = \pi \times 0.295 \times 0.741 = 0.686$ m/s

- $C_v = \dfrac{6.1}{6.1 + v}$ ...12.108/ Pg 176, DHB

$$= \frac{6.1}{6.1 + 0.686}$$

$C_v = 0.8989$

- Face width $b = \dfrac{a^{0.875}}{2}$ ...12.125/ Pg 180, DHB

$$= \frac{180^{0.875}}{2}$$

$b = 47.03$ mm ≈ 50 mm

- $F_t = \dfrac{2 M_{te}}{d_2} = \dfrac{2 M_t K_l}{d_2}$ ...Eq. (ii) 12.109/ Pg 177, DHB

$K_l = 1$ – load factor (assumed)

Also
$$P = 2\pi n_2 M_t$$
$$3.75 \times 10^3 = 2\pi \times 0.7415 \times M_t$$
$$M_t = 805.44 \text{ N-m} = 805.44 \times 10^3 \text{ N-mm}$$

∴ Eq. (ii) yields... $F_t = \dfrac{2 \times 805.44 \times 10^3 \times 1}{295}$

$F_t = 5460.61$ N

For $\alpha = 14.5°$, Lewis form factor, $y = 0.1$ ...Table 12.29/Pg 199, DHB
For $i' > 20$, $z_1 = 1$ ...Table 12.28/ Pg 199, DHB
∴ $z_2 = i'z_1 = 27 \times 1 = 27$ teeth
∴ Eq. (i) yields... $5460.61 = 52 \times 0.8989 \times 50 \times \pi \times 0.1 \times m$

$m = 7.44$

Therefore, standard module, $m = 8$ mm ...Tb. 12.30/ Pg 200, DHB

c. Lead angle:

We know that, $\tan \gamma = \dfrac{mz_1}{d_1}$ ...12.97a/ Pg 175, DHB

$= \dfrac{8 \times 1}{65}$

$\gamma = 7.02°$

d. To find dynamic tooth load:

We know that, $F_s = \sigma_d bYm$ ...12.110/Pg 177, DHB

$= 52 \times 50 \times \pi \times 0.1 \times 8$

$F_s = F_d = 6534.51$ N

e. To find wear tooth load:

The limiting load of wear, $F_w = d_2 bK$ ...12.122/ Pg 179, DHB

for $\gamma = 7.2°$, load stress factor, $K = 0.549$

...Table 12.31/Pg 202, DHB

$= 295 \times 50 \times 0.549$

$F_w = 8097.75$ N

Since $F_w > F_s$, the material is safe against wear.

f. To find efficiency

When the worm drives the worm gear, $\eta = \dfrac{\cos \theta - \mu \tan \gamma}{\cos \theta + \mu \cot \gamma}$

...Eq. (iii) 12.115/ Pg 177, DHB

- $\tan \theta = \tan \alpha \cos \gamma$

  $= \tan (14.5) \times \cos (7.02)$

  $\theta = 14.39°$

- μ–depends upon rubbing velocity v_r

$v_r = \dfrac{\pi d_1 n_1}{1000 \times \cos \gamma}$ ...12.121/Pg 179 DHB

$$= \frac{\pi \times 65 \times 20}{1000 \times \cos 7.02}$$

$$v_r = 4.11 \text{ m/s}$$

And
$$v = \frac{\pi d_1 n_1}{1000} = \frac{\pi \times 65 \times 20}{1000} = 4.08 \text{ m/s}$$

$$\therefore \mu = 0.025 + \frac{3.281 v_r}{1000} \text{ — for } v > 2.8 \text{ m/s} \qquad \text{...12.120b/Pg 178, DHB}$$

$$= 0.025 + \frac{3.281 \times 4.11}{1000}$$

$$\mu = 0.0385$$

∴ Eq. (iii) yields...
$$\eta = \frac{\cos 14.39 - (0.0385 \times \tan 7.02)}{\cos 14.39 + (0.0385 \times \cot 7.02)} = 0.7523$$

$$\eta = 75.23\%$$

g. Heat generated:

We know that heat generated $Q_g = \dfrac{\mu F_n v_r}{\cos \gamma}$ ...Eq. (iv) **12.124a/ Pg 179, DHB**

$$F_n = \frac{F_t}{\cos \gamma \cos \alpha}$$

$$= \frac{5460.61}{\cos 7.02 \times \cos 14.5}$$

$$F_n = 5682.87 \text{ N}$$

∴ Eq. (iv) yields...
$$Q_g = \frac{0.0385 \times 5682.87 \times 4.11}{\cos 7.02}$$

$$= 906 \text{ W}$$

$$Q_g = 0.906 \text{ kW}$$

h. Heat dissipated:

We know that heat dissipated $Q_d = 1000 \text{ (kW)} (1 - \eta)$ ...**12.124b/ Pg 180, DHB**

$$= 1000 \times 3.75 \times (1 - 0.7523)$$

$$= 928.88 \text{ W}$$

$$Q_d = 0.928 \text{ kW}$$

Since $Q_d > Q_g$, artificial cooling is not necessary

20. Design a worm gear drive to transmit 2 kW of power at 1000 rpm. The speed ratio is 20 and center distance is 200 mm. Assume the number of teeth on worm wheel to be 40 and number of starts on worm to be 2. Assume hardened steel worm and phosphor bronze wheel for which $\sigma_d = 55 \text{ N/mm}^2$. Check the gear from stand

point of strength and wear if load stress factor, $K = 0.69$ MPa. If the amount of heat generated is 1.7 KW, check whether artificial cooling is necessary or not for a temperature rise of 40°C.   *VTU – June/ July 2009 – 15 Marks*

Solution: $P = 2$ kW, $N_1 = 1000$ rpm $\Rightarrow n_1 = 16.67$ rps, $i' = 20$, $a = 200$ mm, $z_1 = 2$, $z_2 = 40$, worm material – hardened steel, worm wheel – phosphor bronze, $\sigma_{d2} = 55$ MPa, load stress factor, $K = 0.69$ MPa, $Q_g = 1.7$ kW, $\Delta_t = [t_2 - t_1] = 40°C$. *Design*.

We know that, $i' = \dfrac{n_1}{n_2} = \dfrac{d_2}{d_1} = \dfrac{z_2}{z_1}$ ...**12.130b/ Pg 180, DHB**

$$20 = \dfrac{16.67}{n_2}$$

$$n_2 = 0.8335 \text{ rps}$$

Identifying weaker part (pinion/gear):

The worm gear is assumed to be weaker than the worm since it is subjected to sliding action, thereby resulting in overheating and leading to failure.

a. To find diameters:

- Pitch diameter of the worm $d_1 = \dfrac{a^{0.875}}{1.466}$ ...**12.103/ Pg 176, DHB**

$$= \dfrac{200^{0.875}}{1.466}$$

$$d_1 = 70.35 \text{ mm} \approx 75 \text{ mm}$$

- The pitch diameter of the worm gear is, $d_2 = 2a - d_1$ $\left[\because a = \dfrac{d_1 + d_2}{2} \right]$

$$= (2 \times 200) - 75$$

$$d_2 = 325 \text{ mm}$$

b. To find module:

We know that, $F_t = \sigma_d C_v bYm = \sigma_d C_v b\pi ym$ ...Eq. (i) **12.106/ Pg 176, DHB**

- $v = \pi d_2 n_2 = \pi \times 0.325 \times 0.8335 = 0.851$ m/s

- $C_v = \dfrac{6.1}{6.1 + v}$ ...**12.108/ Pg 176, DHB**

$$= \dfrac{6.1}{6.1 + 0.851}$$

$$C_v = 0.8776$$

- face width $b = \dfrac{a^{0.875}}{2}$ ...**12.125/ Pg 180, DHB**

$$= \dfrac{200^{0.875}}{2}$$

$$b = 51.58 \text{ mm} \approx 55 \text{ mm}$$

- $F_t = \dfrac{2M_{te}}{d_2} = \dfrac{2M_t K_l}{d_2}$ ...Eq. (ii) 12.109/ Pg 177, DHB

   $K_l = 1$ – load factor (assumed)
   Also $P = 2\pi n_2 M_t$
   $2 \times 10^3 = 2\pi \times 0.8335 \times Mt$
   $M_t = 382$ N-m $= 382 \times 10^3$ N-mm

   ∴ Eq. (ii) yields... $F_t = \dfrac{2 \times 382 \times 10^3 \times 1}{325}$

   $F_t = 2350.77$ N

Given: $z_1 = 2$
For $z_1 = 2, \alpha = 145°$ ...Table 12.26/ Pg 199, DHB
For $\alpha = 14.5°$, Lewis form factor, $y = 0.1$
                 ...Table 12.29/ Pg 199, DHB

∴ Eq. (i) yields... $2350.77 = 55 \times 0.8776 \times 55 \times \pi \times 0.1 \times m$
                      $m = 2.88$
Therefore, standard module, $m = 3$ mm   ...Tb. 12.30/ Pg 200, DHB

c. Lead angle:

We know that, $\tan \gamma = \dfrac{mz_1}{d_1}$ ...12.97a/ Pg 175, DHB

$= \dfrac{3 \times 2}{75}$

$\gamma = 4.57°$

d. To find dynamic tooth load:

We know that, $F_s = \sigma_d b Y m$ ...12.110/ Pg 177, DHB
                 $= 55 \times 55 \times \pi \times 0.1 \times 3$
                 $F_s = F_d = 2851$ N

e. To find wear tooth load:

The limiting load of wear, $F_w = d_2 b K$ ...12.122/ Pg 179, DHB
                 $K = 0.69$ (data)
                 $F_w = 325 \times 55 \times 0.69 = 12.33$ kN
                 $F_w = 12.33$ kN
Since $F_w > F_s$, the material is safe against wear.

f. To find efficiency:

When the worm drives the worm gear, $\eta = \dfrac{\cos \theta - \mu \tan \gamma}{\cos \theta + \mu \cot \gamma}$

...Eq. (iii) 12.115/ Pg 177, DHB

- $\tan \theta = \tan \alpha \cos \gamma$
  $= \tan(14.5) \times \cos(4.57)$
  $\theta = 14.46°$
- $\mu =$ depends upon rubbing velocity v_r

$$v_r = \frac{\pi d_1 n_1}{1000 \times \cos \gamma} \qquad \text{...12.121/ Pg 179, DHB}$$

$$= \frac{\pi \times 75 \times 16.67}{1000 \times \cos 4.57}$$

$$v_r = 3.94 \text{ m/s}$$

And $\quad v = \dfrac{\pi d_1 n_1}{1000} = \dfrac{\pi \times 75 \times 16.67}{1000} = 3.93$ m/s

$\therefore \quad \mu = 0.025 + \dfrac{3.281\, v_r}{1000}$ – for speed > m/s $\quad$ ...12.120b/ Pg 178, DHB

$$= 0.025 + \frac{3.281 \times 3.94}{1000}$$

$\mu = 0.0379$

$\therefore$ Eq. (*iii*) yields... $\quad \eta = \dfrac{\cos 14.46 - (0.0379 \times \tan 4.57)}{\cos 14.46 + (0.0379 \times \cot 4.57)} = 0.6692$

$$\eta = 66.92 \%$$

g. Heat generated:

Heat generated $\quad Q_g = 1.7$ kW $\qquad$ (data)

h. Heat dissipated:

We know that heat dissipated $Q_d = \dfrac{0.407}{1000}(A_g + A_w)(t_2 - t_1)$ ...12.124c/ Pg 180, DHB

where, $\qquad \Delta t = [t_2 - t_1] = 40°C \qquad$ (data)

$$A_g = \frac{\pi d_2^2}{4} = \frac{\pi \times 325^2}{4} = 82.96 \times 10^3 \text{ mm}^2$$

$L_w = (14.14 + 0.063 z_1)\, m \qquad$ ...Table 12.25/ Pg 198, DHB

$\qquad = (14.14 + 0.063 \times 2) 3$

$L_w = 42.80$ mm

$A_w = L_w d_1 = 42.80 \times 75 = 3210$ mm^2

$\therefore \quad Q_d = \dfrac{0.407}{1000}(82.96 \times 10^3 + 3210) \times 40$

$\qquad = 1402.85$ W

$\therefore \quad Q_d = 1.403$ kW

Since $Q_d < Q_g$, artificial cooling is necessary.

5.36 CENTER DISTANCE IS UNKNOWN

21. Design a worm gear drive for a speed reduction ratio of 25. The pinion rotates at 600 rpm and transmits 35 kW.

Solution: $i' = 25$, $N_1 = 600$ rpm $\Rightarrow n_1 = 10$ rps, $P = 35$ kW. *Design.*

We know that, $\quad i' = \dfrac{n_1}{n_2} = \dfrac{d_2}{d_1} = \dfrac{z_2}{z_1}$ ...**12.130b/ Pg 180, DHB**

$$25 = \dfrac{10}{n_2}$$

$$n_2 = 0.4 \text{ rps}$$

Identifying weaker part (pinion/gear):

Since the material is not specified, let us assume the following materials:
Worm/ Pinion: C30 heat treated steel, having σ_{d1} = 220.6 MPa
Worm Gear/ wheel: Phosphor bronze, having σ_{d2} = 82.4 MPa
...**Tb. 12.7/ Pg 186, DHB**

The worm gear is assumed to be weaker than the worm since it is subjected to sliding action, thereby resulting in overheating and leading to failure.

a. To find center distance:

We know that power, $\quad P(\text{kW}) = \dfrac{0.02905\, a^{1.7}}{(i' + 5)}$ ...**12.130a/ Pg 180, DHB**

$$35 = \dfrac{0.02905\, a^{1.7}}{(25 + 5)}$$

$$a = 480 \text{ mm}$$

b. To find diameters:

- Pitch diameter of the worm $\quad d_1 = \dfrac{a^{0.875}}{1.466}$ ...**12.103/ Pg 176, DHB**

$$= \dfrac{480^{0.875}}{1.466}$$

$$d_1 = 151.34 \text{ mm} \approx 155 \text{ mm}$$

- The pitch diameter of the worm gear is, $d_2 = 2a - d_1$ $\left[\because a = \dfrac{d_1 + d_2}{2}\right]$

$$= (2 \times 480) - 155$$

$$d_2 = 805 \text{ mm}$$

c. To find module:

We know that, $\quad F_t = \sigma_d C_v b Y m$ ...Eq. (i) **12.106/ Pg 176, DHB**

- $v = \pi d_2 n_2 = \pi \times 0.805 \times 0.4 = 1.012 \text{ m/s}$

- $C_v = \dfrac{6.1}{6.1 + v}$ ...**12.108/ Pg 176, DHB**

$$= \dfrac{6.1}{6.1 + 1.012}$$

$$C_v = 0.8578$$

- face width $b = \dfrac{a^{0.875}}{2}$ ...**12.125/ Pg 180, DHB**

$$= \frac{480^{0.875}}{2}$$
$$b = 111 \text{ mm} \approx 115 \text{ mm}$$

- $$F_t = \frac{2M_{te}}{d_2} = \frac{2M_t K_l}{d_2} \qquad \text{...Eq. (ii) } 12.109/ \text{ Pg 177, DHB}$$

$K_l = 1$ – load factor (assumed)

Also
$$P = 2\pi n_2 M_t$$
$$35 \times 10^3 = 2\pi \times 0.4 \times M_t$$
$$M_t = 13.93 \times 10^3 \text{ N-m} = 13.93 \times 10^6 \text{ N-mm}$$

∴ Eq. (ii) yields... $$F_t = \frac{2 \times 13.93 \times 10^6 \times 1}{805}$$
$$F_t = 34.61 \times 10^3 \text{ N}$$

For $i' > 20$, $z_1 = 1$ ...Table 12.28/ Pg 199, DHB
For $z_1 = 1$, $\alpha = 14.5°$ ...Table 12.26/ Pg 199, DHB
For $\alpha = 14.5°$, Lewis form factor, $y = 0.1$ ...Table 12.29/ Pg 199, DHB

∴ Eq. (i) yields... $34.61 \times 10^3 = 82.4 \times 0.8578 \times 115 \times \pi \times 0.1 \times m$
$$m = 13.26 \text{ mm}$$

Therefore, standard module, $m = 16$ mm ...Tb. 12.30/ Pg 200, DHB

d. Lead angle:

We know that, $$\gamma = \frac{mz_1}{d_1} \qquad \text{...12.97a/ Pg 175, DHB}$$
$$= \frac{16 \times 1}{155}$$
$$\gamma = 5.89°$$

e. To find dynamic tooth load:

We know that, $$F_s = \sigma_d bYm \qquad \text{...12.110/ Pg 177, DHB}$$
$$= 82.4 \times 115 \times \pi \times 0.1 \times 16$$
$$F_s = F_d = 47.63 \text{ kN}$$

f. To find wear tooth load:

The limiting load of wear, $F_w = d_2 bK$ ...12.122/ Pg 179, DHB
For $\gamma = 5.89°$, $K = 0.549$ ...Tb. 12.31/ Pg 202, DHB
$$= 805 \times 115 \times 0.549$$
$$F_w = 50.82 \text{ kN}$$

Since $F_w > F_s$, the material is safe against wear.

g. To find efficiency:

When the worm drives the worm gear, $$\eta = \frac{\cos\theta - \mu \tan\gamma}{\cos\theta + \mu \cot\gamma}$$
...Eq. (iii) 12.115/ Pg 177, DHB

- $\tan\theta = \tan\alpha \cos\gamma$
$$= \tan(14.5) \times \cos(5.89)$$
$$\theta = 14.43°$$

- μ = depends upon rubbing velocity v_r

$$v_r = \frac{\pi d_1 n_1}{1000 \times \cos \gamma} \qquad \text{...12.121/ Pg 179, DHB}$$

$$= \frac{\pi \times 155 \times 10}{1000 \times \cos 5.89}$$

$$v_r = 4.89 \text{ m/s}$$

And $v = \dfrac{\pi d_1 n_1}{1000} = \dfrac{\pi \times 155 \times 10}{1000} = 4.87$ m/s

$\therefore \quad \mu = 0.025 + \dfrac{3.281 v_r}{1000}$ – for speeds > 2.8 m/s ...12.120b/ Pg 178, DHB

$$= 0.025 + \frac{3.281 \times 4.89}{1000}$$

$$\mu = 0.0411$$

$\therefore$ Eq. (*iii*) yields... $\eta = \dfrac{\cos 14.43 - (0.0411 \times \tan 5.89)}{\cos 14.43 + (0.0411 \times \cot 5.89)} = 0.7054$

$$\eta = 70.54 \%$$

h. Heat generated:

We know that heat generated $Q_g = \dfrac{\mu F_n v_r}{\cos \gamma}$ ...Eq. (*iv*) **12.124a/ Pg 179, DHB**

$$F_n = \frac{F_t}{\cos \gamma \cos \alpha}$$

$$= \frac{34.61 \times 10^3}{\cos 5.89 \times \cos 14.5}$$

$$F_n = 35.94 \text{ kN}$$

$\therefore$ Eq. (*iv*) yields... $Q_g = \dfrac{0.0411 \times 35.94 \times 10^3 \times 4.89}{\cos 5.89}$

$$= 7261.52 \text{ W}$$

$$Q_g = 7.26 \text{ kW}$$

i. Heat dissipated:

We know that heat dissipated $Q_d = 1000(\text{kW})(1 - \eta)$ ...**12.124b/ Pg 180, DHB**
$$= 1000 \times 35 \times (1 - 0.7054)$$
$$= 10311 \text{ W}$$
$$Q_d = 10.31 \text{ kW}$$

Since $Q_d > Q_g$, artificial cooling is not necessary.

22. Design a worm drive for a speed reducer to transmit 30 kW at a worm speed of 600 rpm. The required velocity ratio is 25:1. The worm is made of C30 heat treated steel and the worm wheel is made of phosphor bronze. The service conditions are intermittent operations with medium shock loads. Also calculate the heat dissipation through the drive.

[VTU – June/ July 09 – 20 Marks; Dec.08/ Jan. 09 – 20 Marks; Jan./ Feb. 2005 – 20 Marks ; (Similar) Dec.07/ Jan. 08 – 20 Marks; (Similar) June 2012 – 15 Marks.]

Solution: $i' = 25$, $N_1 = 600$ rpm $\Rightarrow n_1 = 10$ rps, $P = 30$ kW. *Design*

We know that, $\qquad i' = \dfrac{n_1}{n_2} = \dfrac{d_2}{d_1} = \dfrac{z_2}{z_1}$ ...**12.130b/ Pg 180, DHB**

$$25 = \dfrac{10}{n_2}$$

$$n_2 = 0.4 \text{ rps}$$

Material properties:

Worm/ Pinion: C30 heat treated steel, having $\sigma_{d1} = 220.6$ MPa
Worm Gear/ wheel: Phosphor bronze, having $\sigma_{d2} = 82.4$ MPa

...**Tb. 12.7/ Pg 186, DHB**

The worm gear is assumed to be weaker than the worm since it is subjected to sliding action, thereby resulting in overheating and leading to failure.

a. To find center distance:

We know that power, $\quad P(kW) = \dfrac{0.02905 \, a^{1.7}}{(i' + 5)}$ ...**12.130a/ Pg 180, DHB**

$$30 = \dfrac{0.02905 \, a^{1.7}}{(25 + 5)}$$

$$a = 438 \text{ mm} \approx 450 \text{ mm}$$

b. To find diameters:

- Pitch diameter of the worm $\quad d_1 = \dfrac{a^{0.875}}{1.466}$ ...**12.103/ Pg 176, DHB**

$$= \dfrac{450^{0.875}}{1.466}$$

$$143 \text{ mm} \approx 150 \text{ mm}$$

- The pitch diameter of the worm gear is, $\quad d_2 = 2a - d_1 \qquad \left[\because a = \dfrac{d_1 + d_2}{2}\right]$

$$= (2 \times 450) - 150$$

$$d_2 = 750 \text{ mm}$$

c. To find module:

We know that, $\qquad F_t = \sigma_d C_v b Y m = \sigma_d C_v b Y m \quad$ ...Eq. (i) **12.106/ Pg 176, DHB**

- $v = \pi d_2 n_2 = \pi \times 0.750 \times 0.4 = 0.9425$ m/s

- $C_v = \dfrac{6.1}{6.1 + v}$ ...**12.108/ Pg 176, DHB**

$$= \dfrac{6.1}{6.1 + 0.9425}$$

$$C_v = 0.8662$$

- face width $b = \dfrac{a^{0.875}}{2}$ ...**12.125/ Pg 180, DHB**

$$= \frac{450^{0.875}}{2}$$
$$b = 104.8 \text{ mm} \approx 105 \text{ mm}$$

- $$F_t = \frac{2M_{te}}{d_2}C_s = \frac{2M_t K_l}{d_2}C_s \qquad \text{...Eq. (ii) 12.109/ Pg 177, DHB}$$

  $K_l = 1$ – load factor (assumed)
  C_s – service condition
  $\quad\quad = 1.25$ for intermittent operation and medium shocks
  $\hfill$ ...Tb. 12.8/ Pg 187, DHB

  Also $\quad P = 2\pi n_2 M_t$
  $\quad 30 \times 10^3 = 2\pi \times 0.4 \times M_t$
  $\quad M_t = 11.94 \times 10^3$ N-m $\;11.94 \times 10^6$ N-mm

  $\therefore\quad$ Eq. (ii) yields... $F_t = \dfrac{2 \times 11.94 \times 10^6 \times 1 \times 1.25}{750}$

  $$F_t = 39.79 \text{ kN}$$

For $i' > 20$, $z_1 = 1$ $\hfill$ ...Table 12.28/ Pg 199, DHB
For $z_1 = 1$, $\alpha = 14.5°$ $\hfill$ ...Table 12.26/ Pg 199, DHB
For $\alpha = 14.5°$, Lewis form factor, $y = 0.1$ $\hfill$ ...Table 12.29/ Pg 199, DHB
$\therefore\quad$ Eq. (i) yields... $39.79 \times 10^3 = 82.4 \times 0.8662 \times 105 \times \pi \times 0.1 \times m$
$\quad\quad\quad m = 16.90$ mm
Therefore, standard module, $m = 20$ mm $\hfill$ ...Tb. 12.30/ Pg 200, DHB

d. Lead angle:

We know that, $\quad\quad \gamma = \dfrac{mz_1}{d_1}$ $\hfill$ ...12.97a/ Pg 175, DHB

$$= \frac{20 \times 1}{150}$$

$$\gamma = 7.59°$$

e. To find dynamic tooth load:

We know that, $\quad\quad F_s = \sigma_d b Y m$ $\hfill$ ...12.110/ Pg 177, DHB
$\quad\quad\quad\quad\quad = 82.4 \times 105 \times \pi \times 0.1 \times 20$
$\quad\quad F_s = F_d = 54.36$ kN

f. To find wear tooth load:

The limiting load of wear, $\quad F_w = d_2 b K$ $\hfill$ ...12.122/ Pg 179, DHB
$\quad\quad$ For $\gamma = 7.59°$, $K = 0.549$
$\quad\quad\quad = 750 \times 105 \times 0.549$
$\quad\quad F_w = 43.23$ kN $\hfill$ ...Tb. 12.31/ Pg 202, DHB

Since $F_w < F_s$, the gear is subjected to rapid wear and hence has to be surface hardened to higher *BHN*.

g. To find efficiency:

When the worm drives the worm gear, $\eta = \dfrac{\cos\theta - \mu\tan\gamma}{\cos\theta + \mu\cot\gamma}$

$\hfill$ ...Eq. (iii) 12.115/ Pg 177, DHB

- $$\tan \theta = \tan \alpha \cos \gamma$$
  $$= \tan(14.5) \times \cos(7.59)$$
  $$\theta = 14.38°$$

- μ = depends upon rubbing velocity v_r

$$v_r = \frac{\pi d_1 n_1}{1000 \times \cos \gamma} \qquad \text{...12.121/ Pg 179, DHB}$$

$$= \frac{\pi \times 150 \times 10}{1000 \times \cos 7.59}$$

$$v_r = 4.75 \text{ m/s}$$

And $v = \dfrac{\pi d_1 n_1}{1000} = \dfrac{\pi \times 150 \times 10}{1000} = 4.71$ m/s

$\therefore \quad \mu = 0.025 + \dfrac{3.281 v_r}{1000}$ — for speed > m/s ...12.120b/ Pg 178, DHB

$$= 0.025 + \frac{3.281 \times 4.75}{1000}$$

$$\mu = 0.0405$$

$\therefore$ Eq. (*iii*) yields... $\eta = \dfrac{\cos 14.38 - (0.0405 \times \tan 7.59)}{\cos 14.38 + (0.0405 \times \cot 7.59)} = 0.7569$

$$\eta = 75.69 \%$$

h. Heat generated:

We know that heat generated $Q_g = \dfrac{\mu F_n v_r}{\cos \gamma}$ ...Eq. (*iv*) **12.124a/ Pg 179, DHB**

$$F_n = \frac{F_t}{\cos \gamma \cos \alpha}$$

$$= \frac{39.79 \times 10^3}{\cos 7.59 \times \cos 14.5}$$

$$F_n = 41.46 \text{ kN}$$

$\therefore$ Eq. (*iv*) yields... $Q_g = \dfrac{0.0405 \times 41.46 \times 10^3 \times 4.75}{\cos 7.59}$

$$= 8046.36 \text{ W}$$
$$Q_g = 8.05 \text{ kW}$$

i. Heat dissipated:

We know that heat dissipated $Q_d = 1000(\text{kW})(1-\eta)$ ...**12.124b/ Pg 180, DHB**
$$= 1000 \times 30 \times (1 - 0.7569)$$
$$= 7293 \text{ W}$$
$$Q_d = 7.29 \text{ kW}$$

Since $Q_d < Q_g$, artificial cooling is necessary.

Bevel and Worm Gears 495

VTU QUESTION PAPERS

Feb. 2002 (ME6T2)

1. a. Explain briefly the formative number of teeth of bevel gear. **(06 Marks)**
   b. A pair of bevel gear wheels with 20° pressure angle consist of 20 teeth pinion meshing with 30 teeth gear. The module is 4 mm while the face width is 20 mm. The surface hardness of both pinion and gear is 400 BHN. The pinion rotates at 500 rpm and receives power from an electric motor. The starting torque of the motor is 150 percent of rated torque. Determine the safe power that can be transmitted considering the dynamic load, wear strength and endurance strength. The allowable bending stress may be taken as 240 MPa. **(14 Marks)**

July/ Aug. 2002 (ME6T2)

2. A bevel gear of 200 mm diameter receives 20 kW power at 300 rpm, the pinion on the motor shaft rotates at 1500 rpm. The bearing supporting the gear shaft 60 mm in diameter and 600 mm apart. The bearing on the left side is 350 mm from the gear. The radial load on the gear is shared by both the bearings while the axial load is taken entirely by the bearing on the right side. Select rolling contact bearing if the expected life is 20000 hours. Take shock and impact factors $f_k = 1.3$ and $f_d = 1.3$. **(20 Marks)**

3. b. A two teeth right hand worm transmits 2 kW at 1500 rpm to a 36 teeth wheel. The module of the wheel is 5 mm and the pitch diameter of the worm is 60 mm. The pressure angle is 14.5°. The coefficient of friction is found to be 0.06.
   i. Find the center distance, the load, and the load angle
   ii. Determine the forces
   iii. Determine the efficiency of the drive. **(10 Marks)**

Jan./ Feb 2003 (ME6T2)

4. Two steel bevel gears connect shafts at 90°. The pinion has a hardness of 300 BHN and gear has a hardness of 200 BHN. The teeth are 20° full depth and module is 3 mm. The number of teeth on pinion is 40 and gear has 64 teeth. The face width is 40 mm. The pinion rotates at 900 rpm. Determine the power that can be transmitted by strength consideration. Check for dynamic wear strength. **(20 Marks)**

5. A hardened steel worm gear rotating at 1250 rpm transmits power to phosphor bronze gear with a transmission ratio of 15 to 1. The center distance is 225 mm. Determine the remaining design and give estimated power input ratings from the standpoint of strength, endurance and heat dissipation. The teeth are 14.5° involute full depth profile. **(20 Marks)**

July/ Aug. 2003 (ME6T2)

6. A pair of mitre gears having pitch diameter 280 mm and face width of 36 mm run at 250 rpm. The teeth are 14½° involute and accurately cut and transmit 6 kW. Neglect friction angle, find the following:
   i. Outside diameter the gears
   ii. Resultant tooth load tangent to pitch cone
   iii. Resultant radial load on the bearings and
   iv. Resultant thrust on shafts. **(20 Marks)**

7. Complete the design and determine the input capacity of a worm gear speed reducer unit which consists of a hardened steel worm and a phosphor bronze gear having 20° stub involute teeth. The center distance is to be 200 mm and the transmission ratio is 10 and the worm speed is 2000 rpm. **(20 Marks)**

July/ Aug. 2004 (ME6T2)

8. a. Two steel bevel gears connect shafts at 90°, the pinion has a surface hardness of 300 *BHN* and the gear has a surface hardness of 200 *BHN*. The tooth profile is to be 14 ½° full depth involute profile and the module is 4 mm. The number of teeth on the pinion is 30 and the gear has 48 teeth. The face width is 40 mm. Determine the wear strength of the pair. What would be the power that can be transmitted based on the above wear strength, if the pinion rotates at 1440 rpm? **(08 Marks)**

   b. The following data refer to a worm and worm gear drive:
   Center distance = 200 mm, pitch circle diameter of the worm = 80 mm, number of starts = 4, axial module = 8 mm, transmission ratio = 20; the worm gear is made of phosphor bronze with an allowable bending stress of 55 MPa. The worm is made of hardened and ground steel. Tooth form is 20° FDI. Determine the following:
   i. Number of teeth on the worm gear
   ii. Lead angle
   iii. Face width of the worm gear to transmit 15 kW of power at 1750 rpm of the worm based on beam strength of the worm gear. **(12 Marks)**

Jan./ Feb. 2005 (ME6T2)

9. A pump is driven by a 30 kW motor through a pair of right angled bevel gears. The speed of the motor is 1200 rpm. The pinion of the motor has a pitch circle diameter of 150 mm and carries 30 teeth and the gear on the pump shaft carries 40 teeth. The pinion is made of C45 steel untreated whereas the gear is made of 0.2% carbon steel untreated. The teeth are generated to have 20° full depth involute. Check whether the gear pair is safe from standpoint of bending strength. **(14 Marks)**

10. Design a worm drive for a speed reducer to transmit 30 kW at a worm speed of 600 rpm. The required velocity ratio is 25:1. The worm is made of C30 heat treated steel and the worm wheel is made of phosphor bronze. The service conditions are intermittent operations with medium shock loads. Also calculate heat dissipation through the drive. **(20 Marks)**

Jan./ Feb. 2005 (AU53)

11. Design a pair of right-angled bevel gears to transmit a power of 15 kW from a shaft running at 750 rpm to a perpendicular shaft to be run at 250 rpm. Suggest suitable surface hardness for the gear pair. **(20 Marks)**

July/ Aug. 2005 (AU53)

12. Design a pair of straight bevel gears to transmit 2 kW power at 1200 rpm. Tooth form is 14 ½° FDI. The velocity ratio is 4:1. The pinion is made of forged steel heat treated and gear material is CI grade 35. **(20 Marks)**

Jan./ Feb. 2006 (AU53)

13. Design a pair of bevel gears to transmit a power of 25 kW from a shaft rotating at 1200 rpm to a perpendicular shaft to be rotated at 400 rpm. **(20 Marks)**

July 2006 (AU53)

14. Determine the proportions of a worm gear drive to transmit 15 kW power from a motor shaft rotating at 2880 rpm. The wheel shaft rotates at 240 rpm. The gear is made from phosphor bronze with permissible strength of 82.4 MPa and hardness 100 BHN, while the worm is made from hardened steel. Determine:
    i. The efficiency of the drive and
    ii. Whether the drive requires cooling. **(20 Marks)**

Dec. 06/ Jan. 2007 (AU53)

15. a. A pair of straight bevel gears transmits 15 kW at 1250 rpm of 120 mm diameter pinion. The speed reduction is 3.5. Use 14.5° involute tooth system. The angle between the shaft axes is 90°. The pinion is made of case hardened alloy steel with allowable static stress of 343.34 MPa and gear is cast steel of 0.20%C heat treated with allowable static stress of 191.295 MPa. Determine module, face width, number of teeth on pinion and gear. Suggest suitable surface hardness for the gear pair. Take the service factor as 1.5 and assume the teeth are generated. **(17 Marks)**
    b. Explain formative number of teeth in bevel gears. **(03 Marks)**

July 2007 (AU53)

16. A pair of 20° full depth involute teeth bevel gears connect two shafts at right angles having velocity ratio 3:1. The gear is made of cast steel, 0.20% untreated and the pinion material is of steel, C30 heat treated. The pinion has 20 number of teeth and transmits 40 kW at 750 rpm. Determine: i) module, ii) face width, iii) pitch diameters. Assume width of gear face as 1/3rd of the length of pitch cone. **(20 Marks)**

Dec. 07/ Jan. 2008 (AU53)

17. Design a worm gear drive for a speed of 500 rpm of the worm transmitting 20 kW. The velocity ratio is 25:1. The material of the gear is phosphor bronze and the worm is hardened steel. Determine the efficiency of the drive also. **(20 Marks)**

Dec. 07/ Jan. 2008 (ME6T2)

18. Design a worm gear to transmit 20 kW at a worm speed of 720 rpm. Speed reduction desired is 30:1. Check the gear pair for heating capacity. **(20 Marks)**

June/ July 2008 (AU53)

19. A pair of straight tooth bevel gears at right angles is to transmit 5 kW at 1200 rpm of the pinion. The diameter of the pinion is 80 mm and the velocity ratio is 3.5. The tooth form is 14 ½°. Both the pinion and gear are cast iron with allowable stress of 55 MN/m². Determine the module, face width from the standpoint of strength and also check the design from standpoint of dynamic load and wear. **(20 Marks)**

Dec. 08/ Jan. 2009 (ME6T2)

20. Design a worm drive for a speed reducer to transmit 30 kW at a worm speed of 600 rpm. The required velocity ratio is 25:1. The worm is made of C30 heat treated steel and the worm wheel is made of phosphor bronze. The service conditions are intermittent operations with medium shocks loads. Also calculate heat dissipation through the drive. **(20 Marks)**

21. One kilowatt power at 740 rpm is supplied to worm shaft. The number of starts for threads of worm are 6 with a 60 mm pitch circle diameter. The worm has 32 teeth with a 6 mm module. The normal pressure angle is 20°. Calculate the efficiency of the worm gear drive and the power lost in friction. **(06 Marks)**

June/ July 2009 (ME6T2)

22. The vertical spindle of a drilling machine is to be driven by a pair of straight bevel gears with 20° involute teeth. The speed reduction is 4:1. The drill requires a power of 50 kW at 720 rpm. A service factor of 1.35 may be taken, and choose suitable materials for the gear and pinion. Design the gear pair. **(15 Marks)**

23. Design a worm drive for a speed reducer to transmit 30 kW at a worm speed of 600 rpm. The required velocity ratio is 25:1. The worm is made of C30 heat treated steel and the worm wheel is made of phosphor bronze. The service conditions are intermittent operations with medium shock loads. Also calculate the heat dissipation through the drive. **(20 Marks)**

Dec. 08/ Jan. 2009 (AU53)

24. a. A hardened steel worm rotating at 1250 rpm transmits power to phosphor bronze gear with transmission ratio 15:1. The center distance of the drive is 225 mm. Design the gear drive, and estimate the power rating of the drive from stand point of strength and heat dissipation. The teeth are 14 ½° full depth involute form. **(15 Marks)**
    b. Explain the meaning of "Formative number of teeth" as referred to bevel gears. **(05 Marks)**

June/ July 2009 (AU53)

25. a. Derive expressions for pitch angles of bevel gear drive. **(06 Marks)**
    b. A triple threaded worm has teeth of 6 mm module and pitch circle diameter of 50 mm. If the worm gear has 30 teeth of 14 ½ and coefficient of friction of the worm gearing is 0.05, find:
       i. The lead angle of the worm,
       ii. Velocity ratio,
       iii. Center distance,
       iv. Efficiency of the worm gearing. **(14 Marks)**

June/ July 2009 (06ME61)

26. a. Under what circumstances the bevel gears are used? Give a detailed classification of bevel gears. **(05 Marks)**
    b. Design a worm gear drive to transmit 2 kW of power at 1000 rpm. The speed ratio is 20 and center distance is 200 mm. Assume the number of teeth on worm wheel to be 40 and number of starts on worm to be 2. Assume hardened steel worm and phosphor bronze wheel for which $\sigma_d = 55$ N/mm².
    Check the gear from stand point of strength and wear if load stress factor, $K = 0.6$ MPa. If the amount of heat generated is 1.7 KW, check whether artificial cooling is necessary or not for a temperature rise of 40° C. **(15 Marks)**

Dec. 09/ Jan. 2010 (06ME61)

27. a. A pair of bevel gears transmitting 7.5 kW at 300 rpm of the pinion. The pressure angle is 20°. The pitch diameters of the pinion and gear at their large ends are

150 mm and 200 mm respectively. The face width of the gears is 40 mm. Determine the components of the resultant gear tooth force and draw free body diagram of the forces acting on the pinion and the gear. **(10 Marks)**

b. A two teeth right hand worm transmits 2 kW at 1500 rpm to a 36 teeth wheel. The module of the wheel is 5 mm and the pitch diameter of the worm is 60 mm. The pressure angle is 14.5°. The coefficient of friction is found to be 0.06.
  i. Find the center distance, the lead and the lead angle
  ii. Determine the forces. **(10 Marks)**

May/ June 2010 (AU53)

28. A pair of cast iron bevel gears connect two shafts at right angles. The pitch diameters of the pinion and gear are 80 mm and 100 mm respectively. The tooth profiles of the gears are 14 ½° composite form. The allowable static stress for both the gears is 55 MPa. If the pinion transmits 2.5 kW at 1000 rpm, find the module and number of teeth on each gear from the standpoint of strength and check the design from the standpoint of wear. Take surface endurance limit as 630 MPa and modulus of elasticity for cast iron as 84 kN/mm². **(20 Marks)**

Dec. 2010 (AU53)

29. a. Explain briefly formulative number of teeth of bevel gears. **(06 Marks)**
   b. A pump is driven by a 30 kW through a pair of right angled bevel gears. The speed of the motor is 1200 rpm. The pinion on the motor has a pitch circle diameter of 150 mm and carries 30 teeth and the gear on the pump shaft carries 40 teeth. The pinion is made of C45 steel untreated whereas the gear is made of 0.2% carbon steel untreated. The teeth are generated to have 20° full depth involute. Check whether the gear pair is safe from the standpoint of bending strength. **(14 Marks)**

May/ June 2010 (06ME61)

30. a. List the advantages and disadvantages of worm gear drives. **(03 Marks)**
   b. A pair of straight tooth bevel gears at right angles is to transmit 5 kW at 1500 rpm of the pinion at a speed ratio of 3. Diameter of pinion is 75 mm. The tooth form is 14 ½° involute. Pinion is made of steel (σ_d = 160 MPa) and gear of CI (σ_d = 80 MPa). Design the gear pair and check the design for dynamic load wear. **(17 Marks)**

Dec. 2010 (06ME61)

31. Design a pair of bevel gears to connect two shafts at 60°. The power transmitted is 25 kW at 900 rpm of pinion. The reduction ratio is 5:1. The teeth are 20° full depth involute and pinion has 24 teeth. Check the design for dynamic and wear considerations. **(20 Marks)**

June/ July 2011 (06ME61)

32. a. A pair of straight bevel gears are to transmit 15 kW at 1500 rpm input speed. The number of teeth on pinion is 20 and the speed ratio is 5. Design the gears for strength only assuming 14 ½° full depth form. **(20 Marks)**

Dec. 2011 (06ME61)

33. a. Explain with a sketch, the formulative number of teeth based on bevel gears. **(04 Marks)**

500 Design of Machine Elements II (DME II)

b. A pump is driven by a 30kW motor through a pair of right angled bevel gear. The speed of the motor is 1200 rpm. The pinion on the motor has a pitch circle diameter of 150 mm and carries 30 teeth and the gear on the pump shaft carries 40 teeth. The pinion is made of C45 steel untreated whereas the gear is made of 0.2% carbon steel untreated. The teeth are generated to have 20° full depth involute. Check whether the gear pair is safe from standpoint of bending strength. **(16 Marks)**

June 2012 (06ME61)

34. a. Explain the advantages of worm drive. Write a note on materials used for worm and worm wheel. **(05 Marks)**
    b. A speed reducer unit is to be designed for an input power of 0.75 kW with a transmission ratio of 27. The speed of the hardened worm is 1750 r/min. The worm wheel is made of phosphor bronze. The tooth form is 14 ½° involute. The allowable stress for the wheel may be taken as 80 MPa. **(15 Marks)**

December 2012 (06ME12)

35. a. A pair of mitre gears have pitch diameter 280 mm and face width of 36 mm and run at 250 rpm. The teeth are 14.5° involute and accurately cut and transmit 6 kW. Neglecting friction angle, find the following:
    i. Outside diameters of gears   ii. Resultant tooth load tangent to pitch cone
    iii. Radial load on the pinion   iv. Thrust on the pinion.
    Assume low carbon cast steel 0.2%C heat treated as the material for both the gears. **(10 Marks)**
    b. The following data refer to a worm and worm gear drive:
    i. Center distance = 200 mm   ii. Pitch circle diameter of the worm = 80 mm
    iii. Number of start = 4   iv. Axial module = 8 mm
    v. Transmission ratio = 20
    vi. The worm gear is made of phosphor bronze with an allowable bending stress = 55 MPa
    vii. The worm is made of hardened and ground steel
    viii. Tooth form is 20° full depth involute. Determine:
       i. Number of teeth on the worm gear
       ii. Lead angle
       iii. Face width of worm gear to transmit 15 kW of power at 1750 rpm of the worm based on beam strength of the worm gear. **(10 Marks)**

June/ July 2013 (AU53)

36. a. A pair of straight bevel gears is mounted on shafts which are intersecting at right angles. The gears are made of steel and the surface hardness is 300 BHN. The number of teeth on pinion and gear are 40 and 65 respectively. The module at the outside diameter is 3 mm while the face width of the tooth is 35 mm. Calculate the wear strength of the tooth. **(10 Marks)**
    b. A gear and 20° involute worm is to transmit 10 kW with worm rotating at 1400 rpm and to obtain a speed reduction of 12:1. The distance between the shafts is 225 mm. Calculate the tangential and dynamic loads. **(10 Marks)**

June/ July 2013 (06ME61)

37. a. A pair of bevel gears transmits 7.5 kW at 300 rpm of the pinion. The pitch diameters of the pinion and gear at their larger ends are 150 mm and 200 mm respectively, and the pressure angle is 20°. Determine the components of resultant gear tooth force and draw a free boy diagram of the forces acting on the pinion and gear, assuming face width of 40 mm. **(10 Marks)**

b. The following data refer to worm and worm gear drive that has to transmit 15 kW at 1750 rpm of the worm:
Center distance = 200 mm   Pitch circle diameter of the worm = 80 mm
No. of starts = 4   Axial module = 8 mm
Transmission ratio = 20   tooth form = 20° FDI.
The work gear has an allowable bending stress of 55 MPa. The worm is made of hardened and ground steel. Determine:
  i. Number of teeth on the worm gear
  ii. The lead angle
  iii. Face width of worm gear based on the beam strength of the worm gear.
(10 Marks)

June/ July 2013 (10ME62)

38. Complete the design and determine the input capacity of worm and gear speed reducer unit which consists of hardened worm and phosphor bronze gear having 20° stub involute teeth. The center distance is to be 200 mm and the transmission ratio is 10, speed of the worm is 2000 rpm. **(20 Marks)**

Dec.2013/ Jan.2014 (10ME62)

39. a. Write a note on formative number of teeth in bevel gear. **(04 Marks)**

b. Hardened steel worm rotates at 1250 r/min and transmit power to a phosphor bronze gear with a transmission ratio of 15:1. The center distance is to be 225 mm. Design the gear drive and give estimated power input ratings from the stand point of strength, endurance and heat dissipation. The teeth are 14 ½° full depth involute. **(16 Marks)**

Dec. 2013/ Jan. 2014 (AU53)

40. a. Two steel bevel gears connect shafts at right angles. The pinion has a Brinell hardness of 250 and the gear of 250. The teeth are 14 ½ degree full depth involute and the module is 4 mm. The number of teeth on the pinion is 30 and gear has 48 teeth. The face width is 40 mm. Determine the wear strength (wear load). **(10 Marks)**

b. A worm drive has the following details:
Pressure angle = 20 degree involute profile, center distance = 200 mm, speed ratio = 10, axial module = 8 mm, rotational speed of the worm = 1750 r/min, face width = 60 mm, pitch circle diameter of the gear = 320 mm, number of starts = 4.
Calculate the following:
  i. Pitch circle diameter of the worm
  ii. Lead angle
  iii. The input power capacity based on heat dissipating capacity. **(10 Marks)**

6

Clutches and Brakes

INTRODUCTION TO CLUTCHES AND BRAKES

Brakes and clutches are referred to as high friction devices. The performance analysis of clutches and brakes involves determination of actuating force, torque transmitted, energy absorption and rise in temperature. The torque to be transmitted is associated with the coefficient of friction, the actuating force and the geometry of the device; while the rise in temperature is associated with the energy absorbed in the form of friction due to the action of clutch and brake.

DESIGN OF CLUTCHES

6.1 INTRODUCTION

Clutches and brakes provide frictional, magnetic, hydraulic –or- mechanical connection between two machine elements, usually shafts (driver and driven). A clutch is a machine member used to connect a driving shaft to a driven shaft so that the driven shaft may be started –or- stopped at will, without stopping the driving shaft.

There are significant similarities between clutches and brakes. If both shafts rotate then the machine element will be classed as a clutch and the usual function is to connect –or- disconnect a driven load from a driving shaft. If one shaft rotates and the other is stationary then the machine element is classed as a brake and the likely function is to decelerate a shaft. In reality, however, the same device can function as a brake –or- clutch by fixing its output element to a shaft that can rotate –or- to ground, respectively.

6.2 CLASSIFICATION OF CLUTCHES

Following are the two main types of clutches commonly used in engineering practice:
1. Positive clutches, and
2. Friction clutches.
   A. Axial friction clutches:
      a. Plate/disc clutch:
         i. Single plate clutch.
         ii. Multi plate clutch.
      b. Cone clutches.
   B. Radial friction clutches:
      Centrifugal clutches.

6.2.1 Positive Clutches

The positive clutches are used when a positive drive is required. The simplest type of a positive clutch is the jaw –or- claw clutch. The jaw clutch permits one shaft to drive another through a direct contact of interlocking jaws. This is used when a sudden starting action is required and when the inertia of the driven parts is relatively small.

It consists of two halves/ segments, one of which is permanently fastened to the driving shaft, while the other half of the clutch is movable and is free to slide axially on the driven shaft, but it is prevented from turning relatively to its shaft by means of feather key. The jaws of the clutch may be of square type –or- of spiral type. **Fig 13.7/ 234, DHB** shoes a square jaw clutch.

Applications: Power presses, punches, etc.

6.2.2 Friction Clutches

Friction clutches transmit torque by virtue of frictional force developed. Friction clutches are designed to reduce coupling shock by slipping during the engagement period. They also serve as safety devices by slipping when the torque exceeds their maximum rating. Hence friction clutches can be engaged when driving member is rotating and the driven member is stationary.

In the axial type of clutches, the engagement –or- disengagement of clutch is achieved by axial movement of parts attached to the driven shaft. Whereas in radial type of clutches, the contact pressure is applied in a direction perpendicular to shaft axis.

6.3 SINGLE PLATE/ DISC CLUTCH

A single plate clutch is shown in **Fig. 6.1.** It essentially consists of two flanges A and B. One of the flanges is fitted rigidly to the shaft, while the other is mounted on the driven shaft by means of splines. Torque is transmitted by friction between the flanges. The amount of torque transmitted depends upon the axial pressure, coefficient of friction and the radius of friction surfaces. These are used where the amount of torque transmitted is less. These clutches are operated in dry condition and hence does not require lubrication.

Applications: Heavy motor vehicles like trucks, busses, etc.

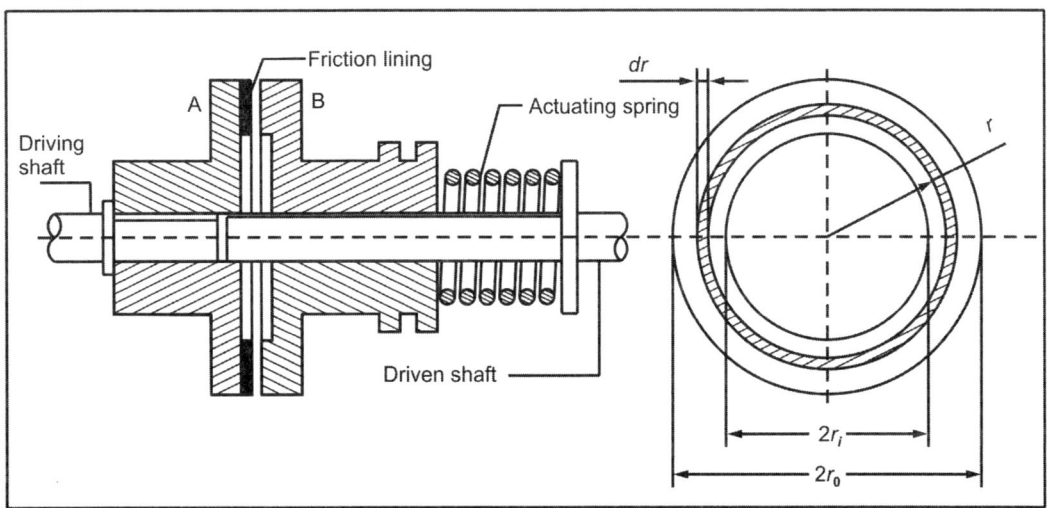

Fig. 6.1: Plate/ Disc clutch (Fig. 13.9/Pg 234, DHB)

6.4 MULTI PLATE CLUTCH

Figure 6.2 shows a line diagram of a multi plate clutch. The plates shown as 'A' are made of steel and are mounted on the driven shaft by splines to permit axial motion, while plates 'B' made of bronze are mounted on the driving shaft. These are used where a large amount of torque has to be transmitted. These clutches are operated in wet condition and hence the face of the clutch plate has to be provided with radial groove/slots –or- spiral grooves for proper lubrication,

Applications: Machine tools and light motor vehicles such as scooters.

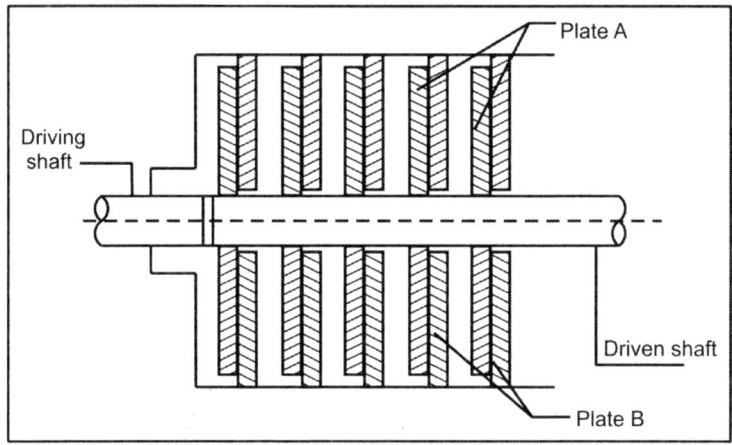

Fig. 6.2: Multi plate/ disc clutch

6.5 DIFFERENCE BETWEEN SINGLE PLATE AND MULTI PLATE CLUTCHES

Sl No.	Single plate clutch	Multi plate clutch
1.	The number of contacting surfaces is limited to one or a maximum of two.	The number of contacting surfaces is more than two.
2.	Heat dissipated is less due to less number of contacting surfaces.	Heat dissipation is more due to more number of contacting surfaces.
3.	Single plate clutches are run dry and hence does not require lubrication	Multi plate clutches are run wet and hence require lubrication.
4.	Requires more space.	Requires less space.
5.	**Applications:** Heavy motor vehicles like trucks, busses, etc.	**Applications:** Machine tools and light motor vehicles such as scooters.
6.	–	For a given torque, the size of multi plate clutch is smaller.

6.6 CONE CLUTCH

A cone clutch shown in **Fig. 6.3** is a simple device to couple two shafts by friction without the use of excessive axial pressure. It is suitable for loads that are connected and disconnected frequently. Here the driver is keyed to the driving shaft by a sunk key, while the inner conical face slides axially on the driven shaft by splines. The clutch parts are held together by springs thereby producing the axial force. The driven member is lined with asbestos, leather, cork –or- wood. The semi cone angle may vary from 10° to 15°, but normally 12.5° is used.

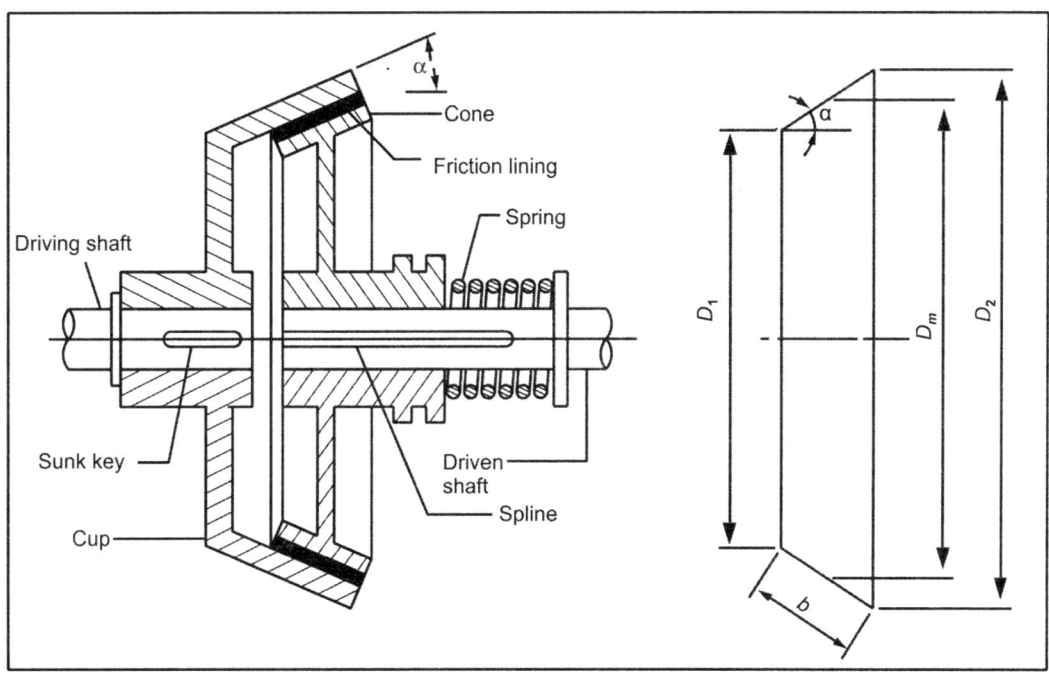

Fig. 6.3: Torque analysis in single plate clutch

Due to increased frictional area and the wedging action of the parts, cone clutches convey large torque than disc clutches for the same diameter and actuating force.

These are used in low speed applications.

6.7 TORQUE ANALYSIS OF PLATE/DISC CLUTCH

Consider a single plate clutch as shown in **Fig. 6.4**.

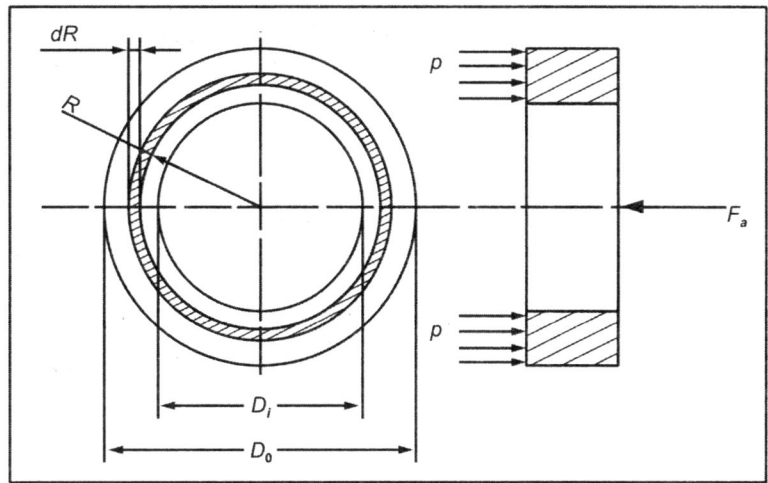

Fig. 6.4: Torque analysis in single plate clutch

Let, R_i = inner radius of contact surface or friction disk
           R_0 = outer radius of contact surface or friction disk
           p = pressure intensity
           F_a = axial force or axial thrust
           f = coefficient of friction

Consider a elementary ring of thickness dR at a radius R as shown in **Fig. 6.4**.

Area of the elemental ring, $dA = 2\pi R \cdot dR$

Axial force on the ring, $dF_a = p \cdot dA = p\,(2\pi R \cdot dR)$ ...(Eq. 6.1)

Frictional force on the ring, $dF_f = f \cdot dF_a$

$dF_f = f \cdot p\,(2\pi R \cdot dR)$ ...(Eq. 6.2)

Frictional torque on the ring, $dT = dF_f \cdot R$

$= f \cdot p\,(2\pi R \cdot dR)R$

$dT = 2\pi f p R^2 \cdot dR$ ...(Eq. 6.3)

Integrating Eqs (6.1) and (6.3), we have

Eq. (6.1) yields... $F_a = \int_{R_i}^{R_0} p(2\pi R) \cdot dR$ ...(Eq. 6.4)

Eq. (6.3) yields... $T = \int_{R_i}^{R_0} \left(2\pi f p R^2\right) \cdot dR$ ...(Eq. 6.5)

For disc clutches, we have two theories for obtaining the torque, i.e.
 a. Uniform pressure theory
 b. Uniform wear theory

a. Uniform Pressure Theory:

This theory is applicable when the **friction lining is new,** since the pressure remains constant over the entire surface of the disc **(Fig. 6.5(a))**.

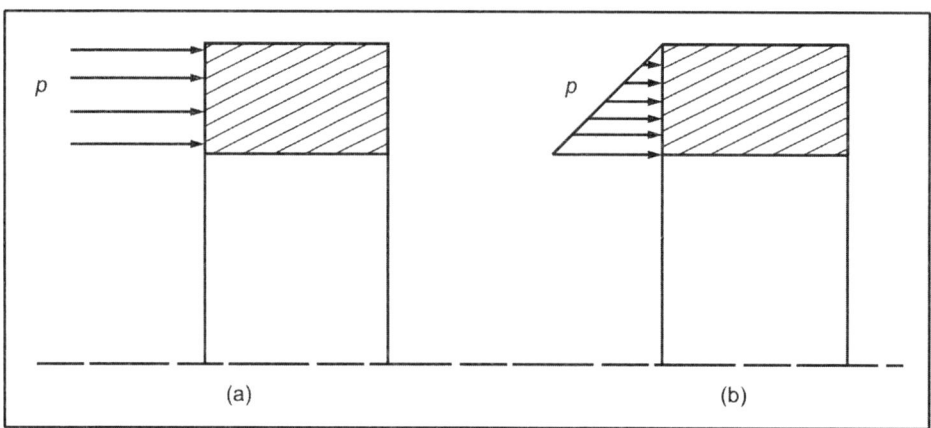

Fig. 6.5: (a) Uniform pressure (b) uniform wear

Eq. (6.4) yields ... $F_a = 2\pi p \int_{R_i}^{R_0} R\,dR$

$= 2\pi p \left(\dfrac{R^2}{2}\right)_{R_i}^{R_0}$

$F_a = \pi p\,(R_0^2 - R_i^2)$ -or- ...(Eq. 6.6)

$F_a = \dfrac{\pi p}{4}\left(D_0^2 - D_i^2\right)$ ...(Eq. 6.6a)

Eq. (6.5) yields ... $T = 2\pi fp \int_{R_i}^{R_0} R^2 \, dR$

$$= 2\pi fp \left(\frac{R^3}{3}\right)_{R_i}^{R_0}$$

$$T = \frac{2}{3}\pi fp \left(R_0^3 - R_i^3\right) \quad \text{...(Eq. 6.7)}$$

But $p = \dfrac{F_a}{\pi \left(R_0^2 - R_i^2\right)}$ ...(Eq. 6.8) ...*using (Eq. 6.6a)*

∴ Eq. (6.7) yields ... $T = \dfrac{2}{3}\pi f \left(R_0^3 - R_i^3\right)\left[\dfrac{F_a}{\pi \left(R_0^2 - R_i^2\right)}\right]$

$$T = \frac{2}{3} fF_a \left[\frac{R_0^3 - R_i^3}{R_0^2 - R_i^2}\right] \quad \text{-or-} \quad \text{...(Eq. 6.9)}$$

$$T = \frac{2fF_a}{3}\left[\frac{\left(D_0^3 - D_i^3\right)/8}{\left(D_0^2 - D_i^2\right)/4}\right]$$

$$T = \frac{2fF_a}{6}\left[\frac{D_0^3 - D_i^3}{D_0^2 - D_i^2}\right] \quad \text{...(Eq. 6.9a)}$$

$$T = \frac{1}{2} fF_a D_m \quad \text{...(Eq. 6.10)} \quad \textbf{13.33a/ Pg 213, DHB}$$

Where, D_m – mean diameter of friction surface

$$= \frac{2}{3}\left[\frac{D_0^3 - D_i^3}{D_0^2 - D_i^2}\right], \text{ for uniform pressure} \quad \text{...13.34/ Pg 213, DHB}$$

F_a = The axial force = $\dfrac{\pi p}{4} (D_0^2 - D_i^2)$ ... *To remember*

b. Uniform Wear Theory:

This theory is applicable for **worn out clutches** which are based on the assumption that the wear is uniformly distributed over the entire surface area of the disc **(Fig. 6.5(b))**. The work of friction is proportional to the product of pressure and sliding velocity.

i.e. wear $\propto p \cdot v$
$\propto p(\omega R)$ ω – angular speed
wear $\propto pR$ (assuming speed to be constant) ...(Eq. 6.11)
If the wear is uniform, then $pR = C$ = constant

$$p = \frac{C}{R} \quad \text{...(Eq. 6.12)}$$

∴ Eq. (6.4) yields ... $F_a = \int_{R_i}^{R_0} (2\pi R) p \, dR$

$$= 2\pi \int_{R_i}^{R_0} R.p \, dR$$

$$= 2\pi \int_{R_i}^{R_0} C \, dR$$

$$F_a = 2\pi C(R_0 - R_i) \quad \text{..(Eq. 6.13)}$$

and Eq. (6.5) yields ... $T = 2\pi f p \int_{R_i}^{R_0} p.R^2 \, dR$

$$= 2\pi f \int_{R_i}^{R_0} CR \, dR$$

$$= 2\pi f C \left(\frac{R^2}{2}\right)_{R_i}^{R_0}$$

$$T = 2\pi f C \left[\frac{R_0^2 - R_i^2}{2}\right]$$

$$T = \pi f C \left(R_0^2 - R_i^2\right) \quad \text{...(Eq. 6.14)}$$

Substituting $C = \dfrac{F_a}{2\pi(R_0 - R_i)}$ ... using (Eq. 6.13)

$$T = \pi f (R_0^2 - R_i^2) \frac{F_a}{2\pi(R_0 - R_i)}$$

$$T = \frac{1}{2} f F_a (R_0 + R_i) \quad \text{-or-} \quad \text{...(Eq. 6.15)}$$

$$T = \frac{1}{2} f F_a \left[\frac{D_0 + D_i}{2}\right]$$

$$T = \frac{1}{2} f F_a D_m \quad \text{[Same as Eq. (6.10)] ...(Eq. 6.16)} \; \textbf{13.33a/ Pg 213, DHB}$$

Where, D_m = mean diameter of friction surface

$= \left[\dfrac{D_0 + D_i}{2}\right]$, for uniform wear ...**13.34/ Pg 213, DHB**

F_a = The axial force,

$= \dfrac{\pi}{2} p D_i (D_0 - D_i)$ ...**13.32/ Pg 213, DHB**

Note: Since uniform pressure theory gives higher value of frictional torque, therefore unless otherwise stated, uniform wear theory should be used.

- Values of coefficient of friction, f ...Table 13.2a/ Pg 228, DHB
- Service factor for clutches ...Table 13.2b/ Pg 229, DHB
- The torque calculated using the above equations is called the *"Frictional torque"*.
    But $T_f = \beta \times$ design torque $= \beta T$ ...(Eq. 6.17) **13.33b/ Pg 213, DHB**
    Where, β = engagement factor, which should guarantee that the clutch operates without slipping under intermediate loads -or- when $f-$ or $-r$ is reduced from designed values due to the nature of contact between friction surfaces.
    = 1.25 to 1.50 – for metal cutting machine tools
    = 1.20 to 1.50 – for automobiles
    = 2 to 2.5 – for tractors
    > 1.5 – for cranes.
- As the ratio D_i/D_0 increases, torque and pressure increases while the contact area decreases **(Fig. 6.6)**.
- In general $T = \dfrac{1}{2} f F_a D_m n'$ ...(Eq. 6.18) **13.34/ Pg 213, DHB**

    n' = number of pairs of friction surfaces
    = 2 – for a single plate clutch, since both sides are effective
    $n' = n_1 + n_2 - 1$
    n_1 = number of discs on the driving shaft
    n_2 = number of discs on the driven shaft.

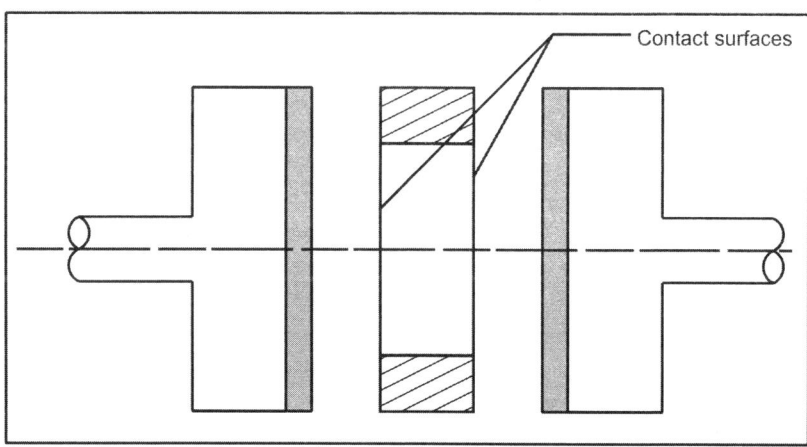

Fig. 6.6: Number of contact surfaces for a single plate clutch ($n' = 2$)

- The pressure intensity is maximum at the inner radius, $p_{max} R_i = C$ ...(Eq. 6.19)
- The pressure intensity is minimum at the outer radius, $p_{min} R_0 = C$ ...(Eq. 6.20)
- The average pressure is calculated as, $p_{avg} = \dfrac{F_a}{2\pi \left(R_0^2 - R_i^2 \right)}$ ...(Eq. 6.21)
- The axial force, $F_a = \dfrac{\pi}{2} p D_i (D_0 - D_i)$ (uniform wear) ...(Eq. 6.22) **13.32/ Pg 213, DHB**

6.8 BASIC PROBLEMS ON PLATE CLUTCH

1. A single plate friction clutch of both sides effective has 0.3 m outer diameter and 0.16 m inner diameter. The coefficient of friction is 0.2 and it runs at 1000 rpm. Find the power transmitted for uniform wear and uniform pressure distribution cases if the allowable maximum pressure is 0.08 MPa.

   [VTU – Dec. 09/ Jan. 2010 – 10 Marks]

Solution: $n' = 2$, outside diameter $D_0 = 0.3$ m $= 300$ mm, inside diameter $D_i = 0.16$ m $= 160$ mm, $f = 0.2$, $N = 1000$ rpm, $P = ?$, $p = 0.08$ MPa.

We know that power, $\quad P = \dfrac{2\pi NT}{60} \quad$ ...Eq. (*i*)

But $\quad T = \dfrac{1}{2} f F_a D_m n' \quad$ ...Eq. (*ii*) **13.34/ Pg 213, DHB**

a. Uniform pressure:

Axial force, $\quad F_a = \dfrac{\pi p}{4}(D_0^2 - D_i^2)$

$= \dfrac{\pi \times 0.08}{4}(300^2 - 160^2)$

$F_a = 4046.37$ N

Mean diameter, $\quad D_m = \dfrac{2}{3}\left[\dfrac{D_0^3 - D_i^3}{D_0^2 - D_i^2}\right] \quad$ ...**13.34/ Pg 213, DHB**

$= \dfrac{2}{3}\left[\dfrac{300^3 - 160^3}{300^2 - 160^2}\right]$

$D_m = 237$ mm $= 0.237$ m

∴ Eq. (*ii*) yields ... $T = \dfrac{1}{2} \times 0.2 \times 4046.37 \times 0.237 \times 2$

$T = 191.80$ N-m

∴ Eq. (*i*) yields ... $P = \dfrac{2\pi \times 1000 \times 191.80}{60}$

$P = 20.08$ kW

b. Uniform wear:

Axial force, $\quad F_a = \dfrac{\pi}{2} p D_i (D_0 - D_i) \quad$ ...**13.32/ Pg 213, DHB**

$= \dfrac{\pi \times 0.08 \times 160}{2}(300 - 160)$

$F_a = 2814.87$ N

Mean diameter, $\quad D_m = \left[\dfrac{D_0 + D_i}{2}\right] \quad$ ...**13.34/ Pg 213, DHB**

$$= \left[\frac{300+160}{2}\right]$$

$$D_m = 230 \text{ mm} = 0.230 \text{ m}$$

∴ Eq. (*ii*) yields ... $T = \frac{1}{2} \times 0.2 \times 2814.87 \times 0.230 \times 2$

$$T = 129.48 \text{ N-m}$$

∴ Eq. (*i*) yields ... $P = \frac{2\pi \times 1000 \times 129.48}{60}$

$$P = 13.56 \text{ kW.}$$

2. A multiple disc clutch has five plate having four pairs of active friction surfaces. If the intensity of pressure is not to exceed 0.127 N/mm², find the power transmitted at 500 rpm. The outer and inner radii of friction surfaces are 125 mm and 75 mm respectively. Assume uniform wear and take coefficient of friction as 0.3. *[VTU – June/ July 2009 – 05 Marks]*

Solution: Number of clutches $n_1 + n_2 = 5$, number of active pairs $n' = 4$, $p = 0.127$ N/mm², $P = ?$, $N = 500$ rpm, $R_0 = 125$ mm, $R_i = 75$ mm, $f = 0.3$.

We know that power, $P = \dfrac{2\pi NT}{60}$ ...Eq. (*i*)

But $T = \dfrac{1}{2} f F_a D_m n'$ ...Eq. (*ii*) **13.34/ Pg 213, DHB**

Uniform wear:

Axial force, $F_a = \dfrac{\pi}{2} p D_i (D_0 - D_i)$ ...**13.32/ Pg 213, DHB**

$$= \frac{\pi \times 0.127 \times 150}{2} (250 - 150)$$

$$F_a = 2992.37 \text{ N}$$

Mean diameter, $D_m = \left[\dfrac{D_0 + D_i}{2}\right]$ ...**13.34/ Pg 213, DHB**

$$= \left[\frac{250+150}{2}\right]$$

$$D_m = 200 \text{ mm} = 0.20 \text{ m}$$

∴ Eq. (*ii*) yields ... $T = \dfrac{1}{2} \times 0.3 \times 2992.37 \times 0.20 \times 4$

$$T = 359.08 \text{ N-m}$$

∴ Eq. (*i*) yields ... $P = \dfrac{2\pi \times 500 \times 359.08}{60}$

$$P = 18.80 \text{ kW.}$$

3. **A single plate clutch both sides effective is required to transmit 25 kW at 1600 rpm. The outer diameter of the plate is limited to 0.3 m and the intensity of pressure is not to exceed 0.07 MPa. Assuming uniform wear and the coefficient of friction 0.3, determine the diameter of the plate and the axial force necessary to engage the clutch.** *[VTU – June/July 2008 – 10 Marks]*

Solution: $n' = 2$, $P = 25$ kW, $N = 1600$ rpm, outside diameter $D_0 = 0.3$ m $= 300$ mm, $p = 0.07$ MPa, $f = 0.3$, $D_i = ?$

Unless otherwise stated, uniform wear theory should be used.

We know that,
$$T = \frac{1}{2} f F_a D_m n' \qquad \text{...Eq. (i) 13.34/ Pg 213, DHB}$$

But $P = \dfrac{2\pi NT}{60}$

$$25 \times 10^3 = \frac{2\pi \times 1600 \times T}{60}$$

$$T = 149.21 \text{ N-m}$$

- Axial force, $F_a = \dfrac{\pi}{2} p D_i (D_0 - D_i)$ \qquad ...13.32/ Pg 213, DHB

$$= \frac{\pi \times 0.07 \times D_i}{2}(D_0 - D_i)$$

$$F_a = 0.1099 \, D_i \, (D_0 - D_i) \qquad \text{...Eq. (ii)}$$

- Mean diameter, $D_m = \left[\dfrac{D_0 + D_i}{2}\right]$ \qquad ...13.34/ Pg 213, DHB

∴ Eq. (i) yields ... $149.21 \times 10^3 = \dfrac{1}{2} \times 0.3 \times 0.1099 \, D_i \, (D_0 - D_i) \times 2 \times \left[\dfrac{D_0 + D_i}{2}\right]$

$$9.05 \times 10^6 = (D_0^2 - D_i^2) \, D_i$$

$$9.05 \times 10^6 = (300^2 - D_i^2) \, D_i$$

$$D_i = 221.80 \text{ mm} \approx 230 \text{ mm}$$

(roots: 221.80, –341.34, 119.53)

And Eq. (ii) yields ... $F_a = 0.1099 \times 230 \times (300 - 230)$

$$F_a = 1769.40 \text{ N}.$$

4. **A single dry plate clutch has a diameter D_0 which is fixed due to space limitations. The permissible pressure intensity is p and coefficient of friction is f. Show that the torque transmitting capacity of the clutch is maximum when $D_i/D_0 = 0.577$.**

Solution: $D_i/D_0 = 0.577$, D_i – inner diameter, D_0 – outer diameter

We know that for a single plate clutch, $T = \dfrac{1}{2} f F_a D_m$ \qquad ...13.33a/ Pg 213, DHB

But \qquad axial force, $F_a = \dfrac{\pi}{2} p D_i (D_0 - D_i)$ \qquad ...13.32/ Pg 213, DHB

Also \qquad mean diameter, $D_m = \left[\dfrac{D_0 + D_i}{2}\right]$ \qquad ...13.34/ Pg 213, DHB

$$\therefore \quad T = \frac{1}{2} f \left[\frac{\pi}{2} p D_i (D_0 - D_i) \right] \left[\frac{D_0 + D_i}{2} \right]$$

$$= \frac{\pi p f}{8} \times (D_0^2 - D_i^2) D_i$$

$$T = \frac{\pi p f}{8} \times D_i D_0^2 \left[1 - \frac{D_i^2}{D_0^2} \right]$$

Let $D_i/D_0 = y$ $\therefore T = \frac{\pi p f}{8} (y D_0)(1 - y^2)$

$$= \frac{\pi p f}{8} \times D_0^3 (y - y^3) \quad \therefore T = \frac{\pi p f}{8} (y D_0)(1 - y^2) \quad \text{...(Eq. (i))}$$

For optimum torque capacity, $\dfrac{dT}{dy} = 0$

i.e. $(y - y^3) = 0$
$(1 - 3y^2) = 0$
$3y^2 = 1$

$$y = 1/\sqrt{3} = 0.577$$

$\therefore \quad y_{max} = D_i/D_0 \leq 0.577.$

5. **A multiple disc clutch is composed of 5 steel and 4 bronze disks. The clutch is required to transmit a maximum torque of 240 N-m. Assume a factor of safety of 2.5 for slippage and full engine torque. If $p = 0.35$ MPa and $f = 0.25$, calculate the diameters of friction lining.**

Solution: $n_1 = 5$, $n_2 = 4$, $T = 240$ N-m $= 240 \times 10^3$ N-mm, $FOS = 2.5$, $p = 0.35$ MPa, $f = 0.25$, $D_i, D_0 = ?$

Here frictional torque, $T_f = T\beta = T \times FOS$
$= (240 \times 10^3) \times 2.5$
$T_f = 6 \times 10^5$ N-mm

We know that, $\quad T = T_f = \dfrac{1}{2} f F_a D_m n'$ ...Eq. (i) **13.34/ Pg 213, DHB**

- But $F_a = \dfrac{\pi}{2} p D_i (D_0 - D_i)$ ...**13.32/ Pg 213, DHB**

$$= \frac{\pi \times 0.35 \times D_i}{2} (D_0 - D_i)$$

$F_a = 0.5497 D_i (D_0 - D_i)$ ...Eq. (ii)

- $D_m = \left[\dfrac{D_0 + D_i}{2} \right]$ ...**13.34/ Pg 213, DHB**

- $n' = n_1 + n_2 - 1$
$= 5 + 4 - 1$
$n' = 8$

$\therefore$ Eq. (i) yields ... $6 \times 10^5 = \dfrac{0.25 \times 8}{2} \times [0.5497 D_i (D_0 - D_i)] \times \left[\dfrac{D_0 + D_i}{2} \right]$

$$= 0.2749 (D_0^2 - D_i^2) D_i$$
$$2.18 \times 10^6 = (D_0^2 - D_i^2) D_i \qquad \text{...Eq. }(iii)$$

Since there are two unknown in Eq. (iii), the problem can't be solved unless some assumption is made for the diameters. We have seen that in the previous problem, $D_i/D_0 \leq 0.577$.

Hence assuming $D_i/D_0 = 0.5$, we have
$$2.18 \times 10^6 = (1 - 0.5^2) \times 0.5 D_0^3$$
$$D_0 = 179.8 \text{ mm} \approx 180 \text{ mm}$$
$$\text{And } D_i = 0.5 \times 180 = 90 \text{ mm}.$$

6. Determine the average, minimum and maximum pressure in a plate clutch subjected to an axial load of 6 kN. The inside radius of contact surface is 60 mm and outside radius is 100 mm. Assume uniform wear.

Solution: $p_{avg} = ?, p_{min} = ?, p_{max} = ?, F_a = 6$ kN, $R_i = 60$ mm, $R_0 = 100$ mm

We know that from the derivation of uniform pressure $p = RC$ ...Eq. (i)

- The average pressure is calculated as, $p_{avg} = \dfrac{F_a}{\pi\left(R_0^2 - R_i^2\right)}$

$$= \dfrac{6000}{\pi(100^2 - 60^2)}$$
$$p_{avg} = 0.2984 \text{ MPa}$$

In general, axial force, $F_a = \dfrac{\pi}{2} pD(D_0 - D_i)$ ...13.32/ Pg 213, DHB

$$F_a = 2\pi R (R_0 - R_i) p \qquad \text{...Eq. }(ii)$$

- The pressure intensity is minimum at the outer radius, $p_{min} R_0 = C$
  i.e. $p = p_{min}$ and $R = R_0$

∴ Eq. (ii) yields ... $F_a = 2\pi R (R_0 - R_i) p_{min}$
$$6000 = 2\pi \times 100 \times (100 - 60) p_{min}$$
$$p_{min} = 0.2387 \text{ MPa}$$

- The pressure intensity is maximum pressure intensity occurs at the inner radius,
  i.e. $p = p_{max}$ and $R = R_i$

∴ Eq. (ii) yields ... $F_a = 2\pi R (R_0 - R_i) p_{max}$
$$6000 = 2\pi \times 60 \times (100 - 60) p_{max}$$
$$p_{max} = 0.3978 \text{ MPa}.$$

7. A multiple disc clutch of steel on bronze category is to transmit 4 kW at 750 rpm. The inner diameter of contact is 80 mm and the outer diameter of contact is 140 mm. The clutch operates in oil with a coefficient of friction of 0.1. The average allowable maximum pressure is 0.35 MPa. Assume uniform wear theory and determine

  i. Number of steel and bronze discs
  ii. Axial force required. *[VTU – Feb. 2002 – 10 Marks]*

Solution: $P = 4$ kW, $N = 750$ rpm, $D_i = 80$ mm, $D_0 = 140$ mm, $f = 0.1, p = 0.35$ MPa

i. $n_1 + n_2 = ?$ ii. $F_a = ?$

i. To find $n_1 + n_2$

We know that, $n' = n_1 + n_2 - 1$

∴ $n_1 + n_2 = n' + 1$ ...Eq. (i)

But $T = \dfrac{1}{2} f F_a D_m n'$ ...Eq. (ii) **13.34/ Pg 213, DHB**

- Also $P = \dfrac{2\pi NT}{60}$

$4 \times 10^3 = \dfrac{2\pi \times 750 \times T}{60}$

$T = 50.93$ N-m $= 50.93 \times 10^3$ N-mm

- $F_a = \dfrac{\pi}{2} p D_i (D_0 - D_i)$ ...**13.32/ Pg 213, DHB**

$= \dfrac{\pi \times 0.35 \times 80}{2}(140 - 80)$

$F_a = 2638.94$ N

- $D_m = \left[\dfrac{D_0 + D_i}{2}\right]$ ...**13.34/ Pg 213, DHB**

$= \left[\dfrac{140 + 80}{2}\right]$

$D_m = 110$ mm

∴ Eq. (ii) yields ... $50.93 \times 10^3 = \dfrac{1}{2} \times 0.1 \times 2638.94 \times 110 \times n'$

$n' = 3.51 \approx 4$

∴ Eq. (i) yields ... $n_1 + n_2 = 4 + 1 = 5$

ii. To find F_a

We know that, $T = \dfrac{1}{2} f F_a D_m n'$ ...**13.34/ Pg 213, DHB**

$50.93 \times 10^3 = \dfrac{1}{2} \times 0.1 \times F_a \times 110 \times 4$

$F_a = 2315$ N.

8. A multiple clutch as steel on bronze is to transmit 8 kW at 1440 rpm. The inner diameter of the contact is 80 mm and the outer diameter of contact is 140 mm. the clutch operates in oil with expected coefficient of friction of 0.1, the average allowable pressure is 0.35 MPa. Assume uniform wear theory and determine the following:
   i. No. of steel and bronze plates.
   ii. Axial force required
   iii. Actual maximum pressure.

   [VTU – Dec. 2011 – 10 Marks; Dec. 06/ Jan. 2007– 10 Marks; July/ Aug. 2004 – 06 Marks.]

Solution: $P = 8$ kW, $N = 1440$ rpm, $D_i = 80$ mm, $D_0 = 140$ mm, $f = 0.1$, $p = 0.35$ MPa
i. $n_1 + n_2 = ?$ ii. $F_a = ?$ iii. $p_{max} = ?$

i. To find $n_1 + n_2$

We know that, $n' = n_1 + n_2 - 1$

$\therefore n_1 + n_2 = n' + 1$ ...Eq. (i)

But $T = \dfrac{1}{2} f F_a D_m n'$ ...Eq. (ii) **13.34/ Pg 213, DHB**

- Also $P = \dfrac{2\pi NT}{60}$

$$8 \times 10^3 = \dfrac{2\pi \times 1440 \times T}{60}$$

$T = 53.05$ N-m $= 53.05 \times 10^3$ N-mm

- $F_a = \dfrac{\pi}{2} p D_i (D_0 - D_i)$ ...**13.32/ Pg 213, DHB**

$$= \dfrac{\pi \times 0.35 \times 80}{2}(140 - 80)$$

$F_a = 2638.94$ N

- $D_m = \left[\dfrac{D_0 + D_i}{2}\right]$ ...**13.34/ Pg 213, DHB**

$$= \left[\dfrac{140 + 80}{2}\right]$$

$D_m = 110$ mm

$\therefore$ Eq. (ii) yields ... $53.05 \times 10^3 = \dfrac{1}{2} \times 0.1 \times 2638.94 \times 110 \times n'$

$n' = 3.66 \approx 4$

$\therefore$ Eq. (i) yields ... $n_1 + n_2 = 4 + 1 = 5$

ii. To find F_a

We know that, $T = \dfrac{1}{2} f F_a D_m n'$ ...**13.34/ Pg 213, DHB**

$$53.05 \times 10^3 = \dfrac{1}{2} \times 0.1 \times F_a \times 110 \times 4$$

$F_a = 2411.36$ N

iii. To find p_{max}

We know that from the derivation of uniform pressure $p = RC$ ...Eq. (iii)
The pressure intensity is maximum pressure intensity occurs at the inner radius, $p_{max} R_i = C$.

i.e. $p = p_{max}$ and $R = R_i$

$\therefore$ Eq. (iii) yields ... $F_a = 2\pi R(R_0 - R_i) p_{max}$

$2411.36 = 2\pi \times 40 \times (70 - 40) p_{max}$

$p_{max} = 0.3198$ MPa.

6.9 DESIGN PROBLEMS ON PLATE CLUTCH

9. A single dry plate clutch transmits 8 kW at 1200 rpm. The axial pressure is limited to 0.07 MPa. If $f = 0.25$, find:

a. Mean radius and face width of friction lining assuming the ratio of mean radius to face width as 4.

b. Inner and outer diameters of friction lining.

Solution: $n' = 2$, $P = 8$ kW, $N = 1200$ rpm, $p = 0.07$ MPa, $f = 0.25$

a. $R_m, b = ?$, if $\dfrac{R_m}{b} = 4$

b. $D_i, D_0 = ?$

a. To find R_m, b:

We know that, $\quad T = \dfrac{1}{2} f F_a D_m n'$ ...Eq. (i) **13.34/ Pg 213, DHB**

- $D_m = 2R_m \Rightarrow R_m = \dfrac{D_m}{2}$

- Axial force, $F_a = pA = p(\pi D_m b) = p(2\pi R_m b)$

$$= 0.07 \times (2\pi R_m) \dfrac{R_m}{4}$$

$$F_a = 0.110 R_m^2$$

- Also $\quad P = \dfrac{2\pi NT}{60}$

$$8 \times 10^3 = \dfrac{2\pi \times 1200 \times T}{60}$$

$$T = 63.66 \text{ N-m} = 63.66 \times 10^3 \text{ N-mm}$$

∴ Eq. (i) yields ... $63.66 \times 10^3 = \dfrac{1}{2} \times 0.25 \times 0.110 R_m^2 \times 2R_m \times 2$

$$R_m = 105 \text{ mm}$$

And $b = 105/4 = 26.25$ mm ≈ 30 mm.

b. To find D_i, D_0:

We know that, $\quad R_m = \dfrac{R_i + R_0}{2}$

$R_0 + R_i = 2R_m = 2 \times 105 = 210$ mm ...Eq. (ii)

Also $\quad b = R_0 - R_i$

$R_0 - R_i = 30$ mm ...Eq. (iii)

Solving Eqs (ii) and (iii), we have

$$R_0 = 118.25 \approx 120 \text{ mm}$$
$$R_i = 90 \text{ mm}.$$

10. Give a complete design analysis for a single plate clutch, with both sides effective to transmit 22 kW at 2800 rpm, allowing an overload of 25%. The pressure intensity is not to exceed 0.08 MPa and surface speed at mean radius is not to exceed 2000 rpm. Take $f = 0.35$ and the ratio of $D_0/D_i = 1.5$. The axial thrust is provided by 6 springs of 24 mm coil diameter. Take shear stress = 420 MPa and $G = 84$ GPa for the spring material.

Solution: $n' = 2$, $P = 22$ kW, $N = 2800$ rpm, overload = 25%, $p = 0.08$ MPa, mean speed $N_m = 2000$ rpm, $f = 0.35$ and the ratio $D_0/D_i = 1.5$, number of springs = 6, coil diameter $D = 24$ mm, $\tau = 420$ MPa, $G = 84$ GPa
a. $D_i, D_0, b = ?$ (Dimensions of the clutch)
b. Dimensions of the spring

a) Dimensions of the clutch: (D_i, D_0, b)

We know that,
$$T = \frac{1}{2} f F_a D_m n' \quad \text{...Eq. (i) 13.34/ Pg 213, DHB}$$

- $$D_m = \left[\frac{D_0 + D_i}{2}\right] \quad \text{...13.34/ Pg 213, DHB}$$

$$= \frac{D_i}{2}\left[\frac{D_0}{D_i} + 1\right]$$

$$= 0.5 D_i [1.5 + 1]$$

$$D_m = 1.25 D_i \quad \text{...Eq. (ii)}$$

- Axial force, $$F_a = \frac{\pi}{2} p D_i (D_0 - D_i)$$

$$= \frac{\pi p D_i^2}{2}\left[\frac{D_0}{D_i} - 1\right]$$

$$= \frac{\pi \times 0.08 \times D_i^2}{2}[1.5 - 1]$$

$$F_a = 0.06283 D_i^2 \quad \text{...Eq. (iii)}$$

- Also $$P = \frac{2\pi N_m T}{60}$$

$$22 \times 10^3 = \frac{2\pi \times 2000 \times T}{60}$$

$$T = 105.04 \text{ N-m} = 105.04 \times 10^3 \text{ N-mm}$$

∴ Eq. (i) yields ... $105.04 \times 10^3 = \frac{1}{2} \times 0.35 \times 0.06283 D_i^2 \times 1.25 D_i \times 2$

$$= 0.0785 D_i^3$$

$$D_i = 156.34 \text{ mm} \approx 160 \text{ mm}$$

$$D_0 = 1.5 \times 160 = 240 \text{ mm}$$

∴ Eq. (iii) yields ... $F_a = 0.06283 \times 160^2$

$$F_a = 1608.45 \text{ N}$$

∴ Eq. (ii) yields ... $D_m = 1.25 \times 160 = 200$ mm

b) Dimensions of the spring: (d, D, y, l_0, p)

i. To find d, D:

Let d = diameter of spring wire
D = Mean diameter of spring

We know that, $\tau = \dfrac{8FDK}{\pi d^3} = \dfrac{8FCK}{\pi d^2}$ ...Eq. (iv) **11.1a/ Pg 139, DHB**

- Load on each spring, $F = \dfrac{F_a}{\text{No. of springs}}$

Given overload = 25%

$$F = \dfrac{1.25 F_a}{\text{No. of springs}}$$

$$= \dfrac{1.25 \times 1608.45}{6}$$

$$F = 335 \text{ N}$$

∴ Eq. (iv) yields ... $420 = \dfrac{8 \times 335 \times 24 \times K}{\pi \times d^3}$

$$K = (20.51 \times 10^{-3}) d^3 \qquad \text{...Eq. (v)}$$

Also $K = 2\left(\dfrac{d}{D}\right)^{0.25}$ ...**11.2d/ Pg 139, DHB**

$$= 2\left(\dfrac{d}{24}\right)^{0.25}$$

$$K = (0.9036) d^{0.25} \qquad \text{...Eq. (vi)}$$

Equating Eq. (v) and Eq. (vi) we have

$$(20.51 \times 10^{-3}) d^3 = (0.9036) d^{0.25}$$

$$d = 3.96 \text{ mm} \approx 4 \text{ mm}$$

Therefore, standard wire diameter, $d = 4$ mm ...**Tb. 11.3a/ Pg 150, DHB**

ii. To find y:

We know that deflection, $y = \dfrac{8FC^3 i}{Gd}$ ...**11.5a/ Pg 139, DHB**

i = active number of coils
  = number of springs – 2
$i = 6 - 2 = 4$

$$= \dfrac{8 \times 335 \times 6^3 \times 6}{84 \times 10^3 \times 4} \qquad (C = D/d = 24/4 = 6)$$

$$y = 10.33 \text{ mm}$$

iii. To find l_0:

For square and ground ends deflection, $l_0 = (i+1)d + y + a$. ...**11.20b/ Pg 142, DHB**

$a = 1$ mm *per coil*
  $= (i - 1) \times 1$ mm
  $= (6 - 1) \times 1$
$a = 5$ mm

∴ $l_0 = ip + 2d$
$l_0 = 43.33$ mm.

iv. To find p:

We know that, $l_0 = ip + 2d$ ...Tb. 11.7/ Pg 152, DHB

$$433 = 6p + 2 \times 4$$
$$p = 5.89 \text{ mm} \approx 6 \text{ mm}.$$

11. The following data are given for a dry single plate clutch:

Power = 18.65 kW, speed = 1500 rpm, number of springs = 6, ratio of mean radius to radial width = 4.5, find:

i. Mean radius and width of friction surfaces.
ii. Dimensions of clutch plate.
iii. Dimensions of springs.

[VTU – Dec. 2010 – 10 Marks]

Solution: $n' = 2$, $P = 18.65$ kW, $N = 1500$ rpm, number of springs = 6, $\dfrac{R_m}{b} = 4.5$

i. $R_m, b = ?$,
ii. $D_i, D_0, b = ?$ (dimensions of the clutch)
iii. Dimensions of the spring

Material properties:

Since the coefficient of friction is not given, let us assume that the clutch plates are made of cast iron, having:

$f = 0.15$ to 0.2 $p_{max} = 0.98$ to 1.18 MPa   ...Tb 13.2a/ Pg228, DHB

Assume $f = 0.2$, $p_{allow} = p_{max}/4 = 0.245$ MPa

i. To find R_m, b:

We know that, $T = \dfrac{1}{2} f F_a D_m n'$ ...Eq. (i) 13.34/ Pg 213, DHB

- $D_m = 2R_m \Rightarrow R_m = \dfrac{D_m}{2}$

- Axial force, $F_a = pA = p(\pi D_m b) = p(2\pi R_m b)$

$$= 0.245 \times (2\pi R_m) \dfrac{R_m}{4.5}$$

$$F_a = 0.3421 R_m^2$$

- Also $P = \dfrac{2\pi NT}{60}$

$$18.65 \times 10^3 = \dfrac{2\pi \times 1500 \times T}{60}$$

$$T = 118.73 \text{ N-m} = 118.73 \times 10^3 \text{ N-mm}$$

∴ Eq. (i) yields... $118.73 \times 10^3 = \dfrac{1}{2} \times 0.2 \times 0.3421 R_m^2 \times 2R_m \times 2$

$$R_m = 95.38 \text{ mm} \approx 100 \text{ mm}$$
And $b = 100/4.5 = 22.23 \text{ mm} \approx 25 \text{ mm}$

ii. Dimensions of the clutch (D_i, D_0, b):

We know that, $R_m = \dfrac{R_i + R_0}{2}$

$R_0 + R_i = 2R_m = 2 \times 100 = 200$ mm ...Eq. (ii)

Also $b = R_0 - R_i$

$R_0 - R_i = 25$ mm ...Eq. (iii)

Solving Eqs (ii) and (iii), we have

$R_0 = 112.5 \approx 120$ mm

$R_i = 95$ mm

iii. Dimensions of the spring (d, D, y, l_0, p):

a. To find d, D:

Let d = diameter of spring wire
D = Mean diameter of spring

We know that, $\tau = \dfrac{8FDK}{\pi d^3} = \dfrac{8FCK}{\pi d^2}$ ...Eq. (iv) **11.1a/ Pg 139, DHB**

- Assume $C = D/d = 6$, $\tau = 420$ MPa, $G = 84$ GPa

- $K = \dfrac{4C-1}{4C-4} + \dfrac{0.615}{C}$ ...**11.2b/ Pg 139, DHB**

  $= \dfrac{4 \times 6 - 1}{4 \times 6 - 4} + \dfrac{0.615}{6}$

  $K = 1.2525$

- Load on each spring, $F = \dfrac{F_a}{\text{No. of springs}}$

Assuming 25% overload, we have

$F = \dfrac{1.25 F_a}{\text{No. of springs}}$

$= \dfrac{1.25(2\pi R_m b p)}{\text{No. of springs}}$

$= \dfrac{1.25(2\pi \times 100 \times 25 \times 0.245)}{6}$

$F = 801.76$ N

∴ Eq. (i) yields ... $420 = \dfrac{8 \times 801.76 \times 6 \times 1.2525}{\pi d^2}$

$d = 6.04$ mm

Therefore, standard wire diameter, $d = 6.00$ mm ...**Tb. 11.3a/ Pg 150, DHB**

Mean diameter of spring, $D = 6 \times 6 = 36$ mm

b. To find y:

We know that deflection, $y = \dfrac{8FC^3 i}{Gd}$ ...**11.5a/ Pg 139, DHB**

i = active number of coils
= number of springs – 2
$i = 6 – 2 = 4$

$$= \frac{8 \times 801.76 \times 6^3 \times 4}{84 \times 10^3 \times 6}$$

$y = 11$ mm.

c. To find l_0:

For square and ground ends deflection, $l_0 = (i + 1)d + y + a$ ...**11.20b/ Pg 142, DHB**

$a = 1$ mm *per coil*
$= (i – 1) \times 1$ mm
$= (6 – 1) \times 1$
$a = 5$ mm

∴ $l_0 = (6 + 1) \times 6 + 11 + 5$
$l_0 = 58$ mm

d. To find p:

We know that, $l_0 = ip + 2d$ ...**Tb. 11.7/ Pg 152, DHB**
$58 = 6p + 2 \times 6$
$p = 7.67$ mm.

12. Design a single plate clutch having both sides effective from the following data: Power transmitted = 30 kW; speed of shaft = 1500 rpm; allowable lining pressure = 0.147 MPa; maximum diameter of the clutch = 300 mm; service factor = 1.5; number of springs = 9; compression of spring during engagement = 2.5 mm.
[VTU – Dec. 2010 – 12 Marks]

Solution: $n' = 2$, $P = 30$ kW, $N = 1500$ rpm, $p = 0.147$ MPa, maximum diameter of clutch, $D_0 = 300$ mm, service factor = 1.5, number of springs = 9, spring compression during engagement = 2.5 mm
a. D_i, D_0, b = ? (Dimensions of the clutch) b. Dimensions of the spring.

a) Dimensions of the clutch: (D_i, D_0, b)

We know that, $T = \frac{1}{2} f F_a D_m n'$ ...Eq. (i) **13.34/ Pg 213, DHB**

- $D_m = \left[\dfrac{D_0 + D_i}{2}\right]$ ...**13.34/ Pg 213, DHB**

  $D_m = 0.5[300 + D_i]$ ...Eq. (ii)

- Axial force, $F_a = \dfrac{\pi}{2} p D_i (D_0 – D_i)$

  $= \dfrac{\pi \times 0.147 D_i}{2}[300 – D_i]$

  $F_0 = 0.2309 D_i [300 – D_i]$ ...Eq. (iii)

- Also $P = \dfrac{2\pi N T}{60} \times (1/C_s)$ ($\because F_t = 1000 P C_s / v$) ... (gears)

$$30 \times 10^3 = \frac{2\pi \times 1500 \times T}{60 \times 1.5}$$

$$T = 286.48 \text{ N-m} = 286.48 \times 10^3 \text{ N-mm}$$

∴ Eq. (*i*) yields ... $286.48 \times 10^3 = \frac{1}{2} \times 0.3 \times 0.2309 D_i [300 - D_i] \times 0.5[300 + D_i] \times 2$

$$= 0.03464 \, D_i \, [300^2 - D_i^2] \qquad \text{(assume } f = 0.3\text{)}$$

$$D_i[300^2 - D_i^2] = 8.27 \times 10^6$$

$$90000 D_i - D_i^3 = 8.27 \times 10^6$$

$$D_i^3 - 90000 D_i + 8.27 \times 10^6 = 0$$

$$D_i = 233.7 \approx 240 \text{ mm} \qquad \text{(roots: 233.7, –338.3, 104.6)}$$

∴ Eq. (*ii*) yields ... $D_m = 0.5[300 + 240]$

$$D_m = 270 \text{ mm}$$

∴ Eq. (*iii*) yields ... $F_a = 0.2309 \times 240 \times [300 - 240]$

$$F_a = 3325 \text{ N.}$$

b. Dimensions of the spring (d, D, y, l_0, p):

i. To find d, D:

We know that, $\quad \tau = \dfrac{8FDK}{\pi d^3} = \dfrac{8FCK}{\pi d^2} \qquad$ ...Eq. (*iv*) **11.1a/ Pg 139, DHB**

- Assume $C = D/d = 6$, $\tau = 420$ MPa, $G = 80$ GPa

- $K = \dfrac{4C - 1}{4C - 4} + \dfrac{0.615}{C} \qquad$ ...**11.2b/ Pg 139, DHB**

$$= \frac{4 \times 6 - 1}{4 \times 6 - 4} + \frac{0.615}{6}$$

$$K = 1.2525$$

- Load on each spring, $F = \dfrac{F_a}{\text{No. of springs}}$

Assuming 25% overload, we have

$$F = \frac{1.25 \, F_a}{\text{No. of springs}}$$

$$= \frac{1.25 \times 3325}{9}$$

$$F = 461.81 \text{ N}$$

∴ Eq. (*iv*) yields ... $420 = \dfrac{8 \times 461.81 \times 6 \times 1.2525}{\pi d^2}$

$$d = 4.58 \text{ mm}$$

Therefore, standard wire diameter, $d = 4.75$ mm ...**Tb. 11.3a/ Pg 150, DHB**

Mean diameter of spring, $D = 6 \times 4.75 = 28.5$ mm

ii. To find y:

We know that deflection, $y = \dfrac{8FC^3 i}{Gd}$ ...11.5a/ Pg 139, DHB

i = active number of coils
= number of springs – 2
$i = 9 - 2 = 7$

$$= \dfrac{8 \times 461.81 \times 6^3 \times 7}{80 \times 10^3 \times 4.75}$$

∴ $y = 14.70$ mm

iii. To find l_0:

For square and ground ends deflection, $l_0 = (i+1)d + y + a$ ...11.20b/ Pg 142, DHB
= 1 mm *per coil*
= $(i – 1) \times 1$ mm
= $(9 – 1) \times 1$
$a = 8$ mm

∴ $l_0 = (9 + 1) \times 4.75 + 2.5 + 8$ ($y = 2.5$ mm, data)
$l_0 = 58$ mm.

iv. To find p:

We know that, $l_0 = ip + 2d$ ...Tb. 11.7/ Pg 152, DHB
$58 = 6p + 2 \times 4.75$
$p = 8.08$ mm.

13. A plate clutch with a maximum diameter of 600 mm has maximum lining pressure of 0.35 MPa. The power to be transmitted at 400 rpm is 135 kW and $f = 0.3$. Find inside diameter and spring force required to engage the clutch, if the springs with spring index 6 and material of spring is steel with safe shear stress 600 MPa is used. Find the wire diameter, if 6 springs are used.

[VTU – Jan./ Feb 2003 – 10 Marks]

Solution: maximum diameter of clutch, $D_0 = 600$ mm, $p = 0.35$ MPa $P = 135$ kW, $N = 400$ rpm, $f = 0.3$, $C = 6$, $\tau = 600$ MPa, $d = ?$, number of springs = 6, $n' = 2$
a. Minimum diameter of clutch, $D_i = ?, F_a = ?$
b. Wire diameter, $d = ?$

a. Minimum diameter of clutch: D_i

We know that, $T = \dfrac{1}{2} f F_a D_m n'$ ...Eq. (i) 13.34/ Pg 213, DHB

- $D_m = \left[\dfrac{D_0 + D_i}{2}\right]$ ...13.34/ Pg 213, DHB

  $D_m = 0.5 [600 + D_i]$ ...Eq. (ii)

- Axial force, $F_a = \dfrac{\pi}{2} p D_i (D_0 - D_i)$

  $= \dfrac{\pi \times 0.35 \times D_i}{2}[600 - D_i]$

  $F_a = 0.5498 D_i [600 - D_i]$ ...Eq. (iii)

- Also $P = \dfrac{2\pi NT}{60}$

$$135 \times 10^3 = \dfrac{2\pi \times 400 \times T}{60}$$

$$T = 3.22 \times 10^3 \text{ N-m} = 3.22 \times 10^6 \text{ N-mm}$$

∴ Eq. (*i*) yields ... $3.22 \times 10^6 = \dfrac{1}{2} \times 0.3 \times 0.5498 D_i[600 - D_i] \times 0.5[600 + D_i] \times 2$

$$= 0.0825 D_i [600^2 - D_i^2]$$

$$D_i[600^2 - D_i^2] = 39 \times 10^6$$
$$360000 D_i - D_i^3 = 39 \times 10^6$$
$$D_i^3 = 360000 D_i + 39 \times 10^6 = 0$$
$$D_i = 536.7 \approx 540 \text{ mm} \qquad \text{(roots: 536, –648, 112)}$$

∴ Eq. (*ii*) yields ... $D_m = 0.5[600 + 540]$
$$D_m = 570 \text{ mm}$$

∴ Eq. (*iii*) yields ... $F_a = 0.5498 \times 540 \times [600 - 540]$
$$F_a = 17.81 \text{ kN}.$$

b. Wire diameter d:

We know that, $\tau = \dfrac{8FDK}{\pi d^3} = \dfrac{8FCK}{\pi d^2}$ ...Eq. (*iv*) **11.1a/ Pg 139, DHB**

- $C = D/d = 6.$ (data)

- $K = \dfrac{4C - 1}{4C - 4} + \dfrac{0.615}{C}$ ...**11.2b/ Pg 139, DHB**

$$= \dfrac{4 \times 6 - 1}{4 \times 6 - 4} + \dfrac{0.615}{6}$$

$$K = 1.2525$$

- Load on each spring, $F = \dfrac{F_a}{\text{No. of springs}}$

Assuming 25% overload, we have

$$F = \dfrac{1.25 F_a}{\text{No. of springs}}$$

$$= \dfrac{1.25 \times 17.81 \times 10^3}{6}$$

$$F = 3711.15 \text{ N}$$

∴ Eq. (*iv*) yields ... $600 = \dfrac{8 \times 3711.15 \times 6 \times 1.2525}{\pi d^2}$

$$d = 10.87 \text{ mm}$$

Therefore, standard wire diameter, $d = 11$ mm ...**Tb. 11.3a/ Pg 150, DHB**

Mean diameter of spring, $D = 6 \times 11 = 66$ mm.

6.10 TORQUE ANALYSIS OF CONE CLUTCH

Consider a single plate clutch as shown in **Fig. 6.7**.

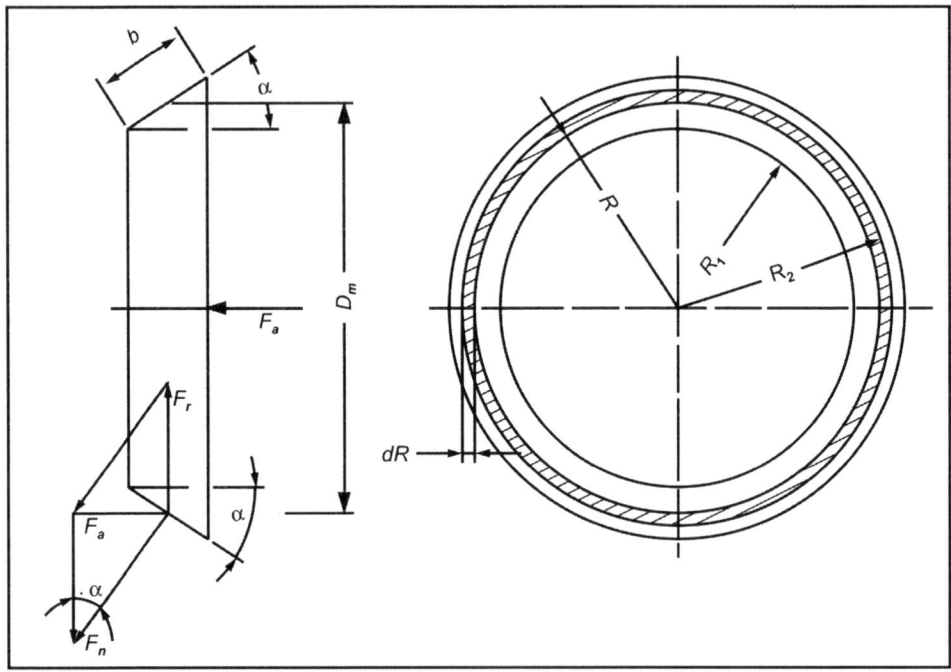

Fig. 6.7: Torque analysis in a cone clutch
(Fig. 13.10/ Pg 235, DHB)

Let, D_2 – Outer diameter of cone D_1 – Inner diameter of cone
D_m – Mean diameter of cone p – pressure intensity
α – semi angle of cone –or- face angle b – breadth/ width of cone
f – coefficient of friction F_a – Axial force or axial thrust

F_b – frictional force F_n – normal force = $\dfrac{F_a}{\sin \alpha}$

Consider a elementary ring of thickness at a radius as shown in **Fig. 6.7**.

Area of the elemental ring, $dA = 2\pi R \cdot \left(\dfrac{dR}{\sin \alpha}\right) = 2\pi R \cdot dR \, \text{cosec} \, \alpha$ ...(Eq. 6.23)

Normal force on the ring, $dF_n = p \cdot dA = p \, (2\pi R \cdot dR \, \text{cosec} \, \alpha)$ ...(Eq. 6.24)

Axial force on the ring, $dF_a = (p \cdot dA) \times \sin \alpha$
$= p(2\alpha R \cdot dR \, \text{cosec} \, \alpha) \times \sin \alpha$
$dF_a = 2\pi p R \cdot dR$ ...(Eq. 6.25)

Frictional force on the ring, $dF_b = f \cdot dF_n$
$dF_b = f \cdot p \, (2\pi R \cdot dR \, \text{cosec} \, \alpha)$ ...(Eq. 6.26)

Frictional torque on the ring $dT = dF_b \cdot R$
$= [f \cdot p \, (2\pi R \cdot dR \, \text{cosec} \, \alpha)] R$
$dT = 2p f p R^2 \cdot dR \cdot \text{cosec} \, \alpha$ ...(Eq. 6.27)

Integrating Eqs (6.25) and (6.27), we have

Eq. (6.25) yields ... $F_a = \int_{R_1}^{R_2} p(2\pi R).dR$

$$F_a = 2\pi \int_{R_1}^{R_2} pR.dR \qquad \text{...(Eq. 6.28)}$$

Eq. (6.27) yields ... $T = \int_{R_1}^{R_2} (2\pi f p R^2 \text{cosec } \alpha).dR$

$$T = T = 2\pi f \text{cosec } \alpha \int_{R_1}^{R_2} pR^2.dR \qquad \text{...(Eq. 6.29)}$$

a. Uniform Pressure Theory:

Eq. (6.28) yields ... $F_a = 2\pi p \int_{R_1}^{R_2} R\, dR$

$$= 2\pi p \left(\frac{R^2}{2}\right)_{R_1}^{R_2}$$

$$F_a = \pi p (R_2^2 - R_1^2) \qquad \text{-or-} \qquad \text{...(Eq. 6.30)}$$

$$F_a = \frac{\pi p}{4}(R_2^2 - R_1^2) \qquad \text{...(Eq. 6.30a)}$$

Eq. (6.29) yields ... $T = 2\pi f p \text{ cosec } \alpha \int_{R_1}^{R_2} R^2.dR$

$$= \frac{2\pi f p}{\sin \alpha}\left(\frac{R^3}{3}\right)_{R_1}^{R_2}$$

$$T = \frac{2\pi f p}{3 \sin \alpha}(R_2^3 - R_1^3) \qquad \text{...(Eq. 6.31)}$$

$$\text{But } p = \frac{F_a}{\pi(R_2^2 - R_1^2)} \qquad \text{...(Eq. 6.32)}$$

$\therefore$ Eq. (6.31) yields ... $T = \dfrac{2\pi f}{3\sin\alpha}(R_2^3 - R_1^3)\left[\dfrac{F_a}{\pi(R_2^2 - R_1^2)}\right]$

$$T = \frac{2fF_a}{3\sin\alpha}\left[\frac{R_2^3 - R_1^3}{R_2^2 - R_1^2}\right] \qquad \text{-or-} \qquad \text{...(Eq. 6.33)}$$

$$T = \frac{2fF_a}{3\sin\alpha}\left[\frac{(D_2^3 - D_1^3)/8}{(D_2^2 - D_1^2)/4}\right]$$

$$= \frac{2fF_a}{6\sin\alpha}\left[\frac{D_2^3 - D_1^3}{D_2^2 - D_1^2}\right]$$

$$T = \frac{fF_a}{2\sin\alpha}\left\{\frac{2}{3}\left[\frac{D_2^3 - D_1^3}{D_2^2 - D_1^2}\right]\right\} \quad \text{...(Eq. 6.33a)}$$

$$T = \frac{fF_a D_m}{2\sin\alpha} = \frac{F_b D_m}{2} \quad \text{...(Eq. 6.34)} \;\; \textbf{13.38/ Pg 214, DHB}$$

Where, D_m – mean diameter of friction surface

$$= \frac{2}{3}\left[\frac{D_2^3 - D_1^3}{D_2^2 - D_1^2}\right]$$

and
$$F_b = \frac{fF_a}{\sin\alpha} \quad \text{...13.36/Pg 214, DHB}$$

b. Uniform Wear Theory:

We know that,
$$p = \frac{C}{R} \quad \text{...using (Eq. 6.12)}$$

$\therefore$ Eq. (6.28) yields ...$F_a = 2\pi\int_{R_1}^{R_2} pR.dR$

$$= 2\pi\int_{R_1}^{R_2} C.dR$$

$$= 2\pi C\,(R)_{R_1}^{R_2}$$

$$F_a = 2\pi C\,(R_2 - R_1) \quad \text{...(Eq. 6.35)}$$

and Eq. (6.29) yields ... $T = 2\pi f \operatorname{cosec}\alpha \int_{R_1}^{R_2} pR^2.dR$

$$= 2\pi f\operatorname{cosec}\alpha \int_{R_1}^{R_2} CR.dR$$

$$= 2\pi fC \operatorname{cosec}\alpha \int_{R_1}^{R_2} R.dR$$

$$= \frac{2\pi fC}{\sin\alpha}\left(\frac{R^2}{2}\right)_{R_1}^{R_2}$$

$$T = \frac{\pi fC}{\sin\alpha}\left(R_2^2 - R_1^2\right) \quad \text{...(Eq. 6.36)}$$

Substituting $C = \dfrac{F_a}{2\pi C(R_2 - R_1)}$ \quad ...using (Eq. 6.35)

$$T = \frac{\pi f}{\sin\alpha}\frac{F_a}{2\pi(R_2 - R_1)}\left(R_2^2 - R_1^2\right)$$

$$T = \frac{fF_a}{2\sin\alpha}(R_2 + R_1) \qquad \text{-or-} \qquad \ldots\text{(Eq. 6.37)}$$

$$T = \frac{fF_a}{2\sin\alpha}\left[\frac{D_1 + D_2}{2}\right]$$

$$T = \frac{fF_a D_m}{2\sin\alpha} = \frac{F_b D_m}{2} \quad \text{[same as Eq. (6.34)]} \ldots\text{(Eq. 6.38)} \; \textbf{13.38/ Pg 214, DHB}$$

Where, D_m = mean diameter of friction surface

$$= \left[\frac{D_2 + D_1}{2}\right] \qquad \ldots\textbf{13.38/ Pg 214, DHB}$$

α = Semi-cone angle
 = 12.5°, ...for leather faced cones
 = 15° – 25°, ...for industrial clutches faced with wood.

Note:

→ We know that, $F_a = 2\pi C(R_2 - R_1)$ ...*using (Eq. 6.35)*
$= 2\pi p R(R_2 - R_1)$

At mean radius, $R = R_m = \dfrac{D_m}{2}$

∴ $$F_a = 2\pi p \frac{D_m}{2}\left(\frac{D_2 - D_1}{2}\right)$$

$$F_a = \pi p D_m \left(\frac{D_2 - D_1}{2}\right) \qquad \ldots\text{(Eq. 6.39)}$$

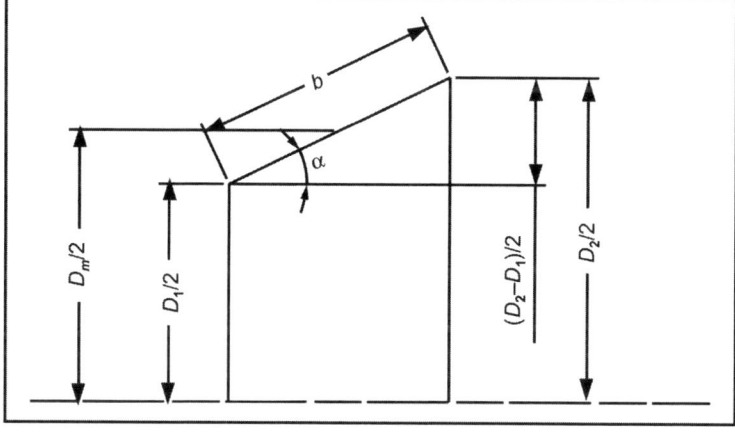

Fig. 6.7(a)

From **Fig. 6.7(a)**, $\sin\alpha = \left[\dfrac{(D_2 - D_1)/2}{b}\right] = \left(\dfrac{D_2 - D_1}{2b}\right)$

$$= \left[\frac{(D_2 - D_m)/2}{b/2}\right] = \left(\frac{D_2 - D_m}{b}\right)$$

$$= \left[\frac{(D_m - D_1)/2}{b/2}\right] = \left(\frac{D_m - D_1}{b}\right)$$

$\therefore \quad \left(\dfrac{D_2 - D_1}{2}\right) = b \sin \alpha$

$\therefore$ Eq. (6.39) yields ... $F_a = \pi D_m b p \sin \alpha$ ...(Eq. 6.40) **13.37/ Pg 214, DHB**
- For mean/ average pressure, $p = p_{avg}$ and $D_m = D_m$
- For maximum pressure, $\quad p = p_{max}$ and $D_m = D_1$ (inner surface)
- For minimum pressure, $\quad p = p_{min}$ and $D_m = D_2$ (outer surface)

→ The ratio of $\quad \dfrac{D_m}{b} = 4.5$ to 8 ...**13.41/ Pg 214, DHB**

→ For commercial clutches, $D_m = 5D$ to $10D$ ...**13.42/ Pg 215, DHB**

$\qquad D$ – diameter of the shaft

→ Frictional force, $\quad F_b = f F_n = \dfrac{f F_a}{\sin \alpha}$ ...**13.36/ Pg 214, DHB**

→ Force necessary to engage the clutch,
$$F_a' = F_n (\sin \alpha + f \cos \alpha)$$
$$= \pi D_m b p (\sin \alpha + f \cos \alpha) \quad \text{...13.40/ Pg 214, DHB}$$

f = coefficient of friction
$\quad = 0.15$, for cast iron on cast iron
$\quad = 0.20$, for a surface faced with leather or wood
$\quad = 0.30$, for a surface faced with asbestos
$\quad = 0.25$ for cone surfaces with cork inserts.

→ Power transmitted, $P = \dfrac{2\pi N T}{60}$ (watts)

$$= \dfrac{2\pi N}{60} \left(\dfrac{f F_a D_m}{2 \sin \alpha}\right) \quad \text{...using 13.38/ Pg 214, DHB}$$

$$= \pi n \left(\dfrac{f D_m}{\sin \alpha}\right) \pi D_m b p \sin \alpha \quad (n = N/60) \quad \text{...using 13.37/ Pg 214, DHB}$$

$P = \pi^2 D_m^2 b p f n \quad$ N-mm/s

$$= \dfrac{\pi^2 D_m^2 b p f n}{10^3} \quad \text{N-m/s}$$

$$P = \frac{\pi^2 D_m^2 bpfn}{10^6} \quad \text{kN-m/s} = \text{kJ/s} = \text{kW}$$

i.e. $P(kW) = \dfrac{\pi^2 D_m^2 bpfn}{10^6 \times K_l}$ ...(Eq. 6.41) **13.39a/ Pg 214, DHB**

K_l = load factor ...**Tb. 12.34/ Pg 203, DHB**
n = speed (rps)
  = 5 to 16.5 for clutches with metal to metal contact
  ...**13.44/ Pg 215, DHB**
v = peripheral velocity
  = 13 to 25, for high speed leather faced couplings
  ...**13.43/ Pg 215, DHB**

6.11 BASIC PROBLEMS ON CONE CLUTCH

14. An engine develops 30 kW at 900 rpm. The cone has a face angle of 12.5° and a mean diameter of 400 mm with coefficient of friction as 0.2. The normal pressure on the clutch is not to exceed 0.15 MPa. Determine:
  a. Face width.
  b. Axial spring force required to engage the clutch.

Solution: P = 30 kW, N = 900 rpm $\Rightarrow n$ = 15 rps, α = 12.5°, D_m = 400 mm, f = 0.2, p = 0.15 MPa
a. b = ?   b. F_a = ?

a. To find b:

We know that, $P(kW) = \dfrac{\pi^2 D_m^2 bpfn}{10^6 \times K_l}$ ...**13.3ab/ Pg 214, DHB**

Assume $K_l = 1$

$$30 = \frac{\pi^2 \times 400^2 \times b \times 0.15 \times 0.2 \times 15}{10^6 \times 1}$$

b = 42.22 mm ≈ 45 mm

b. Axial force to engage the clutch:

We know that, $F_a' = \pi D_m bp(\sin \alpha + f \cos \alpha)$ ...**13.40/ Pg 214, DHB**
  = $\pi \times 400 \times 45 \times 0.15 \times (\sin 12.5 + 0.2 \times \cos 12.5)$
F_a' = 3492.15 N.

15. An engine developing 50 kW at 1000 rpm is fitted with a cone clutch built inside the flywheel. The cone has a face angle of 12.5° and a maximum mean diameter of 550 mm. The coefficient of friction is 0.2. The normal pressure on the clutch face is not to exceed 0.12 N/mm². Determine:
  i. The face width required.
  ii. The axial spring force necessary to engage the clutch.
  [VTU – May/ June 2010 – 10 Marks]

Solution: P = 50 kW, N = 1000 rpm $\Rightarrow n$ = 16.67 rps, α = 12.5°, D_m = 550 mm, f = 0.2, p = 0.12 MPa
a. F_a = ?   b. F_a' = ?

a. To find b:

We know that, $\quad P \text{ (kW)} = \dfrac{\pi^2 D_m^2 b p f n}{10^6 \times K_l} \quad$ ...13.39a/ Pg 214, DHB

Assume $K_l = 1$

$$50 = \dfrac{\pi^2 \times 550^2 \times b \times 0.12 \times 0.2 \times 16.67}{10^6 \times 1}$$

$b = 41.86 \text{ mm} \approx 45 \text{ mm}$

b. Axial force to engage the clutch:

We know that, $\quad F_a' = \pi D_m b p (\sin \alpha + f \cos \alpha) \quad$ ...13.40/ Pg 214, DHB

$\qquad = \pi \times 550 \times 45 \times 0.12 \times (\sin 12.5 + 0.2 \times \cos 12.5)$

$F_a' = 3841.37 \text{ N}.$

16. A cone clutch transmits 180 N-m of torque at 1200 rpm. The larger diameter of the clutch is 300 mm and face angle of the cone is 12.5° with a face width of 60 mm and $f = 0.2$. Determine:
    a. Axial force required to transmit the torque.
    b. Axial force required to engage the clutch.
    c. Average normal pressure when maximum torque is transmitted.
    d. Maximum and minimum normal pressures.

Solution: $T = 180$ N-m $= 180 \times 10^3$ N-mm, $N = 1200$ rpm, $D_2 = 300$ mm, $\alpha = 12.5°$, $b = 60$ mm, $f = 0.2$.
a. $F_a = ?$ b. $F_a' = ?$ c. $p_{avg} = ?$ d. $p_{max}, p_{min} = ?$

a. Axial force required to transmit the torque:

We know that, $\quad T = \dfrac{f F_a D_m}{2 \sin \alpha} \quad$ ...Eq. (i) 13.38/ Pg 214, DHB

- But $\sin \alpha = \left[\dfrac{(D_2 - D_m)/2}{b/2}\right] = \left(\dfrac{D_2 - D_m}{b}\right)$

    i.e. $\sin 12.5 = \left(\dfrac{300 - D_m}{60}\right)$

    $D_m = 287$ mm

- Also $D_m = \left[\dfrac{D_2 + D_1}{2}\right] \quad$ ...13.38/ Pg 214, DHB

    $287 = \left[\dfrac{300 + D_1}{2}\right]$

    $D_1 = 274$ mm

$\therefore$ Eq. (i) yields ... $180 \times 10^3 = \dfrac{0.2 \times F_a \times 287}{2 \times \sin 12.5}$

$F_a = 1357.46$ N.

b. Axial force to engage the clutch:

We know that, $\quad F_a' = F_n(\sin\alpha + f\cos\alpha)$ ...13.40/ Pg 214, DHB

$$= \frac{F_a}{\sin\alpha}(\sin\alpha + f\cos\alpha)$$

$$= \frac{1357.46}{\sin 12.5}(\sin 12.5 + 0.2 \times 12.5)$$

$$F_a' = 2582.08 \text{ N}$$

c. Average normal pressure:

We know that, $\quad F_a = \pi D_m bp \sin\alpha \quad$ ...Eq. (ii) 13.37/ Pg 214, DHB

Since average pressure occurs at mean radius, thus we have $p = p_{avg}$ and $D_m = D_m$

$$F_a = \pi D_m b p_{avg} \sin\alpha$$
$$1357.46 = \pi \times 287 \times 60 \times p_{avg} \times \sin 12.5$$
$$p_{avg} = 0.1159 \text{ MPa}$$

d. Maximum and minimum normal pressures:

- Maximum pressure occurs at inner radius, thus we have $p = p_{max}$ and $D_m = D_1$

  ∴ Eq. (ii) yields ... $F_a = \pi D_1 b p_{max} \sin\alpha$
  $$1357.46 = \pi \times 274 \times 60\, p_{max} \times \sin 12.5$$
  $$p_{max} = 0.1214 \text{ MPa}$$

- Minimum pressure occurs at inner radius, thus we have $p = p_{min}$ and $D_m = D_2$

  ∴ Eq. (ii) yields ... $F_a = \pi D_2 b p_{min} \sin\alpha$
  $$1357.46 = p \times 300 \times 60 \times p_{min} \times \sin 12.5$$
  $$p_{max} = 0.1109 \text{ MPa}.$$

17. A cone clutch with a face angle of 14° has to transmit 286 N-m of torque at a speed of 600 rev/min. The larger diameter of the clutch is 250 mm, face width is 60 mm and coefficient of friction is 0.18. Determine:
   i. Axial force required to transmit the torque.
   ii. Average normal pressure
   iii. Maximum normal pressure.
   Assume uniform wear conditions. *[VTU – Jan./ Feb. 2005 – 10 Marks]*

Solution: $\alpha = 14°$, 286 N-m = 286 × 10³ N-mm, $N = 600$ rpm, $D_2 = 250$ mm, $b = 60$ mm, $f = 0.18$.
a. $F_a = ?$ b. $p_{avg} = ?$ c. $p_{max} = ?$

a. Axial force required to transmit the torque:

We know that, $\quad T = \dfrac{f F_a D_m}{2\sin\alpha} \quad$ ...Eq. (i) 13.38/ Pg 214, DHB

- But $\sin\alpha = \left[\dfrac{(D_2 - D_m)/2}{b/2}\right] = \left(\dfrac{D_2 - D_m}{b}\right)$

  i.e. $\sin 14 = \left(\dfrac{250 - D_m}{60}\right)$

  $D_m = 235.48\text{mm} \approx 235 \text{ mm}$

- Also $D_m = \left[\dfrac{D_2 + D_1}{2}\right]$ ...13.38/ Pg 214, DHB

$$235 = \left[\dfrac{250 + D_1}{2}\right]$$

$$D_1 = 220 \text{ mm}$$

∴ Eq. (i) yields ... $286 \times 10^3 = \dfrac{0.18 \times F_a \times 235}{2 \times \sin 14}$

$$F_a = 3271.38 \text{ N}$$

b. Average normal pressure:

We know that, $F_a = \pi D_m b p \sin \alpha$ ...Eq. (ii) **13.37/ Pg 214, DHB**

Since average pressure occurs at mean radius, thus we have

$$p = p_{avg} \text{ and } D_m = D_m$$
$$F_a = \pi D_m b p_{avg} \sin \alpha$$
$$3271.38 = \pi \times 235 \times 60 \times p_{avg} \times \sin 14$$
$$p_{avg} = 0.3053 \text{ MPa}$$

c. Maximum pressure:

- Maximum pressure occurs at inner radius, thus we have

$$p = p_{max} \text{ and } D_m = D_1$$

∴ Eq. (ii) yields ... $F_a = \pi D_1 b p_{max} \sin \alpha$

$$3271.38 = \pi \times 220 \times 60 \times p_{max} \times \sin 12.5$$
$$p_{max} = 0.3261 \text{ MPa}.$$

18. A friction cone clutch has to transmit a torque of 200 N-m at 1440 rpm. The larger diameter of the cone is 350 mm; the cone pitch angle is 6.25°. The face width is 65 mm. The coefficient if friction is 0.2. Determine:
   i. The axial force required to transmit the torque.
   ii. The average normal pressure on the contact surfaces when the maximum torque is transmitted.

[VTU – Dec. 2011 – 10 Marks; July/ Aug. 2004 – 06 Marks]

Solution: $T = 200$ N-m $= 200 \times 10^3$ N-mm, $N = 1440$ rpm, $D_2 = 350$ mm, $\alpha = 6.25°$, $b = 65$ mm, $f = 0.2$.
i. $F_a = ?$ ii. $p_{avg} = ?$

i. Axial force required to transmit the torque:

We know that, $T = \dfrac{f F_a D_m}{2 \sin \alpha}$ ...Eq. (i) **13.38/ Pg 214, DHB**

But $\sin \alpha = \left[\dfrac{(D_2 - D_m)/2}{b/2}\right] = \left(\dfrac{D_2 - D_m}{b}\right)$

i.e. $\sin 6.25 = \left(\dfrac{350 - D_m}{65}\right)$

$$D_m = 343 \text{ mm}$$

∴ Eq. (i) yields ... $200 \times 10^3 = \dfrac{0.2 \times F_a \times 343}{2 \times \sin 6.25}$

$$F_a = 634.8 \text{ N}$$

ii. Average normal pressure:

We know that, $\qquad F_a = \pi D_m b p \sin \alpha \qquad$ ...13.37/ Pg 214, DHB

Since average pressure occurs at mean radius, thus we have

$$F_a = \pi D_m b p_{avg} \sin \alpha$$
$$643.8 = \pi \times 343 \times 65 \times p_{avg} \times \sin 6.25$$
$$p_{avg} = 0.08325 \text{ MPa}.$$

19. A cone clutch is to be designed to transmit 40 N-m of torque. The semi-cone angle is 12.5°. The mean radius of clutch is twice the face width, coefficient of friction, 0.18, normal intensity of pressure between contacting surfaces should not exceed 0.1 N/mm². Considering uniform wear calculate:

i. The inner and outer diameter of friction layer;
ii. Face width of friction layer; and
iii. Force required to engage the clutch. **[VTU – Dec. 08/ Jan. 2009 – 09 Marks]**

Solution: $T = 40$ N-m $= 40 \times 10^3$ N-mm, $\alpha = 12.5°$, $R_m = 2b, f = 0.18, p = 0.1$ N/mm².

i. $D_1, D_2 = ?\qquad$ ii. $b = ?\quad$ iii. $F_a' = ?$

i. To find D_1, D_2

We know that, $\qquad T = \dfrac{f F_a D_m}{2 \sin \alpha} \qquad$ ...Eq. (i) 13.38/ Pg 214, DHB

But $\quad F_a = \pi D_m b p \sin \alpha$

∴ $\qquad T = \dfrac{f D_m}{2 \sin \alpha} \times \pi D_m b p \sin \alpha$

$\qquad = \dfrac{f D_m^2 \pi b p}{2} = \dfrac{\pi f b p (2 R_m)^2}{2} \qquad (\because R_m = 2b)$ ... (data)

$\qquad = 2 \pi f b p\, R_m^2 = 2 \pi f b p\, (2b)^2$
$\qquad = 8 \pi f b^3 p$
$40 \times 10^3 = 8 \pi \times 0.18 \times b^3 \times 0.1$
$b = 44.6 \text{ mm} \approx 45 \text{ mm}$

And $R_m = 90 \text{ mm} \Rightarrow D_m = 180 \text{ mm}$

- But $\sin \alpha = \left[\dfrac{(D_2 - D_m)/2}{b/2}\right] = \left(\dfrac{D_2 - D_m}{b}\right)$

i.e. $\sin 12.5 = \left(\dfrac{D_2 - 180}{45}\right)$

$D_2 = 189.74 \text{ mm} \approx 190 \text{ mm}$

- Similarly, $\sin \alpha = \left[\dfrac{(D_m - D_1)/2}{b/2}\right] = \left(\dfrac{D_m - D_1}{b}\right)$

i.e. $\sin 12.5 = \left(\dfrac{180 - D_1}{45}\right)$

$D_1 \approx 170$ mm.

ii. To find face width:

$b = 45$ mm

iii. Force to engage the clutch:

We know that, $\quad F_a' = \pi D_m b p (\sin \alpha + f \cos \alpha) \quad$ ...**13.40/ Pg 214, DHB**
$\qquad\qquad\qquad = \pi \times 180 \times 45 \times 0.1 \times (\sin 12.5 + 0.185 \cos 12.5)$
$\qquad\qquad F_a' = 998$ N.

20. **Determine the dimensions of a simple cone clutch to transmit 20 kW at 1000 rpm. The minimum diameter is to be 300 mm and the cone angle 20°. Assume 0.2 and permissible pressure $f = 0.1$ N/mm². Also determine the axial force required to engage the clutch.**

[VTU – June/ July 2011 – 12 Marks; (Similar) July 2007 – 10 Marks]

Solution: $P = 20$ kW, $N = 1000$ rpm $\Rightarrow n = 16.67$ rps, $D_1 = 300$ mm, $2\alpha = 20° \Rightarrow \alpha = 10°, f = 0.2, p = 0.1$ N/mm².
a. Dimensions $(D_m, b, D_1, D_2) = ?$ b. $F_a' = ?$

a. To find clutch dimensions: (D_m, b, D_1, D_2)

We know that, $\quad P(\text{kW}) = \dfrac{\pi^2 D_m^2 b p f n}{10^6 \times K_l} \quad$ ...Eq. (i) **13.39a/ Pg 214, DHB**

- But $\sin \alpha = \left[\dfrac{(D_m - D_1)/2}{b/2}\right] = \left(\dfrac{D_m - D_1}{b}\right)$

  $D_m = b \sin \alpha + D_1$
  $\qquad = b \sin 10 + 300$
  $D_m = 0.1736\, b + 300 \qquad$ ...Eq. (ii)

- Assume, $K_l = 1$

∴ Eq. (i) yields ... $20 = \dfrac{\pi^2 \times (0.1736 b + 300)^2 \times b \times 0.1 \times 0.2 \times 16.67}{10^6 \times 1}$

$6.078 \times 10^6 = (0.1736\, b + 300)^2 \times b$
$\qquad\qquad\quad = (0.03\, b^2 + 90000 + 104.16\, b) \times b$
$\qquad\qquad\quad = 0.03\, b^3 + 90000\, b + 104.16\, b^2$

$0.03\, b^3 + 104.16\, b^2 + 90000\, b - 6.078 \times 10^6 = 0$

$\qquad\qquad\qquad b = 62.87$ mm
$\qquad\qquad\qquad b \approx 65$ mm

∴ Eq. (ii) yields ... $D_m = (0.1736 \times 65) + 300$
$\qquad\qquad\qquad D_m = 311.3$ mm ≈ 310 mm

Also $\sin \alpha = \left[\dfrac{(D_2 - D_m)/2}{b/2}\right] = \left(\dfrac{D_2 - D_m}{b}\right)$

i.e. $\sin 10 = \left(\dfrac{D_2 - 310}{65}\right)$

$D_2 = 321.28$ mm ≈ 320 mm

Thus the dimensions are: $D_1 = 300$ mm, $D_2 = 320$ mm, $D_m = 310$ mm, $b = 65$ mm

b. Axial force to engage the clutch:

We know that, $\quad F_a' = \pi D_m b p (\sin \alpha + f \cos \alpha) \quad$ ...13.40/ Pg 214, DHB

$\qquad = \pi \times 310 \times 65 \times 0.1 \times (\sin 10 + 0.2 \times \cos 10)$

$F_a' = 2346.07$ N.

21. A cone clutch with face angle 12.5° is to transmit 7.5 kW at 900 rpm. The width of the face is half of mean radius and the normal pressure between the contact faces is not to exceed 0.09 MN/m². Assuming uniform wear and the coefficient of friction between the contact faces as 0.2, determine the dimensions of the clutch and the axial force required to engage the clutch.

[VTU – Dec. 07/ Jan. 2008 – 10 Marks]

Solution: *Similar to previous problem.*

Dimensions: $D_m = 224$ mm, $b = 56$ mm, $D_1 \approx 212$ mm, $D_2 \approx 236$ mm,

$F_a' = 1460.19$ N

6.12 DESIGN OF CONE CLUTCH

1. Find the diameter (D) of the shaft using $\tau = \dfrac{16T}{\pi D^3} \quad$ ...3.1/ Pg 42, DHB

$$P = 2\pi n T = \dfrac{2\pi N T}{60} \text{ (watts)}$$

Standardize the shaft diameter using $\qquad$ ...Table 3.5a/ Pg 48, DHB

2. Find the mean diameter of clutch using the relation $D_m = 5D$ to $10D$

...13.42/ Pg 215, DHB

(Select $D_m = 10D$)

3. Material selection: (f, p, α)

- Calculate the velocity as: $v = \dfrac{\pi . D_m . N}{60}$ -or- $= \pi D_m . n$, and

    Check the velocity range in $\qquad$ ...13.43/ Pg 215, DHB
    -or- the speed range (n), based on given speed (rps) $\quad$ ...13.44/ Pg 215, DHB
- Based on **13.43 or 13.44**, select suitable combination of lining over disc material, from **Table 13.2a/ Pg 228, DHB** and note down the values of f (generally wet) and p.
- The value of semi cone angle (α) is obtained under $\quad$ ...13.38/ Pg 214, DHB

4. Find the face width (b) using the power equation:

$$P(\text{kW}) = \dfrac{\pi^2 D_m^2 b p f n}{10^6 \times K_l} \qquad \text{...13.39a/ Pg 214, DHB}$$

$n = N/60$ rps

- The value of load factor (K_l) is obtained from **Table 12.34/ Pg 203, DHB** for suitable combination of driver and driven machines; **else assume** $K_l = 1$
- Check the ratio of $D_m/b = 4.5$ to $8.0 \qquad$ ...13.41/ Pg 214, DHB

If the ratio is not within the range, change the value (range) of D_m in step 3- or- **Increase D**, accordingly.

5. Find the dimensions of the clutch: (D_1, D_2)
   - Inner diameter of the clutch, $D_1 = D_m - b.\sin\alpha$.
   - Outer diameter of the clutch, $D_2 = D_m + b.\sin\alpha$

6. Calculate the axial force to transmit the torque:
$$F_a = \pi D_m b p \sin\alpha \qquad \text{...13.37/ Pg 214, DHB}$$

7. Calculate the normal force:
$$F_n = \frac{F_a}{\sin\alpha} \qquad \text{...13.35/ Pg 214, DHB}$$

8. Calculate the frictional force:
$$F_b = f F_n \qquad \text{...13.36/ Pg 214, DHB}$$

9. Find the axial force to engage the clutch:
$$F_a' = F_n(\sin\alpha + f\cos\alpha) = \pi D_m b p(\sin\alpha + f\cos\alpha)$$
...13.40/ Pg 214, DHB

22. Design a cone clutch to transmit 20 kW of power at 900 rpm. Assume a shear stress of 42 MPa.

Solution: $P = 20$ kW, $N = 900$ rpm $\Rightarrow n = 15$ rps, $\tau = 42$ MPa. *Design*

a. To find shaft diameter:

We know that, $\tau = \dfrac{16T}{\pi D^3}$ ...Eq. (i) 3.1/ Pg 42, DHB

But $P = \dfrac{2\pi NT}{60}$ -or- $T = \dfrac{9.55 \times 10^6 (P)}{n(\text{rpm})}$ N-mm ...3.3a/ Pg 42, DHB

$$20 \times 10^3 = \frac{2\pi \times 900 \times T}{60}$$

$T = 212.21$ N-m
$T = 212.21 \times 10^3$ N-mm

∴ Eq. (i) yields ... $42 = \dfrac{16 \times 212.21 \times 10^3}{\pi D^3}$

$D = 29.52$ mm

Therefore, standard shaft diameter, $D = 32$ mm ...Tb. 3.5a/ Pg 48, DHB

b. To find mean diameter of clutch:

We know that, $D_m = 5D$ to $10D$ ...13.42/ Pg 215, DHB

Assuming $D_m = 10D$
$= 10 \times 32$
$D_m = 320$ mm

c. Material selection:

- Velocity
$$v = \frac{\pi.D_m.N}{60}$$
$$= \frac{\pi \times 0.32 \times 900}{60}$$
$$v = 15.08 \text{ m/s}$$

Check the velocity range:

The velocity range is $13 \leq v \leq 25$ ...13.43/ Pg 215, DHB

$\therefore$ $\qquad 13 \leq 15.08 \leq 25$ ...Safe.

- Assuming leather faced lining on cast iron, we have

$\qquad f = 0.12$ to 0.15 (wet) and $p = 0.07$ to 0.29 ...Tb.13.2a/ Pg 228, DHB

$\therefore$ $\qquad f = 0.14$ and $p = 0.18$ MPa

- The value of semi cone angle $\alpha = 12.5°$ ...13.38/ Pg 214, DHB

d. To find module:

We know that, $\qquad P(\text{kW}) = \dfrac{\pi^2 D_m^2 bpfn}{10^6 \times K_l}$ ...13.39a/ Pg 214, DHB

Since the driver and driven machines combination is not specified, assume $K_l = 1$

$$20 = \dfrac{\pi^2 \times 320^2 \times b \times 0.18 \times 0.14 \times 15}{10^6 \times 1}$$

$$b = 52.35 \text{ mm} \approx 55 \text{ mm}$$

Check for b:

We know that, $\qquad 4.5 \leq \dfrac{D_m}{b} \leq 8$ ...13.41/ Pg214, DHB

$$\dfrac{D_m}{b} = \dfrac{320}{55} = 5.82$$

$\therefore \qquad 4.5 \leq 5.82 \leq 8$ ...Safe.

e. Clutch diameters:

- Inner diameter of the clutch:

We know that, $\qquad \sin \alpha = \left(\dfrac{D_m - D_1}{b}\right)$

i.e. $D_1 = D_m - b.\sin \alpha$

$D_1 = 308$ mm $= 320 - (55 \times \sin 12.5)$

- Outer diameter of the clutch:

We know that, $\qquad \sin \alpha = \left(\dfrac{D_2 - D_m}{b}\right)$

i.e. $D_2 = D_m + b.\sin \alpha$

$\qquad = 320 + (55 \times \sin 12.5)$

$D_2 = 332$ mm

f. Axial force to transmit the torque:

$\qquad F_a = \pi D_m bp \sin \alpha$ ...13.37/ Pg 214, DHB

$\qquad = \pi \times 320 \times 55 \times 0.18 \times \sin 12.5$

$\qquad F_a = 154.13$ N

g. Normal force:

$$F_n = \dfrac{F_a}{\sin \alpha}$$ ...13.35/ Pg 214, DHB

$$= \dfrac{2154.13}{\sin 12.5}$$

$F_n = 9952.57$ N

540 Design of Machine Elements II (DME II)

h. Frictional force:
$$F_b = fF_n \qquad \text{...13.36/ Pg 214, DHB}$$
$$= 0.14 \times 9952.57$$
$$F_b = 1393.36 \text{ N}$$

i. Axial force to engage the clutch:
$$F_a' = F_n (\sin \alpha + f \cos \alpha) \qquad \text{...13.40/ Pg 214, DHB}$$
$$= 9952.57 \times (\sin 12.5 + 0.14 \times \cos 12.5)$$
$$F_a' = 3514.46 \text{ N}.$$

23. Design a cone clutch to transmit 40 kW at 750 rpm. Also determine the i. axial force required to transmit the torque, ii. axial force required to engage the clutch. Assume $f = 0.4$ and $p = 0.2$ N/mm² for the friction material ($\alpha = 12.5°$). Take $D_m/b = 6$.

[VTU – June/ July 2013 – 10 Marks; Jan./ Feb. 2006 – 10 Marks; Jan./ Feb. 2005 – 10 Marks]

Solution: $P = 40$ kW, $N = 750$ rpm $\Rightarrow n = 12.5$ rps, $f = 0.4$ and $p = 0.2$ N/mm², $\alpha = 12.5°$, $D_m/b = 6$. *Design*.

a. To find shaft diameter:

We know that, $\tau = \dfrac{16T}{\pi D^3}$ \qquad ...Eq. (i) **3.1/ Pg 42, DHB**

But $P = \dfrac{2\pi NT}{60}$ -or- $T = \dfrac{9.55 \times 10^6 (P)}{n(\text{rpm})}$ N-mm \qquad ...**3.3a/ Pg 42, DHB**

$$40 \times 10^3 = \dfrac{2\pi \times 750 \times T}{60}$$
$$T = 509.29 \text{ N-m}$$
$$T = 509.29 \times 10^3 \text{ N-m}$$

∴ Eq. (i) yields ... $46 = \dfrac{16 \times 509.29 \times 10^3}{\pi D^3}$ \qquad Assuming $\tau = 46$ MPa

$$D = 38.35 \text{ mm}$$

Therefore, standard shaft diameter, $D \approx 40$ mm \qquad ...**Tb. 3.5a/ Pg 48, DHB**

b. To find mean diameter of clutch:

Given $D_m/b = 6$
$$D_m = 6b \qquad \text{...Eq. (ii)}$$

c. Material selection: (f, p, α)
- Given, $\qquad f = 0.4$ and $p = 0.2$ MPa
- $\alpha = 12.5°$

d. To find module:

We know that, $P(\text{kW}) = \dfrac{\pi^2 D_m^2 b p f n}{10^6 \times K_l}$ \qquad ...**13.39a/ Pg 214, DHB**

Since the driver and driven machines combination is not specified, assume $K_l = 1$

$$40 = \dfrac{\pi^2 \times (6b)^2 \times b \times 0.2 \times 0.4 \times 12.5}{10^6 \times 1}$$
$$b = 48.28 \text{ mm} \approx 50 \text{ mm}$$

∴ Eq. (ii) yields ... $D_m = 6 \times 50$
$$D_m = 300 \text{ mm}$$

e. Clutch diameters:

- Inner diameter of the clutch:

We know that, $\sin \alpha = \left(\dfrac{D_m - D_1}{b}\right)$

i.e. $D_1 = D_m - b \cdot \sin \alpha$
$= 300 - (50 \times \sin 12.5)$
$D_1 = 289.17 \text{ mm} \approx 290 \text{ mm}$

- Outer diameter of the clutch:

We know that, $\sin \alpha = \left(\dfrac{D_2 - D_m}{b}\right)$

i.e. $D_2 = D_m + b \cdot \sin \alpha$
$= 300 + (50 \times \sin 12.5)$
$D_2 = 310.82 \text{ mm} \approx 310 \text{ mm}$

f. Axial force to transmit the torque:

$F_a = \pi D_m b p \sin \alpha$ ...13.37/ Pg 214, DHB
$= \pi \times 300 \times 50 \times 0.2 \sin 12.5$
$F_a = 2039.9 \text{ N}$

g. Normal force:

$F_n = \dfrac{F_a}{\sin \alpha}$ ...13.35/ Pg 214, DHB

$= \dfrac{2039.9}{\sin 12.5}$

$F_n = 9424.8 \text{ N}$

h. Frictional force:

$F_n = f F_n$ ...13.36/ Pg 214, DHB
$= 0.4 \times 9428.8$
$F_b = 3770 \text{ N}$

i. Axial force to engage the clutch:

$F_a' = F_n (\sin \alpha + f \cos \alpha)$ ...13.40/ Pg 214, DHB
$= 9424.8 \times (\sin 12.5 + 0.4 \times \cos 12.5)$
$F_a' = 5720.46 \text{ N}.$

DESIGN OF BRAKES

6.13 INTRODUCTION TO BRAKES

A brake is a device by means of which artificial frictional resistance is applied to a moving vehicle, in order to retard or stop the motion of the machine. In performing this function, the brake absorbs kinetic energy and dissipates it in the form of heat by means of friction. This heat is dissipated to the surrounding air so that excessive heating of the brake lining does not occur.

→ *Basic requirements of a brake:*
  - In consistent with safety, the brakes must be strong enough to stop the vehicle during emergency within the shortest distance. This is possible when there is no skidding and the rider has proper control over the vehicle.
  - The fade characteristics of the brakes should be quite good, i.e. the effectiveness of the brakes should remain constant with prolonged application.

→ *Purpose of brakes:*
  The brakes have the following two purposes:
  - To help in speed control of the vehicle as well as to stop it as desired quickly and efficiently, without skidding.
  - To keep the vehicle in any position after it had been actually brought to rest.

→ *The design or capacity of a brake* depends upon the following factors:
  - The unit pressure between the braking surfaces,
  - The coefficient of friction between the braking surfaces,
  - The peripheral velocity of the brake drum,
  - The projected area of the friction surfaces, and
  - The ability of the brake to dissipate heat equivalent to the energy being absorbed.

6.14 CLASSIFICATION OF BRAKES

Brakes are classified as follows:
1. According to application:
   a. Service or running or foot brakes.   b. Parking or emergency or hand brakes.
2. According to number of wheels:
   a. Two wheel brakes.   b. Four wheel brakes.
3. According to method of braking contact:
   a. Internal expanding brakes.   b. External contracting or band brakes.
4. According to method of applying the braking force:
   a. Single acting brakes.   b. Double acting brakes.
5. According to brake gear:
   a. Mechanical brake.   b. Power brake.
6. According to nature of power employed:
   a. Vacuum brakes.   b. Air brakes.
   c. Hydraulic brakes.   d. Hydrostatic brakes.
   e. Electric brakes.
7. According to power transmission:
   a. Direct acting brakes.   b. Geared brakes.
8. According to power unit:
   a. Cylinder brakes   b. Diaphragm brakes.

6.14.1 Mechanical Brakes

Mechanical brakes incorporate cables which link the brake pedal with the brake shoe operating device. Here rods and shafts or cables and shafts are used to transmit pressure from the brake pedal to the wheel brakes. Further these brakes may be hand operated or foot operated.

The mechanical brakes are classified as:
1. Single block or shoe brake.
2. Pivoted block or shoe brake.
3. Double block or shoe brake.
4. Simple band brake
5. Differential band brake.
6. Band and block brake.
7. Internal expanding brake.

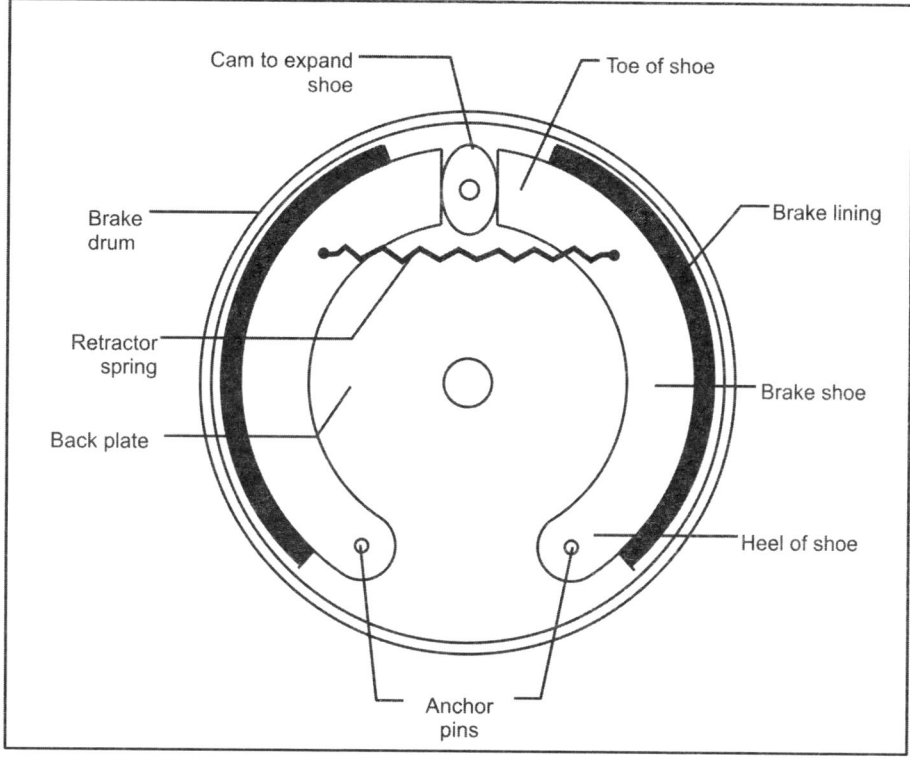

Fig. 6.8: Details of brake drum

6.15 BRAKE SHOE

Brake shoes are a part of the braking system. They are attached with the brake lining and are located at the wheels. These are operated by means of cam or toggle lever which is actuated through various mechanical linkages. When brakes are applied, automotive brake shoes are opened and the lining comes in contact with the brake drum **(Fig. 6.8)**. Due to friction between the drum and the lining, the vehicle slows down or stops.

6.16 BRAKE LINING

Brake lining is attached to brake shoe which contacts the brake drum when the brakes are applied and accomplishes the work of stopping or slowing down the vehicle. The linings are secured to the shoes either by means of riveting or by using synthetic resin adhesives.

The most commonly used lining materials are wood, asbestos, leather, cork, felt, Ferodo.

6.17 ENERGY EQUATIONS

The energy absorbed by a brake depends upon the type of motion of the moving body. The motion can be either
1. Pure translation,
2. Pure rotation or
3. Combined translation and rotation.

The energy corresponding to these motions is kinetic energy.

1. Pure Translation: If m is the mass of the body of mass moving with a velocity v_1, and if v_2 is the velocity of the body after the brakes are applied, then the change (decrease) in kinetic energy/ amount of energy absorbed by the brake is given as:

$$E_k = \frac{W(v_1^2 - v_2^2)}{2g} \text{ Joules } \quad ...(Eq. 6.42) \textbf{ 13.62/ Pg 218, DHB}$$

W = weight of the body (N) = mg
v_1, v_2 = velocity of live load before and after the application of the brakes (m/s).

2. Pure Rotation: If 'I' is the mass moment of inertia of the body rotating about its axis with angular velocity of ω_1 rad/s and if ω_2 rad/s is the angular velocity of the body after the brakes are applied, then the change (decrease) in kinetic energy is given as:

$$E_r = \frac{I(\omega_1^2 - \omega_2^2)}{2g} = \frac{Wk_0^2(\omega_1^2 - \omega_2^2)}{2g}$$

$$E_r = \sum \left[\frac{Wk_0^2(\omega_1^2 - \omega_2^2)}{2g} \right] \text{ Joules} \quad ...(Eq. 6.43) \textbf{ 13.64/ Pg 218, DHB}$$

I = mass moment of inertia = Wk_0^2
W = Weight of the body (N).
k_0 = radius of gyration (m).
Σ = refers to the kinetic energy of all rotating parts such as hoist drum, gears, sheaves, etc.

1.3. Combined Translation and Rotation: For a rolling body the total energy is the sum of energies of translation and rotation.

If the potential energy of the moving part changes during the braking period, then the change in potential energy has to be added to the change in kinetic energy so as to obtain the total energy to be dissipated.

Hence the change of potential energy absorbed by the brake during the time t seconds,

$$E_p = \frac{W}{2}(v_1 + v_2)t \text{ Joules } \quad ...(Eq. 6.44) \textbf{ 13.63/ Pg 218, DHB}$$

Thus, the total energy absorbed by the brake = $E_k + E_r + E_p$ ...(Eq. 6.45)

But the frictional work done by the brake in time 't' seconds,

$$W_k = F_t \pi D t \left(\frac{n_1 + n_2}{2}\right)$$

$$W_k = \frac{\pi D F_t (n_1 + n_2) t}{1000 \times 2} \quad \text{Joules} \quad \text{...(Eq. 6.46) 13.65/ Pg 218, DHB}$$

F_t = Tangential braking/ frictional force (N).
D = Diameter of the brake drum (mm).
n_1 = Speed of the brake drum before the brake is applied (rps).
n_2 = Speed of the brake drum after the brake is applied (rps).

Since the total energy absorbed should be equal to the frictional work done by the brake, equating Eq. (6.45) and Eq. (6.46), we have

$$E_k + E_r + E_p = \frac{\pi D F_t (n_1 + n_2) t}{1000 \times 2}$$

∴ The tangential force, $F_t = \dfrac{2000(E_k + E_r + E_p)}{\pi D(n_1 + n_2)t}$ Joules ...(Eq. 6.47) **13.66/ Pg 218, DHB**

Torque transmitted when the blocks are pressed against a flat –or- conical surface,

$$T = f F_n r_m \text{ N-mm} \quad \text{...(Eq. 6.48) 13.67/ Pg 218, DHB}$$

F_n = total normal force (N)
r_m = mean radius of braking surface (mm)
f = coefficient of friction

- When $\theta < 30°$ (i.e. $2\theta < 60°$), $T = fFr = (fbF_n r^2)\theta$ Joules
  ...(Eq. 6.49) **13.70/ Pg 219, DHB**
- When $\theta > 30°$ (i.e. $2\theta > 60°$), $T = f'F$ Joules ...(Eq. 6.50) **13.69/ Pg 219, DHB**

$$f' = f\left[\frac{4\sin\theta}{2\theta + \sin 2\theta}\right] \quad \text{...equivalent coefficient of friction}$$

6.18 HEATING OF BRAKES

Heat generated during the application of the brake should be dissipated to the surroundings in order to avoid overheating of the lining due to increase in temperature. The rate of heat generation depends upon the braking area, the radiating surface, unit pressure and the air circulation.

- The heat radiated is given as, $H = f F_n v$ J/s   ...(Eq. 6.51) **13.112/ Pg 226, DHB**

  Where, $F_n = pA$
  p = unit pressure (MPa or N/mm²)
  A = area (mm²) v = velocity (m/s)

  Since $F_t = f F_n$, Eq. (6.51) can be written as
  $H = f p A v = F_t v$ ...(Eq. 6.52)

- For a brake lowering the load, the amount of heat dissipated due to absorption of kinetic energy,

$$H = \frac{Wh}{t_1} \quad \text{J/s} \quad \text{...(Eq. 6.53) 13.113/ Pg 226, DHB}$$

W = weight lowered (N)
h = mean height of the load lowered (m)
t_1 = lowering time (sec)

- Heat dissipated is also given by the relation,
$$H_d = HK_L \text{ J/s} \quad \text{...(Eq. 6.54)} \quad \textbf{13.114/ Pg 227, DHB}$$
K_L – load factor
$$= \frac{\text{Actual brake operating time}}{\text{Total time of operation of the cycle.}}$$

- The rate of heat dissipation,
$$H_d = KTA_r \text{ J/s} \quad \text{...(Eq. 6.55)} \quad \textbf{13.115/ Pg 227, DHB}$$
K = radiation factor (J/mm²/s/°C) ...**Table 13.7/ Pg 232, DHB**
A_r = radiating surface (mm²)
T = temperature difference b/w the radiating surface and the surrounding air (°C).

From Eqs (6.54) and (6.55) radiating surface,
$$A_r = \frac{HK_L}{KT} \quad \text{...(Eq. 6.56)} \quad \textbf{13.116/ Pg 227, DHB}$$

The ability of a brake drum to absorb heat is proportional to the mass and the specific heat of the material. Hence from thermodynamics, we have,
$$H = m \cdot C \cdot T \quad \text{...(Eq. 6.57)}$$
m = mass of brake drum (kg)
C = specific heat (J/kg°C)
T = change in temperature (°C)

6.19 OTHER RELATIONS (TO REMEMBER)

- Number of turns or revolutions, that $n' = \dfrac{E}{2\pi T} = \dfrac{E}{\pi D F_t} = \dfrac{h}{\pi D}$

$$= \frac{\theta}{360} \quad \text{...(Eq. 6.58)}$$

- Distance travelled, $h = \dfrac{E}{F_t}$ ...(Eq. 6.59)

- Torque, $T = F_t r$
$$= \frac{E}{\theta} = \frac{E}{\omega_{avg} t}$$
$$= I\alpha = (mk_0^2)\alpha \quad \text{...(Eq. 6.60)}$$

- Number of turns, $n' = \dfrac{\theta}{360} = \dfrac{\omega t}{360 \times \left(\dfrac{\pi}{180}\right)}$ ...(Eq. 6.61)

24. A 40 kg wheel, 400 mm in diameter turning at 200 rpm is brought to rest by pressing a brake shoe radially against a rim with a force of 120 N. If radius of gyration is 0.25 m and $f = 0.3$, how many revolutions will the wheel make before coming to rest?

Solution: $m = 40$ kg, $D = 400$ mm, $N = 200$ rpm, $F = 120$ N, $k_0 = 0.25$ m, $f = 0.3$, number of revolutions $n' = ?$

We know that, $\quad n' = \dfrac{E}{2\pi T} = \dfrac{E}{\pi D F_t}$ ...Eq. (i)

- $F_t = Ff$
 $= 120 \times 0.3$
 $F_t = 36$ N

- Energy absorbed by brake –or- decrease in KE

$$E_r = \sum \left[\frac{W k_o^2 \left(\omega_1^2 - \omega_2^2 \right)}{2g} \right] \qquad \text{...13.64/ Pg 218, DHB}$$

$$= \frac{(mg) k_o^2 \left(\omega_1^2 - \omega_2^2 \right)}{2g}$$

- $\omega_1 = \dfrac{2\pi N}{60}$

$$= \frac{2\pi \times 200}{60}$$

$\omega_1 = 20.94$ rad/s
- $\omega_2 = 0$

$$\therefore E_r = \frac{(40 \times 9.81) \times 0.25^2 \times \left(20.94^2 - 0 \right)}{2 \times 9.81}$$

$E_r = 548.10$ N

∴ Eq. (i) yields ... $n' = \dfrac{548.1}{\pi \times 0.4 \times 36}$

$n' \approx 12$ turns.

25. A bicycle and a rider of mass 95 kg are travelling at 12 kmph on a level road. A brake is applied to the rare wheel which is 0.8 m in diameter and this is the only resistance acting. How far will the bicycle travel and how many turns will it make before coming to rest? The pressure applied on the brake is 100 N and $f = 0.04$.

Solution: $m = 95$ kg, $v = 12$ kmph $= 3.34$ m/s, $D = 0.8$ m, $F = 100$ N, $f = 0.04$.
a. Distance travelled $h = ?$
b. Number of turns $n' = ?$

a. Distance travelled:

We know that, $\quad h = \dfrac{E}{F_t} \qquad$ ...Eq. (i)

- $F_t = Ff$
  $= 100 \times 0.4$
  $F_t = 4$ N

- Energy absorbed by brake –or- decrease in KE

$$E_p = \frac{W \left(v_1^2 - v_2^2 \right)}{2g} \qquad \text{...13.62/ Pg 218, DHB}$$

$$= \frac{(mg) \left(v_1^2 - v_2^2 \right)}{2g}$$

- $v_1 = 3.34$ m/s
- $v_2 = 0$

$$= \frac{(95 \times 9.81) \times (3.34^2 - 0)}{2 \times 9.81}$$

$$E_p = 529.89 \text{ N}$$

∴ Eq. (*i*) yields ... $h = \frac{529.89}{4}$

$$h = 132.47 \text{ m}$$

b. Number of turns:

We know that, $n' = \frac{E}{\pi D F_t} = \frac{h}{\pi D}$

$$= \frac{132.47}{\pi \times 0.8}$$

$$n' = 52.71 \text{ turns} \approx 53 \text{ turns}.$$

26. A cast iron disc of 0.9 m in diameter and 200 mm thick is used as a flywheel which rotates at 400 rpm. It is brought to rest in 2.2 sec by means of a brake. Calculate:
    a. Energy absorbed by the brake.
    b. Torque capacity of the brake.
    c. Number of turns. Take density of CI as 7200 kg/m³ and radius of gyration = 0.125 m.

Solution: $D = 0.9$ m, $b = 200$ mm $= 0.2$ m, $N = 400$ rpm, $t = 2.2$ sec, $\rho = 7200$ kg/m³, 0.125 m.
a. $E = ?$ b. $T = ?$ c. $n' = ?$

a. Energy absorbed by the brake:

We know that, $E_r = \sum \left[\frac{W k_o^2 (\omega_1^2 - \omega_2^2)}{2g} \right]$ ...13.64/ Pg 218, DHB

$$= \frac{(mg) k_o^2 (\omega_1^2 - \omega_2^2)}{2g} \quad \text{...Eq. (}i\text{)}$$

- $\omega_1 = \frac{2\pi N}{60}$

$$= \frac{2\pi \times 400}{60}$$

$$\omega_1 = 41.88 \text{ rad/s}$$

- $\omega_2 = 0$
- $\rho = \frac{m}{V}$

$$m = \left(\frac{\pi D^2 b}{4} \right)$$

$$= \left(\frac{7200 \times \pi \times 0.9^2 \times 0.2}{4}\right)$$

$$m = 916.08 \text{ kg}$$

$\therefore$ Eq. (i) yields ... $E_r = \dfrac{(916.08 \times 9.81) \times 0.125^2 \times (41.88^2 - 0)}{2 \times 9.81}$

$$E_r = 12.55 \text{ kN}$$

b. Torque capacity of the brake:

Torque is defined as $\quad E = T\theta$

$$T = \frac{E}{\theta} = \frac{E}{\omega_{avg} t} \qquad \text{...Eq. (ii)}$$

$$\omega_{avg} = \frac{\omega_1 + \omega_2}{2}$$

$$= \frac{41.88 + 0}{2}$$

$$\omega_{avg} = 20.94 \text{ rad/s}$$

$\therefore$ Eq. (ii) yields ... $T = \dfrac{12.55 \times 10^3}{20.94 \times 2.2}$

$$T = 272.42 \text{ N-m}$$

c. Number of turns:

For rotary motion, $\quad n' = \dfrac{\theta}{360} = \dfrac{\omega t}{360 \times \left(\dfrac{\pi}{180}\right)}$

$$= \frac{20.94 \times 2.2}{360 \times \left(\dfrac{\pi}{180}\right)}$$

$$n' = 7.33.$$

27. A mass of 2000 kg is lowered at a velocity of 2 m/s from a drum of 1.2 m diameter. The mass of the drum is 40 kg having a radius of gyration of 0.8 m. On applying the brakes, the mass is brought to rest in a distance of 0.5 m. Calculate the torque capacity of the brake.

Solution: $m = 2000$ kg, $v = 2$ m/s, $D = 1.2$ m, mass of drum $m_d = 40$ kg, $k_0 = 0.8$ m, distance $h = 0.5$ m, $T = ?$

We know that torque, $\quad T = F_t r \qquad$ ...Eq. (i)

Also distance travelled, $h = \dfrac{E}{F_t}$

$$F_t = \frac{E}{h} \qquad \text{...Eq. (ii)}$$

Referring to **Fig. 6.9**, the total energy is the sum of translation as well as rotation

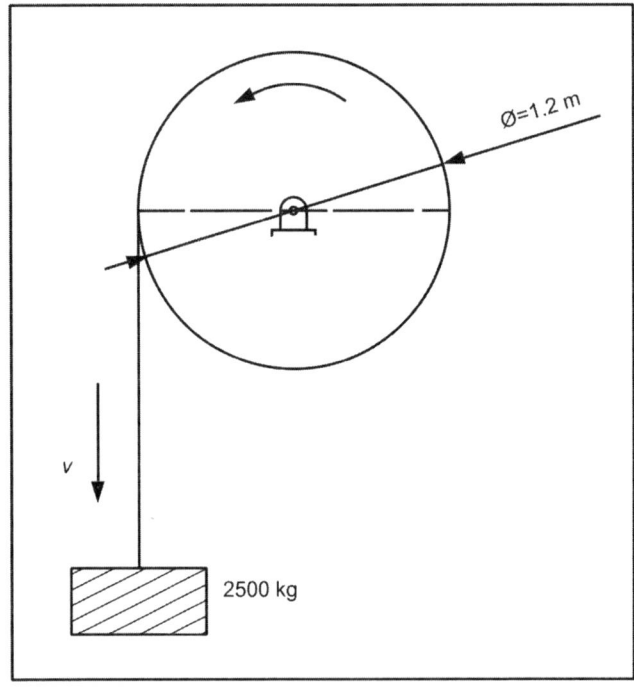

Fig. 6.9: Problem 27

i.e. $E = E_p + E_k$ ...Eq. (*iii*)

- $E_p = mgh$

  $= 2000 \times 9.81 \times 0.5$

  $E_p = 9810$ N

- $E_k = E_{(k) \text{ mass}} + E_{(k) \text{ drum}}$

$$= \frac{W(v_1^2 - v_2^2)}{2g} + \left[\frac{Wk_o^2(\omega_1^2 - \omega_2^2)}{2g}\right] \quad \text{...13.62 \& 13.64/ Pg 218, DHB}$$

$$E_k = \frac{(mg)(v_1^2 - v_2^2)}{2g} + \left[\frac{(m_d g)k_o^2(\omega_1^2 - \omega_2^2)}{2g}\right] \quad \text{...Eq. (}iv\text{)}$$

But $v = \omega r$

$\therefore \omega_1 = \dfrac{v}{r} = \dfrac{2}{0.6} = 3.34$ rad/s

$\omega_1 = 0$

$\therefore$ Eq. (*iv*) yields ... $E_k = \dfrac{2000(2^2 - 0)}{2} + \left[\dfrac{40 \times 0.8^2 \times (3.34^2 - 0)}{2}\right]$

$E_k = 4142.8$ N-m

$\therefore$ Eq. (*iii*) yields ... $E = 9810 + 4142.8$

$E = 13952.8$ N-m

∴ Eq. (ii) yields ... $F_t = \dfrac{13952.8}{0.5}$

$F_t = 27905.6$ N

∴ Eq. (i) yields ... $T = 27905.6 \times 0.6$

$T = 16743.36$ N-m.

6.20 BLOCK/ SHOE BRAKES

A single block or shoe brake is shown in **Fig. 6.10**. It consists of a block or shoe pressed against the rim of a revolving brake wheel drum. The friction between the block and the wheel causes a tangential braking force to act on the wheel, which retards the rotation of the wheel. The block is pressed against the wheel by a force applied to one end of a lever to which the block is rigidly fixed as shown in **Fig. 6.10**. The other end of the lever is pivoted on a fixed fulcrum O.

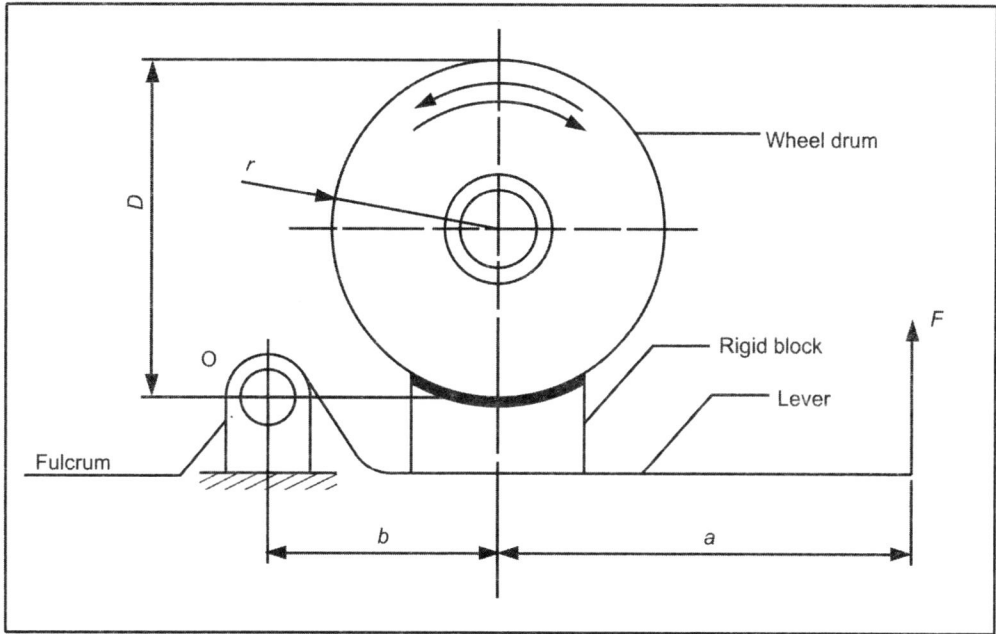

Fig. 6.10: Line of action of the tangential force passing through the fulcrum
(Fig. a/ Pg 219, DHB)

Let, F = Force applied at the end of the lever (brake handle).

f = Coefficient of friction between the brake block and brake wheel.

r = Radius of brake wheel (= $D/2$)

F_t = Tangential braking force at the rim of the wheel. (= $f.F_n$)

F_n = Normal force pressing the brake block on the wheel.

2θ = Angle of contact surface of the block.

a = Distance between fulcrum and applied force

b = Distance between fulcrum and center of the shoe.

Case 1: When line of action of tangential force passes through the fulcrum (Figs 6.10 (a) and (b))

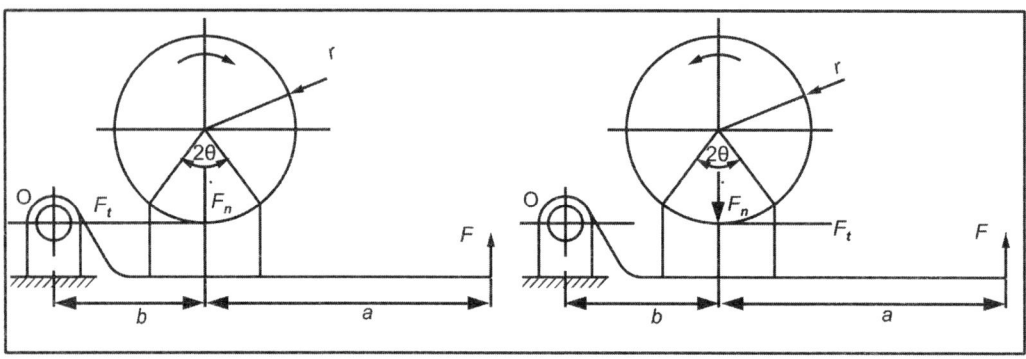

Fig. 6.10: (a) Clockwise rotation of brake wheel **Fig. 6.10:** (b) Anticlockwise rotation of brake wheel

Clockwise rotation:

Taking moments about the fulcrum (O)
$$F(a+b) = F_n \cdot b$$
But $F_t = fF_n$
$$\therefore F_n = \frac{F_t}{f}$$
$$F(a+b) = \frac{F_t \cdot b}{f}$$
$$\therefore F = \frac{F_t \cdot b}{f(a+b)}$$
...13.71/ Pg 219, DHB

Counter clockwise rotation:

Taking moments about the fulcrum (O)
$$F(a+b) = F_n \cdot b$$
But $F_1 = fF_n$
$$\therefore F_n = \frac{F_t}{f}$$
$$F(a+b) = \frac{F_t \cdot b}{f}$$
$$\therefore F = \frac{F_t \cdot b}{f(a+b)}$$
...13.71/ Pg 219, DHB

Thus when the line of action of tangential force (F_t) passes through the fulcrum, the value of F is same in CW and CCW directions.

Case 2: When line of action of tangential force is between the fulcrum and the axis of the drum (Fig. 6.11)

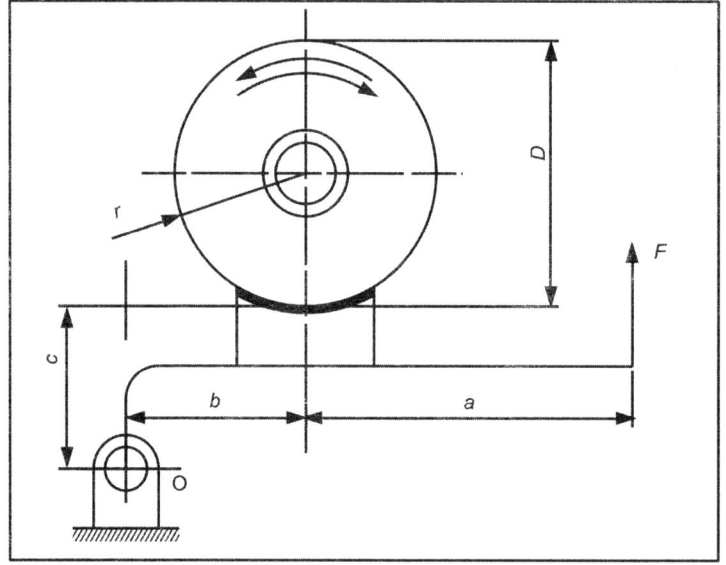

Fig. 6.11: Line of action of tangential force is between the fulcrum and the axis of the drum (Fig. b/Pg 219, DHB)

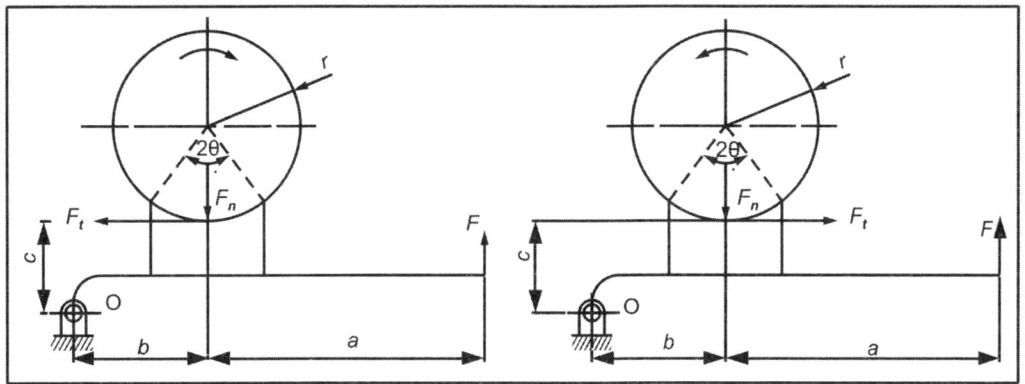

Fig. 6.11: (a) Clockwise rotation of brake wheel   **Fig. 6.11:** (b) Anticlockwise rotation of brake wheel

Clockwise rotation (Fig. 6.11(a):
Taking moments about the fulcrum (O)
$$F(a+b) = F_n \cdot b - F_t \cdot c$$
But $F_t = fF_n$
$$\therefore F_n = \frac{F_t}{f}$$
$$F(a+b) = \frac{F_t \cdot b}{f} - F_t \cdot c$$
$$= F_t\left(\frac{b}{f} - c\right)$$
$$= F_t b\left(\frac{1}{f} - \frac{c}{b}\right)$$
$$\therefore F = \frac{F_t b}{(a+b)}\left(\frac{1}{f} - \frac{c}{b}\right)$$
...13.72a/ Pg 219, DHB

Counter clockwise rotation (Fig. 6.11(b):
Taking moments about the fulcrum (O)
$$F(a+b) = F_n \cdot b + F_t \cdot c$$
But $F_t = fF_n$
$$\therefore F_n = \frac{F_t}{f}$$
$$F(a+b) = \frac{F_t \cdot b}{f} + F_t \cdot c$$
$$= F_t\left(\frac{b}{f} + c\right)$$
$$= F_t b\left(\frac{1}{f} + \frac{c}{b}\right)$$
$$\therefore F = \frac{F_t b}{(a+b)}\left(\frac{1}{f} + \frac{c}{b}\right)$$
...13.72b/ Pg 219, DHB

Case 3: When fulcrum is between the axis of the drum and the line of action of tangential force (Fig. 6.12)

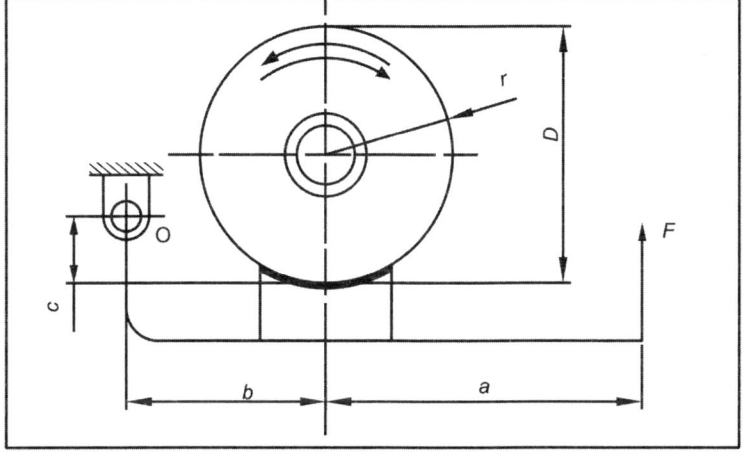

Fig. 6.12: Fulcrum is between the axis of the drum and the line of action of tangential force
(Fig. c/Pg 219, DHB)

Clockwise rotation:
Taking moments about the fulcrum (O)
$$F(a+b) = F_n \cdot b + F_t \cdot c$$
But $F_t = fF_n$
$$\therefore F_n = \frac{F_t}{f}$$
$$F(a+b) = \frac{F_t \cdot b}{f} + F_t \cdot c$$
$$= F_t\left(\frac{b}{f} + c\right)$$
$$= F_t b\left(\frac{1}{f} + \frac{c}{b}\right)$$
$$\therefore F = \frac{F_t b}{(a+b)}\left(\frac{1}{f} + \frac{c}{b}\right)$$
...13.73a/ Pg 219, DHB

Counter clockwise rotation:
Taking moments about the fulcrum (O)
$$F(a+b) = F_n \cdot b - F_t \cdot c$$
But $F_t = fF_n$
$$\therefore F_n = \frac{F_t}{f}$$
$$F(a+b) = \frac{F_t \cdot b}{f} - F_t \cdot c$$
$$= F_t\left(\frac{b}{f} - c\right)$$
$$= F_t b\left(\frac{1}{f} - \frac{c}{b}\right)$$
$$\therefore F = \frac{F_t b}{(a+b)}\left(\frac{1}{f} - \frac{c}{b}\right)$$
...13.73b/ Pg 219, DHB

Note:
1. In the cases discussed above, the normal pressure between the block and the wheel is assumed to be uniform whenever $2\theta < 60°$. (i.e. for $2\theta < 60°$, pressure is uniform) Hence the braking torque, $T = F_t r = fF_n r$
   F_t = tangential force
   r = radius of the wheel.
2. When $2\theta > 60°$, the unit pressure normal to the surface of contact is less at the ends than at the center. In such cases, the block/ shoe is *"pivoted"* to the lever as shown in **Fig. 6.13**, rather than being rigidly attached to the lever, thereby providing uniform wear of the lining in the direction of applied force.
   Hence the braking torque, $T = f' F_n r$
   $$f' = f\left(\frac{4\sin\theta}{2\theta + \sin 2\theta}\right) \quad \text{...equivalent coefficient of friction}$$
   ...13.69/ Pg 219, DHB

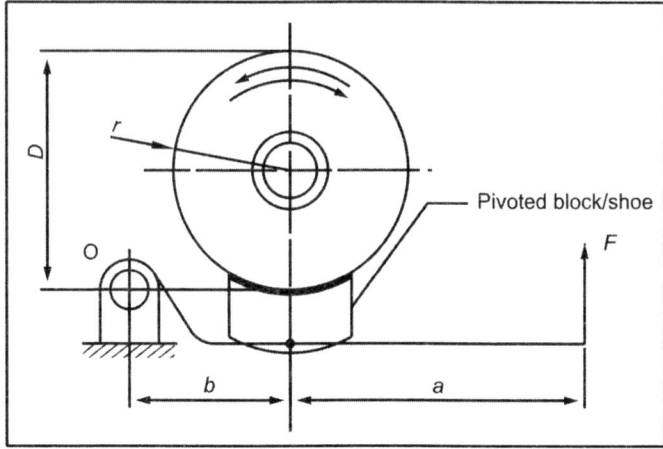

Fig. 6.13: Piovoted shoe

Clutches and Brakes **555**

Values of $\left(\dfrac{4\sin\theta}{2\theta + \sin 2\theta}\right)$ *against semi block angle (θ) are plotted on a graph*

...Fig. 13.16/ Pg 236, DHB

3. The brake is said to be *"self energizing"*, if the frictional force (F_t) helps in applying the brake to the wheel.
4. The brake is said to be *"self locking"*, if the frictional force (F_t) is large enough to apply the brake without any external force.
   i.e. the condition for self locking is $b \le fc$
5. In general the brake should be self energizing and not self locking.
   To avoid self locking, $b \ge fc$.
6. The normal bearing pressure on the shoe is

$$p = \dfrac{F_n}{\text{Projected area of the block- or- shoe}}$$

$$p = \dfrac{F_n}{\text{width} \times (\text{projected shoe length})}$$

$$p = \dfrac{F_n}{b'(2r\sin\theta)} \qquad \text{...(Eq. 6.62)}$$

b' – width of the shoe

7. *Working pressure for brake blocks* ...Table 13.4/ Pg 231, DHB
   Design values for brake facings based on the facing/ lining material.
   ...Table 13.5/ Pg 231, DHB
   Values of $e^{f\theta}$ ...Table 13.6/ Pg 232, DHB
8. *While solving problems, compare the direction of rotation of the given problem with that of DHB and choose the formula accordingly.*
   i.e. if direction of rotation of the drum is in the direction of load applied ⇒ *CCW rotation and if direction of rotation of the drum is against the direction of load applied* ⇒ *CW rotation*
9. Assume $2\theta < 60°$, if not given.
   $$T = F_t r = f F_n r \qquad \text{... for } 2\theta < 60°, (f)$$
   $$T = F_t r = f' F_n r \qquad \text{... for } 2\theta > 60°, (f')$$

28. Determine the torque required for the block brake shown in Fig. 6.14 below. Take $f = 0.3$.

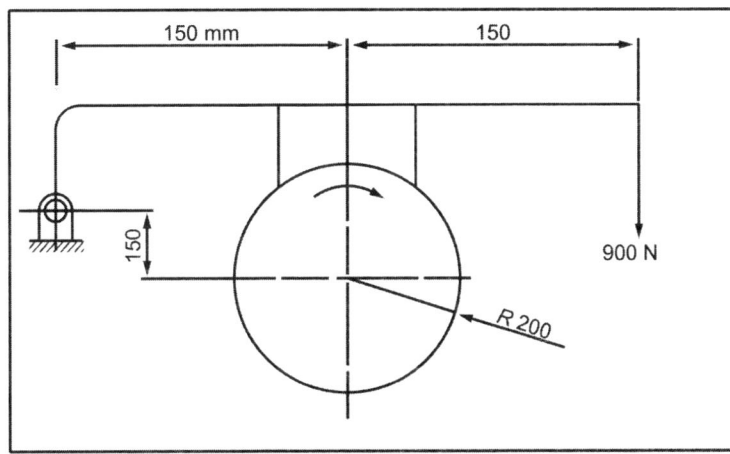

Fig. 6.14: Problem 28

Solution: Here the fulcrum is in between the tangential load and axis of the drum. Comparing the given problem with **DHB**, we have CCW rotation as shown in **Fig. c/ Pg 219, DHB.**

$F = 900$ N, $a = b = 150$ mm, $r = 200$ mm, $c = r - 150 = 50$ mm, $f = 0.3$, $T = ?$

We know that, $\quad T = F_t r$ ...Eq. (i)

For CCW rotation, $\quad T = \dfrac{F_t b}{(a+b)}\left(\dfrac{1}{f} - \dfrac{c}{b}\right)$ ...13.73b/ Pg 219, DHB

Since θ is not given, assume $2\theta < 60°$, so that $f = f$

$\therefore \quad 900 = \dfrac{F_t \times 150}{(150+150)}\left(\dfrac{1}{0.3} - \dfrac{50}{150}\right)$

$F_t = 600$ N

$\therefore$ Eq. (i) yields ... $T = 600 \times 0.2$

$T = 120$ N-m.

29. Determine the torque that may be resisted by the single block brake shown in Fig. 6.15 for a coefficient of friction of 0.3.

[VTU – July/ Aug. 2004 – 08 Marks; Dec. 2010 – 08 Marks]

Solution: Here the fulcrum is in between the tangential load and axis of the drum. Comparing the given problem with **DHB**, we have CCW rotation as shown in **Fig. c/ Pg 219, DHB.**

$F = 625$ N, $a = b = 180$ mm, $r = 125$ mm, $c = r - 100 = 25$ mm, $f = 0.3$, $T = ?$

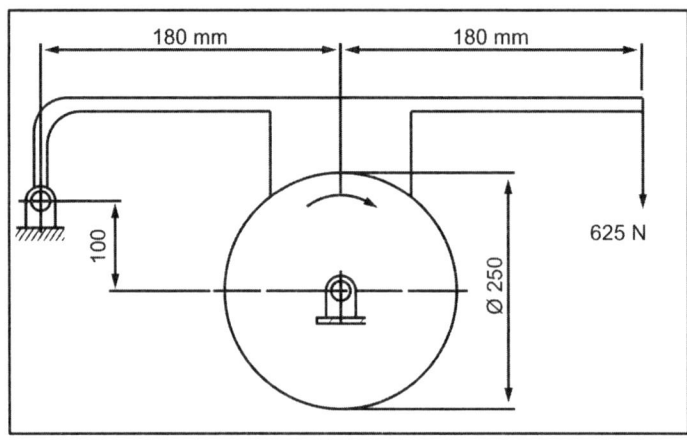

Fig. 6.15: Problem 29

We know that, $\quad T = F_t r$ ...Eq. (i)

For CCW rotation, $\quad F = \dfrac{F_t b}{(a+b)}\left(\dfrac{1}{f} - \dfrac{c}{b}\right)$ ...13.73b/ Pg 219, DHB

Since θ is not given, assume $2\theta < 60°$, so that

$\therefore \quad 625 = \dfrac{F_t \times 180}{(180+180)}\left(\dfrac{1}{0.3} - \dfrac{25}{180}\right)$

$F_t = 391.3$ N

$\therefore$ Eq. (i) yields ... $T = 391.3 \times 0.125$

$T = 48.91$ N-m.

30. The diameter of the drum of a single block brake shown in Fig. 6.16 is 200 mm and the angle of contact is 90°. If the operating force of 700 N is applied at the end of a lever and the coefficient of friction between the drum and the lining is 0.35, determine the torque that may be transmitted by the block brake.

[VTU – July 2007 – 10 Marks; (similar)Feb. 2002 – 08 Marks]

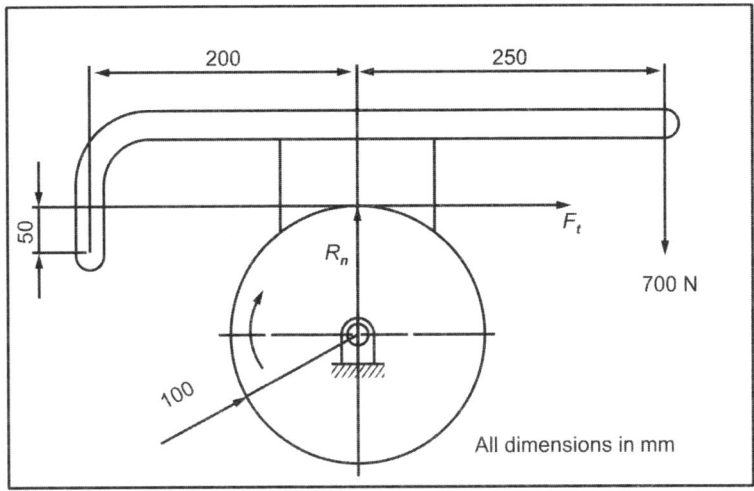

Fig. 6.16: Problem 30

Solution: Here the fulcrum is in between the tangential load and axis of the drum. Comparing the given problem with **DHB**, we have CCW rotation as shown in **Fig. c/ Pg 219, DHB**.

$F = 700$ N, $a = 250$ mm, $b = 200$ mm, $r = 100$ mm, $c = 50$ mm, $f = 0.35$, $2\theta = 90°$ $\Rightarrow$ $\theta = 45° = 0.7854$ rad, $T = ?$

We know that, $\qquad T = F_t r$ ...Eq. (i)

For CCW rotation, $F = \dfrac{F_t b}{(a+b)}\left(\dfrac{1}{f'} - \dfrac{c}{b}\right)$ ...Eq. (ii) **13.73b/ Pg 219, DHB**

Since $2\theta > 60°$, therefore $f = f'$

i.e. equivalent coefficient of friction $f' = f\left(\dfrac{4\sin\theta}{2\theta + \sin 2\theta}\right)$ ...**13.69/ Pg 219, DHB**

$$= 0.35 \times \left(\dfrac{4 \times \sin 45}{(2 \times 0.7854) + \sin 2 \times 45}\right)$$

$f' = 0.385$

∴ Eq. (ii) yields ... $700 = \dfrac{F_t \times 200}{(200 + 250)}\left(\dfrac{1}{0.385} - \dfrac{50}{200}\right)$

$F_t = 671$ N

∴ Eq. (i) yields ... $T = 671 \times 0.100$

$T = 67.11$ N-m.

31. Figure 6.17 shown is a cast iron brake shoe. The coefficient of friction is 0.30. The braking torsional moment is to be 346 N. Determine:
   a. The force P, for anticlockwise rotation.
   b. The force P, for clockwise rotation.
   c. Where must be the pivot be placed to make the brake self-energizing with the counter clockwise direction.   [VTU – Dec. 2010 – 10 Marks]

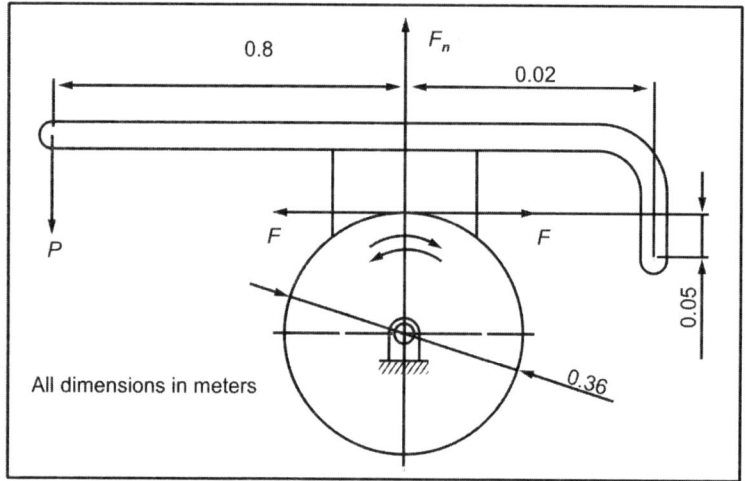

Fig. 6.17: Problem 31

Solution: Here the fulcrum is in between the tangential load and axis of the drum. Comparing the given problem with **DHB**, we have **Fig. c/ Pg 219, DHB**.
$F = P = ?$, $a = 0.8\ m = 800$ mm, $b = 0.02\ m = 20$ mm, $D = 0.36\ m \Rightarrow r = 0.18$ m $= 180$ mm, $c = 0.05$ m $= 50$ mm, $f = 0.30$, $T = 346$ N-m
a. $F - CCW = ?$ b. $F - CW = ?$ c. $c = ?$, for self energizing in CCW

a. Force for CCW rotation of drum:

We know that, $T = F_t r$

$\therefore\quad F_t = \dfrac{346 \times 10^3}{180}$

$F_t = 1922.22$ N

For CCW rotation, $F = \dfrac{F_t b}{(a+b)}\left(\dfrac{1}{f} - \dfrac{c}{b}\right)$ ...13.73b/ Pg 219, DHB

Since $2\theta < 60°$, therefore $f = f$

$F = \dfrac{1922.22 \times 20}{(800 + 20)}\left(\dfrac{1}{0.3} - \dfrac{50}{20}\right)$

$F = 39.07$ N

b. Force for CW rotation of drum:

For CW rotation, $F = \dfrac{F_t b}{(a+b)}\left(\dfrac{1}{f} + \dfrac{c}{b}\right)$ ...13.73a/ Pg 219, DHB

$= \dfrac{1922.22 \times 20}{(800 + 20)}\left(\dfrac{1}{0.3} + \dfrac{50}{20}\right)$

$F = 273.49$ N.

c. Self-energizing:

For the brake to be self energizing the condition is $b \geq fc$

∴ $$c = \frac{b}{f} = \frac{20}{0.3}$$

$c = 66.67$ mm.

32. A block brake of drum radius 250 mm contacts a single shoe as shown in Fig. 6.18 and sustains a torque of 200 N-m at 750 rpm. For $f = 0.25$, determine:
  a. Normal force on the shoe.
  b. Operating force for clockwise rotation of drum.
  c. Operating force for counter clock wise rotation of drum.
  d. Heat generated.
  e. What value of would make the brake self locking?

Solution: Here the tangential load is in between the fulcrum and axis of the drum. Comparing the given problem with **DHB**, we have **Fig. b/ Pg 219, DHB**.
$r = 250$ mm, $T = 200$ N-m, $N = 750$ rpm, $f = 0.25$, $a = 250$ mm, $b = 250$ mm, $c = 75$ mm
a. $F_n = ?$ b. $F - CW = ?$ c. $F - CCW = ?$ d. $H = ?$ e. $c = ?$

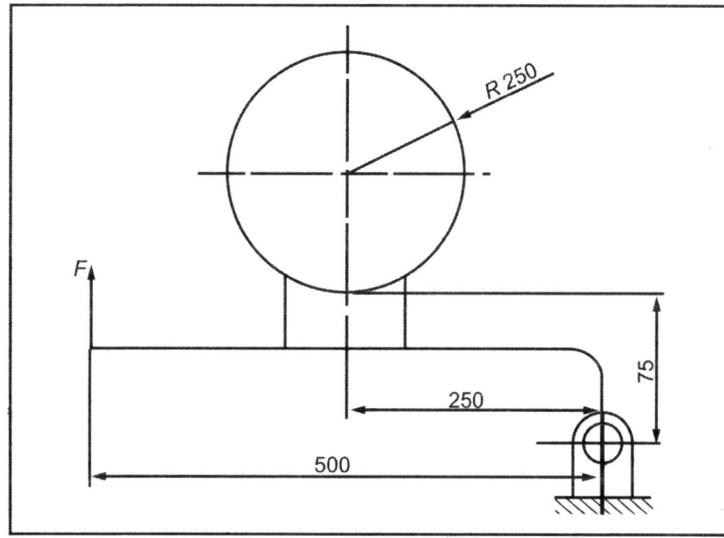

Fig. 6.18: Problem 32

a. To find normal force:

We know that, $T = fF_n r_m$ ...13.67/ Pg 218, DHB

Here $r_m = r = 250$ mm

$200 \times 10^3 = 0.25 \times F_n \times 250$

$F_n = 3200$ N

Also tangential force $F_t = fF_n$

$= 0.25 \times 3200$

$F_t = 800$ N

b. Operating force for CW rotation of drum:

$$F = \frac{F_t b}{(a+b)}\left(\frac{1}{f} + \frac{c}{b}\right)$$ ...13.72b/ Pg 219, DHB

Since θ is not given, assume $2\theta < 60°$, so that $f = f$

∴
$$F = \frac{800 \times 250}{(250 + 250)} \left[\frac{1}{0.25} + \frac{75}{250} \right]$$

$$F = 1720 \text{ N}$$

c. Operating force for CCW rotation of drum:

$$F = \frac{F_t b}{(a+b)} \left(\frac{1}{f} - \frac{c}{b} \right) \qquad \text{...13.72a/ Pg 219, DHB}$$

$$= \frac{800 \times 250}{(250+250)} \left(\frac{1}{0.25} - \frac{75}{250} \right)$$

$$F = 1480 \text{ N}$$

d. Heat generated:

We know that, $\quad H = f F_n v \qquad \text{...13.112/ Pg 226, DHB}$

$$= 0.25 \times 3200 \times \left(\frac{\pi \times 0.5 \times 750}{60} \right)$$

$$H = 15.71 \text{ kJ/s}$$

e. To find c:

For self locking, $\quad b \le fc$

∴
$$c = \frac{b}{f} = \frac{250}{0.25}$$

$$c = 1000 \text{ mm.}$$

33. A single block brake with a torque capacity of 250 N-m is shown in Fig. 6.19. The brake drum rotates at 100 rpm and the coefficient of friction is 0.35. Calculate:
   i. The actuating force and the hinge-pin reaction.
   ii. The rate of heat generated during the braking action and
   iii. The dimensions of the block, if the intensity of pressure between the block and brake drum is 1 MPa.
   The length of the block is twice the width. [VTU – May/ June 2010 – 10 Marks]

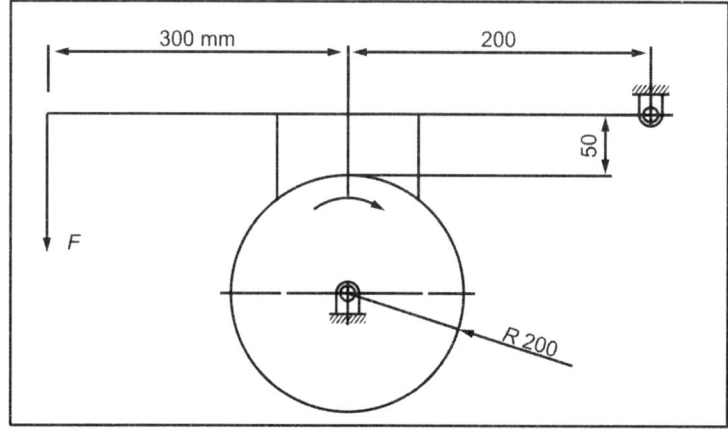

Fig. 6.19: Problem 33

Solution: $T = 250$ N-m, $N = 100$ rpm, $f = 0.35$, $r = 200$ mm, $p = 1$ MPa, $l = 2b'$
a. $F = ?$ and reactions   b. $H = ?$ c. $h, b' = ?$

Here the tangential load is in between the fulcrum and axis of the drum. Comparing the given problem with **DHB**, we have CW rotation as shown in **Fig. b/ Pg 219, DHB.**
$$R = 200 \text{ mm}, a = 300 \text{ mm}, b = 200 \text{ mm}, c = 50 \text{ mm}$$

a. Actuating force and the hinge-pin reaction:

We know that, $\quad T = F_t r$

$\therefore \quad F_t = \dfrac{250 \times 10^3}{200}$

$F_t = 1250$ N

For CW rotation of drum, $F = \dfrac{F_t b}{(a+b)} \left(\dfrac{1}{f} + \dfrac{c}{b} \right)$ ...13.73b/ Pg 219, DHB

Since θ is not given, assume $2\theta < 60°$, so that $f = f$

$$F = \dfrac{1250 \times 200}{(300+200)} \left(\dfrac{1}{0.35} + \dfrac{50}{200} \right)$$

Actuating force, $\quad F = 1553.57$ N
Also $\quad T = f F_n r_m$ ...13.67/ Pg 218, DHB
Here $\quad r_m = r = 200$ mm
$\quad 250 \times 10^3 = 0.35 \times F_n \times 200$
$\quad F_n = 3571.43$ N

Reactions:

$R_x = F_t = f F_n = 1250$ N
$R_y = F_n - F = 3571.43 - 1533.57 = 2017.86$ N

b. Heat generated:

We know that, $\quad H = f F_n v$ ...13.112/ Pg 226, DHB

$$= 0.35 \times 3571.43 \times \left(\dfrac{\pi \times 0.4 \times 100}{60} \right)$$

$H = 2618$ J/s

c. Dimensions of the block:

We know that the normal bearing pressure on the shoe is

$$p = \dfrac{F_n}{b'(2r \sin \theta)}$$

$$1 = \dfrac{3571.43}{b'(2 \times 200 \times \sin 30)}$$

$b' = 17.86$ mm ≈ 20 mm

Length of the block, $\quad l = 2b' \quad$ (data)
$\quad = 2 \times 20$
$\quad l = 40$ mm.

6.21 DOUBLE BLOCK OR SHOE BRAKE

The major drawback in single block brake is that when the load is applied, the unbalanced normal force exerts an additional load on the shaft bearing, thereby causing the shaft to bend. In order to overcome this drawback, a double block brake is used as shown in **Fig. 6.20**.

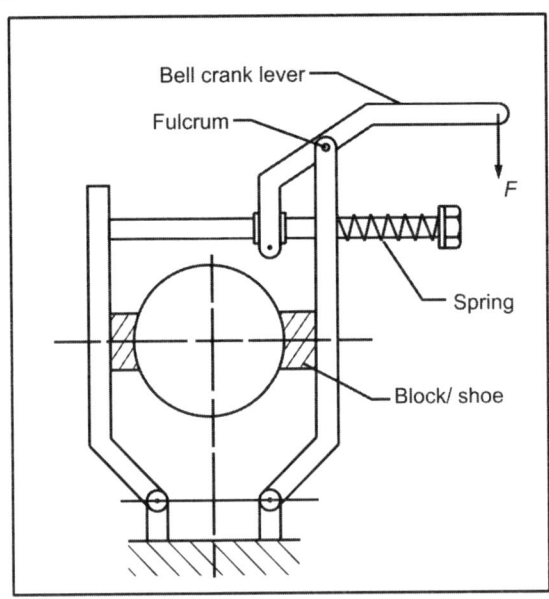

Fig. 6.20: Double block brake

The analysis of the double shoe brake is very similar to the single shoe brake.
Since we have two blocks, the braking action is double.
Therefore, torque, $\quad T = (F_{t1} + F_{t2}) \cdot r \quad$ ...(Eq. 6.62a)
$\quad F_{t1}$ and F_{t2} = tangential forces on respective shoes.

Applications: Electric cranes.

34. The block diagram shown in Fig. 6.21 is set by a spring that produces a force on each arm equal to 2800 N. The diameter of the wheel is 320 mm and angle of contact for each block is 110°. If $f = 0.4$, determine:
   a. The maximum torque the brake is capable of absorbing.
   b. Width of shoe, if bearing pressure is not to exceed 0.28 MPa.

Solution: $F = 2800$ N, $D = 320$ mm, $2\theta = 110° \Rightarrow \theta = 55° = 0.956$ rad, $f = 0.4$, $p = 0.28$ MPa
a. $T = ?$ b. $b' = ?$

a. To find torque:

We know that, $\quad T = (F_{t_1} + F_{t_2})r \quad$ ...Eq. (i)

Since $2\theta > 60°$, therefore $f = f'$

i.e. $f' = f\left(\dfrac{4\sin\theta}{2\theta + \sin 2\theta}\right) \quad$ ...13.69/ Pg 219, DHB

$\quad = 0.4 \times \left(\dfrac{4 \times \sin 55}{(2 \times 0.956) + \sin 2 \times 55}\right)$

$f' = 0.4596$

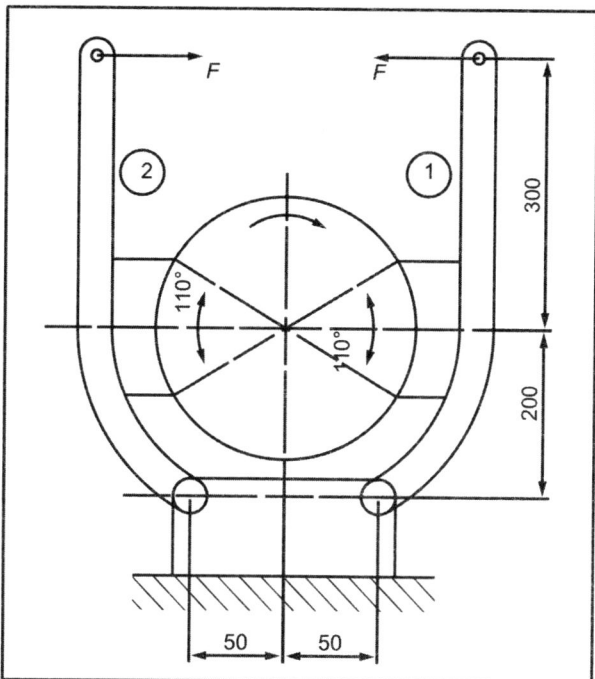

Fig. 6.21: Problem 34

Considering right shoe:

Here the fulcrum is in between the tangential load and axis of the drum. Comparing the given problem with **DHB**, we have CW rotation as shown in **Fig. c/ Pg 219, DHB**.

$$a = 300 \text{ mm}, b = 200 \text{ mm}, c = r - 50 = 160 - 50 = 110 \text{ mm}$$

For CW rotation,
$$F = \frac{F_{t_1} b}{(a+b)}\left(\frac{1}{f'} + \frac{c}{b}\right) \quad \text{...Eq. (ii) 13.73a/ Pg 219, DHB}$$

$$2800 = \frac{F_{t_1} \times 200}{(300 + 200)}\left(\frac{1}{0.4596} + \frac{110}{200}\right)$$

$$F_{t_1} = 2568 \text{ N}.$$

Considering left shoe:

Here the fulcrum is in between the tangential load and axis of the drum. Comparing the given problem with **DHB**, we have CCW rotation as shown in **Fig. c/ Pg 219, DHB**.

For CCW rotation,
$$F = \frac{F_{t_2} b}{(a+b)}\left(\frac{1}{f'} - \frac{c}{b}\right) \quad \text{...Eq. (iii) 13.73a/ Pg 219, DHB}$$

$$2800 = \frac{F_{t_2} \times 200}{(300 + 200)}\left(\frac{1}{0.4596} - \frac{110}{200}\right)$$

$$F_{t_2} = 4305.56 \text{ N}$$

∴ Eq. (i) yields ... $T = (2568 + 4305.56) \times 0.16$

$$T = 1099.78 \text{ N-m}$$

b. Width of shoe:

We know that the normal bearing pressure on the shoe is

$$p = \frac{F_n}{\text{projected area of the block – or– shoe}}$$

$$p = \frac{F_n}{\text{width} \times \text{projected shoe length}}$$

$$p = \frac{F_{n\,max}}{b'(2r \sin \theta)} \qquad \text{...Eq. (iv)}$$

b' – width of the shoe

But $F_{n_1} = \dfrac{F_{t_1}}{f'} = \dfrac{2568}{0.4596} = 5587.47\ \text{N}$

$F_{n_2} = \dfrac{F_{t_2}}{f'} = \dfrac{4305.56}{0.4596} = 9368\ \text{N}$

∴ Eq. (iv) yields ... $0.28 = \dfrac{9368}{b'(2 \times 160 \times \sin 55)} = 127.64\ \text{mm}$

$b' = 128\ \text{mm}.$

35. If in the above problem, the torque absorbed is 2000 N-m, determine the force necessary to set the brake.

Solution: $T = 2000$ N-m

From **Problem 34,** $f' = 0.4596$

Considering right shoe:

∴ Eq. (ii) yields ... $F = \dfrac{F_{t1} \times 200}{(300+200)}\left(\dfrac{1}{0.4596} + \dfrac{110}{200}\right)$

$F_{t_1} = 0.9172\ F$ ...Eq. (v)

Considering left shoe:

∴ Eq. (ii) yields ... $F = \dfrac{F_{t_2} \times 200}{(300+200)}\left(\dfrac{1}{0.4596} - \dfrac{110}{200}\right)$

$F_{t_1} = 1.5377\ F$ ...Eq. (vi)

∴ Eq. (i) yields ... $2000 = (0.9172 + 1.5377)\ F \times 0.16$

$F = 5091.86\ \text{N}.$

36. A spring closed thrustor operated double shoe brake is to be designed for a maximum torque capacity of 3000 N-m. The brake drum diameter is not to exceed 1m and the shoes are to be lined with Ferrodo having a coefficient of friction of 0.3. The rest of the dimensions are shown in Fig. 6.22.
  a. Find the spring force necessary to set the brake.
  b. Find the width of the brakes if the bearing pressure on the lining material is not to exceed 0.5 N/mm², and
  c. Calculate the force required to be exerted by the thrust or to release the brake.

[VTU – June/ July 2009 – 14 Marks]

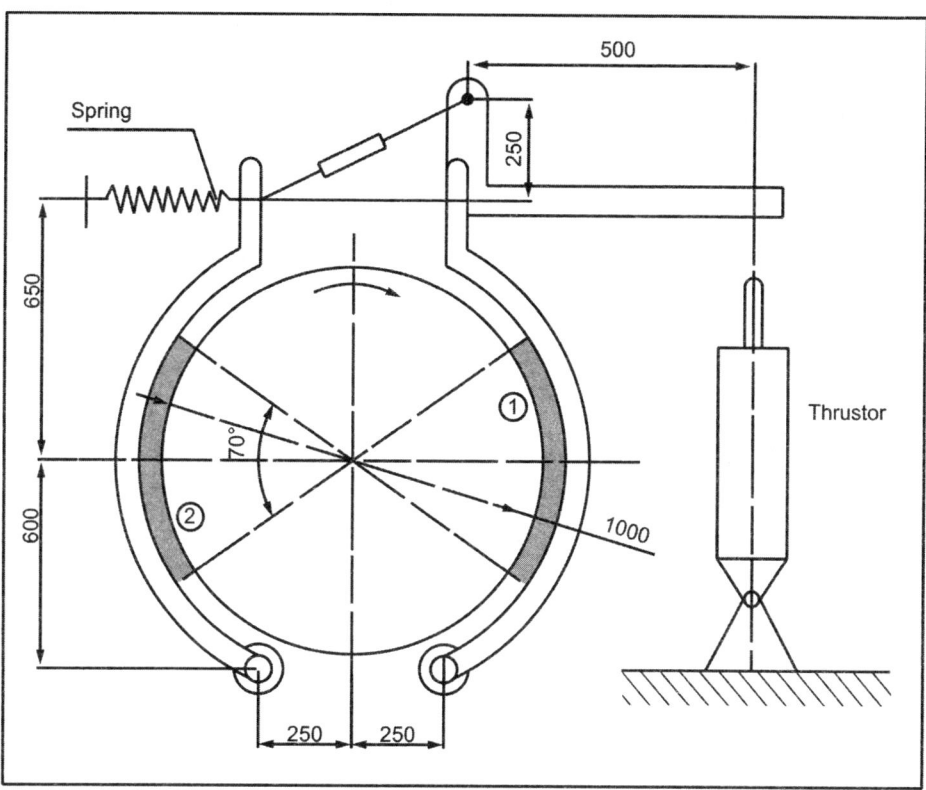

Fig. 6.22: Problem 36

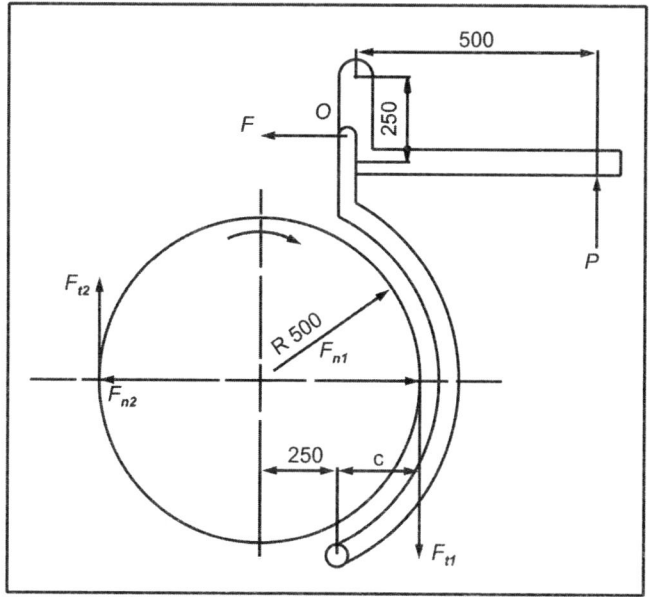

Fig. 6.22: (a) Problem 36 (right shoe)

Solution: $T = 3000$ N-m, $D = 1$ m, $f = 0.3$, $2\theta = 70° \Rightarrow \theta = 35° = 0.6109$ rad, $p = 0.5$ N/mm^2
a. $F = ?$ b. width, $b' = ?$ c. $P = ?$

a. Spring force:

We know that,
$$T = (F_{t_1} + F_{t_2})r$$
$$3000 = (F_{t_1} + F_{t_2}) \times 0.5$$
$$(F_{t_1} + F_{t_2}) = 6000 \text{ N} \quad \text{...Eq. (i)}$$

Since $2\theta > 60°$, therefore $f = f'$

i.e. $f' = f\left(\dfrac{4\sin\theta}{2\theta + \sin 2\theta}\right)$ ...13.69/ Pg 219, DHB

$$= 0.3 \times \left(\dfrac{4 \times \sin 35}{(2 \times 0.6109) + \sin 2 \times 35}\right)$$

$$f' = 0.3184.$$

Considering right shoe (Fig. 6.22a):

Here the fulcrum is in between the tangential load and axis of the drum. Comparing the given problem with **DHB**, we have CW rotation as shown in **Fig. c/ Pg 219, DHB**.

$a = 650$ mm, $b = 600$ mm, $c = r - 250$ mm $= 500 - 250 = 250$ mm

For CW rotation, $F = \dfrac{F_{t_1} b}{(a+b)}\left(\dfrac{1}{f'} + \dfrac{c}{b}\right)$ ...13.73a/ Pg 219, DHB

$$F = \dfrac{F_{t_1} \times 600}{(650 + 600)}\left(\dfrac{1}{0.3184} + \dfrac{250}{600}\right)$$

$$F_{t_1} = 0.5856 \text{ N} \quad \text{...Eq. (ii)}$$

Considering left shoe:

Here the fulcrum is in between the tangential load and axis of the drum. Comparing the given problem with **DHB**, we have CCW rotation as shown in **Fig. c/ Pg 219, DHB**.

For CCW rotation, $F = \dfrac{F_{t_2} b}{(a+b)}\left(\dfrac{1}{f'} - \dfrac{c}{b}\right)$ ...13.73b/ Pg 219, DHB

$$F = \dfrac{F_{t_2} \times 600}{(650 + 600)}\left(\dfrac{1}{0.3184} - \dfrac{250}{600}\right)$$

$$F_{t_2} = 0.7648 \text{ F} \quad \text{...Eq. (iii)}$$

∴ Eq. (i) yields ... $6000 = (0.5856 + 0.7648)F$

$$F = 4443.12 \text{ N}$$

∴ Eq. (iii) yields ... $F_{t_2} = 0.7648 \times 4443.12 = 3398$ N
∴ Eq. (ii) yields ... $F_{t_1} = 0.5856 \times 4443.12 = 2601.90$ N

b. Width of shoe:

We know that the normal bearing pressure on the shoe is

$$p = \dfrac{F_n}{\text{width} \times \text{projected shoe length}}$$

$$p = \dfrac{F_{n\ max}}{b'(2r\sin\theta)} \quad \text{...Eq. (iv)}$$

b' – width of the shoe

$$\text{But } F_{n_1} = \frac{F_{t_1}}{f'} = \frac{2601.90}{0.3184} = 8171.80 \text{ N}$$

$$F_{n_2} = \frac{F_{t_2}}{f'} = \frac{3398}{0.3184} = 10672.11 \text{ N}$$

$\therefore$ Eq. (iv) yields ... $1 = \dfrac{10672.44}{b'(2 \times 500 \times \sin 35)} = 18.61$ mm

$b' = 20$ mm

c. Force exerted by the thrustor to release the brake:

Taking moments about 'O', we have

$P \times 500 + F_{n_1} \times 650 = [F_{n_2} \times 650] + [F_{t_1} \times (500 - 250)] + [F_{t_2} \times (500 + 250)]$

$P \times 500 + [8171.80 \times 650] = [10672.11 \times 650] + [2601.90 \times (500 - 250)] +$
$[3398 \times (500 + 250)]$

$P = 9648.35$ N.

6.22 BAND BRAKES

These are used in power excavators and hoisting machines. Here the band is made of steel and lined with a woven friction material. The braking action is secured by tightening the band wrapped around the drum that has to be stopped or slowed down. The difference in tensions at each end of the band ascertains the torque capacity. The angle of embrace is around 270°. The brake capacity depends upon the angle of wrap, the coefficient of friction and the tensions in the band.

Band brakes are more effective with one direction of rotation than with the other direction of rotation. The advantage of this feature is that the band will release itself when the drum rotates in one direction and locks itself in the opposite direction, known as *"back stop"*. The example of this feature is found in bucket elevators where the band locks itself due to power shut down. Band brakes which are effective in one direction of rotation are classified as:
- Simple band brake
- Differential band brake

6.22.1 Simple Band Brake

A Simple band brake as shown in **Fig. 6.23 and/or Fig. 6.24**, is one in which one end of the band is attached to a fixed pin/ fulcrum of the lever, while the other end is attached to the lever at a distance b from the fulcrum.

Let, F = Force at the end of brake handle,
F_t = Tangential force at the rim of brake wheel,
F_1 = Force on high-tension side [tension in the tight side of the band],
F_2 = Force on low-tension side [tension in the slack side of the band],
θ = Angle of contact of the band on the drum, (also called angle of lap/ embrace),
f = Coefficient of friction between the band and the drum,
r = Radius of the drum,
h = Thickness of the band,
a = Distance between fulcrum and applied force,
b = Distance between fulcrum and center of the shoe.

Case 1: Fulcrum is away from the load (Fig. 6.23)

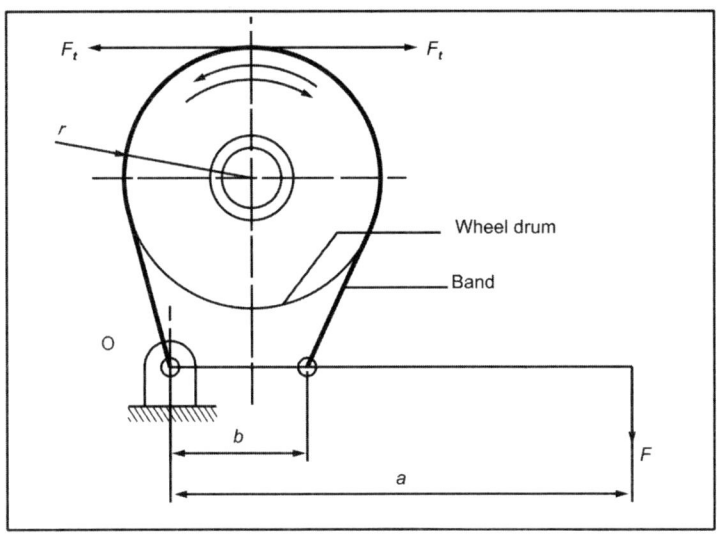

Fig. 6.23: Simple band brake (Fig. e/Pg 220, DHB)

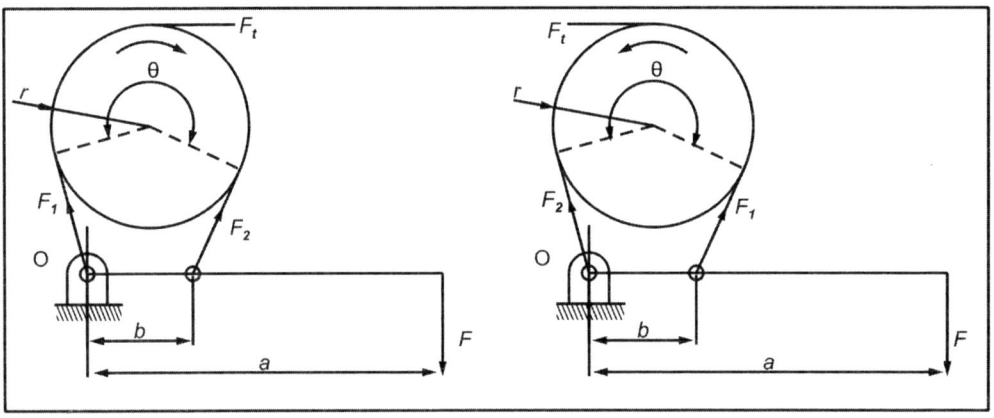

Fig. 6.23 (a): Clockwise rotation of drum   **Fig. 6.23 (b):** Anticlockwise rotation of drum

Since the steel bands act similar to that of belt drive, hence the ratio of tensions is given as,

$$\frac{F_1}{F_2} = e^{f\theta} \qquad \text{...(Eq. 6.63) Pg 220, DHB}$$

The tension in the band decreases from a value F_1 at the pivot side of the band to F_2 at the lever side, hence the braking torque is,

$$T = (F_1 - F_2)\, r \qquad \text{...(Eq. 6.64) Pg 220, DHB}$$

Clockwise rotation:	Counter clockwise rotation:
Taking moments about (O)	Taking moments about (O)
$F \cdot a = F_2 \cdot b$	$F \cdot a = F_1 \cdot b$
Hence the operating force is $F = F_2 \left(\dfrac{b}{a}\right)$ ...(Eq. 6.65)	Hence the operating force is $F = F_1 \left(\dfrac{b}{a}\right)$ ...(Eq. 6.67)
Also $\quad F_t = F_1 - F_2$	Also $\quad F_t = F_1 - F_2$

$$= F_2\left\{\frac{F_1}{F_2} - 1\right\}$$

$$= F_2\left(e^{f\theta} - 1\right)$$

$$\therefore \quad F_2 = \frac{F_t}{\left(e^{f\theta} - 1\right)} \quad \text{...(Eq. 6.66)}$$

$$\therefore \text{Eq. (6.65) yields ... } \mathbf{F} = \frac{F_t b}{a}\left(\frac{1}{e^{f\theta} - 1}\right)$$

...13.75a/ Pg 220, DHB

$$= F_1\left\{1 - \frac{F_2}{F_1}\right\}$$

$$= F_1\left\{1 - \frac{1}{e^{f\theta}}\right\}$$

$$\therefore \quad F_1 = \frac{F_t \cdot e^{f\theta}}{\left(e^{f\theta} - 1\right)} \quad \text{...(Eq. 6.68)}$$

$$\therefore \text{(Eq. 6.67) yields ... } \mathbf{F} = \frac{F_t b}{a}\left(\frac{e^{f\theta}}{e^{f\theta} - 1}\right)$$

...13.75b/ Pg 220, DHB

Case 2: Fulcrum is nearer to the load (Fig. 6.24)

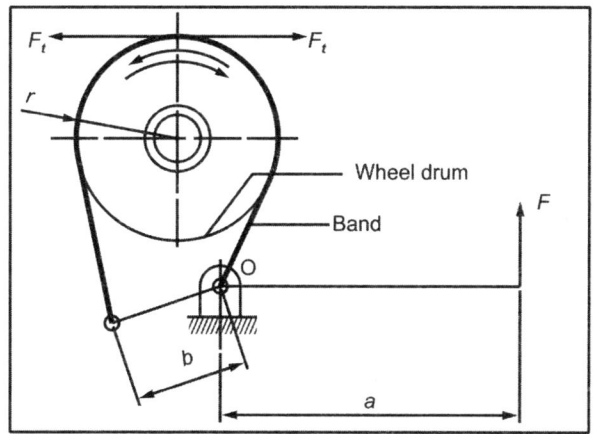

Fig. 6.24: Simple band brake (Fig. d/Pg 220, DHB)

On similar lines we have:

Clockwise rotation:
Taking moments about (O)

$$F \cdot a = F_2 \cdot b$$

Hence the operating force $F = F_2\left(\dfrac{b}{a}\right)$

...(Eq. 6.69)

Also, $F_t = F_1 - F_2$

$$= F_2\left(\frac{F_1}{F_2} - 1\right)$$

$$= F_2(e^{f\theta} - 1)$$

$$\therefore \quad F_2 = \frac{F_t}{\left(e^{f\theta} - 1\right)}$$

...(Eq. 6.70)

$$\therefore \text{Eq. (6.69) yields ... } \mathbf{F} = \frac{F_t b}{a}\left(\frac{1}{e^{f\theta} - 1}\right)$$

...13.74b/ Pg 220, DHB

Counter clockwise rotation:
Taking moments about (O)

$$F \cdot a = F_1 \cdot b$$

Hence the operating force $F = F_1\left(\dfrac{b}{a}\right)$

...(Eq. 6.71)

Also, $F_t = F_1 - F_2$

$$= F_1\left(1 - \frac{F_2}{F_1}\right)$$

$$= F_1\left(1 - \frac{1}{e^{f\theta}}\right)$$

$$F_1 = \frac{F_t \cdot e^{f\theta}}{\left(e^{f\theta} - 1\right)}$$

...(Eq. 6.72)

$$\therefore \text{Eq. (6.71) yields ... } \mathbf{F} = \frac{F_t b}{a}\left(\frac{e^{f\theta}}{e^{f\theta} - 1}\right)$$

...13.74a/ Pg 220, DHB

Notes: **[Applicable for both simple and differential band brakes]**

1. The average pressure b/w the band and the brake sheave,

$$p = \frac{F_1 + F_2}{Db}$$ ...13.78/ Pg 221, DHB

   b – band width (mm)

2. Pressure at high tension end of the band, $p_1 = \frac{2F_1}{Db}$ ...13.79/ Pg 221, DHB

3. Pressure at low tension end of the band, $p_2 = \frac{2F_2}{Db}$ ...13.80/ Pg 221, DHB

4. The band thickness, $h = 0.005D$ ...13.81/ Pg 221, DHB

5. The band width, $b = \frac{F_1}{h\sigma_d}$ ...13.82/ Pg 221, DHB

   σ_d – design stress for the band (in selecting the design stress, a reliability factor of 4 should be used)

6. $F_1 = F_t \left(\frac{e^{f\theta}}{e^{f\theta} - 1} \right)$ 7. $F_2 = F_t \left(\frac{1}{e^{f\theta} - 1} \right)$ 8. $\frac{F_1}{F_2} = e^{f\theta}$

...Pg 220, DHB

37. A simple band brake is shown in Fig. 6.25. The diameter of the drum is 900 mm and the band thickness is 5 mm. The coefficient if friction is 0.25 and arc of contact is 270°. The brake drum is attached to a hoisting drum that sustains a load of 9 kN. The operating force has a moment arm of 1.5 m and the band is attached 200 mm from pivot point. Determine:
    a. Force required to just support the load.
    b. Force when the direction of rotation is reversed.
    c. Band width. Take 50 MPa.

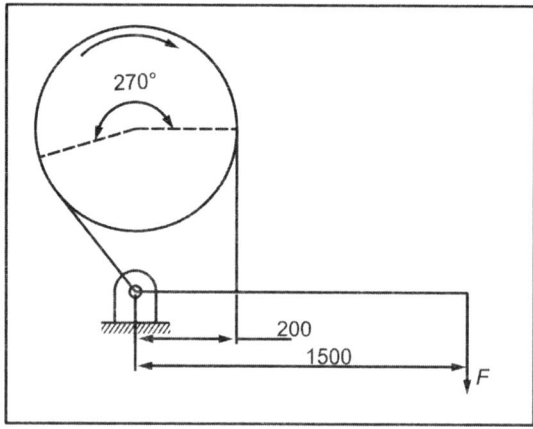

Fig. 6.25: Problem 37

Solution: $D = 600$ mm, $h = 5$ mm, $f = 0.25$, $W = F_t = F_1 - F_2 = 9$ kN, $\sigma_d = 50$ MPa
a. $F_{min} = ?$ b. $F = ?$ c. $b = ?$

a. Force required to just support the load:

Comparing the given problem with **DHB**, we have CW rotation as shown in **Fig. e/ Pg 220, DHB**.

$a = 1500$ mm, $b = 200$ mm, $\theta = 270° = 4.712$ rad.

For CW rotation, $\quad F = \dfrac{F_t b}{a}\left(\dfrac{1}{e^{f\theta}-1}\right) \quad$ ...Eq. (i) **13.75a/ Pg 220, DHB**

- $e^{f\theta} = e^{0.25 \times 4.712} = 3.248$
- Also, $\quad F_t = F_1 - F_2 = 9$ kN $\quad$ ...Eq. (ii)
- Also $\quad \dfrac{F_1}{F_2} = e^{f\theta} \quad$ ...Pg 220, DHB

$F_1 = 3.248\, F_2 \quad$ ...Eq. (iii)

∴ Eq. (ii) yields ... $9000 = 3.248\, F_2 - F_2$

$F_2 = 4003.56$ N

∴ Eq. (iii) yields ... $F_1 = 13003.56$ N

∴ Eq. (i) yields ... $F = F_{min} = \dfrac{9000 \times 200}{1500}\left(\dfrac{1}{3.248-1}\right)$

$F_{min} = 533.81$ N.

b. Force when the direction of rotation is reversed:

For CCW rotation, $\quad F = \dfrac{F_t b}{a}\left(\dfrac{e^{f\theta}}{e^{f\theta}-1}\right) \quad$ ...**13.75b/ Pg 220, DHB**

$= \dfrac{9000 \times 200}{1500}\left(\dfrac{3.248}{3.248-1}\right)$

$F = 1733.81$ N.

c. Band width:

We know that band width, $b = \dfrac{F_1}{h\sigma_d} \quad$ ...**13.82/ Pg 221, DHB**

$= \dfrac{13003.56}{5 \times 50}$

$b = 52$ mm.

38. In a simple band brake, the length of the lever is 440 mm. The tight end of the band is attached to the fulcrum of the lever and the slack end to a pin 50 mm from the fulcrum. The diameter of the brake drum is 1 m and arc of contact is 300°. The coefficient of friction between the band and the drum is 0.35. The brake drum is attached to a hoisting drum of diameter 0.65 m that sustains a load of 20 kN (Fig. 6.26). Determine:
  i. Force required at the end of lever to just support the load.
  ii. Width of steel band if the tensile stress is limited to 50 N/mm².

  [VTU – Dec. 09/ Jan. 2010 – 10 Marks]

Solution: $D = 1$ m $= 1000$ mm, $\theta = 5.236$ rad, $f = 0.35$, $D_{bar} = 0.65$ m $= 650$ mm, $W = 20$ kN, $\sigma_d = 50$ N/mm².
a. $F_{min} = ?$ b. $b = ?$

572 Design of Machine Elements II (DME II)

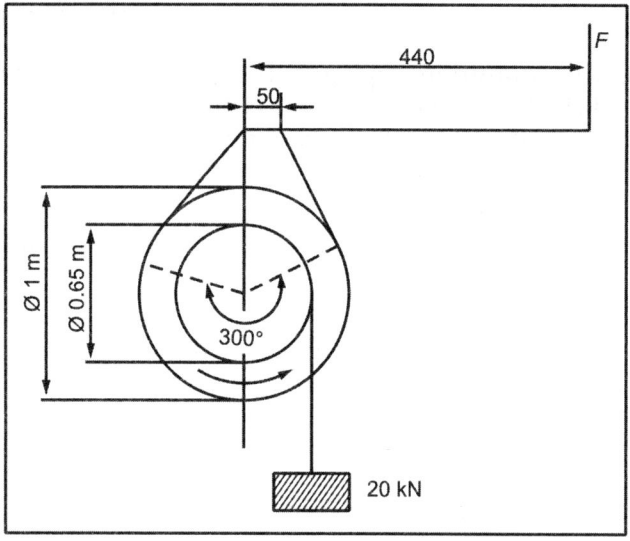

Fig. 6.26: Problem 38

a. Force required to just support the load:

Comparing the given problem with **DHB**, we have CW rotation as shown in **Fig. e/ Pg 220, DHB**.

$$a = 440 \text{ mm}, b = 50 \text{ mm},$$

For CW rotation, $\quad F = \dfrac{F_t b}{a}\left(\dfrac{1}{e^{f\theta}-1}\right) \quad$ ...Eq. (i) **13.75a/ Pg 220, DHB**

- $e^{f\theta} = e^{0.35 \times 5.5236} = 6.25$
- Since barrel and drum are mounted on the same shaft, their torques should be equal.

$$\text{i.e. } T = T_{bar}$$
$$F_t r = W \cdot R_{bar}$$
$$F_t \times 500 = 20 \times 10^3 \times (650/2)$$
$$F_t = 13000 \text{ N} = (F_1 - F_2) \quad \text{...Eq. (ii)}$$

- Also $\quad \dfrac{F_1}{F_2} = e^{f\theta} \quad$ ...**Pg 220, DHB**

$$F_1 = 6.25 \, F_2 \quad \text{...Eq. (iii)}$$

∴ Eq. (ii) yields ... $13000 = 6.25 \, F_2 - F_2$
$$F_2 = 2476.2 \text{ N}$$

∴ Eq. (iii) yields ... $F_1 = 6.25 \times 2476.20$
$$F_1 = 15476.2 \text{ N}$$

∴ Eq. (i) yields ... $F = F_{min} = \dfrac{13000 \times 50}{440}\left(\dfrac{1}{6.25-1}\right)$

$$F_{min} = 281.39 \text{ N.}$$

b. Band width:

We know that band width, $b = \dfrac{F_1}{h\sigma_d} \quad$ ...Eq. (iv) **13.82/ Pg 221, DHB**

Band thickness, $h = 0.005D$ ...13.81/ Pg 221, DHB
$= 0.005 \times 1000$
$h = 5$ mm

∴ Eq. (iv) yields ... $b = \dfrac{15476.2}{5 \times 50}$

$b = 62$ mm.

39. A simple band brake as shown in Fig. 6.27 is to be designed to absorb a power of 30 kW at a rated speed of 750 rpm. Determine:
   i. The effort required to stop clockwise rotation of the brake drum.
   ii. The effort required to stop counter clockwise rotation of the brake drum.
   iii. The dimensions of the rectangular cross-section of the brake lever assuming its depth to be twice the width.
   iv. The dimensions of the cross-section of the band assuming its width to be ten times the thickness.

[VTU – Jan./ Feb. 2005 – 10 Marks]

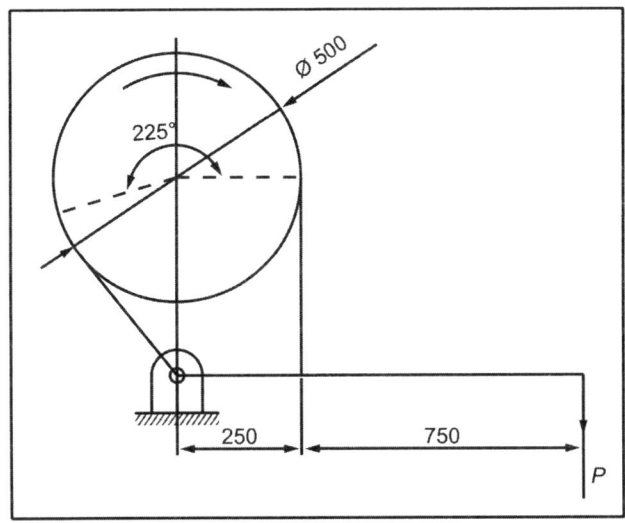

Fig. 6.27: Problem 39

Solution: $P = 30$ kW, $N = 750$ rpm.
   i. $F_{CW} = P_{CW} = ?$
   ii. $P_{CCW} = F_{CCW} = ?$
   iii. Lever dimensions $b_1, h_1 = ?$, if $h_1 = 2b_1$
   iv. Band dimensions $b, h = ?$, if $b = 10h$

i. Effort in CW rotation:
Comparing the given problem with **DHB**, we have **Fig. e/ Pg 220, DHB.**
$D = 500$ mm, $a = 750 + 250 = 1000$ mm, $b = 250$ mm, $\theta = 225° = 3.927$ rad

For CW rotation, $F = \dfrac{F_t b}{a}\left(\dfrac{1}{e^{f\theta}-1}\right)$ ...Eq. (i) **13.75a/ Pg 220, DHB**

- $e^{f\theta} = e^{0.25 \times 3.927} = 2.67$ (assume $f = 0.25$)
- But $T = F_t r$ ...Eq. (ii)

$$P = \frac{2\pi NT}{60}$$

$$30 \times 10^3 = \frac{2\pi \times 750 \times T}{60}$$

$$T = 382 \text{ N-m} = 382 \times 10^3 \text{ N-mm}$$

∴ Eq. (ii) yields ... $382 \times 10^3 = F_t \times 250$

$$F_t = 1528 \text{ N}$$

∴ Eq. (i) yields ... $F = \frac{1528 \times 250}{1000}\left(\frac{1}{2.67-1}\right)$

$$F = 228.74 \text{ N}$$

ii. Effort in CCW rotation:

For CCW rotation, $\quad F = \frac{F_t b}{a}\left(\frac{e^{f\theta}}{e^{f\theta}-1}\right) \qquad$ ...13.75b/ Pg 220, DHB

$$= \frac{1528 \times 250}{1000}\left(\frac{2.67}{2.67-1}\right)$$

$$F = 610.74 \text{ N}.$$

iii. Lever dimensions: (b_1, h_1)

Given depth to be twice the width, i.e. $h_1 = 2b_1 \qquad$ ...Eq. (iii)

Let $\quad h_1 =$ depth of the lever
$\quad b_1 =$ width of the lever

We know that, $\quad \dfrac{M}{I} = \dfrac{E}{R} = \dfrac{\sigma}{c} \qquad$ ...1.16/ Pg 3, DHB

i.e. $\quad \dfrac{M}{I} = \dfrac{\sigma}{c} \qquad$ ...Eq. (iv)

- $\quad I = \dfrac{b_1 h_1^3}{12}$

$$= \frac{b_1(2b_1)^3}{12}$$

$$I = 0.67\, b_1^4$$

- $\quad c = \dfrac{h_1}{2} = \dfrac{2b_1}{2} = b_1$

- Assume $\sigma = 80$ MPa

$$M = F_{max} \cdot a$$
$$= 610.74 \times 1000$$
$$M = 610.74 \times 10^3 \text{ N-mm}$$

∴ Eq. (iv) yields ... $\dfrac{610.74 \times 10^3}{0.67 b_1^4} = \dfrac{80}{b_1}$

$$b_1 = 22.5 \text{ mm} \approx 25 \text{ mm}$$

∴ Eq. (iii) yields ... $h_1 = 2 \times 25 = 50$ mm.

iv. Dimensions of the band:

Given width to be ten times the depth, i.e. $b = 10h$ ...Eq. (v)

Let h = depth of the lever
b = width of the lever

We know that band thickness, $h = 0.005D$ ...13.81/ Pg 221, DHB
$$= 0.005 \times 500$$
$$h = 2.5 \text{ mm}$$

∴ Eq. (v) yields ... 25 mm $b = 10h = 10 \times 2.5 = 25$ mm.

40. A simple band brake of drum diameter 600 mm has a band passing over it with an angle of contact of 225°, while one end is connected to the fulcrum, the other end is connected to the brake lever at a distance of 400 mm from the fulcrum. The brake lever is 1m long. The brake is to absorb a power of 15 kW at 720 rpm. Design the brake lever of rectangular cross-section, assuming depth to be thrice the width. Take allowable stress as 80 MPa (Fig. 6.28).

[VTU – July/ Aug. 2003 – 10 Marks; June/ July 2013 – 10 Marks; (similar) June/ July 2009 – 10 Marks]

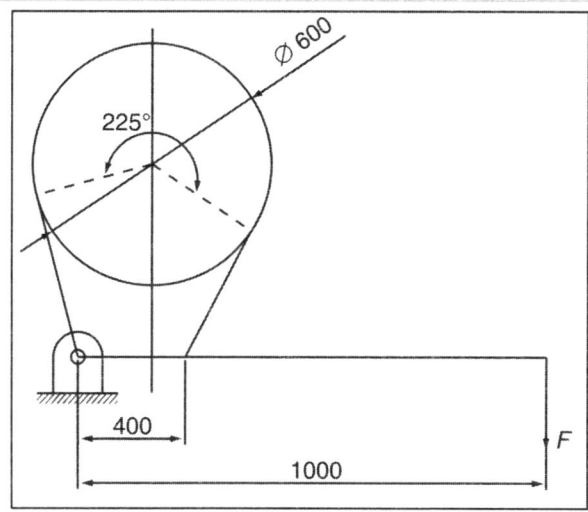

Fig. 6.28: Problem 40

Solution: $D = 600$ mm, $\theta = 225° = 3.927$ rad, $a = 1000$ mm, $b = 400$ mm, $P = 15$ kW, $N = 720$ rpm, $\sigma = 80$ MPa

Lever dimensions $b_1, h_1 = ?$, if $h_1 = 3b_1$

Given depth to be thrice the width, i.e. $h_1 = 3b_1$ ...Eq. (i)

Let h_1 = depth of the lever
b_1 = width of the lever

We know that, $\dfrac{M}{I} = \dfrac{E}{R} = \dfrac{\sigma}{c}$ ...1.16/ Pg 3, DHB

i.e. $\dfrac{M}{I} = \dfrac{\sigma}{c}$ ...Eq. (ii)

- $I = \dfrac{b_1 h_1^3}{12}$

$$= \frac{b_1(3b_1)^3}{12}$$
$$I = 2.25\, b_1^4$$

- $c = \dfrac{h_1}{2} = \dfrac{3b_1}{2} = 1.5\, b_1$
- $M = F_{max} \cdot a$ ...Eq. (iii)

To find F_{max}

Comparing the given problem with **DHB**, we have **Fig. e/ Pg 220, DHB.**

→ For CW rotation, $\quad F = \dfrac{F_t b}{a}\left(\dfrac{1}{e^{f\theta}-1}\right)$ ...Eq. (iv) **13.75a/ Pg 220, DHB**

- $e^{f\theta} = e^{0.25 \times 0.927} = 2.67$ (assume $f = 0.25$)
- But $T = F_t r$ ...Eq.(v)

$$P = \frac{2\pi N T}{60}$$

$$15 \times 10^3 = \frac{2\pi \times 720 \times T}{60}$$

$T = 198.94$ N-m $= 198.94 \times 10^3$ N-mm

∴ Eq. (v) yields ... $198.94 \times 10^3 = F_t \times 300$

$F_t = 663.15$ N

∴ Eq. (iv) yields ... $F = \dfrac{663.15 \times 400}{1000}\left(\dfrac{1}{2.67-1}\right)$

$F = 158.84$ N ...Eq. (vi)

→ For CCW rotation, $\quad F = \dfrac{F_t b}{a}\left(\dfrac{e^{f\theta}}{e^{f\theta}-1}\right)$ ...**13.75b/ Pg 220, DHB**

$$= \frac{663.15 \times 400}{1000}\left(\frac{2.67}{2.67-1}\right)$$

$F = 424.1$ N ...Eq. (vii)

Comparing Eqs (vi) and (vii), we have $F_{max} = 424.1$ N

∴ Eq. (iii) yields ... $M = 424.1 \times 1000 = 424.1 \times 10^3$ N-mm

∴ Eq. (ii) yields ... $\dfrac{424.1 \times 10^3}{2.25\, b_1^4} = \dfrac{80}{1.5\, b_1}$

$h_1 = 15.23$ mm ≈ 15 mm

∴ Eq. (i) yields ... $h_1 = 3 \times 15 = 45$ mm.

41. A simple band brake shown in Fig. 6.29 is to be designed to stop the rotation of a shaft transmitting a power of 45 kW at a rated speed of 500 rpm. Selecting suitable materials determine:

   i. Dimensions of rectangular cross-section of the band.
   ii. Dimensions of rectangular cross-section of the brake lever.
   iii. Diameter of the fulcrum pin. *[VTU – Jan./ Feb. 2006 – 10 Marks.]*

Solution: $D = 600$ mm, $\theta = 225° = 3.927$ rad, $a = 1000$ mm, $b = 300$ mm, $P = 45$ kW, $N = 500$ rpm.

    i. Band dimensions?   ii. Lever dimensions = ?,
    iii. Diameter of fulcrum pin = ?

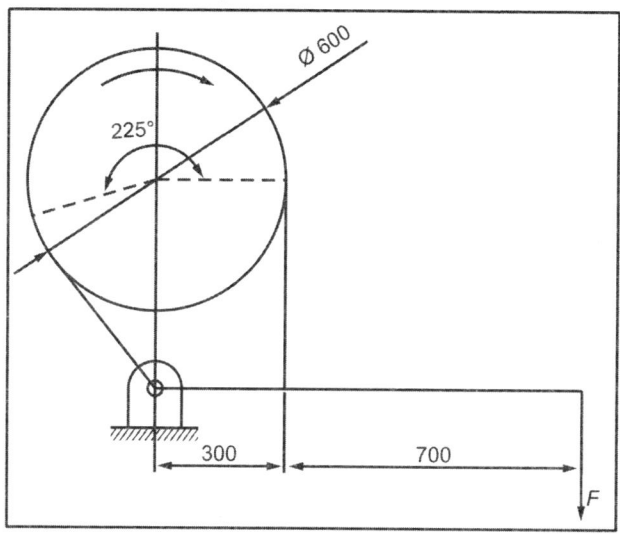

Fig. 6.29: Problem 41

i. Dimensions of the band:

We know that band width, $b = \dfrac{F_1}{h\sigma_d}$ ...Eq. (i) **13.82/ Pg 221, DHB**

-     band thickness, $h = 0.005D$ ...**13.81/ Pg 221, DHB**

$$= 0.005 \times 600$$
$$\therefore h = 3 \text{ mm}$$

- Assume $\sigma_d = 60$ MPa
- But $T = F_t r$ ...Eq. (ii)

$$P = \dfrac{2\pi NT}{60}$$

$$45 \times 10^3 = \dfrac{2\pi \times 500 \times T}{60}$$

$$T = 859.44 \text{ N-m} = 859.44 \times 10^3 \text{ N-mm}$$

$\therefore$ Eq. (ii) yields ... $859.44 \times 10^3 = F_t \times 300$

$$F_t = 2864.79 \text{ N}$$

- Force on high-tension side, $F_1 = F_t \left(\dfrac{e^{f\theta}}{e^{f\theta} - 1} \right)$ ...**Pg 220, DHB**

$$e^{f\theta} = e^{0.25 \times 3.927} = 2.67 \quad \text{(assume } f = 0.25\text{)}$$

$$= 2864.79 \left(\dfrac{2.67}{2.67 - 1} \right)$$

$$F_1 = 4580.23 \text{ N}$$

- Force on low-tension side, $F_2 = F_t\left(\dfrac{1}{e^{f\theta}-1}\right)$ ...Pg 220, DHB

$$= 2864.79\left(\dfrac{1}{2.67-1}\right)$$

$$F_2 = 1715.44 \text{ N}$$

∴ Eq. (i) yields ... $b = \dfrac{4580.23}{3 \times 60}$

$$b = 25.45 \text{ mm.}$$

ii. Lever dimensions:

Let h_1 = depth of the lever
h_2 = width of the lever

We know that, $\dfrac{M}{I} = \dfrac{E}{R} = \dfrac{\sigma}{c}$ ...1.16/ Pg 3, DHB

i.e. $\dfrac{M}{I} = \dfrac{\sigma}{c}$ ...Eq. (iii)

- $I = \dfrac{b_1 h_1^3}{12}$ (assuming $h_1 = 3b_1$)

$$= \dfrac{b_1(3b_1)^3}{12}$$

$$I = 2.25\, b_1^4$$

- $c = \dfrac{h_1}{2} = \dfrac{3b_1}{2} = 1.5\, b_1$

- Assuming that the material used for lever is C45 steel, we have σ_y = 353 MPa
...Tb. 1.8/ Pg 419, DHB

Assuming FOS = 4, we have $FOS = \dfrac{\sigma_y}{\sigma}$

$$4 = \dfrac{353}{\sigma}$$

$$\sigma = 88.25 \text{ MPa}$$

- $M = F_{max} \cdot a$ ...Eq. (iv)

To find F_{max}

Comparing the given problem with **DHB**, we have **Fig. e/ Pg 220, DHB.**

→ For CW rotation, $F = \dfrac{F_t b}{a}\left(\dfrac{1}{e^{f\theta}-1}\right)$ ...Eq. (v) **13.75a/ Pg 220, DHB**

$$= \dfrac{2864.79 \times 300}{1000}\left(\dfrac{1}{2.67-1}\right)$$

$$F = 514.63 \text{ N}$$ ...Eq. (vi)

→ For CCW rotation, $F = \dfrac{F_t b}{a}\left(\dfrac{e^{f\theta}}{e^{f\theta}-1}\right)$ ...13.75b/ Pg 220, DHB

$$= \dfrac{2864.79 \times 300}{1000}\left(\dfrac{2.67}{2.67-1}\right)$$

$F = 1374.1$ N ...Eq. (vii)

Comparing Eqs (vi) and (vii), we have $F_{max} = 1374.1$ N

∴ Eq. (iv) yields ... $M = 1374.1 \times 1000 = 1374.1 \times 10^3$ N-mm

∴ Eq. (iii) yields ... $\dfrac{1374.1 \times 10^3}{2.25 b_1^4} = \dfrac{88.25}{1.5 b_1}$

$b_1 = 21.81$ mm ≈ 22 mm

and $h_1 = 3 \times 22 = 66$ mm

iii. Diameter of the fulcrum pin:

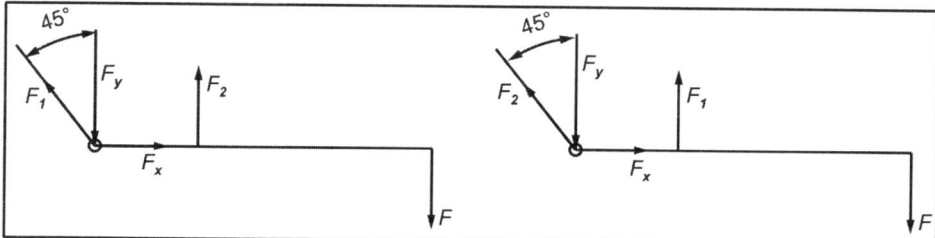

Fig. 6.29 (a): CW rotation, problem 41   **Fig. 6.29 (b):** CCW rotation, problem 41

We know that reaction at fulcrum $R = \sqrt{F_x^2 + F_y^2}$ ...Eq. (viii)

→ For CW rotation:

Vertical forces $F_1 \cos 45 - F_y + F_2 - F = 0$

$(4580.23 \times \cos 45) - F_y + 1715.44 - 514.63 = 0$

∴ $F_y = 4439.52$ N

Horizontal forces: $F_1 \sin 45 - F_x = 0$

$(4580.23 \times \sin 45) = F_x$

∴ $F_x = 3238.71$ N

∴ Eq. (viii) yields ... $R = \sqrt{3238.71^2 + 4439.52^2}$

$R = 5495.32$ N ...Eq. (ix)

→ For CCW rotation:

Vertical forces: $F_2 \cos 45 - F_y + F_1 - F = 0$

$(1715.44 \times \cos 45) - F_y + 4580.23 - 1374.1 = 0$

∴ $F_y = 4419.13$ N

Horizontal forces: $F_2 \sin 45 - F_x = 0$

$1715.44 \times \sin 45 = F_x$

∴ $F_x = 1213$ N

∴ Eq. (viii) yields ... $R = \sqrt{1213^2 + 4419.13^2}$

$R = 4582.58$ N ...Eq. (x)

Since bearing pressure is not given. Let us use the shear stress formula to calculate the diameter.

580 Design of Machine Elements II (DME II)

Here the pin in is subjected to double shear, hence $R_{max} = \dfrac{2\pi}{4} d_f^2 \times \tau$

$$\tau = 0.5\sigma = 0.5 \times 88.25 = 44.125 \text{ MPa}$$

$$5495.32 = \dfrac{2\pi}{4} d_f^2 \times 44.125$$

$$d_f = 8.9 \text{ mm} \approx 9 \text{ mm}.$$

42. **A band brake uses a V-belt as shown in Fig. 6.30. The pitch diameter of the V-grooved sheave is 500 mm. The groove angle is 45° and coefficient of friction is 0.25. Determine the power rating at 300 rev/min.**
    [VTU – Jan./ Feb. 2005 – 10 Marks; (similar) Dec. 07/ Jan. 2008 – 10 Marks.]

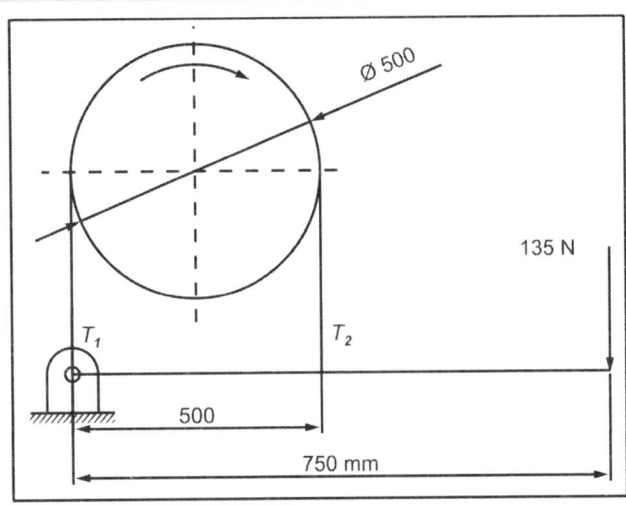

Fig. 6.30: Problem 42

Solution: $D = 500$ mm, **groove angle** $\alpha = 45°, f = 0.25, P = ?, N = 300$ rpm

We know that, $\qquad P = \dfrac{2\pi NT}{60} \qquad$ ...Eq. (i)

But $T = F_t r \qquad$ ...Eq. (ii)

Comparing the given problem with **DHB**, we have CW rotation as shown in **Fig. e/ Pg 220, DHB**.

$a = 750$ mm, $b = 500$ mm, $F = 135$ N, $\theta = 180° = 3.142$ rad.

For CW rotation, $\qquad F = \dfrac{F_t b}{a} \left(\dfrac{1}{e^{f\theta} - 1} \right) \qquad$ ...13.75a/ Pg 220, DHB

Since a V-belt is used, the pulley will be a grooved pulley.

$$F = \dfrac{F_t b}{a} \left(\dfrac{1}{e^{f_1 \theta} - 1} \right) \qquad \text{...Eq. (iii)}$$

- But $f_1 = \dfrac{f}{\sin(\alpha/2)} \qquad$ ...14.26/ Pg 242, DHB

$$= \dfrac{0.25}{\sin(45/2)}$$

$$f_1 = 0.6533$$

$$e^{f_1\theta} = e^{0.6533 \times 3.142} = 7.7866$$

∴ Eq. (iii) yields ... $135 = \dfrac{F_t \times 500}{750}\left(\dfrac{1}{7.7866-1}\right)$

$F_t = 1374.28$ N

∴ Eq. (ii) yields ... $T = 1374.28 \times 0.25$

$T = 343.57$ N-mm

∴ Eq. (i) yields ... $P = \dfrac{2\pi \times 300 \times 343.57}{60}$

$P = 10.79$ kW.

6.22.2 Differential Band Brake

A differential band brake **Fig. 6.31,** is one in which the two ends of the band are attached to points on opposite sides of the fulcrum. This gives the band a differential moment about the fulcrum. Sometimes the bands are also connected as shown in **Fig. 6.32.**

Let, F = Force at the end of brake handle

F_t = Tangential force at the rim of brake wheel.

F_1 = Force on high-tension side [Tension in the tight side of the band],

F_2 = Force on low-tension side [Tension in the slack side of the band],

θ = Angle of contact of the band on the drum, (also called angle of lap/embrace),

f = Coefficient of friction between the band and the drum,

r = Radius of the drum,

h = Thickness of the band.

a = Distance between fulcrum and applied force

b = Distance between fulcrum and center of the shoe

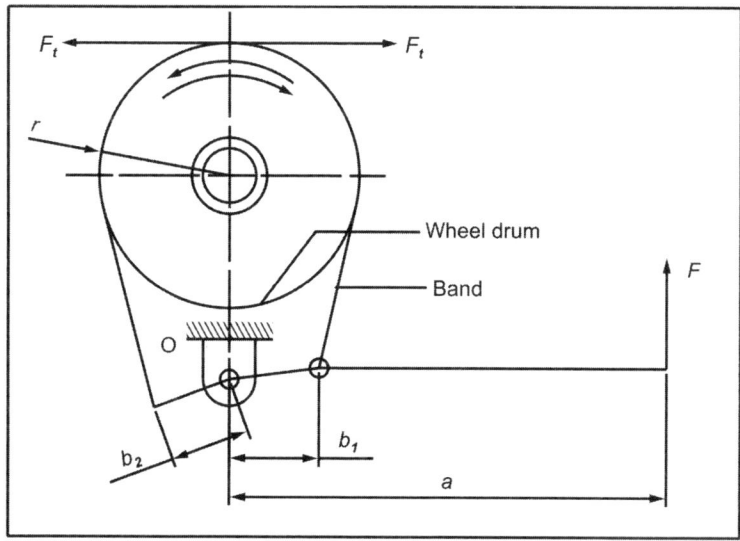

Fig. 6.31: Differential band brake (Fig. f/Pg 220, DHB)

Case 1: Fulcrum is away from the load (Fig. 6.31)

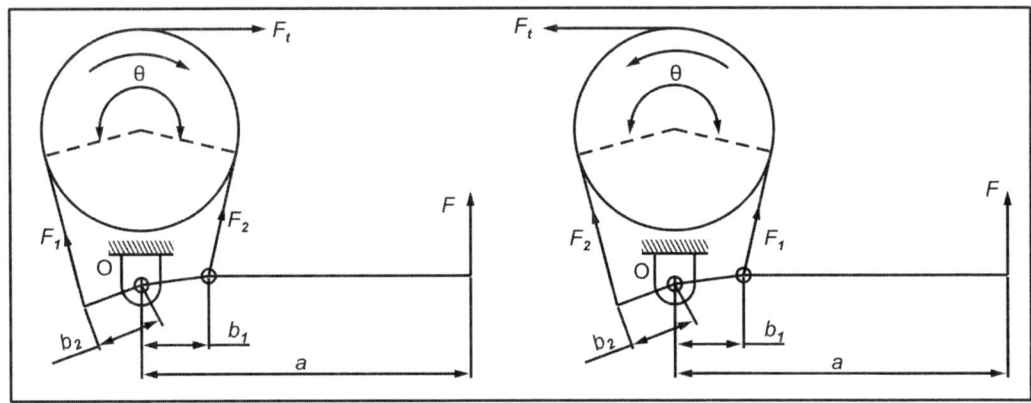

Fig. 6.31 (a): Clockwise rotation of the drum   **Fig. 6.31 (b):** Anticlockwise rotation of the drum

Since the steel bands act similar to that of belt drive, hence the ratio of tensions is given as,

$$\frac{F_1}{F_2} = e^{f\theta} \qquad \text{...using (Eq. 6.63) Pg 220, DHB}$$

The tension in the band decreases from a value at the pivot side of the band to the lever side, hence the braking torque is,

$$T = (F_1 - F_2)r \qquad \text{...using (Eq. 6.64) Pg 220, DHB}$$

Clockwise rotation:	Counter clockwise rotation:
Taking moments about (O)	Taking moments about (O)
$F.a + F_2.b_1 = F_1.b_2$	$F.a = F_1.b_1 = F_2.b_2$
Hence the operating force is	Hence the operating force is
$F = \left(\dfrac{b_2 F_1 - b_1 F_2}{a}\right)$ ...(Eq. 6.73)	$F = \left(\dfrac{b_2 F_2 - b_1 F_1}{a}\right)$ ...(Eq. 6.76)
$= \dfrac{F_2}{a}\left(b_2 \dfrac{F_1}{F_2} - b_1\right)$	$= \dfrac{F_1}{a}\left(b_2 \dfrac{F_2}{F_1} - b_1\right)$
$\therefore F = \dfrac{F_2}{a}(b_2.e^{f\theta} - b_1)$ ...(Eq. 6.74)	$= \dfrac{F_1}{a}\left(\dfrac{b_2}{e^{f\theta}} - b_1\right)$
	$\therefore F = \dfrac{F_1}{a}\left\{\dfrac{(b_2 - b_1.e^{f\theta})}{e^{f\theta}}\right\}$ ...(Eq. 6.77)
Also, $F_t = F_1 - F_2$	Also $F_t = F_1 - F_2$
$= F_2\left(\dfrac{F_1}{F_2} - 1\right)$	$= F_1\left(1 - \dfrac{F_2}{F_1}\right)$
$= F_2(e^{f\theta} - 1)$	$= F_1\left(1 - \dfrac{1}{e^{f\theta}}\right)$
$\therefore F_2 = \dfrac{F_t}{(e^{f\theta} - 1)}$ ...(Eq. 6.75)	$F_1 = \dfrac{F_t.e^{f\theta}}{(e^{f\theta} - 1)}$ ...(Eq. 6.78)

∴ Eq. (6.74) yields ...

$$F = \frac{F_t}{a(e^{f\theta} - 1)}(b_2 \cdot e^{f\theta} - b_1)$$

$$F = \frac{F_t}{a}\left\{\frac{(b_2 \cdot e^{f\theta} - b_1)}{(e^{f\theta} - 1)}\right\}$$

...13.76a/ Pg 220, DHB

∴ Eq. (6.77) yields ...

$$F = \frac{F_t \cdot e^{f\theta}}{a(e^{f\theta} - 1)}\left\{\frac{(b_2 - b_1 \cdot e^{f\theta})}{e^{f\theta}}\right\}$$

$$F = \frac{F_t}{a}\left\{\frac{(b_2 - b_1 \cdot e^{f\theta})}{(e^{f\theta} - 1)}\right\}$$

...13.76b/Pg 220, DHB

Note:
- If in **Eq. 13.76b**, $b_2 \leq b_1 \cdot e^{f\theta}$, then the force F will be negative –or- equal to zero, and thus the band brake works automatically (self locking).
- **If the load is in the opposite direction, then use CW relation for CCW rotation and vice versa.**
  [*check direction of load with rotation of drum while solving the problems*]

Case 2: Fulcrum is nearer to the load Fig. 6.32

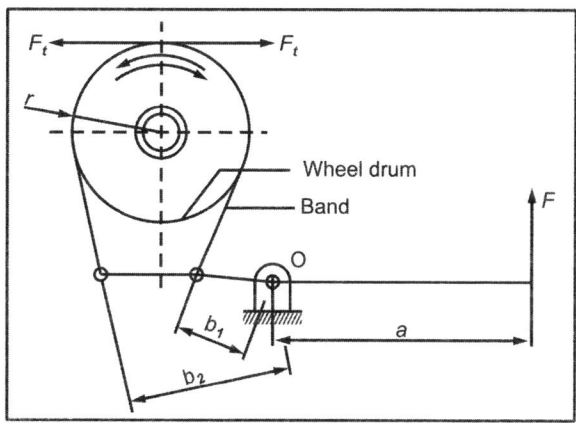

Fig. 6.32: Differential band brake with bands connected (Fig. g/ Pg 221, DHB)

Clockwise rotation: $$F = \frac{F_t}{a}\left\{\frac{(b_2 \cdot e^{f\theta} + b_1)}{(e^{f\theta} - 1)}\right\}$$ ...13.77a/ Pg 221, DHB

Counter clockwise rotation:

$$F = \frac{F_t}{a}\left\{\frac{(b_1 \cdot e^{f\theta} + b_2)}{(e^{f\theta} - 1)}\right\}$$ ...13.77b/ Pg 221, DHB

Note:
- In **Eqs. 13.77 a, and 13.77 b, DHB**, if $b_2 = b_1$ then the force F will be

$$F = \frac{F_t b_1}{a}\left\{\frac{(e^{f\theta} + 1)}{(e^{f\theta} - 1)}\right\}$$ ...(Eq. 6.79)

i.e. the same force is required for CW and CCW rotation.
- *Students are requested/advised to solve the problems by taking the moments about the fulcrum, rather than using the relations.*

43. The band brake shown in **Fig. 6.33** below has an angle of contact of 260° and is to sustain a torque of 300 N-m. The diameter of the drum is 300 mm. Determine:
   a. The operating force assuming $f = 0.25$.
   b. The tensions in the band.
   c. For what value of b_2 will the brake be self-locking?

Solution: $D = 300$ mm, $\theta = 260° = 4.538$ rad, $T = 300$ N-m, $f = 0.25$
   a. $F = ?$ b. $T_1, T_2 = ?$ c. $b_2 = ?$
From **Fig. 6.33**, $a = 600$ mm, $b_1 = 40$ mm, $b_2 = 160$ mm

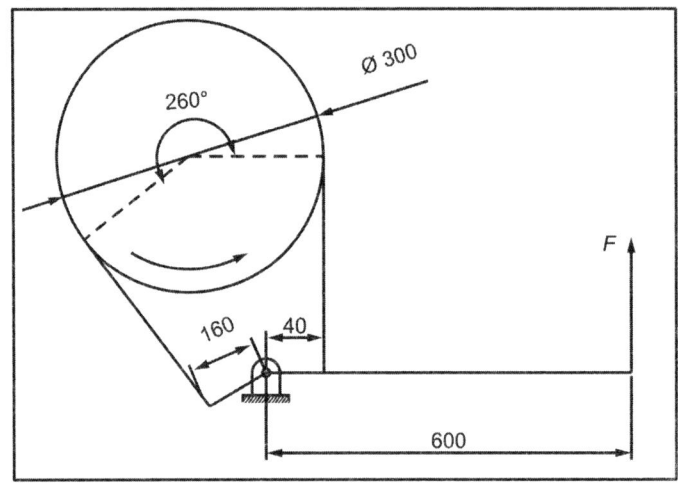

Fig. 6.33: Problem 43

a. To find operating force:
   Taking moments about the fulcrum in CCW direction,
   $F \times 600 + F_1 \times 40 = F_2 \times 160$

$$F = \left(\frac{160 F_2 - 40 F_1}{600}\right) \quad \text{...Eq. }(i)$$

- $e^{f\theta} = e^{0.25 \times 4.538} = 3.11$
- But $T = (F_1 - F_2) r$ ...Pg 220, DHB
  $300 \times 10^3 = (F_1 - F_2) \times 150$
  $(F_1 - F_2) = 2000$ N ...Eq. (ii)

also, $\dfrac{F_1}{F_2} = e^{f\theta}$ ...Pg 220, DHB

$F_1 = 3.11 F_2$ ...Eq. (iii)

∴ Eq. (ii) yields ... $(3.11 F_2 - F_2) = 2000$ N
$F_2 = 947.87$ N

∴ Eq. (iii) yields ... $F_1 = 3.11 \times 947.87$
$F_1 = 2947.87$ N

∴ Eq. (i) yields ... $F = \left(\dfrac{160 \times 947.87 - 40 \times 2947.87}{600}\right)$

$F = 56.24$ N.

-OR- Comparing the given problem with **DHB**, we have **Fig. f/ Pg 220, DHB**.

$$F = \frac{F_t}{a}\left\{\frac{(b_2 - b_1 \cdot e^{f\theta})}{(e^{f\theta} - 1)}\right\} \qquad \ldots 13.76b/\text{ Pg 220, DHB}$$

$$= \frac{2000}{600}\left\{\frac{(160 - 40 \times 3.11)}{(3.11 - 1)}\right\}$$

$$F = 56.24 \text{ N}$$

b. To find tensions:

$$F_2 = 947.87 \text{ N and } F_1 = 2947.87 \text{ N}$$

c. Value of b_2 for self-locking:

For self-locking, $\quad b_2 \geq b_1 \cdot e^{f\theta}$

$$\geq 40 \times 3.11$$

$$b_2 \geq 124.4 \text{ mm.}$$

44. A differential band brake as shown in Fig. 6.34 has an angle of contact of 225°. The band has a compressed woven lining and bears against a cast iron drum of 350 mm diameter. The brake is to sustain a torque of 350 N-m and the coefficient of friction between the band and the drum is 0.3. Find:
    i. The necessary force, P for clockwise rotation and anti clockwise rotation of the drum.
    ii. The value of OA for the brake to be self-locking, when the drum rotates clockwise. *[VTU – June/ July 2009 – 15 Marks]*

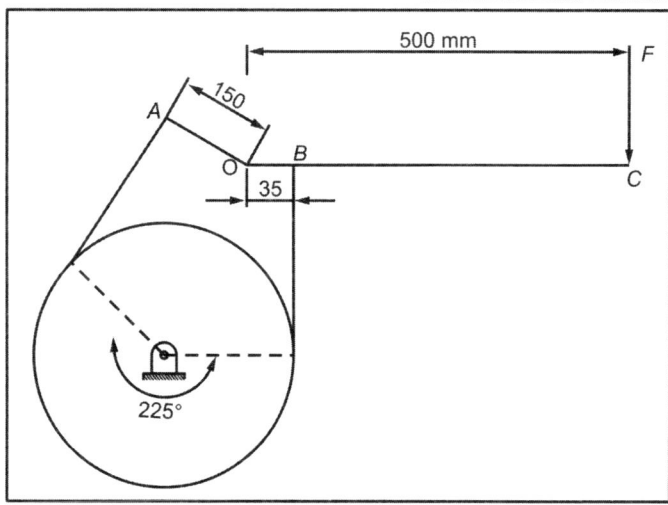

Fig. 6.34: Problem 44

Solution: $D = 350$ mm, $\theta = 225° = 3.927$ rad., $T = 350$ N-m, $f = 0.3$
   i. $F_{CW} = ?, F_{CCW} = ?$ ii. $OA = b_2 = ?$

i. Force in CW rotation:

Comparing the given problem with **DHB**, we have **Fig. f/ Pg 220, DHB**.

$$D = 500 \text{ mm}, a = 500 \text{ mm}, b_1 = 35 \text{ mm}, b_2 = 150 \text{ mm}$$

→ For CW rotation of the drum (in the direction of load), according to **DHB**, we have CCW rotation.

$$F = \frac{F_t}{a}\left\{\frac{(b_2 - b_1 \cdot e^{f\theta})}{(e^{f\theta} - 1)}\right\} \qquad \text{...Eq. (i) 13.76b/Pg 220, DHB}$$

- $e^{f\theta} = e^{0.3 \times 3.927} = 3.25$
- But $T = (F_1 - F_2) r$ ...Pg 220, DHB

$$350 \times 10^3 = (F_1 - F_2) \times 175$$
$$(F_1 - F_2) = 2000 \text{ N} \qquad \text{...Eq.(ii)}$$

Also $\quad \dfrac{F_1}{F_2} = e^{f\theta} \qquad \text{...Pg 220, DHB}$

$$F_1 = 3.25\, F_2 \qquad \text{...Eq. (iii)}$$

∴ Eq. (ii) yields ... $(3.25\, F_2 - F_2) = 2000$ N
$$F_2 = 888.89 \text{ N}$$

∴ Eq. (iii) yields ... $F_1 = 3.25 \times 888.89$
$$F_1 = 2888.89 \text{ N}$$

∴ Eq. (i) yields ... $F = \dfrac{2000}{500}\left\{\dfrac{(150 - 35 \times 3.25)}{(3.25 - 1)}\right\}$

$$F = F_{CW} = 64.44 \text{ N}$$

Force in CCW rotation:

→ For CCW rotation of the drum (against the direction of load), according to **DHB**, we have CW rotation.

$$F = \frac{F_t}{a}\left\{\frac{(b_2 \cdot e^{f\theta} - b_1)}{(e^{f\theta} - 1)}\right\} \qquad \text{...13.76a/ Pg 220, DHB}$$

$$= \frac{2000}{500}\left\{\frac{(150 \times 3.25 - 35)}{(3.25 - 1)}\right\}$$

$$F = F_{CCW} = 804.45 \text{ N}$$

ii. Value of OA for self-locking in CW direction:

For CW rotation of the drum (in the direction of load), according to **DHB**, we have CCW rotation

For self locking, $\quad F = 0$

i.e. $b_2 F_2 - b_1 F_1 = 0 \qquad \text{...13.76b/ Pg 220, DHB}$

$$b_2 F_2 = b_1 F_1$$
$$\frac{b_2}{b_1} = \frac{F_1}{F_2}$$
$$\frac{b_2}{b_1} = e^{f\theta}$$
∴ $b_2 = b_1 \cdot e^{f\theta}$
$$= 35 \times 3.25$$
$$b_2 \geq 113.75 \text{ mm} \qquad \text{-or-}$$

For self locking, $\quad b_2 \geq b_1 \cdot e^{f\theta}$
$$\geq 35 \times 3.25$$
$$b_2 \geq 113.75 \text{ mm}$$

Clutches and Brakes **587**

45. A differential band brake shown in Fig. 6.35 operates on a drum of diameter 600 mm. The band is 3.2 mm × 100 mm and coefficient of friction is 0.22. Determine
  i. Least force required at the end of operating lever when the band is subjected to a stress of 55 N/mm².
  ii. Torque applied to the brake drum shaft.
  iii. Is the brake self locking? Prove your answer.

[VTU – Dec. 06/ Jan. 2007 – 10 Marks]

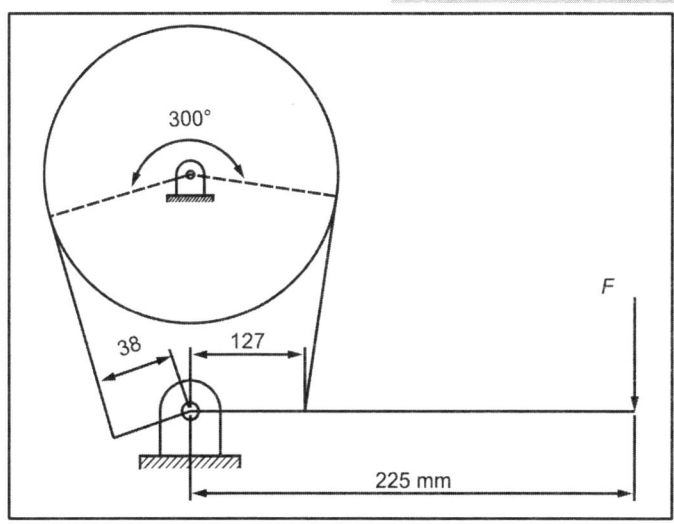

Fig. 6.35: Problem 45

Solution: $D = 600$ mm, $\theta = 300° = 5.236$ rad, $h = 3.2$ mm, $b = 100$ mm, $f = 0.22$, $\sigma = 55$ N/mm²
i. $F_{min} = ?$,   ii. $T = ?$ iii. self locking = ?

i. Minimum force:

→ **CW rotation of drum**

Comparing the given problem with **DHB**, we have **Fig. f/ Pg 220, DHB**.
$$a = 225 \text{ mm}, b_1 = 127 \text{ mm}, b_2 = 38 \text{ mm}$$
Taking moments about the fulcrum in CW direction, we have
$$Fa + F_1 b_2 - F_2 b_1 = 0$$
$$F = \left(\frac{F_2 b_1 - F_1 b_2}{a} \right) \qquad \text{...Eq. } (i)$$

- $e^{f\theta} = e^{0.22 \times 5.236} = 3.164$

- But band width, $\quad b = \dfrac{F_1}{h\sigma_d}$ \qquad ...13.82/ Pg 221, DHB

$$100 = \frac{F_1}{3.2 \times 55}$$
$$F_1 = 17600 \text{ N}$$

- Also $\quad \dfrac{F_1}{F_2} = e^{f\theta}$ \qquad ...Pg 220, DHB

$$\frac{17600}{F_2} = 3.164$$
$$F_2 = 5562.58 \text{ N}$$
$$F_t = F_1 - F_2$$
$$= 17600 - 5562.58$$
$$F_t = 12037.42 \text{ N}$$

∴ Eq. (i) yields ... $F = \left(\dfrac{5562.58 \times 127 - 17600 \times 38}{225}\right)$

$$F = 167.32 \text{ N}.$$

→ **CCW rotation:**
Taking moments about the fulcrum in CW direction, we have
$$Fa + F_2 b_2 - F_1 b_1 = 0$$
$$F = \left(\frac{F_1 b_1 - F_2 b_2}{a}\right)$$
$$= \left(\frac{17600 \times 127 - 5562.58 \times 38}{225}\right)$$
$$F = 8994.76 \text{ N}.$$

Note: Use of relations from DHB yields negative values of "F", since the load is acting downwards, while that as per DHB is acting upward. In such cases neglect the sign.

i.e. neglecting the sign, we have $F_{min} = 167.32$ N

ii. Torque applied:
We know that, $T = F_t r = (F_1 - F_2) r$
$$= 12037.42 \times 0.3$$
$$T = 3611.23 \text{ N}$$

iii. Self-locking:
→ For CW rotation:
For self locking, $F = 0$
From **Fig. 6.35**, $b_1 F_2 - b_2 F_1 = 0$
$$b_1 F_2 \leq b_2 F_1$$
$$\frac{b_1}{b_2} \leq \frac{F_1}{F_2}$$
$$\frac{b_1}{b_2} \leq e^{f\theta}$$
$$\frac{127}{38} \leq e^{f\theta}$$
$$3.342 \nleq 3.164$$

Hence self-locking does not occur.
→ For CCW rotation:
For self locking, $F = 0$

From **Fig. 6.35**, $b_1F_1 - b_2F_2 = 0$

$$b_1F_1 \leq b_2F_2$$

$$\frac{F_1}{F_2} \leq \frac{b_2}{b_1}$$

$$e^{f\theta} \leq \frac{b_2}{b_1}$$

$$e^{f\theta} \leq \frac{38}{127}$$

$$3.164 \nless 0.299$$

Hence self-locking does not occur.

46. A differential band brake is as shown in Fig. 6.36. The width and thickness of the steel band are 100 mm and 3 mm respectively and the maximum tensile stress in the band is 50 N/mm². The coefficient of friction between the friction lining and the brake drum is 0.25. Calculate:
    i. The tensions in the band.
    ii. The actuating force.
    iii. The torque capacity of the brake.
        Also check for self-locking.
        [VTU – Dec. 08/ Jan. 09 – 06 Marks; June/ July 2011 – 08 Marks; June 2012 – 10 Marks; June/ July 2013 – 10 Marks]

Solution: $r = 300$ mm, $\theta = 240° = 4.189$ rad, $b = 100$ mm, $h = 3$ mm, $\sigma = 50$ N/mm², $f = 0.25$.
i. $T_1, T_2 = ?$ ii. $F = ?$ iii. $T = ?$

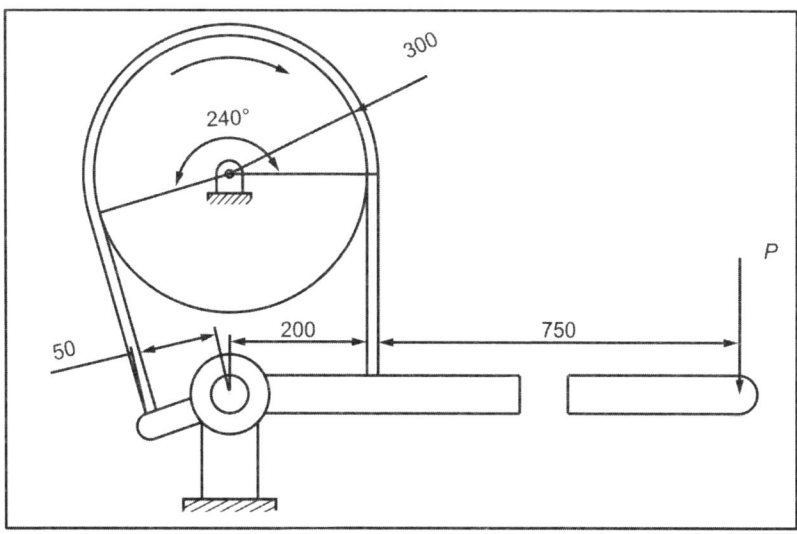

Fig. 6.36: Problem 46

i. The tensions in the band:

We know that, $\dfrac{F_1}{F_2} = e^{f\theta}$ ...Eq. (*i*) **Pg 220, DHB**

- $$e^{f\theta} = e^{0.25 \times 4.189} = 2.85$$

- But $b = \dfrac{F_1}{h\sigma_d}$ ...**13.82/ Pg 221, DHB**

$$100 = \dfrac{F_1}{3 \times 50}$$

$$F_1 = 15000 \text{ N}$$

∴ Eq. (*i*) yields ... $\dfrac{15000}{F_2} = 2.85$

$$F_2 = 5263.16 \text{ N}.$$

ii. The actuating force:

Comparing the given problem with **DHB**, we have **Fig. f/ Pg 220, DHB**.

$$a = 950 \text{ mm}, b_1 = 200 \text{ mm}, b_2 = 50 \text{ mm}$$

Taking moments about the fulcrum in CW direction, we have

$$Fa + F_1 b_2 - F_2 b_1 = 0$$

$$F = \left(\dfrac{F_2 b_1 - F_1 b_2}{a}\right)$$

$$= \left(\dfrac{5263.16 \times 200 - 15000 \times 50}{950}\right)$$

$$F = 318.56 \text{ N}$$

iii. Torque:

We know that, $T = F_t \cdot r = (F_1 - F_2) r$

$$= (15000 - 5263.16) \times 0.3$$

$$T = 2921.05 \text{ N-m}$$

iv. Self locking:

For self locking, $F = 0$

From **Fig. 6.35**, $F_1 b_2 - F_2 b_1 = 0$

$$\dfrac{b_1}{b_2} \leq \dfrac{F_1}{F_2}$$

$$\dfrac{200}{50} \leq e^{f\theta}$$

$$4 \not\leq 2.85$$

Hence self-locking does not occur.

VTU QUESTION PAPERS

Feb. 2002 (ME6T2)

1. a. Explain briefly the uniform pressure theory and uniform wear theory applicable to friction clutches and brakes. **(05 Marks)**
   b. A multiple disc clutch of steel on bronze category is to transmit 4 kW at 750 rpm. The inner diameter of contact is 80 mm and the outer diameter of contact is 140 mm. The clutch operates in oil with a coefficient of friction of 0.1. The average allowable maximum pressure is 0.35 MPa. Assume uniform wear theory and determine:
      i. Number of steel and bronze discs.
      ii. Axial force required. **(10 Marks)**
   c. A single block brake is shown in **Fig. 6.37**. The drum diameter is 250 mm. The contact angle is 90°. If an operating force of 700 N is applied at the end of the lever and the coefficient of friction is 0.35, determine the torque that may be sustained by the brake. **(08 Marks)**s

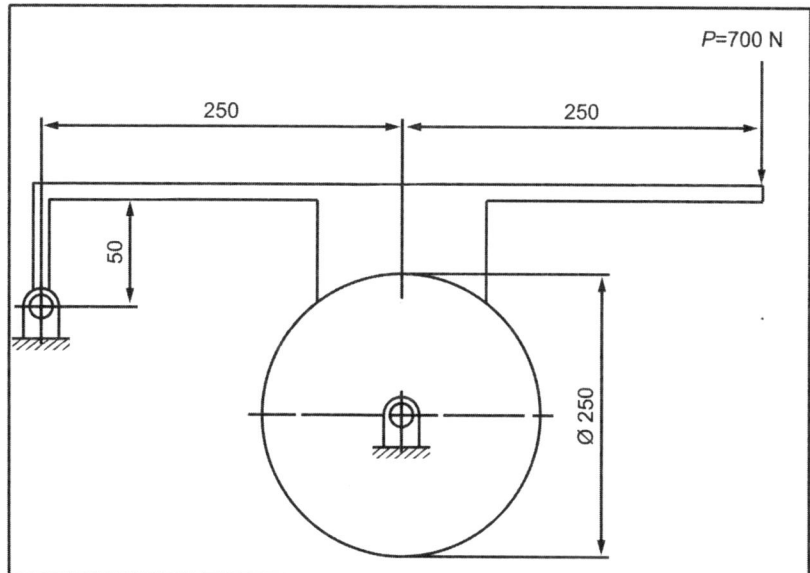

Fig. 6.37

July/ Aug. 2002 (ME6T2)

2. Determine the power transmitted by a single pair plate clutch assuming uniform pressure distribution. The friction surfaces have an outside diameter of 350 mm and an inner diameter of 280 mm. The coefficient of friction is 0.25 and the maximum allowable pressure is 0.85 MPa. **(10 Marks)**

Jan./ Feb 2003 (ME6T2)

3. A plate clutch with a maximum diameter of 600 mm has maximum lining pressure of 0.35 MPa. The power to be transmitted at 400 rpm is 135 kW and $\mu = 0.3$. Find inside diameter and spring force required to engage the clutch, if the springs with spring index 6 and material of spring is steel with safe shear stress 600 MPa is used. Find the wire diameter, if 6 springs are used. **(10 Marks)**

July/ Aug. 2003 (ME6T2)

4. a. In a multiple disc clutch, the radial width of the friction material is to be 0.2 of maximum radius. The coefficient of friction is 0.25. The clutch is to transmit 60 kW at 3000 rpm. Its maximum diameter is 250 mm and the axial force is limited to 600 N. determine:
   i. Number of diving and driven discs and
   ii. Mean unit pressure on each contact surface. Assume uniform wear.
   (10 Marks)

   b. A simple band brake of drum diameter 600 mm has a band passing over it with an angle of contact of 225°, while one end is connected to the fulcrum, the other end is connected to the brake lever at a distance of 400 mm from the fulcrum. The brake lever is 1m long. The brake is to absorb a power of 15 kW at 720 rpm. Design the brake lever of rectangular cross-section, assuming depth to be thrice the width. Take allowable stress as 80 MPa. **(10 Marks)**

July/ Aug. 2004 (ME6T2)

5. a. Determine the torque that may be resisted by the single block brake shown in **Fig. 6.38** for a coefficient of friction of 0.3. **(08 Marks)**

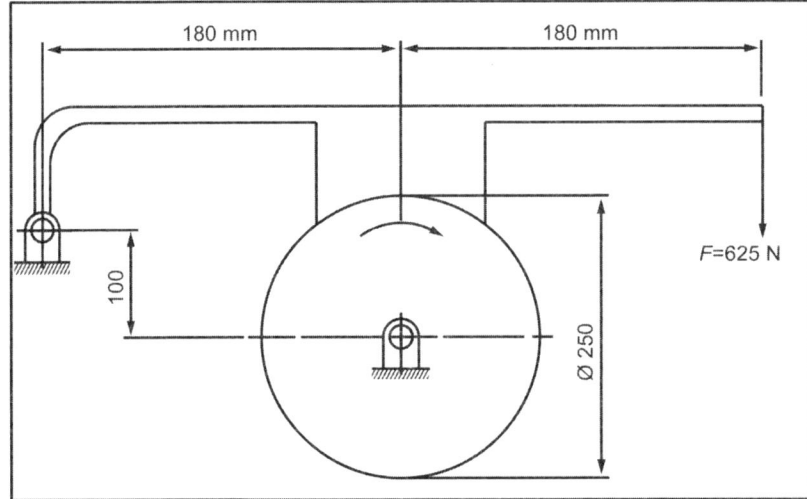

Fig. 6.38

   b. A multiple plate clutch has steel on bronze to resist 8 kW at 1440 rpm. The inner diameter of contact is 80 mm and the outer diameter of contact is 140 mm. The clutch operates in oil with expected coefficient of friction of 0.1 and average allowable pressure = 0.35 MPa. Assume uniform wear theory and determine the following:
   i. Number of steel and bronze plates
   ii. Axial force required
   iii. Actual maximum pressure. **(06 Marks)**

   c. A friction cone clutch has to transmit a torque of 200 N-m at 1440 rpm. The larger diameter of the cone is 350 mm; the cone pitch angle is 6.25°. The face width is 65 mm. The coefficient if friction is 0.2. Determine:
   i. The axial force required to transmit the torque.
   ii. The average normal pressure on the contact surfaces when the maximum torque is transmitted. **(06 Marks)**

Jan./ Feb. 2005 (ME6T2)

6. a. A cone clutch with a face angle of 14° has to transmit 286 N-m of torque at a speed of 600 rev/min. The larger diameter of the clutch is 250 mm, face width is 60 mm and coefficient of friction is 0.18. Determine:
   i. Axial force required to transmit the torque.
   ii. Average normal pressure.
   iii. Maximum normal pressure.
   Assume uniform wear conditions. (10 Marks)

   b. A band brake uses a V-belt as shown in **Fig. 6.39**. The pitch diameter of the V-grooved sheave is 500 mm. The groove angle is 45° and coefficient of friction is 0.25. Determine the power rating at 300 rev/min. (10 Marks)

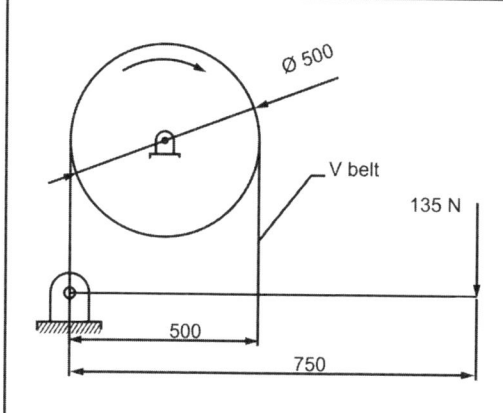

Fig. 6.39

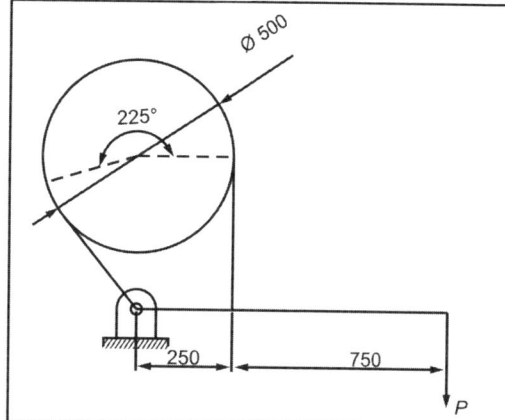

Fig. 6.40

Jan./ Feb. 2005 (AU53)

7. a. Design a cone clutch to transmit a power of 40 kW at a rated speed of 750 rpm. Also determine the
   i. Axial force capacity
   ii. The axial force necessary to transmit the torque
   iii. The axial force necessary to engage the cone clutch. (10 Marks)

   b. A simple band brake as shown in **Fig. 6.40** is to be designed to absorb a power of 30 kW at a rated speed of 750 rpm. Determine:
   i. The effort required to stop clockwise rotation of the brake drum.
   ii. The effort required to stop counter clockwise rotation of the brake drum.
   iii. The dimensions of the rectangular cross-section of the brake lever assuming its depth to be twice the width.
   iv. The dimensions of the cross-section of the band assuming its width to be ten times the thickness. (10 Marks)

July/ Aug. 2005 (AU53)

8. A multi disc plate clutch consists of 5 steel plates and 4 bronze plates. The inner and outer diameters of the friction disc are 75 mm and 150 mm respectively. The coefficient of friction is 0.1. Intensity of pressure is limited to 0.3 MPa. Assuming uniform wear theory, calculate the following:

i. The required operating force.
ii. The power transmitting capacity at 750 rpm. **(10 Marks)**

Jan./ Feb. 2006 (AU53)

9. a. Design a cone clutch to transmit a power of 40 kW at a rated speed of 750 rpm. Also determine
    i. Axial force necessary to transmit torque
    ii. Axial force necessary to engage the cone clutch. **(10 Marks)**
  b. A simple band brake shown in **Fig. 6.41** is to be designed to stop the rotation of a shaft transmitting a power of 45 kW at a rated speed of 500 rpm. Selecting suitable materials determine
    i. Dimensions of rectangular cross-section of the band.
    ii. Dimensions of rectangular cross-section of the brake lever.
    iii. Diameter of the fulcrum pin. **(10 Marks)**

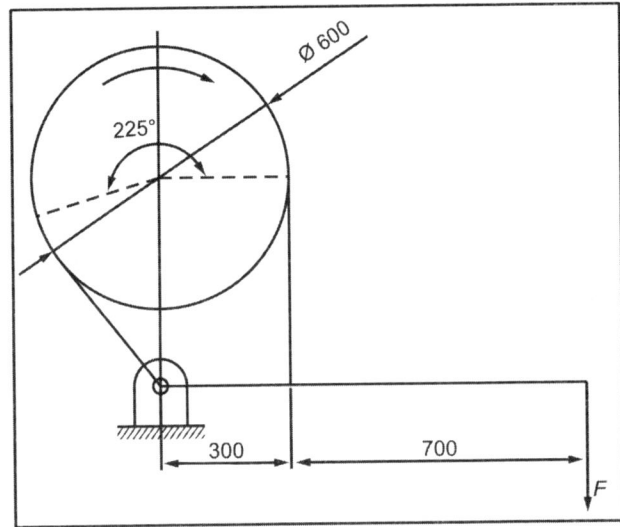

Fig. 6.41

Dec. 06/ Jan. 2007 (AU53)

10. a. A multi plate clutch with steel on bronze is to transmit 8 kW at 1440 rpm. The inner diameter of contact is 80 mm and the outer diameter of contact is 140 mm. The clutch operates in oil with expected coefficient of friction 0.1 and allowable pressure of 0.35 MPa. Assume uniform wear theory and determine the number of steel and bronze plates. **(10 Marks)**
   b. A differential band brake shown in **Fig. 6.42** operates on a drum of diameter 600 mm. The band is 3.2 mm × 100 mm and coefficient of friction is 0.22. Determine
     i. Least force required at the end of operating lever when the band is subjected to a stress of 55 N/mm².
     ii. Torque applied to the brake drum shaft.
     iii. Is the brake self locking? Prove your answer. **(10 Marks)**

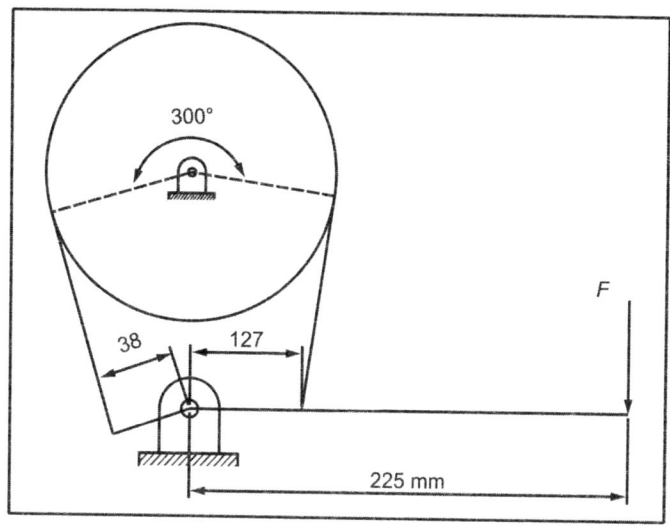

Fig. 6.42

July 2007 (AU53)

11. a. An engine developing 50 kW at 1000 rpm is fitted with a cone clutch. The cone has a face angle of 12.5° and width of face is one-fourth of mean diameter of friction lining. If the normal intensity of pressure between the contact surface is not to exceed 0.1 N/mm², assuming uniform wear criterion and taking $\mu = 0.2$, calculate the dimensions of the clutch. **(10 Marks)**

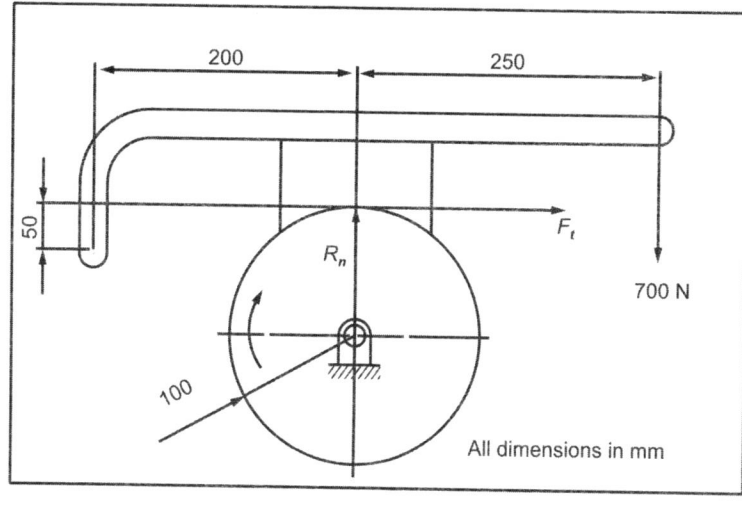

Fig. 6.43

b. The diameter of the drum of a single block brake shown in **Fig. 6.43** is 200 mm and the angle of contact is 90°. If an operating force of 700 N is applied at the end of a lever and the coefficient of friction between the drum and the lining is 0.35, determine the torque that may be transmitted by the block brake. **(10 Marks)**

Dec. 07/ Jan. 2008 (AU53)

12. a. A cone clutch with face angle 12.5° is to transmit 7.5 kW at 900 rpm. The width of the face is half of mean radius and the normal pressure between the contact

faces is not to exceed 0.09 MN/m². Assuming uniform wear and the coefficient of friction between the contact faces as 0.2, determine the dimensions of the clutch and the axial force required to engage the clutch. **(10 Marks)**

b. A band brake as shown in **Fig. 6.44** uses a V-belt. The pitch diameter of the V-grooved pulley is 400 mm. The groove angle is 45° and the coefficient of friction is 0.3. Determine the power rating. **(10 Marks)**

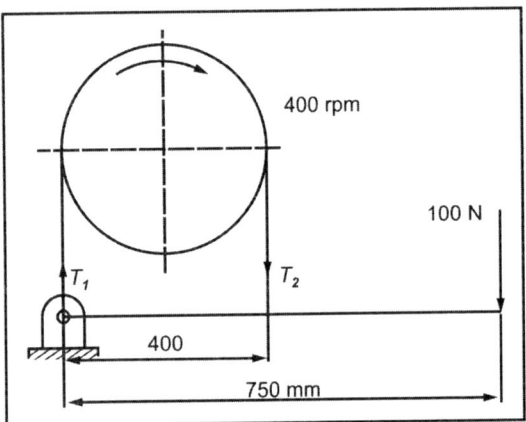

Fig. 6.44

June/ July 2008 (AU53)

13. A single plate clutch both sides effective is required to transmit 25 kW at 1600 rpm. The outer diameter of the plate is limited to 0.3 m and the intensity of pressure is not to exceed 0.07 MPa. Assuming uniform wear and the coefficient of friction 0.3, determine the diameter of the plate and the axial force necessary to engage the clutch. **(10 Marks)**

June/ July 2009 (ME6T2)

14. a. Design a cone clutch from the following data:
    Power transmitted = 8 kW;
    Speed of driving shaft = 900 rpm;
    Coefficient of lining = 0.3;
    Allowable pressure for lining = 0.25 N/mm²;
    Maximum clutch diameter = 300 mm.
    Cone angle = 20°. **(10 Marks)**

    b. A simple band brake for a drum diameter 700 mm has the band passing over it with an angle of contact of 240°, while one end is connected to a brake lever at a distance of 450 mm from the fulcrum. The brake lever is 1000 mm long. The brake is to absorb a power of 17 kW at 900 rpm. Design the brake band if the allowable stress in the band is limited to 40 MPa. **(10 Marks)**

Dec. 08/ Jan. 2009 (AU53)

15. a. With the help of a neat sketch derive an equation for torque transmitting capacity of a single plate clutch, considering uniform wear. **(05 Marks)**

    b. A cone clutch is to be designed to transmit 40 N-m of torque. The semi-cone angle is 12.5°. The mean radius of clutch is twice the face width, coefficient of friction, μ = 0.18, normal intensity of pressure between contacting surfaces should not exceed 0.1 N/mm². Considering uniform wear calculate:

i. The inner and outer diameter of friction layer;
ii. Face width of friction layer; and
iii. Force required to engage the clutch. **(09 Marks)**

c. A band brake shown in **Fig. 6.45**, the width and thickness of the band are 100 mm and 3 mm respectively. Permissible stress in the band material is limited to 50 N/mm^2, coefficient of friction between band and drum is 0.25. Calculate:
   i. Tensions in the band
   ii. Actuating force
   iii. Torque capacity of the brake.
   iv. Also check for self locking **(06 Marks)**

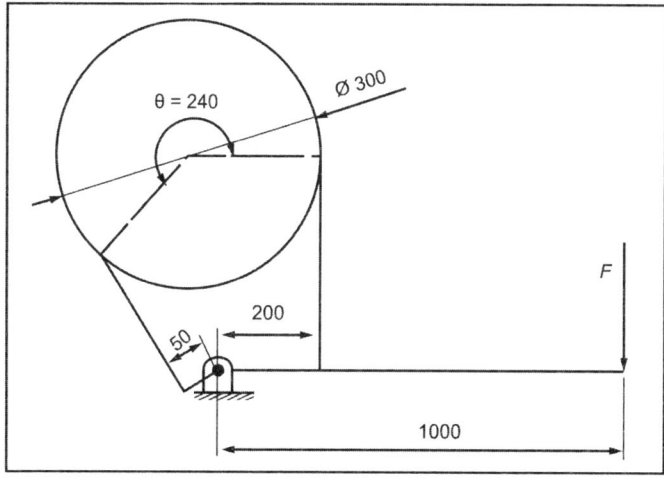

Fig. 6.45

June/ July 2009 (AU53)

16. a. Show that the mean radius of friction surface is given by $R = (r_1 + r_2)/2$ where r_1 and r_2 are the minimum and maximum radii of friction disc, under uniform wear conditions. **(06 Marks)**

b. A spring closed thrustor operated double shoe brake is to be designed for a maximum torque capacity of 3000 N-m. The brake drum diameter is not to exceed 1m and the shoes are to be lined with Ferrodo having a coefficient of friction of 0.3. The rest of the dimensions are shown in **Fig. 6.46**.

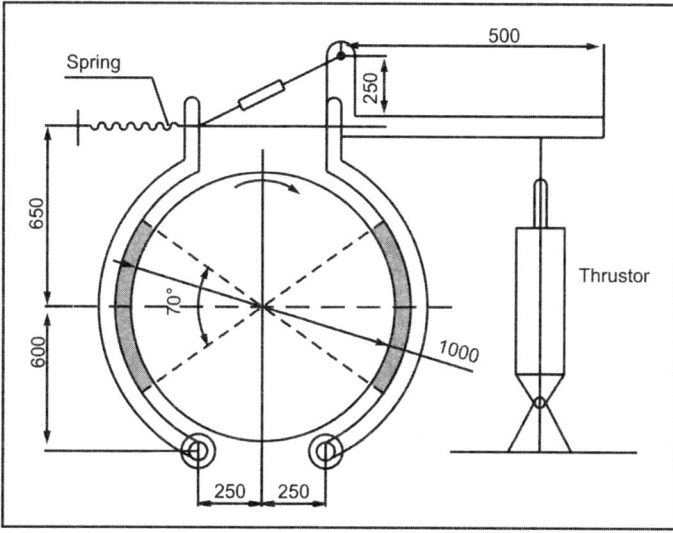

Fig. 6.46

i. Find the spring force necessary to set the brake.
ii. Find the width of the brakes if the bearing pressure on the lining material is not to exceed 0.5 N/mm^2,
iii. Calculate the force required to be exerted by the thrustor to release the brake. **(14 Marks)**

June/ July 2009 (06ME61)

17. a. A multiple disc clutch has five plates having four pairs of active friction surfaces. If the intensity of pressure is not to exceed 0.127 N/mm^2, find the power transmitted at 500 rpm. The outer and inner radii of friction surfaces are 125 mm and 75 mm respectively. Assume uniform wear and take coefficient of friction as 0.3. **(05 Marks)**

b. A differential band brake as shown in **Fig. 6.47** has an angle of contact of 225°. The band has a compressed woven lining and bears against a cast iron drum of 350 mm diameter. The brake is to sustain a torque of 350 N-m and the coefficient of friction between the band and the drum is 0.3. Find:
i. The necessary force, P for clockwise rotation and anti clockwise rotation of the drum.
ii. The value of OA for the brake to be self locking, when the drum rotates clockwise. **(15 Marks)**

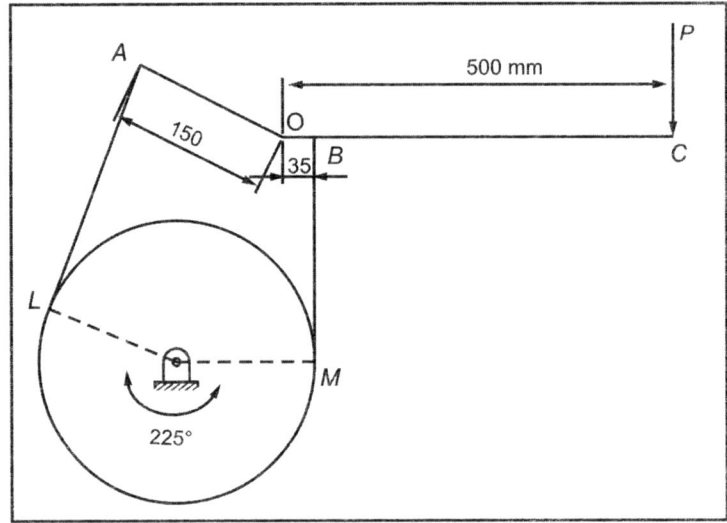

Fig. 6.47

Dec. 09/ Jan. 2010 (06ME61)

18. a. A single plate friction clutch of both sides effective has 0.3 m outer diameter and 0.16 m inner diameter. The coefficient of friction is 0.2 and it runs at 1000 rpm. Find the power transmitted for uniform wear and uniform pressure distribution cases if the allowable maximum pressure is 0.08 MPa. **(10 Marks)**

b. In a simple band brake, the length of the lever is 440 mm. The tight end of the band is attached to the fulcrum of the lever and the slack end to a pin 50 mm from the fulcrum. The diameter of the brake drum is 1 m and arc of contact is 300°. The coefficient of friction between the band and the drum is 0.35. The brake drum is attached to a hoisting drum of diameter 0.65 m that sustains a load of 20 kN. Determine:

i. Force required at the end of lever to just support the load.
ii. Width of steel band if the tensile stress is limited to 50 N/mm².

(10 Marks)

May/ June 2010 (AU53)

19. An engine developing 50 kW at 1000 rpm is fitted with a cone clutch built inside the flywheel. The cone has a face angle of 12.5° and a maximum mean diameter of 550 mm. The coefficient of friction is 0.2. The normal pressure on the clutch face is not to exceed 0.12 N/mm². Determine:
    i the face width required
    ii the axial spring force necessary to engage the clutch. **(10 Marks)**

Dec. 2010 (AU53)

20. a. The following data are given for a dry single plate clutch:
    Power = 18.65 kW, speed = 1500 rpm, number of springs = 6, ratio of mean radius to radial width = 4.5, find:
    i. Mean radius and width of friction surfaces.
    ii. Dimensions of clutch plate.
    iii. Dimensions of springs (only load/ spring). **(10 Marks)**
    b. **Figure 6.48** shown is a cast iron brake shoe. The coefficient of friction is 0.30. The braking torsional moment is to be 346 N. Determine:
    i The force P, for anticlockwise rotation
    ii The force P, for clockwise rotation
    iii. Where must be the pivot be placed to make the brake self-energizing with the counter clockwise direction. **(10 Marks)**

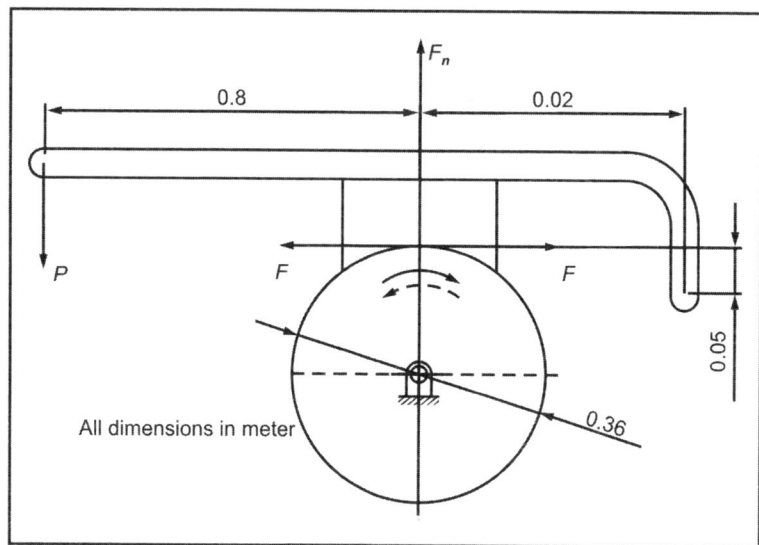

Fig. 6.48

May/ June 2010 (06ME61)

21. a. Derive power transmitting capacity of a single plate clutch for
    i. Uniform pressure condition and   ii. Uniform wear condition.

(10 Marks)

b. A single block brake with a torque capacity of 250 N-m is shown in **Fig. 6.49**. The brake drum rotates at 100 rpm and the coefficient of friction is 0.35. Calculate:
   i. The actuating force and the hinge-pin reaction;
   ii. The rate of heat generated during the braking action; and
   iii. The dimensions of the block, if the intensity of pressure between the block and brake drum is 1 MPa. The length of the block is twice the width.
   (10 Marks)

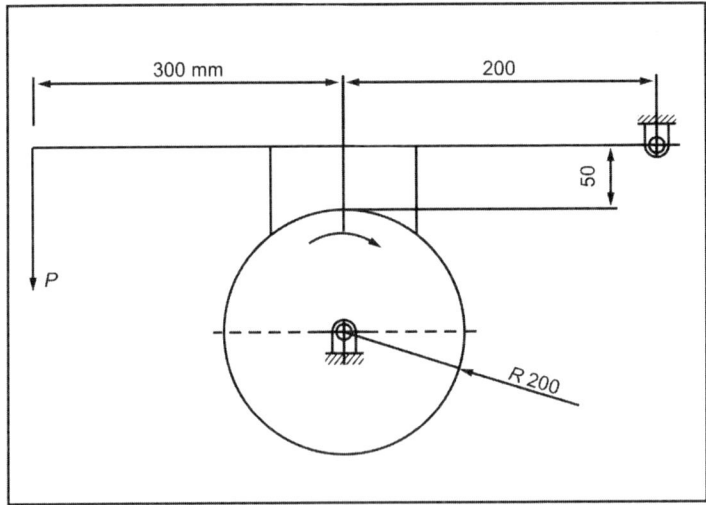

Fig. 6.49

Dec. 2010 (06ME61)

22. a. Design a single plate clutch having both sides effective from the following data:
   Power transmitted = 30 kW;
   Speed of shaft = 1500 rpm;
   Allowable lining pressure = 0.147 MPa;
   Maximum diameter of the clutch = 300 mm;
   Service factor = 1.5; Number of springs = 9;
   Compression of spring during engagement = 2.5 mm. **(12 Marks)**

   b. Determine the torque that may be resisted by a single block brake shown in **Fig. 6.50** below for a coefficient of friction 0.3. **(08 Marks)**

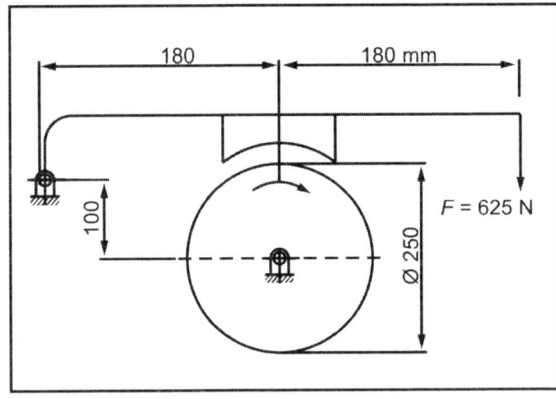

Fig. 6.50

June/ July 2011 (06ME61)

23. a. Determine the dimensions of a simple cone clutch to transmit 20 kW at 1000 rpm. The minimum diameter is to be 300 mm and the cone angle 20°. Assume $\mu = 0.2$ and permissible pressure = 0.1 N/mm^2. Also determine the axial force required to engage the clutch. **(12 Marks)**

b. A differential band brake is as shown in **Fig. 6.51**. The width and thickness of the steel band are 100 mm and 3 mm respectively and the maximum tensile stress in the band is 50 N/mm^2. The coefficient of friction between the friction lining and the brake drum is 0.25. Calculate:
   i. The tensions in the band;
   ii. The actuating force;
   iii. The torque capacity of the brake. **(08 Marks)**

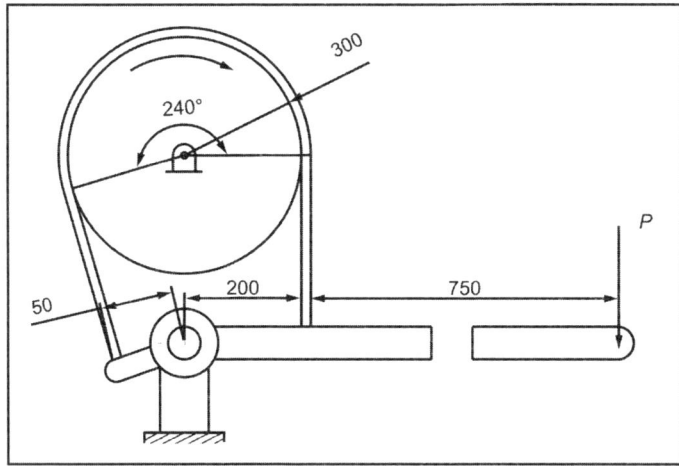

Fig. 6.51

Dec. 2011 (06ME61)

24. a. A multiple clutch has steel on bronze is to transmit 8 kW at 1440 rpm. The inner diameter of the contact is 80 mm and the outer diameter of contact is 140 mm. The clutch operates in oil with expected coefficient of friction of 0.1, the average allowable pressure is 0.35 MPa. Assume uniform wear theory and determine the following:
   i. No. of steel and bronze plates.
   ii. Axial force required.
   iii. Actual maximum pressure. **(10 Marks)**

b. A frictional cone clutch has to transmit a torque of 200 N/m at 1440 rpm. The larger diameter of the cone is 350 mm, the pitch angle is 6.254°. The face width is 65 mm. The coefficient of friction is 0.2. Determine:
   i. The axial force required to transmit the torque.
   ii. The average normal pressure on the contact surface with the maximum torque is transmitted. **(10 Marks)**

June 2012 (06ME61)

25. a. A multi plate clutch consists of 5 steel plates and four bronze plates. The inner and outer diameter of friction disks are 75 mm and 150 mm respectively. The coefficient of friction is 0.1 and the intensity of pressure is limited to 0.3 N/mm^2. Assuming uniform wear theory, calculate:

i. The required operating force;
ii. power transmitting capacity at 750 r/min. (10 Marks)

b. A differential band brake is shown in **Fig. 6.52**. The width and thickness of the steel band are 100 mm and 3 mm respectively. The permissible tensile stress in the band is limited to 50 MPa. The coefficient of friction between the friction lining and the drum is 0.25. Calculate:
  i. Tensions in the band.
  ii. the actuating force.
  iii. Torque capacity of the brake. (10 Marks)

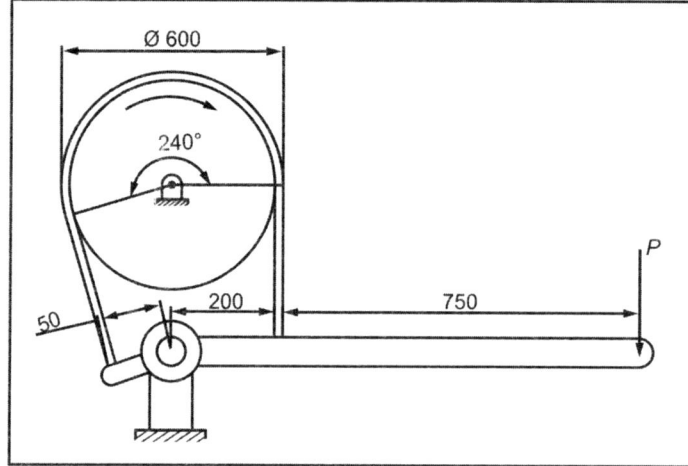

Fig. 6.52

December 2012 (06ME12)

26. a. In a multiple disc clutch, the radial width of the friction material is to be 0.2 of the maximum radius. The coefficient of friction is 0.25. The clutch is to transmit 60 kW at 3000 rpm. Its maximum diameter is 250 mm and the axial force is limited to 600 N. Determine:
  i. Number of driving and driven discs.
  ii. Mean unit pressure on each contact surface.
  Assume uniform wear. (10 Marks)

b. In a band and block brake $\theta = 15°$ and effective diameter is 800 mm. $P = 0.4$, $a = 100$ mm, $b = 25$ mm. The power absorbed at 600 rpm is 450 kW when the force applied at the end of lever at a distance of 1.20 m from the fulcrum is 200 N. Find the number of blocks. (10 Marks)

June/ July 2013 (AU53)

27. a. A clutch is 300 mm, while the face width of the contacting surface of the friction lining is 100 mm. The coefficient of friction is 0.2 and maximum intensity of pressure is limited to 0.07 MPa. Calculate the operating force and the power transmitting capacity. (10 Marks)

b. A differential band brake is shown in **Fig. 6.53**. The width and thickness of the steel band is 100 mm and 3 mm respectively. The permissible tensile stress in the band is limited to 50 MPa. The coefficient of friction between the friction lining and the drum is 0.25. Calculate:

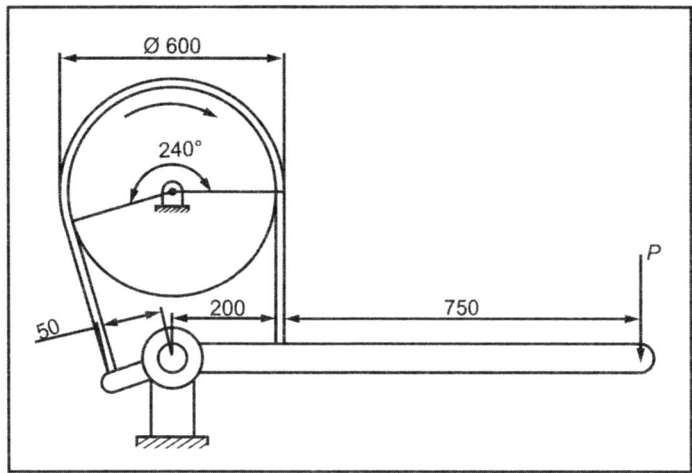

Fig. 6.53

   i. Tensions in the band.
   ii. Actuating force.
   iii. Torque capacity of the brake, and
   iv. Find out whether the brake is self locking. (10 Marks)

June/ July 2013 (06ME61)

28. a. Design a cone clutch to transmit 40 kW at 750 rpm. Also determine the
    i. axial force required to transmit the torque,
    ii. axial force required to engage the clutch.
    Assume $\mu = 0.4$ and $p = 0.2$ N/mm² for the friction material ($\alpha = 12.5°$). Take $D_m/b = 6$. (10 Marks)
 b. The band brake shown in **Fig. 6.54** uses a V-belt. The pitch diameter of the V-grooved pulley is 400 mm, the groove angle is 45° and coefficient of friction is 0.3. Determine the power rating of the brake. (10 Marks)

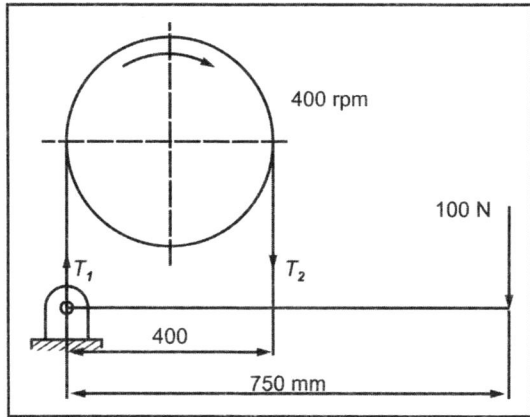

Fig. 6.54

June/ July 2013 (10ME62)

29. a. A multiple clutch has steel on bronze is to transmit 8 kW at 1440 rev/min. The inner diameter of contact is 80 mm and the outer diameter of contact is 140 mm.

The clutch operates in oil with expected coefficient of friction of 0.1. The allowable pressure is 0.35 MPa. Assume uniform wear theory and determine the following:
  i. Number of steel and bronze plates.
  ii. Axial force required.
  iii. Actual maximum pressure. **(10 Marks)**
b. A simple band brake of drum diameter 600 mm has a band passing over it with an angle of contact of 225°, while one end is connected to the fulcrum, the other end is connected to the brake lever at a distance of 400 mm from the fulcrum. The brake lever is 1 m long. The brake is to absorb a power of 15 kW at 720 rpm. Design the brake lever of rectangular cross-section assuming depth to be thrice the width. Take allowable stress as 80 MPa. **(10 Marks)**

Dec.2013/ Jan.2014 (10ME62)

30. a. A cone clutch has a semi cone angle of 12°. It is to transmit 10 kW power at 750 r/min, the width of the face is one-fourth the mean diameter of friction lining. If normal intensity of pressure between contacting surfaces is not to exceed 0.085 N/mm² and coefficient of friction is 0.2, assuming uniform wear conditions, calculate the dimensions of the clutch. **(10 Marks)**
  b. A band brake arrangement is as shown in **Fig. 6.55**. It is used to generate a maximum braking torque of 200 N-m. Determine the actuating force 'P', if the coefficient of friction is 0.25. The angle of wrap of the band is 270°. Determine the maximum pressure intensity, if the band width is 30 mm. **(10 Marks)**

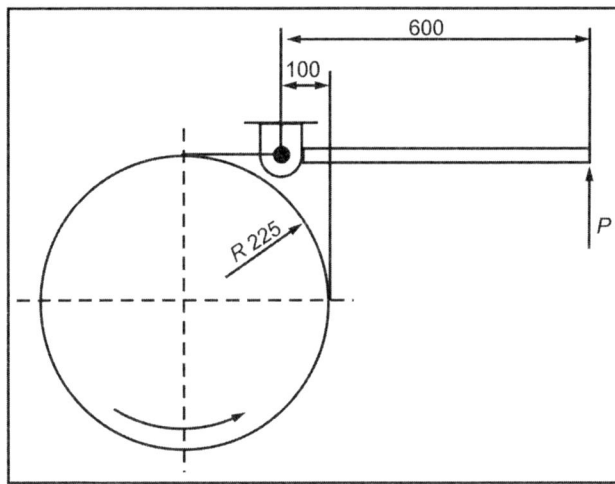

Fig. 6.55

Dec. 2013/ Jan. 2014 (AU53)

31. a. A soft surface cone clutch has an inclined angle of 20 degrees, mean diameter of cone is 300 mm, face width is 100 mm, expected coefficient of friction is 0.2 and the average (mean) pressure is limited to 70 kPa. Calculate the following:
  i. minimum and maximum diameter of the cone;
  ii. axial force required to transmit the torque;
  iii. power that can be transmitted at 710 r/min iv. axial force needed to engage the clutch. **(08 Marks)**

b. A multi plate clutch consists of 5 steel and 4 bronze plates. The torque to be transmitted is 18.5 N-m. The inner diameter of the plate is 50 mm and the outer diameter is 100 mm. The coefficient of friction is 0.1. Determine the axial force needed to transmit the above torque. Determine the maximum normal pressure.

(04 Marks)

c. A band brake is shown in **Fig. 6.56**. What is the power that the brake can sustain? The allowable tensile stress for the band material is 200 MPa and the thickness of the band is 4 mm. Determine the breadth of the band and the power that the brake can sustain. Ratio of tight side to slack side tension is 1.75.

(08 Marks)

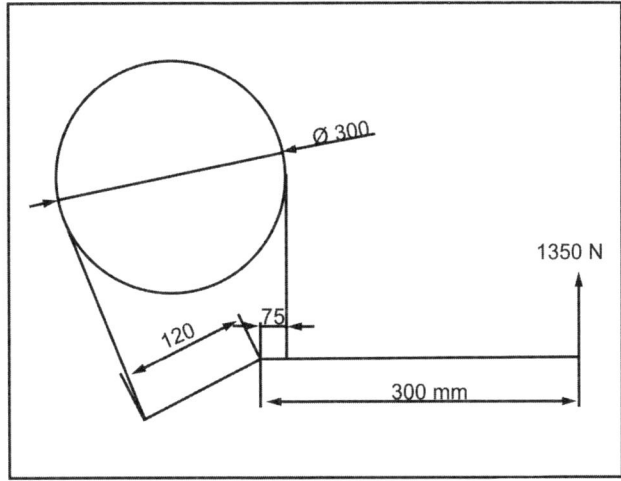

Fig. 6.56

7 Lubrication and Bearings

7.1 INTRODUCTION TO LUBRICATION

Lubrication is the process of reducing the friction and wear between two rubbing surfaces by the introduction of a substance called lubricant. Lubricants are classified as:

1. Solids
2. Liquids
3. Semi-liquids and
4. Gas films

Solid lubricants are often used to reduce dry or boundary friction, but they do not contribute to the heat transfer of the dissipated friction energy. Greases and waxes are widely used for light-duty bearings, as are solid lubricants such as graphite and molybdenum disulphide (MoS_2). In addition, coatings of polymers such as PTFE (Teflon) and polyethylene can reduce friction and are used successfully in light-duty applications.

On the other hand, **liquid lubricants** are used in much larger quantities in industry and transportation because they have several advantages over solid lubricants. The most important advantages of liquid lubricants are the formation of hydrodynamic films, the cooling of the bearing by effective convection heat transfer, and finally their relative convenience for use in bearings. The most common liquid lubricants are mineral oils and synthetic oils.

Mineral oils are made from petroleum. Mineral oils are blends of base oils with many different additives to improve the lubrication characteristics. These are widely used because they are available at relatively low cost. In addition, they contain many additives to improve performance, such as oxidation inhibitors, rust-prevention additives, antifoaming agents, and high-pressure agents. A long list of additives is used, based on each particular application.

The synthetic oils are more expensive, and they are applied only whenever the higher cost can be financially justified. Blends of mineral and synthetic base oils are used for specific applications where unique lubrication characteristics are required.

Grease is a **semi-liquid** lubricant having higher viscosity than oils. Greases are employed where slow speed and heavy pressure exist and where oil drip from the bearing is undesirable. This is widely used, particularly for the lubrication of rolling-element bearings and gears.

Gas can also be used as a lubricant in the same way as oil is used in a hydrodynamic bearing. The main difference arises from the fact that gas has a much lower viscosity than that of oil.

7.2 PURPOSE OF LUBRICANTS

- Keep moving parts apart
- Reduce friction
- Transfer heat
- Carry away contaminants and debris
- Transmit power
- Protect against wear
- Prevent corrosion
- Seal for gases
- Stop the risk of smoke and fire of objects

7.3 SELECTION OF THE PROPER LUBRICANT

This is an important design function in the use of bearings, since lubricant affects bearing life and operation. The major functions of lubrication in bearing application are:

- To minimize friction at points of contact within the bearing.
- To protect the precision finishes on bearing surfaces from becoming corroded.
- To dissipate heat generated within the bearing.
- To remove or prevent the entry of foreign matter within the bearing.

7.4 LUBRICATION REGIMES

The thickness of the fluid film determines the lubrication regime, or the type of lubrication. The basic regimes of fluid film lubrication are:

1. Hydrodynamic lubrication – two surfaces are separated by a fluid film,
2. Elasto-hydrodynamic lubrication – two surfaces are separated by a very thin fluid film,
3. Mixed lubrication – two surfaces are partly separated, partly in contact, and,
4. Boundary lubrication – two surfaces mostly are in contact with each other even though a fluid is present.

7.4.1 Hydrodynamic or Full Fluid Film Lubrication

When a fluid lubricant is present between two rolling and/or sliding surfaces, a thicker pressurized film can be generated by the movement of the surfaces (velocities). The non-compressible nature of this film separates the surfaces resulting in no metal to metal contact.

The condition in which surfaces are completely separated by a continuous film of lubricating fluid is commonly referred to as **Hydrodynamic –or- Full Fluid Film Lubrication,** as shown in **Fig. 7.1**. In this regime, the lubricant adjacent to each surface travels at the same speed and direction of each surface.

Hydrodynamic film thickness can be formed by wedging the lubricant through a convergent gap with the tangential surface velocities, known as wedging film action, (similar to a car tire hydroplaning on a wet road surface).

Factors which affect hydrodynamic lubrication include:

- Lubricant viscosity,
- Rotation speed or rpm,

- Oil supply pressure and component loading.
- An increase in speed or viscosity increases oil film thickness.
- An increase in load decreases oil film thickness.

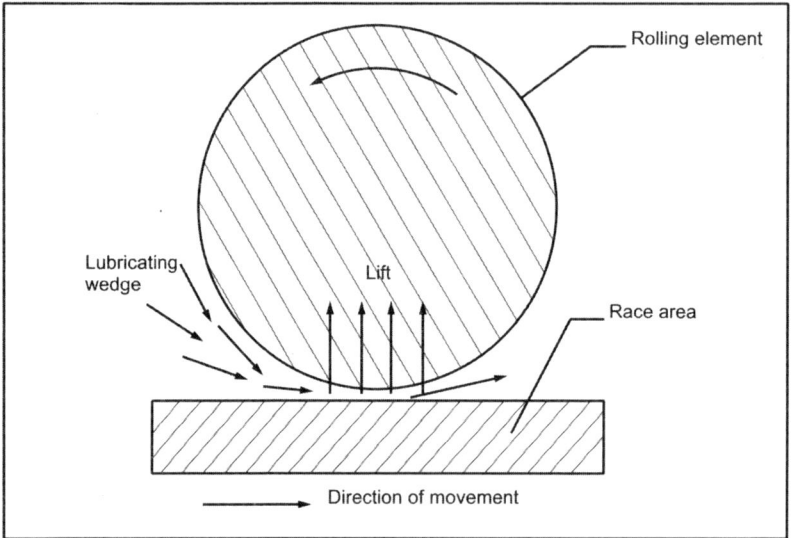

Fig. 7.1: Hydrodynamic lubrication

7.4.2 Boundary Lubrication –or– Thin Film Lubrication

Boundary lubrication as shown in **Fig. 7.2**, is a condition in which the lubricant film becomes too thin to provide total separation. This may be due to excessive loading, speeds –or– a change in the fluid's characteristics. In such a situation, contact between surface asperities (peaks and valleys) occurs.

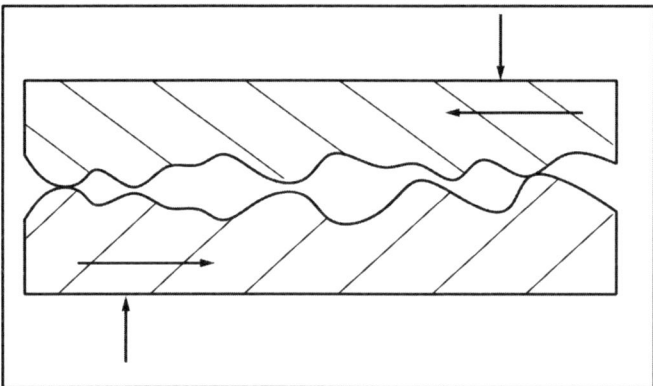

Fig. 7.2: Boundary lubrication

Friction reduction and wear protection is then provided via chemical compounds rather than properties of the lubricating fluid. Boundary lubrication often occurs during the start up and shut down of equipment or when loading becomes excessive.

7.4.3 Mixed Film Lubrication

This is a combination of both hydrodynamic and boundary lubrication. In such a situation only occasional asperity contact occurs.

7.4.4 Elastohydrodynamic Lubrication (EHD –or– EHL)

Figure 7.3 represents elastohydrodynamic lubrication. This occurs as pressure or load increases to a level where the viscosity of the lubricant provides higher shear strength than the metal surface it supports. This regime can occur in roller bearings or gears as the lubricant is carried into the convergent zone approaching a contact area or the intersection of two asperities. As a result the metal surfaces deform elastically in preference to the highly pressurized lubricant, which increases the contact area and thus increasing the effectiveness of the lubricant.

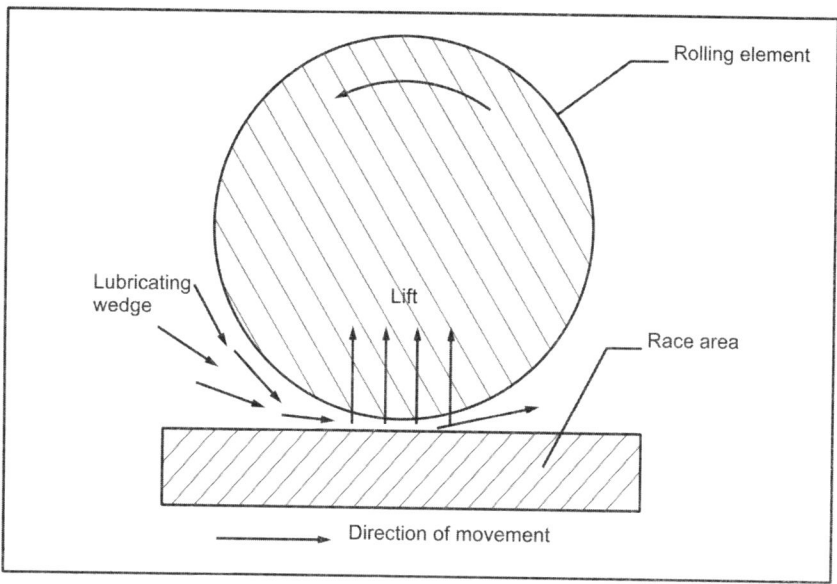

Fig. 7.3: Elastohydrodynamic lubrication

Note: Hydrodynamic lubrication principle can be applied to full and partial journal bearings as well as thrust bearings, the basic requirement being a converging space between the stationary and moving parts.

7.5 PROPERTIES OF LUBRICANTS

The main properties of lubricants, which are usually indicated in the technical characteristics of the product, are:

1. **Viscosity:** It is the ability of a fluid to resist change in shape. This resistance is due to internal friction and its molecular phenomenon. The ability of a fluid film to carry load depends upon the viscosity of the lubricant. As the fluid resists flow, work done on fluid is converted into heat and hence the temperature of the fluid and its surroundings increases.

   It is of two types:

   a. Viscosity/Absolute viscosity/Dynamic viscosity   b. Kinematic viscosity

   a. **Viscosity/Absolute viscosity/Dynamic viscosity:** It may be defined as the force required in moving a plane surface having unit area over another plate with unit velocity, separated by a layer of fluid of unit thickness.

   According to Newton's law of viscous flow, "the shear stress in a fluid is directly proportional to the rate of change of velocity –or– velocity gradient –or– rate of shear.

$$\tau \propto \frac{dv}{dy}$$

i.e. $\quad\quad \tau = Z\dfrac{dv}{dy} \quad\quad$ ...(Eq. 7.1)

In general, $\quad\quad \tau = \dfrac{F}{A} \quad\quad$ ...(Eq. 7.2)

From Eqs (7.1) and (7.2), we have

$$\tau = \frac{F}{A} = Z\frac{dv}{dy} \quad \text{MPa} \quad \text{...(Eq. 7.3)} \; \mathbf{15.1a/\ Pg\ 301,\ DHB}$$

F – frictional force (N), $\quad A$ – area (mm²)
Z – absolute or dynamic viscosity (N-s/m² –or– Pa-s)

$\dfrac{dv}{dy}$ = rate of change of velocity with distance or velocity gradient
 –or– rate of shear (m/s²)

If the rate of shear is constant, then

$$\frac{dv}{dy} = \frac{v}{y} = \frac{v}{h}$$

∴ Eq. (7.3) yields ... $\quad\quad \tau = Z\left(\dfrac{v}{h}\right) \quad\quad$ ...(Eq. 7.3a)

$$\tau = \frac{Z}{1000}\left(\frac{v}{h}\right) \text{ (MPa)} \quad \text{...(Eq. 7.4)} \; \mathbf{15.1b/\ Pg\ 301,\ DHB}$$

v = velocity (m/s),
h = thickness of the lubricant (mm)

Note: $\tau = \left(\dfrac{N-s}{m^2}\right)\left(\dfrac{m/s}{mm}\right) = \left(\dfrac{N}{m}\right)\left(\dfrac{1}{mm}\right) = \left(\dfrac{N}{(1000)\,mm}\right)\left(\dfrac{1}{mm}\right) = \left(\dfrac{1}{1000}\right)\dfrac{N}{mm^2}$

b. **Kinematic viscosity:** It is defined as the ratio of absolute viscosity to mass density of the fluid.

$$Z_k = \frac{Z}{\rho} \times 10^{-3} \quad (m^2/s) \quad \text{...(Eq. 7.5)} \; \mathbf{15.2a/\ Pg\ 301,\ DHB}$$

Z_k = Kinematic viscosity (N-s/m² or Pa-s)
ρ = Specific gravity

Since the most widely used unit of measurement of viscosity is the centistokes (cSt).

$$Z_k = Z'_k \times 10^{-6} \quad (m^2/s) \quad \text{...(Eq. 7.6a)} \; \mathbf{15.2b/\ Pg\ 301,\ DHB}$$

Kinematic viscosity, $Z'_k = \dfrac{Z(cP)}{\rho}$ (cSt) $\quad\quad$ ...(Eq. 7.6b) $\mathbf{15.2b/\ Pg\ 301,\ DHB}$

cP – centipoise

- The specific gravity of oil at any temperature is found as
$$\rho_t = \rho_{15} - 0.00063 (t° - 15) \quad \text{...(Eq. 7.7)} \; \textbf{15.3/ Pg 301, DHB}$$
Value of ρ_{15} obtained from **Table 15.1/ Pg 308, DHB**, based on **Fig. 15.1/Pg 316, DHB**.

- The kinematic viscosity in centistokes from **Saybolt seconds:**

$$Z'_k = \left(0.226 S' - \frac{195}{S'}\right) \quad \text{for } 32 < S' < 100 \quad \text{...(Eq. 7.8a)} \; \textbf{15.4a/ Pg 301, DHB}$$

$$Z'_k = \left(0.220 S' - \frac{135}{S'}\right) \quad \text{for } S' > 100 \quad \text{...(Eq. 7.8b)} \; \textbf{15.4b/ Pg 301, DHB}$$

S' – the number of Saybolt seconds

- The kinematic viscosity in centistokes from **Redwood units:**

→ **For Redwood No. 1:**

$$Z'_k = \left(0.260 R - \frac{179}{R}\right) \quad \text{for } 34 < R < 100 \quad \text{...(Eq. 7.9a)} \; \textbf{15.5a/ Pg 301, DHB}$$

$$Z'_k = \left(0.247 R - \frac{50}{R}\right) \quad \text{for } R > 100 \quad \text{...(Eq. 7.9b)} \; \textbf{15.5b/ Pg 301, DHB}$$

→ **For Redwood Admiralty:**

$$Z'_k = \left(2.7 R - \frac{2000}{R}\right) \quad \text{...(Eq. 7.10)} \; \textbf{15.5c/ Pg 302, DHB}$$

R – the number of Redwood seconds

- The kinematic viscosity in centistokes from **Engler number:**

$$Z'_k = \left(0.147 E - \frac{347}{E}\right) \quad \text{...(Eq. 7.11)} \; \textbf{15.6/ Pg 301, DHB}$$

E – Engler number

Note: From **Pg 300/ DHB**, we have

- $1 \; poise \; (P) = 10^{-1} \frac{N-s}{m^2}$ $\left[1 \frac{N-s}{m^2} = 1 Pa - s\right]$

- $1 \; centpoise \; (cP) = 10^{-3} \frac{N-s}{m^2}$

- $1 \; stoke \; (St) = 10^{-4} \frac{m^2}{s}$

- $1 \; centistoke \; (cSt) = 10^{-6} \frac{m^2}{s}$

2. **Viscosity index:** The viscosity index is a characteristic, expressed on a conventional scale, to indicate variations in the viscosity of lubricating oils with changes in temperature. In other words, the viscosity index measures the variations in the viscosity with changes in temperature; the higher the level of the viscosity index, the lower the variation in viscosity at temperature.

3. **Flash point:** Flash point is the lowest temperature at which application of a flame causes oil vapors to give a momentary flash. Flash point is used to assess the overall hazard of a material.

4. **Fire point:** It is the lowest temperature at which the application of a flame causes the oil vapors to burn continuously.

5. **Pour point:** Refers to the lowest temperature at which the lubricant operates and flows continuously. Below the pour point, the oil tends to thicken and ceases to flow freely. The lower the pour point, the more useful the lubricant is in cold temperatures.

6. **Oiliness:** It is defined as the property of a lubricant to arrange its molecules so as to decrease the resistance of the layers to sliding.

7.6 BEARINGS

Bearing is a machine part whose function is to support a secondary member preventing its motion in the direction of applied load but at the same time allowing the motion in another predetermined direction. The portion of the shaft supported by the bearing is called the '**Journal**'. –OR–

A **bearing** is a connector that permits the connected members to rotate –or– to move relative to one another. Often one of the members is fixed, and the bearing acts as a support for the moving member. Most bearings support rotating shafts against either radial (transverse) –or– axial (thrust) forces.

To minimize friction, the contacting surfaces in a bearing may be partially –or– completely separated by a film of liquid (usually oil) –or– gas. These are *sliding bearings*, and the part of the shaft that turns in the bearing is the journal.

Under certain combinations of force, speed, fluid viscosity, and bearing geometry, a fluid film forms and separates the contacting surfaces in a sliding bearing, and this is known as a **hydrodynamic film**. An oil film can also be developed with a separate pumping unit that supplies pressurized oil to the bearing, and this is known as a **hydrostatic film**.

The surfaces in a bearing may also be separated by balls, rollers, –or– needles; these are known as **rolling bearings**. Further when metal-to-metal contact occurs, low-friction bearing materials such as bronze alloys and babbit metals are used to reduce the friction.

The principal advantage of these bearings is the ability to operate at friction levels considerably lower at startup, the friction coefficient having the values $\mu = 0.001 \pm 0.003$.

7.6.1 Classification of Bearings

1. Depending upon the direction of load to be supported:

    a. Radial bearings, and

    b. Thrust bearings.

    In radial bearings, the load acts perpendicular to the direction of motion of the moving element (perpendicular to shaft axis) as shown in **Fig. 7.4 (a)**. In thrust bearings, the load acts along the axis of rotation (parallel to the shaft axis) as shown in **Fig. 7.4 (b)**.

2. Depending upon the nature of contact:

    a. Sliding contact/Journal/Plain bearings, and

    b. Rolling contact/Antifriction bearings.

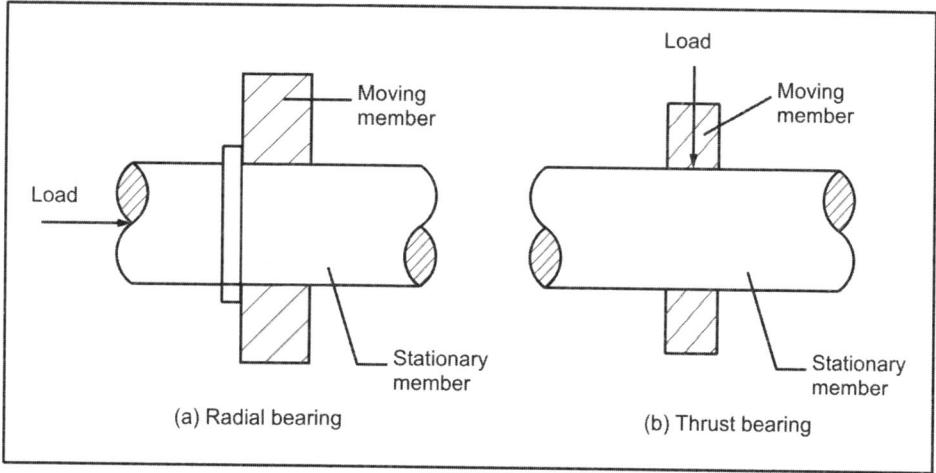

Fig. 7.4: Radial and thrust bearings

In sliding contact bearings, as shown in **Fig. 7.5 (a)**, the sliding takes place along the surfaces of contact between the moving element and the fixed element. The sliding contact bearings are also known as **plain bearings**. In rolling contact bearings, as shown in **Fig. 7.5 (b)**, the steel balls –or- rollers, are interposed between the moving and fixed elements. The balls offer rolling friction at two points for each ball or roller.

The sliding contact bearings in which the sliding action is along the circumference of a circle or an arc of a circle and carrying radial loads are known as **journal –or- sleeve bearings**.

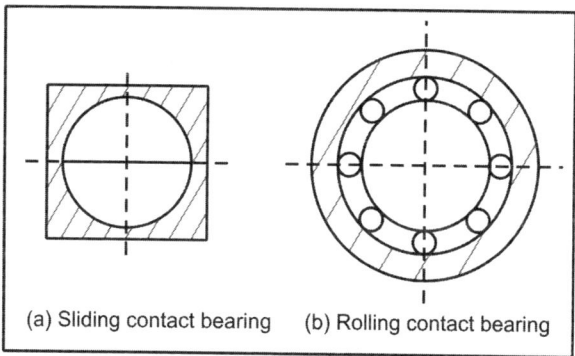

Fig. 7.5: Sliding and rolling contact bearings

When the angle of contact of the bearing with the journal is 360° as shown in **Fig. 7.6 (a)**, then the bearing is called a **full journal bearing**. This type of bearing is commonly used in industrial machinery to accommodate bearing loads in any radial direction.

When the angle of contact of the bearing with the journal is 120°, as shown in **Fig. 7.6 (b),** then the bearing is said to be **partial journal bearing**. This type of bearing has less friction than full journal bearing, but it can be used only where the load is always in one direction. The most common application of the partial journal bearings is found in rail road car axles. The full and partial journal bearings may be called as **clearance bearings** because the diameter of the journal is less than that of bearing.

When a partial journal bearing has no clearance i.e. the diameters of the journal and bearing are equal, then the bearing is called a **fitted bearing**, as shown in **Fig. 7.6 (c)**.

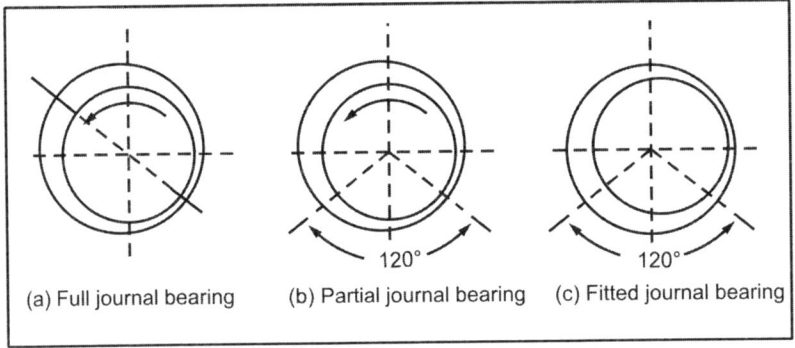

(a) Full journal bearing (b) Partial journal bearing (c) Fitted journal bearing

Fig. 7.6: Sliding contact bearings

Applications: Crank shaft bearings, steam and gas turbines, centrifugal pumps, concrete mixers, rope conveyors, etc

7.6.2 Formation of Continuous Oil Film in a Journal Bearing

A full journal bearing with clearance is as shown in **Fig. 7.7**. Assume that the space between the journal and the bearing is filled with fluid lubricant. In **Fig. 7.7 (a)**, the journal is at rest and is loaded by a vertical load (W). In this case the metal-to-metal contact between the surfaces is at point '1' on the line of action of load. If the journal rotates slowly in the direction as shown in **Fig. 7.7 (b)**, it tends to roll up the bearing surface due to friction between the surfaces. The point of contact at this instant is indicated by '2'. If the speed is so low that the pressure built up in the film can be neglected, the angle α (w.r.t vertical) is equal to the angle of sliding friction between the surfaces. The friction in this case corresponds to boundary/extreme conditions.

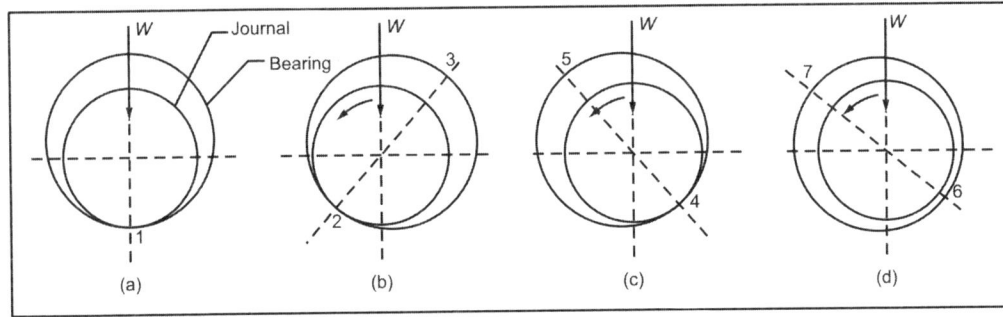

Fig. 7.7: Formation of continuous oil film in a journal bearing

Here the continuous film consists of two parts: a converging part above the line '2-3' and a diverging part below this line. Under these conditions a positive pressure is developed in the converging part of the oil film and tends to move the journal to the right. Now if the journal speed is increased, the pressure forces will overcome the friction at the point of contact and will move the journal towards the right as shown in **Fig. 7.7 (c)**.

As the journal achieves a certain speed, the oil pressure will separate the surfaces of the journal and the bearing, lift the journal and move it to position as shown in **Fig. 7.7 (d)**. The centre of the journal has moved to such a position that the minimum film thickness is now at point '6'. From '6' to '7', in the direction of motion, the oil film is a diverging film while from '7' to '6' it is a converging film and therefore supports the load.

In order to form and maintain the fluid film, it is necessary to supply a sufficient quantity of lubricant to replace that lost due to end leakage from the bearing and to prevent rupture of the continuous film around the journal.

7.7 BEARING MATERIALS

Bearing materials can be metallic or nonmetallic. Included in the metallic category are several types of white metals also called Babbit (tin and lead-based alloys), bronzes, aluminum alloys, and porous metals. Certain thin metallic coatings are widely used, such as white metals, silver, and indium. The nonmetallic bearing materials include plastics, rubber, carbon-graphite, ceramics, cemented carbides, metal oxides, glass, and composites, such as glass-fiber- and carbon-fiber-reinforced PTFE (Teflon).

Nonmetallic materials are widely used for bearings because they offer diversified characteristics that can be applied in a wide range of applications. Generally, they have lower heat conductivity, in comparison to metals; therefore, they are implemented in applications that have a low PV (load–speed product) value. Nonmetallic bearings are selected where self-lubrication and low cost are required (plastic materials) and where high temperature stability must be maintained as well as chemical resistance (e.g., carbon graphite). Nonmetallic bearing materials include the following groups:

- Plastics: PTFE (Teflon), nylon, phenolics, fiber-reinforced plastics, etc.
- Ceramics
- Carbon graphite
- Rubber
- Other diverse materials, such as wood and glass

7.7.1 Properties of Bearing Materials

The bearing materials should have the following properties:

- The material should have good anti-weld and anti-scoring properties.
- Should have high thermal conductivity.
- Good machinability.
- Low cost.
- Resistance to corrosion.
- High fatigue strength
- Low modulus of elasticity.
- Good coefficient of thermal expansion.

Note:

- **Table 15.2/ Pg 308, DHB** *gives data regarding journal bearing materials and applications.*
- **Table 15.3/ Pg 310, DHB** *gives data regarding permissible bearing pressure on journal bearing.*
- **Table 15.4/ Pg 310, DHB** *gives data regarding recommended speeds for some machinery in rpm.*

- **Table 15.5/ Pg 311, DHB** *gives data regarding product of pressure and velocity.*
- **Table 15.6/ Pg 311, DHB** *gives values of C (Bearing characteristic No.) for various combinations of journal & bearings.*
- **Table 15.11/ Pg 314, DHB** *gives design data for bearings.*
- **Table 15.12/ Pg 315, DHB** *gives values of Sommerfeld No. for various h_0/c and L/d ratios.*

7.8 SELECTION OF JOURNAL –OR-ANTIFRICTION BEARING

- When space is a constraint, rolling bearing is preferred.
- Roller bearings produce noise prior to failure, while that of journal bearing is sudden.
- Ball bearings are preferred for small and medium radial loads, while roller bearings are preferred for heavy loads.
- Roller bearings can take a combination of radial and thrust loads.
- For high overloads rolling bearings are preferred.
- Rolling bearings are noisy compared to journal bearings.

7.9 PETROFF'S EQUATION

Consider a vertical shaft rotating in a guide bearing as shown in **Fig. 7.8 (Fig. 15.3/ Pg 316, DHB).**

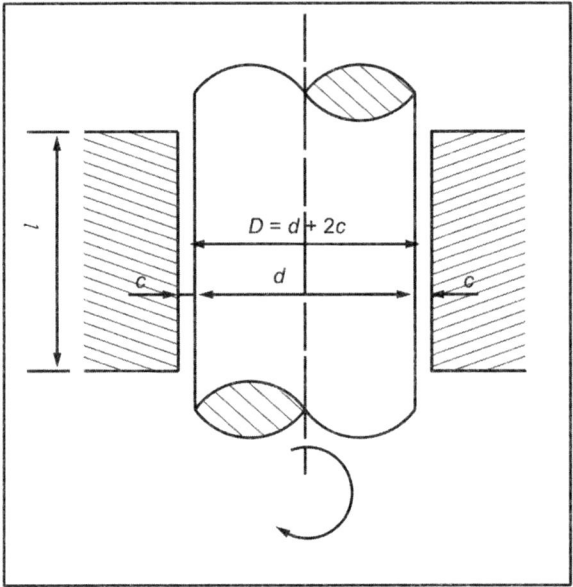

Fig. 7.8: Petroff's equation (Fig. 15.3/Pg 316, DHB)

Let

D = diameter of the bearing = $(d + 2c)$ (mm)
d = diameter of journal or shaft (mm)
c = radial clearance (mm)
l = length of the bearing (mm)

N = speed of the journal (rpm)
n = speed of journal = $N/60$ (rps)
Z = absolute or dynamic viscosity (Pa-s)

Petroff's equation is derived based on the following assumptions:
- The load on the bearing is small or light.
- Leakage (if any) is negligible.
- Clearance between the journal and the bearing is filled with lubricant (oil).
- Viscosity is constant throughout the oil film.

1. **Frictional force:**

We know that, $\tau = \dfrac{F}{A} = Z\left(\dfrac{v}{h}\right)$ ...(Eq. 7.12) **15.1a & b/ Pg 301, DHB**

i.e. $\quad F = \dfrac{ZAv}{h}$ ...(Eq. 7.13)

$\qquad v = \pi d n$ (m/s)
$\qquad A = \pi d l = 2\pi r l$ – surface area (mm²)
$\qquad h = c$ – clearance (mm)

$\therefore \quad F = \dfrac{Z(\pi d l)(\pi d n)}{c}$

$\qquad = \dfrac{\pi^2 d^2 l n Z}{c}$

$\qquad = \dfrac{\pi^2 (2r)^2 l n Z}{c}$

$\qquad = \dfrac{4\pi^2 r^2 l n Z}{c}$

$\qquad = \dfrac{2\pi^2 r^2 l n Z}{c/2}$

$\therefore \quad F = \dfrac{2\pi^2 r^2 l n Z}{0.5 c}$ ...(Eq. 7.14)

All parameters except Z (N – s/m²) are in mm

$\therefore \quad F = \dfrac{2\pi^2 r^2 l n Z}{0.5 \times 10^6 c}$ (N) ...(Eq. 7.14a) **15.8/ Pg 302, DHB**

2. **Shear force:**

$\therefore$ Eq. (7.12) yields... $\quad \tau = \dfrac{F}{A}$

$\qquad = \left(\dfrac{2\pi^2 r^2 l n Z}{0.5 \times 10^6 c}\right)\left(\dfrac{1}{2\pi r l}\right)$

∴ $$\tau = \frac{\pi r n Z}{0.5 \times 10^6 c} \quad \text{(MPa)} \quad \text{...(Eq. 7.15) } \textbf{15.7/ Pg 302, DHB}$$

3. Torque:

We know that torque = frictional force × radius of shaft

$$T = F \times r$$

∴ $$T = \frac{2\pi^2 r^3 l n Z}{0.5 \times 10^6 c} \quad \text{(N-mm)} \quad \text{...(Eq. 7.16) } \textbf{15.9/ Pg 302, DHB}$$

Also frictional torque, $T = fWr$ (N-mm)   ...(Eq. 7.17) **15.10/ Pg 302, DHB**
-or- ...**15.21/ Pg 303, DHB**

W = load = bearing pressure × projected are of bearing = $p \times ld$

$W = 2prl = p.l.d.$ ...**15.18/ Pg 303, DHB**

∴ Eq. (7.17) yields... $T = 2fpr^2 l$ ...(Eq. 7.18) **15.10/ Pg 302, DHB**

Equating Eqs (7.16) and (7.18), we have

$$\frac{2\pi^2 r^3 l n Z}{0.5 \times 10^6 c} = 2fpr^2 l$$

$$\frac{\pi^2 r n Z}{0.5 \times 10^6 c} = fp$$

$$f = \frac{\pi^2 r n Z}{(0.5 \times 10^6) c.p}$$

$$f = \left(\frac{\pi^2}{0.5 \times 10^6}\right)\left(\frac{Zn}{p}\right)\left(\frac{r}{c}\right) \quad \text{...(Eq. 7.19) } \textbf{15.11/ Pg 302, DHB}$$

Equation (7.19) is called the *Petroff's equation for lightly loaded bearing.*

- *The parameter (r/c) is called the radial clearance ratio.*

- *The parameter $\frac{Zn}{p}$ is called the Bearing Modulus, represented by (C).*

→ **For well lubricated bearings:**

According to McKee

$$f = \left[K_a \left(\frac{Zn}{p}\right)\left(\frac{r}{c}\right) \times 10^{-10} + \Delta f\right] \quad \text{...(Eq. 7.20) } \textbf{15.12/ Pg 302, DHB}$$

$K_a = 541.33 \beta$

β = circumferential length of the bearing in degree.

= 0.195×10^6 for full journal bearing [i.e. $\beta = 360°$]

$\Delta f = 0.002$ = Correction factor for bearing having $\frac{l}{d}$ = 0.75 to 2.8

...**Fig. 15.4/ Pg 317, DHB**

→ **For partially lubricated bearings (Fig. 15.5/ Pg 317, DHB):**
According to Louis Illmer,

$$f = \frac{C_1 C_2}{269.44} \sqrt[4]{p_a/v} \qquad \text{...(Eq. 7.21) 15.13/ Pg 302, DHB}$$

C_1 = a constant ...Table 15.7/ Pg 312, DHB
C_2 = a constant ...Table 15.8/ Pg 312, DHB
p_a = average pressure on projected area (MPa)
v = rubbing velocity of journal (m/s)

Power:
- The power loss is given as:

$$P = \frac{2\pi n T}{10^6} \quad (kW) \qquad \text{...(Eq. 7.22) 15.22a/ Pg 304, DHB}$$

T = Torque (N-mm)
n = speed of the journal (rps)

- Also power loss –or– heat generated is calculated as:

$$H_g = fWv \quad (J/s) \qquad \text{(Eq. 7.23) 15.23/ Pg 304, DHB}$$
$$\text{Or ...15.36/ Pg 305, DHB}$$

Rubbing velocity, $v = \dfrac{\pi d n}{1000}$ (m/s)

d – diameter of the journal (mm)

7.10 BEARING CHARACTERISTIC NUMBER –OR– BEARING MODULUS FOR A JOURNAL BEARING

As the journal starts rotating from its initial position (rest), it takes time for the fluid film to build sufficient pressure in the clearance space. During this time period there is partial metal to metal contact and the lubrication is *partial lubrication*. As the speed increases, more of the fluid flows into the wedge shaped space thereby sufficient pressure is built up, separating the bearing and journal surfaces. This is called *thick film lubrication*.

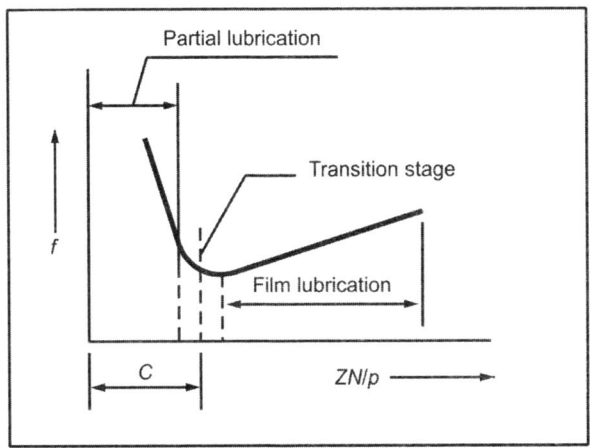

Fig. 7.9: Variation of coefficient of friction with bearing modulus [Fig. 15.5/Pg 317, DHB]

Figure 7.9 shows variation of bearing modulus ($C = ZN/p$) with coefficient of friction (f). It is observed that there exists a minimum value of f for a particular value of C. Values of $ZN/p > C$ indicate that the bearing may operate with complete film lubrication.

At values < C the rapid raise in f indicates that the oil film has ruptured resulting in metal-to-metal contact and consequent higher friction and wear. Thus value of ZN/p at which the oil film ruptures is called "bearing modulus".

When the bearing operates near this value, a slight increase in pressure or decrease in speed may be accompanied by an increase in friction, wear and heating. To prevent such conditions, the bearing should operate at values of ZN/p at least three times the minimum value of C and if the load fluctuations are large with heavy impacts, values as high as 15C may be used.

Table 15.6/ Pg 311, DHB – *gives the values of C, for various materials.*

7.11 SOMMERFELD NUMBER

Sommerfeld number is a dimensionless parameter most commonly used in the design of journal bearings, denoted as S. It is given by the following relations:

a. Without side leakage:

$$S = \left(\frac{r}{c}\right)^2 \left(\frac{ZN}{p}\right) \times 10^{-6} \quad \text{(s/min)} \quad \text{...(Eq. 7.24)} \; \textbf{15.17a/ Pg 303, DHB}$$

b. With side leakage:

$$S_0 = \left(\frac{r}{c}\right)^2 \left(\frac{ZN}{p}\right) K_w \times 10^{-6} \quad \text{(s/min)} \quad \text{...(Eq. 7.25)} \; \textbf{15.17b/ Pg 303, DHB}$$

K_w = correction factor for side leakage ...**Fig. 15.10/ Pg 320, DHB**
N = speed (rpm)
p = bearing pressure (MPa)

Note:
- **Fig. 15.6/ Pg 317, DHB** *gives values of "f", based on no side flow.*
- **Fig. 15.7/ Pg 318, DHB** *gives minimum oil film thickness based on no side flow.*
- **Fig. 15.8/ Pg 319, DHB** *gives values of oil flow, based on no side flow.*

These three figures/graphs are called as "RAIMONDI AND BOYD CURVES"

7.12 OPERATING PRESSURE

The pressure at which oil film breaks down so that metal-to-metal contact begins is called the critical operating pressure or the minimum operating pressure.

- According to Tatarinoff, $p = \dfrac{13.30 Zn}{10^6} \left(\dfrac{d}{c}\right)^2 \left(\dfrac{l}{d+l}\right)$ ...(Eq. 7.26) **15.15/ Pg 303, DHB**

- According to Moore, for unit pressure, $p = 0.726 \sqrt{v}$

  ...(Eq. 7.27) **15.16/ Pg 303, DHB**
- According to General electric company, for designing motor and generator bearings,

$$p = 0.622 \sqrt[3]{v} \qquad \text{...(Eq. 7.28)} \ \mathbf{15.14/ \ Pg \ 303, \ DHB}$$

7.13 TERMS AND DEFINITIONS

- **Radial clearance (c):** It is defined as the distance between the radii of bearing and the journal.

$$c = R - r = \frac{D-d}{2} \qquad \text{...(Eq. 7.29)}$$

- **Radial clearance ratio:** It is defined as the ratio of radial clearance to the radius of the journal.

$$\text{Radial clearance ratio} = \frac{c}{r} = \frac{2c}{d} \qquad \text{...(Eq. 7.30)}$$

- **Eccentricity (e):** It is defined as the radial distance between the centers of the journal and the bearing.
- **Attitude/Eccentricity ratio ($\in$):** It is defined as the ratio of eccentricity to the radial clearance.

$$\in = \frac{e}{c} \qquad \text{...(Eq. 7.31a)}$$

Referring to **Fig. 7.10**,

$$\cos\theta = \frac{e}{c} = \in = 1 - \frac{h_0}{c} \qquad \text{...(Eq. 7.31b)} \ \mathbf{15.25/ \ Pg \ 304, \ DHB}$$

The relation between eccentricity ratio and a constant K for different values of β **(Fig. 15.12/ Pg 321 & Fig. 15.13/ Pg 322, DHB)** is given as

$$K = 5884 \left(\frac{Zn}{p}\right)\left(\frac{r}{c}\right)^2 \qquad \text{...(Eq. 7.32)} \ \mathbf{15.26/ \ Pg \ 304, \ DHB}$$

Referring to **Fig. 15.13/ Pg 322, DHB**, the x co-ordinate is $\dfrac{K}{C_L 10^6}$

Based on $\left(\dfrac{l}{d}\right)$, the value of C_L is obtained from ...**Fig. 15.14/ Pg 322, DHB**

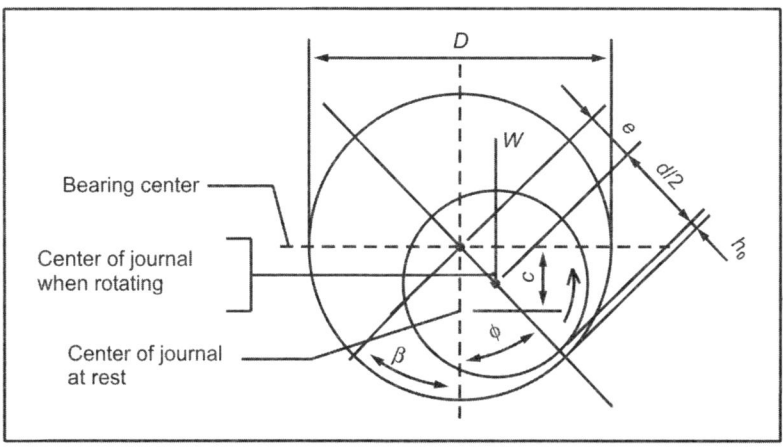

Fig. 7.10: Operating condition of a loaded journal [Fig. 15.12/Pg 321, DHB]

- **Minimum oil film thickness (MFT):** The criteria to determine whether the bearing operates satisfactorily or not is a function of minimum oil thickness.

    It is defined as the minimum distance between the bearing and the journal under the condition of complete lubrication, so as to prevent metal-to-metal contact. Its value depends upon the surface finish of the parts, cleanliness of lubricant, deflection of parts, etc. The surface determines the required oil film thickness. The rougher the surface, the thicker would be the film required.

$$MFT = \frac{h_0}{c} \qquad \text{...(Eq. 7.33)} \quad \textbf{15.24/ Pg 304, DHB}$$

Fig. 15.7/ Pg 318, DHB *gives minimum oil film thickness based on no side flow.*

- **Length to diameter ratio:** It is defined as the ratio of length to the journal of the diameter of the journal.

If $\frac{l}{d} < 1$, the bearing is a short bearing

$\frac{l}{d} > 1$, the bearing is a long bearing

$\frac{l}{d} = 1$, the bearing is a square bearing.

The standard value of $\frac{l}{d} = 2$.

7.14 HEAT GENERATED IN BEARINGS

The power lost to friction in the bearing is converted into heat and must be radiated from the housing without producing excessive temperatures. If the temperature of the bearing increases, the viscosity of the oil decreases as a result the oil squeezes out and the bearing seizes.

The frictional work or heat dissipated, $H_g = fWv$ (J/s)

...(Eq. 7.34) **15.36/ Pg 305, DHB**

Rubbing velocity, $v = \frac{\pi d n}{1000}$ (m/s)

Where, d = diameter of the journal (mm)

n = speed of the journal (rps)

Load $W = 2prl = pdl$ ...**15.18/ Pg 303, DHB**

7.15 HEAT DISSIPATED BY BEARINGS

The amount of heat dissipated or radiated by the bearing depends on the temperature difference, radiating surface, mass of the bearing and the amount of oil flowing around the bearing.

The bearing temperature is given as:

$$t_B = t_A + t_R \qquad \text{...(Eq. 7.35)} \quad \textbf{15.37/ Pg 306, DHB}$$

Where, t_A = ambient temperature, (°C)

t_B = temperature rise of the bearing wall, (°C)

The temperature of the oil film in the bearing is given as:
$$t_o = t_A + 2t_R \quad \text{...(Eq. 7.36)} \textbf{ 15.38/ Pg 306, DHB}$$

For force feed lubrication, $(t_o - t_B) \leq 10°C$

t_o = oil temperature (°C)

Case 1: Based on area of housing:

Heat dissipated from the bearing,
$$H_D = C'A = K_1 A (t_B - t_A) \quad (J/s) \quad \text{...(Eq. 7.37)} \textbf{ 15.39/ Pg 306, DHB}$$

C' = a coefficient = $K_1 (t_B - t_A)$

Value of C' ...Table 15.9/ Pg 313, -or- Fig. 15.15/ Pg 323, DHB

$(t_B - t_A)$ = temperature difference between bearing housing nas surrounding air in °C

$A = 20dl$ = surface area of bearing housing or pedestal (mm²)

Case 2: Based on projected area of bearing:

- Heat dissipated from the bearing,
$$H_D = C'' ld = K_2 ld (t_B - t_A) \quad (J/s) \quad \text{(Eq. 7.38)} \textbf{ 15.40/ Pg 306, DHB}$$

C'' = a coefficient = $K_2 (t_B - t_A)$

Value of C'' ...Table 15.10/ Pg 313, -or- Fig. 15.16/ Pg 323, DHB

(K_1, K_2) = surface dissipation constants

- Another formula as given by O. Lasche (Pedersson) is:
$$H_D = \frac{ld(T+18)^2}{K_3} \quad (J/s) \quad \text{...(Eq. 7.39)} \textbf{ 15.41/ Pg 306, DHB}$$

$K_3 = 0.2674 \times 10^6$, for bearings of heavy construction and well ventilated.

$\quad = 0.4743 \times 10^6$, for bearings of light construction in still air (i.e. unventilated).

$T = (t_B - t_A)$ (°C)

If $H_D < H_g$, then artificial cooling has to be provided.

If bearing conditions are such that the work of friction is high, then artificial cooling has to be provided in any one of the following two ways:

a. By circulating excess oil (lubricant) to the bearing, and

b. By cooling the bearing shell using water.

Note:

- For all practical purposes, $(t_B - t_A) = \dfrac{1}{2} (t_o - t_A)$

- Figs. 15.6/Pg 317, DHB, 15.7/Pg 318, DHB, and 15.8/Pg 319, DHB are called "RAIMONDI AND BOYD CURVES"

- $1\ reyn = \dfrac{1}{1.45 \times 10^{-7}}\ cP$

1. A lightly loaded journal bearing has the following specifications:
   Bearing diameter = 80 mm, bearing length = 60 mm,

diametral clearance = 0.12 mm,   journal speed = 24000 rpm,
radial load = 900 N,   absolute viscosity = 4 cP.

Determine: a. Frictional force   b. Torque   c. Coefficient of friction
            d. Power loss

Solution: $D = 80$ mm, $l = 60$ mm, $2c = 0.12$ mm, $N = 24000$ rpm $\Rightarrow n = 400$ rps, $W = 900$ N, $Z = 4\,cP = 4 \times 10^{-3}$ N-s/m²

a. $F = ?$ b. $T = ?$ c. $f = ?$ d. $P = ?$

a. Frictional force:

We know that, $F = \dfrac{2\pi^2 r^2 l n Z}{0.5 \times 10^6 c}$ ...15.8/ Pg 302, DHB

But $D = d + 2c$ ...Fig. 15.3/ Pg316, DHB

$80 = d + 0.12$

$d = 79.88$ mm

∴ $r = 39.94$ mm

$$F = \frac{2\pi^2 \times 39.94^2 \times 60 \times 400 \times 4 \times 10^{-3}}{0.5 \times 10^6 \times 0.06}$$

$F = 100.76$ N

b. Torque:

We know that torque $T = Fr$

$= 100.76 \times 39.94$

$T = 4024.42$ N-mm

-or-

$$T = \frac{2\pi^2 r^3 l n Z}{0.5 \times 10^6 c}$$ ...15.9/ Pg 302, DHB

$$= \frac{2\pi^2 \times 39.94^3 \times 60 \times 400 \times 4 \times 10^{-3}}{0.5 \times 10^6 \times 0.06}$$

$T = 4024.42$ N-mm

c. Coefficient of friction:

We know that, $f = \left(\dfrac{\pi^2}{0.5 \times 10^6}\right)\left(\dfrac{Zn}{p}\right)\left(\dfrac{r}{c}\right)$ ...Eq. (i) 15.11/ Pg 302, DHB

But $p = \dfrac{W}{2rl}$ ...15.18/ Pg 303, DHB

$$= \frac{900}{2 \times 39.94 \times 60}$$

$p = 0.188$ MPa

∴ Eq. (*i*) yields...
$$f = \left(\frac{\pi^2}{0.5 \times 10^6}\right)\left(\frac{4 \times 10^{-3} \times 400}{0.188}\right)\left(\frac{39.94}{0.06}\right)$$

$$f = 0.1118$$

d. Power loss:

We know that, $P = \dfrac{2\pi n T}{10^6}$ ...15.22a/ Pg 304, DHB

$$= \frac{2\pi \times 400 \times 4024.43}{10^6}$$

$$P = 10.11 \text{ kW}$$

2. A full journal bearing has the following specifications:

Shaft diameter = 45 mm, bearing length = 66 mm,
clearance ratio = 0.0015, speed = 2800 rpm,
load = 800 N, absolute viscosity = 8.27 × 10⁻³ Pa-s.

Determine: a. Frictional torque b. Coefficient of friction c. Power loss

Solution: d = 45 mm, l = 66 mm, $\dfrac{c}{r}$ = 0.0015 ⇒ c = 0.0015 × $\left(\dfrac{45}{2}\right)$ = 0.03375 mm,

N = 2800 rpm ⇒ n = 46.67 rps, W = 800 N, Z = 8.27 × 10⁻³ Pa-s.

a. T = ? b. f = ? c. P = ?

a. Torque:

We know that torque $T = \dfrac{2\pi^2 r^3 l n Z}{0.5 \times 10^6 c}$ ...15.9/ Pg 302, DHB

$$= \frac{2\pi^2 \times 22.5^3 \times 66 \times 46.67 \times 8.27 \times 10^{-3}}{0.5 \times 10^6 \times 0.03375}$$

$$T = 339.41 \text{ N-mm}$$

b. Coefficient of friction:

We know that, $f = \left(\dfrac{\pi^2}{0.5 \times 10^6}\right)\left(\dfrac{Zn}{p}\right)\left(\dfrac{r}{c}\right)$ ...15.11/ Pg 302, DHB

-or-

$$T = fWr$$ ...15.10/ Pg 302, DHB

$$339.41 = f \times 800 \times 22.5$$

$$f = 0.0189$$

c. Power loss:

We know that, $P = \dfrac{2\pi n T}{10^6}$ ...15.22a/ Pg 304, DHB

$$= \frac{2\pi \times 46.67 \times 339.41}{10^6}$$

$$P = 0.0995 \text{ kW}$$

3. A lightly loaded bearing of 70 mm long and 70 mm in diameter is acted on by 1.5 kN radial load. The radial clearance is 0.07 mm and the journal bearing is rotating at 25000 rpm. The viscosity of the oil is 3.45 × 10⁻³ Pa-s. Determine the frictional power loss using Petroff's equation.

VTU – Dec. 09/ Jan. 2010 – 10 Marks

Solution: $d = 70$ mm, $l = 70$ mm, $W = 1500$ N, $c = 0.07$ mm, $N = 25000$ rpm $\Rightarrow n = 416.67$ rps, $Z = 3.45 \times 10^{-3}$ Pa-s, $P = ?$

We know that, $P = \dfrac{2\pi n T}{10^6}$ ...Eq. (i) **15.22a/ Pg 304, DHB**

But, $T = \dfrac{2\pi^2 r^3 l n Z}{0.5 \times 10^6 c}$ ...**15.9/ Pg 302, DHB**

$$= \dfrac{2\pi^2 \times 35^3 \times 70 \times 416.67 \times 3.45 \times 10^{-3}}{0.5 \times 10^6 \times 0.07}$$

$T = 2433.19$ N-mm

∴ Eq. (i) yields... $P = \dfrac{2\pi \times 416.67 \times 2433.19}{10^6}$

$P = 6.37$ kW

4. An engine oil has a kinematic viscosity at 80°C corresponding to 62 seconds as found from Saybolt viscometer. Calculate the absolute viscosity.

Solution: $t = 80°$ C, $S' = 62$ sec, $Z = ?$

We know that, $Z_k = \dfrac{Z}{\rho} \times 10^{-3}$ ...Eq. (i) **15.2a/ Pg 301, DHB**

but, $Z_k = Z'_k \times 10^{-6}$ ...Eq. (ii) **15.2b/ Pg 301, DHB**

$Z'_k = \left(0.226\, S' - \dfrac{195}{S'}\right)$ for $32 < S' < 100$ **15.4a/ Pg 301, DHB**

$= \left(0.226 \times 62 - \dfrac{195}{62}\right)$

$Z'_k = 10.86$ cSt

∴ Eq. (ii) yields... $Z_k = 10.86 \times 10^{-6}$ m²/s

For $S' = 62$ sec @ 80°C, we have	Curve No: 3 Sp. gravity @ 15°C, $\rho_{15} = 0.890$	...Tb. 15.1/ Pg 308, DHB

The specific gravity of oil at any temperature is found as

$\rho_t = \rho_{15} - 0.00063\,(t° - 15)$ ...**15.3/ Pg 301, DHB**

$= 0.890 - 0.00063\,(80 - 15)$

$\rho_t = 0.8491$

∴ Eq. (i) yields... $10.86 \times 10^{-6} = \dfrac{Z}{0.8491} \times 10^{-3}$

$Z = 9.22 \times 10^{-3}$ m²/s

5. A lightly loaded journal bearing has the following specifications:
Shaft diameter = 60 mm, bearing length = 80 mm,
radial load = 1 kN, Diametral clearance = 0.1 mm.
The oil used is heavy steam cylinder oil at 70°C having $f = 0.042$.
Determine: a. Journal speed b. Power loss

Solution: $d = 60$ mm, $l = 80$ mm, $W = 1000$ N, $2c = 0.01$ mm $\Rightarrow c = 0.005$ mm, $f = 0.042$
Oil – heavy steam cylinder oil, $t = 70°C, f = 0.042$

a. Journal speed:

We know that, $F = \dfrac{2\pi^2 r^2 l n Z}{0.5 \times 10^6 c}$ ...Eq. (i) **15.8/ Pg 302, DHB**

But $\quad T = Fr$ ...Eq. (ii)
Also frictional torque, $T = fWr$ ...Eq. (iii) **15.10/ Pg 302, DHB**
Equating Eq. (ii) and Eq. (iii), we have,
$$F = fW$$
$$= 0.042 \times 1000$$
$$F = 42 \text{ N}$$

To find Z:

We know that, $Z_k = \dfrac{Z}{\rho} \times 10^{-3}$ (m²/s) ...Eq. (iv) **15.2a/ Pg 301, DHB**

But $\quad Z_k = Z'_k \times 10^{-6}$ (m²/s) ...Eq. (v) **15.2b/ Pg 301, DHB**
Z'_k = kinematic viscosity (cSt)

For the given type of oil, i.e. heavy steam cylinder oil, we have	Curve No: 11 Sp. gravity @ 15°C, $\rho_{15} = 0.930$	...Tb. 15.1/ Pg 308, DHB
For curve No. 11 @ 70°C, we have	Kinematic viscosity, $Z'_k = 300$ cSt	...Fig. 15.1/ Pg 316, DHB

∴ Eq. (v) yields... $\quad Z_k = 300 \times 10^{-6} = 0.0003$ m²/s
The specific gravity of oil at any temperature is found as
$$\rho_t = \rho_{15} - 0.00063 (t° - 15) \quad \text{...15.3/ Pg 301, DHB}$$
$$= 0.930 - 0.00063 (70 - 15)$$
$$\rho_t = 0.8955$$

∴ Eq. (iv) yields... $\quad 0.0003 = \dfrac{Z}{0.8955} \times 10^{-3}$

$$Z = 0.2687 \text{ N-s/m}^2$$

∴ Eq. (i) yields... $\quad 42 = \dfrac{2\pi^2 \times 30^2 \times 80 \times n \times 0.2687}{0.5 \times 10^6 \times 0.05}$

$$n = 2.75 \text{ rps}$$
$$N = 165 \text{ rpm}$$

b. Power loss:

We know that, $P = \dfrac{2\pi n T}{10^6}$ ...15.22a/ Pg 304, DHB

$= \dfrac{2\pi \times 2.75 \times (42 \times 30)}{10^6}$ ($\because T = Fr$)

$P = 0.0218$ kW

6. A 80 mm diameter shaft is supported by a full journal bearing of 120 mm length with a radial clearance of 0.05 mm. It is lubricated with SAE 10 (curve 2) at 70°C. The shaft rotates at 1200 rpm and has a radial load of 600 N. Using Petroff's equation, find

a. Friction coefficient b. Frictional torque c. Power loss

Solution: $d = 80$ mm, $l = 120$ mm, $c = 0.05$ mm, Oil SAE 10 (curve 2) at 70°C, $N = 1200$ rpm $\Rightarrow n = 20$ rps, $W = 600$ N

a. $f = ?$ b. $T = ?$ c. $P = ?$

a. Coefficient of friction:

We know that, $f = \left(\dfrac{\pi^2}{0.5 \times 10^6}\right)\left(\dfrac{Zn}{p}\right)\left(\dfrac{r}{c}\right)$ ...Eq. (i) 15.11/ Pg 302, DHB

But $p = \dfrac{W}{2rl}$ ...15.18/ Pg 303, DHB

$= \dfrac{600}{2 \times 40 \times 120}$

$p = 0.0625$ MPa

Also $Z_k = \dfrac{Z}{\rho} \times 10^{-3}$ ...Eq. (ii) 15.2a/ Pg 301, DHB

But $Z_k = Z'_k \times 10^{-6}$ ...Eq. (iii) 15.2b/ Pg 301, DHB

Z'_k = kinematic viscosity (cSt)

For the given type of oil, i.e. heavy steam cylinder oil, we have	Curve No: 2 Sp. gravity @ 15°C, $\rho_{15} = 0.880$	...Tb. 15.1/ Pg 308, DHB
For curve No. 2 @ 70°C, we have	Kinematic viscosity, $Z'_k = 11.25$ cSt	...Fig. 15.1/ Pg 316, DHB

$\therefore$ Eq. (iii) yields... $Z_k = 11.25 \times 10^{-6}$ m²/s

The specific gravity of oil at any temperature is found as

$\rho_t = \rho_{15} - 0.00063 (t° - 15)$ ...15.3/ Pg 301, DHB

$= 0.880 - 0.00063 (70 - 15)$

$\rho_t = 0.8454$

∴ Eq. (ii) yields...$11.25 \times 10^{-6} = \dfrac{Z}{0.8554} \times 10^{-3}$

$$Z = 0.00951 \text{ N-s/m}^2$$

∴ Eq. (i) yields... $f = \left(\dfrac{\pi^2}{0.5 \times 10^6}\right)\left(\dfrac{0.00951 \times 20}{0.0625}\right)\left(\dfrac{40}{0.05}\right)$

$$f = 0.0481$$

b. Torque:

We know that, $T = fWr$ ...15.10/ Pg 302, DHB

$$= 0.0486 \times 600 \times 40$$
$$T = 1154.4 \text{ N-mm}$$

c. Power loss:

We know that, $P = \dfrac{2\pi n T}{10^6}$ ...15.22a/ Pg 304, DHB

$$= \dfrac{2\pi \times 20 \times (1154.4)}{10^6} \quad (\because T = Fr)$$

$$P = 0.145 \text{ kW}$$

7. Solve the above prolem using Saybolt seconds.

Solution:

a. Coefficient of friction:

On similar lines, we have

For the given type of oil, i.e. heavy steam cylinder oil, we have	Curve No: 2 Sp. gravity @ 15°C, $\rho_{15} = 0.890$	...Tb. 15.1/ Pg 308, DHB
For curve No. 2 @ 70°C, we have	Saybolt seconds, $S' = 65$ seconds	...Fig. 15.1/ Pg 316, DHB

$$Z'_k = \left(0.226 S' - \dfrac{195}{S'}\right) \quad \text{for } 32 < S' < 100 \quad \text{...Eq. (iv) 15.4a/ Pg 301, DHB}$$

$$= \left(0.226 \times 65 - \dfrac{195}{65}\right)$$

$$Z'_k = 11.69 \text{ cSt}$$

∴ Eq. (iii) yields... $Z_k = 11.69 \times 10^{-6} \text{ m}^2/\text{s}$

∴ Eq. (ii) yields ...$11.69 \times 10^{-6} = \dfrac{Z}{0.8554} \times 10^{-3}$

$$Z = 9.99 \times 10^{-3} \text{ N-s/m}^2$$

∴ Eq. (i) yields... $f = \left(\dfrac{\pi^2}{0.5 \times 10^6}\right)\left(\dfrac{9.99 \times 10^{-3} \times 20}{0.0625}\right)\left(\dfrac{40}{0.05}\right)$

$$f = 0.0505$$

b. Torque:

We know that, $T = fWr$ ...15.10/ Pg 302, DHB

$\qquad = 0.0505 \times 600 \times 40$

$\qquad T = 1212$ N-mm

c. Power loss:

We know that, $P = \dfrac{2\pi nT}{10^6}$ ...15.22a/ Pg 304, DHB

$\qquad = \dfrac{2\pi \times 20 \times (1212)}{10^6}$

$\qquad P = 0.1523$ kW

8. **Determine the power loss in a bearing, the diameter of the journal is 60 mm and length 80 mm. The diametral clearance is 0.12 mm. The bearing supports a load of 5000 N and the journal rotates at a speed of 2500 rpm. The kinematic viscosity and the specific gravity of the oil used at the operating temperature of the bearing are 50 and 0.9 centistokes, respectively.** *VTU-July 2007-07 Marks*

Solution: $P = ?$, $d = 60$ mm, $l = 80$ mm, $W = 1500$ N, $2c = 0.12$ mm $\Rightarrow c = 0.06$ mm, $W = 5000$ N, $N = 2500$ rpm $\Rightarrow n = 41.67$ rps, $Z'_k = 50$ cSt, $\rho = 0.9$ (at operating temperature)

We know that, $P = \dfrac{2\pi nT}{10^6}$ ...Eq. (*i*) **15.22a/ Pg 304, DHB**

But $\qquad T = \dfrac{2\pi^2 r^3 ln Z}{0.5 \times 10^6 c}$ ...Eq. (*ii*) **15.9/ Pg 302, DHB**

Also $\qquad Z_k = \dfrac{Z}{\rho} \times 10^{-3}$ ...Eq. (*iii*) **15.2a/ Pg 301, DHB**

But $\qquad Z_k = Z'_k \times 10^{-6}$

$\qquad Z_k = 50 \times 10^{-6}$ m²/s

∴ Eq. (*iii*) yields... $50 \times 10^{-6} = \dfrac{Z}{0.9} \times 10^{-3}$

$\qquad Z = 0.045$ N-s/m²

∴ Eq. (*ii*) yields... $T = \dfrac{2\pi^2 \times 30^3 \times 80 \times 41.67 \times 0.045}{0.5 \times 10^6 \times 0.06}$

$\qquad T = 2665$ N-mm

∴ Eq. (*i*) yields... $P = \dfrac{2\pi \times 41.67 \times 2665}{10^6}$

$\qquad P = 0.697$ kW

9. **A journal bearing 80 mm long supports a load of 7.5 kN on a 50 mm diameter journal rotating at 900 rpm. The diametral clearance is 0.08 mm. What should be the viscosity, if the oil temperature of the bearing is limited to 75°C, when in still air at 20°C, using McKee's equation?**

Solution: $l = 80$ mm, $W = 7.5$ kN, $d = 50$ mm, $W = 12$ kN, $N = 900$ rpm $\Rightarrow n = 15$ rps, $2c = 0.08$ mm $\Rightarrow c = 0.04$ mm, $Z = ?$, if $t_B = 75°C$, if $t_A = 20°C$, based on McKee's equation,

According to McKee

$$f = \left[K_a \left(\frac{Zn}{p}\right) \left(\frac{r}{c}\right) \times 10^{-10} + \Delta f \right] \qquad \text{...Eq. (i) 15.12/ Pg 302, DHB}$$

- Δf = Correction factor for bearing for $0.75 < \dfrac{l}{d} < 2.8$ ...Fig. 15.4/ Pg 317, DHB

- Now $\dfrac{l}{d} = \dfrac{80}{50} = 1.6$

Since $0.75 < \dfrac{l}{d} < 2.8$, $\Delta f = 0.002$,

- $K_a = 0.195 \times 10^6$ for full journal bearing [i.e. $\beta = 360°$]

- But $p = \dfrac{W}{2rl} = \dfrac{W}{ld}$ \qquad ...15.18/ Pg 303, DHB

$$= \frac{7500}{80 \times 50}$$

$p = 1.875$ MPa

$\therefore$ Eq. (i) yields... $\qquad f = \left[0.195 \times 10^6 \times \left(\dfrac{Z \times 15}{1.875}\right) \times \left(\dfrac{25}{0.04}\right) \times 10^{-10} + 0.002 \right]$

$f = 0.0975 Z + 0.002$ \hfill ...Eq. (ii)

We know that heat generated $H_g = fWv$ \hfill ...15.36/ Pg 305, DHB

$$= (0.0975 Z + 0.002) \times 7.5 \times 10^3 \times \left(\frac{\pi \times 50 \times 15}{1000}\right)$$

$H_g = (0.0975 Z + 0.002) \times 17.67 \times 10^3$ \hfill ...Eq. (iii)

Also heat dissipated $H_D = \dfrac{ld(T+18)^2}{K_3}$ \hfill ...15.41/ Pg 306, DHB

$K_3 = 0.4743 \times 10^6$

...for bearings of light construction in still air (i.e. unventilated).

$T = (t_B - t_A) = (75 - 20) = 55°C$

$\therefore \quad H_D = \dfrac{80 \times 50 \times (55+18)^2}{0.4743 \times 10^6}$

$H_D = 44.94$ W \hfill ...Eq. (iv)

Assuming $H_g = H_D$

$(0.0975 Z + 0.002) \times 17.67 \times 10^3 = 44.94$

$Z = 5.573 \times 10^{-3}$ Pa-s (N-s/m²)

10. A 75 mm long full journal bearing of diameter 75 mm supports a radial load of 12 kN at a shaft speed of 1800 rpm. Assume ratio of diameter to the diametral clearance as 1000. The viscosity of oil is 0.01 Pa-s at the operating temperature. Determine:

a. Coefficient of friction on McKee's equation.
b. Coefficient of friction based on Raimondi & Boyd curves.
c. The probable temperature of the bearing assuming that the heat generated is dissipated in still air at 20°C, using McKee's equation.

VTU – Dec. 06/ Jan. 2007 – 12 Marks; Dec. 07/ Jan. 2008 – 12 Marks; June/ July 2011 – 12 Marks; July/ Aug. 2004 – 08 Marks.

Solution: $d = l = 75$ mm, $W = 12$ kN, $N = 1800$ rpm $\Rightarrow n = 30$ rps, $d/2c = 1000 \Rightarrow r/c = 1000$, $Z = 0.01$ Pa-s

a. $f = ?$ -based on McKee's equation b. $f = ?$ -based on Raimondi & Boyd curves.
c. $t_B = ?$ if $t_A = 20°C$

a. Coefficient of friction based on McKee's equation:

According to McKee

$$f = \left[K_a \left(\frac{Zn}{p} \right) \left(\frac{r}{c} \right) \times 10^{-10} + \Delta f \right] \quad \text{...Eq. (i) 15.12/ Pg 302, DHB}$$

- Δf = Correction factor for bearing for $0.75 < \dfrac{l}{d} < 2.8$ ...**Fig. 15.4/ Pg 317, DHB**

- Now $\dfrac{l}{d} = \dfrac{75}{75} = 1$

  Since $0.75 < 1 < 2.8$, $\Delta f = 0.002$,

- $K_a = 0.195 \times 10^6$ for full journal bearing [i.e. $\beta = 360°$]

- But $p = \dfrac{W}{2rl} = \dfrac{W}{ld}$ ...**15.18/ Pg 303, DHB**

  $= \dfrac{12000}{75 \times 75}$

  $p = 2.13$ MPa

∴ Eq. (i) yields... $f = \left[0.195 \times 10^6 \times \left(\dfrac{0.01 \times 30}{2.13} \right) \times 1000 \times 10^{-10} + 0.002 \right]$

$f = 4.746 \times 10^{-3}$

b. Coefficient of friction based on Raimondi & Boyd curves:

Figs. 15.6/Pg 317, DHB, 15.7/Pg 318, DHB, and 15.8/319, DHB are called "Raimondi and Boyd curves"

We know that Sommerfeld No. $S = \left(\dfrac{r}{c} \right)^2 \left(\dfrac{ZN}{p} \right) \times 10^{-6}$ ...**15.17a/ Pg 303, DHB**

$= 1000^2 \times \left(\dfrac{0.01 \times 1800}{2.13} \right) \times 10^{-6}$

$S = 8.438$ s/min
$S = 0.1406$ (unitless)

For $S = 8.45$ and $\beta = 360°$ (full journal bearing), $f\left(\dfrac{r}{c}\right) = 3$ ...**Fig. 15.6/ Pg 317, DHB**

$$f(1000) = 3$$
$$f = 0.003$$

c. Temperature of the bearing - McKee's equation:

We know that, $H_g = fWv$ ...**15.36/ Pg 305, DHB**

$$= 4.746 \times 10^{-3} \times (12 \times 10^3) \times \left(\dfrac{\pi \times 75 \times 30}{1000}\right)$$

$$H_g = 402.57 \text{ W}$$

Also $H_D = \dfrac{ld(T+18)^2}{K_3}$

$K_3 = 0.4743 \times 10^6$

...for bearings of light construction in still air (i.e. unventilated).

$T = (t_B - t_A) = (t_B - 20)$

$\therefore 402.57 = \dfrac{75 \times 75 \times (t_B - 20 + 18)^2}{0.4743 \times 10^6}$ (since $H_g = H_d$ ... data)

$t_B = 186.1°C$

11. A full journal bearing of diameter 80 mm and 120 mm long supports a radial load of 6000 N. The shaft rotates at 600 rpm and $\dfrac{r}{c} = 1000$. The room temperature is 30°C and the surface of the bearing is limited to 60°C.

Determine the viscosity of the oil to satisfy the above requirements, if the bearing is well ventilated and if no artificial cooling is required. Also determine the temperature of the oil.

Solution: $d = 80$ mm, $l = 120$ mm, $W = 6000$ N, $N = 600$ rpm $\Rightarrow n = 10$ rps, $r/c = 1000 \Rightarrow c = 0.04$ mm, $t_A = 30°C$, $t_B = 60°C$, bearing is well ventilated and if no artificial cooling is required, $z = z$, $t_0 = ?$

According to McKee

$$f = \left[K_a\left(\dfrac{Zn}{p}\right)\left(\dfrac{r}{c}\right) \times 10^{-10} + \Delta f\right]$$ ...Eq. (i) **15.12/ Pg 302, DHB**

- Δf = Correction factor for bearing for $0.75 < \dfrac{l}{d} < 2.8$ ...**Fig. 15.4/ Pg 317, DHB**

- Now $\dfrac{l}{d} = \dfrac{120}{80} = 1.5$

Since $0.75 < 1.5 < 2.8$, $\Delta f = 0.002$,

- $K_a = 0.195 \times 10^6$ ...for full journal bearing [i.e. $\beta = 360°$]

- But $p = \dfrac{W}{2rl} = \dfrac{W}{ld}$ ...15.18/ Pg 303, DHB

$$= \dfrac{6000}{80 \times 120}$$

$$p = 0.625 \text{ MPa}$$

∴ Eq. (*i*) yields... $\quad f = \left[0.195 \times 10^6 \times \left(\dfrac{Z \times 10}{0.625}\right) \times 1000 \times 10^{-10} + 0.002\right]$

$$f = 0.312\, Z + 0.002 \qquad \text{...Eq. (}ii\text{)}$$

We know that heat generated $H_g = fWv$ ...15.36/ Pg 305, DHB

$$= (0.312\, Z + 0.002) \times 6000 \times \left(\dfrac{\pi \times 80 \times 10}{1000}\right)$$

$$H_g = (0.312\, Z + 0.002) \times 15080 \qquad \text{...Eq. (}iii\text{)}$$

Also heat dissipated $H_D = \dfrac{ld\,(T+18)^2}{K_3}$ ...15.41/ Pg 306, DHB

$K_3 = 0.2674 \times 10^6$, ...for bearings that are well ventilated

$T = (t_B - t_A) = (60 - 30) = 30°C$

∴ $\quad H_D = \dfrac{120 \times 80 \times (30+18)^2}{0.2674 \times 10^6}$

$$H_D = 82.72 \text{ W} \qquad \text{...Eq. (}iv\text{)}$$

Since no artificial cooling is required (data), equating $H_g = H_D$

$$(0.312\,Z + 0.002) \times 15080 = 82.71$$

$$Z = 0.01117 \text{ Pa-s}$$

$$= \dfrac{0.01117}{10^{-3}}$$

$$Z = 11.17 \text{ cP}$$

Temperature of oil:

We know that for all practical purposes, $(t_B - t_A) = \dfrac{1}{2}(t_o - t_A)$

$$30 = \dfrac{1}{2}(t_o - 30)$$

Oil temperature, $t_o = 90°C$

12. A tentative design for a journal bearing calls for a full journal bearing calls for an 80 mm diameter shaft and 100 mm length to support a load of 18 kN at 1200 rpm. It is desired to operate at a bearing surface temperature of 70°C in a room temperature of 30°C. The oil used has a viscosity of 0.01 Pa-s at 110°C. Determine the amount of artificial cooling required. Assume $\dfrac{d}{2c} = 1000$.

Solution: $d = 80$ mm, $l = 100$ mm, $W = 18$ kN, $N = 1200$ rpm $\Rightarrow n = 20$ rps, $t_A = 30°C$, $t_B = 70°C$, $Z = 0.01$ Pa-s, $t_o = 110°C$, $\dfrac{d}{2c} = \dfrac{r}{c} = 1000 \Rightarrow c = 0.04$, amount of artificial cooling = ?

We know that amount of artificial cooling = $H_g - H_D$ ...Eq. (i)
But heat generated $H_g = fWv$ ...Eq. (ii) **15.36/ Pg 305, DHB**

- $v = \left(\dfrac{\pi d n}{1000}\right) = \left(\dfrac{\pi \times 80 \times 20}{1000}\right) = 5.03$ m/s

- According to McKee $f = \left[K_a\left(\dfrac{Zn}{p}\right)\left(\dfrac{r}{c}\right) \times 10^{-10} + \Delta f\right]$ ...**15.12/ Pg 302, DHB**

- Δf = Correction factor for bearing for $0.75 < \dfrac{l}{d} < 2.8$ ...**Fig. 15.4/ Pg 317, DHB**

- Now $\dfrac{l}{d} = \dfrac{100}{80} = 1.25$

  Since $0.75 < 1.25 < 2.8$, $\Delta f = 0.002$,

- $K_a = 0.195 \times 10^6$ ...for full journal bearing [i.e. $\beta = 360°$]

- But $p = \dfrac{W}{2rl} = \dfrac{W}{ld}$ ...**15.18/ Pg 303, DHB**

  $= \dfrac{18000}{80 \times 100}$

  $p = 2.25$ MPa

  $f = \left[0.195 \times 10^6 \times \left(\dfrac{0.01 \times 20}{2.25}\right) \times 1000 \times 10^{-10} + 0.002\right]$

  $f = 0.00373$

∴ Eq. (ii) yields... $H_g = 0.00373 \times 18000 \times 5.03$
$H_g = 337.71$ W

Also heat dissipated $H_D = \dfrac{ld(T+18)^2}{K_3}$ ...**15.41/ Pg 306, DHB**

$K_3 = 0.4743 \times 10^6$, for bearings that are well ventilated
$T = (t_B - t_A) = (70 - 30) = 40$ °C

∴ $H_D = \dfrac{100 \times 80 \times (40+18)^2}{0.4743 \times 10^6}$

$H_D = 56.74$ W

∴ Eq. (i) yields... Amount of artificial cooling = $337.71 - 56.74 = 280.97$ W

13. A shaft running at 900 rpm is supported by bearings of 50 mm diameter and 75 m length. The bearing operates in still air at 30°C. The oil has a viscosity of

0.013 Pa-s at 130°C, while the diametral clearance is 0.05 mm. Determine the permissible load on the bearing and the power lost if no artificial cooling is used.

Solution: $N = 900$ rpm $\Rightarrow n = 15$ rps, $d = 50$ mm, $l = 75$ mm, $t_A = 30°C$, $Z = 0.013$ Pa-s, $t_o = 130°C$, $2c = 0.05$ mm $\Rightarrow c = 0.25$ mm, $W = ?$, $P = ?$

a. Permissible load:

We know that amount of artificial cooling = $H_g - H_D$

Since no artificial cooling is required, $H_g = H_D$ ...Eq. (*i*)

But heat generated $H_g = fWv$ ...Eq. (*ii*) **15.36/ Pg 305, DHB**

- $v = \left(\dfrac{\pi d n}{1000}\right) = \left(\dfrac{\pi \times 50 \times 15}{1000}\right) = 2.356$ m/s

- According to McKee $f = \left[K_a\left(\dfrac{Zn}{p}\right)\left(\dfrac{r}{c}\right) \times 10^{-10} + \Delta f\right]$ ...**15.12/ Pg 302, DHB**

- Δf = Correction factor for bearing for $0.75 < \dfrac{l}{d} < 2.8$ ...**Fig. 15.4/ Pg 317, DHB**

- Now $\dfrac{l}{d} = \dfrac{75}{50} = 1.5$

  Since $0.75 < 1.5 < 2.8$, $\Delta f = 0.002$,

- $K_a = 0.195 \times 10^6$ ...[assuming full journal bearing, i.e. $\beta = 360°$]

- But $p = \dfrac{W}{2rl} = \dfrac{W}{ld}$ ...**15.18/ Pg 303, DHB**

  $= \dfrac{W}{50 \times 75}$

  $p = (2.67 \times 10^{-4})\, W$ MPa

$\therefore f = \left[0.195 \times 10^6 \times \left(\dfrac{0.013 \times 15}{2.67 \times 10^{-4}\, W}\right) \times \left(\dfrac{25}{0.025}\right) \times 10^{-10} + 0.002\right]$

$f = \dfrac{14.24}{W} + 0.002$ ...Eq. (*iii*)

$\therefore$ Eq. (*ii*) yields... $H_g = \left[\dfrac{14.24}{W} + 0.002\right] \times W \times 2.356$

$H_g = 33.55 + (4.712 \times 10^{-3})\, W$ ...Eq. (*iv*)

Also heat dissipated $H_D = \dfrac{ld(T+18)^2}{K_3}$ ...**15.41/ Pg 306, DHB**

$K_3 = 0.4743 \times 10^6$, for bearings that are well ventilated

$$T = (t_B - t_A) = \frac{t_o - t_A}{2}$$

$$T = 50°C$$

$$\therefore H_D = \frac{75 \times 50 \times (50+18)^2}{0.4743 \times 10^6}$$

$H_D = 36.56$ W

∴ Eq. (*i*) yields... $33.55 + (4.712 \times 10^{-3}) W = 36.56$

$$W = 638.79 \text{ N}$$

∴ Eq. (*iii*) yields... $f = \dfrac{14.24}{638.79} + 0.002$

$$f = 0.02429$$

b. Power loss:

We know that, $P = \dfrac{2\pi nT}{10^6}$ ...Eq. (*v*) **15.22a/ Pg 304, DHB**

But $\quad\quad T = fWr$ ...**15.10/ Pg 302, DHB**

$\quad\quad\quad = 0.02429 \times 638.79 \times 25$

$\quad\quad T = 387.94$ N-mm

∴ Eq. (*v*) yields... $\quad P = \dfrac{2\pi \times 15 \times 387.94}{10^6}$

$$P = 0.0366 \text{ kW}$$

14. A shaft of 150 mm diameter has a speed of 2400 rpm and runs in a bearing which has a length of 1.2d. The bearing pressure is 0.8 MPa and the coefficient of friction at bearing surface is 0.006. Calculate the heat generated.

If the difference between the outlet and inlet temperatures is 20°C, find the quantity of oil required whose specific heat is 1.92 kJ/kg°C.

Solution: $d = 150$ mm, $N = 2400$ rpm $\Rightarrow n = 40$ rps, $l = 1.2d = 1.2 \times 150 = 180$ mm, $p = 0.8$ MPa, $f = 0.006$, $H_g = ?$, $\Delta t = 20°C$, $C_p = 1.92$ kJ/kg°C, $m = ?$

a. Heat generated:

We know that, $H_g = fWv$

- $v = \left(\dfrac{\pi d n}{1000}\right) = \left(\dfrac{\pi \times 150 \times 40}{1000}\right) = 18.85$ m/s

- $p = \dfrac{W}{2rl}$

$\quad W = 2prl$

$\quad\quad = 2 \times 0.8 \times 75 \times 180$

$\quad W = 21600$ N

$\quad\quad \therefore H_g = 0.006 \times 21600 \times 18.85$

$\quad\quad H_g = 2443$ J/s $= 2.443$ kJ/s

b. Quantity of oil required

We know that, $H_g = mCp\Delta t$

$$2.443 = m \times 1.92 \times 20$$

$$m = 0.0636 \text{ kg/s} = 3.817 \text{ kg/min}$$

15. A full journal bearing of 50 mm diameter and 100 mm long has a bearing pressure of 1.4 N/mm². The speed of the journal is 900 rpm and the ratio of journal diameter to the diametrical clearance is 1000. The bearing is lubricated with oil whose absolute viscosity at the operating temperature of 75°C may be taken as 0.011 kg/m-s. The room temperature is 35°C. Find:
  a. The amount of artificial cooling required.
  b. The mass of lubricating oil required, if the difference between the outlet and the inlet temperature of the oil is 10°C, take specific heat of oil as 1850 J/kg°C.

VTU – June/ July 2009 – 14 Marks; (similar) May/ June 2010 – 15 Marks; (similar) July 2007– 15 Marks

Solution: $d = 50$ mm, $l = 100$ mm, $p = 1.4$ N/mm², $N = 900$ rpm $\Rightarrow n = 15$ rps, $d/2c = 1000 = r/c$, $Z = 0.011$ kg/m-s, $t_o = 75°C$, $t_A = 35°C$.

  a. Amount of artificial cooling = ?
  b. Mass of oil, m = ?, if $\Delta t = 10°C$, $C_p = 1850$ J/kg°C

a. Amount of artificial cooling:

We know that amount of artificial cooling = $H_g - H_D$ ...Eq. (i)

But heat generated $H_g = fWv$ ...Eq. (ii) **15.36/ Pg 305, DHB**

- $v = \left(\dfrac{\pi d n}{1000}\right) = \left(\dfrac{\pi \times 50 \times 15}{1000}\right) = 0.2356$ m/s

- According to McKee $f = \left[K_a\left(\dfrac{Zn}{p}\right)\left(\dfrac{r}{c}\right) \times 10^{-10} + \Delta f\right]$ ...**15.12/ Pg 302, DHB**

- Δf = Correction factor for bearing for $0.75 < \dfrac{l}{d} < 2.8$ ...**Fig. 15.4/ Pg 317, DHB**

- Now $\dfrac{l}{d} = \dfrac{100}{50} = 2$

  Since $0.75 < 2 < 2.8$, $\Delta f = 0.002$,

- $K_a = 0.195 \times 10^6$ ...for full journal bearing [i.e. $\beta = 360°$]

- But $p = \dfrac{W}{2rl} = \dfrac{W}{ld}$ ...**15.18/ Pg 303, DHB**

$$1.4 = \dfrac{W}{100 \times 50}$$

$$W = 7000 \text{ N}$$

$$\therefore f = \left[0.195 \times 10^6 \times \left(\frac{0.011 \times 15}{1.4}\right) \times 1000 \times 10^{-10} + 0.002\right]$$

$$f = 4.298 \times 10^{-3}$$

∴ Eq. (ii) yields... $H_g = 4.298 \times 10^{-3} \times 7000 \times 2.356$

$$H_g = 70.88 \text{ W}$$

Also heat dissipated $H_D = \dfrac{ld(T+18)^2}{K_3}$ ...**15.41/ Pg 306, DHB**

$$K_3 = 0.4743 \times 10^6$$

$$T = (t_B - t_A) = \frac{t_o - t_A}{2}$$

$$= \frac{75 - 35}{2}$$

$$T = 20°C$$

$$\therefore H_D = \frac{100 \times 50 \times (20 + 18)^2}{0.4743 \times 10^6}$$

$H_D = 15.22$ W

∴ Eq. (i) yields... Amount of artificial cooling = 70.88 − 15.22 = 55.66 W

b. Mass of oil:

We know that, $H_g = mC_p \Delta t$

$70.88 = m \times 1850 \times 10$

$m = 0.00383$ kg/s = 0.230 kg/min

16. A 100 mm long bearing supports a load of 3000 N on a 60 mm diameter shaft. The radial clearance is 0.05 mm and the viscosity of oil is 0.021 Pa-s at operating temperature. If the bearing dissipates 100 W, determine the safe speed.

Solution: $l = 100$ mm, $W = 3000$ N, $d = 60$ mm, $c = 0.05$ mm, $Z = 0.021$ Pa-s, $H_g = 100$ W, $N = ?$

We know that heat generated $H_g = fWv$ ...Eq. (i) **15.36/Pg 305, DHB**

- $v = \left(\dfrac{\pi d n}{1000}\right) = \left(\dfrac{\pi \times 60 \times n}{1000}\right) = 0.1885\, n$

- According to McKee $f = \left[K_a \left(\dfrac{Zn}{p}\right)\left(\dfrac{r}{c}\right) \times 10^{-10} + \Delta f\right]$ ...**15.12/ Pg 302, DHB**

- Δf = Correction factor for bearing for $0.75 < \dfrac{l}{d} < 2.8$ ...**Fig. 15.4/ Pg 317, DHB**

- Now $\dfrac{l}{d} = \dfrac{100}{60} = 1.67$

Since $0.75 < 1.67 < 2.8$, $\Delta f = 0.002$,

- $K_a = 0.195 \times 10^6$ ...[assuming full journal bearing, i.e. $\beta = 360°$]

- But $p = \dfrac{W}{2rl} = \dfrac{W}{ld}$ ...15.18/ Pg 303, DHB

$$p = \dfrac{3000}{100 \times 60}$$

$$p = 0.5 \text{ MPa}$$

$$f = \left[0.195 \times 10^6 \times \left(\dfrac{0.021 \times n}{0.5}\right) \times \left(\dfrac{30}{0.05}\right) \times 10^{-10} + 0.002\right]$$

$$f = (4.914 \times 10^{-4})n + 0.002 \quad \text{...Eq. (ii)}$$

∴ Eq. (i) yields... $\quad 100 = [(4.914 \times 10^{-4})n + 0.002] \times 3000 \times 0.1885\, n$

$$100 = 0.2779\, n^2 + 1.131\, n$$

$$0.2779\, n^2 + 1.131\, n - 100 = 0$$

$$n = 17.04, -21.13 \text{ rps}$$

$$n = 17.04 \text{ rps} \quad \text{(taking positive value)}$$

$$\Rightarrow N = 1022.4 \text{ rpm}$$

∴ Eq. (ii) yields... $\quad f = (4.914 \times 10^{-4}) \times 17.04 + 0.002$

$$f = 0.01037$$

17. A 75 mm journal bearing of diameter 75 mm supports a load of 15 kN. The ratio of $\dfrac{d}{c} = 1000$ and the viscosity of oil is 25×10^{-3} Pa-s. The heat generated in the bearing is 442 watts. Determine the maximum speed of the journal using McKee's equation. **VTU – Dec. 12 – 10 Marks**

Solution: $l = 75$ mm, $d = 75$ mm, $W = 15000$ N, $d/c = 1000 = 2r/c \Rightarrow c = 0.075$ mm, $Z = 25 \times 10^{-3}$ Pa-s, $H_g = 442$ W, $N = ?$

We know that heat generated $H_g = fWv$ ...Eq. (i) 15.36/Pg 305, DHB

- $v = \left(\dfrac{\pi d n}{1000}\right) = \left(\dfrac{\pi \times 75 \times n}{1000}\right) = 0.2356\, n$

- According to McKee $f = \left[K_a\left(\dfrac{Zn}{p}\right)\left(\dfrac{r}{c}\right) \times 10^{-10} + \Delta f\right]$ ...15.12/ Pg 302, DHB

- Δf = Correction factor for bearing for $0.75 < \dfrac{l}{d} < 2.8$ ...Fig. 15.4/ Pg 317, DHB

- Now $\dfrac{l}{d} = \dfrac{75}{75} = 1$

Since $0.75 < 1 < 2.8$, $\Delta f = 0.002$,

- $K_a = 0.195 \times 10^6$ ...[assuming full journal bearing, i.e. $\beta = 360°$]

- But $p = \dfrac{W}{2rl} = \dfrac{W}{ld}$ ...15.18/ Pg 303, DHB

$$p = \dfrac{15000}{75 \times 75}$$

$$p = 2.67 \text{ MPa}$$

$$f = \left[0.195 \times 10^6 \times \left(\dfrac{25 \times 10^{-3} \times n}{2.67}\right) \times \left(\dfrac{37.5}{0.075}\right) \times 10^{-10} + 0.002\right]$$

$$f = (9.129 \times 10^{-5})n + 0.002 \qquad ...\text{Eq. }(ii)$$

∴ Eq. (i) yields... $442 = [(9.129 \times 10^{-5})n + 0.002] \times 15000 \times 0.2356\, n$

$$442 = 0.3226\, n^2 + 7.068\, n$$

$$0.3226\, n^2 + 7.068\, n - 442 = 0$$

$$n = 27.65, -49.56 \text{ rps}$$

$$n = 27.65 \text{ rps} \quad \text{(taking positive value)}$$

$$\Rightarrow N = 1659 \text{ rpm}$$

∴ Eq. (ii) yields... $f = ((9.129 \times 10^{-5})) \times 27.65 + 0.002$

$$f = 0.004524$$

18. **A 80 mm long journal bearing supports a load of 2800 N on a 50 mm diameter shaft. The bearing has a clearance of 0.05 mm and the viscosity of oil is 0.021 kg/m-s at the operating temperature of the bearing is capable of dissipating 80 J/s. Determine the maximum safe speed.** *VTU – June/ July 2013 – 10 Marks*

Solution: $l = 80$ mm, $d = 50$ mm, $W = 2800$ N, $c = 0.05$ mm, $Z = 0.021$ kg/m-s, $H_g = 80$ J/s $= 80$ W, $N = ?$

We know that heat generated $H_g = fWv$ ...Eq. (i) **15.36/Pg 305, DHB**

- $v = \left(\dfrac{\pi d n}{1000}\right) = \left(\dfrac{\pi \times 50 \times n}{1000}\right) = 0.1571\, n$

- According to McKee $f = \left[K_a \left(\dfrac{Zn}{p}\right)\left(\dfrac{r}{c}\right) \times 10^{-10} + \Delta f\right]$ ...15.12/ Pg 302, DHB

- $\Delta f =$ Correction factor for bearing for $0.75 < \dfrac{l}{d} < 2.8$ ...Fig. 15.4/ Pg 317, DHB

- Now $\dfrac{l}{d} = \dfrac{80}{50} = 1.6$

Since $0.75 < 1.6 < 2.8$, $\Delta f = 0.002$,

- $K_a = 0.195 \times 10^6$ ...[assuming full journal bearing, i.e. $\beta = 360°$]

- But $p = \dfrac{W}{2rl} = \dfrac{W}{ld}$ ...15.18/ Pg 303, DHB

$$p = \dfrac{2800}{80 \times 50}$$

$$p = 0.7 \text{ MPa}$$

$$f = \left[0.195 \times 10^6 \times \left(\dfrac{0.021 \times n}{0.7}\right) \times \left(\dfrac{25}{0.05}\right) \times 10^{-10} + 0.002\right]$$

$$f = (2.925 \times 10^{-4})n + 0.002 \qquad \text{...Eq. (ii)}$$

∴ Eq. (i) yields... $\quad 80 = [(2.925 \times 10^{-4})n + 0.002] \times 2800 \times 0.1571\, n$

$$80 = 0.1287\, n^2 + 0.8798\, n$$
$$0.1287\, n^2 + 0.8798\, n - 80 = 0$$
$$n = 21.75,\ -28.58 \text{ rps}$$
$$n = 21.75 \text{ rps} \quad \text{(taking positive value)}$$
$$N = 1305 \text{ rpm}$$

∴ Eq. (ii) yields... $\quad f = (2.925 \times 10^{-4}) \times 21.75 + 0.002$

$$f = 0.00836$$

19. A full journal bearing 50 mm in diameter and 50 mm long operates at 1000 rpm and carries a load of 5 kN. The radial clearance is 0.025 mm. The bearing is lubricated with SAE 30 oil and the operating temperature of oil is 80°C. Assume the attitude angle as 60°, determine:

   i. Bearing pressure
   ii. Sommerfeld number
   iii. Attitude
   iv. Minimum film thickness
   v. Heat generated
   vi. Heat dissipated, if the ambient temperature is 20°C and
   vii. Amount of artificial cooling if necessary. Use McKnee's and Pederson's equations. **VTU – Dec. 2010 – 16 Marks**

Solution: $d = 50$ mm, $l = 50$ mm, $N = 1000$ rpm $\Rightarrow n = 16.67$ rps, $W = 5000$ N, $c = 0.025$ mm, Oil - SAE 30, $t_o = 80°C$, $\beta = 60°$, $t_A = 20°C$

   i. $p = ?$
   ii. $S = ?$
   iii. $\epsilon = ?$
   iv. $h_0 = ?$
   v. $H_g = ?$
   vi. $H_D = ?$, if $t_A = 20°C$
   vii. amount of artificial cooling = ?

i. Bearing pressure:

We know that, $p = \dfrac{W}{2rl}$

$$= \dfrac{5000}{50 \times 50}$$

$$p = 2 \text{ MPa}$$

ii. Sommerfeld number:

We know that Sommerfeld No. $S = \left(\dfrac{r}{c}\right)^2 \left(\dfrac{ZN}{p}\right) \times 10^{-6}$

...Eq. (i) **15.17a/ Pg 303, DHB**

Also $\quad Z_k = \dfrac{Z}{\rho} \times 10^{-3}$ ...Eq. (ii) **15.2a/ Pg 301, DHB**

But $\quad Z_k = Z'_k \times 10^{-6}$ ...Eq. (iii) **15.2b/ Pg 301, DHB**

Z'_k = Kinematic viscosity (cSt)

For the given type of oil, i.e. SAE 30, we have	Curve No: F Sp. gravity @ 15°C, ρ_{15} = 0.926
For curve No. F @ 80°C, we have	Kinematic viscosity, Z'_k = 19 cSt

∴ Eq. (iii) yields... $\quad Z_k = 19 \times 10^{-6} \text{ m}^2/\text{s}$

The specific gravity of oil at any temprature is found as

$\rho_t = \rho_{15} - 0.00063\,(t° - 15)$ ...**15.3/ Pg 301, DHB**

$= 0.926 - 0.00063\,(80 - 15)$

$\rho_t = 0.8851$

∴ Eq. (ii) yields... $\quad 19 \times 10^{-6} = \dfrac{Z}{0.8851} \times 10^{-3}$

$Z = 0.01682 \text{ N-s}/\text{m}^2$

∴ Eq. (i) yields... $\quad S = \left(\dfrac{25}{0.025}\right)^2 \times \left(\dfrac{0.01682 \times 1000}{2}\right) \times 10^{-6}$

$S = 8.41 \text{ s/min}$

$S = 0.14017 \text{ (unit less)}$

iii. Attitude:

We know that attitude, $\epsilon = 1 - \dfrac{h_o}{c}$ ...**15.25/ Pg 304, DHB**

$= 1 - 0.27$

$\epsilon = 0.73$

iv. Minimum film thickness:

At $S = 8.41$ and $\beta = 60°$, $\left(\dfrac{h_o}{c}\right) = 0.27$ ...**Fig. 15.7/ Pg 318, DHB**

∴ $\quad h_o = 0.27 \times 0.025$

$h_o = 6.75 \times 10^{-3} \text{ mm}$

v. Heat generated:

We know that heat generated $H_g = fWv$ ...Eq. (iv) **15.36/ Pg 305, DHB**

- $v = \left(\dfrac{\pi d n}{1000}\right) = \left(\dfrac{\pi \times 50 \times 16.67}{1000}\right) = 2.618$ m/s

- According to McKee $f = \left[K_a\left(\dfrac{Zn}{p}\right)\left(\dfrac{r}{c}\right) \times 10^{-10} + \Delta f\right]$ ...**15.12/ Pg 302, DHB**

- Δf = Correction factor for bearing for $0.75 < \dfrac{l}{d} < 2.8$ ...**Fig. 15.4/ Pg 317, DHB**

- Now $\dfrac{l}{d} = \dfrac{50}{50} = 1$

  Since $0.75 < 1 < 2.8$, $\Delta f = 0.002$,

- $K_a = 0.195 \times 10^6$ ...for full journal bearing, [i.e. $\beta = 360°$]

$$f = \left[0.195 \times 10^6 \times \left(\dfrac{0.01682 \times 16.67}{2}\right) \times \left(\dfrac{25}{0.05}\right) \times 10^{-10} + 0.002\right]$$

$f = 0.00473$

∴ Eq. (*iv*) yields... $H_g = 0.00473 \times 5000 \times 2.618$

$H_g = 61.96$ W

vi. Heat dissipated:

We know that, $H_D = \dfrac{ld(T+18)^2}{K_3}$

$K_3 = 0.47434 \times 10^6$

$T = (t_B - t_A) = \dfrac{t_o - t_A}{2}$

$= \dfrac{80 - 20}{2}$

$T = 30°C$

∴ $H_D = \dfrac{50 \times 50 \times (30+18)^2}{0.4743 \times 10^6}$

$H_D = 12.14$ W

vii. Amount of artificial cooling:

We know that amount of artificial cooling = $H_g - H_D$

$= 61.96 - 12.14 = 49.82$ W

20. **Following specifications refer to idealized full journal bearing:**

    Diameter of journal = 50 mm, length of journal = 65 mm, speed of journal = 1200 rpm, attitude = 0.8, diametral clearance = 0.06 mm, absolute viscosity = 11 cP.

Determine:
a. minimum film thickness
b. Sommerfeld number
c. load carrying capacity
d. coefficient of friction
e. power loss
f. frictional force

Solution: $d = 50$ mm, $l = 65$ mm, $N = 120$ rpm $\Rightarrow n = 20$ rps, $\epsilon = 0.8$, $2c = 0.06$ mm $\Rightarrow$ $c = 0.03$ mm, $Z = 11$ cP $= 11 \times 10^{-3}$ Pa-s.

a. Minimum film thickness:

We know that attitude, $\epsilon = 1 - \dfrac{h_o}{c}$ ...15.25/ Pg 304, DHB

$$0.8 = 1 - \dfrac{h_o}{c}$$

$$\dfrac{h_o}{c} = 0.2$$

$$h_o = 0.2 \times 0.03 = 0.006$$

b. Sommerfeld number:

For $\dfrac{h_o}{c} = 0.2$ and $\beta = 360°$ (full journal bearing), $S = 1$ s/min

...Fig. 15.7/ Pg 318, DHB

$$S = 0.01667$$

c. Load carrying capacity:

We know that, $p = \dfrac{W}{2rl}$ ...Eq. (i) 15.18/ Pg 303, DHB

but $S = \left(\dfrac{r}{c}\right)^2 \left(\dfrac{ZN}{p}\right) \times 10^{-6}$ ...15.17a/ Pg 303, DHB

$$1 = \left(\dfrac{25}{0.03}\right)^2 \left(\dfrac{11 \times 10^{-3} \times 1200}{p}\right) \times 10^{-6}$$

$$p = 9.167 \text{ MPa}$$

$\therefore$ Eq. (i) yields... $9.167 = \dfrac{W}{2 \times 25 \times 65}$

$$W = 29.79 \text{ kN}$$

d. Coefficient of friction:

We know that According to McKee $f = \left[K_a \left(\dfrac{Zn}{p}\right)\left(\dfrac{r}{c}\right) \times 10^{-10} + \Delta f\right]$

...15.12/ Pg 302, DHB

- Δf = Correction factor for bearing for $0.75 < \dfrac{l}{d} < 2.8$ ...Fig. 15.4/ Pg 317, DHB

- Now $\dfrac{l}{d} = \dfrac{65}{50} = 1.3$

Since $0.75 < 1.3 < 2.8$, $\Delta f = 0.002$,

- $K_a = 0.195 \times 10^6$ ...for full journal bearing, [i.e. $\beta = 360°$]

$$f = \left[0.195 \times 10^6 \times \left(\dfrac{11 \times 10^{-3} \times 20}{9.167} \right) \times \left(\dfrac{25}{0.05} \right) \times 10^{-10} + 0.002 \right]$$

$f = 0.002390$

e. Power loss:

We know that, $P = \dfrac{2\pi n T}{10^6}$ ...Eq. (ii) **15.22a/ Pg 304, DHB**

But
$T = fWr$
$= 0.002390 \times (29.79 \times 10^3) \times 25$
$T = 1779.36$ N-m

∴ Eq. (ii) yields...
$P = \dfrac{2\pi \times 20 \times 1779.36}{10^6}$

$P = 0.2236$ kW

f. Frictional force:

We know that, $T = Fr$
$1779.36 = F \times 25$
$F = 71.97$ N

21. Following data refers to a 360° hydrodynamic bearing:
Radial load = 3.2 kN, Journal speed = 1500 rpm, Radial clearance = 0.05 mm
Journal diameter = bearing length = 50 mm, viscosity of lubricant = 25 cP
Assume that the total heat generated in the bearing is carried away by total oil flow in the bearing. Calculate:
i. coefficient of friction
ii. power loss in friction
iii. minimum film thickness
iv. flow requirement
v. temperature rise

VTU – May/ June 2010 – 14 Marks

Solution: $\beta = 360°$, $W = 3.2$ kN, $N = 1500$ rpm $\Rightarrow n = 25$ rps, $c = 0.05$ mm, $d = l = 50$ mm, $Z = 25$ cP $= 25 \times 10^{-3}$ Pa-s

i. $f = ?$ ii. $P = ?$ iii. $h_o = ?$ iv. $m = ?$ v. $\Delta t = ?$

We know that, $S = \left(\dfrac{r}{c}\right)^2 \left(\dfrac{ZN}{p}\right) \times 10^{-6}$ ...**15.17a/ Pg 303, DHB**

But
$p = \dfrac{W}{2rl} = \dfrac{W}{ld}$ ...**15.18/ Pg 303, DHB**

$$= \frac{3200}{50 \times 50}$$
$$p = 1.28 \text{ MPa}$$

$$\therefore \quad S = \left(\frac{25}{0.05}\right)^2 \left(\frac{25 \times 10^{-3} \times 1500}{1.28}\right) \times 10^{-6}$$

$$S = 7.32 \text{ s/min}$$
$$= 0.1221$$

For $S = 7.32$ s/min and $\beta = 360°$	$f(r/c) = 2.6$	...Tb. 15.6/ Pg 317, DHB
	$MFT = h_o/c = 0.85$	...Tb. 15.7/ Pg 318, DHB
	$FLV = Q/rcNl = 3.05$	...Tb. 15.8/ Pg 319, DHB

i. Coefficient of friction:

From **DHB**, $f(r/c) = 2.6$

$$f = 2.6 \times \left(\frac{0.05}{25}\right) = 0.0052$$

$$f = 0.0052$$

ii. Power loss in friction:

We know that, $P = \dfrac{2\pi n T}{60}$ ...Eq. (i) 15.22a/ Pg 304, DHB

But
$$T = fWr \quad \text{...15.10/ Pg 302, DHB}$$
$$= 0.0052 \times 3.2 \times 10^3 \times 25$$
$$T = 416 \text{ N-m}$$

$\therefore$ Eq. (i) yields...
$$P = \frac{2\pi \times 25 \times 416}{10^6}$$
$$P = 0.0653 \text{ kW}$$

iii. Minimum film thickness:

From **DHB**, $h_o/c = 0.85$
$$h_o = 0.85 \times 0.05$$
$$h_o = 0.0425 \text{ mm}$$

iv. Flow requirement:

We know that flow (without side leakage), $FLV = \dfrac{Q}{rcNl}$ ...15.27/ Pg 304, DHB

$$3.05 = \frac{Q}{25 \times 0.05 \times 1500 \times 50}$$

$$Q = 285.94 \times 10^3 \text{ mm}^3/\text{min}$$
$$= 2.859 \times 10^{-4} \text{ m}^3/\text{min}$$

$$= 4.766 \times 10^{-6} \text{ m}^3/\text{s} \quad (1 \text{ m}^3 = 1000 \text{ l})$$
$$Q = 4.765 \times 10^{-3} \text{ litres/sec}$$

v. Temperature rise:

Give heat generated in the bearing is carried away by total oil flow in the bearing
i.e.
$$H_g = mC_p \Delta t$$
$$fWv = (\rho Q)C_p \Delta t$$

Assume $\rho = 0.86$ and $C_p = 2 \text{ kJ/kg}°\text{C}$

$$0.0052 \times (3.2 \times 10^3) \times \left(\frac{\pi \times 50 \times 25}{1000}\right) = 0.86 \times (4.766 \times 10^{-3}) \times 2000 \times \Delta t$$

$$\Delta t = 7.97°\text{C}$$

22. A 80 mm diameter bearing carries a load of 7000 N while the shaft rotates at 1200 rpm. The oil used has a Saybolt viscosity of 58.4 sec at the temperature of the film which is 75 °C. The curve of ZN/p and f is a straight line passing through the points

$$\frac{ZN}{p} = 10.55 \text{ at } f = 0.015; \quad \frac{ZN}{p} = 53.55 \text{ at } f = 0.0455$$

Assuming $l = 2d$, determine the power lost in the bearing. Take specific gravity at 15°C as 0.899.

Solution: $d = 80$ mm, $W = 7000$ N, $N = 1200$ rpm $\Rightarrow n = 20$ rps, $S' = 58.4$ sec, $t_o = 75$ °C, $l = 2d = 160$ mm, $\rho_{15} = 0.899$, $P = ?$

$$\left(\frac{ZN}{p}\right)_1 = 10.55 \text{ at } f_1 = 0.015 \quad \left(\frac{ZN}{p}\right)_2 = 53.55 \text{ at } f_2 = 0.0455$$

We know that power loss, $P = H_g = fwv$ ...Eq. (*i*) **15.36/ Pg 305, DHB**

- $v = \left(\dfrac{\pi d n}{1000}\right) = \left(\dfrac{\pi \times 80 \times 20}{1000}\right) = 5.026 \text{ m/s}$

To find f:

We know that, $Z_k = \dfrac{Z}{\rho} \times 10^{-3}$ ...Eq. (*ii*) **15.2a/ Pg 301, DHB**

But $Z_k = Z'_k \times 10^{-6}$ ...Eq. (*iii*) **15.2b/ Pg 301, DHB**

Also $Z'_k = \left(0.226 S' - \dfrac{195}{S'}\right)$ for $32 < S' < 100$ ...**15.4a/ Pg 301, DHB**

$$= \left(0.226 \times 58.4 - \frac{195}{58.4}\right)$$

$Z'_k = 9.86$ cSt

∴ Eq. (*iii*) yields... $Z_k = 9.86 \times 10^{-6} \text{ m}^2/\text{s}$

Also $\rho_t = \rho_{15} - 0.00063 (t° - 15)$ ...**15.3/ Pg 301, DHB**
$= 0.899 - 0.00063 (75 - 15)$
$\rho_t = 0.8612$

∴ Eq. (ii) yields... $9.86 \times 10^{-6} = \dfrac{Z}{0.8612} \times 10^{-3}$

$$Z = 8.491 \times 10^{-3} \text{ m}^2/\text{s}$$

∴ $\dfrac{ZN}{p} = \dfrac{8.491 \times 10^{-3} \times 1200}{(7000/160 \times 80)} = 18.63$ (say X)

Given:

	ZN/p	f	
A_1	10.55	0.015	B_1
A_2	53.55	0.0455	B_2

Now $f_X = B_1 - \dfrac{(B_1 - B_2)(X - A_1)}{(A_2 - A_1)}$

$f_{18.63} = 0.015 - \dfrac{(0.015 - 0.0455)(18.63 - 10.55)}{(53.55 - 10.55)}$

$f_{18.63} = 0.02073$

∴ Eq. (i) yields... $P = 0.02073 \times 7000 \times 5.026$

$$P = 729.36 \text{ W}$$

23. The oiliness curve for a 75 mm × 150 mm long bearing happens to be a straight line passing through the points $\dfrac{\eta n'}{P} = 191 \times 10^{-9}$ and $\mu = 0.002$ and another point $\dfrac{\eta n'}{P} = 956 \times 10^{-9}$ and $\mu = 0.0065$. The load supported by the bearing is 6 kN and speed of the journal is 1200 rpm. Calculate the friction loss in kW at the bearing, if the oil film has a temperature of 80°C and the viscosity of the lubricant is 8.7 cP at the operating temperature. Assume $\psi = 0.001$.

VTU – July/ Aug. 2003 – 10 Marks

Solution: $d = 75$ mm, $l = 150$ mm, $W = 6000$ N, $N = 1200$ rpm $\Rightarrow n = n' = 20$ rps, $t_o = 80°C$, $Z = 8.7$ cP $= 8.7 \times 10^{-3}$ N-s/m^2, $P = ?$, $\psi = 0.001$ **(superfluous data)**.

$\left(\dfrac{ZN}{p}\right)_1 = \left(\dfrac{\eta n'}{P}\right)_1 = 191 \times 10^{-9}$ at $f_1 = \mu_1 = 0.002$

$\left(\dfrac{ZN}{p}\right)_2 = \left(\dfrac{\eta n'}{P}\right)_2 = 956 \times 10^{-9}$ at $f_2 = \mu_2 = 0.0065$ (Here p is in N/m^2)

We know that power loss, $P = H_g = fwv$ ...Eq. (i) **15.36/ Pg 305, DHB**

- $v = \left(\dfrac{\pi d n}{1000}\right) = \left(\dfrac{\pi \times 75 \times 20}{1000}\right) = 4.712$ m/s

- $p = \dfrac{W}{ld} = \dfrac{6000}{150 \times 75} = 0.533$ MPa $= 0.533 \times 10^6$ N/m^2

$$\therefore \frac{Zn}{p} = \frac{8.7 \times 10^{-3} \times 20}{0.533 \times 10^6} = 3.265 \times 10^{-7} \quad \text{(say X)}$$

Given:

	ZN/p	f	
A_1	191×10^{-9}	0.002	B_1
A_2	956×10^{-9}	0.0065	B_2

Now $\quad f_X = B_1 - \dfrac{(B_1 - B_2)(X - A_1)}{(A_2 - A_1)}$

$$f_{3.265 \times 10^{-7}} = 0.002 - \frac{(0.002 - 0.0069)(3.265 \times 10^{-7} - 191 \times 10^{-9})}{(956 \times 10^{-9} - 191 \times 10^{-9})}$$

$$f_{3.265 \times 10^{-7}} = 2.797 \times 10^{-3}$$

$\therefore$ Eq. (i) yields... $\quad P = 2.797 \times 10^{-3} \times 6000 \times 4.712$

$$P = 79.08 \text{ W} = 0.0798 \text{ kW}$$

24. A bearing of 75 mm diameter has a shaft speed of 300 rpm and a lubricating oil of viscosity of 0.06 Pa-s. With a bearing clearance of 0.2 mm and a bearing pressure of 1.4 MPa, this oil is satisfactory in operation.
    a. Determine the pressure at which the bearing should operate, if it is necessary to change the speed to 400 rpm.
    b. What should be the viscosity of oil if bearing clearance is 0.15 mm, $N = 300$ rpm, $p = 1.4$ MPa?
    c. What should be the viscosity of oil if bearing clearance is 0.15 mm, $N = 500$ rpm, $p = 2$ MPa?

Solution: $d = 75$ mm, $N = 300$ rpm $\Rightarrow n = 50$ rps, $Z = 0.06$ Pa-s, $2c = 0.2$ mm $\Rightarrow c = 0.01$ mm, $p = 1.4$ MPa

   a. $p_2 = ?$ if $N = 400$ rpm
   b. $Z_2 = ?$ if $2c = 0.15$ mm, $N = 300$ rpm, $p = 1.4$ MPa
   c. $Z_2 = ?$ if $2c = 0.15$ mm, $N = 500$ rpm, $p = 2$ MPa

a. To find p_2, if $N_2 = 400$ rpm:

For the bearing to operate satisfactorily, $\left(\dfrac{ZN}{p}\right)_1 = \left(\dfrac{ZN}{p}\right)_2$

Since $\quad Z_1 = Z_2$

$$\left(\frac{N}{p}\right)_1 = \left(\frac{N}{p}\right)_2$$

$$\frac{300}{1.4} = \frac{400}{p_2}$$

$$p_2 = 1.87 \text{ MPa}$$

b. To find Z_2, if $2c = 0.15$, $N_2 = 300$ rpm and $p_2 = 1.4$ MPa:

We know that, $S = \left(\dfrac{r}{c}\right)^2 \left(\dfrac{ZN}{p}\right) \times 10^{-6}$ ...15.17a/ Pg 303, DHB

Now $\qquad S_1 = S_2$

$$\left(\dfrac{r}{c}\right)^2 \left(\dfrac{ZN}{p}\right) \times 10^{-6} = \left(\dfrac{r}{c}\right)^2 \left(\dfrac{ZN}{p}\right) \times 10^{-6} \qquad \text{...Eq. (i)}$$

As per the given data, $p_1 = p_2$ and $N_1 = N_2$

$$\left(\dfrac{r}{c}\right)^2 \times Z_1 = \left(\dfrac{r}{c}\right)^2 \times Z_2$$

$$\left(\dfrac{37.5}{0.1}\right)^2 \times 0.06 = \left(\dfrac{37.5}{0.075}\right)^2 \times Z_2$$

$$Z_2 = 0.03375 \text{ Pa-s}$$

c. To find Z_2, if $2c = 0.15$, $N_2 = 500$ rpm and $p_2 = 2$ MPa:

Now, $\left(\dfrac{r}{c}\right)^2 \left(\dfrac{ZN}{p}\right) \times 10^{-6} = \left(\dfrac{r}{c}\right)^2 \left(\dfrac{ZN}{p}\right) \times 10^{-6}$ ...using Eq. (i)

$$\left(\dfrac{37.5}{0.1}\right)^2 \left(\dfrac{300}{1.4}\right) \times 0.06 = \left(\dfrac{37.5}{0.075}\right)^2 \left(\dfrac{500}{1.4}\right) \times Z_2$$

$$Z_2 = 0.02893 \text{ Pa-s}$$

25. A diesel engine crank shaft running at 2400 rpm has a flywheel weighing 30 kN overhangs the bearing by 250 mm. The maximum torque in the shaft is 3.2×10^6 N-mm, average load on the bearing is 45 kN, allowable shear stress on the shaft is 42 MPa.

   a. Select a suitable diameter of the shaft   b. Check the pV value.
   c. Determine the value of Z.   d. Calculate the heat generated

Solution: $N = 2400$ rpm $\Rightarrow n = 40$ rps, $F = 30$ kN, $x = 250$ mm, $T = 3.2 \times 10^6$ N-mm, $W = 45$ kN, $\tau = 42$ MPa.

a. $d = ?$ b. $pV = ?$ c. $Z = ?$ d. $H_g = ?$ e. $P = ?$

a. To find shaft diameter:

We know that, $\tau = \dfrac{16 T_e}{\pi d^3}$ ...Eq. (i) 3.1/ Pg 42, DHB

But $\qquad T_e = \sqrt{T^2 + M^2}$

$\qquad\qquad = \sqrt{(3.2 \times 10^6)^2 + (30000 \times 250)^2} \qquad (M = F \cdot x)$

$\qquad T_e = 8.154 \times 10^6$ N-mm

∴ Eq. (i) yields... $42 = \dfrac{16 \times 8.154 \times 10^6}{\pi d^3}$

$d = 99.96$ mm

∴ Standard shaft diameter, $d = 100$ mm ...Tb. 3.5a/ Pg 48, DHB

b. pV value:

For diesel engine, $pV = 35$ MN/m² ...Tb. 15.5/ Pg 311, DHB

Also From **Tb 15.11/ Pg 314, DHB**, we have

$p = 4.8 - 8.2$ MN/m²

$Z = 0.020 - 0.065$ N-s/m²

$ZN/p = 1.45$

$c/r = 0.001$

$l/d = 0.6 - 1.5$ Take $l/d = 1.5 = 1.5 \times 100 = 150$ mm

- Now $p = \dfrac{W}{ld}$ ...15.18/ Pg 303, DHB

$= \dfrac{45000}{150 \times 100}$

$p = 3$ MN/m²

- $v = \left(\dfrac{\pi d n}{1000}\right) = \left(\dfrac{\pi \times 100 \times 40}{1000}\right) = 12.56$ m/s

∴ $pV = 3 \times 12.56 = 37.68$ MN/m² > 35 MN/m²

Hence safe.

c. To find Z:

According to Tatarinoff, $p = \dfrac{13.30 Zn}{10^6}\left(\dfrac{d}{c}\right)^2\left(\dfrac{l}{d+l}\right)$ ...15.15/ Pg 303, DHB

$c/r = 0.001 \Rightarrow r/c = 1000 \Rightarrow d/c = 2000$

$3 = \dfrac{13.30 \times Z \times 40}{10^6} \times 2000^2 \times \left(\dfrac{150}{100 + 150}\right)$

$Z = 2.349 \times 10^{-3}$ Pa-s

d. Heat generated:

We know that heat generated $H_g = fWv$ ...Eq. (ii) 15.36/ Pg 305, DHB

- According to McKee $f = \left[K_a\left(\dfrac{Zn}{p}\right)\left(\dfrac{r}{c}\right) \times 10^{-10} + \Delta f\right]$ ...15.12/ Pg 302, DHB

- $\Delta f =$ Correction factor for bearing for $0.75 < \dfrac{l}{d} < 2.8$ ...**Fig. 15.4/ Pg 317, DHB**

- Now $\dfrac{l}{d} = 1.5$

  Since $0.75 < 1.5 < 2.8$, $\Delta f = 0.002$,

- $K_a = 0.195 \times 10^6$ ...for full journal bearing, [i.e. $\beta = 360°$]

$$f = \left[0.195 \times 10^6 \times \left(\dfrac{2.349 \times 10^{-3} \times 40}{3}\right) \times 1000 \times 10^{-10} + 0.002\right]$$

$$f = 0.00261$$

∴ Eq. (*ii*) yields... $H_g = 0.00261 \times 45000 \times 12.56$

$$H_g = 1475.17 \text{ W} = 1.47 \text{ kW}$$

26. A 75 mm journal bearing supports a radial load of 3500 N. The bearing is 75 mm long and the shaft operates at 400 rpm. Assume a permissible minimum film thickness of 0.02 mm and a normal running fit for a bearing bore. Determine:
  a. Viscosity of suitable oil   b. Coefficient of friction
  c. Heat generated   d. Amount of oil pumped through the bearing
  e. Amount of end leakage   f. Temperature rise of oil.

Solution: $d = l = 75$ mm, $W = 3500$ N, $N = 400$ rpm $\Rightarrow n = 6.67$ rps, $h_o = 0.02$ mm, fit - normal running fit

  a. $Z = ?$ b. $f = ?$ c. $H_g = ?$ d. $Q = ?$ e. $Q_s = ?$ f. $t_o = ?$

	Go (G)	No-go (N)	
Hole: H7	0 microns = 0.00 mm	30×10^{-3} microns = 0.03 mm	...Tb. 22.3/ Pg 399, DHB
Shaft: f7	-30×10^{-3} microns = -0.03 mm	-60×10^{-3} microns = -0.06 mm	

∴ Maximum hole size = 75 + 0.03 = 75.03 mm

  Maximum shaft size = 75 − 0.03 = 74.97 mm

  Minimum hole size = 75 − 0.00 = 75 mm

  Minimum shaft size = 75 − 0.06 = 74.94 mm

  Maximum Clearance, $2c = 75.03 − 74.94 = 0.09$ mm

  $c = 0.045$

a. To find viscosity:

  We know that, $S = \left(\dfrac{r}{c}\right)^2 \left(\dfrac{ZN}{p}\right) \times 10^{-6}$ Eq. (*i*) **15.17a/ Pg 303, DHB**

- Now $\dfrac{h_o}{c} = \dfrac{0.02}{0.045} = 0.444$

  At $h_o/c = 0.44$, & $\beta = 360°$, $S = 1.8$ s/min   ...**Fig. 15.7/Pg 318, DHB**

- Now $p = \dfrac{W}{ld}$ ...15.18/ Pg 303, DHB

$$= \dfrac{3500}{75 \times 75}$$

$$p = 0.62 \text{ MPa}$$

∴ Eq. (i) yields... $1.8 = \left(\dfrac{37.5}{0.045}\right)^2 \left(\dfrac{Z \times 400}{0.62}\right) \times 10^{-6}$

$$Z = 4.018 \times 10^{-3} \text{ Pa-s}$$

b. To find coefficient of friction:
At $S = 1.8$ & $\beta = 360^0$, $f(r/c) = 0.95$ ...Fig. 15.6/Pg 317, DHB

$$f = 0.95 \times \left(\dfrac{0.045}{37.5}\right)$$

$$f = 0.00114$$

c. Heat generated:
We know that heat generated $H_g = fWv$ ...15.36/ Pg 305, DHB

$$v = \left(\dfrac{\pi d n}{1000}\right) = \left(\dfrac{\pi \times 75 \times 6.67}{1000}\right) = 1.57 \text{ m/s}$$

∴ $H_g = 0.00114 \times 3500 \times 1.57$
$H_g = 6.27$ W

d. Amount of oil pumped through the bearing:
At $S = 1.8$ & $\beta = 360°$, $FLV = Q/rcNl = 1.9$ ...Fig. 15.8/Pg 319, DHB

But, $FLV = \dfrac{Q}{rcNl}$ ...15.27/ Pg 304, DHB

$$1.9 = \dfrac{Q}{37.5 \times 0.045 \times 400 \times 75}$$

$Q = 96.18 \times 10^3$ mm³/min
$= 1.603 \times 10^{-6}$ m³/s (1 m³ = 1000 lts)
$Q = 1.603 \times 10^{-3}$ liters/sec

e. Amount of end leakage (amount of oil supplied to the bearing):
We know that, $Q_s = (FLV)\, rcNlK_Q = QK_Q$ ...Eq. (ii) 15.28/ Pg 304, DHB
K_Q depends upon h_o/c and B/l

but, $\dfrac{B}{l} = \dfrac{2\pi r \times (\beta/360)}{l}$ ...Fig. 15.10/Pg 320, DHB

$$= \dfrac{2\pi \times 37.5 \times (360/360)}{75}$$

∴ $\dfrac{B}{l} = 3.142$

At $\dfrac{B}{l} = 3.142$ and $h_o/c = 0.44$, $K_Q = 1.8$ ...Fig. 15.11/Pg 321, DHB

∴ Eq. (ii) yields... $Q_s = 1.603 \times 10^{-6} \times 1.8$

$Q_s = 2.88 \times 10^{-6} \text{ m}^3/\text{s}$

f. Temperature rise of oil:

Assuming that $H_g = H_D$

$$H_g = \dfrac{ld(T+18)^2}{K_3}$$ ...15.41/ Pg 306, DHB

$K_3 = 0.4743 \times 10^6$

$$6.27 = \dfrac{75 \times 75 (T+18)^2}{0.4743 \times 10^6}$$

$T = 5°C$

27. The following data are given for a full journal bearing:

Radial load = 25 kN   L/d ratio = 1:1

unit bearing pressure = 2.5 MPa,

viscosity of the lubricant = 20 cP,   class of fit = H7e7.

Calculate: i. Dimensions of the bearing   ii. Minimum oil film thickness
       iii. Requirement of flow.

Assume that the process to clearance is centered.   *VTU – June 2012 – 14 Marks*

Solution: $W = 25$ kN, $l = d$, $p = 2.5$ MPa, $Z = 20$ cP = 20×10^{-3} Pa-s, fit: H7e7

a. $l = d = ?$ b. $h_0 = ?$ c. flow requirement = ?

i. Dimensions of the bearing:

We know that, $p = \dfrac{W}{ld}$ ...15.18/ Pg 303, DHB

$2.5 = \dfrac{25000}{d^2}$ $(\because l = d)$

$d = 100$ mm

∴ $d = l = 100$ mm

ii. Minimum oil film thickness:

We know that, $S = \left(\dfrac{r}{c}\right)^2 \left(\dfrac{ZN}{p}\right) \times 10^{-6}$ ...Eq. (i) **15.17a/ Pg 303, DHB**

To find clearance (c):

For a normal running fit, we have H7e7   ...Tb. 22.2/ Pg 397, DHB

Based on diameter, we have

	Go (G)	No-go (N)	
Hole: H7	0 microns = 0.00 mm	35×10^{-3} microns = 0.035 mm	...Tb. 22.3/ Pg 399, DHB
Shaft: e7	-72×10^{-3} microns = -0.072 mm	-170×10^{-3} microns = -0.107 mm	

∴ Maximum hole size = 100 + 0.035 = 100.035 mm

Maximum shaft size = 100 − 0.072 = 99.928 mm

Minimum hole size = 100 − 0.00 = 100 mm

Minimum shaft size = 100 − 0.107 = 99.893 mm

Since the manufacturing process is centered,

$$\text{Maximum Clearance, } 2c = \left(\frac{100.035 + 100}{2} - \frac{99.928 + 99.893}{2}\right)$$

$$2c = 0.107 \text{ mm}$$
$$c = 0.0535 \text{ mm}$$

∴ Eq. (i) yields... $S = \left(\frac{50}{0.0535}\right)^2 \left(\frac{20 \times 10^{-3} \times 1000}{2.5}\right) \times 10^{-6}$

(Assume $N = 1000$ rpm)

$S = 6.98$ s/min

$S = 0.116$

For $S = 6.98$ s/min and $\beta = 360°$	$f(r/c) = 2.4$	...Fig. 15.6/ Pg 317, DHB
	$MFT = h_o/c = 0.845$	...Fig. 15.7/ Pg 318, DHB
	$FLV = Q/rcNl = 3.05$	...Fig. 15.8/ Pg 319, DHB

∴ Minimum oil film thickness From **DHB** $h_o/c = 0.845$

$h_o = 0.845 \times 0.0535$
$h_o = 0.0452$ mm

iii. Requirement of flow:

We know that flow (without side leakage), $FLV = \dfrac{Q}{rcNl}$ ...15.27/ Pg 304, DHB

$$3.05 = \frac{Q}{50 \times .00535 \times 1000 \times 100}$$

$Q = 815.88 \times 10^3$ mm^3/min

$\quad = 1.360$ m^3/s   (1 m^3 = 1000 l)

$Q = 0.0136$ liters/sec

28. SAE 20 oil is used to lubricate a hydrodynamic journal bearing of diameter 75 mm and length 75 mm, oil enters at 40°C. The journal rotates at 1200 rpm. The diametral clearance is 75 μm (0.075 mm). Assume operating temperatures of the oil as 53°C and determine:
    a. Magnitude and location of the minimum oil film thickness b. Power loss
    c. Oil flow through the bearing.   d. Side leakage.

VTU – June/ July 2013 – 20 Marks; Feb. 2002 – 12 Marks

Solution: Oil – SAE 20, $d = l = 75$ mm, $t_A = 40°C$, $N = 1200$ rpm $\Rightarrow n = 20$ rps, $2c = 0.075$ mm $\Rightarrow c = 0.0375$ mm, $t_o = 53°C$.

  a. $h_{min} = h_o = ?, \varnothing = ?$ b. $P = ?$ c. $Q = ?$ d. $Q_s = ?$

a. Magnitude and location of the minimum oil film thickness:

We know that, $MFT = \dfrac{h_o}{c}$ ...15.24/ Pg 304, DHB

$$h_o = (MFT) \cdot c \quad \text{...Eq. (i)}$$

But $S = \left(\dfrac{r}{c}\right)^2 \left(\dfrac{ZN}{p}\right) \times 10^{-6}$ ...Eq.(ii) 15.17a/ Pg 303, DHB

- $p = 0.622 \sqrt[3]{v}$

$= 0.622 \sqrt[3]{\dfrac{\pi d n}{1000}}$

$= 0.622 \sqrt[3]{\dfrac{\pi \times 75 \times 20}{1000}}$

$p = 1.043$ MPa

- Also $Z_k = \dfrac{Z}{\rho} \times 10^{-3}$ ...Eq. (iii) 15.2a/ Pg 301, DHB

But $Z_k = Z'_k \times 10^{-6}$ ...Eq. (iv) 15.2b/ Pg 301, DHB

Z'_k = kinematic viscosity (cSt)

For the given type of oil, i.e. SAE 20, we have	Curve No: 5 Sp. gravity @ 15°C, $\rho_{15} = 0.925$	...Tb. 15.1/ Pg 308, DHB
For curve No. 5 @ 53°C, we have	kinematic viscosity, $Z'_k = 62$ cSt	...Fig. 15.1/ Pg 316, DHB

∴ Eq. (iii) yields... $Z_k = 62 \times 10^{-6}$ m²/s

The specific gravity of oil at any temprature is found as

$\rho_t = \rho_{15} - 0.00063 (t° - 15)$ ...15.3/ Pg 301, DHB

$= 0.926 - 0.00063 (53 - 15)$

$\rho_t = 0.9011$

∴ Eq. (iv) yields... $62 \times 10^{-6} = \dfrac{Z}{0.9011} \times 10^{-3}$

$Z = 0.0559$ N-s/m²

∴ Eq. (ii) yields... $S = \left(\dfrac{37.5}{0.0375}\right)^2 \times \left(\dfrac{0.0559 \times 1200}{1.043}\right) \times 10^{-6}$

$S = 64.31$ s/min

$= 0.0719$ (unit less)

For S = 64.31 s/min and β = 360°	$f(r/c) = 22$	...Fig. 15.6/ Pg 317, DHB
	$MFT = h_o/c = 0.95$	...Fig. 15.7/ Pg 318, DHB
	$FLV = Q/rcNl = 3.1$	...Fig. 15.8/ Pg 319, DHB

∴ Eq. (i) yields... $h_o = 0.95 \times 0.0375$
$h_o = 0.035625$ mm $= 3.56265 \times 10^{-5}$ m

Location:

We know that, $\cos \theta = 1 - \dfrac{h_o}{c}$ ...15.25/ Pg 304, DHB

$\cos \theta = 1 - 0.95$

$\theta = 87.13°$

b. Power loss or heat generated:

We know that, $H_g = fWv$

- $v = \left(\dfrac{\pi d n}{1000}\right) = \left(\dfrac{\pi \times 75 \times 20}{1000}\right) = 4.712$ m/s

- From **DHB**, $f(r/c) = 22$

$$f = 22 \times \left(\dfrac{0.0375}{37.5}\right)$$

$$f = 0.022$$

∴ $H_g = 0.022 \times (1.043 \times 75 \times 75) \times 4.712$ $(W = p.ld)$

$H_g = 608.18$ W

c. Oil flow through the bearing:

From **DHB**, $FLV = Q/rcNl = 3.1$

$Q = 3.1 \times 37.5 \times 0.0375 \times 1200 \times 75$

$Q = 392.34 \times 10^3$ mm³/min

$= 6.54 \times 10^{-6}$ m³/s   (neglecting side leakage)

d. Side leakage:

We know that, $Q_s = (FVL) rcNlK_Q = QK_Q$ ...Eq. (v)

K_Q depends upon h_o/c and B/l

but, $\dfrac{B}{l} = \dfrac{2\pi r \times (\beta/360)}{l}$ ...Fig. 15.10/ Pg 320, DHB

$= \dfrac{2\pi \times 37.5 \times (360/360)}{75}$

∴ $\dfrac{B}{l} = 3.142$

At $\dfrac{B}{l} = 3.142$ and $h_o/c = 0.95$, $K_Q = 1.1$ ... Fig. 15.11/Pg 321, DHB

∴ Eq. (v) yields... $Q_s = 6.54 \times 10^{-6} \times 1.1$

$Q_s = 7.194 \times 10^{-6}$ m³/s

7.16 DESIGN PROCEDURE FOR JOURNAL BEARINGS

The bearing load, speed is given

a. Based on given machinery, note down the parameters from **Tb. 15.11/ Pg 314, DHB**

   i.e. p_{max}, Z, $ZN/p)_{min}$, $\dfrac{c}{r}$, and l/d

b.
   - If diameter is unknown, calculate d as $\dfrac{W}{ld} = \dfrac{W}{2rl} = p$ ...**15.18/ Pg 303, DHB**
   - If diameter is known calculate p and check with the table value, i.e. ($p < p_{max}$)

c. Type of oil: Based on Z from **Tb. 15.11/ Pg 314, DHB**, determine the type of oil using **Fig. 15.1/Pg 316, DHB**, assuming suitable value of oil temperature (t_o).

d. Bearing modulus:
   Calculate $C = ZN/p$ and compare with that of table value in step (a) i.e. $ZN/p)_{min}$
   Since the minimum value of C at which the film breaks is 3 times the calculated value –or– table value/3, we have

   $$C_{min} = \dfrac{ZN/p}{3}$$

   If $C \geq C_{min}$, bearing operates under hydrodynamic lubrication.

e. Calculate Sommerfeld number as $S = \left(\dfrac{r}{c}\right)^2 \left(\dfrac{ZN}{p}\right) \times 10^{-6}$ ...**15.17a/ Pg 303, DHB**

f. Calculate coefficient of friction as $f = \left[K_a \left(\dfrac{Zn}{p}\right)\left(\dfrac{r}{c}\right) \times 10^{-10} + \Delta f\right]$

   ...**15.12/ Pg 302, DHB**

g. Calculate minimum film thickness h_o from ...**Fig. 15.7/Pg 318, DHB**

h. Calculate heat generated as $H_g = fWv$ ...**15.36/ Pg 305, DHB**

i. Calculate heat dissipated as $H_D = \dfrac{ld(T+18)^2}{K_3}$ ...**15.41/ Pg 306, DHB**

   $$T = (t_B - t_A) = \dfrac{t_o - t_A}{2}$$

j. Calculate amount of artificial cooling as $= H_g - H_D$
   If $H_D < H_g$, artificial cooling is required

7.16.1 When Diameter is Unknown

29. Design a journal bearing for a centrifugal pump from the following data:
   Load on the journal = 10 kN
   Speed of the journal = 900 rpm
   Ambient temperature = 15°C

VTU – June/ July 2008 – 14 Marks

Solution: Application: centrifugal pump, W = 10 kN, N = 900 rpm $\Rightarrow n$ = 15 rps, t_A = 15 °C

660 Design of Machine Elements II (DME II)

a. Parameters:

From **Tb. 15.11/ Pg 314, DHB**, for centrifugal pump, we have

$p_{max} = 0.7 - 1.4$ MPa, $Z = 0.025$ N-s/m², $ZN/p)_{min} = 29.01$, $c/r = 0.0013$, $l/d = 1.0 - 2.0$

Let $p_{max} = 1.4$ MPa and $l = 1.5d$

b. To find d:

We know that, $p = \dfrac{W}{ld}$ ...**15.18/ Pg 303, DHB**

$$1.4 = \dfrac{10000}{1.5 \times d^2}$$

$d = 69$ mm

$d \approx 70$ mm and $l = 1.5 \times 70 = 105$ mm

c. Type of oil:

We know that, $Z_k = \dfrac{Z}{\rho} \times 10^{-3}$ ...Eq. (i) **15.2a/ Pg 301, DHB**

Here $Z = 0.025$ N-s/m² (from step a)

- Assume $t_o = 70°C$ and $\rho = 0.9$

∴ Eq. (i) yields... $Z_k = \dfrac{0.025}{0.9} \times 10^{-3}$

$Z_k = 2.78 \times 10^{-5}$ m²/s

Also $Z_k = Z'_k \times 10^{-6}$ ...Eq. (ii) **15.2b/ Pg 301, DHB**

Z'_k = kinematic viscosity (cSt)

$2.78 \times 10^{-5} = Z'_k - 10^{-6}$

$Z'_k = 27.78$ cSt

At $t_o = 70°C$ and $Z'_k = 27.78$ cSt type of curve is	Curve No: 5	...**Fig. 15.1/ Pg 316, DHB**
For curve No. 5 @ 70°C, type of oil is	SAE 20	...**Tb. 15.1/ Pg 308, DHB**

d. Bearing modulus C:

$C = \dfrac{ZN}{p} = \dfrac{0.025 \times 900}{1.4} = 16.07$

From **Tb. 15.11/ Pg 314, DHB**, $ZN/p_{min} = 29.01$

But the minimum value of C at which the film breaks is 3 times the calculated value –or– table value/3, we have

$$C_{min} = \dfrac{ZN/p}{3} = \dfrac{29.01}{3} = 9.67$$

Since $C \geq C_{min}$, bearing operates under hydrodynamic lubrication.

e. Sommerfeld number:

We know that, $S = \left(\dfrac{r}{c}\right)^2 \left(\dfrac{ZN}{p}\right) \times 10^{-6}$ ...15.17a/ Pg 303, DHB

$= \left(\dfrac{1}{0.0013}\right)^2 \times 16.07 \times 10^{-6}$

$S = 9.509 \text{ s/min}$

f. Coefficient of friction:

According to McKee $f = \left[K_a \left(\dfrac{Zn}{p}\right)\left(\dfrac{r}{c}\right) \times 10^{-10} + \Delta f \right]$ ...15.12/ Pg 302, DHB

- Δf = Correction factor for bearing for $0.75 < \dfrac{l}{d} < 2.8$ ...Fig. 15.4/ Pg 317, DHB

- Now $\dfrac{l}{d} = 1.5$

 Since $0.75 < 1.5 < 2.8$, $\Delta f = 0.002$,

- $K_a = 0.195 \times 10^6$ ...for full journal bearing, [i.e. $\beta = 360°$]

$f = \left[0.195 \times 10^6 \times \left(\dfrac{16.07}{60}\right) \times \left(\dfrac{1}{0.0013}\right) \times 10^{-10} + 0.002 \right]$

$f = 0.00602$

g. Minimum film thickness:

For $S = 9.509$ s/min and $\beta = 360°$	MFT = h_o/c = 0.9	...Fig. 15.7/ Pg 318, DHB

∴ $h_o = 0.9 \times (0.0013 \times 35)$
$h_o = 0.04095$ mm

h. Heat generated:

We know that, $H_g = fWv$ ...15.36/ Pg 305, DHB

$v = \left(\dfrac{\pi d n}{1000}\right) = \left(\dfrac{\pi \times 70 \times 15}{1000}\right) = 3.30 \text{ m/s}$

∴ $H_g = 0.00602 \times 10000 \times 3.30$
$H_g = 198.66$ W

i. Heat dissipated:

We know that, $H_D = \dfrac{ld(T+18)^2}{K_3}$ ...15.41/ Pg 306, DHB

$K_3 = 0.4743 \times 10^6$, Assume $t_o = 70°C$

$$T = (t_B - t_A) = \frac{t_o - t_A}{2}$$

$$= \frac{70 - 15}{2}$$

$$T = 27.5°C$$

$$\therefore \quad H_D = \frac{105 \times 70 \times (27.5 + 18)^2}{0.4743 \times 10^6}$$

$$H_D = 32.08 \text{ W}$$

j. Amount of artificial cooling:

Since $H_D < H_g$, artificial cooling is required.

We know that amount of artificial cooling $= H_g - H_D$

$$= 198.66 - 32.08 = 166.62 \text{ W}$$

30. **Design a full journal bearing subjected to 6 kN at 1000 rpm of the journal. The journal is of hardened steel and the bearing is of babbit material. The bearing is operated with SAE40 oil at 70°C and the ambient temperature is 30°C. Also determine the amount of artificial cooling required.**

VTU – June/ July 2009 – 15 Marks; Dec. 07/ Jan. 2008 – 14 Marks

Solution: $W = 6$ kN, $N = 1000$ rpm $\Rightarrow n = 16.67$ rps, oil – SAE 40, $t_A = 30°C$, $t_o = 70°C$

Material: Journal – Hardened steel   Bearing – Babbit

a. To find Z:

We know that, $Z_k = \dfrac{Z}{\rho} \times 10^{-3}$ ...Eq. (i) 15.2a/ Pg 301, DHB

But $\quad Z_k = Z'_k \times 10^{-6}$ ...Eq. (ii) 15.2b/ Pg 301, DHB

Z'_k = kinematic viscosity (cSt)

For the given type of oil, i.e. SAE 40, we have	Curve No: 6 Sp. gravity @ 15°C, $\rho_{15} = 0.930$	...Tb. 15.1/ Pg 308, DHB
For curve No. 6 @ 70°C, we have	Kinematic viscosity, $Z'_k = 42$ cSt	...Fig. 15.1/ Pg 316, DHB

$\therefore$ Eq. (ii) yields... $\quad Z_k = 42 \times 10^{-6}$ m^2/s

The specific gravity of oil at any temprature is found as

$$\rho_t = \rho_{15} - 0.00063 \, (t° - 15) \qquad \text{...15.3/ Pg 301, DHB}$$

$$= 0.930 - 0.00063 \, (70 - 15)$$

$$\rho_t = 0.8954$$

$\therefore$ Eq. (i) yields... $\quad 42 \times 10^{-6} = \dfrac{Z}{0.8954} \times 10^{-3}$

$$Z = 0.0376 \text{ N-s/m}^2$$

b. To find p:

For the given material combination, $\dfrac{ZN}{p} = C = 2.902$ ...Tb. 15.6/ Pg 311, DHB

$$\dfrac{0.0376 \times 1000}{p} = 2.902$$

$$p = 12.96 \text{ MPa}$$

c. To find d:

We know that, $p = \dfrac{W}{ld}$ ...15.18/ Pg 303, DHB

Assume $l = d$

$$12.96 = \dfrac{6000}{d^2}$$

$$d = 21.52 \text{ mm}$$

$$d \approx 25 \text{ mm} = l$$

d. Type of oil:

Given: type of oil is SAE 40

e. Bearing modulus C:

Here $C = \dfrac{ZN}{p} = 2.902$ ...Tb. 15.6/ Pg 311, DHB

But the minimum value of C at which the film breaks is 3 times the calculated value –or- table value/3, we have

$$C_{min} = \dfrac{ZN/p}{3} = \dfrac{2.902}{3} = 0.9673$$

Since $C \geq C_{min}$, bearing operates under hydrodynamic lubrication.

f. Sommerfeld number:

We know that, $S = \left(\dfrac{r}{c}\right)^2 \left(\dfrac{ZN}{p}\right) \times 10^{-6}$ ...15.17a/ Pg 303, DHB

Assume $\dfrac{r}{c} = 1000$

$$= 1000^2 \times 2.902 \times 10^{-6}$$

$$S = 2.902 \text{ s/min}$$

g. Coefficient of friction:

According to McKee $f = \left[K_a \left(\dfrac{Zn}{p}\right)\left(\dfrac{r}{c}\right) \times 10^{-10} + \Delta f\right]$ ...15.12/ Pg 302, DHB

- Δf = Correction factor for bearing for $0.75 < \dfrac{l}{d} < 2.8$ ...**Fig. 15.4/ Pg 317, DHB**

- Now $\dfrac{l}{d} = 1$

  Since $0.75 < 1 < 2.8$, $\Delta f = 0.002$,

- $K_a = 0.195 \times 10^6$ ...for full journal bearing, [i.e. $\beta = 360°$]

$$f = \left[0.195 \times 10^6 \times \left(\dfrac{2.902}{60}\right) \times 1000 \times 10^{-10} + 0.002\right]$$

$$f = 2.493 \times 10^{-3}$$

h. Minimum film thickness:

For $S = 2.902$ s/min and $\beta = 360°$	$MFT = h_o/c = 0.66$	...**Fig. 15.7/ Pg 318, DHB**

$\therefore \quad h_o = 0.66c$

$\qquad = 0.66 \times \dfrac{12.5}{1000} \qquad$ Since $\dfrac{r}{c} = 1000$

$h_o = 0.00825$ mm

i. Heat generated:

We know that, $H_g = fWv$ ...**15.36/ Pg 305, DHB**

$$v = \left(\dfrac{\pi d n}{1000}\right) = \left(\dfrac{\pi \times 25 \times 16.67}{1000}\right) = 1.31 \text{ m/s}$$

$\therefore \quad H_g = 2.943 \times 10^{-3} \times 6000 \times 1.31$

$\qquad H_g = 23.11$ W

j. Heat dissipated:

We know that, $H_D = \dfrac{ld(T+18)^2}{K_3}$ ...**15.41/ Pg 306, DHB**

$\qquad K_3 = 0.4743 \times 10^6$

$\qquad T = (t_B - t_A) = \dfrac{t_o - t_A}{2}$

$\qquad\quad = \dfrac{70 - 30}{2}$

$\qquad T = 20°C$

$\therefore \quad H_D = \dfrac{25 \times 25 \times (20 + 18)^2}{0.4743 \times 10^6}$

$\qquad H_D = 1.90$ W

k. Amount of artificial cooling:

Since $H_D < H_g$, artificial cooling is required.

We know that amount of artificial cooling = $H_g - H_D$
$$= 23.11 - 1.90 = 21.21 \text{ W}$$

31. Design a journal bearing to withstand a load of 5886 N. Speed of the journal is 1000 rpm. The journal is made of hardened steel and bearing is made of babbit. Operating temperature is 70°C and ambient temperature is 30°C. Check the design for thermal equilibrium and also determine the power loss at the bearing. The lubricant used is of grade SAE 40, $l/d = 1.5$.

VTU – Dec. 2011 – 16 Marks; Dec. 2010 – 14 Marks; June/ July 2009 – 14 Marks; Jan./ Feb. 2005 – 10 Marks

Solution: $W = 5886$ N, $N = 1000$ rpm $\Rightarrow n = 16.67$ rps, $t_A = 30°C$, $t_o = 70°C$, oil – SAE 40, $l/d = 1.5$

Material: Journal – Hardened steel   Bearing – Babbit

a. To find Z:

We know that, $Z_k = \dfrac{Z}{\rho} \times 10^{-3}$ ...Eq. (i) 15.2a/ Pg 301, DHB

But $Z_k = Z'_k \times 10^{-6}$ ...Eq. (ii) 15.2b/ Pg 301, DHB

Z'_k = kinematic viscosity (cSt)

For the given type of oil, i.e. SAE 40, we have	Curve No: 6 Sp. gravity @ 15°C, $\rho_{15} = 0.930$	...Tb. 15.1/ Pg 308, DHB
For curve No. 6 @ 70°C, we have	Kinematic viscosity, $Z'_k = 42$ cSt	...Fig. 15.1/ Pg 316, DHB

∴ Eq. (ii) yields... $Z_k = 42 \times 10^{-6}$ m²/s

The specific gravity of oil at any temperature is found as

$$\rho_t = \rho_{15} - 0.00063 (t° - 15) \quad \text{...15.3/ Pg 301, DHB}$$
$$= 0.930 - 0.00063 (70 - 15)$$
$$\rho_t = 0.8954$$

∴ Eq. (i) yields... $42 \times 10^{-6} = \dfrac{Z}{0.8954} \times 10^{-3}$

$$Z = 0.0376 \text{ N-s/m}^2$$

b. To find p:

For the given material combination, $\dfrac{ZN}{p} = C = 2.902$ ...Tb. 15.6/ Pg 311, DHB

$$\dfrac{0.0376 \times 1000}{p} = 2.902$$

$$p = 12.96 \text{ MPa}$$

c. To find d:

We know that, $p = \dfrac{W}{ld}$ ...15.18/ Pg 303, DHB

Given $\qquad l = 1.5d$

$$12.96 = \dfrac{5886}{1.5 \times d^2}$$

$$d = 17.40 \text{ mm}$$
$$d \approx 20 \text{ mm}$$
$$l = 1.5 \times 20 = 30 \text{ mm}$$

d. Type of oil:

Given: type of oil is SAE 40

e. Bearing modulus C:

Here $C = \dfrac{ZN}{p} = 2.902$ ...Tb. 15.6/ Pg 311, DHB

But the minimum value of C at which the film breaks is 3 times the calculated value –or– table value/3, we have

$$C_{min} = \dfrac{ZN/p}{3} = \dfrac{2.902}{3} = 0.9673$$

Since $C \geq C_{min}$, bearing oprates under hydrodynamic lubrication.

f. Sommerfeld number:

We know that, $S = \left(\dfrac{r}{c}\right)^2 \left(\dfrac{ZN}{p}\right) \times 10^{-6}$ ...15.17a/ Pg 303, DHB

Assume $\quad \dfrac{r}{c} = 1000$

$$= 1000^2 \times 2.902 \times 10^{-6}$$
$$S = 2.902 \text{ s/min}$$

g. Coefficient of friction:

According to McKee $f = \left[K_a \left(\dfrac{Zn}{p}\right)\left(\dfrac{r}{c}\right) \times 10^{-10} + \Delta f\right]$ ...15.12/ Pg 302, DHB

- Δf = Correction factor for bearing for $0.75 < \dfrac{l}{d} < 2.8$ ...Fig. 15.4/ Pg 317, DHB

- Now $\dfrac{l}{d} = 1.5$

Since $0.75 < 1.5 < 2.8$, $\Delta f = 0.002$,

- $K_a = 0.195 \times 10^6$ ...for full journal bearing, [i.e. $\beta = 360°$]

$$f = \left[0.195 \times 10^6 \times \left(\frac{2.902}{60}\right) \times 1000 \times 10^{-10} + 0.002\right]$$

$$f = 2.943 \times 10^{-3}$$

h. Minimum film thickness:

For $S = 2.902$ s/min and $\beta = 360°$	$MFT = h_o/c = 0.66$	...Fig. 15.7/ Pg 318, DHB

$\therefore \quad h_o = 0.66c$

$= 0.66 \times \dfrac{10}{1000}$ \quad Since $\dfrac{r}{c} = 1000$

$h_o = 0.0066$ mm

i. Heat generated:

We know that, $H_g = fWv$ \hfill ...15.36/ Pg 305, DHB

$$v = \left(\frac{\pi d n}{1000}\right) = \left(\frac{\pi \times 20 \times 16.67}{1000}\right) = 1.05 \text{ m/s}$$

$\therefore \quad H_g = 2.943 \times 10^{-3} \times 5886 \times 1.05$

$H_g = 18.18$ W

j. Heat dissipated:

We know that, $H_D = \dfrac{ld(T+18)^2}{K_3}$ \hfill ...15.41/ Pg 306, DHB

$K_3 = 0.4743 \times 10^6$

$T = (t_B - t_A) = \dfrac{t_o - t_A}{2}$

$= \dfrac{70 - 30}{2}$

$T = 20°C$

$\therefore \quad H_D = \dfrac{20 \times 30 \times (20+18)^2}{0.4743 \times 10^6}$

$H_D = 1.83$ W

k. Amount of artificial cooling:

Since $H_D < H_g$, artificial cooling is required.

We know that amount of artificial cooling $= H_g - H_D$

$= 18.18 - 1.83 = 1.35$ W

7.16.2 Diameter is Known

32. Design a journal bearing for a centrifugal pump running at 1200 rpm. Diameter of the journal is 100 mm and load on the bearing is 15 kN. Take $l/d = 1.5$, bearing temperature 50° and ambient temperature 30°. Find whether artificial cooling is required. *VTU – Dec. 08/ Jan. 2009 – 14 Marks*

Solution: Application: Centrifugal pump, $N = 1200$ rpm $\Rightarrow n = 20$ rps, $d = 100$ mm, $l/d = 1.5$, $l = 150$ mm, $t_B = 50°C$, $t_A = 30°C$, $W = 15$ kN

a. Parameters:

From **Tb. 15.11/ Pg 314, DHB**, for centrifugal pump, we have

$p_{max} = 0.7 – 1.4$ MPa, $Z = 0.025$ N-s/m², $ZN/p)_{min} = 29.01$, $c/r = 0.0013$, $l/d = 1.0 – 2.0$

Let $p_{max} = 1.4$ MPa and $l = 1.5d = 1.5 \times 100 = 150$ mm

b. To find p:

We know that, $p = \dfrac{W}{ld}$ ...**15.18/ Pg 303, DHB**

$$= \dfrac{15000}{150 \times 100}$$

$p = 1$ MPa

Since $p < p_{max}$, the value of l & d are safe.

c. Type of oil:

We know that, $Z_k = \dfrac{Z}{\rho} \times 10^{-3}$ ...Eq. (i) **15.2a/ Pg 301, DHB**

- Here $Z = 0.025$ N-s/m² (from step *a*)

- $T = (t_B - t_A) = \dfrac{t_o - t_A}{2}$

$(50 - 30) = \dfrac{t_o - 30}{2}$

$t_o = 70°C$

- Assume $\rho = 0.9$

∴ Eq. (7.1) yields... $Z_k = \dfrac{0.025}{0.9} \times 10^{-3}$

$Z_k = 2.78 \times 10^{-5}$ m²/s

Also $Z_k = Z_k' \times 10^{-6}$ ...**15.2b/ Pg 301, DHB**

Z_k' = kinematic viscosity (cSt)

$2.78 \times 10^{-5} = Z_k' \times 10^{-6}$

$Z_k' = 27.78$ cSt

At $t_o = 70°C$ and $Z'_k = 27.78$ cSt, type of curve is	Curve No: 5	...Fig. 15.1/ Pg 316, DHB
For curve No. 5 @ 70°C, type of oil is	SAE 20	...Tb. 15.1/ Pg 308, DHB

d. Bearing modulus C:

$$C = \frac{ZN}{p} = \frac{0.025 \times 1200}{1} = 30$$

From **Tb. 15.11/ Pg 314, DHB**, $ZN/p)_{min} = 29.01$

But the minimum value of C at which the film breaks is 3 times the calculated value –or– table value/3, we have

$$C_{min} = \frac{ZN/p}{3} = \frac{29.01}{3} = 9.67$$

Since $C \geq C_{min}$, bearing operates under hydrodynamic lubrication.

e. Sommerfeld number:

We know that, $S = \left(\frac{r}{c}\right)^2 \left(\frac{ZN}{p}\right) \times 10^{-6}$ ...15.17a/ Pg 303, DHB

$$= \left(\frac{1}{0.0013}\right)^2 \times 30 \times 10^{-6}$$

$S = 17.75$ s/min

f. Coefficient of friction:

According to McKee $f = \left[K_a \left(\frac{Zn}{p}\right)\left(\frac{r}{c}\right) \times 10^{-10} + \Delta f\right]$ ...15.12/ Pg 302, DHB

- Δf = Correction factor for bearing for $0.75 < \frac{l}{d} < 2.8$ ...Fig. 15.4/ Pg 317, DHB

- Now $\frac{l}{d} = 1.5$

  Since $0.75 < 1.5 < 2.8$, $\Delta f = 0.002$,

- $K_a = 0.195 \times 10^6$ ...for full journal bearing [i.e. $\beta = 360°$]

$$f = \left[0.195 \times 10^6 \times \left(\frac{30}{60}\right) \times \left(\frac{1}{0.0013}\right) \times 10^{-10} + 0.002\right]$$

$f = 0.0095$

g. Minimum film thickness:

For **S = 17.75** s/min and $\beta = 360°$	$MFT = h_o/c = 0.94$	...Fig. 15.7/ Pg 318, DHB

$\therefore \quad h_o = 0.94 \times (0.0013 \times 50)$

$h_o = 0.0611$ mm

h. Heat generated:

We know that, $H_g = fWv$ ...15.36/ Pg 305, DHB

$$v = \left(\frac{\pi d n}{1000}\right) = \left(\frac{\pi \times 100 \times 20}{1000}\right) = 6.28 \text{ m/s}$$

$\therefore \quad H_g = 0.0095 \times 15000 \times 6.28$

$H_g = 895$ W

i. Heat dissipated:

We know that, $H_D = \dfrac{ld(T+18)^2}{K_3}$ ...15.41/ Pg 306, DHB

$K_3 = 0.4743 \times 10^6$

$T = (t_B - t_A) = 50 - 30 = 20°C$

$\therefore \quad H_D = \dfrac{105 \times 100 \times (20+18)^2}{0.4743 \times 10^6}$

$H_D = 45.67$ W

j. Amount of artificial cooling:

Since $H_D < H_g$, artificial cooling is required.

We know that amount of artificial cooling = $H_g - H_D$

$= 895 - 45.67 = 849.33$ W

33. **A journal bearing is required to be designed for a rotary compressor for operation at a speed of 1500 rpm. The bearing is to sustain a load of 4500 N and the diameter of the main shaft is 50 mm. Determine:**
   a. length and diameter of bearing.
   b. viscosity of oil to be used as a lubricant and hence suggest a lubricating oil.
   c. the coefficient of friction.
   d. heat generated.
   e. heat dissipating capacity.
   f. amount of heat to be removed by artificial cooling.
   g. sommerfeld number.

VTU – Jan./ Feb. 2005 – 14 Marks

Solution: Application: Rotary compressor, $N = 1500$ rpm $\Rightarrow n = 25$ rps, $W = 4500$ N, $d = 50$ mm,

a. $l = ?$ b. $Z = ?$ c. $f = ?$ d. $H_g = ?$ e. $H_D = ?$
f. Artificial cooling g. $S = ?$

Parameters:

From **Tb. 15.11/ Pg 314, DHB**, for rotary compressor, we have

$p_{max} = 1.8$ MPa, $Z = 0.030 - 0.080$ N-s/m², $ZN/p_{min} = 4.36$, $c/r = 0.001$, $l/d = 1.0 - 2.2$

Let $p_{max} = 1.8$ MPa and $l = 1.6d$

a. To find l:

Let $l = 1.6d = 16 \times 50 = 80$ mm

Check for p:

We know that, $p = \dfrac{W}{ld}$ ...15.18/ Pg 303, DHB

$$= \dfrac{4500}{80 \times 50}$$

$p = 1.13$ MPa

Since $p < p_{max}$, the value of l & d are safe.

b. Type of oil:

We know that, $Z_k = \dfrac{Z}{\rho} \times 10^{-3}$ ...Eq. (i) 15.2a/ Pg 301, DHB

- Here $Z = 0.030$ N-s/m² (from step a)
- Assume $t_o = 70°C$, $t_A = 25°C$ $\rho = 0.9$

∴ Eq. (i) yields... $Z_k = \dfrac{0.03}{0.9} \times 10^{-3}$

$Z_k = 3.33 \times 10^{-5}$ m²/s

Also $Z_k = Z'_k \times 10^{-6}$ ...15.2b/ Pg 301, DHB

Z'_k = kinematic viscosity (cSt)

$3.33 \times 10^{-5} = Z'_k - 10^{-6}$

$Z'_k = 33.33$ cSt

At $t_o = 70°C$ and $Z'_k = 33.33$ cSt, type of curve is	Curve No: 5	...Fig. 15.1/ Pg 316, DHB
For curve No. 5 @ 70°C, type of oil is	SAE 20	...Tb. 15.1/ Pg 308, DHB

c. Coefficient of friction:

According to McKee $f = \left[K_a \left(\dfrac{Zn}{p} \right) \left(\dfrac{r}{c} \right) \times 10^{-10} + \Delta f \right]$ ...15.12/ Pg 302, DHB

- Δf = Correction factor for bearing for $0.75 < \dfrac{l}{d} < 2.8$ ...Fig. 15.4/ Pg 317, DHB

- Now $\dfrac{l}{d} = 1.6$

  Since $0.75 < 1.6 < 2.8$, $\Delta f = 0.002$,

- $K_a = 0.195 \times 10^6$ ...for full journal bearing [i.e. $\beta = 360°$]

$$f = \left[0.195 \times 10^6 \times \left(\dfrac{0.03 \times 25}{1.13} \right) \times \left(\dfrac{1}{0.001} \right) \times 10^{-10} + 0.002 \right]$$

$f = 0.015$

d. Heat generated:

We know that, $H_g = fWv$ ...15.36/ Pg 305, DHB

$$v = \left(\frac{\pi d n}{1000}\right) = \left(\frac{\pi \times 50 \times 25}{1000}\right) = 3.93 \text{ m/s}$$

$\therefore \quad H_g = 0.015 \times 4500 \times 3.93$

$H_g = 265.07$ W

e. Heat dissipated:

We know that, $H_D = \dfrac{ld(T+18)^2}{K_3}$ ...15.41/ Pg 306, DHB

$K_3 = 0.4743 \times 10^6$

$T = (t_B - t_A) = \dfrac{t_o - t_A}{2}$

$T = \dfrac{70 - 25}{2}$

$\therefore \quad H_D = \dfrac{80 \times 50 \times (22.5 + 18)^2}{0.4743 \times 10^6}$

$H_D = 13.83$ W

f. Amount of artificial cooling:

Since $H_D < H_g$, artificial cooling is required.

We know that amount of artificial cooling $= H_g - H_D$

$= 265.07 - 13.83 = 251.2$ W

g. Sommerfeld number:

We know that, $S = \left(\dfrac{r}{c}\right)^2 \left(\dfrac{ZN}{p}\right) \times 10^{-6}$ ...15.17a/ Pg 303, DHB

$$= \left(\frac{1}{0.001}\right)^2 \times \left(\frac{0.03 \times 1500}{1.13}\right) \times 10^{-6}$$

$S = 39.82$ s/min $= 0.664$

34. It is required to design a main bearing of a 4 stroke oil engine to sustain a load of 6 kN over a shaft of diameter 50 mm. The operating speed of the shaft is 1000 rpm and the operating temperature is 50°C. Determine:
   i. dimensions of the bearing.
   ii. the viscosity of the oil to be used for the bearing and hence suggest appropriate oil.
   iii. coefficient of friction.
   iv. heat generated.
   v. heat dissipated.

vi. heat to be removed by artificial cooling if necessary.
vii. sommerfeld number.

VTU – Jan./ Feb. 2006 – 14 Marks

Solution: Application: 4 stroke oil engine, $W = 6000$ N, $d = 50$ mm, $N = 1000$ rpm $\Rightarrow$ $n = 16.67$ rps

a. $d, l = ?$ b. $Z = ?$ c. $f = ?$ d. $H_g = ?$ e. $H_D = ?$
f. Artificial cooling g. $S = ?$

Parameters:

From **Tb. 15.11/ Pg 314, DHB**, for rotary compressor, we have

$p_{max} = 4.8 - 8.2$ MPa, $Z = 0.02 - 0.065$ N-s/m², $ZN/p_{min} = 2.90$, $c/r = 0.001$, $l/d = 0.6 - 2.0$

Let $p_{max} = 8.2$ MPa and $l = 1.3d$

i. To find d, l:

Given $d = 50$ mm
Let $l = 1.3d = 1.3 \times 50 = 65$ mm

Check for p:

We know that, $p = \dfrac{W}{ld}$ ...**15.18/ Pg 303, DHB**

$= \dfrac{6000}{65 \times 50}$

$p = 1.85$ MPa

Since $p < p_{max}$, the value of l & d are safe.

ii. Type of oil:

We know that, $Z_k = \dfrac{Z}{\rho} \times 10^{-3}$ ...**Eq. (i) 15.2a/ Pg 301, DHB**

- Here $Z = 0.020$ N-s/m² (from step a)
- Assume $t_o = 60°C$, $t_A = 25°C$ $\rho = 0.9$

∴ Eq. (i) yields... $Z_k = \dfrac{0.02}{0.9} \times 10^{-3}$

$Z_k = 2.22 \times 10^{-5}$ m²/s

Also $Z_k = Z'_k \times 10^{-6}$ ...**15.2b/ Pg 301, DHB**

Z'_k = Kinematic viscosity (cSt)
$2.22 \times 10^{-5} = Z'_k - 10^{-6}$
$Z'_k = 22.22$ cSt

At $t_o = 60°C$ and $Z'_k = 22.22$ cSt, type of curve is	Curve No: 4	...**Fig. 15.1/ Pg 316, DHB**
For curve No. 4 @ 60°C, type of oil is	Extra light motor oil	...**Tb. 15.1/ Pg 308, DHB**

iii. Coefficient of friction:

According to McKee $f = \left[K_a \left(\dfrac{Zn}{p} \right) \left(\dfrac{r}{c} \right) \times 10^{-10} + \Delta f \right]$ ...15.12/ Pg 302, DHB

- Δf = Correction factor for bearing for $0.75 < \dfrac{l}{d} < 2.8$ ...Fig. 15.4/ Pg 317, DHB

- Now $\dfrac{l}{d} = 1.3$

  Since $0.75 < 1.3 < 2.8$, $\Delta f = 0.002$,

- $K_a = 0.195 \times 10^6$ ...for full journal bearing [i.e. $\beta = 360°$]

$$f = \left[0.195 \times 10^6 \times \left(\dfrac{0.02 \times 16.67}{1.85} \right) \times \left(\dfrac{1}{0.001} \right) \times 10^{-10} + 0.002 \right]$$

$f = 0.0055$

iv. Heat generated:

We know that, $H_g = fWv$ ...15.36/ Pg 305, DHB

$$v = \left(\dfrac{\pi d n}{1000} \right) = \left(\dfrac{\pi \times 50 \times 16.67}{1000} \right) = 2.62 \text{ m/s}$$

∴ $H_g = 0.0055 \times 6000 \times 2.62$
$H_g = 86.41$ W

v. Heat dissipated:

We know that, $H_D = \dfrac{ld(T+18)^2}{K_3}$ ...15.41/ Pg 306, DHB

$K_3 = 0.4743 \times 10^6$

$T = (t_B - t_A) = \dfrac{t_o - t_A}{2}$

$= \dfrac{60 - 25}{2}$

$T = 17.5°C$

∴ $H_D = \dfrac{65 \times 50 \times (17.5 + 18)^2}{0.4743 \times 10^6}$

$H_D = 8.64$ W

vi. Amount of artificial cooling:

Since $H_D < H_g$, artificial cooling is required.
We know that amount of artificial cooling = $H_g - H_D$
$= 86.41 - 8.64 = 77.77$ W

vii. Sommerfeld number:

We know that, $S = \left(\dfrac{r}{c}\right)^2 \left(\dfrac{ZN}{p}\right) \times 10^{-6}$ ...15.17a/ Pg 303, DHB

$= \left(\dfrac{1}{0.001}\right)^2 \times \left(\dfrac{0.02 \times 1000}{1.85}\right) \times 10^{-6}$

$S = 10.81$ s/min $= 0.180$

7.17 THRUST BEARING

Thrust bearings are used to take axial load in a shaft, the axis of which may be horizontal or vertical. Thrust normally occurs in vertical shafts. The functions of thrust bearing are:
- To prevent the shaft from drifting in the axial direction and
- To transfer thrust loads applied on the shaft

Examples: Machine tools, marine drive shafts, turbines, motors and pumps.

Classification:

Thrust bearings are classified as
1. Foot step -or- pivot bearing
   a. Flat pivot
   b. Conical pivot/conical truncated pivot
2. Collar bearing

7.17.1 Pivot Bearing

The simplest thrust bearing is the flat pivot/ plain thrust bearing as shown in **Fig. 7.11**, used for vertical shafts. Here the wear occurs at the outer radius since the rubbing velocity is maximum. As a result, the pressure at the center becomes excessive thereby leading to overheating and failure of lubricant. This problem can be overcome in two ways:
- By making a hole in the center of the thrust disc of diameter d''.
- By using a pile of discs made of bronze and steel, arranged alternatively thereby leading to reduction in wear by distributing it over all the discs.

Note: In designing thrust bearings, it is assumed that the pressure is uniformly distributed throughout the bearing surface.

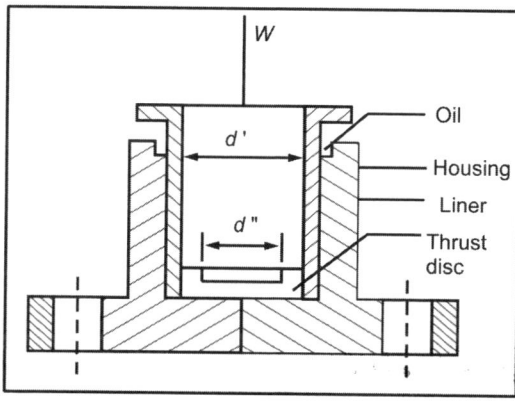

Fig. 7.11: Flat pivot plain thrust bearing

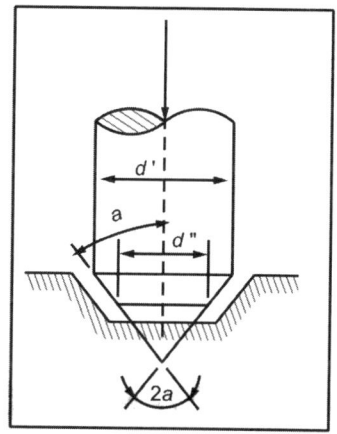

Fig. 7.12: Conical pivot-or-truncated conical pivot bearing

→ Total axial load on the shaft, $W = \dfrac{\pi}{4}(d'^2 - d''^2)p$

→ Power lost in friction, $P = \dfrac{2\pi n T_c}{1000}$ kW

Flat pivot bearing (Fig. 7.11)

In designing a flat pivot bearing, it is assumed that the pressure is uniformly distributed throughout the bearing surface.

→ The frictional torque: $T_c = \dfrac{W f_c d_c}{2}$ ...9.28/ Pg 107, DHB

- d_c = mean diameter of thrust collar

$= \dfrac{2}{3}\left(\dfrac{d'^3 - d''^3}{d'^2 - d''^2}\right)$ ...Based on uniform intensity of pressure

$= \left(\dfrac{d' + d''}{2}\right)$ ...Based on uniform wear.

d' = outer diameter of pivot
d'' = hole diameter in thrust disc.

→ The coefficient of friction for a well lubricated step bearing may be taken as 0.015 to 0.02

Conical pivot (Fig. 7.12)

→ The frictional torque: $T_c = \dfrac{W f_c d_c}{2}$ ...9.28/ Pg 107, DHB

- d_c = mean diameter of thrust collar

$= \dfrac{2}{3 \sin \alpha}\left(\dfrac{d'^3 - d''^3}{d'^2 - d''^2}\right)$ ...Based on uniform intensity of pressure

$= \left(\dfrac{d' + d''}{2 \sin \alpha}\right)$ ...Based on uniform wear.

d' = outer diameter of cone
d'' = inner diameter of cone
α_1 = semi-vertical angle of cone, (normally 60°)

7.17.2 Collar Bearing

A simple multicollar bearing for horizontal shaft is shown in **Fig. 7.13**. The collars are either internal parts of the shaft or rigidly fastened to it.

→ The average intensity of pressure with i collars, $p = \dfrac{4W}{\pi i (d'^2 - d''^2)}$

→ The frictional torque for each collar: $T_c = \dfrac{W f_c d_c}{2i}$ ...9.28/ Pg 107, DHB

- d_c = mean diameter of thrust collar

$$= \frac{2}{3}\left(\frac{d'^3 - d''^3}{d'^2 - d''^2}\right) \quad \text{...Based on uniform intensity of pressure}$$

$$= \left(\frac{d' + d''}{2}\right) \quad \text{...Based on uniform wear.}$$

d' = outer diameter of collar (1.5 d'')
d'' = inner diameter of collar or diameter of shaft
i = number of collars

→ The coefficient of friction for collar bearing is given as, $f = 83.75\left(\dfrac{v^{0.5}}{p^{0.67}}\right)$

v – m/s, p – N/m²

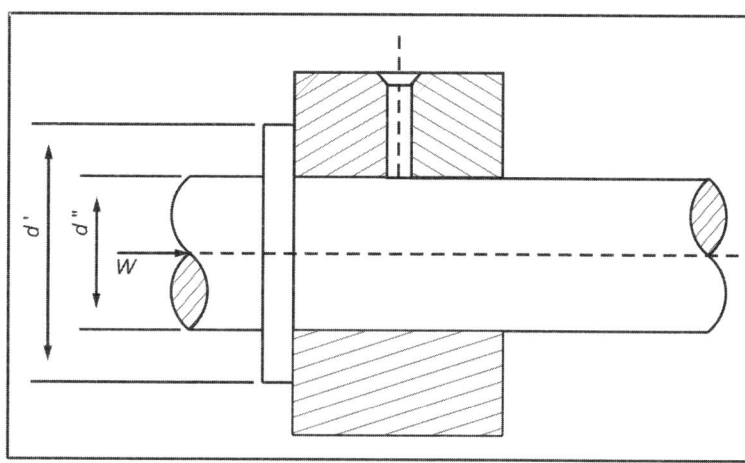

Fig. 7.13: Collar bearing

7.18 ALLOWABLE PRESSURES

For step bearings, single collar and water cooled multi-collar thrust bearings, the allowable bearing pressure may be taken as follows:
- For rubbing speeds (v) from 0.25 to 1 m/s, the bearing pressure should be such that $pv \leq 700$.
  Where p is in kPa and v in m/s.
- For rubbing speeds over 1 m/s, the pressure should not exceed 0.7 MPa.
- For intermittent service, the bearing pressure may be taken as 10.5 MPa.
- For very slow speeds, the bearing pressure may be taken as high as 14 MPa

35. Determine the dimensions of a step bearing required to support a load of 20 kN. The shaft speed is 740 rpm. Assume $d'' = 0.3d'$, $p = 0.45$ MPa, and $f_c = 0.018$. Also calculate the power lost in friction.

Solution: W = 20 kN, N = 740 rpm ⇒ n = 12.33 rps, $d'' = 0.3d'$, $p = 0.45$ MPa, $f = 0.018$.
  a. d', d'' = ?   b. P = ?

a. To find d', d'':

We know that, $W = \dfrac{\pi}{4}(d'^2 - d''^2)p$

$$20000 = \dfrac{\pi}{4}[d'^2 - (0.3d')^2] \times 0.45$$

$$d' = 249.36 \approx 250 \text{ mm}$$

$$d'' = 0.3d' = 0.3 \times 250 = 75 \text{ mm}$$

b. To find P:

Power lost in friction, $P = \dfrac{2\pi n T_c}{1000}$ (kW)

But $T_c = W f_c d_c/2$ ...9.28/Pg 107, DHB

$$d_c = \dfrac{2}{3}\left(\dfrac{d'^3 - d''^3}{d'^2 - d''^2}\right)$$

$$= \dfrac{2}{3}\left(\dfrac{250^3 - 75^3}{250^2 - 75^2}\right)$$

$$d_c = 178.21 \text{ mm}$$

$$T_c = \dfrac{20000 \times 0.018 \times 178.21}{2}$$

$$T_c = 32.08 \times 10^3 \text{ N-mm} = 32.08 \text{ N-m}$$

$$P = \dfrac{2\pi \times 12.33 \times 32.08}{1000}$$

$$P = 2.49 \text{ kW}$$

36. Determine the minimum dimensions of a multi-collar thrust bearing for a propeller shaft of 450 kW marine oil engine. The engine makes 220 rpm and the shaft diameter is 150 mm. The boat speed is 6 m/s.

Solution: $P = 450$ kW, $N = 220$ rpm $\Rightarrow n = 3.67$ rps, $d'' = 150$ mm, $v = 6$ m/s

a. To find W:

Power lost in friction, $P = \dfrac{Wv}{1000}$ $\because P = \dfrac{Fv}{1000}$ ...12.19a/Pg 174, DHB

$$450 = \dfrac{W \times 6}{1000}$$

$$W = 75 \text{ kN}$$

b. To find d', d'':

Given $d'' = 150$ mm

Assume $d' = 1.5d'' = 1.5 \times 150 = 225$ mm

c. Rubbing velocity:

We know that, $v_r = \pi d_c n = \pi d_c n \left(\dfrac{d' + d''}{2} \right)$

$$= \pi \times 3.67 \times \left(\dfrac{0.225 + 0.150}{2} \right)$$

$$v_r = 2.16 \text{ m/s}$$

d. Number of collars:

We know that, $p = \dfrac{4W}{\pi i (d'^2 - d''^2)}$

Assume $p = 0.5$ MPa

$$0.5 = \dfrac{4 \times 75000}{\pi \times i \times (225^2 - 150^2)}$$

$$i = 6.79 \approx 7$$

e. Actual pressure:

We know that, $p_a = \dfrac{4W}{\pi i (d'^2 - d''^2)}$

$$= \dfrac{4 \times 75000}{\pi \times 7 \times (225^2 - 150^2)}$$

$p_a = 0.48$ MPa < assumed value. Hence safe.

f. Coefficient of friction:

According to Louis Illmer, $f = \dfrac{C_1 C_2}{269.44} \sqrt[4]{p_a / v_r}$ ...15.13/ Pg 302, DHB

$C_1 = 2$, a constant ...Table 15.7/ Pg 312, DHB
$C_2 = 4$, a constant ...Table 15.8/ Pg 312, DHB

∴ $$f = \dfrac{2 \times 4}{269.44} \sqrt[4]{0.48/2.16}$$

$$f = 0.0204$$

g. Power lost:

Power lost in friction, $P = \dfrac{2\pi n T_c}{1000}$ (kW)

But $T_c = W f_c d_c / 2$ ...9.28/ Pg 107, DHB

$$= \left(\dfrac{75000 \times 0.0204}{2} \right) \left(\dfrac{0.225 + 0.150}{2} \right)$$

$T_c = 143.44 \times 10^3$ N-mm $= 143.44$ N-m

∴ $P = \dfrac{2\pi \times 3.67 \times 143.44}{1000}$

$P = 3.31$ kW

VTU QUESTION PAPERS

Feb. 2002 (ME6T2)

1. a. Derive Petroff's equation for coefficient of friction for hydrodynamic bearing. **(08 Marks)**
   b. SAE 20 oil is used to lubricate a hydrodynamic journal bearing of diameter 75 mm and length 75 mm, oil enters at 40 °C. The journal rotates at 1200 rpm. The diametral clearance is 75 μm (0.075 mm). Assume operating temperatures of the oil as 53°C and determine:
   a. Magnitude and location of the minimum oil film thickness.
   b. Power loss.
   c. Oil flow through the bearing.
   d. Side leakage. **(12 Marks)**

July/Aug. 2002 (ME6T2)

2. a. Explain the significance of bearing characteristic number in the design of sliding bearing. **(05 Marks)**
   b. A turbine shaft 60 mm in diameter rotates at speed of 10000 rpm. The load on each bearing is estimated at 2 kN and length of the bearing is 80 mm. Taking radial clearance as 0.05 mm and SAE 20 oil for lubrication determine the coefficient of friction, power loss, minimum film thickness and oil flow rate. The temperature of the bearing is not to exceed 50°C. **(15 Marks)**

Jan./Feb 2003 (ME6T2)

3. Design a hydrodynamic journal bearing for the following particulars:
   Diameter of the journal = 70 mm. Speed of the shaft = 250 rpm
   Load on shaft = 7500 N
   Viscosity of oil- Saybolt of 270 sec at 38°C and specific gravity 0.905 at 35°C.
   Determine:
   i. Length of the bearing
   ii. Running clearance
   iii. Minimum film thickness
   iv. Heat dissipation capacity of bearing
   v. Whether artificial cooling is required. **(20 Marks)**

July/Aug. 2003 (ME6T2)

4. The oiliness curve for a 75 mm × 150 mm long bearing happens to be a straight line passing through the points $\frac{\eta n'}{P} = 191 \times 10^{-9}$ and μ = 0.002 and another point $\frac{\eta n'}{P} = 956 \times 10^{-9}$ and μ = 0.0065. The load supported by the bearing is 6 kN and speed of the journal is 1200 rpm. Calculate the friction loss in kW at the bearing, if the oil film has a temperature of 80°C and the viscosity of the lubricant is 8.7 cP at the operating temperature. Assume ψ = 0.001. **(10 Marks)**

July/Aug. 2004 (ME6T2)

5. a. What is Sommerfeld number? What is its application in designing hydrodynamic journal bearings? Explain at least four dimensionless parameters, which depend upon the Sommerfeld number as plotted by Raimondi and Boyd. **(08 Marks)**

b. A 75 mm long full journal bearing of diameter 75 mm supports a radial load of 12 kN at the shaft speed of 1800 rpm. Assume the ratio of diameter to the diametral clearance as 1000. The viscosity of oil is 0.01 Pa-s at the operating temperature. Determine the following:
   i. Sommerfeld number.
   ii. The coefficient of friction based on McKee equation.
   iii. Amount of heat generated. **(08 Marks)**

Jan./Feb. 2005 (ME6T2)

6. a. Discuss the mechanism of fluid film lubrication. **(05 Marks)**
   b. Design a journal bearing to withstand a load of 5886 N. Speed of the journal is 1000 rpm. The journal is made of hardened steel and bearing is made of babbit. Operating temperature is 70°C and ambient temperature is 30°C. Check the design for thermal equilibrium and also determine the power loss at the bearing. The lubricant used is of grade SAE 40. $l/d = 1.5$ **(10 Marks)**

Jan./Feb. 2005 (AU53)

7. a. Explain with sketches theory of hydrodynamic bearings **(06 Marks)**
   b. A journal bearing is required to be designed for a rotary compressor for operation at a speed of 1500 rpm. The bearing is to sustain a load of 4500 N and the diameter of the main shaft is 50 mm. Determine:
   i. length and inner diameter of bearing bush.
   ii. viscosity of oil to be used as a lubricant and hence suggest a lubricating oil.
   iii. the coefficient of friction.
   iv. heat generated.
   v. heat dissipating capacity.
   vi. amount of heat to be removed by artificial cooling.
   vii. sommerfeld number. **(14 Marks)**

July/Aug. 2005 (AU53)

8. a. Derive Petroff's equation for a lightly loaded bearing. **(05 Marks)**
   b. A full journal bearing 90 mm diameter and 150 mm long has a radial load of 2 MPa per unit projected area. Shaft speed is 500 rpm. The bearing is operating with SAE 20 oil at 50°C. The specific gravity of the oil at the operating temperature is 0.985. Calculate the following:
   i. the minimum film thickness.   ii. heat loss due to friction.
   iii. whether artificial cooling is necessary? **(15 Marks)**

Jan./Feb. 2006 (AU53)

9. a. Derive Petroff's equation for coefficient of friction of a lightly loaded journal bearing. **(06 Marks)**
   b. It is required to design a main bearing of a 4 stroke oil engine to sustain a load of 6 kN over a shaft of diameter 50 mm. The operating speed of the shaft is 1000 rpm and the operating temperature is 50° C. Determine:
   i. dimensions of the bearing.
   ii. the viscosity of the oil to be used for the bearing and hence suggest appropriate oil.
   iii. coefficient of friction.

682 Design of Machine Elements II (DME II)

   iv. heat generated.
   v. heat dissipated.
   vi. heat to be removed by artificial cooling, if necessary.
   vii. sommerfeld number. **(14 Marks)**

July 2006 (AU53)

10. a. Derive the Petroff's equation for frictional power loss for a lightly loaded journal bearing rotating at high speed concentric to the bearing. **(05 Marks)**
    b. Determine the power loss in a bearing, the diameter of the journal is 60 mm and length is 80 mm. The diametral clearance is 0.12 mm. The bearing supports a load of 5000 N and the journal rotates at a speed of 2500 rpm. The kinematic viscosity and the specific gravity of the oil used at the operating temperature of the bearing are 50 centistokes and 0.9 respectively. **(07 Marks)**

Dec. 06/Jan. 2007 (AU53)

11. a. Explain the bearing modulus. **(03 Marks)**
    b. Derive Petroff's equation for a lightly loaded bearing. **(05 Marks)**
    c. A 75 mm long full journal bearing of diameter 75 mm supports a radial load of 12 kN at a shaft speed of 1800 rpm. Assume ratio of diameter to the diametral clearance as 1000. The viscosity of oil is 0.01 Pa-s at the operating temperature. Determine:
       i. Sommerfeld number.
       ii. Coefficient of friction based on McKee's equation.
       iii. Amount of heat generated. **(12 Marks)**

July 2007 (AU53)

12. a. Explain the significance of the bearing characteristic number in the design of sliding contact bearing. **(05 Marks)**
    b. A full journal bearing of 60 mm diameter and 100 mm long has a bearing pressure of 1.4 N/mm^2. The speed of the journal is 800 rpm and the ratio of journal diameter to the diametral clearance is 1000. The bearing is lubricated with oil whose viscosity at the operating temperature of 75°C may be taken as 0.011kg/ms. The room temperature is 30°C. Find: (i) The amount of artificial cooling required, (ii) The mass of lubricating oil required, if the difference between the outlet and inlet temperate of the oil is 10°C. Take specific heat of the oil as 1850 J/kg/°C. **(15 Marks)**

Dec. 07/Jan. 2008 (AU53)

13. a. Explain with sketch theory of hydrodynamic lubrication. **(06 Marks)**
    b. Design a full journal bearing subjected to 6000 N at 1000 rpm of the journal. The journal is of hardened steel and the bearing is of babbit metal. The bearing is operating with SAE 40 oil at 70°C and the ambient temperature is 30°C. Also determine the amount of artificial cooling required. **(14 Marks)**

Dec. 07/Jan. 2008 (ME6T2)

14. a. What is Sommerfeld number? What is its application in designing hydrodynamic journal bearings? Explain at least four dimensionless parameters, which depend upon the Sommerfeld number as plotted by Raimondi and Boyd. **(08 Marks)**

b. A 75 mm long full journal bearing of diameter 75 mm supports a radial load of 12 kN at the shaft speed of 1800 rpm. Assume the ratio of diameter to the diametral clearance as 1000. The viscosity of oil is 0.01 Poise at the operating temperature. Determine the following:
   i. Sommerfeld number.   ii. Amount of heat generated.
   iii. The coefficient of friction based on McKee's equation. **(12 Marks)**

June/July 2008 (AU53)

15. a. What is bearing modulus? Explain the significance of bearing modulus in the design of bearing. **(06 Marks)**
    b. Design a journal bearing for a centrifugal pump from the following data:
    Load on the journal = 10 kN
    Speed of the journal = 900 rpm
    Ambient temperature = 15°C **(14 Marks)**
16. Explain the different types of bearings. What are the requirements of a lubricant used in the bearings? **(08 Marks)**

June/July 2009 (ME6T2)

17. a. Discuss the mechanism of fluid film lubrication. **(05 Marks)**
    b. Design a journal bearing to withstand a load of 5886 N. Speed of the journal is 1000 rpm. The journal is made of hardened steel and bearing is made of babbit. Operating temperature is 70°C and ambient temperature is 30°C. Check the design for thermal equilibrium and also determine the power loss at the bearing. The lubricant used is of grade SEA40. $l/d = 1.5$. **(15 Marks)**
18. Describe how the friction between the journal and the bearing varies from the instant at which rotation of the journal begins until high speed is attained. **(05 Marks)**

Dec. 08/Jan. 2009 (AU53)

19. a. Explain with a neat sketch, the importance of bearing characteristic number in the design of journal bearing. **(06 Marks)**
    b. Design a journal bearing for a centrifugal pump running at 1200 rpm. Diameter of the journal is 100 mm and load on the bearing is 15 kN. Take $l/d = 1.5$, bearing temperature 50° and ambient temperature 30°. Find whether artificial cooling is required. **(14 Marks)**

June/July 2009 (AU53)

20. a. Explain the three ratios of journal bearing, which influence coefficient of friction. **(06 Marks)**
    b. A full journal bearing of 50 mm diameter and 100 mm long has a bearing pressure of 1.4 N/mm². The speed of the journal is 900 rpm and the ratio of journal diameter to the diametrical clearance is 1000. The bearing is lubricated with oil whose absolute viscosity at the operating temperature of 75°C may be taken as 0.121 kg/ms. The room temperature is 35°C. Find:
    i. The amount of artificial cooling required.
    ii. The mass of lubricating oil required, if the difference between the outlet and the inlet temperature of the oil is 10°C, take specific heat of oil as 1850 J/kg/°C. **(14 Marks)**

June/July 2009 (06ME61)

21. a. Derive Petroff's equation for a lightly loaded bearing. **(05 Marks)**
    b. Design a full journal bearing subjected to 6 kN at 1000 rpm of the journal. The journal is of hardened steel and the bearing is of babbit material. The bearing is operated with SAE40 oil at 70°C and the ambient temperature is 30°C. Also determine the amount of artificial cooling required. **(15 Marks)**

Dec. 09/Jan. 2010 (06ME61)

22. a. Derive Petroff's equation with usual notations. **(10 Marks)**
    b. A lightly loaded bearing of 70 mm long and 70 mm in diameter is acted on by 1.5 kN radial load. The radial clearance is 0.07 mm and the journal bearing is rotating at 25000 rpm. The viscosity of the oil is 3.45×10^{-3} Pa-s. Determine the frictional power loss using Petroff's equation. **(10 Marks)**

May/June 2010 (AU53)

23. a. Explain bearing characteristic number and bearing modulus for journal bearings. **(05 Marks)**
    b. A full journal bearing of 60 mm diameter and 120 mm long has a bearing pressure of 1.4 N/mm². The speed of the journal is 1000 rpm and the ratio of journal diameter to the diametral clearance is 1000. The bearing is lubricated with oil whose absolute viscosity at the operating temperature of 75°C may be taken as 0.011 kg/m.s. The room temperature is 30°C. Find,
    i. The amount of artificial cooling required
    ii. The mass of lubricating oil required, if the difference between the outlet and inlet temperature of the oil is 10°C. Take specific heat of the oil as 1850 J/kg/°C. **(15 Marks)**

Dec. 2010 (AU53)

24. a. Derive Petroff's equation for coefficient of friction for hydrodynamic bearing. **(06 Marks)**
    b. Design a journal bearing to withstand a load of 5886 N. Speed of journal is 1000 rpm. The journal is made of hardened steel and bearing is made of babbit. Operating temperature is 70°C and ambient temperature is 30°C. Check the design for thermal equilibrium and also determine the power loss at the bearing. The lubricant used is of grade SAE 40, $\mu_d = 15$. **(14 Marks)**

May/June 2010 (06ME61)

25. a. Derive the Petroff's equation for coefficient of friction, in a sliding contact. **(06 Marks)**
    b. Following data refers to a 360° hydrodynamic bearing:
    Radial load = 3.2 kN, Journal speed = 1500 rpm, Radial clearance = 0.05 mm
    Journal diameter = bearing length = 50 mm, viscosity of lubricant = 25 cP.
    Assume that the total heat generated in the bearing is carried away by total oil flow in the bearing. Calculate:
    i. coefficient of friction;   ii. power loss in friction;
    iii. minimum film thickness; iv. flow requirement;
    v. temperature rise. **(14 Marks)**

Dec. 2010 (06ME61)

26. a. Explain mechanism of hydrodynamic journal bearing. **(04 Marks)**
    b. A full journal bearing 50 mm in diameter and 50 mm long operates at 1000 rpm and carries a load of 5 kN. The radial clearance is 0.025 mm. The bearing is lubricated with SAE 30 oil and the operating temperature of oil is 80°C. Assume the attitude angle as 60°, determine:
    i. Bearing pressure
    ii. Sommerfeld number
    iii. Attitude
    iv. Minimum film thickness
    v. Heat generated
    vi. Heat dissipated if the ambient temperature is 20°C and
    vii. Amount of artificial cooling if necessary. Use McKee's and Pederson's equations. **(16 Marks)**

June/July 2011 (06ME61)

27. a. A 75 mm long full journal bearing of diameter 75 mm supports a radial load of 12 kN at the shaft speed of 1800 rpm. Assume the ratio of diameter to the diametral clearance as 1000. The viscosity of oil is $0.001 \dfrac{\text{N-sec}}{\text{m}^2}$ at the operating temperature. Determine:
    i. sommerfeld number
    ii. coefficient of friction
    iii. amount of heat generated. **(12 Marks)**
    b. Derive Petroff's equation for coefficient of friction in journal bearing. **(08 Marks)**

Dec. 2011 (06ME61)

28. a. Discuss the mechanism of fluid film lubrication. **(04 Marks)**
    b. Design a journal bearing to withstand a load of 5886 N speed of the journal is 1000 rpm. The journal is made of hardened steel and bearing is made of babbit. Operating temperature is 70°C and ambient temperature is 30°C. Check the design for thermal equilibrium and also determine the power los at the bearing. The lubricant used is of grade SAE 40, $l/d = 1.5$. **(16 Marks)**

June 2012 (06ME61)

29. a Explain the properties a good bearing material should possess. List the different types of bearing materials. **(06 Marks)**
    b. The following data are given for a full journal bearing:
    Radial load = 25 kN, L/d ratio = 1:1 unit bearing pressure = 2.5 MPa, viscosity of the lubricant = 20 cP, class of fit = $H7e7$.
    Calculate:
    i. Dimensions of the bearing
    ii. Minimum oil film thickness
    iii. Requirement of flow. Assume that the process to clearance is centered **(14 Marks)**

December 2012 (06ME61)

30. a. Explain the meaning of
    i. Oiliness
    ii. Flash point
    iii. Fire point
    iv. Pour point
    v. Cloud point. **(05 Marks)**

b. Write a note on bearing modulus. **(05 Marks)**

c. A 75 mm journal bearing of diameter 75 mm supports a load of 15 kN. The ratio of $\frac{d}{c} = 1000$ and the viscosity of oil is 25×10^{-3} Pa-s. The heat generated in the bearing is 442 watts. Determine the maximum speed of the journal using McKee's equation. **(10 Marks)**

June/July 2013 (AU53)

31. a. Explain the factors that influence most the formulation and maintenance of oil film in hydrodynamic bearings. **(05 Marks)**

b. List and explain any three required properties of sliding contact bearing materials. **(05 Marks)**

c. A 80 mm long journal bearing supports a load of 2800 N on a 50 mm diameter shaft. The bearing has a clearance of 0.05 mm and the viscosity of oil is 0.021 kg/m-s at the operating temperature. The bearing is capable of dissipating 80 J/s. Determine the maximum safe speed. **(10 Marks)**

June/July 2013 (06ME61)

32. SAE 20 oil is used to lubricate a hydrodynamic journal bearing of diameter 75 mm and length 75 mm. The journal rotates at 1200 rpm, the diametral clearance is 0.075 mm, the operating temperature of the oil is 53°C and the oil enters at 40°C. Determine:
   i. The magnitude and location of minimum oil film thickness
   ii. Power loss
   iii. Oil flow through the bearing
   iv. Side leakage. **(20 Marks)**

June/July 2013 (10ME62)

33. a. Derive Petroff's equation for coefficient of friction in journal bearings. **(08 Marks)**

b. The main bearing of a steam turbine runs at 1500 rpm and has a diameter of 40 mm. The load on the bearing is estimated to be 3 kN. Assume clearance ratio of 0.001 mm, length to diameter ratio is 1.5 and well ventilated. The operating temperature of the oil film is 60°C and oil used is turbine oil SAE 10. Determine whether,
   i. Fluid film lubrication can be expected.
   ii. Artificial cooling is necessary.
   iii. The amount of oil flow. **(12 Marks)**

Dec. 2013/Jan. 2014 (10ME62)

34. a. Explain the following types of lubrication:
   i. Hydrodynamic lubrication
   ii. Hydrostatic lubrication
   iii. Boundary lubrication
   iv. Elastohydrodynamic lubrication **(08 Marks)**

b. The following data are given for a 360° hydro dynamic bearing:
   Bearing diameter = 50.02 mm   Journal diameter = 49.93 mm
   Bearing length = 50 mm   Journal speed = 1440 rpm
   Radial load = 8 kN   Viscosity of lubricant = 12 cP.

The bearing is machined on a lathe from bronze casing, while the steel journal is hardened and ground. The surface roughness values for turning and grinding are 0.8 and 0.4 microns respectively. For thick film lubrication the minimum film thickness should be five times the sum of surface roughness values for the journal and the bearing. Calculate:
i. The permissible film thickness
ii. The actual film thickness under operating conditions
iii. Power loss in friction
iv. Flow requirement. **(12 Marks)**

Dec. 2013/Jan. 2014 (AU53)

35. a. Mention atleast three advantages of hydrodynamic bearings over antifriction bearings. **(02 Marks)**
    b. A 75 mm diameter full length bearing has to support a load of 3500 N. The bearing is 75 mm long and the shaft rotates at 400 r/min. Assume a permissible minimum film thickness of 0.02 mm and a diametral clearance of 0.016 mm. Using Raimondi and Boyd curves or tables, determine the following:
       i. viscosity of oil
       ii. coefficient of friction
       iii. heat generated
       iv. amount of oil pumped through the bearing
       v. end leakage
       vi. temperature rise of oil
       vii. Sommerfeld number. **(14 Marks)**

8
IC Engine Parts

8.1 PISTON—AN INTRODUCTION

A piston reciprocates within a cylinder of an IC engine and is moved by the expanding combustion gas and also moves the gas or fluid that enters the cylinder and compresses it. It receives the impulse and energy from the expanding gas due to combustion and transmits this energy to the crank through the connecting rod. It is provided with piston rings to provide a good seal between the piston and cylinder wall.

8.1.1 Functions of Piston

- To compress the gas during compression stroke.
- To transmit the force to the connecting rod through crankshaft due to gas pressure inside the cylinder.
- To dissipate large amount of heat from the combustion chamber to the cylinder wall.
- To receive the thrust generated by the explosion of the gas in the cylinder and transmit it to the connecting rod.
- To form a guide and bearing to the small end of the connecting rod and to take the side thrust due to obliquity of the rod.
- To seal the inner portion of cylinder by means of piston rings.

8.2 PARTS OF A PISTON

Pistons may be classified as double acting piston and single acting piston. The later is called *trunk piston*. **Figure 8.1** represents a trunk type piston commonly used in IC engines. It consists of the following parts:

→ **Piston head or crown:** It refers to the top portion of the piston and withstands the gas pressures inside the cylinder. It may be of flat type, dished or domed type.

→ **Skirt:** It refers to lower portion of the piston below the piston rings. It acts as a bearing and receives the side thrust created by the movement of the crank and connecting rod. In addition to receiving thrust, the skirt aids in keeping the piston in proper alignment within the cylinder.

→ **Land:** The portions of the piston that separate the grooves are called lands. Some pistons have a groove in the top land called as a heat dam which reduces heat transfer to the rings.

→ **Piston rings:** Piston rings must perform following three functions:

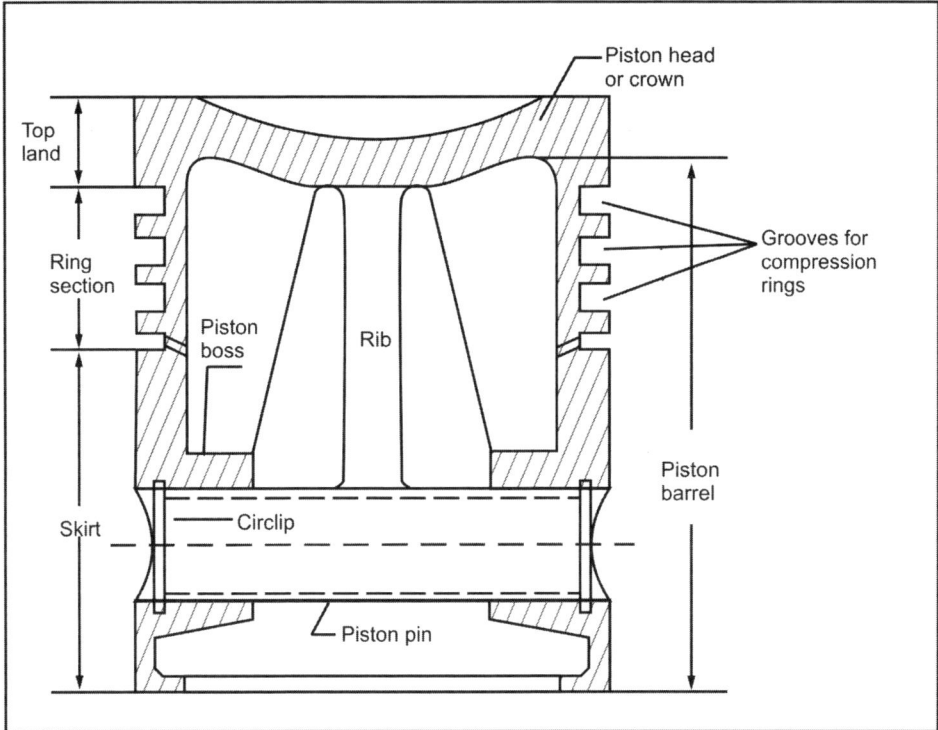

Fig. 8.1: Trunk type piston

- seal the cylinder,
- distribute and control lubricating oil on the cylinder wall, and
- transfer heat from the piston to the cylinder wall.

All rings on a piston perform the last, but two general types of rings: compression and oil are required to perform the first two functions.

- **Compression rings:** The principal function of compression rings is to seal the cylinder and combustion space so that the gases within the space cannot escape until they have performed their function.
- **Oil rings:** These are also called *oil scrapper rings*. It performs two functions
- distribute enough oil to the cylinder wall to prevent metal-to-metal contact, and
- control the amount of oil distributed.

Both the rings are located toward the crown or combustion end of the piston. The oil rings are placed below the compression rings.

In general two compression rings and one oil ring is used. The purpose of providing two compression rings is that during power stroke the pressure is very high and a single compression ring would give up. On the other hand if two compression rings are provided the pressure is distributed among the two rings.

→ **Piston pin:** It is also known as *gudgeon pin* or *wrist pin* and connects the piston to the connecting rod.

8.3 MATERIALS FOR PISTON

The most commonly used materials for IC engine pistons are cast iron (CI), cast steel, forged steel, cast aluminium alloys, and forged aluminium alloy.

Aluminium alloy pistons are mainly used because the thermal conductivity of aluminium is three-times that of cast iron piston, light in weight and has less variation in temperature. Further the density of aluminium alloy is one-third that of cast iron thereby reducing its weight which in turn results in reduction of inertia forces. Since the thermal expansion of aluminium alloy is approximately twice that of cast iron, a greater clearance is to be provided between the cylinder walls and the piston.

On the other hand, cast iron pistons have high strength compared to that of aluminium alloy pistons. Cast iron gives longer service since the wear strength of cast iron is more than the aluminium alloy.

Cast iron pistons are moderately rated (speed) engines with piston speed below 6 m/s, while the aluminium alloy pistons are highly rated engines with piston speeds above 6 m/s.

8.4 BASIC DESIGN CONSIDERATIONS

- The piston must have the strength to resist the impulse and inertia forces.
- Ability to disperse the heat of combustion and avoid thermal distortion.
- Sealing the gas and oil.
- Sufficient bearing area to work for large number of reciprocating cycles.
- Minimum weight.
- Smooth noiseless operation.
- Provide adequate support for piston pin.

8.5 DESIGN OF PISTON

8.5.1 Thickness of Piston Head

Piston heads are of two types:
- flat type piston head **(Fig. 8.2(a))** and
- cup type piston head **(Fig. 8.2 (b))**

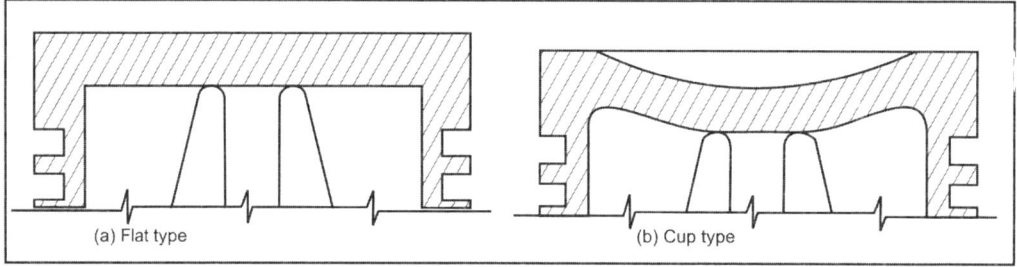

Fig. 8.2: Types of piston heads

The thickness of piston head is calculated based on the following two criteria:
1. Strength
2. Heat dissipation

- Based on the *first criteria (strength)*, the piston head is treated as a flat circular plate of uniform thickness fixed at the outer edges and subjected to a uniformly distributed load due to the gas pressure (p) over the entire cross-section.
  - According to Grashoff's formula, the thickness of the piston head is given by

$$t_1 = \sqrt{\frac{3pD^2}{16\sigma_t}} = 0.43D\sqrt{\frac{p}{\sigma_t}} \text{ (mm)} \qquad \text{...(Eq. 8.1) } \textbf{18.18a/ Pg 361, DHB}$$

Where, D – diameter of the cylinder bore or piston (mm)

$p(=p_{max})$ – Fluid pressure inside the cylinder (MN/m²) *or* (MPa)

σ_t – allowable tensile stress or bending stress.

= 38 MN/m² for good closed grain cast iron or aluminium alloys, having ultimate tensile strength of 137 MN/m².

= 55 MN/m² for Nickel cast iron, semi-steel or special aluminium alloy having ultimate tensile strength of 206 MN/m²

= 82.5 MN/m² for forged steel

- Another formula recommended by Held and Favary for calculating the thickness of piston head is given as

$$t_1 = 0.032\ D + 1.5\ \text{mm} \quad \text{...(Eq. 8.2)} \ \textbf{18.18b/ Pg 361, DHB}$$

♦ On the basis of *second criteria (heat dissipation)*, the thickness of the piston head should be such that the heat absorbed by the piston due to combustion of fuel is quickly transferred to the cylinder walls. On the basis of heat dissipation, the thickness of piston head is given by,

$$t_1 = \frac{D^2 q}{1600 K (T_c - T_e)} \quad \text{...(Eq. 8.3)} \ \textbf{18.19/ Pg 361, DHB}$$

Where, θ = Heat flow from gases (J/s), depends upon material of the piston, mean effective pressure and stroke – bore ratio.

= 32000 to 128000 for CI pistons in 4 stroke engines.

= 64000 to 256000 for aluminium pistons

K – Heat conductivity (J/s m² °C/mm length)

= 460 for CI

= 1600 for aluminium

T_c – Temperature at center of head, (°C)

= 444 °C for CI

= 275 °C for aluminium

T_e – Temperature at edge of head, (°C)

$(T_c - T_e)$ – Permissible difference in temperature

= 222 °C for CI

= 111 °C for aluminium

Based on Eqs (8.1) and (8.3), higher value of is taken for design.

Note:
- *The thickness of piston head for Spark Ignition (SI) and Compression Ignition (CI) engines are given in.* ...**Table 18.5/ Pg 366, DHB**
- The amount of heat conducted through piston head may also be calculated as:

$$q = (HCV \times C \times m \times BP)/A \quad (W) \quad \text{...(Eq. 8.4)}$$

HCV = Higher calorific value (J/kg) = 44×10^6 J/kg

m = Mass of fuel used per brake power per sec. (kg/ BP/s)

A = Area of piston head = $\pi D^2/4$ (m²)

C = Constant representing that part of the heat supplied to the engine which is absorbed by the piston. Usually taken 5% i.e. (C = 0.05)

BP – Brake power of engine per cylinder (kW)

$$= \frac{p_m L_s A n}{60 \times 1000} \text{ (kW)}$$

p_m – Mean effective pressure (N/mm²)
L_s – Stroke length (m)
n – Number of strokes per min
  = N, for 2- stroke engines
  = $N/2$, for 4- stroke engines
N – Speed (rpm)
A – Area of piston head (mm²)

8.5.2 Piston Rings

Figure 8.3 shows a piston ring. These are usually made of gray cast iron. The compression springs have rectangular cross-section as shown in **Fig. 8.3(a)**. It is preferred to provide more number of thin piston rings than a small number of thick rings since thin rings have better sealing action and reduce frictional loss due to wear.

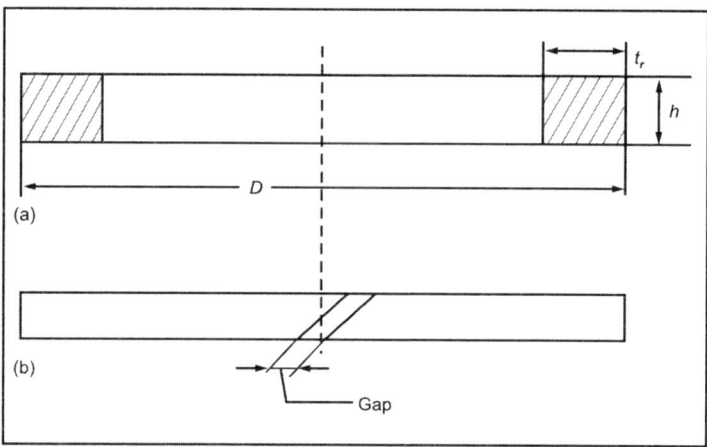

Fig. 8.3: Piston ring

- The radial thickness or width of the ring is:

$$h = D\sqrt{\frac{3p_r}{\sigma}} \text{ (mm)} \qquad \text{...(Eq. 8.5)} \textbf{ 18.27/ Pg 363, DHB}$$

  Where, D – diameter of the cylinder bore or piston (mm)
  σ – allowable (tensile/ bending) stress for cast iron (CI)
    = 82 to 110 MN/m²
  p_r – magnitude of radial pressure on the piston rings (MN/m²)
  ...**Table 18.6/ Pg 366, DHB**

- The depth or axial thickness (h) of the piston ring is given by,
  $h = 0.7\, t_r$ to t_r \qquad ...(Eq. 8.6) **18.28a/ Pg 363, DHB**

- The number of rings is found as $h = \dfrac{D}{10i}$ \qquad ...(Eq. 8.7) **18.28b/ Pg 363, DHB**

  Number of piston rings = i
  Number of lands = $i - 1$

- The minimum thickness is given by

$$h_{min} = \frac{D}{10i} \quad \text{...(Eq. 8.7a) } \textbf{18.28b/ Pg 363, DHB}$$

- The distance from the top of piston to the first ring groove *(top land)* should be cut at a distance of

$$t_g = t_1 \text{ to } 1.2\, t_1 \quad \text{...(Eq. 8.8) } \textbf{18.30/ Pg 363, DHB}$$

- The distance/lands between the ring grooves (consecutive rings) should be

$$t_{land} = h \text{ or slightly less than } h \quad \text{...(Eq. 8.9) } \textbf{18.31/ Pg 363, DHB}$$

- The total height of ring section is found as

Based on i, $h_{total} = [i + (i - 1)]\, h$ ...(Eq. 8.10)

- The total depth of piston rings is given as:

$$h_{total} = \left(\frac{D}{15}\right) + 15.2 \text{ mm, for steam engines}$$

$$= \left(\frac{D}{7}\right) + 6 \text{ mm, for gas and oil engines}$$

$$= \left(\frac{D}{5.5}\right), \text{ for petrol engines} \quad \text{...(Eq. 8.11) } \textbf{18.29/ Pg 363, DHB}$$

8.5.3 Piston Barrel (Thickness)

- The maximum thickness of the piston barrel **(Fig. 8.4)** is given by

$$t_3 = 0.03\, D + b + 4.5 \text{ (mm)} \quad \text{...(Eq. 8.12) } \textbf{18.20/ Pg 362, DHB}$$

Where, b = depth of ring grooves (mm)

$$= t_r + 0.4 \text{ mm}$$

t_r = radial thickness or width of piston ring (mm)

- The thickness of piston barrel towards the open end of piston is given by

$$t_4 = 0.25\, t_3 \text{ to } 0.35\, t_3 \text{ (mm)} \quad \text{...(Eq. 8.13) } \textbf{18.21/ Pg 362, DHB}$$

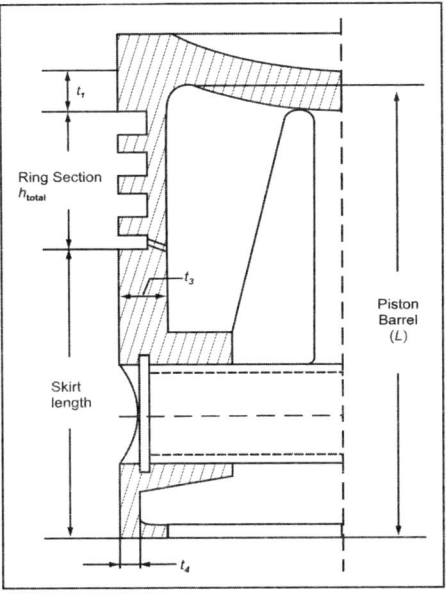

Fig. 8.4: Piston barrel

8.5.4 Piston Skirt

It refers to lower portion of the piston below the piston rings, as shown in **Fig. 8.4**. It acts as a bearing and receives the side thrust created by the movement of the crank and connecting rod. In addition to receiving thrust, the skirt aids in keeping the piston in proper alignment within the cylinder.

The length of the piston skirt should be such that the bearing pressure on the piston barrel due to the side thrust does not exceed 0.25 MPa of the projected area for low speed engines and 0.5 MPa for high speed engines.
- The length of the piston is given as $L = D$ ...(Eq. 8.14) **18.22/ Pg 362, DHB**
   - For aero engines, $L = 0.75\ D$
   - For medium and high speed engine, $L = 1.5D$
   - For diesel and marine engines, $L = 2.5\ D$
- Length of skirt = barrel length – piston head thickness – ring section
   $$= L - t_1 - h_{\text{total}} \qquad \text{...(Eq. 8.15)}$$

8.5.5 Piston Pin

It is also known as *gudgeon pin* or *wrist pin* and connects the piston to the connecting rod. It is usually made hollow to reduce its weight. It is tapered on the inside and the smallest diameter being at the centre of the pin, as shown in **Fig. 8.5**. The piston pin passes through the bosses provided on the inside of the piston skirt and the bush of the small end of the connecting rod. The end movement of the piston pin is restricted by means of circlips.

Pins are made of alloy steel, machined, hardened, and precision-ground to fit the bearings. The bearings or bushings are made of bronze or similar material.

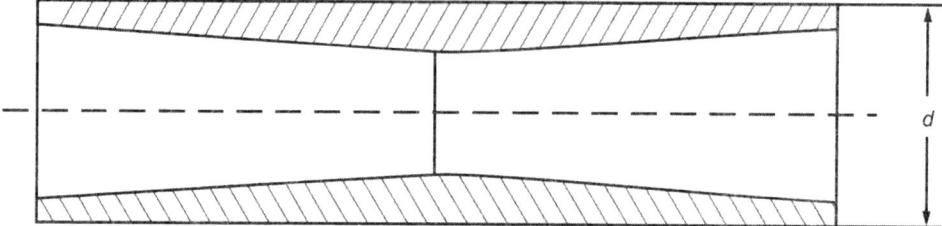

Fig. 8.5: Piston pin (the smallest diameter at the center of the pin)

The connection between the piston pin and the small end of the connecting rod may be of two types:
i. **Full floating type:** Here the piston pin is free to turn both in the piston bosses and the bush of the small end of the connecting rod. The end movements of the piston pin should be secured by means of spring circlips in order to prevent the pin from touching and scoring the cylinder liner.
ii. **Semi floating type:** Here the piston pin is either free to turn in the piston bosses and rigidly fixed to the small end of the connecting rod, or free to turn in the bush of the small end of the connecting rod and is rigidly secured in the piston bosses by means of a screw.

There are two criteria for designing the piston pin – bearing consideration and bending failure:
- **Bearing consideration:**
   Based on bearing pressure, the diameter of the piston pin is calculated as:
   $$d = \frac{\pi D^2 p_{\max}}{4 l_1 p_b} \qquad \text{...(Eq. 8.16) } \mathbf{18.24/\ Pg\ 362,\ DHB}$$

Where, l_1 = length of gudgeon pin bearing (mm)
$= k_1 d$
$k_1 = 1.5$ for petrol and gas engines
$= 2$ for oil engines
p_b = bearing pressure
$= 12.4$ MN/m² for gas engines
$= 15$ MN/m² for oil engines
$= 15.7$ MN/m² for automotive engines

- Another formula to determine the length of the gudgeon pin bearing is given by,

$l_1 = 0.45\,D$ to $0.5\,D$, if it oscillates in the connecting rod
$= 0.62\,D$, if it oscillates in the piston bosses
...(Eq. 8.17) **18.25/ Pg 363, DHB**

- **Bending consideration:**
The maximum bending stress in the piston pin is checked using the relation,

$$\sigma_b = \frac{F_p D}{8Z} \text{ (MN/m}^2\text{)} \qquad \text{...(Eq. 8.18)} \textbf{ 18.26/ Pg 363, DHB}$$

Where, σ_b = bending stress
≤ 82 MN/m², for case hardened carbon steel
≤ 137 MN/m², for heat treated alloy steel
F_p = force on the piston

$$= p \cdot A = \frac{p \pi D^2}{4} \text{ (N)} \qquad \text{...(Eq. 8.19)}$$

$$Z = \text{section modulus} = \frac{\pi D^3}{32} \text{ (mm}^3\text{)} \qquad \text{...(Eq. 8.20)}$$

1. **Design a trunk piston for an IC engine. The piston is made of cast iron with an allowable stress of 38.5 MPa. The bore of the cylinder is 200 mm and the maximum explosion pressure is 0.4 MPa. The permissible bending stress of the material of the gudgeon pin is 100 MPa. The bearing pressure in the gudgeon pin bearing of the connecting rod is to be taken as 200 MPa.**

[VTU – Dec. 2013/ Jan. 2014 – 15 Marks]

Solution: $\sigma_t = 38.5$ MPa, $D = 200$ mm, $p = p_{max} = 0.4$ MPa, $\sigma_b = 100$ MPa, $p_b = 200$ MPa

a. Thickness of piston head:

- **Based on strength:**

$$t_1 = 0.43 D \sqrt{\frac{p}{\sigma_t}} \qquad \text{...18.18a/ Pg 361, DHB}$$

$\sigma_t = 38.5$ MPa (Data)

$$= 0.43 \times 200 \times \sqrt{\frac{0.4}{38.5}}$$

$t_1 = 8.76$ mm ...Eq. (i)

- **Based on heat dissipation:**

$$t = \frac{D^2 q}{1600 K (T_c - T_e)} \qquad \text{...18.19/ Pg 361, DHB}$$

q = Heat flow from gases (J/s)
  = 128000 (higher value) for CI pistons in 4 stroke engines.
K = Heat conductivity
  = 460 J/s m² °C/mm length for CI
$(T_c - T_e)$ = Permissible difference in temperature = 222 °C for CI

$$= \frac{200^2 \times 128000}{1600 \times 460 \times 222}$$

t_1 = 31.33 mm   ...Eq. (ii)

Based on Eqs (i) and (ii), adopt higher value for design
i.e. thickness of piston head, t_1 = 31.33 mm
$\therefore t_1 \simeq 32$ mm.

b. Piston rings:

i. Radial thickness or width of the ring:

$$t_r = D\sqrt{\frac{3p_r}{\sigma}} \qquad \text{...18.27/ Pg 363, DHB}$$

σ = allowable stress for cast iron = 82 to 110 MPa
  = 96 MPa (average value)
p_r = magnitude of radial pressure on the piston rings
  = 0.02746 MPa for oil engines (average value)
                                                            ...Tb 18.6/ Pg 366, DHB

$$= 200 \times \sqrt{\frac{3 \times 0.02746}{96}}$$

t_r = 5.86 mm
$t_r \approx 6$ mm

ii. Depth or axial thickness of the piston ring:

$h = 0.7\, t_r$ to t_r ...18.28a/ Pg 363, DHB
$h = t_r = 6$ mm

- **Number of rings:**

  The number of rings is found as $h = \dfrac{D}{10i}$ ...18.28b/ Pg 363, DHB

  $$6 = \frac{200}{10i}$$

  $i = 3.33 \approx 4$

  i.e. Number of piston rings, $i = 4$
  Number of lands = $i - 1 = 4 - 1 = 3$

- **Check for h:**

  The minimum thickness is given by $h_{\min} = \dfrac{D}{10i}$ ...18.28b/ Pg 363, DHB

  $$= \frac{200}{10 \times 4}$$

  $h_{\min} = 5$ mm

  Since $h \geq h_{\min}$, h is satisfactory.

iii. Distance from the top of piston to the first groove:

$$t_g = t_1 \text{ to } 1.2\, t_1$$
$$= 1.2 \times 32$$
$$t_g = 38.4 \text{ mm}$$

...18.30/ Pg 363, DHB

iv. Distance/lands between the ring grooves:

$$t_{land} = h$$
$$t_{land} = h = 6 \text{ mm}$$

...18.31/ Pg 363, DHB

v. Total height of ring section:

Based on i, $h_{total} = [i + (i-1)]\, h$
$$= [4 + (4-1)] \times 6$$
$$h_{total} = 42 \text{ mm}$$

- **Check for h_{total}:**

The total depth of piston rings is given as:

$$h_{total} = \left(\frac{D}{7}\right) + 6 \text{ mm, for gas and oil engines}$$

...18.29/ Pg 363, DHB

$$= \left(\frac{200}{7}\right) + 6 \text{ mm}$$
$$h_{total} = 34.57 \text{ mm (minimum value)}$$

Since h_{total} > table (minimum) value, hence safe.

c. Piston barrel:

i. Maximum thickness of the piston barrel:

$$t_3 = 0.03\, D + b + 4.5 \text{ mm}$$

...18.20/ Pg 362, DHB

b – depth of ring grooves (mm)
$$= t_r + 0.4 \text{ mm}$$
$$= 6 + 0.4$$
$$b = 6.4 \text{ mm}$$
$$t_3 = (0.03 \times 200) + 6.4 + 4.5 \text{ mm}$$
$$t_3 = 16.9 \text{ mm} \approx 17 \text{ mm}$$

ii. Thickness of piston barrel towards the open end of piston:

$$t_4 = 0.25\, t_3 \text{ to } 0.35\, t_3$$

...18.21/ Pg 362, DHB

$$= (0.25 \times 17) \text{ to } (0.35 \times 17)$$
$$t_4 = 4.25 \text{ to } 5.95 \text{ mm}$$
$$t_4 = 5.10 \text{ mm}$$

d. Piston skirt:

i. Length of the piston:

$$L = 1.5\, D$$

...18.22/ Pg 362, DHB

$$= 1.5 \times 200$$
$$L = 300 \text{ mm}$$

ii. Length of skirt:

Length of skirt = *barrel length – piston head thickness – ring section*
$$= L - t_1 - h_{total}$$
$$= 300 - 32 - 42$$
$$= 226 \text{ mm}$$

e. Piston pin:

i. Diameter of piston pin—Bearing consideration:
The diameter of the piston is calculated as:

$$d = \frac{\pi D^2 p_{max}}{4 l_1 p_b} \qquad \text{...18.24/ Pg 362, DHB}$$

Where, t_1 = length of gudgeon pin bearing (mm)
$= k_1 d$
$k_1 = 2$ for oil engines
$p_b = 200$ MPa (data)

$$d = \frac{\pi \times 200^2 \times 0.4}{4 \times (2d) \times 200}$$

$d = 5.6$ mm ≈ 6 mm

ii. Bending consideration:
The maximum bending stress in the piston pin is checked using the relation,

$$\sigma_b = \frac{F_p D}{8Z} \quad (MN/m^2) \qquad \text{...18.26/ Pg 363, DHB}$$

Where, $\sigma_b = 100$ MPa (data)
F_p – force on the piston

$$= p.A = \frac{p \pi D^2}{4} = \frac{0.4 \times \pi \times 200^2}{4}$$

$F_p = 12.56 \times 10^3$ N
Z = section modulus

$$= \frac{\pi D^3}{32} = \frac{\pi \times 200^3}{32}$$

$\therefore Z = 785.3 \times 10^3$ mm^3

$$\sigma_b = \frac{12.56 \times 10^3 \times 200}{8 \times 785.3 \times 10^3}$$

$\sigma_b = 0.4$ MPa < 100 MPa, hence safe.

2. **Design an aluminum alloy piston for a single acting four stroke petrol engine for the following data:**

Cylinder bore = 0.3 m, Stroke = 0.375 m,
Maximum gas pressure = 8 MPa, Speed = 50 rev/min.
Break mean effective pressure = 1.15 MPa, Fuel consumption = 0.22 kg/kW/h

Solution: $D = 0.3$ m $= 300$ mm, $L_s = 0.375$ m, $p(= p_{max}) = 8$ MPa, $N = 50$ rpm, (Bmep) $p_m = 1.15$ MPa, $m = 0.22$ kg /BP/per hour = 6.11×10^{-5} kg/BP/s

a. Thickness of piston head:
- **Based on strength:**

$$t_1 = 0.43 D \sqrt{\frac{p}{\sigma_t}} \qquad \text{...18.18a/ Pg 361, DHB}$$

$$\sigma_t = 38 \text{ MPa for aluminium alloys}$$

$$= 0.43 \times 300 \times \sqrt{\frac{8}{38}}$$

$$t_1 = 59.19 \text{ mm} \quad \text{...Eq. }(i)$$

- **Based on heat dissipation:**

$$t_1 = \frac{D^2 q}{1600 K (T_c - T_e)} \quad \text{...Eq. }(ii) \text{ 18.19/ Pg 361, DHB}$$

K = Heat conductivity = 1600 J/s m² °C/mm length
$(T_c - T_e)$ = Permissible difference in temperature = 111°C for aluminium
The amount of heat (q) conducted through piston head is calculated as:

$$q = (HCV \times C \times m \times BP)/A \text{ (W)} \quad \text{...Eq. }(iii)$$

HCV = Higher calorific value = 44 × 10⁶ J/kg
$m = 6.11 \times 10^{-5}$ kg/BP/s
A = Area of piston head = $\pi D^2/4 = \pi \times 0.32/4 = 0.0707$ m²
= 0.0707 × 10⁶ mm²
C = Constant representing that part of the heat supplied to the engine which is absorbed by the piston.

$$BP = \frac{p_m L_s A n}{60 \times 1000} \text{ (kW)}$$

n = Number of strokes per min
= $N/2$, for 4- stroke engines
= 50/2
n = 25 strokes/min
$A = 0.0707 \times 10^6$ mm²

$$BP = \frac{1.15 \times 0.375 \times 0.0707 \times 10^6 \times 25}{60 \times 1000}$$

$$BP = 12.70 \text{ kW.}$$

Eq. (iii) yields ... $q = \dfrac{\left(44 \times 10^6 \times 0.05 \times 6.11 \times 10^{-5} \times 12.70\right)}{0.0707} = 24146.17 \text{ W}$

Eq. (ii) yields ... $t_1 = \dfrac{300^2 \times 24146.17}{1600 \times 1600 \times 111}$

$$t_1 = 7.65 \text{ mm} \quad \text{...Eq. }(iv)$$

Based on Eqs (i) and (ii), adopt higher value for design
i.e. thickness of piston head, $t_1 = 59.19$ mm
$$t_1 \approx 60 \text{ mm.}$$

b. Piston rings:

i. Radial thickness or width of the ring:

$$t_r = D\sqrt{\frac{3 p_r}{\sigma}} \quad \text{...18.27/ Pg 363, DHB}$$

σ = allowable stress = 100 MPa *(assume)*
p_r = magnitude of radial pressure on the piston rings
= 0.03089 MPa for petrol engines (average value)

...Tb 18.6/ Pg 366, DHB

$$= 300 \times \sqrt{\frac{3 \times 0.03089}{100}}$$

$t_r \approx 9.13$ mm
$t_r = 10$ mm.

ii. **Depth or axial thickness of the piston ring:**
$h = 0.7\, t_r$ to t_r ...18.28a/ Pg 363, DHB
$h = t_r = 10$ mm

- **Number of rings:**

The number of rings is found as $h = \dfrac{D}{10i}$ ...18.28b/ Pg 363, DHB

$$10 = \frac{300}{10i}$$

$i = 3.$

i.e. Number of piston rings, $i = 3$
Number of lands = $i - 1 = 3 - 1 = 2$

- **Check for h:**

The minimum thickness is given by

$$h_{min} = \frac{D}{10i}$$ ...18.28b/ Pg 363, DHB

$$= \frac{300}{10 \times 3}$$

$h_{min} = 10$ mm

Since $h \geq h_{min}$, h is satisfactory

iii. **Distance from the top of piston to the first groove:**
$t_g = t_1$ to $1.2\, t_1$ ...18.30/ Pg 363, DHB
$= 1.2 \times 60$
$t_g = 72$ mm

iv. **Distance/lands between the ring grooves:**
$t_{land} = h$ ...18.31/ Pg 363, DHB
$t_{land} = h = 10$ mm

v. **Total height of ring section:**
Trial 1: Based on i, $h_{total} = [i + (i - 1)]\, h$
$= [3 + (3 - 1)] \times 10$
$h_{total} = 50$ mm.

Check for h_{total}:
The total depth of piston rings is given as:

$$h_{total} = \left(\frac{D}{5.5}\right), \text{ for petrol engines}$$ ...18.29/ Pg 363, DHB

$$= \left(\frac{300}{5.5}\right)$$

$h_{total} = 54.55$ mm (minimum value)

Since h_{total} < table (minimum) value, **hence not safe**.

Trial 2: Change the number of rings to $i = 4$
i.e. Number of piston rings, $i = 4$
Number of lands $= i - 1 = 4 - 1 = 3$

$\therefore \quad h_{total} = [i + (i - 1)] h$
$= [4 + (4 - 1)] \times 10$
$h_{total} = 70$ mm

Since h_{total} > table (minimum) value, **hence safe**.

c. Piston barrel:
i. Maximum thickness of the piston barrel:
$t_3 = 0.03 D + b + 4.5$ mm ...18.20/ Pg 362, DHB
b = depth of ring grooves (mm)
$= t_r + 0.4$ mm
$= 10 + 0.4$ mm
$b = 10.4$ mm
$t_3 = (0.03 \times 300) + 10.4 + 4.5$ mm
$t_3 = 23.9$ mm $= 24$ mm

ii. Thickness of piston barrel towards the open end of piston:
$t_4 = 0.25 t_3$ to $0.35 t_3$ ...18.21/ Pg 362, DHB
$= (0.25 \times 24)$ to (0.35×24)
$t_4 = 6$ to 8.4 mm
$t_4 = 7$ mm

d. Piston skirt:
i. Length of the piston:
$L = 1.5 D$ ...18.22/ Pg 362, DHB
$= 1.5 \times 300$
$L = 450$ mm

ii. Length of skirt:
Length of skirt = *barrel length – piston head thickness – ring section*
$= L - t_1 - h_{total}$
$= 450 - 60 - 70$
$= 320$

e. Piston pin:
i. Diameter of piston pin–Bearing consideration:
The diameter of the piston is calculated as:

$$d = \frac{\pi D^2 p_{max}}{4 l_1 p_b}$$ ...18.24/ Pg 362, DHB

Where, l_1 = length of gudgeon pin bearing (mm)
$= k_1 d$
$k_1 = 1.5$ for oil engines
p_b = bearing pressure
$= 15.7$ MN/m² for automotive engines

$$= \frac{\pi \times 300^2 \times 8}{4 \times (1.5 d) \times 15.7}$$

$d = 155$ mm

ii. Bending consideration:

The maximum bending stress in the piston pin is checked using the relation,

$$\sigma_b = \frac{F_p D}{8Z} \quad (MN/m^2) \qquad \ldots 18.26/\ Pg\ 363,\ DHB$$

= 155 mm

Where, σ_b = bending stress
$\leq 82\ MN/m^2$, for case hardened carbon steel
F_p – force on the piston

$$= p.A = \frac{p\pi D^2}{4} = \frac{8 \times \pi \times 300^2}{4}$$

$F_p = 565.49 \times 10^3$ N
Z – section modulus

$$= \frac{\pi D^3}{32} = \frac{\pi \times 300^3}{32}$$

$Z = 2.65 \times 10^6\ mm^3$

$$\sigma_b = \frac{565.49 \times 10^3 \times 300}{8 \times 2.65 \times 10^6}$$

$\sigma_b = 7.98$ MPa < 82 MPa, hence safe.

3. **Design a cast iron piston for a single acting four stroke diesel engine with the following data:**
   Cylinder bore = 200 mm,   Length of stroke = 250 mm,
   Speed = 600 rpm,   Brake mean effective pressure = 0.60 MPa,
   Maximum gas pressure = 4 MPa,   Fuel consumption = 0.25 kg per BP per hour,
   μd ratio for bush in small end of connecting rod = 1.5

   [VTU – June/ July 2013 – 20 Marks]

Solution: $D = 200$ mm, $L_s = 250$ mm, $N = 600$ rpm, (Bmep) $p_m = 0.60$ MPa, $p(= p_{max}) = 4$ MPa, $m = 0.25$ kg /BP/ per hour = 6.94×10^{-5} kg/BP/s

a. Thickness of piston head:
- **Based on strength:**

$$t_1 = 0.43D\sqrt{\frac{p}{\sigma_t}} \qquad \ldots 18.18a/\ Pg\ 361,\ DHB$$

$\sigma_t = 38$ MPa for closed grain CI

$$= 0.43 \times 200 \times \sqrt{\frac{4}{38}}$$

$t_1 = 27.90$ mm ...Eq. (i)

- **Based on heat dissipation:**

$$t_1 = \frac{D^2 q}{1600K(T_c - T_e)} \qquad \ldots Eq.\ (ii)\ 18.19/\ Pg\ 361,\ DHB$$

K = Heat conductivity = 460 J/s m² °C/mm length for CI
$(T_c - T_e)$ = Permissible difference in temperature = 222°C for CI

The amount of heat (q) conducted through piston head is calculated as:
$$q = (HCV \times C \times m \times BP)/A \quad (W) \quad \text{...Eq. (iii)}$$
HCV = Higher calorific value = 44×10^6 J/kg
$m = 6.94 \times 10^{-5}$ kg/BP/s
A = Area of piston head = $\pi D^2/4 = \pi \times 0.2^2/4 = 0.0314$ m^2
    = 0.0314×10^6 mm^2
$C = 0.05$ – Constant representing that part of the heat supplied to the engine which is absorbed by the piston.

$$BP = \frac{p_m L_s A n}{60 \times 1000} \quad (kW)$$

$n = N/2$, for 4-stroke engines
  = $600/2$,
$n = 300$ strokes/min
$A = 0.0314 \times 10^6$ mm^2

$$BP = \frac{0.6 \times 0.25 \times 0.0314 \times 10^6 \times 300}{60 \times 1000}$$

$BP = 23.55$ W.

Eq. (iii) yields ... $q = \dfrac{(44 \times 10^6 \times 0.05 \times 6.94 \times 10^{-5} \times 23.55)}{0.0314} = 114675$ W

Eq. (ii) yields ... $t_1 = \dfrac{200^2 \times 114675}{1600 \times 460 \times 222}$

$t_1 = 28.07$ mm   ...Eq. (iv)

Based on Eq. (i) and (iv), adopt higher value for design
i.e. thickness of piston head, $t_1 = 28.07$ mm
$t_1 \approx 30$ mm

b. Piston rings:

i. Radial thickness or width of the ring:

$$t_r = D\sqrt{\frac{3p_r}{\sigma}} \quad \text{...18.27/ Pg 363, DHB}$$

σ = allowable stress for cast iron = 82 MPa to 110 MPa
  = 96 MPa (average value)
p_r = magnitude of radial pressure on the piston rings
  = 0.02746 MPa for oil engines (average value)
...Tb 18.6/ Pg 366, DHB

$$= 200 \times \sqrt{\frac{3 \times 0.02746}{96}}$$

$t_r = 5.86$ mm
$t_r \approx 6$ mm

ii. Depth or axial thickness of the piston ring:

$h = 0.7\, t_r$ to t_r ...18.28a/ Pg 363, DHB
$h = t_r = 6$ mm

- **Number of rings:**

  The number of rings is found as $h = \dfrac{D}{10i}$ ...18.28b/ Pg 363, DHB

  $= \dfrac{200}{10i}$

  $i = 3.33 \approx 4$

  i.e. Number of piston rings, $i = 4$

  Number of lands $= i - 1 = 4 - 1 = 3$

- **Check for h:**

  The minimum thickness is given by $h_{min} = \dfrac{D}{10i}$ ...18.28b/ Pg 363, DHB

  $= \dfrac{200}{10 \times 4}$

  $h_{min} = 5$ mm

  Since $h \geq h_{min}$, h is satisfactory.

iii. **Distance from the top of piston to the first groove:**

   $t_g = t_1$ to $1.2\, t_1$ ...18.30/ Pg 363, DHB

   $= 1.2 \times 30$

   $t_g = 36$ mm

iv. **Distance/lands between the ring grooves:**

   $t_{land} = h$ ...18.31/ Pg 363, DHB

   $t_{land} = h = 6$ mm

v. **Total height of ring section:**

   Based on i, $h_{total} = [i + (i - 1)]\, h$

   $= [4 + (4 - 1)] \times 6$

   $h_{total} = 42$ mm

Check for h_{total}:

The total depth of piston rings is given as:

$h_{total} = \left(\dfrac{D}{7}\right) + 6$ mm, for gas and oil engines ...18.29/ Pg 363, DHB

$= \left(\dfrac{200}{7}\right) + 6$ mm

$h_{total} = 34.57$ mm (minimum value)

Since $h_{total} >$ table (minimum) value, hence safe.

c. Piston barrel:

i. **Maximum thickness of the piston barrel:**

   $t_3 = 0.03\, D + b + 4.5$ mm ...18.20/ Pg 362, DHB

   b – depth of ring grooves (mm)

   $= t_r + 0.4$ mm

   $= 6 + 0.4$ mm

   $b = 6.4$ mm

   $t_3 = (0.03 \times 200) + 6.4 + 4.5$ mm

   $t_3 = 16.9$ mm ≈ 17 mm

ii. **Thickness of piston barrel towards the open end of piston:**

$$t_4 = 0.25\, t_3 \text{ to } 0.35\, t_3 \qquad \text{...18.21/ Pg 362, DHB}$$
$$= (0.25 \times 17) \text{ to } (0.35 \times 17)$$
$$t_4 = 4.25 \text{ to } 5.95 \text{ mm}$$
$$t_4 = 5.5 \text{ mm}$$

d. Piston skirt:

i. **Length of the piston:**

$$L = 1.5\, D \qquad \text{...18.22/ Pg 362, DHB}$$
$$= 1.5 \times 200$$
$$L = 300 \text{ mm}$$

ii. **Length of skirt:**

Length of skirt = *barrel length – piston head thickness – ring section*
$$= L - t_1 - h_{total}$$
$$= 300 - 30 - 42$$
$$= 228 \text{ mm}$$

e. Piston pin:

i. **Diameter of piston pin–Bearing consideration:**

The diameter of the piston is calculated as:

$$d = \frac{\pi D^2 p_{max}}{4 l_1 p_b} \qquad \text{...18.24/ Pg 362, DHB}$$

Where, l_1 = length of gudgeon pin bearing (mm)
$$= k_1 d$$
k_1 = 2 for oil engines
p_b = bearing pressure
$\quad$ = 15.7 MN/m² for automotive engines

$$d = \frac{\pi \times 200^2 \times 4}{4 \times (2d) \times 15.7}$$

$$d = 63.26 \text{ mm} \approx 65 \text{ mm}.$$

ii. **Bending consideration:**

The maximum bending stress in the piston pin is checked using the relation,

$$\sigma_b = \frac{F_p D}{8Z} \text{ (MN/m}^2\text{)} \qquad \text{...18.26/ Pg 363, DHB}$$

Where, σ_b = bending stress
$\quad \leq 82$ MN/m², for case hardened carbon steel
F_p = force on the piston

$$= p \cdot A = \frac{p \pi D^2}{4} = \frac{4 \times \pi \times 200^2}{4}$$

$F_p = 125.66 \times 10^3$ N
Z = section modulus

$$= \frac{\pi D^3}{32} = \frac{\pi \times 200^3}{32}$$

$$\therefore Z = 785.3 \times 10^3 \text{ mm}^3$$

$$\sigma_b = \frac{125.66 \times 10^3 \times 200}{8 \times 785.4 \times 10^3}$$

$\sigma_b = 4$ MPa. < 82 MPa, hence safe.

8.6 CONNECTING ROD

The connecting rod is the connecting link between the piston and the crankshaft. Its primary function is to transmit the push and pull from the piston pin to the crank pin and thus convert the reciprocating motion of the piston into the rotary motion of the crank **(Fig. 8.6)**.

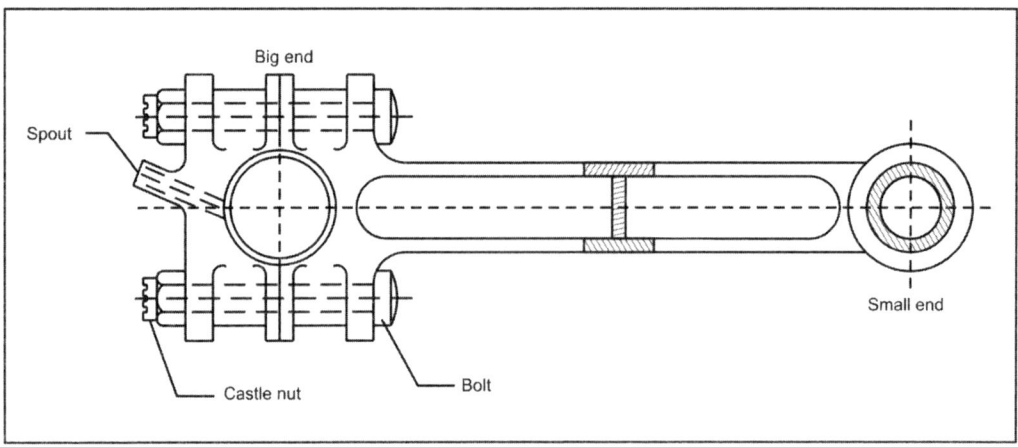

Fig. 8.6: Connecting rod

The connecting rod is one of the most highly stressed parts of an engine. Rods are generally made of drop-forged, heat-treated carbon steel (alloy steel forging). The cross-section of the shank may be rectangular, circular, tubular, I-section or H-section. Generally circular section is used for low speed engines while I-section is preferred for high speed engines.

The small end of the connecting rod (bore at the piston end) is generally forged as an integral part of the rod and is provided with a bush of phosphor bronze. It is connected to the piston by means of a *piston pin gudgeon pin* or *wrist pin*.

The big end of the connecting rod (bore at the crankshaft end) is made by two parts: one an integral part of the rod and the other a removable cap. The split cap is fastened to the big end with two cap bolts. The bearing shells of the big end are made of steel, brass or bronze with a thin lining of white metal or babbit metal.

The length (l) of connecting rod is distance between the centres of small end and big end of the connecting rod. An important consideration is designing the connecting rod is its length. If the length is small compared to its crank radius (r), the angularity of the connecting rod increases, which in turn increases the side thrust of the piston.

8.7 FORCE ANALYSIS IN CONNECTING ROD

8.7.1 Force on the Piston due to Gas Pressure and Inertia of the Reciprocating Parts

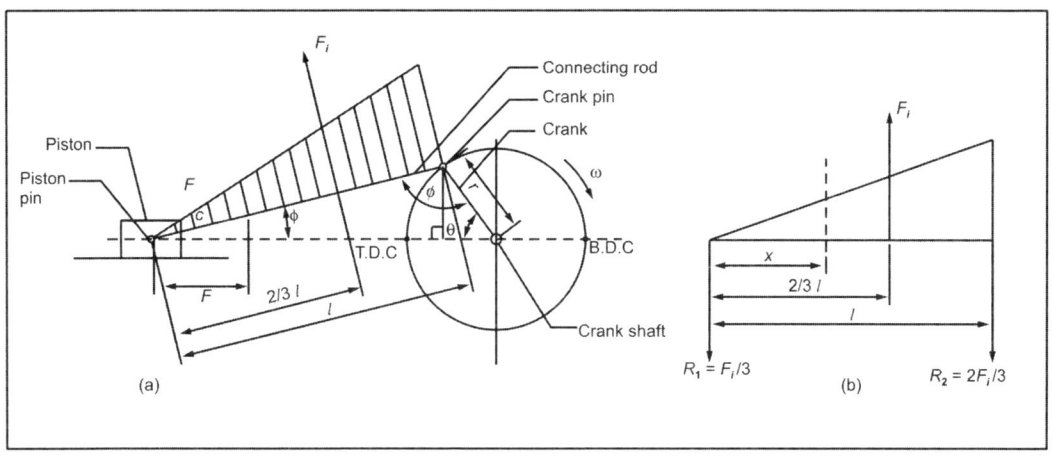

Fig. 8.7: Forces acting on a connecting rod [Fig. 19.1/ Pg 372, DHB)

Force on the piston due to pressure of gas,

$$F_p = p_{max} \frac{\pi D^2}{4} \qquad \text{...(Eq. 8.21)}$$

$p (= p_{max})$ = maximum gas or steam pressure
D = diameter of piston

Inertia force of reciprocating parts is given as,

$$F = \frac{1000 W_r v^2}{gr}\left(\cos\theta \pm \frac{\cos 2\theta}{n'}\right) \qquad \text{...(Eq. 8.22)} \; \textbf{19.8a/ Pg 370, DHB}$$

Where, W_r = mg = weight of reciprocating parts (N)
= weight of (piston + piston rings + piston pins + 1/3rd of connecting rod)
m = mass of reciprocating parts (kg)
g = acceleration due to gravity = 9.81 (m/s^2)
v = $\pi d n$ = $2\pi r n$ = crank velocity (m/s)
r = $L_s/2$ crank radius (mm)
L_s = stroke length (mm)
n = crank speed (rps)
θ = Angle of inclination of the crank from top dead centre.
= Positive sign to be taken from inner dead center while negative sign from outer dead center.

$n' = \dfrac{l}{r}$ = Ratio of length of connecting rod to radius of crank

= 5 to 7 for satisfactory steam engines
= 4 to 5 for ordinary marine engines
= 5.4 to 6 for locomotive engines
= 3.2 to 4 for IC engines
= 3 to 4 for aero engines ...**19.7/Pg 370, DHB**
l = length of connecting rod (mm)

Net force acting on the connecting rod, $F_{net} = F_p \pm F$ ...(Eq. 8.23)

This force F gives rise to a force F_c in the connecting rod and a thrust F_i on the sides of the cylinder walls. From **Fig. 8.8,** force in the connecting rod at any instant,

The force component acting along the axis of connecting rod,

$$F_c = \frac{F}{\cos \phi} = \frac{F}{\sqrt{1-\sin^2 \phi}} \qquad \text{...(Eq. 8.24) } \textbf{3.12/ Pg 45, DHB}$$

$$\text{But } \sin \theta = \frac{l}{r} \sin \phi \qquad \text{...(Eq. 8.24a)}$$

$$\therefore \sin \phi = \frac{\sin \theta}{l/r} = \frac{\sin \theta}{n'}$$

$$\therefore F_c = \frac{F}{\cos \phi} = \frac{F}{\sqrt{1-\left(\frac{\sin \theta}{n'}\right)^2}} \qquad \text{... (Eq. 8.25)}$$

The force in the connecting rod will be maximum when the crank and the connecting rod are perpendicular to each other (i.e. when $\theta = 90°$).

Note:

$$v = \left(\frac{\pi d n}{1000}\right) = \left(\frac{2\pi r n}{1000}\right) \text{ (m/s) in Eq. (8.22), we have}$$

Eq. (8.22) yields ... $F = \dfrac{1000 W_r}{gr} \left(\dfrac{2\pi r n}{1000}\right)^2 \left(\cos \theta \pm \dfrac{\cos 2\theta}{ng'}\right)$

$$F = 4.03 \times 10^{-3} W_r n^2 r \left(\cos \theta \pm \frac{\cos 2\theta}{n'}\right)$$

...(Eq. 8.26) **19.8b/ Pg 370, DHB**

8.7.2 Force due to Inertia of the Connecting Rod

The inertia force of connecting rod has two components: longitudinal (parallel) and transverse (perpendicular). The longitudinal component is accounted for 1/3rd of its mass at the piston pin and 2/3rd at the crank pin. The transverse component acts on every part of the rod.

The small end of connecting rod has pure translatory motion and the big end has rotary motion, while all the intermediate points on the rod move in elliptical orbit. This lateral oscillation of the rod results in inertia bending forces all along the length of the rod. This type of action is referred to as *whipping stress -or- bending force due to inertia.*

For the purpose of analysis, the rod is assumed to be of uniform cross-section throughout its length without any appreciable error, in which case the resultant inertia due to acceleration of the oscillating rod will act at a distance of 2/3 from the piston pin as shown in **Fig. 8.7 (a).**

At the crank pin the force acting on unit length of the rod is

$$F' = \rho A\omega^2 r \sin(\theta + \phi) \qquad \text{...(Eq. 8.27)}$$

$$= \frac{wA\omega^2 r}{g} \sin(\theta + \phi) \quad (\because w = \rho g)$$

This force will be maximum when the crank and connecting rod are at right angles,

i.e. $$F'_{max} = \frac{wA\omega^2 r}{g} \qquad \text{...(Eq. 8.28)}$$

Thus, the resulting normal force acting on the rod is

$$F_i = \left(\frac{1}{2}\right) F'_{max} \cdot l \qquad \text{...(Eq. 8.29)}$$

$$F_i = \frac{wA\omega^2 rl}{2g} \qquad \text{...(Eq. 8.30)}$$

$$F_i = \frac{wA\omega^2 rl}{2g} \times 10^{-12} \qquad \text{...(Eq. 8.31)} \; \textbf{19.1/ Pg 369, DHB}$$

Where, $w = \rho g$ = weight of unit volume of rod (N/m^3)
ρ = density of material (kg/m^3)
g = acceleration due to gravity = 9.81 (m/s^2)
A = cross-sectional area (mm^2)
r = crank radius (mm)
n = crank speed (rps)
l = length of connecting rod (mm)
$\omega = 2\pi n$ = angular velocity of crank (rad/s)

Since it has been assumed that 1/3rd mass of the connecting rod is concentrated at piston pin (i.e. small end of connecting rod) and 2/3rd at the crankpin (i.e. big end of connecting rod), therefore, the reaction at these two ends are:

$$R_1 = \frac{F_i}{3} \text{ and } R_2 = \frac{2F_i}{3} \qquad \text{[Center of gravity of triangle]} \qquad \text{...(Eq. 8.32)}$$

Now the bending moment acting on the rod at a distance from piston pin is

$$M_x = R_1 x - \left(\frac{1}{2}\right)\left(\frac{F'_{max} x}{l}\right) x \left(\frac{x}{3}\right)$$

$$= \frac{F_i}{3} x - \left(\frac{1}{2}\right)\left(\frac{x^3}{3l}\right) F'_{max}$$

$$= \frac{F_i x}{3} - \left(\frac{1}{2}\right)\left(\frac{x^3}{3l}\right)\left(\frac{2F_i}{l}\right) \qquad \text{... using (Eq. 8.29)}$$

$$= \frac{F_i x}{3} - \left(\frac{F_i x^3}{3l^2}\right)$$

$$\therefore M_x = \frac{F_i}{3}\left(x - \frac{x^3}{l^2}\right) \qquad \text{...(Eq. 8.33)}$$

For maximum bending moment, $\dfrac{dM_x}{dx} = 0$

$$\dfrac{d}{dx}\left[\dfrac{F_i}{3}\left(x - \dfrac{x^3}{l^2}\right)\right] = 0$$

$$\dfrac{F_i}{3}\left(1 - \dfrac{3x^2}{l^2}\right) = 0$$

$$\left(1 - \dfrac{3x^2}{l^2}\right) = 0$$

$$l^2 = 3x^2$$

$$\therefore x = \dfrac{l}{\sqrt{3}} \qquad \ldots\text{(Eq. 8.34)}$$

i.e. the maximum bending moment occurs at a distance of $\dfrac{l}{\sqrt{3}}$ from piston pin.

Eq. (8.33) yields ... $M_{max} = \dfrac{F_i}{3}\left(\dfrac{l}{\sqrt{3}} - \dfrac{(l/\sqrt{3})^3}{l^2}\right)$

$$= \dfrac{F_i}{3}\left(\dfrac{l}{\sqrt{3}} - \dfrac{l^3}{3\sqrt{3}\,l^2}\right)$$

$$= \dfrac{F_i}{3}\left(\dfrac{l}{\sqrt{3}} - \dfrac{l}{3\sqrt{3}}\right)$$

$$= \dfrac{F_i l}{3\sqrt{3}}\left(1 - \dfrac{1}{3}\right)$$

$$M_{max} = \dfrac{2F_i l}{9\sqrt{3}} \qquad \ldots\text{(Eq. 8.35) } \mathbf{19.2/\ Pg\ 369,\ DHB}$$

Thus the maximum bending stress,

$$\sigma_b = \dfrac{M_{max}}{Z}$$

$$= \left(\dfrac{2F_i l}{9\sqrt{3}}\right) \times \left(\dfrac{1}{Z}\right)$$

But $F_i = \dfrac{wA\omega^2 rl}{2g} \times 10^{-12} \qquad \ldots\mathbf{19.1/\ Pg\ 369,\ DHB}$

$$= \left(\dfrac{1}{Z}\right)\left(\dfrac{2l}{9\sqrt{3}}\right)\left[\dfrac{wA\omega^2 rl}{2g} \times 10^{-12}\right]$$

Also $\omega = 2\pi n \quad n - \text{speed (rps)}$

$$= \left(\dfrac{1}{Z}\right)\left(\dfrac{2l}{9\sqrt{3}}\right)\left[\dfrac{wA(2\pi n)^2 rl}{2g} \times 10^{-12}\right]$$

$$\therefore \quad \sigma_b = \frac{(0.2584 \times 10^{-12})wArn^2 l^2}{Z} \quad \text{(MPa)} \quad \text{...(Eq. 8.36) } \mathbf{19.3/ Pg\ 369,\ DHB}$$

According to BB Low, the value of crank angle (θ) at which the bending moment is maximum, is given by

$$\theta = 90 - \frac{3500}{(n'+7.82)^2} \quad \text{(deg)} \quad \text{...(Eq. 8.37) } \mathbf{19.4/ Pg\ 369,\ DHB}$$

8.8 DESIGN OF CONNECTING ROD

In designing a connecting rod the following dimensions are required to be determined:
1. Dimension of cross-section of connecting rod
2. Dimension of the crank pin at the big end and the piston pin at the small end.
3. Size of the bolts for securing the big end cap and
4. Thickness of the big end cap.

8.8.1 Dimension of Cross-section of Connecting Rod

The most commonly used cross-section for connecting rods in IC engines is the I-section due to its lightness and capacity to withstand high gas pressures. It is subjected to axial compressive force which is equal to the maximum gas load on the piston. Hence the connecting rod is designed as a strut or column. Due to this compressive force, the rod can buckle. The buckling of the rod is considered under the following cases:
- In the plane of motion (X-axis as neutral axis)
- In a plane perpendicular to the plane of motion (Y-axis as neutral axis)

In the plane of motion, the ends of the rod are direction free and so freely hinged at the piston and crank pin. Hence for buckling about the neutral axis X-X, the strut is freely hinged.

In the plane perpendicular to the plane of motion, the strut has fixed ends due to constraining effects of bearings at the crank and gudgeon pin. Hence for buckling about the neutral axis Y-Y, the connecting rod is four times stronger than that about X-X axis. To achieve this condition, the necessary condition for the rod to be equally resistant to buckling in either plane is:

$$I_{xx} = 4I_{yy} \quad \text{...(Eq. 8.38) } \mathbf{19.6/ Pg\ 370,\ DHB}$$
or $\quad k_{xx}^2 = 4k_{yy}^2 \quad$ ...(Eq. 8.39)

I = moment of inertia (mm^4)
$I = Ak^2$
A = area of the cross-section (mm^2)
k = radius of gyration (mm)

Proof:

Fig 8.8 (**Table 1.3-Fig. (c)/ Pg 8, DHB** –or– **Appendix II – Fig. (b)/Pg 431, DHB** –or– **Fig. 19.2/ Pg 372, DHB**) shows standard proportions of an I-section commonly used for IC engines.

Let t = thickness of the flange and web
B = Width of the section (= $4t$)
D or H = depth of the section (= $5t$)
I_{xx} = Moment of inertia of the section about X-axis
I_{yy} = Moment of inertia of the section about Y-axis

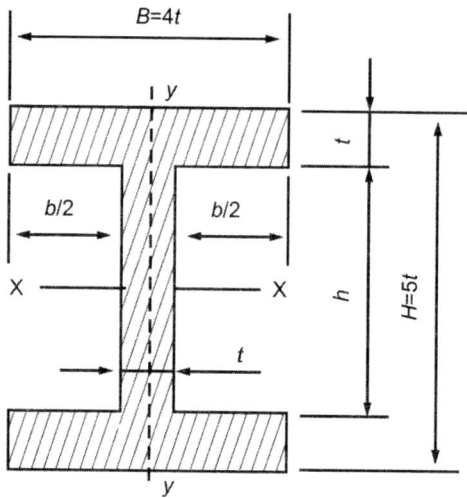

Fig. 8.8: Standard proportions of I-section

→ $$I_{xx} = \frac{BH^3 - bh^3}{12} \qquad \text{...Tb 1.3-Fig. (c)/ Pg 8, DHB}$$

$$= \frac{(4t)(5t)^3 - (3t)(3t)^3}{12}$$

$$I_{xx} = \frac{419t^4}{12} \qquad \text{...(Eq. 8.40)}$$

→ $I_{yy} = 2I_{yy\text{flanges}} + I_{yy\text{web}}$

$$= 2\left[\frac{(t)(4t)^3}{12}\right] + \left[\frac{(3t)(t)^3}{12}\right]$$

$$I_{yy} = \frac{131t^4}{12} \qquad \text{...(Eq. 8.41)}$$

∴ $$\frac{I_{xx}}{I_{yy}} = \frac{419t^4/12}{131t^4/12} = \mathbf{3.1985} \qquad \text{...(Eq. 8.42)}$$

→ Also radius of gyration, $k = \sqrt{\dfrac{I}{A}}$ ...Tb 1.3-Fig. (c)/ Pg 8, DHB

Area $A = 2[(4t)t] + (t)(3t) = 11t^2$ ...(Eq. 8.43)

i.e. $$k_{xx}^2 = \frac{I_{xx}}{A} = \frac{419t^4/12}{11t^2} = 3.1742t^2 \Rightarrow k_{xx} = 1.782t$$

$$k_{yy}^2 = \frac{I_{yy}}{A} = \frac{131t^4/12}{11t^2} = 0.9924t^2 \Rightarrow k_{yy} = 0.9962t$$

∴ $$\frac{k_{xx}^2}{k_{xx}^2} = \frac{3.1742t^2}{0.9924t^2} = 3.1985 \qquad \ldots(Eq.\ 8.44)$$

From Eqs (8.42) and (8.44) it is observed that the proportions of the I-section are satisfactory (i.e. < 4).

The buckling load may be calculated by Rankine-Gordon formula as:

$$f_{cr} = \frac{F_c}{A} = \frac{f_c}{1 + K(l/k)^2} \qquad \ldots(Eq.\ 8.45)\ \mathbf{19.5/\ Pg\ 369,\ DHB}$$

Where, F_c = crippling load i.e. axial load on the rod due to steam or gas pressure (N)
– Taken equal to the maximum force acting on piston due to gas pressure

i.e. $$F_c = F_p = p_{max} \frac{\pi D^2}{4} \qquad \ldots using\ (Eq.\ 8.21)$$

$p = p_{max})$ – maximum gas or steam pressure
D = diameter of piston
f_c = allowable unit stress for designing (N/mm²)
$$= \frac{\text{Yield point stress}}{\text{FOS}}$$

Values of yield point stress   ...**Table 19.1/ Pg 371, DHB**

FOS = factor of safety = 5 or 6
K = constant
 = 1/25000, for steel rod having both ends fixed
 = 4/25000, for steel rod – pin connected at both ends so that the rod is free to bend in any plane
$k = k_{xx}$ = radius of gyration about of an axis parallel to the pins of the end joints   ...**Fig. 19.2/ Pg 372, DHB**
 = $d/4$, for circular section of diameter   ...**Tb 1.3-Fig. (g)/ Pg 8, DHB**
 = $0.289h$, for rectangular section of depth   ...**Tb 1.3-Fig. (a)/ Pg 8, DHB**
$$= \sqrt{\frac{BH^3 - bh^3}{12(BH - bh)}},\ \text{for an I-section} \qquad \ldots\mathbf{Tb\ 1.3\text{-}Fig.\ (g)/\ Pg\ 8,\ DHB}$$

8.8.2 Dimension of the Crank Pin at the Big End and the Piston Pin at the Small End Small End

The dimensions of small end may be obtained based on bearing consideration as discussed in design of piston pin. Based on bearing pressure, the diameter of the piston pin is calculated as:

$$d_p = \frac{\pi D^2 p_{max}}{4 l_1 p_b} \qquad \ldots using\ (Eq.\ 8.16)\ \mathbf{18.24/\ Pg\ 362,\ DHB}$$

i.e. diameter of piston pin $$d_p = \left(\frac{\pi D^2}{4}\right) \frac{p_{max}}{l_p p_{bp}} \qquad \ldots(Eq.\ 8.46)$$

But $F_p = p_{max} \dfrac{\pi D^2}{4}$ ...using (8.21)

$$d_p = \dfrac{F_p}{l_p p_b}$$

or $F_p = F_c = l_p d_p p_{bp}$ ...(Eq. 8.47)

Where, $l_p (= l_1)$ = length of piston pin (mm)
$= k_1 d_p$
$k_1 = 1.5$ for petrol and gas engines
$= 2$ for oil engines
$p_{bp} (= p_b)$ = bearing pressure
$= 12.4$ MN/m² for gas engines
$= 15$ MN/m² for oil engines
$= 15.7$ MN/m² for automotive engines
$p (= p_{max})$ = maximum gas or steam pressure (MPa)
D = diameter of piston (mm)

Big End

On similar lines to small end, we have

$F_p = F_c = l_c d_c p_{bc}$ ...(Eq. 8.48)

l_c = length of crank pin (mm)
d_c = diameter of crank pin

Note: In general

	l_p/d_p	p_{bp}
Small end	1.5 to 2	10 to14 MPa
Big end	1.25 to 1.5	5 to 10 MPa

8.8.3 Size of the Bolts for Big End Cap

The maximum load to be taken by the bolts and cap consists only of inertia force at the top dead center (TDC) on the exhaust stroke. The explosion and compression loads and also the inertia load at the bottom dead center (BDC) are compressive. Hence do not affect these components. The inertia force is given in Eq. (8.22 or 8.26) **(19.8 a or b/ Pg 370, DHB)**.

i.e. $F = 4.03 \times 10^{-3} W_r n^2 r \left(\cos\theta \pm \dfrac{\cos 2\theta}{n'} \right)$ ... using (Eq. 8.26) **19.8b/ Pg 370, DHB**

The maximum value of inertia force occurs at $\theta = 0$, at the top dead center.

i.e. $F_{1max} = 4.03 \times 10^{-3} W_r n^2 r \left(1 + \dfrac{1}{n'} \right)$ ...(Eq. 8.49) **19.9/ Pg 371, DHB**

$W_r = mg$ = weight of reciprocating parts (N)
= weight of (piston + piston rings + piston pins + 1/3rd of connecting rod)
m = mass of reciprocating parts (kg)
g = acceleration due to gravity = 9.81 (m/s²)
$r = L_s/2$ = crank radius (mm)
L_s = stroke length (mm)
n' = Ratio of length of connecting rod to radius of crank = l/r

The bolts are under repeated stresses but not alternating stresses. Since there are two bolts, each shares the inertia force equally.

$$\therefore \quad F_{1max} = 2\left(\frac{\pi d_b^2}{4}\right)\sigma_t \qquad \ldots\text{(Eq. 8.50)}$$

Where, d_b = core diameter of the bolts (mm)
σ_t = permissible tensile stress for bolt material (N/mm²)

The nominal diameter of the bolt is calculated as $d = \dfrac{d_b}{0.84}$ ...(Eq. 8.51)

8.8.4 Thickness of the Big End Cap

The cap is subjected to inertia force. It is treated as a beam freely supported at the bolt centers and loaded in manner intermediate between uniformly distributed load and centrally concentrated load. The maximum bending moment is given as

$$M_b = \frac{F_{1max} l_0}{6} \qquad \ldots\text{(Eq. 8.52)}$$

l_0 – distance between bolt centers
= dia. of crank pin + 2[thickness of liner (3 mm)] + nominal dia. of bolt + clearance (3 mm)
= $d_c + 2(3) + d + 3$
$l_0 = d_c + d + 9$ mm   ...(Eq. 8.53)

The thickness of the cap is obtained as:

$$\sigma_b = \frac{M_b}{Z} = \frac{6M_b}{bh^2} \qquad \ldots\text{(Eq. 8.54)}$$

Where, Z = section modulus = $\dfrac{I}{y} = \dfrac{bh^2}{6}$

$I = \dfrac{bh^3}{12}$ and $y = \dfrac{h}{2}$

b = width of cap (mm)-taken equal to length of crank pin or big end bearing
i.e. $b = l_c$
h = thickness of cap (mm)

8.8.5 Whipping Stress or Bending Force Due to Inertia

The whipping stress is calculated as

$$\sigma_b = \frac{\left(0.2584 \times 10^{-12}\right) w A r n^2 l^2}{Z} \quad \text{(MPa)} \qquad \ldots \text{using (8.36)} \; \mathbf{19.3/\, Pg\, 369,\, DHB}$$

Where, $w = \rho g$ = weight of unit volume of rod (N/m³)
π = density of material (kg/m³)
g = acceleration due to gravity = 9.81 (m/s²)
A = cross-sectional area (mm²)
r = crank radius (mm)
n = crank speed (rps)
l = length of connecting rod (mm)
$\omega = 2\pi n$ = angular velocity of crank (rad/s)

n = crank speed (rps)

$$Z = \text{section modulus} = \frac{I_{xx}}{y} \quad \ldots(\text{Eq. 8.55})$$

$$I_{xx} = \frac{419t^4}{12} \quad (mm^4) \quad \ldots \text{using (Eq. 8.40)}$$

and $y = \dfrac{5t}{2}$ (mm)

t = thickness of connecting rod (mm).

4. A connecting rod of length l may be considered as a strut with the ends free to turn on the crank pin and the gudgeon pin. In the directions of the axes of these pins, however, it may be considered as having fixed ends. Assuming that Euler's formula is applicable, determine the ratios of the sides of the rectangular cross-section so that the connecting rod is equally strong in both planes of buckling.

Solution: Consider an I – section as shown in **Fig. 8.8**

Let t – thickness of the flange and web

B – Width of the section (= $4t$)

D or H – depth of the section (= $5t$)

For the connecting rod to be equally strong in buckling about both the axes (planes), the condition is

$$I_{xx} = 4 I_{yy} \quad \ldots \text{using (Eq. 8.38)} \; \mathbf{19.6/\; Pg\; 370,\; DHB}$$

Repeat steps in Eqs (8.39), (8.40), and (8.41)

$$\therefore \quad \frac{I_{xx}}{I_{yy}} = \frac{419t^4/12}{131t^4/12} = 3.1985 \quad \ldots \text{using (Eq. 8.42)}$$

Since Eq. (8.42) is < Eq. (8.38), hence the assumed values of dimensions are satisfactory.

5. Design a connecting rod for a IC engine using the following data:

diameter of piston = 140 mm, stroke = 160 mm,
weight of reciprocating parts = 3 kg, length of connecting rod = 400 mm,
maximum speed = 2000 rpm, maximum explosion pressure = 2.25 MPa

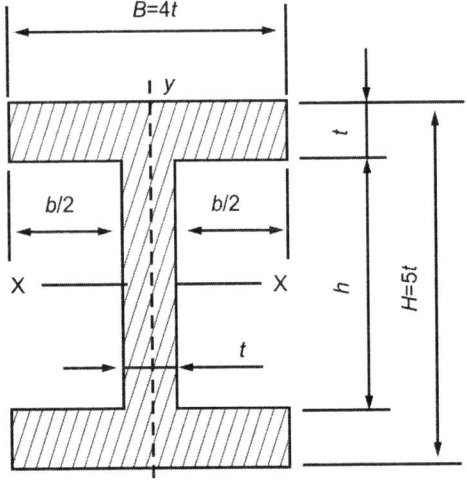

Fig. 8.9: Problem 5

Solution: $D = 140$ mm, $L_s = 160$ mm, $m = 3$ kg, $l = 400$ mm, $N = 2000$ rpm $\Rightarrow n = 33.34$ rps, $p = p_{max} = 2.25$ MPa

1. Dimensions of connecting rod:

Consider an I-section of the connecting rod, as shown in **Fig. 8.9**
Let t = thickness of the flange and web
B = Width of the section ($= 4t$)
D or H = depth of the section ($= 5t$)
I_{xx} = Moment of inertia of the section about X-axis
I_{yy} = Moment of inertia of the section about Y-axis

For the connecting rod to be equally strong in buckling about both the axes (planes), the condition is

$$I_{xx} = 4I_{yy} \qquad \text{...Eq. (}i\text{) 19.6/ Pg 370, DHB}$$

• $$I_{xx} = \frac{BH^3 - bh^3}{12} \qquad \text{...Tb 1.3-Fig. (c)/ Pg 8, DHB}$$

$$= \frac{(4t)(5t)^3 - (3t)(3t)^3}{12}$$

$$I_{xx} = \frac{419t^4}{12}$$

→ $$I_{yy} = 2I_{yy\,\text{flanges}} + I_{yy\,\text{web}} \qquad \text{...Eq. (}ii\text{)}$$

$$= 2\left[\frac{(t)(4t)^3}{12}\right] + \left[\frac{(3t)(t)^3}{12}\right]$$

$$I_{yy} = \frac{131t^4}{12} \qquad \text{...Eq. (}iii\text{)}$$

∴ $$\frac{I_{xx}}{I_{yy}} = \frac{I_{xx}}{I_{yy}} = \frac{419t^4/12}{131t^4/12} = 3.1985 \qquad \text{...Eq. (}iv\text{)}$$

Since $\dfrac{I_{xx}}{I_{yy}} = 3.2 < 4$, the section chosen is quite satisfactory.

→ Also radius of gyration, $k = \sqrt{\dfrac{I}{A}}$ ...Tb 1.3-Fig. (c)/ Pg 8, DHB

Area $A = 2[(4t)t] + (t)(3t) = 11t^2$ ...Eq. (v)

i.e. $$k_{xx} = \sqrt{\frac{I_{xx}}{A}} = \sqrt{\frac{419t^4/12}{11t^2}} = 1.78t \qquad \text{...Eq.(}vi\text{)}$$

The buckling load $f_{cr} = \dfrac{F_c}{A} = \dfrac{f_c}{1 + K(l/k)^2}$ ...19.5/ Pg 369, DHB

$$F_c = \frac{f_c A}{1 + K\left(\dfrac{l}{k_{xx}}\right)^2} \qquad \text{...Eq.(}vii\text{)}$$

- $$F_c = F_p = p_{max} \frac{\pi D^2}{4}$$
  $$= 2.25 \times \frac{\pi \times 140^2}{4}$$
  $\therefore \quad F_c = F_p = 34636.06 \text{ N}$

- Allowable unit stress for designing, $f_c = \dfrac{\text{Yield point stress}}{\text{FOS}}$

  Assume carbon steel (C 0.35% to 0.45%), yield point stress = 378 MPa

  ...Tb 19.1/ Pg 371, DHB

  Assume a factor of safety (FOS) = 5

  i.e. $\quad f_c = \dfrac{378}{5}$

  $\therefore \quad f_c = 75.6$ MPa

- $K = 4/25000$, for steel rod – pin connected at both ends so that the rod is free to bend in any plane

$\therefore$ Eq. (vii) yields ... $34636.06 = \dfrac{75.6 \times 11t^2}{1 + \left(\dfrac{4}{25000}\right)\left(\dfrac{400}{1.78t}\right)^2}$

$$1 + \frac{8.08}{t^2} = 0.024t^2$$

$$t^2 + 8.08 = 0.024t^4$$

i.e. $\quad t^4 - 41.64t^2 - 336.53 = 0$

$$t^2 = \frac{-(-41.64) \pm \sqrt{(-41.64)^2 - [4 \times 1 \times (-336.53)]}}{2 \times 1}$$

$t^2 = 48.56, -6.93$

$\therefore \quad t = 6.97$ mm = 7 mm

Thus the dimensions of the connecting rod are:
→ Thickness of the flange and web, $t = 7$ mm
→ Width of the section, $B = 4t = 4 \times 7 = 28$ mm
→ Depth of the section, $H = 5t = 5 \times 7 = 35$ mm
→ Area, $A = 11t^2 = 11 \times 7^2 = 539$ mm²
→ Radius of gyration, $k_{xx} = 1.78\, t = 1.78 \times 7 = 12.46$ mm.

2. Dimension of the piston pin at the small end

Load on piston pin or small end bearing,
$$F_p = F_c = l_p d_p p_{bp}$$
Assume $l_p = 1.5\, d_p$ and $p_{bp} = 15$ MPa
$$34636.06 = (1.5\, d_p)\, d_p \times 15$$

$\therefore$ Diameter of piston pin, $d_p = 39.23$ mm ≈ 40 mm

and length of piston pin, $l_p = 1.5 \times 40 = 60$ mm

-OR-

The diameter of the piston is calculated as:

$$d_p = \frac{\pi D^2 p_{max}}{4 l_1 p_b} \qquad \text{...18.24/ Pg 362, DHB}$$

$$d_p = \left(\frac{\pi D^2}{4}\right) \frac{p_{max}}{l_p p_{bp}}$$

But $F_p = p_{max} \dfrac{\pi D^2}{4}$ ...using (8.21)

$$d_p = \frac{F_p}{l_p p_b}$$

i.e. $\quad F_p = F_c = l_p d_p p_{bp}$

Where, $l_p (= l_1)$ – length of gudgeon pin bearing (mm)
$\qquad = k_1 d_p$
$\qquad k_1 = 1.5$ for petrol and gas engines
$\qquad p_{bp}(= p_b) = 15 \text{ MN/m}^2$ for oil engines

i.e. $\quad 34636.06 = (1.5\, d_p)\, d_p \times 15$

Diameter of piston pin, $d_p = 39.23$ mm ≈ 40 mm
Length of piston pin, $l_p = 1.5 \times 40 = 60$ mm.

3. Dimension of the crank pin at the big end:

Load on piston pin or small end bearing, $F_p = F_c = l_c d_c p_{bc}$

Assume $l_p = 1.3\, d_p$ and $p_{bp} = 10$ MPa

$$34636.06 = (1.3\, d_c)\, d_c \times 10$$

∴ Diameter of crank pin, $d_c = 51.62$ mm ≈ 52 mm
and length of crank pin, $l_c = 1.3 \times 52 = 67.6$ mm ≈ 68 mm

4. Size of the bolts for big end cap:

The maximum value of inertia force occurs at $\theta = 0$, at the top dead center.

i.e. $\quad F_{1max} = 4.03 \times 10^{-3}\, W_r n^2 r \left(1 + \dfrac{1}{n'}\right) \qquad \text{...19.9/ Pg 370, DHB}$

- Weight of reciprocating parts, $W_r = mg = 3 \times 9.81 = 29.43$ N
- Crank radius, $r = \dfrac{L_s}{2} = \dfrac{160}{2} = 80$ mm
- $n' = \dfrac{l}{r} = \dfrac{400}{80} = 5$
- $n = 33.34$ rps

$$F_{1max} = 4.03 \times 10^{-3} \times 29.43 \times (33.34)^2 \times 80 \times \left(1 + \dfrac{1}{5}\right)$$

∴ $\quad F_{1max} = 12656.04$ N ...Eq. (*viii*)

'Since there are two bolts, each shares the inertia force equally.

i.e. $\quad F_{1max} = 2\left(\dfrac{\pi d_b^2}{4}\right)\sigma_t$ ...Eq. (*ix*)

Equating Eq. (*viii*) and Eq. (*ix*), we have

$$12656.04 = 2\left(\frac{\pi d_b^2}{4}\right) \times 60, \quad \text{assume } \sigma_t = 60 \text{ MPa}$$

∴ Core diameter of the bolts, $d_b = 11.59$ mm
Comparing the above value in **Tb. 9.8/ Pg 113, DHB** under *column 5*, the nominal diameter of the bolt is $d = 14$ mm ... *(column 3)* **Tb. 9.8/ Pg 113, DHB**

-OR- The nominal diameter of the bolt is calculated as $d = \dfrac{d_b}{0.84}$

$$= \frac{11.59}{0.84}$$

$$d = 13.79 \text{ mm} = 14 \text{ mm (round off)}$$

5. Thickness of the big end cap:

The thickness of the cap is calculated as:

$$\sigma_b = \frac{M_b}{Z} = \frac{6M_b}{bh^2} \qquad \text{...Eq. }(x)$$

- b = width of cap (mm) - taken equal to length of crank pin or big end bearing i.e. $b = l_c = 68$ mm
- $M_b = \dfrac{F_{1\max} l_o}{6}$

  l_0 = distance between bolt centers
  = dia. of crank pin + 2[thickness of liner (3 mm)] + nominal dia. of bolt + clearance (3 mm)
  $l_0 = d_c + 2(3 \text{ mm}) + d + 3$ mm
  = 52 + 6 mm + 14 + 3 mm
  $l_0 = 75$ mm

$$M_b = \frac{12656.04 \times 75}{6}$$

i.e. $M_b = 158.2 \times 10^3$ N-mm

- Assume that the material for cap and bolt has $\sigma_b = \sigma_t = 60$ MPa

∴ Eq. (*x*) yields ... $60 = \dfrac{6 \times 158.2 \times 10^3}{68 \times h^2}$

$$h = 15.25 \text{ mm} \approx 16 \text{ mm}$$

6. Whipping stress -or- bending force due to inertia:

The whipping stress is calculated as

$$\sigma_b = \frac{\left(0.2584 \times 10^{-12}\right) w A r n^2 l^2}{Z} \qquad \text{...19.3/ Pg 369, DHB}$$

- Assume density of material, $\rho = 8000$ kg/m^3
- Assume that the material for cap and bolt has $\sigma_b = \sigma_t = 60$ MPa
- Weight of unit volume of rod, $w = \rho g = 8000 \times 9.81 = 78480$ N/m^3

- Section modulus, $Z = \dfrac{I_{xx}}{y}$

$$I_{xx} = \dfrac{419t^4}{12} = \dfrac{419 \times 7^4}{12} = 83835 \text{ mm}^4$$

and $\quad y = \dfrac{5t}{2} = \dfrac{5 \times 7}{2} = 17.5 \text{ mm}$

$$Z = \dfrac{83835}{17.5} = 4790.57 \text{ mm}^3$$

$$\sigma_b = \dfrac{(0.2584 \times 10^{-12}) \times 78480 \times 539 \times 80 \times 33.34^2 \times 400^2}{4790.57}$$

$\sigma_b = 32$ MPa < 60 MPa, hence safe.

6. Design a connecting rod for a diesel engine using the following data:
   Cylinder bore = 100 mm, length of connecting rod = 350 mm, maximum gas pressure = 3.5 MPa, Allowable unit stress for rod = 330 MPa, FOS against buckling pressure = 5, stroke length = 180 mm, mass of reciprocating parts = 2 kg, engine speed = 1800 rpm, thickness of bearing bush = 3 mm, (l/d) 1.5 and 1.25 for bearings of piston pin and crank pin respectively, allowable bearing pressure for piston pin bearing = 13 MPa, allowable bearing pressure for crank pin baring = 10 MPa, yield strength of cap material and bolt material = 380 MPa and 450 MPa respectively, FOS for cap material and bolt material = 4 and 5 respectively, density of rod = 7800 kg/m³.

Solution: $D = 100$ mm, $l = 350$ mm, $p = p_{max} = 3.5$ MPa, $f_c = 330$ MPa, FOS = 5, $L_s = 180$ mm, $m = 2$ kg, $N = 1800$ rpm $\Rightarrow n = 30$ rps, bearing = 3 mm thick,

Piston pin: $\quad (l/d)p = 1.5, p_{bp} = 13$ MPa
Crank pin: $\quad (l/d)_c = 1.25, p_{bc} = 10$ MPa
Cap: $\quad$ FOS = 4, $\sigma_{by} = 380$ MPa, $\sigma_b = 95$ MPa
Bolt: $\quad$ FOS = 5, $\sigma_{ty} = 450$ MPa, $\sigma_t = 90$ MPa

1. Dimensions of connecting rod:

   Repeat steps from Eq. (i) to Eq. (vi), from problem 5

   $\rightarrow \quad I_{xx} = \dfrac{419t^4}{12}$ ... using Eq. (ii)

   $\rightarrow \quad$ Area $A = 2[4t)t] + (t)(3t) = 11t^2$ ... using Eq. (v)

   $\rightarrow \quad k_{xx} = \sqrt{\dfrac{I_{xx}}{A}} = \sqrt{\dfrac{419t^4/12}{11t^2}} = 1.78\,t$ ... using Eq. (vi)

   The buckling load $\quad f_{cr} = \dfrac{F_c}{A} = \dfrac{f_c}{1 + K(l/k)^2}$ ...19.5/ Pg 369, DHB

   $$F_c = \dfrac{f_c A}{1 + K\left(\dfrac{l}{k_{xx}}\right)^2}$$ ...Eq. (vii)

- $$F_c = p_{max} \frac{\pi D^2}{4}$$

$$= 3.5 \times \frac{\pi \times 100^2}{4}$$

$\therefore \quad F_c = F_p = 27489 \text{ N}$

- Allowable unit stress for rod, $f_c = \dfrac{\text{Yield point stress}}{\text{FOS}}$

i.e. $f_c = \dfrac{330}{5}$

$\therefore \quad f_c = 66 \text{ MPa}$

- $K = 4/25000$, for steel rod – pin connected at both ends so that the rod is free to bend in any plane

$\rightarrow \quad k = k_{xx} = 1.78\, t$

$\therefore$ Eq. (vii) yields ... $27489 = \dfrac{66 \times 11 t^2}{1 + \left(\dfrac{4}{25000}\right)\left(\dfrac{350}{1.78 t}\right)^2}$

$$1 + \frac{6.19}{t^2} = 0.0264 t^2$$

$$t^2 + 6.19 = 0.0264 t^4$$

i.e. $\quad t^4 - 37.89 t^2 - 234.47 = 0$

$$t^2 = \frac{-(-37.89) \pm \sqrt{(-37.89)^2 - [4 \times 1 \times (-234.47)]}}{2 \times 1}$$

$t^2 = 43.30, -5.41$

$\therefore \quad t = 6.58 \text{ mm} \approx 7 \text{ mm}$

Thus the dimensions of the connecting rod are:
- $\rightarrow$ Thickness of the flange and web, $t = 7$ mm
- $\rightarrow$ Width of the section, $B = 4t = 4 \times 7 = 28$ mm
- $\rightarrow$ Depth of the section, $H = 5t = 5 \times 7 = 35$ mm
- $\rightarrow$ Area, $A = 11 t^2 = 11 \times 7^2 = 539$ mm²
- $\rightarrow$ Radius of gyration, $k_{xx} = 1.78\, t = 1.78 \times 7 = 12.46$ mm.

2. Dimension of the piston pin at the small end:

Load on piston pin or small end bearing, $F_p = F_c = l_p d_p p_{bp}$

$27489 = (1.5\, d_p)\, d_p \times 13$

$\therefore \quad$ Diameter of piston pin, $d_p = 37.54$ mm ≈ 38 mm

and length of piston pin, $l_p = 1.5 \times 38 = 57$ mm

3. Dimension of the crank pin at the big end:

Load on piston pin or small end bearing, $F_p = F_c = l_c d_c p_{bc}$

$27489 = (1.25\, d_c)\, d_c \times 10$

$\therefore \quad$ Diameter of crank pin, $d_c = 46.89$ mm ≈ 48 mm

and length of crank pin, $l_c = 1.25 \times 48 = 60$ mm.

4. Size of the bolts for big end cap:

The maximum value of inertia force occurs at $\theta = 0$, at the top dead center.

i.e. $\quad F_{1max} = 4.03 \times 10^{-3} W_r n^2 r \left(1 + \dfrac{1}{n'}\right)$ ...19.9/ Pg 371, DHB

- Weight of reciprocating parts $W_r = mg = 2 \times 9.81 = 19.62$ N
- Crank radius, $r = \dfrac{L_s}{2} = \dfrac{180}{2} = 90$ mm
- $n' = \dfrac{l}{r} = \dfrac{350}{90} = 3.89$
- $n = 30$ rps

$$F_{1max} = 4.03 \times 10^{-3} \times 19.62 \times (30)^2 \times 90 \times \left(1 + \dfrac{1}{3.89}\right)$$

$\therefore \quad F_{1max} = 8051$ N Eq. (*viii*)

Since there are two bolts, each shares the inertia force equally.

i.e. $\quad F_{1max} = 2\left(\dfrac{\pi d_b^2}{4}\right) \sigma_t$ ...Eq. (*ix*)

Equating Eq. (*viii*) and Eq. (*ix*), we have

$$8051 = 2\left(\dfrac{\pi d_b^2}{4}\right) \times 90$$

$\therefore$ Core diameter of the bolts, $d_b = 7.55$ mm

Comparing the above value in **Tb. 9.8/ Pg 113, DHB** under *column 5*,
the nominal diameter of the bolt is $d = 10$ mm ...*(Column 3)* **Tb. 9.8/ Pg 113, DHB**

5. Thickness of the big end cap:

The thickness of the cap is calculated as:

$$\sigma_b = \dfrac{M_b}{Z} = \dfrac{6M_b}{bh^2} \qquad \text{...Eq. }(x)$$

- b – width of cap (mm)-taken equal to length of crank pin or big end bearing
  i.e. $b = l_c = 60$ mm

- $M_b = \dfrac{F_{1max} l_0}{6}$

  l_0 = distance between bolt centers
  = dia. of crank pin + 2[thickness of liner (3 mm)] + nominal dia. of bolt + clearance (3 mm)
  $l_0 = d_c + 2(3 \text{ mm}) + d + 3$ mm
  $= 48 + 6$ mm $+ 10 + 3$ mm
  $l_0 = 67$ mm

  i.e. $M_b = \dfrac{8051 \times 67}{6}$

$\therefore \quad M_b = 89.90 \times 10^3$ N-mm

- Assume that the material for cap and bolt has $\sigma_b = \sigma_t = 60$ MPa

$$\therefore \quad \text{Eq. } (x) \text{ yields } ... \; 95 = \frac{6 \times 89.90 \times 10^3}{60 \times h^2}$$

$$h = 9.72 \text{ mm} \approx 10 \text{ mm}$$

6. Whipping stress -or- bending force due to inertia:

The whipping stress is calculated as

$$\sigma_b = \frac{(0.2584 \times 10^{-12}) w A r n^2 l^2}{Z} \quad \text{...19.3/ Pg 369, DHB}$$

- Weight of unit volume of rod, $w = \rho g = 7800 \times 9.81 = 76518$ N/m³
- Section modulus, $Z = \dfrac{I_{xx}}{y}$

$$I_{xx} = \frac{419 t^4}{12} = \frac{419 \times 7^4}{12} = 83835 \text{ mm}^4$$

and

$$y = \frac{5t}{2} = \frac{5 \times 7}{2} = 17.5 \text{ mm}$$

$$Z = \frac{83835}{17.5} = 4790.57 \text{ mm}^3$$

$$\sigma_b = \frac{(0.2584 \times 10^{-12}) \times 76518 \times 539 \times 90 \times 30^2 \times 350^2}{4790.57}$$

$\sigma_b = 22.07$ MPa < 95 MPa,

Hence safe.

8.9 DESIGN OF CRANKSHAFT

A crankshaft is used to convert reciprocating motion of the piston into rotary motion or *vice versa*. The crankshaft consists of three portions:
- Shaft parts, which revolve in the main bearings,
- Crank pins to which the big ends of the connecting rod are connected,
- Crank arms or webs or crank cheeks, which connect the crankpins, and the shaft parts.

8.9.1 Classification

1. Depending upon the position of crank:

    a. Side crankshaft or overhung crankshaft, as shown in **Fig. 8.10(a)** and
    b. Centre crankshaft, as shown in **Fig. 8.10(b)**.

The side crankshaft has only one web and requires two bearings for support. It is widely used in medium sized engines as well as large horizontal engines.

The center crankshaft has two webs and three bearings for support. It is used in radial aircraft, stationary engines and marine engines and is more popular in automotive engines.

2. Depending upon the number of throw:
   a. Single throw or
   b. Multi-throw crankshafts.

A crankshaft with only one side crank or centre crank is called a single throw crankshaft, whereas, the crankshaft with two side cranks, one on each end or with two or more centre cranks is known as multi-throw crankshaft.

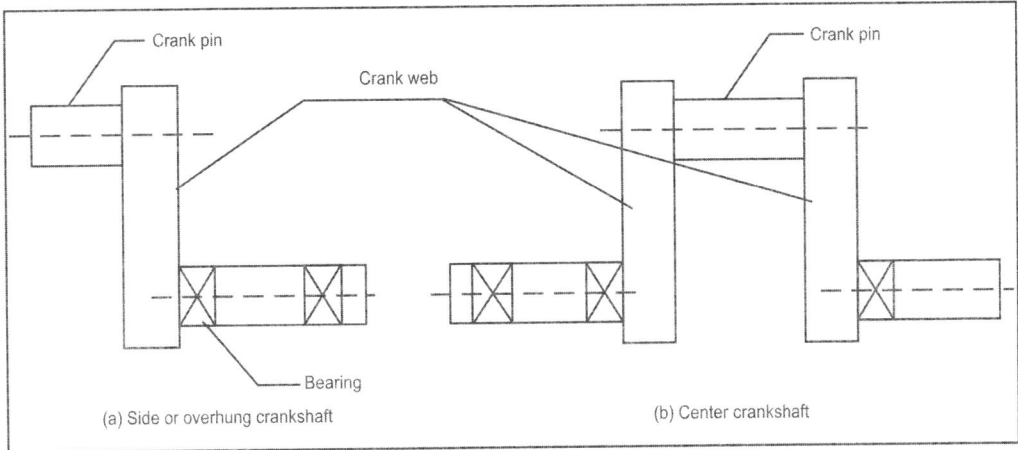

Fig. 8.10: Types of crankshafts

8.9.2 Materials

The crankshafts are made by drop forging process. These are made much heavier and stronger than necessary from strength point of view so as to satisfy the requirements of rigidity and vibrations. The material to be selected will also depend upon the method of manufacture i.e. cast, forged, or built up. Built up crank shafts are sometimes used in aero engines where light weight is very important.

- For industrial engines, the crankshafts are commonly made from carbon steel such as 40C8, 55C8 and 60C4.
- In transport engines, manganese steel such as $20Mn_2$, $27Mn_2$ and $37Mn_2$ are used.
- In aero engines, nickel chromium steel such as 35Ni1Cr60 and 40Ni2Cr1Mo28 are extensively used.

Note:
- **Table 3.2/ Pg 47, DHB** .... *Gives properties used for shafts.*
- **Table 3.5a/ Pg 48, DHB** .... *Gives standard sizes for shaft.*
- **Table 3.5b/ Pg 48, DHB** .... *Gives maximum permissible working stresses for shafts.*
- **Table 3.6/ Pg 49, DHB** .... *Gives allowable bearing pressures for various engines.*
- **Table 19.1/ Pg 371, DHB** .... *Gives strength of various steels.*
- **Also refer Tables 1.1 to 1.18/ Pg 412 – 430, DHB** *for different material properties.*

726 Design of Machine Elements II (DME II)

8.10 DESIGN OF CENTRE CRANKSHAFT

Figure 8.11 shows a forged centre crank (**Fig. 3.5/ Pg 50, DHB**). In general a crankshaft is subjected to bending and torsional moments due to the following forces:

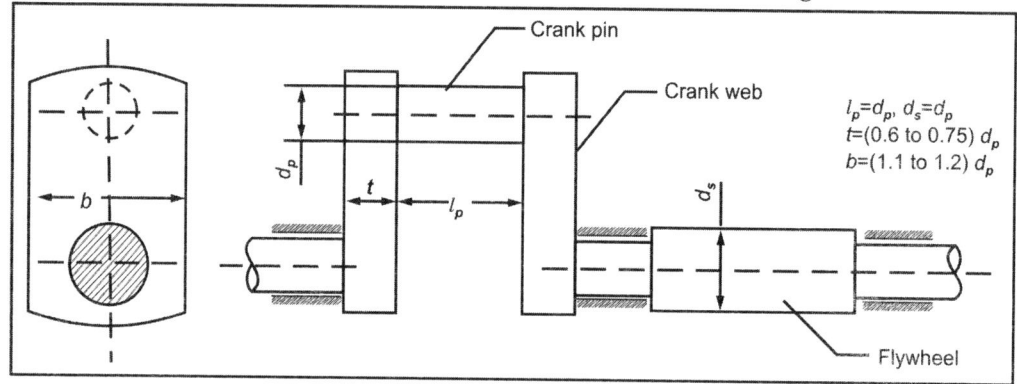

Fig. 8.11: Forged center crank (Fig. 3.5/ Pg 50, DHB)

- Force exerted by the connecting rod on the crank pin.
- Weight of the flywheel acting vertically downwards.
- Belt tensions in horizontal direction.

In designing the crankshaft, two positions of the crank are considered:
1. The crank is at top dead center (TDC) and subjected to maximum bending moment.
2. The crank is at an angle with the line of dead centre position and subjected to maximum torsional moment.

8.10.1 Case 1: Centre Crankshaft at Top Dead Center Position

Consider a single throw three bearing crankshaft as shown in **Fig. 8.12**, representing forces acting on the crankshaft when the crank is at TDC.

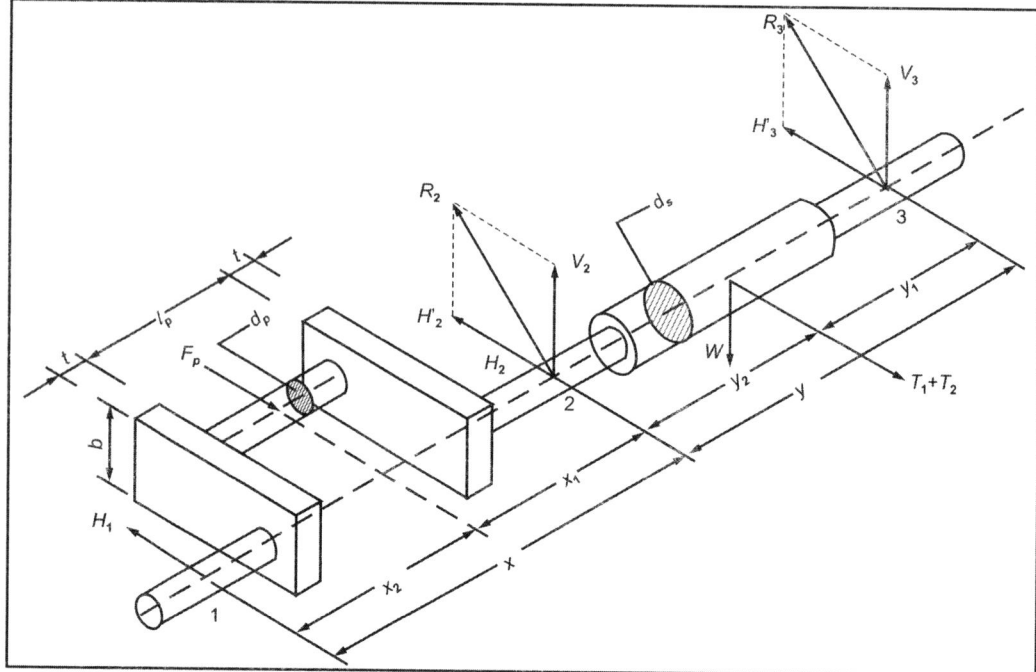

Fig. 8.12: Center crankshaft at dead center

IC Engine Parts

Assumptions
- The engine is vertical and the crank is at TDC position.
- The belt drive is horizontal
- The crankshaft is simply supported at the bearings.

Let F_p = force acting on crank pin (N)
D = diameter of piston (mm)
$p\ (= p_{max})$ = maximum gas or steam pressure (MPa)
W = weight of flywheel, acting vertically downwards (N)
$T_1 + T_2$ = belt pull acting in horizontal direction (N)
T_1 = tension on tight side of belt (N)
T_2 = tension on slack side of belt (N)
d_p = diameter of crank pin (mm)
l_p = length of crank pin (mm)
d_s = diameter of flywheel (mm)
b = width of crank web (mm)
t = thickness of crank web (mm)
x = distance between bearings 1 and 2 (mm)
y = distance between bearings 2 and 3 (mm)

a. Bearing reactions:

When the crank is on dead center as shown in **Fig. 8.12**, the bending moment is maximum and the torque is zero. The thrust in the connecting rod will be equal to the force acting on the piston due to gas pressure.

i.e. Force on the piston due to pressure of gas,

$$F_p = p_{max}\left(\frac{\pi D^2}{4}\right) \quad \text{...(Eq. 8.56) [same as [8.21]]}$$

- **Reactions at bearings 1 and 2:**
  It is assumed that the portion of the crankshaft between the bearings 1 and 2 is simply supported on the bearings and subjected to vertical force as shown in **Fig. 8.13(a)**.

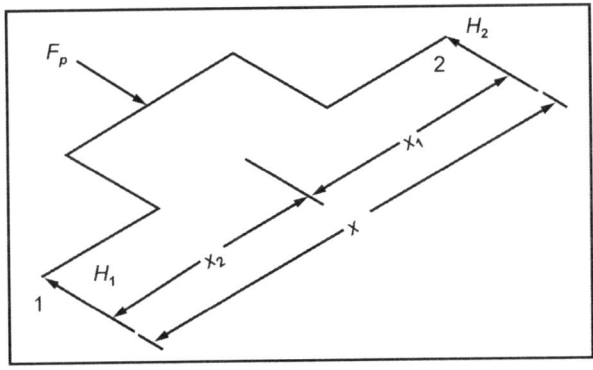

Fig. 8.13(a): Reactions at bearings 1 and 2

Now $\quad H_1 + H_2 = F_p \quad$ ...(Eq. 8.57)

Taking moments about bearing 1, we have

$$H_2 \cdot x = F_p \cdot x_2$$

$$H_2 = \frac{F_p \cdot x_2}{x} \qquad \text{...(Eq. 8.58)}$$

∴ Eq. (8.57) yields ... $H_1 = F_p - \dfrac{F_p \cdot x_2}{x}$

$$= F_p \left(1 - \frac{x_2}{x}\right)$$

$$= F_p \left(\frac{x - x_2}{x}\right)$$

$$H_1 = \frac{F_p \cdot x_1}{x} \qquad \text{...(Eq. 8.59)}$$

Thus the resultant reactions at bearings 1 is $R_1 = H_1$ ...(Eq. 8.60)

- **Reactions at bearings 2 and 3:**

  Similarly it is assumed that the portion of the crankshaft between the bearings 2 and 3 is simply supported on the bearings and subjected to vertical force W and horizontal force or pull $T_1 + T_2$ due to belt as shown in **Fig. 8.13(b)**.

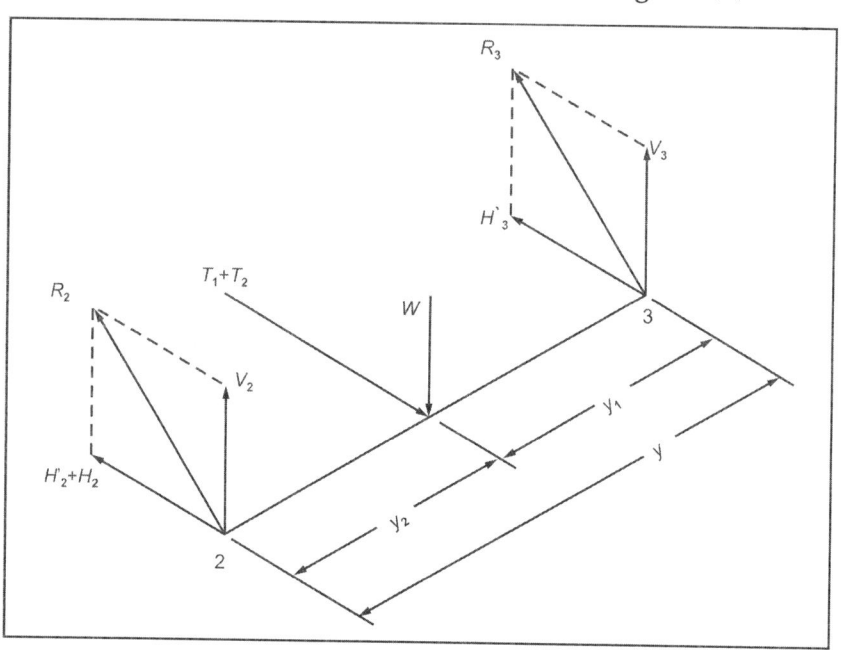

Fig. 8.13(b): Reactions at beanings 2 and 3

→ **Reactions due to weight of flywheel:**

$$V_2 + V_3 = W \qquad \text{...(Eq. 8.61)}$$

Taking moments about bearing 2, we have

$$V_3 \cdot y = W \cdot y^2$$

$$V_3 = \frac{W \cdot y_2}{y} \qquad \text{...(Eq. 8.62)}$$

∴ Eq. (8.61) yields ... $V_2 = W - \dfrac{W \cdot y_2}{y}$

$$= W\left(1 - \dfrac{y_2}{y}\right)$$

$$= W\left(\dfrac{y - y_2}{y}\right) \qquad \text{...(Eq. 8.63)}$$

$$V_2 = \dfrac{W \cdot y_1}{y}$$

→ **Reactions due to belt pull:**
$$H_2' + H_3' = (T_1 + T_2) \qquad \text{...(Eq. 8.64)}$$
Taking moments about bearing 2, we have
$$H_3' \cdot y = (T_1 + T_2) \cdot y_2$$

$$\boldsymbol{H_3' = \dfrac{(T_1 + T_2) \cdot y_2}{y}} \qquad \text{...(Eq. 8.65)}$$

Eq. (8.64) yields ... $H_2' = (T_1 + T_2) - \dfrac{(T_1 + T_2) \cdot y_2}{y}$

$$= (T_1 + T_2)\left(1 - \dfrac{y_2}{y}\right)$$

$$= (T_1 + T_2)\left(\dfrac{y - y_2}{y}\right)$$

$$\boldsymbol{H_2' = \dfrac{(T_1 + T_2) \cdot y_1}{y}} \qquad \text{...(Eq. 8.66)}$$

→ Thus the resultant reactions at bearings 2 and 3 are
$$R_2 = \sqrt{(H_2 + H_2')^2 + V_2^2} \qquad \text{...(Eq. 8.67)}$$
$$R_3 = \sqrt{(H_3')^2 + V_3^2} \qquad \text{...(Eq. 8.68)}$$

b. Design of crank pin:

→ The bending moment at the center of crank pin is given as
$$M_p = H_1 \cdot x_2 = \dfrac{\pi d_p^3}{32} = \sigma_b \qquad \text{...(Eq. 8.69)}$$
Where, d_p = diameter of crank pin (mm)
σ_b = allowable bending stress for crank pin (MPa)
...**Tb. 3.5b/ Pg 48, DHB**

Eq. (8.69) gives the diameter of crank pin (d_p).
→ The length of crank pin is calculated as
$$F_p = l_p \cdot d_p \cdot p_{bc} \qquad \text{...(Eq. 8.70)}$$
p_{bc} = permissible bearing pressure for crank pin (MPa)
...**Tb 3.6/ Pg 49, DHB**

Note: If the ratio is taken as $l_p/d_p = 1$ (i.e. $l_p = d_p$) then check for p_{bc}

...Fig. 3.5/ Pg 50, DHB

c. Design of left hand crank web:

→ The dimensions of web are given in **Fig. 3.5/ Pg 50, DHB**

Width of web, $b = (1.1 \text{ to } 1.2) d_p$

Thickness of web, $t = (0.6 \text{ to } 0.75).d_p$ ...(Eq. 8.71) **Fig. 3.5/ Pg 50, DHB**

The left crank web is subjected to eccentric loading. Due to this there will be two stresses acting on it, one direct compressive stress and the other bending stress due to gas load (F_p).

→ **Direct compressive stress:** $\sigma_c = \dfrac{H_1}{b.t}$ (MPa) ...(Eq. 8.72)

→ **Bending stress:** $\sigma_{b1} = \dfrac{M_1}{Z_1} = \dfrac{6M_1}{b.t^2}$ (MPa) ...(Eq. 8.73)

b = width of crank web (mm)

t = thickness of crank web (mm)

The bending moment at the center of crank pin is given as

$$M_1 = H_1.\left(x_2 - \dfrac{t}{2} - \dfrac{l_p}{2}\right)$$ ...(Eq. 8.74)

→ Thus, the total stress on the web, $(\sigma_c)_t = \sigma_c + \sigma_{b1} \leq \sigma_b$ ...(Eq. 8.75)

d. Design of right hand crank web:

The dimensions of the right hand crank web (i.e. thickness and width) are made equal to left hand crank web from the balancing point of view.

e. Design of shaft under flywheel:

- The bending moment due to weight of flywheel, $M_W = V_3.y_1$ ...(Eq. 8.76)
- The bending moment due to belt tension, $M_T = H_3'.y_1$ ..(Eq. 8.77)
- Thus the resultant bending moment at the flywheel,

$$M_S = \dfrac{\pi d_s^3}{32}\sigma_b$$ ...(Eq. 8.78)

$$M_S = R_3.y_1 = \sqrt{M_W^2 + M_T^2} = \sqrt{(V_3.y_1)^2 + (H_3'.y_1)^2}$$ ...(Eq. 8.79)

σ_b = allowable bending stress for crank pin (MPa)

...**Tb. 3.5b/ Pg 48, DHB**

The diameter of shaft (d_s) is found using **(Eqs 8.78 and 8.79)**

Round off the obtained value of d_s using ...**Tb 3.5a/ Pg 48, DHB**

Note: Length of bearings are taken equal as

$$l_1 = l_2 = l_3 = 2\left(\dfrac{x}{2} - \dfrac{l_p}{2} - t\right)$$ ...(Eq. 8.79a)

8.10.2 Case 2: Centre Crankshaft at an Angle of Maximum Torque

Consider a position of the crank at an angle of maximum twisting moment as shown in **Fig. 8.14**. The twisting moment on the crankshaft will be maximum when the tangential force on the crank (F_t) is maximum. The maximum value of tangential force lies when the crank is at angle of 25° to 30° from the dead centre for petrol engines (i.e. constant volume combustion engines) and 30° to 40° for diesel engines (i.e. constant pressure combustion engines).

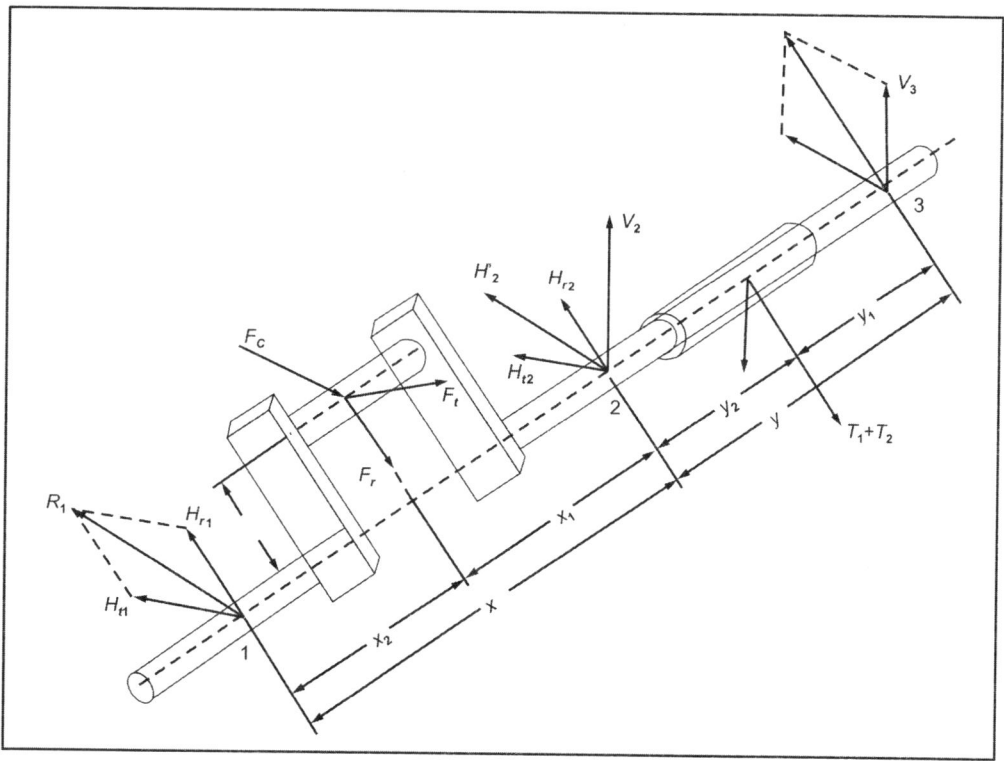

Fig. 8.14: Crank at angle of maximum torque

a. Force components on crank pin:

The position of the crank at an angle of θ with the line of dead centers is shown in **Fig. 8.15 [Fig. 3.1/Pg 50, DHB]**.

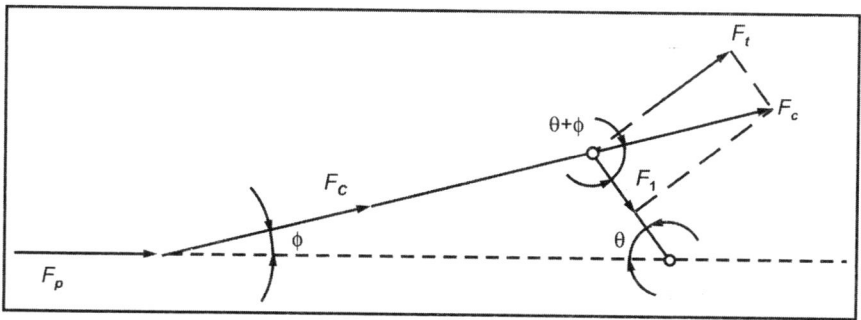

Fig. 8.15: Forces on crank arm [Fig. 3.1/ Pg 50, DHB]

Let F_p = force acting on piston due to gas pressure (N)
F_c = thrust on connecting rod (N)
F_t = tangential component of force on crank pin (N)
ϕ = Angle of inclination of the connecting rod with the line of dead centers (deg)
θ = Angle of inclination of the crank with the line of dead centers (deg)

→ If p' is the intensity of gas pressure on the piston at this instant, then for maximum torque condition,
Force on the piston due to pressure of gas,

$$F_p = p'\left(\frac{\pi D^2}{4}\right) \qquad \text{...(Eq. 8.80)}$$

→ The thrust on the connecting rod is $F_c = \dfrac{F_p}{\cos \phi}$ ...(Eq. 8.81) **3.12/ Pg 45, DHB**

→ The components of F_c are:
- Tangential component or rotative effort on crank, $F_t = F_c \sin(\theta + \phi)$

$$= F_p \frac{\cos(\theta + \phi)}{\cos \phi} \qquad \text{...(Eq. 8.82)} \ \textbf{3.13/ Pg 45, DHB}$$

- Radial component or force along the crank, $F_r = F_c \cos(\theta + \phi)$

$$= F_p \frac{\sin(\theta + \phi)}{\cos \phi} \qquad \text{...(Eq. 8.83)} \ \textbf{3.14/ Pg 45, DHB}$$

Where, $\sin \phi = \dfrac{\sin \theta}{l/r}$ ...*using (Eq. 8.24a)*

b. Bearing reactions:

- **Reactions at bearings 1 and 2:**
It is assumed that the portion of the crankshaft between the bearings 1 and 2 is simply supported on the bearings and subjected to vertical force F_p as shown in **Fig. 8.16**.

→ **Radial forces:**
Now $\qquad H_{r1} + H_{r2} = F_r \qquad$ ...(Eq. 8.84)

Taking moments about bearing 1, we have
$$H_{r2} \cdot x = F_r \cdot x_2$$

$$H_{r2} = \frac{F_r \cdot x_2}{x} \qquad \text{...(Eq. 8.85)}$$

∴ Eq. (8.84) yields... $\quad H_{r1} = F_r - \dfrac{F_r \cdot x_2}{x}$

$$= F_r - \left(1 - \frac{x_2}{x}\right)$$

$$= F_r \left(\frac{x - x_2}{x}\right)$$

$$H_{r1} = \frac{F_r \cdot x_1}{x} \qquad \ldots(8.86)$$

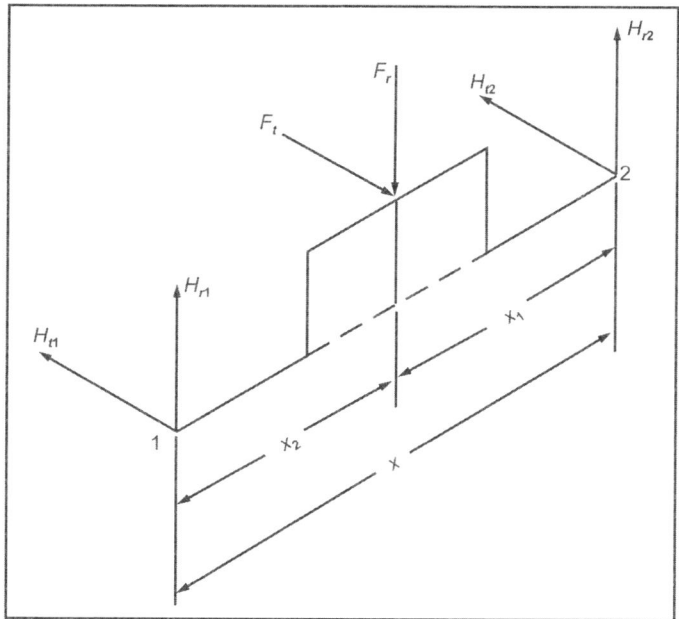

Fig. 8.16: Reactions at bearings 1 and 2

→ **Tangential forces:**
Now $\qquad H_{t1} + H_{t2} = F_t \qquad \ldots$(Eq. 8.87)
Taking moments about bearing 1, we have
$$H_{t2} \cdot x = F_t \cdot x_2$$
$$H_{t2} = \frac{F_t \cdot x_2}{x} \qquad \ldots(Eq.\ 8.88)$$

∴ Eq. (8.87) yields... $H_{t1} = F_t - \dfrac{F_t \cdot x_2}{x}$

$$= F_t \left(1 - \frac{x_2}{x}\right)$$

$$= F_t \left(\frac{x - x_2}{x}\right)$$

$$H_{t1} = \frac{F_t \cdot x_1}{x} \qquad \ldots(Eq.\ 8.89)$$

- **Reactions at bearings 2 and 3:**
  The reactions at the bearings 2 and 3, due to weight of the flywheel (W) and resultant belt pull ($T_1 + T_2$) are same as discussed in Section **8.10.1; Case 1:** *[Eqs 8.61 to 8.66]*
  → **Reactions due to weight of flywheel:**
  $\qquad V_2 + V_3 = W \qquad \ldots$*using (Eq. 8.61)*

Taking moments about bearing 2, we have
$$V_3 \cdot y = W \cdot y_2$$
$$V_3 = \frac{W \cdot y_2}{y} \qquad \text{...using (Eq. 8.62)}$$

∴ Eq. (8.61) yields...
$$V_2 = W - \frac{W \cdot y_2}{y}$$
$$= W - \left(1 - \frac{y_2}{y}\right)$$
$$= W\left(\frac{y - y_2}{y}\right)$$
$$V_2 = \frac{W \cdot y_1}{y} \qquad \text{...using (Eq. 8.63)}$$

→ **Reactions due to belt pull:**
$$H_2' + H_3' = (T_1 + T_2) \qquad \text{...using (Eq. 8.64)}$$
Taking moments about bearing 2, we have
$$H_3' \cdot y = (T_1 + T_2) \cdot y_2$$
$$H_3' = \frac{(T_1 + T_2) \cdot y_2}{y} \qquad \text{...using (Eq. 8.65)}$$

Eq. (8.64) yields...
$$H_2' = (T_1 + T_2) - \frac{(T_1 + T_2) \cdot y_2}{y}$$
$$= (T_1 + T_2)\left(1 - \frac{y_2}{y}\right)$$
$$= (T_1 + T_2)\left(\frac{y - y_2}{y}\right)$$
$$H_2' = \frac{(T_1 + T_2) \cdot y_1}{y} \qquad \text{...using (Eq. 8.66)}$$

→ Thus the resultant reactions at bearings are
$$R_1 = \sqrt{H_{r1}^2 + H_{t1}^2} \qquad \text{...(Eq. 8.90)}$$
$$R_2 = \sqrt{\left(H_{t2} + H_2'\right)^2 + \left(H_{r2} + V_2\right)^2} \qquad \text{...(Eq. 8.91)}$$
$$R_3 = \sqrt{\left(H_3'\right)^2 + V_3^2} \qquad \text{...(Eq. 8.92)}$$

c. Design of crank pin:
→ The bending moment at the center of crank pin is $M_p = H_{r1} \cdot x_2$ ...(Eq. 8.93)
→ The twisting moment on the crankpin is, $T_p = H_{t1} \cdot r$ ...(Eq. 8.94)

→ Thus the equivalent torque on the crank pin is,

$$T_e = \sqrt{M_p^2 + T_p^2} = \frac{\pi d_p^3}{16}\tau \qquad \text{...(Eq. 8.95)}$$

Where, d_p = diameter of crank pin (mm)
τ = allowable shear stress in crank pin (MPa) **[40 MPa – if not given]**

$r = \dfrac{L_s}{2}$ = crank radius (mm), L_s = stroke length (mm)

Eq. (8.95) gives the diameter of crank pin (d_p).
Compare this value with that of case 1 and adopt higher value for design.

→ The length of crank pin is calculated as $F_p = l_p \cdot d_p \cdot p_{bc}$ ...(Eq. 8.96)
Ratio of $l_p/d_p = 1$ [i.e. $l_p = d_p$] ...Fig. 3.5/ Pg 50, DHB
p_{bc} – permissible bearing pressure for crank pin (MPa) ...Tb 3.6/ Pg 49, DHB

d. Design of shaft under flywheel:

→ The bending moment on the shaft, $M_s = R_3 \cdot y_1$ ...(Eq. 8.97)
→ The twisting moment on the shaft, $T_s = F_t \cdot r$ ...(Eq. 8.98)
→ Thus the equivalent twisting moment on the shaft is,

$$T_{es} = \sqrt{M_s^2 + T_s^2} = \frac{\pi d_s^3}{16}\tau \qquad \text{...(Eq. 8.99)}$$

Where, d_s = diameter of shaft under flywheel (mm)
τ = allowable shear stress in crank pin (MPa) **[40 MPa – if not given]**
Eq. (8.99) gives the diameter of shaft under flywheel (d_s).
Round off the obtained value d_s of using ...Tb 3.5a/ Pg 48, DHB
Compare this value with that of case 1 and adopt higher value for design.

e. Design of shaft at the juncture of right hand crank arm:

→ The bending moment at the juncture of the right hand crank arm,

$$M_{s1} = R_1 \cdot \left(x_2 + \frac{l_p}{2} + \frac{t}{2}\right) - F_c \cdot \left(\frac{l_p}{2} + \frac{t}{2}\right) \qquad \text{...(Eq. 8.100)}$$

→ The twisting moment at the juncture of the right hand crank arm,
$$T_{s1} = F_t \cdot r \qquad \text{...(Eq. 8.101)}$$

→ Thus the equivalent twisting moment at the juncture of the right hand crank arm,

$$T_{es1} = \sqrt{M_{s1}^2 + T_{s1}^2} = \frac{\pi d_{s1}^3}{16}\tau \qquad \text{...(Eq. 8.102)}$$

Where, d_{s1} = diameter of shaft at the juncture of the right hand crank arm (mm)
τ = allowable shear stress in the shaft (MPa) **[40 MPa – if not given]**

$$R_1 = \sqrt{H_{r1}^2 + H_{t1}^2} \qquad \text{...using (Eq. 8.90)}$$

Eq. (8.102) gives the diameter of shaft at the juncture of the right hand crank arm (d_{s1}).

Round off the obtained value of d_s using ...Tb 3.5a/ Pg 48, DHB

f. Design of right hand crank web:

The right hand crank web is subjected to the following stresses:
  i. Bending stresses in two planes normal to each other, due to the radial and tangential components of F_p
  ii. Direct compressive stress due to F_r, and
  iii. Torsional stress.

→ The bending moment due to the radial component of F_r is

$$M_r = H_{r2} \cdot \left(x_1 - \frac{l_p}{2} - \frac{t}{2}\right) = \frac{b \cdot t^2}{6} \cdot \sigma_{br} \quad \text{...(Eq. 8.103)}$$

Eq. (8.103) gives the value of bending stress (σ_{br}) due to radial component.
→ The bending moment due to the tangential component of F_t is

$$M_t = F_t \cdot \left(r - \frac{d_{s1}}{2}\right) = \frac{t \cdot b^2}{6} \cdot \sigma_{bt} \quad \text{...(Eq. 8.104)}$$

Eq. (8.104) gives the value of bending stress (σ_{bt}) due to tangential component.
→ The direct compressive stress is given by

$$\sigma_{dc} = \frac{F_r}{2bt} \quad \text{...(Eq. 8.105)}$$

Where, d_{s1} = diameter of shaft at the juncture of the right hand crank arm (mm)
b = width of crank web (mm)
t = thickness of crank web (mm)

→ The maximum compressive stress (σ_c) will occur at the upper left corner of the cross-section of the crank.
  i.e. $\sigma_c = \sigma_{br} + \sigma_{bt} + \sigma_{dc}$ ...(Eq. 8.106)
→ The twisting moment on the arm,

$$T = H_{t1} \cdot \left(x_2 + \frac{l_p}{2}\right) - F_t \cdot \left(\frac{l_p}{2}\right) = H_{t2} \cdot \left(x_1 - \frac{l_p}{2}\right) \quad \text{...(Eq. 8.107)}$$

But shear stress on the arm, $\tau = \dfrac{T}{Z_p} = \dfrac{4.5T}{b \cdot t^2}$ ...(Eq. 8.108)

Where, Z_p = polar section modulus = $\dfrac{b \cdot t^2}{4.5}$

→ Thus the maximum or total combined stress,

$$(\sigma_c)_{max} = \frac{\sigma_c}{2} + \sqrt{\left(\frac{\sigma_c}{2}\right)^2 + \tau^2} < \sigma_b \quad \text{...(Eq. 8.109)} \quad \textbf{1.11a / Pg 2, DHB}$$

σ_b – allowable bending stress for crank pin (MPa) ...Tb. 3.5b/ Pg 48, DHB

Note: The value of $(\sigma_c)_{max}$ should be within safe limits. If it exceeds the safe value, then the dimension b may be increased because it does not affect other dimensions.

g. Design of left hand crank web:

The left hand crank web is not stressed to the extent as the right hand crank web. Hence the dimensions for the left hand crank web may be made same as for right hand crank web.

h. Design of crankshaft bearings:

→ Bearing 2 is the most heavily loaded and should be checked for the safe bearing pressure.

We know that the total reaction at the bearing 2 is

$$R_2 = \sqrt{(H_{t2} + H_2')^2 + (H_{r2} + V_2)^2} \qquad \text{...using (Eq. 8.91)}$$

→ The length of crank pin is calculated as $R_2 = l_2 \cdot d_{s1} \cdot p_{bc}$ ...(Eq. 8.110)

Where, l_2 = Length of bearing 2 (mm)

p_{bc} = permissible bearing pressure for crank pin (MPa)

...Tb 3.6/ Pg 49, DHB

7. **Design a center crankshaft for a single cylinder vertical engine using the following data:**
Cylinder bore = 125 mm, l/r ratio = 4.5, maximum gas pressure = 2.5 MPa, stroke length = 150 mm, weight of flywheel cum belt pulley = 1 kN, total belt pull = 2 kN, width of hub for flywheel cum belt pulley = 200 mm, allowable bending stress = 75 MPa, bearing pressure = 10 MPa.
The torque on the crankshaft is maximum when the crank turns through 25° from the top dead centre and at this position, the gas pressure inside the cylinder is on the piston is 2 MPa. The belts are in horizontal direction.

Solution: D = 125 mm, l/r = 4.5, $p = (p_{max})$ = 2.5 MPa, L_s = 150 mm, W = 1 kN, $T_1 + T_2$ = 2 kN, width of flywheel hub = 200 mm, σ_b = 75 MPa, p_{bc} = 10 MPa, θ = 25°, p' = 2 MPa.

Case 1: Centre crankshaft at top dead center position:

a. Bearing reactions:

→ Force on the piston due to gas pressure, $F_p = p_{max}\left(\dfrac{\pi D^2}{4}\right) = 2.5 \times \left(\dfrac{\pi \times 125^2}{4}\right)$

$= 30679.6$ N

i. Reactions at bearings 1 and 2:

It is assumed that the portion of the crankshaft between the bearings 1 and 2 is simply supported on the bearings and subjected to vertical force F_p as shown in Fig. 8.17(a).

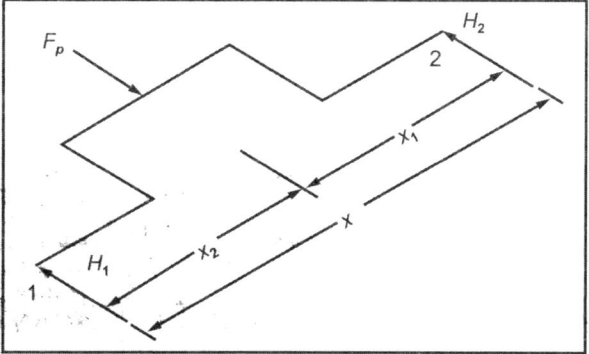

Fig. 8.17(a): Reactions at bearings 1 and 2

Assume
→ $x = 2D = 2 \times 125 = 250$ mm
→ $x_1 = x_2 = x/2 = 250/2 = 125$ mm
Due to symmetry

$$H_1 = \frac{F_p \cdot x_1}{x} = \frac{30679.6 \times 125}{250} = 15339.81 \text{ N}$$

$$H_2 = \frac{F_p \cdot x_2}{x} = \frac{30679.6 \times 125}{250} = 15339.81 \text{ N}$$

Thus the resultant reactions at bearings 1 is $R_1 = H_1 = 15339.81$ N

ii. **Reactions at bearings 2 and 3:**

Similarly it is assumed that the portion of the crankshaft between the bearings 2 and 3 is simply supported on the bearings and subjected to vertical force W and horizontal force or pull $T_1 + T_2$ due to belt as shown in **Fig. 8.17(b)**.

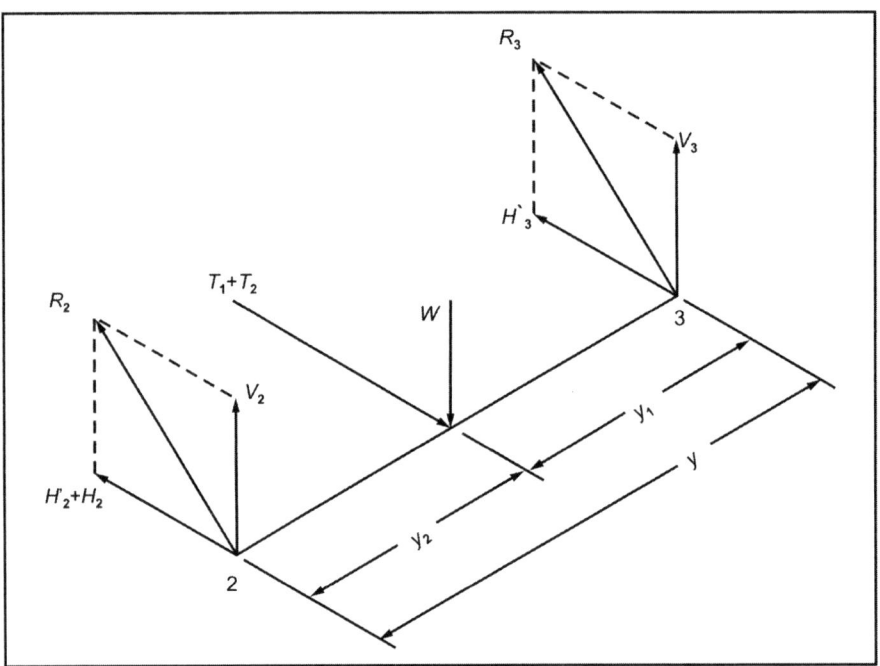

Fig. 8.17(b): Reactions at bearings 2 and 3

Assume
→ $y_1 = y_2 = y/2$

→ **Reactions due to weight of flywheel:**

Due to symmetry

$$V_2 = \frac{W \cdot y_1}{y} = \frac{1000 \times (y/2)}{y} = 500 \text{ N}$$

$$V_3 = \frac{W \cdot y_2}{y} = \frac{1000 \times (y/2)}{y} = 500 \text{ N}$$

→ **Reactions due to belt pull:**

Due to symmetry

$$H_2' = \frac{(T_1 + T_2) \cdot y_1}{y} = \frac{2000 \times (y/2)}{y} = 1000 \text{ N}$$

$$H_3' = \frac{(T_1 + T_2) \cdot y_2}{y} = \frac{2000 \times (y/2)}{y} = 1000 \text{ N}$$

→ Thus the resultant reactions at bearings 2 and 3 are

$$R_2 = \sqrt{(H_2 + H_2')^2 + V_2^2} = \sqrt{(15339.81 + 1000)^2 + 500^2} = 16347.46 \text{ N}$$

$$R_3 = \sqrt{(H_3')^2 + V_3^2} = \sqrt{1000^2 + 500^2} = 1118 \text{ N}$$

b. Design of crank pin:

→ *Diameter of crank pin:*

The bending moment at the center of crank pin is $M_p = H_1 \cdot x_2 = \dfrac{\pi d_p^3}{32} \sigma_b$

$$15339.81 \times 125 = \frac{\pi d_p^3}{32} \times 75$$

$$d_p = 63.85 \text{ mm} \approx 65 \text{ mm}$$

...Eq. (i)

→ *Length of crank pin:*

The length of crank pin is calculated as $F_p = l_p \cdot d_p \cdot p_{bc}$

$$30679.6 = l_p \times 65 \times 10$$

$$l_p = 47.2 \text{ mm} \approx 48 \text{ mm}$$

Note: *If the ratio is taken as $l_p/d_p = 1$ [i.e $l_p = d_p$], then check for p_{bc}*

...Fig. 3.5/ Pg 50, DHB

c. Design of left hand crank web:

→ The dimensions of web are given in **Fig. 3.5/ Pg 50, DHB**

Width of web, $b = 1.2 \, d_p = 1.2 \times 65 = 78$ mm

Thickness of web, $t = 0.7 \, d_p = 0.7 \times 65 = 45.5$ mm ≈ 46 mm

→ The left crank web is subjected to eccentric loading. Due to this there will be two stresses acting on it, one direct compressive stress and the other bending stress due to gas load (F_p).

→ Direct compressive stress: $\sigma_c = \dfrac{H_1}{bt} = \dfrac{15339.81}{78 \times 46} = 4.28$ MPa

→ Bending stress: $\sigma_{b1} = \dfrac{6M_1}{b \cdot t^2}$

The bending moment at the center of crank pin is given as

$$M_1 = H_1 \cdot \left(x_2 - \frac{t}{2} - \frac{l_p}{2}\right)$$

$$= 15339.1 \times \left(125 - \frac{46}{2} - \frac{48}{2}\right)$$

$$M_1 = 1.2 \times 10^6 \text{ N-mm}$$

$$\therefore \sigma_{b1} = \frac{6M_1}{b \cdot t^2} = \frac{6 \times 1.2 \times 10^6}{78 \times 46^2} = 43.49 \text{ MPa}$$

→ Thus the total stress on the web, $\sigma_{c)t} = \sigma_c + \sigma_{b1} \leq \sigma_b$

$$= 4.28 + 43.49$$

$$\sigma_{c)t} = 47.77 \text{ MPa} < 75 \text{ MPa}.$$

Hence design of crank web is safe.

d. Design of right hand crank web:

The dimensions of the right hand crank web (i.e. thickness and width) are made equal to left hand crank web from the balancing point of view.

e. Design of shaft under flywheel:

→ length of bearings are taken equal as $l_1 = l_2 = l_3 = 2\left(\frac{x}{2} - \frac{l_p}{2} - t\right)$

$$= 2 \times \left(\frac{250}{2} - \frac{48}{2} - 46\right)$$

$$l_1 = l_2 = l_3 = 110 \text{ mm}$$

Therefore, $y = 110 + 200 = 310$ mm

And $y_1 = y_2 = y/2 = 310/2 = 155$ mm

→ The bending moment due to weight of flywheel, $M_W = V_3 \cdot y_1 = 500 \times 155 = 77500$ N-mm
→ The bending moment due to belt tension, $M_T = H'_3 \cdot y_1 = 1000 \times 155 = 155000$ N-mm
→ Thus, the resultant bending moment at the flywheel, $M_s = \sqrt{M_W^2 + M_T^2}$

$$= \sqrt{77500^2 + 155000^2}$$

$$M_s = 173.29 \times 10^3 \text{ N-mm}$$

also, $M_s = \dfrac{\pi d_s^3}{32} \sigma_b$

$$173.29 \times 10^3 = \frac{\pi d_s^3}{32} \times 75$$

$$d_s = 28.66 \text{ mm} \qquad \qquad \text{...Eq. }(ii)$$

$\therefore$ Standard shaft size, $d_s = 32$ mm **Tb 3.5a/ Pg 48, DHB**

Case 2: Centre crankshaft at an angle of maximum torque:

a. Force components on crank pin:

→ If p' is the intensity of gas pressure on the piston at this instant, then for maximum torque condition,

Force on the piston due to pressure of gas, $F_p = p'\left(\dfrac{\pi D^2}{4}\right) = 2 \times \left(\dfrac{\pi \times 125^2}{4}\right)$

$$= 24543.70 \text{ N}$$

→ The thrust on the connecting rod is $F_c = \dfrac{F_p}{\cos \phi}$ ...3.12/ Pg 45, DHB

But $\sin \phi = \dfrac{\sin \theta}{l/r} = \dfrac{\sin 25}{4.5} = 0.094$

$\phi = 5.39°$

∴ $F_c = \dfrac{24543.70}{\cos 5.39} = 24652.70 \text{ N}$

→ The components of F_c are:
- Tangential component or rotative effort on crank, $F_t = F_c \sin(\theta + \phi)$
  ...3.13/ Pg 45, DHB
  $= 24652.70 \times \sin(25 + 5.39)$
  $F_t = 12471.39 \text{ N}$
- Radial component or force along the crank, $F_r = F_c \cos(\theta + \phi)$
  ...3.14/ Pg 45, DHB
  $= 24652.70 \times \cos(25 + 5.39)$
  $F_r = 21265.48 \text{ N}$

b. Bearing reactions:

- **Reactions at bearings 1 and 2:**
  It is assumed that the portion of the crankshaft between the bearings 1 and 2 is simply supported on the bearings and subjected to vertical force F_p as shown in Fig. 8.18.

  From Case 1:
  - $x_1 = x_2 = x/2 = 250/2 = 125$ mm
  - $y_1 = y_2 = y/2 = 310/2 = 155$ mm
  - Width of web, $b = 78$ mm
  - Thickness of web, $t = 46$ mm

- **Radial forces:**
  Due to symmetry

  $H_{r1} = \dfrac{F_r \cdot x_1}{x} = \dfrac{21265.48 \times 125}{250} = 10632.74 \text{ N}$

  $H_{r2} = \dfrac{F_r \cdot x_2}{x} = \dfrac{21265.48 \times 125}{250} = 10632.74 \text{ N}$

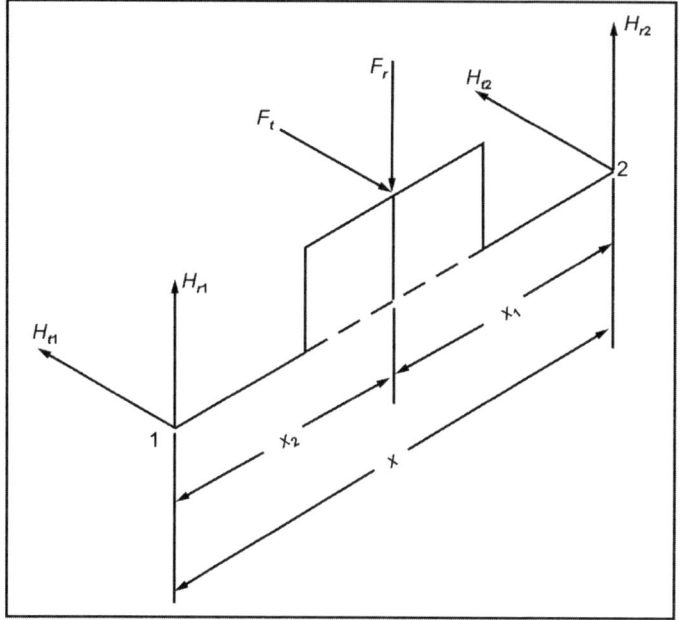

Fig. 8.18: Reactions at bearings 1 and 2

→ **Tangential forces:**
Due to symmetry

$$H_{t1} = \frac{F_t \cdot x_1}{x} = \frac{12471.39 \times 125}{250} = 6235.70 \text{ N}$$

$$H_{t2} = \frac{F_t \cdot x_2}{x} = \frac{12471.39 \times 125}{250} = 6235.70 \text{ N}$$

- **Reactions at bearings 2 and 3:**
  The reactions at the bearings 2 and 3, due to weight of the flywheel (W) and resultant belt pull are same as discussed in **Case 1**.
  → **Reactions due to weight of flywheel:**
  Due to symmetry

$$V_2 = \frac{W \cdot y_1}{y} = \frac{1000 \times 155}{310} = 500 \text{ N}$$

$$V_3 = \frac{W \cdot y_2}{y} = \frac{1000 \times 155}{310} = 500 \text{ N}$$

→ **Reactions due to belt pull:**
Due to symmetry

$$H'_2 = \frac{(T_1 + T_2) \cdot y_1}{y} = \frac{2000 \times 155}{310} = 1000 \text{ N}$$

$$H'_3 = \frac{(T_1 + T_2) \cdot y_2}{y} = \frac{2000 \times 155}{310} = 1000 \text{ N}$$

→ Thus the resultant reactions at bearings are

$$R_1 = \sqrt{H_{r1}^2 + H_{t1}^2} = \sqrt{10632.74^2 + 6235.70^2} = 12326.36 \text{ N}$$

$$R_2 = \sqrt{(H_{t2} + H_2')^2 + (H_{r2} + V_2)^2}$$

$$= \sqrt{(6235.70 + 1000)^2 + (10632.74 + 500)^2} = 13277.5 \text{ N}$$

$$R_3 = \sqrt{(H_3')^2 + V_3^2} = \sqrt{1000^2 + 500^2} = 1118.03 \text{ N}$$

c. Design of crank pin:

→ Bending moment at the center of crank pin is $M_p = H_{r1} \cdot x_2 = 10632.74 \times 125 = 1.33 \times 10^6$ N-mm

→ The twisting moment on the crankpin is, $T_p = H_{t1} \cdot r$
$$r = L_s/2 = 150/2 = 75 \text{ mm}$$
$$= 6235.70 \times 75$$
$$T_p = 4.68 \times 10^5 \text{ N-mm}$$

→ Thus the equivalent torque on the crank pin is, $T_e = \sqrt{M_p^2 + T_p^2}$

$$= \sqrt{(1.33 \times 10^6)^2 + (4.68 \times 10^5)^2}$$
$$T_e = 1.41 \times 10^6 \text{ N-mm}$$

Also
$$T_e = \frac{\pi d_p^3}{16} \tau$$

Assume $\tau = 0.5\sigma_b = 0.5 \times 75 = 37.5$ MPa ≈ 40 MPa

$$1.41 \times 10^6 = \frac{\pi d_p^3}{16} \times 40$$
$$d_p = 56.41 \text{ mm} \qquad \ldots\text{Eq. }(iii)$$

Compare Eqs (i) and (iii), and adopt higher value for design.

i.e. $\qquad d_p = 65$ mm and $l_p = 48$ mm

d. Design of shaft under flywheel:

→ The bending moment on the shaft, $M_s = R_3 \cdot y_1 = 1118.03 \times 115 = 1.73 \times 10^5$ N-mm
→ The twisting moment on the shaft, $T_s = F_t \cdot r = 1471.39 \times 75 = 9.35 \times 10^5$ N-mm

→ Thus the equivalent twisting moment on the shaft is, $T_{es} = \sqrt{M_s^2 + T_s^2}$

$$= \sqrt{(1.73 \times 10^5)^2 + (9.35 \times 10^5)^2}$$
$$T_{es} = 9.51 \times 10^5 \text{ N-mm}$$

Also
$$T_{es} = \frac{\pi d_s^3}{16} \tau$$

$$9.51 \times 10^5 = \frac{\pi d_p^3}{16} \times 40$$
$$d_s = 49.47 \text{ mm} \qquad \ldots\text{Eq. }(iv)$$

Compare Eqs (ii) and (iv), and adopt higher value for design.

i.e. $d_s = 49.47$ mm

∴ Standard shaft size, $d_s = 50$ mm ...Tb 3.5a/ Pg 48, DHB

e. Design of shaft at the juncture of right hand crank arm:

→ The bending moment at the juncture of the right hand crank arm,

$$M_{s1} = R_1 \cdot \left(x_2 + \frac{l_p}{2} + \frac{t}{2} \right) - F_c \cdot \left(\frac{l_p}{2} + \frac{t}{2} \right)$$

$$= 12326.36 \times \left(125 + \frac{48}{2} + \frac{46}{2} \right) - 24652.70 \times \left(\frac{48}{2} + \frac{46}{2} \right)$$

$M_{s1} = 9.61 \times 10^5$ N-mm

→ The twisting moment at the juncture of the right hand crank arm, $T_{s1} = F_t \cdot r$
$= 12471.39 \times 75 = 9.35 \times 10^5$ N-mm

→ Thus the equivalent twisting moment at the juncture of the right hand crank arm

$$T_{es1} = \sqrt{M_{s1}^2 + T_{s1}^2} = \sqrt{(9.61 \times 10^5)^2 + (9.35 \times 10^5)^2} = 1.34 \times 10^6 \text{ N-mm}$$

Also $\quad T_{es1} = \dfrac{\pi d_{s1}^3}{16} \tau$

$$1.34 \times 10^6 = \frac{\pi d_{s1}^3}{16} \times 40$$

$d_{s1} = 55.47$ mm

∴ Standard shaft size, $d_{s1} = 56$ mm ...Tb 3.5a/ Pg 48, DHB

f. Design of right hand crank web:

The right hand crank web is subjected to the following stresses:

(i) Bending stresses in two planes normal to each other, due to the radial and tangential components of F_p

(ii) Direct compressive stress due to F_r, and

(iii) Torsional stress.

→ The bending moment due to the radial component of F_r is

$$M_r = \frac{b \cdot t^2}{6} \cdot \sigma_{br}$$

But $\quad M_r = H_{r2} \cdot \left(x_1 - \dfrac{l_p}{2} - \dfrac{t}{2} \right)$

$$= 10632.74 \times \left(125 - \frac{48}{2} - \frac{46}{2} \right)$$

$M_r = 8.29 \times 10^5$ N-mm

$$\therefore \quad 8.29 \times 10^5 = \frac{78 \times 46^2}{6} \times \sigma_{br}$$

$$\sigma_{br} = 30.14 \text{ MPa}$$

- The bending moment due to the tangential component of F_t is

$$M_t = \frac{t \cdot b^2}{6} \times \sigma_{bt}$$

But

$$M_t = F_t \cdot \left(r - \frac{d_{s1}}{2}\right)$$

$$= 12471.39 \times \left(75 - \frac{56}{2}\right)$$

$$M_r = 5.86 \times 10^5 \text{ N-mm}$$

$$\therefore \quad 5.86 \times 10^5 = \frac{46 \times 78^2}{6} \times \sigma_{bt}$$

$$\sigma_{bt} = 12.57 \text{ MPa}$$

→ The direct compressive stress is given by

$$\sigma_{dc} = \frac{F_r}{2bt} = \frac{21265.48}{2 \times 78 \times 46} = 2.96 \text{ MPa}$$

→ The maximum compressive stress (σ_c) will occur at the upper left corner of the cross-section of the crank.

i.e.
$$\sigma_c = \sigma_{br} + \sigma_{bt} + \sigma_{dc}$$
$$= 30.14 + 12.57 + 2.96$$
$$\sigma_c = 45.67 \text{ MPa}$$

→ The twisting moment on the arm,

$$\tau = \frac{T}{Z_p} = \frac{4.5T}{b \cdot t^2}$$

But

$$T = H_{t2} \cdot \left(x_1 - \frac{l_p}{2}\right)$$

$$= 6235.70 \times \left(125 - \frac{48}{2}\right)$$

$$T = 6.30 \times 10^5 \text{ N-mm}$$

$$\therefore \tau = \frac{4.5 \times 6.30 \times 10^5}{78 \times 46^2}$$

$$\tau = 17.17 \text{ MPa}$$

→ Thus the maximum or total combined stress,

$$(\sigma_c)_{max} = \frac{\sigma_c}{2} + \sqrt{\left(\frac{\sigma_c}{2}\right)^2 + \tau^2} < \sigma_b \qquad \text{...1.11a / Pg 2, DHB}$$

$$= \frac{45.67}{2} + \sqrt{\left(\frac{45.67}{2}\right)^2 + 17.17^2}$$

$(\sigma_c)_{max} = 51.41$ MPa < 75 MPa

Hence design of crank web is safe.

g. Design of left hand crank web:

The left hand crank web is not stressed to the extent as the right hand crank web. Hence the dimensions for the left hand crank web may be made same as for right hand crank web.

h. Design of crankshaft bearings:

→ Bearing 2 is the most heavily loaded and should be checked for the safe bearing pressure.

We know that the total reaction at the bearing 2 is

$$R_2 = \sqrt{(H_{t2} + H_2')^2 + (H_{r2} + V_2)^2} = 13277.5 \text{ N}$$

→ The length of crank pin is calculated as

$$R_2 = l_2 \cdot d_{s1} \cdot p_{bc}$$
$$13277.5 = 110 \times 56 \times p_{bc}$$
$$p_{bc} = 2.16 \text{ MPa} < 10 \text{ MPa}$$

Hence the design is safe.

8. Design a plain carbon steel centre crankshaft for a single acting four stroke single cylinder engine for the following data: Piston diameter = 400 mm, stroke = 600 mm, engine speed = 200 rpm, mean effective pressure = 0.5 MPa, maximum combustion pressure = 2.5 MPa, weight of flywheel used as a pulley = 50 kN, total belt pull = 6.5 kN.

When the crank has turned through 35° from the top dead centre, the pressure on the piston is 1 MPa and the torque on the crank is maximum. The ratio of the connecting rod length to the crank radius is 5. Assume any other data required for the design.

Solution: $D = 400$ mm, $L_s = 600$ mm, $N = 600$ rpm, Bmep = 0.5 MPa, $p = (p_{max}) = 2.5$ MPa, $W = 50$ kN, $T_1 + T_2 = 6.5$ kN, $\theta = 35°$, $p' = 1$ MPa, $l/r = 5$.

Case 1: Centre crankshaft at top dead center position:

a. Bearing reactions:

→ Force on the piston due to gas pressure, $F_p = p_{max}\left(\frac{\pi D^2}{4}\right) = 2.5 \times \left(\frac{\pi \times 400^2}{4}\right)$

$$= 314159.26 \text{ N}$$

i. Reactions at bearings 1 and 2:

It is assumed that the portion of the crankshaft between the bearings 1 and 2 is simply supported on the bearings and subjected to vertical force F_p as shown in Fig. 8.19(a).

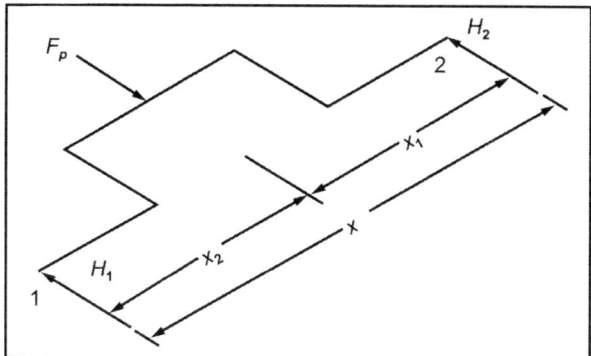

Fig. 8.19(a): Reactions at bearings 1 and 2

Assume
→ $x = 2D = 2 \times 400 = 800$ mm
→ $x_1 = x_2 = x/2 = 800/2 = 400$ mm

Due to symmetry

$$H_1 = \frac{F_p \cdot x_1}{x} = \frac{314159.26 \times 400}{800} = 157.1 \text{ kN}$$

$$H_2 = \frac{F_p \cdot x_2}{x} = \frac{314159.26 \times 400}{800} = 157.1 \text{ kN}$$

Thus the resultant reactions at bearings 1 is $R_1 = H_1 = 15339.81$ N

ii. Reactions at bearings 2 and 3:

Similarly it is assumed that the portion of the crankshaft between the bearings 2 and 3 is simply supported on the bearings and subjected to vertical force W and horizontal force or pull $T_1 + T_2$ due to belt as shown in **Fig. 8.19(b)**.

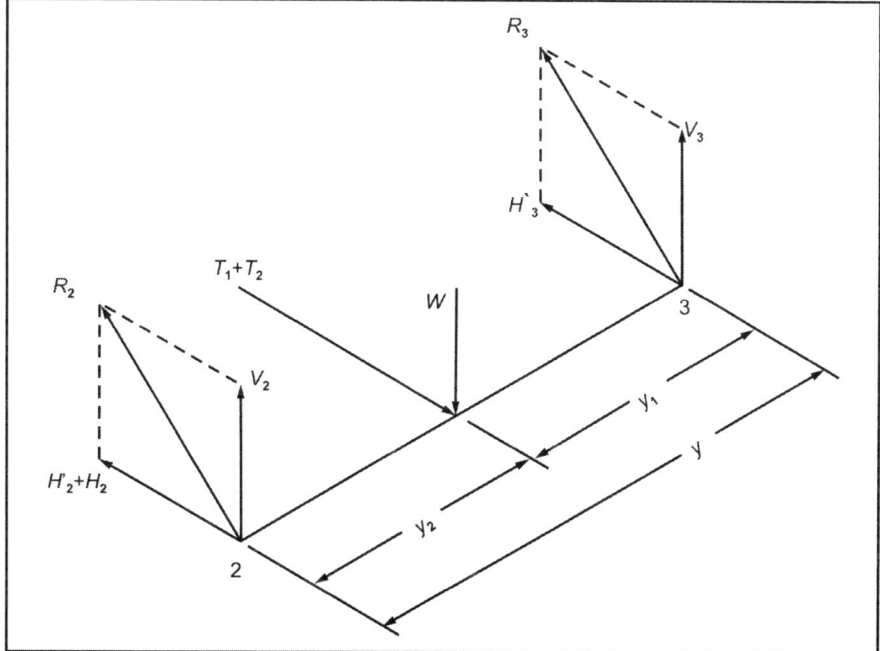

Fig. 8.19(b): Reactions at bearings 2 and 3

Assume
→ $y_1 = y_2 = y/2$

→ **Reactions due to weight of flywheel:**
Due to symmetry
$$V_2 = \frac{W \cdot y_1}{y} = \frac{50000 \times (y/2)}{y} = 25000 \text{ N}$$

$$V_3 = \frac{W \cdot y_2}{y} = \frac{50000 \times (y/2)}{y} = 25000 \text{ N}$$

→ **Reactions due to belt pull:**
Due to symmetry
$$H_2' = \frac{(T_1 + T_2) \cdot y_1}{y} = \frac{6500 \times (y/2)}{y} = 3250 \text{ N}$$

$$H_3' = \frac{(T_1 + T_2) \cdot y_2}{y} = \frac{6500 \times (y/2)}{y} = 3250 \text{ N}$$

→ Thus the resultant reactions at bearings 2 and 3 are
$$R_2 = \sqrt{(H_2 + H_2')^2 + V_2^2} = \sqrt{(157.1 \times 10^3 + 3250)^2 + 25000^2} = 162287.16 \text{ N}$$

$$R_3 = \sqrt{(H_3')^2 + V_3^2} = \sqrt{3250^2 + 25000^2} = 25210.36 \text{ N}$$

b. Design of crank pin:

→ *Diameter of crank pin:*

The bending moment at the center of crank pin $M_p = H_1 \cdot x_2 = \frac{\pi d_p^3}{32} \sigma_b$

Bending stress $\sigma_b = 83$ MPa
...**Tb 3.5b/ Pg 48, DHB**

Bearing pressure $p_{bc} = 10$ MPa
...**Tb 15.11/ Pg 314, DHB**

$$157.1 \times 10^3 \times 400 = \frac{\pi d_p^3}{32} \times 83$$

$$d_p = 197.57 \text{ mm} \approx 200 \text{ mm}$$
...Eq. (*i*)

→ *Length of crank pin:*
The length of crank pin is calculated as $F_p = l_p \cdot d_p \cdot p_{bc}$
$$314159.26 = l_p \times 200 \times 10$$
$$l_p = 157 \text{ mm}$$

Note: *If the ratio is taken as $l_p/d_p = 1$ [i.e $l_p = d_p$], then check for p_{bc}*
...**Fig. 3.5/ Pg 50, DHB**

c. Design of left hand crank web:

→ The dimensions of web are given in **Fig. 3.5/ Pg 50, DHB**
Width of web, $b = 1.2\, d_p = 1.2 \times 200 = 240$ mm
Thickness of web, $t = 0.7\, d_p = 0.7 \times 200 = 140$ mm

→ The left crank web is subjected to eccentric loading. Due to this there will be two stresses acting on it, one direct compressive stress and the other bending stress due to gas load (F_p).

→ Direct compressive stress: $\sigma_c = \dfrac{H_1}{bt} = \dfrac{157.1 \times 10^3}{240 \times 140} = 4.67$ MPa

→ Bending stress: $\sigma_{b1} = \dfrac{6M_1}{b.t^2}$

The bending moment at the center of crank pin is given as

$$M_1 = H_1 \cdot \left(x_2 - \dfrac{t}{2} - \dfrac{l_p}{2} \right)$$

$$= 157.1 \times 10^3 \times \left(400 - \dfrac{140}{2} - \dfrac{157}{2} \right)$$

$M_1 = 39.5 \times 10^6$ N-mm

$$\therefore \sigma_{b1} = \dfrac{6M_1}{b.t^2} = \dfrac{6 \times 39.5 \times 10^6}{240 \times 140^2} = 50.38 \text{ MPa}$$

→ Thus the total stress on the web, $\sigma_{c)t} = \sigma_c + \sigma_{b1} \leq \sigma_b$
$= 4.67 + 50.38$
$\sigma_{c)t} = 55.05$ MPa < 83 MPa.

Hence design of crank web is safe.

d. Design of right hand crank web:

The dimensions of the right hand crank web (i.e. thickness and width) are made equal to left hand crank web from the balancing point of view.

e. Design of shaft under flywheel:

→ Length of bearings are taken equal as $l_1 = l_2 = l_3 = 2\left(\dfrac{x}{2} - \dfrac{l_p}{2} - t \right)$

$$= 2 \times \left(\dfrac{800}{2} - \dfrac{157}{2} - 140 \right)$$

$l_1 = l_2 = l_3 = 363$ mm

Assume width of flywheel as 250 mm
Therefore, $y = 363 + 250 = 613$ mm ≈ 620 mm
And $\quad y_1 = y_2 = y/2 = 620/2 = 310$ mm

→ The bending moment due to weight of flywheel, $M_W = V_3 \cdot y_1 = 25000 \times 310$
$= 7.75 \times 10^6$ N-mm

→ The bending moment due to belt tension, $M_T = H'_3 \cdot y_1 = 3250 \times 310 = 1 \times 10^6$ N-mm

→ Thus the resultant bending moment at the flywheel, $M_S = \sqrt{M_W^2 + M_T^2}$

$$= \sqrt{(7.75 \times 10^6)^2 + (1 \times 10^6)^2}$$

$$M_S = 7.81 \times 10^6 \text{ N-mm}$$

Also $$M_S = \frac{\pi d_s^3}{32} \sigma_b$$

$$7.81 \times 10^6 = \frac{\pi d_s^3}{32} \times 83$$

$$d_s = 98.60 \text{ mm} \qquad \text{...Eq. (ii)}$$

∴ Standard shaft size, $d_s = 100$ mm ...Tb 3.5a/ Pg 48, DHB

Case 2: Centre crankshaft at an angle of maximum torque:

a. Force components on crank pin:

→ If p' is the intensity of gas pressure on the piston at this instant, then for maximum torque condition,
force on the piston due to pressure of gas,

$$F_p = p'\left(\frac{\pi D^2}{4}\right) = 1 \times \left(\frac{\pi \times 400^2}{4}\right) = 125.66 \times 10^3 \text{ N}$$

→ The thrust on the connecting rod is $F_c = \dfrac{F_p}{\cos \phi}$ .... 3.12/ Pg 45, DHB

But $$\sin \phi = \frac{\sin \theta}{l/r} = \frac{\sin 35}{5} = 0.1147$$

$$\phi = 6.59 \text{ deg}$$

∴ $$F_c = \frac{125.66 \times 10^3}{\cos 6.59} = 126.5 \times 10^3 \text{ N}$$

→ The components of F_c are:
- Tangential component or rotative effort on crank,
$$F_t = F_c \sin \sin (\theta + \phi) \qquad \text{...3.13/ Pg 45, DHB}$$
$$= 126.5 \times 10^3 \times \sin (35 + 6.59)$$
$$F_t = 83.79 \times 10^3 \text{ N}$$
- Radial component or force along the crank,
$$F_r = F_c \cos (\theta + \phi) \qquad \text{...3.14/ Pg 45, DHB}$$
$$= 126.5 \times 10^3 \times \cos (35 + 6.59)$$
$$F_r = 94.61 \times 10^3 \text{ N}$$

b. Bearing reactions:

- **Reactions at bearings 1 and 2:**
It is assumed that the portion of the crankshaft between the bearings 1 and 2 is simply supported on the bearings and subjected to vertical force F_p as shown in **Fig. 8.20**.

From Case 1:
- $x_1 = x_2 = x/2 = 800/2 = 400$ mm
- $y_1 = y_2 = y/2 = 620/2 = 310$ mm

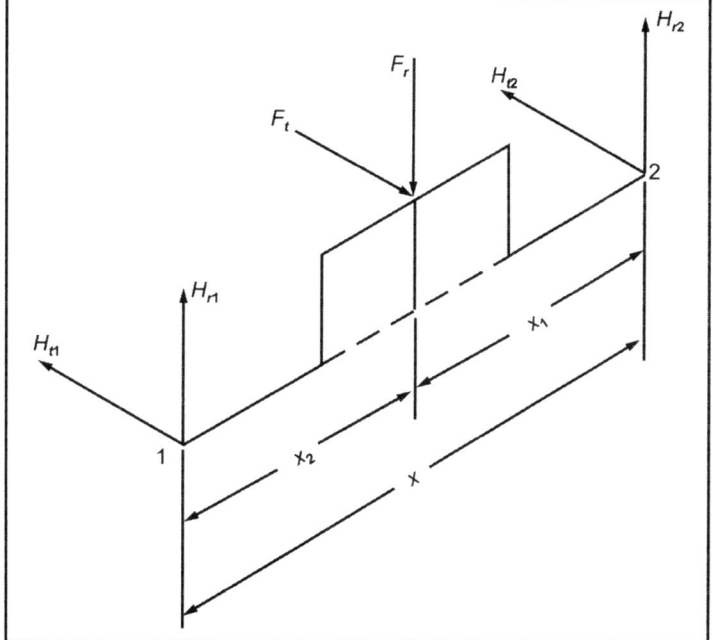

Fig. 8.20: Reactions at bearings 1 and 2

- Width of web, $b = 240$ mm
- Thickness of web, $t = 140$ mm
- **Radial forces:**
  Due to symmetry

$$H_{r1} = \frac{F_r \cdot x_1}{x} = \frac{94.61 \times 10^3 \times 400}{800} = 47305.56 \text{ N}$$

$$H_{r2} = \frac{F_r \cdot x_2}{x} = \frac{94.61 \times 10^3 \times 400}{800} = 47305.56 \text{ N}$$

→ **Tangential forces:**
  Due to symmetry

$$H_{t1} = \frac{F_t \cdot x_1}{x} = \frac{83.97 \times 10^3 \times 400}{800} = 41985 \text{ N}$$

$$H_{t2} = \frac{F_t \cdot x_2}{x} = \frac{83.97 \times 10^3 \times 400}{800} = 41985 \text{ N}$$

- **Reactions at bearings 2 and 3:**
  The reactions at the bearings 2 and 3, due to weight of the flywheel (W) and resultant belt pull are same as discussed in **Case 1**.

→ **Reactions due to weight of flywheel:**
Due to symmetry

$$V_2 = \frac{W \cdot y_1}{y} = \frac{50{,}000 \times 310}{620} = 25000 \text{ N}$$

$$V_3 = \frac{W \cdot y_2}{y} = \frac{50{,}000 \times 310}{620} = 25000 \text{ N}$$

→ **Reactions due to belt pull:**
Due to symmetry

$$H_2' = \frac{(T_1 + T_2) \cdot y_1}{y} = \frac{6500 \times 310}{620} = 3250 \text{ N}$$

$$H_3' = \frac{(T_1 + T_2) \cdot y_2}{y} = \frac{6500 \times 310}{620} = 3250 \text{ N}$$

→ Thus the resultant reactions at bearings are

$$R_1 = \sqrt{H_{r1}^2 + H_{t1}^2} = \sqrt{47305.56^2 + 41985^2} = 63250 \text{ N}$$

$$R_2 = \sqrt{(H_{t2} + H_2')^2 + (H_{r2} + V_2)^2}$$

$$= \sqrt{(41985 + 3250)^2 + (47305.56 + 25000)^2} = 85289.50 \text{ N}$$

$$R_3 = \sqrt{(H_3')^2 + V_3^2} = \sqrt{3250^2 + 25000^2} = 25210.36 \text{ N}$$

c. Design of crank pin:

→ Bending moment at the center of crank pin is $M_p = H_{r1} \cdot x_2 = 47305.56 \times 400 = 18.92 \times 10^6$ N-mm

→ The twisting moment on the crankpin is, $T_p = H_{t1} \cdot r$

$$r = L_s/2 = 600/2 = 300 \text{ mm}$$

$$= 41985 \times 300 \text{ mm}$$

$$T_p = 12.60 \times 10^6 \text{ N-mm}$$

→ Thus, the equivalent torque on the crank pin is, $T_e = \sqrt{M_p^2 + T_p^2}$

$$= \sqrt{(18.92 \times 10^6)^2 + (12.60 \times 10^6)^2}$$

$$T_e = 22.73 \times 10^6 \text{ N-mm}$$

Also $T_e = \dfrac{\pi d_p^3}{16} \tau$

Assume $\tau = 0.5\sigma_b = 0.5 \times 83 = 41.5$ MPa ≈ 42 MPa

$$22.73 \times 10^6 = \frac{\pi d_p^3}{16} \times 42$$

$$d_p = 140.21 \text{ mm} \qquad \ldots \text{Eq. }(iii)$$

Compare Eqs (*i*) and (*iii*), and adopt higher value for design.
i.e. $d_p = 200$ mm and $l_p = 157$ mm

d. Design of shaft under flywheel:

→ The bending moment on the shaft, $M_s = R_3 \cdot y_1 = 25210.36 \times 310 = 7.81 \times 10^6$ N-mm
→ The twisting moment on the shaft, $T_s = F_t \cdot r = 83.79 \times 10^3 \times 300 = 25.19 \times 10^6$ N-mm
→ Thus the equivalent twisting moment on the shaft is,

$$T_{es} = \sqrt{M_s^2 + T_s^2}$$

$$= \sqrt{(7.81 \times 10^6)^2 + (25.19 \times 10^6)^2}$$

$$T_{es} = 26.37 \times 10^6 \text{ N-mm}$$

Also $T_{es} = \dfrac{\pi d_s^3}{16} \tau$

$$26.37 \times 10^6 = \frac{\pi d_s^3}{16} \times 42$$

$$d_s = 147.33 \text{ mm} \qquad \ldots \text{Eq. }(iv)$$

Compare Eqs (*ii*) and (*iv*), and adopt higher value for design.
i.e. $d_s = 147.33$ mm
∴ Standard shaft size, $d_s = 160$ mm   …Tb 3.5a/ Pg 48, DHB

e. Design of shaft at the juncture of right hand crank arm:

→ The bending moment at the juncture of the right hand crank arm,

$$M_{s1} = R_1 \cdot \left(x_2 + \frac{l_p}{2} + \frac{t}{2} \right) - F_c \cdot \left(\frac{l_p}{2} + \frac{t}{2} \right)$$

$$= 63250 \times \left(400 + \frac{157}{2} + \frac{140}{2} \right) - 126.5 \times 10^3 \times \left(\frac{157}{2} + \frac{140}{2} \right)$$

$$M_{s1} = 15.91 \times 10^6 \text{ N-mm}$$

→ The twisting moment at the juncture of the right hand crank arm,
$T_{s1} = F_t \cdot r = 83.97 \times 10^3 \times 300$
$= 25.19 \times 10^6$ N-mm

→ Thus the equivalent twisting moment at the juncture of the right hand crank arm

$$T_{es1} = \sqrt{M_{s1}^2 + T_{s1}^2} = \sqrt{(15.91 \times 10^6)^2 + (25.19 \times 10^6)^2}$$

$$= 29.79 \times 10^6 \text{ N-mm}$$

Also $T_{es1} = \dfrac{\pi d_{s1}^3}{16} \times \tau$

$$29.79 \times 10^6 = \frac{\pi d_{s1}^3}{16} \times 42$$

$$d_{s1} = 153.44 \text{ mm}$$

∴ Standard shaft size, $d_{s1} = 160$ mm ...Tb 3.5a/ Pg 48, DHB

f. Design of right hand crank web:

The right hand crank web is subjected to the following stresses:
  i. Bending stresses in two planes normal to each other, due to the radial and tangential components of F_p
  ii. Direct compressive stress due to F_r, and
  iii. Torsional stress.

→ The bending moment due to the radial component of F_r is

$$M_r = \frac{b.t^2}{6}.\sigma_{br}$$

But $M_r = H_{r2}.\left(x_1 - \frac{l_p}{2} - \frac{t}{2}\right)$

$$= 47305.56 \times \left(400 - \frac{157}{2} - \frac{140}{2}\right)$$

$$M_r = 11.89 \times 10^6 \text{ N-mm}$$

∴ $11.89 \times 10^6 = \frac{240 \times 140^2}{6} \times \sigma_{br}$

$$\sigma_{br} = 15.16 \text{ MPa}$$

• The bending moment due to the tangential component of F_t is

$$M_t = \frac{t.b^2}{6}.\sigma_{bt}$$

But $M_t = F_t.\left(r - \frac{d_{s1}}{2}\right)$

$$= 83.97 \times 10^3 \times \left(300 - \frac{160}{2}\right)$$

$$M_r = 18.47 \times 10^6 \text{ N-mm}$$

∴ $18.74 \times 10^6 = \frac{140 \times 240^2}{6} \times \sigma_{bt}$

$$\sigma_{bt} = 13.74 \text{ MPa}$$

→ The direct compressive stress is given by

$$\sigma_{dc} = \frac{F_r}{2bt} = \frac{94.61 \times 10^3}{2 \times 240 \times 140} = 1.41 \text{ MPa}$$

→ The maximum compressive stress (σ_c) will occur at the upper left corner of the cross-section of the crank.

i.e. $\sigma_c = \sigma_{br} + \sigma_{bt} + \sigma_{dc}$
$= 15.16 + 13.74 + 1.41$
$\sigma_c = 30.31$ MPa

→ The twisting moment on the arm,

$$\tau = \frac{T}{Z_p} = \frac{4.5T}{b.t^2}$$

But $T = H_{t2} \cdot \left(x_1 - \frac{l_p}{2} \right)$

$= 41985 \times \left(400 - \frac{157}{2} \right)$

$T = 13.50 \times 10^6$ N-mm

∴ $\tau = \dfrac{4.5 \times 13.50 \times 10^6}{240 \times 140^2}$

$\tau = 12.91$ MPa

→ Thus, the maximum or total combined stress,

$$(\sigma_c)_{max} = \frac{\sigma_c}{2} + \sqrt{\left(\frac{\sigma_c}{2}\right)^2 + \tau^2} < \sigma_b \qquad \ldots 1.11a\,/\,Pg\,2,\,DHB$$

$= \dfrac{30.31}{2} + \sqrt{\left(\dfrac{30.31}{2}\right)^2 + 12.91^2}$

$(\sigma_c)_{max} = 35.06$ MPa < 83 MPa

Hence design of crank web is safe.

g. Design of left hand crank web:

The left hand crank web is not stressed to the extent as the right hand crank web. Hence the dimensions for the left hand crank web may be made same as for right hand crank web.

h. Design of crankshaft bearings:

→ Bearing 2 is the most heavily loaded and should be checked for the safe bearing pressure.

We know that the total reaction at bearing 2 is

$$R_2 = \sqrt{(H_{t2} + H'_2)^2 + (H_{r2} + V_2)^2} = 85289.50 \text{ N}$$

→ The length of crank pin is calculated as
$R_2 = l_2 \cdot d_{s1} \cdot p_{bc}$
$85289.50 = 363 \times 160 \times p_{bc}$
$p_{bc} = 1.46$ MPa < 10 MPa

Hence the design is safe.

8.11 DESIGN OF SIDE CRANKSHAFT

The side crankshaft has only one web and requires two bearings for support. It is widely used in medium sized engines as well as large horizontal engines. The design procedure for the side or overhung crankshaft is same as that for centre crankshaft **(Fig. 8.21)**.

In designing the crankshaft, two positions of the crank are considered:
1. The crank is at top dead center (TDC) and subjected to maximum bending moment.
2. The crank is at an angle with the line of dead centre position and subjected to maximum torsional moment.

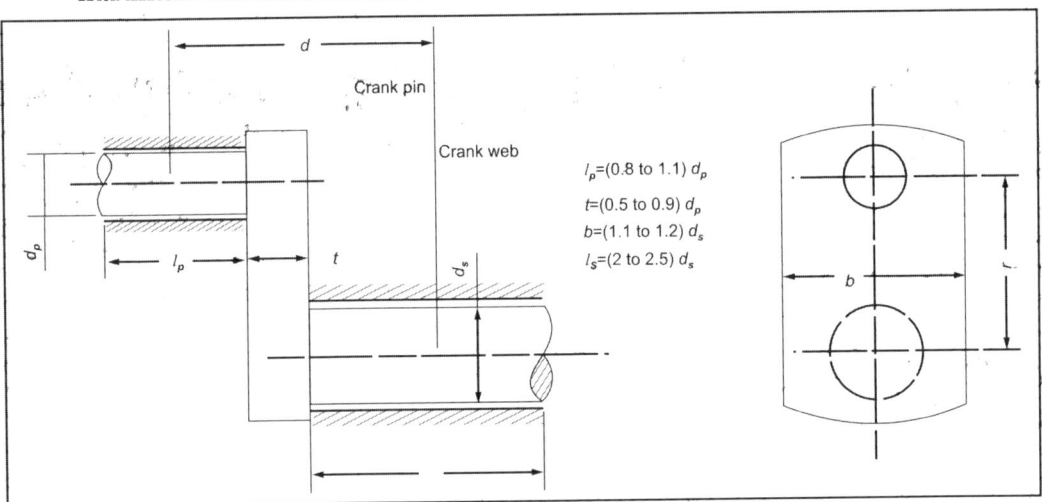

Fig. 8.21: Forged overhung crankshaft (Fig 3.3/Pg 50, DHB)

8.11.1 Case 1: Side Crankshaft at Top Dead Center Position

Figure 8.22 represents forces acting on the side crankshaft when the crank is at TDC. The crank is supported on two bearings.

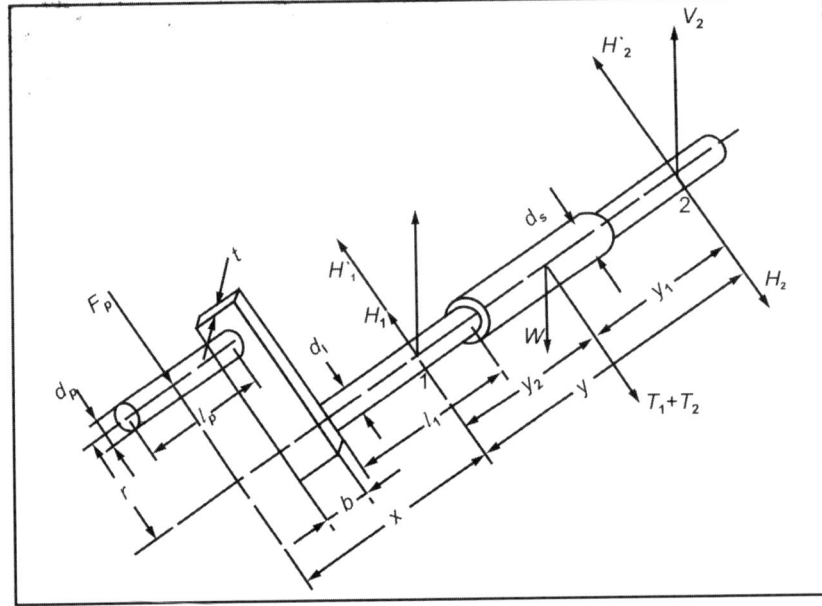

Fig. 8.22: Side crank at dead center

Assumptions

- The engine is vertical and the crank is at TDC position.
- The belt drive is horizontal.
- The crankshaft is simply supported at the bearings.

Let F_p = force acting on crank pin (N)
D = diameter of piston (mm)
$p\ (= p_{max})$ = maximum gas or steam pressure (MPa)
W = weight of flywheel, acting vertically downwards (N)
$T_1 + T_2$ = belt pull acting in horizontal direction (N)
T_1 = tension on tight side of belt (N)
T_2 = tension on slack side of belt (N)
d_p = diameter of crank pin (mm)
l_p = length of crank pin (mm)
d_s = diameter of flywheel (mm)
b = width of crank web (mm)
t = thickness of crank web (mm)
x = overhang distance of force F_p from bearing 1 (mm)
y = distance between bearings 1 and 2 (mm)

a. Bearing reactions:

→ The thrust in the connecting rod will be equal to the force acting on the piston due to gas pressure.
i.e. Force on the piston due to pressure of gas,

$$F_p = p_{max} \left(\frac{\pi D^2}{4} \right) \qquad \text{...(Eq. 8.111) [same 8.21]}$$

→ It is assumed that the portion of the crankshaft between the bearings 1 and 2 is simply supported on the bearings and subjected to vertical force as shown in **Fig. 8.23(a)**.

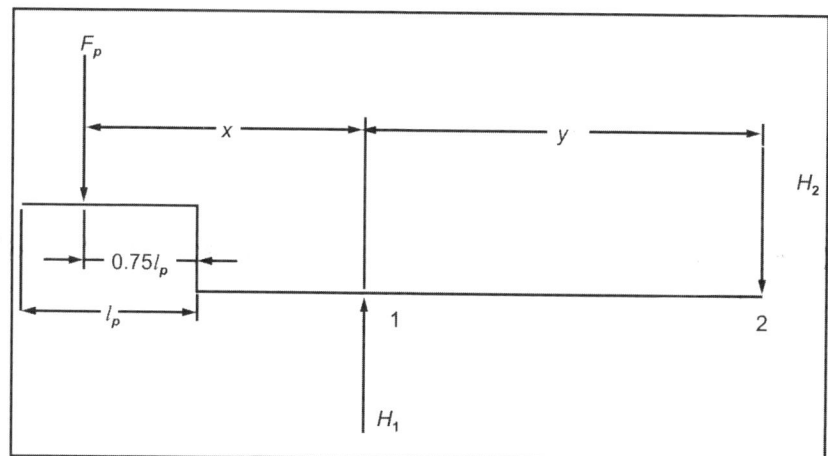

Fig. 8.23: (a) Reactions at bearings 1 and 2

→ **Horizontal reactions: [Fig. 8.23 (a)]**

$$\text{Now } H_1 = F_p + H_2 \qquad \text{...(Eq. 8.112)}$$

Taking moments about bearing 2, we have

$$F_p \cdot (x+y) = H_1 \cdot y$$

$$H_1 = \frac{F_p \cdot (x+y)}{y} \qquad \text{...(Eq. 8.113)}$$

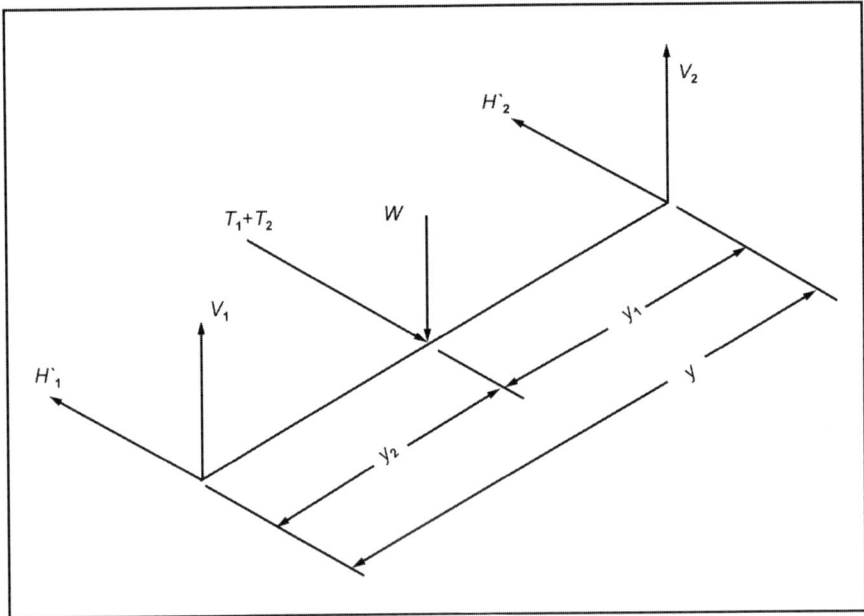

Fig. 8.23: (b) Reactions at bearings 1 and 2

$$\therefore \quad \text{Eq. (8.112) yields ... } H_2 = \frac{F_p \cdot (x+y)}{y} - F_p$$

$$= F_p \left(\frac{x+y}{y} - 1 \right)$$

$$= F_p \left(\frac{x+y-y}{y} \right)$$

$$H_2 = \frac{F_p \cdot x}{y} \qquad \text{...(Eq. 8.114)}$$

→ **Reactions due to weight of flywheel: [Fig. 8.23 (b)]**

$$V_1 + V_2 = W \qquad \text{...(Eq. 8.115)}$$

Taking moments about bearing 1, we have

$$V_2 \cdot y = W \cdot y_2$$

$$V_2 = \frac{W \cdot y_2}{y} \qquad \text{...(Eq. 8.116)}$$

$$\therefore \quad \text{Eq. (8.116) yields ... } V_1 = W - \frac{W \cdot y_2}{y}$$

$$= W\left(1 - \frac{y_2}{y}\right)$$

$$= W\left(\frac{y - y_2}{y}\right)$$

$$V_1 = \frac{W \cdot y_1}{y} \qquad \ldots \text{(Eq. 8.117)}$$

→ **Reactions due to belt pull: [Fig. 8.23 (b)]**

$$H_1' + H_2' = (T_1 + T_2) \qquad \ldots \text{(Eq. 8.118)}$$

Taking moments about bearing 1, we have

$$H_2' \cdot y = (T_1 + T_2) \cdot y_2$$

$$H_2' = \frac{(T_1 + T_2) \cdot y_2}{y} \qquad \ldots \text{(Eq. 8.119)}$$

Eq. (8.118) yields ... $H_1' = (T_1 + T_2) - \dfrac{(T_1 + T_2) \cdot y_2}{y}$

$$= (T_1 + T_2)\left(1 - \frac{y_2}{y}\right)$$

$$= (T_1 + T_2)\left(\frac{y - y_2}{y}\right)$$

$$H_1' = \frac{(T_1 + T_2) \cdot y_1}{y} \qquad \ldots \text{(Eq. 8.120)}$$

From **Fig. 8.22**, $x = 0.75\, l_p + t + \left(\dfrac{l_1}{2}\right)$

$$y = \left(\frac{l_1}{2}\right) + \text{fly wheel width} + \left(\frac{l_2}{2}\right) + \text{clearence}$$

$l_1 = 1.75 d_p = l_2$

l_1, l_2 = length of bearings 1 & 2 respectively

b. Design of crank pin:

The dimensions of the crankpin are obtained by considering the crankpin in bearing and then checked for bending stress

→ The bearing pressure at the crank pin is $F_p = l_p \cdot d_p \cdot p_{bc}$ ...(Eq. 8.121)

Where, d_p = diameter of crank pin (mm)

l_p = length of crank pin (mm)

= (0.8 to 1.1) d_p ...**Fig. 3.3/ Pg 50, DHB**

p_{bc} − permissible bearing pressure for crank pin (MPa)

...**Tb 3.6/ Pg 49, DHB**

Eq. (8.121) gives the diameter of crank pin (d_p) and length of crank pin (l_p).

→ Check for bending stress:

If it is assumed that the crankpin acts as a cantilever and the load on the crankpin is uniformly distributed, then maximum bending moment will be

$$M_p = F_p \left(\frac{l_p}{2}\right) \qquad \text{...(a)}$$

On the other hand, if we assume that the load is not uniformly distributed and loacated at the end of crank pin, then the maximum bending moment is given by

$$M_p = F_p \cdot l_p \qquad \text{...(b)}$$

Eqs (a) and (b) indicate the limiting values in two conditions. So, a mean value of bending moment is taken for calculations.

$$M_p = 0.75 \, F_p \cdot l_p \qquad \text{...(c)}$$

i.e. we assume that the mean value of bending moment acts at a distance of $(0.75 \, l_p)$ from the crank web.

→ Assuming that the gas force to be acting at $0.75 \, l_p$ from the crank web, the bending moment at the center of crank pin is given as

$$M_p = F_p \times (0.75 \, l_p) = \frac{\pi d_p^3}{32} \qquad \text{...(Eq. 8.122)}$$

σ_b – allowable bending stress for crank pin (MPa)
...**Tb. 3.5b/ Pg 48, DHB**

c. Design of bearings:

→ The dimensions of web are given in **Fig. 3.3/ Pg 50, DHB**
Length of crank pin, $l_p = (0.8 \text{ to } 1.1) d_p$
Thickness of web, $t = (0.5 \text{ to } 0.9) d_p$
Width of web, $b = (1.1 \text{ to } 1.2) d_s$
Length of crankshaft, $l_s = (2 \text{ to } 2.5) d_s$ ...(Eq. 8.123) **Fig. 3.3/ Pg 50, DHB**
d_s – diameter of crankshaft

→ The bending moment at bearing 1 is given by

$$M_b = F_p \cdot x = F_p \times \left(0.75 l_p + t + \frac{l_1}{2}\right) = \frac{\pi d_1^3}{32} \sigma_b \qquad \text{...(Eq. 8.124)}$$

d_1 = diameter of shaft or journal at bearing 1 (mm)
t_1 = length of bearing (mm)
= $1.75 \, d_p$

d. Design of crank web:

The crank web is subjected to eccentric loading. Due to this there will be two stresses acting on it, one direct compressive stress and the other bending stress due to gas load (F_p).

→ Direct compressive stress: $\sigma_c = \dfrac{F_p}{b.t}$ (MPa) ...(Eq. 8.125)

→ Bending stress: $\sigma_{b1} = \dfrac{M_1}{Z_1} = \dfrac{6 M_1}{b.t^2}$ (MPa) ...(Eq. 8.126)

Where, b = width of crank web (mm)
t = thickness of crank web (mm)

The bending moment at the center of crank pin is given as

$$M_1 = F_p \times \left(0.75 l_p + \frac{t}{2}\right) \qquad \text{...(Eq. 8.127)}$$

→ Thus the total stress on the web, $(\sigma_c)_t = \sigma_c + \sigma_{b1} \leq \sigma_b$ ...(Eq. 8.128)

e. Design of shaft under flywheel:

The total bending moment at the flywheel location will be the resultant of horizontal bending moment due to the gas load and belt pull and the vertical bending moment due to the flywheel weight.

→ **Horizontal bending moment:**
- Horizontal bending moment at flywheel due to gas load:
$$M_W = F_p \cdot (x + y_2) - (H_1 + H_1') y_2 = H_2 y_1 \qquad \text{...(Eq. 8.129)}$$
- Horizontal bending moment at flywheel due to belt tension:
$$M_T = H_1' \cdot y_2 = H_2' \cdot y_1 = \frac{(T_1 + T_2) \cdot y_1 \cdot y_2}{y} \qquad \text{...(Eq. 8.130)}$$
- Thus the resultant horizontal bending moment is
$$M_H = M_W + M_T \qquad \text{...(Eq. 8.131)}$$

→ **Vertical bending moment:**
$$M_V = \frac{W \cdot y_1 \cdot y_2}{y} \qquad \text{...(Eq. 8.132)}$$

→ Thus the resultant bending moment is, $M_s = \sqrt{M_H^2 + M_V^2} = \frac{\pi d_s^3}{32} \sigma_b$ ...(Eq. 8.133)

Eq. (8.133) gives the diameter of shaft at flywheel. The value of $d_s > d_1$, if not adopt higher value.

8.11.2 Case 2: Side Crankshaft at an Angle of Maximum Torque

Consider a position of the crank at an angle of maximum twisting moment as shown in **Fig. 8.24.** The twisting moment on the crankshaft will be maximum when the tangential force on the crank (F_t) is maximum. The maximum value of tangential force lies when the crank is at angle of 25° to 30° from the dead centre for petrol engines (i.e. constant volume combustion engines) and 30° to 40° for diesel engines (i.e. constant pressure combustion engines).

a. Force components on crank pin:

The position of the crank at an angle of θ with the line of dead centers is shown in **Fig. 8.16 [Fig. 3.1/Pg 50, DHB].**

Let F_p = force acting on piston due to gas pressure (N)
F_c = thrust on connecting rod (N)
F_t = tangential component of force on crank pin (N)
φ = Angle of inclination of the connecting rod with the line of dead centers (deg)
θ = Angle of inclination of the crank with the line of dead centers (deg)

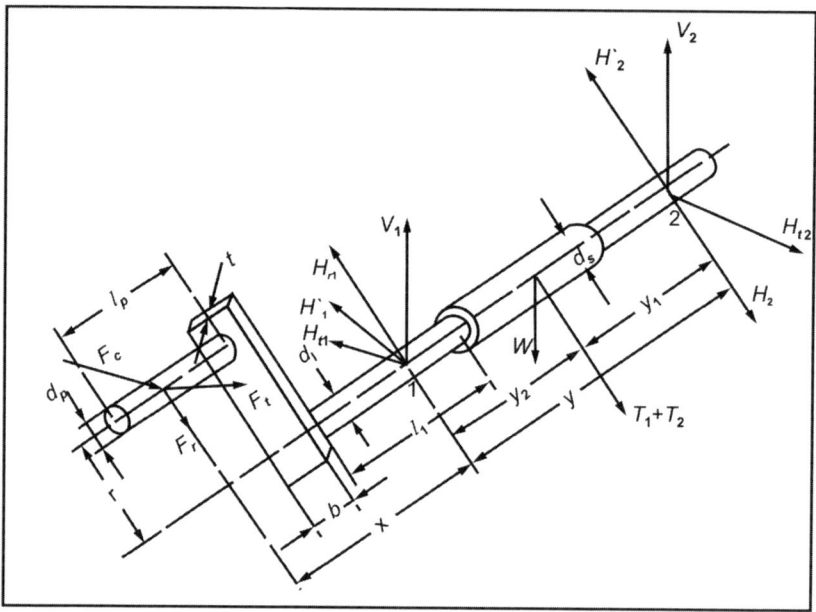

Fig. 8.24: Crank at angle of maximum torque

→ If p' is the intensity of gas pressure on the piston at this instant, then for maximum torque condition,
force on the piston due to pressure of gas,

$$F_p = p'\left(\frac{\pi D^2}{4}\right) \qquad \text{...using (Eq. 8.80)}$$

→ The thrust on the connecting rod is $F_c = \dfrac{F_p}{\cos \phi}$ ...using (Eq. 8.81) **3.12/ Pg 45, DHB**

→ The components of F_c are:
 • Tangential component or rotative effort on crank, $F_t = F_c \sin(\theta + \phi)$

$$= F_p \frac{\cos(\theta + \phi)}{\cos \phi} \qquad \text{... using (Eq. 8.82)} \textbf{ 3.13/ Pg 45, DHB}$$

 • Radial component or force along the crank, $F_r = F_c \cos(\theta + \phi) = F_p \dfrac{\cos(\theta + \phi)}{\cos \phi}$
 ...using (Eq. 8.83) **3.14/ Pg 45, DHB**

Where, $\sin \phi = \dfrac{\sin \theta}{l/r}$ ...using (Eq. 8.24a)

b. Bearing reactions:

It is assumed that the portion of the crankshaft between the bearings 1 and 2 is simply supported on the bearings and subjected to vertical force F_p as shown in **Fig. 8.25**.

→ **Radial forces:**
 Now $\qquad H_{r1} = F_r + H_{r2} \qquad$ ...(Eq. 8.134)
 Taking moments about bearing 1, we have
 $\qquad H_{r2} \cdot y = F_r \cdot x$

$$H_{r2} = \frac{F_r \cdot x}{y} \qquad \text{...(Eq. 8.135)}$$

∴ Eq. (8.134) yields...
$$H_{r1} = F_r + \frac{F_r \cdot x}{y}$$
$$= F_r \left(1 + \frac{x}{y}\right)$$
$$H_{r1} = F_r \left(\frac{x+y}{y}\right) \qquad \text{...(Eq. 8.136)}$$

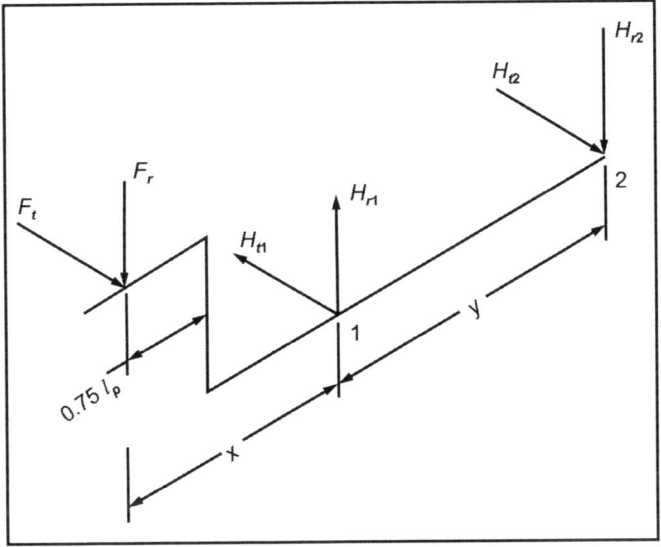

Fig. 8.25: Reactions at bearings 1 and 2

→ **Tangential forces:**
Now
$$H_{t1} = F_t + H_{t2} \qquad \text{...(Eq. 8.137)}$$
Taking moments about bearing 1, we have
$$H_{t2} \cdot y = F_t \cdot x$$
$$H_{t2} = \frac{F_t \cdot x}{y} \qquad \text{...(Eq. 8.138)}$$

∴ Eq. (8.137) yields...
$$H_{t1} = F_t + \frac{F_t \cdot x}{x}$$
$$= F_t \left(1 + \frac{x}{y}\right)$$
$$H_{t1} = F_t \left(\frac{x+y}{y}\right) \qquad \text{...(Eq. 8.139)}$$

- The reactions at the bearings 1 and 2, due to weight of the flywheel (W) and resultant belt pull are same as discussed in Section **8.11.1; Case 1** *[Eqs (115) to (120)]*.

→ **Reactions due to weight of flywheel: [Fig. 8.23 (b)]**
$$V_1 + V_2 = W \qquad \text{...using (Eq. 8.115)}$$

Taking moments about bearing 1, we have
$$V_2 \cdot y = W \cdot y_2$$
$$V_2 = \frac{W \cdot y_2}{y} \quad \text{...using (Eq. 8.116)}$$

$\therefore$ Eq. (8.116) yields... $V_1 = W - \dfrac{W \cdot y_2}{y}$

$$= W\left(1 - \frac{y_2}{y}\right)$$

$$= W\left(\frac{y - y_2}{y}\right)$$

$$V_1 = \frac{W \cdot y_1}{y} \quad \text{...using (Eq. 8.117)}$$

→ **Reactions due to belt pull: [Fig. 8.23 (b)]**
$$H_1' + H_2' = (T_1 + T_2) \quad \text{...using (Eq. 8.118)}$$
Taking moments about bearing 1, we have
$$H_2' \cdot y = (T_1 + T_2) \cdot y_2$$
$$H_2' = \frac{(T_1 + T_2) \cdot y_2}{y} \quad \text{...using (Eq. 8.119)}$$

Eq. (8.118) yields... $H_1' = (T_1 + T_2) - \dfrac{(T_1 + T_2) \cdot y_2}{y}$

$$= (T_1 + T_2)\left(1 - \frac{y_2}{y}\right)$$

$$= (T_1 + T_2)\left(\frac{y - y_2}{y}\right)$$

$$H_1' = \frac{(T_1 + T_2) \cdot y_1}{y} \quad \text{...using (Eq. 8.120)}$$

c. Design of crank pin:

Check for shear stress:
→ The bending moment in the crank pin is, $M_p = F_r \times (0.75\, l_p)$ ...(Eq. 8.140)
→ The twisting moment on the crankpin is, $T_p = F_t \cdot r$ ...(Eq. 8.141)
→ Thus the equivalent torque on the crank pin is,

$$T_e = \sqrt{M_p^2 + T_p^2} = \frac{\pi d_p^3}{16}\tau \quad \text{...(Eq. 8.142)}$$

Where, d_p = diameter of crank pin (mm)

τ = allowable shear stress in crank pin (MPa) **[40 MPa – if not given]**

$r = \dfrac{L_s}{2}$ – crank radius (mm), $\quad L_s$ = stroke length (mm)

d. Design of crank web:

The crank web is subjected to the following stresses:

i. Bending stresses in two planes normal to each other, due to the radial and tangential components of F_p.

ii. Direct compressive stress due to F_r, and

iii. Torsional stress.

Check for maximum compressive stress:

→ The bending moment due to the radial component of F_r is

$$M_r = F_r \cdot \left(0.75 \, l_p + \frac{t}{2}\right) = \frac{b \cdot t^2}{6} \cdot \sigma_{br} \quad \ldots(\text{Eq. 8.143})$$

Eq. (8.143) gives the value of bending stress (σ_{br}) due to radial component.

→ The bending moment due to the tangential component of F_t is

$$M_t = F_t \cdot \left(r - \frac{d_1}{2}\right) = \frac{t \cdot b^2}{6} \cdot \sigma_{bt} \quad \ldots(\text{Eq. 8.144})$$

Eq. (8.144) gives the value of bending stress (σ_{bt}) due to tangential component.

→ The direct compressive stress is given by

$$\sigma_{dc} = \frac{F_r}{bt} \quad \ldots(\text{Eq. 8.145})$$

Where, d_1 = diameter of shaft/journal at bearing 1 (mm)
b = width of crank web (mm)
t = thickness of crank web (mm)

→ The maximum compressive stress (σ_c) is calculated as:

$$\sigma_c = \sigma_{br} + \sigma_{bt} + \sigma_{dc} \quad \ldots(\text{Eq. 8.146})$$

→ The twisting moment on the arm,

$$T = F_t \cdot \left(0.75 \, l_p + \frac{t}{2}\right) \quad \ldots(\text{Eq. 8.147})$$

But shear stress on the arm, $\tau = \dfrac{T}{Z_p} = \dfrac{4.5T}{b \cdot t^2} \quad \ldots(\text{Eq. 8.148})$

Where, Z_p = polar section modulus = $\dfrac{b \cdot t^2}{4.5}$

→ Thus the maximum or total combined stress,

$$(\sigma_c)_{max} = \frac{\sigma_c}{2} + \sqrt{\left(\frac{\sigma_c}{2}\right)^2 + \tau^2} < \sigma_b \quad \ldots(\text{Eq. 8.149}) \quad \textbf{1.11a / Pg 2, DHB}$$

σ_b – allowable bending stress for crank pin (MPa) **Tb. 3.5b/ Pg 48, DHB**

Note: The value of $(\sigma_c)_{max}$ should be within safe limits. If it exceeds the safe value, then the dimension b may be increased because it does not affect other dimensions.

e. Design of shaft at the juncture of crank arm/web:

Check for shear stress:

→ The bending moment bending moment at the junction of the crank,

$$M_{s1} = F_c \cdot (0.75 \, l_p + t) \quad \ldots(\text{Eq. 8.150})$$

→ The twisting moment, $T_{s1} = F_t \cdot r$ ...(Eq. 8.151)
→ Thus the equivalent twisting moment at the juncture of crank arm

$$T_{es1} = \sqrt{M_{s1}^2 + T_{s1}^2} = \frac{\pi d_{s1}^3}{16} \tau \qquad \text{...(Eq. 8.152)}$$

Where, d_{s1} = diameter of shaft at the juncture of crank arm (mm)
(assume $d_{s1} = d_1$)
τ = allowable shear stress in the shaft (MPa) **[30 to 40 MPa – if not given]**

f. Design of shaft under flywheel:
Check for shear stress:

The total bending moment at the flywheel location will be the resultant of horizontal bending moment due to the gas load and belt pull and the vertical bending moment due to the flywheel weight.

→ **Horizontal bending moment:**
  - Horizontal bending moment due to weight of flywheel:
    $$M_W = F_r \cdot (x + y_2) - (H_{r1} + V_1)y_2 \qquad \text{...(Eq. 8.153)}$$
  - Horizontal bending moment due to belt tension:
    $$M_T = F_t \cdot (x + y_2) - (H_{t1} + H_1')y_2 \qquad \text{...(Eq. 8.154)}$$
  - Thus the resultant horizontal bending moment is
    $$M_H = M_W + M_T \qquad \text{...using (8.131)}$$

→ **Vertical bending moment:**
  $$M_V = \frac{W \cdot y_1 \cdot y_2}{y} \qquad \text{...using (Eq. 8.132)}$$

→ Thus the resultant bending moment is, $M_s = \sqrt{M_H^2 + M_V^2}$ ...using (Eq. 8.133)
→ The twisting moment on the shaft, $T_s = F_t \cdot r$ ...using (Eq. 8.98)
→ Thus the equivalent twisting moment on the shaft is,

$$T_{es} = \sqrt{M_s^2 + T_s^2} = \frac{\pi d_s^3}{16} \tau \qquad \text{...using (Eq. 8.99)}$$

Where, d_s = diameter of shaft under flywheel (mm)
τ = allowable shear stress in crank pin (MPa) **[40 MPa – if not given]**

9. **Design an overhung crankshaft for a 300 mm × 350 mm single cylinder vertical engine using the following data:**
Maximum gas pressure = 2.5 MPa, l/r = 4.5, weight of flywheel = 10 kN, total belt pull = 5 kN, width of hub for flywheel cum belt pulley = 150 mm, allowable bending stress = 75 MPa, bearing pressure = 10 MPa.
The torque on the crankshaft is maximum when the crank turns through 35° from TDC and at this position the gas pressure inside the cylinder is 1 MPa. The belts are in horizontal position.

Solution: D = 300 mm, L_s = 350 mm, $p = (p_{max})$ = 2.5 MPa, l/r = 4.5, W = 10 kN, $T_1 + T_2$ = 5 kN, θ = 35°, p' = 1 MPa, σ_b = 75 MPa, p_{bc} = 10 MPa, flywheel width = 150 mm

Case 1: Centre crankshaft at top dead center position:

a. Design of crank pin:

→ Force on the piston due to gas pressure, $F_p = p_{max}\left(\dfrac{\pi D^2}{4}\right) = 2.5 \times \left(\dfrac{\pi \times 300^2}{4}\right)$

   $= 176714.59$ N

→ Diameter of crank pin:
   The bearing pressure at the crank pin is $F_p = l_p \cdot d_p \cdot p_{bc}$
   l_p = length of crank pin
   $= (0.8 \text{ to } 1.1) d_p$ ...Fig. 3.3/ Pg 50, DHB

   Assume $l_p = d_p$
   $176714.59 = d_p^2 \times 10$
   $d_p = 133$ mm ≈ 135 mm

→ Length of crank pin: $l_p = d_p = 135$ mm

→ **Check for bending stress:**
   Assuming that the gas force to be acting at $0.75\, l_p$ from the crank web, the bending moment at the center of crank pin is given as
   $M_p = F_p \times (0.75\, l_p) = 176714.59 \times (0.75 \times 135) = 17.89 \times 10^6$ N-mm

   Also $M_p = \dfrac{\pi d_p^3}{32} \sigma_b$

   $17.89 \times 10^6 = \dfrac{\pi \times 135^3}{32} \sigma_b$

   $\sigma_b = 74.07$ MPa < 75 MPa

   Hence design of crank pin is safe.

b. Design of bearings:

→ The dimensions of web are given in **Fig. 3.3/ Pg 50, DHB**
   Thickness of web, $t = 0.6\, d_p = 0.6 \times 135 = 81$ mm ≈ 85 mm
- Assume the length of bearing as $l_1 = 1.75\, d_p = 1.75 \times 135 = 236.25$ mm ≈ 240 mm

→ The bending moment at bearing 1 is given by, $M_b = F_p \times \left(0.75\, l_p + t + \dfrac{l_1}{2}\right)$

   $= 176714.59 \times \left(0.75 \times 135 + 84 + \dfrac{240}{2}\right)$

   $M_b = 54.12 \times 10^6$ N-mm

   Also $M_b = \dfrac{\pi d_1^3}{32} \sigma_b$

   $54.12 \times 10^6 = \dfrac{\pi d_1^3}{32} \times 75$

   $d_1 = 194$ mm ≈ 200 mm

c. Bearing reactions:

→ It is assumed that the portion of the crankshaft between the bearings 1 and 2 is simply supported on the bearings and subjected to vertical force F_p as shown in **Fig. 8.26(a)**.

→ From **Fig. 8.25**

$x = 0.75\, l_p + t + (l_1/2) = (0.75 \times 135) + 85 + (240/2) = 306.25$ mm ≈ 310 mm

$y = (l_1/2) + \text{flywheel width} + (l_1/2) + \text{clearence}$

$\quad = (240/2) + 150 + (240/2) + 10$

$y = 400$ mm

$y_1 = y_2 = y/2 = 400/2 = 200$ mm

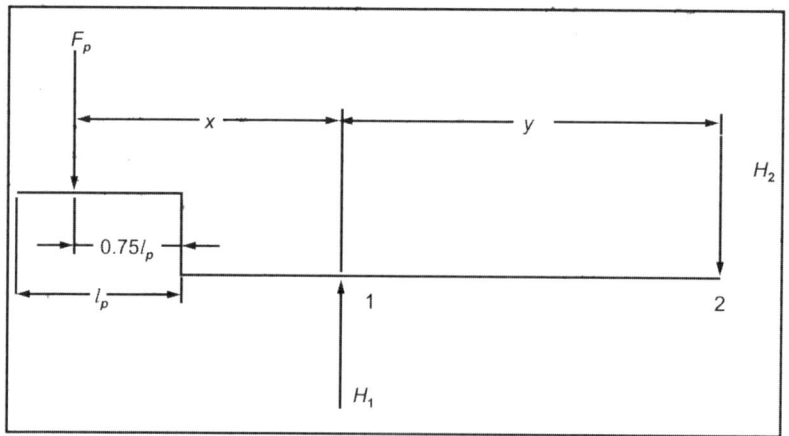

Fig. 8.26: (a) Reactions at bearings 1 and 2

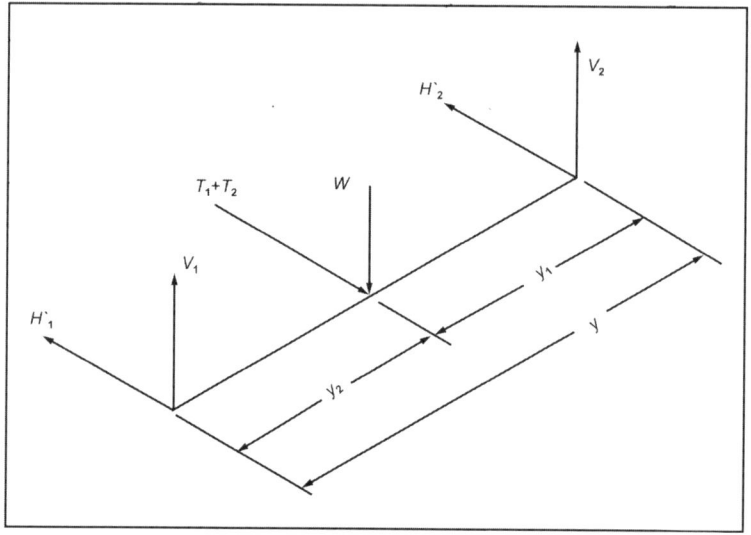

Fig. 8.26: (b) Reactions at bearings 1 and 2

→ **Horizontal reactions: [Fig. 8.26 (a)]**

$$H_1 = \frac{F_p \cdot (x+y)}{y} = \frac{176714.59 \times (310+400)}{400} = 313.57 \times 10^3 \text{ N}$$

$$H_2 = \frac{F_p \cdot x}{y} = \frac{176714.59 \times 310}{400} = 137 \times 10^3 \text{ N}$$

→ **Reactions due to weight of flywheel: [Fig. 8.26 (b)]**
Due to symmetry

$$V_1 = \frac{W \cdot y_1}{y} = \frac{10 \times 10^3 \times 200}{400} = 5000 \text{ N}$$

$$V_2 = \frac{W \cdot y_2}{y} = \frac{10 \times 10^3 \times 200}{400} = 5000 \text{ N}$$

→ **Reactions due to belt pull: [Fig. 8.26 (b)]**
Due to symmetry

$$H_1' = \frac{(T_1 + T_2) \cdot y_1}{y} = \frac{5000 \times 200}{400} = 2500 \text{ N}$$

$$H_2' = \frac{(T_1 + T_2) \cdot y_2}{y} = \frac{5000 \times 200}{400} = 2500 \text{ N}$$

d. Design of crank web:

To find width of web b

The crank web is subjected to eccentric loading. Due to this there will be two stresses acting on it, one direct compressive stress and the other bending stress due to gas load (F_p).

→ **Direct compressive stress:** $\sigma_c = \dfrac{F_p}{b \cdot t} = \dfrac{176714.59}{85b} = \dfrac{2079}{b}$ ...Eq. (i)

→ **Bending stress:** $\sigma_{b1} = \dfrac{M_1}{Z_1} = \dfrac{6 M_1}{b \cdot t^2}$ ...Eq. (ii)

The bending moment at the center of crank pin is given as

$$M_1 = F_p \times \left(0.75 l_p + \frac{t}{2}\right) = 176714.59 \times \left(0.75 \times 135 + \frac{85}{2}\right) = 25.4 \times 10^6 \text{ N-mm}$$

∴ $\sigma_{b1} = \dfrac{6 \times 25.4 \times 10^6}{b \times 85^2} = \dfrac{21095.69}{b}$ ...Eq. (iii)

→ Thus the total stress on the web, $\sigma_{c)t} = \sigma_c + \sigma_{b1} \leq \sigma_b$

$$75 = \frac{2079}{b} + \frac{21095.69}{b}$$

$$b = 309 \text{ mm} \approx 310 \text{ mm}$$

e. Design of shaft under flywheel:

The total bending moment at the flywheel location will be the resultant of horizontal bending moment due to the gas load and belt pull and the vertical bending moment due to the flywheel weight.

→ **Horizontal bending moment:**
- Horizontal bending moment at flywheel due to gas load:
$$M_W = F_p \cdot (x + y_2) - (H_1 + H_1')y_2 \approx H_2 y_1$$
$$= 176714.59 \times (310 + 200) - (313.57 \times 103 + 2500) \times 200$$
$$M_W = 26.91 \times 10^6 \text{ N-mm}$$

- Horizontal bending moment at flywheel due to belt tension:
$$M_T = \frac{(T_1 + T_2) \cdot y_1 \cdot y_2}{y} = \frac{5000 \times 200 \times 200}{400} = 500 \times 10^3 \text{ N-mm}$$

- Thus the resultant horizontal bending moment is
$$M_H = M_W + M_T$$
$$= 26.91 \times 10^6 + 500 \times 10^3$$
$$M_H = 27.41 \times 10^6 \text{ N-mm}$$

→ **Vertical bending moment:**
$$M_V = \frac{W \cdot y_1 \cdot y_2}{y} = \frac{10000 \times 200 \times 200}{400} = 1 \times 10^6 \text{ N-mm}$$

→ Thus the resultant bending moment is, $M_s = \sqrt{M_H^2 + M_V^2}$
$$= \sqrt{(27.41 \times 10^6)^2 + (1 \times 10^6)^2}$$
$$M_s = 27.43 \times 10^6 \text{ N-mm}$$

Also
$$M_s = \frac{\pi d_s^3}{32} \sigma_b$$

$$27.43 \times 10^6 = \frac{\pi d_s^3}{32} \times 75$$

$$d_s = 155 \text{ mm}$$

The value of $d_s > d_1$, if not adopt higher value.

Let us assume $d_s = 250$ mm.

Case 2: Side crankshaft at an angle of maximum torque:

a. Force components on crank pin:

→ If p' is the intensity of gas pressure on the piston at this instant, then for maximum torque condition,

force on the piston due to pressure of gas, $F_p = p' \left(\frac{\pi D^2}{4} \right) = 1 \times \left(\frac{\pi \times 300^2}{4} \right)$

$= 70.68 \times 10^3$ N

→ The thrust on the connecting rod is $F_c = \dfrac{F_p}{\cos \phi}$ ...**3.12/ Pg 45, DHB**

But $\sin \phi = \dfrac{\sin \theta}{l/r} = \dfrac{\sin 35}{4.5} = 0.1275$

$$\phi = 7.32 \text{ deg}$$

$$\therefore \quad F_c = \frac{70.68 \times 10^3}{\cos 7.32} = 71.27 \times 10^3 \text{ N}$$

→ The components of F_c are:
- Tangential component or rotative effort on crank, $F_t = F_c \sin(\theta + \phi)$
  ..3.13/ Pg 45, DHB

$$= 71.27 \times 10^3 \times \sin(35 + 7.32)$$
$$F_t = 47.98 \times 10^3 \text{ N}$$

- Radial component or force along the crank, $F_r = F_c \cos(\theta + \phi)$
  ...3.14/ Pg 45, DHB

$$= 71.27 \times 10^3 \times \cos(35 + 7.32)$$
$$F_r = 52.69 \times 10^3 \text{ N}$$

b. Bearing reactions:

It is assumed that the portion of the crankshaft between the bearings 1 and 2 is simply supported on the bearings and subjected to vertical force F_p as shown in **Fig. 8.27**.

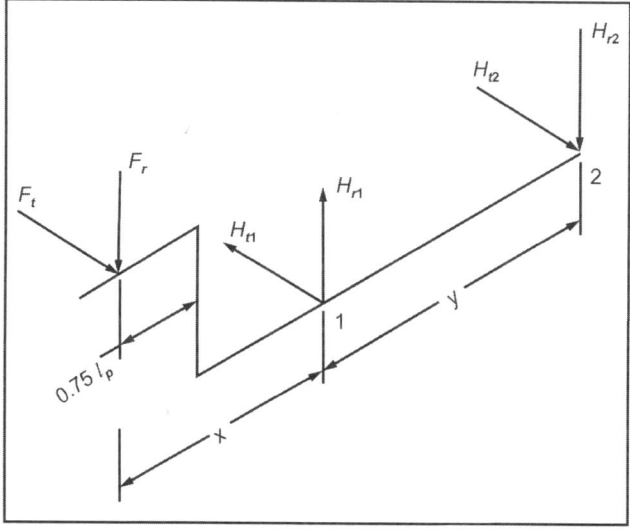

Fig. 8.27: Reactions at bearings 1 and 2

From Case 1:
- $x = 310$ mm
- $y = 400$ mm
- $y_1 = y_2 = y/2 = 400/2 = 200$ mm
- $d_p = l_p = 135$ mm
- $d_1 = 200$ mm
- $l_1 = 240$ mm
- $d_1 = 250$ mm
- Width of web, $b = 210$ mm
- Thickness of web, $t = 85$ mm

→ **Radial forces:**

$$H_{r1} = F_r \cdot \left(\frac{x+y}{z}\right) = 52.69 \times 10^3 \times \left(\frac{310+400}{400}\right) = 93.52 \times 10^3 \text{ N}$$

$$H_{r2} = \frac{F_r \cdot x}{y} = \frac{52.69 \times 10^3 \times 310}{400} = 40.83 \times 10^3 \text{ N}$$

→ **Tangential forces:**

$$H_{t1} = F_t \left(\frac{x+y}{y}\right) = 47.98 \times 10^3 \times \left(\frac{310+400}{400}\right) = 85.16 \times 10^3 \text{ N}$$

$$H_{t2} = \frac{F_t \cdot x}{y} = \frac{47.98 \times 10^3 \times 310}{400} = 37.18 \times 10^3 \text{ N}$$

- The reactions at the bearings 1 and 2, due to weight of the flywheel (W) and resultant belt pull are same as discussed in Section **8.12.1; Case 1** *(Eqs 8.115 to 8.120)*

→ **Reactions due to weight of flywheel: [Fig. 8.26 (b)]**

Due to symmetry

$$V_1 = \frac{W \cdot y_1}{y} = \frac{10 \times 10^3 \times 200}{400} = 5000 \text{ N}$$

$$V_2 = \frac{W \cdot y_2}{y} = \frac{10 \times 10^3 \times 200}{400} = 5000 \text{ N}$$

→ **Reactions due to belt pull: [Fig. 8.26 (b)]**

Due to symmetry

$$H_1' = \frac{(T_1+T_2) \cdot y_1}{y} = \frac{5000 \times 200}{400} = 2500 \text{ N}$$

$$H_2' = \frac{(T_1+T_2) \cdot y_2}{y} = \frac{5000 \times 200}{400} = 2500 \text{ N}$$

c. Design of crank pin:

Check for shear stress

→ The bending moment in the crank pin is

$$M_p = F_r \cdot (0.75 l_p) = 52.69 \times 10^3 \times (0.75 \times 135) = 5.33 \times 10^6 \text{ N-mm}$$

→ The twisting moment on the crankpin is, $T_p = F_t \cdot r$

$$r = L_s / 2 = 350/2 = 175 \text{ mm}$$
$$= 47.98 \times 10^3 \times 175$$
$$T_p = 8.39 \times 10^6 \text{ N-mm}$$

→ Thus, the equivalent torque on the crank pin is, $T_e = \sqrt{M_p^2 + T_p^2}$

$$= \sqrt{(5.33 \times 10^6)^2 + (8.39 \times 10^6)^2}$$

$$T_e = 9.94 \times 10^6 \text{ N-mm}$$

Also $\quad T_e = \dfrac{\pi d_p^3}{16} \tau$

Assume $\tau = 0.5\sigma_b = 0.5 \times 75 = 37.5$ MPa ≈ 40 MPa

$$9.94 \times 10^6 = \dfrac{\pi \times 135^3}{16} = 20.57 \text{ MPa} < 40 \text{ MPa}$$

$$\tau = 20.57 \text{ MPa} < 40 \text{ MPa}$$

Hence design of crank pin is safe.

d. Design of crank web:

The crank web is subjected to the following stresses:
i. Bending stresses in two planes normal to each other, due to the radial and tangential components of F_p.
ii. Direct compressive stress due to F_r, and
iii. Torsional stress.

Check for maximum compressive stress:

→ The bending moment due to the radial component is

$$M_r = \dfrac{b.t^2}{6} \cdot \sigma_{br}$$

But $\quad M_r = F_r \cdot \left(0.75 l_p + \dfrac{t}{2}\right)$

$$= 52.69 \times 10^3 \times \left(0.75 \times 135 + \dfrac{85}{2}\right)$$

$$M_r = 7.57 \times 10^6 \text{ N-mm}$$

$\therefore \quad 7.57 \times 10^6 = \dfrac{210 \times 85^2}{6} \times \sigma_{br}$

$$\sigma_{br} = 29.95 \text{ MPa}$$

→ The bending moment due to the tangential component is

$$M_t = \dfrac{t.b^2}{6} \cdot \sigma_{bt}$$

But $\quad M_t = F_t \cdot \left(r - \dfrac{d_1}{2}\right)$

$$= 47.98 \times 10^3 \times \left(175 - \dfrac{200}{2}\right)$$

$$M_t = 3.60 \times 10^6 \text{ N-mm}$$

$\therefore \quad 3.60 \times 10^6 = \dfrac{85 \times 210^2}{6} \times \sigma_{bt}$

$$\sigma_{bt} = 5.76 \text{ MPa}$$

→ The direct compressive stress is given by, $\sigma_{dc} = \dfrac{F_r}{bt} = \dfrac{52.69 \times 10^3}{210 \times 85} = 2.95$ MPa

→ The maximum compressive stress is calculated as
$$\sigma_c = \sigma_{br} + \sigma_{bt} + \sigma_{dc}$$
$$= 29.95 + 5.76 + 2.95$$
$$\sigma_c = 38.66 \text{ MPa}$$

→ The twisting moment on the arm,
$$\tau = \dfrac{T}{Z_p} = \dfrac{4.5T}{b.t^2}$$

But $T = F_t \cdot \left(0.75 l_p + \dfrac{t}{2}\right)$

$$= 47.98 \times 10^3 \times \left(0.75 \times 135 + \dfrac{85}{2}\right)$$

$$T = 6.89 \times 10^6 \text{ N-mm}$$

∴ $\tau = \dfrac{4.5 \times 6.89 \times 10^6}{210 \times 85^2}$

$\tau = 20.46$ MPa

→ Thus, the maximum or total combined stress,

$$(\sigma_c)_{max} = \dfrac{\sigma_c}{2} + \sqrt{\left(\dfrac{\sigma_c}{2}\right)^2 + \tau^2} \qquad \text{...1.11a / Pg 2, DHB}$$

$$= \dfrac{38.66}{2} + \sqrt{\left(\dfrac{38.66}{2}\right)^2 + 20.46^2}$$

$(\sigma_c)_{max} = 47.48$ MPa < 75 MPa

Hence design of crank web is safe.

Note: The value of (σ_c) should be within safe limits. If it exceeds the safe value, then the dimension b may be increased because it does not affect other dimensions.

e. Design of shaft at the juncture of crank arm/web:

Check for shear stress:

→ The bending moment bending moment at the junction of the crank,
$$M_{s1} = F_c \cdot (0.75\, l_p + t)$$
$$= 71.27 \times 10^3 \times (0.75 \times 135 + 85)$$
$$M_{s1} = 13.27 \times 10^6 \text{ N-mm}$$

→ The twisting moment $T_{s1} = F_t \cdot r = (47.98 \times 10^3) \times 175 = 8.40 \times 10^6$ N-mm

→ Thus the equivalent twisting moment at the juncture of crank arm

$$T_{es1} = \sqrt{M_{s1}^2 + T_{s1}^2}$$

$$= \sqrt{(13.27 \times 10^6)^2 + (8.40 \times 10^6)^2}$$

$$T_{es1} = 15.71 \times 10^6 \text{ N-mm}$$

Also
$$T_{es1} = \frac{\pi d_{s1}^3}{16} \tau \text{ (assume } d_{s1} = d_1 = 200 \text{ mm)}$$

$$15.71 \times 10^6 = \frac{\pi \times 200^3}{16} \times \tau$$

$$\tau = 10 \text{ MPa} < 40 \text{ MPa}$$

Hence safe.

f. Design of shaft under flywheel:

Check for shear stress:

The total bending moment at the flywheel location will be the resultant of horizontal bending moment due to the gas load and belt pull and the vertical bending moment due to the flywheel weight.

→ **Horizontal bending moment:**
- Horizontal bending moment due to radial component:
$$M_W = F_r \cdot (x + y^2) - (H_{r1} + V_1) y^2$$
$$= 52.69 \times 10^3 \times (310 + 200) - (93.52 \times 10^3 + 5000) \times 200$$
$$M_W = 7.16 \times 10^6 \text{ N-mm}$$
- Horizontal bending moment due to tangential component:
$$M_T = F_t \cdot (x + y_2) - (H_{t1} + H_1') y_2$$
$$= 47.98 \times 10^3 \times (310 + 200) - (85.16 \times 10^3 + 2500) \times 200$$
$$M_T = 6.94 \times 10^6 \text{ N-mm}$$
- Thus, the resultant horizontal bending moment is
$$M_H = M_W + M_T$$
$$= 7.16 \times 10^6 + 6.94 \times 10^6$$
$$M_H = 14.09 \times 10^6 \text{ N-mm}$$

→ **Vertical bending moment:**
$$M_V = \frac{W \cdot y_1 \cdot y_2}{y} = \frac{10000 \times 200 \times 200}{400} = 1 \times 10^6 \text{ N-mm}$$

→ Thus, the resultant bending moment is,
$$M_S = \sqrt{M_H^2 + M_V^2}$$
$$= \sqrt{(14.09 \times 10^6)^2 + (1 \times 10^6)^2}$$
$$M_S = 14.125 \times 10^6 \text{ N-mm}$$

→ The twisting moment on the shaft, $T_s = F_t \cdot r = 47.98 \times 10^3 \times 175 = 8.40 \times 10^6$ N-mm

→ Thus, the equivalent twisting moment on the shaft is,
$$T_{es} = \sqrt{M_s^2 + T_s^2}$$

$$= \sqrt{(14.125 \times 10^6)^2 + (8.40 \times 10^6)^2}$$

$$T_S = 16.43 \times 10^6 \text{ N-mm}$$

Also $\quad T_{es} = \dfrac{\pi d_s^3}{16} \tau$

$$16.43 \times 10^6 = \dfrac{\pi \times 250^3}{16} \times \tau$$

$$\tau = 5.36 \text{ MPa} < 40 \text{ MPa}$$

Hence safe.

VTU QUESTION PAPERS

June/ July 2013 (10ME62)

1. Design a cast iron piston for a single acting four stroke diesel engine with the following data:
Cylinder bore = 200 mm, length of stroke = 250 mm, speed = 600 rpm, brake mean effective pressure = 0.60 MPa, maximum gas pressure = 4 MPa, fuel consumption = 0.25 kg per BP per hour, μd ratio for bush in small end of connecting rod = 1.5
(20 Marks)

Dec.2013/ Jan.2014 (10ME62)

2. a. Explain the considerations given in the design of pistons for IC engines.
(05 Marks)
   b. Design a trunk piston for an IC engine. The piston is made of cast iron with an allowable stress of 38.5 MPa. The bore of the cylinder is 200 mm and the maximum explosion pressure is 0.4 MPa. The permissible bending stress of the material of the gudgeon pin is 100 MPa. The bearing pressure in the gudgeon pin bearing of the connecting rod is to be taken as 200 MPa. **(15 Marks)**

ADDENDUM FOR DESIGN DATA HANDBOOK

Design Data Handbook (Third edition) (Old edition)		Design Data Handbook (Fourth edition) (New edition)	
Equation/Table/Fig. No.	Page No.	Equation/Table/Fig. No.	Page No.
Design of Curved Beams			
Eq. 10.1	132	Eq. 10.1(a)	159
Eq. 10.2a	132	Eq. 10.1(c)	159
Eq. 10.2b	132	Eq. 10.1(b)	159
Eq. 10.3a	132	Eq. 10.2(a)	159
Eq. 10.3b	132	Eq. 10.2(b)	159
Eq. 10.5	133	Eq. 10.5	160
Eq. 10.6	133	Eq. 10.6	161
Eq. 10.7	133	Eq. 10.6	161
Eq. 10.8	133	Eq. 10.8	161
Fig. 10.2	137	Fig. 10.1	160
Fig. 10.3	137	Fig. 10.3	160
Fig. 10.4	137	Fig. 10.5	161
Fig. 10.5	137	Fig. 10.5	161
Table 10.1	134	Table 10.1	162
Cylinders and Cylinder Heads			
Cylinders			
Eq. 7.1	75	Eq. 7.1(a)	99
Eq. 7.2a	75	Eq. 7.1(b)	99
Eq. 7.2b	75	Eq. 7.1(c)	99
Eq. 7.3	75	Eq. 7.1(d)	100
Eq. 7.6	75	Eq. 7.3	100
Eq. 7.14	78	Eq. 7.10(a)	102
Eq. 7.15	79	Eq. 7.10(b)	102
Eq. 7.15a	79	Eq. 7.10(c)	102
Eq. 7.15b	79	Eq. 7.10(c)	102
Eq. 7.16	79	Eq. 7.11(a)	103
Eq. 7.17	79	Eq. 7.11(b)	103
Eq. 7.18	79	Eq. 7.11(c)	103
Eq. 7.19	79	Eq. 7.11(d)	103
Eq. 7.20	79	Eq. 7.11(e)	103
Eq. 7.21	79	Eq. 7.11(f)	103
Eq. 7.22	79	Eq. 7.11(g)	103
Eq. 7.23	79	Eq. 7.11(h)	103
Eq. 7.24	79	Eq. 7.12(a)	103
Eq. 7.25	80	Eq. 7.12(b)	103
Eq. 7.26	80	Eq. 7.12(c)	103
Eq. 7.27	80	Eq. 7.13(a)	103

Design Data Handbook (Third edition) (Old edition)		Design Data Handbook (Fourth edition) (New edition)	
Equation/Table/Fig. No.	Page No.	Equation/Table/Fig. No.	Page No.
Cylinder Heads			
Eq. 7.28	80	Eq. 7.13(b)	104
Eq. 7.29	80	Eq. 7.13(c)	104
Eq. 7.30	80	Eq. 7.13(d)	104
Eq. 7.31	80	Eq. 7.14(a)	104
Eq. 7.32	80	Eq. 7.14(b)	104
Eq. 7.33	80	Eq. 7.15(a)	104
Eq. 7.35	81	Eq. 7.16(a)	104
Eq. 7.36	81	Eq. 7.16(b)	104
Eq. 7.37	81	Eq. 7.16(c)	105
Eq. 7.38	81	Eq. 7.16(d)	105
Eq. 7.39	81	Eq. 7.17(a)	105
Eq. 7.40	82	Eq. 7.17(b)	105
Eq. 7.41	82	Eq. 7.18(a)	105
Eq. 7.42	82	Eq. 7.18(b)	105
Eq. 7.43	82	Eq. 7.19(a)	105
Eq. 7.44	82	Eq. 7.19(b)	106
Table 7.1	83	Table 7.1	107
Table 7.2	84	Table 7.2	108
Eq. 8.1	86	Eq. 8.1	110
Eq. 8.2	86	Eq. 8.2	110
Eq. 8.6	87	Eq. 8.6	111
Eq. 8.7	87	Eq. 8.7	111
Eq. 8.8	87	Eq. 8.8	111
Eq. 8.9	88	Eq. 8.9	111
Eq. 8.10	88	Eq. 8.10	113
Eq. 8.11	88	Eq. 8.11	113
Eq. 8.12	88	Eq. 8.12	113
Eq. 8.14	88	Eq. 8.14	113
Eq. 8.15	88	Eq. 8.15	113
Eq. 8.16	89	Eq. 8.16	113
Eq. 8.17	89	Eq. 8.17	113
Table 8.1	90	Table 8.1	114
Table 8.2	93	Table 8.2	117
Table 8.5	97	Table 8.5	121
Table 8.7	98	Table 8.7	122
Fig. 8.1	101	Fig. 8.1	112
Fig. 8.2	101	Fig. 8.2	112
Fig. 8.3	102	Fig. 8.3	112

Contd...

Addendum

Design Data Handbook (Third edition) (Old edition)		Design Data Handbook (Fourth edition) (New edition)	
Equation/Table/Fig. No.	Page No.	Equation/Table/Fig. No.	Page No.
Belts, Ropes and Chain Drives			
Flat Belts			
Eq. 14.1a	238	Eq. 14.1(a)	289
Eq. 14.1b	238	Eq. 14.1(b)	289
Eq. 14.2	238	Eq. 14.2(a)	289
Eq. 14.3	238	Eq. 14.2(b)	290
Eq. 14.4	238	Eq. 14.2(c)	290
Eq. 14.5	238	Eq. 14.2(d)	290
Eq. 14.6a	238	Eq. 14.3(a)	290
Eq. 14.6b	238	Eq. 14.3(b)	290
Eq. 14.6c	238	Eq. 14.3(c)	290
Eq. 14.6d	238	Eq. 14.3(d)	290
Eq. 14.7a	239	Eq. 14.3(e)	291
Eq. 14.7b	239	Eq. 14.3(f)	291
Eq. 14.8	239	Eq. 14.4	291
Eq. 14.9a	239	Eq. 14.5(a)	291
Eq. 14.10a	239	Eq. 14.6(a)	291
Eq. 14.10c	239	Eq. 14.6(c)	291
Eq. 14.11	240	Eq. 14.7	291
Eq. 14.12	240	Eq. 14.8	291
Eq. 14.13a	240	Eq. 14.9(a)	292
Eq. 14.13b	240	Eq. 14.9(b)	292
Table 14.1	251	Table 14.1	305
Table 14.2	252	Table 14.3	306
Table 14.3	253	Table 14.2(a)	305
Table 14.4	253	Table 14.2(b)	305
Table 14.5	254	Table 14.4	307
Table 14.6	254	Table 14.5	307
Table 14.7	255	Table 14.6	308
Table 14.9	257	Table 14.8	310
Table 14.10a	258	Table 14.9(a)	311
Table 14.10b	258	Table 14.9(b)	311
Table 14.10e	259	Table 14.12	312
V Belts			
Eq. 14.26	242	Eq. 14.12	294
Eq. 14.27a to 14.27e	243	Eq. 14.13(a) to 14.13(e)	295
Eq. 14.28	244	Eq. 14.14	295
Eq. 14.29	244	Eq. 14.15(a)	295
Eq. 14.30	244	Eq. 14:15(b)	295
Eq. 14.31a	244	Eq. 14.16(a)	295
Table 14.12	261	Table 14.14	314
Table 14.13	262	Table 14.17	315
Table 14.14	264	Table 14.18(a)	317
Table 14.15	265	Table 14.18(b)	318
Table 14.16	266	Table 14.18(c)	319

Contd...

Design Data Handbook (Third edition) (Old edition)		Design Data Handbook (Fourth edition) (New edition)	
Equation/Table/Fig. No.	Page No.	Equation/Table/Fig. No.	Page No.
Table 14.17	267	Table 14.18(d)	320
Table 14.18	268	Table 14.18(e)	321
Table 14.19	269	Table 14.15	314
Table 14.20	269	Table 14.19	322
Table 14.21	271	Table 14.20	323
Table 14.22	273	Table 14.21	325
Table 14.23	274	Table 14.16	314
Table 14.24	274	Table 14.24	328
Table 14.25	275	Table 14.22	326
Wire Ropes			
Eq. 14.44	246	Eq. 14.20(b)	298
Table 14.27	277	Table 14.25	328
Table 14.27a	279	Table 14.26(a)	331
Table 14.28	280	Table 14.27	332
Table 14.29	281	Table 14.28	333
Table 14.30	282	Table 14.29	334
Table 14.31	283	Table 14.30	336
Table 14.32	284	Table 14.31	337
Table 14.33	285	Table 14.33	338
Table 14.34	285	Table 14.32	337
Chain Drives			
Eq. 14.49	247	Eq. 14.22(a)	300
Eq. 14.50	247	Eq. 14.22(b)	300
Eq. 14.51a	247	Eq. 14.22(c)	300
Eq. 14.52	247	Eq. 14.22(e)	300
Eq. 14.53a	248	Eq. 14.22(f)	300
Eq. 14.54	248	Eq. 14.22(h)	301
Eq. 14.55	248	Eq. 14.22(i)	301
Eq. 14.56	248	Eq. 14.22(j)	301
Eq. 14.57a	248	Eq. 14.22(k)	301
Eq. 14.27b	248	Eq. 14.22(l)	301
Eq. 14.58	248	Eq. 14.22(m)	301
Eq. 14.59	248	Eq. 14.22(n)	301
Eq. 14.60	249	Eq. 14.22(o)	301
Table 14.11b	260	Table 14.13(b)	313
Table 14.36	286	Table 14.35	338
Table 14.37a	286	Table 14.36(a)	339
Table 14.37b	286	Table 14.36(b)	339
Table 14.38	287	Table 14.37	339
Table 14.39	287A	Table 14.38	339
Table 14.40a	287B	Table 14.39(a)	340
Table 14.40b	288	Table 14.39(b)	341
Table 14.41	289	Table 14.40	342
Table 14.42	290	Table 14.41	343
Table 14.43	293	Table 14.43	346
Table 14.44	295	Table 14.44	348
Fig. 14.14	298	Fig. 14.13(b)	304
Fig. 14.16	298	Fig. 14.13(a)	303
Fig. 14.19	299	Fig. 14.14	304

Contd...

Design Data Handbook (Third edition) (Old edition)		Design Data Handbook (Fourth edition) (New edition)	
Equation/Table/Fig. No.	Page No.	Equation/Table/Fig. No.	Page No.
Springs			
Eq. 11.1a	139	Eq. 11.1(d)	169
Eq. 11.2a	139	Eq. 11.2(b)	169
Eq. 11.2b	139	Eq. 11.2(a)	169
Eq. 11.2c	139	Eq. 11.2(c)	169
Eq. 11.2d	139	Eq. 11.2(d)	169
Eq. 11.4	139	Eq. 11.4	170
Eq. 11.5a	139	Eq. 11.5(a)	170
Eq. 11.5b	139	Eq. 11.5(b)	170
Eq. 11.6	139	Eq. 11.6	170
Eq. 11.7a	139	Eq. 11.7(a)	170
Eq. 11.7b	139	Eq. 11.7(b)	170
Eq. 11.8	139	Eq. 11.8	171
Eq. 11.9	140	Eq. 11.9	171
Eq. 11.13b	140	Eq. 11.12(b)	171
Eq. 11.14	140	Eq. 11.13(a)	171
Eq. 11.14a	141	Eq. 11.13(b)	172
Eq. 11.14b	141	Eq. 11.13(c)	172
Eq. 11.16	141	Eq. 11.15(a)	173
Eq. 11.17	141	Eq. 11.15(b)	173
Eq. 11.18f	142	Eq. 11.116(f)	173
Eq. 11.18g	142	Eq. 11.116(g)	173
Eq. 11.20a	142	Eq. 11.18(a)	174
Eq. 11.20b	142	Eq. 11.18(b)	174
Eq. 11.20c	142	Eq. 11.18(c)	174
Eq. 11.24a	143	Eq. 11.22(a)	177
Eq. 11.24b	144	Eq. 11.22(b)	177
Eq. 11.24c	144	Eq. 11.22(c)	177
Eq. 11.24d	144	Eq. 11.22(d)	178
Eq. 11.28	144A	Eq. 11.26	179
Eq. 11.29a	144A	Eq. 11.25(a)	179
Eq. 11.29b	144A	Eq. 11.25(b)	179
Eq. 11.30	144A	Eq. 11.26	179
Eq. 11.31	144A	Eq. 11.27(a)	179
Eq. 11.32	144A	Eq. 11.27(b)	179
Eq. 11.33	144A	Eq. 11.27(c)	179
Eq. 11.34	144A	Eq. 11.27(d)	180
Eq. 11.35	145	Eq. 11.28(a)	180
Eq. 11.36	145	Eq. 11.28(b)	180
Eq. 11.37	145	Eq. 11.28(c)	180
Eq. 11.38	145	Eq. 11.29(a)	181

Contd...

Design Data Handbook (Third edition) (Old edition)		Design Data Handbook (Fourth edition) (New edition)	
Equation/Table/Fig. No.	Page No.	Equation/Table/Fig. No.	Page No.
Eq. 11.39a	145	Eq. 11.29(b)	181
Eq. 11.39b	145	Eq. 11.29(c)	181
Eq. 11.39c	145	Eq. 11.29(d)	181
Eq. 11.40a	145	Eq. 11.30(a)	182
Eq. 11.40b	145	Eq. 11.30(b)	182
Eq. 11.40c	145	Eq. 11.30(c)	182
Eq. 11.41a	145	Eq. 11.31(a)	182
Eq. 11.41b	145	Eq. 11.31(b)	182
Eq. 11.41c	145	Eq. 11.31(c)	182
Eq. 11.42a	145	Eq. 11.32(a)	182
Eq. 11.42b	146	Eq. 11.32(b)	182
Eq. 11.42c	146	Eq. 11.32(c)	182
Eq. 11.44	146	Eq. 11.33(a)	183
Eq. 11.45a	146	Eq. 11.33(b)	183
Eq. 11.45b	146	Eq. 11.33(c)	183
Eq. 11.45c	146	Eq. 11.33(d)	183
Eq. 11.45d	146	Eq. 11.33(e)	183
Eq. 11.45e	146	Eq. 11.33(f)	183
Table 11.1	149	Table 11.9	198
Table 11.2	149	Table 11.1	188
Table 11.3a	150	Table 11.2	189
Table 11.4	150	Table 11.10(a)	198
Table 11.5	151	Table 11.10(b)	198
Table 11.6	151	Table 11.3	189
Table 11.7	152	Table 11.4	189
Table 11.8	153	Table 11.5	190
Table 11.12	155B	Table 11.6(d)	194
Table 11.13	155B	Table 11.6(e)	194
Table 11.14	155C	Table 11.7	195
Fig. 11.1	156	Fig. 11.3	169
Fig. 11.2a	156	Fig. 11.4	170
Fig. 11.2b	156	Fig. 11.5	172
Fig. 11.3h	157B	Fig. 11.9(a)	178
Fig. 11.3i	157B	Fig. 11.9(b)	178
Fig. 11.6	157C	Fig. 11.10	180
Fig. 11.7	157C	Fig. 11.13	184
Fig. 11.7a	157C	Fig. 11.13(e)	168
Others			
Eq. 2.19a	17	Eq. 2.15(a)	23
Eq. 2.17a	17	Eq. 2.13(a)	23
Table 1.4	10	Table 1.4	15

Contd...

Addendum

Design Data Handbook (Third edition) (Old edition)		Design Data Handbook (Fourth edition) (New edition)	
Equation/Table/Fig. No.	Page No.	Equation/Table/Fig. No.	Page No.
Spur Gears			
Eq. 12.1	162	Eq. 12.1(a)	203
Eq. 12.2	162	Eq. 12.1(b)	203
Eq. 12.3	162	Eq. 12.1(c)	203
Eq. 12.4	162	Eq. 12.1(d)	203
Eq. 12.5	163	Eq. 12.1(e)	203
Eq. 12.14a	163	Eq. 12.4(a)	205
Eq. 12.15	163	Eq. 12.5(a)	204
Eq. 12.16	163	Eq. 12.5(b)	204
Eq. 12.17a	163	Eq. 12.15(c)	204
Eq. 12.17b	163	Eq. 12.15(d)	204
Eq. 12.17c	163	Eq. 12.15(e)	204
Eq. 12.18	164	Eq. 12.5(f)	205
Eq. 12.19a	164	Eq. 12.6(a)	205
Eq. 12.19b	164	Eq. 12.6(b)	205
Eq. 12.19c	164	Eq. 12.6(c)	205
Eq. 12.19d	164	Eq. 12.6(d)	205
Eq. 12.19e	164	Eq. 12.6(e)	205
Eq. 12.20a	164	Eq. 12.7(a)	205
Eq. 12.22	165	Eq. 12.8(a)	206
Eq. 12.23	165	Eq. 12.8(b)	206
Eq. 12.4a	165	Eq. 12.8(c)	206
Eq. 12.24b	165		
Eq. 12.25	165	Eq. 12.9(a)	206
Eq. 12.26	165	Eq. 12.9(b)	206
Eq. 12.33	166	Eq. 12.12	207
Eq. 12.34	166	Eq. 12.13(a)	207
Eq. 12.35a	166	Eq. 12.13(b)	208
Eq. 12.35b	166	Eq. 12.13(c)	208
Eq. 12.35c	166	Eq. 12.13(d)	208
Eq. 12.36a	167	Eq. 12.15(a)	208
Eq. 12.36b	167	Eq. 12.15(b)	208
Eq. 12.36c	167	Eq. 12.15(c)	208
Eq. 12.36d	167	Eq. 12.15(d)	208
Table 12.2	182	Table 12.2	229
Table 12.7	186	Table 12.7	234
Table 12.8	187	Table 12.8	235
Table 12.8a	187	Table 12.9	235
Table 12.9	188	Table 12.4(c)	231
Table 12.12	190	Table 12.12	236
Table 12.13	191	Table 12.13	237
Table 12.14	191	Table 12.14	237
Table 12.15	192	Table 12.15	238
Table 12.16	193	Table 12.16	239
Table 12.17	194	Table 12.17	240
Fig. 12.4	205	Fig. 12.5	209

Contd…

Design Data Handbook (Third edition) (Old edition)		Design Data Handbook (Fourth edition) (New edition)	
Equation/Table/Fig. No.	Page No.	Equation/Table/Fig. No.	Page No.
Helical Gears			
Eq. 12.43	168	Eq. 12.19(a)	211
Eq. 12.44	168	Eq. 12.19(b)	211
Eq. 12.45	168	Eq. 12.19(c)	211
Eq. 12.46	168	Eq. 12.19(d)	211
Eq. 12.47	168	Eq. 12.19(e)	211
Ea. 12.50	169	Eq. 12.20	211
Eq. 12.51	169	Eq. 12.21	211
Eq. 12.52a	169	Eq. 12.22(a)	211
Eq. 12.52b	169	Eq. 12.22(b)	211
Eq. 12.54	169	Eq. 12.23(b)	213
Eq. 12.56	169	Eq. 12.23(d)	213
Eq. 12.58a	169	Eq. 12.23(f)	213
Eq. 12.58b	169	Eq. 12.23(g)	213
Eq. 12.59	169	Eq. 12.24(a)	214
Eq. 12.60	170	Eq. 12.24(b)	214
Eq. 12.61a	170	Eq. 12.25(a)	214
Eq. 12.61b	170	Eq. 12.25(b)	214
Eq. 12.61c	170	Eq. 12.25(c)	214
Eq. 12.61d	170	Eq. 12.25(d)	214
Eq. 12.61e	170	Eq. 12.25(e)	214
Eq. 12.62	170	Eq. 12.26(a)	214
Eq. 12.63	170	Eq. 12.26(b)	214
Eq. 12.64	170	Eq. 12.26(c)	214
Eq. 12.65	170		214
Table 12.2	182	Table 12.2	229
Table 12.7	186	Table 12.7	234
Table 12.8	187	Table 12.8	235
Table 12.8a	187	Table 12.9	235
Table 12.9	188	Table 12.4(c)	231
Table 12.12	190	Table 12.12	236
Table 12.13	191	Table 12.13	237
Table 12.14	191	Table 12.14	237
Table 12.15	192	Table 12.15	238
Table 12.16	193	Table 12.16	239
Table 12.17	194	Table 12.17	240
Table 12.20	195	Table 12.20	241
Table 12.21	196	Table 12.21	241

Contd…

Note: Some of the equations and tables are common to both spur and helical gears.

Addendum **785**

Design Data Handbook (Third edition) (Old edition)		Design Data Handbook (Fourth edition) (New edition)	
Equation/Table/Fig. No.	Page No.	Equation/Table/Fig. No.	Page No.
Bevel Gears			
Eq. 12.67	171	Eq. 12.29(a)	215
Eq. 12.68	171	Eq. 12.29(b)	215
Eq. 12.72a	172	Eq. 12.32(a)	217
Eq. 12.72b	172	Eq. 12.32(b)	217
Eq.12.73a	172	Eq. 12.31(a)	217
Eq. 12.73b	172	Eq. 12.31(b)	217
Eq. 12.74	172	Eq. 12.33	217
Eq. 12.75	172	Eq. 12.34(a)	217
Eq. 12.76	172	Eq. 12.34(b)	217
Eq. 12.77	173	Eq. 12.34(c)	219
Eq. 12.81	173	Eq. 12.35(d)	218
Eq. 12.82	173	Eq. 12.35(e)	218
Eq. 12.83a	173	Eq. 12.36(a)	219
Eq. 12.83b	173	Eq. 12.36(b)	219
Eq. 12.84	173	Eq. 12.36(c) & (d)	218
Eq. 12.85	173	Eq. 12.37	218
Eq. 12.86a	174	Eq. 12.38(a)	219
Eq. 12.86b	174	Eq. 12.38(b)	219
Eq. 12.87	174	Eq. 12.39	219
Eq. 12.88	174	Eq. 12.40	219
Eq. 12.89	174	Eq. 12.41	219
Eq. 12.91a	174	Eq. 12.43(a)	219
Eq. 12.92	175	Eq. 12.45(a)	219
Eq. 12.93	175	Eq. 12.45(d)	219
Eq. 12.94	175	Eq. 12.45(e)	219
Table 12.22	196	Table 12.23(a)	242
Table 12.23	197	Table 12.24	242
Table 12.24	197	Table 12.25	242
Fig. 12.7	206	Fig. 12.9(b)	216
Fig. 12.8	207	Fig. 12.10	217
Fig. 12.9	207	Fig. 12.11	218
Fig. 12.10	207	Fig. 12.12	218
Worm Gears			
Eq. 12.96	175	Eq. 12.46(g)	221
Eq. 12.97a	175	Eq. 12.46(h)	221
Eq. 12.97b	175	Eq. 12.46(i)	221

Contd…

Design of Machine Elements II (DME II)

Design Data Handbook (Third edition) (Old edition)		Design Data Handbook (Fourth edition) (New edition)	
Equation/Table/Fig. No.	Page No.	Equation/Table/Fig. No.	Page No.
Eq. 12.98	175	Eq. 12.46(b)	220
Eq. 12.99	175	Eq. 12.46(d)	221
Eq. 12.100	175	Eq. 12.46(e)	221
Eq. 12.101	175	Eq. 12.49	223
Eq. 12.102	176	Eq. 12.50	223
Eq. 12.103	176	Eq. 12.51(a)	223
Eq. 12.104	176	Eq. 12.52(a)	223
Eq. 12.105	176	Eq. 12.52(b)	223
Eq. 12.106	176	Eq. 12.53(a)	223
Eq. 12.107	176	Eq. 12.53(b)	223
Eq. 12.108	176	Eq. 12.53(c)	223
Eq. 12.109	177	Eq. 12.53(d)	223
Eq. 12.110	177	Eq. 12.54	223
Eq. 12.115	177	Eq. 12.57(b)	225
Eq. 12.116	177	Eq. 12.57(c)	225
Eq. 12.117	177	Eq. 12.57(d)	225
Eq. 12.118a	178	Eq. 12.58(a)	225
Eq. 12.118b	178	Eq. 12.58(b)	225
Eq. 12.120a	178	Eq. 12.60(a)	226
Eq. 12.120b	178	Eq. 12.60(b)	226
Eq. 12.121	179	Eq. 12.61	226
Eq. 12.122	179	Eq. 12.62(a)	227
Eq. 12.123	179	Eq. 12.62(b)	227
Eq. 12.124a	179	Eq. 12.63(a)	227
Eq. 12.124b	180	Eq. 12.63(b)	227
Eq. 12.124c	180	Eq. 12.63(c)	227
Eq. 12.125	180	Eq. 12.64	227
Eq. 12.130a	180	Eq. 12.68(a)	228
Table 12.25	198	Table 12.26	243
Table 12.26	199	Table 12.27	244
Table 12.27	199	Table 12.28(a)	244
Table 12.28	199	Table 12.28(b)	244
Table 12.29	199	Table 12.28(c)	244
Table 12.30	200	Table 12.29	245
Table 12.31	202	Table 12.30	246
Table 12.32	202	Table 12.31	247
Table 12.33	203	Table 12.32	247
Table 12.34	203	Table 12.33	248

Contd...

Note: Some of the equations and tables are common to spur, helical, bevel and worm gears.

Design Data Handbook (Third edition) (Old edition)		Design Data Handbook (Fourth edition) (New edition)	
Equation/Table/Fig. No.	Page No.	Equation/Table/Fig. No.	Page No.
Clutches and Brakes			
Clutches			
Eq. 13.32	213	Eq. 13.9(d)	258
Eq. 13.33a	213	Eq. 13.9(b)	258
Eq. 13.33b	213	Eq. 13.9(g)	259
Eq. 13.34	213	Eq. 13.9(c) & (f)	258, 259
Eq. 13.36	214	Eq. 13.10(b)	259
Eq. 13.37	214	Eq. 13.10(c)	259
Eq. 13.38	214	Eq. 13.10(d)	259
Eq. 13.39a	214	Eq. 13.10(e)	260
Eq. 13.40	214	Eq. 13.10(g)	260
Eq. 13.41	214	Eq. 13.10(h)	260
Eq. 13.42	215	Eq. 13.10(j)	260
Eq. 13.43	215	Eq. 13.10(k)	260
Eq. 13.44	215	Eq. 13.10(l)	260
Table 13.2a	228	Table 13.4	283
Table 13.2b	229	Table 13.5	284
Fig. 13.9	234	Fig. 13.10	258
Fig. 13.10	235	Fig. 13.11	259
Others			
Eq. 3.1	42	Eq. 3.1	50
Table 3.5a	48	Table 3.5(a)	57
Table 12.34	203	Table 12.33	248
Brakes			
Eq. 13.62	218	Eq. 13.15(a)	264
Eq. 13.63	218	Eq. 13.15(b)	264
Eq. 13.64	218	Eq. 13.15(c)	264
Eq. 13.65	218	Eq. 13.15(d)	264
Eq. 13.66	218	Eq. 13.15(f)	264
Eq. 13.67	218	Eq. 13.16(a)	264
Eq. 13.69	219	Eq. 13.16(m)	266
Eq. 13.70	219	Eq. 13.16(n)	266
Eq. 13.71a	219	Eq. 13.17(a)	267
Eq. 13.71b	219	Eq. 13.17(a)	267
Eq. 13.72a	219	Eq. 13.17(b)	267
Eq. 13.72b	219	Eq. 13.17(c)	267

Contd...

Design of Machine Elements II (DME II)

Design Data Handbook (Third edition) (Old edition)		Design Data Handbook (Fourth edition) (New edition)	
Equation/Table/Fig. No.	Page No.	Equation/Table/Fig. No.	Page No.
Eq. 13.73a	219	Eq. 13.17(d)	267
Eq. 13.73b	219	Eq. 13.17(e)	267
Eq. 13.74a	220	Eq. 13.19(b)	270
Eq. 13.74b	220	Eq. 13.19(a)	270
Eq. 13.75a	220	Eq. 13.19(c)	270
Eq. 13.75b	220	Eq. 13.19(d)	270
Eq. 13.76a	220	Eq. 13.19(e)	270
Eq. 13.76b	220	Eq. 13.19(f)	270
Eq. 13.77a	221	Eq. 13.19(g)	270
Eq. 13.77b	221	Eq. 13.19(h) & (i)	270
Eq. 13.78	221	Eq. 13.18(k)	268
Eq. 13.79	221	Eq. 13.18(l)	269
Eq. 13.80	221	Eq. 13.18(m)	269
Eq. 13.81	221	Eq. 13.18(n)	269
Eq. 13.82	221	Eq. 13.18(o)	269
Eq. 13.83b	222	Eq. 13.18(q)	269
Eq. 13.112	226	Eq. 13.24(h)	276
Eq. 13.113	226	Eq. 13.24(i)	276
Eq. 13.114	227	Eq. 13.24(j)	276
Eq. 13.115	227	Eq. 13.24(k)	276
Eq. 13.116	227	Eq. 13.24(l)	276
Table 13.2a	228	Table 13.4	283
Table 13.2b	229	Table 13.5	284
Table 13.4	231	Table 13.7	285
Table 13.5	231	Table 13.8	286
Table 13.6	232	Table 13.10	287
Table 13.7	232	Table 13.9	286
Fig. a	219	Fig. a	267
Fig. b	219	Fig. b	267
Fig. c	219	Fig. c	267
Fig. d	220	Fig. d	270
Fig. e	220	Fig. e	270
Fig. f	220	Fig. f	270
Fig. g	221	Fig. g	270
Fig. 13.16	236	Fig. 13.17(c)	266

Contd...

Note: Some of the parameter(s), representations have been changed in 4th edition.

Addendum **789**

Design Data Handbook (Third edition) (Old edition)		Design Data Handbook (Fourth edition) (New edition)	
Equation/Table/Fig. No.	Page No.	Equation/Table/Fig. No.	Page No.
Lubrication and Bearings			
Eq. 15.1a	301	Eq. 15.1(a)	350
Eq. 15.1b	301	Eq. 15.1(b)	350
Eq. 15.2b	301	Eq. 15.1(e)	350
Eq. 15.3	301	Eq. 15.1(f)	350
Eq. 15.4a	301	Eq. 15.1(c)	351
Eq. 15.4b	301	Eq. 15.1(d)	351
Eq. 15.5a	301	Eq. 15.2(a)	351
Eq. 15.5b	301	Eq. 15.2(b)	351
Eq. 15.5c	302	Eq. 15.2(c)	351
Eq. 15.6	302	Eq. 15.2(d)	351
Eq. 15.7	302	Eq. 15.3 (a)	351
Eq. 15.8	302	Eq. 15.3 (b)	351
Eq. 15.9	302	Eq. 15.3 (c)	351
Eq. 15.10 & 15.21	302 & 303	Eq. 15.3 (d)	351
Eq. 15.11	302	Eq. 15.4 (a)	353
Eq. 15.12	302	Eq. 15.4 (b)	353
Eq. 15.13	302	Eq. 15.4 (c)	353
Eq. 15.14	303	Eq. 15.5 (a)	354
Eq. 15.15	303	Eq. 15.5 (b)	354
Eq. 15.16	303	Eq. 15.5 (c)	354
Eq. 15.17a	303	Eq. 15.6 (a)	354
Eq. 15.17b	303	Eq. 15.6 (b)	354
Eq. 15.18	303	Eq. 15.6 (c)	355
Eq. 15.22a	304	Eq. 15.6 (h)	355
Eq. 15.23	304	Eq. 15.6 (j)	356
Eq. 15.24	304	Eq. 15.7 (a)	356
Eq. 15.25	304	Eq. 15.17 (b)	357
Eq. 15.26	304	Eq. 15.17 (c)	357
Eq. 15.27	304	Eq. 15.8 (a)	358
Eq. 15.28a	304	Eq. 15.8 (b)	358
Eq. 15.28b	304	Eq. 15.8 (c)	358
Eq. 15.36	305	Eq. 15.6 (j)	356
Eq. 15.39	306	Eq. 15.11 (b)	360

Contd...

Design of Machine Elements II (DME II)

Design Data Handbook (Third edition) (Old edition)		Design Data Handbook (Fourth edition) (New edition)	
Equation/Table/Fig. No.	Page No.	Equation/Table/Fig. No.	Page No.
Eq. 15.40	306	Eq. 15.11(c)	360
Eq. 15.41	306	Eq. 15.11(c)	240
Table 15.1	308	Table 15.1	363
Table 15.2	308	Table 15.3	364
Table 15.3	310	Table 15.10	368
Table 15.4	310	Table 15.2	363
Table 15.5	311	Table 15.12	369
Table 15.6	311	Table 15.6	365
Table 15.7	312	Table 15.4	365
Table 15.8	312	Table 15.5	365
Table 15.11	314	Table 15.7	366
Table 15.12	315	Table 15.11	368
Fig. 15.1	316	Fig. 15.3	352
Fig. 15.3	316	Fig. 15.2(a)	350
Fig. 15.4	317	Fig. 15.5(b)	353
Fig. 15.5	317	Fig. 15.5(a)	353
Fig. 15.6	317	Fig. 15.7	355
Fig. 15.7	318	Fig. 15.9	356
Fig. 15.8	319	Fig. 15.13	358
Fig. 15.9	320	Fig. 15.8	356
Fig. 15.10	320	Fig. 15.6	354
Fig. 15.11	321	Fig. 15.14	358
Fig. 15.12	321	Fig. 15.10	357
Fig. 15.13	322	Fig. 15.12	357
Fig. 15.14	322	Fig. 15.11	357
–	–	Fig. 15.15	359
–	–	Fig. 15.16	361
–	–	Fig. 15.17	361
Pivot Bearing			
Eq. 9.28	107	Eq. 9.11 (g)	134

Contd...

Note: Some of the parameter(s), representations have been changed in 4th edition.

Addendum **791**

Design Data Handbook (Third edition) (Old edition)		Design Data Handbook (Fourth edition) (New edition)	
Equation/Table/Fig. No.	Page No.	Equation/Table/Fig. No.	Page No.
IC Engine Parts			
Piston			
Eq. 18.18a	361	Eq. 18.13 (a)	409
Eq. 18.18b	361	Eq. 18.13 (b)	409
Eq. 18.19	361	Eq. 18.13 (c)	409
Eq. 18.20	362	Eq. 18.13 (d)	410
Eq. 18.21	362	Eq. 18.13 (f)	410
Eq. 18.22	362	Eq. 18.14 (a)	410
Eq. 18.23	362	Eq. 18.14 (b)	410
Eq. 18.24	362	Eq. 18.15 (a)	411
Eq. 18.25	363	Eq. 18.15 (b)	411
Eq. 18.26	363	Eq. 18.16	411
Eq. 18.27	363	Eq. 18.17 (a)	411
Eq. 18.28a	363	Eq. 18.17 (b)	444
Eq. 18.28b	363	Eq. 18.17 (c)	411
Eq. 18.29	363	Eq. 18.17 (d)	411
Eq. 18.30	363	Eq. 18.18	411
Eq. 18.31	363	Eq. 18.19	411
Table 18.1	364	Table 18.5	413
Table 18.2	364	Table 18.6	413
Table 18.5	366	Table 18.4	412
Table 18.6	366	Table 18.9	414
Connecting Rod			
Eq. 19.1	369	Eq. 19.1 (b)	415
Eq. 19.2	369	Eq. 19.1 (c)	415
Eq. 19.3	369	Eq. 19.1 (d)	415
Eq. 19.4	369	Eq. 19.2	415
Eq. 19.5	369	Eq. 19.3	416
Eq. 19.6	370	Eq. 19.11	417
Eq. 19.7	370	Eq. 19.10	417
Eq. 19.8a	370	Eq. 19.8 (a)	417
Eq. 19.8b	370	Eq. 19.8 (b)	417
Eq. 19.9	371	Eq. 19.9	417
Table 19.1	371	Table 19.1	419
Fig. 19.1	372	Fig. 19.1	415
Fig. 19.2	372	Fig. 19.2	416
Others			
Table 1.3	8	Table 1.3	12
Appendix II	431	Appendix II	476
Crankshaft			
Eq. 3.12	45	Eq. 3.12 (a)	52
Eq. 3.13	45	Eq. 3.12 (b)	52
Eq. 3.14	45	Eq. 3.12 (c)	52
Table 3.2	47	Table 3.3	56
Table 3.5a	48	Table 3.5a	57
Table 3.5b	48	Table 3.5b	57
Table 3.6	49	Table 3.6	58
Table 19.1	371	Table 19.1	419
Tables 1.1 to 1.18	412–430	Tables 1.1 to 1.18	458–475
Fig. 3.3	50	Fig. 3.4	54
Fig. 3.5	50	Fig. 3.6	55

Index

Absolute viscosity 609
Angle of contact for belts 121, 123
Autofrettage 69

Barth's formula for
   belt friction 127
Bearing pressure 614, 620
Bearings 612
   clearance 616
   coefficient of friction (f) 618
   eccentricity ratio (ε) 621
   flow variable (FLV) 647
   heat dissipation 622
   journal bearing 612, 613
   length-diameter ratio 622
   minimum oil film thickness (MFT) 622
   modulus 619
   pressure 615, 618
   projected area of bearing 618
   side flow 620
   Sommerfeld number 620
   thrust 675
Belleville or Disk springs 290
Belts 119
   coefficient of friction 125
   flat belts 120
   length of belt-open 120
   length of belt-cross 122
   power ratings, V-belt 156
   power transmitted for 131, 156
   rubber 119, 135
   tension ratio of 125
   thickness of 124
   V-belt 154
Bevel gears 419
Birnie's equation for cylinders 68
Brakes 542
   band-simple 567
   band-differential 581
   block 551
   coefficient of friction for 545
   energy equation 544
   heating of 545
   self locking of 555
Bush chains 199

Centipoise 610
Centrifugal tension in belts 127
Chains 196
   bush 199
   length of 198
   power transmitted 198
Chain links 37
Closed rings 29
Clutches 502
   cone 504
   plate 503
Compound cylinders 76
Connecting rods 706
Crank shaft 724
   center 726
   side 756
Curved beams 3
Cylinders equations
   Barlow's formula 68
   Birnie's equation 68
   Clavarino's equation 68
   Lame's equation 61
   radial pressure between 65
Cylinder heads 99

Dished heads 101
Disk or belleville springs 290
Dynamic tooth load for
   bevel gear 426
   helical gear 370
   spur gear 332
   worm gear 472

Efficiency of worm gears 473
Energy stored in springs 228
Equalized stresses in springs or nipping 301
Endurance strength
   bevel 427
   helical 371
   spur 333

Fits
   press and shrink 81

Flat
  belts 120
  plates 100, 298
  springs 294
Formative number of teeth (z_e) 366

Gears
  Bevel 419
    design methodology 428
    design procedure 429
    dynamic load 426
    Lewis equation for 425
    strength of 424
    wear formula for 427
  Helical 364
    AGMA system of 472
    design methodology 369
    design procedure 372
    dynamic tooth load 370
    formative number of teeth (z_e) 366
    strength of 369
    wear formula for 371
  Herringbone gears 371
  Spur gears 324
    design methodology 330
    design procedure 334
    dynamic tooth load 332
    Lewis equation 327
    velocity factor 330
    wear formula for 333
  Worm gear 468
    design procedure 481
    designation 469
    dynamic strength 472
    efficiency of 473
    heating of 474
    lead angle 470
    power rating 474
    strength of 472
    wear formula for 473

Heads
  dished 101
  flat 99
  unstayed flat 101
Heat dissipation from
  bearings 622
  brakes 545
  worm gears 474
Helical
  gears 364
  springs 225

Herringbone gears 371
Hoop stress 58

Index-spring 222
Initial tension in belts 133

Journal bearing 613, 614

Kinematic viscosity 610

Lame's cylinder equation 61
Laminated springs 297
  cantilever springs 294
  semi-elliptical springs 298
Leaf springs 294
Lewis equation 327, 425
Lewis form factor 329, 331, 372, 425, 481
Longitudinal stress 59

Mechanisms of lubrication 614
Methods of gear drive 326
Minimum film thickness (MFT) 622
Multi-leaf springs 298

Natural frequency of spring 222
Newton's law of viscous flow 609

Oil
  film thickness-minimum (MFT) 622
  flow variable 641
  viscosities 609–611

Petroff's equation 616
Piston 688
  design 690
  rings 688, 692
    compression rings 689
    oil rings 689
  trunk type 688
Pitch angle for bevel gears 422
Plate clutch
  single 503
  multi 504
Plates, flat 100
Poisson's ratio 68, 79

Rate of spring 222
Rectangular section springs 272
Roller chain 196, 201
Rope
  sheaves for 185
  wire 183, 186

Rubber
   belts 119, 135
   springs 220

Self locking of brakes 555
Semi-elliptical springs 298
Shells 57, 101
Shrink fits 81
Sommerfeld number 620
Spring index 222
Springs 220
   angular deflection 227, 285
   axial deflection 222, 227
   belleville springs or disc spring 290
   compression spring 221
   free length of spring 220
   helical spring 225
   leaf spring 294
      flat 294
      multi-leaf 298
      laminated spring 297
         cantilever springs 298
         semi-elliptical springs 298
   natural frequency 222
   rectangular section springs 272
   rubber springs 220
   square section spring 272
   torsion spring-helical 220
   Wahl's stress factor 227

Spring scale 222, 227
Sprockets, chain 196
Spur gears 324
Stresses in
   curved beam-bending 7
   thick cylinder 62
   thin cylinder 57

Thick cylinders 60
Torsion springs-helical 283

V-belts 154
Virtual number of teeth 366
Viscosity
   absolute viscosity 609
   kinematic viscosity 610
   Redwood units 611
   Saybolt units 611

Wahl's correction factor 227
Wear load for
   bevel gear 427
   helical gear 371
   spur gear 333
   worm gear 473
Wire rope 183
Worm gear 468

Reader's Notes

Reader's Notes